Computer Graphics with OpenGL

THIRD EDITION

Computer Graphics with OpenGL

Donald Hearn

M. Pauline Baker

Computer Science Department and Pervasive Technology Lab
for Visualization and Interactive Spaces
Indiana University—Purdue University

Pearson Education International

Vice President and Editorial Director, ECS: *Marcia J. Horton*
Publisher: *Alan R. Apt*
Associate Editor: *Toni Dianne Holm*
Editorial Assistant: *Patrick Lindner*
Vice President and Director of Production and Manufacturing, ESM: *David W. Riccardi*
Executive Managing Editor: *Vince O'Brien*
Managing Editor: *Camille Trentacoste*
Production Editor: *Kathy Ewing*
Production Assistant: *Daniela Petrilli*
Director of Creative Services: *Paul Belfanti*
Creative Director: *Carole Anson*
Art Director: *Heather Scott*
Cover Designer: *John Christiana*
Interior Designer: *Carmella Pereira*
Cover Image: *Courtesy of Deborah R. Fowler, Przemyslaw Prusininkiewicz, and Johannes Battjes, University of Calgary. © 1992.*
Managing Editor, AV Management and Production: *Patricia Burns*
Art Editor: *Xiaohong Zhu*
Image Researcher: *Kathryn Kasturas*
Image Permission Coordinators: *Joanne Dippel and Cynthia Vincenti*
Manufacturing Manager: *Trudy Pisciotti*
Manufacturing Buyer: *Lynda Castillo*
Marketing Manager: *Pamela Shaffer*

Published by Pearson Prentice Hall
Pearson Education, Inc.
Upper Saddle River, NJ 07458

Printed in the United States of America

10 9 8 7 6 5 4 3 2

PIE ISBN: 0-13-120238-3

Pearson Education LTD.
Pearson Education Australia PTY. Limited
Pearson Education Singapore, Pte. Ltd.
Pearson Education North Asia Ltd.
Pearson Education Canada, Ltd.
Pearson Educación de Mexico, S.A. de C.V.
Pearson Education—Japan
Pearson Education Malaysia, Pte. Ltd.
Pearson Education, Upper Saddle River, New Jersey

To Our Folks

Dwight, Rose, Jay, and Millie

Contents

10 Illumination Models and Surface-Rendering Methods 556

Preface

Computer graphics remains one of the most exciting and rapidly growing areas of modern technology. Since the appearance of the first edition of this book, computer graphics has become a standard feature in applications software and computer systems in general. Computer-graphics methods are routinely applied in the design of most products, in training simulators, in the production of music videos and television commercials, in motion pictures, in data analysis, in scientific studies, in medical procedures, and in numerous other applications. A great variety of techniques and hardware devices are now in use or under development for these diverse application areas. In particular, much of today's computer-graphics research is concerned with improving the effectiveness, realism, and speed of picture generation. To produce a realistic view of a natural scene, a graphics program must simulate the effects of actual light reflections and refractions from physical objects. Therefore, the current trend in computer graphics is to incorporate improved approximations of physics principles into graphics algorithms, to better simulate the complex interactions between objects and a lighting environment.

Features of the Third Edition

The material in this third edition evolved from notes used in a variety of courses we have taught over the years, including introductory computer graphics, advanced computer graphics, scientific visualization, special topics, and project courses. When we wrote the first edition of this book, many graphics courses and applications dealt only with two-dimensional methods, so we separated the discussions of two-dimensional and three-dimensional graphics techniques. A solid foundation in two-dimensional computer-graphics procedures was given in the first half of the book, and three-dimensional methods were discussed in the second half. Now, however, three-dimensional graphics applications are commonplace, and many initial computer-graphics courses either deal primarily with three-dimensional methods or introduce three-dimensional graphics at an early stage. Therefore, a major feature of this third edition is the integration of three-dimensional and two-dimensional topics.

We have also expanded the treatment of most topics to include discussions of recent developments and new applications. General subjects covered in this third edition include: current hardware and software components of graphics systems, fractal geometry, ray tracing, splines, illumination models, surface rendering, computer animation, virtual reality, parallel implementations for graphics algorithms, antialiasing, superquadrics, BSP trees, particle systems, physically based modeling, scientific visualization, radiosity, bump mapping, and morphing. Some of the major expansion areas are animation, object representations, the three-dimensional viewing pipeline, illumination models, surface-rendering techniques, and texture mapping.

Another significant change in this third edition is the introduction of the OpenGL set of graphics routines, which is now widely used and available on most computer systems. The OpenGL package provides a large and efficient collection of device-independent functions for creating computer-graphics displays, using a program written in a general-purpose language such as C or C++. Auxiliary libraries are available in OpenGL for handling input and output operations, which require device interactions, and for additional graphics procedures such as generating cylinder shapes, spherical objects, and B-splines.

Programming Examples

More than twenty complete C++ programs are provided in this third edition, using the library of graphics routines available in the popular OpenGL package. These programs illustrate applications of basic picture-construction techniques, two-dimensional and three-dimensional geometric transformations, two-dimensional and three-dimensional viewing methods, perspective projections, spline generation, fractal methods, interactive mouse input, picking operations, menu and submenu displays, and animation techniques. In addition, over one hundred C++/OpenGL program segments are given to demonstrate the implementation of computer-graphics algorithms for clipping, lighting effects, surface rendering, texture mapping, and many other computer-graphics methods.

Required Background

We assume no prior familiarity with computer graphics, but we do assume that the reader has some knowledge of computer programming and basic data structures, such as arrays, pointer lists, files, and record organizations. A variety of mathematical methods are used in computer-graphics algorithms, and these methods are discussed in some detail in the appendix. Mathematical topics covered in the appendix include techniques from analytic geometry, linear algebra, vector and tensor analysis, complex numbers, quaternions, basic calculus, and numerical analysis.

This third edition can be used both as a text for students with no prior background in computer graphics and as a reference for graphics professionals. The emphasis is on the basic principles needed to design, use, and understand computer-graphics systems, along with numerous example programs to illustrate the methods and applications for each topic.

Suggested Course Outlines

For a one-semester course, a subset of topics dealing with either two-dimensional methods or a combination of two-dimensional and three-dimensional topics can be chosen, depending on the requirements of a particular course. A two-semester course sequence can cover the basic graphics concepts and algorithms in the first semester and advanced three-dimensional methods in the second. For the self-study reader, early chapters can be used to provide an understanding of graphics concepts, supplemented with selected topics from the later chapters.

At the undergraduate level, an introductory computer-graphics course can be organized using selected material from Chapters 2 through 6, 11, and 13. Sections could be chosen from these chapters to cover two-dimensional methods only, or three-dimensional topics could be added from these chapters along with limited selections from Chapters 7 and 10. Other topics, such as fractal representations, spline curves, texture mapping, depth-buffer methods, or color models, could be introduced in a first computer-graphics course. For an introductory graduate or upper-level undergraduate course, more emphasis could be given to three-dimensional viewing, three-dimensional modeling illumination models, and surface-rendering methods. In general, however, a two-semester sequence provides a better framework for adequately covering the fundamentals of two-dimensional and three-dimensional computer-graphics methods, including spline representations, surface rendering, and ray tracing. Special-topics courses, with an introductory computer-graphics prerequisite, can be offered in one or two areas, selected from visualization techniques, fractal geometry, spline methods, ray tracing, radiosity, and computer animation.

Chapter 1 illustrates the diversity of computer-graphics applications by taking a look at the many different kinds of pictures that people have generated with graphics software. In Chapter 2, we present the basic vocabulary of computer graphics, along with an introduction to the hardware and software components of graphics systems, a detailed introduction to OpenGL, and a complete OpenGL example program. The fundamental algorithms for the representation and display of simple objects are given in Chapters 3 and 4. These two chapters examine methods for producing basic picture components such as polygons and circles; for setting the color, size, and other attributes of objects; and for implementing these methods in OpenGL. Chapter 5 discusses the algorithms for performing geometric transformations such as rotation and scaling. In Chapters 6 and 7, we give detailed explanations of the procedures for displaying views of two-dimensional and three-dimensional scenes. Methods for generating displays of complex objects, such as quadric surfaces, splines, fractals, and particle systems are discussed in Chapter 8. In Chapter 9 we explore the various computer-graphics techniques for identifying the visible objects in a three-dimensional scene. Illumination models and the methods for applying lighting conditions to a scene are examined in Chapter 10. Methods for interactive graphics input and for designing graphical user interfaces are given in Chapter 11. The various color models useful in computer graphics are discussed in Chapter 12, along with color-design considerations. Computer-animation techniques are explored in Chapter 13. Methods for the hierarchical modeling of complex systems are presented in Chapter 14. And, in Chapter 15, we survey the major graphics file formats.

Acknowledgments

Many people have contributed to this project in a variety of ways over the years. To the organizations and individuals who furnished pictures and other materials, we again express our appreciation. We also acknowledge the many helpful comments received from our students in various computer-graphics and visualization courses and seminars. We are indebted to all those who provided comments, reviews, suggestions for improving the material covered in this book, and other input, and we extend our apologies to anyone we may have failed to mention. Our thanks to Ed Angel, Norman Badler, Phillip Barry, Brian Barsky,

Hedley Bond, Bart Braden, Lara Burton, Robert Burton, Greg Chwelos, John Cross, Steve Cunningham, John DeCatrel, Victor Duvaneko, Gary Eerkes, Parris Egbert, Tony Faustini, Thomas Foley, Thomas Frank, Don Gillies, Andrew Glassner, Jack Goldfeather, Georges Grinstein, Eric Haines, Robert Herbst, Larry Hodges, Carol Hubbard, Eng-Kiat Koh, Mike Krogh, Michael Laszlo, Suzanne Lea, Michael May, Nelson Max, David McAllister, Jeffrey McConnell, Gary McDonald, C. L. Morgan, Greg Nielson, James Oliver, Lee-Hian Quek, Laurence Rainville, Paul Ross, David Salomon, Günther Schrack, Steven Shafer, Cliff Shaffer, Pete Shirley, Carol Smith, Stephanie Smullen, Jeff Spears, William Taffe, Wai Wan Tsang, Spencer Thomas, Sam Uselton, David Wen, Bill Wicker, Andrew Woo, Angelo Yfantis, Marek Zaremba, Michael Zyda, and the many anonymous reviewers. We also thank our editor Alan Apt, Toni Holm, and the Colorado staff for their help, suggestions, encouragement, and, above all, their patience during the preparation of this third edition. And to our production editors and staff, Lynda Castillo, Camille Trentacoste, Heather Scott, Xiaohong Zhu, Vince O'Brien, Patricia Burns, Kathy Ewing, and David Abel, we extend our sincere appreciation for their many talented contributions and careful attention to detail.

Computer Graphics with OpenGL

CHAPTER 1

A Survey of Computer Graphics

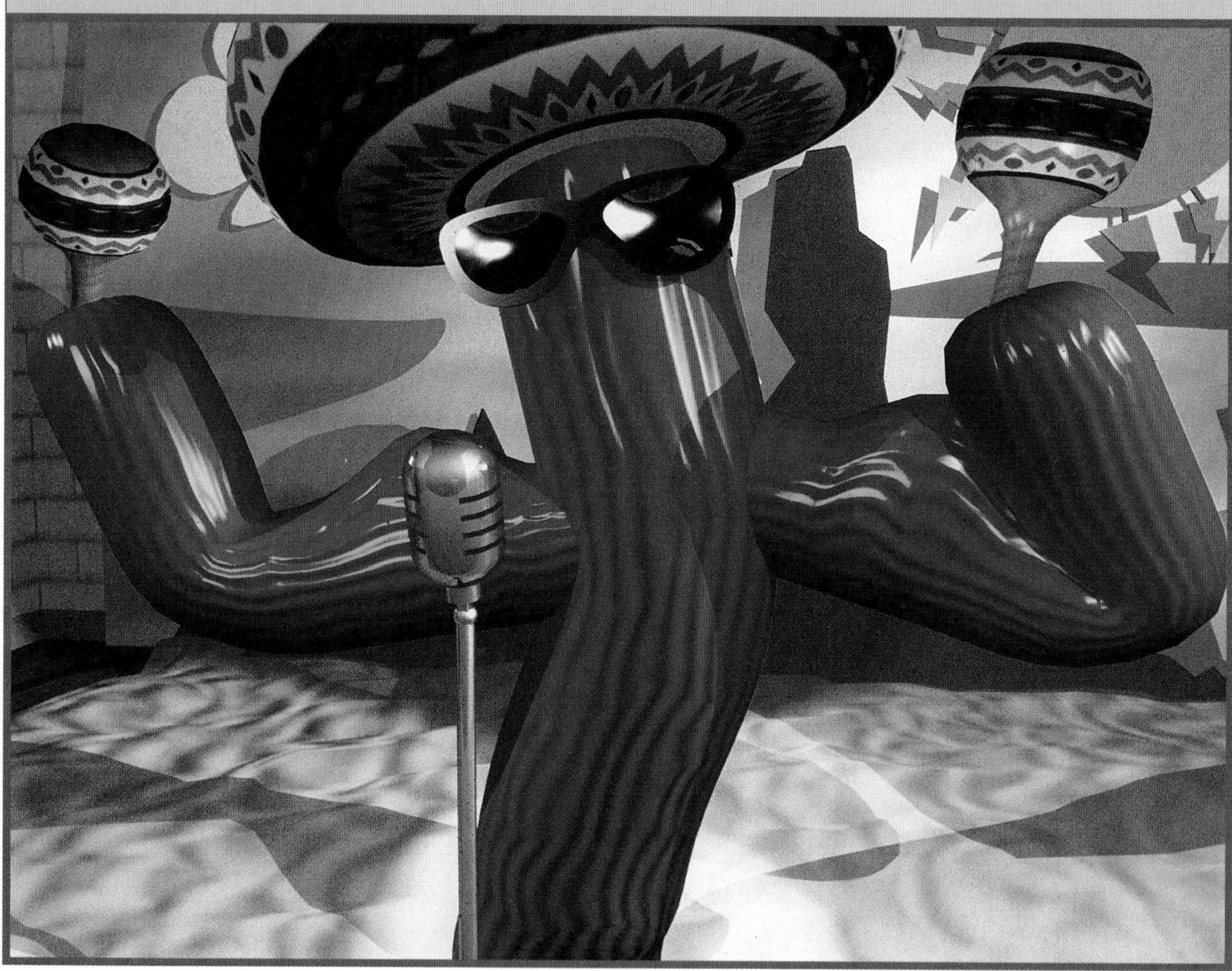

A saguaro-entertainer scene from a computer-generated cartoon animation.
(Courtesy of SOFTIMAGE, Inc.)

Computers have become a powerful tool for the rapid and economical production of pictures. There is virtually no undertaking in which graphical displays cannot be used to some advantage, and so it is not surprising to find the use of computer graphics so widespread. Although early applications in engineering and science had to rely on expensive and cumbersome equipment, advances in computer technology have made interactive computer graphics a practical tool. Today, we find computer graphics used routinely in such diverse fields as science, art, engineering, business, industry, medicine, government, entertainment, advertising, education, training, and home applications. And we can even transmit graphical images around the world using the Internet. Figure 1-1 gives a compact summary of the many applications of graphics in simulations, training, and data plotting. Before we get into the details of how to do computer graphics, we first take a short tour through a gallery of graphics applications.

1-1 GRAPHS AND CHARTS

An early application for computer graphics is the display of simple data graphs, usually plotted on a character printer. Data plotting is still one of the most common graphics applications, but today we can easily generate graphs showing highly complex data relationships for printed reports or for presentations using 35 mm slides, transparencies, or animated videos. Graphs and charts are commonly used

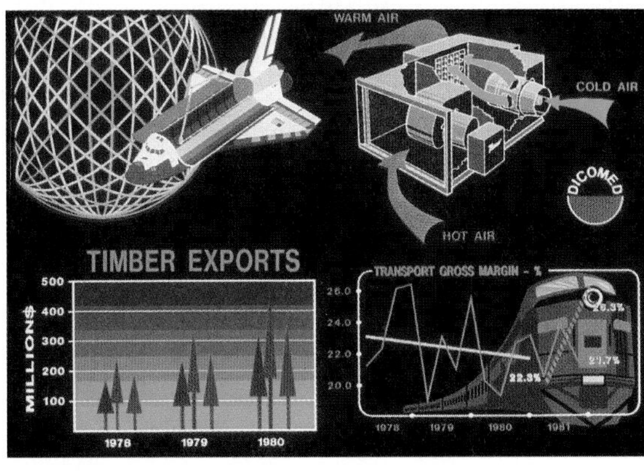

FIGURE 1-1 Examples of computer-graphics applications in various areas. (*Courtesy of the DICOMED Corporation.*)

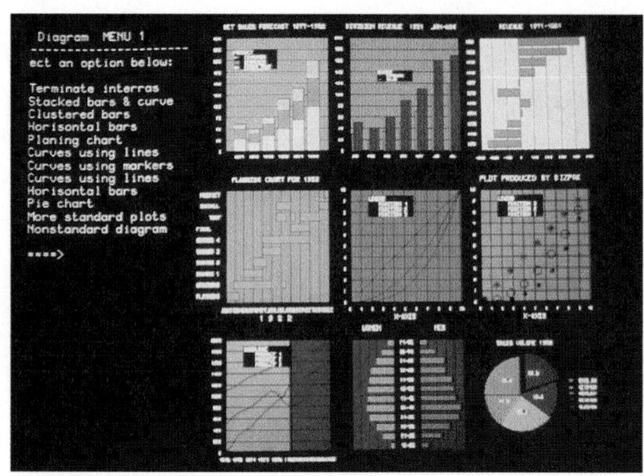

FIGURE 1-2 Two-dimensional line graphs, bar charts, and a pie chart. (*Courtesy of UNIRAS, Inc.*)

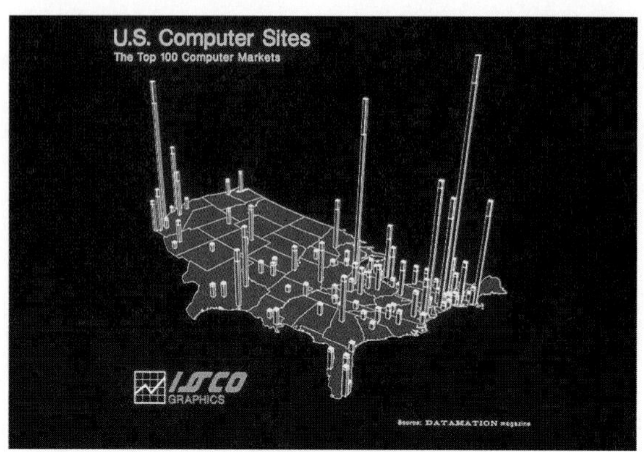

FIGURE 1-3 Two color-coded data sets displayed as a three-dimensional bar chart on the surface of a geographical region. (*Reprinted with permission from ISSCO Graphics, San Diego, California.*)

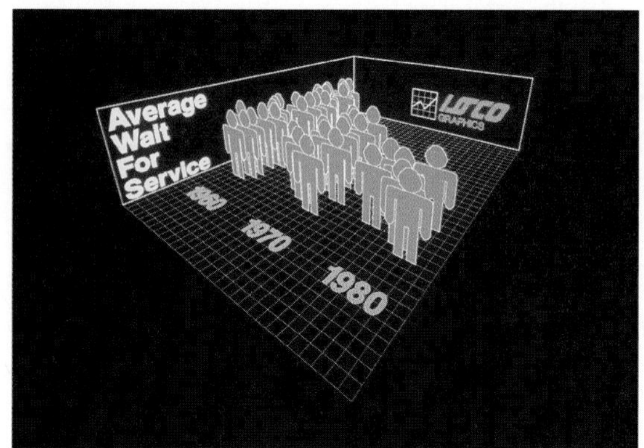

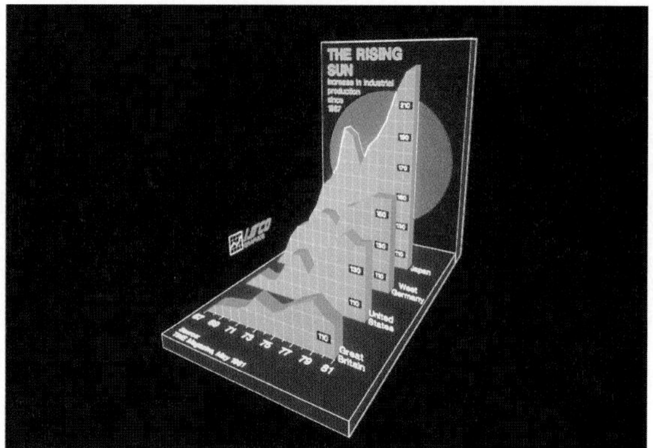

FIGURE 1-4 Two three-dimensional graphs designed for dramatic effect. (*Reprinted with permission from ISSCO Graphics, San Diego, California.*)

to summarize financial, statistical, mathematical, scientific, engineering, and economic data for research reports, managerial summaries, consumer information bulletins, and other types of publications. A variety of commercial graphing packages are available, and workstation devices and service bureaus exist for converting screen displays into film, slides, or overhead transparencies for use in presentations or archiving. Typical examples of data plots are line graphs, bar charts, pie charts, surface graphs, contour plots, and other displays showing relationships between multiple parameters in two dimensions, three dimensions, or higher-dimensional spaces.

Figures 1-1 and 1-2 give examples of two-dimensional data plots. These two figures illustrate basic line graphs, bar charts, and a pie chart. One or more sections of a pie chart can be emphasized by displacing the sections radially to produce an "exploded" pie chart.

Three-dimensional graphs and charts are used to display additional parameter information, although they are sometimes used simply for effect, providing more dramatic or more attractive presentations of the data relationships. Figure 1-3 shows a three-dimensional bar chart combined with geographical information. And Figure 1-4 provides examples of dramatic three-dimensional data

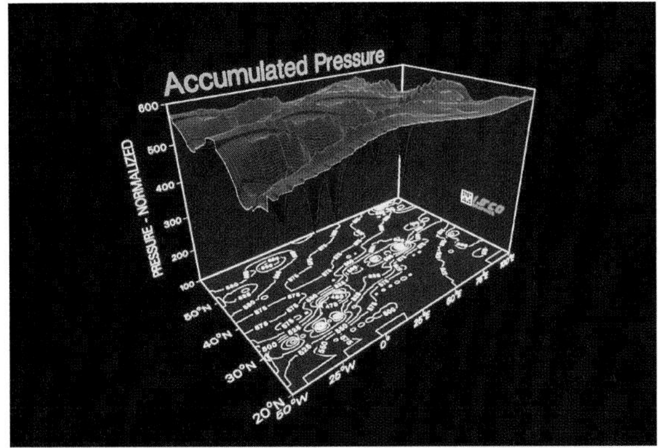

FIGURE 1-5 Plotting two-dimensional contours in a ground plane, with a height field plotted as a surface above the ground plane. *(Reprinted with permission from ISSCO Graphics, San Diego, California.)*

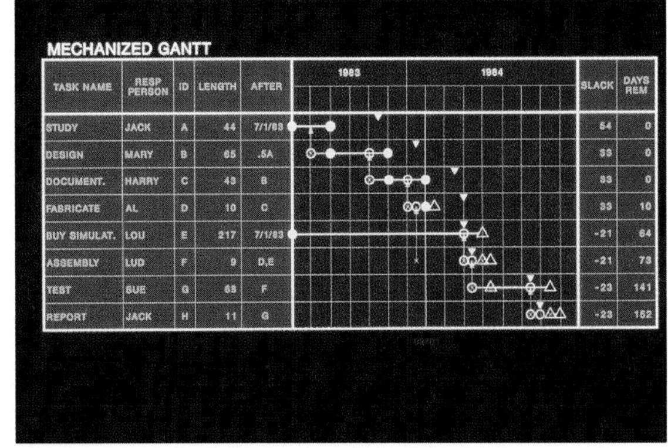

FIGURE 1-6 A time chart displaying scheduling and other relevant information about project tasks. *(Reprinted with permission from ISSCO Graphics, San Diego, California.)*

graphs. Another example of three-dimensional graphing is a surface plot, as illustrated in Fig. 1-5, which shows a height surface and its projected two-dimensional contour plot.

Figure 1-6 illustrates a time chart used in task planning. Time charts and task network layouts are used in project management to schedule and monitor the progress of projects.

1-2 COMPUTER-AIDED DESIGN

A major use of computer graphics is in design processes—particularly for engineering and architectural systems, although most products are now computer designed. Generally referred to as **CAD, computer-aided design,** or **CADD, computer-aided drafting and design,** these methods are now routinely used in the design of buildings, automobiles, aircraft, watercraft, spacecraft, computers, textiles, home appliances, and a multitude of other products.

For some design applications, objects are first displayed in a wire-frame outline that shows the overall shape and internal features of the objects. Wire-frame displays also allow designers to quickly see the effects of interactive adjustments to design shapes without waiting for the object surfaces to be fully generated. Figures 1-7 and 1-8 give examples of wire-frame images in design applications.

Software packages for CAD applications typically provide the designer with a multiwindow environment, as in Figs. 1-9 and 1-10. The various windows can show enlarged sections or different views of objects.

Circuits, such as the one shown in Fig. 1-10, and networks for communications, water supply, or other utilities are constructed with repeated placement of a few graphical shapes. The shapes used in a design represent the different network or circuit components. Standard shapes for mechanical, electrical, electronic, and logic circuits are often supplied by the design package. For other applications, a designer can create personalized symbols that are to be used to construct the network or circuit. The system is then designed by successively placing copies of the components into the layout, with the graphics package automatically providing

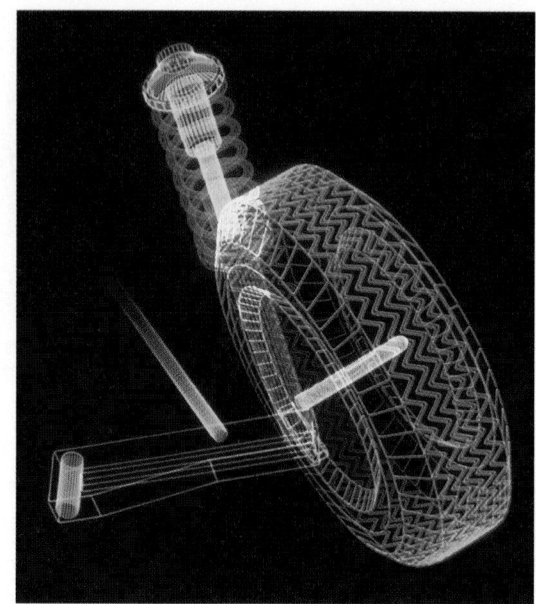

FIGURE 1-7 Color-coded, wire-frame display for an automobile wheel assembly. (*Courtesy of Evans & Sutherland.*)

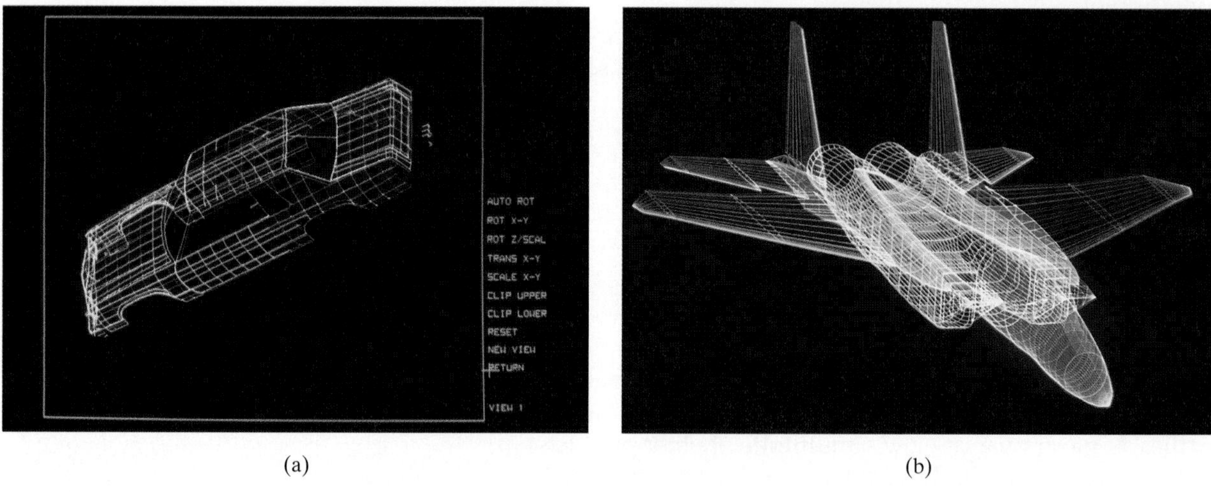

(a) (b)

FIGURE 1-8 Color-coded, wire-frame outlines of body designs for an automobile and an aircraft. (*Courtesy of* (a) *Peritek Corporation and* (b) *Evans & Sutherland.*)

the links between components. This allows the designer to quickly test alternate circuit schematics for minimization of the number of components or the space required for the system.

Animations are often used in CAD applications. Real-time, computer animations using wire-frame shapes are useful for quickly testing the performance of a vehicle or system, as demonstrated in Fig. 1-11. Because a wire-frame image is not displayed with rendered surfaces, the calculations for each segment of the animation can be performed quickly to produce a smooth motion on the screen. Also, wire-frame displays allow the designer to see into the interior of the vehicle and to watch the behavior of inner components during motion.

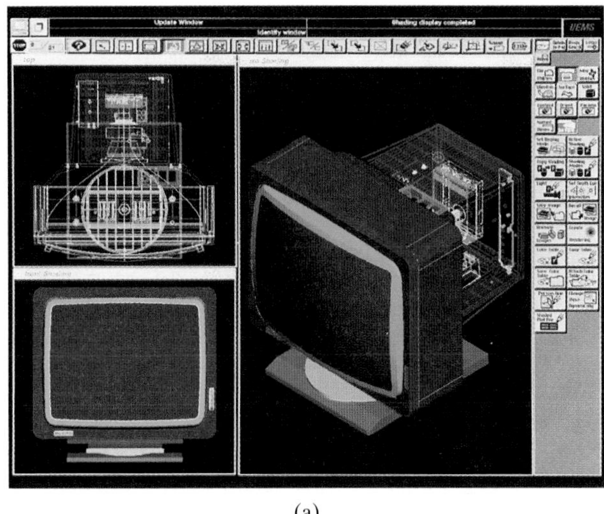

(a)

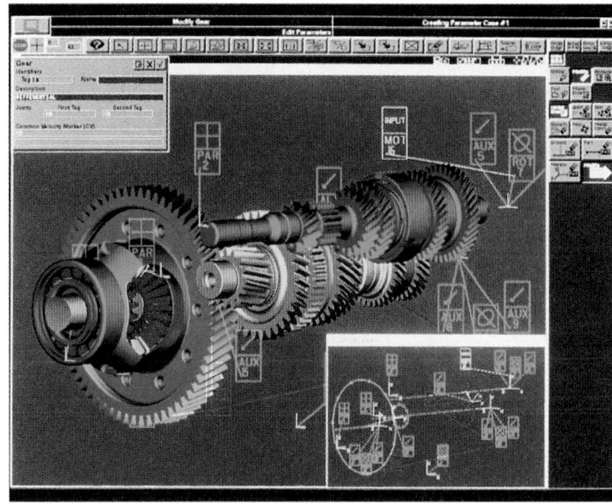

(b)

FIGURE 1-9 Multiple-window, color-coded CAD workstation displays. (*Courtesy of Intergraph Corporation.*)

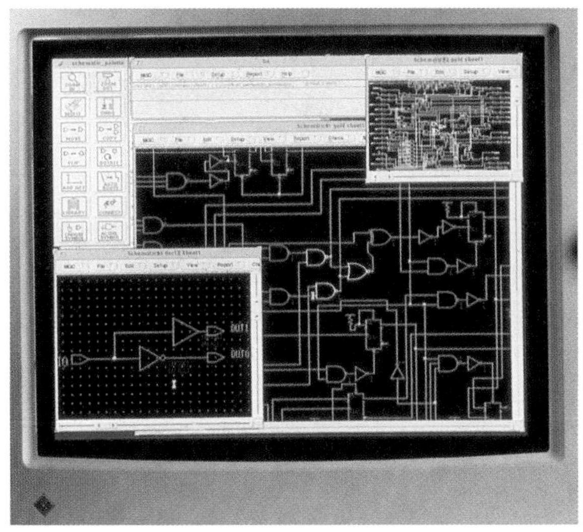

FIGURE 1-10 A circuit design application, using multiple windows and color-coded logic components. (*Courtesy of Sun Microsystems.*)

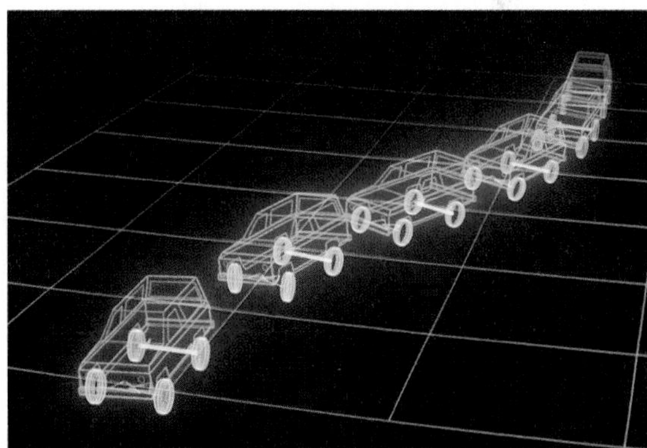

FIGURE 1-11 Simulation of vehicle performance during lane changes. (*Courtesy of Evans & Sutherland and Mechanical Dynamics, Inc.*)

When object designs are complete, or nearly complete, realistic lighting conditions and surface rendering are applied to produce displays that will show the appearance of the final product. Examples of this are given in Fig. 1-12. Realistic displays are also generated for advertising of automobiles and other vehicles using special lighting effects and background scenes (Fig. 1-13).

The manufacturing process is also tied in to the computer description of designed objects so that the fabrication of a product can be automated, using methods that are referred to as **CAM, computer-aided manufacturing.** A circuit

(a)

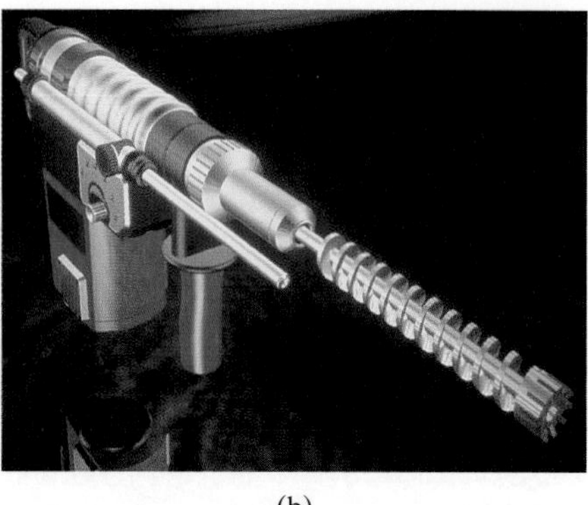

(b)

FIGURE 1-12 Realistic renderings of engineering designs. (*Courtesy of* (a) *Intergraph Corporation and* (b) *Evans & Sutherland.*)

FIGURE 1-13 Studio lighting effects and realistic surface-rendering techniques are applied by computer-graphics programs to produce advertising pieces for finished products. This computer-generated image of a Chrysler Laser automobile was produced from data supplied by the Chrysler Corporation. (*Courtesy of Eric Haines, Autodesk, Inc.*)

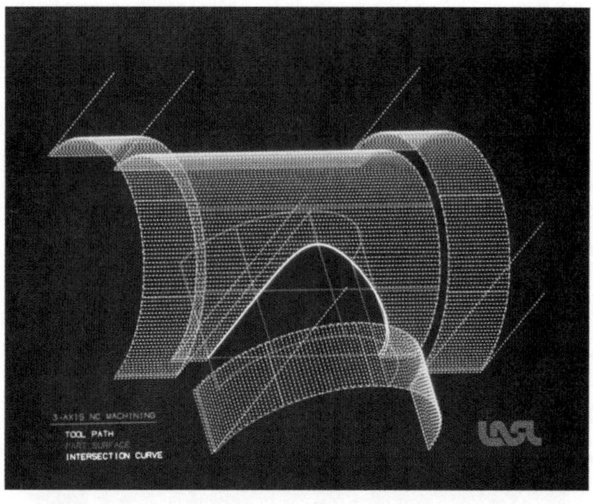

FIGURE 1-14 A CAD layout for describing the numerically controlled machining of a part. The part surface is displayed in one color and the tool path in another color. (*Courtesy of Los Alamos National Laboratory.*)

board layout, for example, can be transformed into a description of the individual processes needed to construct the electronics network. Some mechanical parts are manufactured from descriptions of how the surfaces are to be formed with the machine tools. Figure 1-14 shows the path to be taken by machine tools over the surfaces of an object during its construction. Numerically controlled machine tools are then set up to manufacture the part according to these construction layouts.

Architects use interactive computer-graphics methods to lay out floor plans, such as Fig. 1-15, that show the positioning of rooms, doors, windows, stairs, shelves, counters, and other building features. Working from the display of a building layout on a video monitor, an electrical designer can try out

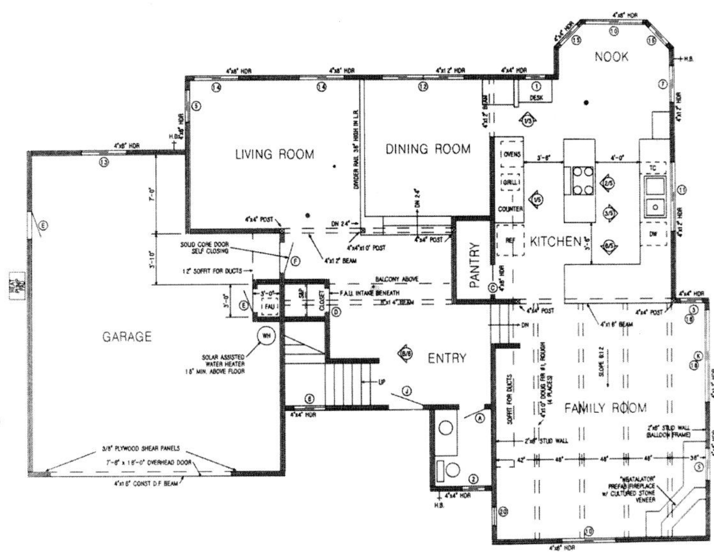

FIGURE 1-15 Architectural CAD layout for a building design. (*Courtesy of Precision Visuals, Inc., Boulder, Colorado.*)

(a)

(b)

FIGURE 1-16 Realistic, three-dimensional renderings of building designs. (a) A street-level perspective for the World Trade Center project. (*Courtesy of Skidmore, Owings, & Merrill.*) (b) Architectural visualization of an atrium, created for a computer animation by Marialine Prieur, Lyon, France. (*Courtesy of Thomson Digital Image, Inc.*)

arrangements for wiring, electrical outlets, and fire-warning systems. Also, facility-layout packages can be used to optimize space utilization in an office or within a manufacturing facility.

Realistic displays of architectural designs, as in Fig. 1-16, permit both architects and their clients to study the appearance of a single building or a group of buildings, such as a campus or industrial complex. In addition to realistic exterior building displays, architectural CAD packages also provide facilities for experimenting with three-dimensional interior layouts and lighting (Fig. 1-17).

Many other kinds of systems and products are designed using either general CAD packages or specially developed CAD software. Figure 1-18, for example, shows a rug pattern designed with a CAD system.

FIGURE 1-17 A hotel corridor that provides a sense of movement by positioning light fixtures along an undulating path and creates a sense of entry by placing a light tower at the entrance to each room. (*Courtesy of Skidmore, Owings, & Merrill.*)

FIGURE 1-18 Oriental rug pattern created with computer-graphics design methods. (*Courtesy of Lexidata Corporation.*)

1-3 VIRTUAL-REALITY ENVIRONMENTS

A more recent application of computer graphics is in the creation of **virtual-reality environments** in which a user can interact with the objects in a three-dimensional scene. Specialized hardware devices provide three-dimensional viewing effects and allow the user to "pick up" objects in a scene.

Animations in virtual-reality environments are often used to train heavy-equipment operators or to analyze the effectiveness of various cabin configurations and control placements. As the tractor operator in Fig. 1-19 manipulates the

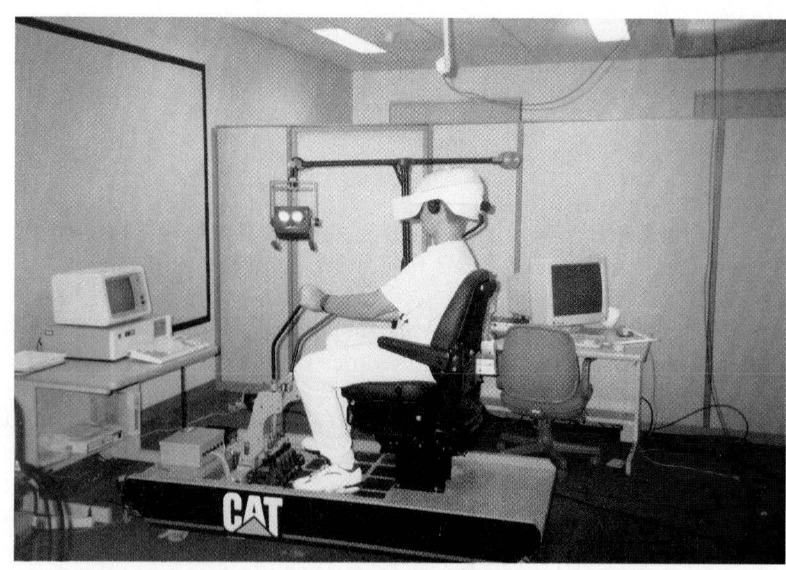

FIGURE 1-19 Operating a tractor in a virtual-reality environment. As the controls are moved, the operator views the front loader, backhoe, and surroundings through the headset. (*Courtesy of the National Center for Supercomputing Applications, University of Illinois at Urbana-Champaign, and Caterpillar, Inc.*)

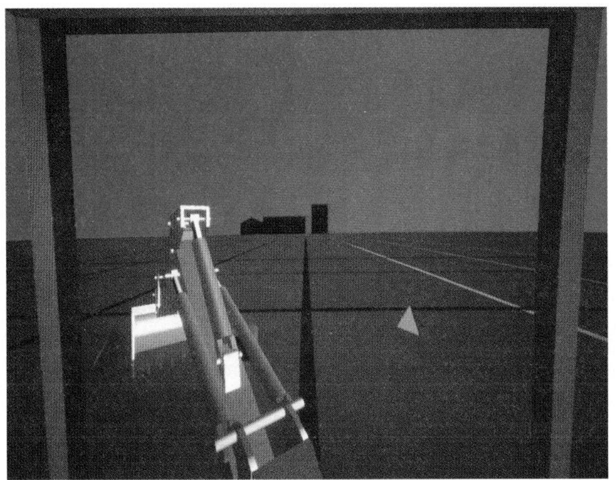

FIGURE 1-20 A headset view of the backhoe presented to a tractor operator in a virtual-reality environment. (*Courtesy of the National Center for Supercomputing Applications, University of Illinois at Urbana-Champaign, and Caterpillar, Inc.*)

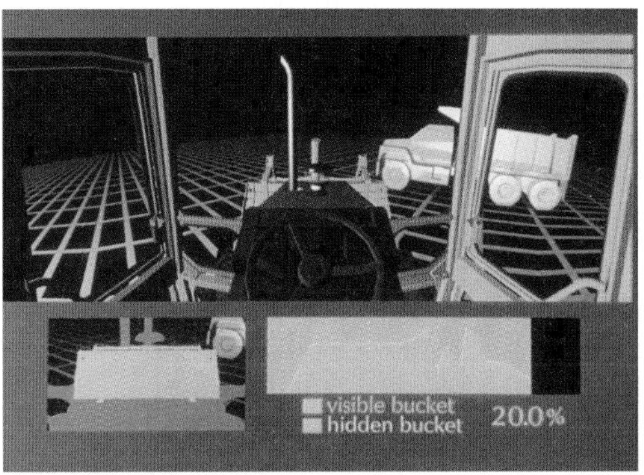

FIGURE 1-21 Operator's view of the tractor bucket, composited in several sections to form a wide-angle view on a standard monitor. (*Courtesy of the National Center for Supercomputing Applications, University of Illinois at Urbana-Champaign, and Caterpillar, Inc.*)

FIGURE 1-22 View of the tractor displayed on a standard monitor. (*Courtesy of the National Center for Supercomputing Applications, University of Illinois at Urbana-Champaign, and Caterpillar, Inc.*)

controls, the headset presents a stereoscopic view (Fig. 1-20) of the front-loader bucket or the backhoe, just as if the operator were in the tractor seat. This allows the designer to explore various positions of the bucket or backhoe that might obstruct the operator's view, which can then be taken into account in the overall tractor design. Figure 1-21 shows a composite, wide-angle view from the tractor seat, displayed on a standard video monitor instead of in a virtual, three-dimensional scene. And Fig. 1-22 shows a view of the tractor that can be displayed in a separate window or on another monitor.

With virtual-reality systems, designers and others can move about and interact with objects in various ways. Architectural designs can be examined by taking a simulated "walk" through the rooms or around the outsides of buildings to better appreciate the overall effect of a particular design. And with a special glove, we can even "grasp" objects in a scene and turn them over or move them from one place to another.

1-4 DATA VISUALIZATIONS

Producing graphical representations for scientific, engineering, and medical data sets and processes is another fairly new application of computer graphics, which is generally referred to as **scientific visualization.** And the term **business visualization** is used in connection with data sets related to commerce, industry, and other nonscientific areas.

Researchers, analysts, and others often need to deal with large amounts of information or to study the behavior of highly complex processes. Numerical computer simulations, for example, frequently produce data files containing thousands and even millions of values. Similarly, satellite cameras and other recording sources are amassing large data files faster than they can be interpreted. Scanning these large sets of numbers to determine trends and relationships is a tedious and ineffective process. But if the data are converted to a visual form, the trends and patterns are often immediately apparent. Figure 1-23 shows an example of a large data set that has been converted to a color-coded display of relative heights above a ground plane. Once we have plotted the density values in this way, we can easily see the overall pattern of the data.

There are many different kinds of data sets, and effective visualization schemes depend on the characteristics of the data. A collection of data can contain scalar values, vectors, higher-order tensors, or any combination of these data types. And data sets can be distributed over a two-dimensional region of space, a three-dimensional region, or a higher-dimensional space. Color coding is just one way to visualize a data set. Other visualization techniques include contour plots, renderings for constant-value surfaces or other spatial regions, and specially designed shapes that are used to represent different data types.

Visual techniques are also used to aid in the understanding and analysis of complex processes and mathematical functions. A color plot of mathematical curve functions is shown in Fig. 1-24, and a surface plot of a function is shown in Fig. 1-25. Fractal procedures using quaternions generated the object shown in Fig. 1-26, and a topological structure is displayed in Fig. 1-27. Scientists are also

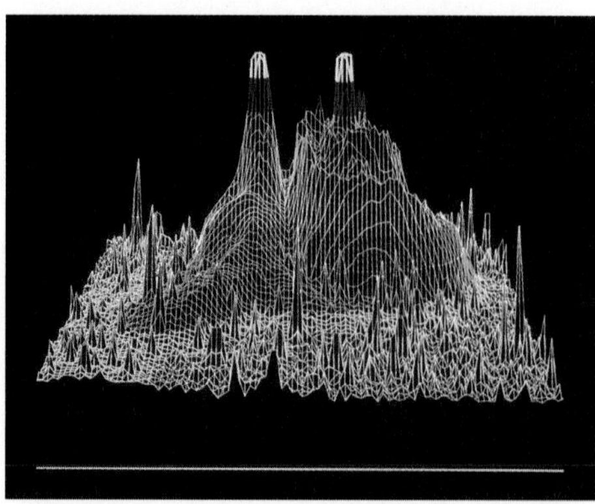

FIGURE 1-23 A color-coded plot with sixteen million density points of relative brightness observed for the Whirlpool Nebula reveals two distinct galaxies. (*Courtesy of Los Alamos National Laboratory.*)

FIGURE 1-24 Mathematical curve functions plotted in various color combinations. (*Courtesy of Melvin L. Prueitt, Los Alamos National Laboratory.*)

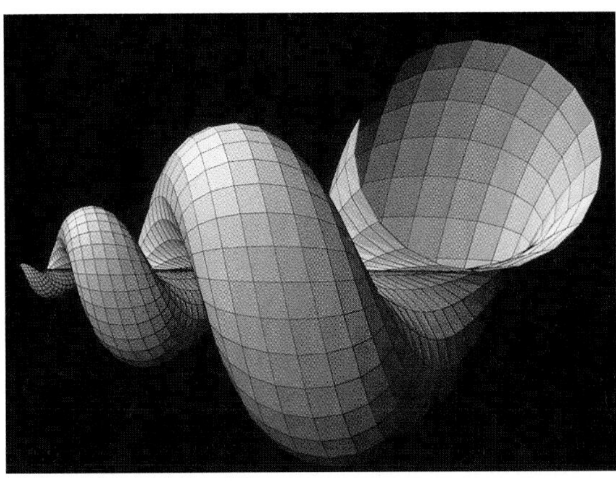

FIGURE 1-25 Lighting effects and surface-rendering techniques were applied to produce this surface representation for a three-dimensional function. *(Courtesy of Wolfram Research, Inc., The Maker of Mathematica.)*

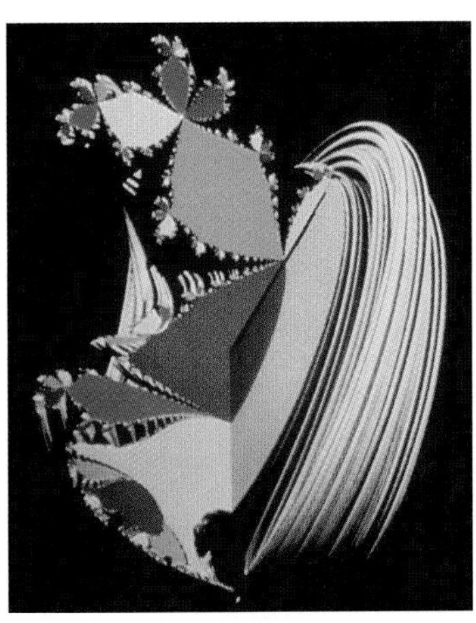

FIGURE 1-26 A four-dimensional object projected into three-dimensional space, then projected to the two-dimensional screen of a video monitor and color coded. The object was generated using quaternions and fractal squaring procedures, with an octant subtracted to show the complex Julia set. *(Courtesy of John C. Hart, Department of Computer Science, University of Illinois at Urbana-Champaign.)*

FIGURE 1-27 Four views from a real-time, interactive computer-animation study of minimal surfaces ("snails") in the 3-sphere projected to three-dimensional Euclidean space. *(Courtesy of George Francis, Department of Mathematics and the National Center for Supercomputing Applications, University of Illinois at Urbana-Champaign. © 1993.)*

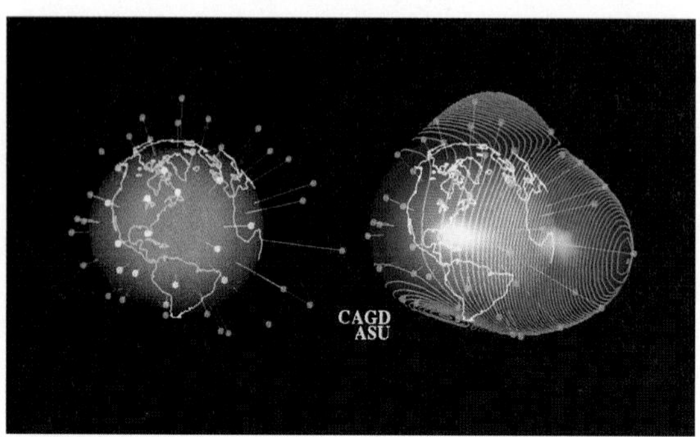

FIGURE 1-28 A method for graphing and modeling data distributed over a spherical surface. (*Courtesy of Greg Nielson, Computer Science Department, Arizona State University.*)

FIGURE 1-29 A visualization of stream surfaces flowing past a space shuttle, devised by Jeff Hultquist and Eric Raible, NASA Ames. (*Courtesy of Sam Uselton, NASA Ames Research Center.*)

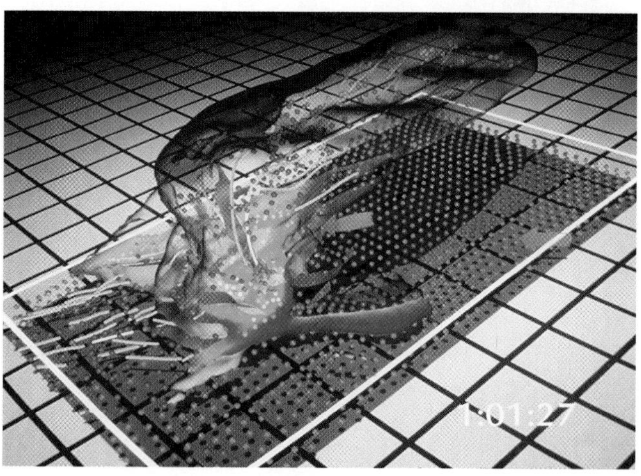

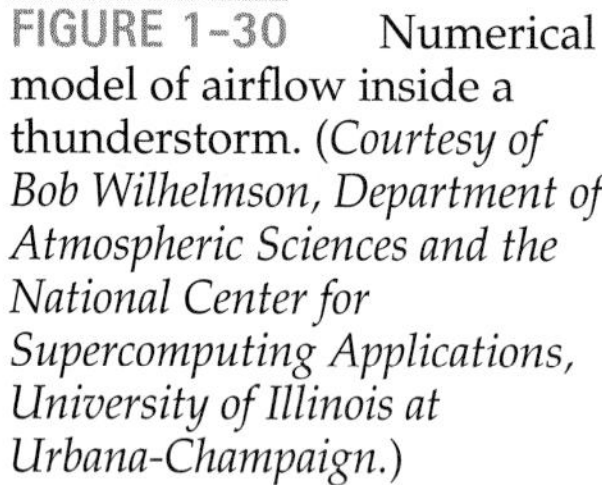

FIGURE 1-30 Numerical model of airflow inside a thunderstorm. (*Courtesy of Bob Wilhelmson, Department of Atmospheric Sciences and the National Center for Supercomputing Applications, University of Illinois at Urbana-Champaign.*)

developing methods for visualizing general classes of data. Figure 1-28 shows a general technique for graphing and modeling data distributed over a spherical surface.

A few of the many other visualization applications are shown in Figs. 1-29 through 1-42. These figures show: airflow over the surface of a space shuttle, numerical modeling of thunderstorms, a display of the effects of crack propagation in metals, a color-coded plot of fluid density over an airfoil, a cross-sectional slicer for data sets, protein modeling, interactive viewing of molecular structures within a virtual-reality environment, a model of the ocean floor, a Kuwaiti oil-fire simulation, an air-pollution study, a corn-growing study, reconstruction of Arizona's Chaco Canyon ruins, and a graph of automobile accident statistics.

FIGURE 1-31 Numerical model of the surface of a thunderstorm. (*Courtesy of Bob Wilhelmson, Department of Atmospheric Sciences and the National Center for Supercomputing Applications, University of Illinois at Urbana-Champaign.*)

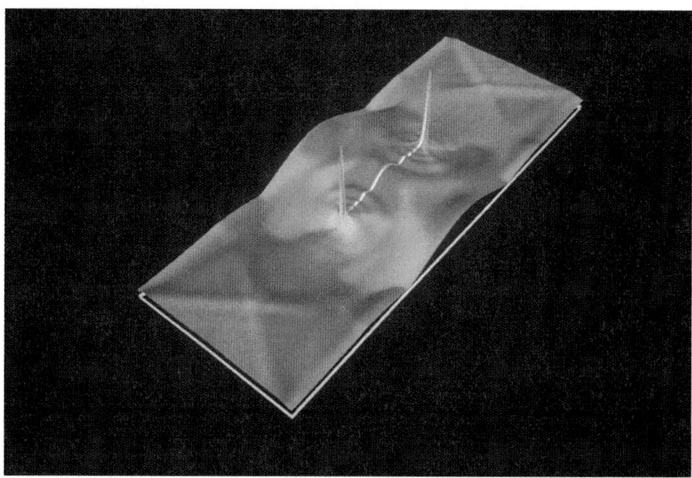

FIGURE 1-32 Color-coded visualization of stress energy density in a crack propagation study for metal plates, modeled by Bob Haber. (*Courtesy of the National Center for Supercomputing Applications, University of Illinois at Urbana-Champaign.*)

FIGURE 1-33 A fluid-dynamic simulation, showing a color-coded plot of fluid density over a span of grid planes around an aircraft wing, developed by Lee-Hian Quek, John Eickemeyer, and Jeffery Tan. (*Courtesy of the Information Technology Institute, Republic of Singapore.*)

FIGURE 1-34 Commercial slicer-dicer software, showing color-coded data values over cross-sectional slices of a data set. (*Courtesy of Spyglass, Inc.*)

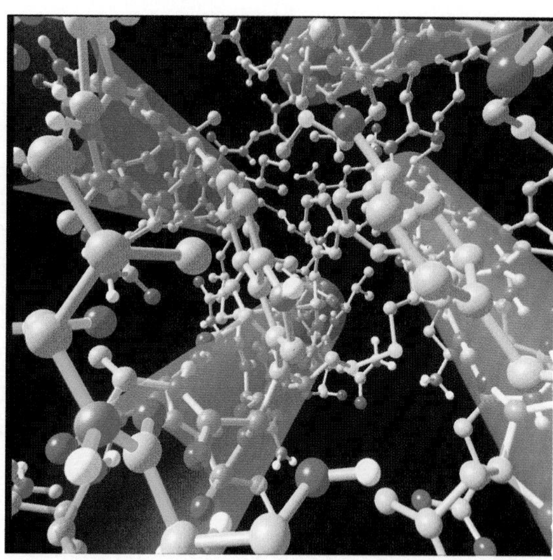

FIGURE 1-35 Visualization of a protein structure, created by Jay Siegel and Kim Baldridge, SDSC. (*Courtesy of Stephanie Sides, San Diego Supercomputer Center.*)

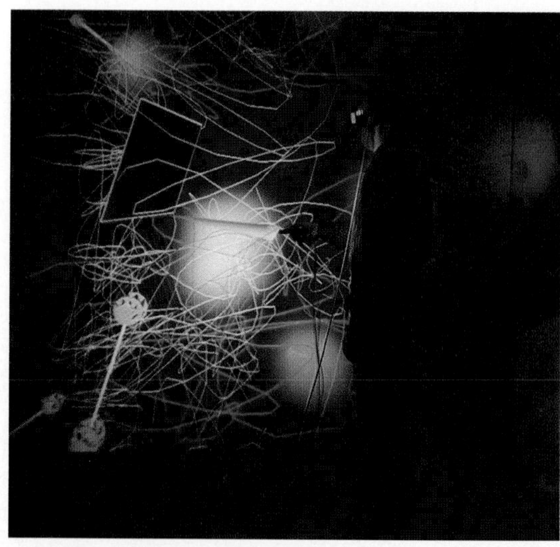

FIGURE 1-36 A scientist interacting with stereoscopic views of molecular structures within a virtual-reality environment called the "CAVE". (*Courtesy of William Sherman and the National Center for Supercomputing Applications, University of Illinois at Urbana-Champaign.*)

FIGURE 1-37 One image from a stereoscopic pair, showing a visualization of the ocean floor obtained from satellite data, created by David Sandwell and Chris Small, Scripps Institution of Oceanography, and Jim Mcleod, SDSC. (*Courtesy of Stephanie Sides, San Diego Supercomputer Center.*)

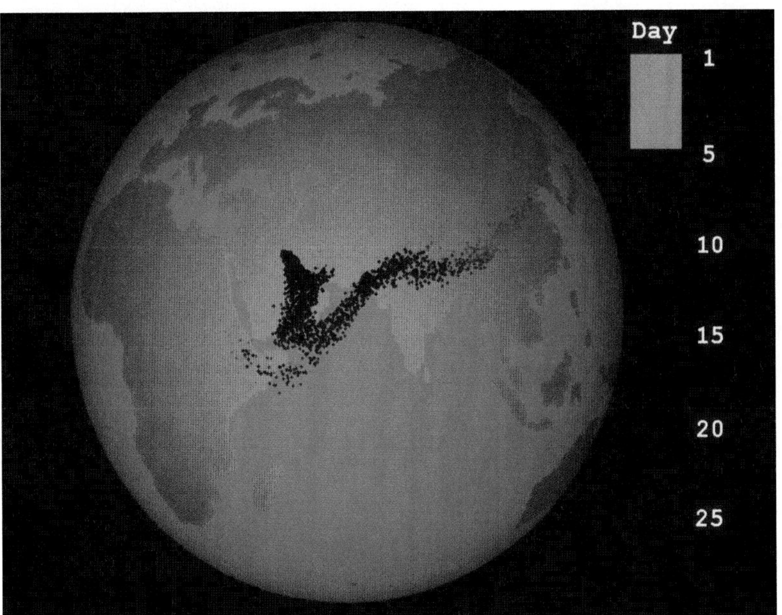

FIGURE 1-38 A simulation of the effects of the 1991 Kuwaiti oil fires, developed by Gary Glatzmeier, Chuck Hanson, and Paul Hinker. (*Courtesy of Mike Krogh, Advanced Computing Laboratory at the Los Alamos National Laboratory.*)

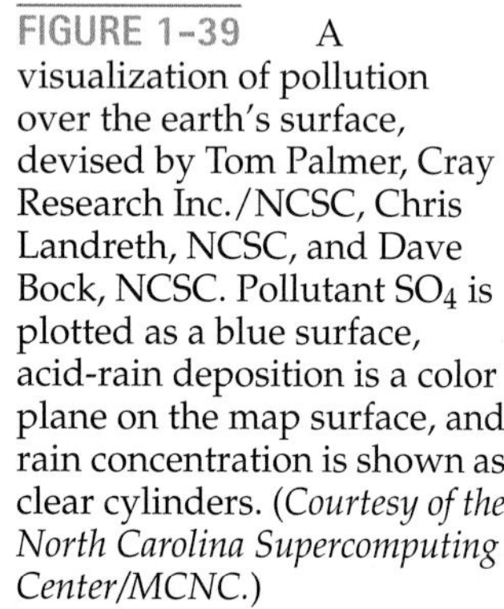

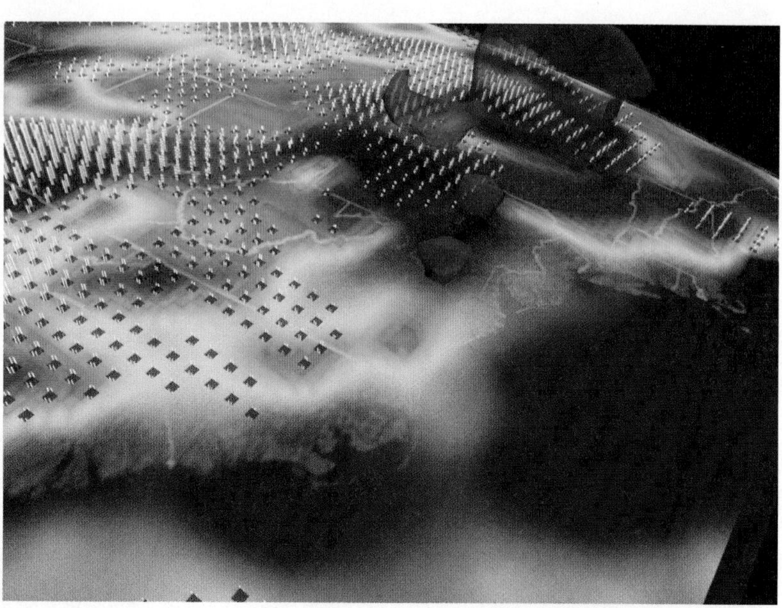

FIGURE 1-39 A visualization of pollution over the earth's surface, devised by Tom Palmer, Cray Research Inc./NCSC, Chris Landreth, NCSC, and Dave Bock, NCSC. Pollutant SO_4 is plotted as a blue surface, acid-rain deposition is a color plane on the map surface, and rain concentration is shown as clear cylinders. (*Courtesy of the North Carolina Supercomputing Center/MCNC.*)

FIGURE 1-40 One frame of an animation sequence showing the development of a corn ear. (*Courtesy of the National Center for Supercomputing Applications, University of Illinois at Urbana-Champaign.*)

FIGURE 1-41 A visualization of the reconstruction of the ruins at Chaco Canyon, Arizona. (*Courtesy of Melvin L. Prueitt, Los Alamos National Laboratory. Data supplied by Stephen H. Lekson.*)

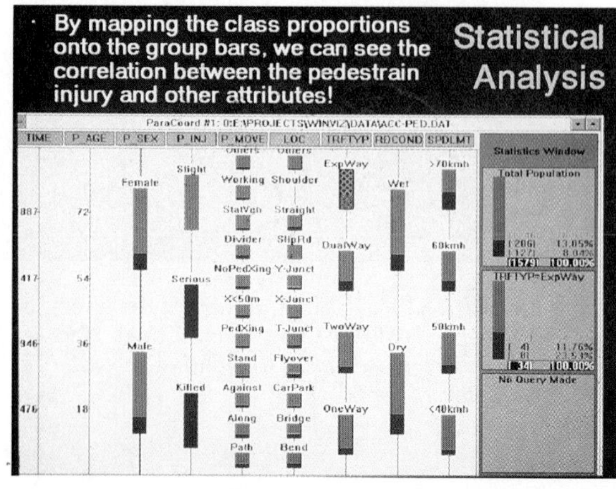

FIGURE 1-42 A prototype technique for visualizing tabular multidimensional data, called WinViz and developed by a visualization team at the Information Technology Institute, Republic of Singapore, is used here to correlate statistical information on pedestrians involved in automobile accidents. (*Courtesy of Lee-Hian Quek, Oracle Corporation, Redwood Shores, California.*)

1-5 EDUCATION AND TRAINING

Computer-generated models of physical, financial, political, social, economic, and other systems are often used as educational aids. Models of physical processes, physiological functions, population trends, or equipment, such as the color-coded diagram in Fig. 1-43, can help trainees to understand the operation of a system.

For some training applications, special hardware systems are designed. Examples of such specialized systems are the simulators for practice sessions or training of ship captains, aircraft pilots, heavy-equipment operators, and air traffic-control personnel. Some simulators have no video screens; for example, a flight simulator with only a control panel for instrument flying. But most simulators provide screens for visual displays of the external environment. Two examples of large simulators with internal viewing systems are shown in Figs. 1-44 and 1-45. Another type of viewing system is shown in Fig. 1-46(b) and (c). Here a viewing screen with multiple panels is mounted in front of the simulator, and color projectors display the flight scene on the screen panels. Figure 1-47 shows the instructor's area that can be situated behind the cockpit of a flight simulator. The keyboard is used by the instructor to input parameters affecting the airplane performance or the environment, and the path of the aircraft and other data is viewed on the monitors during a training or testing session.

Scenes generated for aircraft, naval, and spacecraft simulators are shown in Figs. 1-48 through 1-50. An automobile simulator and associated imagery is given in Fig. 1-51. Part (a) of this figure shows the interior of the simulator and the viewing screen visible through the windshield. A typical traffic street scene is shown in Fig. 1-51 (b). Although automobile simulators can be used as training systems, they are commonly employed to study the behavior of drivers in critical situations. Driver reactions in various traffic conditions can then used as a basis for optimizing vehicle design to maximize traffic safety.

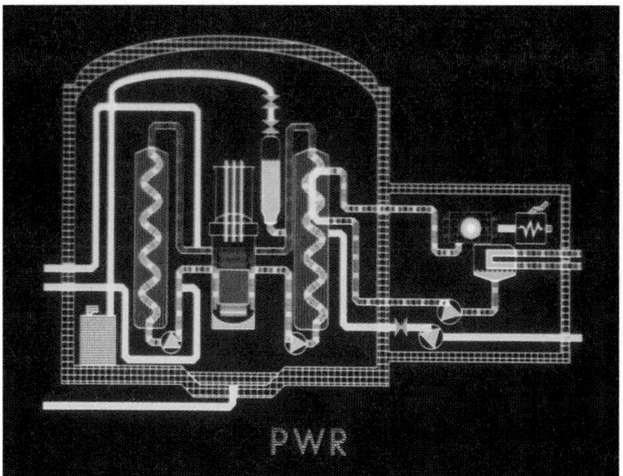

FIGURE 1-43 Color-coded diagram used to explain the operation of a nuclear reactor. (*Courtesy of Los Alamos National Laboratory.*)

FIGURE 1-44 A large, enclosed flight simulator with a full-color visual system and six degrees of freedom in its motion. (*Courtesy of Frasca International.*)

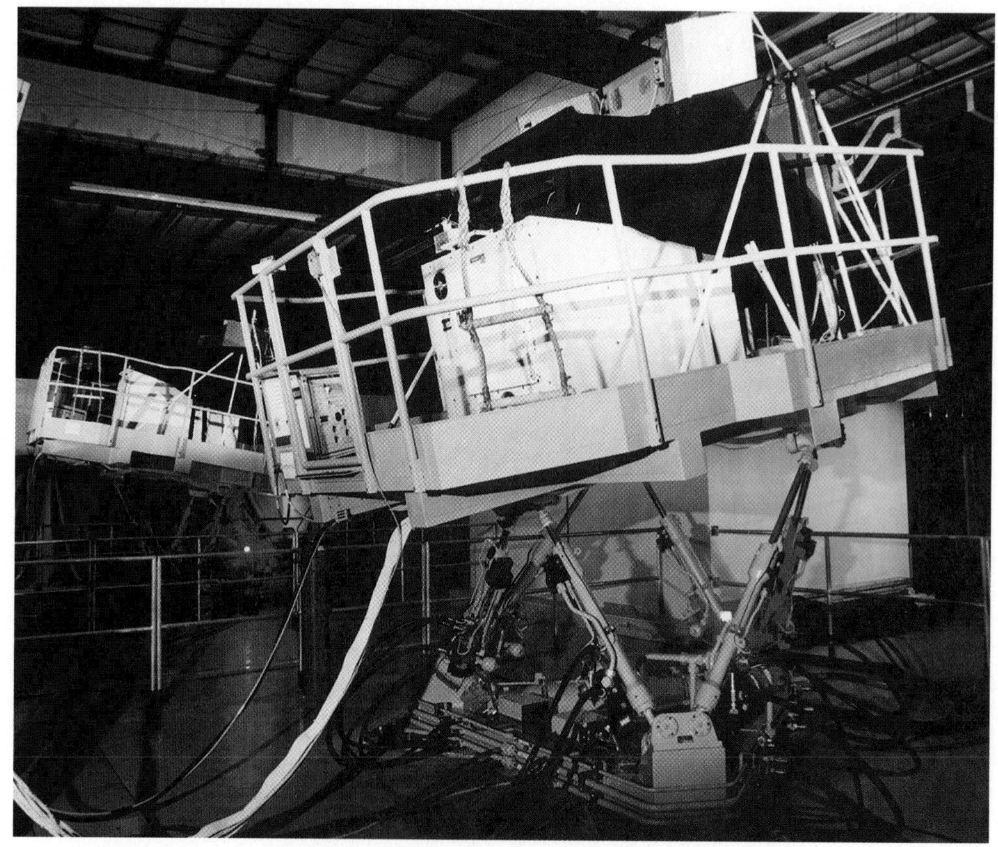

FIGURE 1-45 A military tank simulator with a visual imagery system. (*Courtesy of Mediatech and GE Aerospace.*)

(a)

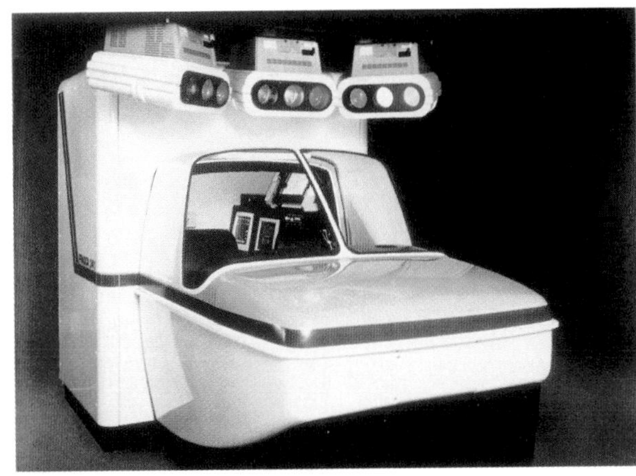

(b)

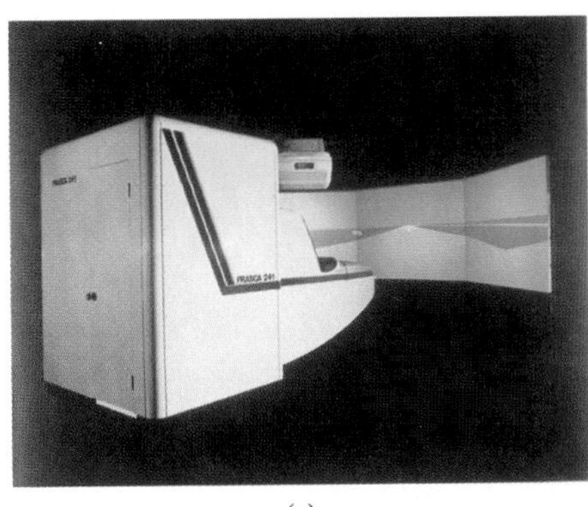

(c)

FIGURE 1-46 The cabin interior (a) of a dual-control flight simulator, and an external full-color viewing system (b) and (c) for a small flight simulator. (*Courtesy of Frasca International.*)

FIGURE 1-47 An instructor's area behind the cabin of a small flight simulator. The equipment allows the instructor to monitor flight conditions and to set airplane and environment parameters. (*Courtesy of Frasca International.*)

FIGURE 1-48 Flight-simulator imagery. (*Courtesy of Evans & Sutherland.*)

FIGURE 1-49 Imagery generated for a naval simulator. (*Courtesy of Evans & Sutherland.*)

FIGURE 1-50 Space-shuttle imagery. (*Courtesy of Mediatech and GE Aerospace.*)

(a)

(b)

FIGURE 1-51 The interior of an automobile-simulator (a) and a street-scene view (b) that can be presented to a driver. *(Courtesy of Evans & Sutherland.)*

1-6 COMPUTER ART

Both fine art and commercial art make use of computer-graphics methods. Artists now have available a variety of computer methods and tools, including specialized hardware, commercial software packages (such as Lumena), symbolic mathematics programs (such as Mathematica), CAD packages, desktop publishing software, and animation systems that provide facilities for designing object shapes and specifying object motions.

Figure 1-52 gives a figurative representation of the use of a **paintbrush program** that allows an artist to "paint" pictures on the screen of a video monitor.

FIGURE 1-52 Cartoon drawing produced with a paintbrush program, symbolically illustrating an artist at work on a video monitor. *(Courtesy of Gould Inc., Imaging & Graphics Division, and Aurora Imaging.)*

(a)

(b)

FIGURE 1-53 Cartoon demonstrations of an "artist" creating a picture with a paintbrush system. In (a), the picture is drawn on a graphics tablet as elves watch the development of the image on the video screen. In (b), the artist and elves are superimposed on the famous Thomas Nast drawing of Saint Nicholas, which was input to the system with a video camera, then scaled and positioned. (*Courtesy of Gould Inc., Imaging & Graphics Division, and Aurora Imaging.*)

FIGURE 1-54 A Van Gogh look-alike created by graphics artist Elizabeth O'Rourke with a cordless, pressure-sensitive stylus. (*Courtesy of Wacom Technology Corporation.*)

Actually, the picture is usually painted electronically on a graphics tablet (digitizer) using a stylus, which can simulate different brush strokes, brush widths, and colors. Using a paintbrush program, a cartoonist created the characters in Fig. 1-53, who seem to be busy on a creation of their own.

A paintbrush system, with a Wacom cordless, pressure-sensitive stylus, was used to produce the electronic painting in Fig. 1-54 that simulates the brush strokes of Van Gogh. The stylus translates changing hand pressure into variable line widths, brush sizes, and color gradations. Figure 1-55 shows a watercolor painting produced with this stylus and with software that allows the artist to create watercolor, pastel, or oil brush effects that simulate different drying times, wetness, and footprint. Figure 1-56 gives an example of paintbrush methods combined with scanned images.

FIGURE 1-55 An electronic watercolor, painted by John Derry of Time Arts, Inc. using a cordless, pressure-sensitive stylus and Lumena gouache-brush software. (*Courtesy of Wacom Technology Corporation.*)

FIGURE 1-56 The artist of this picture, entitled *Electronic Avalanche,* makes a statement about our entanglement with technology, using a personal computer with a graphics tablet and Lumena software to combine renderings of leaves, flower petals, and electronics components with scanned images. (*Courtesy of the Williams Gallery. © 1991 Joan Truckenbrod, The School of the Art Institute of Chicago.*)

Fine artists use a variety of other computer technologies to produce images. To create pictures such as the one shown in Fig. 1-57, the artist uses a combination of three-dimensional modeling packages, texture mapping, drawing programs, and CAD software. In Fig. 1-58, we have a painting produced on a pen plotter using specially designed software that can create "automatic art" without intervention from the artist.

Figure 1-59 shows an example of "mathematical" art. This artist uses a combination of mathematical functions, fractal procedures, Mathematica software, ink-jet printers, and other systems to create a variety of three-dimensional and two-dimensional shapes and stereoscopic image pairs. Another example of electronic art created with the aid of mathematical relationships is shown in Fig. 1-60. The artwork of this composer is often designed in relation to frequency variations and other parameters in a musical composition to produce a video that integrates visual and aural patterns.

Commercial art also uses these "painting" techniques for generating logos and other designs, page layouts combining text and graphics, TV advertising spots, and other applications. A workstation for producing page layouts that combine text and graphics is illustrated in Fig. 1-61.

FIGURE 1-57 From a series called "Spheres of Influence", this electronic painting (entitled *Whigmalaree*) was created with a combination of methods using a graphics tablet, three-dimensional modeling, texture mapping, and a series of geometric transformations. (*Courtesy of the Williams Gallery. © 1992 Wynne Ragland, Jr.*)

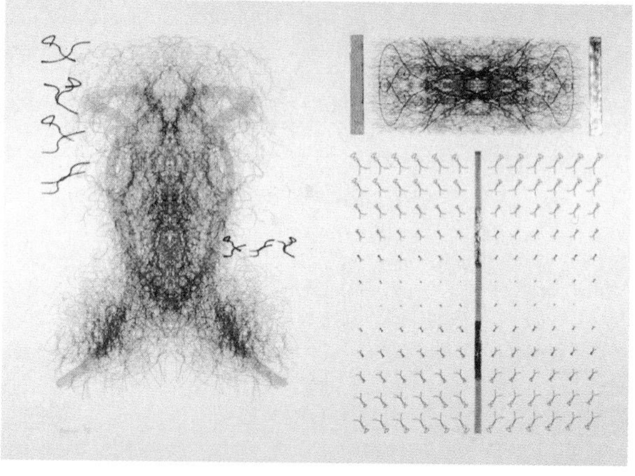

FIGURE 1-58 Electronic art output to a pen plotter from software specially designed by the artist to emulate his style. The pen plotter includes multiple pens and painting instruments, including Chinese brushes. (*Courtesy of the Williams Gallery. © Roman Verostko, Minneapolis College of Art & Design.*)

FIGURE 1-59 This creation is based on a visualization of Fermat's Last Theorem, $x^n + y^n = z^n$, with $n = 5$, by Andrew Hanson, Department of Computer Science, Indiana University. The image was rendered using Mathematica and Wavefront software. (*Courtesy of the Williams Gallery. © 1991 Stewart Dickson.*)

FIGURE 1-60 Using mathematical functions, fractal procedures, and supercomputers, this artist-composer experiments with various designs to synthesize form and color with musical composition. (*Courtesy of Brian Evans, Vanderbilt University.*)

FIGURE 1-61 Page-layout workstation. (*Courtesy of Visual Technology.*)

FIGURE 1-62 Three-dimensional rendering for a logo. (*Courtesy of Vertigo Technology, Inc.*)

As in many other computer-graphics applications, commercial-art displays often employ photo-realistic techniques to render images of a design, product, or scene. Figure 1-62 shows an example of three-dimensional logo design, and Fig. 1-63 gives three computer-graphics images for product advertising.

Computer-generated animations are also frequently used in producing television commercials. These advertising spots are generated frame by frame, where each frame of the motion is rendered and saved as a separate image file. In each successive frame, object positions are displaced slightly to simulate the motions involved in the animation. When all frames in the animation sequence have been rendered, the frames are transferred to film or stored in a video buffer for playback. Film animations require 24 frames for each second in the animation sequence. If the animation is to be played back on a video monitor, at least 30 frames per second are required.

A common graphics method employed in many television commercials is *morphing*, where one object is transformed (metamorphosed) into another. This method has been used in TV commercials to turn an oil can into an automobile

(a)

(b)

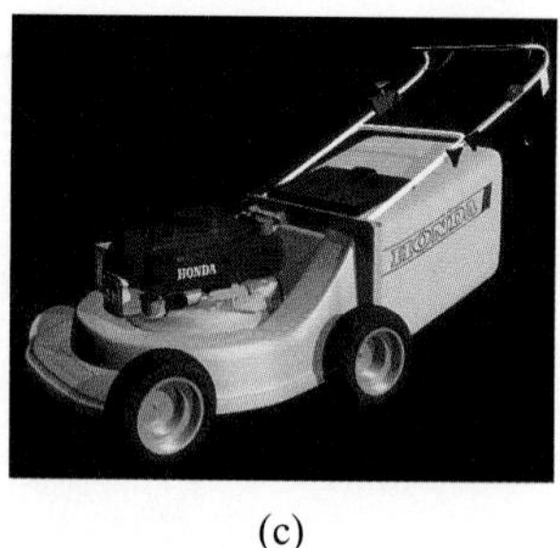

(c)

FIGURE 1-63 Product advertising using computer-generated images. (*Courtesy of* (a) *Audrey Fleisher and* (b) *and* (c) *SOFTIMAGE, Inc.*)

engine, an automobile into a tiger, a puddle of water into a tire, and one person's face into another face. An example of morphing is given in the next section (Fig. 1-69).

1-7 ENTERTAINMENT

Television productions, motion pictures, and music videos routinely use computer-graphics methods. Sometimes graphics images are combined with live actors and scenes, and sometimes the films are completely generated using computer-rendering and animation techniques.

Many TV series regularly employ computer-graphics methods to produce special effects, such as the scene in Figure 1-64 from the television series *Deep Space Nine*. Some television programs also use animation techniques to combine computer-generated figures of people, animals, or cartoon characters with the live actors in a scene or to transform an actor's face into another shape. And many programs employ computer graphics to generate buildings, terrain features, or other backgrounds for a scene. Figure 1-65, shows a highly realistic computer-generated view of thirteenth-century Dadu (now Beijing) for a Japanese television broadcast.

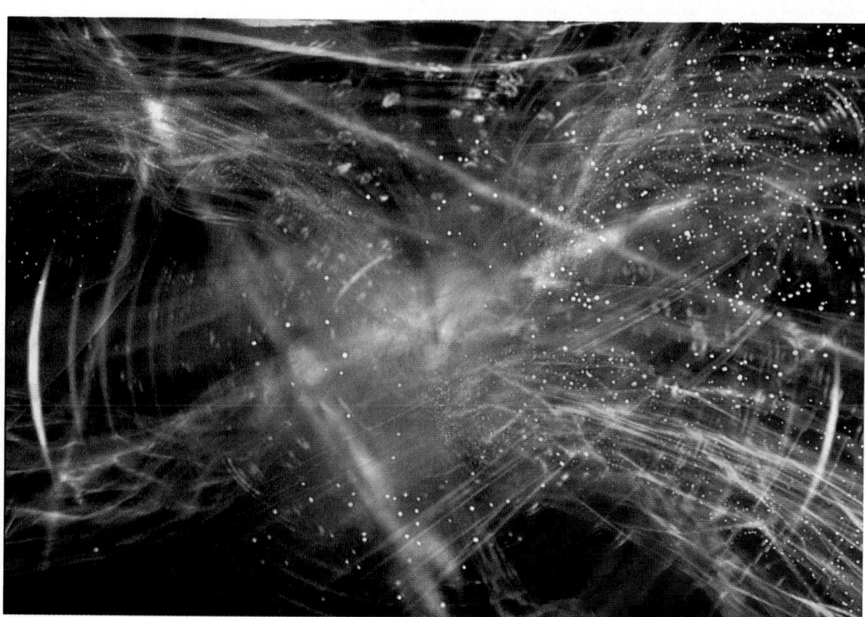

FIGURE 1-64 A graphics scene from the TV series *Deep Space Nine*. (*Courtesy of Rhythm & Hues Studios.*)

FIGURE 1-65 An image from a computer-generated reconstruction of thirteenth-century Dadu (Beijing today), created for a Japanese broadcast by Taisei Corporation (Tokyo, Japan) and rendered with TDI software. *(Courtesy of Thomson Digital Image, Inc.)*

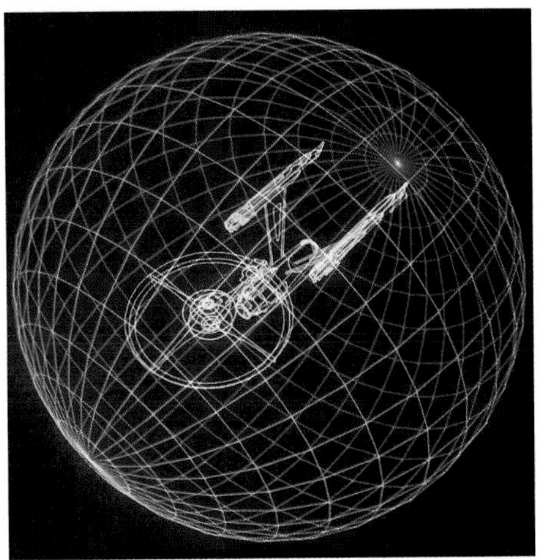

FIGURE 1-66 Graphics developed for the Paramount Pictures movie *Star Trek—The Wrath of Khan.* *(Courtesy of Evans & Sutherland.)*

(a)

(b)

FIGURE 1-67 Computer-generated film scenes: (a) *Red's Dream*, *(Courtesy of Pixar.* Copyright © Pixar 1987.), and (b) *Knickknack*, *(Courtesy of Pixar.* Copyright © Pixar 1989.)

Computer-generated special effects, animations, characters, and scenes are widely used in todays motion pictures. Figure 1-66 illustrates a preliminary computer-graphics scene generated for the movie *Star Trek—The Wrath of Khan.* Rendering methods are then applied to the wire-frame forms for the planet and spaceship in this illustration to produce the final surface appearances of the objects that are shown in the film. Advanced computer-modeling and surface-rendering methods were employed in two award-winning short films to produce the scenes shown in Fig. 1-67. Other films employ computer modeling, rendering, and animation to produce an entire human-like cast of characters. Photo-realistic techniques are employed in such films to give the computer-generated "actors" flesh tones,

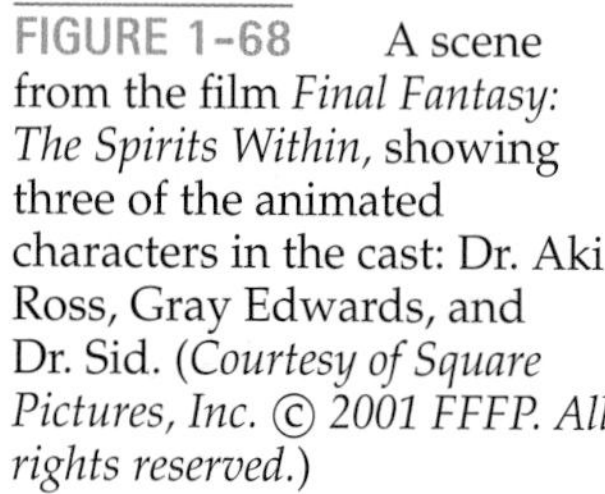

FIGURE 1-68 A scene from the film *Final Fantasy: The Spirits Within,* showing three of the animated characters in the cast: Dr. Aki Ross, Gray Edwards, and Dr. Sid. (*Courtesy of Square Pictures, Inc. © 2001 FFFP. All rights reserved.*)

(a)

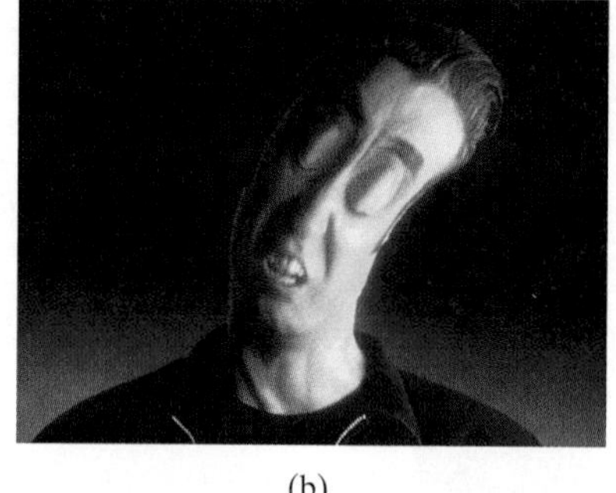

(b)

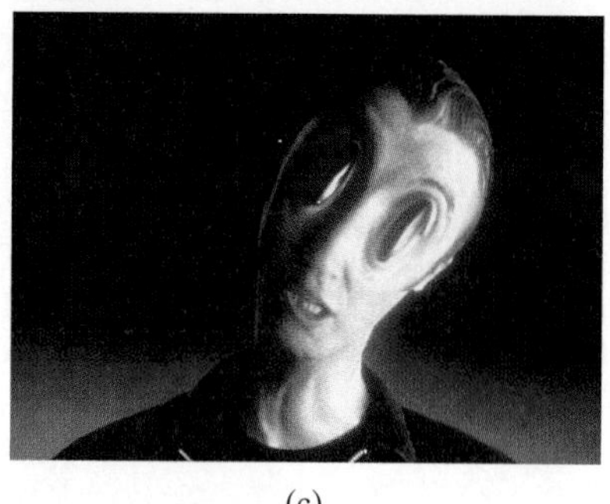

(c)

(d)

(e)

FIGURE 1-69 Examples of morphing from the David Byrne video *She's Mad.* (*Courtesy of David Byrne, Index Video, and Pacific Data Images.*)

realistic facial features, and skin imperfections such as moles, sunspots, freckles, and acne. Figure 1-68 shows a scene from the film *Final Fantasy: The Spirits Within,* which employed these photo-realistic techniques to closely simulate the appearance of a cast of human actors.

Computer-graphics methods can also be employed to simulate a human actor. Using digital files of an actor's facial features, an animation program can generate film sequences that contain a computer-generated replica of that person. In the event of an illness or accident during the filming of a motion picture, these simulation methods can be used to replace the actor in subsequent film scenes.

Music videos use computer graphics in several ways. Graphics objects can be combined with the live action, or graphics and image-processing techniques can be used to produce a transformation of one person or object into another (morphing). An example of morphing is given in the sequence of scenes in Fig. 1-69, produced for the David Byrne video *She's Mad*.

1-8 IMAGE PROCESSING

The modification or interpretation of existing pictures, such as photographs and TV scans, is called **image processing.** Although methods used in computer graphics and image processing overlap, the two areas are concerned with fundamentally different operations. In computer graphics, a computer is used to create a picture. Image-processing techniques, on the other hand, are used to improve picture quality, analyze images, or recognize visual patterns for robotics applications. However, image-processing methods are often used in computer graphics, and computer-graphics methods are frequently applied in image processing.

Typically, a photograph or other picture is digitized into an image file before image-processing methods are employed. Then digital methods can be used to rearrange picture parts, to enhance color separations, or to improve the quality of shading. An example of the application of image-processing methods to enhance the quality of a picture is shown in Fig. 1-70. These techniques are used extensively in commercial-art applications that involve the retouching and rearranging of sections of photographs and other artwork. Similar methods are used to analyze satellite photos of the earth and telescopic recordings of galactic star distributions.

Medical applications also make extensive use of image-processing techniques for picture enhancements in tomography and in simulations of surgical operations. Tomography is a technique of X-ray photography that allows cross-sectional views of physiological systems to be displayed. *Computed X-ray tomography* (CT), *position emission tomography* (PET), and *computed axial tomography* (CAT) use projection methods to reconstruct cross sections from digital data. These techniques are also used to monitor internal functions and to show cross sections

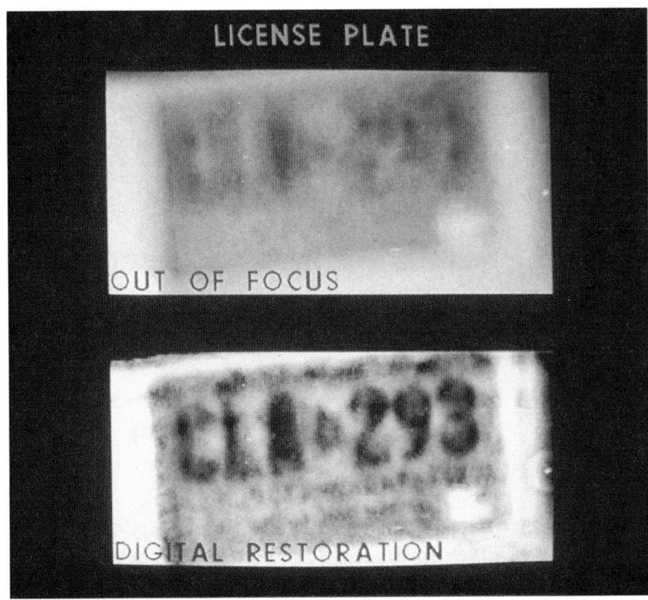

FIGURE 1-70 A blurred photograph of a license plate becomes legible after the application of image-processing techniques. *(Courtesy of Los Alamos National Laboratory.)*

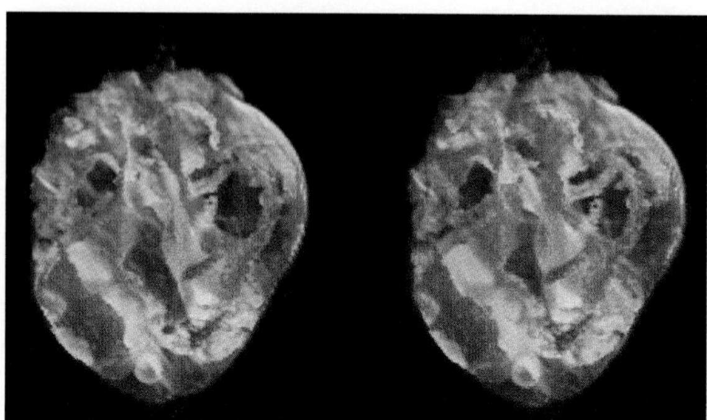

FIGURE 1-71 One frame from a computer animation visualizing cardiac activation levels within regions of a semitransparent volume-rendered dog heart. Medical data furnished by William Smith, Ed Simpson, and G. Allan Johnson, Duke University. Image-rendering software provided by Tom Palmer, Cray Research, Inc./NCSC. (*Courtesy of Dave Bock, North Carolina Supercomputing Center/MCNC.*)

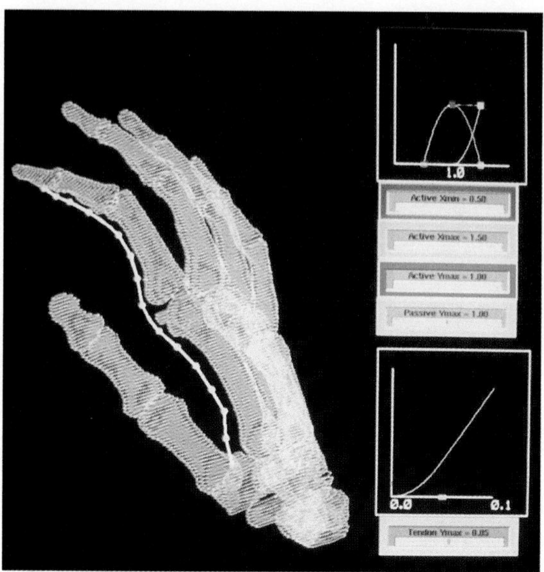

FIGURE 1-72 One image from a stereoscopic pair, showing the bones of a human hand, rendered by Inmo Yoon, D. E. Thompson, and W. N. Waggenspack, Jr., LSU, from a data set obtained with CT scans by Rehabilitation Research, GWLNHDC. These images show a possible tendon path for reconstructive surgery. (*Courtesy of IMRLAB, Mechanical Engineering, Louisiana State University.*)

during surgery. Other medical imaging techniques include ultrasonics and nuclear medicine scanners. With ultrasonics, high-frequency sound waves are used instead of X-rays to generate digital data. Nuclear medicine scanners collect digital data from radiation that is emitted by ingested radionuclides, and the data is then plotted as color-coded images.

Image processing and computer graphics are often combined in medical applications to model and study physical functions, to design artificial limbs, and to plan and practice surgery. The last application is generally referred to as *computer-aided surgery*. Two-dimensional cross sections of the body are obtained using imaging techniques. Then the slices are viewed and manipulated using graphics methods to simulate actual surgical procedures and to try out different surgical cuts. Examples of these medical applications are shown in Figs. 1-71 and 1-72.

1-9 GRAPHICAL USER INTERFACES

It is common now for applications software to provide a **graphical user interface** (GUI). A major component of a graphical interface is a window manager that allows a user to display multiple, rectangular screen areas, called display windows. Each screen display area can contain a different process, showing graphical or nongraphical information, and various methods can be used to activate a display window. Using an interactive pointing device, such as a mouse, we can active a display window on some systems by positioning the screen cursor within the window display area and pressing the left mouse button. With other systems, we may need to click on the title bar at the top of the display window.

FIGURE 1-73 A graphical user interface, showing multiple display windows, menus, and icons. (*Courtesy of Image-In Corporation.*)

Interfaces also display menus and icons for selection of a display window, a processing option, or a parameter value. An **icon** is a graphical symbol that is often designed to suggest the option it represents. The advantages of icons are that they take up less screen space than corresponding textual descriptions and they can be understood more quickly if well designed. A display window can often be converted to or from an icon representation, and menus can contain lists of both textual descriptions and icons.

Figure 1-73 illustrates a typical graphical interface, containing multiple display windows, menus, and icons. In this example, the menus allow selection of processing options, color values, and graphics parameters. The icons represent options for painting, drawing, zooming, typing text strings, and other operations connected with picture construction.

1-10 SUMMARY

We have surveyed many of the areas in which computer graphics is applied, including data graphing, CAD, virtual reality, scientific visualization, education, art, entertainment, image processing, and graphical user interfaces. However, many other fields were not mentioned, and we could have filled this book with examples from the many other applications areas. In the following chapters, we explore the equipment and methods used in the applications discussed in this chapter, as well as various other applications.

REFERENCES

Applications of graphical methods in various areas, including art, science, mathematics, and technology, are treated in Bouquet (1978), Yessios (1979), Gardner and Nelson (1983), Grotch (1983), Tufte (1983 and 1990), Wolfram (1984), Huitric and Nahas (1985), Glassner (1989), and Hearn and Baker (1991). Graphics methods for visualizing music are given in Mitroo, Herman, and Badler (1979). Detailed discussions of computer-aided design and manufacturing (CAD/CAM) in various industries are presented in Pao (1984). Graphics techniques for flight simulators are presented in Schachter (1983). Fu and Rosenfeld (1984) discuss simulation of vision, and Weinberg (1978) gives an account of space-shuttle simulation. Graphics icon and symbol concepts are presented in Lodding (1983) and in Loomis, et al. (1983). For additional information on medical applications see Hawrylyshyn, Tasker, and Organ (1977); Preston, Fagan, Huang, and Pryor (1984); and Rhodes, et al. (1983).

CHAPTER 2

Overview of Graphics Systems

A wide, curved-screen, computer-graphics presentation system and its control desk.
(Courtesy of Silicon Graphics, Inc. and Trimension Systems. © 2003 SGI. All rights reserved.)

The power and utility of computer graphics is widely recognized, and a broad range of graphics hardware and software systems are now available for applications in virtually all fields. Graphics capabilities for both two-dimensional and three-dimensional applications are now common, even on general-purpose computers and handheld calculators. With personal computers, we can use a variety of interactive input devices and graphics software packages. For higher-quality applications, we can choose from a number of sophisticated special-purpose graphics hardware systems and technologies. In this chapter, we explore the basic features of graphics hardware components and graphics software packages.

2-1 VIDEO DISPLAY DEVICES

Typically, the primary output device in a graphics system is a video monitor (Fig. 2-1). The operation of most video monitors is based on the standard **cathode-ray tube** (**CRT**) design, but several other technologies exist and solid-state monitors may eventually predominate.

FIGURE 2-1 A computer-graphics workstation. *(Courtesy of Silicon Graphics, Inc., Why Not Films, and 525 Post Production. © 2003 SGI. All rights reserved.)*

Refresh Cathode-Ray Tubes

Figure 2-2 illustrates the basic operation of a CRT. A beam of electrons (*cathode rays*), emitted by an electron gun, passes through focusing and deflection systems that direct the beam toward specified positions on the phosphor-coated screen. The phosphor then emits a small spot of light at each position contacted by the electron beam. Because the light emitted by the phosphor fades very rapidly, some method is needed for maintaining the screen picture. One way to do this is to store the picture information as a charge distribution within the CRT. This charge distribution can then be used to keep the phosphors activated. However, the most common method now employed for maintaining phosphor glow is to redraw the picture repeatedly by quickly directing the electron beam back over the same screen points. This type of display is called a **refresh CRT,** and the frequency at which a picture is redrawn on the screen is referred to as the **refresh rate.**

The primary components of an electron gun in a CRT are the heated metal cathode and a control grid (Fig. 2-3). Heat is supplied to the cathode by directing a current through a coil of wire, called the filament, inside the cylindrical cathode structure. This causes electrons to be "boiled off" the hot cathode surface. In the vacuum inside the CRT envelope, the free, negatively charged electrons are then accelerated toward the phosphor coating by a high positive voltage. The accelerating voltage can be generated with a positively charged metal coating on the inside of the CRT envelope near the phosphor screen, or an accelerating anode, as in Fig. 2-3, can be used to provide the positive voltage. Sometimes the electron gun is designed so that the accelerating anode and focusing system are within the same unit.

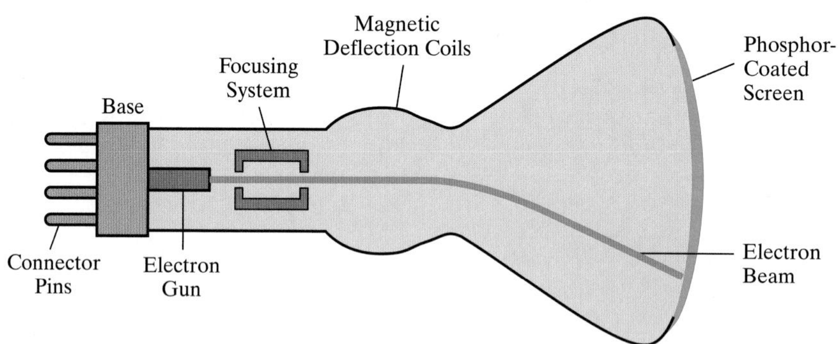

FIGURE 2-2 Basic design of a magnetic-deflection CRT.

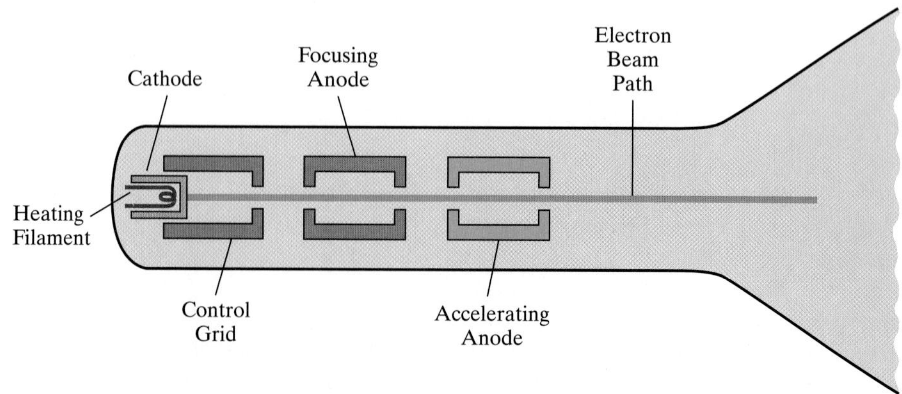

FIGURE 2-3 Operation of an electron gun with an accelerating anode.

Intensity of the electron beam is controlled by the voltage at the control grid, which is a metal cylinder that fits over the cathode. A high negative voltage applied to the control grid will shut off the beam by repelling electrons and stopping them from passing through the small hole at the end of the control-grid structure. A smaller negative voltage on the control grid simply decreases the number of electrons passing through. Since the amount of light emitted by the phosphor coating depends on the number of electrons striking the screen, the brightness of a display point is controlled by varying the voltage on the control grid. This brightness, or intensity level, is specified for individual screen positions with graphics software commands, as discussed in Chapter 3.

The focusing system in a CRT forces the electron beam to converge to a small cross section as it strikes the phosphor. Otherwise, the electrons would repel each other, and the beam would spread out as it approaches the screen. Focusing is accomplished with either electric or magnetic fields. With electrostatic focusing, the electron beam is passed through a positively charged metal cylinder so that electrons along the centerline of the cylinder are in an equilibrium position. This arrangement forms an electrostatic lens, as shown in Fig. 2-3, and the electron beam is focused at the center of the screen in the same way that an optical lens focuses a beam of light at a particular focal distance. Similar lens focusing effects can be accomplished with a magnetic field set up by a coil mounted around the outside of the CRT envelope, and magnetic lens focusing usually produces the smallest spot size on the screen.

Additional focusing hardware is used in high-precision systems to keep the beam in focus at all screen positions. The distance that the electron beam must travel to different points on the screen varies because the radius of curvature for most CRTs is greater than the distance from the focusing system to the screen center. Therefore, the electron beam will be focused properly only at the center of the screen. As the beam moves to the outer edges of the screen, displayed images become blurred. To compensate for this, the system can adjust the focusing according to the screen position of the beam.

As with focusing, deflection of the electron beam can be controlled with either electric or magnetic fields. Cathode-ray tubes are now commonly constructed with magnetic-deflection coils mounted on the outside of the CRT envelope, as illustrated in Fig. 2-2. Two pairs of coils are used for this purpose. One pair is mounted on the top and bottom of the CRT neck, and the other pair is mounted on opposite sides of the neck. The magnetic field produced by each pair of coils results in a transverse deflection force that is perpendicular to both the direction of the magnetic field and the direction of travel of the electron beam. Horizontal deflection is accomplished with one pair of coils, and vertical deflection with the other pair. The proper deflection amounts are attained by adjusting the current through the coils. When electrostatic deflection is used, two pairs of parallel plates are mounted inside the CRT envelope. One pair of plates is mounted horizontally to control vertical deflection, and the other pair is mounted vertically to control horizontal deflection (Fig. 2-4).

Spots of light are produced on the screen by the transfer of the CRT beam energy to the phosphor. When the electrons in the beam collide with the phosphor coating, they are stopped and their kinetic energy is absorbed by the phosphor. Part of the beam energy is converted by friction into heat energy, and the remainder causes electrons in the phosphor atoms to move up to higher quantum-energy levels. After a short time, the "excited" phosphor electrons begin dropping back to their stable ground state, giving up their extra energy as small quantums of light energy called photons. What we see on the screen is the combined effect of all

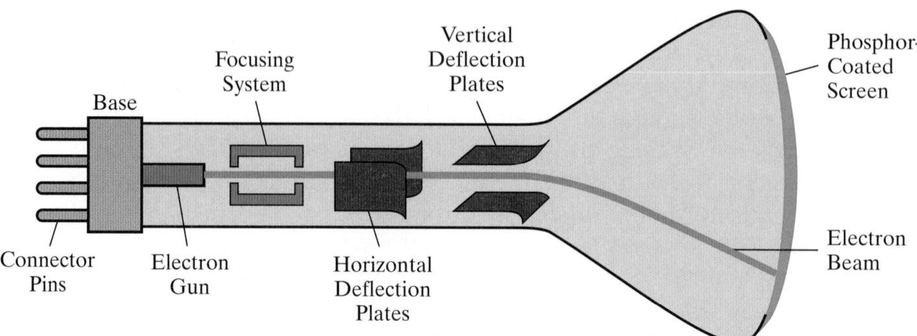

FIGURE 2-4 Electrostatic deflection of the electron beam in a CRT.

the electron light emissions: a glowing spot that quickly fades after all the excited phosphor electrons have returned to their ground energy level. The frequency (or color) of the light emitted by the phosphor is proportional to the energy difference between the excited quantum state and the ground state.

Different kinds of phosphors are available for use in CRTs. Besides color, a major difference between phosphors is their **persistence:** how long they continue to emit light (that is, how long before all excited electrons have returned to the ground state) after the CRT beam is removed. Persistence is defined as the time that it takes the emitted light from the screen to decay to one-tenth of its original intensity. Lower-persistence phosphors require higher refresh rates to maintain a picture on the screen without flicker. A phosphor with low persistence can be useful for animation, while high-persistence phosphors are better suited for displaying highly complex, static pictures. Although some phosphors have persistence values greater than 1 second, general-purpose graphics monitors are usually constructed with persistence in the range from 10 to 60 microseconds.

FIGURE 2-5 Intensity distribution of an illuminated phosphor spot on a CRT screen.

Figure 2-5 shows the intensity distribution of a spot on the screen. The intensity is greatest at the center of the spot, and it decreases with a Gaussian distribution out to the edges of the spot. This distribution corresponds to the cross-sectional electron density distribution of the CRT beam.

The maximum number of points that can be displayed without overlap on a CRT is referred to as the **resolution.** A more precise definition of resolution is the number of points per centimeter that can be plotted horizontally and vertically, although it is often simply stated as the total number of points in each direction. Spot intensity has a Gaussian distribution (Fig. 2-5), so two adjacent spots will appear distinct as long as their separation is greater than the diameter at which each spot has an intensity of about 60 percent of that at the center of the spot. This overlap position is illustrated in Fig. 2-6. Spot size also depends on intensity. As more electrons are accelerated toward the phosphor per second, the diameters of the CRT beam and the illuminated spot increase. In addition, the increased excitation energy tends to spread to neighboring phosphor atoms not directly in the path of the beam, which further increases the spot diameter. Thus, resolution of a CRT is dependent on the type of phosphor, the intensity to be displayed, and the focusing and deflection systems. Typical resolution on high-quality systems is 1280 by 1024, with higher resolutions available on many systems. High-resolution systems are often referred to as *high-definition systems*. The physical size of a graphics monitor, on the other hand, is given as the length of the screen diagonal, with sizes varying from about 12 inches to 27 inches or more. A CRT monitor can be attached to a variety of computer systems, so the number of screen points that can actually be plotted also depends on the capabilities of the system to which it is attached.

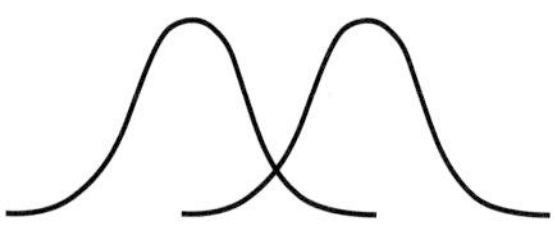

FIGURE 2-6 Two illuminated phosphor spots are distinguishable when their separation is greater than the diameter at which a spot intensity has fallen to 60 percent of maximum.

Raster-Scan Displays

The most common type of graphics monitor employing a CRT is the **raster-scan display,** based on television technology. In a raster-scan system, the electron beam is swept across the screen, one row at a time, from top to bottom. Each row is referred to as a **scan line.** As the electron beam moves across a scan line, the beam intensity is turned on and off (or set to some intermediate value) to create a pattern of illuminated spots. Picture definition is stored in a memory area called the **refresh buffer** or **frame buffer,** where the term **frame** refers to the total screen area. This memory area holds the set of color values for the screen points. These stored color values are then retrieved from the refresh buffer and used to control the intensity of the electron beam as it moves from spot to spot across the screen. In this way, the picture is "painted" on the screen one scan line at a time, as demonstrated in Fig. 2-7. Each screen spot that can be illuminated by the electron beam is referred to as a **pixel** or **pel** (shortened forms of **picture element**). Since the refresh buffer is used to store the set of screen color values, it is also sometimes called a **color buffer.** Also, other kinds of pixel information, besides color, are stored in buffer locations, so all the different buffer areas are sometimes referred to collectively as the "frame buffer". The capability of a raster-scan system to store color information for each screen point makes it well suited for the realistic display of scenes containing subtle shading and color patterns. Home television sets and printers are examples of other systems using raster-scan methods.

Raster systems are commonly characterized by their resolution, which is the number of pixel positions that can be plotted. Another property of video monitors is **aspect ratio,** which is now often defined as the number of pixel columns divided by the number of scan lines that can be displayed by the system. (Sometimes the term aspect ratio is used to refer to the number of scan lines divided by the number of pixel columns.) Aspect ratio can also be described as the number of horizontal

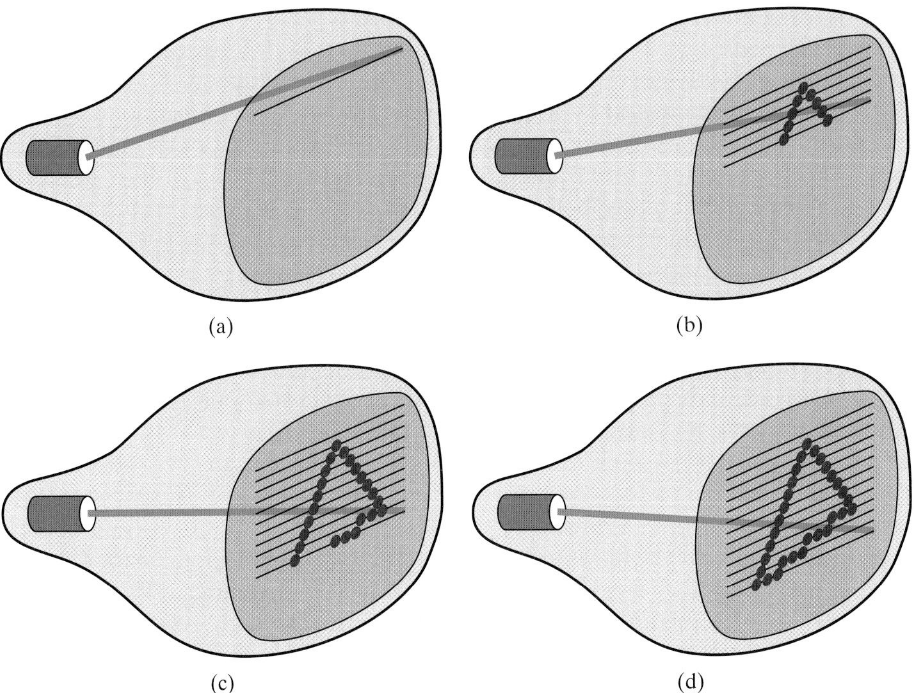

FIGURE 2-7 A raster-scan system displays an object as a set of discrete points across each scan line.

points to vertical points (or vice versa) necessary to produce equal-length lines in both directions on the screen. Thus, an aspect ratio of 4/3, for example, means that a horizontal line plotted with four points has the same length as a vertical line plotted with three points, where line length is measured in some physical units such as centimeters. Similarly, the aspect ratio of any rectangle (including the total screen area) can be defined to be the width of the rectangle divided by its height.

The range of colors or shades of gray that can be displayed on a raster system depends on both the types of phosphor used in the CRT and the number of bits per pixel available in the frame buffer. For a simple black-and-white system, each screen point is either on or off, so only one bit per pixel is needed to control the intensity of screen positions. A bit value of 1, for example, indicates that the electron beam is to be turned on at that position, and a value of 0 turns the beam off. Additional bits allow the intensity of the electron beam to be varied over a range of values between "on" and "off". Up to 24 bits per pixel are included in high-quality systems, which can require several megabytes of storage for the frame buffer, depending on the resolution of the system. For example, a system with 24 bits per pixel and a screen resolution of 1024 by 1024 requires 3 megabytes of storage for the refresh buffer. The number of bits per pixel in a frame buffer is sometimes referred to as either the **depth** of the buffer area or the number of **bit planes.** Also, a frame buffer with one bit per pixel is commonly called a **bitmap,** and a frame buffer with multiple bits per pixel is a **pixmap.** But the terms bitmap and pixmap are also used to describe other rectangular arrays, where a bitmap is any pattern of binary values and a pixmap is a multicolor pattern.

As each screen refresh takes place, we tend to see each frame as a smooth continuation of the patterns in the previous frame, as long as the refresh rate is not too low. Below about 24 frames per second, we can usually perceive a gap between successive screen images, and the picture appears to flicker. Old silent films, for example, show this effect because they were photographed at a rate of 16 frames per second. When sound systems were developed in the 1920s, motion-picture film rates increased to 24 frames per second, which removed flickering and the accompanying jerky movements of the actors. Early raster-scan computer systems were designed with a refresh rate of about 30 frames per second. This produces reasonably good results, but picture quality is improved, up to a point, with higher refresh rates on a video monitor because the display technology on the monitor is basically different from that of film. A film projector can maintain the continuous display of a film frame until the next frame is brought into view. But on a video monitor, a phosphor spot begins to decay as soon as it is illuminated. Therefore, current raster-scan displays perform refreshing at the rate of 60 to 80 frames per second, although some systems now have refresh rates of up to 120 frames per second. And some graphics systems have been designed with a variable refresh rate. For example, a higher refresh rate could be selected for a stereoscopic application so that two views of a scene (one from each eye position) can be alternately displayed without flicker. But other methods, such as multiple frame buffers, are typically used for such applications.

Sometimes, refresh rates are described in units of cycles per second, or Hertz (Hz), where a cycle corresponds to one frame. Using these units, we would describe a refresh rate of 60 frames per second as simply 60 Hz. At the end of each scan line, the electron beam returns to the left side of the screen to begin displaying the next scan line. The return to the left of the screen, after refreshing each scan line, is called the **horizontal retrace** of the electron beam. And at the end of each frame (displayed in $\frac{1}{80}$ to $\frac{1}{60}$ of a second), the electron beam returns to the top left corner of the screen (**vertical retrace**) to begin the next frame.

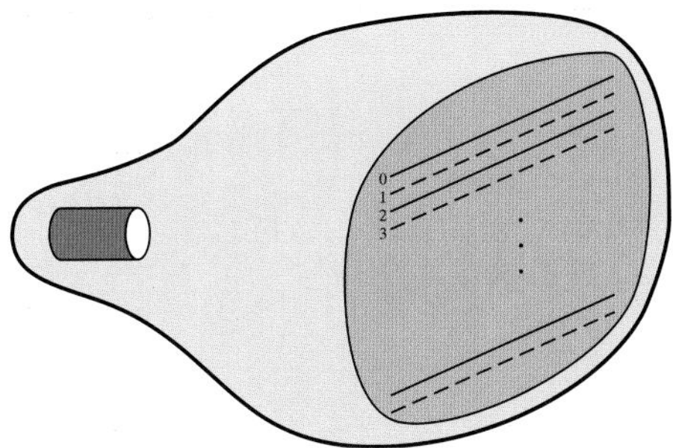

FIGURE 2-8 Interlacing scan lines on a raster-scan display. First, all points on the even-numbered (solid) scan lines are displayed; then all points along the odd-numbered (dashed) lines are displayed.

On some raster-scan systems and TV sets, each frame is displayed in two passes using an *interlaced* refresh procedure. In the first pass, the beam sweeps across every other scan line from top to bottom. After the vertical retrace, the beam then sweeps out the remaining scan lines (Fig. 2-8). Interlacing of the scan lines in this way allows us to see the entire screen displayed in one-half the time it would have taken to sweep across all the lines at once from top to bottom. This technique is primarily used with slower refresh rates. On an older, 30 frame-per-second, non-interlaced display, for instance, some flicker is noticeable. But with interlacing, each of the two passes can be accomplished in $\frac{1}{60}$ of a second, which brings the refresh rate nearer to 60 frames per second. This is an effective technique for avoiding flicker—provided that adjacent scan lines contain similar display information.

Random-Scan Displays

When operated as a **random-scan display** unit, a CRT has the electron beam directed only to those parts of the screen where a picture is to be displayed. Pictures are generated as line drawings, with the electron beam tracing out the component lines one after the other. For this reason, random-scan monitors are also referred to as **vector displays** (or **stroke-writing displays** or **calligraphic displays**). The component lines of a picture can be drawn and refreshed by a random-scan system in any specified order (Fig. 2-9). A pen plotter operates in a similar way and is an example of a random-scan, hard-copy device.

Refresh rate on a random-scan system depends on the number of lines to be displayed on that system. Picture definition is now stored as a set of line-drawing commands in an area of memory referred to as the **display list, refresh display file, vector file,** or **display program.** To display a specified picture, the system cycles through the set of commands in the display file, drawing each component line in turn. After all line-drawing commands have been processed, the system cycles back to the first line command in the list. Random-scan displays are designed to draw all the component lines of a picture 30 to 60 times each second, with up to 100,000 "short" lines in the display list. When a small set of lines is to be displayed, each refresh cycle is delayed to avoid very high refresh rates, which could burn out the phosphor.

Random-scan systems were designed for line-drawing applications, such as architectural and engineering layouts, and they cannot display realistic shaded scenes. Since picture definition is stored as a set of line-drawing instructions rather than as a set of intensity values for all screen points, vector displays generally have higher resolutions than raster systems. Also, vector displays produce smooth line drawings because the CRT beam directly follows the line path. A raster system, by

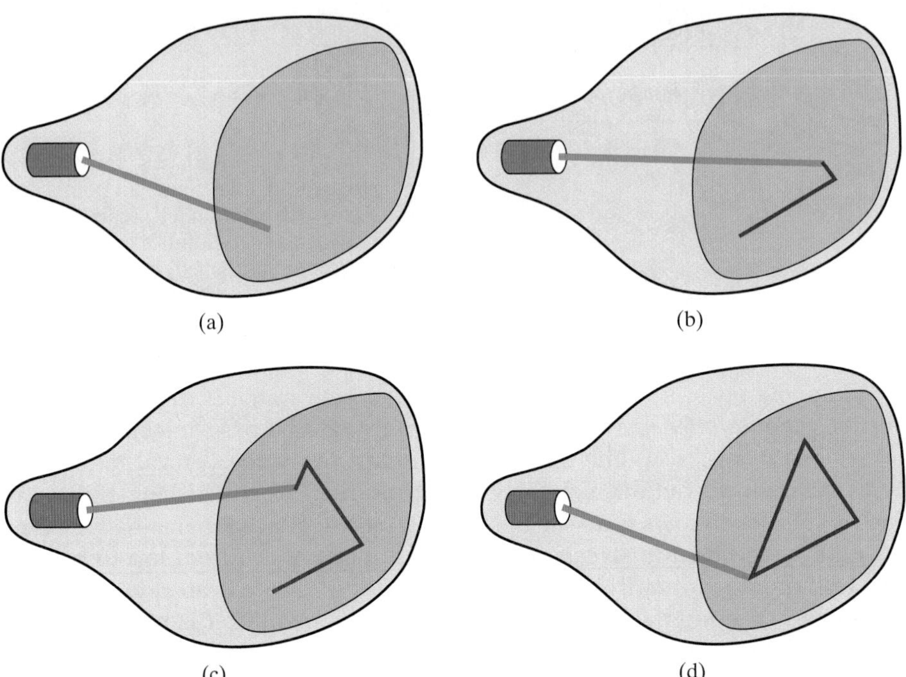

FIGURE 2-9 A random-scan system draws the component lines of an object in any specified order.

contrast, produces jagged lines that are plotted as discrete point sets. However, the greater flexibility and improved line-drawing capabilities of raster systems have resulted in the abandonment of vector technology.

Color CRT Monitors

A CRT monitor displays color pictures by using a combination of phosphors that emit different-colored light. The emitted light from the different phosphors merges to form a single perceived color, which depends on the particular set of phosphors that have been excited.

One way to display color pictures is to coat the screen with layers of different-colored phosphors. The emitted color depends on how far the electron beam penetrates into the phosphor layers. This approach, called the **beam-penetration** method, typically used only two phosphor layers: red and green. A beam of slow electrons excites only the outer red layer, but a beam of very fast electrons penetrates through the red layer and excites the inner green layer. At intermediate beam speeds, combinations of red and green light are emitted to show two additional colors, orange and yellow. The speed of the electrons, and hence the screen color at any point, is controlled by the beam acceleration voltage. Beam penetration has been an inexpensive way to produce color, but only a limited number of colors are possible, and picture quality is not as good as with other methods.

Shadow-mask methods are commonly used in raster-scan systems (including color TV) since they produce a much wider range of colors than the beam-penetration method. This approach is based on the way that we seem to perceive colors as combinations of red, green, and blue components, called the **RGB color model.** Thus, a shadow-mask CRT uses three phosphor color dots at each pixel position. One phosphor dot emits a red light, another emits a green light, and the third emits a blue light. This type of CRT has three electron guns, one for each

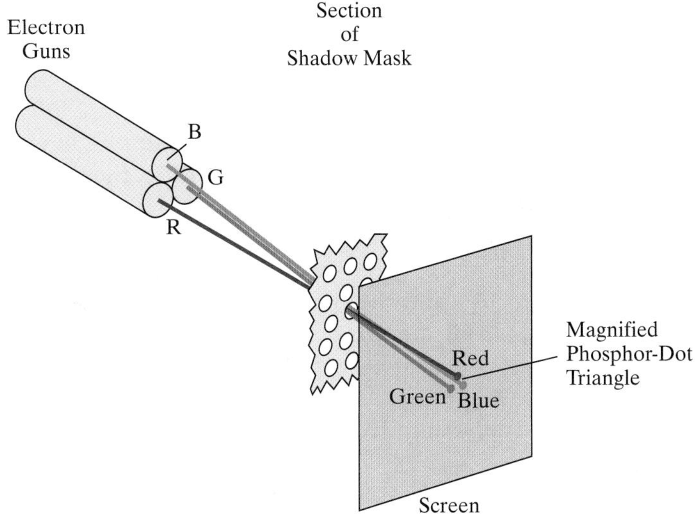

FIGURE 2-10 Operation of a delta-delta, shadow-mask CRT. Three electron guns, aligned with the triangular color-dot patterns on the screen, are directed to each dot triangle by a shadow mask.

color dot, and a shadow-mask grid just behind the phosphor-coated screen. The light emitted from the three phosphors results in a small spot of color at each pixel position, since our eyes tend to merge the light emitted from the three dots into one composite color. Figure 2-10 illustrates the *delta-delta* shadow-mask method, commonly used in color CRT systems. The three electron beams are deflected and focused as a group onto the shadow mask, which contains a series of holes aligned with the phosphor-dot patterns. When the three beams pass through a hole in the shadow mask, they activate a dot triangle, which appears as a small color spot on the screen. The phosphor dots in the triangles are arranged so that each electron beam can activate only its corresponding color dot when it passes through the shadow mask. Another configuration for the three electron guns is an *in-line* arrangement in which the three electron guns, and the corresponding red-green-blue color dots on the screen, are aligned along one scan line instead of in a triangular pattern. This in-line arrangement of electron guns is easier to keep in alignment and is commonly used in high-resolution color CRTs.

We obtain color variations in a shadow-mask CRT by varying the intensity levels of the three electron beams. By turning off two of the three guns, we get only the color coming from the single activated phosphor (red, green, or blue). When all three dots are activated with equal beam intensities, we see a white color. Yellow is produced with equal intensities from the green and red dots only, magenta is produced with equal blue and red intensities, and cyan shows up when blue and green are activated equally. In an inexpensive system, each of the three electron beams might be restricted to either on or off, limiting displays to eight colors. More sophisticated systems can allow intermediate intensity levels to be set for the electron beams, so that several million colors are possible.

Color graphics systems can be used with several types of CRT display devices. Some inexpensive home-computer systems and video games have been designed for use with a color TV set and an RF (radio-frequency) modulator. The purpose of the RF modulator is to simulate the signal from a broadcast TV station. This means that the color and intensity information of the picture must be combined and superimposed on the broadcast-frequency carrier signal that the TV requires as input. Then the circuitry in the TV takes this signal from the RF modulator, extracts the picture information, and paints it on the screen. As we might expect, this extra handling of the picture information by the RF modulator and TV circuitry decreases the quality of displayed images.

Composite monitors are adaptations of TV sets that allow bypass of the broadcast circuitry. These display devices still require that the picture information be combined, but no carrier signal is needed. Since picture information is combined into a composite signal and then separated by the monitor, the resulting picture quality is still not the best attainable.

Color CRTs in graphics systems are designed as **RGB monitors.** These monitors use shadow-mask methods and take the intensity level for each electron gun (red, green, and blue) directly from the computer system without any intermediate processing. High-quality raster-graphics systems have 24 bits per pixel in the frame buffer, allowing 256 voltage settings for each electron gun and nearly 17 million color choices for each pixel. An RGB color system with 24 bits of storage per pixel is generally referred to as a **full-color system** or a **true-color system.**

Flat-Panel Displays

Although most graphics monitors are still constructed with CRTs, other technologies are emerging that may soon replace CRT monitors. The term **flat-panel display** refers to a class of video devices that have reduced volume, weight, and power requirements compared to a CRT. A significant feature of flat-panel displays is that they are thinner than CRTs, and we can hang them on walls or wear them on our wrists. Since we can even write on some flat-panel displays, they are also available as pocket notepads. Some additional uses for flat-panel displays are as small TV monitors, calculator screens, pocket video-game screens, laptop computer screens, armrest movie-viewing stations on airlines, advertisement boards in elevators, and graphics displays in applications requiring rugged, portable monitors.

We can separate flat-panel displays into two categories: **emissive displays** and **nonemissive displays.** The emissive displays (or **emitters**) are devices that convert electrical energy into light. Plasma panels, thin-film electroluminescent displays, and light-emitting diodes are examples of emissive displays. Flat CRTs have also been devised, in which electron beams are accelerated parallel to the screen and then deflected 90° onto the screen. But flat CRTs have not proved to be as successful as other emissive devices. Nonemissive displays (or **nonemitters**) use optical effects to convert sunlight or light from some other source into graphics patterns. The most important example of a nonemissive flat-panel display is a liquid-crystal device.

Plasma panels, also called **gas-discharge displays,** are constructed by filling the region between two glass plates with a mixture of gases that usually includes neon. A series of vertical conducting ribbons is placed on one glass panel, and a set of horizontal conducting ribbons is built into the other glass panel (Fig. 2-11). Firing voltages applied to an intersecting pair of horizontal and vertical conductors cause the gas at the intersection of the two conductors to break down into a glowing plasma of electrons and ions. Picture definition is stored in a refresh buffer, and the firing voltages are applied to refresh the pixel positions (at the intersections of the conductors) 60 times per second. Alternating-current methods are used to provide faster application of the firing voltages and, thus, brighter displays. Separation between pixels is provided by the electric field of the conductors. Figure 2-12 shows a high-definition plasma panel. One disadvantage of plasma panels has been that they were strictly monochromatic devices, but systems are now available with multicolor capabilities.

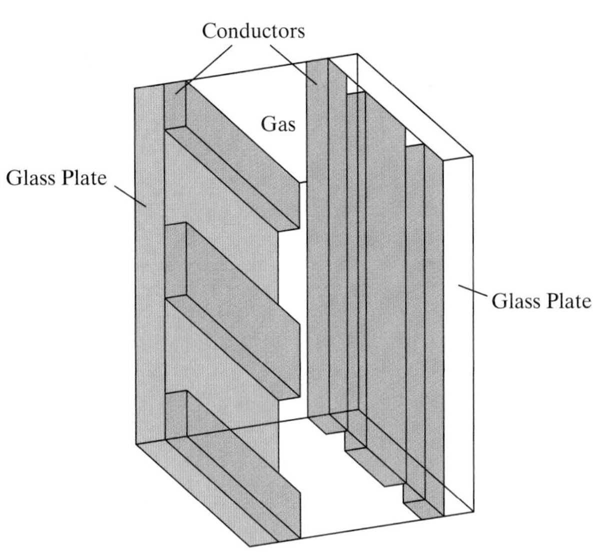

FIGURE 2-11 Basic design of a plasma-panel display device.

FIGURE 2-12 A plasma-panel display with a resolution of 2048 by 2048 and a screen diagonal of 1.5 meters. (*Courtesy of Photonics Systems.*)

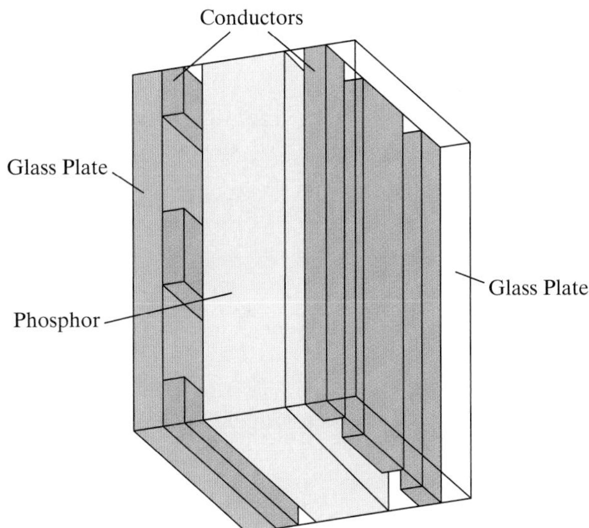

FIGURE 2-13 Basic design of a thin-film electroluminescent display device.

Thin-film electroluminescent displays are similar in construction to plasma panels. The difference is that the region between the glass plates is filled with a phosphor, such as zinc sulfide doped with manganese, instead of a gas (Fig. 2-13). When a sufficiently high voltage is applied to a pair of crossing electrodes, the phosphor becomes a conductor in the area of the intersection of the two electrodes. Electrical energy is absorbed by the manganese atoms, which then release the energy as a spot of light similar to the glowing plasma effect in a plasma panel.

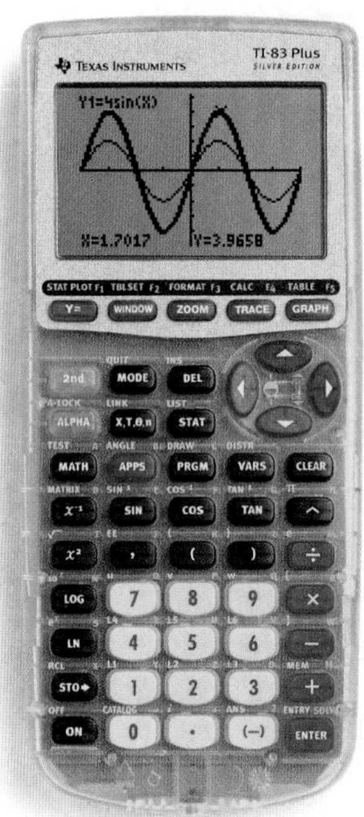

FIGURE 2-14 A handheld calculator with an LCD screen. (*Courtesy of Texas Instruments.*)

Electroluminescent displays require more power than plasma panels, and good color displays are harder to achieve.

A third type of emissive device is the **light-emitting diode** (**LED**). A matrix of diodes is arranged to form the pixel positions in the display, and picture definition is stored in a refresh buffer. As in scan-line refreshing of a CRT, information is read from the refresh buffer and converted to voltage levels that are applied to the diodes to produce the light patterns in the display.

Liquid-crystal displays (**LCDs**) are commonly used in small systems, such as laptop computers and calculators (Fig. 2-14). These nonemissive devices produce a picture by passing polarized light from the surroundings or from an internal light source through a liquid-crystal material that can be aligned to either block or transmit the light.

The term *liquid crystal* refers to the fact that these compounds have a crystalline arrangement of molecules, yet they flow like a liquid. Flat-panel displays commonly use nematic (threadlike) liquid-crystal compounds that tend to keep the long axes of the rod-shaped molecules aligned. A flat-panel display can then be constructed with a nematic liquid crystal, as demonstrated in Fig. 2-15. Two glass plates, each containing a light polarizer that is aligned at a right angle to the other plate, sandwich the liquid-crystal material. Rows of horizontal, transparent conductors are built into one glass plate, and columns of vertical conductors are put into the other plate. The intersection of two conductors defines a pixel position. Normally, the molecules are aligned as shown in the "on state" of Fig. 2-15. Polarized light passing through the material is twisted so that it will pass through the opposite polarizer. The light is then reflected back to the viewer. To turn off the

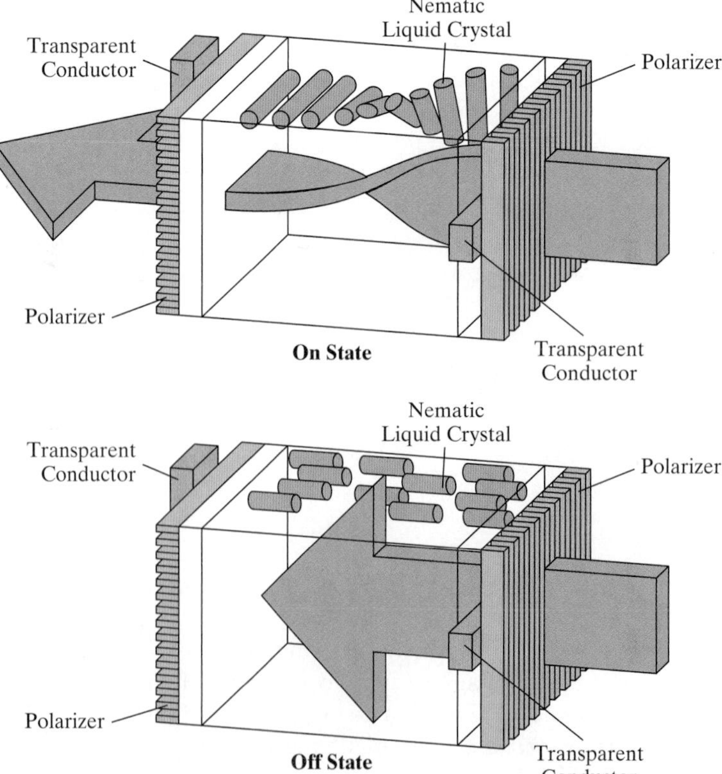

FIGURE 2-15 The light-twisting, shutter effect used in the design of most liquid-crystal display devices.

pixel, we apply a voltage to the two intersecting conductors to align the molecules so that the light is not twisted. This type of flat-panel device is referred to as a **passive-matrix** LCD. Picture definitions are stored in a refresh buffer, and the screen is refreshed at the rate of 60 frames per second, as in the emissive devices. Backlighting is also commonly applied using solid-state electronic devices, so that the system is not completely dependent on outside light sources. Colors can be displayed by using different materials or dyes and by placing a triad of color pixels at each screen location. Another method for constructing LCDs is to place a transistor at each pixel location, using thin-film transistor technology. The transistors are used to control the voltage at pixel locations and to prevent charge from gradually leaking out of the liquid-crystal cells. These devices are called **active-matrix** displays.

Three-Dimensional Viewing Devices

Graphics monitors for the display of three-dimensional scenes have been devised using a technique that reflects a CRT image from a vibrating, flexible mirror (Fig. 2-16). As the varifocal mirror vibrates, it changes focal length. These vibrations are synchronized with the display of an object on a CRT so that each point on the object is reflected from the mirror into a spatial position corresponding to the distance of that point from a specified viewing location. This allows us to walk around an object or scene and view it from different sides.

Figure 2-17 shows the Genisco SpaceGraph system, which uses a vibrating mirror to project three-dimensional objects into a 25-cm by 25-cm by 25-cm volume. This system is also capable of displaying two-dimensional cross-sectional

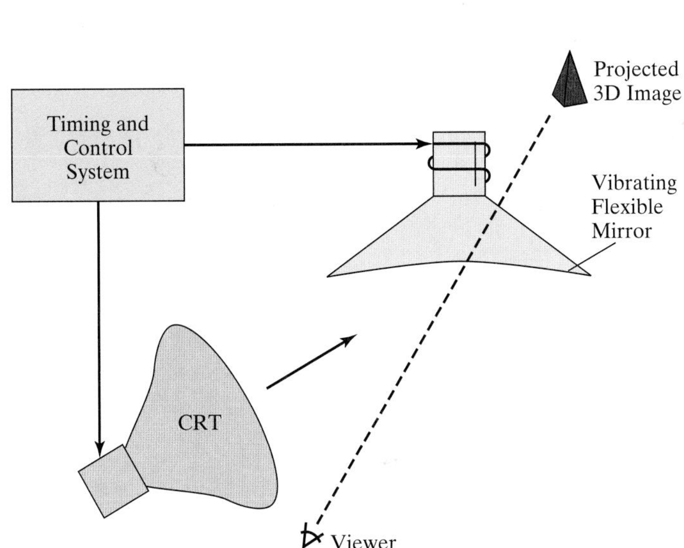

FIGURE 2-16 Operation of a three-dimensional display system using a vibrating mirror that changes focal length to match the depths of points in a scene.

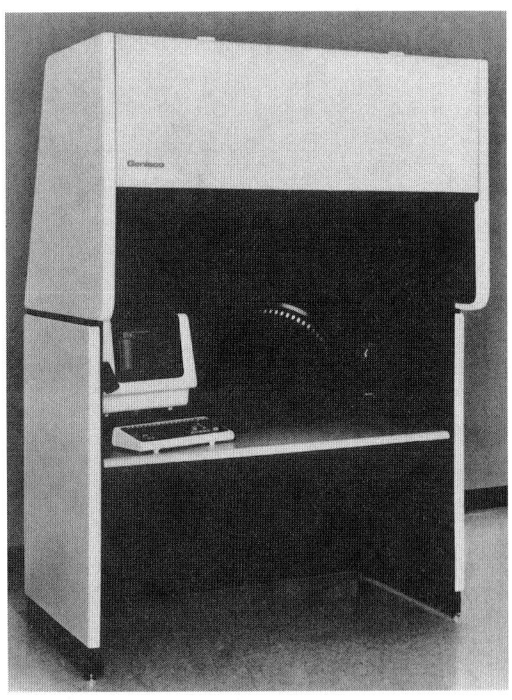

FIGURE 2-17 The SpaceGraph interactive graphics system displays objects in three dimensions using a vibrating, flexible mirror. *(Courtesy of Genisco Computers Corporation.)*

"slices" of objects selected at different depths. Such systems have been used in medical applications to analyze data from ultrasonography and CAT scan devices, in geological applications to analyze topological and seismic data, in design applications involving solid objects, and in three-dimensional simulations of systems, such as molecules and terrain.

Stereoscopic and Virtual-Reality Systems

Another technique for representing a three-dimensional object is to display stereoscopic views of the object. This method does not produce true three-dimensional images, but it does provide a three-dimensional effect by presenting a different view to each eye of an observer so that scenes do appear to have depth (Fig. 2-18).

To obtain a stereoscopic projection, we must obtain two views of a scene generated with viewing directions along the lines from the position of each eye (left and right) to the scene. We can construct the two views as computer-generated scenes with different viewing positions, or we can use a stereo camera pair to photograph an object or scene. When we simultaneously look at the left view with the left eye and the right view with the right eye, the two views merge into a single image and we perceive a scene with depth. Figure 2-19 shows two views of a computer-generated scene for stereoscopic projection. To increase viewing comfort, the areas at the left and right edges of this scene that are visible to only one eye have been eliminated.

One way to produce a stereoscopic effect on a raster system is to display each of the two views on alternate refresh cycles. The screen is viewed through glasses, with each lens designed to act as a rapidly alternating shutter that is synchronized to block out one of the views. Figure 2-20 shows a pair of stereoscopic glasses constructed with liquid-crystal shutters and an infrared emitter that synchronizes the glasses with the views on the screen.

Stereoscopic viewing is also a component in **virtual-reality** systems, where users can step into a scene and interact with the environment. A headset (Fig. 2-21) containing an optical system to generate the stereoscopic views can

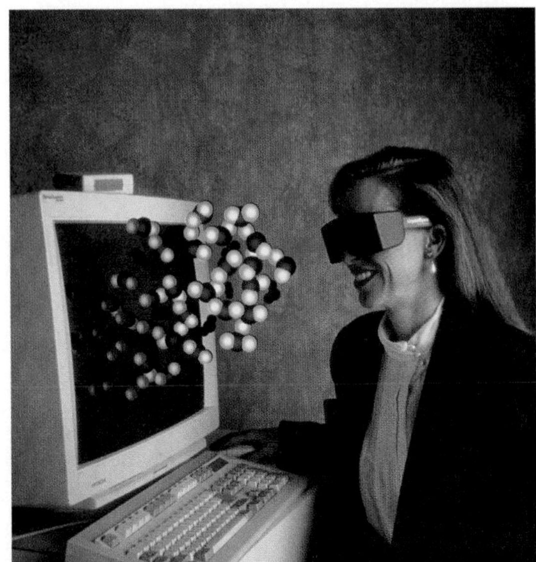

FIGURE 2-18 Simulated viewing of a stereoscopic projection. (*Courtesy of StereoGraphics Corporation.*)

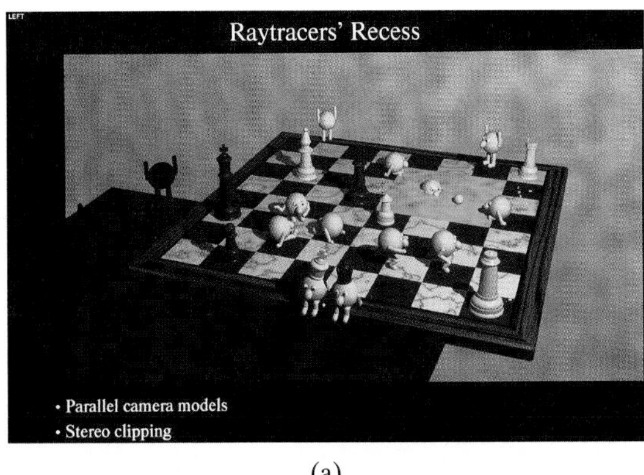

(a)

(b)

FIGURE 2-19 A stereoscopic viewing pair. (*Courtesy of Jerry Farm.*)

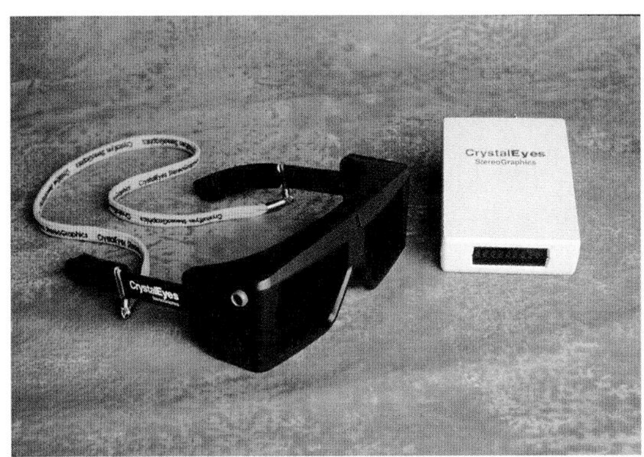

FIGURE 2-20 Glasses for viewing a stereoscopic scene and an infrared synchronizing emitter. (*Courtesy of StereoGraphics Corporation.*)

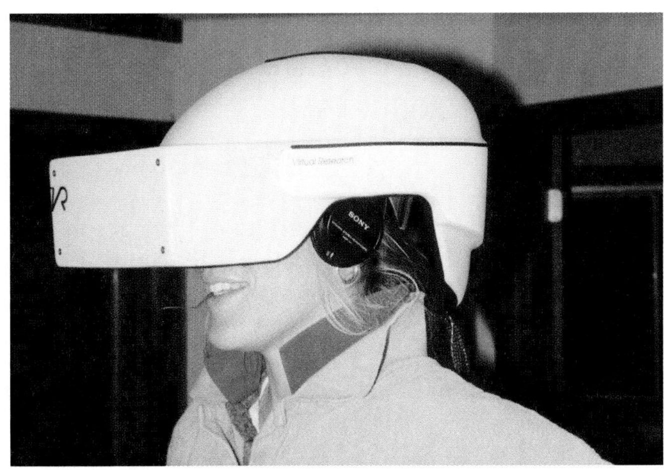

FIGURE 2-21 A headset used in virtual-reality systems. (*Courtesy of Virtual Research.*)

be used in conjunction with interactive input devices to locate and manipulate objects in the scene. A sensing system in the headset keeps track of the viewer's position, so that the front and back of objects can be seen as the viewer "walks through" and interacts with the display. Another method for creating a virtual-reality environment is to use projectors to generate a scene within an arrangement of walls, as in Figure 2-22, where a viewer interacts with a virtual display using stereoscopic glasses and data gloves (Section 2-4).

Lower-cost, interactive virtual-reality environments can be set up using a graphics monitor, stereoscopic glasses, and a head-tracking device. Figure 2-23 shows an ultrasound tracking device with six degrees of freedom. The tracking device is placed above the video monitor and is used to record head movements, so that the viewing position for a scene can be changed as head position changes.

FIGURE 2-22 A molecular biologist analyzing molecular structures inside a virtual-reality system called the Trimension ReaCTor. The "Fakespace Pinch gloves" enable the scientist to grasp and rearrange virtual objects in a projected scene. (*Courtesy Silicon Graphics, Inc. and Trimension Systems ReaCTor. © 2003 SGI. All rights reserved.*)

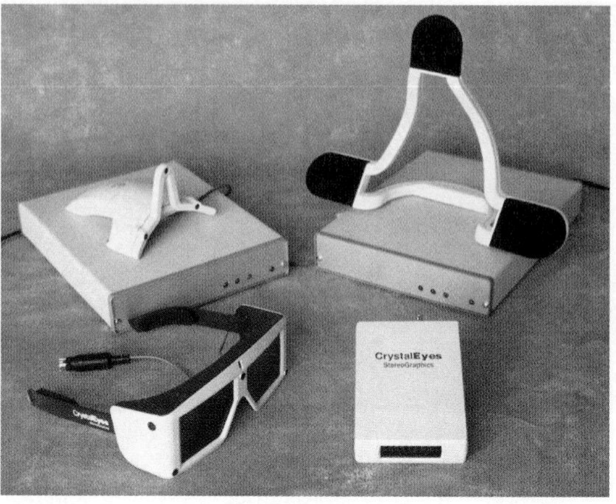

FIGURE 2-23 An ultrasound tracking device used with stereoscopic glasses to record changes in a viewer's head position. (*Courtesy of StereoGraphics Corporation.*)

2-2 RASTER-SCAN SYSTEMS

Interactive raster-graphics systems typically employ several processing units. In addition to the central processing unit, or CPU, a special-purpose processor, called the **video controller** or **display controller,** is used to control the operation of the display device. Organization of a simple raster system is shown in Fig. 2-24. Here, the frame buffer can be anywhere in the system memory, and the video controller accesses the frame buffer to refresh the screen. In addition to the video controller, more sophisticated raster systems employ other processors as coprocessors and accelerators to implement various graphics operations.

Video Controller

Figure 2-25 shows a commonly used organization for raster systems. A fixed area of the system memory is reserved for the frame buffer, and the video controller is given direct access to the frame-buffer memory.

Frame-buffer locations, and the corresponding screen positions, are referenced in Cartesian coordinates. In an application program, we use the commands

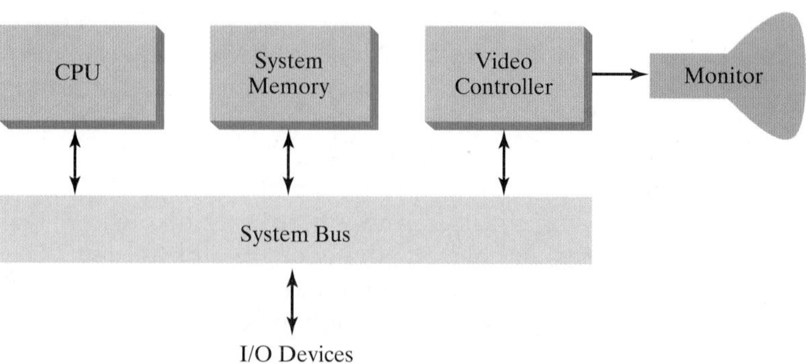

FIGURE 2-24 Architecture of a simple raster-graphics system.

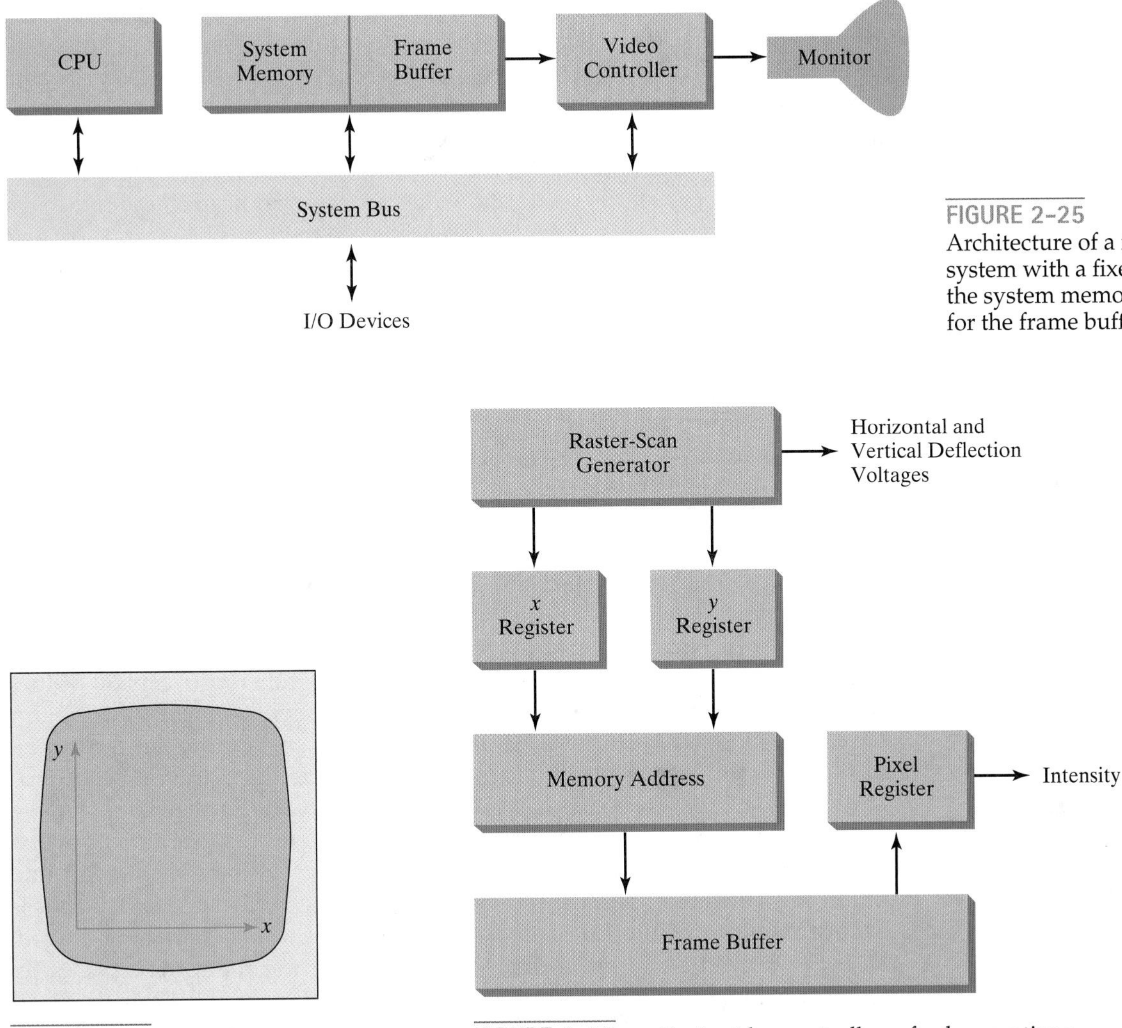

FIGURE 2-25 Architecture of a raster system with a fixed portion of the system memory reserved for the frame buffer.

FIGURE 2-26 A Cartesian reference frame with origin at the lower-left corner of a video monitor.

FIGURE 2-27 Basic video-controller refresh operations.

within a graphics software package to set coordinate positions for displayed objects relative to the origin of the Cartesian reference frame. Often, the coordinate origin is referenced at the lower-left corner of a screen display area by the software commands, although we can typically set the origin at any convenient location for a particular application. Figure 2-26 shows a two-dimensional Cartesian reference frame with the origin at the lower-left screen corner. The screen surface is then represented as the first quadrant of a two-dimensional system, with positive x values increasing from left to right and positive y values increasing from the bottom of the screen to the top. Pixel positions are then assigned integer x values that range from 0 to x_{max} across the screen, left to right, and integer y values that vary from 0 to y_{max}, bottom to top. However, hardware processes such as screen refreshing, as well as some software systems, reference the pixel positions from the top-left corner of the screen.

In Fig. 2-27, the basic refresh operations of the video controller are diagrammed. Two registers are used to store the coordinate values for the screen pixels. Initially, the x register is set to 0 and the y register is set to the value for the top scan line. The contents of the frame buffer at this pixel position are then retrieved and used to set the intensity of the CRT beam. Then the x register is incremented by 1, and the process is repeated for the next pixel on the top scan line. This procedure continues for each pixel along the top scan line. After the last pixel on the top scan line has been processed, the x register is reset to 0 and the y register is set to the value for the next scan line down from the top of the screen. Pixels along this scan line are then processed in turn, and the procedure is repeated for each successive scan line. After cycling through all pixels along the bottom scan line, the video controller resets the registers to the first pixel position on the top scan line and the refresh process starts over.

Since the screen must be refreshed at a rate of at least 60 frames per second, the simple procedure illustrated in Fig. 2-27 may not be accommodated by typical RAM chips if the cycle time is too slow. To speed up pixel processing, video controllers can retrieve multiple pixel values from the refresh buffer on each pass. The multiple pixel intensities are then stored in a separate register and used to control the CRT beam intensity for a group of adjacent pixels. When that group of pixels has been processed, the next block of pixel values is retrieved from the frame buffer.

A video controller can be designed to perform a number of other operations. For various applications, the video controller can retrieve pixel values from different memory areas on different refresh cycles. In some systems, for example, multiple frame buffers are often provided so that one buffer can be used for refreshing while pixel values are being loaded into the other buffers. Then the current refresh buffer can switch roles with one of the other buffers. This provides a fast mechanism for generating real-time animations, for example, since different views of moving objects can be successively loaded into a buffer without interrupting a refresh cycle. Another video-controller task is the transformation of blocks of pixels, so that screen areas can be enlarged, reduced, or moved from one location to another during the refresh cycles. In addition, the video controller often contains a lookup table, so that pixel values in the frame buffer are used to access the lookup table instead of controlling the CRT beam intensity directly. This provides a fast method for changing screen intensity values, and lookup tables are discussed in more detail in Chapter 4. Finally, some systems are designed to allow the video controller to mix the frame-buffer image with an input image from a television camera or other input device.

Raster-Scan Display Processor

Figure 2-28 shows one way to organize the components of a raster system that contains a separate **display processor,** sometimes referred to as a **graphics controller** or a **display coprocessor.** The purpose of the display processor is to free the CPU from the graphics chores. In addition to the system memory, a separate display-processor memory area can be provided.

A major task of the display processor is digitizing a picture definition given in an application program into a set of pixel values for storage in the frame buffer. This digitization process is called **scan conversion.** Graphics commands specifying straight lines and other geometric objects are scan converted into a set

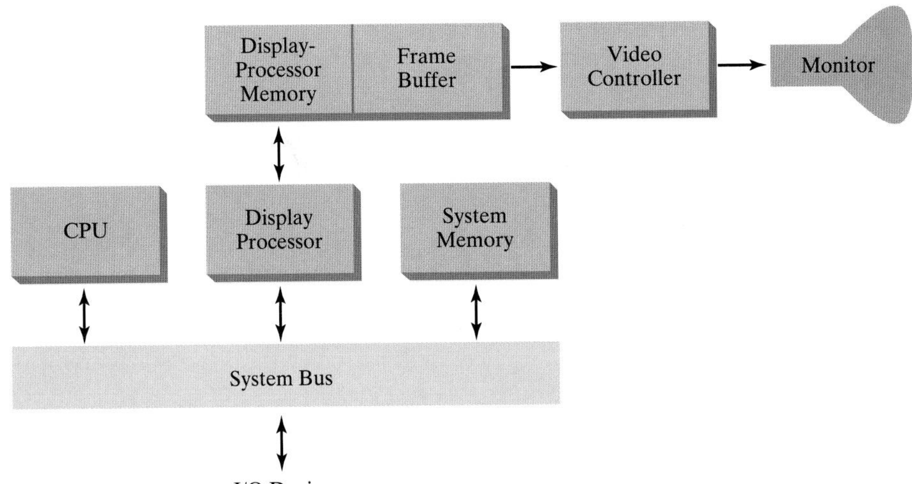

FIGURE 2-28 Architecture of a raster-graphics system with a display processor.

of discrete points, corresponding to screen pixel positions. Scan converting a straight-line segment, for example, means that we have to locate the pixel positions closest to the line path and store the color for each position in the frame buffer. Similar methods are used for scan converting other objects in a picture definition. Characters can be defined with rectangular pixel grids, as in Fig. 2-29, or they can be defined with outline shapes, as in Fig. 2-30. The array size for character grids can vary from about 5 by 7 to 9 by 12 or more for higher-quality displays. A character grid is displayed by superimposing the rectangular grid pattern into the frame buffer at a specified coordinate position. For characters that are defined as outlines, the shapes are scan converted into the frame buffer by locating the pixel positions closest to the outline.

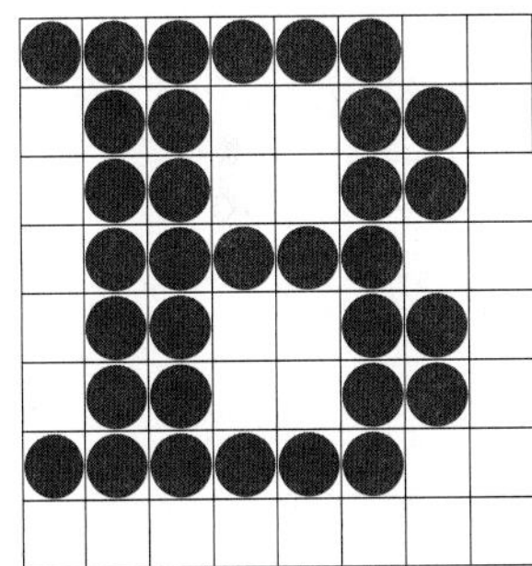

FIGURE 2-29 A character defined as a rectangular grid of pixel positions.

Display processors are also designed to perform a number of additional operations. These functions include generating various line styles (dashed, dotted, or solid), displaying color areas, and applying transformations to the objects in a scene. Also, display processors are typically designed to interface with interactive input devices, such as a mouse.

In an effort to reduce memory requirements in raster systems, methods have been devised for organizing the frame buffer as a linked list and encoding the color information. One organization scheme is to store each scan line as a set of number pairs. The first number in each pair can be a reference to a color value, and the second number can specify the number of adjacent pixels on the scan line that are to be displayed in that color. This technique, called **run-length encoding,** can result in a considerable saving in storage space if a picture is to be constructed mostly with long runs of a single color each. A similar approach can be taken when pixel colors change linearly. Another approach is to encode the raster as a set of rectangular areas (**cell encoding**). The disadvantages of encoding runs are that color changes are difficult to record and storage requirements increase as the lengths of the runs decrease. In addition, it is difficult for the display controller to process the raster when many short runs are involved. Moreover, the size of the frame buffer is no longer a major concern, because of sharp declines in memory costs. Nevertheless, encoding methods can be useful in the digital storage and transmission of picture information.

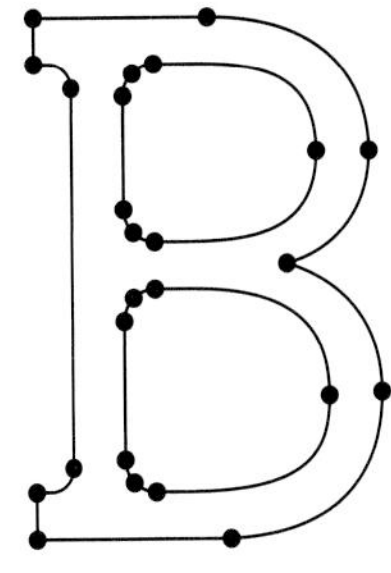

FIGURE 2-30 A character defined as an outline shape.

2-3 GRAPHICS WORKSTATIONS AND VIEWING SYSTEMS

Most graphics monitors today operate as raster-scan displays, and both CRT and flat-panel systems are in common use. Graphics workstations range from small general-purpose computer systems to multi-monitor facilities, often with ultra-large viewing screens. For a personal computer, screen resolutions vary from about 640 by 480 to 1280 by 1024, and diagonal screen lengths measure from 12 inches to over 21 inches. Most general-purpose systems now have considerable color capabilities, and many are full-color systems. For a desktop workstation specifically designed for graphics applications, the screen resolution can vary from 1280 by 1024 to about 1600 by 1200, with a typical screen diagonal of 18 inches or more. Commercial workstations can also be obtained with a variety of devices for specific applications. Figure 2-31 shows the features in one type of artist's workstation.

High-definition graphics systems, with resolutions up to 2560 by 2048, are commonly used in medical imaging, air-traffic control, simulation, and CAD. A 2048 by 2048 flat-panel display is shown in Fig. 2-32.

Many high-end graphics workstations also include large viewing screens, often with specialized features. Figure 2-33 shows a large-screen system for stereoscopic viewing, and Fig. 2-34 is a multi-channel wide-screen system.

Multi-panel display screens are used in a variety of applications that require "wall-sized" viewing areas. These systems are designed for presenting graphics displays at meetings, conferences, conventions, trade shows, retail stores, museums, and passenger terminals. A multi-panel display can be used to show a large view of a single scene or several individual images. Each panel in the system displays one section of the overall picture, as illustrated in Fig. 2-35. Large graphics displays can also be presented on curved viewing screens, such as the system in Fig. 2-36. A large, curved-screen system can be useful for viewing by a group of people studying a particular graphics application, such as the examples in Figs. 2-37 and 2-38. A control center, featuring a battery of

FIGURE 2-31 An artist's workstation, featuring a monitor, a keyboard, a graphics tablet with a hand cursor, and a light table, in addition to data storage and telecommunications devices. (*Courtesy of DICOMED Corporation.*)

FIGURE 2-32 A high-resolution (2048 by 2048) graphics monitor. (*Courtesy of BarcoView.*)

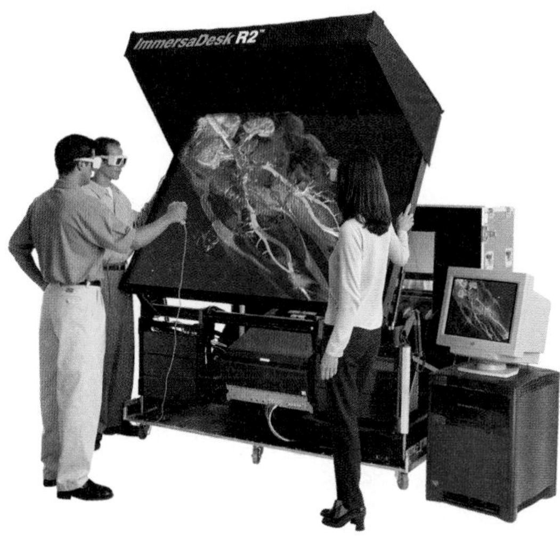

FIGURE 2-33 The SGI Reality Center 2000D, featuring an ImmersaDesk R2 and displaying a large-screen stereoscopic view of pressure contours in a vascular blood-flow simulation superimposed on a volume-rendered anatomic data set. (*Courtesy of Silicon Graphics, Inc. and Professor Charles Taylor, Stanford University. © 2003 SGI. All rights reserved.*)

FIGURE 2-34 A wide-screen view of a molecular system displayed on the three-channel SGI Reality Center 3300W. (*Courtesy of Silicon Graphics, Inc. and Molecular Simulations. © 2003 SGI. All rights reserved.*)

FIGURE 2-35 A multi-panel display system called the "Super Wall". (*Courtesy of RGB Spectrum.*)

FIGURE 2-36 A homeland security study displayed using a system with a large curved viewing screen. (*Courtesy of Silicon Graphics, Inc. © 2003. All rights reserved.*)

standard monitors, allows an operator to view sections of the large display and to control the audio, video, lighting, and projection systems using a touch-screen menu. The system projectors provide a seamless, multichannel display that includes edge blending, distortion correction, and color balancing. And a surround-sound system is used to provide the audio environment. Fig 2-39 shows a 360° paneled viewing system in the NASA control-tower simulator, which is used for training and for testing ways to solve air-traffic and runway problems at airports.

FIGURE 2-37 A curved-screen graphics system displaying an interactive walk-through of a natural gas plant. (*Courtesy of Silicon Graphics, Inc., Trimension Systems, and the Cadcentre, Cortaillod, Switzerland. © 2003 SGI. All rights reserved.*)

FIGURE 2-38 A geophysical visualization presented on a 25-foot semicircular screen, which provides a 160° horizontal and 40° vertical field of view. (*Courtesy of Silicon Graphics, Inc., the Landmark Graphics Corporation, and Trimension Systems. © 2003 SGI. All rights reserved.*)

FIGURE 2-39 The 360° viewing screen in the NASA airport control-tower simulator, called the FutureFlight Central Facility. (*Courtesy of Silicon Graphics, Inc. and NASA. © 2003 SGI. All rights reserved.*)

2-4 INPUT DEVICES

Graphics workstations can make use of various devices for data input. Most systems have a keyboard and one or more additional devices specifically designed for interactive input. These include a mouse, trackball, spaceball, and joystick. Some other input devices used in particular applications are digitizers, dials, button boxes, data gloves, touch panels, image scanners, and voice systems.

Keyboards, Button Boxes, and Dials

An alphanumeric **keyboard** on a graphics system is used primarily as a device for entering text strings, issuing certain commands, and selecting menu options. The keyboard is an efficient device for inputting such nongraphic data as picture labels associated with a graphics display. Keyboards can also be provided with features to facilitate entry of screen coordinates, menu selections, or graphics functions.

Cursor-control keys and function keys are common features on general-purpose keyboards. Function keys allow users to select frequently accessed operations with a single keystroke, and cursor-control keys are convenient for selecting a displayed object or a location by positioning the screen cursor. A keyboard can also contain other types of cursor-positioning devices, such as a trackball or joystick, along with a numeric keypad for fast entry of numeric data. In addition to these features, some keyboards have an ergonomic design (Fig. 2-40) that provides adjustments for relieving operator fatigue.

For specialized tasks, input to a graphics application may come from a set of buttons, dials, or switches that select data values or customized graphics operations. Figure 2-41 gives an example of a **button box** and a set of **input dials.** Buttons and switches are often used to input predefined functions, and dials are common devices for entering scalar values. Numerical values within some defined range are selected for input with dial rotations. A potentiometer is used to measure dial rotation, which is then converted to the corresponding numerical value.

Mouse Devices

Figure 2-40 illustrates a typical design for one-button **mouse,** which is a small hand-held unit that is usually moved around on a flat surface to position the screen cursor. Wheels or rollers on the bottom of the mouse can be used to record the amount and direction of movement. Another method for detecting mouse

FIGURE 2-40
Ergonomically designed keyboard with removable palm rests. The slope of each half of the keyboard can be adjusted separately. A one-button mouse, shown in front of the keyboard, has a cable attachment for connection to the main computer unit. *(Courtesy of Apple Computer, Inc.)*

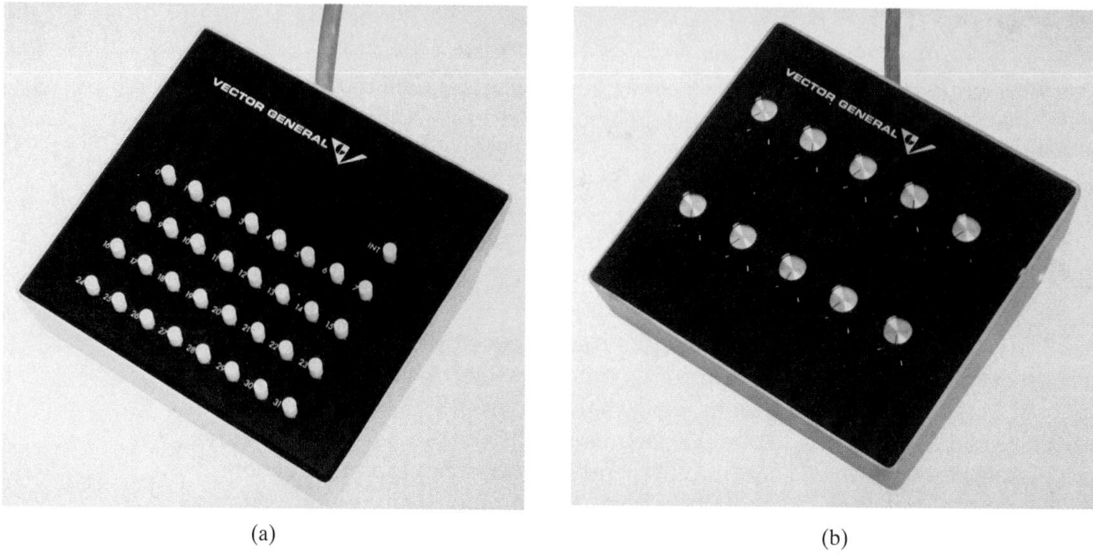

(a) (b)

FIGURE 2-41 A button box (a) and a set of input dials (b). (*Courtesy of Vector General.*)

FIGURE 2-42 The Z mouse features three buttons, a mouse ball underneath, a thumbwheel on the side, and a trackball on top. (*Courtesy of the Multipoint Technology Corporation.*)

motion is with an optical sensor. For some optical systems, the mouse is moved over a special mouse pad that has a grid of horizontal and vertical lines. The optical sensor detects movement across the lines in the grid. Other optical mouse systems can operate on any surface. And some are cordless, communicating with computer processors using digital radio technology.

Since a mouse can be picked up and put down at another position without change in cursor movement, it is used for making relative changes in the position of the screen cursor. One, two, three, or four buttons are included on the top of the mouse for signaling the execution of operations, such as recording cursor position or invoking a function. Most general-purpose graphics systems now include a mouse and a keyboard as the primary input devices.

Additional features can be included in the basic mouse design to increase the number of allowable input parameters. The Z mouse in Fig. 2-42 has three buttons, a thumbwheel on the side, a trackball on the top, and a standard mouse ball underneath. This design provides six degrees of freedom to select spatial positions, rotations, and other parameters. With the Z mouse, we can select an object displayed on a video monitor, rotate it, and move it in any direction. We could also use the Z mouse to navigate our viewing position and orientation through a three-dimensional scene. Applications of the Z mouse include virtual reality, CAD, and animation.

Trackballs and Spaceballs

A **trackball** is a ball device that can be rotated with the fingers or palm of the hand to produce screen-cursor movement. Potentiometers, connected to the ball, measure the amount and direction of rotation. Laptop keyboards are often equipped with a trackball to eliminate the extra space required by a mouse. A trackball can be mounted also on other devices, such as the Z mouse shown in Fig. 2-42, or it can be obtained as a separate add-on unit that contains two or three control buttons.

An extension of the two-dimensional trackball concept is the **spaceball** (Fig. 2-44), which provides six degrees of freedom. Unlike the trackball, a spaceball does not actually move. Strain gauges measure the amount of pressure applied to the spaceball to provide input for spatial positioning and orientation as the ball is pushed or pulled in various directions. Spaceballs are used for three-dimensional positioning and selection operations in virtual-reality systems, modeling, animation, CAD, and other applications.

Joysticks

Another positioning device is the **joystick,** which consists of a small, vertical lever (called the stick) mounted on a base. We use the joystick to steer the screen cursor around. Most joysticks, such as the unit in Fig. 2-43, select screen positions with actual stick movement; others respond to pressure on the stick. Some joysticks are mounted on a keyboard, and some are designed as stand-alone units.

The distance that the stick is moved in any direction from its center position corresponds to the relative screen-cursor movement in that direction.

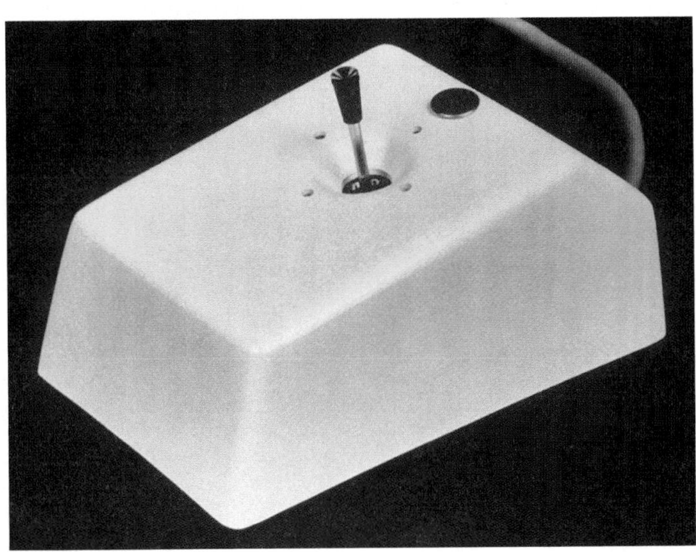

FIGURE 2-43 A movable joystick. (*Courtesy of the CalComp Group, Sanders Associates, Inc.*)

Potentiometers mounted at the base of the joystick measure the amount of movement, and springs return the stick to the center position when it is released. One or more buttons can be programmed to act as input switches to signal actions that are to be executed once a screen position has been selected.

In another type of movable joystick, the stick is used to activate switches that cause the screen cursor to move at a constant rate in the direction selected. Eight switches, arranged in a circle, are sometimes provided so that the stick can select any one of eight directions for cursor movement. Pressure-sensitive joysticks, also called *isometric joysticks,* have a non-movable stick. A push or pull on the stick is measured with strain gauges and converted to movement of the screen cursor in the direction of the applied pressure.

Data Gloves

Figure 2-44 shows a **data glove** that can be used to grasp a "virtual object". The glove is constructed with a series of sensors that detect hand and finger motions. Electromagnetic coupling between transmitting antennas and receiving antennas are used to provide information about the position and orientation of the hand. The transmitting and receiving antennas can each be structured as a set of three mutually perpendicular coils, forming a three-dimensional Cartesian reference system. Input from the glove is used to position or manipulate objects in a virtual scene. A two-dimensional projection of the scene can be viewed on a video monitor, or a three-dimensional projection can be viewed with a headset.

Digitizers

A common device for drawing, painting, or interactively selecting positions is a **digitizer.** These devices can be designed to input coordinate values in either a two-dimensional or a three-dimensional space. In engineering or architectural applications, a digitizer is often used to scan a drawing or object and to input a set of discrete coordinate positions. The input positions are then joined with straight-line segments to generate an approximation of a curve or surface shape.

One type of digitizer is the **graphics tablet** (also referred to as a *data tablet*), which is used to input two-dimensional coordinates by activating a hand cursor or stylus at selected positions on a flat surface. A hand cursor contains cross hairs for sighting positions, while a stylus is a pencil-shaped device that is pointed at positions on the tablet. Figures 2-45 and 2-46 show examples of desktop and

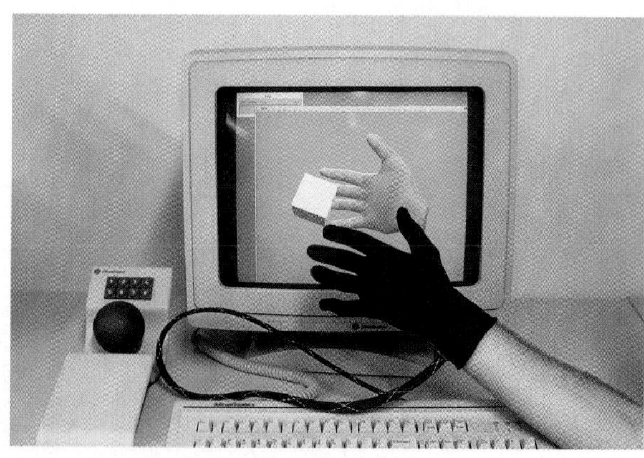

FIGURE 2-44 A virtual-reality scene, displayed on a two-dimensional video monitor, with input from a data glove and a spaceball. *(Courtesy of The Computer Graphics Center, Darmstadt, Germany.)*

FIGURE 2-45 The SummaSketch III desktop tablet with a sixteen-button hand cursor. (*Courtesy of Summagraphics Corporation.*)

FIGURE 2-46 The Microgrid III tablet with a sixteen-button hand cursor, designed for digitizing larger drawings. (*Courtesy of Summagraphics Corporation.*)

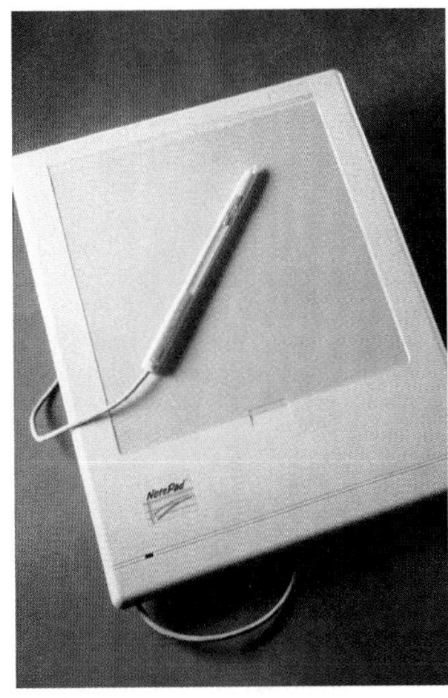

FIGURE 2-47 The NotePad desktop tablet with stylus. (*Courtesy of CalComp Digitizer Division, a part of CalComp, Inc.*)

FIGURE 2-48 An artist's digitizer system, with a pressure-sensitive, cordless stylus. (*Courtesy of Wacom Technology Corporation.*)

floor-model tablets, using hand cursors that are available with two, four, or sixteen buttons. Examples of stylus input with a tablet are shown in Figs. 2-47 and 2-48. The artist's digitizing system in Fig. 2-48 uses electromagnetic resonance to detect the three-dimensional position of the stylus. This allows an artist to produce different brush strokes by applying different pressures to the tablet surface. Tablet size varies from 12 by 12 inches for desktop models to 44 by 60 inches or larger for floor models. Graphics tablets provide a highly accurate method for selecting coordinate positions, with an accuracy that varies from about 0.2 mm on desktop models to about 0.05 mm or less on larger models.

Many graphics tablets are constructed with a rectangular grid of wires embedded in the tablet surface. Electromagnetic pulses are generated in sequence along the wires, and an electric signal is induced in a wire coil in an activated stylus or hand-cursor to record a tablet position. Depending on the technology, signal strength, coded pulses, or phase shifts can be used to determine the position on the tablet.

An *acoustic* (or *sonic*) *tablet* uses sound waves to detect a stylus position. Either strip microphones or point microphones can be employed to detect the sound emitted by an electrical spark from a stylus tip. The position of the stylus is calculated by timing the arrival of the generated sound at the different microphone positions. An advantage of two-dimensional acoustic tablets is that the microphones can be placed on any surface to form the "tablet" work area. For example, the microphones could be placed on a book page while a figure on that page is digitized.

Three-dimensional digitizers use sonic or electromagnetic transmissions to record positions. One electromagnetic transmission method is similar to that employed in the data glove: a coupling between the transmitter and receiver is used to compute the location of a stylus as it moves over an object surface. Figure 2-49 shows a digitizer recording the locations of positions on the surface of a three-dimensional object. As the points are selected on a nonmetallic object, a wire-frame outline of the surface is displayed on the computer screen. Once the surface outline is constructed, it can be rendered using lighting effects to produce a realistic display of the object. Resolution for this system is from 0.8 mm to 0.08 mm, depending on the model.

Image Scanners

Drawings, graphs, photographs, or text can be stored for computer processing with an **image scanner** by passing an optical scanning mechanism over the

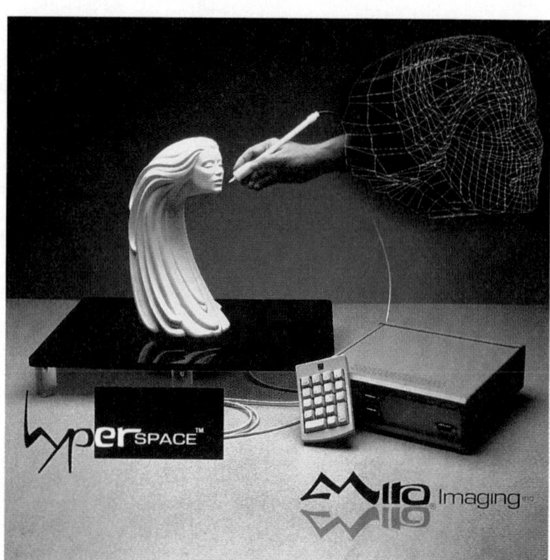

FIGURE 2-49 A three-dimensional digitizing system for use with Apple Macintosh computers. (*Courtesy of Mira Imaging.*)

information to be stored. The gradations of gray scale or color are then recorded and stored in an array. Once we have the internal representation of a picture, we can apply transformations to rotate, scale, or crop the picture to a particular screen area. We can also apply various image-processing methods to modify the array representation of the picture. For scanned text input, various editing operations can be performed on the stored documents. Scanners are available in a variety of sizes and capabilities. A small hand-model scanner is shown in Fig. 2-50, while Figs. 2-51 and 2-52 show larger models.

FIGURE 2-50 A hand-held scanner that can be used to input either text or graphics images. (*Courtesy of Thunderware, Inc.*)

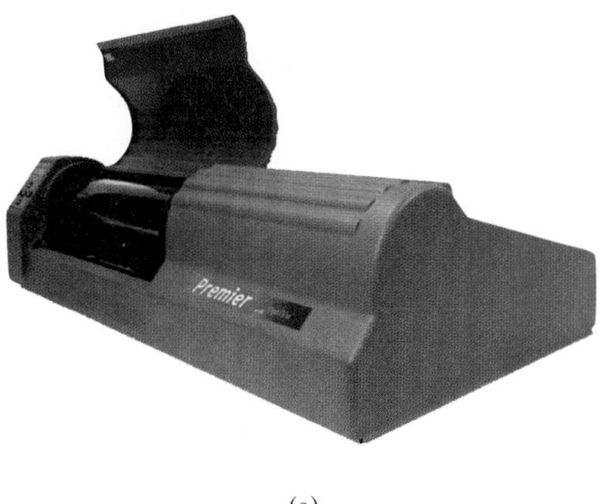

(a)

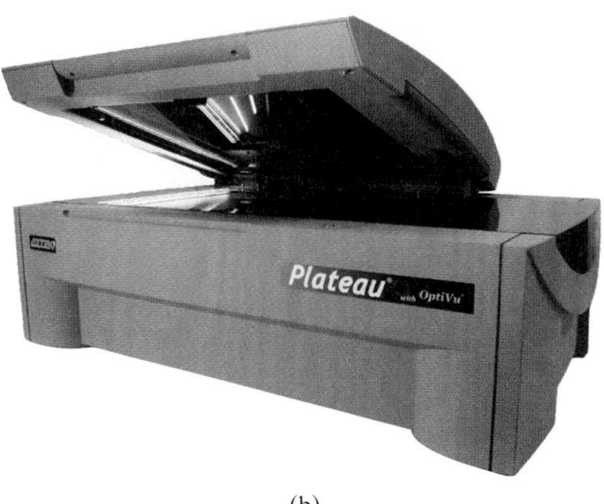

(b)

FIGURE 2-51 Desktop scanners: (a) drum scanner and (b) flatbed scanner. (*Courtesy of Aztek, Inc., Lake Forest, California.*)

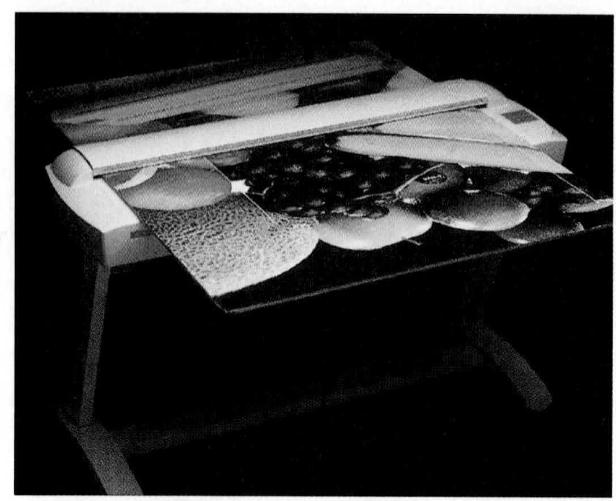

FIGURE 2-52
A wide-format scanner. (*Courtesy of Aztek, Inc., Lake Forest, California.*)

(a)

(b)

FIGURE 2-53 Plasma panels with touch screens. (*Courtesy of Photonics Systems.*)

Touch Panels

As the name implies, **touch panels** allow displayed objects or screen positions to be selected with the touch of a finger. A typical application of touch panels is for the selection of processing options that are represented as a menu of graphical icons. Some monitors, such as the plasma panels shown in Fig. 2-53, are designed with touch screens. Other systems can be adapted for touch input by fitting a transparent device (Fig. 2-54) containing a touch-sensing mechanism over the video monitor screen. Touch input can be recorded using optical, electrical, or acoustical methods.

Optical touch panels employ a line of infrared light-emitting diodes (LEDs) along one vertical edge and along one horizontal edge of the frame. Light detectors are placed along the opposite vertical and horizontal edges. These detectors are used to record which beams are interrupted when the panel is touched. The two crossing beams that are interrupted identify the horizontal and vertical coordinates of the screen position selected. Positions can be selected with an accuracy of about 1/4 inch. With closely spaced LEDs, it is possible to break two horizontal or two vertical beams simultaneously. In this case, an average position between the two interrupted beams is recorded. The LEDs operate at infrared frequencies so that the light is not visible to a user.

An electrical touch panel is constructed with two transparent plates separated by a small distance. One of the plates is coated with a conducting material, and

FIGURE 2-54 Resistive touch-screen overlays. (*Courtesy of Elo TouchSystems, Inc.*)

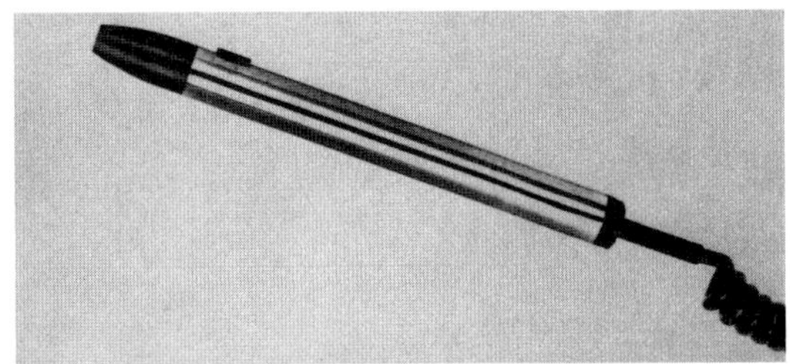

FIGURE 2-55 A light pen with a button activator. (*Courtesy of Interactive Computer Products.*)

the other plate is coated with a resistive material. When the outer plate is touched, it is forced into contact with the inner plate. This contact creates a voltage drop across the resistive plate that is converted to the coordinate values of the selected screen position.

In acoustical touch panels, high-frequency sound waves are generated in horizontal and vertical directions across a glass plate. Touching the screen causes part of each wave to be reflected from the finger to the emitters. The screen position at the point of contact is calculated from a measurement of the time interval between the transmission of each wave and its reflection to the emitter.

Light Pens

Figure 2-55 shows the design of one type of **light pen.** Such pencil-shaped devices are used to select screen positions by detecting the light coming from points on the CRT screen. They are sensitive to the short burst of light emitted from the phosphor coating at the instant the electron beam strikes a particular point. Other light sources, such as the background light in the room, are usually not detected by a light pen. An activated light pen, pointed at a spot on the screen as the electron beam lights up that spot, generates an electrical pulse that causes the coordinate position of the electron beam to be recorded. As with cursor-positioning devices, recorded light-pen coordinates can be used to position an object or to select a processing option.

Although light pens are still with us, they are not as popular as they once were since they have several disadvantages compared to other input devices that have been developed. For example, when a light pen is pointed at the screen, part of the screen image is obscured by the hand and pen. And prolonged use of the light pen can cause arm fatigue. Also, light pens require special implementations for some applications since they cannot detect positions within black areas. To be able to select positions in any screen area with a light pen, we must have some nonzero light intensity emitted from each pixel within that area. In addition, light pens sometimes give false readings due to background lighting in a room.

Voice Systems

Speech recognizers are used with some graphics workstations as input devices for voice commands. The **voice system** input can be used to initiate graphics

FIGURE 2-56 A speech-recognition system. (*Courtesy of Threshold Technology, Inc.*)

operations or to enter data. These systems operate by matching an input against a predefined dictionary of words and phrases.

A dictionary is set up by speaking the command words several times. The system then analyzes each word and establishes a dictionary of word frequency patterns, along with the corresponding functions that are to be performed. Later, when a voice command is given, the system searches the dictionary for a frequency-pattern match. A separate dictionary is needed for each operator using the system. Input for a voice system is typically spoken into a microphone mounted on a headset, as in Fig. 2-56, and the microphone is designed to minimize input of background sounds. Voice systems have some advantage over other input devices, since the attention of the operator need not switch from one device to another to enter a command.

2-5 HARD-COPY DEVICES

We can obtain hard-copy output for our images in several formats. For presentations or archiving, we can send image files to devices or service bureaus that will produce overhead transparencies, 35mm slides, or film. And we can put our pictures on paper by directing graphics output to a printer or plotter.

The quality of the pictures obtained from an output device depends on dot size and the number of dots per inch, or lines per inch, that can be displayed. To produce smooth patterns, higher-quality printers shift dot positions so that adjacent dots overlap.

Printers produce output by either impact or nonimpact methods. *Impact* printers press formed character faces against an inked ribbon onto the paper. A line printer is an example of an impact device, with the typefaces mounted on bands, chains, drums, or wheels. *Nonimpact* printers and plotters use laser techniques, ink-jet sprays, electrostatic methods, and electrothermal methods to get images onto paper.

Character impact printers often have a *dot-matrix* print head containing a rectangular array of protruding wire pins, with the number of pins dependent upon the quality of the printer. Individual characters or graphics patterns are obtained by retracting certain pins so that the remaining pins form the pattern to be printed. Figure 2-57 shows a picture printed on a dot-matrix printer.

In a *laser* device, a laser beam creates a charge distribution on a rotating drum coated with a photoelectric material, such as selenium. Toner is applied to the drum and then transferred to paper. *Ink-jet* methods produce output by squirting ink in horizontal rows across a roll of paper wrapped on a drum. The electrically charged ink stream is deflected by an electric field to produce dot-matrix patterns. And an *electrostatic* device places a negative charge on the paper, one complete

FIGURE 2-57 A picture generated on a dot-matrix printer, illustrating how the density of dot patterns can be varied to produce light and dark areas. (*Courtesy of Apple Computer, Inc.*)

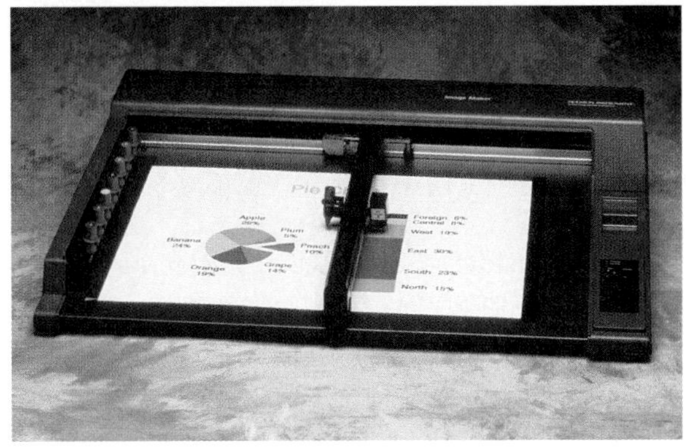

FIGURE 2-58 A desktop pen plotter with a resolution of 0.025 mm. (*Courtesy of Summagraphics Corporation.*)

row at a time across the sheet. Then the paper is exposed to a positively charged toner. This causes the toner to be attracted to the negatively charged areas, where it adheres to produce the specified output. Another output technology is the *electrothermal* printer. With these systems, heat is applied to a dot-matrix print head to output patterns on heat-sensitive paper.

We can get limited color output on some impact printers by using different-colored ribbons. Nonimpact devices use various techniques to combine three different color pigments (cyan, magenta, and yellow) to produce a range of color patterns. Laser and electrostatic devices deposit the three pigments on separate passes; ink-jet methods shoot the three colors simultaneously on a single pass along each print line.

Drafting layouts and other drawings are typically generated with ink-jet or pen plotters. A pen plotter has one or more pens mounted on a carriage, or crossbar, that spans a sheet of paper. Pens with varying colors and widths are used to produce a variety of shadings and line styles. Wet-ink, ball-point, and felt-tip pens are all possible choices for use with a pen plotter. Plotter paper can lie flat or it can be rolled onto a drum or belt. Crossbars can be either movable or stationary, while the pen moves back and forth along the bar. The paper is held in position using clamps, a vacuum, or an electrostatic charge. An example of a table-top, flatbed pen plotter is given in Figure 2-58, and a larger, roll-feed pen plotter is shown in Fig. 2-59.

FIGURE 2-59 A large, roll-feed pen plotter with an automatic multicolor eight-pen changer and a resolution of 0.0127 mm. (*Courtesy of Summagraphics Corporation.*)

2-6 GRAPHICS NETWORKS

So far, we have mainly considered graphics applications on an isolated system with a single user. However, multiuser environments and computer networks are now common elements in many graphics applications. Various resources, such as processors, printers, plotters, and data files, can be distributed on a network and shared by multiple users.

A graphics monitor on a network is generally referred to as a **graphics server,** or simply a **server.** Often, the monitor includes standard input devices such as a keyboard and a mouse or trackball. In that case, the system can provide input, as well as being an output server. The computer on the network that is executing a graphics application program is called the **client,** and the output of the program is displayed on a server. A workstation that includes processors, as well as a monitor and input devices, can function as both a server and a client.

When operating on a network, a client computer transmits the instructions for displaying a picture to the monitor (server). Typically, this is accomplished by collecting the instructions into packets before transmission, instead of sending the individual graphics instructions one at a time over the network. Thus, graphics software packages often contain commands that affect packet transmission, as well as the commands for creating pictures.

2-7 GRAPHICS ON THE INTERNET

A great deal of graphics development is now done on the **Internet,** which is a global network of computer networks. Computers on the Internet communicate using TCP/IP (*transmission control protocol/internetworking protocol*). In addition, the **World Wide Web** provides a hypertext system that allows users to locate and view documents that can contain text, graphics, and audio. Resources, such as graphics files, are identified by a *uniform resource locator* (*URL*). Each URL, sometimes also referred to as a universal resource locator, contains two parts: (1) the protocol for transferring the document, and (2) the server that contains the document and, optionally, the location (directory) on the server. For example, the URL *http://www.siggraph.org* indicates a document that is to be transferred with the *hypertext transfer protocol* (*http*) and that the server is www.siggraph.org, which is the home page of the Special Interest Group in Graphics (SIGGRAPH) of the Association for Computing Machinery. Another common type of URL begins with *ftp://*. This identifies an "ftp site", where programs or other files can be downloaded using the *file-transfer protocol*.

Documents on the Internet can be constructed with the *Hypertext Markup Language* (*HTML*). The development of HTML provided a simple method for describing a document containing text, graphics, and references (hyperlinks) to other documents. Although resources could be made available using HTML and URL addressing, it was difficult originally to find information on the Internet. Subsequently, the National Center for Supercomputing Applications (NCSA) developed a "browser" called Mosaic that made it easier for users to search for Web resources. The Mosaic browser later evolved into the browser called Netscape Navigator.

The Hypertext Markup Language provides a simple method for developing graphics on the Internet, but it has limited capabilities. Therefore, other languages have been developed for internet graphics applications, and we discuss these languages in Section 2-8.

2-8 GRAPHICS SOFTWARE

There are two broad classifications for computer-graphics software: special-purpose packages and general programming packages. Special-purpose packages are designed for nonprogrammers who want to generate pictures, graphs, or charts in some application area without worrying about the graphics procedures that might be needed to produce such displays. The interface to a special-purpose package is typically a set of menus that allows users to communicate with the programs in their own terms. Examples of such applications include artist's painting programs and various architectural, business, medical, and engineering CAD systems. By contrast, a general programming package provides a library of graphics functions that can be used in a programming language such as C, C++, Java, or Fortran. Basic functions in a typical graphics library include those for specifying picture components (straight lines, polygons, spheres, and other objects), setting color values, selecting views of a scene, and applying rotations or other transformations. Some examples of general graphics programming packages are GL (Graphics Library), OpenGL, VRML (Virtual-Reality Modeling Language), Java 2D, and Java 3D. A set of graphics functions is often called a **computer-graphics application programming interface** (**CG API**), because the library provides a software interface between a programming language (such as C++) and the hardware. So when we write an application program in C++, the graphics routines allow us to construct and display a picture on an output device.

Coordinate Representations

To generate a picture using a programming package, we first need to give the geometric descriptions of the objects that are to be displayed. These descriptions determine the locations and shapes of the objects. For example, a box is specified by the positions of its corners (vertices), and a sphere is defined by its center position and radius. With few exceptions, general graphics packages require geometric descriptions to be specified in a standard, right-handed, Cartesian-coordinate reference frame (Appendix A). If coordinate values for a picture are given in some other reference frame (spherical, hyperbolic, etc.), they must be converted to Cartesian coordinates before they can be input to the graphics package. Some packages that are designed for specialized applications may allow use of other coordinate frames that are appropriate for those applications.

In general, several different Cartesian reference frames are used in the process of constructing and displaying a scene. First, we can define the shapes of individual objects, such as trees or furniture, within a separate coordinate reference frame for each object. These reference frames are called **modeling coordinates,** or sometimes **local coordinates** or **master coordinates.** Once the individual object shapes have been specified, we can construct ("model") a scene by placing the objects into appropriate locations within a scene reference frame called **world coordinates.** This step involves the transformation of the individual modeling-coordinate frames to specified positions and orientations within the world-coordinate frame. As an example, we could construct a bicycle by defining each of its parts (wheels, frame, seat, handle bars, gears, chain, pedals) in a separate modeling-coordinate frame. Then, the component parts are fitted together in world coordinates. If both bicycle wheels are the same size, we only need to describe one wheel in a local-coordinate frame. Then the wheel description is fitted into the world-coordinate bicycle description in two places. For scenes that are not too complicated, object components can be set up directly within the overall world-coordinate object structure, bypassing the modeling-coordinate and modeling-transformation steps. Geometric descriptions in modeling coordinates and world coordinates can be given in any convenient floating-point or integer values, without regard for the constraints of a particular output device. For some scenes, we might want to specify object geometries in fractions of a foot, while for other applications we might want to use millimeters, or kilometers, or light-years.

After all parts of a scene have been specified, the overall world-coordinate description is processed through various routines onto one or more output-device reference frames for display. This process is called the **viewing pipeline.** World-coordinate positions are first converted to *viewing coordinates* corresponding to the view we want of a scene, based on the position and orientation of a hypothetical camera. Then object locations are transformed to a two-dimensional projection of the scene, which corresponds to what we will see on the output device. The scene is then stored in **normalized coordinates,** where each coordinate value is in the range from -1 to 1 or in the range from 0 to 1, depending on the system. Normalized coordinates are also referred to as *normalized device coordinates,* since using this representation makes a graphics package independent of the coordinate range for any specific output device. We also need to identify visible surfaces and eliminate picture parts outside of the bounds for the view we want to show on the display device. Finally, the picture is scan converted into the refresh buffer of a raster system for display. The coordinate systems for display devices are generally called **device coordinates,** or **screen coordinates** in the case of a video monitor. Often, both normalized coordinates and screen coordinates are specified in a left-handed coordinate reference frame so that increasing positive distances from the xy plane (the screen, or viewing plane) can be interpreted as being farther from the viewing position.

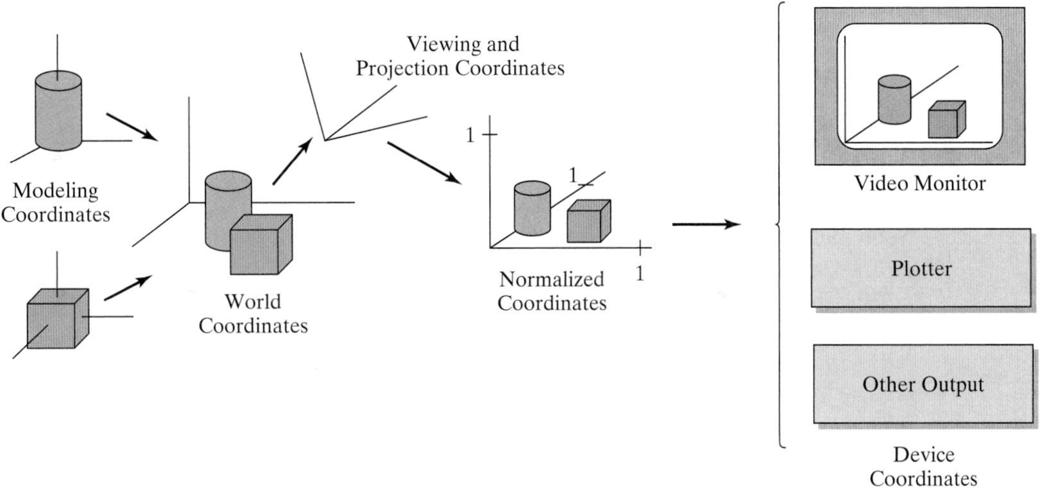

FIGURE 2-60 The transformation sequence from modeling coordinates to device coordinates for a three-dimensional scene. Object shapes can be individually defined in modeling-coordinate reference systems. Then the shapes are positioned within the world-coordinate scene. Next, world-coordinate specifications are transformed through the viewing pipeline to viewing and projection coordinates and then to normalized coordinates. At the final step, individual device drivers transfer the normalized-coordinate representation of the scene to the output devices for display.

Figure 2-60 briefly illustrates the sequence of coordinate transformations from modeling coordinates to device coordinates for a display that is to contain a view of two three-dimensional objects. An initial modeling-coordinate position (x_{mc}, y_{mc}, z_{mc}) in this illustration is transferred to world coordinates, then to viewing and projection coordinates, then to left-handed normalized coordinates, and finally to a device-coordinate position (x_{dc}, y_{dc}) with the sequence:

$$(x_{mc}, y_{mc}, z_{mc}) \rightarrow (x_{wc}, y_{wc}, z_{wc}) \rightarrow (x_{vc}, y_{vc}, z_{vc}) \rightarrow (x_{pc}, y_{pc}, z_{pc})$$
$$\rightarrow (x_{nc}, y_{nc}, z_{nc}) \rightarrow (x_{dc}, y_{dc})$$

Device coordinates (x_{dc}, y_{dc}) are integers within the range (0, 0) to $(x_{\max}, y_{\max})$ for a particular output device. In addition to the two-dimensional positions (x_{dc}, y_{dc}) on the viewing surface, depth information for each device-coordinate position is stored for use in various visibility and surface-processing algorithms.

Graphics Functions

A general-purpose graphics package provides users with a variety of functions for creating and manipulating pictures. These routines can be broadly classified according to whether they deal with graphics output, input, attributes, transformations, viewing, subdividing pictures, or general control.

The basic building blocks for pictures are referred to as **graphics output primitives.** They include character strings and geometric entities, such as points, straight lines, curved lines, filled color areas (usually polygons), and shapes defined with arrays of color points. Additionally, some graphics packages provide functions for displaying more complex shapes such as spheres, cones, and cylinders. Routines for generating output primitives provide the basic tools for constructing pictures.

Attributes are properties of the output primitives; that is, an attribute describes how a particular primitive is to be displayed. This includes color specifications, line styles, text styles, and area-filling patterns.

We can change the size, position, or orientation of an object within a scene using **geometric transformations.** Some graphics packages provide an additional set of functions for performing **modeling transformations,** which are used to construct a scene where individual object descriptions are given in local coordinates. Such packages usually provide a mechanism for describing complex objects (such as an electrical circuit or a bicycle) with a tree (hierarchical) structure. Other packages simply provide the geometric-transformation routines and leave modeling details to the programmer.

After a scene has been constructed, using the routines for specifying the object shapes and their attributes, a graphics package projects a view of the picture onto an output device. **Viewing transformations** are used to select a view of the scene, the type of projection to be used, and the location on a video monitor where the view is to be displayed. Other routines are available for managing the screen display area by specifying its position, size, and structure. For three-dimensional scenes, visible objects are identified and the lighting conditions are applied.

Interactive graphics applications make use of various kinds of input devices, including a mouse, a tablet, or a joystick. **Input functions** are used to control and process the data flow from these interactive devices.

Some graphics packages also provide routines for subdividing a picture description into a named set of component parts. And other routines may be available for manipulating these picture components in various ways.

Finally, a graphics package contains a number of housekeeping tasks, such as clearing a screen display area to a selected color and initializing parameters. We can lump the functions for carrying out these chores under the heading **control operations.**

Software Standards

The primary goal of standardized graphics software is portability. When packages are designed with standard graphics functions, software can be moved easily from one hardware system to another and used in different implementations and applications. Without standards, programs designed for one hardware system often cannot be transferred to another system without extensive rewriting of the programs.

International and national standards-planning organizations in many countries have cooperated in an effort to develop a generally accepted standard for computer graphics. After considerable effort, this work on standards led to the development of the **Graphical Kernel System** (**GKS**) in 1984. This system was adopted as the first graphics software standard by the *International Standards Organization* (*ISO*) and by various national standards organizations, including the *American National Standards Institute* (*ANSI*). Although GKS was originally designed as a two-dimensional graphics package, a three-dimensional GKS extension was soon developed. The second software standard to be developed and approved by the standards organizations was **PHIGS** (**Programmer's Hierarchical Interactive Graphics Standard**), which is an extension of GKS. Increased capabilities for hierarchical object modeling, color specifications, surface rendering, and picture manipulations are provided in PHIGS. Subsequently, an extension of PHIGS, called PHIGS+, was developed to provide three-dimensional surface-rendering capabilities not available in PHIGS.

As the GKS and PHIGS packages were being developed, the graphics workstations from Silicon Graphics, Inc. (SGI) became increasingly popular. These workstations came with a set of routines called **GL** (**Graphics Library**), which very soon became a widely used package in the graphics community. Thus GL became a de facto graphics standard. The GL routines were designed for fast, real-time rendering, and soon this package was being extended to other hardware systems. As a result, OpenGL was developed as a hardware-independent version of GL in the early 1990s. This graphics package is now maintained and updated by the **OpenGL Architecture Review Board,** which is a consortium of representatives from many graphics companies and organizations. The OpenGL library is specifically designed for efficient processing of three-dimensional applications, but it can also handle two-dimensional scene descriptions as a special case of three dimensions where all the z coordinate values are 0.

Graphics functions in any package are typically defined as a set of specifications that are independent of any programming language. A **language binding** is then defined for a particular high-level programming language. This binding gives the syntax for accessing the various graphics functions from that language. Each language binding is defined to make best use of the corresponding language capabilities and to handle various syntax issues, such as data types, parameter passing, and errors. Specifications for implementing a graphics package in a particular language are set by the International Standards Organization. The OpenGL bindings for the C and C++ languages are the same. Other OpenGL bindings are also available, such as those for Ada and Fortran.

In the following chapters, we use the C/C++ binding for OpenGL as a framework for discussing basic graphics concepts and the design and application of graphics packages. Example programs in C++ illustrate applications of OpenGL and the general algorithms for implementing graphics functions.

Other Graphics Packages

Many other computer-graphics programming libraries have been developed. Some provide general graphics routines, and some are aimed at specific applications or particular aspects of computer graphics, such as animation, virtual reality, or graphics on the Internet.

A package called *Open Inventor* furnishes a set of object-oriented routines for describing a scene that is to be displayed with calls to OpenGL. The *Virtual-Reality Modeling Language* (*VRML*), which began as a subset of Open Inventor, allows us to set up three-dimensional models of virtual worlds on the Internet. We can also construct pictures on the Web using graphics libraries developed for the Java language. With *Java 2D,* we can create two-dimensional scenes within Java applets, for example. Or we can produce three-dimensional web displays with *Java 3D*. And with the *Renderman Interface* from the Pixar Corporation, we can generate scenes using a variety of lighting models. Finally, graphics libraries are often provided in other types of systems, such as Mathematica, MatLab, and Maple.

2-9 INTRODUCTION TO OpenGL

A basic library of functions is provided in OpenGL for specifying graphics primitives, attributes, geometric transformations, viewing transformations, and many other operations. As we noted in the last section, OpenGL is designed to be hardware independent, therefore many operations, such as input and output routines, are not included in the basic library. However, input and output routines and many additional functions are available in auxiliary libraries that have been developed for OpenGL programs.

Basic OpenGL Syntax

Function names in the **OpenGL basic library** (also called the **OpenGL core library**) are prefixed with `gl`, and each component word within a function name has its first letter capitalized. The following examples illustrate this naming convention.

```
glBegin,   glClear,   glCopyPixels,   glPolygonMode
```

Certain functions require that one (or more) of their arguments be assigned a symbolic constant specifying, for instance, a parameter name, a value for a parameter, or a particular mode. All such constants begin with the uppercase letters GL. In addition, component words within a constant name are written in capital letters, and the underscore (_) is used as a separator between all component words in the name. Following are a few examples of the several hundred symbolic constants available for use with OpenGL functions.

```
GL_2D,  GL_RGB,  GL_CCW,  GL_POLYGON,  GL_AMBIENT_AND_DIFFUSE
```

The OpenGL functions also expect specific data types. For example, an OpenGL function parameter might expect a value that is specified as a 32-bit integer. But the size of an integer specification can be different on different machines. To indicate a specific data type, OpenGL uses special built-in, data-type names, such as

```
GLbyte,  GLshort,  GLint,  GLfloat,  GLdouble,  GLboolean
```

Each data-type name begins with the capital letters `GL` and the remainder of the name is a standard data-type designation, written in lower-case letters.

Some arguments of OpenGL functions can be assigned values using an array that lists a set of data values. This is an option for specifying a list of values as a pointer to an array, rather than specifying each element of the list explicitly as a parameter argument. A typical example of the use of this option is in specifying *xyz* coordinate values.

Related Libraries

In addition to the OpenGL basic (core) library, there are a number of associated libraries for handling special operations. The **OpenGL Utility** (**GLU**) provides routines for setting up viewing and projection matrices, describing complex objects with line and polygon approximations, displaying quadrics and B-splines using linear approximations, processing the surface-rendering operations, and other complex tasks. Every OpenGL implementation includes the GLU library, and all GLU function names start with the prefix `glu`. There is also an object-oriented toolkit based on OpenGL, called **Open Inventor,** which provides routines and predefined object shapes for interactive three-dimensional applications. This toolkit is written in C++.

To create a graphics display using OpenGL, we first need to set up a **display window** on our video screen. This is simply the rectangular area of the screen in which our picture will be displayed. We cannot create the display window directly with the basic OpenGL functions, since this library contains only device-independent graphics functions, and window-management operations depend on the computer we are using. However, there are several window-system libraries that support OpenGL functions for a variety of machines. The **OpenGL Extension to the X Window System** (**GLX**) provides a set of routines that are prefixed with the letters `glX`. Apple systems can use the **Apple GL** (**AGL**) interface for window-management operations. Function names for this library are prefixed with `agl`. For Microsoft Windows systems, the **WGL** routines provide a **Windows-to-OpenGL** interface. These routines are prefixed with the letters `wgl`. The **Presentation Manager to OpenGL** (**PGL**) is an interface for the IBM OS/2, which uses the prefix `pgl` for the library routines. And the **OpenGL Utility Toolkit** (**GLUT**) provides a library of functions for interacting with any screen-windowing system. The GLUT library functions are prefixed with `glut`, and this library also contains methods for describing and rendering quadric curves and surfaces.

Since GLUT is an interface to other device-specific window systems, we can use GLUT so that our programs will be device independent. Information regarding the latest version of GLUT and download procedures for the source code are available at the Web site:

```
http://reality.sgi.com/opengl/glut3/glut3.html
```

Header Files

In all of our graphics programs, we will need to include the header file for the OpenGL core library. For most applications we will also need GLU. And we need to include the header file for the window system. For instance, with Microsoft Windows, the header file that accesses the WGL routines is `windows.h`. This header file must be listed before the OpenGL and GLU header files because it contains macros needed by the Microsoft Windows version of the OpenGL libraries. So the source file in this case would begin with

```
#include <windows.h>
#include <GL/gl.h>
#include <GL/glu.h>
```

However, if we use GLUT to handle the window-managing operations, we do not need to include `gl.h` and `glu.h` because GLUT ensures that these will be included correctly. Thus, we can replace the header files for OpenGL and GLU with

```
#include <GL/glut.h>
```

We could include `gl.h` and `glu.h` as well, but doing so would be redundant and could affect program portability.

In addition, we will often need to include header files that are required by the C++ code. For example,

```
#include <stdio.h>
#include <stdlib.h>
#include <math.h>
```

With the new ISO/ANSI standard for C++, these header files are called `cstdio`, `cstdlib`, and `cmath`.

Display-Window Management Using GLUT

To get started, we can consider a simplified, minimal number of operations for displaying a picture. Since we are using the OpenGL Utility Toolkit, our first step is to initialize GLUT. This initialization function could also process any command-line arguments, but we will not need to use these parameters for our first example programs. We perform the GLUT initialization with the statement

```
glutInit (&argc, argv);
```

Next, we can state that a display window is to be created on the screen with a given caption for the title bar. This is accomplished with the function

```
glutCreateWindow ("An Example OpenGL Program");
```

where the single argument for this function can be any character string we want to use for the display-window title.

Then we need to specify what the display window is to contain. For this, we create a picture using OpenGL functions and pass the picture definition to the GLUT routine `glutDisplayFunc`, which assigns our picture to the display window. As an example, suppose we have the OpenGL code for describing a line segment in a procedure called `lineSegment`. Then the following function call passes the line-segment description to the display window.

```
glutDisplayFunc (lineSegment);
```

But the display window is not yet on the screen. We need one more GLUT function to complete the window-processing operations. After execution of the following statement, all display windows that we have created, including their graphic content, are now activated.

```
glutMainLoop ( );
```

This function must be the last one in our program. It displays the initial graphics and puts the program into an infinite loop that checks for input from devices such as a mouse or keyboard. Our first example will not be interactive, so the program will just continue to display our picture until we close the display window. In later chapters, we consider how we can modify our OpenGL programs to handle interactive input.

Although the display window that we created will be in some default location and size, we can set these parameters using additional GLUT functions. We use the `glutInitWindowPosition` function to give an initial location for the top-left corner of the display window. This position is specified in integer screen coordinates, whose origin is at the upper-left corner of the screen. For instance, the following statement specifies that the top-left corner of the display window should be placed 50 pixels to the right of the left edge of the screen and 100 pixels down from the top edge of the screen.

```
glutInitWindowPosition (50, 100);
```

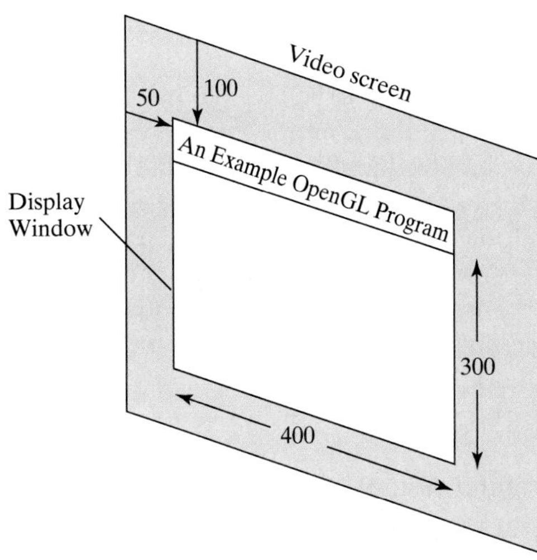

FIGURE 2-61 A 400 by 300 display window at position (50, 100) relative to the top-left corner of the video display.

Similarly, the `glutInitWindowSize` function is used to set the initial pixel width and height of the display window. Thus, we specify a display window with an initial width of 400 pixels and a height of 300 pixels (Fig. 2-61) with the statement

```
glutInitWindowSize (400, 300);
```

After the display window is on the screen, we can reposition and resize it.

We can also set a number of other options for the display window, such as buffering and a choice of color modes, with the `glutInitDisplayMode` function. Arguments for this routine are assigned symbolic GLUT constants. For example, the following command specifies that a single refresh buffer is to be used for the display window and that the RGB (red, green, blue) color mode is to be used for selecting color values.

```
glutInitDisplayMode (GLUT_SINGLE | GLUT_RGB);
```

The values of the constants passed to this function are combined using a logical *or* operation. Actually, single buffering and RGB color mode are the default options. But we will use the function now as a reminder that these are the options that are set for our display. Later, we discuss color modes in more detail, as well as other display options such as double buffering for animation applications and selecting parameters for viewing three-dimensional scenes.

A Complete OpenGL Program

There are still a few more tasks to perform before we have all the parts we need for a complete program. For the display window, we can choose a background color. And we need to construct a procedure that contains the appropriate OpenGL functions for the picture that we want to display.

Using RGB color values, we set the background color for the display window to be white, as in Fig. 2-61, with the OpenGL function

```
glClearColor (1.0, 1.0, 1.0, 0.0);
```

The first three arguments in this function set each of the red, green, and blue component colors to the value 1.0. Thus we get a white color for the display window. If, instead of 1.0, we set each of the component colors to 0.0, we would get a black background. And if each of the red, green, and blue components were set to the same intermediate value between 0.0 and 1.0, we would get some shade of gray. The fourth parameter in the `glClearColor` function is called the *alpha value* for the specified color. One use for the alpha value is as a "blending" parameter. When we activate the OpenGL blending operations, alpha values can be used to determine the resulting color for two overlapping objects. An alpha value of 0.0 indicates a totally transparent object, and an alpha value of 1.0 indicates an opaque object. Blending operations will not be used for a while, so the value of alpha is irrelevant to our early example programs. For now, we simply set alpha to 0.0.

Although the `glClearColor` command assigns a color to the display window, it does not put the display window on the screen. To get the assigned window color displayed, we need to invoke the following OpenGL function.

```
glClear (GL_COLOR_BUFFER_BIT);
```

The argument `GL_COLOR_BUFFER_BIT` is an OpenGL symbolic constant specifying that it is the bit values in the color buffer (refresh buffer) that are to be set to the values indicated in the `glClearColor` function. (We discuss other buffers in later chapters.)

In addition to setting the background color for the display window, we can choose a variety of color schemes for the objects we want to display in a scene. For our initial programming example, we will simply set object color to be red and defer further discussion of the various color options until Chapter 4:

```
glColor3f (1.0, 0.0, 0.0);
```

The suffix 3f on the `glColor` function indicates that we are specifying the three RGB color components using floating-point (`f`) values. These values must be in the range from 0.0 to 1.0, and we have set red = 1.0 and green = blue = 0.0.

For our first program, we simply display a two-dimensional line segment. To do this, we need to tell OpenGL how we want to "project" our picture onto the display window, because generating a two-dimensional picture is treated by OpenGL as a special case of three-dimensional viewing. So, although we only want to produce a very simple two-dimensional line, OpenGL processes our picture through the full three-dimensional viewing operations. We can set the projection type (mode) and other viewing parameters that we need with the following two functions.

```
glMatrixMode (GL_PROJECTION);
gluOrtho2D (0.0, 200.0, 0.0, 150.0);
```

This specifies that an orthogonal projection is to be used to map the contents of a two-dimensional (2D) rectangular area of world coordinates to the screen, and that the x-coordinate values within this rectangle range from 0.0 to 200.0 with y-coordinate values ranging from 0.0 to 150.0. Whatever objects we define within this world-coordinate rectangle will be shown within the display window. Anything outside this coordinate range will not be displayed. Therefore, the GLU function `gluOrtho2D` defines the coordinate reference frame within the

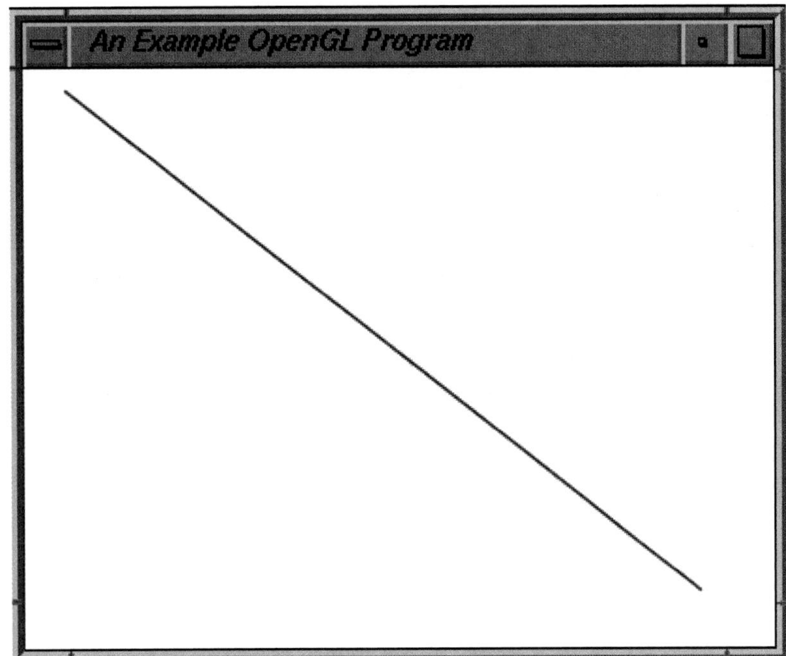

FIGURE 2-62 The display window and line segment produced by the example program.

display window to be (0.0, 0.0) at the lower-left corner of the display window and (200.0, 150.0) at the upper-right window corner. Since we are only describing a two-dimensional object, the orthogonal projection has no other effect than to "paste" our picture into the display window that we defined earlier. For now, we will use a world-coordinate rectangle with the same aspect ratio as the display window, so that there is no distortion of our picture. Later, we will consider how we can maintain an aspect ratio that is not dependent upon the display-window specification.

Finally, we need to call the appropriate OpenGL routines to create our line segment. The following code defines a two-dimensional, straight-line segment with integer, Cartesian endpoint coordinates (180, 15) and (10, 145). In Chapter 3, we present a detailed explanation of these functions and the other OpenGL functions for generating graphics primitives.

```
glBegin (GL_LINES);
    glVertex2i (180, 15);
    glVertex2i (10, 145);
glEnd ( );
```

Now we are ready to put all the pieces together. The following OpenGL program is organized into three procedures. We place all initializations and related one-time parameter settings in procedure `init`. Our geometric description of the "picture" we want to display is in procedure `lineSegment`, which is the procedure that will be referenced by the GLUT function `glutDisplayFunc`. And the `main` procedure contains the GLUT functions for setting up the display window and getting our line segment onto the screen. Figure 2-62 shows the display window and red line segment generated by this program.

```
#include <GL/glut.h>      // (or others, depending on the system in use)

void init (void)
{
    glClearColor (1.0, 1.0, 1.0, 0.0);  // Set display-window color to white.

    glMatrixMode (GL_PROJECTION);       // Set projection parameters.
    gluOrtho2D (0.0, 200.0, 0.0, 150.0);
}

void lineSegment (void)
{
    glClear (GL_COLOR_BUFFER_BIT);  // Clear display window.

    glColor3f (1.0, 0.0, 0.0);      // Set line segment color to red.
    glBegin (GL_LINES);
        glVertex2i (180, 15);       // Specify line-segment geometry.
        glVertex2i (10, 145);
    glEnd ( );

    glFlush ( );     // Process all OpenGL routines as quickly as possible.
}

void main (int argc, char** argv)
{
    glutInit (&argc, argv);                         // Initialize GLUT.
    glutInitDisplayMode (GLUT_SINGLE | GLUT_RGB);   // Set display mode.
    glutInitWindowPosition (50, 100);   // Set top-left display-window position.
    glutInitWindowSize (400, 300);      // Set display-window width and height.
    glutCreateWindow ("An Example OpenGL Program"); // Create display window.

    init ( );                            // Execute initialization procedure.
    glutDisplayFunc (lineSegment);       // Send graphics to display window.
    glutMainLoop ( );                    // Display everything and wait.
}
```

At the end of procedure `lineSegment` is a function, `glFlush`, that we have not yet discussed. This is simply a routine to force execution of our OpenGL functions, which are stored by computer systems in buffers in different locations, depending on how OpenGL is implemented. On a busy network, for example, there could be delays in processing some buffers. But the call to `glFlush` forces all such buffers to be emptied and the OpenGL functions to be processed.

The procedure `lineSegment` that we set up to describe our picture is referred to as a *display callback function*. And this procedure is described as being "registered" by `glutDisplayFunc` as the routine to invoke whenever the display window might need to be redisplayed. This can occur, for example, if the display window is moved. In subsequent chapters we will take a look at other types of callback functions and the associated GLUT routines that we use to register them. In general, OpenGL programs are organized as a set of callback functions that are to be invoked when certain actions occur.

2-10 SUMMARY

In this introductory chapter, we surveyed the major hardware and software features of computer-graphics systems. Hardware components include video monitors, hardcopy output devices, various kinds of input devices, and components for interacting with virtual environments. Some software systems, such as CAD packages and paint programs, are designed for particular applications. Other software systems provide a library of general graphics routines that can be used within a programming language such as C++ to generate pictures for any application.

The predominant graphics display device is the raster refresh monitor, based on television technology. A raster system uses a frame buffer to store the color value for each screen position (pixel). Pictures are then painted onto the screen by retrieving this information from the frame buffer (also called a refresh buffer) as the electron beam in the CRT sweeps across each scan line, from top to bottom. Older vector displays construct pictures by drawing straight-line segments between specified endpoint positions. Picture information is then stored as a set of line-drawing instructions.

Many other video display devices are available. In particular, flat-panel display technology is developing at a rapid rate, and these devices are now used in a variety of systems, including both desktop and laptop computers. Plasma panels and liquid-crystal devices are two examples of flat-panel displays. Other display technologies include three-dimensional and stereoscopic-viewing systems. Virtual-reality systems can include either a stereoscopic headset or a standard video monitor.

For graphical input, we have a range of devices to choose from. Keyboards, button boxes, and dials are used to input text, data values, or programming options. The most popular "pointing" device is the mouse, but trackballs, spaceballs, joysticks, cursor-control keys, and thumbwheels are also used to position the screen cursor. In virtual-reality environments, data gloves are commonly used. Other input devices are image scanners, digitizers, touch panels, light pens, and voice systems.

Hardcopy devices for graphics workstations include standard printers and plotters, in addition to devices for producing slides, transparencies, and film output. Printers produce hardcopy output using dot-matrix, laser, inkjet, electrostatic, or electrothermal methods. Graphs and charts can be produced with an ink-pen plotter or with a combination printer-plotter device.

Standard graphics-programming packages developed and approved through ISO and ANSI are GKS, 3D GKS, PHIGS, and PHIGS+. Other packages that have evolved into standards are GL and OpenGL. Many other graphics libraries are available for use in a programming language, including Open Inventor, VRML, RenderMan, Java 2D, and Java 3D. Other systems, such as Mathematica, MatLab, and Maple, often provide a set of graphics-programming functions.

Normally, graphics-programming packages require coordinate specifications to be given in Cartesian reference frames. Each object for a scene can be defined in a separate modeling Cartesian-coordinate system, which is then mapped to a world-coordinate location to construct the scene. From world coordinates, three-dimensional objects are projected to a two-dimensional plane, converted to normalized device coordinates, and then transformed to the final display-device coordinates. The transformations from modeling coordinates to normalized device coordinates are independent of particular output devices that might be used in an application. Device drivers are then used to convert normalized coordinates to integer device coordinates.

Functions that are available in graphics programming packages can be divided into the following categories: graphics output primitives, attributes, geometric and modeling transformations, viewing transformations, input functions, picture-structuring operations, and control operations.

The OpenGL system consists of a device-independent set of routines (called the core library), the utility library (GLU), and the utility toolkit (GLUT). In the auxiliary set of routines provided by GLU, functions are available for generating complex objects, for parameter specifications in two-dimensional viewing applications, for dealing with surface-rendering operations, and for performing some other supporting tasks. In GLUT, we have an extensive set of functions for managing display windows, interacting with screen-window systems, and for generating some three-dimensional shapes. We can use GLUT to interface with any computer system, or we can use GLX, Apple GL, WGL, or another system-specific software package.

REFERENCES

A general treatment of electronic displays is available in Tannas (1985) and in Sherr (1993). Flat-panel devices are discussed in Depp and Howard (1993). Additional information on raster-graphics architecture can be found in Foley, van Dam, Feiner, and Hughes (1990). Three-dimensional and stereoscopic displays are discussed in Johnson (1982) and in Grotch (1983). Head-mounted displays and virtual-reality environments are discussed in Chung, et al. (1989).

Standard sources for information on OpenGL are Woo, Neider, Davis, and Shreiner (1999) and Shreiner (2000). Open Inventor is explored in Wernecke (1994). McCarthy and Descartes (1998) can be consulted for discussions of VRML. A presentation on RenderMan can be found in Upstill (1989). Examples of graphics programming in Java 2D are given in Knudsen (1999), Hardy (2000), and Horstmann and Cornell (2001). Graphics programming using Java 3D is explored in Sowizral, Rushforth, and Deering (2000); Palmer (2001); Selman (2002); and Walsh and Gehringer (2002).

For information on PHIGS and PHIGS+, see Howard, Hewitt, Hubbold, and Wyrwas (1991); Hopgood and Duce (1991); Gaskins (1992); and Blake (1993). Information on the two-dimensional GKS standard and on the evolution of graphics standards is available in Hopgood, Duce, Gallop, and Sutcliffe (1983). An additional reference for GKS is Enderle, Kansy, and Pfaff (1984).

EXERCISES

2-1 List the operating characteristics for the following display technologies: raster refresh systems, vector refresh systems, plasma panels, and LCDs.

2-2 List some applications appropriate for each of the display technologies in Exercise 2-1.

2-3 Determine the resolution (pixels per centimeter) in the x and y directions for the video monitor in use on your system. Determine the aspect ratio, and explain how relative proportions of objects can be maintained on your system.

2-4 Consider three different raster systems with resolutions of 640 by 480, 1280 by 1024, and 2560 by 2048. What size frame buffer (in bytes) is needed for each of these systems to store 12 bits per pixel? How much storage is required for each system if 24 bits per pixel are to be stored?

2-5 Suppose an RGB raster system is to be designed using an 8 inch by 10 inch screen with a resolution of 100 pixels per inch in each direction. If we want to store 6 bits per pixel in the frame buffer, how much storage (in bytes) do we need for the frame buffer?

2-6 How long would it take to load a 640-by-480 frame buffer with 12 bits per pixel, if 10^5 bits can be transferred per second? How long would it take to load a 24-bit-per-pixel frame buffer with a resolution of 1280 by 1024 using this same transfer rate?

2-7 Suppose we have a computer with 32 bits per word and a transfer rate of 1 mip (one million instructions per second). How long would it take to fill the frame buffer of a 300 dpi (dot per inch) laser printer with a page size of $8\,^1/_2$ inches by 11 inches?

2-8 Consider two raster systems with resolutions of 640 by 480 and 1280 by 1024. How many pixels could be accessed per second in each of these systems by a display controller that refreshes the screen at a rate of 60 frames per second? What is the access time per pixel in each system?

2-9 Suppose we have a video monitor with a display area that measures 12 inches across and 9.6 inches high. If the resolution is 1280 by 1024 and the aspect ratio is 1, what is the diameter of each screen point?

2-10 How much time is spent scanning across each row of pixels during screen refresh on a raster system with a resolution of 1280 by 1024 and a refresh rate of 60 frames per second?

2-11 Consider a noninterlaced raster monitor with a resolution of n by m (m scan lines and n pixels per scan line), a refresh rate of r frames per second, a horizontal retrace time of t_{horiz}, and a vertical retrace time of t_{vert}. What is the fraction of the total refresh time per frame spent in retrace of the electron beam?

2-12 What is the fraction of the total refresh time per frame spent in retrace of the electron beam for a noninterlaced raster system with a resolution of 1280 by 1024, a refresh rate of 60 Hz, a horizontal retrace time of 5 microseconds, and a vertical retrace time of 500 microseconds?

2-13 Assuming that a certain full-color (24-bit-per-pixel) RGB raster system has a 512-by-512 frame buffer, how many distinct color choices (intensity levels) would we have available? How many different colors could we display at any one time?

2-14 Compare the advantages and disadvantages of a three-dimensional monitor using a varifocal mirror to those of a stereoscopic system.

2-15 List the different input and output components that are typically used with virtual-reality systems. Also, explain how users interact with a virtual scene displayed with different output devices, such as two-dimensional and stereoscopic monitors.

2-16 Explain how virtual-reality systems can be used in design applications. What are some other applications for virtual-reality systems?

2-17 List some applications for large-screen displays.

2-18 Explain the differences between a general graphics system designed for a programmer and one designed for a specific application, such as architectural design.

2-19 Explain the differences between the OpenGL core library, the OpenGL Utility, and the OpenGL Utility Toolkit.

2-20 What command could we use to set the color of an OpenGL display window to light gray? What command would we use to set the color of the display window to black?

2-21 List the statements needed to set up an OpenGL display window whose lower-right corner is at pixel position (200, 200), with a window width of 100 pixels and a height of 75 pixels.

2-22 Explain what is meant by the term "OpenGL display callback function".

CHAPTER 3

Graphics Output Primitives

A scene from the wolfman video. The animated figure of this primitive lycanthrope is modeled with 61 bones and eight layers of fur. Each frame of the computer animation contains 100,000 surface polygons. *(Courtesy of the NVIDIA Corporation.)*

A general software package for graphics applications, sometimes referred to as a computer-graphics application programming interface (CG API), provides a library of functions that we can use within a programming language such as C++ to create pictures. As we noted in Section 2-8, the set of library functions can be subdivided into several categories. One of the first things we need to do when creating a picture is to describe the component parts of the scene to be displayed. Picture components could be trees and terrain, furniture and walls, storefronts and street scenes, automobiles and billboards, atoms and molecules, or stars and galaxies. For each type of scene, we need to describe the structure of the individual objects and their coordinate locations within the scene. Those functions in a graphics package that we use to describe the various picture components are called the **graphics output primitives,** or simply **primitives.** The output primitives describing the geometry of objects are typically referred to as **geometric primitives.** Point positions and straight-line segments are the simplest geometric primitives. Additional geometric primitives that can be available in a graphics package include circles and other conic sections, quadric surfaces, spline curves and surfaces, and polygon color areas. And most graphics systems provide some functions for displaying character strings. After the geometry of a picture has been specified within a selected coordinate reference frame, the output primitives are projected to a two-dimensional plane, corresponding to the display area of an output device, and scan converted into integer pixel positions within the frame buffer.

In this chapter, we introduce the output primitives available in OpenGL, and we also discuss the device-level algorithms for implementing the primitives. Exploring the implementation algorithms for a graphics library will give us valuable insight into the capabilities of these packages. It will also provide us with an understanding of how the functions work, perhaps how they could be improved, and how we might implement graphics routines ourselves for some special application. Research in computer graphics is continually discovering new and improved implementation techniques to provide us with methods for special applications, such as Internet graphics, and for developing faster and more realistic graphics displays in general.

3-1 COORDINATE REFERENCE FRAMES

To describe a picture, we first decide upon a convenient Cartesian coordinate system, called the world-coordinate reference frame, which could be either two-dimensional or three-dimensional. We then describe the objects in our picture by giving their geometric specifications in terms of positions in world coordinates. For instance, we define a straight-line segment with two endpoint positions, and a polygon is specified with a set of positions for its vertices. These coordinate positions are stored in the scene description along with other information about the objects, such as their color and their **coordinate extents,** which are the minimum and maximum x, y, and z values for each object. A set of coordinate extents is also described as a **bounding box** for an object. For a two-dimensional figure, the coordinate extents are sometimes called an object's **bounding rectangle.** Objects are then displayed by passing the scene information to the viewing routines, which identify visible surfaces and ultimately map the objects to positions on the video monitor. The scan-conversion process stores information about the scene, such as color values, at the appropriate locations in the frame buffer, and the objects in the scene are displayed on the output device.

Screen Coordinates

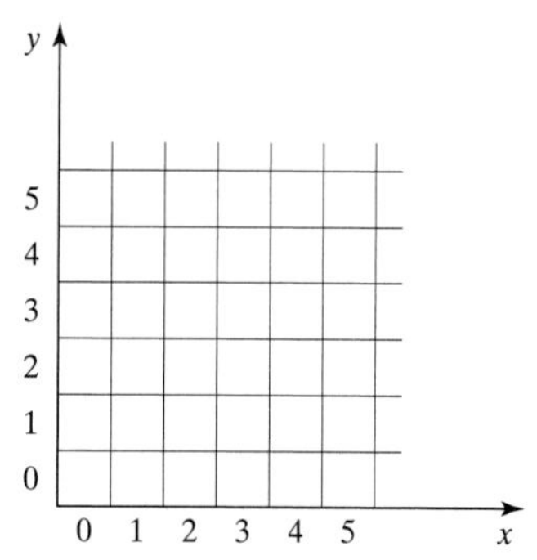

FIGURE 3-1 Pixel positions referenced with respect to the lower-left corner of a screen area.

Locations on a video monitor are referenced in integer **screen coordinates,** which correspond to the pixel positions in the frame buffer. Pixel coordinate values give the *scan line number* (the y value) and the *column number* (the x value along a scan line). Hardware processes, such as screen refreshing, typically address pixel positions with respect to the top-left corner of the screen. Scan lines are then referenced from 0, at the top of the screen, to some integer value, y_{max}, at the bottom of the screen, and pixel positions along each scan line are numbered from 0 to x_{max}, left to right. However, with software commands, we can set up any convenient reference frame for screen positions. For example, we could specify an integer range for screen positions with the coordinate origin at the lower-left of a screen area (Fig. 3-1), or we could use noninteger Cartesian values for a picture description. The coordinate values we use to describe the geometry of a scene are then converted by the viewing routines to integer pixel positions within the frame buffer.

Scan-line algorithms for the graphics primitives use the defining coordinate descriptions to determine the locations of pixels that are to be displayed. For example, given the endpoint coordinates for a line segment, a display algorithm must calculate the positions for those pixels that lie along the line path between the endpoints. Since a pixel position occupies a finite area of the screen, the finite size of a pixel must be taken into account by the implementation algorithms. For the present, we assume that each integer screen position references the center of a pixel area. (In Section 3-13, we consider alternative pixel-addressing schemes.)

Once pixel positions have been identified for an object, the appropriate color values must be stored in the frame buffer. For this purpose, we will assume that we have available a low-level procedure of the form

```
setPixel (x, y);
```

This procedure stores the current color setting into the frame buffer at integer position (x, y), relative to the selected position of the screen-coordinate origin. We sometimes also will want to be able to retrieve the current frame-buffer setting for a pixel location. So we will assume that we have the following low-level function for obtaining a frame-buffer color value.

```
getPixel (x, y, color);
```

In this function, parameter `color` receives an integer value corresponding to the combined RGB bit codes stored for the specified pixel at position (x, y).

Although, we need only specify color values at (x, y) positions for a two-dimensional picture, additional screen-coordinate information is needed for three-dimensional scenes. In this case, screen coordinates are stored as three-dimensional values, where the third dimension references the depth of object positions relative to a viewing position. For a two-dimensional scene, all depth values are 0.

Absolute and Relative Coordinate Specifications

So far, the coordinate references that we have discussed are stated as **absolute coordinate** values. This means that the values specified are the actual positions within the coordinate system in use.

However, some graphics packages also allow positions to be specified using **relative coordinates.** This method is useful for various graphics applications, such as producing drawings with pen plotters, artist's drawing and painting systems, and graphics packages for publishing and printing applications. Taking this approach, we can specify a coordinate position as an offset from the last position that was referenced (called the **current position**). For example, if location (3, 8) is the last position that has been referenced in an application program, a relative coordinate specification of $(2, -1)$ corresponds to an absolute position of $(5, 7)$. An additional function is then used to set a current position before any coordinates for primitive functions are specified. To describe an object, such as a series of connected line segments, we then need to give only a sequence of relative coordinates (offsets), once a starting position has been established. Options can be provided in a graphics system to allow the specification of locations using either relative or absolute coordinates. In the following discussions, we will assume that all coordinates are specified as absolute references unless explicitly stated otherwise.

3-2 SPECIFYING A TWO-DIMENSIONAL WORLD-COORDINATE REFERENCE FRAME IN OpenGL

In our first example program (Section 2-9), we introduced the `gluOrtho2D` command, which is a function we can use to set up any two-dimensional Cartesian reference frame. The arguments for this function are the four values defining the x and y coordinate limits for the picture we want to display. Since the

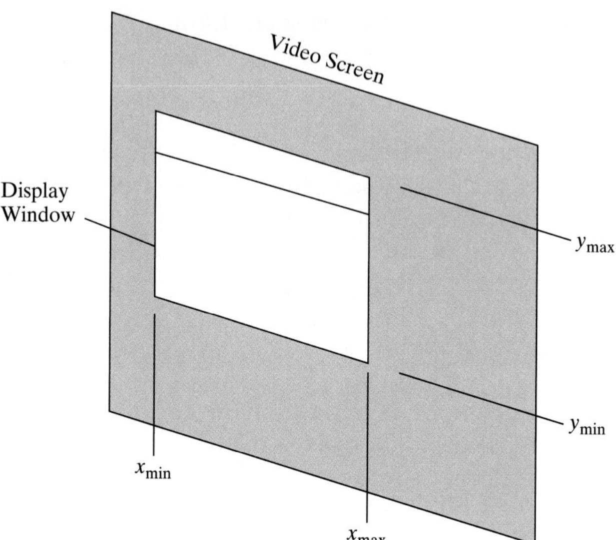

FIGURE 3-2
World-coordinate limits for a display window, as specified in the glOrtho2D function.

gluOrtho2D function specifies an orthogonal projection, we need also to be sure that the coordinate values are placed in the OpenGL projection matrix. In addition, we could assign the identity matrix as the projection matrix before defining the world-coordinate range. This would ensure that the coordinate values were not accumulated with any values we may have previously set for the projection matrix. Thus, for our initial two-dimensional examples, we can define the coordinate frame for the screen display window with the following statements.

```
glMatrixMode (GL_PROJECTION);
glLoadIdentity ( );
gluOrtho2D (xmin, xmax, ymin, ymax);
```

The display window will then be referenced by coordinates (*xmin*, *ymin*) at the lower-left corner and by coordinates (*xmax*, *ymax*) at the upper-right corner, as shown in Fig. 3-2.

We can then designate one or more graphics primitives for display using the coordinate reference specified in the gluOrtho2D statement. If the coordinate extents of a primitive are within the coordinate range of the display window, all of the primitive will be displayed. Otherwise, only those parts of the primitive within the display-window coordinate limits will be shown. Also, when we set up the geometry describing a picture, all positions for the OpenGL primitives must be given in absolute coordinates, with respect to the reference frame defined in the gluOrtho2D function.

3-3 OpenGL POINT FUNCTIONS

To specify the geometry of a point, we simply give a coordinate position in the world reference frame. Then this coordinate position, along with other geometric descriptions we may have in our scene, is passed to the viewing routines. Unless we specify other attribute values, OpenGL primitives are displayed with a default size and color. The default color for primitives is white and the default point size is equal to the size of one screen pixel.

We use the following OpenGL function to state the coordinate values for a single position

```
glVertex* ( );
```

where the asterisk (*) indicates that suffix codes are required for this function. These suffix codes are used to identify the spatial dimension, the numerical data type to be used for the coordinate values, and a possible vector form for the coordinate specification. A `glVertex` function must be placed between a `glBegin` function and a `glEnd` function. The argument of the `glBegin` function is used to identify the kind of output primitive that is to be displayed, and `glEnd` takes no arguments. For point plotting, the argument of the `glBegin` function is the symbolic constant `GL_POINTS`. Thus, the form for an OpenGL specification of a point position is

```
glBegin (GL_POINTS);
   glVertex* ( );
glEnd ( );
```

Although the term *vertex* strictly refers to a "corner" point of a polygon, the point of intersection of the sides of an angle, a point of intersection of an ellipse with its major axis, or other similar coordinate positions on geometric structures, the `glVertex` function is used in OpenGL to specify coordinates for any point position. In this way, a single function is used for point, line, and polygon specifications—and, most often, polygon patches are used to describe the objects in a scene.

Coordinate positions in OpenGL can be given in two, three, or four dimensions. We use a suffix value of 2, 3, or 4 on the `glVertex` function to indicate the dimensionality of a coordinate position. A four-dimensional specification indicates a *homogeneous-coordinate* representation, where the *homogeneous parameter* h (the fourth coordinate) is a scaling factor for the Cartesian-coordinate values. Homogeneous-coordinate representations are useful for expressing transformation operations in matrix form, and they are discussed in detail in Chapter 5. Since OpenGL treats two dimensions as a special case of three dimensions, any (x, y) coordinate specification is equivalent to $(x, y, 0)$ with $h = 1$.

We need to state also which data type is to be used for the numerical-value specifications of the coordinates. This is accomplished with a second suffix code on the `glVertex` function. Suffix codes for specifying a numerical data type are `i` (integer), `s` (short), `f` (float), and `d` (double). Finally, the coordinate values can be listed explicitly in the `glVertex` function, or a single argument can be used that references a coordinate position as an array. If we use an array specification for a coordinate position, we need to append a third suffix code: `v` (for "vector").

In the following example, three equally spaced points are plotted along a two-dimensional straight-line path with a slope of 2 (Fig. 3-3). Coordinates are given as integer pairs.

```
glBegin (GL_POINTS);
  glVertex2i (50, 100);
  glVertex2i (75, 150);
  glVertex2i (100, 200);
glEnd ( );
```

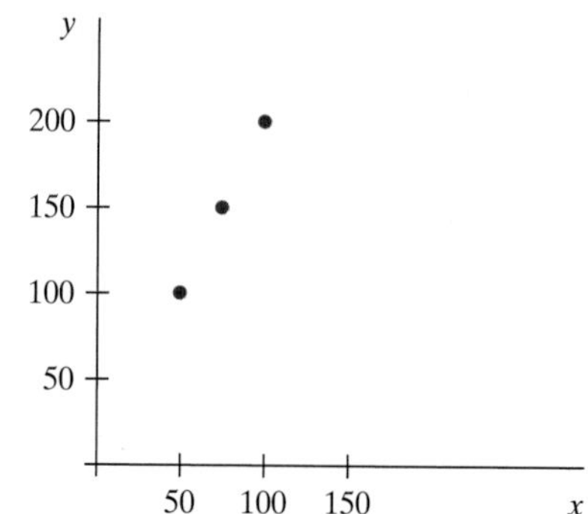

FIGURE 3-3 Display of three point positions generated with glBegin (GL_POINTS).

Alternatively, we could specify the coordinate values for the preceding points in arrays such as

```
int point1 [ ] = {50, 100};
int point2 [ ] = {75, 150};
int point3 [ ] = {100, 200};
```

and call the OpenGL functions for plotting the three points as

```
glBegin (GL_POINTS);
  glVertex2iv (point1);
  glVertex2iv (point2);
  glVertex2iv (point3);
glEnd ( );
```

And here is an example of specifying two point positions in a three-dimensional world reference frame. In this case, we give the coordinates as explicit floating-point values.

```
glBegin (GL_POINTS);
  glVertex3f (-78.05, 909.72, 14.60);
  glVertex3f (261.91, -5200.67, 188.33);
glEnd ( );
```

We could also define a C++ class or structure (`struct`) for specifying point positions in various dimensions. For example,

```
class wcPt2D {
public:
   GLfloat x, y;
};
```

Using this class definition, we could specify a two-dimensional, world-coordinate point position with the statements

```
wcPt2D pointPos;

pointPos.x = 120.75;
pointPos.y = 45.30;
glBegin (GL_POINTS);
   glVertex2f (pointPos.x, pointPos.y);
glEnd ( );
```

And we can use the OpenGL point-plotting functions within a C++ procedure to implement the `setPixel` command.

3-4 OpenGL LINE FUNCTIONS

Graphics packages typically provide a function for specifying one or more straight-line segments, where each line segment is defined by two endpoint coordinate positions. In OpenGL, we select a single endpoint coordinate position using the `glVertex` function, just as we did for a point position. And we enclose a list of `glVertex` functions between the `glBegin/glEnd` pair. But now we use a symbolic constant as the argument for the `glBegin` function that interprets a list of positions as the endpoint coordinates for line segments. There are three symbolic constants in OpenGL that we can use to specify how a list of endpoint positions should be connected to form a set of straight-line segments. By default, each symbolic constant displays solid, white lines.

A set of straight-line segments between each successive pair of endpoints in a list is generated using the primitive line constant `GL_LINES`. In general, this will result in a set of unconnected lines unless some coordinate positions are repeated. Nothing is displayed if only one endpoint is specified, and the last endpoint is not processed if the number of endpoints listed is odd. For example, if we have five coordinate positions, labeled `p1` through `p5`, and each is represented as a two-dimensional array, then the following code could generate the display shown in Fig. 3-4(a).

```
glBegin (GL_LINES);
   glVertex2iv (p1);
   glVertex2iv (p2);
   glVertex2iv (p3);
   glVertex2iv (p4);
   glVertex2iv (p5);
glEnd ( );
```

Thus, we obtain one line segment between the first and second coordinate positions, and another line segment between the third and fourth positions. In this case, the number of specified endpoints is odd, so the last coordinate position is ignored.

With the OpenGL primitive constant `GL_LINE_STRIP`, we obtain a **polyline.**

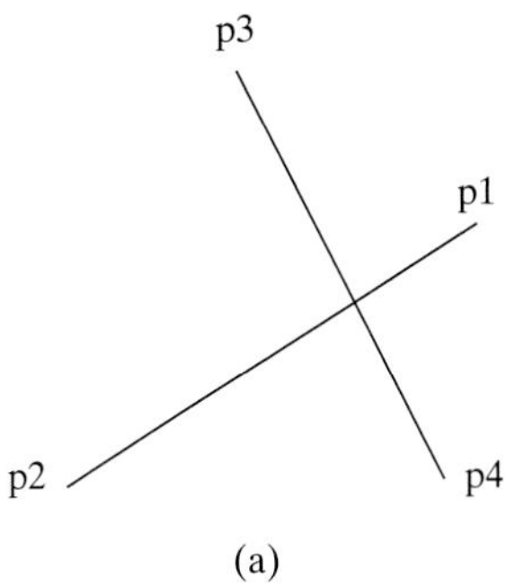

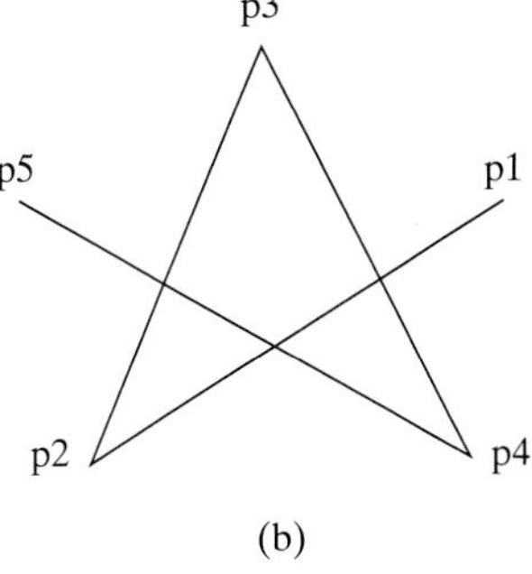

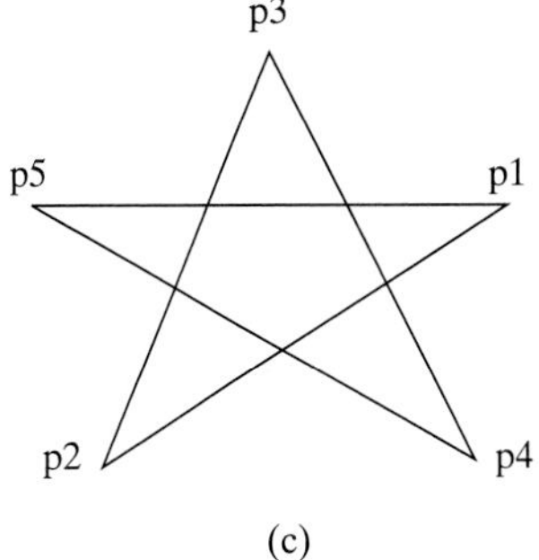

FIGURE 3-4 Line segments that can be displayed in OpenGL using a list of five endpoint coordinates. (a) An unconnected set of lines generated with the primitive line constant `GL_LINES`. (b) A polyline generated with `GL_LINE_STRIP`. (c) A closed polyline generated with `GL_LINE_LOOP`.

In this case, the display is a sequence of connected line segments between the first endpoint in the list and the last endpoint. The first line segment in the polyline is displayed between the first endpoint and the second endpoint; the second line segment is between the second and third endpoints; and so forth, up to the last line endpoint. Nothing is displayed if we do not list at least two coordinate positions. Using the same five coordinate positions as in the previous example, we obtain the display in Fig. 3-4(b) with the code

```
glBegin (GL_LINE_STRIP);
   glVertex2iv (p1);
   glVertex2iv (p2);
   glVertex2iv (p3);
   glVertex2iv (p4);
   glVertex2iv (p5);
glEnd ( );
```

The third OpenGL line primitive is `GL_LINE_LOOP`, which produces a **closed polyline.** An additional line is added to the line sequence from the previous example, so that the last coordinate endpoint in the sequence is connected to the first coordinate endpoint of the polyline. Figure 3-4(c) shows the display of our endpoint list when we select this line option.

```
glBegin (GL_LINE_LOOP);
   glVertex2iv (p1);
   glVertex2iv (p2);
   glVertex2iv (p3);
   glVertex2iv (p4);
   glVertex2iv (p5);
glEnd ( );
```

As noted earlier, picture components are described in a world-coordinate reference frame that is eventually mapped to the coordinate reference for the output device. Then the geometric information about the picture is scan converted to pixel positions. In the next section, we take a look at the scan-conversion algorithms for implementing the OpenGL line functions.

3-5 LINE-DRAWING ALGORITHMS

A straight-line segment in a scene is defined by the coordinate positions for the endpoints of the segment. To display the line on a raster monitor, the graphics system must first project the endpoints to integer screen coordinates and determine the nearest pixel positions along the line path between the two endpoints. Then the line color is loaded into the frame buffer at the corresponding pixel coordinates. Reading from the frame buffer, the video controller plots the screen pixels. This process digitizes the line into a set of discrete integer positions that, in general, only approximates the actual line path. A computed line position of (10.48, 20.51), for example, is converted to pixel position (10, 21). This rounding of coordinate values to integers causes all but horizontal and vertical lines to be displayed with a stair-step appearance ("the jaggies"), as represented in Fig. 3-5. The characteristic stair-step shape of raster lines is particularly noticeable on systems with low resolution, and we can improve their appearance somewhat by displaying them

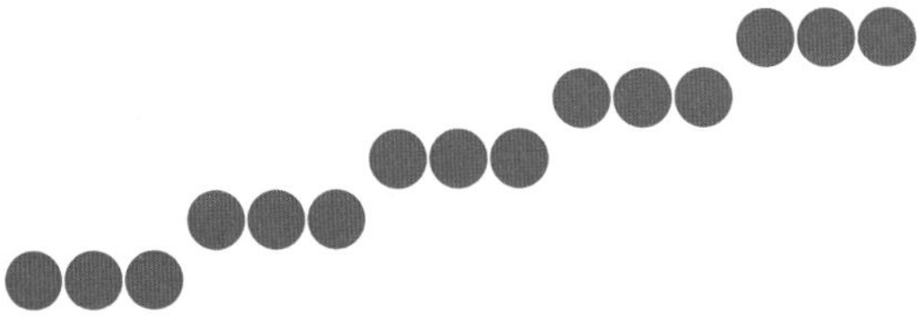

FIGURE 3-5 Stair-step effect (jaggies) produced when a line is generated as a series of pixel positions.

on high-resolution systems. More effective techniques for smoothing a raster line are based on adjusting pixel intensities along the line path (Section 4-17).

Line Equations

We determine pixel positions along a straight-line path from the geometric properties of the line. The Cartesian *slope-intercept equation* for a straight line is

$$y = m \cdot x + b \tag{3-1}$$

with m as the slope of the line and b as the y intercept. Given that the two endpoints of a line segment are specified at positions (x_0, y_0) and $(x_{\text{end}}, y_{\text{end}})$, as shown in Fig. 3-6, we can determine values for the slope m and y intercept b with the following calculations:

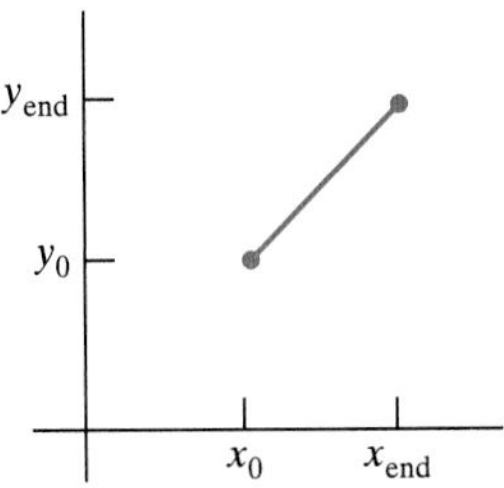

FIGURE 3-6 Line path between endpoint positions (x_0, y_0) and $(x_{\text{end}}, y_{\text{end}})$.

$$m = \frac{y_{\text{end}} - y_0}{x_{\text{end}} - x_0} \tag{3-2}$$

$$b = y_0 - m \cdot x_0 \tag{3-3}$$

Algorithms for displaying straight lines are based on the line equation 3-1 and the calculations given in Eqs. 3-2 and 3-3.

For any given x interval δx along a line, we can compute the corresponding y interval δy from Eq. 3-2 as

$$\delta y = m \cdot \delta x \tag{3-4}$$

Similarly, we can obtain the x interval δx corresponding to a specified δy as

$$\delta x = \frac{\delta y}{m} \tag{3-5}$$

These equations form the basis for determining deflection voltages in analog displays, such as a vector-scan system, where arbitrarily small changes in deflection voltage are possible. For lines with slope magnitudes $|m| < 1$, δx can be set proportional to a small horizontal deflection voltage, and the corresponding vertical deflection is then set proportional to δy as calculated from Eq. 3-4. For lines whose slopes have magnitudes $|m| > 1$, δy can be set proportional to a small vertical deflection voltage with the corresponding horizontal deflection voltage set proportional to δx, calculated from Eq. 3-5. For lines with $m = 1$, $\delta x = \delta y$ and the horizontal and vertical deflections voltages are equal. In each case, a smooth line with slope m is generated between the specified endpoints.

On raster systems, lines are plotted with pixels, and step sizes in the horizontal and vertical directions are constrained by pixel separations. That is, we must "sample" a line at discrete positions and determine the nearest pixel to the line at each sampled position. This scan-conversion process for straight lines is illustrated in Fig. 3-7 with discrete sample positions along the x axis.

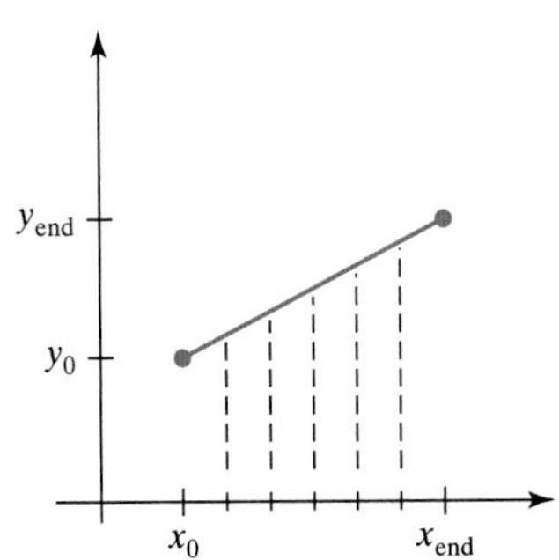

FIGURE 3-7 Straight-line segment with five sampling positions along the x axis between x_0 and x_{end}.

DDA Algorithm

The *digital differential analyzer* (DDA) is a scan-conversion line algorithm based on calculating either δy or δx, using Eq. 3-4 or Eq. 3-5. A line is sampled at unit intervals in one coordinate and the corresponding integer values nearest the line path are determined for the other coordinate.

We consider first a line with positive slope, as shown in Fig. 3-6. If the slope is less than or equal to 1, we sample at unit x intervals ($\delta x = 1$) and compute successive y values as

$$y_{k+1} = y_k + m \tag{3-6}$$

Subscript k takes integer values starting from 0, for the first point, and increases by 1 until the final endpoint is reached. Since m can be any real number between 0.0 and 1.0, each calculated y value must be rounded to the nearest integer corresponding to a screen pixel position in the x column we are processing.

For lines with a positive slope greater than 1.0, we reverse the roles of x and y. That is, we sample at unit y intervals ($\delta y = 1$) and calculate consecutive x values as

$$x_{k+1} = x_k + \frac{1}{m} \tag{3-7}$$

In this case, each computed x value is rounded to the nearest pixel position along the current y scan line.

Equations 3-6 and 3-7 are based on the assumption that lines are to be processed from the left endpoint to the right endpoint (Fig. 3-6). If this processing is reversed, so that the starting endpoint is at the right, then either we have $\delta x = -1$ and

$$y_{k+1} = y_k - m \tag{3-8}$$

or (when the slope is greater than 1) we have $\delta y = -1$ with

$$x_{k+1} = x_k - \frac{1}{m} \tag{3-9}$$

Similar calculations are carried out using equations 3-6 through 3-9 to determine pixel positions along a line with negative slope. Thus, if the absolute value of the slope is less than 1 and the starting endpoint is at the left, we set $\delta x = 1$ and calculate y values with Eq. 3-6. When the starting endpoint is at the right (for the same slope), we set $\delta x = -1$ and obtain y positions using Eq. 3-8. For a negative slope with absolute value greater than 1, we use $\delta y = -1$ and Eq. 3-9 or we use $\delta y = 1$ and Eq. 3-7.

This algorithm is summarized in the following procedure, which accepts as input two integer screen positions for the endpoints of a line segment. Horizontal and vertical differences between the endpoint positions are assigned to parameters `dx` and `dy`. The difference with the greater magnitude determines the value of parameter `steps`. Starting with pixel position (`x0, y0`), we determine the offset needed at each step to generate the next pixel position along the line path. We loop through this process `steps` times. If the magnitude of `dx` is greater than the magnitude of `dy` and `x0` is less than `xEnd`, the values for the increments in the x and y directions are 1 and m, respectively. If the greater change is in the x direction, but `x0` is greater than `xEnd`, then the decrements -1 and $-m$ are used to generate each new point on the line. Otherwise, we use a unit increment (or decrement) in the y direction and an x increment (or decrement) of $\frac{1}{m}$.

```
#include <stdlib.h>
#include <math.h>

inline int round (const float a)  { return int (a + 0.5); }

void lineDDA (int x0, int y0, int xEnd, int yEnd)
{
   int dx = xEnd - x0,  dy = yEnd - y0,  steps,  k;
   float xIncrement, yIncrement, x = x0, y = y0;

   if (fabs (dx) > fabs (dy))
      steps = fabs (dx);
   else
      steps = fabs (dy);
   xIncrement = float (dx) / float (steps);
   yIncrement = float (dy) / float (steps);

   setPixel (round (x), round (y));
   for (k = 0; k < steps; k++) {
      x += xIncrement;
      y += yIncrement;
      setPixel (round (x), round (y));
   }
}
```

The DDA algorithm is a faster method for calculating pixel positions than one that directly implements Eq. 3-1. It eliminates the multiplication in Eq. 3-1 by making use of raster characteristics, so that appropriate increments are applied in the x or y directions to step from one pixel position to another along the line path. The accumulation of round-off error in successive additions of the floating-point increment, however, can cause the calculated pixel positions to drift away from the true line path for long line segments. Furthermore, the rounding operations and floating-point arithmetic in this procedure are still time consuming. We can improve the performance of the DDA algorithm by separating the increments m and $\frac{1}{m}$ into integer and fractional parts so that all calculations are reduced to integer operations. A method for calculating $\frac{1}{m}$ increments in integer steps is discussed in Section 4-10. And in the next section, we consider a more general scan-line approach that can be applied to both lines and curves.

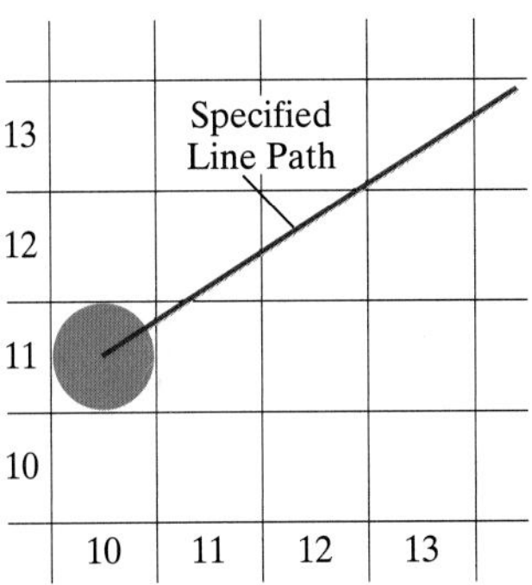

FIGURE 3-8 A section of a display screen where a straight-line segment is to be plotted, starting from the pixel at column 10 on scan line 11.

Bresenham's Line Algorithm

In this section, we introduce an accurate and efficient raster line-generating algorithm, developed by Bresenham, that uses only incremental integer calculations. In addition, Bresenham's line algorithm can be adapted to display circles and other curves. Figures 3-8 and 3-9 illustrate sections of a display screen where straight-line segments are to be drawn. The vertical axes show scan-line positions, and the horizontal axes identify pixel columns. Sampling at unit x intervals in these examples, we need to decide which of two possible pixel positions is closer to the line path at each sample step. Starting from the left endpoint shown in Fig. 3-8, we need to determine at the next sample position whether to plot the pixel at position (11, 11) or the one at (11, 12). Similarly, Fig 3-9 shows a negative-slope line path

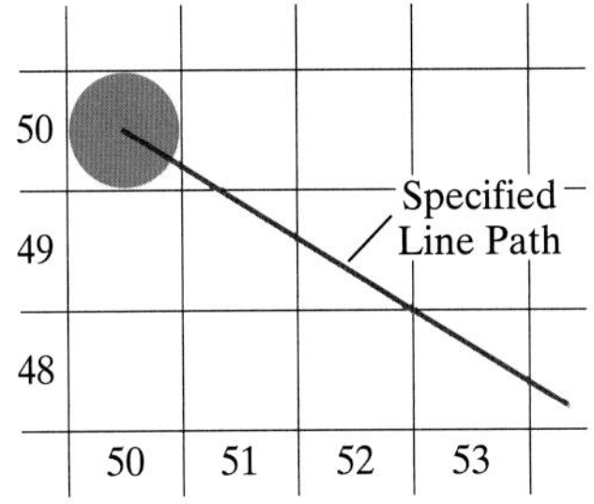

FIGURE 3-9 A section of a display screen where a negative slope line segment is to be plotted, starting from the pixel at column 50 on scan line 50.

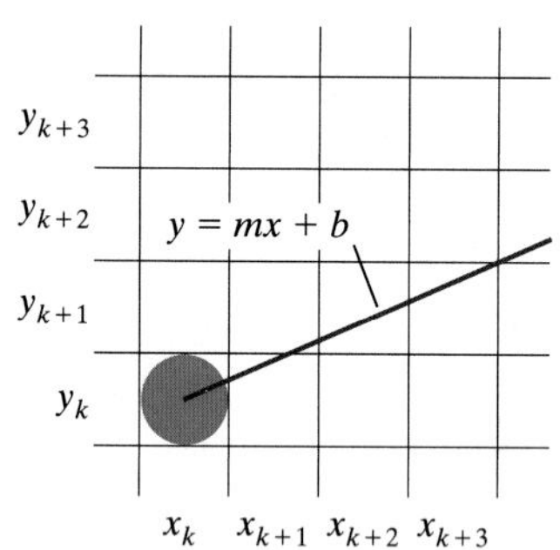

FIGURE 3-10 A section of the screen showing a pixel in column x_k on scan line y_k that is to be plotted along the path of a line segment with slope $0 < m < 1$.

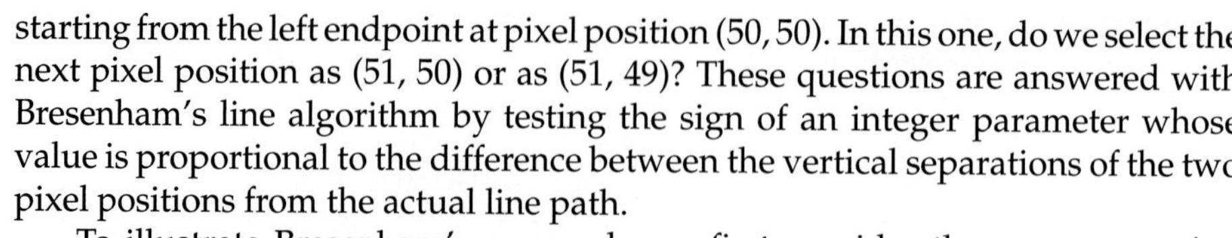

starting from the left endpoint at pixel position (50, 50). In this one, do we select the next pixel position as (51, 50) or as (51, 49)? These questions are answered with Bresenham's line algorithm by testing the sign of an integer parameter whose value is proportional to the difference between the vertical separations of the two pixel positions from the actual line path.

To illustrate Bresenham's approach, we first consider the scan-conversion process for lines with positive slope less than 1.0. Pixel positions along a line path are then determined by sampling at unit x intervals. Starting from the left endpoint (x_0, y_0) of a given line, we step to each successive column (x position) and plot the pixel whose scan-line y value is closest to the line path. Figure 3-10 demonstrates the kth step in this process. Assuming we have determined that the pixel at (x_k, y_k) is to be displayed, we next need to decide which pixel to plot in column $x_{k+1} = x_k + 1$. Our choices are the pixels at positions $(x_k + 1, y_k)$ and $(x_k + 1, y_k + 1)$.

At sampling position $x_k + 1$, we label vertical pixel separations from the mathematical line path as d_{lower} and d_{upper} (Fig. 3-11). The y coordinate on the mathematical line at pixel column position $x_k + 1$ is calculated as

$$y = m(x_k + 1) + b \tag{3-10}$$

Then

$$\begin{aligned} d_{\text{lower}} &= y - y_k \\ &= m(x_k + 1) + b - y_k \end{aligned} \tag{3-11}$$

and

$$\begin{aligned} d_{\text{upper}} &= (y_k + 1) - y \\ &= y_k + 1 - m(x_k + 1) - b \end{aligned} \tag{3-12}$$

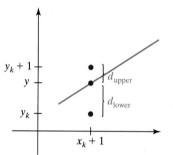

FIGURE 3-11 Vertical distances between pixel positions and the line y coordinate at sampling position $x_k + 1$.

To determine which of the two pixels is closest to the line path, we can set up an efficient test that is based on the difference between the two pixel separations:

$$d_{\text{lower}} - d_{\text{upper}} = 2m(x_k + 1) - 2y_k + 2b - 1 \tag{3-13}$$

A decision parameter p_k for the kth step in the line algorithm can be obtained by rearranging Eq. 3-13 so that it involves only integer calculations. We accomplish this by substituting $m = \Delta y/\Delta x$, where Δy and Δx are the vertical and horizontal separations of the endpoint positions, and defining the decision parameter as

$$\begin{aligned} p_k &= \Delta x(d_{\text{lower}} - d_{\text{upper}}) \\ &= 2\Delta y \cdot x_k - 2\Delta x \cdot y_k + c \end{aligned} \tag{3-14}$$

The sign of p_k is the same as the sign of $d_{\text{lower}} - d_{\text{upper}}$, since $\Delta x > 0$ for our example. Parameter c is constant and has the value $2\Delta y + \Delta x(2b - 1)$, which is independent of the pixel position and will be eliminated in the recursive calculations for p_k. If the pixel at y_k is "closer" to the line path than the pixel at $y_k + 1$ (that is, $d_{\text{lower}} < d_{\text{upper}}$), then decision parameter p_k is negative. In that case, we plot the lower pixel; otherwise we plot the upper pixel.

Coordinate changes along the line occur in unit steps in either the x or y directions. Therefore, we can obtain the values of successive decision parameters using incremental integer calculations. At step $k + 1$, the decision parameter is evaluated from Eq. 3-14 as

$$p_{k+1} = 2\Delta y \cdot x_{k+1} - 2\Delta x \cdot y_{k+1} + c$$

Subtracting Eq. 3-14 from the preceding equation, we have

$$p_{k+1} - p_k = 2\Delta y(x_{k+1} - x_k) - 2\Delta x(y_{k+1} - y_k)$$

But $x_{k+1} = x_k + 1$, so that

$$p_{k+1} = p_k + 2\Delta y - 2\Delta x(y_{k+1} - y_k) \tag{3-15}$$

where the term $y_{k+1} - y_k$ is either 0 or 1, depending on the sign of parameter p_k.

This recursive calculation of decision parameters is performed at each integer x position, starting at the left coordinate endpoint of the line. The first parameter, p_0, is evaluated from Eq. 3-14 at the starting pixel position (x_0, y_0) and with m evaluated as $\Delta y/\Delta x$:

$$p_0 = 2\Delta y - \Delta x \tag{3-16}$$

We summarize Bresenham line drawing for a line with a positive slope less than 1 in the following outline of the algorithm. The constants $2\Delta y$ and $2\Delta y - 2\Delta x$ are calculated once for each line to be scan converted, so the arithmetic involves only integer addition and subtraction of these two constants.

Bresenham's Line-Drawing Algorithm for $|m| < 1.0$

1. Input the two line endpoints and store the left endpoint in (x_0, y_0).
2. Set the color for frame-buffer position (x_0, y_0); i.e., plot the first point.
3. Calculate the constants Δx, Δy, $2\Delta y$, and $2\Delta y - 2\Delta x$, and obtain the starting value for the decision parameter as

$$p_0 = 2\Delta y - \Delta x$$

4. At each x_k along the line, starting at $k = 0$, perform the following test. If $p_k < 0$, the next point to plot is $(x_k + 1, y_k)$ and

$$p_{k+1} = p_k + 2\Delta y$$

Otherwise, the next point to plot is $(x_k + 1, y_k + 1)$ and

$$p_{k+1} = p_k + 2\Delta y - 2\Delta x$$

5. Perform step 4 $\Delta x - 1$ times.

EXAMPLE 3-1 Bresenham Line Drawing

To illustrate the algorithm, we digitize the line with endpoints (20, 10) and (30, 18). This line has a slope of 0.8, with

$$\Delta x = 10, \qquad \Delta y = 8$$

The initial decision parameter has the value:

$$p_0 = 2\Delta y - \Delta x$$
$$= 6$$

and the increments for calculating successive decision parameters are

$$2\Delta y = 16, \qquad 2\Delta y - 2\Delta x = -4$$

We plot the initial point $(x_0, y_0) = (20, 10)$, and determine successive pixel positions along the line path from the decision parameter as:

k	p_k	(x_{k+1}, y_{k+1})
0	6	(21, 11)
1	2	(22, 12)
2	−2	(23, 12)
3	14	(24, 13)
4	10	(25, 14)

k	p_k	(x_{k+1}, y_{k+1})
5	6	(26, 15)
6	2	(27, 16)
7	−2	(28, 16)
8	14	(29, 17)
9	10	(30, 18)

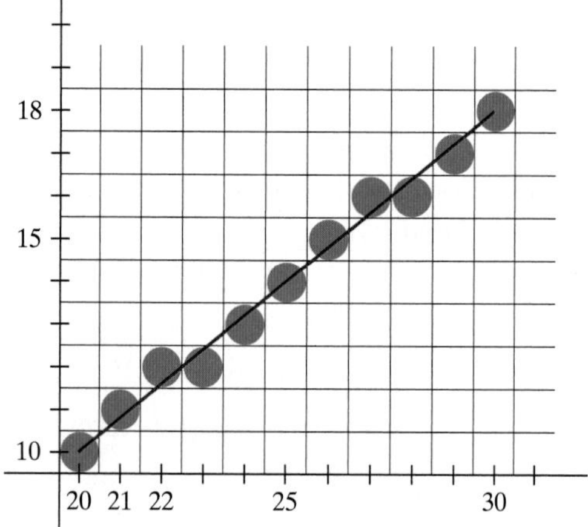

FIGURE 3-12 Pixel positions along the line path between endpoints (20, 10) and (30, 18), plotted with Bresenham's line algorithm.

A plot of the pixels generated along this line path is shown in Fig. 3-12. ■

An implementation of Bresenham line drawing for slopes in the range $0 < m < 1.0$ is given in the following procedure. Endpoint pixel positions for the line are passed to this procedure, and pixels are plotted from the left endpoint to the right endpoint.

```
#include <stdlib.h>
#include <math.h>

/*  Bresenham line-drawing procedure for |m| < 1.0.  */
void lineBres (int x0, int y0, int xEnd, int yEnd)
{
   int dx = fabs (xEnd - x0),  dy = fabs(yEnd - y0);
   int p = 2 * dy - dx;
   int twoDy = 2 * dy,  twoDyMinusDx = 2 * (dy - dx);
   int x, y;

   /* Determine which endpoint to use as start position.  */
   if (x0 > xEnd) {
      x = xEnd;
      y = yEnd;
      xEnd = x0;
   }
```

```
    else {
       x = x0;
       y = y0;
    }
    setPixel (x, y);

    while (x < xEnd) {
       x++;
       if (p < 0)
          p += twoDy;
       else {
          y++;
          p += twoDyMinusDx;
       }
       setPixel (x, y);
    }
}
```

Bresenham's algorithm is generalized to lines with arbitrary slope by considering the symmetry between the various octants and quadrants of the xy plane. For a line with positive slope greater than 1.0, we interchange the roles of the x and y directions. That is, we step along the y direction in unit steps and calculate successive x values nearest the line path. Also, we could revise the program to plot pixels starting from either endpoint. If the initial position for a line with positive slope is the right endpoint, both x and y decrease as we step from right to left. To ensure that the same pixels are plotted regardless of the starting endpoint, we always chose the upper (or the lower) of the two candidate pixels whenever the two vertical separations from the line path are equal ($d_{\text{lower}} = d_{\text{upper}}$). For negative slopes, the procedures are similar, except that now one coordinate decreases as the other increases. Finally, special cases can be handled separately: Horizontal lines ($\Delta y = 0$), vertical lines ($\Delta x = 0$), and diagonal lines ($|\Delta x| = |\Delta y|$) can each be loaded directly into the frame buffer without processing them through the line-plotting algorithm.

Displaying Polylines

Implementation of a polyline procedure is accomplished by invoking a line-drawing routine $n - 1$ times to display the lines connecting the n endpoints. Each successive call passes the coordinate pair needed to plot the next line section, where the first endpoint of each coordinate pair is the last endpoint of the previous section. Once the color values for pixel positions along the first line segment have been set in the frame buffer, we process subsequent line segments starting with the next pixel position following the first endpoint for that segment. In this way, we can avoid setting the color of some endpoints twice. We discuss methods for avoiding overlap of displayed objects in more detail in Section 3-13.

3-6 PARALLEL LINE ALGORITHMS

The line-generating algorithms we have discussed so far determine pixel positions sequentially. Using parallel processing, we can calculate multiple pixel positions along a line path simultaneously by partitioning the computations among the various processors available. One approach to the partitioning problem is to adapt an existing sequential algorithm to take advantage of multiple processors. Alternatively, we can look for other ways to set up the processing so that pixel positions can be calculated efficiently in parallel. An important consideration in devising a parallel algorithm is to balance the processing load among the available processors.

Given n_p processors, we can set up a parallel Bresenham line algorithm by subdividing the line path into n_p partitions and simultaneously generating line segments in each of the subintervals. For a line with slope $0 < m < 1.0$ and left endpoint coordinate position (x_0, y_0), we partition the line along the positive x direction. The distance between beginning x positions of adjacent partitions can be calculated as

$$\Delta x_p = \frac{\Delta x + n_p - 1}{n_p} \tag{3-17}$$

where Δx is the width of the line, and the value for partition width Δx_p is computed using integer division. Numbering the partitions, and the processors, as 0, 1, 2, up to $n_p - 1$, we calculate the starting x coordinate for the kth partition as

$$x_k = x_0 + k\Delta x_p \tag{3-18}$$

As an example, if we have $n_p = 4$ processors, with $\Delta x = 15$, the width of the partitions is 4 and the starting x values for the partitions are x_0, $x_0 + 4$, $x_0 + 8$, and $x_0 + 12$. With this partitioning scheme, the width of the last (rightmost) subinterval will be smaller than the others in some cases. In addition, if the line endpoints are not integers, truncation errors can result in variable width partitions along the length of the line.

To apply Bresenham's algorithm over the partitions, we need the initial value for the y coordinate and the initial value for the decision parameter in each partition. The change Δy_p in the y direction over each partition is calculated from the line slope m and partition width Δx_p:

$$\Delta y_p = m\Delta x_p \tag{3-19}$$

At the kth partition, the starting y coordinate is then

$$y_k = y_0 + \text{round}(k\Delta y_p) \tag{3-20}$$

The initial decision parameter for Bresenham's algorithm at the start of the kth subinterval is obtained from Eq. 3-14:

$$p_k = (k\Delta x_p)(2\Delta y) - \text{round}(k\Delta y_p)(2\Delta x) + 2\Delta y - \Delta x \tag{3-21}$$

Each processor then calculates pixel positions over its assigned subinterval using the preceding starting decision parameter value and the starting coordinates (x_k, y_k). Floating-point calculations can be reduced to integer arithmetic in the computations for starting values y_k and p_k by substituting $m = \Delta y/\Delta x$ and rearranging terms. We can extend the parallel Bresenham algorithm to a line with slope greater than 1.0 by partitioning the line in the y direction and calculating beginning x values for the partitions. For negative slopes, we increment coordinate values in one direction and decrement in the other.

Another way to set up parallel algorithms on raster systems is to assign each processor to a particular group of screen pixels. With a sufficient number of processors, we can assign each processor to one pixel within some screen region. This approach can be adapted to line display by assigning one processor to each of the pixels within the limits of the coordinate extents of the line and calculating pixel distances from the line path. The number of pixels within the bounding box of a line is $\Delta x \cdot \Delta y$ (Fig. 3-13). Perpendicular distance d from the line in Fig. 3-13 to a pixel with coordinates (x, y) is obtained with the calculation

$$d = A\,x + B\,y + C \tag{3-22}$$

where

$$A = \frac{-\Delta y}{\text{linelength}}$$

$$B = \frac{\Delta x}{\text{linelength}}$$

$$C = \frac{x_0 \Delta y - y_0 \Delta x}{\text{linelength}}$$

with

$$\text{linelength} = \sqrt{\Delta x^2 + \Delta y^2}$$

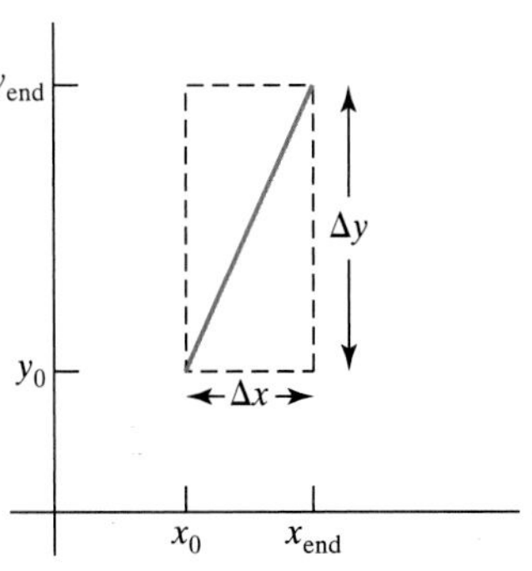

FIGURE 3-13 Bounding box for a line with endpoint separations Δx and Δy.

Once the constants A, B, and C have been evaluated for the line, each processor must perform two multiplications and two additions to compute the pixel distance d. A pixel is plotted if d is less than a specified line thickness parameter.

Instead of partitioning the screen into single pixels, we can assign to each processor either a scan line or a column of pixels depending on the line slope. Each processor then calculates the intersection of the line with the horizontal row or vertical column of pixels assigned to that processor. For a line with slope $|m| < 1.0$, each processor simply solves the line equation for y, given an x column value. For a line with slope magnitude greater than 1.0, the line equation is solved for x by each processor, given a scan line y value. Such direct methods, although slow on sequential machines, can be performed efficiently using multiple processors.

3-7 SETTING FRAME-BUFFER VALUES

A final stage in the implementation procedures for line segments and other objects is to set the frame-buffer color values. Since scan-conversion algorithms generate pixel positions at successive unit intervals, incremental operations can also be used to access the frame buffer efficiently at each step of the scan-conversion process.

As a specific example, suppose the frame buffer array is addressed in row-major order and that pixel positions are labeled from (0, 0) at the lower-left screen corner to (x_{max}, y_{max}) at the top-right corner (Fig. 3-14). For a bilevel system (one bit per pixel), the frame-buffer bit address for pixel position (x, y) is calculated as

$$\text{addr}(x, y) = \text{addr}(0, 0) + y(x_{max} + 1) + x \tag{3-23}$$

Moving across a scan line, we can calculate the frame-buffer address for the pixel at $(x + 1, y)$ as the following offset from the address for position (x, y):

$$\text{addr}(x + 1, y) = \text{addr}(x, y) + 1 \tag{3-24}$$

Stepping diagonally up to the next scan line from (x, y), we get to the frame-buffer

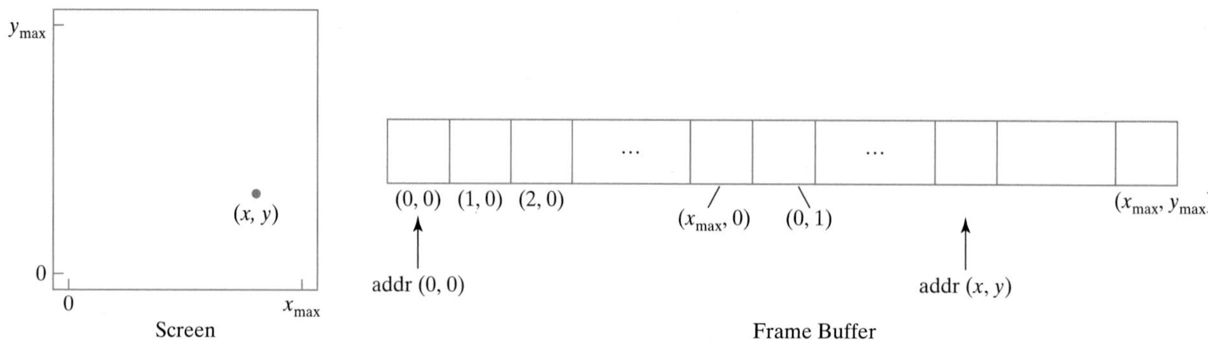

FIGURE 3-14 Pixel screen positions stored linearly in row-major order within the frame buffer.

address of $(x + 1, y + 1)$ with the calculation

$$\text{addr}(x + 1, y + 1) = \text{addr}(x, y) + x_{\text{max}} + 2 \qquad (3\text{-}25)$$

where the constant $x_{\text{max}} + 2$ is precomputed once for all line segments. Similar incremental calculations can be obtained from Eq. 3-23 for unit steps in the negative x and y screen directions. Each of the address calculations involves only a single integer addition.

Methods for implementing these procedures depend on the capabilities of a particular system and the design requirements of the software package. With systems that can display a range of intensity values for each pixel, frame-buffer address calculations include pixel width (number of bits), as well as the pixel screen location.

3-8 OpenGL CURVE FUNCTIONS

Routines for generating basic curves, such as circles and ellipses, are not included as primitive functions in the OpenGL core library. But this library does contain functions for displaying Bézier splines, which are polynomials that are defined with a discrete point set. And the OpenGL Utility (GLU) has routines for three-dimensional quadrics, such as spheres and cylinders, as well as routines for producing rational B-splines, which are a general class of splines that include the simpler Bézier curves. Using rational B-splines, we can display circles, ellipses, and other two-dimensional quadrics. In addition, there are routines in the OpenGL Utility Toolkit (GLUT) that we can use to display some three-dimensional quadrics, such as spheres and cones, and some other shapes. However, all these routines are more involved than the basic primitives we introduce in this chapter, so we defer further discussion of this group of functions until Chapter 8.

Another method we can use to generate a display of a simple curve is to approximate it using a polyline. We just need to locate a set of points along the curve path and connect the points with straight-line segments. The more line sections we include in the polyline, the smoother the appearance of the curve. As an example, Fig. 3-15 illustrates various polyline displays that could be used for a circle segment.

A third alternative is to write our own curve-generation functions based on the algorithms presented in the following sections. We first discuss efficient methods for circle and ellipse generation, then we take a look at procedures for displaying other conic sections, polynomials, and splines.

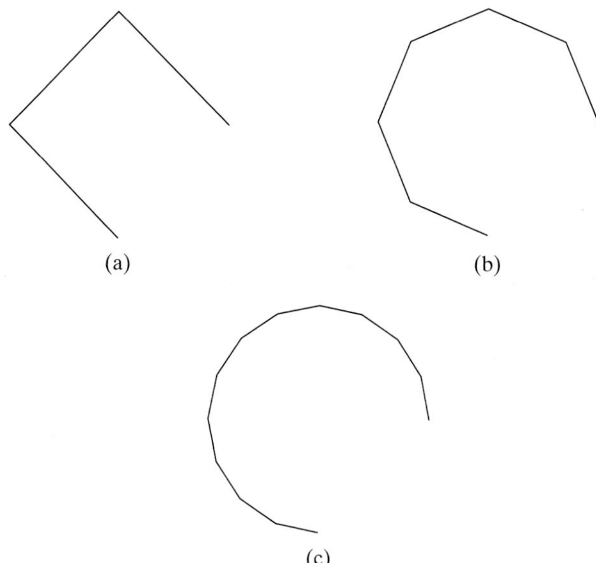

FIGURE 3-15 A circular arc approximated with (a) three straight-line segments, (b) six line segments, and (c) twelve line segments.

3-9 CIRCLE-GENERATING ALGORITHMS

Since the circle is a frequently used component in pictures and graphs, a procedure for generating either full circles or circular arcs is included in many graphics packages. And sometimes a general function is available in a graphics library for displaying various kinds of curves, including circles and ellipses.

Properties of Circles

A circle (Fig. 3-16) is defined as the set of points that are all at a given distance r from a center position (x_c, y_c). For any circle point (x, y), this distance relationship is expressed by the Pythagorean theorem in Cartesian coordinates as

$$(x - x_c)^2 + (y - y_c)^2 = r^2 \tag{3-26}$$

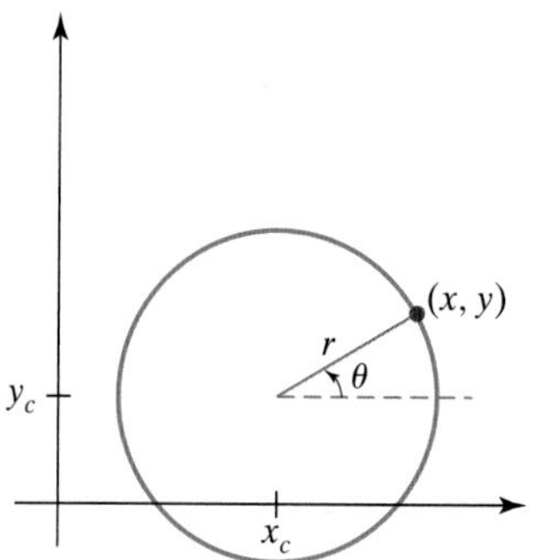

FIGURE 3-16 Circle with center coordinates (x_c, y_c) and radius r.

We could use this equation to calculate the position of points on a circle circumference by stepping along the x axis in unit steps from $x_c - r$ to $x_c + r$ and calculating the corresponding y values at each position as

$$y = y_c \pm \sqrt{r^2 - (x_c - x)^2} \tag{3-27}$$

But this is not the best method for generating a circle. One problem with this approach is that it involves considerable computation at each step. Moreover, the spacing between plotted pixel positions is not uniform, as demonstrated in Fig. 3-17. We could adjust the spacing by interchanging x and y (stepping through y values and calculating x values) whenever the absolute value of the slope of the circle is greater than 1. But this simply increases the computation and processing required by the algorithm.

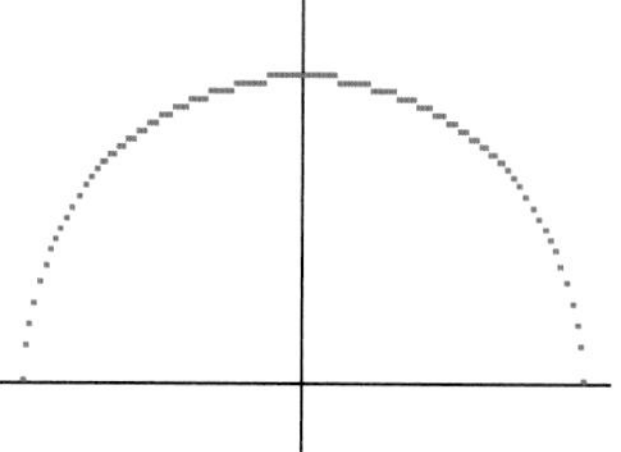

FIGURE 3-17 Upper half of a circle plotted with Eq. 3-27 and with $(x_c, y_c) = (0, 0)$.

Another way to eliminate the unequal spacing shown in Fig. 3-17 is to calculate points along the circular boundary using polar coordinates r and θ (Fig. 3-16). Expressing the circle equation in parametric polar form yields the pair of equations

$$x = x_c + r \cos\theta$$
$$y = y_c + r \sin\theta \qquad (3\text{-}28)$$

When a display is generated with these equations using a fixed angular step size, a circle is plotted with equally spaced points along the circumference. To reduce calculations, we can use a large angular separation between points along the circumference and connect the points with straight-line segments to approximate the circular path. For a more continuous boundary on a raster display, we can set the angular step size at $\frac{1}{r}$. This plots pixel positions that are approximately one unit apart. Although polar coordinates provide equal point spacing, the trigonometric calculations are still time consuming.

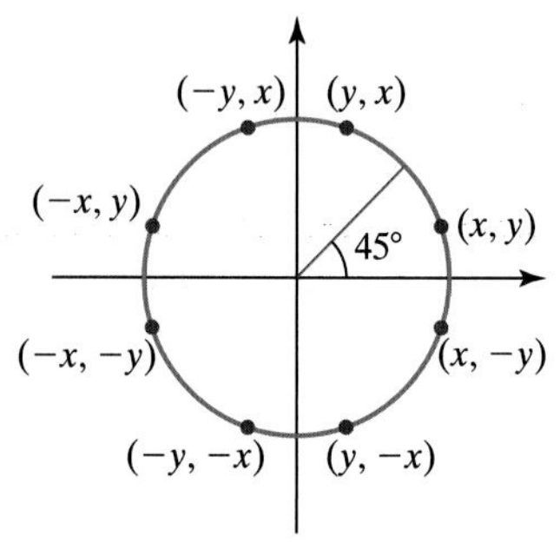

FIGURE 3-18 Symmetry of a circle. Calculation of a circle point (x, y) in one octant yields the circle points shown for the other seven octants.

For any of the previous circle-generating methods, we can reduce computations by considering the symmetry of circles. The shape of the circle is similar in each quadrant. Therefore, if we determine the curve positions in the first quadrant, we can generate the circle section in the second quadrant of the xy plane by noting that the two circle sections are symmetric with respect to the y axis. And circle sections in the third and fourth quadrants can be obtained from sections in the first and second quadrants by considering symmetry about the x axis. We can take this one step further and note that there is also symmetry between octants. Circle sections in adjacent octants within one quadrant are symmetric with respect to the 45° line dividing the two octants. These symmetry conditions are illustrated in Fig. 3-18, where a point at position (x, y) on a one-eighth circle sector is mapped into the seven circle points in the other octants of the xy plane. Taking advantage of the circle symmetry in this way, we can generate all pixel positions around a circle by calculating only the points within the sector from $x = 0$ to $x = y$. The slope of the curve in this octant has a magnitude less than or equal to 1.0. At $x = 0$, the circle slope is 0, and at $x = y$, the slope is -1.0.

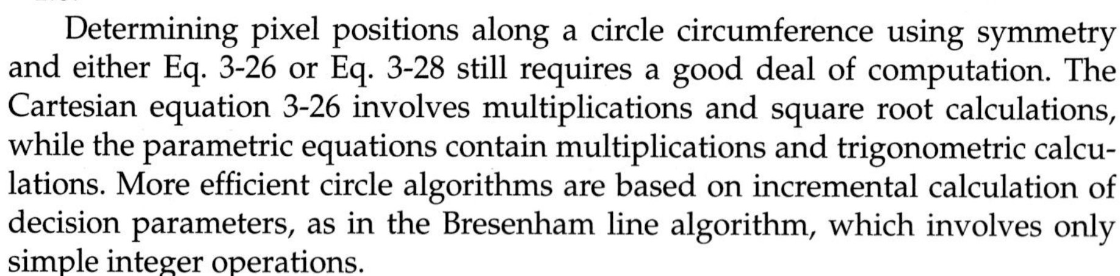

Determining pixel positions along a circle circumference using symmetry and either Eq. 3-26 or Eq. 3-28 still requires a good deal of computation. The Cartesian equation 3-26 involves multiplications and square root calculations, while the parametric equations contain multiplications and trigonometric calculations. More efficient circle algorithms are based on incremental calculation of decision parameters, as in the Bresenham line algorithm, which involves only simple integer operations.

Bresenham's line algorithm for raster displays is adapted to circle generation by setting up decision parameters for finding the closest pixel to the circumference at each sampling step. The circle equation 3-26, however, is nonlinear, so that square root evaluations would be required to compute pixel distances from a circular path. Bresenham's circle algorithm avoids these square-root calculations by comparing the squares of the pixel separation distances.

However, it is possible to perform a direct distance comparison without a squaring operation. The basic idea in this approach is to test the halfway position between two pixels to determine if this midpoint is inside or outside the circle boundary. This method is more easily applied to other conics; and for an integer circle radius, the midpoint approach generates the same pixel positions as the Bresenham circle algorithm. For a straight-line segment, the midpoint method is equivalent to the Bresenham line algorithm. Also, the error involved in locating pixel positions along any conic section using the midpoint test is limited to one-half the pixel separation.

Midpoint Circle Algorithm

As in the raster line algorithm, we sample at unit intervals and determine the closest pixel position to the specified circle path at each step. For a given radius r and screen center position (x_c, y_c), we can first set up our algorithm to calculate pixel positions around a circle path centered at the coordinate origin (0, 0). Then each calculated position (x, y) is moved to its proper screen position by adding x_c to x and y_c to y. Along the circle section from $x = 0$ to $x = y$ in the first quadrant, the slope of the curve varies from 0 to -1.0. Therefore, we can take unit steps in the positive x direction over this octant and use a decision parameter to determine which of the two possible pixel positions in any column is vertically closer to the circle path. Positions in the other seven octants are then obtained by symmetry.

To apply the midpoint method, we define a circle function as

$$f_{\text{circ}}(x, y) = x^2 + y^2 - r^2 \tag{3-29}$$

Any point (x, y) on the boundary of the circle with radius r satisfies the equation $f_{\text{circ}}(x, y) = 0$. If the point is in the interior of the circle, the circle function is negative. And if the point is outside the circle, the circle function is positive. To summarize, the relative position of any point (x, y) can be determined by checking the sign of the circle function:

$$f_{\text{circ}}(x, y) \begin{cases} < 0, & \text{if } (x, y) \text{ is inside the circle boundary} \\ = 0, & \text{if } (x, y) \text{ is on the circle boundary} \\ > 0, & \text{if } (x, y) \text{ is outside the circle boundary} \end{cases} \tag{3-30}$$

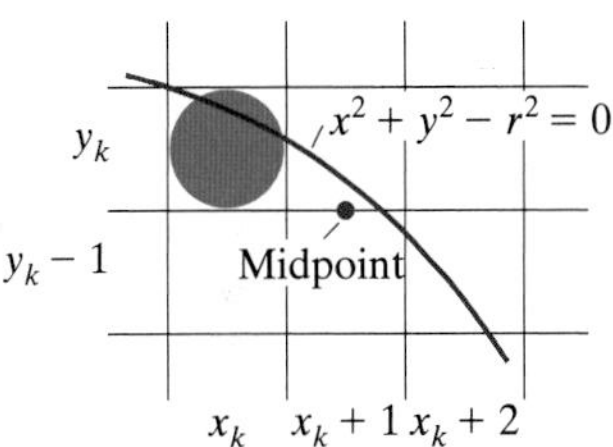

FIGURE 3-19 Midpoint between candidate pixels at sampling position $x_k + 1$ along a circular path.

The tests in 3-30 are performed for the midpositions between pixels near the circle path at each sampling step. Thus, the circle function is the decision parameter in the midpoint algorithm, and we can set up incremental calculations for this function as we did in the line algorithm.

Figure 3-19 shows the midpoint between the two candidate pixels at sampling position $x_k + 1$. Assuming that we have just plotted the pixel at (x_k, y_k), we next need to determine whether the pixel at position $(x_k + 1, y_k)$ or the one at position $(x_k + 1, y_k - 1)$ is closer to the circle. Our decision parameter is the circle function 3-29 evaluated at the midpoint between these two pixels:

$$\begin{aligned} p_k &= f_{\text{circ}}\left(x_k + 1, y_k - \frac{1}{2}\right) \\ &= (x_k + 1)^2 + \left(y_k - \frac{1}{2}\right)^2 - r^2 \end{aligned} \tag{3-31}$$

If $p_k < 0$, this midpoint is inside the circle and the pixel on scan line y_k is closer to the circle boundary. Otherwise, the midposition is outside or on the circle boundary, and we select the pixel on scan line $y_k - 1$.

Successive decision parameters are obtained using incremental calculations. We obtain a recursive expression for the next decision parameter by evaluating the circle function at sampling position $x_{k+1} + 1 = x_k + 2$:

$$\begin{aligned} p_{k+1} &= f_{\text{circ}}\left(x_{k+1} + 1, y_{k+1} - \frac{1}{2}\right) \\ &= [(x_k + 1) + 1]^2 + \left(y_{k+1} - \frac{1}{2}\right)^2 - r^2 \end{aligned}$$

or

$$p_{k+1} = p_k + 2(x_k + 1) + \left(y_{k+1}^2 - y_k^2\right) - (y_{k+1} - y_k) + 1 \tag{3-32}$$

where y_{k+1} is either y_k or $y_k - 1$, depending on the sign of p_k.

Increments for obtaining p_{k+1} are either $2x_{k+1} + 1$ (if p_k is negative) or $2x_{k+1} + 1 - 2y_{k+1}$. Evaluation of the terms $2x_{k+1}$ and $2y_{k+1}$ can also be done incrementally as

$$2x_{k+1} = 2x_k + 2$$
$$2y_{k+1} = 2y_k - 2$$

At the start position $(0, r)$, these two terms have the values 0 and $2r$, respectively. Each successive value for the $2x_{k+1}$ term is obtained by adding 2 to the previous value, and each successive value for the $2y_{k+1}$ term is obtained by subtracting 2 from the previous value.

The initial decision parameter is obtained by evaluating the circle function at the start position $(x_0, y_0) = (0, r)$:

$$\begin{aligned} p_0 &= f_{\text{circ}}\left(1, r - \frac{1}{2}\right) \\ &= 1 + \left(r - \frac{1}{2}\right)^2 - r^2 \end{aligned}$$

or

$$p_0 = \frac{5}{4} - r \tag{3-33}$$

If the radius r is specified as an integer, we can simply round p_0 to

$$p_0 = 1 - r \qquad \text{(for } r \text{ an integer)}$$

since all increments are integers.

As in Bresenham's line algorithm, the midpoint method calculates pixel positions along the circumference of a circle using integer additions and subtractions, assuming that the circle parameters are specified in integer screen coordinates. We can summarize the steps in the midpoint circle algorithm as follows.

Midpoint Circle Algorithm

1. Input radius r and circle center (x_c, y_c), then set the coordinates for the first point on the circumference of a circle centered on the origin as

$$(x_0, y_0) = (0, r)$$

2. Calculate the initial value of the decision parameter as

$$p_0 = \frac{5}{4} - r$$

3. At each x_k position, starting at $k = 0$, perform the following test. If $p_k < 0$, the next point along the circle centered on $(0, 0)$ is (x_{k+1}, y_k) and

$$p_{k+1} = p_k + 2x_{k+1} + 1$$

Otherwise, the next point along the circle is $(x_k + 1, y_k - 1)$ and

$$p_{k+1} = p_k + 2x_{k+1} + 1 - 2y_{k+1}$$

where $2x_{k+1} = 2x_k + 2$ and $2y_{k+1} = 2y_k - 2$.

4. Determine symmetry points in the other seven octants.
5. Move each calculated pixel position (x, y) onto the circular path centered at (x_c, y_c) and plot the coordinate values:

$$x = x + x_c, \qquad y = y + y_c$$

6. Repeat steps 3 through 5 until $x \geq y$.

EXAMPLE 3-2 Midpoint Circle Drawing

Given a circle radius $r = 10$, we demonstrate the midpoint circle algorithm by determining positions along the circle octant in the first quadrant from $x = 0$ to $x = y$. The initial value of the decision parameter is

$$p_0 = 1 - r = -9$$

For the circle centered on the coordinate origin, the initial point is $(x_0, y_0) = (0, 10)$, and initial increment terms for calculating the decision parameters are

$$2x_0 = 0, \qquad 2y_0 = 20$$

Successive midpoint decision parameter values and the corresponding coordinate positions along the circle path are listed in the following table.

k	p_k	(x_{k+1}, y_{k+1})	$2x_{k+1}$	$2y_{k+1}$
0	−9	(1, 10)	2	20
1	−6	(2, 10)	4	20
2	−1	(3, 10)	6	20
3	6	(4, 9)	8	18
4	−3	(5, 9)	10	18
5	8	(6, 8)	12	16
6	5	(7, 7)	14	14

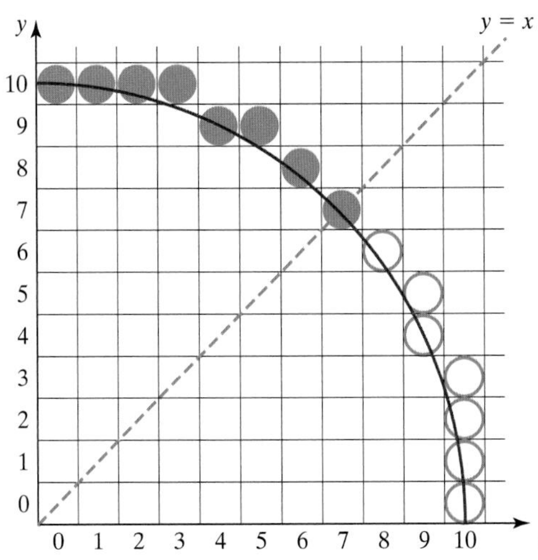

FIGURE 3-20 Pixel positions (solid circles) along a circle path centered on the origin and with radius $r = 10$, as calculated by the midpoint circle algorithm. Open ("hollow") circles show the symmetry positions in the first quadrant.

A plot of the generated pixel positions in the first quadrant is shown in Fig. 3-20. ■

The following code segment illustrates procedures that could be used to implement the midpoint circle algorithm. Values for a circle radius and for the center coordinates of the circle are passed to procedure `circleMidpoint`. A pixel position along the circular path in the first octant is then computed and passed to procedure `circlePlotPoints`. This procedure sets the circle color in the frame buffer for all circle symmetry positions with repeated calls to the `setPixel` routine, which is implemented with the OpenGL point-plotting functions.

```
#include <GL/glut.h>

class screenPt
{
    private:
       GLint x, y;

    public:
       /*  Default Constructor: initializes coordinate position to (0, 0).  */
       screenPt ( )  {
           x = y = 0;
       }
       void setCoords (GLint xCoordValue, GLint yCoordValue)  {
           x = xCoordValue;
           y = yCoordValue;
       }

       GLint getx ( ) const  {
           return x;
       }

       GLint gety ( ) const  {
           return y;
       }
       void incrementx ( )  {
           x++;
       }
       void decrementy ( )  {
           y--;
       }
};

void setPixel (GLint xCoord, GLint yCoord)
{
    glBegin (GL_POINTS);
        glVertex2i (xCoord, yCoord);
    glEnd ( );
}

void circleMidpoint (GLint xc, GLint yc, GLint radius)
{
    screenPt circPt;

    GLint p = 1 - radius;          //  Initial value for midpoint parameter.

    circPt.setCoords (0, radius); //  Set coords for top point of circle.

    void circlePlotPoints (GLint, GLint, screenPt);
```

```
    /*  Plot the initial point in each circle quadrant.  */
    circlePlotPoints (xc, yc, circPt);
    /*  Calculate next point and plot in each octant.  */
    while (circPt.getx ( ) < circPt.gety ( )) {
        circPt.incrementx ( );
        if (p < 0)
            p += 2 * circPt.getx ( ) + 1;
        else {
            circPt.decrementy ( );
            p += 2 * (circPt.getx ( ) - circPt.gety ( )) + 1;
        }
        circlePlotPoints (xc, yc, circPt);
    }
}

void circlePlotPoints (GLint xc, GLint yc, screenPt circPt)
{
    setPixel (xc + circPt.getx ( ), yc + circPt.gety ( ));
    setPixel (xc - circPt.getx ( ), yc + circPt.gety ( ));
    setPixel (xc + circPt.getx ( ), yc - circPt.gety ( ));
    setPixel (xc - circPt.getx ( ), yc - circPt.gety ( ));
    setPixel (xc + circPt.gety ( ), yc + circPt.getx ( ));
    setPixel (xc - circPt.gety ( ), yc + circPt.getx ( ));
    setPixel (xc + circPt.gety ( ), yc - circPt.getx ( ));
    setPixel (xc - circPt.gety ( ), yc - circPt.getx ( ));
}
```

3-10 ELLIPSE-GENERATING ALGORITHMS

Loosely stated, an ellipse is an elongated circle. We can also describe an ellipse as a modified circle whose radius varies from a maximum value in one direction to a minimum value in the perpendicular direction. The straight-line segments through the interior of the ellipse in these two perpendicular directions are referred to as the major and minor axes of the ellipse.

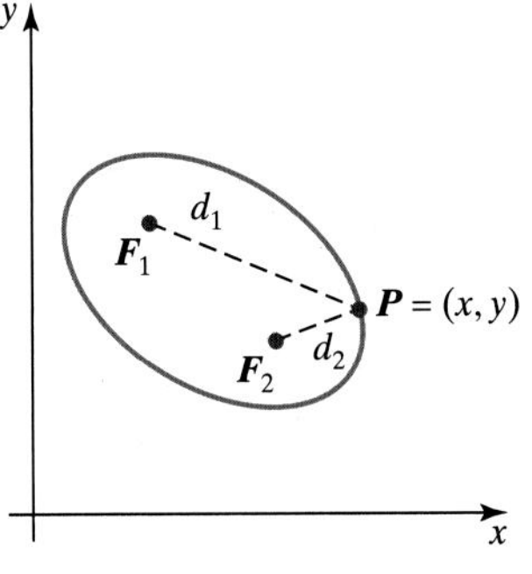

FIGURE 3-21 Ellipse generated about foci $\mathbf{F}_1$ and $\mathbf{F}_2$.

Properties of Ellipses

A precise definition of an ellipse can be given in terms of the distances from any point on the ellipse to two fixed positions, called the foci of the ellipse. The sum of these two distances is the same value for all points on the ellipse (Fig. 3-21). If the distances to the two focus positions from any point $\mathbf{P} = (x, y)$ on the ellipse are labeled d_1 and d_2, then the general equation of an ellipse can be stated as

$$d_1 + d_2 = \text{constant} \tag{3-34}$$

Expressing distances d_1 and d_2 in terms of the focal coordinates $\mathbf{F}_1 = (x_1, y_1)$ and $\mathbf{F}_2 = (x_2, y_2)$, we have

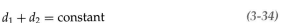

$$\sqrt{(x - x_1)^2 + (y - y_1)^2} + \sqrt{(x - x_2)^2 + (y - y_2)^2} = \text{constant} \tag{3-35}$$

By squaring this equation, isolating the remaining radical, and squaring again, we can rewrite the general ellipse equation in the form

$$A\,x^2 + B\,y^2 + C\,x\,y + D\,x + E\,y + F = 0 \tag{3-36}$$

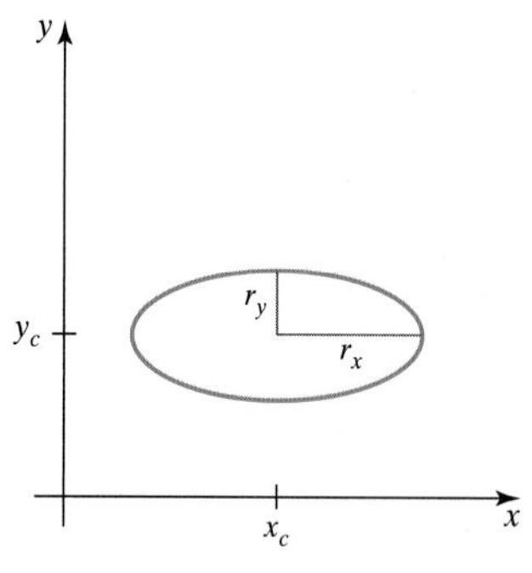

FIGURE 3-22 Ellipse centered at (x_c, y_c) with semimajor axis r_x and semiminor axis r_y.

where the coefficients A, B, C, D, E, and F are evaluated in terms of the focal coordinates and the dimensions of the major and minor axes of the ellipse. The major axis is the straight-line segment extending from one side of the ellipse to the other through the foci. The minor axis spans the shorter dimension of the ellipse, perpendicularly bisecting the major axis at the halfway position (ellipse center) between the two foci.

An interactive method for specifying an ellipse in an arbitrary orientation is to input the two foci and a point on the ellipse boundary. With these three coordinate positions, we can evaluate the constant in Eq. 3-35. Then, the values for the coefficients in Eq. 3-36 can be computed and used to generate pixels along the elliptical path.

Ellipse equations are greatly simplified if the major and minor axes are oriented to align with the coordinate axes. In Fig. 3-22, we show an ellipse in "standard position" with major and minor axes oriented parallel to the x and y axes. Parameter r_x for this example labels the semimajor axis, and parameter r_y labels the semiminor axis. The equation for the ellipse shown in Fig. 3-22 can be written in terms of the ellipse center coordinates and parameters r_x and r_y as

$$\left(\frac{x - x_c}{r_x}\right)^2 + \left(\frac{y - y_c}{r_y}\right)^2 = 1 \tag{3-37}$$

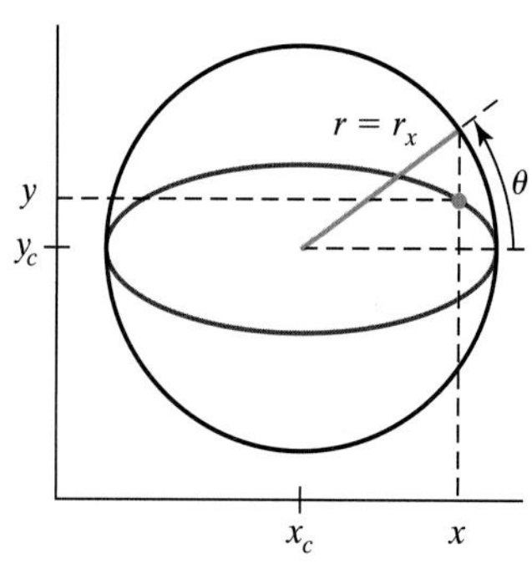

FIGURE 3-23 The bounding circle and eccentric angle θ for an ellipse with $r_x > r_y$.

Using polar coordinates r and θ, we can also describe the ellipse in standard position with the parametric equations

$$\begin{aligned} x &= x_c + r_x \cos\theta \\ y &= y_c + r_y \sin\theta \end{aligned} \tag{3-38}$$

Angle θ, called the *eccentric angle* of the ellipse, is measured around the perimeter of a bounding circle. If $r_x > r_y$, the radius of the bounding circle is $r = r_x$ (Fig. 3-23). Otherwise, the bounding circle has radius $r = r_y$.

As with the circle algorithm, symmetry considerations can be used to reduce computations. An ellipse in standard position is symmetric between quadrants, but, unlike a circle, it is not symmetric between the two octants of a quadrant. Thus, we must calculate pixel positions along the elliptical arc throughout one quadrant, then use symmetry to obtain curve positions in the remaining three quadrants (Fig. 3-24).

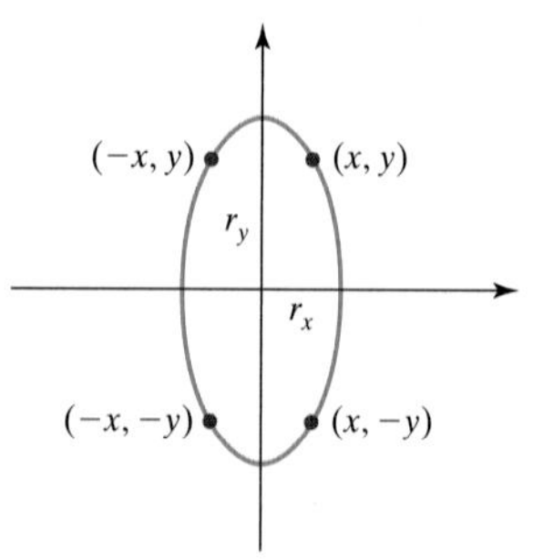

FIGURE 3-24 Symmetry of an ellipse. Calculation of a point (x, y) in one quadrant yields the ellipse points shown for the other three quadrants.

Midpoint Ellipse Algorithm

Our approach here is similar to that used in displaying a raster circle. Given parameters r_x, r_y, and (x_c, y_c), we determine curve positions (x, y) for an ellipse in standard position centered on the origin, then we shift all the points using a fixed offset so that the ellipse is centered at (x_c, y_c). If we wish also to display the ellipse in nonstandard position, we could rotate the ellipse about its center coordinates to reorient the major and minor axes in the desired directions. For the present, we consider only the display of ellipses in standard position. We discuss general methods for transforming object orientations and positions in Chapter 5.

The midpoint ellipse method is applied throughout the first quadrant in two parts. Figure 3-25 shows the division of the first quadrant according to the slope of an ellipse with $r_x < r_y$. We process this quadrant by taking unit steps in the x direction where the slope of the curve has a magnitude less than 1.0, and then we take unit steps in the y direction where the slope has a magnitude greater than 1.0.

Regions 1 and 2 (Fig. 3-25) can be processed in various ways. We can start at position $(0, r_y)$ and step clockwise along the elliptical path in the first quadrant, shifting from unit steps in x to unit steps in y when the slope becomes less than -1.0. Alternatively, we could start at $(r_x, 0)$ and select points in a counterclockwise order, shifting from unit steps in y to unit steps in x when the slope becomes greater than -1.0. With parallel processors, we could calculate pixel positions in the two regions simultaneously. As an example of a sequential implementation of the midpoint algorithm, we take the start position at $(0, r_y)$ and step along the ellipse path in clockwise order throughout the first quadrant.

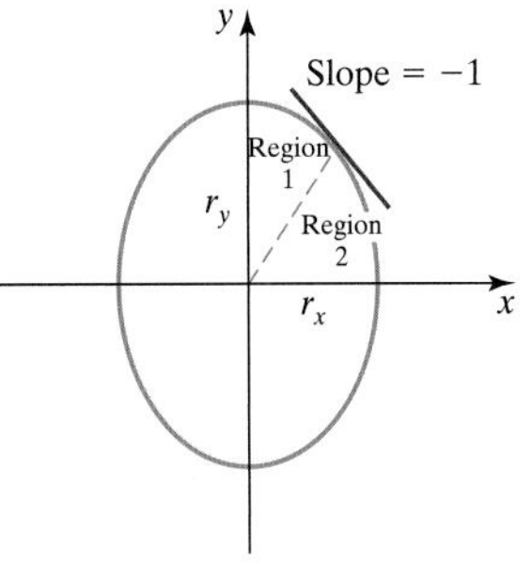

FIGURE 3-25 Ellipse processing regions. Over region 1, the magnitude of the ellipse slope is less than 1.0; over region 2, the magnitude of the slope is greater than 1.0.

We define an ellipse function from Eq. 3-37 with $(x_c, y_c) = (0, 0)$ as

$$f_{\text{ellipse}}(x, y) = r_y^2 x^2 + r_x^2 y^2 - r_x^2 r_y^2 \tag{3-39}$$

which has the following properties:

$$f_{\text{ellipse}}(x, y) \begin{cases} < 0, & \text{if } (x, y) \text{ is inside the ellipse boundary} \\ = 0, & \text{if } (x, y) \text{ is on the ellipse boundary} \\ > 0, & \text{if } (x, y) \text{ is outside the ellipse boundary} \end{cases} \tag{3-40}$$

Thus, the ellipse function $f_{\text{ellipse}}(x, y)$ serves as the decision parameter in the midpoint algorithm. At each sampling position, we select the next pixel along the ellipse path according to the sign of the ellipse function evaluated at the midpoint between the two candidate pixels.

Starting at $(0, r_y)$, we take unit steps in the x direction until we reach the boundary between region 1 and region 2 (Fig. 3-25). Then we switch to unit steps in the y direction over the remainder of the curve in the first quadrant. At each step we need to test the value of the slope of the curve. The ellipse slope is calculated from Eq. 3-39 as

$$\frac{dy}{dx} = -\frac{2r_y^2 x}{2r_x^2 y} \tag{3-41}$$

At the boundary between region 1 and region 2, $dy/dx = -1.0$ and

$$2r_y^2 x = 2r_x^2 y$$

Therefore, we move out of region 1 whenever

$$2r_y^2 x \geq 2r_x^2 y \tag{3-42}$$

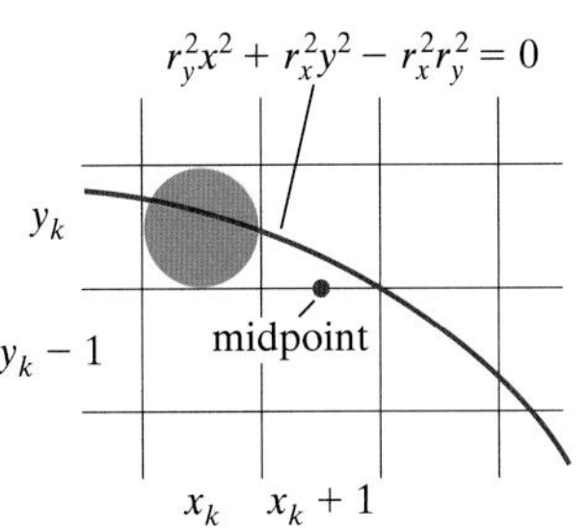

FIGURE 3-26 Midpoint between candidate pixels at sampling position $x_k + 1$ along an elliptical path.

Figure 3-26 shows the midpoint between the two candidate pixels at sampling position x_k+1 in the first region. Assuming position (x_k, y_k) has been selected in the previous step, we determine the next position along the ellipse path by evaluating the decision parameter (that is, the ellipse function 3-39) at this midpoint:

$$\begin{aligned} p1_k &= f_{\text{ellipse}}\left(x_k + 1, y_k - \frac{1}{2}\right) \\ &= r_y^2(x_k + 1)^2 + r_x^2\left(y_k - \frac{1}{2}\right)^2 - r_x^2 r_y^2 \end{aligned} \tag{3-43}$$

If $p1_k < 0$, the midpoint is inside the ellipse and the pixel on scan line y_k is closer to the ellipse boundary. Otherwise, the midposition is outside or on the ellipse boundary, and we select the pixel on scan line $y_k - 1$.

At the next sampling position ($x_{k+1} + 1 = x_k + 2$), the decision parameter for region 1 is evaluated as

$$p1_{k+1} = f_{\text{ellipse}}\left(x_{k+1} + 1, y_{k+1} - \frac{1}{2}\right)$$
$$= r_y^2[(x_k + 1) + 1]^2 + r_x^2\left(y_{k+1} - \frac{1}{2}\right)^2 - r_x^2 r_y^2$$

or

$$p1_{k+1} = p1_k + 2r_y^2(x_k + 1) + r_y^2 + r_x^2\left[\left(y_{k+1} - \frac{1}{2}\right)^2 - \left(y_k - \frac{1}{2}\right)^2\right] \tag{3-44}$$

where y_{k+1} is either y_k or $y_k - 1$, depending on the sign of $p1_k$.

Decision parameters are incremented by the following amounts:

$$\text{increment} = \begin{cases} 2r_y^2 x_{k+1} + r_y^2, & \text{if } p1_k < 0 \\ 2r_y^2 x_{k+1} + r_y^2 - 2r_x^2 y_{k+1}, & \text{if } p1_k \geq 0 \end{cases}$$

Increments for the decision parameters can be calculated using only addition and subtraction, as in the circle algorithm, since values for the terms $2r_y^2 x$ and $2r_x^2 y$ can be obtained incrementally. At the initial position $(0, r_y)$, these two terms evaluate to

$$2r_y^2 x = 0 \tag{3-45}$$
$$2r_x^2 y = 2r_x^2 r_y \tag{3-46}$$

As x and y are incremented, updated values are obtained by adding $2r_y^2$ to the current value of the increment term in Eq. 3-45 and subtracting $2r_x^2$ from the current value of the increment term in Eq. 3-46. The updated increment values are compared at each step, and we move from region 1 to region 2 when condition 3-42 is satisfied.

In region 1, the initial value of the decision parameter is obtained by evaluating the ellipse function at the start position $(x_0, y_0) = (0, r_y)$:

$$p1_0 = f_{\text{ellipse}}\left(1, r_y - \frac{1}{2}\right)$$
$$= r_y^2 + r_x^2\left(r_y - \frac{1}{2}\right)^2 - r_x^2 r_y^2$$

or

$$p1_0 = r_y^2 - r_x^2 r_y + \frac{1}{4}r_x^2 \tag{3-47}$$

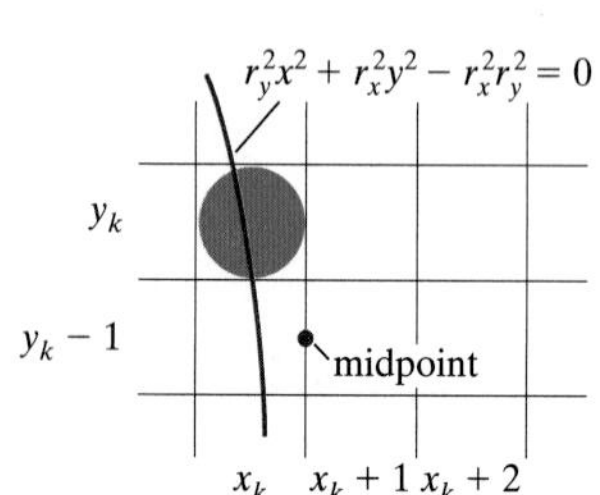

FIGURE 3-27 Midpoint between candidate pixels at sampling position $y_k - 1$ along an elliptical path.

Over region 2, we sample at unit intervals in the negative y direction, and the midpoint is now taken between horizontal pixels at each step (Fig. 3-27). For this region, the decision parameter is evaluated as

$$p2_k = f_{\text{ellipse}}\left(x_k + \frac{1}{2}, y_k - 1\right)$$
$$= r_y^2\left(x_k + \frac{1}{2}\right)^2 + r_x^2(y_k - 1)^2 - r_x^2 r_y^2 \tag{3-48}$$

If $p2_k > 0$, the midposition is outside the ellipse boundary, and we select the pixel at x_k. If $p2_k \leq 0$, the midpoint is inside or on the ellipse boundary, and we select pixel position x_{k+1}.

To determine the relationship between successive decision parameters in region 2, we evaluate the ellipse function at the next sampling step $y_{k+1} - 1 = y_k - 2$:

$$p2_{k+1} = f_{\text{ellipse}}\left(x_{k+1} + \frac{1}{2}, y_{k+1} - 1\right)$$

$$= r_y^2\left(x_{k+1} + \frac{1}{2}\right)^2 + r_x^2[(y_k - 1) - 1]^2 - r_x^2 r_y^2 \tag{3-49}$$

or

$$p2_{k+1} = p2_k - 2r_x^2(y_k - 1) + r_x^2 + r_y^2\left[\left(x_{k+1} + \frac{1}{2}\right)^2 - \left(x_k + \frac{1}{2}\right)^2\right] \tag{3-50}$$

with x_{k+1} set either to x_k or to $x_k + 1$, depending on the sign of $p2_k$.

When we enter region 2, the initial position (x_0, y_0) is taken as the last position selected in region 1 and the initial decision parameter in region 2 is then

$$p2_0 = f_{\text{ellipse}}\left(x_0 + \frac{1}{2}, y_0 - 1\right)$$

$$= r_y^2\left(x_0 + \frac{1}{2}\right)^2 + r_x^2(y_0 - 1)^2 - r_x^2 r_y^2 \tag{3-51}$$

To simplify the calculation of $p2_0$, we could select pixel positions in counterclockwise order starting at $(r_x, 0)$. Unit steps would then be taken in the positive y direction up to the last position selected in region 1.

This midpoint algorithm can be adapted to generate an ellipse in nonstandard position using the ellipse function Eq. 3-36 and calculating pixel positions over the entire elliptical path. Alternatively, we could reorient the ellipse axes to standard position, using transformation methods discussed in Chapter 5, apply the midpoint ellipse algorithm to determine curve positions, and then convert calculated pixel positions to path positions along the original ellipse orientation.

Assuming r_x, r_y, and the ellipse center are given in integer screen coordinates, we need only incremental integer calculations to determine values for the decision parameters in the midpoint ellipse algorithm. The increments r_x^2, r_y^2, $2r_x^2$, and $2r_y^2$ are evaluated once at the beginning of the procedure. In the following summary, we list the steps for displaying an ellipse using the midpoint algorithm.

Midpoint Ellipse Algorithm

1. Input r_x, r_y, and ellipse center (x_c, y_c), and obtain the first point on an ellipse centered on the origin as

$$(x_0, y_0) = (0, r_y)$$

2. Calculate the initial value of the decision parameter in region 1 as

$$p1_0 = r_y^2 - r_x^2 r_y + \frac{1}{4}r_x^2$$

3. At each x_k position in region 1, starting at $k = 0$, perform the following test. If $p1_k < 0$, the next point along the ellipse centered on (0, 0) is (x_{k+1}, y_k) and

$$p1_{k+1} = p1_k + 2r_y^2 x_{k+1} + r_y^2$$

Otherwise, the next point along the ellipse is $(x_k + 1, y_k - 1)$ and

$$p1_{k+1} = p1_k + 2r_y^2 x_{k+1} - 2r_x^2 y_{k+1} + r_y^2$$

with

$$2r_y^2 x_{k+1} = 2r_y^2 x_k + 2r_y^2, \qquad 2r_x^2 y_{k+1} = 2r_x^2 y_k - 2r_x^2$$

and continue until $2r_y^2 x \geq 2r_x^2 y$.

4. Calculate the initial value of the decision parameter in region 2 as

$$p2_0 = r_y^2 \left(x_0 + \frac{1}{2} \right)^2 + r_x^2 (y_0 - 1)^2 - r_x^2 r_y^2$$

where (x_0, y_0) is the last position calculated in region 1.

5. At each y_k position in region 2, starting at $k = 0$, perform the following test. If $p2_k > 0$, the next point along the ellipse centered on (0, 0) is $(x_k, y_k - 1)$ and

$$p2_{k+1} = p2_k - 2r_x^2 y_{k+1} + r_x^2$$

Otherwise, the next point along the ellipse is $(x_k + 1, y_k - 1)$ and

$$p2_{k+1} = p2_k + 2r_y^2 x_{k+1} - 2r_x^2 y_{k+1} + r_x^2$$

using the same incremental calculations for x and y as in region 1. Continue until $y = 0$.

6. For both regions, determine symmetry points in the other three quadrants.

7. Move each calculated pixel position (x, y) onto the elliptical path centered on (x_c, y_c) and plot the coordinate values:

$$x = x + x_c, \qquad y = y + y_c$$

EXAMPLE 3-3 Midpoint Ellipse Drawing

Given input ellipse parameters $r_x = 8$ and $r_y = 6$, we illustrate the steps in the midpoint ellipse algorithm by determining raster positions along the ellipse path in the first quadrant. Initial values and increments for the decision parameter calculations are

$$2r_y^2 x = 0 \qquad \text{(with increment } 2r_y^2 = 72)$$
$$2r_x^2 y = 2r_x^2 r_y \qquad \text{(with increment } -2r_x^2 = -128)$$

For region 1, the initial point for the ellipse centered on the origin is

$(x_0, y_0) = (0, 6)$, and the initial decision parameter value is

$$p1_0 = r_y^2 - r_x^2 r_y + \frac{1}{4} r_x^2 = -332$$

Successive midpoint decision-parameter values and the pixel positions along the ellipse are listed in the following table.

k	$p1_k$	(x_{k+1}, y_{k+1})	$2r_y^2 x_{k+1}$	$2r_x^2 y_{k+1}$
0	−332	(1, 6)	72	768
1	−224	(2, 6)	144	768
2	−44	(3, 6)	216	768
3	208	(4, 5)	288	640
4	−108	(5, 5)	360	640
5	288	(6, 4)	432	512
6	244	(7, 3)	504	384

We now move out of region 1, since $2r_y^2 x > 2r_x^2 y$.
For region 2, the initial point is $(x_0, y_0) = (7, 3)$ and the initial decision parameter is

$$p2_0 = f_{\text{ellipse}}\left(7 + \frac{1}{2}, 2\right) = -151$$

The remaining positions along the ellipse path in the first quadrant are then calculated as

k	$p1_k$	(x_{k+1}, y_{k+1})	$2r_y^2 x_{k+1}$	$2r_x^2 y_{k+1}$
0	−151	(8, 2)	576	256
1	233	(8, 1)	576	128
2	745	(8, 0)	—	—

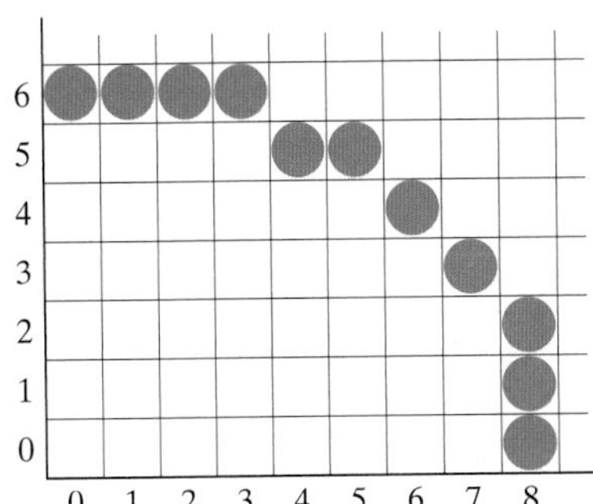

FIGURE 3-28 Pixel positions along an elliptical path centered on the origin with $r_x = 8$ and $r_y = 6$, using the midpoint algorithm to calculate locations within the first quadrant.

A plot of the calculated positions for the ellipse within the first quadrant is shown in Fig. 3-28. ■

In the following code segment, example procedures are given for implementing the midpoint ellipse algorithm. Values for the ellipse parameters `Rx`, `Ry`, `xCenter`, and `yCenter` are input to procedure `ellipseMidpoint`. Positions along the curve in the first quadrant are then calculated and passed to procedure `ellipsePlotPoints`. Symmetry is used to obtain ellipse positions in the other three quadrants, and the `setPixel` routine sets the ellipse color in the frame-buffer locations corresponding to these positions.

```
inline int round (const float a)  { return int (a + 0.5); }

/*  The following procedure accepts values for an ellipse
 *  center position and its semimajor and semiminor axes, then
 *  calculates ellipse positions using the midpoint algorithm.
 */
void ellipseMidpoint (int xCenter, int yCenter, int Rx, int Ry)
{
   int Rx2 = Rx * Rx;
   int Ry2 = Ry * Ry;
   int twoRx2 = 2 * Rx2;
   int twoRy2 = 2 * Ry2;
   int p;
   int x = 0;
   int y = Ry;
   int px = 0;
   int py = twoRx2 * y;
   void ellipsePlotPoints (int, int, int, int);

   /* Plot the initial point in each quadrant. */
   ellipsePlotPoints (xCenter, yCenter, x, y);

   /* Region 1 */
   p = round (Ry2 - (Rx2 * Ry) + (0.25 * Rx2));
   while (px < py) {
      x++;
      px += twoRy2;
      if (p < 0)
         p += Ry2 + px;
      else {
         y--;
         py -= twoRx2;
         p += Ry2 + px - py;
      }
      ellipsePlotPoints (xCenter, yCenter, x, y);
   }

   /* Region 2 */
   p = round (Ry2 * (x+0.5) * (x+0.5) + Rx2 * (y-1) * (y-1) - Rx2 * Ry2);
   while (y > 0) {
      y--;
      py -= twoRx2;
      if (p > 0)
         p += Rx2 - py;
      else {
         x++;
         px += twoRy2;
         p += Rx2 - py + px;
      }
      ellipsePlotPoints (xCenter, yCenter, x, y);
   }
}
```

```
void ellipsePlotPoints (int xCenter, int yCenter, int x, int y);
{
    setPixel (xCenter + x, yCenter + y);
    setPixel (xCenter - x, yCenter + y);
    setPixel (xCenter + x, yCenter - y);
    setPixel (xCenter - x, yCenter - y);
}
```

3-11 OTHER CURVES

Various curve functions are useful in object modeling, animation path specifications, data and function graphing, and other graphics applications. Commonly encountered curves include conics, trigonometric and exponential functions, probability distributions, general polynomials, and spline functions. Displays of these curves can be generated with methods similar to those discussed for the circle and ellipse functions. We can obtain positions along curve paths directly from explicit representations $y = f(x)$ or from parametric forms. Alternatively, we could apply the incremental midpoint method to plot curves described with implicit functions $f(x, y) = 0$.

A simple method for displaying a curved line is to approximate it with straight-line segments. Parametric representations are often useful in this case for obtaining equally spaced positions along the curve path for the line endpoints. We can also generate equally spaced positions from an explicit representation by choosing the independent variable according to the slope of the curve. Where the slope of $y = f(x)$ has a magnitude less than 1, we choose x as the independent variable and calculate y values at equal x increments. To obtain equal spacing where the slope has a magnitude greater than 1, we use the inverse function, $x = f^{-1}(y)$, and calculate values of x at equal y steps.

Straight-line or curve approximations are used to generate a line graph for a set of discrete data values. We could join the discrete points with straight-line segments, or we could use linear regression (least squares) to approximate the data set with a single straight line. A nonlinear least-squares approach is used to display the data set with some approximating function, usually a polynomial.

As with circles and ellipses, many functions possess symmetries that can be exploited to reduce the computation of coordinate positions along curve paths. For example, the normal probability distribution function is symmetric about a center position (the mean), and all points within one cycle of a sine curve can be generated from the points in a 90° interval.

Conic Sections

In general, we can describe a **conic section** (or **conic**) with the second-degree equation

$$A x^2 + B y^2 + C x y + D x + E y + F = 0 \tag{3-52}$$

where values for parameters A, B, C, D, E, and F determine the kind of curve we are to display. Given this set of coefficients, we can determine the particular

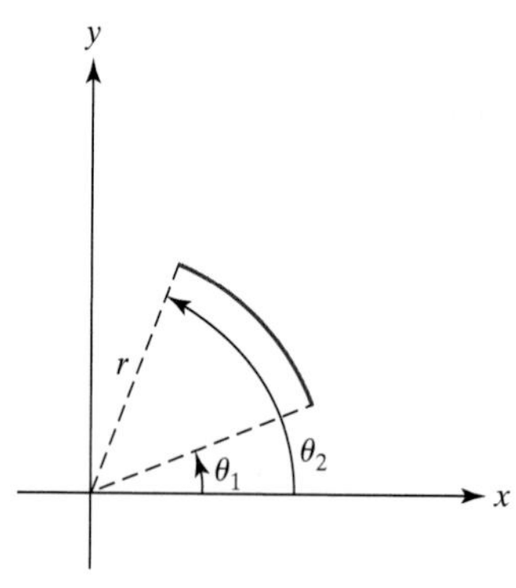

FIGURE 3-29 A circular arc, centered on the origin, defined with beginning angle θ_1, ending angle θ_2, and radius r.

conic that will be generated by evaluating the discriminant $B^2 - 4AC$:

$$B^2 - 4AC \begin{cases} < 0, & \text{generates an ellipse (or circle)} \\ = 0, & \text{generates a parabola} \\ > 0, & \text{generates a hyperbola} \end{cases} \tag{3-53}$$

For example, we get the circle equation 3-26 when $A = B = 1, C = 0, D = -2x_c$, $E = -2y_c$, and $F = x_c^2 + y_c^2 - r^2$. Equation 3-52 also describes the "degenerate" conics: points and straight lines.

In some applications, circular and elliptical arcs are conveniently specified with the beginning and ending angular values for the arc, as illustrated in Fig. 3-29. And such arcs are sometimes defined by their endpoint coordinate positions. For either case, we could generate the arc with a modified midpoint method, or we could display a set of approximating straight-line segments.

Ellipses, hyperbolas, and parabolas are particularly useful in certain animation applications. These curves describe orbital and other motions for objects subjected to gravitational, electromagnetic, or nuclear forces. Planetary orbits in the solar system, for example, are approximated with ellipses; and an object projected into a uniform gravitational field travels along a parabolic trajectory. Figure 3-30 shows a parabolic path in standard position for a gravitational field acting in the negative y direction. The explicit equation for the parabolic trajectory of the object shown can be written as

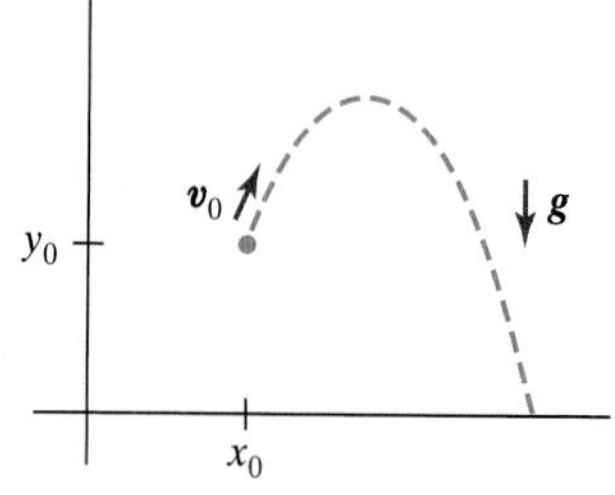

FIGURE 3-30 Parabolic path of an object tossed into a downward gravitational field at the initial position (x_0, y_0).

$$y = y_0 + a(x - x_0)^2 + b(x - x_0) \tag{3-54}$$

with constants a and b determined by the initial velocity $\mathbf{v}_0$ of the object and the acceleration g due to the uniform gravitational force. We can also describe such parabolic motions with parametric equations using a time parameter t, measured in seconds from the initial projection point:

$$\begin{aligned} x &= x_0 + v_{x0}\, t \\ y &= y_0 + v_{y0}\, t - \frac{1}{2} g t^2 \end{aligned} \tag{3-55}$$

Here, v_{x0} and v_{y0} are the initial velocity components, and the value of g near the surface of the earth is approximately 980 cm/sec^2. Object positions along the parabolic path are then calculated at selected time steps.

Hyperbolic curves (Fig. 3-31) are useful in various scientific-visualization applications. Motions of objects along hyperbolic paths occur in connection with the collision of charged particles and in certain gravitational problems. For example, comets or meteorites moving around the sun may travel along hyperbolic paths and escape to outer space, never to return. The particular branch (left or right, in Fig. 3-31) describing the motion of an object depends on the forces involved in the problem. We can write the standard equation for the hyperbola centered on the origin in Fig. 3-31 as

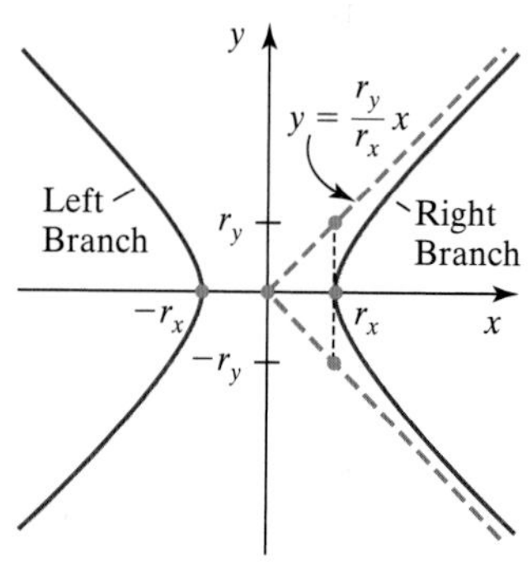

FIGURE 3-31 Left and right branches of a hyperbola in standard position with the symmetry axis along the x axis.

$$\left(\frac{x}{r_x}\right)^2 - \left(\frac{y}{r_y}\right)^2 = 1 \tag{3-56}$$

with $x \le -r_x$ for the left branch and $x \ge r_x$ for the right branch. Since this equation differs from the standard ellipse equation 3-39 only in the sign between the x^2 and y^2 terms, we can generate points along a hyperbolic path with a slightly modified ellipse algorithm.

Parabolas and hyperbolas possess a symmetry axis. For example, the parabola described by Eq. 3-55 is symmetric about the axis

$$x = x_0 + v_{x0}v_{y0}/g$$

The methods used in the midpoint ellipse algorithm can be directly applied to obtain points along one side of the symmetry axis of hyperbolic and parabolic paths in the two regions: (1) where the magnitude of the curve slope is less than 1, and (2) where the magnitude of the slope is greater than 1. To do this, we first select the appropriate form of Eq. 3-52 and then use the selected function to set up expressions for the decision parameters in the two regions.

Polynomials and Spline Curves

A polynomial function of nth degree in x is defined as

$$\begin{aligned} y &= \sum_{k=0}^{n} a_k x^k \\ &= a_0 + a_1 x + \cdots + a_{n-1}x^{n-1} + a_n x^n \end{aligned} \tag{3-57}$$

where n is a nonnegative integer and the a_k are constants, with $a_n \neq 0$. We obtain a quadratic curve when $n = 2$, a cubic polynomial when $n = 3$, a quartic curve when $n = 4$, and so forth. And we have a straight line when $n = 1$. Polynomials are useful in a number of graphics applications, including the design of object shapes, the specification of animation paths, and the graphing of data trends in a discrete set of data points.

Designing object shapes or motion paths is typically accomplished by first specifying a few points to define the general curve contour, then the selected points are fitted with a polynomial. One way to accomplish the curve fitting is to construct a cubic polynomial curve section between each pair of specified points. Each curve section is then described in parametric form as

$$\begin{aligned} x &= a_{x0} + a_{x1}u + a_{x2}u^2 + a_{x3}u^3 \\ y &= a_{y0} + a_{y1}u + a_{y2}u^2 + a_{y3}u^3 \end{aligned} \tag{3-58}$$

where parameter u varies over the interval from 0 to 1.0. Values for the coefficients of u in the preceding equations are determined from boundary conditions on the curve sections. One boundary condition is that two adjacent curve sections have the same coordinate position at the boundary, and a second condition is to match the two curve slopes at the boundary so that we obtain one continuous, smooth curve (Fig. 3-32). Continuous curves that are formed with polynomial pieces are called **spline curves,** or simply **splines.** There are other ways to set up spline curves, and various spline-generating methods are explored in Chapter 8.

FIGURE 3-32 A spline curve formed with individual cubic polynomial sections between specified coordinate positions.

3-12 PARALLEL CURVE ALGORITHMS

Methods for exploiting parallelism in curve generation are similar to those used in displaying straight-line segments. We can either adapt a sequential algorithm by allocating processors according to curve partitions, or we could devise other methods and assign processors to screen partitions.

A parallel midpoint method for displaying circles is to divide the circular arc from 45° to 90° into equal subarcs and assign a separate processor to each subarc.

As in the parallel Bresenham line algorithm, we then need to set up computations to determine the beginning y value and decision parameter p_k value for each processor. Pixel positions are calculated throughout each subarc, and positions in the other circle octants can be obtained by symmetry. Similarly, a parallel ellipse midpoint method divides the elliptical arc over the first quadrant into equal subarcs and parcels these out to separate processors. Again, pixel positions in the other quadrants are determined by symmetry. A screen-partitioning scheme for circles and ellipses is to assign each scan line that crosses the curve to a separate processor. In this case, each processor uses the circle or ellipse equation to calculate curve intersection coordinates.

For the display of elliptical arcs or other curves, we can simply use the scan-line partitioning method. Each processor uses the curve equation to locate the intersection positions along its assigned scan line. With processors assigned to individual pixels, each processor would calculate the distance (or distance squared) from the curve to its assigned pixel. If the calculated distance is less than a predefined value, the pixel is plotted.

3-13 PIXEL ADDRESSING AND OBJECT GEOMETRY

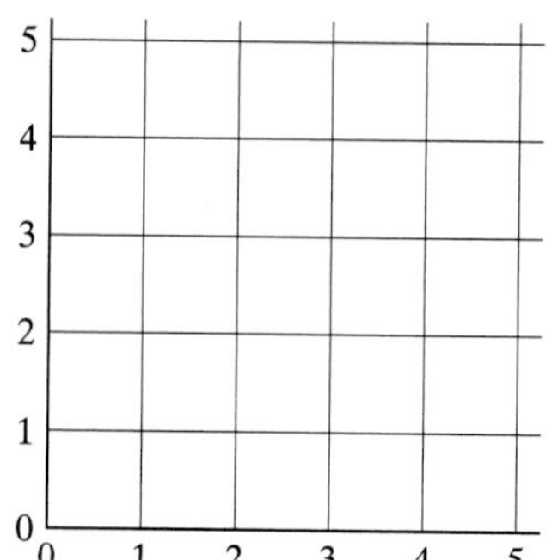

FIGURE 3-33 Lower-left section of a screen area with coordinate positions referenced by grid intersection lines.

In discussing the raster algorithms for displaying graphics primitives, we assumed that frame-buffer coordinates referenced the center of a screen pixel position. We now consider the effects of different addressing schemes and an alternate pixel-addressing method used by some graphics packages, including OpenGL.

An object description that is input to a graphics program is given in terms of precise world-coordinate positions, which are infinitesimally small mathematical points. But when the object is scan converted into the frame buffer, the input description is transformed to pixel coordinates which reference finite screen areas, and the displayed raster image may not correspond exactly with the relative dimensions of the input object. If it is important to preserve the specified geometry of world objects, we can compensate for the mapping of mathematical input points to finite pixel areas. One way to do this is simply to adjust the pixel dimensions of displayed objects so as to correspond to the dimensions given in the original mathematical description of the scene. For example, if a rectangle is specified as having a width of 40 cm, then we could adjust the screen display so that the rectangle has a width of 40 pixels, with the width of each pixel representing one centimeter. Another approach is to map world coordinates onto screen positions between pixels, so that we align object boundaries with pixel boundaries instead of pixel centers.

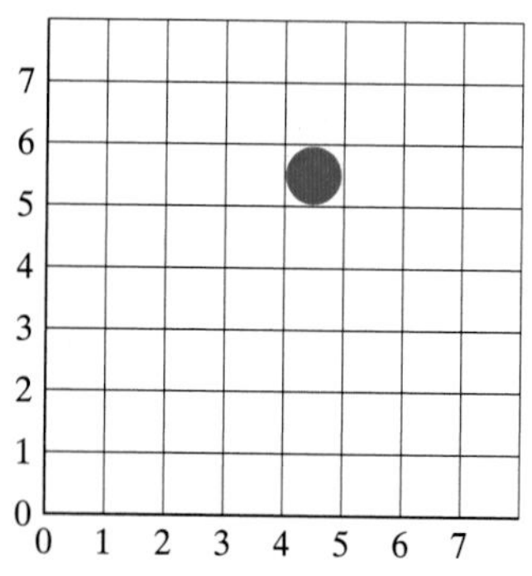

FIGURE 3-34 Illuminated pixel at raster position (4, 5).

Screen Grid Coordinates

Figure 3-33 shows a screen section with grid lines marking pixel boundaries, one unit apart. In this scheme, a screen position is given as the pair of integer values identifying a grid-intersection position between two pixels. The address for any pixel is now at its lower-left corner, as illustrated in Fig. 3-34. And a straight-line path is now envisioned as between grid intersections. For example, the mathematical line path for a polyline with endpoint coordinates (0, 0), (5, 2), and (1, 4) would then be as shown in Fig. 3-35.

Using screen grid coordinates, we now identify the area occupied by a pixel with screen coordinates (x, y) as the unit square with diagonally opposite corners at (x, y) and $(x + 1, y + 1)$. This pixel-addressing method has several advantages:

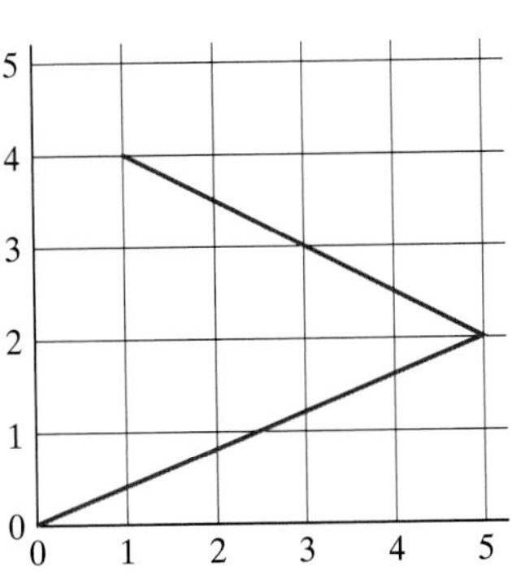

FIGURE 3-35 Line path for two connected line segments between screen grid-coordinate positions.

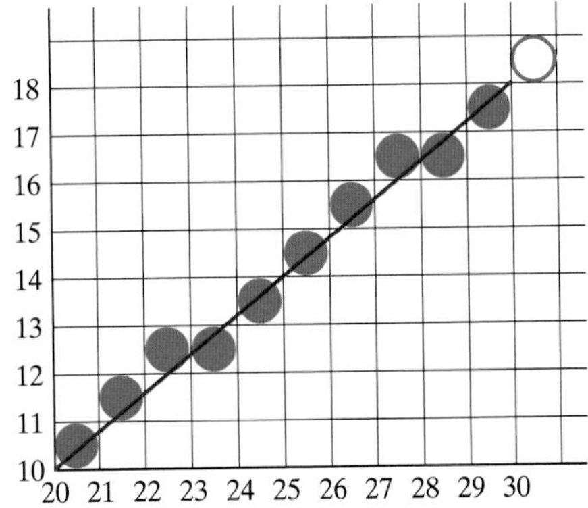

FIGURE 3-36 Line path and corresponding pixel display for grid endpoint coordinates (20, 10) and (30, 18).

it avoids half-integer pixel boundaries, it facilitates precise object representations, and it simplifies the processing involved in many scan-conversion algorithms and other raster procedures.

The algorithms for line drawing and curve generation discussed in the preceding sections are still valid when applied to input positions expressed as screen grid coordinates. Decision parameters in these algorithms would now be a measure of screen grid separation differences, rather than separation differences from pixel centers.

Maintaining Geometric Properties of Displayed Objects

When we convert geometric descriptions of objects into pixel representations, we transform mathematical points and lines into finite screen areas. If we are to maintain the original geometric measurements specified by the input coordinates for an object, we need to account for the finite size of pixels when we transform the object definition to a screen display.

Figure 3-36 shows the line plotted in the Bresenham line-algorithm example of Section 3-5. Interpreting the line endpoints (20, 10) and (30, 18) as precise grid-crossing positions, we see that the line should not extend past screen-grid position (30, 18). If we were to plot the pixel with screen coordinates (30, 18), as in the example given in Section 3-5, we would display a line that spans 11 horizontal units and 9 vertical units. For the mathematical line, however, $\Delta x = 10$ and $\Delta y = 8$. If we are addressing pixels by their center positions, we can adjust the length of the displayed line by omitting one of the endpoint pixels. But if we think of screen coordinates as addressing pixel boundaries, as shown in Fig. 3-36, we plot a line using only those pixels that are "interior" to the line path; that is, only those pixels that are between the line endpoints. For our example, we would plot the leftmost pixel at (20, 10) and the rightmost pixel at (29, 17). This displays a line that has the same geometric magnitudes as the mathematical line from (20, 10) to (30, 18).

For an enclosed area, input geometric properties are maintained by displaying the area using only those pixels that are interior to the object boundaries. The rectangle defined with the screen coordinate vertices shown in Fig. 3-37(a), for example, is larger when we display it filled with pixels up to and including

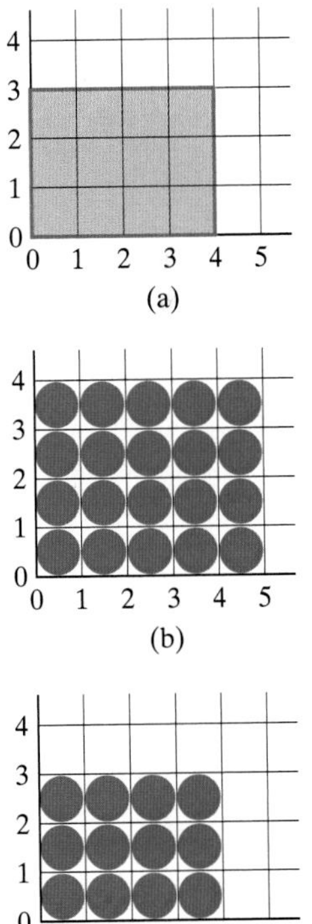

FIGURE 3-37 Conversion of rectangle (a) with vertices at screen coordinates (0, 0), (4, 0), (4, 3), and (0, 3) into display (b) that includes the right and top boundaries and into display (c) that maintains geometric magnitudes.

the border pixel lines joining the specified vertices (Fig. 3-37(b)). As defined, the area of the rectangle is 12 units, but as displayed in Fig. 3-37(b), it has an area of 20 units. In Fig. 3-37(c), the original rectangle measurements are maintained by displaying only the internal pixels. The right boundary of the input rectangle is at $x = 4$. To maintain the rectangle width in the display, we set the rightmost pixel grid coordinate for the rectangle at $x = 3$, since the pixels in this vertical column span the interval from $x = 3$ to $x = 4$. Similarly, the mathematical top boundary of the rectangle is at $y = 3$, so we set the top pixel row for the displayed rectangle at $y = 2$.

These compensations for finite pixel size can be applied to other objects, including those with curved boundaries, so that the raster display maintains the input object specifications. A circle with radius 5 and center position (10, 10), for instance, would be displayed as in Fig 3-38 by the midpoint circle algorithm using pixel centers as screen-coordinate positions. But the plotted circle has a diameter of 11. To plot the circle with the defined diameter of 10, we can modify the circle algorithm to shorten each pixel scan line and each pixel column, as in Fig. 3-39.

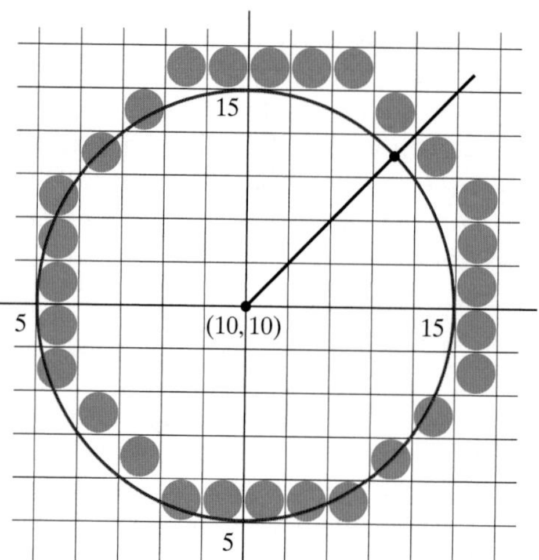

FIGURE 3-38
A midpoint-algorithm plot of the circle equation $(x - 10)^2 + (y - 10)^2 = 5^2$ using pixel-center coordinates.

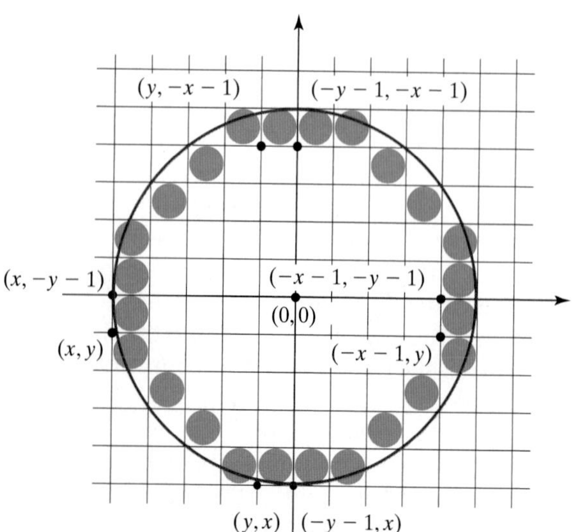

FIGURE 3-39
Modification of the circle plot in Fig. 3-38 to maintain the specified circle diameter of 10.

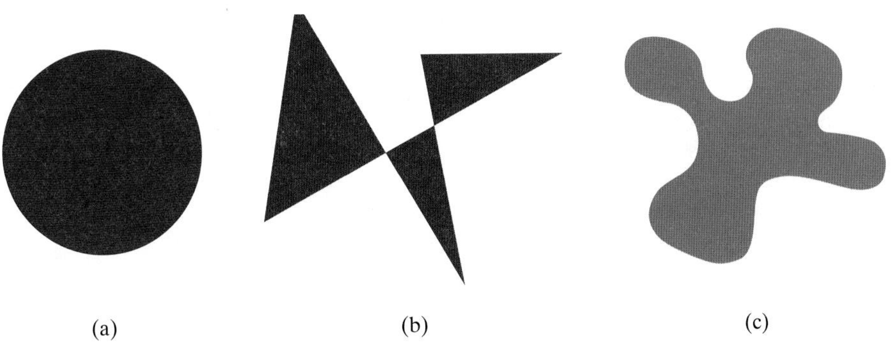

FIGURE 3-40 Solid-color fill areas specified with various boundaries. (a) A circular fill region. (b) A fill area bounded by a closed polyline. (c) A filled area specified with an irregular curved boundary.

One way to do this is to generate points clockwise along the circular arc in the third quadrant, starting at screen coordinates (10, 5). For each generated point, the other seven circle symmetry points are generated by decreasing the x coordinate values by 1 along scan lines and decreasing the y coordinate values by 1 along pixel columns. Similar methods are applied in ellipse algorithms to maintain the specified proportions in the display of an ellipse.

3-14 FILL-AREA PRIMITIVES

Another useful construct, besides points, straight-line segments, and curves, for describing components of a picture is an area that is filled with some solid color or pattern. A picture component of this type is typically referred to as a **fill area** or a **filled area.** Most often, fill areas are used to describe surfaces of solid objects, but they are also useful in a variety of other applications. Also, fill regions are usually planar surfaces, mainly polygons. But, in general, there are many possible shapes for a region in a picture that we might wish to fill with some color option. Figure 3-40 illustrates a few possible fill-area shapes. For the present, we assume that all fill areas are to be displayed with a specified solid color. Other fill options are discussed in Chapter 4.

Although any fill-area shape is possible, graphics libraries generally do not support specifications for arbitrary fill shapes. Most library routines require that a fill area be specified as a polygon. Graphics routines can more efficiently process polygons than other kinds of fill shapes because polygon boundaries are described with linear equations. Moreover, most curved surfaces can be approximated reasonably well with a set of polygon patches, just as a curved line can be approximated with a set of straight-line segments. And when lighting effects and surface-shading procedures are applied, an approximated curved surface can be displayed quite realistically. Approximating a curved surface with polygon facets is sometimes referred to as *surface tessellation,* or fitting the surface with a *polygon mesh.* Figure 3-41 shows the side and top surfaces of a metal cylinder approximated in an outline form as a polygon mesh. Displays of such figures can be generated quickly as *wire-frame* views, showing only the polygon edges to give a general indication of the surface structure. Then the wire-frame model could be shaded to generate a display of a natural-looking material surface. Objects described with a set of polygon surface patches are usually referred to as **standard graphics objects,** or just **graphics objects.**

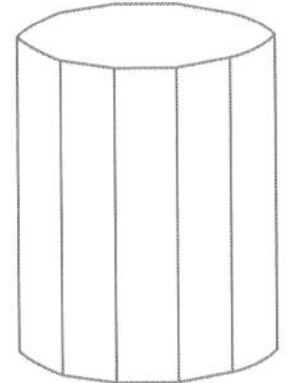

FIGURE 3-41 Wire-frame representation for a cylinder, showing only the front (visible) faces of the polygon mesh used to approximate the surfaces.

In general, we can create fill areas with any boundary specification, such as a circle or connected set of spline-curve sections. And some of the polygon methods discussed in the next section can be adapted to display fill areas with a nonlinear border. Other fill-area methods for objects with curved boundaries are given in Chapter 4.

3-15 POLYGON FILL AREAS

Mathematically defined, a **polygon** is a plane figure specified by a set of three or more coordinate positions, called *vertices,* that are connected in sequence by straight-line segments, called the *edges* or *sides* of the polygon. Further, in basic geometry, it is required that the polygon edges have no common point other than their endpoints. Thus, by definition, a polygon must have all its vertices within a single plane and there can be no edge crossings. Examples of polygons include triangles, rectangles, octagons, and decagons. Sometimes, any plane figure with a closed-polyline boundary is alluded to as a polygon, and one with no crossing edges is referred to as a *standard polygon* or a *simple polygon.* In an effort to avoid ambiguous object references, we will use the term "polygon" to refer only to those planar shapes that have a closed-polyline boundary and no edge crossings.

For a computer-graphics application, it is possible that a designated set of polygon vertices do not all lie exactly in one plane. This can be due to round-off error in the calculation of numerical values, to errors in selecting coordinate positions for the vertices, or, more typically, to approximating a curved surface with a set of polygonal patches. One way to rectify this problem is simply to divide the specified surface mesh into triangles. But in some cases there may be reasons to retain the original shape of the mesh patches, so methods have been devised for approximating a nonplanar polygonal shape with a plane figure. We discuss how these plane approximations are calculated in the subsection on plane equations.

Polygon Classifications

An **interior angle** of a polygon is an angle inside the polygon boundary that is formed by two adjacent edges. If all interior angles of a polygon are less than or equal to 180°, the polygon is **convex.** An equivalent definition of a convex polygon is that its interior lies completely on one side of the infinite extension line of any one of its edges. Also, if we select any two points in the interior of a convex polygon, the line segment joining the two points is also in the interior. A polygon that is not convex is called a **concave** polygon. Figure 3-42 gives examples of convex and concave polygons.

The term **degenerate polygon** is often used to describe a set of vertices that are collinear or that have repeated coordinate positions. Collinear vertices generate a line segment. Repeated vertex positions can generate a polygon shape with extraneous lines, overlapping edges, or edges that have a length equal to 0. Sometimes the term degenerate polygon is also applied to a vertex list that contains fewer than three coordinate positions.

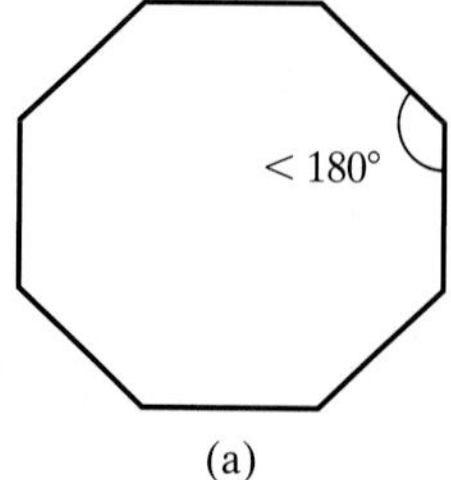

(a)

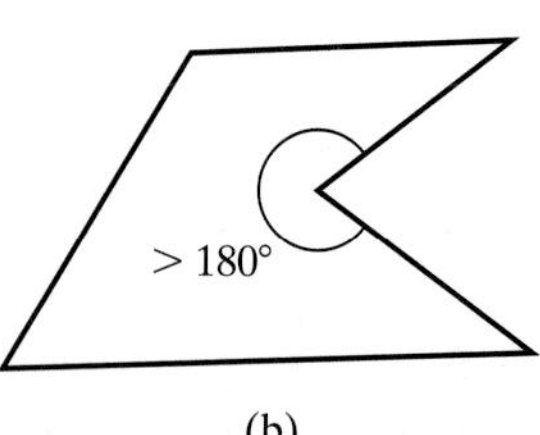

(b)

FIGURE 3-42 A convex polygon (a), and a concave polygon (b).

To be robust, a graphics package could reject degenerate or nonplanar vertex sets. But this requires extra processing to identify these problems, so graphics systems usually leave such considerations to the programmer.

Concave polygons also present problems. Implementations of fill algorithms and other graphics routines are more complicated for concave polygons, so it is generally more efficient to split a concave polygon into a set of convex polygons before processing. As with other polygon preprocessing algorithms, concave polygon splitting is often not included in a graphics library. Some graphics packages, including OpenGL, require all fill polygons to be convex. And some systems accept only triangular fill areas, which greatly simplifies many of the display algorithms.

Identifying Concave Polygons

A concave polygon has at least one interior angle greater than 180°. Also, the extension of some edges of a concave polygon will intersect other edges, and some pair of interior points will produce a line segment that intersects the polygon boundary. Therefore, we can use any one of these characteristics of a concave polygon as a basis for constructing an identification algorithm.

If we set up a vector for each polygon edge, then we can use the cross product of adjacent edges to test for concavity. All such vector products will be of the same sign (positive or negative) for a convex polygon. Therefore, if some cross products yield a positive value and some a negative value, we have a concave polygon. Figure 3-43 illustrates the edge-vector, cross-product method for identifying concave polygons.

Another way to identify a concave polygon is to take a look at the polygon vertex positions relative to the extension line of any edge. If some vertices are on one side of the extension line and some vertices are on the other side, the polygon is concave.

Splitting Concave Polygons

Once we have identified a concave polygon, we can split it into a set of convex polygons. This can be accomplished using edge vectors and edge cross products. Or, we can use vertex positions relative to an edge extension line to determine which vertices are on one side of this line and which are on the other. For the following algorithms, we assume that all polygons are in the xy plane. Of course, the original position of a polygon described in world coordinates may not be in

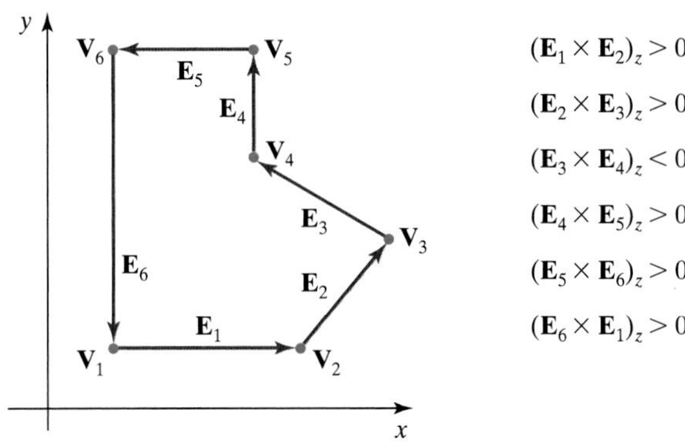

FIGURE 3-43 Identifying a concave polygon by calculating cross products of successive pairs of edge vectors.

the xy plane, but we can always move it into that plane using the transformation methods discussed in Chapter 5.

With the **vector method** for splitting a concave polygon, we first need to form the edge vectors. Given two consecutive vertex positions, $\mathbf{V}_k$ and $\mathbf{V}_{k+1}$, we define the edge vector between them as

$$\mathbf{E}_k = \mathbf{V}_{k+1} - \mathbf{V}_k$$

Next we calculate the cross products of successive edge vectors in order around the polygon perimeter. If the z component of some cross products is positive while other cross products have a negative z component, the polygon is concave. Otherwise, the polygon is convex. This assumes that no series of three successive vertices are collinear, in which case the cross product of the two edge vectors for these vertices would be zero. If all vertices are collinear, we have a degenerate polygon (a straight line). We can apply the vector method by processing edge vectors in a counterclockwise order. If any cross product has a negative z component (as in Fig. 3-43), the polygon is concave and we can split it along the line of the first edge vector in the cross-product pair. The following example illustrates this method for splitting a concave polygon.

EXAMPLE 3-4 Vector Method for Splitting Concave Polygons

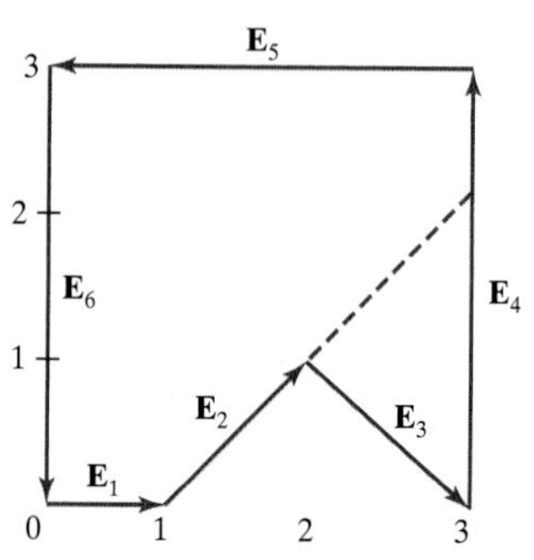

FIGURE 3-44 Splitting a concave polygon using the vector method.

Figure 3-44 shows a concave polygon with six edges. Edge vectors for this polygon can be expressed as

$$\begin{aligned} \mathbf{E}_1 &= (1, 0, 0) & \mathbf{E}_2 &= (1, 1, 0) \\ \mathbf{E}_3 &= (1, -1, 0) & \mathbf{E}_4 &= (0, 2, 0) \\ \mathbf{E}_5 &= (-3, 0, 0) & \mathbf{E}_6 &= (0, -2, 0) \end{aligned}$$

where the z component is 0, since all edges are in the xy plane. The cross product $\mathbf{E}_j \times \mathbf{E}_k$ for two successive edge vectors is a vector perpendicular to the xy plane with z component equal to $E_{jx}E_{ky} - E_{kx}E_{jy}$:

$$\begin{aligned} \mathbf{E}_1 \times \mathbf{E}_2 &= (0, 0, 1) & \mathbf{E}_2 \times \mathbf{E}_3 &= (0, 0, -2) \\ \mathbf{E}_3 \times \mathbf{E}_4 &= (0, 0, 2) & \mathbf{E}_4 \times \mathbf{E}_5 &= (0, 0, 6) \\ \mathbf{E}_5 \times \mathbf{E}_6 &= (0, 0, 6) & \mathbf{E}_6 \times \mathbf{E}_1 &= (0, 0, 2) \end{aligned}$$

Since the cross product $\mathbf{E}_2 \times \mathbf{E}_3$ has a negative z component, we split the polygon along the line of vector $\mathbf{E}_2$. The line equation for this edge has a slope of 1 and a y intercept of -1. We then determine the intersection of this line with the other polygon edges to split the polygon into two pieces. No other edge cross products are negative, so the two new polygons are both convex. ■

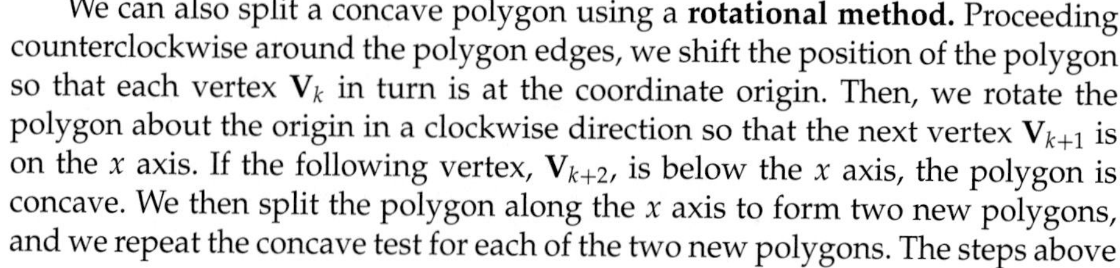

We can also split a concave polygon using a **rotational method.** Proceeding counterclockwise around the polygon edges, we shift the position of the polygon so that each vertex $\mathbf{V}_k$ in turn is at the coordinate origin. Then, we rotate the polygon about the origin in a clockwise direction so that the next vertex $\mathbf{V}_{k+1}$ is on the x axis. If the following vertex, $\mathbf{V}_{k+2}$, is below the x axis, the polygon is concave. We then split the polygon along the x axis to form two new polygons, and we repeat the concave test for each of the two new polygons. The steps above are repeated until we have tested all vertices in the polygon list. Methods for rotating and shifting the position of an object are discussed in detail in Chapter 5. Figure 3-45 illustrates the rotational method for splitting a concave polygon.

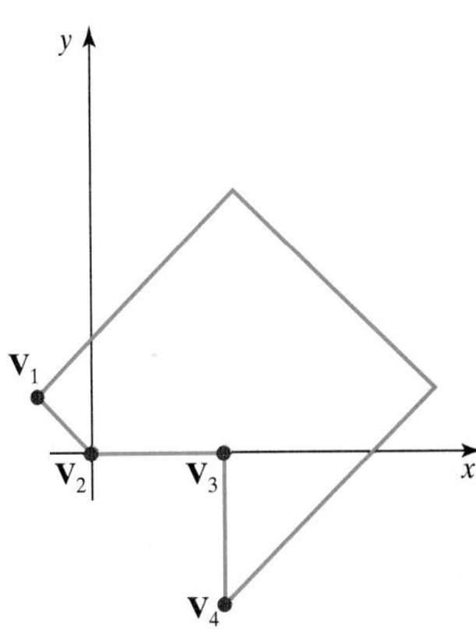

FIGURE 3-45 Splitting a concave polygon using the rotational method. After moving $\mathbf{V}_2$ to the coordinate origin and rotating $\mathbf{V}_3$ onto the x axis, we find that $\mathbf{V}_4$ is below the x axis. So we split the polygon along the line of $\overline{\mathbf{V}_2\mathbf{V}_3}$, which is the x axis.

Splitting a Convex Polygon into a Set of Triangles

Once we have a vertex list for a convex polygon, we could transform it into a set of triangles. This can be accomplished by first defining any sequence of three consecutive vertices to be a new polygon (a triangle). The middle triangle vertex is then deleted from the original vertex list. Then the same procedure is applied to this modified vertex list to strip off another triangle. We continue forming triangles in this manner until the original polygon is reduced to just three vertices, which define the last triangle in the set. A concave polygon can also by divided into a set of triangles using this approach, as long as the three selected vertices at each step form an interior angle that is less than 180° (a "convex" angle).

Inside-Outside Tests

Various graphics processes often need to identify interior regions of objects. Identifying the interior of a simple object, such as a convex polygon, a circle, or a sphere, is generally a straightforward process. But sometimes we must deal with more complex objects. For example, we may want to specify a complex fill region with intersecting edges, as in Fig. 3-46. For such shapes, it is not always clear which regions of the xy plane we should call "interior" and which regions we should designate as "exterior" to the object boundaries. Two commonly used algorithms for identifying interior areas of a plane figure are the odd-even rule and the nonzero winding-number rule.

We apply the **odd-even rule,** also called the *odd-parity rule* or the *even-odd rule,* by first conceptually drawing a line from any position **P** to a distant point outside the coordinate extents of the closed polyline. Then we count the number of line-segment crossings along this line. If the number of segments crossed by this line is odd, then **P** is considered to be an *interior* point. Otherwise, **P** is an *exterior* point. To obtain an accurate count of the segment crossings, we must be sure that the line path we choose does not intersect any line-segment endpoints. Figure 3-46(a) shows the interior and exterior regions obtained using the odd-even rule for a self-intersecting closed polyline. We can use this procedure, for example,

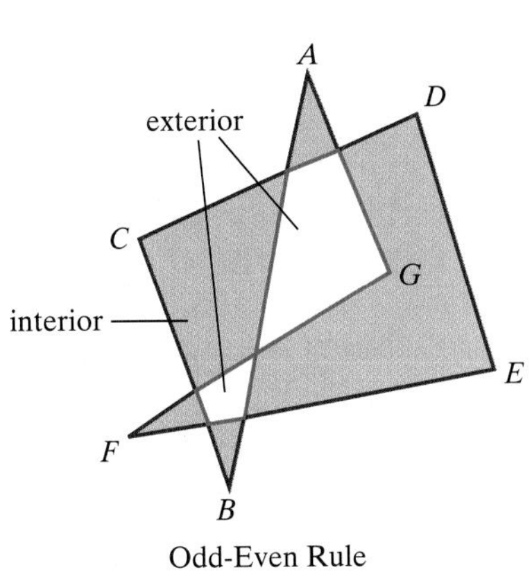

Odd-Even Rule

(a)

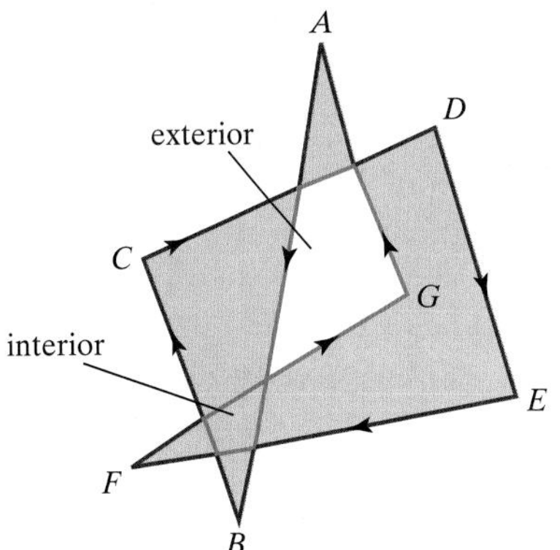

Nonzero Winding-Number Rule

(b)

FIGURE 3-46 Identifying interior and exterior regions of a closed polyline that contains self-intersecting segments.

to fill the interior region between two concentric circles or two concentric polygons with a specified color.

Another method for defining interior regions is the **nonzero winding-number rule,** which counts the number of times the boundary of an object "winds" around a particular point in the counterclockwise direction. This count is called the **winding number,** and the interior points of a two-dimensional object can be defined to be those that have a nonzero value for the winding number. We apply the nonzero winding number rule by initializing the winding number to 0 and again imagining a line drawn from any position **P** to a distant point beyond the coordinate extents of the object. The line we choose must not pass through any endpoint coordinates. As we move along the line from position **P** to the distant point, we count the number of object line segments that cross the reference line in each direction. We add 1 to the winding number every time we intersect a segment that crosses the line in the direction from right to left, and we subtract 1 every time we intersect a segment that crosses from left to right. The final value of the winding number, after all boundary crossings have been counted, determines the relative position of **P**. If the winding number is nonzero, **P** is considered to be an interior point. Otherwise, **P** is taken to be an exterior point. Figure 3-46(b) shows the interior and exterior regions defined by the nonzero winding-number rule for a self-intersecting, closed polyline. For simple objects, such as polygons and circles, the nonzero winding-number rule and the odd-even rule give the same results. But for more complex shapes, the two methods may yield different interior and exterior regions, as in the example of Fig. 3-46.

One way to determine directional boundary crossings is to set up vectors along the object edges (or boundary lines) and along the reference line. Then we compute the vector cross product of the vector **u**, along the line from **P** to a distant point, with an object edge vector **E** for each edge that crosses the line. Assuming that we have a two-dimensional object in the xy plane, the direction of each vector cross product will be either in the $+z$ direction or in the $-z$ direction. If the z component of a cross product $\mathbf{u} \times \mathbf{E}$ for a particular crossing is positive, that segment crosses from right to left and we add 1 to the winding number. Otherwise, the segment crosses from left to right and we subtract 1 from the winding number.

A somewhat simpler way to compute directional boundary crossings is to use vector dot products instead of cross products. To do this, we set up a vector that is perpendicular to vector **u** and that has a right-to-left direction as we look along the line from **P** in the direction of **u.** If the components of **u** are denoted as (u_x, u_y), then the vector that is perpendicular to **u** has components $(-u_y, u_x)$ (Appendix A). Now, if the dot product of this perpendicular vector and a boundary-line vector is positive, that crossing is from right to left and we add 1 to the winding number. Otherwise, the boundary crosses our reference line from left to right, and we subtract 1 from the winding number.

The nonzero winding-number rule tends to classify as interior some areas that the odd-even rule deems to be exterior, and it can be more versatile in some applications. In general, plane figures can be defined with multiple, disjoint components, and the direction specified for each set of disjoint boundaries can be used to designate the interior and exterior regions. Examples include characters (such as letters of the alphabet and punctuation symbols), nested polygons, and concentric circles or ellipses. For curved lines, the odd-even rule is applied by calculating intersections with the curve paths. Similarly, with the nonzero winding-number rule, we need to calculate tangent vectors to the curves at the crossover intersection points with the reference line from position **P**.

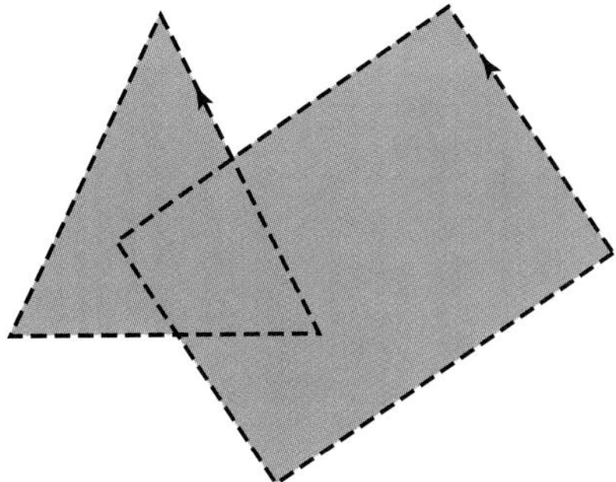

FIGURE 3-47 A fill area defined as a region that has a positive value for the winding number. This fill area is the union of two regions, each with a counterclockwise border direction.

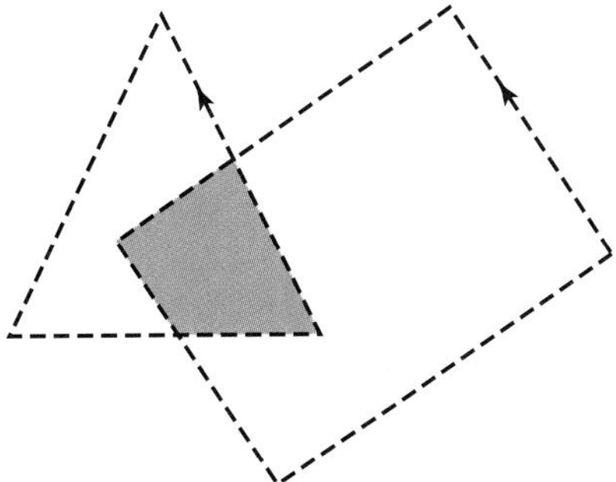

FIGURE 3-48 A fill area defined as a region with a winding number greater than 1. This fill area is the intersection of two regions, each with a counterclockwise border direction.

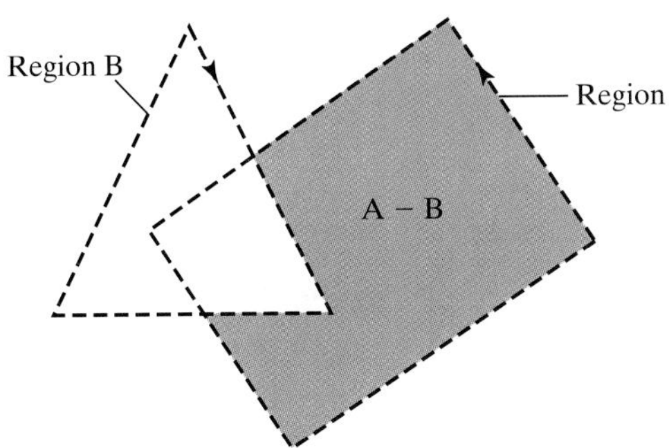

FIGURE 3-49 A fill area defined as a region with a positive value for the winding number. This fill area is the difference, A − B, of two regions, where region A has a positive border direction (counterclockwise) and region B has a negative border direction (clockwise).

Variations of the nonzero winding-number rule can be used to define interior regions in other ways. For example, we could define a point to be interior if its winding number is positive or if it is negative. Or we could use any other rule to generate a variety of fill shapes. Sometimes, Boolean operations are used to specify a fill area as a combination of two regions. One way to implement Boolean operations is by using a variation of the basic winding-number rule. With this scheme, we first define a simple, nonintersecting boundary for each of two regions. Then if we consider the direction for each boundary to be counterclockwise, the union of two regions would consist of those points whose winding number is positive (Fig. 3-47). Similarly, the intersection of two regions with counterclockwise boundaries would contain those points whose winding number is greater than 1, as illustrated in Fig. 3-48. To set up a fill area that is the difference of two regions, say A − B, we can enclose region A with a counterclockwise border and B with a clockwise border. Then the difference region (Fig. 3-49) is the set of all points whose winding number is positive.

Polygon Tables

Typically, the objects in a scene are described as sets of polygon surface facets. In fact, graphics packages often provide functions for defining a surface shape as a mesh of polygon patches. The description for each object includes coordinate information specifying the geometry for the polygon facets and other surface parameters such as color, transparency, and light-reflection properties. As

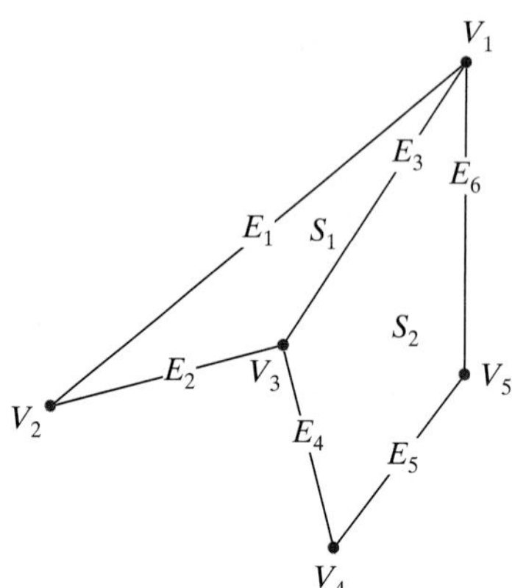

VERTEX TABLE	
V_1:	x_1, y_1, z_1
V_2:	x_2, y_2, z_2
V_3:	x_3, y_3, z_3
V_4:	x_4, y_4, z_4
V_5:	x_5, y_5, z_5

EDGE TABLE	
E_1:	V_1, V_2
E_2:	V_2, V_3
E_3:	V_3, V_1
E_4:	V_3, V_4
E_5:	V_4, V_5
E_6:	V_5, V_1

SURFACE-FACET TABLE	
S_1:	E_1, E_2, E_3
S_2:	E_3, E_4, E_5, E_6

FIGURE 3-50 Geometric data-table representation for two adjacent polygon surface facets, formed with six edges and five vertices.

information for each polygon is input, the data are placed into tables that are to be used in the subsequent processing, display, and manipulation of the objects in the scene. These polygon data tables can be organized into two groups: geometric tables and attribute tables. Geometric data tables contain vertex coordinates and parameters to identify the spatial orientation of the polygon surfaces. Attribute information for an object includes parameters specifying the degree of transparency of the object and its surface reflectivity and texture characteristics.

Geometric data for the objects in a scene are arranged conveniently in three lists: a vertex table, an edge table, and a surface-facet table. Coordinate values for each vertex in the object are stored in the vertex table. The edge table contains pointers back into the vertex table to identify the vertices for each polygon edge. And the surface-facet table contains pointers back into the edge table to identify the edges for each polygon. This scheme is illustrated in Fig. 3-50 for two adjacent polygon facets on an object surface. In addition, individual objects and their component polygon faces can be assigned object and facet identifiers for easy reference.

Listing the geometric data in three tables, as in Fig. 3-50, provides a convenient reference to the individual components (vertices, edges, and surface facets) for each object. Also, the object can be displayed efficiently by using data from the edge table to identify polygon boundaries. An alternative arrangement is to use just two tables: a vertex table and a surface-facet table. But this scheme is less convenient, and some edges could get drawn twice in a wire-frame display. Another possibility is to use only a surface-facet table, but this duplicates coordinate information, since explicit coordinate values are listed for each vertex in each polygon facet. Also the relationship between edges and facets would have to be reconstructed from the vertex listings in the surface-facet table.

We can add extra information to the data tables of Fig. 3-50 for faster information extraction. For instance, we could expand the edge table to include forward pointers into the surface-facet table so that a common edge between polygons could be identified more rapidly (Fig. 3-51). This is particularly useful for rendering procedures that must vary surface shading smoothly across the edges from one polygon to the next. Similarly, the vertex table could be expanded to reference corresponding edges, for faster information retrieval.

Additional geometric information that is usually stored in the data tables includes the slope for each edge and the coordinate extents for polygon edges, polygon facets, and each object in a scene. As vertices are input, we can calculate edge slopes, and we can scan the coordinate values to identify the minimum and maximum x, y, and z values for individual lines and polygons. Edge slopes and bounding-box information are needed in subsequent processing, such as surface rendering and visible-surface identification algorithms.

Since the geometric data tables may contain extensive listings of vertices and edges for complex objects and scenes, it is important that the data be checked for consistency and completeness. When vertex, edge, and polygon definitions are specified, it is possible, particularly in interactive applications, that certain input errors could be made that would distort the display of the objects. The more information included in the data tables, the easier it is to check for errors. Therefore, error checking is easier when three data tables (vertex, edge, and surface facet) are used, since this scheme provides the most information. Some of the tests that could be performed by a graphics package are (1) that every vertex is listed as an endpoint for at least two edges, (2) that every edge is part of at least one polygon, (3) that every polygon is closed, (4) that each polygon has at least one shared edge, and (5) that if the edge table contains pointers to polygons, every edge referenced by a polygon pointer has a reciprocal pointer back to the polygon.

E_1:	V_1, V_2, S_1
E_2:	V_2, V_3, S_1
E_3:	V_3, V_1, S_1, S_2
E_4:	V_3, V_4, S_2
E_5:	V_4, V_5, S_2
E_6:	V_5, V_1, S_2

FIGURE 3-51 Edge table for the surfaces of Fig. 3-50 expanded to include pointers into the surface-facet table.

Plane Equations

To produce a display of a three-dimensional scene, a graphics system processes the input data through several procedures. These procedures include transformation of the modeling and world-coordinate descriptions through the viewing pipeline, identification of visible surfaces, and the application of rendering routines to the individual surface facets. For some of these processes, information about the spatial orientation of the surface components of objects is needed. This information is obtained from the vertex coordinate values and the equations that describe the polygon surfaces.

Each polygon in a scene is contained within a plane of infinite extent. The general equation of a plane is

$$Ax + By + Cz + D = 0 \tag{3-59}$$

where (x, y, z) is any point on the plane, and the coefficients A, B, C, and D (called *plane parameters*) are constants describing the spatial properties of the plane. We can obtain the values of A, B, C, and D by solving a set of three plane equations using the coordinate values for three noncollinear points in the plane. For this purpose, we can select three successive convex-polygon vertices, (x_1, y_1, z_1), (x_2, y_2, z_2), and (x_3, y_3, z_3), in a counterclockwise order and solve the following set of simultaneous linear plane equations for the ratios A/D, B/D, and C/D:

$$(A/D)x_k + (B/D)y_k + (C/D)z_k = -1, \qquad k = 1, 2, 3 \tag{3-60}$$

The solution to this set of equations can be obtained in determinant form, using

Cramer's rule, as

$$A = \begin{vmatrix} 1 & y_1 & z_1 \\ 1 & y_2 & z_2 \\ 1 & y_3 & z_3 \end{vmatrix} \qquad B = \begin{vmatrix} x_1 & 1 & z_1 \\ x_2 & 1 & z_2 \\ x_3 & 1 & z_3 \end{vmatrix}$$
$$C = \begin{vmatrix} x_1 & y_1 & 1 \\ x_2 & y_2 & 1 \\ x_3 & y_3 & 1 \end{vmatrix} \qquad D = - \begin{vmatrix} x_1 & y_1 & z_1 \\ x_2 & y_2 & z_2 \\ x_3 & y_3 & z_3 \end{vmatrix} \tag{3-61}$$

Expanding the determinants, we can write the calculations for the plane coefficients in the form

$$\begin{aligned} A &= y_1(z_2 - z_3) + y_2(z_3 - z_1) + y_3(z_1 - z_2) \\ B &= z_1(x_2 - x_3) + z_2(x_3 - x_1) + z_3(x_1 - x_2) \\ C &= x_1(y_2 - y_3) + x_2(y_3 - y_1) + x_3(y_1 - y_2) \\ D &= -x_1(y_2z_3 - y_3z_2) - x_2(y_3z_1 - y_1z_3) - x_3(y_1z_2 - y_2z_1) \end{aligned} \tag{3-62}$$

These calculations are valid for any three coordinate positions, including those for which $D = 0$. When vertex coordinates and other information are entered into the polygon data structure, values for A, B, C, and D can be computed for each polygon facet and stored with the other polygon data.

It is possible that the coordinates defining a polygon facet may not be contained within a single plane. We can solve this problem by dividing the facet into a set of triangles. Or we could find an approximating plane for the vertex list. One method for obtaining an approximating plane is to divide the vertex list into subsets, where each subset contains three vertices, and calculate plane parameters A, B, C, D for each subset. The approximating plane parameters are then obtained as the average value for each of the calculated plane parameters. Another approach is to project the vertex list onto the coordinate planes. Then we take parameter A proportional to the area of the polygon projection on the yz plane, parameter B proportional to the projection area on the xz plane, and parameter C proportional to the projection area on the xy plane. The projection method is often used in ray-tracing applications.

Front and Back Polygon Faces

Since we are usually dealing with polygon surfaces that enclose an object interior, we need to distinguish between the two sides of each surface. The side of a polygon that faces into the object interior is called the **back face,** and the visible, or outward, side is the **front face.** Identifying the position of points in space relative to the front and back faces of a polygon is a basic task in many graphics algorithms, as, for example, in determining object visibility. Every polygon is contained within an infinite plane that partitions space into two regions. Any point that is not on the plane and that is visible to the front face of a polygon surface section is said to be *in front of* (or *outside*) the plane, and, thus, outside the object. And any point that is visible to the back face of the polygon is *behind* (or *inside*) the plane. A point that is behind (inside) all polygon surface planes is inside the object. We need to keep in mind that this inside/outside classification is relative to the plane containing the polygon, whereas our previous inside/outside tests using the winding-number or odd-even rule were in reference to the interior of some two-dimensional boundary.

Plane equations can be used to identify the position of spatial points relative to the polygon facets of an object. For any point (x, y, z) not on a plane with parameters A, B, C, D, we have

$$Ax + By + Cz + D \neq 0$$

Thus we can identify the point as either behind or in front of a polygon surface contained within that plane according to the sign (negative or positive) of $Ax + By + Cz + D$:

if $Ax + By + Cz + D < 0$, the point (x, y, z) is behind the plane

if $Ax + By + Cz + D > 0$, the point (x, y, z) is in front of the plane

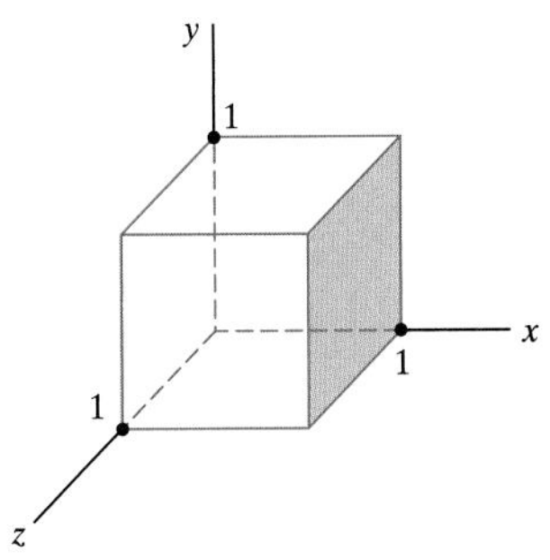

FIGURE 3-52 The shaded polygon surface of the unit cube has plane equation $x - 1 = 0$.

These inequality tests are valid in a right-handed Cartesian system, provided the plane parameters A, B, C, and D were calculated using coordinate positions selected in a strictly counterclockwise order when viewing the surface along a front-to-back direction. For example, in Fig. 3-52, any point outside (in front of) the plane of the shaded polygon satisfies the inequality $x - 1 > 0$, while any point inside (in back of) the plane has an x-coordinate value less than 1.

Orientation of a polygon surface in space can be described with the **normal vector** for the plane containing that polygon, as shown in Fig. 3-53. This surface normal vector is perpendicular to the plane and has Cartesian components (A, B, C), where parameters A, B, and C are the plane coefficients calculated in Eqs. 3-62. The normal vector points in a direction from inside the plane to the outside; that is, from the back face of the polygon to the front face.

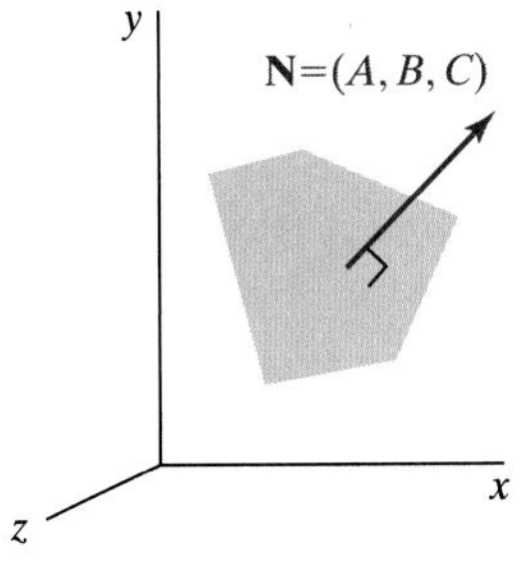

FIGURE 3-53 The normal vector $\mathbf{N}$ for a plane described with the equation $Ax + By + Cz + D = 0$ is perpendicular to the plane and has Cartesian components (A, B, C).

As an example of calculating the components of the normal vector for a polygon, which also gives us the plane parameters, we choose three of the vertices of the shaded face of the unit cube in Fig. 3-52. These points are selected in a counterclockwise ordering as we view the cube from outside looking toward the origin. Coordinates for these vertices, in the order selected, are then used in Eqs. 3-62 to obtain the plane coefficients: $A = 1$, $B = 0$, $C = 0$, $D = -1$. Thus, the normal vector for this plane is $\mathbf{N} = (1, 0, 0)$, which is in the direction of the positive x axis. That is, the normal vector is pointing from inside the cube to the outside and is perpendicular to the plane $x = 1$.

The elements of a normal vector can also be obtained using a vector cross-product calculation. Assuming we have a convex-polygon surface facet and a right-handed Cartesian system, we again select any three vertex positions, $\mathbf{V}_1$, $\mathbf{V}_2$, and $\mathbf{V}_3$, taken in counterclockwise order when viewing from outside the object toward the inside. Forming two vectors, one from $\mathbf{V}_1$ to $\mathbf{V}_2$ and the second from $\mathbf{V}_1$ to $\mathbf{V}_3$, we calculate $\mathbf{N}$ as the vector cross product:

$$\mathbf{N} = (\mathbf{V}_2 - \mathbf{V}_1) \times (\mathbf{V}_3 - \mathbf{V}_1) \tag{3-63}$$

This generates values for the plane parameters A, B, and C. We can then obtain the value for parameter D by substituting these values and the coordinates for one of the polygon vertices into the plane equation 3-59 and solving for D. The plane equation can be expressed in vector form using the normal $\mathbf{N}$ and the position $\mathbf{P}$ of any point in the plane as

$$\mathbf{N} \cdot \mathbf{P} = -D \tag{3-64}$$

For a convex polygon, we could also obtain the plane parameters using the cross product of two successive edge vectors. And with a concave polygon, we can select the three vertices so that the two vectors for the cross product form an angle less than 180°. Otherwise, we can take the negative of their cross product to get the correct normal vector direction for the polygon surface.

3-16 OpenGL POLYGON FILL-AREA FUNCTIONS

With one exception, the OpenGL procedures for specifying fill polygons are similar to those for describing a point or a polyline. A `glVertex` function is used to input the coordinates for a single polygon vertex, and a complete polygon is described with a list of vertices placed between a `glBegin/glEnd` pair. However, there is one additional function that we can use for displaying a rectangle that has an entirely different format.

By default, a polygon interior is displayed in a solid color, determined by the current color settings. As options (which are described in the next chapter), we can fill a polygon with a pattern and we can display polygon edges as line borders around the interior fill. There are six different symbolic constants that we can use as the argument in the `glBegin` function to describe polygon fill areas. These six primitive constants allow us to display a single fill polygon, a set of unconnected fill polygons, or a set of connected fill polygons.

In OpenGL, a fill area must be specified as a convex polygon. Thus, a vertex list for a fill polygon must contain at least three vertices, there can be no crossing edges, and all interior angles for the polygon must be less than 180°. And a single polygon fill area can be defined with only one vertex list, which precludes any specifications that contain holes in the polygon interior, such as that shown in Fig. 3-54. We could describe such a figure using two overlapping convex polygons.

Each polygon that we specify has two faces: a back face and a front face. In OpenGL, fill color and other attributes can be set for each face separately, and back/front identification is needed in both two-dimensional and three-dimensional viewing routines. Therefore, polygon vertices should be specified in a counterclockwise order as we view the polygon from "outside". This identifies the front face for that polygon.

Because graphics displays often include rectangular fill areas, OpenGL provides a special rectangle function that directly accepts vertex specifications in the xy plane. In some implementations of OpenGL, the following routine can be more efficient than generating a fill rectangle using `glVertex` specifications.

```
glRect* (x1, y1, x2, y2);
```

One corner of this rectangle is at coordinate position ($x1$, $y1$), and the opposite corner of the rectangle is at position ($x2$, $y2$). Suffix codes for `glRect` specify the coordinate data type and whether coordinates are to be expressed as array elements. These codes are `i` (for integer), `s` (for short), `f` (for float), `d` (for double), and `v` (for vector). The rectangle is displayed with edges parallel to the xy

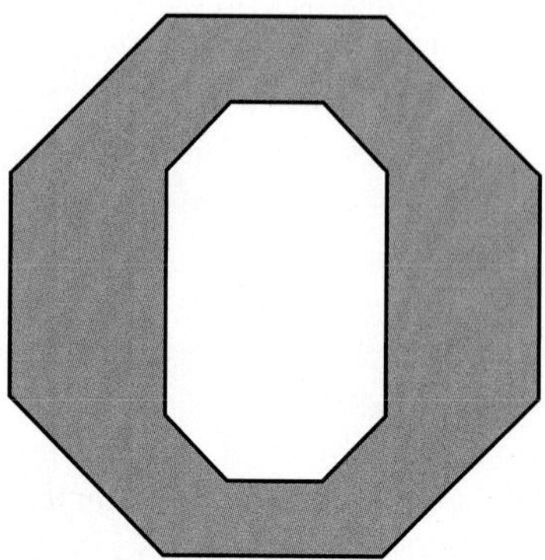

FIGURE 3-54 A polygon with a complex interior, which cannot be specified with a single vertex list.

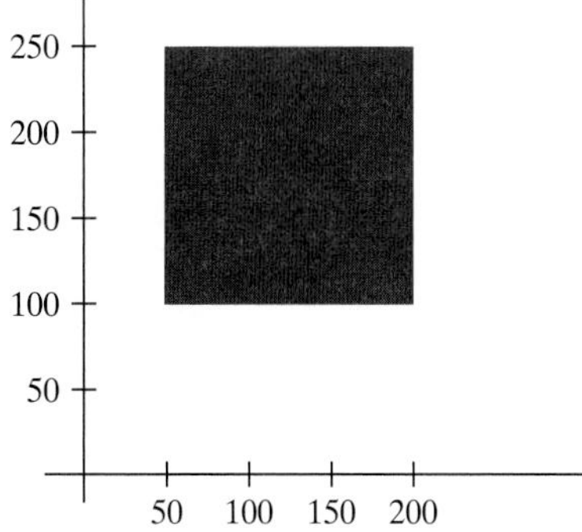

FIGURE 3-55 Display of a square fill area using the `glRect` function.

coordinate axes. As an example, the following statement defines the square shown in Fig. 3-55.

```
glRecti (200, 100, 50, 250);
```

If we put the coordinate values for this rectangle into arrays, we can generate the same square with the following code.

```
int vertex1 [ ] = {200, 100};
int vertex2 [ ] = {50, 250};

glRectiv (vertex1, vertex2);
```

When a rectangle is generated with function `glRect`, the polygon edges are formed between the vertices in the order $(x1, y1)$, $(x2, y1)$, $(x2, y2)$, $(x1, y2)$, and then back to the first vertex. Thus, in our example, we produced a vertex list with a clockwise ordering. In many two-dimensional applications, the determination of front and back faces is unimportant. But if we do want to assign different properties to the front and back faces of the rectangle, then we should reverse the order of the two vertices in this example so that we obtain a counterclockwise ordering of the vertices. In Chapter 4, we discuss another way that we can reverse the specification of front and back polygon faces.

Each of the other six OpenGL polygon fill primitives is specified with a symbolic constant in the `glBegin` function, along with a a list of `glVertex` commands. With the OpenGL primitive constant `GL_POLYGON`, we can display a single polygon fill area such as that shown in Fig. 3-56(a). For this example, we assume that we have a list of six points, labeled p1 through p6, specifying two-dimensional polygon vertex positions in a counterclockwise ordering. Each of the points is represented as an array of (x, y) coordinate values.

```
glBegin (GL_POLYGON);
    glVertex2iv (p1);
    glVertex2iv (p2);
    glVertex2iv (p3);
    glVertex2iv (p4);
    glVertex2iv (p5);
    glVertex2iv (p6);
glEnd ( );
```

A polygon vertex list must contain at least three vertices. Otherwise, nothing is displayed.

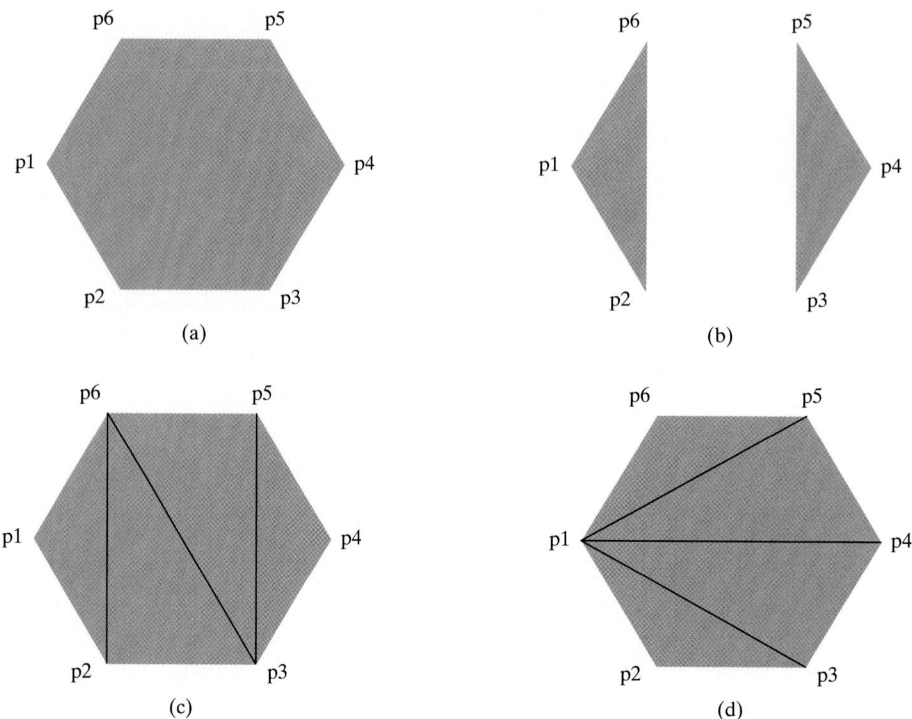

FIGURE 3-56 Displaying polygon fill areas using a list of six vertex positions. (a) A single convex polygon fill area generated with the primitive constant GL_POLYGON. (b) Two unconnected triangles generated with GL_TRIANGLES. (c) Four connected triangles generated with GL_TRIANGLE_STRIP. (d) Four connected triangles generated with GL_TRIANGLE_FAN.

If we reorder the vertex list and change the primitive constant in the previous code example to GL_TRIANGLES, we obtain the two separated triangle fill areas in Fig. 3-56(b).

```
glBegin (GL_TRIANGLES);
    glVertex2iv (p1);
    glVertex2iv (p2);
    glVertex2iv (p6);
    glVertex2iv (p3);
    glVertex2iv (p4);
    glVertex2iv (p5);
glEnd ( );
```

In this case, the first three coordinate points define the vertices for one triangle, the next three points define the next triangle, and so forth. For each triangle fill area, we specify the vertex positions in a counterclockwise order. A set of unconnected triangles is displayed with this primitive constant unless some vertex coordinates are repeated. Nothing is displayed if we do not list at least three vertices. And if the number of vertices specified is not a multiple of three, the final one or two vertex positions are not used.

By reordering the vertex list once more and changing the primitive constant to GL_TRIANGLE_STRIP, we can display the set of connected triangles shown in Fig. 3-56(c).

```
glBegin (GL_TRIANGLE_STRIP);
    glVertex2iv (p1);
    glVertex2iv (p2);
    glVertex2iv (p6);
    glVertex2iv (p3);
    glVertex2iv (p5);
    glVertex2iv (p4);
glEnd ( );
```

Assuming that no coordinate positions are repeated in a list of N vertices, we obtain $N - 2$ triangles in the strip. Clearly, we must have $N \geq 3$ or nothing is displayed. In this example, $N = 6$ and we obtain four triangles. Each successive triangle shares an edge with the previously defined triangle, so the ordering of the vertex list must be set up to ensure a consistent display. One triangle is defined for each vertex position listed after the first two vertices. Thus, the first three vertices should be listed in counterclockwise order, when viewing the front (outside) surface of the triangle. After that, the set of three vertices for each subsequent triangle is arranged in a counterclockwise order within the polygon tables. This is accomplished by processing each position n in the vertex list in the order $n = 1$, $n = 2, \ldots, n = N - 2$ and arranging the order of the corresponding set of three vertices according to whether n is an odd number or an even number. If n is odd, the polygon table listing for the triangle vertices is in the order $n, n+1, n+2$. If n is even, the triangle vertices are listed in the order $n+1, n, n+2$. In the preceding example, our first triangle ($n = 1$) would be listed as having vertices (p1, p2, p6). The second triangle ($n = 2$) would have the vertex ordering (p6, p2, p3). Vertex ordering for the third triangle ($n = 3$) would be (p6, p3, p5). And the fourth triangle ($n = 4$) would be listed in the polygon tables with vertex ordering (p5, p3, p4).

Another way to generate a set of connected triangles is to use the "fan" approach illustrated in Fig. 3-56(d), where all triangles share a common vertex. We obtain this arrangement of triangles using the primitive constant `GL_TRIANGLE_FAN` and the original ordering of our six vertices:

```
glBegin (GL_TRIANGLE_FAN);
    glVertex2iv (p1);
    glVertex2iv (p2);
    glVertex2iv (p3);
    glVertex2iv (p4);
    glVertex2iv (p5);
    glVertex2iv (p6);
glEnd ( );
```

For N vertices, we again obtain $N - 2$ triangles, providing no vertex positions are repeated, and we must list at least three vertices. In addition, the vertices must be specified in the proper order to correctly define front and back faces for each triangle. The first coordinate position listed (in this case, p1) is a vertex for each triangle in the fan. If we again enumerate the triangles and the coordinate positions listed as $n = 1, n = 2, \ldots, n = N - 2$, then vertices for triangle n are listed in the polygon tables in the order $1, n + 1, n + 2$. Therefore, triangle 1 is defined with the vertex list (p1, p2, p3); triangle 2 has the vertex ordering (p1, p3, p4); triangle 3 has its vertices specified in the order (p1, p4, p5); and triangle 4 is listed with vertices (p1, p5, p6).

Besides the primitive functions for triangles and a general polygon, OpenGL provides for the specifications of two types of quadrilaterals (four-sided polygons). With the `GL_QUADS` primitive constant and the following list of eight

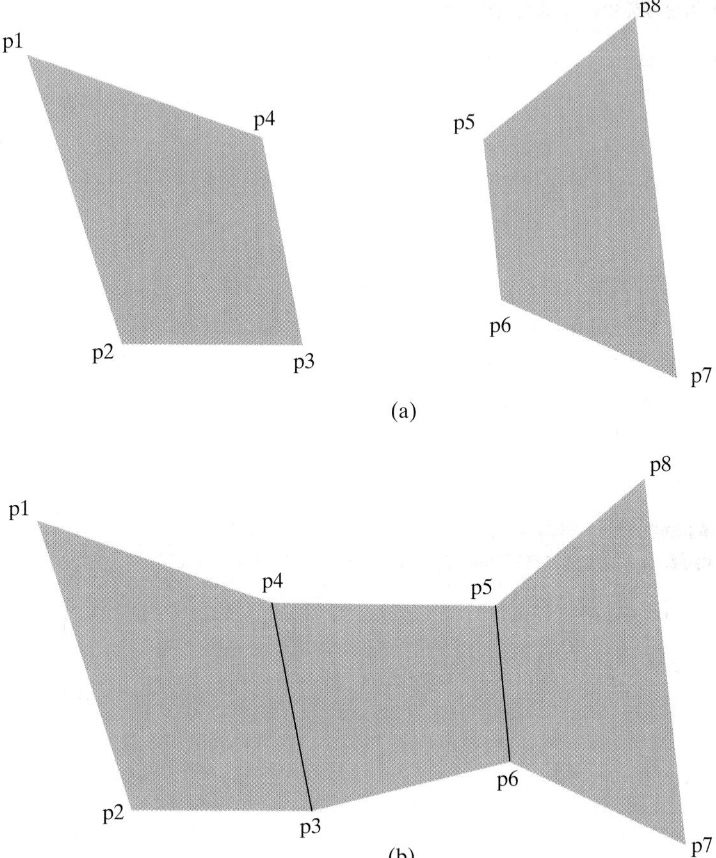

FIGURE 3-57 Displaying quadrilateral fill areas using a list of eight vertex positions. (a) Two unconnected quadrilaterals generated with `GL_QUADS`. (b) Three connected quadrilaterals generated with `GL_QUAD_STRIP`.

vertices, specified as two-dimensional coordinate arrays, we can generate the display shown in Fig. 3-57(a).

```
glBegin (GL_QUADS);
    glVertex2iv (p1);
    glVertex2iv (p2);
    glVertex2iv (p3);
    glVertex2iv (p4);
    glVertex2iv (p5);
    glVertex2iv (p6);
    glVertex2iv (p7);
    glVertex2iv (p8);
glEnd ( );
```

The first four coordinate points define the vertices for one quadrilateral, the next four points define the next quadrilateral, and so on. For each quadrilateral fill area, we specify the vertex positions in a counterclockwise order. If no vertex coordinates are repeated, we display a set of unconnected four-sided fill areas. We must list at least four vertices with this primitive. Otherwise, nothing is displayed. And if the number of vertices specified is not a multiple of four, the extra vertex positions are ignored.

Rearranging the vertex list in the previous quadrilateral code example and changing the primitive constant to `GL_QUAD_STRIP`, we can obtain the set of connected quadrilaterals shown in Fig. 3-57(b).

```
glBegin (GL_QUAD_STRIP);
    glVertex2iv (p1);
    glVertex2iv (p2);
    glVertex2iv (p4);
    glVertex2iv (p3);
    glVertex2iv (p5);
    glVertex2iv (p6);
    glVertex2iv (p8);
    glVertex2iv (p7);
glEnd ( );
```

A quadrilateral is set up for each pair of vertices specified after the first two vertices in the list, and we need to list the vertices so that we generate a correct counterclockwise vertex ordering for each polygon. For a list of N vertices, we obtain $\frac{N}{2} - 1$ quadrilaterals, providing that $N \geq 4$. If N is not a multiple of 4, any extra coordinate positions in the list are not used. We can enumerate these fill polygons and the vertices listed as $n = 1, n = 2, \ldots, n = \frac{N}{2} - 1$. Then polygon tables will list the vertices for quadrilateral n in the vertex order number $2n - 1, 2n, 2n + 2, 2n + 1$. For this example, $N = 8$ and we have 3 quadrilaterals in the strip. Thus, our first quadrilateral ($n = 1$) is listed as having a vertex ordering of (p1, p2, p3, p4). The second quadrilateral ($n = 2$) has the vertex ordering (p4, p3, p6, p5). And the vertex ordering for the third quadrilateral ($n = 3$) is (p5, p6, p7, p8).

Most graphics packages display curved surfaces as a set of approximating plane facets. This is because plane equations are linear, and processing the linear equations is much quicker than processing quadric or other types of curve equations. So OpenGL and other packages provide polygon primitives to facilitate the approximation of a curved surface. Objects are modeled with polygon meshes, and a database of geometric and attribute information is set up to facilitate processing of the polygon facets. In OpenGL, primitives we can use for this purpose are the *triangle strip*, the *triangle fan*, and the *quad strip*. Fast hardware-implemented polygon renderers are incorporated into high-quality graphics systems with the capability for displaying one million or more shaded polygons per second (usually triangles), including the application of surface texture and special lighting effects.

Although the OpenGL core library allows only convex polygons, the OpenGL Utility (GLU) provides functions for dealing with concave polygons and other nonconvex objects with linear boundaries. A set of GLU *polygon tessellation* routines is available for converting such shapes into a set of triangles, triangle meshes, triangle fans, and straight-line segments. Once such objects have been decomposed, they can be processed with basic OpenGL functions.

3-17 OpenGL VERTEX ARRAYS

Although our examples so far have contained relatively few coordinate positions, describing a scene containing several objects can get much more complicated. To illustrate, we first consider describing a single, very basic object: the unit cube shown in Fig. 3-58, with coordinates given in integers to simplify the following discussion. A straightforward method for defining the vertex coordinates is to

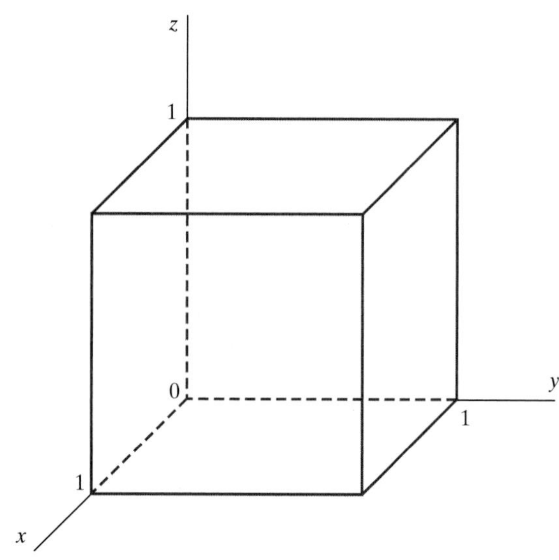

FIGURE 3-58 A cube with an edge length of 1.

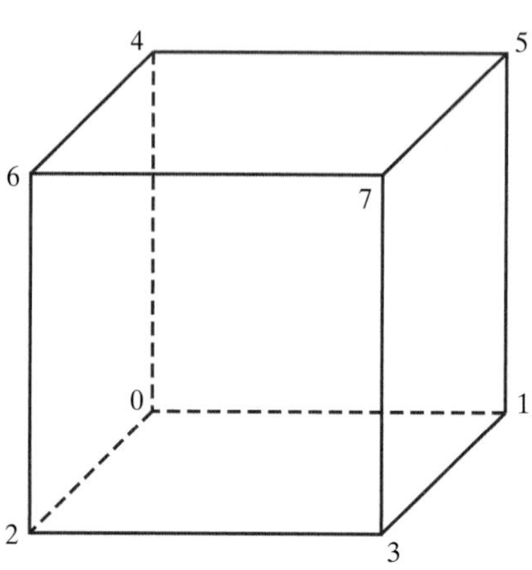

FIGURE 3-59 Subscript values for array pt corresponding to the vertex coordinates for the cube shown in Fig. 3-58.

use a double-subscripted array, such as

```
GLint points [8][3] = { {0, 0, 0}, {0, 1, 0}, {1, 0, 0}, {1, 1, 0},
                        {0, 0, 1}, {0, 1, 1}, {1, 0, 1}, {1, 1, 1} };
```

Or we could first define a data type for a three-dimensional vertex position and then give the coordinates for each vertex position as an element of a single-subscripted array as, for example,

```
typedef GLint vertex3 [3];

 vertex3 pt [8] = { {0, 0, 0}, {0, 1, 0}, {1, 0, 0}, {1, 1, 0},
                    {0, 0, 1}, {0, 1, 1}, {1, 0, 1}, {1, 1, 1} };
```

Next, we need to define each of the six faces of this object. For this, we could make six calls either to `glBegin (GL_POLYGON)` or to `glBegin (GL_QUADS)`. In either case, we must be sure to list the vertices for each face in a counterclockwise order when viewing that surface from the outside of the cube. In the following code segment, we specify each cube face as a quadrilateral and use a function call to pass array subscript values to the OpenGL primitive routines. Figure 3-59 shows the subscript values for array `pt` corresponding to the cube vertex positions.

```
void quad (GLint n1, GLint n2, GLint n3, GLint n4)
{
   glBegin (GL_QUADS);
      glVertex3iv (pt [n1]);
      glVertex3iv (pt [n2]);
      glVertex3iv (pt [n3]);
      glVertex3iv (pt [n4]);
   glEnd ( );
}
```

```
void cube ( )
{
    quad (6, 2, 3, 7);
    quad (5, 1, 0, 4);
    quad (7, 3, 1, 5);
    quad (4, 0, 2, 6);
    quad (2, 0, 1, 3);
    quad (7, 5, 4, 6);
}
```

Thus, the specification for each face requires six OpenGL functions, and we have six faces to specify. When we add color specifications and other parameters, our display program for the cube could easily contain one hundred or more OpenGL function calls. And scenes with many complex objects can require much more.

As we can see from the preceding cube example, a complete scene description could require hundreds or thousands of coordinate specifications. In addition, there are various attribute and viewing parameters that must be set for individual objects. Thus, object and scene descriptions could require an enormous number of function calls, which puts a demand on system resources and can slow execution of the graphics programs. A further problem with complex displays is that object surfaces (such as the cube in Fig. 3-58) usually have shared vertex coordinates. Using the methods we have discussed up to now, these shared positions may need to be specified multiple times.

To alleviate these problems, OpenGL provides a mechanism for reducing the number of function calls needed in processing coordinate information. Using a **vertex array,** we can arrange the information for describing a scene so that we need only a very few function calls. The steps involved are

(1) Invoke the function `glEnableClientState (GL_VERTEX_ARRAY)` to activate the vertex-array feature of OpenGL.

(2) Use the function `glVertexPointer` to specify the location and data format for the vertex coordinates.

(3) Display the scene using a routine such as `glDrawElements`, which can process multiple primitives with very few function calls.

Using the `pt` array previously defined for the cube, we implement these three steps in the following code example.

```
glEnableClientState (GL_VERTEX_ARRAY);
glVertexPointer (3, GL_INT, 0, pt);

GLubyte vertIndex [ ] = (6, 2, 3, 7, 5, 1, 0, 4, 7, 3, 1, 5,
     4, 0, 2, 6, 2, 0, 1, 3, 7, 5, 4, 6);

glDrawElements (GL_QUADS, 24, GL_UNSIGNED_BYTE, vertIndex);
```

With the first command, `glEnableClientState (GL_VERTEX_ARRAY)`, we activate a capability (in this case, a vertex array) on the client side of a client-server system. Because the client (the machine that is running the main program) retains the data for a picture, the vertex array must be there also. As we noted in Chapter 2, the server (our workstation, for example) generates commands and displays the picture. Of course, a single machine can be both client and server.

The vertex-array feature of OpenGL is deactivated with the command:

```
glDisableClientState (GL_VERTEX_ARRAY);
```

We next give the location and format of the coordinates for the object vertices in the function `glVertexPointer`. The first parameter in `glVertexPointer`, 3 in this example, specifies the number of coordinates used in each vertex description. Data type for the vertex coordinates is designated using an OpenGL symbolic constant as the second parameter in this function. For our example, the data type is `GL_INT`. Other data types are specified with the symbolic constants `GL_BYTE`, `GL_SHORT`, `GL_FLOAT`, and `GL_DOUBLE`. With the third parameter we give the byte offset between consecutive vertices. The purpose of this argument is to allow various kinds of data, such as coordinates and colors, to be packed together in one array. Since we are only giving the coordinate data, we assign a value of 0 to the offset parameter. The last parameter in the `glVertexPointer` function references the vertex array, which contains the coordinate values.

All the indices for the cube vertices are stored in array `vertIndex`. Each of these indices is the subscript for array `pt` corresponding to the coordinate values for that vertex. This index list is referenced as the last parameter value in function `glDrawElements` and is then used by the primitive `GL_QUADS`, which is the first parameter, to display the set of quadrilateral surfaces for the cube. The second parameter specifies the number of elements in array `vertIndex`. Since a quadrilateral requires just four vertices and we specified 24, the `glDrawElements` function continues to display another cube face after each successive set of four vertices until all 24 have been processed. Thus, we accomplish the final display of all faces of the cube with this single function call. The third parameter in function `glDrawElements` gives the type for the index values. Since our indices are small integers, we specified a type of `GL_UNSIGNED_BYTE`. The two other index types that can be used are `GL_UNSIGNED_SHORT` and `GL_UNSIGNED_INT`.

Additional information can be combined with the coordinate values in the vertex arrays to facilitate the processing of a scene description. We can specify color values and other attributes for objects in arrays that can be referenced by the `glDrawElements` function. And we can interlace the various arrays for greater efficiency. We take a look at the methods for implementing these attribute arrays in the next chapter.

3-18 PIXEL-ARRAY PRIMITIVES

In addition to straight lines, polygons, circles, and other primitives, graphics packages often supply routines to display shapes that are defined with a rectangular array of color values. We can obtain the rectangular grid pattern by digitizing (scanning) a photograph or other picture or by generating a shape with a graphics program. Each color value in the array is then mapped to one or more screen pixel positions. As we noted in Chapter 2, a pixel array of color values is typically referred to as a *pixmap*.

Parameters for a pixel array can include a pointer to the color matrix, the size of the matrix, and the position and size of the screen area to be affected by the color values. Figure 3-60 gives an example of mapping a pixel-color array onto a screen area.

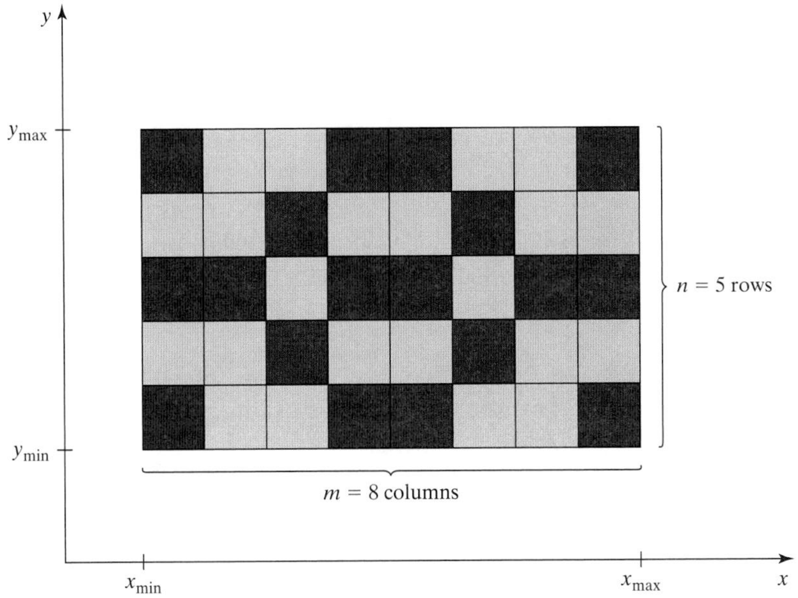

FIGURE 3-60 Mapping an n by m color array onto a region of the screen coordinates.

Another method for implementing a pixel array is to assign either the bit value 0 or the bit value 1 to each element of the matrix. In this case, the array is simply a *bitmap,* which is sometimes called a *mask,* that indicates whether or not a pixel is to be assigned (or combined with) a preset color.

3-19 OpenGL PIXEL-ARRAY FUNCTIONS

There are two functions in OpenGL that we can use to define a shape or pattern specified with a rectangular array. One is a bitmap and the other is a pixmap. Also, OpenGL provides several routines for saving, copying, and manipulating arrays of pixel values.

OpenGL Bitmap Function

A binary array pattern is defined with the function

```
glBitmap (width, height, x0, y0, xOffset, yOffset, bitShape);
```

Parameters `width` and `height` in this function give the number of columns and number of rows, respectively, in the array `bitShape`. Each element of `bitShape` is assigned either a 1 or a 0. A value of 1 indicates that the corresponding pixel is to be displayed in a previously set color. Otherwise, the pixel is unaffected by the bitmap. (As an option, we could use a value of 1 to indicate that a specified color is to be combined with the color value stored in the refresh buffer at that position.) Parameters `x0` and `y0` define the position that is to be considered the "origin" of the rectangular array. This origin position is specified relative to the lower left corner of `bitShape`, and values for `x0` and `y0` can be positive or negative. In addition, we need to designate a location in the frame buffer where the pattern is to be applied. This location is called the **current raster position,** and the bitmap is displayed by positioning its origin, (`x0`, `y0`), at the current raster position. Values assigned to parameters `xOffset` and `yOffset` are used as coordinate offsets to update the frame-buffer current raster position after the bitmap is displayed.

Coordinate values for `x0`, `y0`, `xOffset`, and `yOffset`, as well as the current raster position, are maintained as floating-point values. Of course, bitmaps will be applied at integer pixel positions. But floating-point coordinates allow a set of bitmaps to be spaced at arbitrary intervals, which is useful in some applications such as forming character strings with bitmap patterns.

We use the following routine to set the coordinates for the current raster position.

```
glRasterPos* ( )
```

Parameters and suffix codes are the same as those for the `glVertex` function. Thus, a current raster position is given in world coordinates, and it is transformed to screen coordinates by the viewing transformations. For our two-dimensional examples, we can specify coordinates for the current raster position directly in integer screen coordinates. The default value for the current raster position is the world-coordinate origin (0, 0, 0).

The color for a bitmap is the color that is in effect at the time that the `glRasterPos` command is invoked. Any subsequent color changes do not affect the bitmap.

Each row of a rectangular bit array is stored in multiples of 8 bits, where the binary data is arranged as a set of 8-bit unsigned characters. But we can describe a shape using any convenient grid size. As an example, Fig. 3-61 shows a bit pattern defined on a 10-row by 9-column grid, where the binary data is specified with 16 bits for each row. When this pattern is applied to the pixels in the frame buffer, all bit values beyond the ninth column are ignored.

We apply the bit pattern of Fig. 3-61 to a frame-buffer location with the following code section.

```
GLubyte bitShape [20] = {
    0x1c, 0x00, 0x1c, 0x00, 0x1c, 0x00, 0x1c, 0x00, 0x1c, 0x00,
    0xff, 0x80, 0x7f, 0x00, 0x3e, 0x00, 0x1c, 0x00, 0x08, 0x00};

glPixelStorei (GL_UNPACK_ALIGNMENT, 1);  // Set pixel storage mode.

glRasterPos2i (30, 40);
glBitmap (9, 10, 0.0, 0.0, 20.0, 15.0, bitShape);
```

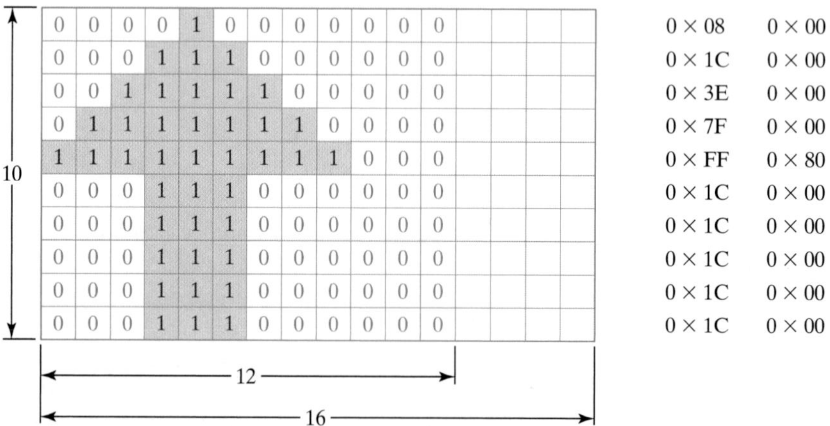

FIGURE 3-61 A bit pattern, specified in an array with 10 rows and 9 columns, is stored in 8-bit blocks of 10 rows with 16 bit values per row.

Array values for bitShape are specified row by row, starting at the bottom of the rectangular-grid pattern. Next we set the storage mode for the bitmap with the OpenGL routine glPixelStorei. The parameter value of 1 in this function indicates that the data values are to be aligned on byte boundaries. With glRasterPos, we set the current raster position to (30, 40). Finally, function glBitmap specifies that the bit pattern is given in array bitShape, and that this array has 9 columns and 10 rows. The coordinates for the origin of this pattern are (0.0, 0.0), which is the lower-left corner of the grid. We illustrate a coordinate offset with the values (20.0, 15.0), although we make no use of the offset in this example.

OpenGL Pixmap Function

A pattern defined as an array of color values is applied to a block of frame-buffer pixel positions with the function

```
glDrawPixels (width, height, dataFormat, dataType, pixMap);
```

Again, parameters width and height give the column and row dimensions, respectively, of the array pixMap. Parameter dataFormat is assigned an OpenGL constant that indicates how the values are specified for the array. For example, we could specify a single blue color for all pixels with the constant GL_BLUE, or we could specify three color components in the order blue, green, red with the constant GL_BGR. A number of other color specifications are possible, and we examine color selections in greater detail in the next chapter. An OpenGL constant, such as GL_BYTE, GL_INT, or GL_FLOAT, is assigned to parameter dataType to designate the data type for the color values in the array. The lower-left corner of this color array is mapped to the current raster position, as set by the glRasterPos function. As an example, the following statement displays a pixmap defined in a 128-by-128 array of RGB color values.

```
glDrawPixels (128, 128, GL_RGB, GL_UNSIGNED_BYTE, colorShape);
```

Since OpenGL provides several buffers, we can paste an array of values into a particular buffer by selecting that buffer as the target of the glDrawPixels routine. Some buffers store color values and some store other kinds of pixel data. A *depth buffer*, for instance, is used to store object distances (depths) from the viewing position, and a *stencil buffer* is used to store boundary patterns for a scene. We select one of these two buffers by setting parameter dataFormat in the glDrawPixels routine to either GL_DEPTH_COMPONENT or GL_STENCIL_INDEX. For these buffers, we would need to set up the pixel array using either depth values or stencil information. We examine both of these buffers in more detail in later chapters.

There are four *color buffers* available in OpenGL that can be used for screen refreshing. Two of the color buffers constitute a left-right scene pair for displaying stereoscopic views. For each of the stereoscopic buffers, there is a front-back pair for double-buffered animation displays. In a particular implementation of OpenGL, either stereoscopic viewing or double buffering, or both, might not be supported. If neither stereoscopic effects nor double buffering is supported, then there is only a single refresh buffer, which is designated as the **front-left color buffer.** This is the default refresh buffer when double buffering is not available or not in effect. If double buffering is in effect, the default is either the back-left and back-right buffers or only the back-left buffer, depending on the current state of stereoscopic viewing. Also, a number of user-defined, auxiliary color buffers are supported that can be used for any nonrefresh purpose, such as saving a picture that is to be copied later into a refresh buffer for display.

We select a single color or auxiliary buffer or a combination of color buffers for storing a pixmap with the following command.

```
glDrawBuffer (buffer);
```

A variety of OpenGL symbolic constants can be assigned to parameter `buffer` to designate one or more "draw" buffers. For instance, we can pick a single buffer with either `GL_FRONT_LEFT`, `GL_FRONT_RIGHT`, `GL_BACK_LEFT`, or `GL_BACK_RIGHT`. We can select both front buffers with `GL_FRONT`, and we can select both back buffers with `GL_BACK`. This is assuming that stereoscopic viewing is in effect. Otherwise, the previous two symbolic constants designate a single buffer. Similarly, we can designate either the left or right buffer pairs with `GL_LEFT` or `GL_RIGHT`. And we can select all the available color buffers with `GL_FRONT_AND_BACK`. An auxiliary buffer is chosen with the constant `GL_AUXk`, where `k` is an integer value from 0 to 3, although more than four auxiliary buffers may be available in some implementations of OpenGL.

OpenGL Raster Operations

In addition to storing an array of pixel values in a buffer, we can retrieve a block of values from a buffer or copy the block into another buffer area. And we can perform a variety of other operations on a pixel array. In general, the term **raster operation** or **raster op** is used to describe any function that processes a pixel array in some way. A raster operation that moves an array of pixel values from one place to another is also referred to as a **block transfer** of pixel values. On a bilevel system, these operations are called **bitblt transfers** (**bit-block transfers**), particularly when the functions are hardware implemented. On a multilevel system, the term **pixblt** is sometimes used for block transfers.

We use the following function to select a rectangular block of pixel values in a designated set of buffers.

```
glReadPixels (xmin, ymin, width, height,
                    dataFormat, dataType, array};
```

The lower-left corner of the rectangular block to be retrieved is at screen-coordinate position (`xmin`, `ymin`). Parameters `width`, `height`, `dataFormat`, and `dataType` are the same as in the `glDrawPixels` routine. The type of data to be saved in parameter `array` depends on the selected buffer. We can choose either the depth buffer or the stencil buffer by assigning either the value `GL_DEPTH_COMPONENT` or the value `GL_STENCIL_INDEX` to parameter `dataFormat`.

A particular combination of color buffers or an auxiliary buffer is selected for the application of the `glReadPixels` routine with the function

```
glReadBuffer (buffer);
```

Symbolic constants for specifying one or more buffers are the same as in the `glDrawBuffer` routine, except that we cannot select all four of the color buffers. The default buffer selection is the front left-right pair or just the front-left buffer, depending on the status of stereoscopic viewing.

We can also copy a block of pixel data from one location to another within the set of OpenGL buffers using the following routine.

```
glCopyPixels (xmin, ymin, width, height, pixelValues);
```

The lower-left corner of the block is at screen-coordinate location (`xmin, ymin`), and parameters `width` and `height` are assigned positive integer values to designate the number of columns and rows, respectively, that are to be copied. Parameter `pixelValues` is assigned either `GL_COLOR`, `GL_DEPTH`, or `GL_STENCIL` to indicate the kind of data we want to copy: color values, depth values, or stencil values. And the block of pixel values is copied from a *source buffer* to a *destination buffer*, with its lower-left corner mapped to the current raster position. We select the source buffer with the `glReadBuffer` command, and we select the destination buffer with the `glDrawBuffer` command. Both the region to be copied and the destination area should lie completely within the bounds of the screen coordinates.

To achieve different effects as a block of pixel values is placed into a buffer with `glDrawPixels` or `glCopyPixels`, we can combine the incoming values with the old buffer values in various ways. As an example, we could apply logical operations, such as *and, or,* and *exclusive or,* to combine the two blocks of pixel values. In OpenGL, we select a bitwise, logical operation for combining incoming and destination pixel color values with the functions

```
glEnable (GL_COLOR_LOGIC_OP);

glLogicOp (logicOp);
```

A variety of symbolic constants can be assigned to parameter `logicOp`, including `GL_AND`, `GL_OR`, and `GL_XOR`. In addition, either the incoming bit values or the destination bit values can be inverted (interchanging 0 and 1 values). We use the constant `GL_COPY_INVERTED` to invert the incoming color bit values and then replace the destination values with the inverted incoming values. And we could simply invert the destination bit values without replacing them with the incoming values using `GL_INVERT`. The various invert operations can also be combined with the logical *and, or,* and *exclusive or* operations. Other options include clearing all the destination bits to the value 0 (`GL_CLEAR`), or setting all the destination bits to the value 1 (`GL_SET`). The default value for the `glLogicOp` routine is `GL_COPY`, which simply replaces the destination values with the incoming values.

Additional OpenGL routines are available for manipulating pixel arrays processed by the `glDrawPixels`, `glReadPixels`, and `glCopyPixels` functions. For example, the `glPixelTransfer` and `glPixelMap` routines can be used to shift or adjust color values, depth values, or stencil values. We return to pixel operations in later chapters as we explore other facets of computer-graphics packages.

3-20 CHARACTER PRIMITIVES

Graphics displays often include textural information such as labels on graphs and charts, signs on buildings or vehicles, and general identifying information for simulation and visualization applications. Routines for generating character primitives are available in most graphics packages. Some systems provide an extensive set of character functions, while other systems offer only minimal support for character generation.

Letters, numbers, and other characters can be displayed in a variety of sizes and styles. The overall design style for a set (or family) of characters is called a **typeface.** Today, there are thousands of typefaces available for computer applications. Examples of a few common typefaces are Courier, Helvetica, New York, Palatino, and Zapf Chancery. Originally, the term **font** referred to a set of cast metal character forms in a particular size and format, such as 10-point Courier Italic or 12-point Palatino Bold. A 14-point font has a total character height of about 0.5 centimeter. In other words, 72 points is about the equivalent of 2.54 centimeters (1 inch). The terms font and typeface are now often used interchangeably, since most printing is no longer done with cast metal forms.

Typefaces (or fonts) can be divided into two broad groups: *serif* and *sans serif.* Serif type has small lines or accents at the ends of the main character strokes, while sans-serif type does not have accents. For example, the text in this book is set in a serif font (Palatino). But this sentence is printed in a sans-serif font (Univers). Serif type is generally more *readable*; that is, it is easier to read in longer blocks of text. On the other hand, the individual characters in sans-serif type are easier to recognize. For this reason, sans-serif type is said to be more *legible.* Since sans-serif characters can be quickly recognized, this typeface is good for labeling and short headings.

Fonts are also classified according to whether they are *monospace* or *proportional.* Characters in a monospace font all have the same width. In a proportional font, character width varies.

Two different representations are used for storing computer fonts. A simple method for representing the character shapes in a particular typeface is to set up a pattern of binary values on a rectangular grid. The set of characters is then referred to as a **bitmap font** (or **bitmapped font**). A bitmapped character set is also sometimes referred to as a **raster font.** Another, more flexible, scheme is to describe character shapes using straight-line and curve sections, as in PostScript, for example. In this case, the set of characters is called an **outline font** or a **stroke font.** Figure 3-62 illustrates the two methods for character representation. When the pattern in Fig. 3-62(a) is applied to an area of the frame buffer, the 1 bits designate which pixel positions are to be displayed in a specified color. To display the character shape in Fig. 3-62(b), the interior of the character outline is treated as a fill area.

Bitmap fonts are the simplest to define and display: we just need to map the character grids to a frame-buffer position. In general, however, bitmap fonts

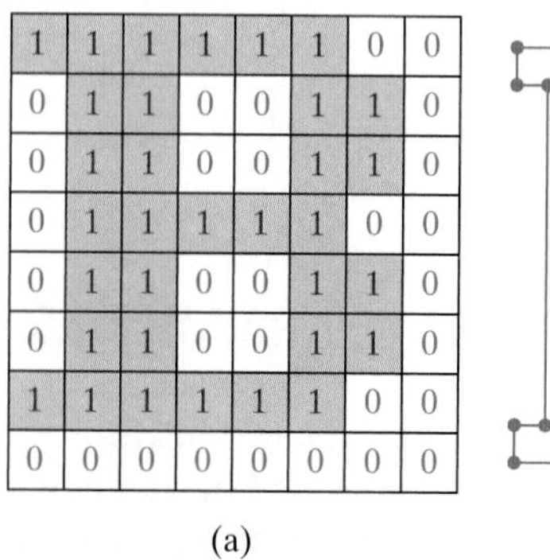

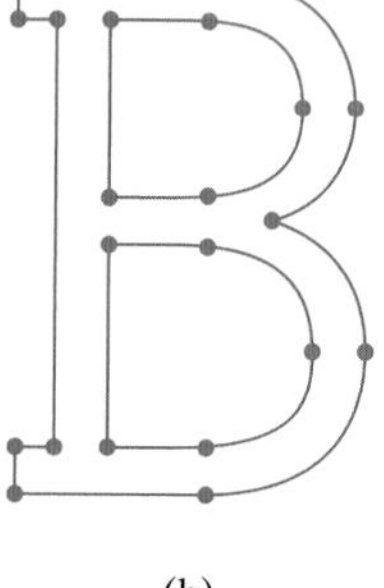

FIGURE 3-62 The letter "B" represented with an 8-by-8 bitmap pattern (a) and with an outline shape defined with straight-line and curve segments (b).

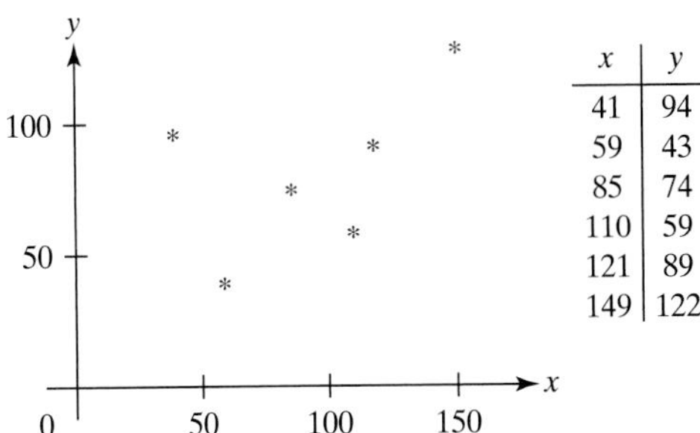

x	y
41	94
59	43
85	74
110	59
121	89
149	122

FIGURE 3-63 A polymarker graph of a set of data values.

require more storage space, since each variation (size and format) must be saved in a *font cache*. It is possible to generate different sizes and other variations, such as bold and italic, from one bitmap font set, but this often does not produce good results. We can increase or decrease the size of a character bitmap only in integer multiples of the pixel size. To double the size of a character, we need to double the number of pixels in the bitmap. And this just increases the ragged appearance of its edges.

In contrast to bitmap fonts, outline fonts can be increased in size without distorting the character shapes. And outline fonts require less storage because each variation does not require a distinct font cache. We can produce boldface, italic, or different sizes by manipulating the curve definitions for the character outlines. But it does take more time to process the outline fonts, since they must be scan converted into the frame buffer.

There are a variety of possible functions for implementing character displays. Some graphics packages provide a function that accepts any character string and a frame-buffer starting position for the string. Another type of function is one that displays a single character at one or more selected positions. Since this character routine is useful for showing markers in a network layout or in displaying a point plot of a discrete data set, the character displayed by this routine is sometimes referred to as a **marker symbol** or **polymarker,** in analogy with a polyline primitive. In addition to standard characters, special shapes such as dots, circles, and crosses are often available as marker symbols. Figure 3-63 shows a plot of a discrete data set using an asterisk as a marker symbol.

Geometric descriptions for characters are given in world coordinates, just as they are for other primitives, and this information is mapped to screen coordinates by the viewing transformations. A bitmap character is described with a rectangular grid of binary values and a grid reference position. This reference position is then mapped to a specified location in the frame buffer. An outline character is defined by a set of coordinate positions that are to be connected with a series of curves and straight-line segments and a reference position that is to be mapped to a given frame-buffer location. The reference position can be specified either for a single outline character or for a string of characters. In general, character routines can allow the construction of both two-dimensional and three-dimensional character displays.

3-21 OpenGL CHARACTER FUNCTIONS

Only low-level support is provided by the basic OpenGL library for displaying individual characters and text strings. We can explicitly define any character as a bitmap, as in the example shape shown in Fig. 3-61, and we can store a set of bitmap characters as a font list. A text string is then displayed by mapping a selected sequence of bitmaps from the font list into adjacent positions in the frame buffer.

However, some predefined character sets are available in the OpenGL Utility Toolkit (GLUT). So we do not need to create our own fonts as bitmap shapes, unless we want to display a font that is not available in GLUT. The GLUT library contains routines for displaying both bitmapped and outline fonts. Bitmapped GLUT fonts are rendered using the OpenGL `glBitmap` function, and the outline fonts are generated with polyline (`GL_LINE_STRIP`) boundaries.

We can display a bitmap GLUT character with

```
glutBitmapCharacter (font, character);
```

where parameter `font` is assigned a symbolic GLUT constant identifying a particular set of type faces, and parameter `character` is assigned either the ASCII code or the specific character we wish to display. Thus, to display the upper-case letter "A", we can either use the ASCII value 65 or the designation `'A'`. Similarly, a code value of 66 is equivalent to `'B'`, code 97 corresponds to the lower-case letter `'a'`, code 98 corresponds to `'b'`, and so forth. Both fixed-width fonts and proportionally spaced fonts are available. We can select a fixed-width font by assigning either `GLUT_BITMAP_8_BY_13` or `GLUT_BITMAP_9_BY_15` to parameter `font`. And we can select a 10-point, proportionally spaced font with either `GLUT_BITMAP_TIMES_ROMAN_10` or `GLUT_BITMAP_HELVETICA_10`. A 12-point Times-Roman font is also available, as well as 12-point and 18-point Helvetica fonts.

Each character generated by `glutBitmapCharacter` is displayed so that the origin (lower-left corner) of the bitmap is at the current raster position. After the character bitmap is loaded into the refresh buffer, an offset equal to the width of the character is added to the x coordinate for the current raster position. As an example, we could display a text string containing 36 bitmap characters with the following code.

```
glRasterPosition2i (x, y);
for (k = 0; k < 36; k++)
   glutBitmapCharacter (GLUT_BITMAP_9_BY_15, text [k]);
```

Characters are displayed in the color that was specified before the execution of the `glutBitmapCharacter` function.

An outline character is displayed with the following function call.

```
glutStrokeCharacter (font, character);
```

For this function, we can assign parameter `font` either the value `GLUT_STROKE_ROMAN`, which displays a proportionally spaced font, or the value `GLUT_STROKE_MONO_ROMAN`, which displays a font with constant spacing. We control the size and position of these characters by specifying transformation operations (Chapter 5) before executing the `glutStrokeCharacter` routine. After each character is displayed, a coordinate offset is automatically applied so that the position for displaying the next character is to the right of the current character. Text strings generated with outline fonts are part of the geometric description for a two-dimensional or three-dimensional scene because they are constructed with line segments. Thus, they can be viewed from various directions, and we can shrink or expand them without distortion, or transform them in other ways. But they are slower to render, compared to bitmapped fonts.

3-22 PICTURE PARTITIONING

Some graphics libraries include routines for describing a picture as a collection of named sections and for manipulating the individual sections of a picture. Using these functions we can create, edit, delete, or move a part of a picture independently of the other picture components. And we can also use this feature of a graphics package for hierarchical modeling (Chapter 14), in which an object description is given as a tree structure composed of a number of levels specifying the object subparts.

Various names are used for the subsections of a picture. Some graphics packages refer to them as `structures`, while other packages call them `segments` or `objects`. Also, the allowable subsection operations vary greatly from one package to another. Modeling packages, for example, provide a wide range of operations that can be used to describe and manipulate picture elements. On the other hand, for any graphics library, we can always structure and manage the components of a picture using procedural elements available in a high-level language such as C++.

3-23 OpenGL DISPLAY LISTS

Often it can be convenient or more efficient to store an object description (or any other set of OpenGL commands) as a named sequence of statements. We can do this in OpenGL using a structure called a **display list.** Once a display list has been created, we can reference the list multiple times with different display operations. On a network, a display list describing a scene is stored on the server machine, which eliminates the need to transmit the commands in the list each time the scene is to be displayed. We can also set up a display list so that it is saved for later execution, or we can specify that the commands in the list be executed immediately. And display lists are particularly useful for hierarchical modeling, where a complex object can be described with a set of simpler subparts.

Creating and Naming an OpenGL Display List

A set of OpenGL commands is formed into a display list by enclosing the commands within the `glNewList/glEndList` pair of functions. For example,

```
glNewList (listID, listMode};
   .
   .
   .
glEndList ( );
```

This structure forms a display list with a positive integer value assigned to parameter `listID` as the name for the list. Parameter `listMode` is assigned an OpenGL symbolic constant that can be either `GL_COMPILE` or

GL_COMPILE_AND_EXECUTE. If we want to save the list for later execution, we use GL_COMPILE. Otherwise, the commands are executed as they are placed into the list, in addition to allowing us to execute the list again at a later time.

As a display list is created, expressions involving parameters such as coordinate positions and color components are evaluated so that only the parameter values are stored in the list. Any subsequent changes to these parameters have no effect on the list. Because display-list values cannot be changed, we cannot include certain OpenGL commands, such as vertex-list pointers, in a display list.

We can create any number of display lists, and we execute a particular list of commands with a call to its identifier. Further, one display list can be embedded within another display list. But if a list is assigned an identifier that has already been used, the new list replaces the previous list that had been assigned that identifier. Therefore, to avoid losing a list by accidentally reusing its identifier, we can let OpenGL generate an identifier for us:

```
listID = glGenLists (1);
```

This statement returns one (1) unused positive integer identifier to the variable listID. A range of unused integer list identifiers is obtained if we change the argument of glGenLists from the value 1 to some other positive integer. For instance, if we invoke glGenLists (6), then a sequence of six contiguous positive integer values is reserved and the first value in this list of identifiers is returned to the variable listID. A value of 0 is returned by the glGenLists function if an error occurs or if the system cannot generate the range of contiguous integers requested. Therefore, before using an identifier obtained from the glGenLists routine, we could check to be sure that it is not 0.

Although unused list identifiers can be generated with the glGenList function, we can independently query the system to determine whether a specific integer value has been used as a list name. The function to accomplish this is

```
glIsList (listID};
```

A value of GL_TRUE is returned if the value of listID is an integer that has already been used as a display-list name. If the integer value has not been used as a list name, the glIsList function returns the value GL_FALSE.

Executing OpenGL Display Lists

We execute a single display list with the statement

```
glCallList (listID);
```

The following code segment illustrates the creation and execution of a display list. We first set up a display list that contains the description for a regular hexagon, defined in the *xy* plane using a set of six equally spaced vertices around the circumference of a circle, whose center coordinates are (200, 200) and whose radius is 150. Then we issue a call to function glCallList, which displays the hexagon.

```
const double TWO_PI = 6.2831853;

GLuint regHex;

GLdouble theta;
GLint x, y, k;

/*  Set up a display list for a regular hexagon.
 *  Vertices for the hexagon are six equally spaced
 *  points around the circumference of a circle.
 */
regHex = glGenLists (1);  //  Get an identifier for the display list.
glNewList (regHex, GL_COMPILE);
   glBegin (GL_POLYGON);
      for (k = 0; k < 6; k++) {
         theta = TWO_PI * k / 6.0;
         x = 200 + 150 * cos (theta);
         y = 200 + 150 * sin (theta);
         glVertex2i (x, y);
      }
   glEnd ( );
glEndList ( );

glCallList (regHex);
```

Several display lists can be executed using the following two statements.

```
glListBase (offsetValue);

glCallLists (nLists, arrayDataType, listIDArray);
```

The integer number of lists that we want to execute is assigned to parameter `nLists`, and parameter `listIDArray` is an array of display-list identifiers. In general, `listIDArray` can contain any number of elements, and invalid display-list identifiers are ignored. Also, the elements in `listIDArray` can be specified in a variety of data formats, and parameter `arrayDataType` is used to indicate a data type, such as `GL_BYTE`, `GL_INT`, `GL_FLOAT`, `GL_3_BYTES`, or `GL_4_BYTES`. A display-list identifier is calculated by adding the value in an element of `listIDArray` to the integer value of `offsetValue` that is given in the `glListBase` function. The default value for `offsetValue` is 0.

This mechanism for specifying a sequence of display lists that are to be executed allows us to set up groups of related display lists, whose identifiers are formed from symbolic names or codes. A typical example is a font set where each display-list identifier is the ASCII value of a character. When several font sets are defined, we use parameter `offsetValue` in the `glListBase` function to obtain a particular font described within the array `listIDArray`.

Deleting OpenGL Display Lists

We eliminate a contiguous set of display lists with the function call

```
glDeleteLists (startID, nLists);
```

Parameter `startID` gives the initial display-list identifier, and parameter `nLists` specifies the number of lists that are to be deleted. For example, the statement

```
glDeleteLists (5, 4);
```

eliminates the four display lists with identifiers 5, 6, 7, and 8. An identifier value that references a nonexistent display list is ignored.

3-24 OpenGL DISPLAY-WINDOW RESHAPE FUNCTION

In our introductory OpenGL program (Section 2-9), we discussed the functions for setting up an initial display window. But after the generation of our picture, we often want to use the mouse pointer to drag the display window to another screen location or to change its size. Changing the size of a display window could change its aspect ratio and cause objects to be distorted from their original shapes.

To allow us to compensate for a change in display-window dimensions, the GLUT library provides the following routine

```
glutReshapeFunc (winReshapeFcn);
```

We can include this function in the `main` procedure in our program, along with the other GLUT routines, and it will be activated whenever the display-window size is altered. The argument for this GLUT function is the name of a procedure that is to receive the new display-window width and height. We can then use the new dimensions to reset the projection parameters and perform any other operations, such as changing the display-window color. In addition, we could save the new width and height values so that they could be used by other procedures in our program.

As an example, the following program illustrates how we might structure the `winReshapeFcn` procedure. The `glLoadIdentity` command is included in the

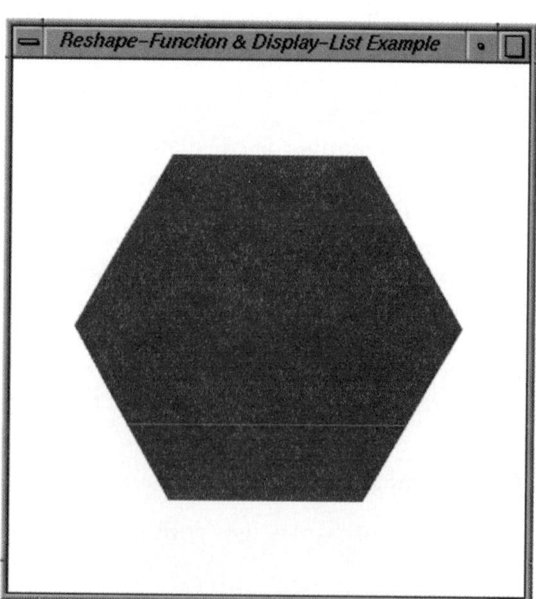

FIGURE 3-64 Display window generated by the example program illustrating the use of the reshape function.

reshape function so that any previous values for the projection parameters will not affect the new projection settings. This program displays the regular hexagon discussed in Section 3-23. Although the hexagon center (at the position of the circle center) in this example is specified in terms of the display-window parameters, the position of the hexagon is unaffected by any changes in the size of the display window. This is because the hexagon is defined within a display list, and only the original center coordinates are stored in the list. If we want the position of the hexagon to change when the display window is resized, we need to define the hexagon in another way or alter the coordinate reference for the display window. The output from this program is shown in Fig. 3-64.

```
#include <GL/glut.h>
#include <math.h>
#include <stdlib.h>

const double TWO_PI = 6.2831853;

/*  Initial display-window size.  */
GLsizei winWidth = 400, winHeight = 400;
GLuint regHex;

class screenPt
{
      private:
         GLint x, y;

      public:
         /*  Default Constructor: initializes coordinate position to (0, 0).  */
         screenPt ( )  {
            x = y = 0;
         }

         void setCoords (GLint xCoord, GLint yCoord)  {
            x = xCoord;
            y = yCoord;
         }

         GLint getx ( ) const  {
            return x;
         }

         GLint gety ( ) const  {
            return y;
         }
};

static void init (void)
{
   screenPt hexVertex, circCtr;
   GLdouble theta;
   GLint k;

   /*  Set circle center coordinates.  */
   circCtr.setCoords (winWidth / 2, winHeight / 2);
```

```
    glClearColor (1.0, 1.0, 1.0, 0.0);   //  Display-window color = white.

    /*  Set up a display list for a red regular hexagon.
     *  Vertices for the hexagon are six equally spaced
     *  points around the circumference of a circle.
     */
    regHex = glGenLists (1);   //  Get an identifier for the display list.
    glNewList (regHex, GL_COMPILE);
       glColor3f (1.0, 0.0, 0.0);   //  Set fill color for hexagon to red.
       glBegin (GL_POLYGON);
          for (k = 0; k < 6; k++) {
             theta = TWO_PI * k / 6.0;
                hexVertex.setCoords (circCtr.getx ( ) + 150 * cos (theta),
                                     circCtr.gety ( ) + 150 * sin (theta));
                glVertex2i (hexVertex.getx ( ), hexVertex.gety ( ));
          }
       glEnd ( );
    glEndList ( );
}

void regHexagon (void)
{
    glClear (GL_COLOR_BUFFER_BIT);

    glCallList (regHex);

    glFlush ( );
}

void winReshapeFcn (int newWidth, int newHeight)
{
    glMatrixMode (GL_PROJECTION);
    glLoadIdentity ( );
    gluOrtho2D (0.0, (GLdouble) newWidth, 0.0, (GLdouble) newHeight);

    glClear (GL_COLOR_BUFFER_BIT);
}

void main (int argc, char** argv)
{
    glutInit (&argc, argv);
    glutInitDisplayMode (GLUT_SINGLE | GLUT_RGB);
    glutInitWindowPosition (100, 100);
    glutInitWindowSize (winWidth, winHeight);
    glutCreateWindow ("Reshape-Function & Display-List Example");

    init ( );
    glutDisplayFunc (regHexagon);
    glutReshapeFunc (winReshapeFcn);

    glutMainLoop ( );
}
```

3-25 SUMMARY

The output primitives discussed in this chapter provide the basic tools for constructing pictures with individual points, straight lines, curves, filled color areas, array patterns, and text. We specify primitives by giving their geometric descriptions in a Cartesian, world-coordinate reference system. Examples of displays generated with output primitives are illustrated in Figs. 3-65 and 3-66.

Three methods that can be used to locate pixel positions along a straight-line path are the DDA algorithm, Bresenham's algorithm, and the midpoint method. Bresenham's line algorithm and the midpoint line method are equivalent, and they are the most efficient. Color values for the pixel positions along the line path are efficiently stored in the frame buffer by incrementally calculating the memory addresses. Any of the line-generating algorithms can be adapted to a parallel implementation by partitioning the line segments and distributing the partitions among the available processors.

Circles and ellipses can be efficiently and accurately scan converted using midpoint methods and taking curve symmetry into account. Other conic sections (parabolas and hyperbolas) can be plotted with similar methods. Spline curves, which are piecewise continuous polynomials, are widely used in animation and in computer-aided design. Parallel implementations for generating curve displays can be accomplished with methods similar to those for parallel line processing.

To account for the fact that displayed lines and curves have finite widths, we can adjust the pixel dimensions of objects to coincide to the specified geometric dimensions. This can be done with an addressing scheme that references pixel positions at their lower left corner, or by adjusting line lengths.

A fill area is a planar region that is to be displayed in a solid color or color pattern. Fill-area primitives in most graphics packages are polygons. But, in general, we could specify a fill region with any boundary. Often, graphics systems allow only convex polygon fill areas. In that case, a concave-polygon fill area can be displayed by dividing it into a set of convex polygons. Triangles are the easiest polygons to fill, since each scan line crossing a triangle intersects exactly two polygon edges (assuming the scan line does not pass through any vertices).

The odd-even rule can be used to locate the interior points of a planar region. Other methods for defining object interiors are also useful, particularly with irregular, self-intersecting objects. A common example is the nonzero winding-number rule. This rule is more flexible than the odd-even rule for handling objects defined with multiple boundaries. We can also use variations of the winding-number rule to combine plane areas using Boolean operations.

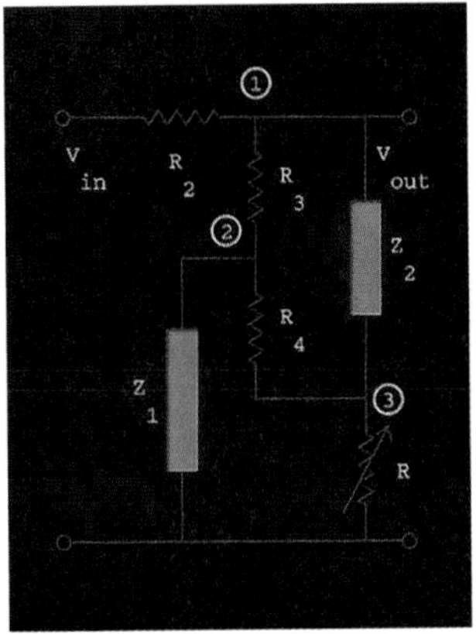

FIGURE 3-66 An electrical diagram drawn with straight-line sections, circles, filled rectangles, and text. (*Courtesy of Wolfram Research, Inc., The Maker of Mathematica.*)

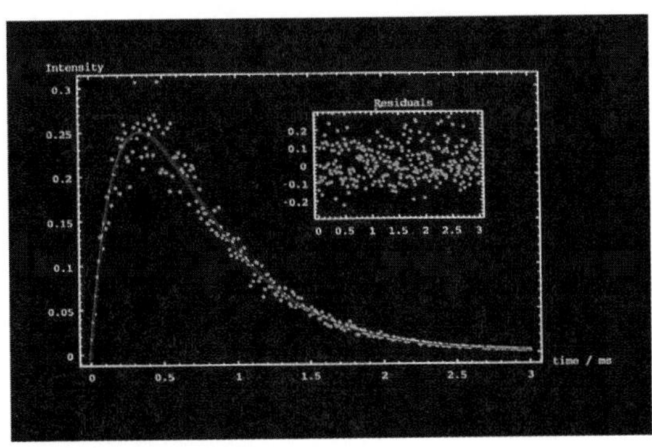

FIGURE 3-65 A data plot generated with straight-line segments, curves, character marker symbols, and text. (*Courtesy of Wolfram Research, Inc., The Maker of Mathematica.*)

TABLE 3-1

SUMMARY OF OpenGL OUTPUT PRIMITIVE FUNCTIONS AND RELATED ROUTINES

Function	Description
`gluOrtho2D`	Specify a 2D world-coordinate reference.
`glVertex*`	Select a coordinate position. This function must be placed within a `glBegin/glEnd` pair.
`glBegin (GL_POINTS);`	Plot one or more point positions, each specified in a `glVertex` function. The list of positions is then closed with a `glEnd` statement.
`glBegin (GL_LINES);`	Display a set of straight-line segments, whose endpoint coordinates are specified in `glVertex` functions. The list of endpoints is then closed with a `glEnd` statement.
`glBegin (GL_LINE_STRIP);`	Display a polyline, specified using the same structure as `GL_LINES`.
`glBegin (GL_LINE_LOOP);`	Display a closed polyline, specified using the same structure as `GL_LINES`.
`glRect*`	Display a fill rectangle in the xy plane.
`glBegin (GL_POLYGON);`	Display a fill polygon, whose vertices are given in `glVertex` functions and terminated with a `glEnd` statement.
`glBegin (GL_TRIANGLES);`	Display a set of fill triangles using the same structure as `GL_POLYGON`.
`glBegin (GL_TRIANGLE_STRIP);`	Display a fill-triangle mesh, specified using the same structure as `GL_POLYGON`.
`glBegin (GL_TRIANGLE_FAN);`	Display a fill-triangle mesh in a fan shape with all triangles connected to the first vertex, specified with same structure as `GL_POLYGON`.
`glBegin (GL_QUADS);`	Display a set of fill quadrilaterals, specified with same structure as `GL_POLYGON`.
`glBegin (GL_QUAD_STRIP);`	Display a fill-quadrilateral mesh, specified with same structure as `GL_POLYGON`.
`glEnableClientState (GL_VERTEX_ARRAY);`	Activate vertex-array features of OpenGL.
`glVertexPointer (size, type, stride, array);`	Specify an array of coordinate values.
`glDrawElements (prim, num, type, array);`	Display a specified primitive type from array data.

Function	*Description*
`glNewList (listID, listMode)`	Define a set of commands as a display list, terminate with a `glEndList` statement.
`glGenLists`	Generate one or more display-list identifiers.
`glIsList`	Query function to determine whether a display-list identifier is in use.
`glCallList`	Execute a single display list.
`glListBase`	Specify an offset value for an array of display-list identifiers.
`glCallLists`	Execute multiple display lists.
`glDeleteLists`	Eliminate a specified sequence of display lists.
`glRasterPos*`	Specify a two-dimensional or three-dimensional current position for the frame buffer. This position is used as a reference for bitmap and pixmap patterns.
`glBitmap (w, h, x0, y0, xShift, yShift, pattern);`	Specify a binary pattern that is to be mapped to pixel positions relative to the current position.
`glDrawPixels (w, h, type, format, pattern);`	Specify a color pattern that is to be mapped to pixel positions relative to the current position.
`glDrawBuffer`	Select one or more buffers for storing a pixmap.
`glReadPixels`	Save a block of pixels in a selected array.
`glCopyPixels`	Copy a block of pixels from one buffer position to another.
`glLogicOp`	Select a logical operation for combining two pixel arrays, after enabling with the constant `GL_COLOR_LOGIC_OP`.
`glutBitmapCharacter (font, char);`	Specify a font and a bitmap character for display.
`glutStrokeCharacter (font, char);`	Specify a font and an outline character for display.
`glutReshapeFunc`	Specify actions to be taken when display-window dimensions are changed.

Each polygon has a front face and a back face, which determines the spatial orientation of the polygon plane. This spatial orientation can be determined from the normal vector, which is perpendicular to the polygon plane and points in the direction from the back face to the front face. We can determine the components of the normal vector from the polygon plane equation or by forming a vector cross product using three points in the plane, where the three points are taken in a counterclockwise order and the angle formed by the three points is less than 180°. All coordinate values, spatial orientations, and other geometric data for a scene are entered into three tables: vertex, edge, and surface-facet tables.

Additional primitives available in graphics packages include pattern arrays and character strings. Pattern arrays can be used to specify two-dimensional shapes, including a character set, using either a rectangular set of binary values or a set of color values. Character strings are used to provide picture and graph labeling.

Using the primitive functions available in the basic OpenGL library, we can generate points, straight-line segments, convex polygon fill areas, and either bitmap or pixmap pattern arrays. Routines for displaying character strings are available in GLUT. Other types of primitives, such as circles, ellipses, and concave-polygon fill areas, can be constructed or approximated with these functions, or they can be generated using routines in GLU and GLUT. All coordinate values are expressed in absolute coordinates within a right-handed Cartesian-coordinate reference system. Coordinate positions describing a scene can be given in either a two-dimensional or a three-dimensional reference frame. We can use integer or floating-point values to give a coordinate position, and we can also reference a position with a pointer to an array of coordinate values. A scene description is then transformed by viewing functions into a two-dimensional display on an output device, such as a video monitor. Except for the `glRect` function, each coordinate position for a set of points, lines, or polygons is specfied in a `glVertex` function. And the set of `glVertex` functions defining each primitive is included between a `glBegin/glEnd` pair of statements, where the primitive type is identified with a symbolic constant as the argument for the `glBegin` function. When describing a scene containing many polygon fill surfaces, we can efficiently generate the display using OpenGL vertex arrays to specify geometric and other data.

In Table 3-1, we list the basic functions for generating output primitives in OpenGL. Some related routines are also listed in this table.

EXAMPLE PROGRAMS

Here, we present a few example OpenGL programs illustrating the use of output primitives. Each program uses one or more of the functions listed in Table 3-1. A display window is set up for the output from each program using the GLUT routines discussed in Chapter 2.

The first program illustrates the use of a polyline, a set of polymarkers, and bit-mapped character labels to generate a line graph for monthly data over a period of one year. A proportionally spaced font is demonstrated, although a fixed-width font is usually easier to align with graph positions. Since the bit maps are referenced at the lower-left corner by the raster-position function, we must shift the reference position to align the center of a text string with a plotted data position. Figure 3-67 shows the output of the line-graph program.

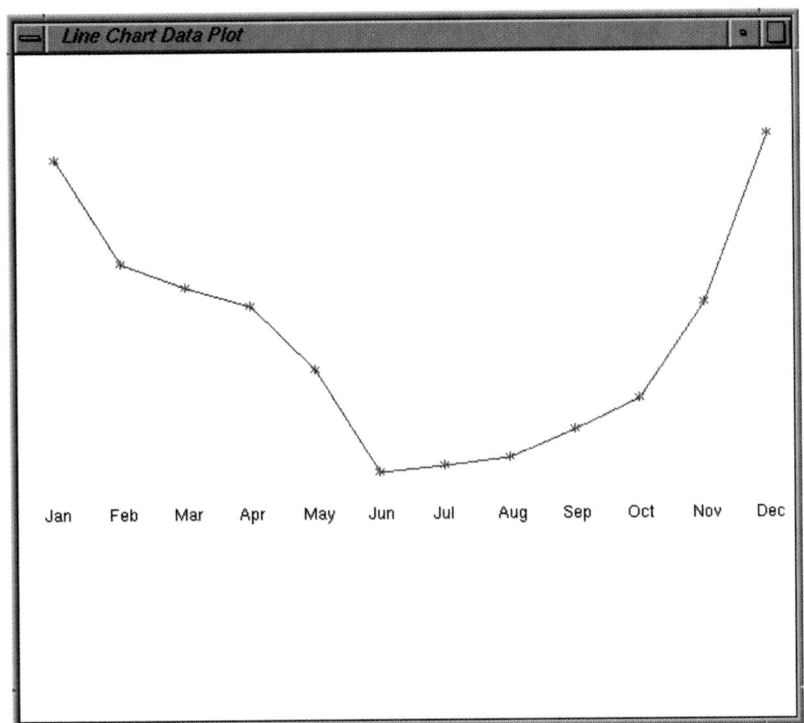

FIGURE 3-67 A polyline and polymarker plot of data points output by the `lineGraph` routine.

```
#include <GL/glut.h>

GLsizei winWidth = 600, winHeight = 500;    // Initial display window size.
GLint xRaster = 25, yRaster = 150;          // Initialize raster position.

GLubyte label [36] = {'J', 'a', 'n',   'F', 'e', 'b',   'M', 'a', 'r',
                      'A', 'p', 'r',   'M', 'a', 'y',   'J', 'u', 'n',
                      'J', 'u', 'l',   'A', 'u', 'g',   'S', 'e', 'p',
                      'O', 'c', 't',   'N', 'o', 'v',   'D', 'e', 'c'};

GLint dataValue [12] = {420, 342, 324, 310, 262, 185,
                        190, 196, 217, 240, 312, 438};

void init (void)
{
    glClearColor (1.0, 1.0, 1.0, 1.0);    // White display window.
    glMatrixMode (GL_PROJECTION);
    gluOrtho2D (0.0, 600.0, 0.0, 500.0);
}

void lineGraph (void)
{
    GLint month, k;
    GLint x = 30;                         // Initialize x position for chart.

    glClear (GL_COLOR_BUFFER_BIT);        //  Clear display window.
```

```
    glColor3f (0.0, 0.0, 1.0);           //  Set line color to blue.
    glBegin (GL_LINE_STRIP);             //  Plot data as a polyline.
        for (k = 0; k < 12; k++)
            glVertex2i (x + k*50, dataValue [k]);
    glEnd ( );

    glColor3f (1.0, 0.0, 0.0);           //  Set marker color to red.
    for (k = 0; k < 12; k++) {           //  Plot data as asterisk polymarkers.
        glRasterPos2i (xRaster + k*50, dataValue [k] - 4);
        glutBitmapCharacter (GLUT_BITMAP_9_BY_15, '*');
    }

    glColor3f (0.0, 0.0, 0.0);           //  Set text color to black.
    xRaster = 20;                        //  Display chart labels.
    for (month = 0; month < 12; month++) {
        glRasterPos2i (xRaster, yRaster);
        for (k = 3*month; k < 3*month + 3; k++)
          glutBitmapCharacter (GLUT_BITMAP_HELVETICA_12, label [k]);
        xRaster += 50;
    }
    glFlush ( );
}

void winReshapeFcn (GLint newWidth, GLint newHeight)
{
    glMatrixMode (GL_PROJECTION);
    glLoadIdentity ( );
    gluOrtho2D (0.0, GLdouble (newWidth), 0.0, GLdouble (newHeight));

    glClear (GL_COLOR_BUFFER_BIT);
}

void main (int argc, char** argv)
{
    glutInit (&argc, argv);
    glutInitDisplayMode (GLUT_SINGLE | GLUT_RGB);
    glutInitWindowPosition (100, 100);
    glutInitWindowSize (winWidth, winHeight);
    glutCreateWindow ("Line Chart Data Plot");

    init ( );
    glutDisplayFunc (lineGraph);
    glutReshapeFunc (winReshapeFcn);

    glutMainLoop ( );
}
```

We use the same data set in the second program to produce the bar chart in Fig. 3-68. This program illustrates an application of rectangular fill areas, as well as bit-mapped character labels.

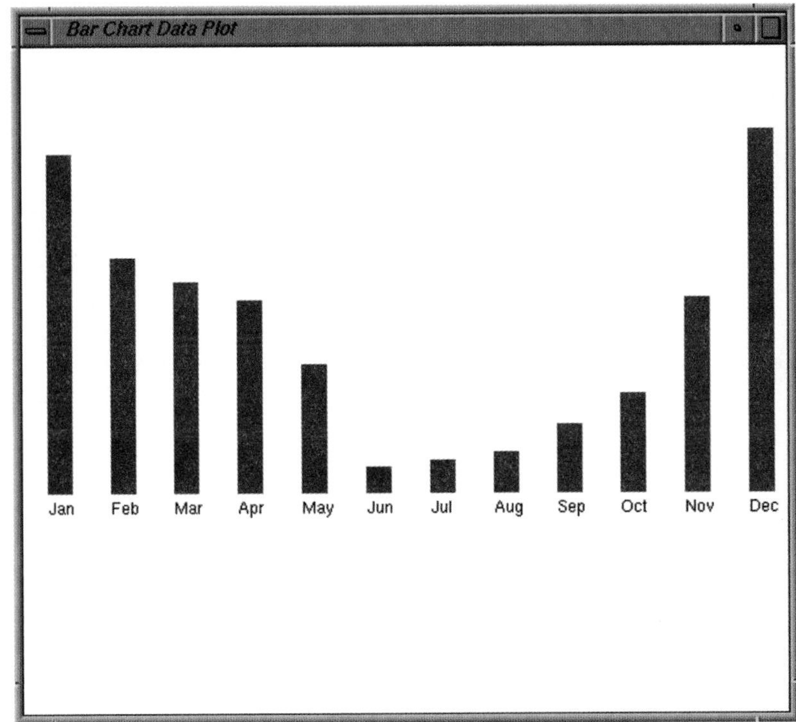

FIGURE 3-68 A bar chart generated by the `barChart` procedure.

```
void barChart (void)
{
   GLint month, k;

   glClear (GL_COLOR_BUFFER_BIT); //  Clear display window.

   glColor3f (1.0, 0.0, 0.0);     //  Set bar color to red.
   for (k = 0; k < 12; k++)
      glRecti (20 + k*50, 165, 40 + k*50, dataValue [k]);

   glColor3f (0.0, 0.0, 0.0);        //  Set text color to black.
   xRaster = 20;                     //  Display chart labels.
   for (month = 0; month < 12; month++) {
      glRasterPos2i (xRaster, yRaster);
      for (k = 3*month; k < 3*month + 3; k++)
         glutBitmapCharacter (GLUT_BITMAP_HELVETICA_12,
                                                label [h]);
      xRaster += 50;
   }
   glFlush ( );
}
```

Pie charts are used to show the percentage contribution of individual parts to the whole. The next program constructs a pie chart, using the midpoint routine for generating a circle. Example values are used for the number and relative sizes of the slices, and the output from this program appears in Fig. 3-69.

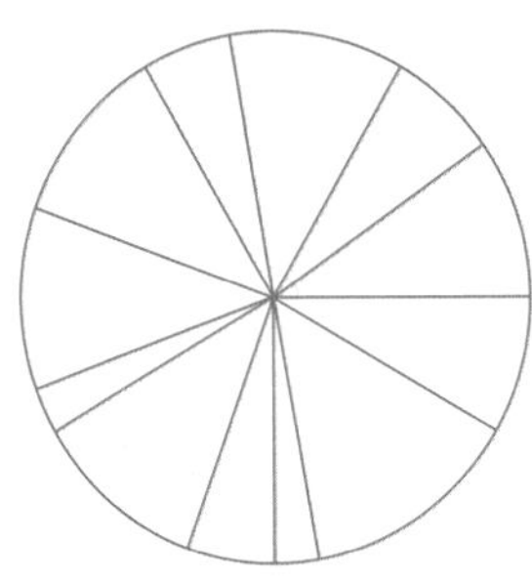

FIGURE 3-69 Output produced with the `pieChart` procedure.

```
#include <GL/glut.h>
#include <stdlib.h>
#include <math.h>

const GLdouble twoPi = 6.283185;

class scrPt {
public:
    GLint x, y;
};

GLsizei winWidth = 400, winHeight = 300;    // Initial display window size.

void init (void)
{
    glClearColor (1.0, 1.0, 1.0, 1.0);

    glMatrixMode (GL_PROJECTION);
    gluOrtho2D (0.0, 200.0, 0.0, 150.0);
}

    .                         //  Midpoint routines for displaying a circle.
    .
    .

void pieChart (void)
{
    scrPt circCtr, piePt;
    GLint radius = winWidth / 4;                  // Circle radius.

    GLdouble sliceAngle, previousSliceAngle = 0.0;

    GLint k, nSlices = 12;                        // Number of slices.
    GLfloat dataValues[12] = {10.0, 7.0, 13.0, 5.0, 13.0, 14.0,
                               3.0, 16.0, 5.0, 3.0, 17.0, 8.0};
    GLfloat dataSum = 0.0;

    circCtr.x = winWidth / 2;                     // Circle center position.
    circCtr.y = winHeight / 2;
    circleMidpoint (circCtr, radius);  // Call a midpoint circle-plot routine.

    for (k = 0; k < nSlices; k++)
        dataSum += dataValues[k];

    for (k = 0; k < nSlices; k++) {
        sliceAngle = twoPi * dataValues[k] / dataSum + previousSliceAngle;
        piePt.x = circCtr.x + radius * cos (sliceAngle);
        piePt.y = circCtr.y + radius * sin (sliceAngle);
        glBegin (GL_LINES);
            glVertex2i (circCtr.x, circCtr.y);
            glVertex2i (piePt.x, piePt.y);
        glEnd ( );
        previousSliceAngle = sliceAngle;
    }
}
```

```
void displayFcn (void)
{
    glClear (GL_COLOR_BUFFER_BIT);    //  Clear display window.

    glColor3f (0.0, 0.0, 1.0);        //  Set circle color to blue.

    pieChart ( );
    glFlush ( );
}

void winReshapeFcn (GLint newWidth, GLint newHeight)
{
    glMatrixMode (GL_PROJECTION);
    glLoadIdentity ( );
    gluOrtho2D (0.0, GLdouble (newWidth), 0.0, GLdouble (newHeight));

    glClear (GL_COLOR_BUFFER_BIT);

    /*  Reset display-window size parameters.  */
    winWidth = newWidth;
    winHeight = newHeight;
}

void main (int argc, char** argv)
{
    glutInit (&argc, argv);
    glutInitDisplayMode (GLUT_SINGLE | GLUT_RGB);
    glutInitWindowPosition (100, 100);
    glutInitWindowSize (winWidth, winHeight);
    glutCreateWindow ("Pie Chart");

    init ( );
    glutDisplayFunc (displayFcn);
    glutReshapeFunc (winReshapeFcn);

    glutMainLoop ( );
}
```

Some variations on the circle equations are displayed by our last example program, which uses the parametric polar equations (3-28) to compute points along the curve paths. These points are then used as the endpoint positions for straight-line sections, displaying the curves as approximating polylines. The curves shown in Fig. 3-70 are generated by varying the radius r of a circle. Depending on how we vary r, we can produce a limaçon, cardioid, spiral, or other similar figure.

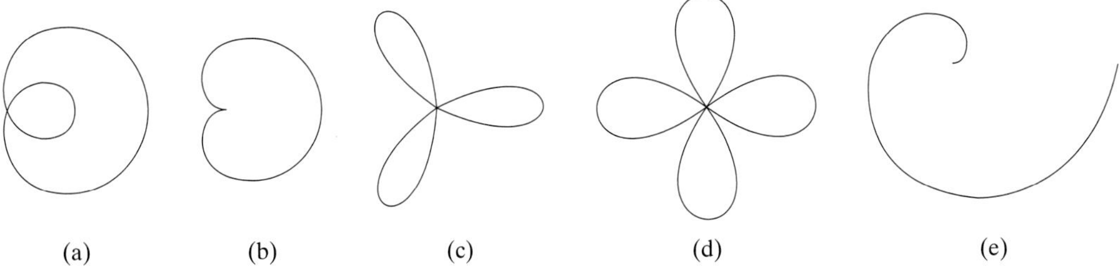

FIGURE 3-70 Curved figures displayed by the `drawCurve` procedure: (a) limaçon, (b) cardiod, (c) three-leaf curve, (d) four-leaf curve, and (e) spiral.

```
#include <GL/glut.h>
#include <stdlib.h>
#include <math.h>

#include <iostream.h>

struct screenPt
{
    GLint x;
    GLint y;
};

typedef enum { limacon = 1, cardioid, threeLeaf, fourLeaf, spiral } curveName;

GLsizei winWidth = 600, winHeight = 500;    // Initial display window size.

void init (void)
{
    glClearColor (1.0, 1.0, 1.0, 1.0);

    glMatrixMode (GL_PROJECTION);
    gluOrtho2D (0.0, 200.0, 0.0, 150.0);
}

void lineSegment (screenPt pt1, screenPt pt2)
{
    glBegin (GL_LINES);
        glVertex2i (pt1.x, pt1.y);
        glVertex2i (pt2.x, pt2.y);
    glEnd ( );
}

void drawCurve (GLint curveNum)
{
    /*  The limacon of Pascal is a modification of the circle equation
     *  with the radius varying as r = a * cos (theta) + b, where a
     *  and b are constants.  A cardiod is a limacon with a = b.
     *  Three-leaf and four-leaf curves are generated when
     *  r = a * cos (n * theta), with n = 3 and n = 2, respectively.
     *  A spiral is displayed when r is a multiple of theta.
     */

    const GLdouble twoPi = 6.283185;
    const GLint a = 175, b = 60;

    GLfloat r, theta, dtheta = 1.0 / float (a);
    GLint x0 = 200, y0 = 250;    // Set an initial screen position.
    screenPt curvePt[2];

    glColor3f (0.0, 0.0, 0.0);       //  Set curve color to black.

    curvePt[0].x = x0;      // Initialize curve position.
    curvePt[0].y = y0;
```

```
    switch (curveNum) {
        case limacon:    curvePt[0].x += a + b;  break;
        case cardioid:   curvePt[0].x += a + a;  break;
        case threeLeaf:  curvePt[0].x += a;      break;
        case fourLeaf:   curvePt[0].x += a;      break;
        case spiral:     break;
        default:         break;
    }

    theta = dtheta;
    while (theta < two_Pi) {
        switch (curveNum) {
            case limacon:
                r = a * cos (theta) + b;    break;
            case cardioid:
                r = a * (1 + cos (theta));  break;
            case threeLeaf:
                r = a * cos (3 * theta);    break;
            case fourLeaf:
                r = a * cos (2 * theta);    break;
            case spiral:
                r = (a / 4.0) * theta;      break;
            default:                        break;
        }

        curvePt[1].x = x0 + r * cos (theta);
        curvePt[1].y = y0 + r * sin (theta);
        lineSegment (curvePt[0], curvePt[1]);

        curvePt[0].x = curvePt[1].x;
        curvePt[0].y = curvePt[1].y;
        theta += dtheta;
    }
}

void displayFcn (void)
{
    GLint curveNum;

    glClear (GL_COLOR_BUFFER_BIT);   //  Clear display window.

    cout << "\nEnter the integer value corresponding to\n";
    cout << "one of the following curve names.\n";
    cout << "Press any other key to exit.\n";
    cout << "\n1-limacon, 2-cardioid, 3-threeLeaf, 4-fourLeaf, 5-spiral:  ";
    cin  >> curveNum;

    if (curveNum == 1 || curveNum == 2 || curveNum == 3 || curveNum == 4
          || curveNum == 5)
        drawCurve (curveNum);
    else
        exit (0);

    glFlush ( );
}
```

```
void winReshapeFcn (GLint newWidth, GLint newHeight)
{
    glMatrixMode (GL_PROJECTION);
    glLoadIdentity ( );
    gluOrtho2D (0.0, (GLdouble) newWidth, 0.0, (GLdouble) newHeight);

    glClear (GL_COLOR_BUFFER_BIT);
}

void main (int argc, char** argv)
{
    glutInit (&argc, argv);
    glutInitDisplayMode (GLUT_SINGLE | GLUT_RGB);
    glutInitWindowPosition (100, 100);
    glutInitWindowSize (winWidth, winHeight);
    glutCreateWindow ("Draw Curves");

    init ( );
    glutDisplayFunc (displayFcn);
    glutReshapeFunc (winReshapeFcn);

    glutMainLoop ( );
}
```

REFERENCES

Basic information on Bresenham's algorithms can be found in Bresenham (1965 and 1977). For midpoint methods, see Kappel (1985). Parallel methods for generating lines and circles are discussed in Pang (1990) and in Wright (1990). Many other methods for generating and processing graphics primitives are discussed in Glassner (1990), Arvo (1991), Kirk (1992), Heckbert (1994), and Paeth (1995).

Additional programming examples using OpenGL primitive functions are given in Woo, Neider, Davis, and Shreiner (1999). A listing of all OpenGL primitive functions is available in Shreiner (2000). For a complete reference to GLUT, see Kilgard (1996).

EXERCISES

3-1 Implement a polyline function using the DDA algorithm, given any number (n) of input points. A single point is to be plotted when $n = 1$.

3-2 Extend Bresenham's line algorithm to generate lines with any slope, taking symmetry between quadrants into account.

3-3 Implement a polyline function, using the algorithm from the previous exercise, to display the set of straight lines connecting a list of n input points. For $n = 1$, the routine displays a single point.

3-4 Use the midpoint method to derive decision parameters for generating points along a straight-line path with slope in the range $0 < m < 1$. Show that the midpoint decision parameters are the same as those in the Bresenham line algorithm.

3-5 Use the midpoint method to derive decision parameters that can be used to generate straight-line segments with any slope.

3-6 Set up a parallel version of Bresenham's line algorithm for slopes in the range $0 < m < 1$.

3-7 Set up a parallel version of Bresenham's algorithm for straight lines with any slope.

3-8 Suppose you have a system with an 8 inch by 10 inch video monitor that can display 100 pixels per inch. If memory is organized in one-byte words, the starting frame buffer address is 0, and each pixel is assigned one byte of storage, what is the frame buffer address of the pixel with screen coordinates (x, y)?

3-9 Suppose you have a system with an 8 inch by 10 inch video monitor that can display 100 pixels per inch. If memory is organized in one-byte words, the starting frame buffer address is 0, and each pixel is assigned 6 bits of storage, what is the frame buffer address (or addresses) of the pixel with screen coordinates (x, y)?

3-10 Incorporate the iterative techniques for calculating frame-buffer addresses (Section 3-7) into the Bresenham line algorithm.

3-11 Revise the midpoint circle algorithm to display circles with input geometric magnitudes preserved (Section 3-13).

3-12 Set up a procedure for a parallel implementation of the midpoint circle algorithm.

3-13 Derive decision parameters for the midpoint ellipse algorithm assuming the start position is $(r_x, 0)$ and points are to be generated along the curve path in counterclockwise order.

3-14 Set up a procedure for a parallel implementation of the midpoint ellipse algorithm.

3-15 Devise an efficient algorithm that takes advantage of symmetry properties to display a sine function over one cycle.

3-16 Modify the algorithm in the preceding exercise to display a sine curve over any specified angular interval.

3-17 Devise an efficient algorithm, taking function symmetry into account, to display a plot of damped harmonic motion:

$$y = Ae^{-kx} \sin(\omega x + \theta)$$

where ω is the angular frequency and θ is the phase of the sine function. Plot y as a function of x for several cycles of the sine function or until the maximum amplitude is reduced to $\frac{A}{10}$.

3-18 Using the midpoint method, and taking symmetry into account, develop an efficient algorithm for scan conversion of the following curve over the interval $-10 \le x \le 10$.

$$y = \frac{1}{12}x^3$$

3-19 Use the midpoint method and symmetry considerations to scan convert the parabola

$$y = 100 - x^2$$

over the interval $-10 \le x \le 10$.

3-20 Use the midpoint method and symmetry considerations to scan convert the parabola

$$x = y^2$$

for the interval $-10 \le y \le 10$.

3-21 Set up a midpoint algorithm, taking symmetry considerations into account to scan convert any parabola of the form

$$y = ax^2 + b$$

with input values for parameters a, b, and the range for x.

3-22 Set up geometric data tables as in Fig. 3-50 for a unit cube.

3-23 Set up geometric data tables for a unit cube using just a vertex table and a surface-facet table, then store the same information using just the surface-facet table. Compare the two methods for representing the unit cube with a representation using the three tables in Exercise 3-22. Estimate the storage requirements for each.

3-24 Define an efficient polygon-mesh representation for a cylinder and justify your choice of representation.

3-25 Set up a procedure for establishing the geometric data tables for any input set of points defining the polygon facets for the surface of a three-dimensional object.

3-26 Devise routines for checking the three geometric data tables in Fig. 3-50 to ensure consistency and completeness.

3-27 Write a program for calculating parameters A, B, C, and D for an input mesh of polygon-surface facets.

3-28 Write a procedure to determine whether an input coordinate position is in front of a polygon surface or behind it, given the plane parameters A, B, C, and D for the polygon.

3-29 If the coordinate reference for a scene is changed from a right-handed system to a left-handed system, what changes could we make in the values of surface plane parameters A, B, C, and D to ensure that the orientation of the plane is correctly described?

3-30 Develop a procedure for identifying a nonplanar vertex list for a quadrilateral.

3-31 Extend the algorithm of the previous exercise to identify a nonplanar vertex list that contains more than four coordinate positions.

3-32 Write a procedure to split a set of four polygon vertex positions into a set of triangles.

3-33 Devise an algorithm for splitting a set of n polygon vertex positions, with $n > 4$, into a set of triangles.

3-34 Set up an algorithm for identifying a degenerate polygon vertex list that may contain repeated vertices or collinear vertices.

3-35 Devise an algorithm for identifying a polygon vertex list that contains intersecting edges.

3-36 Write a routine to identify concave polygons by calculating cross products of pairs of edge vectors.

3-37 Write a routine to split a concave polygon, using the vector method.

3-38 Write a routine to split a concave polygon, using the rotational method.

3-39 Devise an algorithm for determining interior regions for any input set of vertices using the nonzero winding-number rule and cross-product calculations to identify the direction for edge crossings.

3-40 Devise an algorithm for determining interior regions for any input set of vertices using the nonzero winding-number rule and dot-product calculations to identify the direction for edge crossings.

3-41 What regions of the self-intersecting polyline shown in Fig. 3-46 have a positive winding number? What are the regions that have a negative winding number? What regions have a winding number greater than 1?

3-42 Write a routine to implement a text-string function that has two parameters: one parameter specifies a world-coordinate position and the other parameter specifies a text string.

3-43 Write a routine to implement a polymarker function that has two parameters: one parameter is the character that is to be displayed and the other parameter is a list of world-coordinate positions.

3-44 Modify the example program in Section 3-24 so that the displayed hexagon is always at the center of the display window, regardless of how the display window may be resized.

3-45 Write a complete program for displaying a bar chart. Input to the program is to include the data points and the labeling required for the x and y axes. The data points are to be scaled by the program so that the graph is displayed across the full area of a display window.

3-46 Write a program to display a bar chart in any selected area of a display window.

3-47 Write a procedure to display a line graph for any input set of data points in any selected area of the screen, with the input data set scaled to fit the selected screen area. Data points are to be displayed as asterisks joined with straight-line segments, and the x and y axes are to be labeled according to input specifications. (Instead of asterisks, small circles or some other symbols could be used to plot the data points.)

3-48 Using a circle function, write a routine to display a pie chart with appropriate labeling. Input to the routine is to include a data set giving the distribution of the data over some set of intervals, the name of the pie chart, and the names of the intervals. Each section label is to be displayed outside the boundary of the pie chart near the corresponding pie section.

CHAPTER 4

Attributes of Graphics Primitives

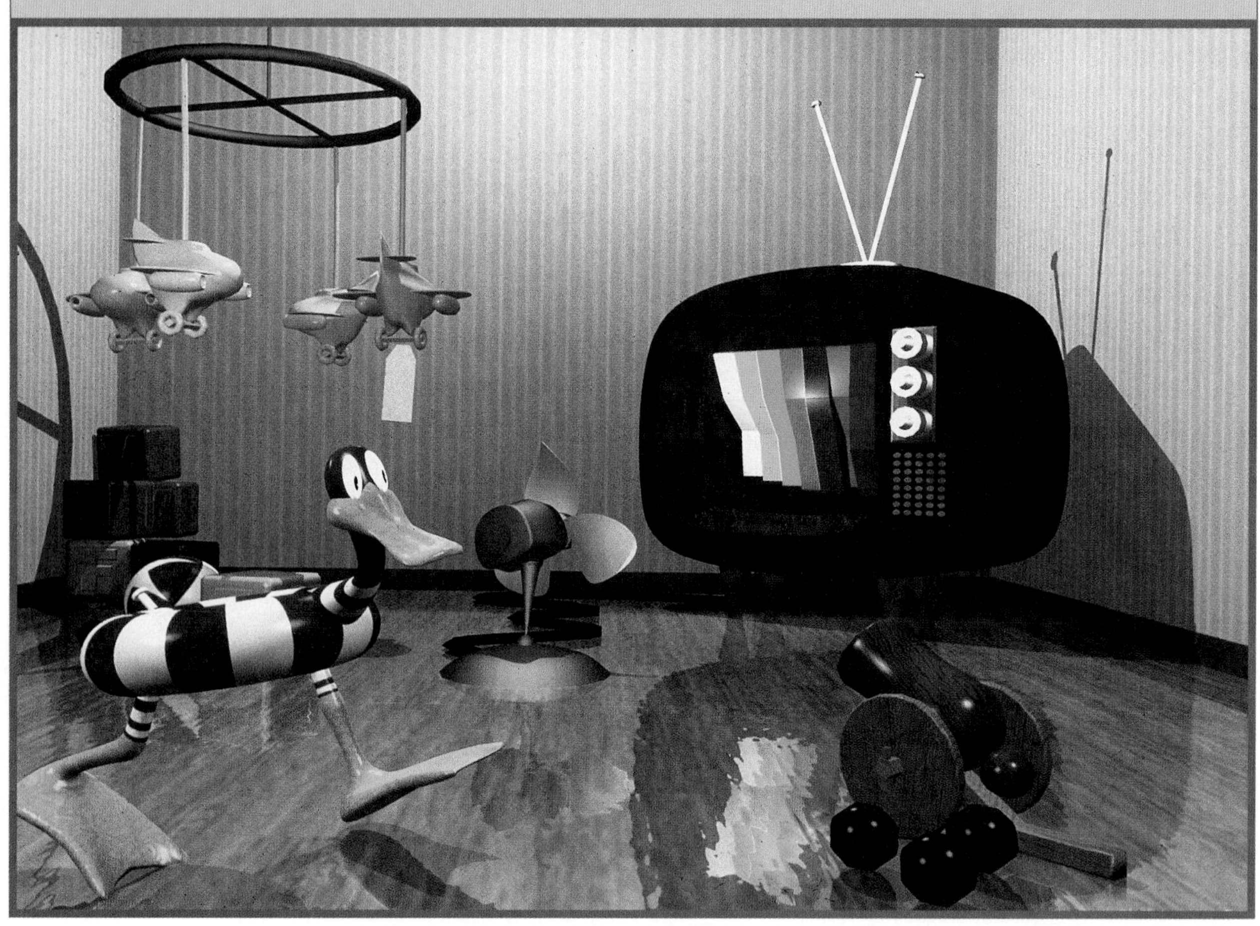

One frame from a computer-generated cartoon illustrating a variety of object colors and other attributes. *(Courtesy of SOFTIMAGE, Inc.)*

In general, a parameter that affects the way a primitive is to be displayed is referred to as an **attribute parameter.** Some attribute parameters, such as color and size, determine the fundamental characteristics of a primitive. Other attributes specify how the primitive is to be displayed under special conditions. Examples of special-condition attributes are the options such as visibility or detectability within an interactive object-selection program. These special-condition attributes are explored in later chapters. Here, we treat only those attributes that control the basic display properties of graphics primitives, without regard for special situations. For example, lines can be dotted or dashed, fat or thin, and blue or orange. Areas might be filled with one color or with a multicolor pattern. Text can appear reading from left to right, slanted diagonally across the screen, or in vertical columns. Individual characters can be displayed in different fonts, colors, and sizes. And we can apply intensity variations at the edges of objects to smooth out the raster stair-step effect.

One way to incorporate attribute options into a graphics package is to extend the parameter list associated with each graphics-primitive function to include the appropriate attribute values. A line-drawing function, for example, could contain additional parameters to set the color, width, and other properties of a line. Another approach is to maintain a system list of current attribute values. Separate functions are then included in the graphics package for setting the current values in the attribute list. To generate a primitive, the system checks the relevant attributes and invokes the display routine for that primitive using the current attribute settings. Some graphics packages use a combination of methods for setting attribute values, and other libraries, including OpenGL, assign attributes using separate functions that update a system attribute list.

A graphics system that maintains a list for the current values of attributes and other parameters is referred to as a **state system** or **state machine.** Attributes of output primitives and some other parameters, such as the current frame-buffer position, are referred to as **state variables** or **state parameters.** When we assign a value to one or more state parameters, we put the system into a particular state. And that state remains in effect until we change the value of a state parameter.

4-1 OpenGL STATE VARIABLES

Attribute values and other parameter settings are specified with separate functions that define the current OpenGL state. The state parameters in OpenGL include color and other primitive attributes, the current matrix mode, the elements of the model-view matrix, the current position for the frame buffer, and the parameters for the lighting effects in a scene. All OpenGL state parameters have default values, which remain in effect until new values are specified. At any time, we can query the system to determine the current value of a state parameter. In the following sections of this chapter, we discuss only the attribute settings for output primitives. Other state parameters are examined in later chapters.

All graphics primitives in OpenGL are displayed with the attributes in the current state list. Changing one or more of the attribute settings affects only those primitives that are specified after the OpenGL state is changed. Primitives that were defined before the state change retain their attributes. Thus we can display a green line, change the current color to red, and define another line segment. Both the green line and the red line will then be displayed. Also, some OpenGL state values can be specified within `glBegin/glEnd` pairs, along with the coordinate values, so that parameter settings can vary from one coordinate position to another.

4-2 COLOR AND GRAY SCALE

A basic attribute for all primitives is color. Various color options can be made available to a user, depending on the capabilities and design objectives of a particular system. Color options can be specified numerically or selected from menus or displayed slider scales. For a video monitor, these color codes are then converted to intensity-level settings for the electron beams. With color plotters, the codes might control ink-jet deposits or pen selections.

RGB Color Components

In a color raster system, the number of color choices available depends on the amount of storage provided per pixel in the frame buffer. Also, color information can be stored in the frame buffer in two ways: We can store RGB color codes directly in the frame buffer, or we can put the color codes into a separate table and use the pixel locations to store index values referencing the color-table entries. With the direct storage scheme, whenever a particular color code is specified in an application program, that color information is placed in the frame buffer at the location of each component pixel in the output primitives to be displayed in that color. A minimum number of colors can be provided in this scheme with 3 bits of storage per pixel, as shown in Table 4-1. Each of the three bit positions is used to control the intensity level (either on or off, in this case) of the corresponding electron gun in an RGB monitor. The leftmost bit controls the red gun, the middle bit controls the green gun, and the rightmost bit controls the blue gun. Adding more bits per pixel to the frame buffer increases the number of color choices we have. With 6 bits per pixel, 2 bits can be used for each gun. This allows four

TABLE 4-1

THE EIGHT RGB COLOR CODES FOR A THREE-BIT PER PIXEL FRAME BUFFER

Color Code	RED	GREEN	BLUE	Displayed Color
	Stored Color Values in Frame Buffer			
0	0	0	0	Black
1	0	0	1	Blue
2	0	1	0	Green
3	0	1	1	Cyan
4	1	0	0	Red
5	1	0	1	Magenta
6	1	1	0	Yellow
7	1	1	1	White

different intensity settings for each of the three color guns, and a total of 64 color options are available for each screen pixel. As more color options are provided, the storage required for the frame buffer also increases. With a resolution of 1024 by 1024, a full-color (24-bit per pixel) RGB system needs 3 megabytes of storage for the frame buffer.

Color tables are an alternate means for providing extended color capabilities to a user without requiring large frame buffers. At one time, this was an important consideration. But today, hardware costs have decreased dramatically and extended color capabilities are fairly common, even in low-end personal computer systems. So most of our examples will simply assume that RGB color codes are stored directly in the frame buffer.

Color Tables

Figure 4-1 illustrates a possible scheme for storing color values in a **color lookup table** (or **color map**). Sometimes a color table is referred to as a **video lookup table.**

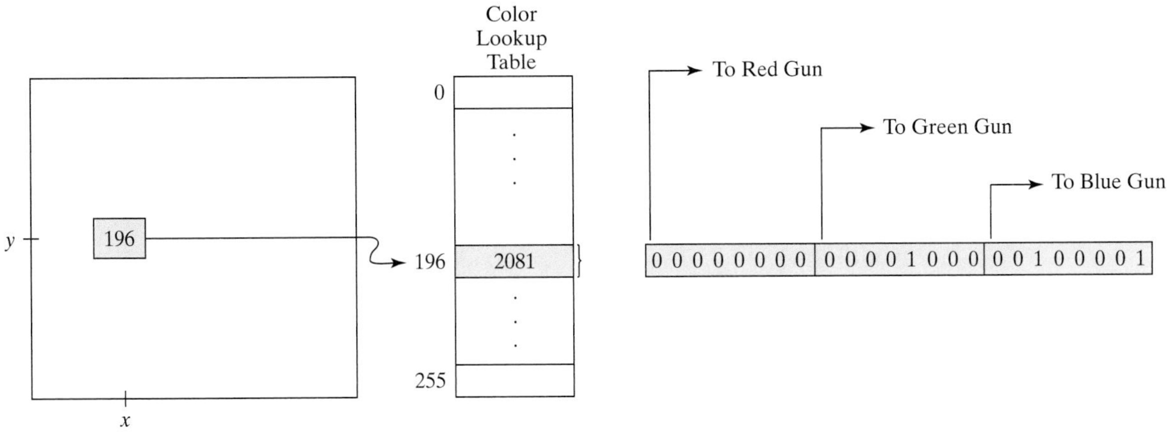

FIGURE 4-1 A color lookup table with 24 bits per entry that is accessed from a frame buffer with 8 bits per pixel. A value of 196 stored at pixel position (x, y) references the location in this table containing the hexadecimal value 0x0821 (a decimal value of 2081). Each 8-bit segment of this entry controls the intensity level of one of the three electron guns in an RGB monitor.

Values stored in the frame buffer are now used as indices into the color table. In this example, each pixel can reference any one of the 256 table positions, and each entry in the table uses 24 bits to specify an RGB color. For the hexadecimal color code 0x0821, a combination green-blue color is displayed for pixel location (x, y). Systems employing this particular lookup table allow a user to select any 256 colors for simultaneous display from a palette of nearly 17 million colors. Compared to a full-color system, this scheme reduces the number of simultaneous colors that can be displayed, but it also reduces the frame-buffer storage requirement to 1 megabyte. Multiple color tables are sometimes available for handling specialized rendering applications, such as antialiasing, and they are used with systems that contain more than one color output device.

A color table can be useful in a number of applications, and it can provide a "reasonable" number of simultaneous colors without requiring large frame buffers. For most applications, 256 or 512 different colors are sufficient for a single picture. Also, table entries can be changed at any time, allowing a user to be able to experiment easily with different color combinations in a design, scene, or graph without changing the attribute settings for the graphics data structure. When a color value is changed in the color table, all pixels with that color index immediately change to the new color. Without a color table, we can only change the color of a pixel by storing the new color at that frame-buffer location. Similarly, data-visualization applications can store values for some physical quantity, such as energy, in the frame buffer and use a lookup table to experiment with various color combinations without changing the pixel values. And in visualization and image-processing applications, color tables are a convenient means for setting color thresholds so that all pixel values above or below a specified threshold can be set to the same color. For these reasons, some systems provide both capabilities for storing color information. A user can then elect either to use color tables or to store color codes directly in the frame buffer.

Gray Scale

Since color capabilities are now common in computer-graphics systems, we use RGB color functions to set shades of gray, or **gray scale,** in an application program. When an RGB color setting specifies an equal amount of red, green, and blue, the result is some shade of gray. Values close to 0 for the color components produce dark gray, and higher values near 1.0 produce light gray. Applications for gray-scale display methods include enhancing black-and-white photographs and generating visualization effects.

Other Color Parameters

In addition to an RGB specification, other three-component color representations are useful in computer-graphics applications. For example, color output on printers is described with cyan, magenta, and yellow color components, and color interfaces sometimes use parameters such as lightness and darkness to choose a color. Also, color, and light in general, is a complex subject, and many terms and concepts have been devised in the fields of optics, radiometry, and psychology to describe the various aspects of light sources and lighting effects. Physically, we can describe a color as electromagnetic radiation with a particular frequency range and energy distribution, but then there are also the characteristics of our perception of the color. Thus, we use the physical term *intensity* to quantify the amount of light energy radiating in a particular direction over a period of time, and we use the psychological term *luminance* to characterize the perceived brightness of the light. We discuss these terms and other color concepts in greater detail when we consider methods for modeling lighting effects (Chapter 10) and the various models for describing color (Chapter 12).

4-3 OpenGL COLOR FUNCTIONS

In the example program at the end of Chapter 2, we introduced a few OpenGL color routines. We used one function to set the color for the display window, and we used another function to specify a color for the straight-line segment. Also, we set the **color display mode** to RGB with the statement

```
glutInitDisplayMode (GLUT_SINGLE | GLUT_RGB);
```

The first parameter in the argument list states that we are using a single buffer for the frame buffer, and the second parameter puts us into the RGB (or RGBA) mode, which is the default color mode. We can use either `GLUT_RGB` or `GLUT_RGBA` to select this color mode. If we wanted to specify colors by an index into a color table, we would replace the OpenGL constant `GLUT_RGB` with `GLUT_INDEX`.

The OpenGL RGB and RGBA Color Modes

Most color settings for OpenGL primitives are made in the **RGB mode,** which is basically the same as the **RGBA mode.** The only difference between RGB and RGBA is whether or not we are employing the alpha value for color blending. When we specify a particular set of color values for primitives, we define the *color state* of OpenGL. The current color is applied to all subsequently defined primitives until we change the color settings. A new color specification affects only the objects we define after the color change.

In RGB mode, we specify values for the red, green, and blue components of a color. As we noted in Section 2-9, the fourth color parameter, the **alpha coefficient,** is optional, and a four-dimensional color specification is called the RGBA color. This fourth color parameter can be used to control color blending for overlapping primitives. An important application of color blending is in the simulation of transparency effects. For these calculations, the value of alpha corresponds to a transparency (or, opacity) setting. In the RGB (or RGBA) mode, we select the current color components with the function:

```
glColor* (colorComponents);
```

Suffix codes are similar to those for the `glVertex` function. We use a code of either 3 or 4 to specify the RGB or RGBA mode along with the numerical data-type code and an optional vector suffix. The suffix codes for the numerical data types are `b` (byte), `i` (integer), `s` (short), `f` (float), and `d` (double), as well as unsigned numerical values. Floating-point values for the color components are in the range from 0.0 to 1.0, and the default color components for `glColor`, including the alpha value, are (1.0, 1.0, 1.0, 1.0), which sets the RGB color to white and the alpha value to 1.0. As an example, the following statement uses floating-point values in RGB mode to set the current color for primitives to cyan (a combination of the highest intensities for green and blue).

```
glColor3f (0.0, 1.0, 1.0);
```

Using an array specification for the three color components, we could set the color in the above example as

```
glColor3fv (colorArray);
```

An OpenGL color selection can be assigned to individual point positions within `glBegin/glEnd` pairs.

Integer specifications for the color components depend on the capabilities of the system. For a full-color system, which allocates 8 bits per pixel (256 levels for each color component), integer color values range from 0 to 255. The corresponding floating-point values for the color components would then be 0.0, 1.0/255.0, $2.0/255.0, \ldots, 255.0/255.0 = 1.0$. With a full-color system, we can specify the cyan color in the previous example using integer values for the color components as

```
glColor3i (0, 255, 255);
```

Frame-buffer positions actually store integer values, so specifying the color values as integers avoids the conversions necessary when floating-point values are given. A specified color value in any format is scaled to an integer within the range of the number of bits available on a particular system.

OpenGL Color-Index Mode

Color specifications in OpenGL can also be given in the **color-index mode,** which references values in a color table. Using this mode, we set the current color by specifying an index into a color table:

```
glIndex* (colorIndex);
```

Parameter `colorIndex` is assigned a nonnegative integer value. This index value is then stored in the frame-buffer positions for subsequently specified primitives. We can specify the color index in any of the following data types: unsigned byte, integer, or floating point. Data type for parameter `colorIndex` is indicated with a suffix code of `ub`, `s`, `i`, `d`, or `f`, and the number of index positions in a color table is always a power of 2, such as 256 or 1024. The number of bits available at each table position depends on the hardware features of the system. As an example of specifying a color in index mode, the following statement sets the current color index to the value 196.

```
glIndexi (196);
```

All primitives defined after this statement will be assigned the color stored at that position in the color table, until the current color is changed.

There are no functions provided in the core OpenGL library for loading values into a color-lookup table, because table-processing routines are part of a window system. Also, some window systems support multiple color tables and full color, while other systems may have only one color table and limited color choices.

However, we do have a GLUT routine that interacts with a window system to set color specifications into a table at a given index position:

```
glutSetColor (index, red, green, blue);
```

Color parameters `red`, `green`, and `blue` are assigned floating-point values in the range from 0.0 to 1.0. This color is then loaded into the table at the position specified by the value of parameter `index`.

Routines for processing three other color tables are provided as extensions to the OpenGL core library. These routines are part of the **Imaging Subset** of OpenGL. Color values stored in these tables can be used to modify pixel values as they are processed through various buffers. Some examples of using these tables are setting camera focusing effects, filtering out certain colors from an image, enhancing certain intensities or making brightness adjustments, converting a gray-scale photograph to color, and antialiasing a display. And we can use these tables to change color models; that is, we can change RGB colors to another specification using three other "primary" colors (such as cyan, magenta, and yellow).

A particular color table in the Imaging Subset of OpenGL is activated with the `glEnable` function using one of the table names: `GL_COLOR_TABLE`, `GL_POST_CONVOLUTION_COLOR_TABLE`, or `GL_POST_COLOR_MATRIX_COLOR_TABLE`. We can then use routines in the Imaging Subset to select a particular color table, set color-table values, copy table values, or specify which component of a pixel's color we want to change and how we want to change it.

OpenGL Color Blending

In many applications, it is convenient to be able to combine the colors of overlapping objects or to blend an object with the background. Some examples are simulating a paintbrush effect, forming a composite image of two or more pictures, modeling transparency effects, and antialiasing the objects in a scene. Most graphics packages provide methods for producing various color-mixing effects, and these procedures are called **color-blending functions** or **image-compositing functions.** In OpenGL, the colors of two objects can be blended by first loading one object into the frame buffer, then combining the color of the second object with the frame-buffer color. The current frame-buffer color is referred to as the OpenGL *destination color* and the color of the second object is the OpenGL *source color*. Blending methods can be performed only in RGB or RGBA mode. To apply color blending in an application, we first need to activate this OpenGL feature using the following function.

```
glEnable (GL_BLEND);
```

And we turn off the color-blending routines in OpenGL with

```
glDisable (GL_BLEND);
```

If color blending is not activated, an object's color simply replaces the frame-buffer contents at the object's location.

Colors can be blended in a number of different ways, depending on the effects we want to achieve, and we generate different color effects by specifying two sets of *blending factors*. One set of blending factors is for the current object in the frame buffer (the "destination object"), and the other set of blending factors is for the incoming ("source") object. The new, blended color that is then loaded into the frame buffer is calculated as

$$(S_r R_s + D_r R_d, S_g G_s + D_g G_d, S_b B_s + D_b B_d, S_a A_s + D_a A_d) \tag{4-1}$$

where the RGBA source color components are (R_s, G_s, B_s, A_s), the destination color components are (R_d, G_d, B_d, A_d), the source blending factors are (S_r, S_g, S_b, S_a), and the destination blending factors are (D_r, D_g, D_b, D_a). Computed values for the combined color components are clamped to the range from 0.0 to 1.0. That is, any sum greater than 1.0 is set to the value 1.0, and any sum less than 0.0 is set to 0.0.

We select the blending-factor values with the OpenGL function

```
glBlendFunc (sFactor, dFactor);
```

Parameters `sFactor` and `dFactor`, the source and destination factors, are each assigned an OpenGL symbolic constant specifying a predefined set of four blending coefficients. For example, the constant `GL_ZERO` yields the blending factors (0.0, 0.0, 0.0, 0.0) and `GL_ONE` gives us the set (1.0, 1.0, 1.0, 1.0). We could set all four blending factors either to the destination alpha value or to the source alpha value using `GL_DST_ALPHA` or `GL_SRC_ALPHA`. Other OpenGL constants that are available for setting the blending factors include `GL_ONE_MINUS_DST_ALPHA`, `GL_ONE_MINUS_SRC_ALPHA`, `GL_DST_COLOR`, and `GL_SRC_COLOR`. These blending factors are often used for simulating transparency, and they are discussed in greater detail in Section 10-19. The default value for parameter `sFactor` is `GL_ONE`, and the default value for parameter `dFactor` is `GL_ZERO`. Hence, the default values for the blending factors result in the incoming color values replacing the current values in the frame buffer.

Additional functions have been included in an OpenGL extension called the Imaging Subset. These functions include a routine to set a blending color and another routine to specify a blending equation.

OpenGL Color Arrays

We can also specify color values for a scene in combination with the coordinate values in a vertex array (Section 3-17). This can be done either in RGB mode or in color-index mode. As with vertex arrays, we must first activate the color-array features of OpenGL:

```
glEnableClientState (GL_COLOR_ARRAY);
```

Then, for RGB color mode, we specify the location and format of the color components with

```
glColorPointer (nColorComponents, dataType, offset, colorArray);
```

Parameter `nColorComponents` is assigned a value of either 3 or 4, depending upon whether we are listing RGB or RGBA color components in the array `colorArray`. An OpenGL symbolic constant such as `GL_INT` or `GL_FLOAT` is assigned to parameter `dataType` to indicate the data type for the color values. For a separate color array, we can assign the value 0 to parameter `offset`. But if we combine color data with vertex data in the same array, the `offset` value is the number of bytes between each set of color components in the array.

As an example of using color arrays, we can modify the vertex-array example in Section 3-17 to include a color array. The following code fragment sets the color of all vertices on the front face of the cube to blue, and all vertices of the back face are assigned the color red.

```
typedef GLint vertex3 [3], color3 [3];

vertex3 pt [8] = { {0, 0, 0}, {0, 1, 0}, {1, 0, 0},
    {1, 1, 0}, {0, 0, 1}, {0, 1, 1}, {1, 0, 1}, {1, 1, 1} };
color3 hue [8] = { {1, 0, 0}, {1, 0, 0}, {0, 0, 1},
    {0, 0, 1}, {1, 0, 0}, {1, 0, 0}, {0, 0, 1}, {0, 0, 1} };

glEnableClientState (GL_VERTEX_ARRAY);
glEnableClientState (GL_COLOR_ARRAY);

glVertexPointer (3, GL_INT, 0, pt);
glColorPointer (3, GL_INT, 0, hue);
```

We can even stuff both the colors and the vertex coordinates into one **interlaced array.** Each of the pointers would then reference the single interlaced array, with an appropriate `offset` value. For example,

```
static GLint hueAndPt [ ] =
    {1, 0, 0, 0, 0, 0, 1, 0, 0, 0, 1, 0,
     0, 0, 1, 1, 0, 0, 0, 0, 1, 1, 1, 0,
     1, 0, 0, 0, 0, 1, 1, 0, 0, 0, 1, 1,
     0, 0, 1, 1, 0, 1, 0, 0, 1, 1, 1, 1};

glVertexPointer (3, GL_INT, 6*sizeof(GLint), hueAndPt [3]);
glColorPointer (3, GL_INT, 6*sizeof(GLint), hueAndPt [0]);
```

The first three elements of this array specify an RGB color value, the next three elements specify a set of (x, y, z) vertex coordinates, and this pattern continues to the last color-vertex specification. We set the `offset` parameter to the number of bytes between successive color, or vertex, values, which is `6*sizeof(GLint)` for both. Color values start at the first element of the interlaced array, which is `hueAndPt [0]`, and vertex values start at the fourth element, which is `hueAndPt [3]`.

Since a scene generally contains several objects, each with multiple planar surfaces, OpenGL provides a function in which we can specify all the vertex and color arrays at once, as well as other types of information. If we change the color and vertex values in the above example to floating point, we use this function in the form

```
glInterleavedArrays (GL_C3F_V3F, 0, hueAndPt);
```

The first parameter is an OpenGL constant that indicates three-element floating-point specifications for both color (C) and vertex coordinates (V). And the elements of array `hueAndPt` are to be interlaced with the color for each vertex listed before the coordinates. This function also automatically enables both vertex and color arrays.

In color-index mode, we define an array of color indices with

```
glIndexPointer (type, stride, colorIndex);
```

Color indices are listed in the array `colorIndex` and the `type` and `stride` parameters are the same as in `glColorPointer`. No `size` parameter is needed since color-table indices are specified with a single value.

Other OpenGL Color Functions

In our first programming example in Section 2-9, we introduced the following function that selects RGB color components for a display window.

```
glClearColor (red, green, blue, alpha);
```

Each color component in the designation (red, green, and blue), as well as the alpha parameter, is assigned a floating-point value in the range from 0.0 to 1.0. The default value for all four parameters is 0.0, which produces the color black. If each color component is set to 1.0, the clear color is white. Shades of gray are obtained with identical values for the color components between 0.0 and 1.0. The fourth parameter, `alpha`, provides an option for blending the previous color with the current color. This can occur only if we activate the blending feature of OpenGL; color blending cannot be performed with values specified in a color table.

As we noted in Section 3-19, there are several *color buffers* in OpenGL that can be used as the current refresh buffer for displaying a scene, and the `glClearColor` function specifies the color for all the color buffers. We then apply the clear color to the color buffers with the command:

```
glClear (GL_COLOR_BUFFER_BIT);
```

We can also use the `glClear` function to set initial values for other buffers that are available in OpenGL. These are the *accumulation buffer,* which stores blended-color information, the *depth buffer,* which stores depth values (distances from the viewing position) for objects in a scene, and the *stencil buffer,* which stores information to define the limits of a picture.

In color-index mode, we use the following function (instead of `glClearColor`) to set the display-window color.

```
glClearIndex (index);
```

The window background color is then assigned the color that is stored at position `index` in the color table. And the window is displayed in this color when we issue the `glClear (GL_COLOR_BUFFER_BIT)` function.

Many other color functions are available in the OpenGL library for dealing with a variety of tasks, such as changing color models, setting lighting effects for a scene, specifying camera effects, and rendering the surfaces of an object. We examine other color functions as we explore each of the component processes in a computer-graphics system. For now, we limit our discussion to those functions relating to color specifications for graphics primitives.

4-4 POINT ATTRIBUTES

Basically, we can set two attributes for points: color and size. In a state system, the displayed color and size of a point is determined by the current values stored in the attribute list. Color components are set with RGB values or an index into a color table. For a raster system, point size is an integer multiple of the pixel size, so that a large point is displayed as a square block of pixels.

4-5 LINE ATTRIBUTES

A straight-line segment can be displayed with three basic attributes: color, width, and style. Line color is typically set with the same function for all graphics primitives, while line width and line style are selected with separate line functions. Additionally, lines may be generated with other effects, such as pen and brush strokes.

Line Width

Implementation of line-width options depends on the capabilities of the output device. A heavy line could be displayed on a video monitor as adjacent parallel lines, while a pen plotter might require pen changes to draw a thick line.

For raster implementations, a standard-width line is generated with single pixels at each sample position, as in the Bresenham algorithm. Thicker lines are displayed as positive integer multiples of the standard line by plotting additional pixels along adjacent parallel line paths. If a line has slope magnitude less than or equal to 1.0, we can modify a line-drawing routine to display thick lines by plotting a vertical span of pixels in each column (x position) along the line. The number of pixels to be displayed in each column is set equal to the integer value of the line width. In Fig. 4-2 we display a double-width line by generating a parallel line above the original line path. At each x sampling position, we calculate the corresponding y coordinate and plot pixels at screen coordinates (x, y) and $(x, y+1)$. We could display lines with a width of 3 or greater by alternately plotting pixels above and below the single-width line path.

With a line slope greater than 1.0 in magnitude, we can display thick lines using horizontal spans, alternately picking up pixels to the right and left of the line path. This scheme is demonstrated in Fig. 4-3, where a line segment with a width of 4 is plotted using multiple pixels across each scan line. Similarly, a thick line with slope less than or equal to 1.0 can be displayed using vertical pixel spans. We can implement this procedure by comparing the magnitudes of the horizontal and vertical separations (Δx and Δy) of the line endpoints. If $|\Delta x| \geq |\Delta y|$,

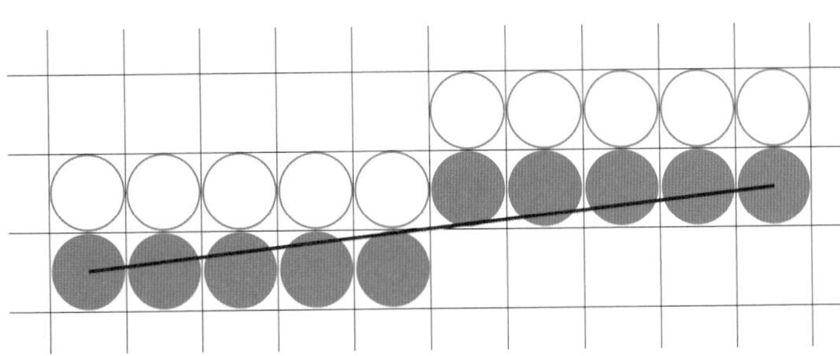

FIGURE 4-2 A double-wide raster line with slope $|m| < 1.0$ generated with vertical pixel spans.

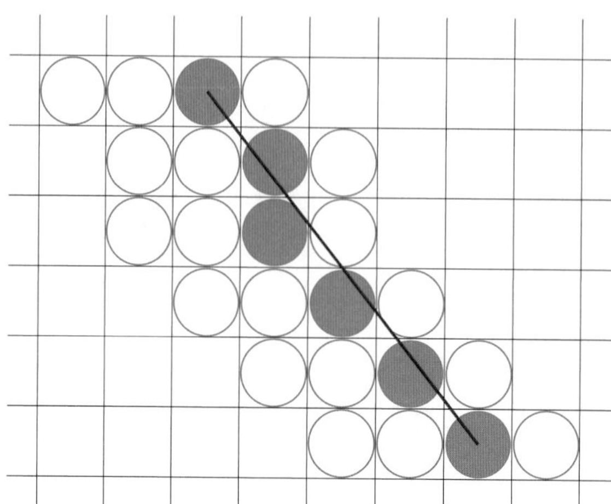

FIGURE 4-3 A raster line with slope $|m| > 1.0$ and a line width of 4 plotted using horizontal pixel spans.

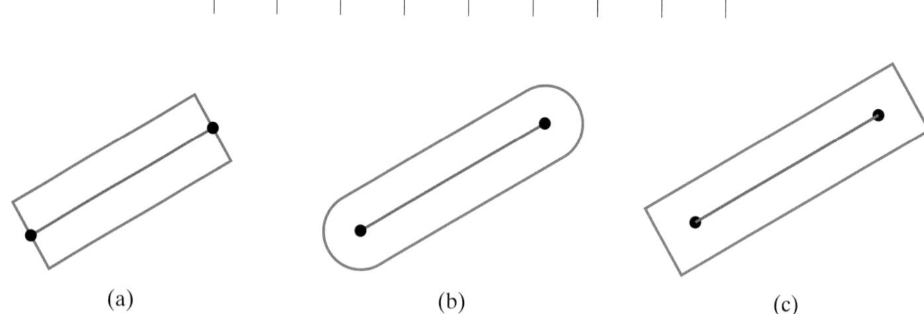

FIGURE 4-4 Thick lines drawn with (a) butt caps, (b) round caps, and (c) projecting square caps.

pixels are replicated along columns. Otherwise, multiple pixels are plotted across rows.

Although thick lines are generated quickly by plotting horizontal or vertical pixel spans, the displayed width of a line (measured perpendicular to the line path) is dependent on its slope. A 45° line will be displayed thinner by a factor of $1/\sqrt{2}$ compared to a horizontal or vertical line plotted with the same-length pixel spans.

Another problem with implementing width options using horizontal or vertical pixel spans is that the method produces lines whose ends are horizontal or vertical regardless of the slope of the line. This effect is more noticeable with very thick lines. We can adjust the shape of the line ends to give them a better appearance by adding **line caps** (Fig. 4-4). One kind of line cap is the *butt cap,* which has square ends that are perpendicular to the line path. If the specified line has slope m, the square ends of the thick line have slope $-1/m$. Each of the component parallel lines is then displayed between the two perpendicular lines at each end of the specified line path. Another line cap is the *round cap* obtained by adding a filled semicircle to each butt cap. The circular arcs are centered at the middle of the thick line and have a diameter equal to the line thickness. A third type of line cap is the *projecting square cap*. Here, we simply extend the line and add butt caps that are positioned one-half of the line width beyond the specified endpoints.

Other methods for producing thick lines include displaying the line as a filled rectangle or generating the line with a selected pen or brush pattern, as discussed in the next section. To obtain a rectangle representation for the line boundary, we calculate the position of the rectangle vertices along perpendiculars to the line path so that the rectangle vertex coordinates are displaced from the original line-endpoint positions by one-half the line width. The rectangular line then appears

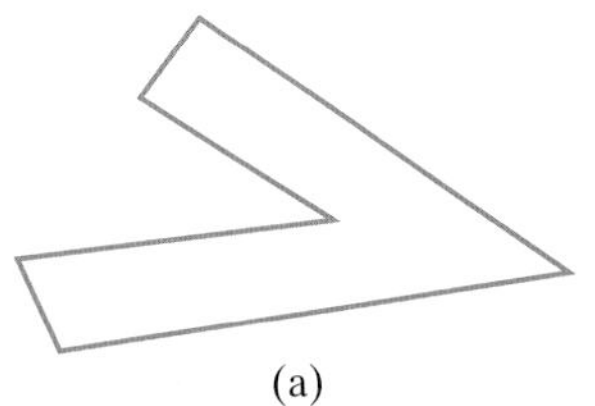
(a)

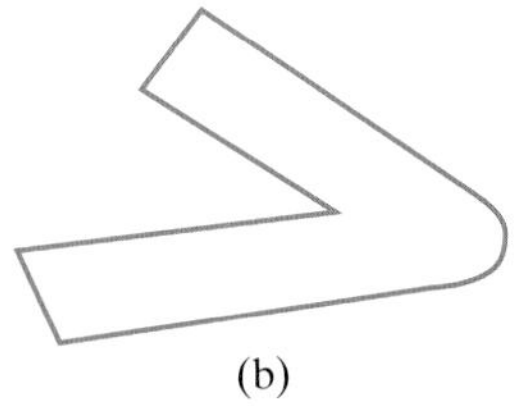
(b)

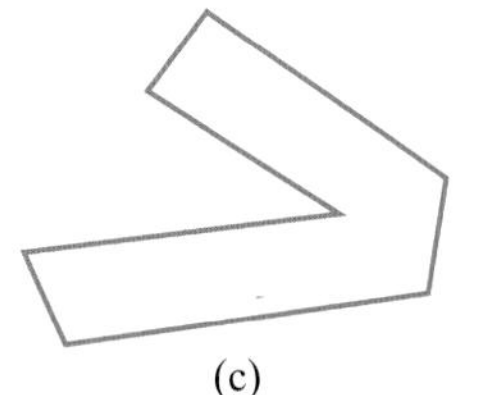
(c)

FIGURE 4-5 Thick line segments connected with a miter join (a), a round join (b), and a bevel join (c).

as in Fig. 4-4 (a). We could add round caps to the filled rectangle, or we could extend its length to display projecting square caps.

Generating thick polylines requires some additional considerations. In general, the methods we have considered for displaying a single line segment will not produce a smoothly connected series of line segments. Displaying thick polylines using horizontal and vertical pixel spans, for example, leaves pixel gaps at the boundaries between line segments with different slopes where there is a shift from horizontal pixel spans to vertical spans. We can generate thick polylines that are smoothly joined at the cost of additional processing at the segment endpoints. Figure 4-5 shows three possible methods for smoothly joining two line segments. A *miter join* is accomplished by extending the outer boundaries of each of the two line segments until they meet. A *round join* is produced by capping the connection between the two segments with a circular boundary whose diameter is equal to the line width. And a *bevel join* is generated by displaying the line segments with butt caps and filling in the triangular gap where the segments meet. If the angle between two connected line segments is very small, a miter join can generate a long spike that distorts the appearance of the polyline. A graphics package can avoid this effect by switching from a miter join to a bevel join when, for example, the angle between any two consecutive segments is small.

Line Style

Possible selections for the line-style attribute include solid lines, dashed lines, and dotted lines. We modify a line-drawing algorithm to generate such lines by setting the length and spacing of displayed solid sections along the line path. With many graphics packages, we can select the length of both the dashes and the inter-dash spacing.

Raster line algorithms display line-style attributes by plotting pixel spans. For dashed, dotted, and dot-dashed patterns, the line-drawing procedure outputs sections of contiguous pixels along the line path, skipping over a number of intervening pixels between the solid spans. Pixel counts for the span length and inter-span spacing can be specified in a **pixel mask,** which is a pattern of binary digits indicating which positions to plot along the line path. The linear mask 11111000, for instance, could be used to display a dashed line with a dash length of five pixels and an inter-dash spacing of three pixels. Pixel positions corresponding to the 1 bits are assigned the current color, and pixel positions corresponding to the 0 bits are displayed in the background color.

Plotting dashes with a fixed number of pixels results in unequal length dashes for different line orientations, as illustrated in Fig. 4-6. Both dashes shown are plotted with four pixels but the diagonal dash is longer by a factor of $\sqrt{2}$. For precision drawings, dash lengths should remain approximately constant for any line orientation. To accomplish this, we could adjust the pixel counts for the solid spans and inter-span spacing according to the line slope. In Fig. 4-6, we can display approximately equal length dashes by reducing the diagonal dash to three pixels.

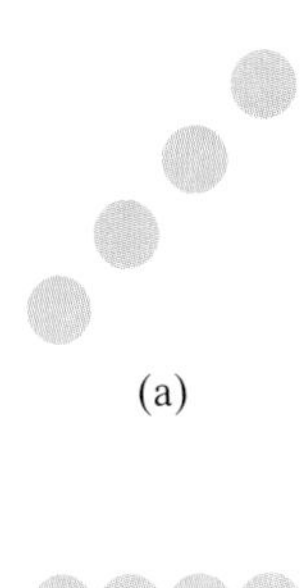
(a)

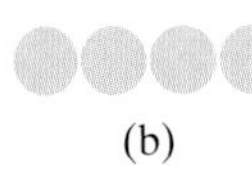
(b)

FIGURE 4-6 Unequal length dashes displayed with the same number of pixels.

Another method for maintaining dash length is to treat dashes as individual line segments. Endpoint coordinates for each dash are located and passed to the line routine, which then calculates pixel positions along the dash path.

Pen and Brush Options

With some packages, particularly painting and drawing systems, we can directly select different pen and brush styles. Options in this category include shape, size, and pattern for the pen or brush. Some example pen and brush shapes are given in Fig. 4-7. These shapes can be stored in a pixel mask that identifies the array of pixel positions that are to be set along the line path. For example, a rectangular pen could be implemented with the mask shown in Fig. 4-8 by moving the center (or one corner) of the mask along the line path, as in Fig. 4-9. To avoid setting pixels more than once in the frame buffer, we can simply accumulate the horizontal spans generated at each position of the mask and keep track of the beginning and ending x positions for the spans across each scan line.

Lines generated with pen (or brush) shapes can be displayed in various widths by changing the size of the mask. For example, the rectangular pen line in Fig. 4-9 could be narrowed with a 2 by 2 rectangular mask or widened with a 4 by 4 mask. Also, lines can be displayed with selected patterns by superimposing the pattern values onto the pen or brush mask.

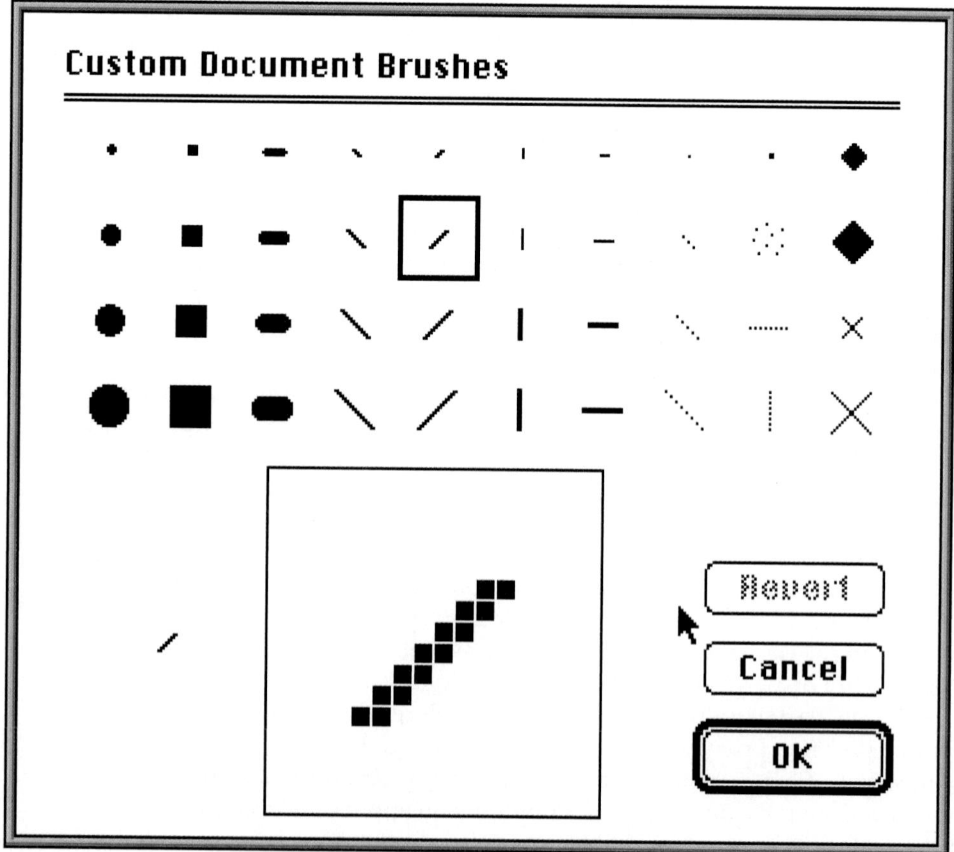

FIGURE 4-7 Pen and brush shapes for line display.

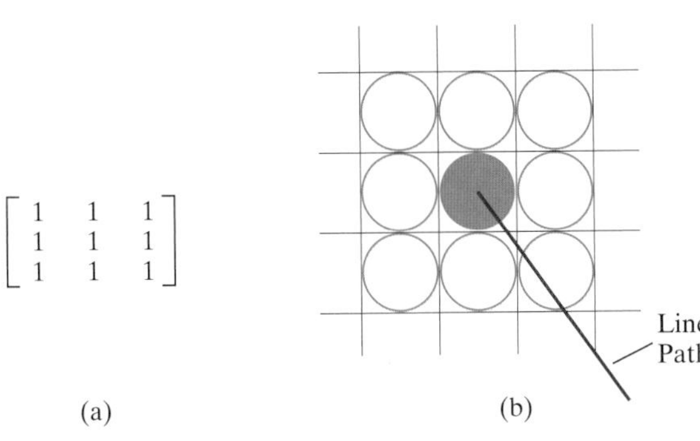

FIGURE 4-8 A pixel mask (a) for a rectangular pen, and the associated array of pixels (b) displayed by centering the mask over a specified pixel position.

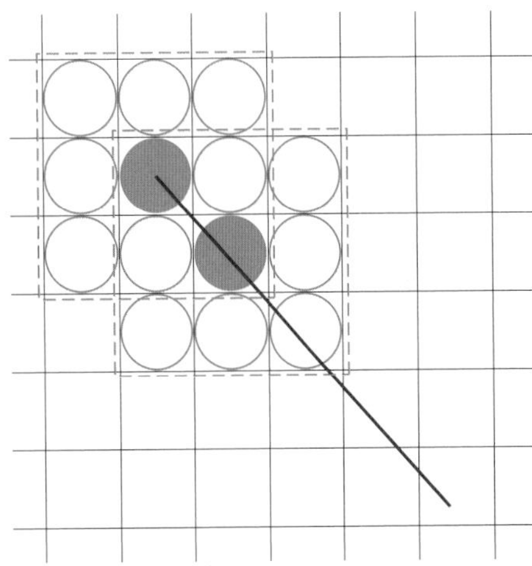

FIGURE 4-9 Generating a line with the pen shape of Fig. 4-8.

4-6 CURVE ATTRIBUTES

Parameters for curve attributes are the same as those for straight-line segments. We can display curves with varying colors, widths, dot-dash patterns, and available pen or brush options. Methods for adapting curve-drawing algorithms to accommodate attribute selections are similar to those for line drawing.

Raster curves of various widths can be displayed using the method of horizontal or vertical pixel spans. Where the magnitude of the curve slope is less than or equal to 1.0, we plot vertical spans; where the slope magnitude is greater than 1.0, we plot horizontal spans. Figure 4-10 demonstrates this method for displaying a circular arc of width 4 in the first quadrant. Using circle symmetry, we generate the circle path with vertical spans in the octant from $x = 0$ to $x = y$, and then reflect pixel positions about the line $y = x$ to obtain the remainder of the curve shown. Circle sections in the other quadrants are obtained by reflecting pixel positions in the first quadrant about the coordinate axes. The thickness of curves displayed with this method is again a function of curve slope. Circles, ellipses, and other curves will appear thinnest where the slope has a magnitude of 1.

Another method for displaying thick curves is to fill in the area between two parallel curve paths, whose separation distance is equal to the desired width. We could do this using the specified curve path as one boundary and setting up the second boundary either inside or outside the original curve path. This approach, however, shifts the original curve path either inward or outward, depending on which direction we choose for the second boundary. We can maintain the original curve position by setting the two boundary curves at a distance of one-half the width on either side of the specified curve path. An example of this approach is shown in Figure 4-11 for a circle segment with radius 16 and a specified width of 4. The boundary arcs are then set at a separation distance of 2 on either side of the radius of 16. To maintain the proper dimensions of the circular arc, as discussed in Section 3-13, we can set the radii for the concentric boundary arcs at $r = 14$ and $r = 17$. Although this method is accurate for generating thick circles,

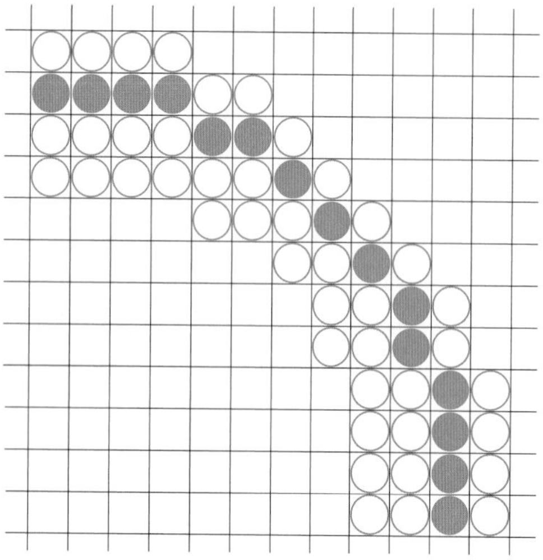

FIGURE 4-10 A circular arc of width 4 plotted with either vertical or horizontal pixel spans, depending on the slope.

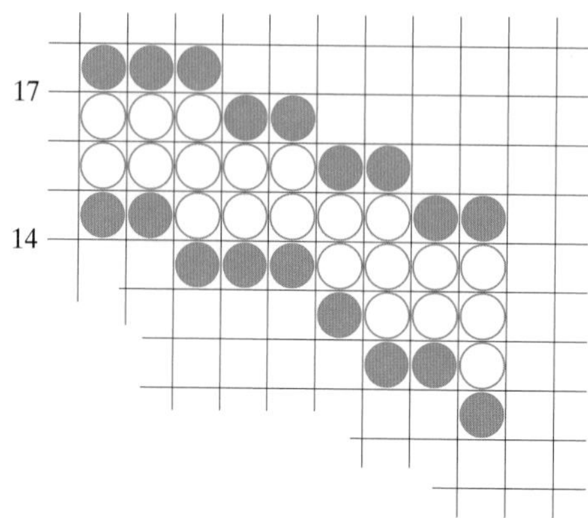

FIGURE 4-11 A circular arc of width 4 and radius 16 displayed by filling the region between two concentric arcs.

it provides, in general, only an approximation to the true area of other thick curves. For example, the inner and outer boundaries of a fat ellipse generated with this method do not have the same foci.

The pixel masks discussed for implementing line-style options could also be used in raster curve algorithms to generate dashed or dotted patterns. For example, the mask 11100 produces the dashed circle shown in Figure 4-12. We can generate the dashes in the various octants using circle symmetry, but we must shift the pixel positions to maintain the correct sequence of dashes and spaces as we move from one octant to the next. Also, as in straight-line algorithms, pixel masks display dashes and inter-dash spaces that vary in length according to the slope of the curve. If we want to display constant length dashes, we need to adjust the number of pixels plotted in each dash as we move around the circle circumference. Instead of applying a pixel mask with constant spans, we plot pixels along equal angular arcs to produce equal-length dashes.

Pen (or brush) displays of curves are generated using the same techniques discussed for straight-line segments. We replicate a pen shape along the line path, as illustrated in Figure 4-13 for a circular arc in the first quadrant. Here, the center of the rectangular pen is moved to successive curve positions to produce the curve shape shown. Curves displayed with a rectangular pen in this manner will be thicker where the magnitude of the curve slope is 1. A uniform curve thickness can be displayed by rotating the rectangular pen to align it with the slope direction as we move around the curve or by using a circular pen shape. Curves drawn with pen and brush shapes can be displayed in different sizes and with superimposed patterns or simulated brush strokes.

Painting and drawing programs allow pictures to be constructed interactively by using a pointing device, such as a stylus and a graphics tablet, to sketch various curve shapes. Some examples of such curve patterns are shown in Fig. 4-14. An additional pattern option that can be provided in a paint package is the display of simulated brush strokes. Figure 4-15 illustrates some patterns that can be produced by modeling different types of brush strokes.

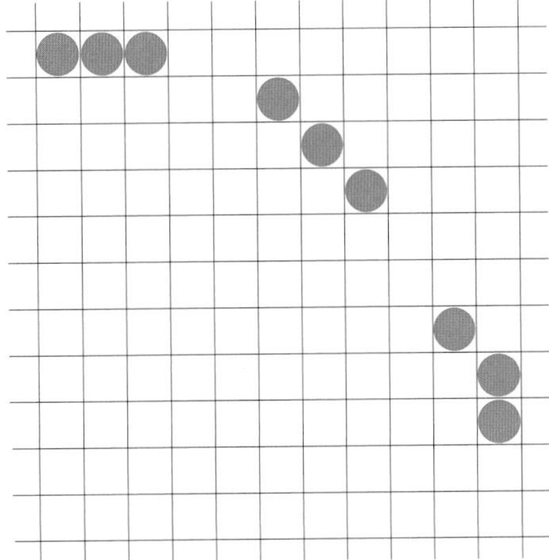

FIGURE 4-12 A dashed circular arc displayed with a dash span of 3 pixels and an inter-dash spacing of 2 pixels.

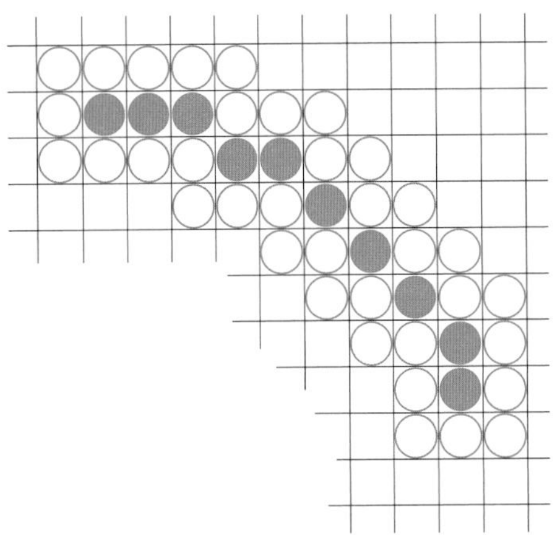

FIGURE 4-13 A circular arc displayed with a rectangular pen.

FIGURE 4-14 Curved lines drawn with a paint program using various shapes and patterns. From left to right, the brush shapes are square, round, diagonal line, dot pattern, and faded airbrush.

FIGURE 4-15 A daruma doll, a symbol of good fortune in Japan, drawn by computer artist Koichi Kozaki using a paintbrush system. Daruma dolls actually come without eyes. One eye is painted in when a wish is made, and the other is painted in when the wish comes true. (*Courtesy of Wacom Technology, Corp.*)

4-7 OpenGL POINT-ATTRIBUTE FUNCTIONS

The displayed color of a designated point position is controlled by the current color values in the state list. And a color is specified with either the `glColor` function or the `glIndex` function.

We set the size for an OpenGL point with

```
glPointSize (size);
```

and the point is then displayed as a square block of pixels. Parameter `size` is assigned a positive floating-point value, which is rounded to an integer (unless the point is to be antialiased). The number of horizontal and vertical pixels in the display of the point is determined by parameter `size`. Thus a point size of 1.0 displays a single pixel, and a point size of 2.0 displays a 2 by 2 pixel array. If we activate the antialiasing features of OpenGL, the size of a displayed block of pixels will be modified to smooth the edges. The default value for point size is 1.0.

Attribute functions may be listed inside or outside of a `glBegin/glEnd` pair. For example, the following code segment plots three points in varying colors and sizes. The first is a standard-size red point, the second is a double-size green point, and the third is a triple-size blue point.

```
glColor3f (1.0, 0.0, 0.0);
glBegin (GL_POINTS);
   glVertex2i (50, 100);
   glPointSize (2.0);
   glColor3f (0.0, 1.0, 0.0);
   glVertex2i (75, 150);
   glPointSize (3.0);
   glColor3f (0.0, 0.0, 1.0);
   glVertex2i (100, 200);
glEnd ( );
```

4-8 OpenGL LINE-ATTRIBUTE FUNCTIONS

We can control the appearance of a straight-line segment in OpenGL with three attribute settings: line color, line width, and line style. We have already seen how to make a color selection, and OpenGL provides a function for setting the width of a line and another function for specifying a line style, such as a dashed or dotted line.

OpenGL Line-Width Function

Line width is set in OpenGL with the function

```
glLineWidth (width);
```

We assign a floating-point value to parameter `width`, and this value is rounded to the nearest nonnegative integer. If the input value rounds to 0.0, the line is displayed with a standard width of 1.0, which is the default width. However, when antialiasing is applied to the line, its edges are smoothed to reduce the raster stair-step appearance and fractional widths are possible. Some implementations of the line-width function might support only a limited number of widths, and some might not support widths other than 1.0.

The OpenGL line-width function is implemented using the methods described in Section 4-5. That is, the magnitude of the horizontal and vertical separations of the line endpoints, Δx and Δy, are compared to determine whether to generate a thick line using vertical pixel spans or horizontal pixel spans.

OpenGL Line-Style Function

By default, a straight-line segment is displayed as a solid line. But we can also display dashed lines, dotted lines, or a line with a combination of dashes and dots. And we can vary the length of the dashes and the spacing between dashes or dots. We set a current display style for lines with the OpenGL function:

```
glLineStipple (repeatFactor, pattern);
```

Parameter `pattern` is used to reference a 16-bit integer that describes how the line should be displayed. A 1 bit in the pattern denotes an "on" pixel position, and a 0 bit indicates an "off" pixel position. The pattern is applied to the pixels along the line path starting with the low-order bits in the pattern. The default pattern is 0xFFFF (each bit position has a value of 1), which produces a solid line. Integer parameter `repeatFactor` specifies how many times each bit in the pattern is to be repeated before the next bit in the pattern is applied. The default repeat value is 1.

With a polyline, a specified line-style pattern is not restarted at the beginning of each segment. It is applied continuously across all the segments, starting at the first endpoint of the polyline and ending at the final endpoint for the last segment in the series.

As an example of specifying a line style, suppose parameter `pattern` is assigned the hexadecimal representation 0x00FF and the repeat factor is 1. This would display a dashed line with eight pixels in each dash and eight pixel positions that are "off" (an eight-pixel space) between two dashes. Also, since low-order bits are applied first, a line begins with an eight-pixel dash starting at the first endpoint. This dash is followed by an eight-pixel space, then another eight-pixel dash, and so forth, until the second endpoint position is reached.

Before a line can be displayed in the current line-style pattern, we must activate the line-style feature of OpenGL. We accomplish this with the following function.

```
glEnable (GL_LINE_STIPPLE);
```

If we forget to include this enable function, solid lines are displayed; that is, the default pattern 0xFFFF is used to display line segments. At any time, we can turn off the line-pattern feature with

```
glDisable (GL_LINE_STIPPLE);
```

This replaces the current line-style pattern with the default pattern (solid lines).

In the following program outline, we illustrate use of the OpenGL line-attribute functions by plotting three line graphs in different styles and widths. Figure 4-16 shows the data plots that could be generated by this program.

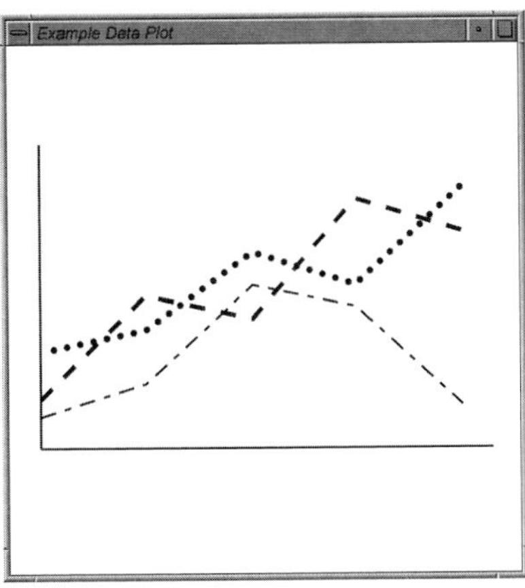

FIGURE 4-16 Plotting three data sets with three different OpenGL line styles and line widths: single-width dash-dot pattern, double-width dash pattern, and triple-width dot pattern.

```
/* Define a two-dimensional world-coordinate data type. */
typedef struct { float x, y; } wcPt2D;

wcPt2D dataPts [5];

void linePlot (wcPt2D dataPts [5])
{
   int k;

   glBegin (GL_LINE_STRIP);
      for (k = 0; k < 5; k++)
         glVertex2f (dataPts [k].x, dataPts [k].y);

   glFlush ( );

   glEnd ( );
}

/* Invoke a procedure here to draw coordinate axes.  */

glEnable (GL_LINE_STIPPLE);

/* Input first set of (x, y) data values. */
glLineStipple (1, 0x1C47);    // Plot a dash-dot, standard-width polyline.
linePlot (dataPts);

/* Input second set of (x, y) data values. */
glLineStipple (1, 0x00FF);    // Plot a dashed, double-width polyline.
glLineWidth (2.0);
linePlot (dataPts);

/* Input third set of (x, y) data values. */
glLineStipple (1, 0x0101);    // Plot a dotted, triple-width polyline.
glLineWidth (3.0);
linePlot (dataPts);

glDisable (GL_LINE_STIPPLE);
```

Other OpenGL Line Effects

In addition to specifying width, style, and a solid color, we can display lines with color gradations. For example, we can vary the color along the path of a solid line by assigning a different color to each line endpoint as we define the line. In the following code segment we illustrate this by assigning a blue color to one endpoint of a line and a red color to the other endpoint. The solid line is then displayed as a linear interpolation of the colors at the two endpoints.

```
glShadeModel (GL_SMOOTH);

glBegin (GL_LINES);
   glColor3f (0.0, 0.0, 1.0);
   glVertex2i (50, 50);
   glColor3f (1.0, 0.0, 0.0);
   glVertex2i (250, 250);
glEnd ( );
```

Function `glShadeModel` can also be given the argument `GL_FLAT`. In that case, the line segment would have been displayed in a single color: the color of the second endpoint, (250, 250). That is, we would have generated a red line. Actually, `GL_SMOOTH` is the default, so we would generate a smoothly interpolated color line segment even if we did not include this function in our code.

We can produce other effects by displaying adjacent lines that have different colors and patterns. And we can also make use of the color-blending features of OpenGL by superimposing lines or other objects with varying alpha values. A brush stroke, and other painting effects, can be simulated with a pixelmap and color blending. The pixelmap can then be moved interactively to generate line segments. Individual pixels in the pixmap can be assigned different alpha values to display lines as brush or pen strokes.

4-9 FILL-AREA ATTRIBUTES

Most graphics packages limit fill areas to polygons, because they are described with linear equations. A further restriction requires fill areas to be convex polygons, so that scan lines do not intersect more than two boundary edges. However, in general, we can fill any specified regions, including circles, ellipses, and other objects with curved boundaries. And applications systems, such as paint programs, provide fill options for arbitrarily shaped regions.

There are two basic procedures for filling an area on raster systems, once the definition of the fill region has been mapped to pixel coordinates. One procedure first determines the overlap intervals for scan lines that cross the area. Then, pixel positions along these overlap intervals are set to the fill color. Another method for area filling is to start from a given interior position and "paint" outward, pixel-by-pixel, from this point until we encounter specified boundary conditions. The scan-line approach is usually applied to simple shapes such as circles or regions with polyline boundaries, and general graphics packages use this fill method. Fill algorithms that use a starting interior point are useful for filling areas with more complex boundaries and in interactive painting systems.

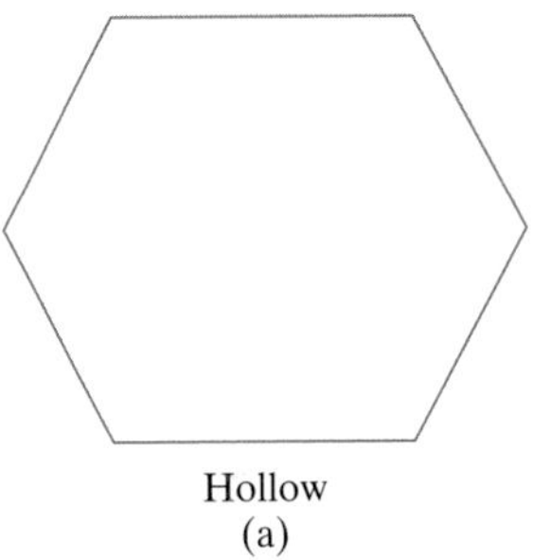

Hollow
(a)

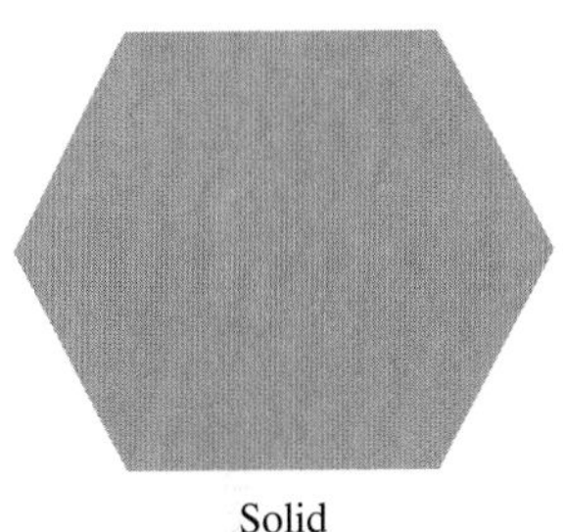

Solid
(b)

Patterned
(c)

FIGURE 4-17 Basic polygon fill styles.

Fill Styles

A basic fill-area attribute provided by a general graphics library is the display style of the interior. We can display a region with a single color, a specified fill pattern, or in a "hollow" style by showing only the boundary of the region. These three fill styles are illustrated in Fig. 4-17. We can also fill selected regions of a scene using various brush styles, color-blending combinations, or textures. Other options include specifications for the display of the boundaries of a fill area. For polygons, we could show the edges in different colors, widths, and styles. And we can select different display attributes for the front and back faces of a region.

Fill patterns can be defined in rectangular color arrays that list different colors for different positions in the array. Or, a fill pattern could be specified as a bit array that indicates which relative positions are to be displayed in a single selected color. An array specifying a fill pattern is a *mask* that is to be applied to the display area. Some graphics systems provide an option for selecting an arbitrary initial position for overlaying the mask. From this starting position, the mask is replicated in the horizontal and vertical directions until the display area is filled with nonoverlapping copies of the pattern. Where the pattern overlaps

Diagonal Hatch Fill

Diagonal Crosshatch Fill

FIGURE 4-18 Areas filled with hatch patterns.

specified fill areas, the array pattern indicates which pixels should be displayed in a particular color. This process of filling an area with a rectangular pattern is called **tiling,** and a rectangular fill pattern is sometimes referred to as a **tiling pattern.** Sometimes, predefined fill patterns are available in a system, such as the *hatch* fill patterns shown in Fig. 4-18.

We can implement a pattern fill by determining where the pattern overlaps those scan lines that cross a fill area. Beginning from a specified start position for a pattern fill, we map the rectangular patterns vertically across scan lines and horizontally across pixel positions on the scan lines. Each replication of the pattern array is performed at intervals determined by the width and height of the mask. Where the pattern overlaps the fill area, pixel colors are set according to the values stored in the mask.

Hatch fill could be applied to regions by drawing sets of line segments to display either single hatching or crosshatching. Spacing and slope for the hatch lines could be set as parameters in a hatch table. Alternatively, hatch fill can be specified as a pattern array that produces sets of diagonal lines.

A reference point (xp, yp) for the starting position of a fill pattern can be set at any convenient position, inside or outside the fill region. For instance, the reference point could be set at a polygon vertex. Or the reference point could be chosen as the lower left corner of the bounding rectangle (or bounding box) determined by the coordinate extents of the region. To simplify selection of the reference coordinates, some packages always use the coordinate origin of the display window as the pattern start position. Always setting (xp, yp) at the coordinate origin also simplifies the tiling operations when each element of a pattern is to be mapped to a single pixel. For example, if the row positions in the pattern array are referenced from bottom to top, starting with the value 1, a color value is then assigned to pixel position (x, y) in screen coordinates from pattern position $(y \bmod ny + 1, x \bmod nx + 1)$. Here, ny and nx specify the number of rows and number of columns in the pattern array. Setting the pattern start position at the coordinate origin, however, effectively attaches the pattern fill to the screen background, rather than to the fill regions. Adjacent or overlapping areas filled with the same pattern would show no apparent boundary between the areas. Also, repositioning and refilling an object with the same pattern can result in a shift in the assigned pixel values over the object interior. A moving object would appear to be transparent against a stationary pattern background, instead of moving with a fixed interior pattern.

Color-Blended Fill Regions

It is also possible to combine a fill pattern with background colors in various ways. A pattern could be combined with background colors using a *transparency factor* that determines how much of the background should be mixed with the object color. Or we could use simple logical or replace operations. Figure 4-19 demonstrates how logical and replace operations would combine a 2 by 2 fill pattern with a background pattern for a binary (black-and-white) system.

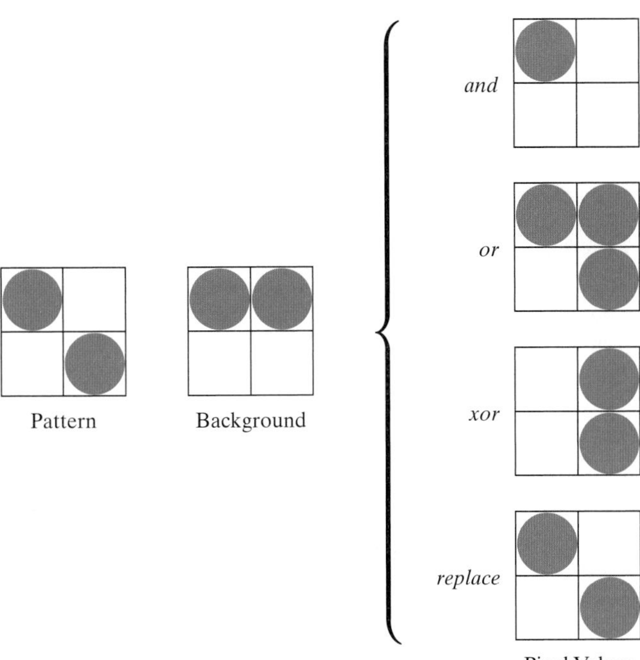

FIGURE 4-19 Combining a fill pattern with a background pattern using logical operations *and, or,* and *xor* (*exclusive or*), and using simple replacement.

Some fill methods using blended colors have been referred to as **soft-fill** or **tint-fill** algorithms. One use for these fill methods is to soften the fill colors at object borders that have been blurred to antialias the edges. Another application of a soft-fill algorithm is to allow repainting of a color area that was originally filled with a semitransparent brush, where the current color is then a mixture of the brush color and the background colors "behind" the area. In either case, we want the new fill color to have the same variations over the area as the current fill color.

As an example of this type of fill, the *linear soft-fill algorithm* repaints an area that was originally painted by merging a foreground color **F** with a single background color **B**, where $\mathbf{F} = B$. Assuming we know the values for **F** and **B**, we can check the current contents of the frame buffer to determine how these colors were combined. The current RGB color **P** of each pixel within the area to be refilled is some linear combination of **F** and **B**:

$$\mathbf{P} = t\mathbf{F} + (1 - t)\mathbf{B} \tag{4-2}$$

where the transparency factor t has a value between 0 and 1 for each pixel. For values of t less than 0.5, the background color contributes more to the interior color of the region than does the fill color. Vector Eq. 4-2 holds for each RGB component of the colors, with

$$\mathbf{P} = (P_R, P_G, P_B), \qquad \mathbf{F} = (F_R, F_G, F_B), \qquad \mathbf{B} = (B_R, B_G, B_B) \tag{4-3}$$

We can thus calculate the value of parameter t using one of the RGB color components as

$$t = \frac{P_k - B_k}{F_k - B_k} \tag{4-4}$$

where $k = R, G,$ or B; and $F_k \neq B_k$. Theoretically, parameter t has the same value for each RGB component, but the round-off calculations to obtain integer codes can result in different values of t for different components. We can minimize this round-off error by selecting the component with the largest difference between **F** and **B**. This value of t is then used to mix the new fill color **NF** with the background color. We can accomplish this mixing using either a modified flood-fill or boundary-fill procedure, as described in Section 4-13.

Similar color-blending procedures can be applied to an area whose foreground color is to be merged with multiple background color areas, such as a checkerboard pattern. When two background colors B_1 and B_2 are mixed with foreground color **F**, the resulting pixel color **P** is

$$\mathbf{P} = t_0\mathbf{F} + t_1\mathbf{B}_1 + (1 - t_0 - t_1)\mathbf{B}_2 \tag{4-5}$$

where the sum of the color-term coefficients t_0, t_1, and $(1 - t_0 - t_1)$ must equal 1. We can set up two simultaneous equations using two of the three RGB color components to solve for the two proportionality parameters, t_0 and t_1. These parameters are then used to mix the new fill color with the two background colors to obtain the new pixel color. With three background colors and one foreground color, or with two background and two foreground colors, we need all three RGB equations to obtain the relative amounts of the four colors. For some foreground and background color combinations, however, the system of two or three RGB equations cannot be solved. This occurs when the color values are all very similar or when they are all proportional to each other.

4-10 GENERAL SCAN-LINE POLYGON-FILL ALGORITHM

A scan-line fill of a region is performed by first determining the intersection positions of the boundaries of the fill region with the screen scan lines. Then the fill colors are applied to each section of a scan line that lies within the interior of the fill region. The scan-line fill algorithm identifies the same interior regions as the odd-even rule (Section 3-15). The simplest area to fill is a polygon, because each scan-line intersection point with a polygon boundary is obtained by solving a pair of simultaneous linear equations, where the equation for the scan line is simply $y =$ constant.

Figure 4-20 illustrates the basic scan-line procedure for a solid-color fill of a polygon. For each scan line that crosses the polygon, the edge intersections are sorted from left to right, and then the pixel positions between, and including, each intersection pair are set to the specified fill color. In the example of Fig. 4-20, the four pixel intersection positions with the polygon boundaries define two stretches of interior pixels. Thus, the fill color is applied to the five pixels from $x = 10$ to $x = 14$ and to the seven pixels from $x = 18$ to $x = 24$. If a pattern fill is to be applied to the polygon, then the color for each pixel along a scan line is determined from its overlap position with the fill pattern.

However, the scan-line fill algorithm for a polygon is not quite as simple as Fig. 4-20 might suggest. Whenever a scan line passes through a vertex, it intersects two polygon edges at that point. In some cases, this can result in an odd number of boundary intersections for a scan line. Figure 4-21 shows two scan lines that cross a polygon fill area and intersect a vertex. Scan line y' intersects an even number of edges, and the two pairs of intersection points along this scan line correctly identify the interior pixel spans. But scan line y intersects five polygon edges. To

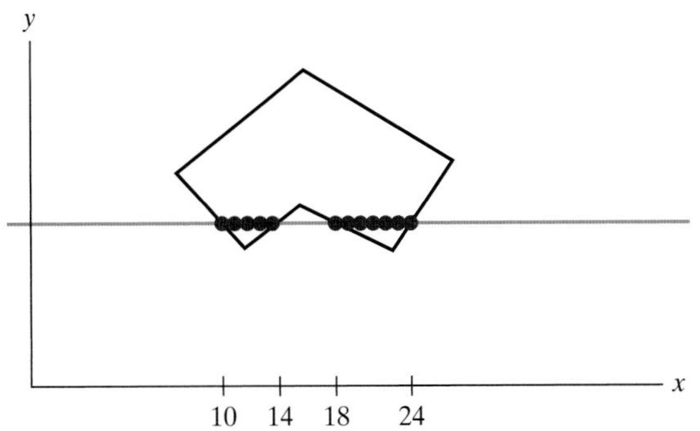

FIGURE 4-20 Interior pixels along a scan line passing through a polygon fill area.

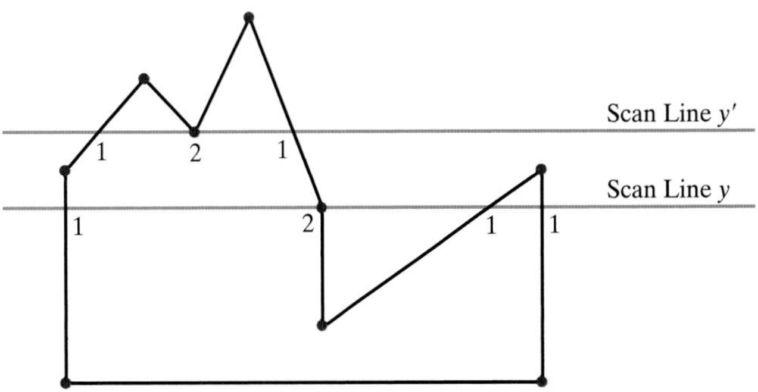

FIGURE 4-21 Intersection points along scan lines that intersect polygon vertices. Scan line y generates an odd number of intersections, but scan line y' generates an even number of intersections that can be paired to identify correctly the interior pixel spans.

identify the interior pixels for scan line y, we must count the vertex intersection as only one point. Thus, as we process scan lines, we need to distinguish between these cases.

We can detect the topological difference between scan line y and scan line y' in Fig. 4-21 by noting the position of the intersecting edges relative to the scan line. For scan line y, the two edges sharing an intersection vertex are on opposite sides of the scan line. But for scan line y', the two intersecting edges are both above the scan line. Thus, a vertex that has adjoining edges on opposite sides of an intersecting scan line should be counted as just one boundary intersection point. We can identify these vertices by tracing around the polygon boundary in either clockwise or counterclockwise order and observing the relative changes in vertex y coordinates as we move from one edge to the next. If the three endpoint y values of two consecutive edges monotonically increase or decrease, we need to count the shared (middle) vertex as a single intersection point for the scan line passing through that vertex. Otherwise, the shared vertex represents a local extremum (minimum or maximum) on the polygon boundary, and the two edge intersections with the scan line passing through that vertex can be added to the intersection list.

One method for implementing the adjustment to the vertex-intersection count is to shorten some polygon edges to split those vertices that should be counted as one intersection. We can process nonhorizontal edges around the polygon boundary in the order specified, either clockwise or counterclockwise. As we process each edge, we can check to determine whether that edge and the next nonhorizontal edge have either monotonically increasing or decreasing endpoint y values. If so, the lower edge can be shortened to ensure that only one intersection point is generated for the scan line going through the common vertex joining the two edges. Figure 4-22 illustrates shortening of an edge. When the endpoint y coordinates of the two edges are increasing, the y value of the upper endpoint for the current edge is decreased by 1, as in Fig. 4-22 (a). When the endpoint y values are monotonically decreasing, as in Fig. 4-22 (b), we decrease the y coordinate of the upper endpoint of the edge following the current edge.

Typically, certain properties of one part of a scene are related in some way to the properties in other parts of the scene, and these **coherence properties** can be used in computer-graphics algorithms to reduce processing. Coherence methods

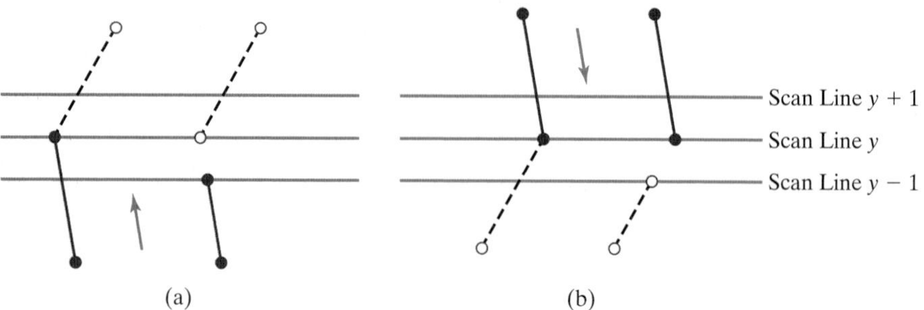

FIGURE 4-22 Adjusting endpoint y values for a polygon, as we process edges in order around the polygon perimeter. The edge currently being processed is indicated as a solid line. In (a), the y coordinate of the upper endpoint of the current edge is decreased by 1. In (b), the y coordinate of the upper endpoint of the next edge is decreased by 1.

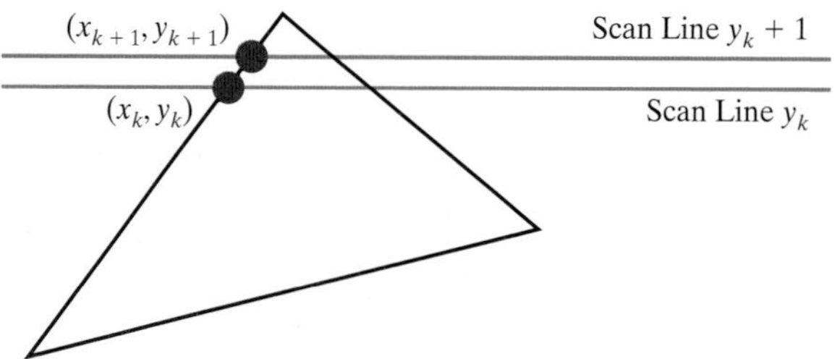

FIGURE 4-23 Two successive scan lines intersecting a polygon boundary.

often involve incremental calculations applied along a single scan line or between successive scan lines. For example, in determining fill-area edge intersections, we can set up incremental coordinate calculations along any edge by exploiting the fact that the slope of the edge is constant from one scan line to the next. Figure 4-23 shows two successive scan lines crossing the left edge of a triangle. The slope of this edge can be expressed in terms of the scan-line intersection coordinates:

$$m = \frac{y_{k+1} - y_k}{x_{k+1} - x_k} \tag{4-6}$$

Since the change in y coordinates between the two scan lines is simply

$$y_{k+1} - y_k = 1 \tag{4-7}$$

the x-intersection value x_{k+1} on the upper scan line can be determined from the x-intersection value x_k on the preceding scan line as

$$x_{k+1} = x_k + \frac{1}{m} \tag{4-8}$$

Each successive x intercept can thus be calculated by adding the inverse of the slope and rounding to the nearest integer.

An obvious parallel implementation of the fill algorithm is to assign each scan line that crosses the polygon to a separate processor. Edge intersection calculations are then performed independently. Along an edge with slope m, the intersection

x_k value for scan line k above the initial scan line can be calculated as

$$x_k = x_0 + \frac{k}{m} \tag{4-9}$$

In a sequential fill algorithm, the increment of x values by the amount $\frac{1}{m}$ along an edge can be accomplished with integer operations by recalling that the slope m is the ratio of two integers:

$$m = \frac{\Delta y}{\Delta x}$$

where Δx and Δy are the differences between the edge endpoint x and y coordinate values. Thus, incremental calculations of x intercepts along an edge for successive scan lines can be expressed as

$$x_{k+1} = x_k + \frac{\Delta x}{\Delta y} \tag{4-10}$$

Using this equation, we can perform integer evaluation of the x intercepts by initializing a counter to 0, then incrementing the counter by the value of Δx each time we move up to a new scan line. Whenever the counter value becomes equal to or greater than Δy, we increment the current x intersection value by 1 and decrease the counter by the value Δy. This procedure is equivalent to maintaining integer and fractional parts for x intercepts and incrementing the fractional part until we reach the next integer value.

As an example of this integer-incrementing scheme, suppose we have an edge with slope $m = \frac{7}{3}$. At the initial scan line, we set the counter to 0 and the counter increment to 3. As we move up to the next three scan lines along this edge, the counter is successively assigned the values 3, 6, and 9. On the third scan line above the initial scan line, the counter now has a value greater than 7. So we increment the x intersection coordinate by 1, and reset the counter to the value $9 - 7 = 2$. We continue determining the scan-line intersections in this way until we reach the upper endpoint of the edge. Similar calculations are carried out to obtain intersections for edges with negative slopes.

We can round to the nearest pixel x intersection value, instead of truncating to obtain integer positions, by modifying the edge-intersection algorithm so that the increment is compared to $\Delta y/2$. This can be done with integer arithmetic by incrementing the counter with the value $2\Delta x$ at each step and comparing the increment to Δy. When the increment is greater than or equal to Δy, we increase the x value by 1 and decrement the counter by the value of $2\Delta y$. In our previous example with $m = \frac{7}{3}$, the counter values for the first few scan lines above the initial scan line on this edge would now be 6, 12 (reduced to −2), 4, 10 (reduced to −4), 2, 8 (reduced to −6), 0, 6, and 12 (reduced to −2). Now x would be incremented on scan lines 2, 4, 6, 9, and so forth, above the initial scan line for this edge. The extra calculations required for each edge are $2\Delta x = \Delta x + \Delta x$ and $2\Delta y = \Delta y + \Delta y$, which are carried out as preprocessing steps.

To efficiently perform a polygon fill, we can first store the polygon boundary in a *sorted edge table* that contains all the information necessary to process the scan lines efficiently. Proceeding around the edges in either a clockwise or a counterclockwise order, we can use a bucket sort to store the edges, sorted on the smallest y value of each edge, in the correct scan-line positions. Only nonhorizontal edges are entered into the sorted edge table. As the edges are processed, we can also shorten certain edges to resolve the vertex-intersection question. Each entry in

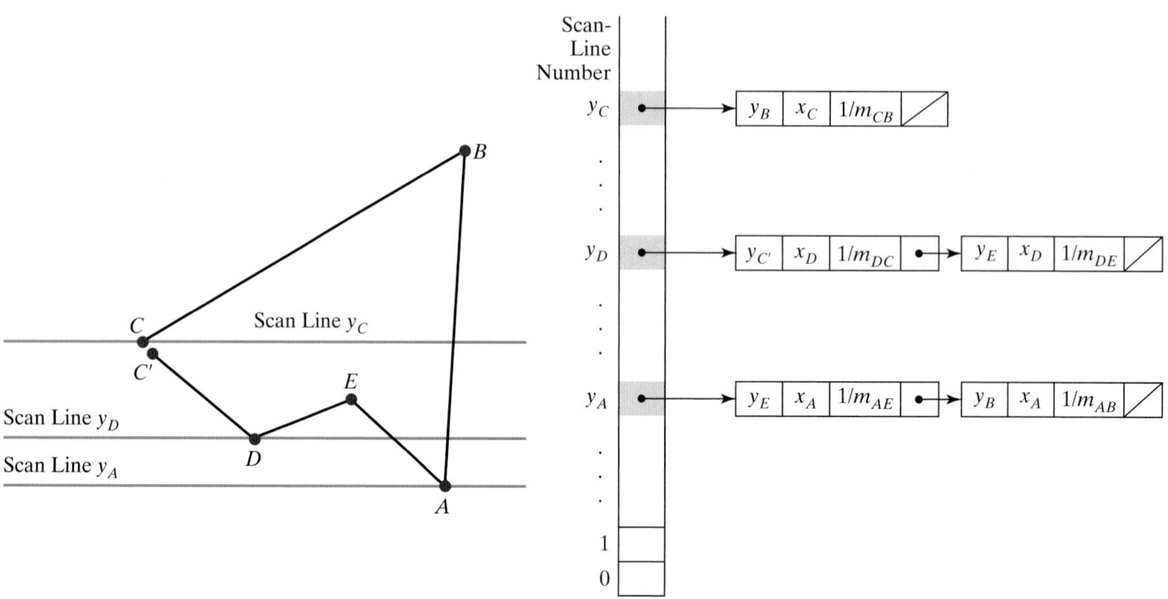

FIGURE 4–24 A polygon and its sorted edge table, with edge $\overline{\mathbf{DC}}$ shortened by one unit in the y direction.

the table for a particular scan line contains the maximum y value for that edge, the x-intercept value (at the lower vertex) for the edge, and the inverse slope of the edge. For each scan line, the edges are in sorted order from left to right. Figure 4-24 shows a polygon and the associated sorted edge table.

Next, we process the scan lines from the bottom of the polygon to its top, producing an *active edge list* for each scan line crossing the polygon boundaries. The active edge list for a scan line contains all edges crossed by that scan line, with iterative coherence calculations used to obtain the edge intersections.

Implementation of edge-intersection calculations can be facilitated by storing Δx and Δy values in the sorted edge list. Also, to ensure that we correctly fill the interior of specified polygons, we can apply the considerations discussed in Section 3-13. For each scan line, we fill in the pixel spans for each pair of x intercepts starting from the leftmost x intercept value and ending at one position before the rightmost x intercept. And each polygon edge can be shortened by one unit in the y direction at the top endpoint. These measures also guarantee that pixels in adjacent polygons will not overlap.

4-11 SCAN-LINE FILL OF CONVEX POLYGONS

When we apply a scan-line fill procedure to a convex polygon, there can be no more than a single interior span for each screen scan line. So we need to process the polygon edges only until we have found two boundary intersections for each scan line crossing the polygon interior.

The general polygon scan-line algorithm discussed in the preceding section can be simplified considerably for convex-polygon fill. We again use coordinate extents to determine which edges cross a scan line. Intersection calculations with these edges then determine the interior pixel span for that scan line, where any vertex crossing is counted as a single boundary intersection point. When a scan line intersects a single vertex (at an apex, for example), we plot only that point. Some graphics packages further restrict fill areas to be triangles. This makes filling even easier, because each triangle has just three edges to process.

4-12 SCAN-LINE FILL FOR REGIONS WITH CURVED BOUNDARIES

Since an area with curved boundaries is described with nonlinear equations, a scan-line fill generally takes more time than a polygon scan-line fill. We can use the same general approach detailed in Section 4-10, but the boundary intersection calculations are performed with curve equations. And the slope of the boundary is continuously changing, so we cannot use the straightforward incremental calculations that are possible with straight-line edges.

For simple curves such as circles or ellipses, we can apply fill methods similar to those for convex polygons. Each scan line crossing a circle or ellipse interior has just two boundary intersections. And we can determine these two intersection points along the boundary of a circle or an ellipse using the incremental calculations in the midpoint method. Then we simply fill in the horizontal pixel spans from one intersection point to the other. Symmetries between quadrants (and between octants for circles) are used to reduce the boundary calculations.

FIGURE 4-25 Interior fill of an elliptical arc.

Similar methods can be used to generate a fill area for a curve section. For example, an area bounded by an elliptical arc and a straight line section (Fig. 4-25) can be filled using a combination of curve and line procedures. Symmetries and incremental calculations are exploited whenever possible to reduce computations.

Filling other curve areas can involve considerably more processing. We could use similar incremental methods in combination with numerical techniques to determine the scan-line intersections, but usually such curve boundaries are approximated with straight-line segments.

4-13 FILL METHODS FOR AREAS WITH IRREGULAR BOUNDARIES

Another approach for filling a specified area is to start at an inside position and "paint" the interior, point by point, out to the boundary. This is a particularly useful technique for filling areas with irregular borders, such as a design created with a paint program. Generally, these methods require an input starting position inside the area to be filled and some color information about either the boundary or the interior.

We can fill irregular regions with a single color or with a color pattern. For a pattern fill, we overlay a color mask, as discussed in Section 4-9. As each pixel within the region is processed, its color is determined by the corresponding values in the overlaid pattern.

Boundary-Fill Algorithm

If the boundary of some region is specified in a single color, we can fill the interior of this region, pixel by pixel, until the boundary color is encountered. This method,

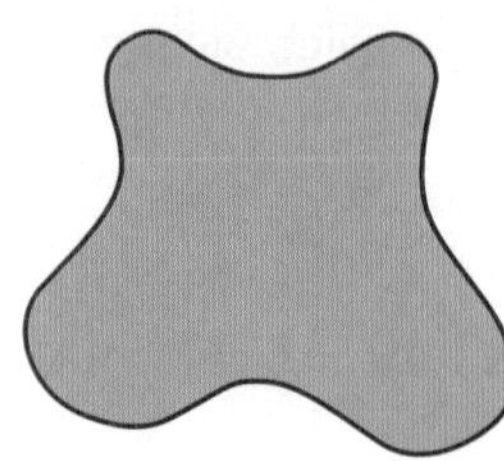
(a)

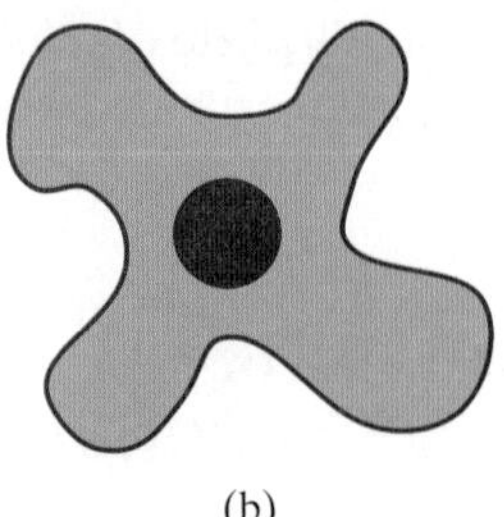
(b)

FIGURE 4-26 Example color boundaries for a boundary-fill procedure.

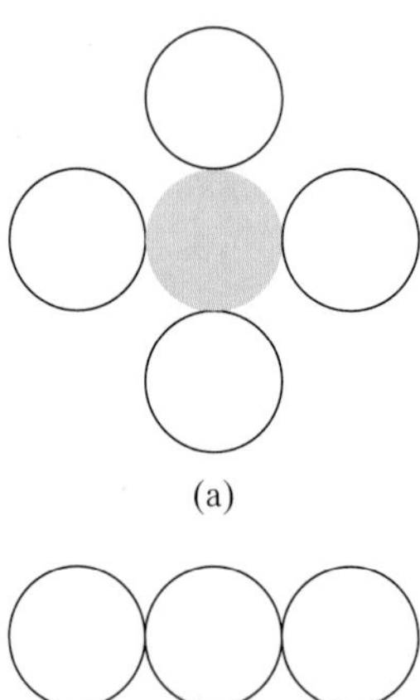
(a)

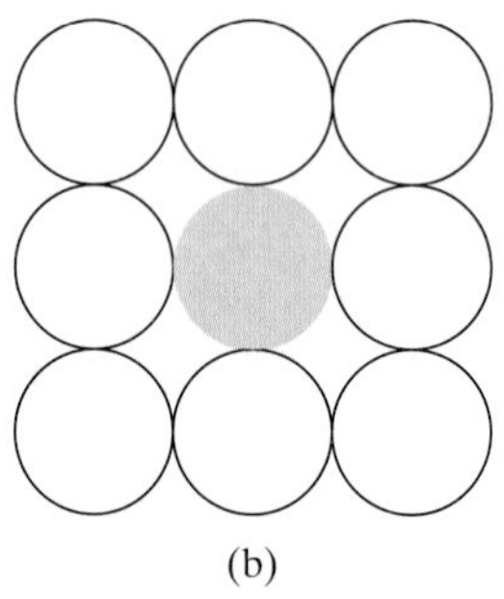
(b)

FIGURE 4-27 Fill methods applied to a 4-connected area (a) and to an 8-connected area (b). Hollow circles represent pixels to be tested from the current test position, shown as a solid color.

called the **boundary-fill algorithm,** is employed in interactive painting packages, where interior points are easily selected. Using a graphics tablet or other interactive device, an artist or designer can sketch a figure outline, select a fill color from a color menu, specify the area boundary color, and pick an interior point. The figure interior is then painted in the fill color. Both inner and outer boundaries can be set up to define an area for boundary fill, and Fig. 4-26 illustrates examples for specifying color regions.

Basically, a boundary-fill algorithm starts from an interior point (x, y) and tests the color of neighboring positions. If a tested position is not displayed in the boundary color, its color is changed to the fill color and its neighbors are tested. This procedure continues until all pixels are processed up to the designated boundary color for the area.

Figure 4-27 shows two methods for processing neighboring pixels from a current test position. In Fig. 4-27(a), four neighboring points are tested. These are the pixel positions that are right, left, above, and below the current pixel. Areas filled by this method are called **4-connected.** The second method, shown in Fig. 4-27(b), is used to fill more complex figures. Here the set of neighboring positions to be tested includes the four diagonal pixels, as well as those in the cardinal directions. Fill methods using this approach are called **8-connected.** An 8-connected boundary-fill algorithm would correctly fill the interior of the area defined in Fig. 4-28, but a 4-connected boundary-fill algorithm would only fill part of that region.

The following procedure illustrates a recursive method for painting a 4-connected area with a solid color, specified in parameter `fillColor`, up to a boundary color specified with parameter `borderColor`. We can extend this

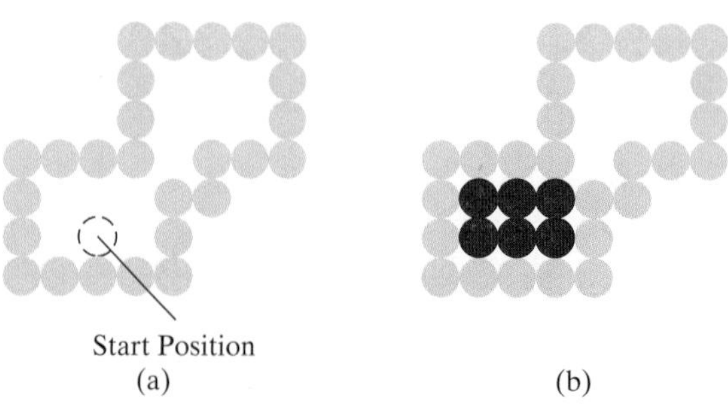

FIGURE 4-28 The area defined within the color boundary (a) is only partially filled in (b) using a 4-connected boundary-fill algorithm.

procedure to fill an 8-connected region by including four additional statements to test the diagonal positions ($x \pm 1, y \pm 1$).

```
void boundaryFill4 (int x, int y, int fillColor, int borderColor)
{
   int interiorColor;

   /* Set current color to fillColor, then perform following oprations. */
   getPixel (x, y, interiorColor);
   if ((interiorColor != borderColor) && (interiorColor != fillColor)) {
      setPixel (x, y);    // Set color of pixel to fillColor.
      boundaryFill4 (x + 1, y , fillColor, borderColor);
      boundaryFill4 (x - 1, y , fillColor, borderColor);
      boundaryFill4 (x , y + 1, fillColor, borderColor);
      boundaryFill4 (x , y - 1, fillColor, borderColor)
   }
}
```

Recursive boundary-fill algorithms may not fill regions correctly if some interior pixels are already displayed in the fill color. This occurs because the algorithm checks next pixels both for boundary color and for fill color. Encountering a pixel with the fill color can cause a recursive branch to terminate, leaving other interior pixels unfilled. To avoid this, we can first change the color of any interior pixels that are initially set to the fill color before applying the boundary-fill procedure.

Also, since this procedure requires considerable stacking of neighboring points, more efficient methods are generally employed. These methods fill horizontal pixel spans across scan lines, instead of proceeding to 4-connected or 8-connected neighboring points. Then we need only stack a beginning position for each horizontal pixel span, instead of stacking all unprocessed neighboring positions around the current position. Starting from the initial interior point with this method, we first fill in the contiguous span of pixels on this starting scan line. Then we locate and stack starting positions for spans on the adjacent scan lines, where spans are defined as the contiguous horizontal string of positions bounded by pixels displayed in the border color. At each subsequent step, we retrieve the next start position from the top of the stack and repeat the process.

An example of how pixel spans could be filled using this approach is illustrated for the 4-connected fill region in Figure 4-29. In this example, we first process scan lines successively from the start line to the top boundary. After all upper scan lines are processed, we fill in the pixel spans on the remaining scan lines in order down to the bottom boundary. The leftmost pixel position for each horizontal span is located and stacked, in left to right order across successive scan lines, as shown in Fig. 4-29. In (a) of this figure, the initial span has been filled, and starting positions 1 and 2 for spans on the next scan lines (below and above) are stacked. In Fig. 4-29(b), position 2 has been unstacked and processed to produce the filled span shown, and the starting pixel (position 3) for the single span on the next scan line has been stacked. After position 3 is processed, the filled spans and stacked positions are as shown in Fig. 4-29(c). And Fig. 4-29(d) shows the filled pixels after processing all spans in the upper right of the specified area. Position 5 is next processed, and spans are filled in the upper left of the region; then position 4 is picked up to continue the processing for the lower scan lines.

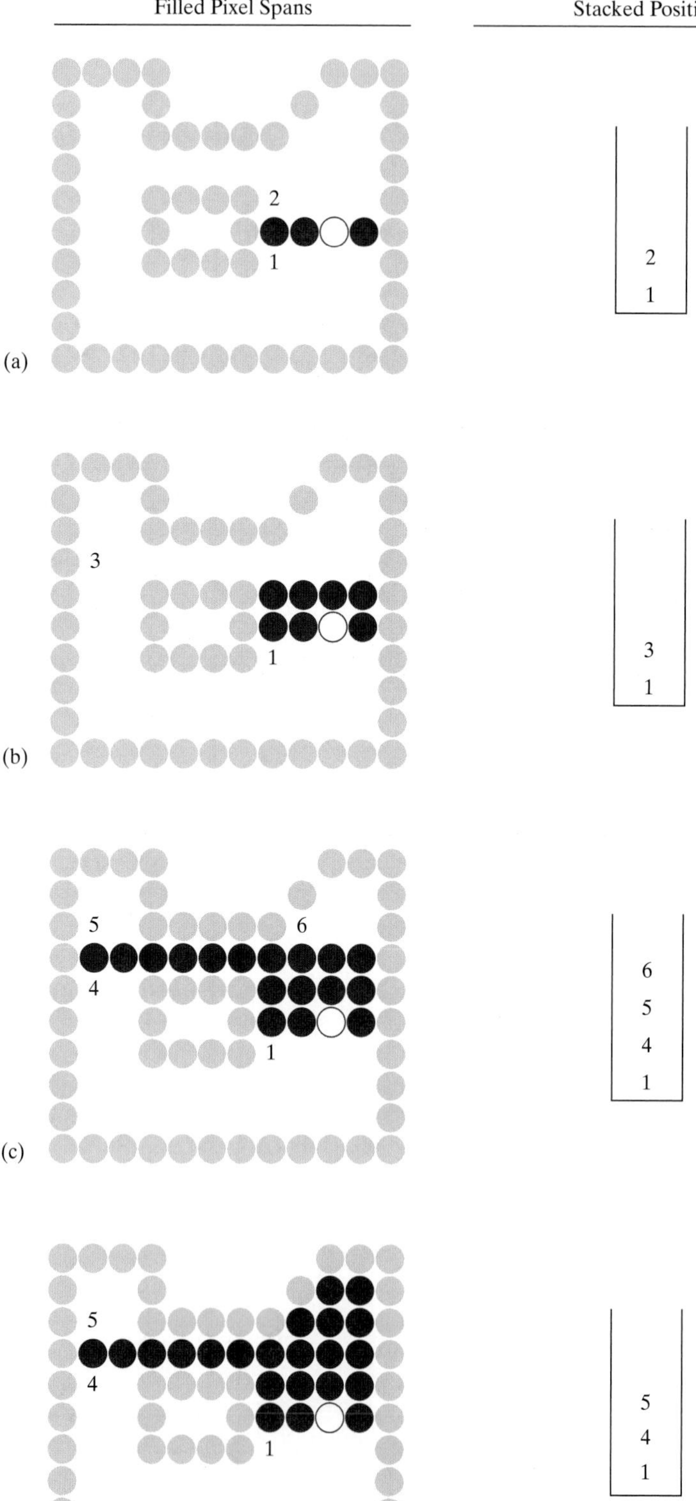

FIGURE 4-29 Boundary fill across pixel spans for a 4-connected area: (a) Initial scan line with a filled pixel span, showing the position of the initial point (hollow) and the stacked positions for pixel spans on adjacent scan lines. (b) Filled pixel span on the first scan line above the initial scan line and the current contents of the stack. (c) Filled pixel spans on the first two scan lines above the initial scan line and the current contents of the stack. (d) Completed pixel spans for the upper-right portion of the defined region and the remaining stacked positions to be processed.

Flood-Fill Algorithm

Sometimes we want to fill in (or recolor) an area that is not defined within a single color boundary. Figure 4-30 shows an area bordered by several different color regions. We can paint such areas by replacing a specified interior color instead of searching for a particular boundary color. This fill procedure is called a **flood-fill algorithm.** We start from a specified interior point (x, y) and reassign all pixel values that are currently set to a given interior color with the desired fill color. If the area we want to paint has more than one interior color, we can first reassign pixel values so that all interior points have the same color. Using either a 4-connected or 8-connected approach, we then step through pixel positions until all interior points have been repainted. The following procedure flood fills a 4-connected region recursively, starting from the input position.

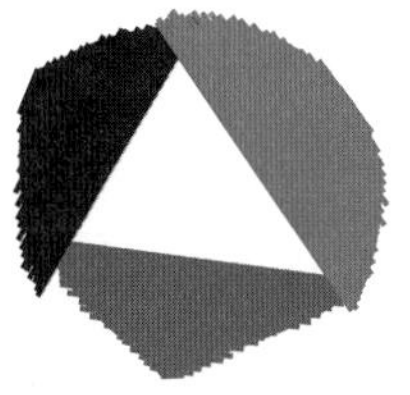

FIGURE 4-30 An area defined within multiple color boundaries.

```
void floodFill4 (int x, int y, int fillColor, int interiorColor)
{
   int color;

   /* Set current color to fillColor, then perform following operations. */
   getPixel (x, y, color);
   if (color = interiorColor) {
      setPixel (x, y);      // Set color of pixel to fillColor.
      floodFill4 (x + 1, y, fillColor, interiorColor);
      floodFill4 (x - 1, y, fillColor, interiorColor);
      floodFill4 (x, y + 1, fillColor, interiorColor);
      floodFill4 (x, y - 1, fillColor, interiorColor)
   }
}
```

We can modify the above procedure to reduce the storage requirements of the stack by filling horizontal pixel spans, as discussed for the boundary-fill algorithm. In this approach, we stack only the beginning positions for those pixel spans having the value `interiorColor`. The steps in this modified flood-fill algorithm are similar to those illustrated in Fig. 4-29 for a boundary fill. Starting at the first position of each span, the pixel values are replaced until a value other than `interiorColor` is encountered.

4-14 OpenGL FILL-AREA ATTRIBUTE FUNCTIONS

In the OpenGL graphics package, fill-area routines are available for convex polygons only. We generate displays of filled convex polygons in four steps:

(1) Define a fill pattern.

(2) Invoke the polygon-fill routine.

(3) Activate the polygon-fill feature of OpenGL.

(4) Describe the polygons to be filled.

A polygon fill pattern is displayed up to and including the polygon edges. Thus, there are no boundary lines around the fill region unless we specifically add them to the display.

In addition to specifying a fill pattern for a polygon interior, there are a number of other options available. One option is to display a hollow polygon, where no interior color or pattern is applied and only the edges are generated. A hollow polygon is equivalent to the display of a closed polyline primitive. Another option is to show the polygon vertices, with no interior fill and no edges. Also, we designate different attributes for the front and back faces of a polygon fill area.

OpenGL Fill-Pattern Function

By default, a convex polygon is displayed as a solid-color region, using the current color setting. To fill the polygon with a pattern in OpenGL, we use a 32-bit by 32-bit mask. A value of 1 in the mask indicates that the corresponding pixel is to be set to the current color, and a 0 leaves the value of that frame-buffer position unchanged. The fill pattern is specified in unsigned bytes using the OpenGL data type `GLubyte`, just as we did with the `glBitmap` function. We define a bit pattern with hexadecimal values as, for example,

```
GLubyte fillPattern [ ] = {
    0xff, 0x00, 0xff, 0x00, ... };
```

The bits must be specified starting with the bottom row of the pattern, and continuing up to the topmost row (32) of the pattern, as we did with `bitShape` in Section 3-19. This pattern is replicated across the entire area of the display window, starting at the lower-left window corner, and specified polygons are filled where the pattern overlaps those polygons (Fig. 4-31).

Once we have set a mask, we can establish it as the current fill pattern with the function

```
glPolygonStipple (fillPattern);
```

Next, we need to enable the fill routines before we specify the vertices for the polygons that are to be filled with the current pattern. We do this with the statement

```
glEnable (GL_POLYGON_STIPPLE);
```

Similarly, we turn off pattern filling with

```
glDisable (GL_POLYGON_STIPPLE);
```

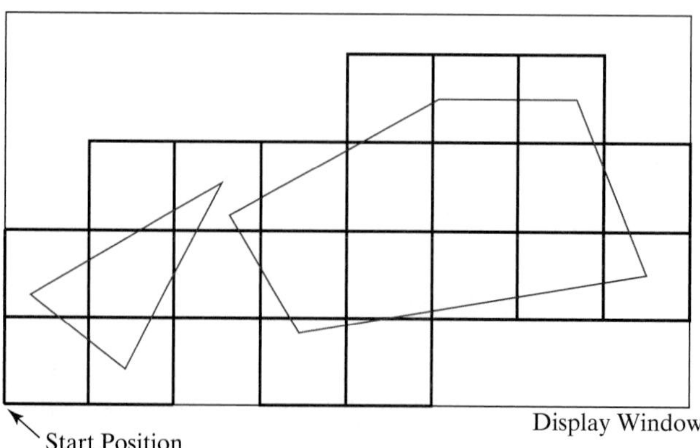

FIGURE 4-31 Tiling a rectangular fill pattern across a display window to fill two convex polygons.

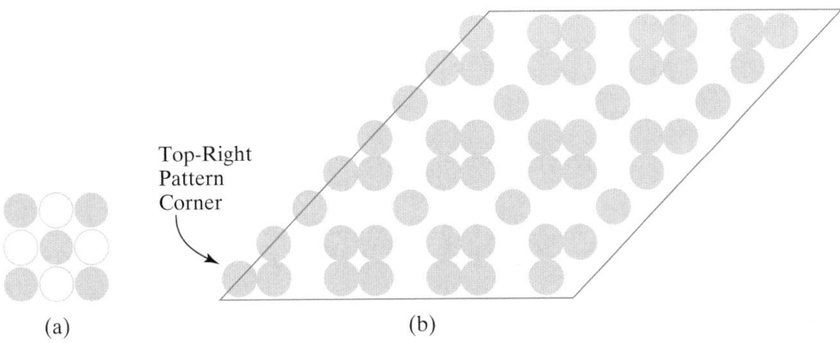

FIGURE 4-32 A 3 by 3 bit pattern (a) superimposed on a parallelogram to produce the fill area in (b), where the top-right corner of the pattern coincides with the lower-left corner of the parallelogram.

Figure 4-32 illustrates how a 3 by 3 bit pattern, repeated over a 32 by 32 bit mask, might be applied to fill a parallelogram.

OpenGL Texture and Interpolation Patterns

Another method for filling polygons is to use texture patterns, as discussed in Chapter 10. This can produce fill patterns that simulate the surface appearance of wood, brick, brushed steel, or some other material. Also, we can obtain an interpolation coloring of a polygon interior just as we did with the line primitive. To do this, we assign different colors to polygon vertices. Interpolation fill of a polygon interior is used to produce realistic displays of shaded surfaces under various lighting conditions.

As an example of an interpolation fill, the following code segment assigns either a blue, red, or green color to each of the three vertices of a triangle. The polygon fill is then a linear interpolation of the colors at the vertices.

```
glShadeModel (GL_SMOOTH);

glBegin (GL_TRIANGLES);
   glColor3f (0.0, 0.0, 1.0);
   glVertex2i (50, 50);
   glColor3f (1.0, 0.0, 0.0);
   glVertex2i (150, 50);
   glColor3f (0.0, 1.0, 0.0);
   glVertex2i (75, 150);
glEnd ( );
```

Of course, if a single color is set for the triangle as a whole, the polygon is filled with that one color. And if we change the argument in the `glShadeModel` function to `GL_FLAT` in this example, the polygon is filled with the last color specified (green). The value `GL_SMOOTH` is the default shading, but we can include that specification to remind us that the polygon is to be filled as an interpolation of the vertex colors.

OpenGL Wire-Frame Methods

We can also choose to show only polygon edges. This produces a wire-frame or hollow display of the polygon. Or we could display a polygon by only plotting a set of points at the vertex positions. These options are selected with the function

```
glPolygonMode (face, displayMode);
```

We use parameter `face` to designate which face of the polygon we want to show as edges only or vertices only. This parameter is then assigned either `GL_FRONT`, `GL_BACK`, or `GL_FRONT_AND_BACK`. Then, if we want only the polygon edges displayed for our selection, we assign the constant `GL_LINE` to parameter `displayMode`. To plot only the polygon vertex points, we assign the constant `GL_POINT` to parameter `displayMode`. A third option is `GL_FILL`. But this is the default display mode, so we usually only invoke `glPolygonMode` when we want to set attributes for the polygon edges or vertices.

Another option is to display a polygon with both an interior fill and a different color or pattern for its edges (or for its vertices). This is accomplished by specifying the polygon twice: once with parameter `displayMode` set to `GL_FILL` and then again with `displayMode` set to `GL_LINE` (or `GL_POINT`). For example, the following code section fills a polygon interior with a green color, and then the edges are assigned a red color.

```
glColor3f (0.0, 1.0, 0.0);
\* Invoke polygon-generating routine. */

glColor3f (1.0, 0.0, 0.0);
glPolygonMode (GL_FRONT, GL_LINE);
\* Invoke polygon-generating routine again. */
```

For a three-dimensional polygon (one that does not have all vertices in the xy plane), this method for displaying the edges of a filled polygon may produce gaps along the edges. This effect, sometimes referred to as **stitching,** is caused by differences between calculations in the scan-line fill algorithm and calculations in the edge line-drawing algorithm. As the interior of a three-dimensional polygon is filled, the depth value (distance from the xy plane) is calculated for each (x, y) position. But this depth value at an edge of the polygon is often not exactly the same as the depth value calculated by the line-drawing algorithm for the same (x, y) position. Therefore, when visibility tests are made, the interior fill color could be used instead of an edge color to display some points along the boundary of a polygon.

One way to eliminate the gaps along displayed edges of a three-dimensional polygon is to shift the depth values calculated by the fill routine so that they do not overlap with the edge depth values for that polygon. We do this with the following two OpenGL functions.

```
glEnable (GL_POLYGON_OFFSET_FILL);
glPolygonOffset (factor1, factor2);
```

The first function activates the offset routine for scan-line filling, and the second function is used to set a couple of floating-point values `factor1` and `factor2` that are used to calculate the amount of depth offset. The calculation for this depth offset is

$$\text{depthOffset} = \text{factor1} \cdot \text{maxSlope} + \text{factor2} \cdot \text{const} \qquad (4\text{-}11)$$

where maxSlope is the maximum slope of the polygon and const is an implementation constant. For a polygon in the xy plane, the slope is 0. Otherwise, the maximum slope is calculated as the change in depth of the polygon divided by either the change in x or the change in y. A typical value for the two factors is either 0.75 or 1.0, although some experimentation with the factor values is often necessary to produce good results. As an example of assigning values to offset factors, we can modify the previous code segment as follows:

```
glColor3f (0.0, 1.0, 0.0);
glEnable (GL_POLYGON_OFFSET_FILL);
glPolygonOffset (1.0, 1.0);
\* Invoke polygon-generating routine. */
glDisable (GL_POLYGON_OFFSET_FILL);

glColor3f (1.0, 0.0, 0.0);
glPolygonMode (GL_FRONT, GL_LINE);
\* Invoke polygon-generating routine again. */
```

Now the interior fill of the polygon is pushed a little farther away in depth, so that it does not interfere with the depth values of its edges. It is also possible to implement this method by applying the offset to the line-drawing algorithm, by changing the argument of the `glEnable` function to `GL_POLYGON_OFFSET_LINE`. In this case, we want to use negative factors to bring the edge depth values closer. And if we just wanted to display different color points at the vertex positions, instead of highlighted edges, the argument in the `glEnable` function would be `GL_POLYGON_OFFSET_POINT`.

Another method for eliminating the stitching effect along polygon edges is to use the OpenGL stencil buffer to limit the polygon interior filling so that it does not overlap the edges. But this approach is more complicated and generally slower, so the polygon depth-offset method is preferred.

To display a concave polygon using OpenGL routines, we must first split it into a set of convex polygons. We typically divide a concave polygon into a set of triangles, using the methods described in Section 3-15. Then we could display the concave polygon as a fill region by filling the triangles. Similarly, if we want to show only the polygon vertices, we plot the triangle vertices. But to display the original concave polygon in a wire-frame form, we cannot just set the display mode to `GL_LINE`, because that would show all the triangle edges that are interior to the original concave polygon (Fig. 4-33).

Fortunately, OpenGL provides a mechanism that allows us to eliminate selected edges from a wire-frame display. Each polygon vertex is stored with a one-bit flag that indicates whether or not that vertex is connected to the next vertex by a boundary edge. So all we need do is set that bit flag to "off" and the edge

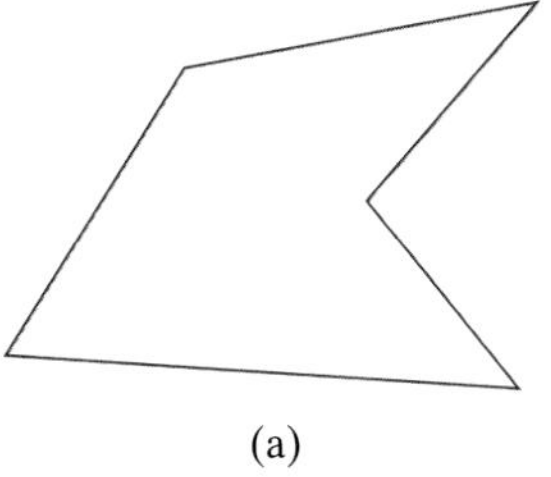
(a)

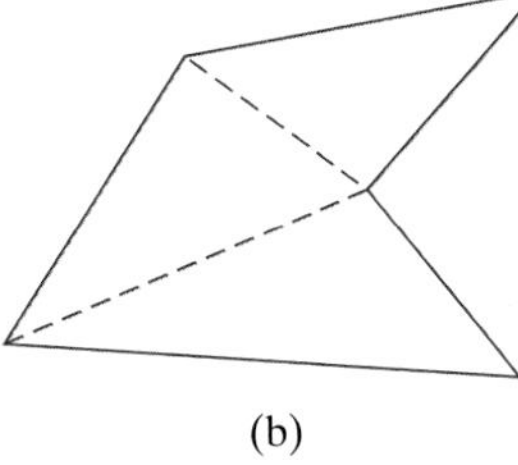
(b)

FIGURE 4-33 Dividing a concave polygon (a) into a set of triangles (b) produces triangle edges (dashed) that are interior to the original polygon.

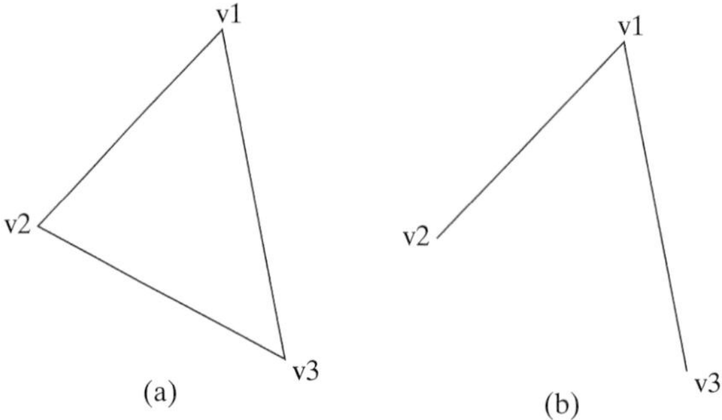

FIGURE 4–34 The triangle in (a) can be displayed as in (b) by setting the edge flag for vertex v2 to the value GL_FALSE, assuming that the vertices are specified in a counterclockwise order.

following that vertex will not be displayed. We set this flag for an edge with the following function.

```
glEdgeFlag (flag);
```

To indicate that a vertex does not precede a boundary edge, we assign the OpenGL constant `GL_FALSE` to parameter `flag`. This applies to all subsequently specified vertices until the next call to `glEdgeFlag` is made. The OpenGL constant `GL_TRUE` turns the edge flag back on again, which is the default. Function `glEdgeFlag` can be placed between `glBegin`/`glEnd` pairs. As an illustration of the use of an edge flag, the following code displays only two edges of the defined triangle (Fig. 4-34).

```
glPolygonMode (GL_FRONT_AND_BACK, GL_LINE);

glBegin (GL_POLYGON);
   glVertex3fv (v1);
   glEdgeFlag (GL_FALSE);
   glVertex3fv (v2);
   glEdgeFlag (GL_TRUE);
   glVertex3fv (v3);
glEnd ( );
```

Polygon edge flags can also be specified in an array that could be combined or associated with a vertex array (Sections 3-17 and 4-3). The statements for creating an array of edge flags are

```
glEnableClientState (GL_EDGE_FLAG_ARRAY);

glEdgeFlagPointer (offset, edgeFlagArray);
```

Parameter `offset` indicates the number of bytes between the values for the edge flags in the array `edgeFlagArray`. The default value for parameter `offset` is 0.

OpenGL Front-Face Function

Although, by default, the ordering of polygon vertices controls the identification of front and back faces, we can independently label selected surfaces in a scene as front or back with the function

```
glFrontFace (vertexOrder);
```

If we set parameter `vertexOrder` to the OpenGL constant `GL_CW`, then a subsequently defined polygon with a clockwise ordering for its vertices is considered to be front facing. This OpenGL feature can be used to swap faces of a polygon for which we have specified vertices in a clockwise order. The constant GL_CCW labels a counterclockwise ordering of polygon vertices as front facing, which is the default ordering.

4-15 CHARACTER ATTRIBUTES

We control the appearance of displayed characters with attributes such as font, size, color, and orientation. In many packages, attributes can be set both for entire character strings (text) and for individual characters that can be used for special purposes such as plotting a data graph.

There are a great many possible text-display options. First of all, there is the choice of font (or typeface), which is a set of characters with a particular design style such as New York, Courier, Helvetica, London, Times Roman, and various special symbol groups. The characters in a selected font can also be displayed with assorted underlining styles (solid, dotted, double), in **boldface,** in *italics,* and in OUTLINE or shadow styles.

Color settings for displayed text can be stored in the system attribute list and used by the procedures that generate character definitions in the frame buffer. When a character string is to be displayed, the current color is used to set pixel values in the frame buffer corresponding to the character shapes and positions.

We could adjust text size by scaling the overall dimensions (height and width) of characters or by scaling only the height or the width. Character size (height) is specified by printers and compositors in *points,* where 1 point is about 0.035146 centimeters (or 0.013837 inch, which is approximately $\frac{1}{72}$ inch). For example, the characters in this book are set in a 10-point font. Point measurements specify the size of the *body* of a character (Fig. 4-35), but different fonts with the same point specifications can have different character sizes, depending on the design of the typeface. The distance between the *bottomline* and the *topline* of the character body is the same for all characters in a particular size and typeface, but the body width may vary. *Proportionally spaced fonts* assign a smaller body width to narrow characters such as i, j, l, and f compared to broad characters such as W or M. *Character height* is defined as the distance between the *baseline* and the *capline* of characters. Kerned characters, such as f and j in Fig. 4-35, typically extend beyond the character body limits, and letters with descenders (g, j, p, q, y) extend below the baseline. Each character is positioned within the character body by a font designer in such a way that suitable spacing is attained along and between print lines when text is displayed with character bodies touching.

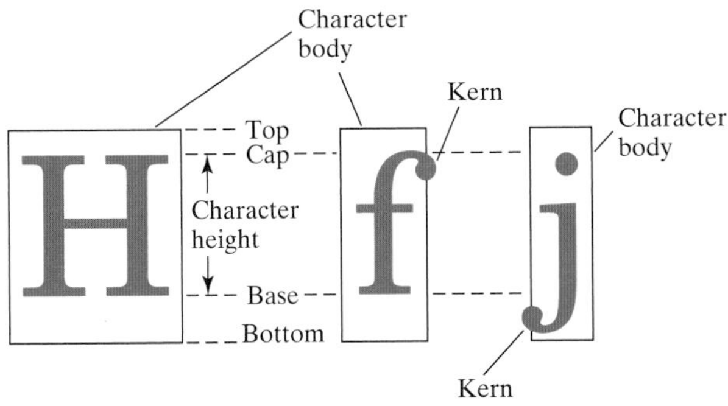

FIGURE 4-35 Examples of character bodies.

Height 1

Height 2

Height 3

FIGURE 4-36 Text strings displayed with different character-height settings and a constant width-to-height ratio.

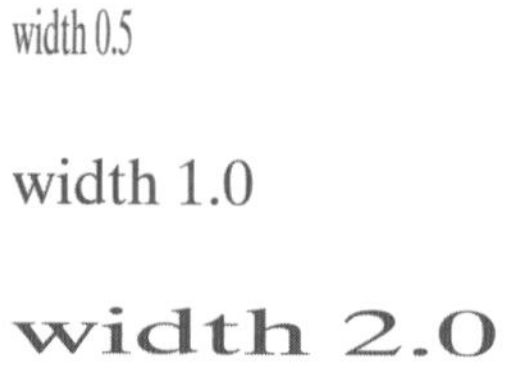

width 0.5

width 1.0

width 2.0

FIGURE 4-37 Text strings displayed with varying sizes for the character widths and a fixed height.

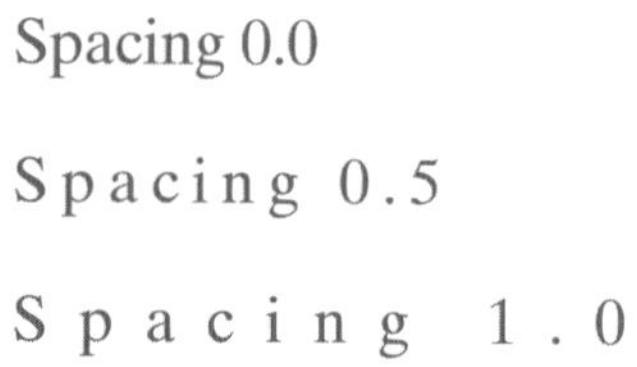

Spacing 0.0

S p a c i n g 0 . 5

S p a c i n g   1 . 0

FIGURE 4-38 Text strings displayed with different character-spacing values.

Up Vector
(a)

SLANTED TEXT

(b)

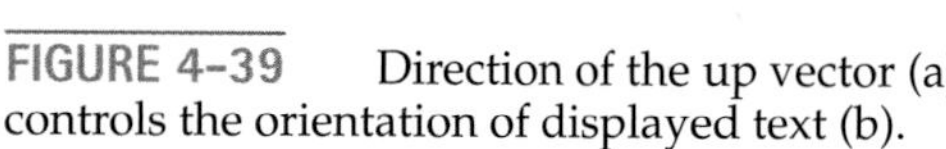

FIGURE 4-39 Direction of the up vector (a) controls the orientation of displayed text (b).

FIGURE 4-40 Text-path attributes can be set to produce horizontal or vertical arrangements of character strings.

Sometimes, text size is adjusted without changing the width-to-height ratio of characters. Figure 4-36 shows a character string displayed with three different character heights, while maintaining the ratio of width to height. Examples of text displayed with a constant height and varying widths are given in Fig. 4-37.

Spacing between characters is another attribute that can often be assigned to a character string. Figure 4-38 shows a character string displayed with three different settings for the intercharacter spacing.

The orientation for a character string can be set according to the direction of a **character up vector.** Text is then displayed so that the orientation of characters from baseline to capline is in the direction of the up vector. For example, with the direction of the up vector at 45°, text would be displayed as shown in Fig. 4-39. A procedure for orienting text could rotate characters so that the sides of character bodies, from baseline to capline, are aligned with the up vector. The rotated character shapes are then scan converted into the frame buffer.

It is useful in many applications to be able to arrange character strings vertically or horizontally. Examples of this are given in Fig. 4-40. We could also arrange the characters in a text string so that the string is displayed forward or backward. Examples of text displayed with these options are shown in Fig. 4-41. A procedure for implementing text-path orientation adjusts the position of the individual characters in the frame buffer according to the option selected.

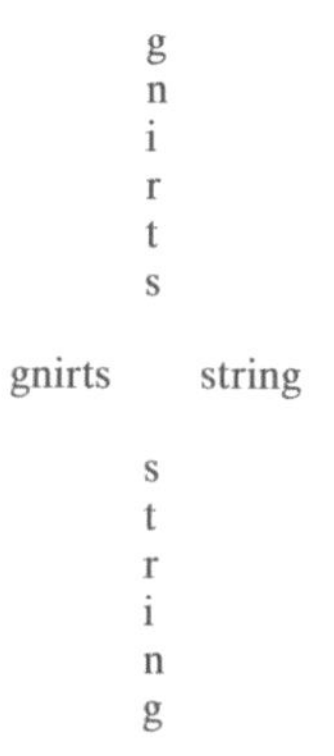

FIGURE 4-41 A text string displayed with the four text-path options: left, right, up, and down.

Character strings could also be oriented using a combination of up-vector and text-path specifications to produce slanted text. Fig. 4-42 shows the directions

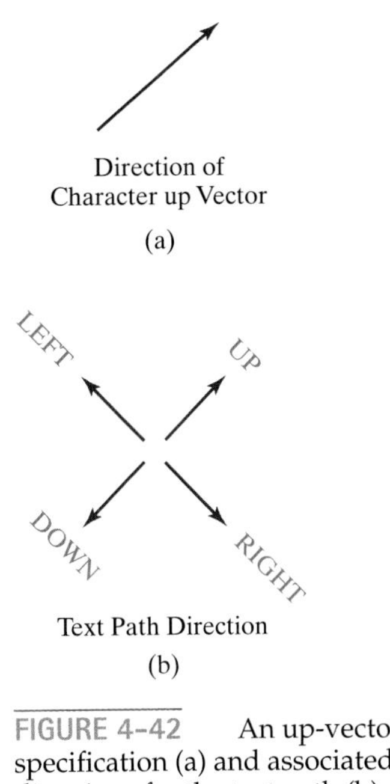

FIGURE 4-42 An up-vector specification (a) and associated directions for the text path (b).

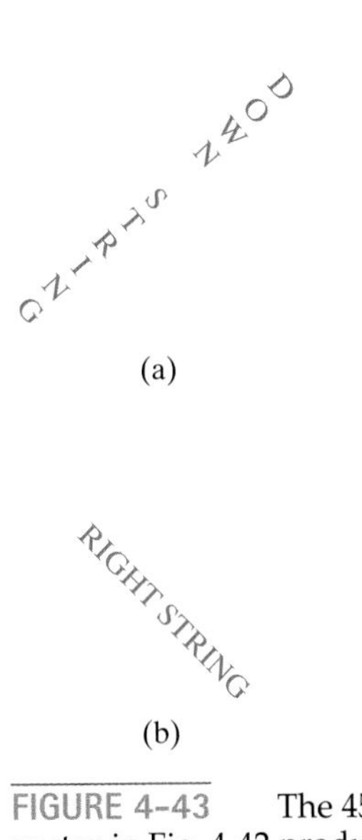

FIGURE 4-43 The 45° up vector in Fig. 4-42 produces the display (a) for a *down* path and the display (b) for a *right* path.

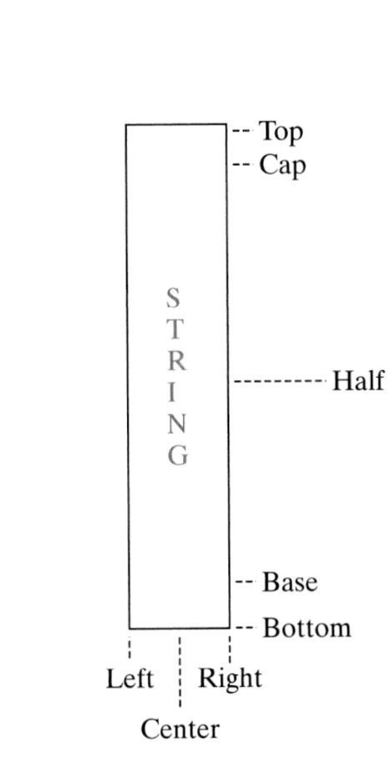

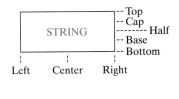

FIGURE 4-44 Character alignments for horizontal and vertical strings.

of character strings generated by various text path settings for a 45° up vector. Examples of character strings generated for text-path values *down* and *right* with this up vector are illustrated in Fig. 4-43.

Another possible attribute for character strings is alignment. This attribute specifies how text is to be displayed with respect to a reference position. For example, individual characters could be aligned according to the base lines or the character centers. Figure 4-44 illustrates typical character positions for horizontal and vertical alignments. String alignments are also possible, and Fig. 4-45 shows common alignment positions for horizontal and vertical text labels.

In some graphics packages, a text-precision attribute is also available. This parameter specifies the amount of detail and the particular processing options that are to be used with a text string. For a low-precision text string, many attribute selections, such as text path, are ignored, and faster procedures are used for processing the characters through the viewing pipeline.

Finally, a library of text-processing routines often supplies a set of special characters, such as a small circle or cross, which are useful in various applications. Most often these characters are used as marker symbols in network layouts or in graphing data sets. The attributes for these marker symbols are typically *color* and *size*.

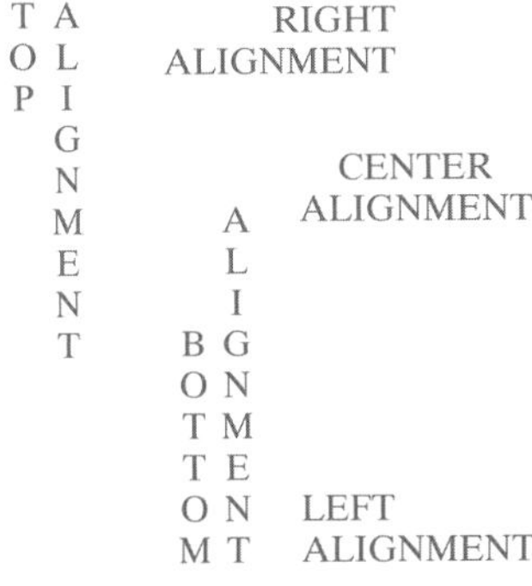

FIGURE 4-45 Character-string alignments.

4-16 OpenGL CHARACTER-ATTRIBUTE FUNCTIONS

We have two methods for displaying characters with the OpenGL package. Either we can design a font set using the bitmap functions in the core library, or we can invoke the GLUT character-generation routines. The GLUT library contains functions for displaying predefined bitmap and stroke character sets. Therefore, the character attributes we can set are those that apply to either bitmaps or line segments.

For either bitmap or outline fonts, the display color is determined by the current color state. In general, the spacing and size of characters is determined by the font designation, such as `GLUT_BITMAP_9_BY_15` and `GLUT_STROKE_MONO_ROMAN`. But we can also set the line width and line type for the outline fonts. We specify the width for a line with the `glLineWidth` function, and we select a line type with the `glLineStipple` function. The GLUT stroke fonts will then be displayed using the current values we specified for the OpenGL line-width and line-type attributes.

We can accomplish some other text-display characteristics using the transformation functions described in Chapter 5. The transformation routines allow us to scale, position, and rotate the GLUT stroke characters in either two-dimensional space or three-dimensional space. In addition, the three-dimensional viewing transformations (Chapter 7) can be used to generate other display effects.

4-17 ANTIALIASING

Line segments and other graphics primitives generated by the raster algorithms discussed in Chapter 3 have a jagged, or stair-step, appearance because the sampling process digitizes coordinate points on an object to discrete integer pixel positions. This distortion of information due to low-frequency sampling (undersampling) is called **aliasing.** We can improve the appearance of displayed raster lines by applying **antialiasing** methods that compensate for the undersampling process.

An example of the effects of undersampling is shown in Fig. 4-46. To avoid losing information from such periodic objects, we need to set the sampling frequency to at least twice that of the highest frequency occurring in the object, referred to as the **Nyquist sampling frequency** (or Nyquist sampling rate) f_s:

$$f_s = 2 f_{\max} \tag{4-12}$$

Another way to state this is that the sampling interval should be no larger than one-half the cycle interval (called the **Nyquist sampling interval**). For x-interval sampling, the Nyquist sampling interval Δx_s is

$$\Delta x_s = \frac{\Delta x_{\text{cycle}}}{2} \tag{4-13}$$

where $\Delta x_{\text{cycle}} = 1/f_{\max}$. In Fig. 4-46, our sampling interval is one and one-half

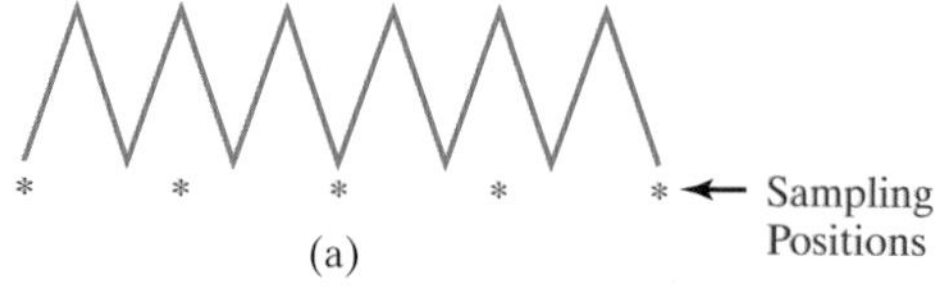

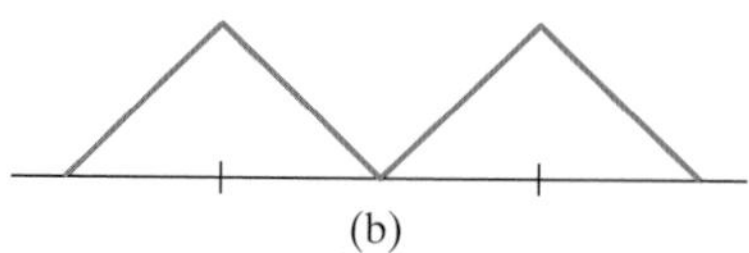

FIGURE 4-46 Sampling the periodic shape in (a) at the indicated positions produces the aliased lower-frequency representation in (b).

times the cycle interval, so the sampling interval is at least three times too large. If we want to recover all the object information for this example, we need to cut the sampling interval down to one-third the size shown in the figure.

One way to increase sampling rate with raster systems is simply to display objects at higher resolution. But even at the highest resolution possible with current technology, the jaggies will be apparent to some extent. There is a limit to how big we can make the frame buffer and still maintain the refresh rate at 60 frames or more per second. And to represent objects accurately with continuous parameters, we need arbitrarily small sampling intervals. Therefore, unless hardware technology is developed to handle arbitrarily large frame buffers, increased screen resolution is not a complete solution to the aliasing problem.

With raster systems that are capable of displaying more than two intensity levels per color, we can apply antialiasing methods to modify pixel intensities. By appropriately varying the intensities of pixels along the boundaries of primitives, we can smooth the edges to lessen their jagged appearance.

A straightforward antialiasing method is to increase sampling rate by treating the screen as if it were covered with a finer grid than is actually available. We can then use multiple sample points across this finer grid to determine an appropriate intensity level for each screen pixel. This technique of sampling object characteristics at a high resolution and displaying the results at a lower resolution is called **supersampling** (or **postfiltering,** since the general method involves computing intensities at subpixel grid positions, then combining the results to obtain the pixel intensities). Displayed pixel positions are spots of light covering a finite area of the screen, and not infinitesimal mathematical points. Yet in the line and fill-area algorithms we have discussed, the intensity of each pixel is determined by the location of a single point on the object boundary. By supersampling, we obtain intensity information from multiple points that contribute to the overall intensity of a pixel.

An alternative to supersampling is to determine pixel intensity by calculating the areas of overlap of each pixel with the objects to be displayed. Antialiasing by computing overlap areas is referred to as **area sampling** (or **prefiltering,** since the intensity of the pixel as a whole is determined without calculating subpixel intensities). Pixel overlap areas are obtained by determining where object boundaries intersect individual pixel boundaries.

Raster objects can also be antialiased by shifting the display location of pixel areas. This technique, called **pixel phasing,** is applied by "micropositioning" the electron beam in relation to object geometry. For example, pixel positions along a straight-line segment can be moved closer to the defined line path to smooth out the raster stair-step effect.

Supersampling Straight-Line Segments

We can perform supersampling in several ways. For a straight-line segment, we can divide each pixel into a number of subpixels and count the number of subpixels that overlap the line path. The intensity level for each pixel is then set to a value that is proportional to this subpixel count. An example of this method is given in Fig. 4-47. Each square pixel area is divided into nine equal-sized square subpixels, and the shaded regions show the subpixels that would be selected by Bresenham's algorithm. This scheme provides for three intensity settings above zero, since the maximum number of subpixels that can be selected within any pixel is three. For this example, the pixel at position (10, 20) is set to the

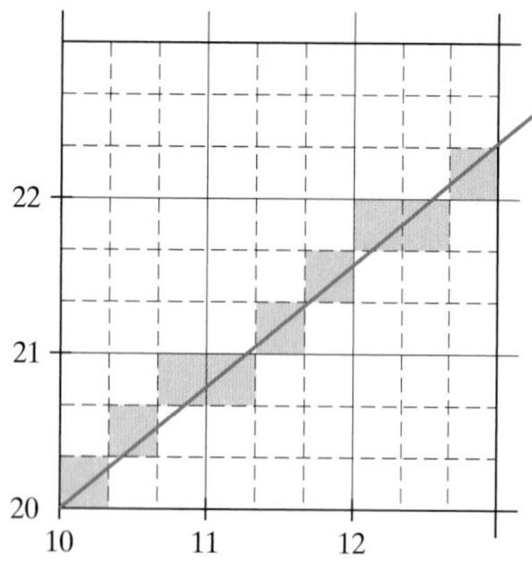

FIGURE 4–47 Supersampling subpixel positions along a straight-line segment whose left endpoint is at screen coordinates (10, 20).

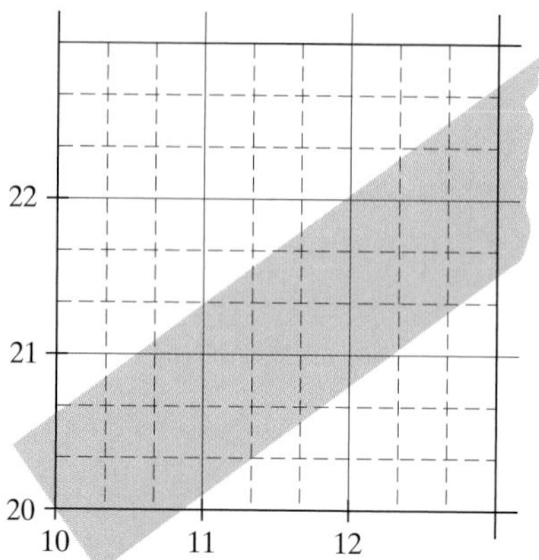

FIGURE 4–48 Supersampling subpixel positions in relation to the interior of a line of finite width.

maximum intensity (level 3); pixels at (11, 21) and (12, 21) are each set to the next highest intensity (level 2); and pixels at (11, 20) and (12, 22) are each set to the lowest intensity above zero (level 1). Thus the line intensity is spread out over a greater number of pixels to smooth the original jagged effect. This procedure displays a somewhat blurred line in the vicinity of the stair steps (between horizontal runs). If we want to use more intensity levels to antialiase the line with this method, we increase the number of sampling positions across each pixel. Sixteen subpixels gives us four intensity levels above zero; twenty-five subpixels gives us five levels; and so on.

In the supersampling example of Fig. 4-47, we considered pixel areas of finite size, but we treated the line as a mathematical entity with zero width. Actually, displayed lines have a width approximately equal to that of a pixel. If we take the finite width of the line into account, we can perform supersampling by setting pixel intensity proportional to the number of subpixels inside the polygon representing the line area. A subpixel can be considered to be inside the line if its lower left corner is inside the polygon boundaries. An advantage of this supersampling procedure is that the number of possible intensity levels for each pixel is equal to the total number of subpixels within the pixel area. For the example in Fig. 4-47, we can represent this line with finite width by positioning the polygon boundaries parallel to the line path as in Fig. 4-48. And each pixel can now be set to one of nine possible brightness levels above zero.

Another advantage of supersampling with a finite-width line is that the total line intensity is distributed over more pixels. In Fig. 4-48, we now have the pixel at grid position (10, 21) turned on (at intensity level 2), and we also pick up contributions from pixels immediately below and immediately to the left of position (10, 21). Also, if we have a color display, we can extend the method to take background colors into account. A particular line might cross several different color areas, and we can average subpixel intensities to obtain pixel color settings. For instance, if five subpixels within a particular pixel area are determined to be inside the boundaries for a red line and the remaining four subpixels fall within a blue background area, we can calculate the color for this pixel as

$$\text{pixel}_{\text{color}} = \frac{(5 \cdot \text{red} + 4 \cdot \text{blue})}{9}$$

The trade-off for these gains from supersampling a finite-width line is that identifying interior subpixels requires more calculations than simply determining which subpixels are along the line path. Also, we need to take into account the positioning of the line boundaries in relation to the line path. This positioning depends on the slope of the line. For a 45° line, the line path is centered on the polygon area; but for either a horizontal or a vertical line, we want the line path to be one of the polygon boundaries. As an example, a horizontal line passing through grid coordinates (10, 20) could be represented as the polygon bounded by horizontal grid lines $y = 20$ and $y = 21$. Similarly, the polygon representing a vertical line through (10, 20) can have vertical boundaries along grid lines $x = 10$ and $x = 11$. For lines with slope $|m| < 1$, the mathematical line path is positioned proportionately closer to the lower polygon boundary; and for lines with slope $|m| > 1$, the line path is placed closer to the upper polygon boundary.

1	2	1
2	4	2
1	2	1

FIGURE 4-49 Relative weights for a grid of 3 by 3 subpixels.

Subpixel Weighting Masks

Supersampling algorithms are often implemented by giving more weight to subpixels near the center of a pixel area, since we would expect these subpixels to be more important in determining the overall intensity of a pixel. For the 3 by 3 pixel subdivisions we have considered so far, a weighting scheme as in Fig. 4-49 could be used. The center subpixel here is weighted four times that of the corner subpixels and twice that of the remaining subpixels. Intensities calculated for each of the nine subpixels would then be averaged so that the center subpixel is weighted by a factor of $\frac{1}{4}$; the top, bottom, and side subpixels are each weighted by a factor of $\frac{1}{8}$; and the corner subpixels are each weighted by a factor of $\frac{1}{16}$. An array of values specifying the relative importance of subpixels is usually referred to as a *weighting mask*. Similar masks can be set up for larger subpixel grids. Also, these masks are often extended to include contributions from subpixels belonging to neighboring pixels, so that intensities can be averaged with adjacent pixels to provide a smoother intensity variation between pixels.

Area Sampling Straight-Line Segments

We perform area sampling for a straight line by setting pixel intensity proportional to the area of overlap of the pixel with the finite-width line. The line can be treated as a rectangle, and the section of the line area between two adjacent vertical (or two adjacent horizontal) screen grid lines is then a trapezoid. Overlap areas for pixels are calculated by determining how much of the trapezoid overlaps each pixel in that column (or row). In Fig. 4-48, the pixel with screen grid coordinates (10, 20) is about 90 percent covered by the line area, so its intensity would be set to 90 percent of the maximum intensity. Similarly, the pixel at (10, 21) would be set to an intensity of about 15 percent of maximum. A method for estimating pixel overlap areas is illustrated by the supersampling example in Fig. 4-48. The total number of subpixels within the line boundaries is approximately equal to the overlap area, and this estimation is improved by using finer subpixel grids.

Filtering Techniques

A more accurate method for antialiasing lines is to use **filtering** techniques. The method is similar to applying a weighted pixel mask, but now we imagine a continuous *weighting surface* (or *filter function*) covering the pixel. Figure 4-50 shows

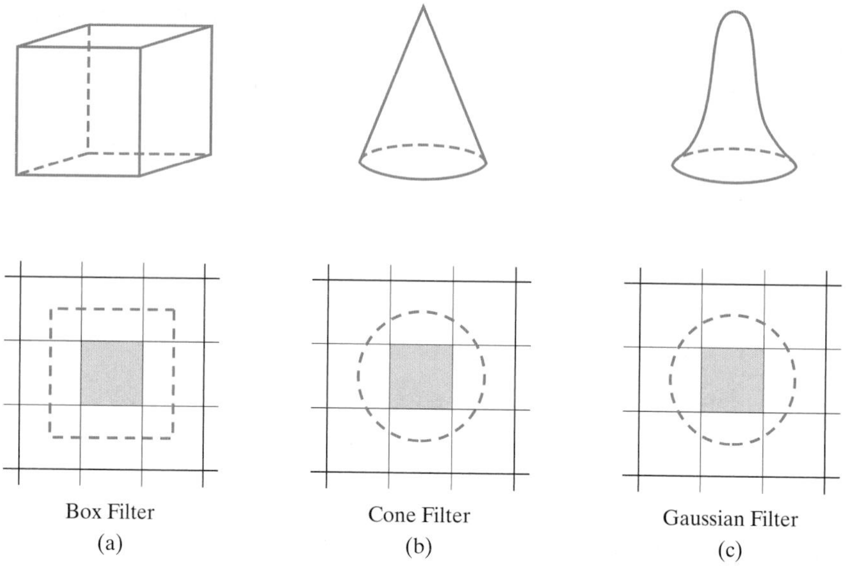

FIGURE 4-50 Common filter functions used to antialias line paths. The volume of each filter is normalized to 1.0, and the height gives the relative weight at any subpixel position.

examples of rectangular, conical, and Gaussian filter functions. Methods for applying the filter function are similar to those for applying a weighting mask, but now we integrate over the pixel surface to obtain the weighted average intensity. To reduce computation, table lookups are commonly used to evaluate the integrals.

Pixel Phasing

On raster systems that can address subpixel positions within the screen grid, pixel phasing can be used to antialias objects. A line display is smoothed with this technique by moving (micropositioning) pixel positions closer to the line path. Systems incorporating *pixel phasing* are designed so that the electron beam can be shifted by a fraction of a pixel diameter. The electron beam is typically shifted by $\frac{1}{4}$, $\frac{1}{2}$, or $\frac{3}{4}$ of a pixel diameter to plot points closer to the true path of a line or object edge. Some systems also allow the size of individual pixels to be adjusted as an additional means for distributing intensities. Figure 4-51 illustrates the antialiasing effects of pixel phasing on a variety of line paths.

Compensating for Line-Intensity Differences

Antialiasing a line to soften the stair-step effect also compensates for another raster effect, illustrated in Fig. 4-52. Both lines are plotted with the same number of pixels, yet the diagonal line is longer than the horizontal line by a factor of $\sqrt{2}$. For example, if the horizontal line had a length of 10 centimeters, the diagonal line would have a length of more than 14 centimeters. The visual effect of this is that the diagonal line appears less bright than the horizontal line, since the diagonal line is displayed with a lower intensity per unit length. A line-drawing algorithm could be adapted to compensate for this effect by adjusting the intensity of each line according to its slope. Horizontal and vertical lines would be displayed with the lowest intensity, while 45° lines would be given the highest intensity. But if antialiasing techniques are applied to a display, intensities are automatically compensated. When the finite width of a line is taken into account, pixel intensities are adjusted so that the line displays a total intensity proportional to its length.

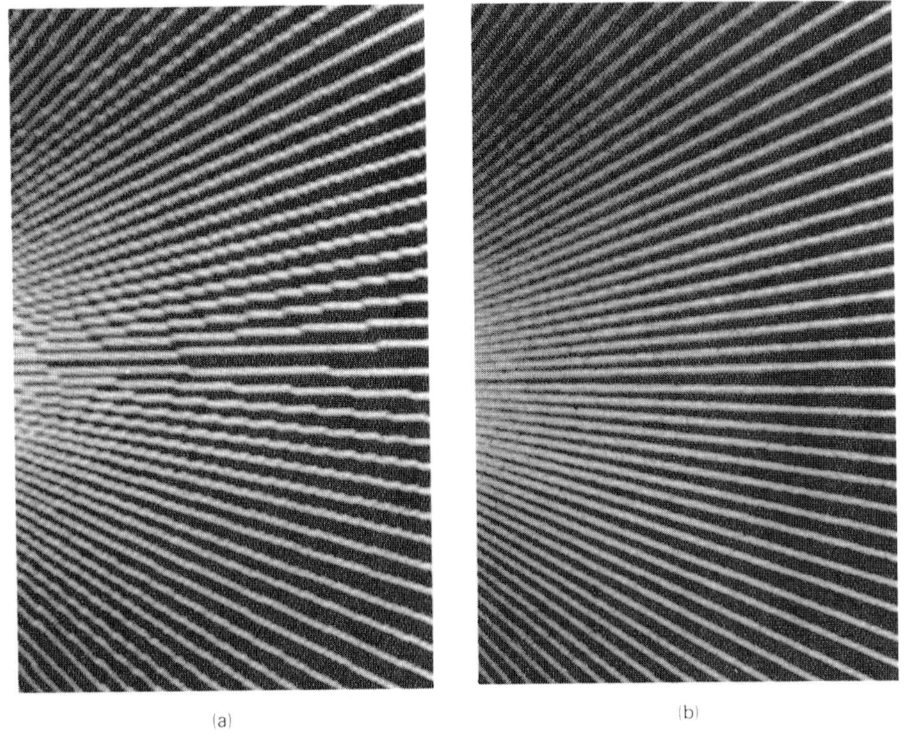

FIGURE 4-51 Jagged lines (a), plotted on the Merlin 9200 system, are smoothed (b) with an antialiasing technique called pixel phasing. This technique increases the number of addressable points on the system from 768 by 576 to 3072 by 2304. (*Courtesy of Peritek Corp.*)

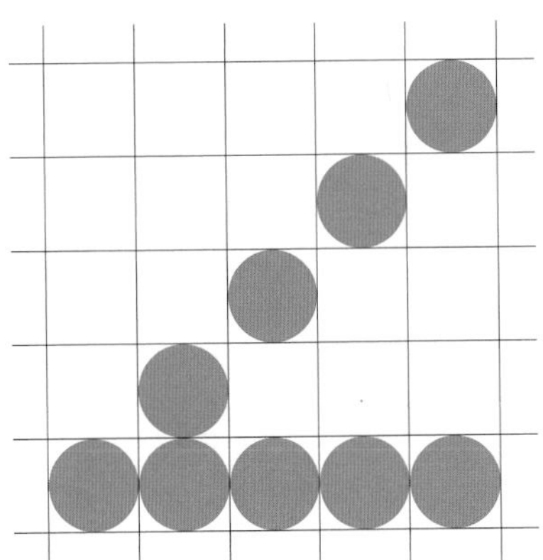

FIGURE 4-52 Unequal length lines displayed with the same number of pixels in each line.

Antialiasing Area Boundaries

The antialiasing concepts we have discussed for lines can also be applied to the boundaries of areas to remove their jagged appearance. We can incorporate these procedures into a scan-line algorithm to smooth the boundaries as the area is generated.

If system capabilities permit the repositioning of pixels, we could smooth area boundaries by shifting pixel positions closer to the boundary. Other methods adjust pixel intensity at a boundary position according to the percent of the pixel area that is interior to the object. In Fig. 4-53, the pixel at position (x, y) has about half its area inside the polygon boundary. Therefore, the intensity at that position would be adjusted to one-half its assigned value. At the next position $(x+1, y+1)$

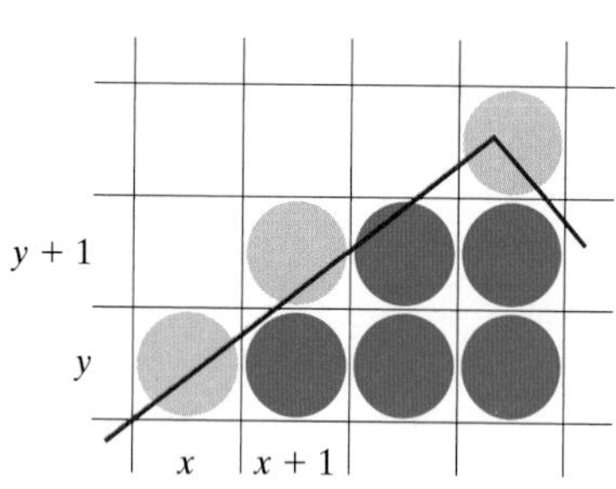

FIGURE 4-53 Adjusting pixel intensities along an area boundary.

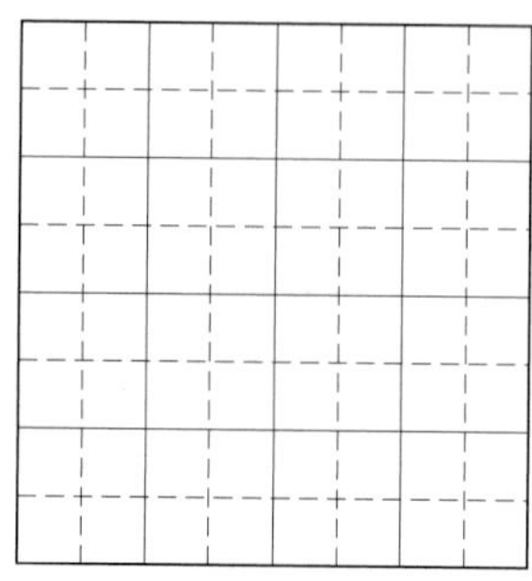

FIGURE 4-54 A 4 by 4 pixel section of a raster display subdivided into an 8 by 8 grid.

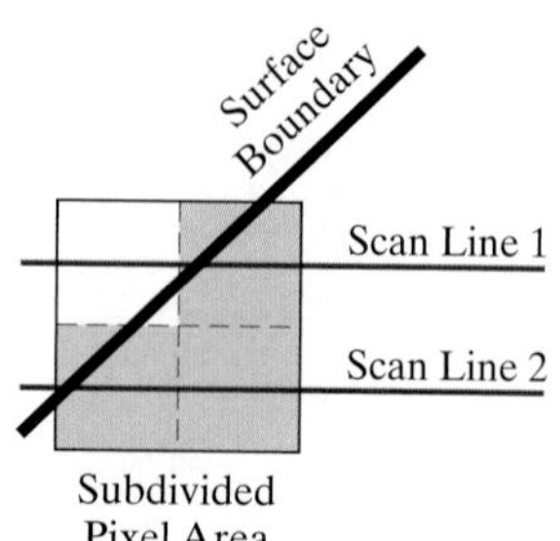

FIGURE 4-55 A subdivided pixel area with three subdivisions inside an object boundary line.

along the boundary, the intensity is adjusted to about one-third the assigned value for that point. Similar adjustments, based on the percent of pixel area coverage, are applied to the other intensity values around the boundary.

Supersampling methods can be applied by determining the number of subpixels that are in the interior of an object. A partitioning scheme with four subareas per pixel is shown in Fig. 4-54. The original 4 by 4 grid of pixels is turned into an 8 by 8 grid, and we now process eight scan lines across this grid instead of four. Figure 4-55 shows one of the pixel areas in this grid that overlaps an object boundary. Along the two scan lines, we determine that three of the subpixel areas are inside the boundary. So we set the pixel intensity at 75 percent of its maximum value.

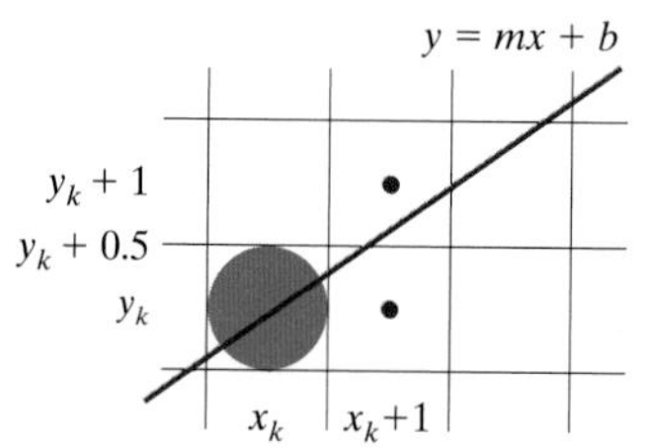

FIGURE 4-56 Boundary edge of a fill area passing through a pixel grid section.

Another method for determining the percentage of pixel area within a fill region, developed by Pitteway and Watkinson, is based on the midpoint line algorithm. This algorithm selects the next pixel along a line by testing the location of the midposition between two pixels. As in the Bresenham algorithm, we set up a decision parameter p whose sign tells us which of the next two candidate pixels is closer to the line. By slightly modifying the form of p, we obtain a quantity that also gives the percentage of the current pixel area that is covered by an object.

We first consider the method for a line with slope m in the range from 0 to 1. In Fig. 4-56, a straight-line path is shown on a pixel grid. Assuming that the pixel at position (x_k, y_k) has been plotted, the next pixel nearest the line at $x = x_k + 1$ is either the pixel at y_k or the one at $y_k + 1$. We can determine which pixel is nearer with the calculation

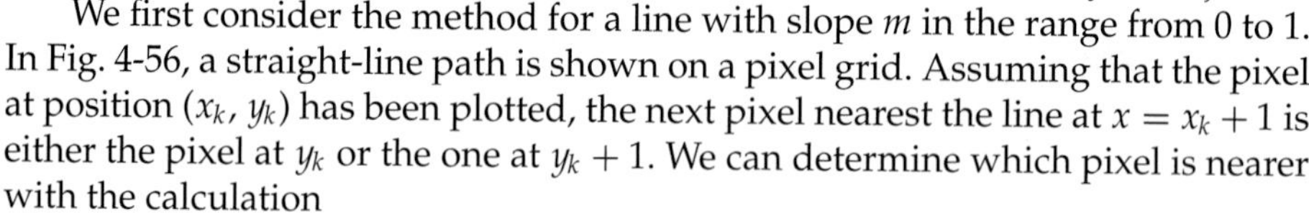

$$y - y_{\text{mid}} = [m(x_k + 1) + b] - (y_k + 0.5) \tag{4-14}$$

This gives the vertical distance from the actual y coordinate on the line to the halfway point between pixels at position y_k and $y_k + 1$. If this difference calculation is negative, the pixel at y_k is closer to the line. If the difference is positive, the pixel at $y_k + 1$ is closer. We can adjust this calculation so that it produces a positive number in the range from 0 to 1 by adding the quantity $1 - m$:

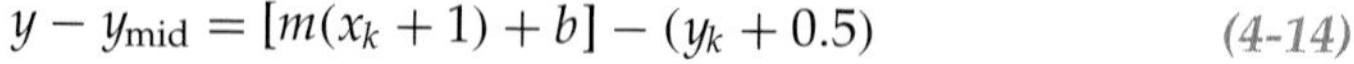

$$p = [m(x_k + 1) + b] - (y_k + 0.5) + (1 - m) \tag{4-15}$$

Now the pixel at y_k is nearer if $p < 1 - m$, and the pixel at $y_k + 1$ is nearer if $p > 1 - m$.

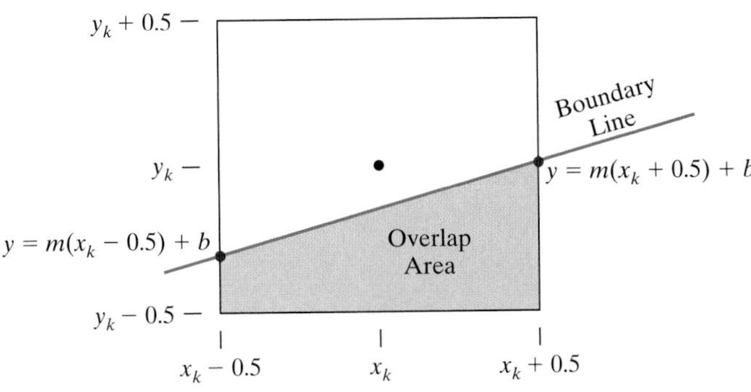

FIGURE 4-57 Overlap area of a pixel rectangle, centered at position (x_k, y_k), with the interior of a polygon fill area.

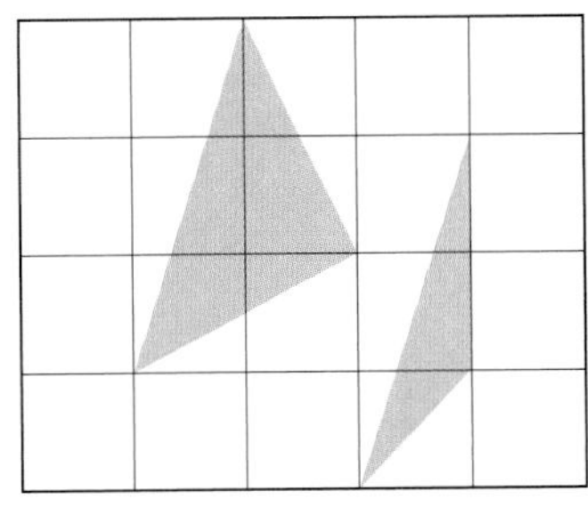

FIGURE 4-58 Polygons with more than one boundary line passing through individual pixel regions.

Parameter p also measures the amount of the current pixel that is overlapped by the area. For the pixel at (x_k, y_k) in Fig. 4-57, the interior part of the pixel has an area that can be calculated as

$$\text{area} = m \cdot x_k + b - y_k + 0.5 \tag{4-16}$$

This expression for the overlap area of the pixel at (x_k, y_k) is the same as that for parameter p in Eq. 4-15. Therefore, by evaluating p to determine the next pixel position along the polygon boundary, we also determine the percentage of area coverage for the current pixel.

We can generalize this algorithm to accommodate lines with negative slopes and lines with slopes greater than 1. This calculation for parameter p could then be incorporated into a midpoint line algorithm to locate pixel positions along a polygon edge and, concurrently, adjust pixel intensities along the boundary lines. Also, we can adjust the calculations to reference pixel coordinates at their lower-left coordinates and maintain area proportions, as discussed in Section 3-13.

At polygon vertices and for very skinny polygons, as shown in Fig. 4-58, we have more than one boundary edge passing through a pixel area. For these cases, we need to modify the Pitteway-Watkinson algorithm by processing all edges passing through a pixel and determining the correct interior area.

Filtering techniques discussed for line antialiasing can also be applied to area edges. And the various antialiasing methods can be applied to polygon areas or to regions with curved boundaries. Equations describing the boundaries are used to estimate the amount of pixel overlap with the area to be displayed, and coherence techniques are used along and between scan lines to simplify the calculations.

4-18 OpenGL ANTIALIASING FUNCTIONS

We activate the antialiasing routines in OpenGL with the function

```
glEnable (primitiveType);
```

where parameter `primitiveType` is assigned one of the symbolic constant values `GL_POINT_SMOOTH`, `GL_LINE_SMOOTH`, or `GL_POLYGON_SMOOTH`.

Assuming we are specifying color values using the RGBA mode, we also need to activate the OpenGL color-blending operations.

```
glEnable (GL_BLEND);
```

Next, we apply the color-blending method described in Section 4-3 using the function

```
glBlendFunc (GL_SRC_ALPHA, GL_ONE_MINUS_SRC_ALPHA);
```

The smoothing operations are more effective if we use large alpha values in the color specifications for the objects.

Antialiasing can also be applied when we use color tables. However, in this color mode, we must create a `color ramp`, which is a table of color graduations from the background color to the object color. This color ramp is then used to antialias object boundaries.

4-19 OpenGL QUERY FUNCTIONS

We can retrieve current values for any of the state parameters, including attribute settings, using OpenGL **query functions.** These functions copy specified state values into an array, which we can save for later reuse or to check the current state of the system if an error occurs.

For current attribute values we use an appropriate "`glGet`" function, such as

```
glGetBooleanv ( )              glGetFloatv ( )
glGetIntegerv ( )              glGetDoublev ( )
```

In each of the preceding functions, we specify two arguments. The first argument is an OpenGL symbolic constant that identifies an attribute or other state parameter. The second argument is a pointer to an array of the data type indicated by the function name. For instance, we can retrieve the current RGBA floating-point color settings with

```
glGetFloatv (GL_CURRENT_COLOR, colorValues);
```

The current color components are then passed to the array `colorValues`. To obtain the integer values for the current color components, we invoke the `glGetIntegerv` function. In some cases, a type conversion may be necessary to return the specified data type.

Other OpenGL constants, such as `GL_POINT_SIZE`, `GL_LINE_WIDTH`, and `GL_CURRENT_RASTER_POSITION`, can be used in these functions to return current state values. And we could check the range of point sizes or line widths that are supported using the constants `GL_POINT_SIZE_RANGE` and `GL_LINE_WIDTH_RANGE`.

Although we can retrieve and reuse settings for a single attribute with the `glGet` functions, OpenGL provides other functions for saving groups of attributes and reusing their values. We consider the use of these functions for saving current attribute settings in the next section.

There are many other state and system parameters that are often useful to query. For instance, to determine how many bits per pixel are provided in the frame buffer on a particular system, we can ask the system how many bits are available for each individual color component, such as

```
glGetIntegerv (GL_RED_BITS, redBitSize);
```

Here, array `redBitSize` is assigned the number of red bits available in each of the buffers (frame buffer, depth buffer, accumulation buffer, and stencil buffer). Similarly, we can make an inquiry for the other color bits using `GL_GREEN_BITS`, `GL_BLUE_BITS`, `GL_ALPHA_BITS`, or `GL_INDEX_BITS`.

We can also find out whether edge flags have been set, whether a polygon face was tagged as a front face or a back face, and whether the system supports double buffering. And we can inquire whether certain routines, such as color blending, line stippling or antialiasing, have been enabled or disabled.

4-20 OpenGL ATTRIBUTE GROUPS

Attributes and other OpenGL state parameters are arranged in **attribute groups.** Each group contains a set of related state parameters. For instance, the **point-attribute group** contains the size and point-smooth (antialiasing) parameters, and the **line-attribute group** contains the width, stipple status, stipple pattern, stipple repeat counter, and line-smooth status. Similarly, the **polygon-attribute group** contains eleven polygon parameters, such as fill pattern, front-face flag, and polygon-smooth status. Since color is an attribute for all primitives, it has its own attribute group. And some parameters are included in more than one group.

About twenty different attribute groups are available in OpenGL, and all parameters in one or more groups can be saved or reset with a single function. We save all parameters within a specified group using the following command.

```
glPushAttrib (attrGroup);
```

Parameter `attrGroup` is assigned an OpenGL symbolic constant that identifies an attribute group, such as `GL_POINT_BIT`, `GL_LINE_BIT`, or `GL_POLYGON_BIT`. To save color parameters, we use the symbolic constant `GL_CURRENT_BIT`. And we can save all state parameters in all attribute groups with the constant `GL_ALL_ATTRIB_BITS`. The `glPushAttrib` function places all parameters within the specified group onto an **attribute stack.**

We can also save parameters within two or more groups by combining their symbolic constants with a logical `OR` operation. The following statement places all parameters for points, lines, and polygons on the attribute stack.

```
glPushAttrib (GL_POINT_BIT | GL_LINE_BIT | GL_POLYGON_BIT);
```

Once we have saved a group of state parameters, we can reinstate all values on the attribute stack with this function:

```
glPopAttrib ( );
```

No arguments are used in the `glPopAttrib` function since it resets the current state of OpenGL using all values on the stack.

These commands for saving and resetting state parameters use a *server attribute stack*. There is also a *client attribute stack* available in OpenGL for saving and resetting client state parameters. The functions for accessing this stack are `glPushClientAttrib` and `glPopClientAttrib`. Only two client attribute groups are available: one for pixel-storage modes and the other for vertex arrays. Pixel-storage parameters include information such as byte alignment and the type of arrays used to store subimages of a display. Vertex-array parameters give information about the current vertex-array state, such as the enable/disable state of various arrays.

4-21 SUMMARY

Attributes control the display characteristics of graphics primitives. In many graphics systems, attribute values are stored as state variables and primitives are generated using the current attribute values. When we change the value of a state variable, it affects only those primitives defined after the change.

A common attribute for all primitives is color, which is most often specified in terms of RGB (or RGBA) components. The red, green, and blue color values are stored in the frame buffer, and they are used to control the intensity of the three electron guns in an RGB monitor. Color selections can also be made using color-lookup tables. In this case, a color in the frame buffer is indicated as a table index, and the table location at that index stores a particular set of RGB color values. Color tables are useful in data-visualization and image-processing applications, and they can also be used to provide a wide range of colors without requiring a large frame buffer. Often, computer-graphics packages provide options for using either color tables or storing color values directly in the frame buffer.

The basic point attributes are color and size. On raster systems, various point sizes are displayed as square pixel arrays. Line attributes are color, width, and style. Specifications for line width are given in terms of multiples of a standard, one-pixel-wide line. The line-style attributes include solid, dashed, and dotted lines, as well as various brush or pen styles. These attributes can be applied to both straight lines and curves.

Fill-area attributes include a solid-color fill, a fill pattern, or a hollow display that shows only the area boundaries. Various pattern fills can be specified in color arrays, which are then mapped to the interior of the region. Scan-line methods are commonly used to fill polygons, circles, and ellipses. Across each scan line, the interior fill is applied to pixel positions between each pair of boundary intersections, left to right. For polygons, scan-line intersections with vertices can result in an odd number of intersections. This can be resolved by shortening some polygon edges. Scan-line fill algorithms can be simplified if fill areas are restricted to convex polygons. A further simplification is achieved if all fill areas in a scene are triangles. The interior pixels along each scan line are assigned appropriate color values, depending on the fill-attribute specifications. Painting programs generally display fill regions using a boundary-fill method or a flood-fill method. Each of these two fill methods requires an initial interior point. The interior is then painted pixel by pixel from the initial point out to the region boundaries.

Areas can also be filled using color blending. This type of fill has applications in antialiasing and in painting packages. Soft-fill procedures provide a new fill color for a region that has the same variations as the previous fill color. One example of this approach is the linear soft-fill algorithm that assumes that the previous fill was a linear combination of foreground and background colors. This same linear relationship is then determined from the frame buffer settings and used to repaint the area in a new color.

TABLE 4-2

SUMMARY OF OpenGL ATTRIBUTE FUNCTIONS

Function	Description
`glutInitDisplayMode`	Select the color mode, which can be either `GLUT_RGB` or `GLUT_INDEX`.
`glColor*`	Specify an RGB or RGBA color.
`glIndex*`	Specify a color using a color-table index.
`glutSetColor (index, r, g, b);`	Load a color into a color-table position.
`glEnable (GL_BLEND);`	Activate color blending.
`glBlendFunc (sFact, dFact);`	Specify factors for color blending.
`glEnableClientState (GL_COLOR_ARRAY);`	Activate color-array features of OpenGL.
`glColorPointer (size, type, stride, array);`	Specify an RGB color array.
`glIndexPointer (type, stride, array);`	Specify a color array using color-index mode.
`glPointSize (size)`	Specify a point size.
`glLineWidth (width);`	Specify a line width.
`glEnable (GL_LINE_STIPPLE);`	Activate line style.
`glEnable (GL_POLYGON_STIPPLE);`	Activate fill style.
`glLineStipple (repeat, pattern);`	Specify a line-style pattern.
`glPolygonStipple (pattern);`	Specify a fill-style pattern.
`glPolygonMode`	Display front or back face as either a set of edges or a set of vertices.
`glEdgeFlag`	Set fill-polygon edge flag to `GL_TRUE` or `GL_FALSE` to determine display status for an edge.
`glFrontFace`	Specify front-face vertex order as either `GL_CCW` or `GL_CW`.
`glEnable`	Activate antialiasing with `GL_POINT_SMOOTH`, `GL_LINE_SMOOTH`, or `GL_POLYGON_SMOOTH`. (Also need to activate color blending.)
`glGet**`	Various query functions, requiring specification of data type, symbolic name of a state parameter, and an array pointer.
`glPushAttrib`	Save all state parameters within a specified attribute group.
`glPopAttrib ( );`	Reinstate all state parameter values that were last saved.

Characters can be displayed in different styles (fonts), colors, sizes, spacing, and orientations. To set the orientation of a character string, we can specify a direction for the character up vector and a direction for the text path. In addition, we can set the alignment of a text string in relation to the start coordinate position. Individual characters, called marker symbols, can be used for applications such as plotting data graphs. Marker symbols can be displayed in various sizes and colors using standard characters or special symbols.

Because scan conversion is a digitizing process on raster systems, displayed primitives have a jagged appearance. This is due to the undersampling of information, which rounds coordinate values to pixel positions. We can improve the appearance of raster primitives by applying antialiasing procedures that adjust pixel intensities. One method for doing this is to supersample. That is, we consider each pixel to be composed of subpixels and we calculate the intensity of the subpixels and average the values of all subpixels. We can also weight the subpixel contributions according to position, giving higher weights to the central subpixels. Alternatively, we can perform area sampling and determine the percentage of area coverage for a screen pixel, then set the pixel intensity proportional to this percentage. Another method for antialiasing is to build special hardware configurations that can shift pixel positions.

In OpenGL, attribute values for the primitives are maintained as state variables. An attribute setting remains in effect for all subsequently defined primitives until that attribute value is changed. Changing an attribute value does not affect previously displayed primitives. We can specify colors in OpenGL using either the RGB (RGBA) color mode or the color-index mode, which uses color-table indices to select colors. Also, we can blend color values using the alpha color component. And we can specify values in color arrays that are to be used in conjunction with vertex arrays. In addition to color, OpenGL provides functions for selecting point size, line width, line style, and convex-polygon fill style, as well as providing functions for the display of polygon fill areas as either a set of edges or a set of vertex points. We can also eliminate selected polygon edges from a display, and we can reverse the specification of front and back faces. We can generate text strings in OpenGL using bitmaps or routines that are available in GLUT. Attributes that can be set for the display of GLUT characters include color, font, size, spacing, line width, and line type. The OpenGL library also provides functions to antialias the display of output primitives. We can use query functions to obtain the current value for state variables, and we can also obtain all values within an OpenGL attribute group using a single function.

Table 4-2 summarizes the OpenGL attribute functions discussed in this chapter. Additionally, the table lists some attribute-related functions.

REFERENCES

Soft-fill techniques are given in Fishkin and Barsky (1984). Antialiasing techniques are discussed in Pitteway and Watinson (1980), Crow (1981), Turkowski (1982), Fujimoto and Iwata (1983), Korein and Badler (1983), Kirk and Arvo (1991), and Wu (1991). Gray-scale applications are explored in Crow (1978). Other discussions of attributes and state parameters are available in Glassner (1990), Arvo (1991), Kirk (1992), Heckbert (1994), and Paeth (1995).

Programming examples using OpenGL attribute functions are given in Woo, Neider, Davis, and Shreiner (1999). A complete listing of OpenGL attribute functions is available in Shreiner (2000), and GLUT character attributes are discussed in Kilgard (1996).

EXERCISES

4-1 Use the `glutSetColor` function to set up a color table for an input set of color values.

4-2 Using vertex and color arrays, set up the description for a scene containing at least six two-dimensional objects.

4-3 Write a program to display the two-dimensional scene description in the previous exercise.

4-4 Using vertex and color arrays, set up the description for a scene containing at least four three-dimensional objects.

4-5 Write a program to display a two-dimensional, gray-scale "cloud" scene, where the cloud shapes are to be described as point patterns on a blue-sky background. The light and dark regions of the clouds are to be modeled using points of varying sizes and interpoint spacing. (For example, a very light region can be modeled with small, widely spaced, light-gray points. Similarly, a dark region can be modeled with larger, more closely spaced, dark-gray points.)

4-6 Modify the program in the previous exercise to display the clouds in red and yellow color patterns as they might be seen at sunrise or at sunset. To achieve a realistic effect, use different shades of red and yellow (and perhaps green) for the points.

4-7 Implement a general line-style function by modifying Bresenham's line-drawing algorithm to display solid, dashed, or dotted lines.

4-8 Implement a line-style function using a midpoint line algorithm to display solid, dashed, or dotted lines.

4-9 Devise a parallel method for implementing a line-style function.

4-10 Devise a parallel method for implementing a line-width function.

4-11 A line specified by two endpoints and a width can be converted to a rectangular polygon with four vertices and then displayed using a scan-line method. Develop an efficient algorithm for computing the four vertices needed to define such a rectangle, with the line endpoints and line width as input parameters.

4-12 Implement a line-width function in a line-drawing program so that any one of three line widths can be displayed.

4-13 Write a program to output a line graph of three data sets defined over the same x-coordinate range. Input to the program is to include the three sets of data values and the labels for the graph. The data sets are to be scaled to fit within a defined coordinate range for a display window. Each data set is to be plotted with a different line style.

4-14 Modify the program in the previous exercise to plot the three data sets in different colors, as well as different line styles.

4-15 Set up an algorithm for displaying thick lines with butt caps, round caps, or projecting square caps. These options can be provided in an option menu.

4-16 Devise an algorithm for displaying thick polylines with a miter join, a round join, or a bevel join. These options can be provided in an option menu.

4-17 Modify the code segments in Section 4-8 for displaying data line plots, so that the line-width parameter is passed to procedure `linePlot`.

4-18 Modify the code segments in Section 4-8 for displaying data line plots, so that the line-style parameter is passed to procedure `linePlot`.

4-19 Complete the program in Section 4-8 for displaying line plots using input values from a data file.

4-20 Complete the program in Section 4-8 for displaying line plots using input values from a data file. In addition, the program should provide labeling for the axes and the coordinates for the display area on the screen. The data sets are to be scaled to fit the coordinate range of the display window, and each plotted line is to be displayed in a different line style, width, and color.

4-21 Implement pen and brush menu options for a line-drawing procedure, including at least two options: round and square shapes.

4-22 Modify a line-drawing algorithm so that the intensity of the output line is set according to its slope. That is, by adjusting pixel intensities according to the value of the slope, all lines are displayed with the same intensity per unit length.

4-23 Define and implement a function for controlling the line style (solid, dashed, dotted) of displayed ellipses.

4-24 Define and implement a function for setting the width of displayed ellipses.

4-25 Write a routine to display a bar graph in any specified screen area. Input is to include the data set, labeling for the coordinate axes, and the coordinates for the screen area. The data set is to be scaled to fit the designated screen area, and the bars are to be displayed in designated colors or patterns.

4-26 Write a procedure to display two data sets defined over the same x-coordinate range, with the data values scaled to fit a specified region of the display screen. The bars for one of the data sets are to be displaced horizontally to produce an overlapping bar pattern for easy comparison of the two sets of data. Use a different color or a different fill pattern for the two sets of bars.

4-27 Devise an algorithm for implementing a color lookup table.

4-28 Suppose you have a system with an 8 inch by 10 inch video screen that can display 100 pixels per inch. If a color lookup table with 64 positions is used with this system, what is the smallest possible size (in bytes) for the frame buffer?

4-29 Consider an RGB raster system that has a 512-by-512 frame buffer with 20 bits per pixel and a color lookup table with 24 bits per pixel. (a) How many distinct gray levels can be displayed with this system? (b) How many distinct colors (including gray levels) can be displayed? (c) How many colors can be displayed at any one time? (d) What is the total memory size? (e) Explain two methods for reducing memory size while maintaining the same color capabilities.

4-30 Modify the scan-line algorithm to apply any specified rectangular fill pattern to a polygon interior, starting from a designated pattern position.

4-31 Write a program to scan convert the interior of a specified ellipse into a solid color.

4-32 Write a procedure to fill the interior of a given ellipse with a specified pattern.

4-33 Write a procedure for filling the interior of any specified set of fill-area vertices, including one with crossing edges, using the nonzero winding number rule to identify interior regions.

4-34 Modify the boundary-fill algorithm for a 4-connected region to avoid excessive stacking by incorporating scan-line methods.

4-35 Write a boundary-fill procedure to fill an 8-connected region.

4-36 Explain how an ellipse displayed with the midpoint method could be properly filled with a boundary-fill algorithm.

4-37 Develop and implement a flood-fill algorithm to fill the interior of any specified area.

4-38 Define and implement a procedure for changing the size of an existing rectangular fill pattern.

4-39 Write a procedure to implement a soft-fill algorithm. Carefully define what the soft-fill algorithm is to accomplish and how colors are to be combined.

4-40 Devise an algorithm for adjusting the height and width of characters defined as rectangular grid patterns.

4-41 Implement routines for setting the character up vector and the text path for controlling the display of character strings.

4-42 Write a program to align text as specified by input values for the alignment parameters.

4-43 Develop procedures for implementing marker attributes (size and color).

4-44 Implement an antialiasing procedure by extending Bresenham's line algorithm to adjust pixel intensities in the vicinity of a line path.

4-45 Implement an antialiasing procedure for the midpoint line algorithm.

4-46 Develop an algorithm for antialiasing elliptical boundaries.

4-47 Modify the scan-line algorithm for area fill to incorporate antialiasing. Use coherence techniques to reduce calculations on successive scan lines.

4-48 Write a program to implement the Pitteway-Watkinson antialiasing algorithm as a scan-line procedure to fill a polygon interior, using the OpenGL point-plotting function.

CHAPTER 5

Geometric Transformations

A computer-graphics scene containing a fractional Brownian-motion landscape and a water reflection of the moon. *(Courtesy of Ken Musgrave and Benoit B. Mandelbrot, Mathematics and Computer Science, Yale University.)*

So far, we have seen how we can describe a scene in terms of graphics primitives, such as line segments and fill areas, and the attributes associated with these primitives. And we have explored the scan-line algorithms for displaying output primitives on a raster device. Now, we take a look at transformation operations that we can apply to objects to reposition or resize them. These operations are also used in the viewing routines that convert a world-coordinate scene description to a display for an output device. In addition, they are used in a variety of other applications, such as computer-aided design and computer animation. An architect, for example, creates a layout by arranging the orientation and size of the component parts of a design, and a computer animator develops a video sequence by moving the "camera" position or the objects in a scene along specified paths. Operations that are applied to the geometric description of an object to change its position, orientation, or size are called **geometric transformations.**

Sometimes geometric-transformation operations are also referred to as *modeling transformations*, but some graphics packages make a distinction between the two. In general, modeling transformations are used to construct a scene or to give the hierarchical description of a complex object that is composed of several parts, which in turn could be composed of simpler parts, and so forth. As an example, an aircraft consists of wings, tail, fuselage, engine, and other components, each of which can be specified in terms of second-level components, and so on, down the hierarchy of component parts. Thus, the aircraft can be described in terms of these components and an associated "modeling" transformation for each one that describes how that component is to be fitted into the overall aircraft design. Geometric transformations, on the other hand, can be used to describe how objects might move around in a scene during an animation sequence or simply to view them from another angle. Therefore, some graphics packages provide two sets of transformation routines, while other packages have a single set of functions that can be used for both geometric transformations and modeling transformations.

5-1 BASIC TWO-DIMENSIONAL GEOMETRIC TRANSFORMATIONS

The geometric-transformation functions that are available in all graphics packages are those for translation, rotation, and scaling. Other useful transformation routines that are sometimes included in a package are reflection and shearing operations. To introduce the general concepts associated with geometric transformations, we first consider operations in two dimensions, then we discuss how these basic ideas can be extended to three-dimensional scenes. Once we understand the basic concepts, we can easily write routines to perform geometric transformations on objects in a two-dimensional scene.

Two-Dimensional Translation

We perform a **translation** on a single coordinate point by adding offsets to its coordinates so as to generate a new coordinate position. In effect, we are moving the original point position along a straight-line path to its new location. Similarly, a translation is applied to an object that is defined with multiple coordinate positions, such as a quadrilateral, by relocating all the coordinate positions by the same displacement along parallel paths. Then the complete object is displayed at the new location.

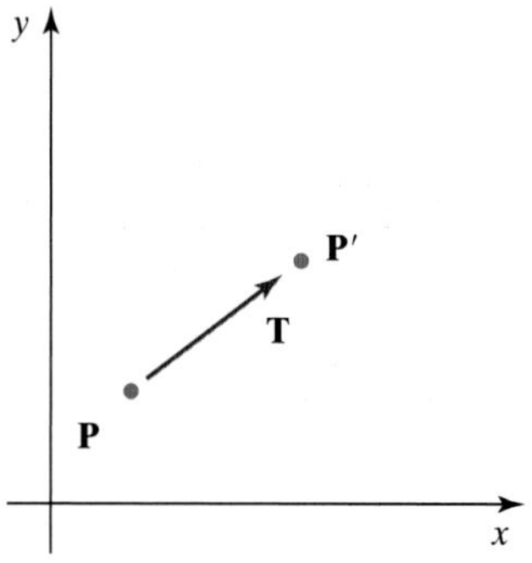

FIGURE 5-1 Translating a point from position **P** to position **P**′ using a translation vector **T**.

To translate a two-dimensional position, we add **translation distances** t_x and t_y to the original coordinates (x, y) to obtain the new coordinate position (x', y') as shown in Fig. 5-1.

$$x' = x + t_x, \qquad y' = y + t_y \tag{5-1}$$

The translation distance pair (t_x, t_y) is called a **translation vector** or **shift vector.**

We can express the translation equations 5-1 as a single matrix equation by using the following column vectors to represent coordinate positions and the translation vector.

$$\mathbf{P} = \begin{bmatrix} x \\ y \end{bmatrix}, \qquad \mathbf{P}' = \begin{bmatrix} x' \\ y' \end{bmatrix}, \qquad \mathbf{T} = \begin{bmatrix} t_x \\ t_y \end{bmatrix} \tag{5-2}$$

This allows us to write the two-dimensional translation equations in the matrix form

$$\mathbf{P}' = \mathbf{P} + \mathbf{T} \tag{5-3}$$

Translation is a *rigid-body transformation* that moves objects without deformation. That is, every point on the object is translated by the same amount. A straight-line segment is translated by applying the transformation equation 5-3 to each of the two line endpoints and redrawing the line between the new endpoint positions. A polygon is translated similarly. We add a translation vector to the coordinate position of each vertex and then regenerate the polygon using the new set of vertex coordinates. Figure 5-2 illustrates the application of a specified translation vector to move an object from one position to another.

The following routine illustrates the translation operations. An input translation vector is used to move the n vertices of a polygon from one world-coordinate position to another, and OpenGL routines are used to regenerate the translated polygon.

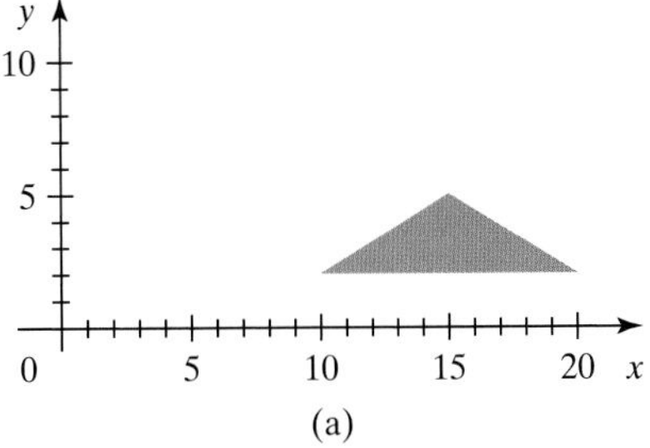

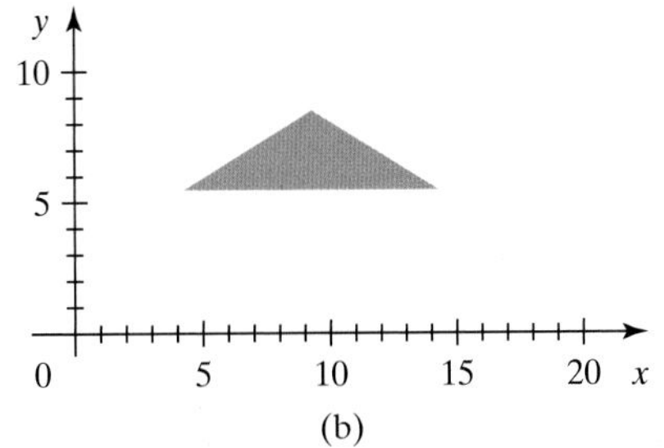

FIGURE 5-2 Moving a polygon from position (a) to position (b) with the translation vector (−5.50, 3.75).

```
class wcPt2D {
   public:
      GLfloat x, y;
};

void translatePolygon (wcPt2D * verts, GLint nVerts, GLfloat tx, GLfloat ty)
{
   GLint k;

   for (k = 0; k < nVerts; k++) {
      verts [k].x = verts [k].x + tx;
      verts [k].y = verts [k].y + ty;
   }
   glBegin (GL_POLYGON);
      for (k = 0; k < nVerts; k++)
         glVertex2f (verts [k].x, verts [k].y);
   glEnd ( );
}
```

If we want to delete the original polygon, we could display it in the background color before translating it. Other methods for deleting picture components are available in some graphics packages. Also, if we want to save the original polygon position, we can store the translated positions in a different array.

Similar methods are used to translate other objects. To change the position of a circle or ellipse, we translate the center coordinates and redraw the figure in the new location. For a spline curve, we translate the points that define the curve path and then reconstruct the curve sections between the new coordinate positions.

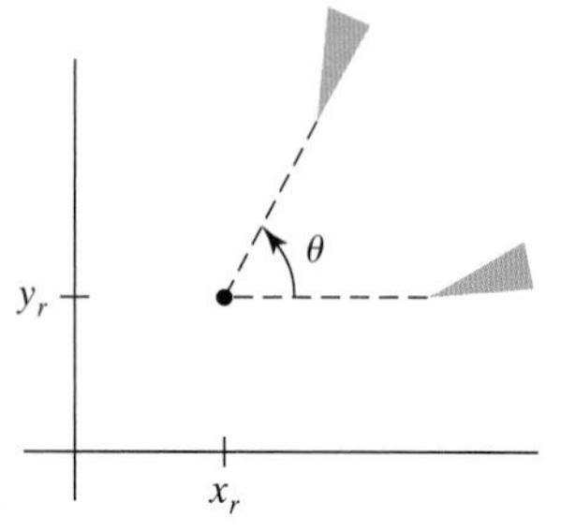

FIGURE 5-3 Rotation of an object through angle θ about the pivot point (x_r, y_r).

Two-Dimensional Rotation

We generate a **rotation** transformation of an object by specifying a **rotation axis** and a **rotation angle**. All points of the object are then transformed to new positions by rotating the points through the specified angle about the rotation axis.

A two-dimensional rotation of an object is obtained by repositioning the object along a circular path in the xy plane. In this case, we are rotating the object about a rotation axis that is perpendicular to the xy plane (parallel to the coordinate z axis). Parameters for the two-dimensional rotation are the rotation angle θ and a position (x_r, y_r), called the **rotation point** (or **pivot point**), about which the object is to be rotated (Fig. 5-3). The pivot point is the intersection position of the rotation axis with the xy plane. A positive value for the angle θ defines a counterclockwise rotation about the pivot point, as in Fig. 5-3, and a negative value rotates objects in the clockwise direction.

To simplify the explanation of the basic method, we first determine the transformation equations for rotation of a point position **P** when the pivot point is at the coordinate origin. The angular and coordinate relationships of the original and transformed point positions are shown in Fig. 5-4. In this figure, r is the constant distance of the point from the origin, angle ϕ is the original angular position of the point from the horizontal, and θ is the rotation angle. Using standard trigonometric identities, we can express the transformed coordinates in terms of angles θ and ϕ as

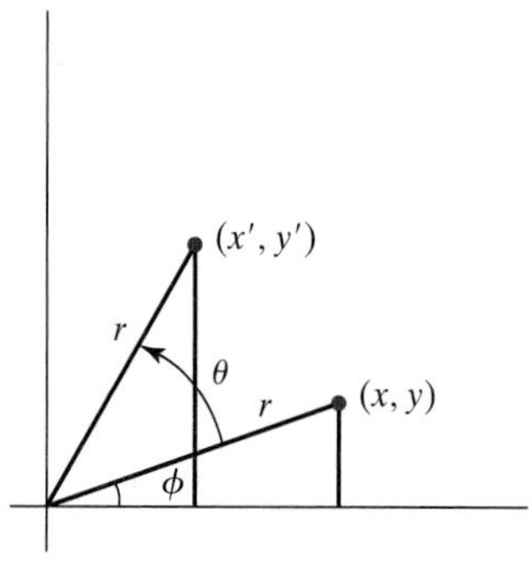

FIGURE 5-4 Rotation of a point from position (x, y) to position (x', y') through an angle θ relative to the coordinate origin. The original angular displacement of the point from the x axis is ϕ.

$$\begin{aligned} x' &= r\cos(\phi + \theta) = r\cos\phi\cos\theta - r\sin\phi\sin\theta \\ y' &= r\sin(\phi + \theta) = r\cos\phi\sin\theta + r\sin\phi\cos\theta \end{aligned} \tag{5-4}$$

The original coordinates of the point in polar coordinates are

$$x = r\cos\phi, \qquad y = r\sin\phi \tag{5-5}$$

Substituting expressions 5-5 into 5-4, we obtain the transformation equations for rotating a point at position (x, y) through an angle θ about the origin:

$$\begin{aligned} x' &= x\cos\theta - y\sin\theta \\ y' &= x\sin\theta + y\cos\theta \end{aligned} \tag{5-6}$$

With the column-vector representations 5-2 for coordinate positions, we can write the rotation equations in the matrix form

$$\mathbf{P}' = \mathbf{R} \cdot \mathbf{P} \tag{5-7}$$

where the rotation matrix is

$$\mathbf{R} = \begin{bmatrix} \cos\theta & -\sin\theta \\ \sin\theta & \cos\theta \end{bmatrix} \tag{5-8}$$

A column-vector representation for a coordinate position **P**, as in equations 5-2, is standard mathematical notation. However, early graphics systems sometimes used a row-vector representation for point positions. This changes the order in which the matrix multiplication for a rotation would be performed. But now, graphics packages such as OpenGL, Java, PHIGS, and GKS all follow the standard column-vector convention.

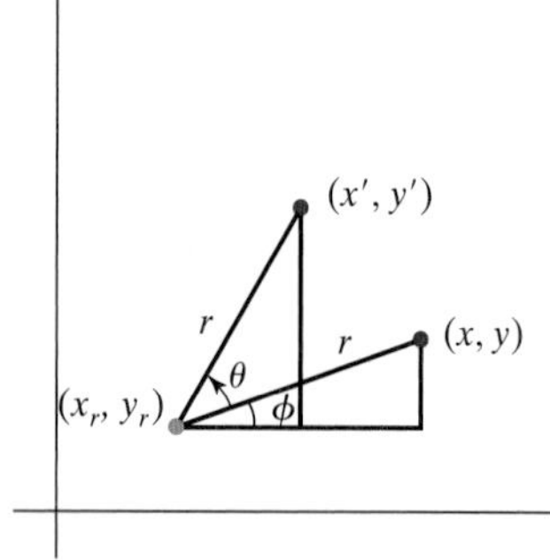

FIGURE 5-5 Rotating a point from position (x, y) to position (x', y') through an angle θ about rotation point (x_r, y_r).

Rotation of a point about an arbitrary pivot position is illustrated in Fig. 5-5. Using the trigonometric relationships indicated by the two right triangles in this figure, we can generalize Eqs. 5-6 to obtain the transformation equations for rotation of a point about any specified rotation position (x_r, y_r):

$$\begin{aligned} x' &= x_r + (x - x_r)\cos\theta - (y - y_r)\sin\theta \\ y' &= y_r + (x - x_r)\sin\theta + (y - y_r)\cos\theta \end{aligned} \tag{5-9}$$

These general rotation equations differ from equations 5-6 by the inclusion of additive terms, as well as the multiplicative factors on the coordinate values. The matrix expression 5-7 could be modified to include pivot coordinates by including the matrix addition of a column vector whose elements contain the additive (translational) terms in equations 5-9. There are better ways, however, to formulate such matrix equations, and in Section 5-2 we discuss a more consistent scheme for representing the transformation equations.

As with translations, rotations are rigid-body transformations that move objects without deformation. Every point on an object is rotated through the same angle. A straight-line segment is rotated by applying the rotation equations 5-9 to each of the two line endpoints and redrawing the line between the new endpoint positions. A polygon is rotated by displacing each vertex using the specified rotation angle and then regenerating the polygon using the new vertices. We rotate a curve by repositioning the defining points for the curve and then redrawing it. A circle or an ellipse, for instance, can be rotated about a noncentral pivot point by moving the center position through the arc that subtends the specified rotation angle. And we could rotate an ellipse about its center coordinates simply by rotating the major and minor axes.

In the following code example, a polygon is rotated about a specified world-coordinate pivot point. Parameters input to the rotation procedure are the original vertices of the polygon, the pivot-point coordinates, and the rotation angle `theta` specified in radians. Following the transformation of the vertex positions, the polygon is regenerated using OpenGL routines.

```
class wcPt2D {
   public:
      GLfloat x, y;
};

void rotatePolygon (wcPt2D * verts, GLint nVerts, wcPt2D pivPt,
                    GLdouble theta)
{
   wcPt2D * vertsRot;
   GLint k;

   for (k = 0; k < nVerts; k++) {
      vertsRot [k].x = pivPt.x + (verts [k].x - pivPt.x) * cos (theta)
                         - (verts [k].y - pivPt.y) * sin (theta);
      vertsRot [k].y = pivPt.y + (verts [k].x - pivPt.x) * sin (theta)
                         + (verts [k].y - pivPt.y) * cos (theta);
   }
   glBegin {GL_POLYGON};
      for (k = 0; k < nVerts; k++)
         glVertex2f (vertsRot [k].x, vertsRot [k].y);
   glEnd ( );
}
```

Two-Dimensional Scaling

To alter the size of an object, we apply a **scaling** transformation. A simple two-dimensional scaling operation is performed by multiplying object positions (x, y) by **scaling factors** s_x and s_y to produce the transformed coordinates (x', y'):

$$x' = x \cdot s_x, \qquad y' = y \cdot s_y \tag{5-10}$$

Scaling factor s_x scales an object in the x direction, while s_y scales in the y direction. The basic two-dimensional scaling equations 5-10 can also be written in the following matrix form.

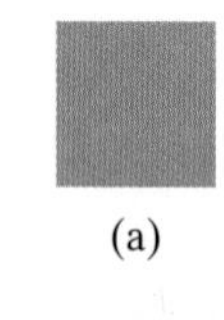

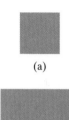

(a)

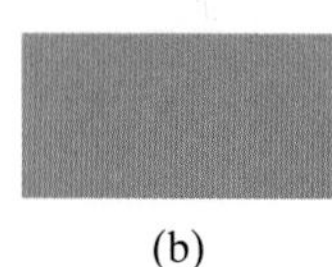

(b)

FIGURE 5-6 Turning a square (a) into a rectangle (b) with scaling factors $s_x = 2$ and $s_y = 1$.

$$\begin{bmatrix} x' \\ y' \end{bmatrix} = \begin{bmatrix} s_x & 0 \\ 0 & s_y \end{bmatrix} \cdot \begin{bmatrix} x \\ y \end{bmatrix} \tag{5-11}$$

or

$$\mathbf{P}' = \mathbf{S} \cdot \mathbf{P} \tag{5-12}$$

where **S** is the 2 by 2 scaling matrix in Eq. 5-11.

Any positive values can be assigned to the scaling factors s_x and s_y. Values less than 1 reduce the size of objects; values greater than 1 produce enlargements. Specifying a value of 1 for both s_x and s_y leaves the size of objects unchanged. When s_x and s_y are assigned the same value, a **uniform scaling** is produced which maintains relative object proportions. Unequal values for s_x and s_y result in a **differential scaling** that is often used in design applications, where pictures are constructed from a few basic shapes that can be adjusted by scaling and positioning transformations (Fig. 5-6). In some systems, negative values can also be specified for the scaling parameters. This not only resizes an object, it reflects it about one or more of the coordinate axes.

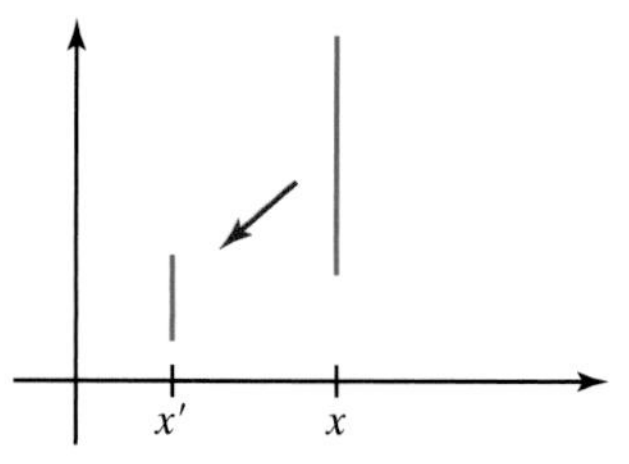

FIGURE 5-7 A line scaled with Eq. 5-12 using $s_x = s_y = 0.5$ is reduced in size and moved closer to the coordinate origin.

Objects transformed with Eq. 5-11 are both scaled and repositioned. Scaling factors with absolute values less than 1 move objects closer to the coordinate origin, while absolute values greater than 1 move coordinate positions farther from the origin. Figure 5-7 illustrates scaling of a line by assigning the value 0.5 to both s_x and s_y in Eq. 5-11. Both the line length and the distance from the origin are reduced by a factor of $\frac{1}{2}$.

We can control the location of a scaled object by choosing a position, called the **fixed point,** that is to remain unchanged after the scaling transformation. Coordinates for the fixed point, (x_f, y_f), are often chosen at some object position, such as its centroid (Appendix A), but any other spatial position can be selected. Objects are now resized by scaling the distances between object points and the fixed point (Fig. 5-8). For a coordinate position (x, y), the scaled coordinates (x', y') are then calculated from the following relationships.

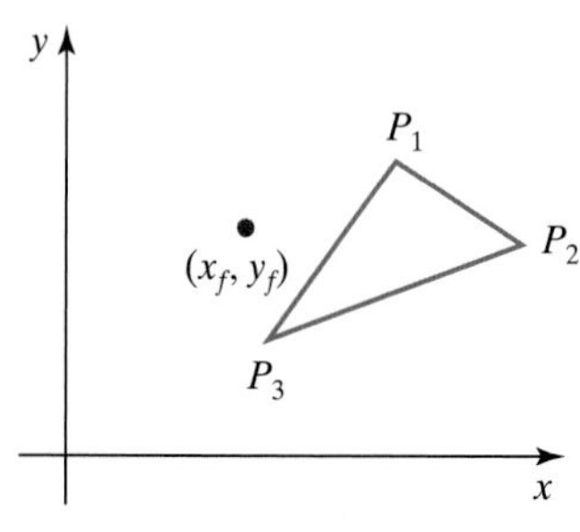

FIGURE 5-8 Scaling relative to a chosen fixed point (x_f, y_f). The distance from each polygon vertex to the fixed point is scaled by transformation equations 5-13.

$$x' - x_f = (x - x_f)s_x, \qquad y' - y_f = (y - y_f)s_y \tag{5-13}$$

We can rewrite Eqs. 5-13 to separate the multiplicative and additive terms as

$$\begin{aligned} x' &= x \cdot s_x + x_f(1 - s_x) \\ y' &= y \cdot s_y + y_f(1 - s_y) \end{aligned} \tag{5-14}$$

where the additive terms $x_f(1 - s_x)$ and $y_f(1 - s_y)$ are constants for all points in the object.

Including coordinates for a fixed point in the scaling equations is similar to including coordinates for a pivot point in the rotation equations. We can set up a column vector whose elements are the constant terms in Eqs. 5-14, then add this column vector to the product $\mathbf{S} \cdot \mathbf{P}$ in Eq. 5-12. In the next section, we discuss a matrix formulation for the transformation equations that involves only matrix multiplication.

Polygons are scaled by applying transformations 5-14 to each vertex, then regenerating the polygon using the transformed vertices. For other objects, we apply the scaling transformation equations to the parameters defining the objects. To change the size of a circle, we can scale its radius and calculate the new coordinate positions around the circumference. And to change the size of an ellipse, we apply scaling parameters to its two axes and then plot the new ellipse positions about its center coordinates.

The following procedure illustrates an application of the scaling calculations for a polygon. Coordinates for the polygon vertices and for the fixed point are input parameters, along with the scaling factors. After the coordinate transformations, OpenGL routines are used to generate the scaled polygon.

```
class wcPt2D {
   public:
      GLfloat x, y;
};

void scalePolygon (wcPt2D * verts, GLint nVerts, wcPt2D fixedPt,
                                     GLfloat sx, GLfloat sy)
{
   wcPt2D vertsNew;
   GLint k;

   for (k = 0; k < nVerts; k++) {
     vertsNew [k].x = verts [k].x * sx + fixedPt.x * (1 - sx);
     vertsNew [k].y = verts [k].y * sy + fixedPt.y * (1 - sy);
   }
   glBegin {GL_POLYGON};
      for (k = 0; k < nVerts; k++)
         glVertex2f (vertsNew [k].x, vertsNew [k].y);
   glEnd ( );
}
```

5-2 MATRIX REPRESENTATIONS AND HOMOGENEOUS COORDINATES

Many graphics applications involve sequences of geometric transformations. An animation might require an object to be translated and rotated at each increment of the motion. In design and picture construction applications, we perform translations, rotations, and scalings to fit the picture components into their proper positions. And the viewing transformations involve sequences of translations and rotations to take us from the original scene specification to the display on an output device. Here we consider how the matrix representations discussed in the previous sections can be reformulated so that such transformation sequences can be efficiently processed.

We have seen in Section 5-1 that each of the three basic two-dimensional transformations (translation, rotation, and scaling) can be expressed in the general matrix form

$$\mathbf{P}' = \mathbf{M}_1 \cdot \mathbf{P} + \mathbf{M}_2 \tag{5-15}$$

with coordinate positions $\mathbf{P}$ and $\mathbf{P}'$ represented as column vectors. Matrix $\mathbf{M}_1$ is a 2 by 2 array containing multiplicative factors, and $\mathbf{M}_2$ is a two-element column matrix containing translational terms. For translation, $\mathbf{M}_1$ is the identity matrix. For rotation or scaling, $\mathbf{M}_2$ contains the translational terms associated with the pivot point or scaling fixed point. To produce a sequence of transformations with these equations, such as scaling followed by rotation then translation, we could calculate the transformed coordinates one step at a time. First, coordinate positions are scaled, then these scaled coordinates are rotated, and finally the rotated coordinates are translated. A more efficient approach, however, is to combine the transformations so that the final coordinate positions are obtained directly from the initial coordinates, without calculating intermediate coordinate values. We can do this by reformulating Eq. 5-15 to eliminate the matrix addition operation.

Homogeneous Coordinates

Multiplicative and translational terms for a two-dimensional geometric transformation can be combined into a single matrix if we expand the representations to 3 by 3 matrices. Then we can use the third column of a transformation matrix for the translation terms, and all transformation equations can be expressed as matrix multiplications. But to do so, we also need to expand the matrix representation for a two-dimensional coordinate position to a three-element column matrix. A standard technique for accomplishing this is to expand each two-dimensional coordinate-position representation (x, y) to a three-element representation (x_h, y_h, h), called **homogeneous coordinates,** where the **homogeneous parameter** h is a nonzero value such that

$$x = \frac{x_h}{h}, \qquad y = \frac{y_h}{h} \tag{5-16}$$

Therefore, a general two-dimensional homogeneous coordinate representation could also be written as $(h \cdot x, h \cdot y, h)$. For geometric transformations, we can choose the homogeneous parameter h to be any nonzero value. Thus, there are an infinite number of equivalent homogeneous representations for each coordinate point (x, y). A convenient choice is simply to set $h = 1$. Each two-dimensional position is then represented with homogeneous coordinates $(x, y, 1)$. Other values for parameter h are needed, for example, in matrix formulations of three-dimensional viewing transformations.

The term *homogeneous coordinates* is used in mathematics to refer to the effect of this representation on Cartesian equations. When a Cartesian point (x, y) is converted to a homogeneous representation (x_h, y_h, h), equations containing x and y, such as $f(x, y) = 0$, become homogeneous equations in the three parameters x_h, y_h, and h. This just means that if each of the three parameters is replaced by any value v times that parameter, the value v can be factored out of the equations.

Expressing positions in homogeneous coordinates allows us to represent all geometric transformation equations as matrix multiplications, which is the standard method used in graphics systems. Two-dimensional coordinate positions are represented with three-element column vectors, and two-dimensional transformation operations are expressed as 3 by 3 matrices.

Two-Dimensional Translation Matrix

Using a homogeneous-coordinate approach, we can represent the equations for a two-dimensional translation of a coordinate position using the following matrix multiplication.

$$\begin{bmatrix} x' \\ y' \\ 1 \end{bmatrix} = \begin{bmatrix} 1 & 0 & t_x \\ 0 & 1 & t_y \\ 0 & 0 & 1 \end{bmatrix} \cdot \begin{bmatrix} x \\ y \\ 1 \end{bmatrix} \tag{5-17}$$

This translation operation can be written in the abbreviated form

$$\mathbf{P}' = \mathbf{T}(t_x, t_y) \cdot \mathbf{P} \tag{5-18}$$

with $\mathbf{T}(t_x, t_y)$ as the 3 by 3 translation matrix in Eq. 5-17. In situations where there is no ambiguity about the translation parameters, we can simply represent the translation matrix as **T**.

Two-Dimensional Rotation Matrix

Similarly, two-dimensional rotation transformation equations about the coordinate origin can be expressed in the matrix form

$$\begin{bmatrix} x' \\ y' \\ 1 \end{bmatrix} = \begin{bmatrix} \cos\theta & -\sin\theta & 0 \\ \sin\theta & \cos\theta & 0 \\ 0 & 0 & 1 \end{bmatrix} \cdot \begin{bmatrix} x \\ y \\ 1 \end{bmatrix} \tag{5-19}$$

or as

$$\mathbf{P}' = \mathbf{R}(\theta) \cdot \mathbf{P} \tag{5-20}$$

The rotation transformation operator $\mathbf{R}(\theta)$ is the 3 by 3 matrix in Eq. 5-19 with rotation parameter θ. We can also write this rotation matrix simply as **R**.

In some graphics libraries, a two-dimensional rotation function generates only rotations about the coordinate origin, as in Eq. 5-19. A rotation about any other pivot point must then be performed as a sequence of transformation operations. An alternative approach in a graphics package is to provide additional parameters in the rotation routine for the pivot-point coordinates. A rotation routine that includes a pivot-point parameter then sets up a general rotation matrix without the need to invoke a succession of transformation functions.

Two-Dimensional Scaling Matrix

Finally, a scaling transformation relative to the coordinate origin can now be expressed as the matrix multiplication

$$\begin{bmatrix} x' \\ y' \\ 1 \end{bmatrix} = \begin{bmatrix} s_x & 0 & 0 \\ 0 & s_y & 0 \\ 0 & 0 & 1 \end{bmatrix} \cdot \begin{bmatrix} x \\ y \\ 1 \end{bmatrix} \tag{5-21}$$

or

$$\mathbf{P}' = \mathbf{S}(s_x, s_y) \cdot \mathbf{P} \tag{5-22}$$

The scaling operator $\mathbf{S}(s_x, s_y)$ is the 3 by 3 matrix in Eq. 5-21 with parameters s_x and s_y. And, in most cases, we can represent the scaling matrix simply as **S**.

Some libraries provide a scaling function that can generate only scaling with respect to the coordinate origin, as in Eq. 5-21. In this case, a scaling transformation relative to another reference position is handled as a succession of transformation operations. However, other systems do include a general scaling routine that can construct the homogeneous matrix for scaling with respect to a designated fixed point.

5-3 INVERSE TRANSFORMATIONS

For translation, we obtain the inverse matrix by negating the translation distances. Thus, if we have two-dimensional translation distances t_x and t_y, the inverse translation matrix is

$$\mathbf{T}^{-1} = \begin{bmatrix} 1 & 0 & -t_x \\ 0 & 1 & -t_y \\ 0 & 0 & 1 \end{bmatrix} \tag{5-23}$$

This produces a translation in the opposite direction, and the product of a translation matrix and its inverse produces the identity matrix.

An inverse rotation is accomplished by replacing the rotation angle by its negative. For example, a two-dimensional rotation through an angle θ about the coordinate origin has the inverse transformation matrix

$$\mathbf{R}^{-1} = \begin{bmatrix} \cos\theta & \sin\theta & 0 \\ -\sin\theta & \cos\theta & 0 \\ 0 & 0 & 1 \end{bmatrix} \tag{5-24}$$

Negative values for rotation angles generate rotations in a clockwise direction, so the identity matrix is produced when any rotation matrix is multiplied by its inverse. Since only the sine function is affected by the change in sign of the rotation angle, the inverse matrix can also be obtained by interchanging rows and columns. That is, we can calculate the inverse of any rotation matrix **R** by evaluating its transpose ($\mathbf{R}^{-1} = \mathbf{R}^T$).

We form the inverse matrix for any scaling transformation by replacing the scaling parameters with their reciprocals. For two-dimensional scaling with parameters s_x and s_y applied relative to the coordinate origin, the inverse transformation matrix is

$$\mathbf{S}^{-1} = \begin{bmatrix} \frac{1}{s_x} & 0 & 0 \\ 0 & \frac{1}{s_y} & 0 \\ 0 & 0 & 1 \end{bmatrix} \tag{5-25}$$

The inverse matrix generates an opposite scaling transformation, so the multiplication of any scaling matrix with its inverse produces the identity matrix.

5-4 TWO-DIMENSIONAL COMPOSITE TRANSFORMATIONS

Using matrix representations, we can set up a sequence of transformations as a **composite transformation matrix** by calculating the product of the individual transformations. Forming products of transformation matrices is often referred to as a **concatenation,** or **composition,** of matrices. Since a coordinate position is represented with a homogeneous column matrix, we must premultiply the column matrix by the matrices representing any transformation sequence. And, since many positions in a scene are typically transformed by the same sequence, it is more efficient to first multiply the transformation matrices to form a single composite matrix. Thus, if we want to apply two transformations to point position **P**, the transformed location would be calculated as

$$\begin{aligned} \mathbf{P}' &= \mathbf{M}_2 \cdot \mathbf{M}_1 \cdot \mathbf{P} \\ &= \mathbf{M} \cdot \mathbf{P} \end{aligned} \tag{5-26}$$

The coordinate position is transformed using the composite matrix **M**, rather than applying the individual transformations $\mathbf{M}_1$ and then $\mathbf{M}_2$.

Composite Two-Dimensional Translations

If two successive translation vectors (t_{1x}, t_{1y}) and (t_{2x}, t_{2y}) are applied to a two-dimensional coordinate position **P**, the final transformed location **P**′ is calculated as

$$\begin{aligned} \mathbf{P}' &= \mathbf{T}(t_{2x}, t_{2y}) \cdot \{\mathbf{T}(t_{1x}, t_{1y}) \cdot \mathbf{P}\} \\ &= \{\mathbf{T}(t_{2x}, t_{2y}) \cdot \mathbf{T}(t_{1x}, t_{1y})\} \cdot \mathbf{P} \end{aligned} \tag{5-27}$$

where **P** and **P**′ are represented as three-element, homogeneous-coordinate column vectors. We can verify this result by calculating the matrix product for the two associative groupings. Also, the composite transformation matrix for this sequence of translations is

$$\begin{bmatrix} 1 & 0 & t_{2x} \\ 0 & 1 & t_{2y} \\ 0 & 0 & 1 \end{bmatrix} \cdot \begin{bmatrix} 1 & 0 & t_{1x} \\ 0 & 1 & t_{1y} \\ 0 & 0 & 1 \end{bmatrix} = \begin{bmatrix} 1 & 0 & t_{1x} + t_{2x} \\ 0 & 1 & t_{1y} + t_{2y} \\ 0 & 0 & 1 \end{bmatrix} \tag{5-28}$$

or

$$\mathbf{T}(t_{2x}, t_{2y}) \cdot \mathbf{T}(t_{1x}, t_{1y}) = \mathbf{T}(t_{1x} + t_{2x}, t_{1y} + t_{2y}) \tag{5-29}$$

which demonstrates that two successive translations are additive.

Composite Two-Dimensional Rotations

Two successive rotations applied to a point **P** produce the transformed position

$$\begin{aligned} \mathbf{P}' &= \mathbf{R}(\theta_2) \cdot \{\mathbf{R}(\theta_1) \cdot \mathbf{P}\} \\ &= \{\mathbf{R}(\theta_2) \cdot \mathbf{R}(\theta_1)\} \cdot \mathbf{P} \end{aligned} \tag{5-30}$$

By multiplying the two rotation matrices, we can verify that two successive rotations are additive:

$$\mathbf{R}(\theta_2) \cdot \mathbf{R}(\theta_1) = \mathbf{R}(\theta_1 + \theta_2) \tag{5-31}$$

so that the final rotated coordinates of a point can be calculated with the composite rotation matrix as

$$\mathbf{P}' = \mathbf{R}(\theta_1 + \theta_2) \cdot \mathbf{P} \tag{5-32}$$

Composite Two-Dimensional Scalings

Concatenating transformation matrices for two successive scaling operations in two dimensions produces the following composite scaling matrix.

$$\begin{bmatrix} s_{2x} & 0 & 0 \\ 0 & s_{2y} & 0 \\ 0 & 0 & 1 \end{bmatrix} \cdot \begin{bmatrix} s_{1x} & 0 & 0 \\ 0 & s_{1y} & 0 \\ 0 & 0 & 1 \end{bmatrix} = \begin{bmatrix} s_{1x} \cdot s_{2x} & 0 & 0 \\ 0 & s_{1y} \cdot s_{2y} & 0 \\ 0 & 0 & 1 \end{bmatrix} \tag{5-33}$$

or

$$\mathbf{S}(s_{2x}, s_{2y}) \cdot \mathbf{S}(s_{1x}, s_{1y}) = \mathbf{S}(s_{1x} \cdot s_{2x},\ s_{1y} \cdot s_{2y}) \tag{5-34}$$

The resulting matrix in this case indicates that successive scaling operations are multiplicative. That is, if we were to triple the size of an object twice in succession, the final size would be nine times that of the original.

General Two-Dimensional Pivot-Point Rotation

When a graphics package provides only a rotate function with respect to the coordinate origin, we can generate a two-dimensional rotation about any other pivot point (x_r, y_r) by performing the following sequence of translate-rotate-translate operations.

(1) Translate the object so that the pivot-point position is moved to the coordinate origin.

(2) Rotate the object about the coordinate origin.

(3) Translate the object so that the pivot point is returned to its original position.

This transformation sequence is illustrated in Fig. 5-9. The composite transformation matrix for this sequence is obtained with the concatenation

$$\begin{bmatrix} 1 & 0 & x_r \\ 0 & 1 & y_r \\ 0 & 0 & 1 \end{bmatrix} \cdot \begin{bmatrix} \cos\theta & -\sin\theta & 0 \\ \sin\theta & \cos\theta & 0 \\ 0 & 0 & 1 \end{bmatrix} \cdot \begin{bmatrix} 1 & 0 & -x_r \\ 0 & 1 & -y_r \\ 0 & 0 & 1 \end{bmatrix}$$

$$= \begin{bmatrix} \cos\theta & -\sin\theta & x_r(1-\cos\theta) + y_r \sin\theta \\ \sin\theta & \cos\theta & y_r(1-\cos\theta) - x_r \sin\theta \\ 0 & 0 & 1 \end{bmatrix} \tag{5-35}$$

which can be expressed in the form

$$\mathbf{T}(x_r, y_r) \cdot \mathbf{R}(\theta) \cdot \mathbf{T}(-x_r, -y_r) = \mathbf{R}(x_r, y_r, \theta) \tag{5-36}$$

where $\mathbf{T}(-x_r, -y_r) = \mathbf{T}^{-1}(x_r, y_r)$. In general, a rotate function in a graphics library could be structured to accept parameters for pivot-point coordinates, as

(x_r, y_r)

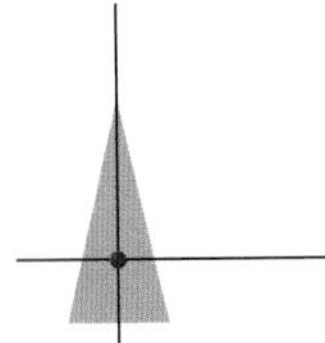

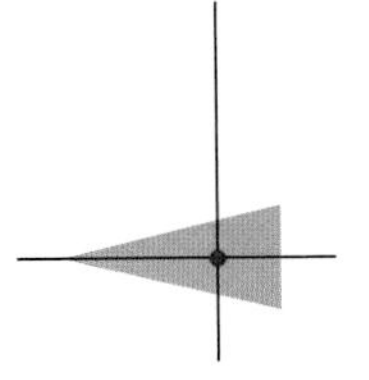

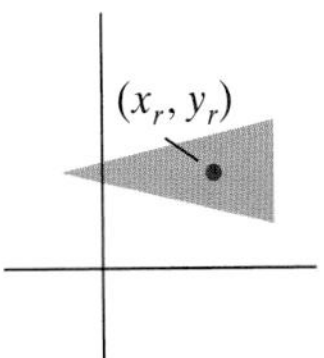

(a) Original Position of Object and Pivot Point

(b) Translation of Object so that Pivot Point (x_r, y_r) is at Origin

(c) Rotation about Origin

(d) Translation of Object so that the Pivot Point is Returned to Position (x_r, y_r)

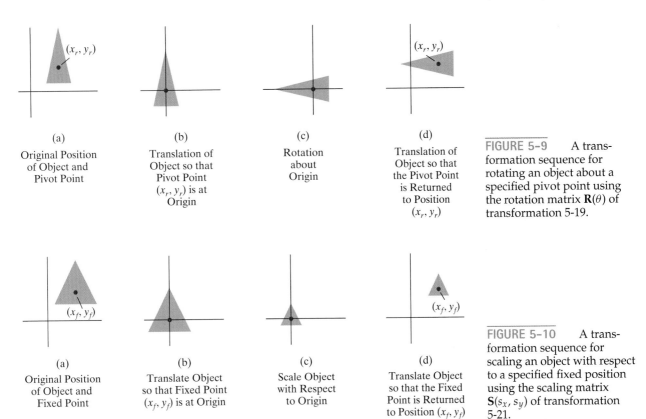

FIGURE 5-9 A transformation sequence for rotating an object about a specified pivot point using the rotation matrix $\mathbf{R}(\theta)$ of transformation 5-19.

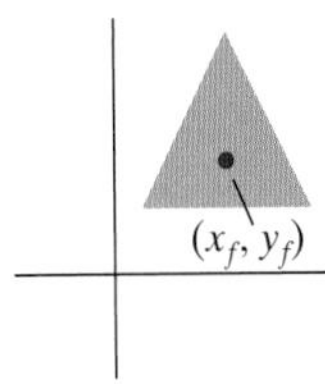

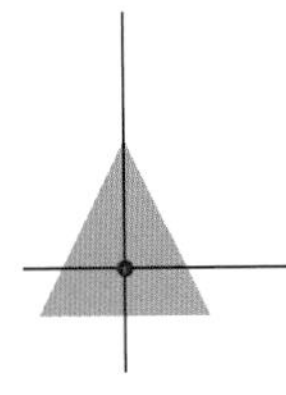

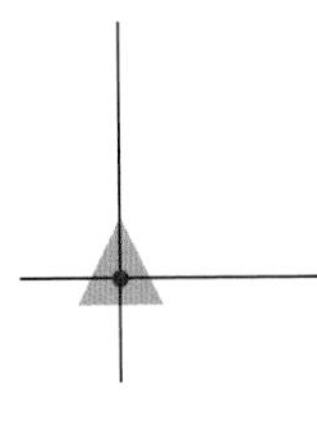

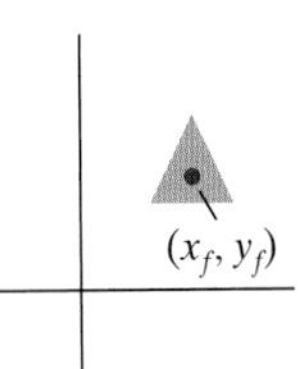

(a) Original Position of Object and Fixed Point

(b) Translate Object so that Fixed Point (x_f, y_f) is at Origin

(c) Scale Object with Respect to Origin

(d) Translate Object so that the Fixed Point is Returned to Position (x_f, y_f)

FIGURE 5-10 A transformation sequence for scaling an object with respect to a specified fixed position using the scaling matrix $\mathbf{S}(s_x, s_y)$ of transformation 5-21.

well as the rotation angle, and to generate automatically the rotation matrix of Eq. 5-35.

General Two-Dimensional Fixed-Point Scaling

Figure 5-10 illustrates a transformation sequence to produce a two-dimensional scaling with respect to a selected fixed position (x_f, y_f), when we have a function that can scale relative to the coordinate origin only. This sequence is

(1) Translate the object so that the fixed point coincides with the coordinate origin.

(2) Scale the object with respect to the coordinate origin.

(3) Use the inverse of the translation in step (1) to return the object to its original position.

Concatenating the matrices for these three operations produces the required scaling matrix:

$$\begin{bmatrix} 1 & 0 & x_f \\ 0 & 1 & y_f \\ 0 & 0 & 1 \end{bmatrix} \cdot \begin{bmatrix} s_x & 0 & 0 \\ 0 & s_y & 0 \\ 0 & 0 & 1 \end{bmatrix} \cdot \begin{bmatrix} 1 & 0 & -x_f \\ 0 & 1 & -y_f \\ 0 & 0 & 1 \end{bmatrix} = \begin{bmatrix} s_x & 0 & x_f(1 - s_x) \\ 0 & s_y & y_f(1 - s_y) \\ 0 & 0 & 1 \end{bmatrix} \tag{5-37}$$

or

$$\mathbf{T}(x_f, y_f) \cdot \mathbf{S}(s_x, s_y) \cdot \mathbf{T}(-x_f, -y_f) = \mathbf{S}(x_f, y_f, s_x, s_y) \tag{5-38}$$

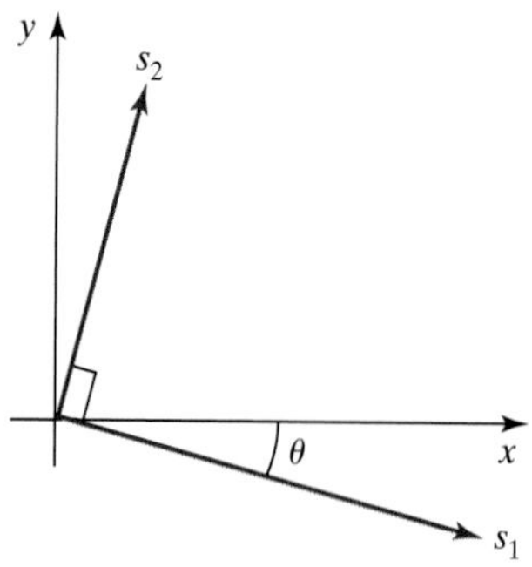

FIGURE 5-11 Scaling parameters s_1 and s_2 along orthogonal directions defined by the angular displacement θ.

This transformation is automatically generated in systems that provide a scale function that accepts coordinates for the fixed point.

General Two-Dimensional Scaling Directions

Parameters s_x and s_y scale objects along the x and y directions. We can scale an object in other directions by rotating the object to align the desired scaling directions with the coordinate axes before applying the scaling transformation.

Suppose we want to apply scaling factors with values specified by parameters s_1 and s_2 in the directions shown in Fig. 5-11. To accomplish the scaling without changing the orientation of the object, we first perform a rotation so that the directions for s_1 and s_2 coincide with the x and y axes, respectively. Then the scaling transformation $\mathbf{S}(s_1, s_2)$ is applied, followed by an opposite rotation to return points to their original orientations. The composite matrix resulting from the product of these three transformations is

$$\mathbf{R}^{-1}(\theta) \cdot \mathbf{S}(s_1, s_2) \cdot \mathbf{R}(\theta) = \begin{bmatrix} s_1 \cos^2\theta + s_2 \sin^2\theta & (s_2 - s_1)\cos\theta \sin\theta & 0 \\ (s_2 - s_1)\cos\theta\sin\theta & s_1 \sin^2\theta + s_2\cos^2\theta & 0 \\ 0 & 0 & 1 \end{bmatrix} \tag{5-39}$$

As an example of this scaling transformation, we turn a unit square into a parallelogram (Fig. 5-12) by stretching it along the diagonal from (0, 0) to (1, 1). We first rotate the diagonal onto the y axis using $\theta = 45^\circ$, then we double its length with the scaling values $s_1 = 1$ and $s_2 = 2$, and then we rotate again to return the diagonal to its original orientation.

In Eq. 5-39, we assumed that scaling was to be performed relative to the origin. We could take this scaling operation one step further and concatenate the matrix with translation operators, so that the composite matrix would include parameters for the specification of a scaling fixed position.

Matrix Concatenation Properties

Multiplication of matrices is associative. For any three matrices, $\mathbf{M}_1$, $\mathbf{M}_2$, and $\mathbf{M}_3$, the matrix product $\mathbf{M}_3 \cdot \mathbf{M}_2 \cdot \mathbf{M}_1$ can be performed by first multiplying $\mathbf{M}_3$ and $\mathbf{M}_2$ or by first multiplying $\mathbf{M}_2$ and $\mathbf{M}_1$:

$$\mathbf{M}_3 \cdot \mathbf{M}_2 \cdot \mathbf{M}_1 = (\mathbf{M}_3 \cdot \mathbf{M}_2) \cdot \mathbf{M}_1 = \mathbf{M}_3 \cdot (\mathbf{M}_2 \cdot \mathbf{M}_1) \tag{5-40}$$

Therefore, depending upon the order in which the transformations are specified, we can construct a composite matrix either by multiplying from left-to-right

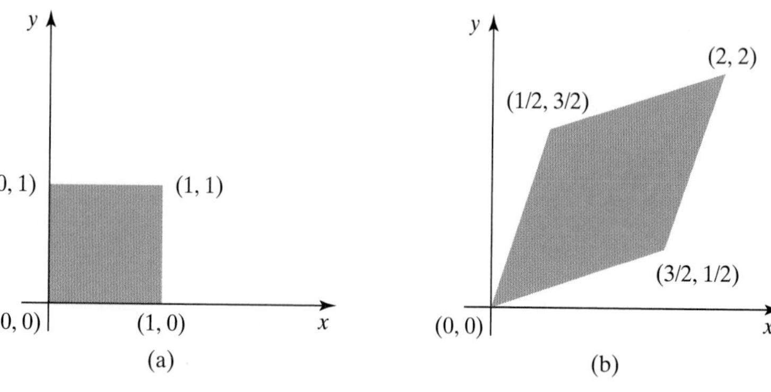

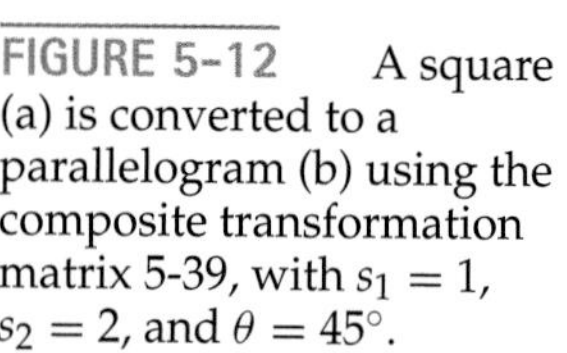

FIGURE 5-12 A square (a) is converted to a parallelogram (b) using the composite transformation matrix 5-39, with $s_1 = 1$, $s_2 = 2$, and $\theta = 45^\circ$.

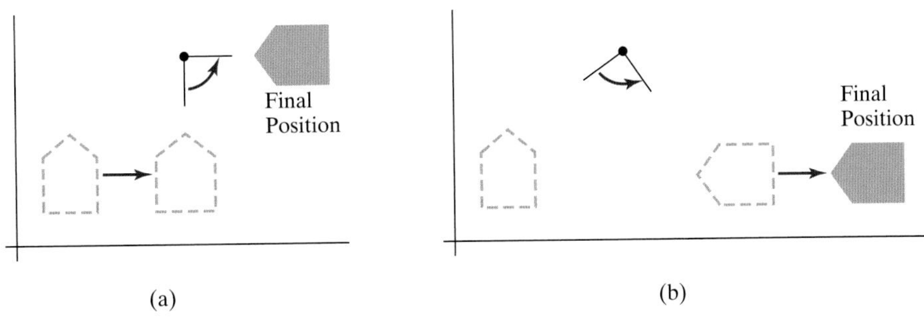

FIGURE 5-13 Reversing the order in which a sequence of transformations is performed may affect the transformed position of an object. In (a), an object is first translated in the x direction, then rotated counterclockwise through an angle of 45°. In (b), the object is first rotated 45° counterclockwise, then translated in the x direction.

(premultiplying) or by multiplying from right-to-left (postmultiplying). Some graphics packages require that transformations be specified in the order in which they are to be applied. In that case, we would first invoke transformation $\mathbf{M}_1$, then $\mathbf{M}_2$, then $\mathbf{M}_3$. As each successive transformation routine is called, its matrix is concatenated on the left of the previous matrix product. Other graphics systems, however, postmultiply matrices, so that this transformation sequence would have to be invoked in the reverse order: the last transformation invoked (which is $\mathbf{M}_1$ for this example) is the first to be applied, and the first transformation that is called ($\mathbf{M}_3$ in this case) is the last to be applied.

Transformation products, on the other hand, may not be commutative. The matrix product $\mathbf{M}_2 \cdot \mathbf{M}_1$ is not equal to $\mathbf{M}_1 \cdot \mathbf{M}_2$, in general. This means that if we want to translate and rotate an object, we must be careful about the order in which the composite matrix is evaluated (Fig. 5-13). For some special cases—such as a sequence of transformations that are all of the same kind—the multiplication of transformation matrices is commutative. As an example, two successive rotations could be performed in either order and the final position would be the same. This commutative property holds also for two successive translations or two successive scalings. Another commutative pair of operations is rotation and uniform scaling ($s_x = s_y$).

General Two-Dimensional Composite Transformations and Computational Efficiency

A two-dimensional transformation, representing any combination of translations, rotations, and scalings, can be expressed as

$$\begin{bmatrix} x' \\ y' \\ 1 \end{bmatrix} = \begin{bmatrix} rs_{xx} & rs_{xy} & trs_x \\ rs_{yx} & rs_{yy} & trs_y \\ 0 & 0 & 1 \end{bmatrix} \cdot \begin{bmatrix} x \\ y \\ 1 \end{bmatrix} \tag{5-41}$$

The four elements rs_{jk} are the multiplicative rotation-scaling terms in the transformation, which involve only rotation angles and scaling factors. Elements trs_x and trs_y are the translational terms, containing combinations of translation distances, pivot-point and fixed-point coordinates, rotation angles, and scaling parameters. For example, if an object is to be scaled and rotated about its centroid coordinates (x_c, y_c) and then translated, the values for the elements of the composite transformation matrix are

$$\mathbf{T}(t_x, t_y) \cdot \mathbf{R}(x_c, y_c, \theta) \cdot \mathbf{S}(x_c, y_c, s_x, s_y)$$

$$= \begin{bmatrix} s_x \cos\theta & -s_y \sin\theta & x_c(1 - s_x \cos\theta) + y_c s_y \sin\theta + t_x \\ s_x \sin\theta & s_y \cos\theta & y_c(1 - s_y \cos\theta) - x_c s_x \sin\theta + t_y \\ 0 & 0 & 1 \end{bmatrix} \tag{5-42}$$

Although matrix equation 5-41 requires nine multiplications and six additions, the explicit calculations for the transformed coordinates are

$$x' = x \cdot rs_{xx} + y \cdot rs_{xy} + trs_x, \qquad y' = x \cdot rs_{yx} + y \cdot rs_{yy} + trs_y \tag{5-43}$$

Thus we need actually perform only four multiplications and four additions to transform coordinate positions. This is the maximum number of computations required for any transformation sequence, once the individual matrices have been concatenated and the elements of the composite matrix evaluated. Without concatenation, the individual transformations would be applied one at a time, and the number of calculations could be significantly increased. An efficient implementation for the transformation operations, therefore, is to formulate transformation matrices, concatenate any transformation sequence, and calculate transformed coordinates using Eqs. 5-43. On parallel systems, direct matrix multiplications with the composite transformation matrix of Eq. 5-41 can be equally efficient.

Since rotation calculations require trigonometric evaluations and several multiplications for each transformed point, computational efficiency can become an important consideration in rotation transformations. In animations and other applications that involve many repeated transformations and small rotation angles, we can use approximations and iterative calculations to reduce computations in the composite transformation equations. When the rotation angle is small, the trigonometric functions can be replaced with approximation values based on the first few terms of their power series expansions. For small enough angles (less than 10°), $\cos\theta$ is approximately 1.0 and $\sin\theta$ has a value very close to the value of θ in radians. If we are rotating in small angular steps about the origin, for instance, we can set $\cos\theta$ to 1.0 and reduce transformation calculations at each step to two multiplications and two additions for each set of coordinates to be rotated. These rotation calculations are

$$x' = x - y\sin\theta, \qquad y' = x\sin\theta + y \tag{5-44}$$

where $\sin\theta$ is evaluated once for all steps, assuming the rotation angle does not change. The error introduced by this approximation at each step decreases as the rotation angle decreases. But even with small rotation angles, the accumulated error over many steps can become quite large. We can control the accumulated error by estimating the error in x' and y' at each step and resetting object positions when the error accumulation becomes too great. Some animation applications automatically reset object positions at fixed intervals, such as every 360° or every 180°.

Composite transformations often involve inverse matrices. For example, transformation sequences for general scaling directions and for some reflections and shears (Section 5-5) require inverse rotations. As we have noted, the inverse matrix representations for the basic geometric transformations can be generated with simple procedures. An inverse translation matrix is obtained by changing the signs of the translation distances, and an inverse rotation matrix is obtained by performing a matrix transpose (or changing the sign of the sine terms). These operations are much simpler than direct inverse matrix calculations.

Two-Dimensional Rigid-Body Transformation

If a transformation matrix includes only translation and rotation parameters, it is a **rigid-body transformation matrix.** The general form for a two-dimensional rigid-body transformation matrix is

$$\begin{bmatrix} r_{xx} & r_{xy} & tr_x \\ r_{yx} & r_{yy} & tr_y \\ 0 & 0 & 1 \end{bmatrix} \tag{5-45}$$

where the four elements r_{jk} are the multiplicative rotation terms, and the elements tr_x and tr_y are the translational terms. A rigid-body change in coordinate position is also sometimes referred to as a **rigid-motion** transformation. All angles and distances between coordinate positions are unchanged by the transformation. In addition, matrix 5-45 has the property that its upper-left 2 by 2 submatrix is an *orthogonal matrix*. This means that if we consider each row (or each column) of the submatrix as a vector, then the two row vectors (r_{xx}, r_{xy}) and (r_{yx}, r_{yy}) (or the two column vectors) form an orthogonal set of unit vectors. Such a set of vectors is also referred to as an *orthonormal* vector set. Each vector has unit length:

$$r_{xx}^2 + r_{xy}^2 = r_{yx}^2 + r_{yy}^2 = 1 \tag{5-46}$$

and the vectors are perpendicular (their dot product is 0):

$$r_{xx}r_{yx} + r_{xy}r_{yy} = 0 \tag{5-47}$$

Therefore, if these unit vectors are transformed by the rotation submatrix, then the vector (r_{xx}, r_{xy}) is converted to a unit vector along the x axis and the vector (r_{yx}, r_{yy}) is transformed into a unit vector along the y axis of the coordinate system:

$$\begin{bmatrix} r_{xx} & r_{xy} & 0 \\ r_{yx} & r_{yy} & 0 \\ 0 & 0 & 1 \end{bmatrix} \cdot \begin{bmatrix} r_{xx} \\ r_{xy} \\ 1 \end{bmatrix} = \begin{bmatrix} 1 \\ 0 \\ 1 \end{bmatrix} \tag{5-48}$$

$$\begin{bmatrix} r_{xx} & r_{xy} & 0 \\ r_{yx} & r_{yy} & 0 \\ 0 & 0 & 1 \end{bmatrix} \cdot \begin{bmatrix} r_{yx} \\ r_{yy} \\ 1 \end{bmatrix} = \begin{bmatrix} 0 \\ 1 \\ 1 \end{bmatrix} \tag{5-49}$$

As an example, the following rigid-body transformation first rotates an object through an angle θ about a pivot point (x_r, y_r) and then translates the object.

$$\mathbf{T}(t_x, t_y) \cdot \mathbf{R}(x_r, y_r, \theta) = \begin{bmatrix} \cos\theta & -\sin\theta & x_r(1-\cos\theta) + y_r\sin\theta + t_x \\ \sin\theta & \cos\theta & y_r(1-\cos\theta) - x_r\sin\theta + t_y \\ 0 & 0 & 1 \end{bmatrix} \tag{5-50}$$

Here, orthogonal unit vectors in the upper-left 2 by 2 submatrix are $(\cos\theta, -\sin\theta)$ and $(\sin\theta, \cos\theta)$, and

$$\begin{bmatrix} \cos\theta & -\sin\theta & 0 \\ \sin\theta & \cos\theta & 0 \\ 0 & 0 & 1 \end{bmatrix} \cdot \begin{bmatrix} \cos\theta \\ -\sin\theta \\ 1 \end{bmatrix} = \begin{bmatrix} 1 \\ 0 \\ 1 \end{bmatrix} \tag{5-51}$$

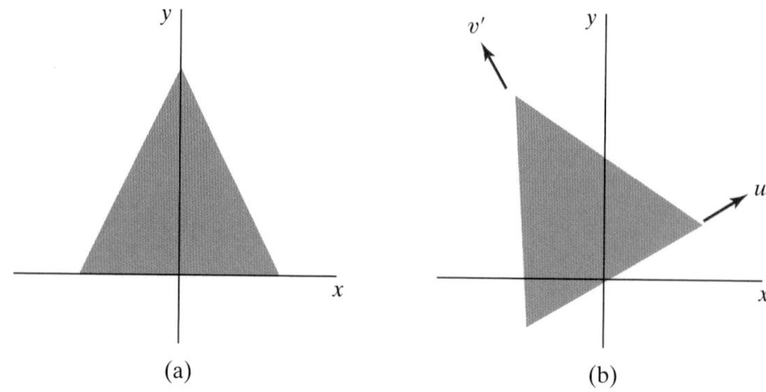

FIGURE 5-14 The rotation matrix for revolving an object from position (a) to position (b) can be constructed with the values of the unit orientation vectors **u**′ and **v**′ relative to the original orientation.

Similarly, unit vector $(\sin\theta, \cos\theta)$ is converted by the preceding transformation matrix to the unit vector (0, 1) in the y direction.

Constructing Two-Dimensional Rotation Matrices

The orthogonal property of rotation matrices is useful for constructing the matrix when we know the final orientation of an object, rather than the amount of angular rotation necessary to put the object into that position. This orientation information could be determined by the alignment of certain objects in a scene or by reference positions within the coordinate system. For example, we might want to rotate an object to align its axis of symmetry with the viewing (camera) direction, or we might want to rotate one object so that it is above another object. Figure 5-14 shows an object that is to be aligned with the unit direction vectors **u**′ and **v**′. Assuming that the original object orientation, as shown in Fig. 5-14(a), is aligned with the coordinate axes, we construct the desired transformation by assigning the elements of **u**′ to the first row of the rotation matrix and the elements of **v**′ to the second row. In a modeling application, for instance, we can use this method to obtain the transformation matrix within an object's local coordinate system when we know what its orientation is to be within the overall world-coordinate scene. A similar transformation is the conversion of object descriptions from one coordinate system to another, and we take up these methods in more detail in Sections 5-8 and 5-15.

Two-Dimensional Composite-Matrix Programming Example

An implementation example for a sequence of geometric transformations is given in the following program. Initially, the composite matrix, `compMatrix`, is constructed as the identity matrix. For this example, a left-to-right concatenation order is used to construct the composite transformation matrix, and we invoke the transformation routines in the order that they are to be executed. As each of the basic transformation routines (scale, rotate, and translate) is invoked, a matrix is set up for that transformation and left-concatenated with the composite matrix. When all transformations have been specified, the composite transformation is applied to transform a triangle. The triangle is first scaled with respect to its centroid position (Appendix A), then the triangle is rotated about its centroid, and, lastly, it is translated. Figure 5-15 shows the original and final positions of the triangle that is transformed by this sequence. Routines in OpenGL are used to display the initial and final position of the triangle.

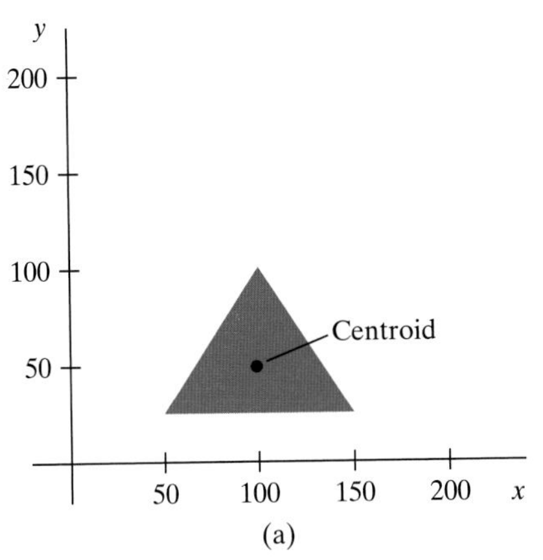

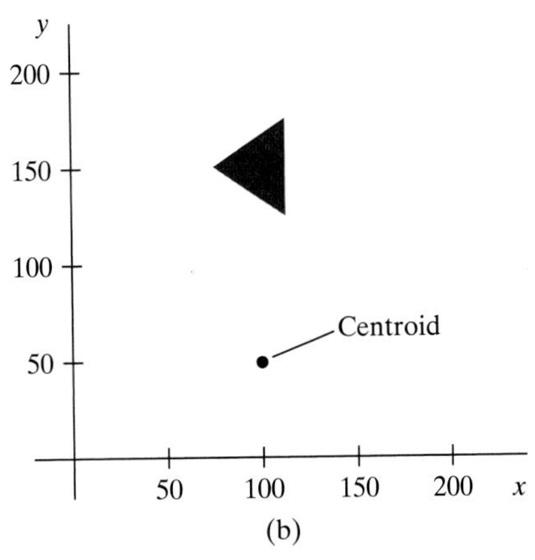

FIGURE 5-15 A triangle (a) is transformed into position (b) using the composite-matrix calculations in procedure `transformVerts2D`.

```
#include <GL/glut.h>
#include <stdlib.h>
#include <math.h>

/*  Set initial display-window size. */
GLsizei winWidth = 600, winHeight = 600;

/*  Set range for world coordinates.  */
GLfloat xwcMin = 0.0, xwcMax = 225.0;
GLfloat ywcMin = 0.0, ywcMax = 225.0;

class wcPt2D {
   public:
      GLfloat x, y;
};

typedef GLfloat Matrix3x3 [3][3];

Matrix3x3 matComposite;

const GLdouble pi = 3.14159;

void init (void)
{
   /*  Set color of display window to white.  */
   glClearColor (1.0, 1.0, 1.0, 0.0);
}

/* Construct the 3 by 3 identity matrix. */
void matrix3x3SetIdentity (Matrix3x3 matIdent3x3)
{
   GLint row, col;

   for (row = 0; row < 3; row++)
      for (col = 0; col < 3; col++)
         matIdent3x3 [row][col] = (row == col);
}
```

```
/* Premultiply matrix m1 times matrix m2, store result in m2. */
void matrix3x3PreMultiply (Matrix3x3 m1, Matrix3x3 m2)
{
   GLint row, col;
   Matrix3x3 matTemp;

   for (row = 0; row < 3; row++)
      for (col = 0; col < 3 ; col++)
         matTemp [row][col] = m1 [row][0] * m2 [0][col] + m1 [row][1] *
                            m2 [1][col] + m1 [row][2] * m2 [2][col];

   for (row = 0; row < 3; row++)
      for (col = 0; col < 3; col++)
         m2 [row][col] = matTemp [row][col];
}

void translate2D (GLfloat tx, GLfloat ty)
{
   Matrix3x3 matTransl;

   /*  Initialize translation matrix to identity.  */
   matrix3x3SetIdentity (matTransl);

   matTransl [0][2] = tx;
   matTransl [1][2] = ty;

   /*  Concatenate matTransl with the composite matrix.  */
   matrix3x3PreMultiply (matTransl, matComposite);
}

void rotate2D (wcPt2D pivotPt, GLfloat theta)
{
   Matrix3x3 matRot;

   /*  Initialize rotation matrix to identity.  */
   matrix3x3SetIdentity (matRot);

   matRot [0][0] = cos (theta);
   matRot [0][1] = -sin (theta);
   matRot [0][2] = pivotPt.x * (1 - cos (theta)) +
                       pivotPt.y * sin (theta);
   matRot [1][0] = sin (theta);
   matRot [1][1] = cos (theta);
   matRot [1][2] = pivotPt.y * (1 - cos (theta)) -
                       pivotPt.x * sin (theta);

   /*  Concatenate matRot with the composite matrix.  */
   matrix3x3PreMultiply (matRot, matComposite);
}

void scale2D (GLfloat sx, GLfloat sy, wcPt2D fixedPt)
{
   Matrix3x3 matScale;
```

```
   /*  Initialize scaling matrix to identity.  */
   matrix3x3SetIdentity (matScale);

   matScale [0][0] = sx;
   matScale [0][2] = (1 - sx) * fixedPt.x;
   matScale [1][1] = sy;
   matScale [1][2] = (1 - sy) * fixedPt.y;

   /*  Concatenate matScale with the composite matrix.  */
   matrix3x3PreMultiply (matScale, matComposite);
}

/* Using the composite matrix, calculate transformed coordinates. */
void transformVerts2D (GLint nVerts, wcPt2D * verts)
{
   GLint k;
   GLfloat temp;

   for (k = 0; k < nVerts; k++) {
      temp = matComposite [0][0] * verts [k].x + matComposite [0][1] *
             verts [k].y + matComposite [0][2];
      verts [k].y = matComposite [1][0] * verts [k].x + matComposite [1][1] *
                    verts [k].y + matComposite [1][2];
         verts [k].x = temp;
   }
}

void triangle (wcPt2D *verts)
{
    GLint k;

    glBegin (GL_TRIANGLES);
       for (k = 0; k < 3; k++)
          glVertex2f (verts [k].x, verts [k].y);
    glEnd ( );
}

void displayFcn (void)
{
   /*  Define initial position for triangle.  */
   GLint nVerts = 3;
   wcPt2D verts [3] = { {50.0, 25.0}, {150.0, 25.0}, {100.0, 100.0} };

   /*  Calculate position of triangle centroid.  */
   wcPt2D centroidPt;

   GLint k, xSum = 0, ySum = 0;
   for (k = 0; k < nVerts;  k++) {
      xSum += verts [k].x;
      ySum += verts [k].y;
   }
   centroidPt.x = GLfloat (xSum) / GLfloat (nVerts);
   centroidPt.y = GLfloat (ySum) / GLfloat (nVerts);
```

```
    /* Set geometric transformation parameters. */
    wcPt2D pivPt, fixedPt;
    pivPt = centroidPt;
    fixedPt = centroidPt;

    GLfloat tx = 0.0, ty = 100.0;
    GLfloat sx = 0.5, sy = 0.5;
    GLdouble theta = pi/2.0;

    glClear (GL_COLOR_BUFFER_BIT);   // Clear display window.

    glColor3f (0.0, 0.0, 1.0);       // Set initial fill color to blue.
    triangle (verts);                // Display blue triangle.

    /* Initialize composite matrix to identity. */
    matrix3x3SetIdentity (matComposite);

    /* Construct composite matrix for transformation sequence. */
    scale2D (sx, sy, fixedPt);   // First transformation: Scale.
    rotate2D (pivPt, theta);     // Second transformation: Rotate
    translate2D (tx, ty);        // Final transformation: Translate.

    /* Apply composite matrix to triangle vertices. */
    transformVerts2D (nVerts, verts);

    glColor3f (1.0, 0.0, 0.0);  // Set color for transformed triangle.
    triangle (verts);           // Display red transformed triangle.

    glFlush ( );
}

void winReshapeFcn (GLint newWidth, GLint newHeight)
{
    glMatrixMode (GL_PROJECTION);
    glLoadIdentity ( );
    gluOrtho2D (xwcMin, xwcMax, ywcMin, ywcMax);

    glClear (GL_COLOR_BUFFER_BIT);
}

void main (int argc, char ** argv)
{
    glutInit (&argc, argv);
    glutInitDisplayMode (GLUT_SINGLE | GLUT_RGB);
    glutInitWindowPosition (50, 50);
    glutInitWindowSize (winWidth, winHeight);
    glutCreateWindow ("Geometric Transformation Sequence");

    init ( );
    glutDisplayFunc (displayFcn);
    glutReshapeFunc (winReshapeFcn);

    glutMainLoop ( );
}
```

5-5 OTHER TWO-DIMENSIONAL TRANSFORMATIONS

Basic transformations such as translation, rotation, and scaling are standard components of graphics libraries. Some packages provide a few additional transformations that are useful in certain applications. Two such transformations are reflection and shear.

Reflection

A transformation that produces a mirror image of an object is called a **reflection.** For a two-dimensional reflection, this image is generated relative to an **axis of reflection** by rotating the object 180° about the reflection axis. We can choose an axis of reflection in the xy plane or perpendicular to the xy plane. When the reflection axis is a line in the xy plane, the rotation path about this axis is in a plane perpendicular to the xy plane. For reflection axes that are perpendicular to the xy plane, the rotation path is in the xy plane. Following are examples of some common reflections.

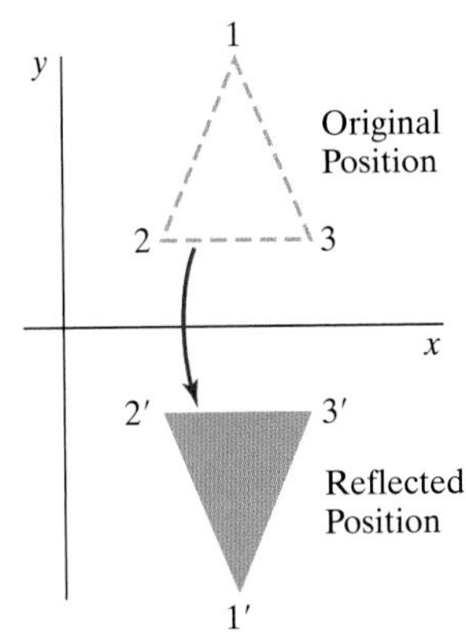

FIGURE 5-16 Reflection of an object about the x axis.

Reflection about the line $y = 0$ (the x axis) is accomplished with the transformation matrix

$$\begin{bmatrix} 1 & 0 & 0 \\ 0 & -1 & 0 \\ 0 & 0 & 1 \end{bmatrix} \tag{5-52}$$

This transformation retains x values, but "flips" the y values of coordinate positions. The resulting orientation of an object after it has been reflected about the x axis is shown in Fig. 5-16. To envision the rotation transformation path for this reflection, we can think of the flat object moving out of the xy plane and rotating 180° through three-dimensional space about the x axis and back into the xy plane on the other side of the x axis.

A reflection about the line $x = 0$ (the y axis) flips x coordinates while keeping y coordinates the same. The matrix for this transformation is

$$\begin{bmatrix} -1 & 0 & 0 \\ 0 & 1 & 0 \\ 0 & 0 & 1 \end{bmatrix} \tag{5-53}$$

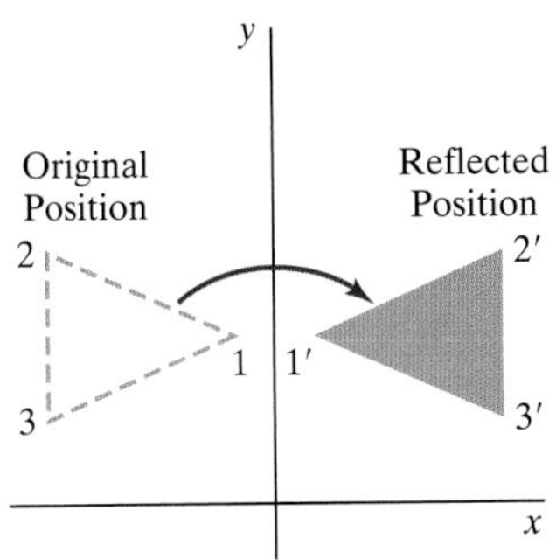

FIGURE 5-17 Reflection of an object about the y axis.

Figure 5-17 illustrates the change in position of an object that has been reflected about the line $x = 0$. The equivalent rotation in this case is 180° through three-dimensional space about the y axis.

We flip both the x and y coordinates of a point by reflecting relative to an axis that is perpendicular to the xy plane and that passes through the coordinate origin. This reflection is sometimes referred to as a reflection relative to the coordinate origin, and it is equivalent to reflecting with respect to both coordinate axes. The matrix representation for this reflection is

$$\begin{bmatrix} -1 & 0 & 0 \\ 0 & -1 & 0 \\ 0 & 0 & 1 \end{bmatrix} \tag{5-54}$$

An example of reflection about the origin is shown in Fig. 5-18. The reflection matrix 5-54 is the same as the rotation matrix $\mathbf{R}(\theta)$ with $\theta = 180°$. We are simply rotating the object in the xy plane half a revolution about the origin.

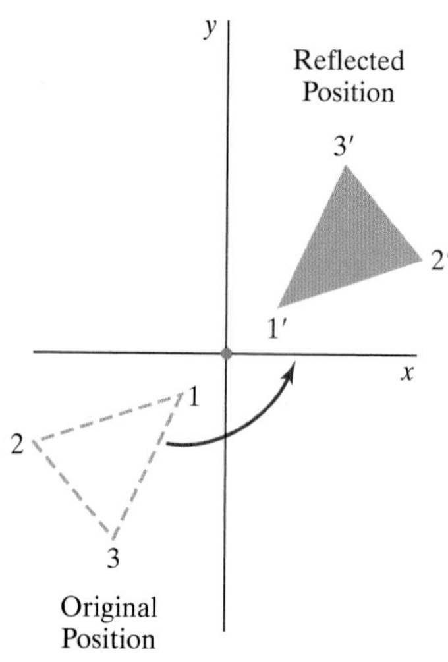

FIGURE 5-18 Reflection of an object relative to the coordinate origin. This transformation can be accomplished with a rotation in the xy plane about the coordinate origin.

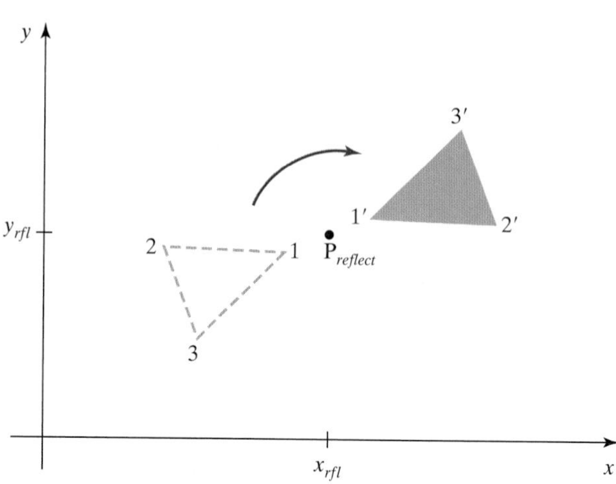

FIGURE 5-19 Reflection of an object relative to an axis perpendicular to the xy plane and passing through point $\mathbf{P}_{\text{reflect}}$.

Reflection 5-54 can be generalized to any reflection point in the xy plane (Fig. 5-19). This reflection is the same as a 180° rotation in the xy plane about the reflection point.

If we choose the reflection axis as the diagonal line $y = x$ (Fig. 5-20), the reflection matrix is

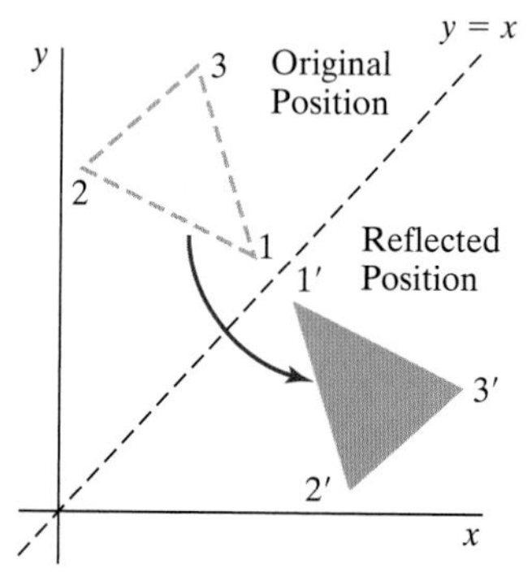

FIGURE 5-20 Reflection of an object with respect to the line $y = x$.

$$\begin{bmatrix} 0 & 1 & 0 \\ 1 & 0 & 0 \\ 0 & 0 & 1 \end{bmatrix} \tag{5-55}$$

We can derive this matrix by concatenating a sequence of rotation and coordinate-axis reflection matrices. One possible sequence is shown in Fig. 5-21. Here, we first perform a clockwise rotation with respect to the origin through a 45° angle, which rotates the line $y = x$ onto the x axis. Next, we perform a reflection with respect to the x axis. The final step is to rotate the line $y = x$ back to its original position with a counterclockwise rotation through 45°. Another equivalent sequence of transformations is to first reflect the object about the x axis, then rotate it counterclockwise 90°.

To obtain a transformation matrix for reflection about the diagonal $y = -x$, we could concatenate matrices for the transformation sequence: (1) clockwise rotation by 45°, (2) reflection about the y axis, and (3) counterclockwise rotation by 45°. The resulting transformation matrix is

$$\begin{bmatrix} 0 & -1 & 0 \\ -1 & 0 & 0 \\ 0 & 0 & 1 \end{bmatrix} \tag{5-56}$$

Figure 5-22 shows the original and final positions for an object transformed with this reflection matrix.

Reflections about any line $y = mx + b$ in the xy plane can be accomplished with a combination of translate-rotate-reflect transformations. In general, we first translate the line so that it passes through the origin. Then we can rotate the line onto one of the coordinate axes and reflect about that axis. Finally, we restore the line to its original position with the inverse rotation and translation transformations.

We can implement reflections with respect to the coordinate axes or coordinate origin as scaling transformations with negative scaling factors. Also, elements of the reflection matrix can be set to values other than ± 1. A reflection parameter with a magnitude greater than 1 shifts the mirror image of a point farther from the reflection axis, and a parameter with magnitude less than 1 brings the mirror image of a point closer to the reflection axis. Thus, a reflected object can also be enlarged, reduced, or distorted.

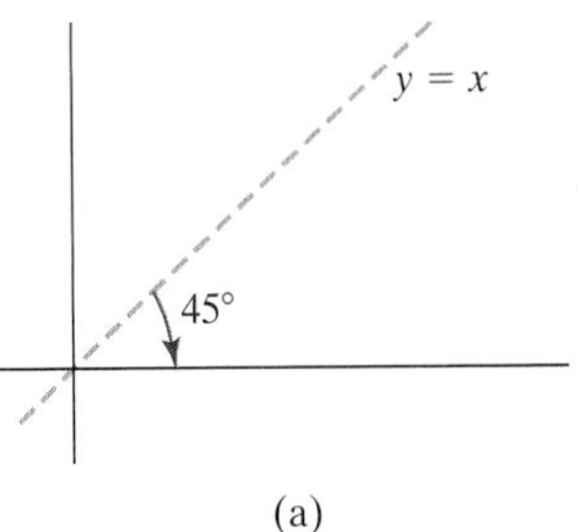

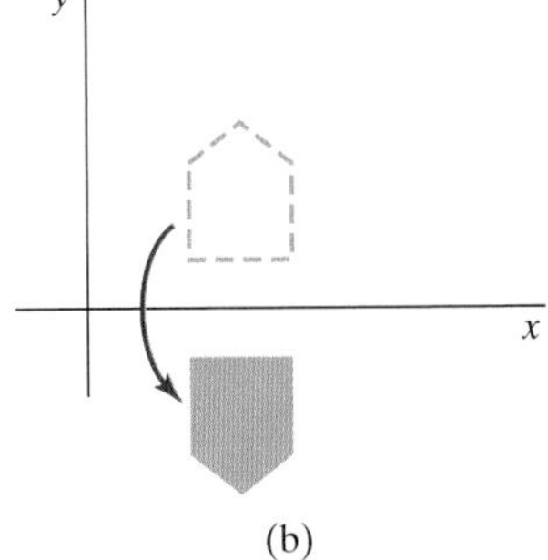

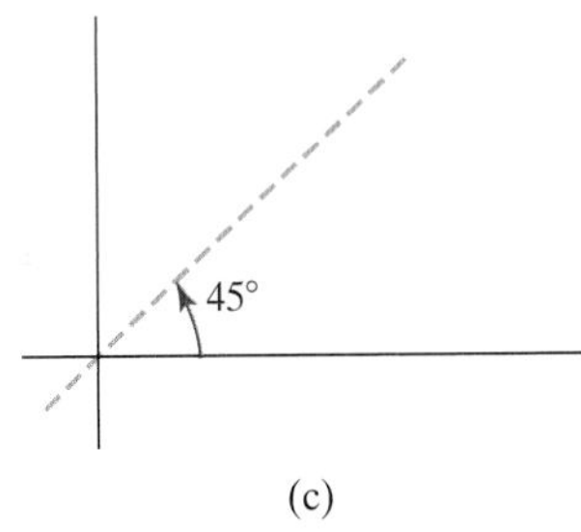

FIGURE 5-21 Sequence of transformations to produce a reflection about the line $y = x$: A clockwise rotation of 45° (a), a reflection about the x axis (b), and a counterclockwise rotation by 45° (c).

Shear

A transformation that distorts the shape of an object such that the transformed shape appears as if the object were composed of internal layers that had been caused to slide over each other is called a **shear.** Two common shearing transformations are those that shift coordinate x values and those that shift y values.

An x-direction shear relative to the x axis is produced with the transformation matrix

$$\begin{bmatrix} 1 & sh_x & 0 \\ 0 & 1 & 0 \\ 0 & 0 & 1 \end{bmatrix} \tag{5-57}$$

which transforms coordinate positions as

$$x' = x + sh_x \cdot y, \qquad y' = y \tag{5-58}$$

Any real number can be assigned to the shear parameter sh_x. A coordinate position (x, y) is then shifted horizontally by an amount proportional to its perpendicular distance (y value) from the x axis. Setting parameter sh_x to the value 2, for example, changes the square in Fig. 5-23 into a parallelogram. Negative values for sh_x shift coordinate positions to the left.

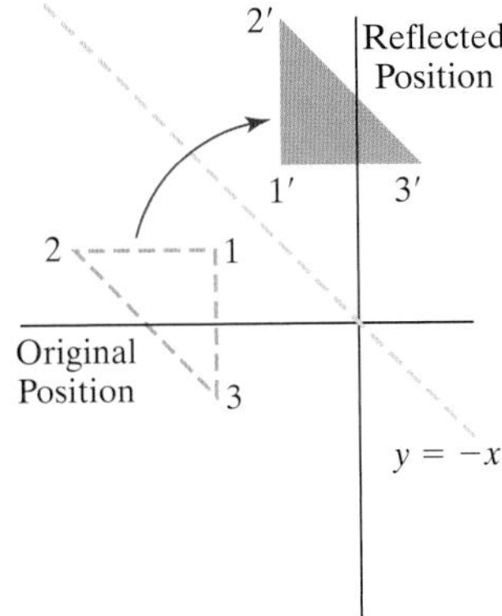

FIGURE 5-22 Reflection with respect to the line $y = -x$.

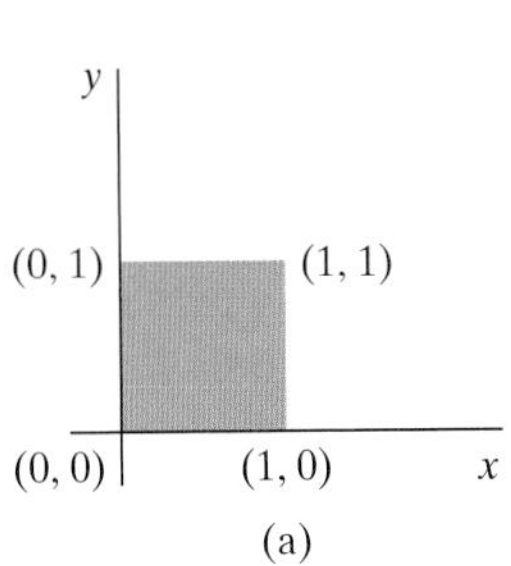

y
(2, 1) (3, 1)
(0, 0) (1, 0) x
(b)

FIGURE 5-23 A unit square (a) is converted to a parallelogram (b) using the x-direction shear matrix 5-57 with $sh_x = 2$.

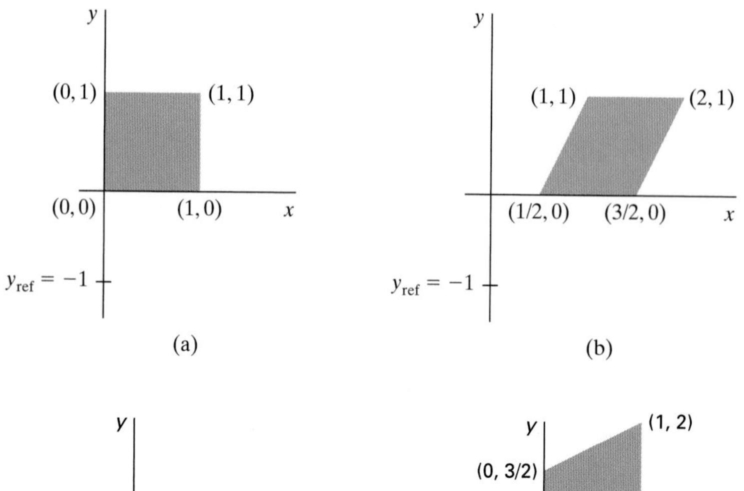

FIGURE 5-24 A unit square (a) is transformed to a shifted parallelogram (b) with $sh_x = 0.5$ and $y_{ref} = -1$ in the shear matrix 5-59.

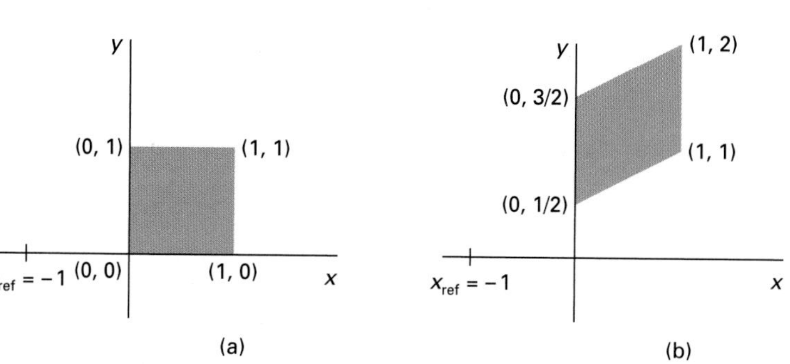

FIGURE 5-25 A unit square (a) is turned into a shifted parallelogram (b) with parameter values $sh_y = 0.5$ and $x_{ref} = -1$ in the y-direction shearing transformation 5-61.

We can generate x-direction shears relative to other reference lines with

$$\begin{bmatrix} 1 & sh_x & -sh_x \cdot y_{ref} \\ 0 & 1 & 0 \\ 0 & 0 & 1 \end{bmatrix} \tag{5-59}$$

Now, coordinate positions are transformed as

$$x' = x + sh_x(y - y_{ref}), \qquad y' = y \tag{5-60}$$

An example of this shearing transformation is given in Fig. 5-24 for a shear parameter value of $\frac{1}{2}$ relative to the line $y_{ref} = -1$.

A y-direction shear relative to the line $x = x_{ref}$ is generated with the transformation matrix

$$\begin{bmatrix} 1 & 0 & 0 \\ sh_y & 1 & -sh_y \cdot x_{ref} \\ 0 & 0 & 1 \end{bmatrix} \tag{5-61}$$

which generates the transformed coordinate values

$$x' = x, \qquad y' = y + sh_y(x - x_{ref}) \tag{5-62}$$

This transformation shifts a coordinate position vertically by an amount proportional to its distance from the reference line $x = x_{ref}$. Fig. 5-25 illustrates the conversion of a square into a parallelogram with $sh_y = 0.5$ and $x_{ref} = -1$.

Shearing operations can be expressed as sequences of basic transformations. The x-direction shear matrix 5-57, for example, can be represented as a composite transformation involving a series of rotation and scaling matrices. This composite transformation scales the unit square of Fig. 5-23 along its diagonal, while maintaining the original lengths and orientations of edges parallel to the x axis. Shifts in the positions of objects relative to shearing reference lines are equivalent to translations.

5-6 RASTER METHODS FOR GEOMETRIC TRANSFORMATIONS

The characteristics of raster systems suggest an alternate method for performing certain two-dimensional transformations. Raster systems store picture information as color patterns in the frame buffer. Therefore, some simple object transformations can be carried out rapidly by manipulating an array of pixel values. Few arithmetic operations are needed, so the pixel transformations are particularly efficient.

As we noted in Section 3-19, functions that manipulate rectangular pixel arrays are called *raster operations,* and moving a block of pixel values from one position to another is termed a *block transfer,* a *bitblt,* or a *pixblt.* Routines for performing some raster operations are usually available in a graphics package.

Figure 5-26 illustrates a two-dimensional translation implemented as a block transfer of a refresh-buffer area. All bit settings in the rectangular area shown are copied as a block into another part of the frame buffer. We can erase the pattern at the original location by assigning the background color to all pixels within that block (assuming that the pattern to be erased does not overlap other objects in the scene).

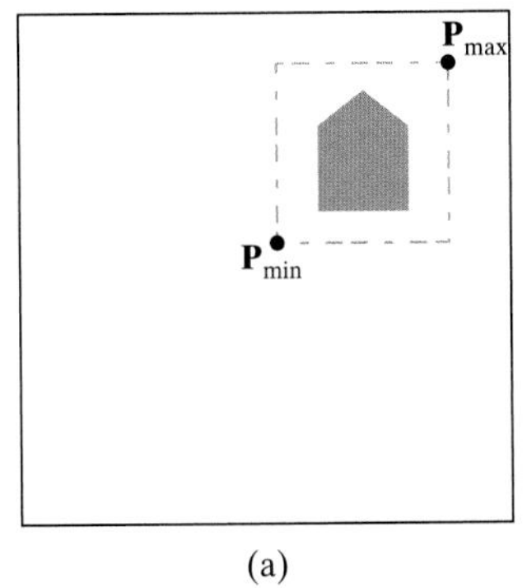

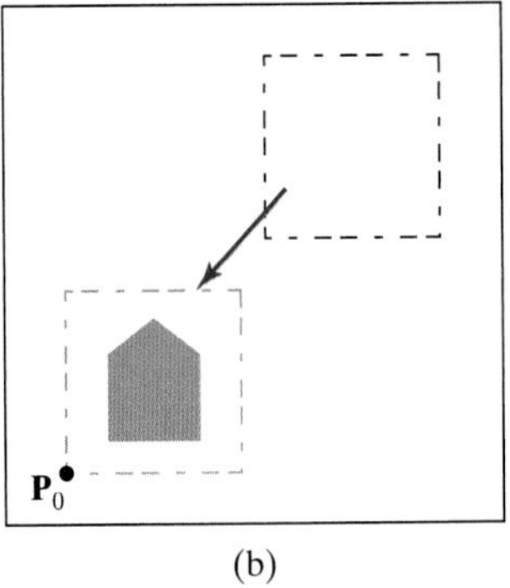

FIGURE 5-26 Translating an object from screen position (a) to the destination position shown in (b) by moving a rectangular block of pixel values. Coordinate positions $\mathbf{P}_{min}$ and $\mathbf{P}_{max}$ specify the limits of the rectangular block to be moved, and $\mathbf{P}_0$ is the destination reference position.

Rotations in 90-degree increments are easily accomplished by rearranging the elements of a pixel array. We can rotate a two-dimensional object or pattern 90° counterclockwise by reversing the pixel values in each row of the array, then interchanging rows and columns. A 180° rotation is obtained by reversing the order of the elements in each row of the array, then reversing the order of the rows. Figure 5-27 demonstrates the array manipulations that can be used to rotate a pixel block by 90° and by 180°.

For array rotations that are not multiples of 90°, we need to do some extra processing. The general procedure is illustrated in Fig. 5-28. Each destination pixel area is mapped onto the rotated array and the amount of overlap with the rotated pixel areas is calculated. A color for a destination pixel can then be computed by averaging the colors of the overlapped source pixels, weighted by their percentage of area overlap. Or, we could use an approximation method, as in antialiasing, to determine the color of the destination pixels.

We can use similar methods to scale a block of pixels. Pixel areas in the original block are scaled, using specified values for s_x and s_y, and then mapped onto a set of destination pixels. The color of each destination pixel is then assigned according to its area of overlap with the scaled pixel areas (Fig. 5-29).

An object can be reflected using raster transformations that reverse row or column values in a pixel block, combined with translations. Shears are produced with shifts in the positions of array values along rows or columns.

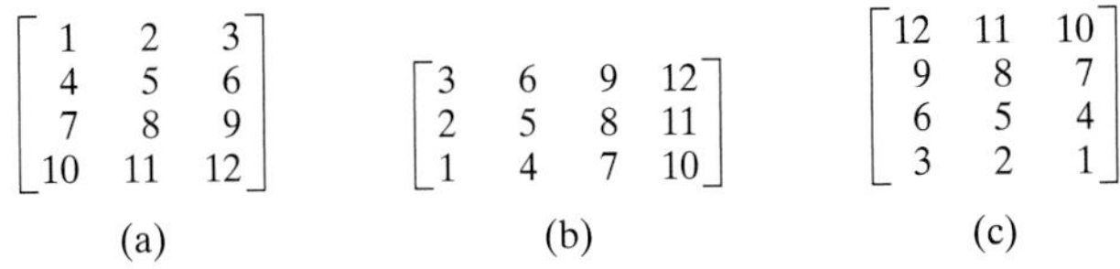

$\begin{bmatrix} 1 & 2 & 3 \\ 4 & 5 & 6 \\ 7 & 8 & 9 \\ 10 & 11 & 12 \end{bmatrix}$
(a)
$\begin{bmatrix} 3 & 6 & 9 & 12 \\ 2 & 5 & 8 & 11 \\ 1 & 4 & 7 & 10 \end{bmatrix}$
(b)
$\begin{bmatrix} 12 & 11 & 10 \\ 9 & 8 & 7 \\ 6 & 5 & 4 \\ 3 & 2 & 1 \end{bmatrix}$
(c)

FIGURE 5-27 Rotating an array of pixel values. The original array is shown in (a), the positions of the array elements after a 90° counterclockwise rotation are shown in (b), and the positions of the array elements after a 180° rotation are shown in (c).

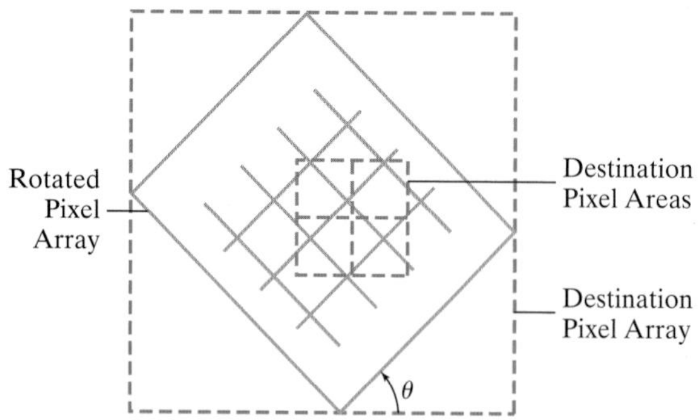

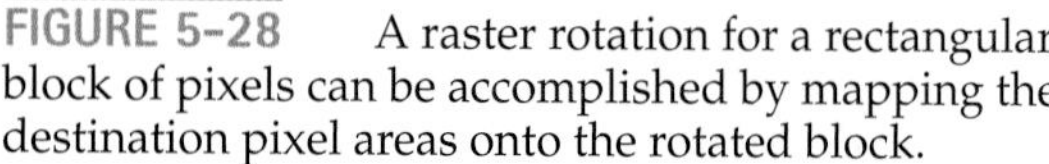
FIGURE 5-28 A raster rotation for a rectangular block of pixels can be accomplished by mapping the destination pixel areas onto the rotated block.

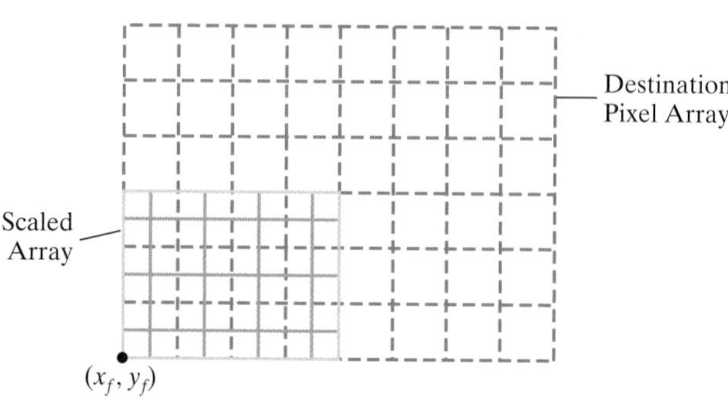

FIGURE 5-29 Mapping destination pixel areas onto a scaled array of pixel values. Scaling factors $s_x = s_y = 0.5$ are applied relative to fixed point (x_f, y_f).

5-7 OpenGL RASTER TRANSFORMATIONS

In Section 3-19, we introduced most of the OpenGL functions for performing raster operations. A translation of a rectangular array of pixel-color values from one buffer area to another can be accomplished in OpenGL as a copy operation:

```
glCopyPixels (xmin, ymin, width, height, GL_COLOR);
```

The first four parameters in this function give the location and dimensions of the pixel block. And the OpenGL symbolic constant `GL_COLOR` specifies that it is color values that are to be copied. This array of pixels is to be copied to a rectangular area of a refresh buffer whose lower-left corner is at the location specified by the current raster position. Pixel-color values are copied as either RGBA values or color-table indices, depending on the current setting for the color mode. Both the region to be copied (the source) and the destination area should lie completely within the bounds of the screen coordinates. This translation can be carried out on any of the OpenGL buffers used for refreshing, or even between different buffers. A source buffer for the `glCopyPixels` function is chosen with the `glReadBuffer` routine, and a destination buffer is selected with the `glDrawBuffer` routine.

We can rotate a block of pixel-color values in 90-degree increments by first saving the block in an array, then rearranging the elements of the array and placing it back in the refresh buffer. As we saw in Section 3-19, a block of RGB color values in a buffer can be saved in an array with the function

```
glReadPixels (xmin, ymin, width, height, GL_RGB,
                    GL_UNSIGNED_BYTE, colorArray);
```

If color-table indices are stored at the pixel positions, we replace the constant `GL_RGB` with `GL_COLOR_INDEX`. To rotate the color values, we rearrange the rows and columns of the color array as described in the previous section. Then we put the rotated array back in the buffer with

```
glDrawPixels (width, height, GL_RGB, GL_UNSIGNED_BYTE,
                    colorArray);
```

The lower-left corner of this array is placed at the current raster position. We select the source buffer containing the original block of pixel values with `glReadBuffer`, and we designate a destination buffer with `glDrawBuffer`.

A two-dimensional scaling transformation can be performed as a raster operation in OpenGL by specifying scaling factors and then invoking either `glCopyPixels` or `glDrawPixels`. For the raster operations, we set the scaling factors with

```
glPixelZoom (sx, sy);
```

where parameters `sx` and `sy` can be assigned any nonzero floating-point values. Positive values greater than 1.0 increase the size of an element in the source array, and positive values less than 1.0 decrease element size. A negative value for `sx` or `sy`, or both, produces a reflection as well as scaling the array elements. Thus, if `sx` = `sy` = −3.0, the source array is reflected with respect to the current raster position and each color element of the array is mapped to a 3 by 3 block of destination pixels. If the center of a destination pixel lies within the rectangular area of a scaled color element of an array, it is assigned the color of that array element. Destination pixels whose centers are on the left or top boundary of the scaled array element are also assigned the color of that element. The default value for both `sx` and `sy` is 1.0.

We can also combine raster transformations with the logical operations discussed in Section 3-19 to produce various effects. With the *exclusive or* operator, for example, two successive copies of a pixel array to the same buffer area restores the values that were originally present in that area. This technique can be used in an animation application to translate an object across a scene without altering the background pixels.

5-8 TRANSFORMATIONS BETWEEN TWO-DIMENSIONAL COORDINATE SYSTEMS

Computer-graphics applications involve coordinate transformations from one reference frame to another during various stages of scene processing. The viewing routines transform object descriptions from world coordinates to device coordinates. For modeling and design applications, individual objects are typically defined in their own local Cartesian references. These local-coordinate descriptions must then be transformed into positions and orientations within the overall scene coordinate system. A facility-management program for office layouts, for instance, has individual coordinate descriptions for chairs and tables and other furniture that can be placed into a floor plan, with multiple copies of the chairs and other items in different positions.

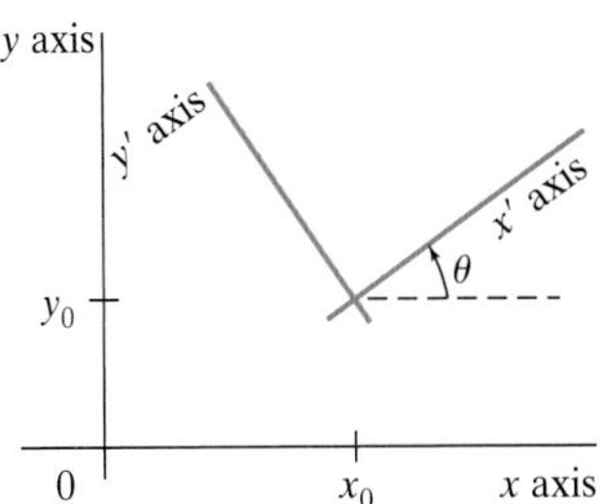

FIGURE 5-30 A Cartesian $x'y'$ system positioned at (x_0, y_0) with orientation θ in an xy Cartesian system.

Also, scenes are sometimes described in non-Cartesian reference frames that take advantage of object symmetries. Coordinate descriptions in these systems must be converted to Cartesian world-coordinates for processing. Some examples of non-Cartesian systems are polar coordinates, spherical coordinates, elliptical coordinates, and parabolic coordinates. Relationships between Cartesian reference systems and some common non-Cartesian systems are given in Appendix A. Here, we consider only the transformations involved in converting from one two-dimensional Cartesian frame to another.

Figure 5-30 shows a Cartesian $x'y'$ system specified with coordinate origin (x_0, y_0) and orientation angle θ in a Cartesian xy reference frame. To transform object descriptions from xy coordinates to $x'y'$ coordinates, we set up a transformation that superimposes the $x'y'$ axes onto the xy axes. This is done in two steps:

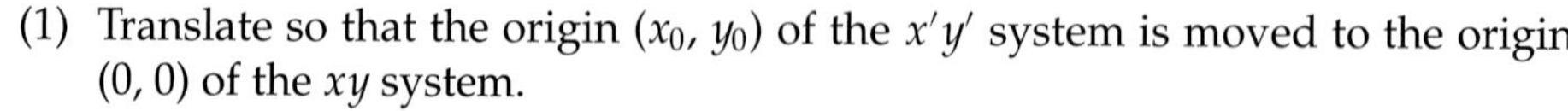

(1) Translate so that the origin (x_0, y_0) of the $x'y'$ system is moved to the origin $(0, 0)$ of the xy system.

(2) Rotate the x' axis onto the x axis.

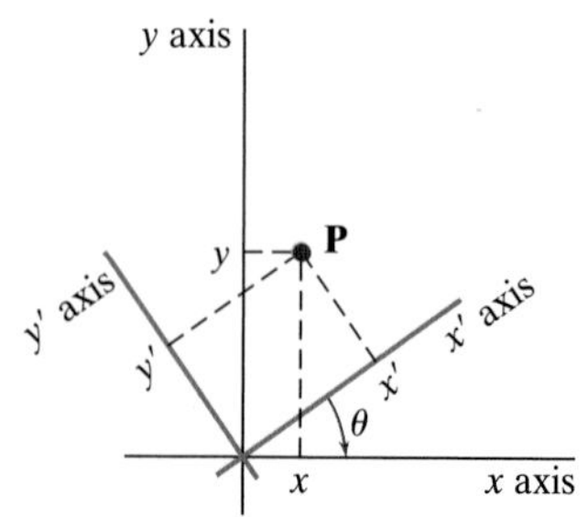

FIGURE 5-31 Position of the reference frames shown in Fig. 5-30 after translating the origin of the $x'y'$ system to the coordinate origin of the xy system.

Translation of the coordinate origin is accomplished with the matrix transformation

$$\mathbf{T}(-x_0, -y_0) = \begin{bmatrix} 1 & 0 & -x_0 \\ 0 & 1 & -y_0 \\ 0 & 0 & 1 \end{bmatrix} \tag{5-63}$$

The orientation of the two systems after the translation operation would then appear as in Fig. 5-31. To get the axes of the two systems into coincidence, we then perform the clockwise rotation

$$\mathbf{R}(-\theta) = \begin{bmatrix} \cos\theta & \sin\theta & 0 \\ -\sin\theta & \cos\theta & 0 \\ 0 & 0 & 1 \end{bmatrix} \tag{5-64}$$

Concatenating these two transformation matrices gives us the complete composite matrix for transforming object descriptions from the xy system to the $x'y'$ system:

$$\mathbf{M}_{xy,x'y'} = \mathbf{R}(-\theta) \cdot \mathbf{T}(-x_0, -y_0) \tag{5-65}$$

An alternate method for describing the orientation of the $x'y'$ coordinate system is to specify a vector $\mathbf{V}$ that indicates the direction for the positive y' axis, as shown in Fig. 5-32. We can specify vector $\mathbf{V}$ as a point in the xy reference frame relative to the origin of the xy system, which we can convert to the unit vector

$$\mathbf{v} = \frac{\mathbf{V}}{|\mathbf{V}|} = (v_x, v_y) \tag{5-66}$$

And we obtain the unit vector $\mathbf{u}$ along the x' axis by applying a 90° clockwise rotation to vector $\mathbf{v}$:

$$\begin{aligned} \mathbf{u} &= (v_y, -v_x) \\ &= (u_x, u_y) \end{aligned} \tag{5-67}$$

In Section 5-4, we noted that the elements of any rotation matrix could be expressed as elements of a set of orthonormal vectors. Therefore, the matrix to rotate the

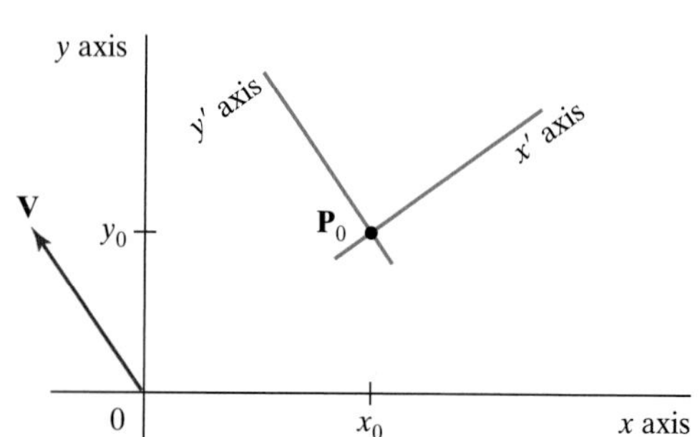

FIGURE 5-32 Cartesian system $x'y'$ with origin at $\mathbf{P}_0 = (x_0, y_0)$ and y' axis parallel to vector $\mathbf{V}$.

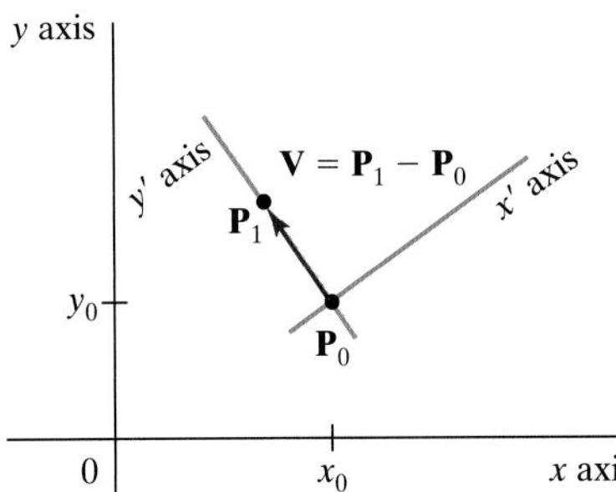

FIGURE 5-33 A Cartesian $x'y'$ system defined with two coordinate positions, $\mathbf{P}_0$ and $\mathbf{P}_1$, within an xy reference frame.

$x'y'$ system into coincidence with the xy system can be written as

$$R = \begin{bmatrix} u_x & u_y & 0 \\ v_x & v_y & 0 \\ 0 & 0 & 1 \end{bmatrix} \tag{5-68}$$

For example, suppose we choose the orientation for the y' axis as $\mathbf{V} = (-1, 0)$. Then the x' axis is in the positive y direction and the rotation transformation matrix is

$$\begin{bmatrix} 0 & 1 & 0 \\ -1 & 0 & 0 \\ 0 & 0 & 1 \end{bmatrix}$$

Equivalently, we can obtain this rotation matrix from Eq. 5-64 by setting the orientation angle as $\theta = 90°$.

In an interactive application, it may be more convenient to choose the direction for $\mathbf{V}$ relative to position $\mathbf{P}_0$ than to specify it relative to the xy-coordinate origin. Unit vectors $\mathbf{u}$ and $\mathbf{v}$ would then be oriented as shown in Fig. 5-33. The components of $\mathbf{v}$ are now calculated as

$$\mathbf{v} = \frac{\mathbf{P}_1 - \mathbf{P}_0}{|\mathbf{P}_1 - \mathbf{P}_0|} \tag{5-69}$$

and $\mathbf{u}$ is obtained as the perpendicular to $\mathbf{v}$ that forms a right-handed Cartesian system.

5-9 GEOMETRIC TRANSFORMATIONS IN THREE-DIMENSIONAL SPACE

Methods for geometric transformations in three dimensions are extended from two-dimensional methods by including considerations for the z coordinate. We now translate an object by specifying a three-dimensional translation vector, which determines how much the object is to be moved in each of the three coordinate directions. Similarly, we scale an object by choosing a scaling factor for each of the three Cartesian coordinates. But the extension from two-dimensional rotation methods to three dimensions is less straightforward.

When we discussed two-dimensional rotations in the xy plane, we needed to consider only rotations about axes that were perpendicular to the xy plane. In three-dimensional space, we can now select any spatial orientation for the rotation axis. Some graphics packages handle three-dimensional rotation as a composite of three rotations, one for each of the three Cartesian axes. Alternatively, we can set up general rotation equations, given the orientation of a rotation axis and the required rotation angle.

A three-dimensional position, expressed in homogeneous coordinates, is represented as a four-element column vector. Thus, each geometric transformation operator is now a 4 by 4 matrix, which premultiplies a coordinate column vector. And, as in two dimensions, any sequence of transformations is represented as a single matrix, formed by concatenating the matrices for the individual transformations in the sequence. Each successive matrix in a transformation sequence is concatenated to the left of previous transformation matrices.

5-10 THREE-DIMENSIONAL TRANSLATION

A position $\mathbf{P} = (x, y, z)$ in three-dimensional space is translated to a location $\mathbf{P}' = (x', y', z')$ by adding translation distances t_x, t_y, and t_z to the Cartesian coordinates of $\mathbf{P}$:

$$x' = x + t_x, \qquad y' = y + t_y, \qquad z' = z + t_z \tag{5-70}$$

Figure 5-34 illustrates three-dimensional point translation.

We can express these three-dimensional translation operations in matrix form as in Eq. 5-17. But now the coordinate positions, $\mathbf{P}$ and $\mathbf{P}'$, are represented in homogeneous coordinates with four-element column matrices, and the translation operator $\mathbf{T}$ is a 4 by 4 matrix:

$$\begin{bmatrix} x' \\ y' \\ z' \\ 1 \end{bmatrix} = \begin{bmatrix} 1 & 0 & 0 & t_x \\ 0 & 1 & 0 & t_y \\ 0 & 0 & 1 & t_z \\ 0 & 0 & 0 & 1 \end{bmatrix} \cdot \begin{bmatrix} x \\ y \\ z \\ 1 \end{bmatrix} \tag{5-71}$$

or

$$\mathbf{P}' = \mathbf{T} \cdot \mathbf{P} \tag{5-72}$$

An object is translated in three dimensions by transforming each of the defining coordinate positions for the object, then reconstructing the object at the new location. For an object represented as a set of polygon surfaces, we translate each vertex for each surface (Fig. 5-35) and redisplay the polygon facets at the translated positions.

The following program segment illustrates construction of a translation matrix, given an input set of translation parameters. To construct the matrices in

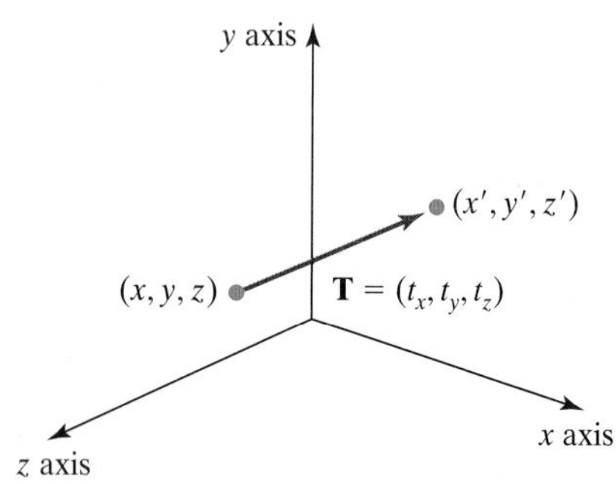

FIGURE 5-34 Moving a coordinate position with translation vector $\mathbf{T} = (t_x, t_y, t_z)$.

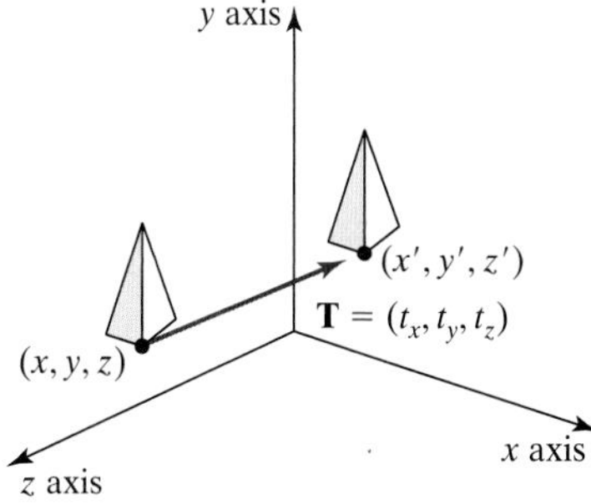

FIGURE 5-35 Shifting the position of a three-dimensional object using translation vector **T**.

these procedures, we use methods similar to those in the example program of Section 5-4.

```
typedef GLfloat Matrix4x4 [4][4];

/* Construct the 4 by 4 identity matrix. */
void matrix4x4SetIdentity (Matrix4x4 matIdent4x4)
{
   GLint row, col;

   for (row = 0; row < 4; row++)
      for (col = 0; col < 4 ; col++)
         matIdent4x4 [row][col] = (row == col);
}

void translate3D (GLfloat tx, GLfloat ty, GLfloat tz)
{
   Matrix4x4 matTransl3D;

   /*  Initialize translation matrix to identity.  */
   matrix4x4SetIdentity (matTransl3D);

   matTransl3D [0][3] = tx;
   matTransl3D [1][3] = ty;
   matTransl3D [2][3] = tz;
}
```

An inverse of a three-dimensional translation matrix is obtained using the same procedures that we applied in a two-dimensional translation. That is, we negate the translation distances t_x, t_y, and t_z. This produces a translation in the opposite direction, and the product of a translation matrix and its inverse is the identity matrix.

5-11 THREE-DIMENSIONAL ROTATION

We can rotate an object about any axis in space, but the easiest rotation axes to handle are those that are parallel to the Cartesian-coordinate axes. Also, we can use combinations of coordinate-axis rotations (along with appropriate translations)

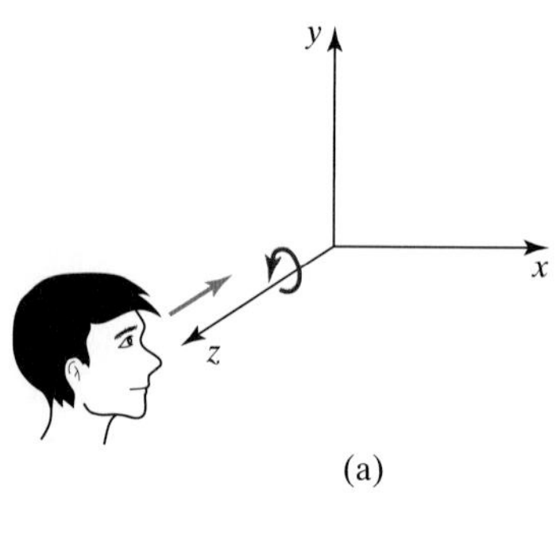

(a)

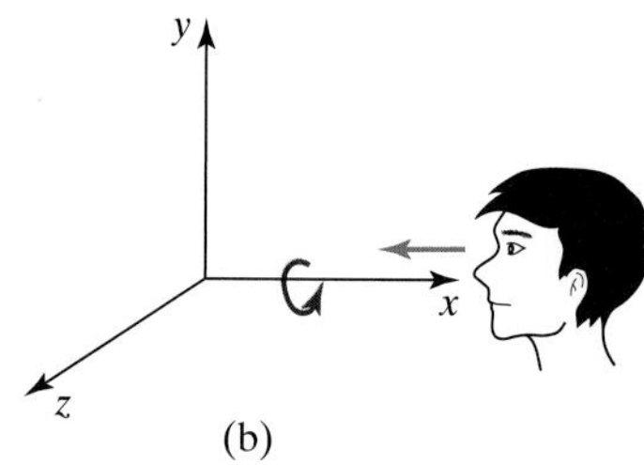

(b)

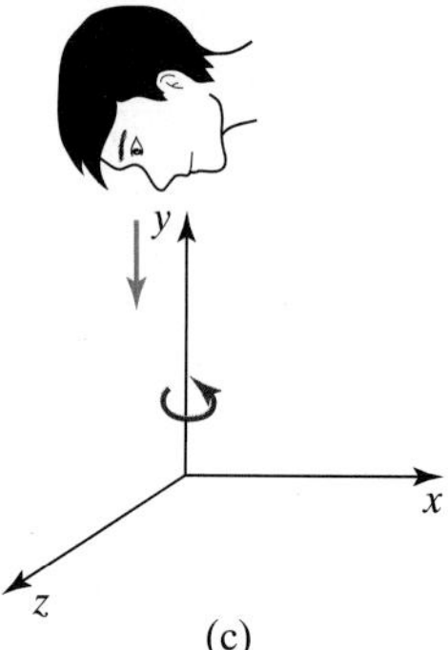

(c)

FIGURE 5-36 Positive rotations about a coordinate axis are counterclockwise, when looking along the positive half of the axis toward the origin.

to specify a rotation about any other line in space. Therefore, we first consider the operations involved in coordinate-axis rotations, then we discuss the calculations needed for other rotation axes.

By convention, positive rotation angles produce counterclockwise rotations about a coordinate axis, assuming that we are looking in the negative direction along that coordinate axis (Fig. 5-36). This agrees with our earlier discussion of rotations in two dimensions, where positive rotations in the xy plane are counterclockwise about a pivot point (an axis that is parallel to the z axis).

Three-Dimensional Coordinate-Axis Rotations

The two-dimensional **z-axis rotation** equations are easily extended to three dimensions:

$$\begin{aligned} x' &= x\cos\theta - y\sin\theta \\ y' &= x\sin\theta + y\cos\theta \\ z' &= z \end{aligned} \tag{5-73}$$

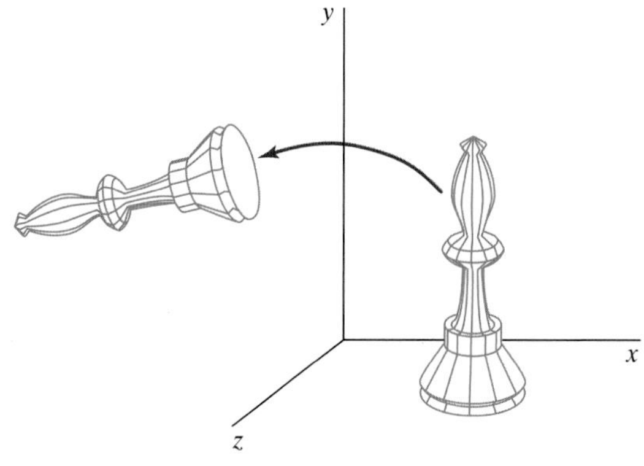

FIGURE 5-37 Rotation of an object about the z axis.

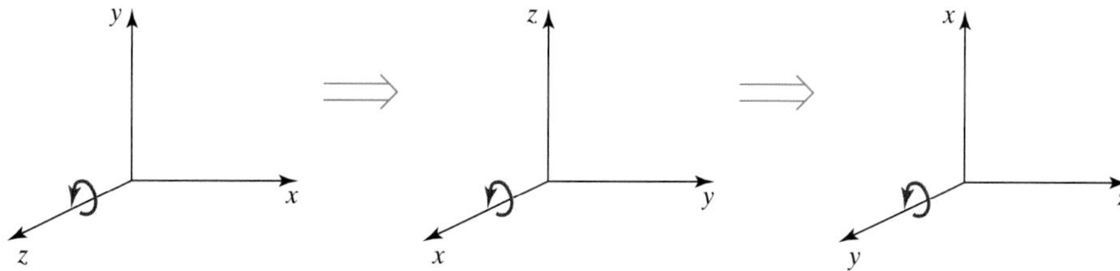

FIGURE 5-38 Cyclic permutation of the Cartesian-coordinate axes to produce the three sets of coordinate-axis rotation equations.

Parameter θ specifies the rotation angle about the z axis, and z-coordinate values are unchanged by this transformation. In homogeneous-coordinate form, the three-dimensional z-axis rotation equations are

$$\begin{bmatrix} x' \\ y' \\ z' \\ 1 \end{bmatrix} = \begin{bmatrix} \cos\theta & -\sin\theta & 0 & 0 \\ \sin\theta & \cos\theta & 0 & 0 \\ 0 & 0 & 1 & 0 \\ 0 & 0 & 0 & 1 \end{bmatrix} \cdot \begin{bmatrix} x \\ y \\ z \\ 1 \end{bmatrix} \tag{5-74}$$

which we can write more compactly as

$$\mathbf{P}' = \mathbf{R}_z(\theta) \cdot \mathbf{P} \tag{5-75}$$

Figure 5-37 illustrates rotation of an object about the z axis.

Transformation equations for rotations about the other two coordinate axes can be obtained with a cyclic permutation of the coordinate parameters x, y, and z in Eqs. 5-73:

$$x \rightarrow y \rightarrow z \rightarrow x \tag{5-76}$$

Thus, to obtain the x-axis and y-axis rotation transformations, we cyclically replace x with y, y with z, and z with x, as illustrated in Fig. 5-38.

Substituting permutations 5-76 into Eqs. 5-73, we get the equations for an **x-axis rotation**:

$$\begin{aligned} y' &= y\cos\theta - z\sin\theta \\ z' &= y\sin\theta + z\cos\theta \\ x' &= x \end{aligned} \tag{5-77}$$

Rotation of an object around the x axis is demonstrated in Fig. 5-39.

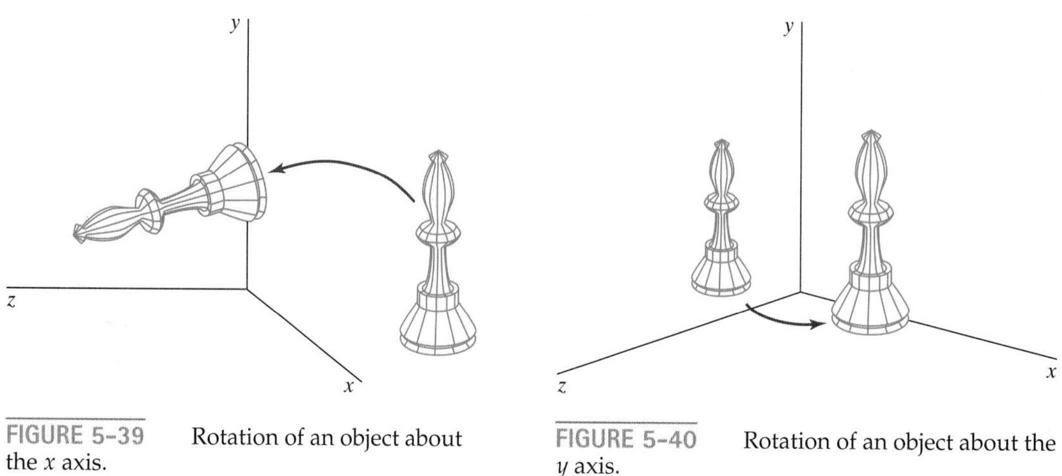

FIGURE 5-39 Rotation of an object about the x axis.

FIGURE 5-40 Rotation of an object about the y axis.

A cyclic permutation of coordinates in Eqs. 5-77 gives us the transformation equations for a ***y*-axis rotation:**

$$\begin{aligned} z' &= z\cos\theta - x\sin\theta \\ x' &= z\sin\theta + x\cos\theta \\ y' &= y \end{aligned} \tag{5-78}$$

An example of y-axis rotation is shown in Fig. 5-40.

An inverse three-dimensional rotation matrix is obtained in the same way as the inverse rotations in two dimensions. We just replace the angle θ with $-\theta$. Negative values for rotation angles generate rotations in a clockwise direction, and the identity matrix is produced when we multiply any rotation matrix by its inverse. Since only the sine function is affected by the change in sign of the rotation angle, the inverse matrix can also be obtained by interchanging rows and columns. That is, we can calculate the inverse of any rotation matrix **R** by forming its transpose ($\mathbf{R}^{-1} = \mathbf{R}^T$).

General Three-Dimensional Rotations

A rotation matrix for any axis that does not coincide with a coordinate axis can be set up as a composite transformation involving combinations of translations and the coordinate-axis rotations. We first move the designated rotation axis onto one of the coordinate axes. Then we apply the appropriate rotation matrix for that coordinate axis. The last step in the transformation sequence is to return the rotation axis to its original position.

In the special case where an object is to be rotated about an axis that is parallel to one of the coordinate axes, we attain the desired rotation with the following transformation sequence.

(1) Translate the object so that the rotation axis coincides with the parallel coordinate axis.

(2) Perform the specified rotation about that axis.

(3) Translate the object so that the rotation axis is moved back to its original position.

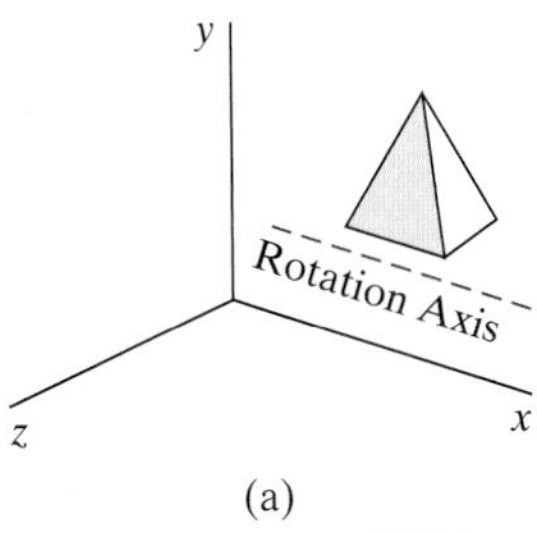

(a)
Original Position of Object

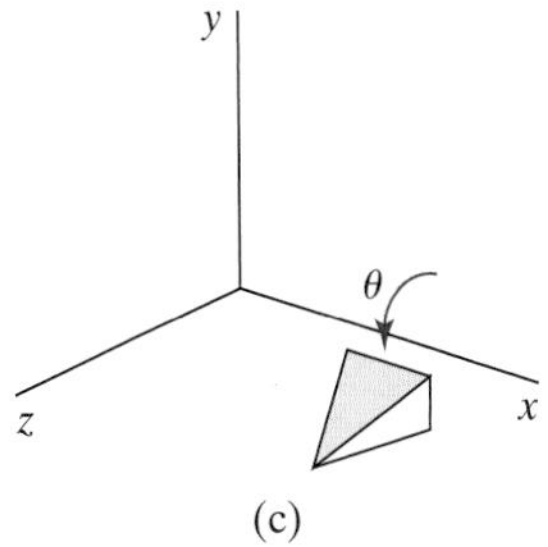

(c)
Rotate Object Through Angle θ

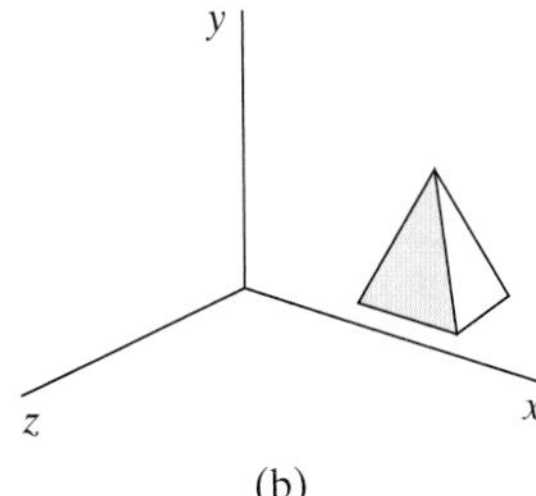

(b)
Translate Rotation Axis onto x Axis

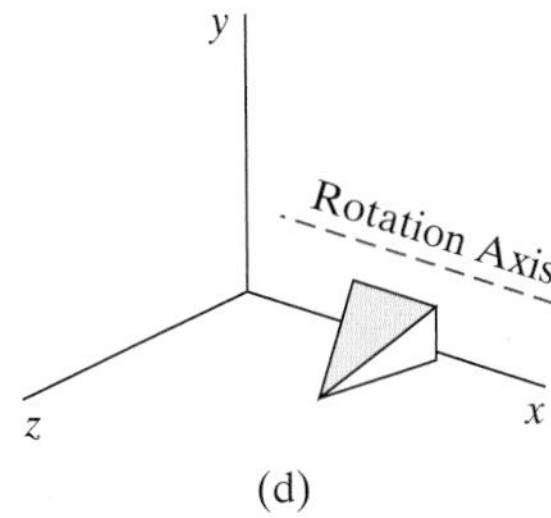

(d)
Translate Rotation Axis to Original Position

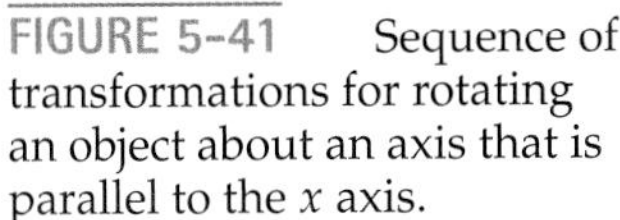

FIGURE 5-41 Sequence of transformations for rotating an object about an axis that is parallel to the x axis.

The steps in this sequence are illustrated in Fig. 5-41. A coordinate position **P** is transformed with the sequence shown in this figure as

$$\mathbf{P}' = \mathbf{T}^{-1} \cdot \mathbf{R}_x(\theta) \cdot \mathbf{T} \cdot \mathbf{P} \tag{5-79}$$

where the composite rotation matrix for the transformation is

$$\mathbf{R}(\theta) = \mathbf{T}^{-1} \cdot \mathbf{R}_x(\theta) \cdot \mathbf{T} \tag{5-80}$$

This composite matrix is of the same form as the two-dimensional transformation sequence for rotation about an axis that is parallel to the z axis (a pivot point that is not at the coordinate origin).

When an object is to be rotated about an axis that is not parallel to one of the coordinate axes, we must perform some additional transformations. In this case, we also need rotations to align the rotation axis with a selected coordinate axis and then to bring the rotation axis back to its original orientation. Given the specifications for the rotation axis and the rotation angle, we can accomplish the required rotation in five steps:

(1) Translate the object so that the rotation axis passes through the coordinate origin.

(2) Rotate the object so that the axis of rotation coincides with one of the coordinate axes.

(3) Perform the specified rotation about the selected coordinate axis.

(4) Apply inverse rotations to bring the rotation axis back to its original orientation.

(5) Apply the inverse translation to bring the rotation axis back to its original spatial position.

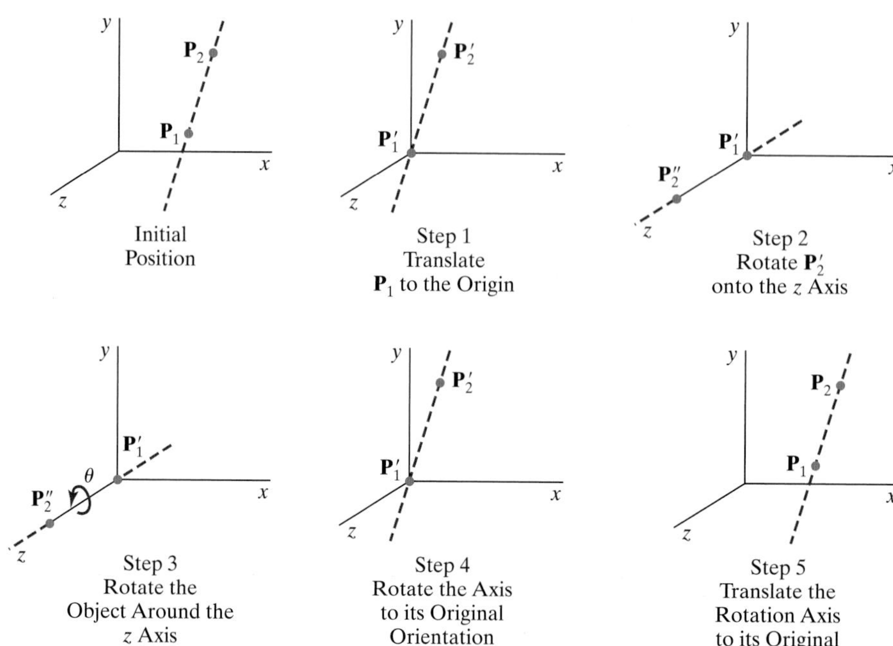

FIGURE 5-42 Five transformation steps for obtaining a composite matrix for rotation about an arbitrary axis, with the rotation axis projected onto the z axis.

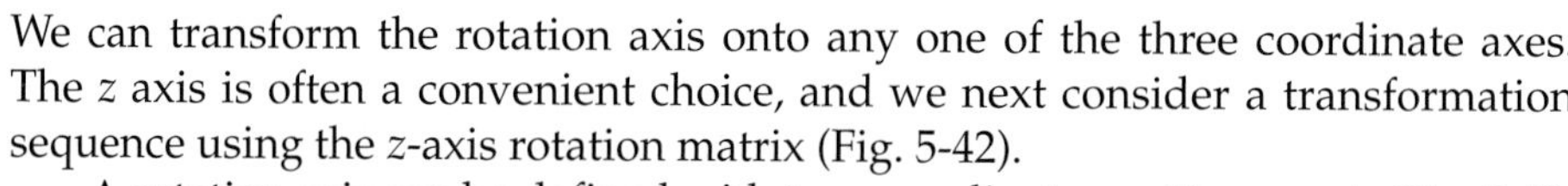

We can transform the rotation axis onto any one of the three coordinate axes. The z axis is often a convenient choice, and we next consider a transformation sequence using the z-axis rotation matrix (Fig. 5-42).

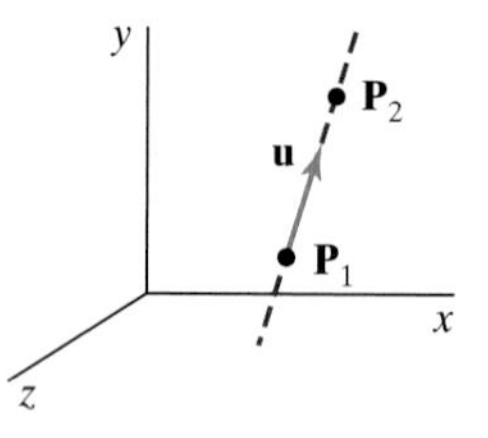

FIGURE 5-43 An axis of rotation (dashed line) defined with points $\mathbf{P}_1$ and $\mathbf{P}_2$. The direction for the unit axis vector $\mathbf{u}$ is determined by the specified rotation direction.

A rotation axis can be defined with two coordinate positions, as in Fig. 5-43, or with one coordinate point and direction angles (or direction cosines) between the rotation axis and two of the coordinate axes. We assume that the rotation axis is defined by two points, as illustrated, and that the direction of rotation is to be counterclockwise when looking along the axis from $\mathbf{P}_2$ to $\mathbf{P}_1$. The components of the rotation-axis vector are then computed as

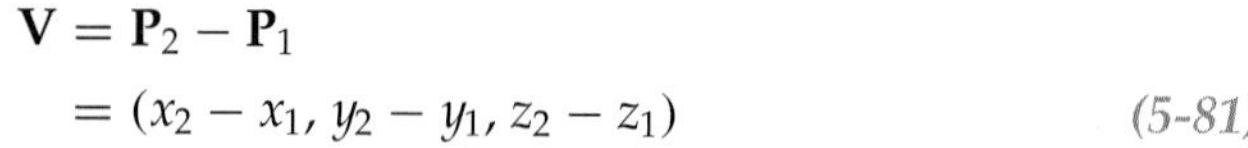

$$\begin{aligned} \mathbf{V} &= \mathbf{P}_2 - \mathbf{P}_1 \\ &= (x_2 - x_1, y_2 - y_1, z_2 - z_1) \end{aligned} \tag{5-81}$$

And the unit rotation-axis vector $\mathbf{u}$ is

$$\mathbf{u} = \frac{\mathbf{V}}{|\mathbf{V}|} = (a, b, c) \tag{5-82}$$

where the components a, b, and c are the direction cosines for the rotation axis:

$$a = \frac{x_2 - x_1}{|\mathbf{V}|}, \qquad b = \frac{y_2 - y_1}{|\mathbf{V}|}, \qquad c = \frac{z_2 - z_1}{|\mathbf{V}|} \tag{5-83}$$

If the rotation is to be in the opposite direction (clockwise when viewing from $\mathbf{P}_2$ to $\mathbf{P}_1$), then we would reverse axis vector $\mathbf{V}$ and unit vector $\mathbf{u}$ so that they point in the direction from $\mathbf{P}_2$ to $\mathbf{P}_1$.

The first step in the rotation sequence is to set up the translation matrix that repositions the rotation axis so that it passes through the coordinate origin. Since we want a counterclockwise rotation when viewing along the axis from $\mathbf{P}_2$ to $\mathbf{P}_1$ (Fig. 5-43), we move the point $\mathbf{P}_1$ to the origin. (If the rotation had been specified in the opposite direction, we would move $\mathbf{P}_2$ to the origin.) This translation matrix is

$$\mathbf{T} = \begin{bmatrix} 1 & 0 & 0 & -x_1 \\ 0 & 1 & 0 & -y_1 \\ 0 & 0 & 1 & -z_1 \\ 0 & 0 & 0 & 1 \end{bmatrix} \tag{5-84}$$

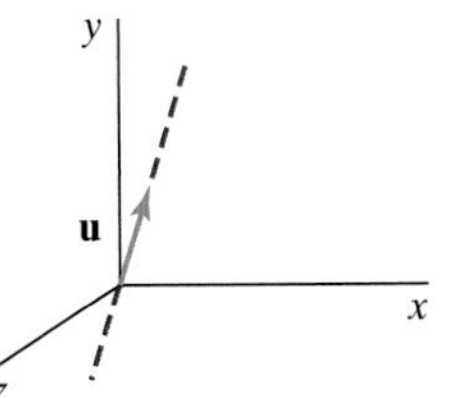

FIGURE 5-44 Translation of the rotation axis to the coordinate origin.

which repositions the rotation axis and the object as shown in Fig. 5-44.

Next, we formulate the transformations that will put the rotation axis onto the z axis. We can use the coordinate-axis rotations to accomplish this alignment in two steps, and there are a number of ways to perform the two steps. For this example, we first rotate about the x axis, then rotate about the y axis. The x-axis rotation gets vector **u** into the xz plane, and the y-axis rotation swings **u** around to the z axis. These two rotations are illustrated in Fig. 5-45 for one possible orientation of vector **u**.

Since rotation calculations involve sine and cosine functions, we can use standard vector operations (Appendix A) to obtain elements of the two rotation matrices. A vector dot product can be used to determine the cosine term, and a vector cross product can be used to calculate the sine term.

We establish the transformation matrix for rotation around the x axis by determining the values for the sine and cosine of the rotation angle necessary to get **u** into the xz plane. This rotation angle is the angle between the projection of **u** in the yz plane and the positive z axis (Fig. 5-46). If we represent the projection of **u** in the yz plane as the vector $\mathbf{u}' = (0, b, c)$, then the cosine of the rotation angle α can be determined from the dot product of $\mathbf{u}'$ and the unit vector $\mathbf{u}_z$ along the z axis:

$$\cos\alpha = \frac{\mathbf{u}' \cdot \mathbf{u}_z}{|\mathbf{u}'|\,|\mathbf{u}_z|} = \frac{c}{d} \tag{5-85}$$

where d is the magnitude of $\mathbf{u}'$:

$$d = \sqrt{b^2 + c^2} \tag{5-86}$$

Similarly, we can determine the sine of α from the cross product of $\mathbf{u}'$ and $\mathbf{u}_z$. The coordinate-independent form of this cross product is

$$\mathbf{u}' \times \mathbf{u}_z = \mathbf{u}_x\,|\mathbf{u}'|\,|\mathbf{u}_z|\sin\alpha \tag{5-87}$$

and the Cartesian form for the cross product gives us

$$\mathbf{u}' \times \mathbf{u}_z = \mathbf{u}_x \cdot b \tag{5-88}$$

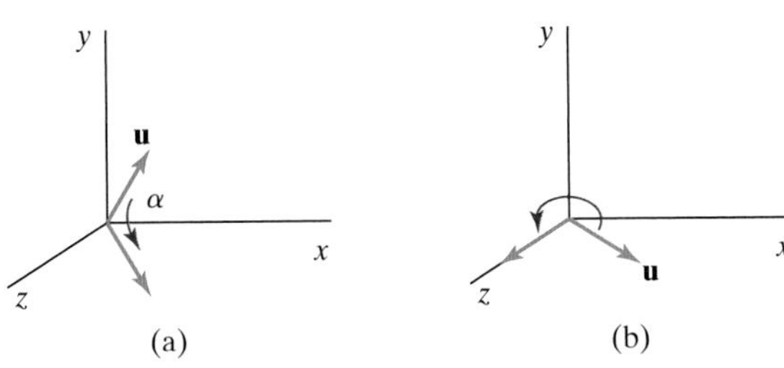

FIGURE 5-45 Unit vector **u** is rotated about the x axis to bring it into the xz plane (a), then it is rotated around the y axis to align it with the z axis (b).

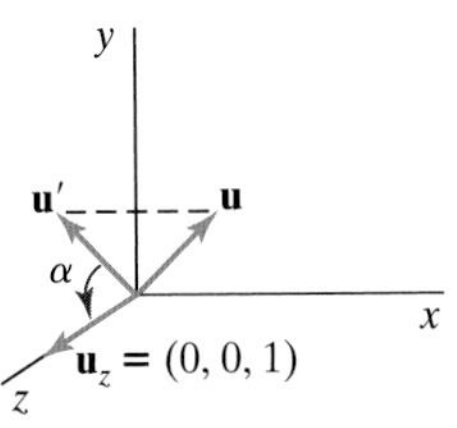

FIGURE 5-46 Rotation of **u** around the x axis into the xz plane is accomplished by rotating $\mathbf{u}'$ (the projection of **u** in the yz plane) through angle α onto the z axis.

Equating the right sides of Eqs. 5-87 and 5-88, and noting that $|\mathbf{u}_z| = 1$ and $|\mathbf{u}'| = d$, we have

$$d \sin\alpha = b$$

or

$$\sin\alpha = \frac{b}{d} \tag{5-89}$$

Now that we have determined the values for $\cos\alpha$ and $\sin\alpha$ in terms of the components of vector $\mathbf{u}$, we can set up the matrix elements for rotation of this vector about the x axis and into the xz plane:

$$\mathbf{R}_x(\alpha) = \begin{bmatrix} 1 & 0 & 0 & 0 \\ 0 & \frac{c}{d} & -\frac{b}{d} & 0 \\ 0 & \frac{b}{d} & \frac{c}{d} & 0 \\ 0 & 0 & 0 & 1 \end{bmatrix} \tag{5-90}$$

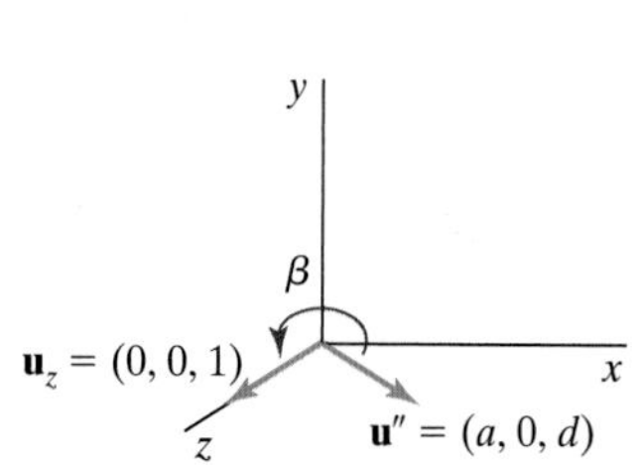

FIGURE 5-47 Rotation of unit vector $\mathbf{u}''$ (vector $\mathbf{u}$ after rotation into the xz plane) about the y axis. Positive rotation angle β aligns $\mathbf{u}''$ with vector $\mathbf{u}_z$.

The next step in the formulation of the transformation sequence is to determine the matrix that will swing the unit vector in the xz plane counterclockwise around the y axis onto the positive z axis. Figure 5-47 shows the orientation of the unit vector in the xz plane, resulting from the rotation about the x axis. This vector, labeled $\mathbf{u}''$, has the value a for its x component, since rotation about the x axis leaves the x component unchanged. Its z component is d (the magnitude of $\mathbf{u}'$), because vector $\mathbf{u}'$ has been rotated onto the z axis. And the y component of $\mathbf{u}''$ is 0, because it now lies in the xz plane. Again, we can determine the cosine of rotation angle β from the dot product of unit vectors $\mathbf{u}''$ and $\mathbf{u}_z$. Thus,

$$\cos\beta = \frac{\mathbf{u}'' \cdot \mathbf{u}_z}{|\mathbf{u}''|\,|\mathbf{u}_z|} = d \tag{5-91}$$

since $|\mathbf{u}_z| = |\mathbf{u}''| = 1$. Comparing the coordinate-independent form of the cross product

$$\mathbf{u}'' \times \mathbf{u}_z = \mathbf{u}_y\,|\mathbf{u}''|\,|\mathbf{u}_z| \sin\beta \tag{5-92}$$

with the Cartesian form

$$\mathbf{u}'' \times \mathbf{u}_z = \mathbf{u}_y \cdot (-a) \tag{5-93}$$

we find that

$$\sin\beta = -a \tag{5-94}$$

Therefore, the transformation matrix for rotation of $\mathbf{u}''$ about the y axis is

$$\mathbf{R}_y(\beta) = \begin{bmatrix} d & 0 & -a & 0 \\ 0 & 1 & 0 & 0 \\ a & 0 & d & 0 \\ 0 & 0 & 0 & 1 \end{bmatrix} \tag{5-95}$$

With transformation matrices 5-84, 5-90, and 5-95, we have aligned the rotation axis with the positive z axis. The specified rotation angle θ can now be applied as a rotation about the z axis:

$$\mathbf{R}_z(\theta) = \begin{bmatrix} \cos\theta & -\sin\theta & 0 & 0 \\ \sin\theta & \cos\theta & 0 & 0 \\ 0 & 0 & 1 & 0 \\ 0 & 0 & 0 & 1 \end{bmatrix} \tag{5-96}$$

To complete the required rotation about the given axis, we need to transform the rotation axis back to its original position. This is done by applying the inverse of transformations 5-84, 5-90, and 5-95. The transformation matrix for rotation about an arbitrary axis can then be expressed as the composition of these seven individual transformations:

$$\mathbf{R}(\theta) = \mathbf{T}^{-1} \cdot \mathbf{R}_x^{-1}(\alpha) \cdot \mathbf{R}_y^{-1}(\beta) \cdot \mathbf{R}_z(\theta) \cdot \mathbf{R}_y(\beta) \cdot \mathbf{R}_x(\alpha) \cdot \mathbf{T} \tag{5-97}$$

A somewhat quicker, but perhaps less intuitive, method for obtaining the composite rotation matrix $\mathbf{R}_y(\beta) \cdot \mathbf{R}_x(\alpha)$ is to make use of the fact that the composite matrix for any sequence of three-dimensional rotations is of the form

$$\mathbf{R} = \begin{bmatrix} r_{11} & r_{12} & r_{13} & 0 \\ r_{21} & r_{22} & r_{23} & 0 \\ r_{31} & r_{32} & r_{33} & 0 \\ 0 & 0 & 0 & 1 \end{bmatrix} \tag{5-98}$$

The upper-left 3 by 3 submatrix of this matrix is orthogonal. This means that the rows (or the columns) of this submatrix form a set of orthogonal unit vectors that are rotated by matrix $\mathbf{R}$ onto the x, y, and z axes, respectively:

$$\mathbf{R} \cdot \begin{bmatrix} r_{11} \\ r_{12} \\ r_{13} \\ 1 \end{bmatrix} = \begin{bmatrix} 1 \\ 0 \\ 0 \\ 1 \end{bmatrix}, \quad \mathbf{R} \cdot \begin{bmatrix} r_{21} \\ r_{22} \\ r_{23} \\ 1 \end{bmatrix} = \begin{bmatrix} 0 \\ 1 \\ 0 \\ 1 \end{bmatrix}, \quad \mathbf{R} \cdot \begin{bmatrix} r_{31} \\ r_{32} \\ r_{33} \\ 1 \end{bmatrix} = \begin{bmatrix} 0 \\ 0 \\ 1 \\ 1 \end{bmatrix} \tag{5-99}$$

Therefore, we can set up a local coordinate system with one of its axes aligned on the rotation axis. Then the unit vectors for the three coordinate axes are used to construct the columns of the rotation matrix. Assuming that the rotation axis is not parallel to any coordinate axis, we could form the following set of local unit vectors (Fig. 5-48).

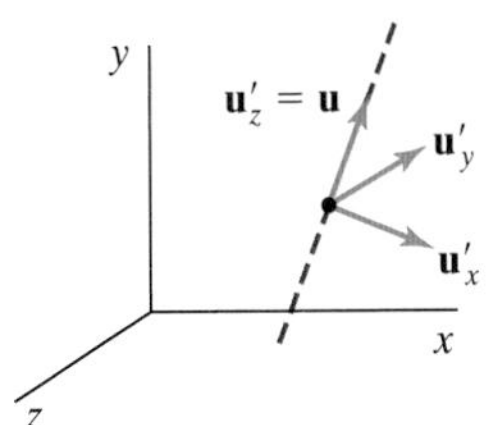

FIGURE 5-48 Local coordinate system for a rotation axis defined by unit vector **u**.

$$\begin{aligned} \mathbf{u}'_z &= \mathbf{u} \\ \mathbf{u}'_y &= \frac{\mathbf{u} \times \mathbf{u}_x}{|\mathbf{u} \times \mathbf{u}_x|} \\ \mathbf{u}'_x &= \mathbf{u}'_y \times \mathbf{u}'_z \end{aligned} \tag{5-100}$$

If we express the elements of the unit local vectors for the rotation axis as

$$\begin{aligned} \mathbf{u}'_x &= (u'_{x1}, u'_{x2}, u'_{x3}) \\ \mathbf{u}'_y &= (u'_{y1}, u'_{y2}, u'_{y3}) \\ \mathbf{u}'_z &= (u'_{z1}, u'_{z2}, u'_{z3}) \end{aligned} \tag{5-101}$$

then the required composite matrix, which is equal to the product $\mathbf{R}_y(\beta) \cdot \mathbf{R}_x(\alpha)$, is

$$\mathbf{R} = \begin{bmatrix} u'_{x1} & u'_{x2} & u'_{x3} & 0 \\ u'_{y1} & u'_{y2} & u'_{y3} & 0 \\ u'_{z1} & u'_{z2} & u'_{z3} & 0 \\ 0 & 0 & 0 & 1 \end{bmatrix} \tag{5-102}$$

This matrix transforms the unit vectors $\mathbf{u}'_x$, $\mathbf{u}'_y$, and $\mathbf{u}'_z$ onto the x, y, and z axes, respectively. And this aligns the rotation axis with the z axis, because $\mathbf{u}'_z = \mathbf{u}$.

Quaternion Methods for Three-Dimensional Rotations

A more efficient method for generating a rotation about an arbitrarily selected axis is to use a quaternion representation (Appendix A) for the rotation transformation. Quaternions, which are extensions of two-dimensional complex numbers, are useful in a number of computer-graphics procedures, including the generation of fractal objects. They require less storage space than 4 by 4 matrices, and it is simpler to write quaternion procedures for transformation sequences. This is particularly important in animations, which often require complicated motion sequences and motion interpolations between two given positions of an object.

One way to characterize a quaternion is as an ordered pair, consisting of a *scalar part* and a *vector part:*

$$q = (s, \mathbf{v})$$

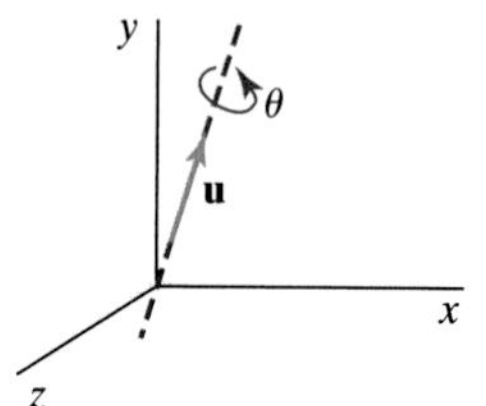

FIGURE 5-49 Unit quaternion parameters θ and $\mathbf{u}$ for rotation about a specified axis.

We can also think of a quaternion as a higher-order complex number with one real part (the scalar part) and three complex parts (the elements of vector $\mathbf{v}$). A rotation about any axis passing through the coordinate origin is accomplished by first setting up a unit quaternion with the scalar and vector parts:

$$s = \cos\frac{\theta}{2}, \qquad \mathbf{v} = \mathbf{u}\sin\frac{\theta}{2} \tag{5-103}$$

where $\mathbf{u}$ is a unit vector along the selected rotation axis and θ is the specified rotation angle about this axis (Fig. 5-49). Any point position $\mathbf{P}$ that is to be rotated by this quaternion can be represented in quaternion notation as

$$\mathbf{P} = (0, \mathbf{p})$$

with the coordinates of the point as the vector part $\mathbf{p} = (x, y, z)$. The rotation of the point is then carried out with the quaternion operation

$$\mathbf{P}' = q\mathbf{P}q^{-1} \tag{5-104}$$

where $q^{-1} = (s, -\mathbf{v})$ is the inverse of the unit quaternion q with the scalar and vector parts given in Eqs. 5-103. This transformation produces the following new quaternion.

$$\mathbf{P}' = (0, \mathbf{p}') \tag{5-105}$$

The second term in this ordered pair is the rotated point position $\mathbf{p}'$, which is evaluated with vector dot and cross products as

$$\mathbf{p}' = s^2\mathbf{p} + \mathbf{v}(\mathbf{p} \cdot \mathbf{v}) + 2s(\mathbf{v} \times \mathbf{p}) + \mathbf{v} \times (\mathbf{v} \times \mathbf{p}) \tag{5-106}$$

Values for parameters s and $\mathbf{v}$ are obtained from the expressions in 5-103. Many computer graphics systems use efficient hardware implementations of these vector calculations to perform rapid three-dimensional object rotations.

Transformation 5-104 is equivalent to rotation about an axis that passes through the coordinate origin. This is the same as the sequence of rotation transformations in Eq. 5-97 that aligns the rotation axis with the z axis, rotates about z, and then returns the rotation axis to its original orientation at the coordinate origin.

We can evaluate the terms in Eq. 5-106 using the definition for quaternion multiplication given in Appendix A. Also, designating the components of the vector part of q as $\mathbf{v} = (a, b, c)$, we obtain the elements for the composite rotation matrix $\mathbf{R}_x^{-1}(\alpha) \cdot \mathbf{R}_y^{-1}(\beta) \cdot \mathbf{R}_z(\theta) \cdot \mathbf{R}_y(\beta) \cdot \mathbf{R}_x(\alpha)$ in a 3 by 3 form as

$$\mathbf{M}_R(\theta) = \begin{bmatrix} 1 - 2b^2 - 2c^2 & 2ab - 2sc & 2ac + 2sb \\ 2ab + 2sc & 1 - 2a^2 - 2c^2 & 2bc - 2sa \\ 2ac - 2sb & 2bc + 2sa & 1 - 2a^2 - 2b^2 \end{bmatrix} \tag{5-107}$$

The calculations involved in this matrix can be greatly reduced by substituting explicit values for parameters a, b, c, and s, and then using the following trigonometric identities to simplify the terms.

$$\cos^2\frac{\theta}{2} - \sin^2\frac{\theta}{2} = 1 - 2\sin^2\frac{\theta}{2} = \cos\theta, \qquad 2\cos\frac{\theta}{2}\sin\frac{\theta}{2} = \sin\theta$$

Thus, we can rewrite matrix 5-107 as

$$\mathbf{M}_R(\theta) = \begin{bmatrix} u_x^2(1-\cos\theta) + \cos\theta & u_x u_y(1-\cos\theta) - u_z\sin\theta & u_x u_z(1-\cos\theta) + u_y\sin\theta \\ u_y u_x(1-\cos\theta) + u_z\sin\theta & u_y^2(1-\cos\theta) + \cos\theta & u_y u_z(1-\cos\theta) - u_x\sin\theta \\ u_z u_x(1-\cos\theta) - u_y\sin\theta & u_z u_y(1-\cos\theta) + u_x\sin\theta & u_z^2(1-\cos\theta) + \cos\theta \end{bmatrix} \tag{5-108}$$

where u_x, u_y, and u_z are the components of the unit axis vector $\mathbf{u}$.

To complete the transformation sequence for rotating about an arbitrarily placed rotation axis, we need to include the translations that move the rotation axis to the coordinate axis and return it to its original position. Thus, the complete quaternion rotation expression, corresponding to Eq. 5-97, is

$$\mathbf{R}(\theta) = \mathbf{T}^{-1} \cdot \mathbf{M}_R \cdot \mathbf{T} \tag{5-109}$$

As an example, we can perform a rotation about the z axis by setting rotation-axis vector $\mathbf{u}$ to the unit z-axis vector (0, 0, 1). Substituting the components of this vector into matrix 5-108, we get the 3 by 3 version of the z-axis rotation matrix $\mathbf{R}_z(\theta)$ in transformation equation 5-74. Similarly, substituting the unit-quaternion rotation values into the transformation equation 5-104 produces the rotated coordinate values in Eqs. 5-73.

In the following code, we give examples of procedures that could be used to construct a three-dimensional rotation matrix. The quaternion representation in Eq. 5-109 is used to set up the matrix elements for a general three-dimensional rotation.

```
class wcPt3D {
   public:
      GLfloat x, y, z;
};
typedef float Matrix4x4 [4][4];

Matrix4x4 matRot;

/* Construct the 4 by 4 identity matrix. */
void matrix4x4SetIdentity (Matrix4x4 matIdent4x4)
{
   GLint row, col;

   for (row = 0; row < 4; row++)
      for (col = 0; col < 4 ; col++)
         matIdent4x4 [row][col] = (row == col);
}

/* Premultiply matrix m1 times matrix m2, store result in m2. */
void matrix4x4PreMultiply (Matrix4x4 m1, Matrix4x4 m2)
{
   GLint row, col;
   Matrix4x4 matTemp;

   for (row = 0; row < 4; row++)
      for (col = 0; col < 4 ; col++)
         matTemp [row][col] = m1 [row][0] * m2 [0][col] + m1 [row][1] *
                              m2 [1][col] + m1 [row][2] * m2 [2][col] +
                              m1 [row][3] * m2 [3][col];
   for (row = 0; row < 4; row++)
      for (col = 0; col < 4; col++)
         m2 [row][col] = matTemp [row][col];
}

void translate3D (GLfloat tx, GLfloat ty, GLfloat tz)
{
   Matrix4x4 matTransl3D;

   /*  Initialize translation matrix to identity.  */
   matrix4x4SetIdentity (matTransl3D);

   matTransl3D [0][3] = tx;
   matTransl3D [1][3] = ty;
   matTransl3D [2][3] = tz;

   /*  Concatenate translation matrix with matRot.  */
   matrix4x4PreMultiply (matTransl3D, matRot);
}

void rotate3D (wcPt3D p1, wcPt3D p2, GLfloat radianAngle)
{
   Matrix4x4 matQuaternionRot;
```

```
   GLfloat axisVectLength = sqrt ((p2.x - p1.x) * (p2.x - p1.x) +
                          (p2.y - p1.y) * (p2.y - p1.y) +
                          (p2.z - p1.z) * (p2.z - p1.z));
   GLfloat cosA = cos (radianAngle);
   GLfloat oneC = 1 - cosA;
   GLfloat sinA = sin (radianAngle);
   GLfloat ux = (p2.x - p1.x) / axisVectLength;
   GLfloat uy = (p2.y - p1.y) / axisVectLength;
   GLfloat uz = (p2.z - p1.z) / axisVectLength;

   /*  Set up translation matrix for moving p1 to origin.  */
   translate3D (-p1.x, -p1.y, -p1.z);

   /*  Initialize matQuaternionRot to identity matrix.  */
   matrix4x4SetIdentity (matQuaternionRot);

   matQuaternionRot [0][0] = ux*ux*oneC + cosA;
   matQuaternionRot [0][1] = ux*uy*oneC - uz*sinA;
   matQuaternionRot [0][2] = ux*uz*oneC + uy*sinA;
   matQuaternionRot [1][0] = uy*ux*oneC + uz*sinA;
   matQuaternionRot [1][1] = uy*uy*oneC + cosA;
   matQuaternionRot [1][2] = uy*uz*oneC - ux*sinA;
   matQuaternionRot [2][0] = uz*ux*oneC - uy*sinA;
   matQuaternionRot [2][1] = uz*uy*oneC + ux*sinA;
   matQuaternionRot [2][2] = uz*uz*oneC + cosA;

   /*  Combine matQuaternionRot with translation matrix.  */
   matrix4x4PreMultiply (matQuaternionRot, matRot);

   /*  Set up inverse matTransl3D and concatenate with
    *  product of previous two matrices.
    */
   translate3D (p1.x, p1.y, p1.z);
}

void displayFcn (void)
{
   /*  Input rotation parameters.  */

   /*  Initialize matRot to identity matrix:  */
   matrix4x4SetIdentity (matRot);

   /*  Pass rotation parameters to procedure rotate3D.  */

   /*  Display rotated object.  */
}
```

5-12 THREE-DIMENSIONAL SCALING

The matrix expression for the three-dimensional scaling transformation of a position $\mathbf{P} = (x, y, z)$ relative to the coordinate origin is a simple extension of two-dimensional scaling. We just include the parameter for z-coordinate scaling in the

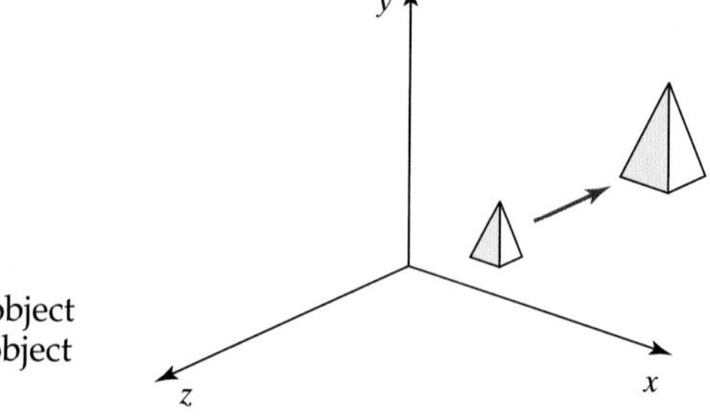

FIGURE 5-50 Doubling the size of an object with transformation 5-110 also moves the object farther from the origin.

transformation matrix:

$$\begin{bmatrix} x' \\ y' \\ z' \\ 1 \end{bmatrix} = \begin{bmatrix} s_x & 0 & 0 & 0 \\ 0 & s_y & 0 & 0 \\ 0 & 0 & s_z & 0 \\ 0 & 0 & 0 & 1 \end{bmatrix} \cdot \begin{bmatrix} x \\ y \\ z \\ 1 \end{bmatrix} \tag{5-110}$$

The three-dimensional scaling transformation for a point position can be represented as

$$\mathbf{P}' = \mathbf{S} \cdot \mathbf{P} \tag{5-111}$$

where scaling parameters s_x, s_y, and s_z are assigned any positive values. Explicit expressions for the scaling transformation relative to the origin are

$$x' = x \cdot s_x, \qquad y' = y \cdot s_y, \qquad z' = z \cdot s_z \tag{5-112}$$

Scaling an object with transformation 5-110 changes the position of the object relative to the coordinate origin. A parameter value greater than 1 moves a point farther from the origin in the corresponding coordinate direction. Similarly, a parameter value less than 1 moves a point closer to the origin in that coordinate direction. Also, if the scaling parameters are not all equal, relative dimensions of a transformed object are changed. We preserve the original shape of an object with a *uniform scaling*: $s_x = s_y = s_z$. The result of scaling an object uniformly with each scaling parameter set to 2 is illustrated in Fig. 5-50.

Since some graphics packages provide only a routine that scales relative to the coordinate origin, we can always construct a scaling transformation with respect to any selected *fixed position* (x_f, y_f, z_f) using the following transformation sequence.

(1) Translate the fixed point to the origin.

(2) Apply the scaling transformation relative to the coordinate origin using Eq. 5-110.

(3) Translate the fixed point back to its original position.

This sequence of transformations is demonstrated in Fig. 5-51. The matrix representation for an arbitrary fixed-point scaling can then be expressed as the concatenation of these translate-scale-translate transformations:

$$\mathbf{T}(x_f, y_f, z_f)\cdot\mathbf{S}(s_x, s_y, s_z)\cdot\mathbf{T}(-x_f, -y_f, -z_f) = \begin{bmatrix} s_x & 0 & 0 & (1-s_x)x_f \\ 0 & s_y & 0 & (1-s_y)y_f \\ 0 & 0 & s_z & (1-s_z)z_f \\ 0 & 0 & 0 & 1 \end{bmatrix} \tag{5-113}$$

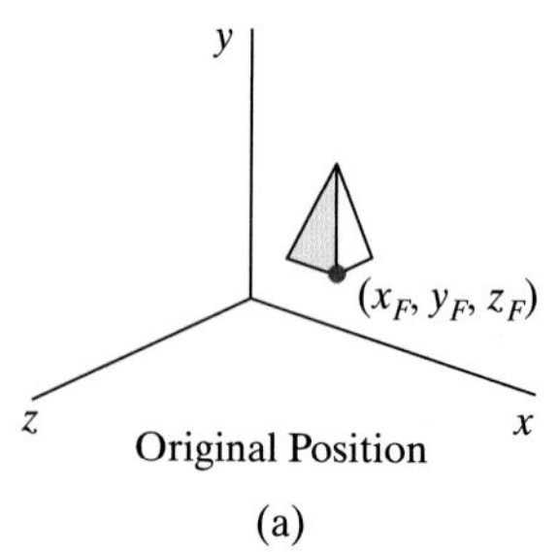

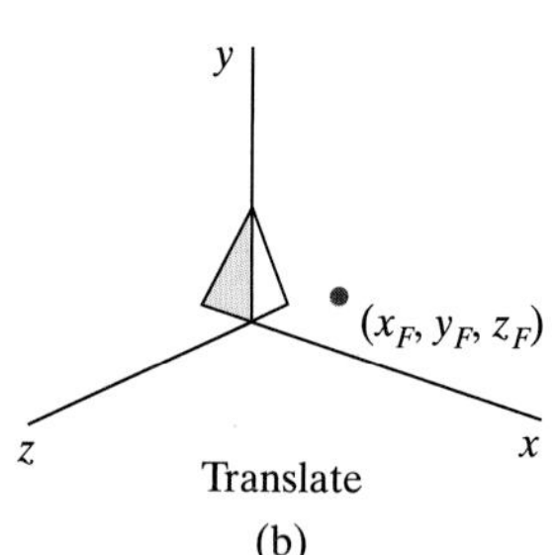

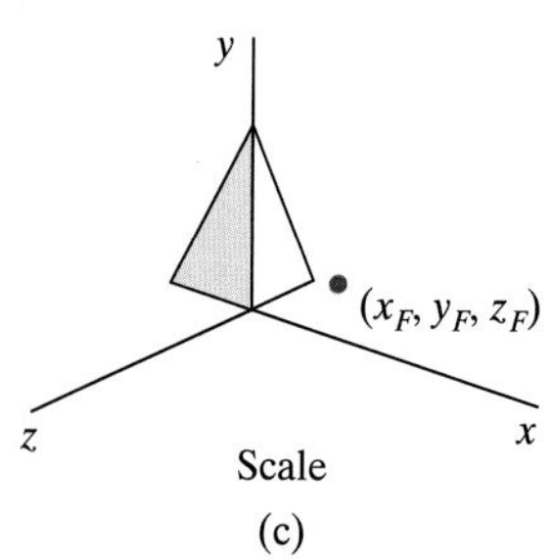

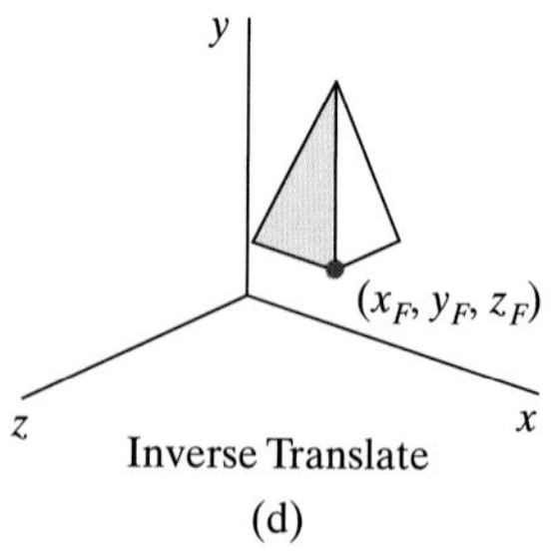

FIGURE 5-51 A sequence of transformations for scaling an object relative to a selected fixed point, using Eq. 5-110.

We can set up programming procedures for constructing a three-dimensional scaling matrix using either a translate-scale-translate sequence or a direct incorporation of the fixed-point coordinates. In the following code example, we demonstrate a direct construction of a three-dimensional scaling matrix relative to a selected fixed point using the calculations in Eq. 5-113.

```
class wcPt3D
{
   private:
      GLfloat x, y, z;

   public:
   /*  Default Constructor:
    *  Initialize position as (0.0, 0.0, 0.0).
    */
   wcPt3D ( ) {
      x = y = z = 0.0;
   }

   setCoords (GLfloat xCoord, GLfloat yCoord, GLfloat zCoord) {
      x = xCoord;
      y = yCoord;
      z = zCoord;
   }

   GLfloat getx ( ) const {
      return x;
   }

   GLfloat gety ( ) const {
      return y;
   }

   GLfloat getz ( ) const {
      return z;
   }
};

typedef float Matrix4x4 [4][4];

void scale3D (GLfloat sx, GLfloat sy, GLfloat sz, wcPt3D fixedPt)
{
   Matrix4x4 matScale3D;

   /*  Initialize scaling matrix to identity.  */
   matrix4x4SetIdentity (matScale3D);

   matScale3D [0][0] = sx;
   matScale3D [0][3] = (1 - sx) * fixedPt.getx ( );
   matScale3D [1][1] = sy;
   matScale3D [1][3] = (1 - sy) * fixedPt.gety ( );
   matScale3D [2][2] = sz;
   matScale3D [2][3] = (1 - sz) * fixedPt.getz ( );
}
```

An inverse, three-dimensional scaling matrix is set up for either Eq. 5-110 or Eq. 5-113 by replacing each scaling parameter (s_x, s_y, and s_z) with its reciprocal. But this inverse transformation is undefined if any scaling parameter is assigned the value 0. The inverse matrix generates an opposite scaling transformation, and the concatenation of a three-dimensional scaling matrix with its inverse yields the identity matrix.

5-13 COMPOSITE THREE-DIMENSIONAL TRANSFORMATIONS

As with two-dimensional transformations, we form a composite three-dimensional transformation by multiplying the matrix representations for the individual operations in the transformation sequence. Any of the two-dimensional transformation sequences discussed in Section 5-4, such as scaling in noncoordinate directions, can be carried out in three-dimensional space.

We can implement a transformation sequence by concatenating the individual matrices from right to left or from left to right, depending on the order in which the matrix representations are specified. Of course, the rightmost term in a matrix product is always the first transformation to be applied to an object and the leftmost term is always the last transformation. We need to use this ordering for the matrix product because coordinate positions are represented as four-element column vectors, which are premultiplied by the composite 4 by 4 transformation matrix.

The following program provides example routines for constructing a three-dimensional composite transformation matrix. The three basic geometric transformations are combined in a selected order to produce a single composite matrix, which is initialized to the identity matrix. For this example, we first rotate, then scale, then translate. We choose a left-to-right evaluation of the composite matrix so that the transformations are called in the order that they are to be applied. Thus, as each matrix is constructed, it is concatenated on the left of the current composite matrix to form the updated product matrix.

```
class wcPt3D {
   public:
      GLfloat x, y, z;
};
typedef GLfloat Matrix4x4 [4][4];

Matrix4x4 matComposite;

/* Construct the 4 by 4 identity matrix. */
void matrix4x4SetIdentity (Matrix4x4 matIdent4x4)
{
   GLint row, col;

   for (row = 0; row < 4; row++)
      for (col = 0; col < 4 ; col++)
         matIdent4x4 [row][col] = (row == col);
}

/* Premultiply matrix m1 times matrix m2, store result in m2. */
void matrix4x4PreMultiply (Matrix4x4 m1, Matrix4x4 m2)
```

```
{
   GLint row, col;
   Matrix4x4 matTemp;

   for (row = 0; row < 4; row++)
      for (col = 0; col < 4 ; col++)
         matTemp [row][col] = m1 [row][0] * m2 [0][col] + m1 [row][1] *
                              m2 [1][col] + m1 [row][2] * m2 [2][col] +
                              m1 [row][3] * m2 [3][col];
   for (row = 0; row < 4; row++)
      for (col = 0; col < 4; col++)
         m2 [row][col] = matTemp [row][col];
}

/*  Procedure for generating 3D translation matrix.  */
void translate3D (GLfloat tx, GLfloat ty, GLfloat tz)
{
   Matrix4x4 matTransl3D;

   /*  Initialize translation matrix to identity.  */
   matrix4x4SetIdentity (matTransl3D);

   matTransl3D [0][3] = tx;
   matTransl3D [1][3] = ty;
   matTransl3D [2][3] = tz;

   /*  Concatenate matTransl3D with composite matrix.  */
   matrix4x4PreMultiply (matTransl3D, matComposite);
}

/*  Procedure for generating a quaternion rotation matrix.  */
void rotate3D (wcPt3D p1, wcPt3D p2, GLfloat radianAngle)
{
   Matrix4x4 matQuatRot;

   float axisVectLength = sqrt ((p2.x - p1.x) * (p2.x - p1.x) +
                          (p2.y - p1.y) * (p2.y - p1.y) +
                          (p2.z - p1.z) * (p2.z - p1.z));
   float cosA = cosf (radianAngle);
   float oneC = 1 - cosA;
   float sinA = sinf (radianAngle);
   float ux = (p2.x - p1.x) / axisVectLength;
   float uy = (p2.y - p1.y) / axisVectLength;
   float uz = (p2.z - p1.z) / axisVectLength;

   /*  Set up translation matrix for moving p1 to origin,
    *  and concatenate translation matrix with matComposite.
    */
   translate3D (-p1.x, -p1.y, -p1.z);

   /*  Initialize matQuatRot to identity matrix.  */
   matrix4x4SetIdentity (matQuatRot);

   matQuatRot [0][0] = ux*ux*oneC + cosA;
   matQuatRot [0][1] = ux*uy*oneC - uz*sinA;
```

```
    matQuatRot [0][2] = ux*uz*oneC + uy*sinA;
    matQuatRot [1][0] = uy*ux*oneC + uz*sinA;
    matQuatRot [1][1] = uy*uy*oneC + cosA;
    matQuatRot [1][2] = uy*uz*oneC - ux*sinA;
    matQuatRot [2][0] = uz*ux*oneC - uy*sinA;
    matQuatRot [2][1] = uz*uy*oneC + ux*sinA;
    matQuatRot [2][2] = uz*uz*oneC + cosA;

    /*  Concatenate matQuatRot with composite matrix.  */
    matrix4x4PreMultiply (matQuatRot, matComposite);

    /*  Construct inverse translation matrix for p1 and
     *  concatenate with composite matrix.
     */
    translate3D (p1.x, p1.y, p1.z);
}

/*  Procedure for generating a 3D scaling matrix.  */
void scale3D (Gfloat sx, GLfloat sy, GLfloat sz, wcPt3D fixedPt)
{
    Matrix4x4 matScale3D;

    /*  Initialize scaling matrix to identity.  */
    matrix4x4SetIdentity (matScale3D);

    matScale3D [0][0] = sx;
    matScale3D [0][3] = (1 - sx) * fixedPt.x;
    matScale3D [1][1] = sy;
    matScale3D [1][3] = (1 - sy) * fixedPt.y;
    matScale3D [2][2] = sz;
    matScale3D [2][3] = (1 - sz) * fixedPt.z;

    /*  Concatenate matScale3D with composite matrix.  */
    matrix4x4PreMultiply (matScale3D, matComposite);
}

void displayFcn (void)
{
    /*  Input object description.  */
    /*  Input translation, rotation, and scaling parameters.  */

    /* Set up 3D viewing-transformation routines. */

    /*  Initialize matComposite to identity matrix:  */
    matrix4x4SetIdentity (matComposite);

    /*  Invoke transformation routines in the order they
     *  are to be applied:
     */
    rotate3D (p1, p2, radianAngle);  //  First transformation: Rotate.
    scale3D (sx, sy, sz, fixedPt);   //  Second transformation: Scale.
    translate3D (tx, ty, tz);        //  Final transformation: Translate.

    /*  Call routines for displaying transformed objects.  */
}
```

5-14 OTHER THREE-DIMENSIONAL TRANSFORMATIONS

In addition to translation, rotation, and scaling, the other transformations discussed for two-dimensional applications are also useful in many three-dimensional situations. These additional transformations include reflection, shear, and transformations between coordinate-reference frames.

Three-Dimensional Reflections

A reflection in a three-dimensional space can be performed relative to a selected *reflection axis* or with respect to a *reflection plane*. In general, three-dimensional reflection matrices are set up similarly to those for two dimensions. Reflections relative to a given axis are equivalent to 180° rotations about that axis. Reflections with respect to a plane are equivalent to 180° rotations in four-dimensional space. When the reflection plane is a coordinate plane (xy, xz, or yz), we can think of the transformation as a conversion between a left-handed frame and a right-handed frame (Appendix A).

An example of a reflection that converts coordinate specifications from a right-handed system to a left-handed system (or vice versa) is shown in Fig. 5-52. This transformation changes the sign of z coordinates, leaving the values for the x and y coordinates unchanged. The matrix representation for this reflection relative to the xy plane is

$$M_{z\text{reflect}} = \begin{bmatrix} 1 & 0 & 0 & 0 \\ 0 & 1 & 0 & 0 \\ 0 & 0 & -1 & 0 \\ 0 & 0 & 0 & 1 \end{bmatrix} \tag{5-114}$$

Transformation matrices for inverting x coordinates or y coordinates are defined similarly, as reflections relative to the yz plane or to the xz plane, respectively. Reflections about other planes can be obtained as a combination of rotations and coordinate-plane reflections.

Three-Dimensional Shears

These transformations can be used to modify object shapes, just as in two-dimensional applications. They are also applied in three-dimensional viewing transformations for perspective projections. Shearing transformations relative to the x or y axes are the same as those discussed in Section 5-5. For three-dimensional applications, we can also generate shears relative to the z axis.

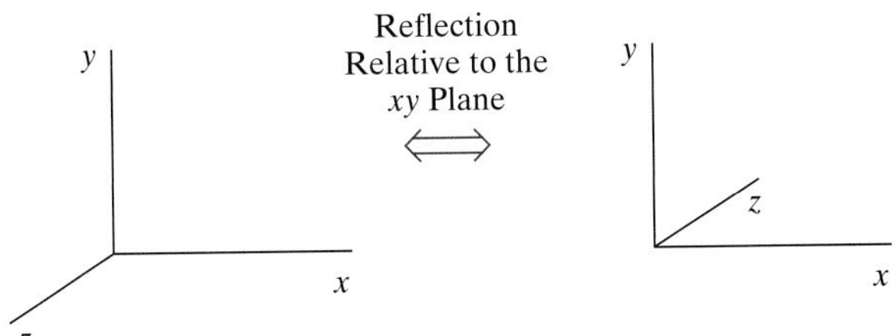

FIGURE 5-52 Conversion of coordinate specifications between a right-handed and a left-handed system can be carried out with the reflection transformation 5-114.

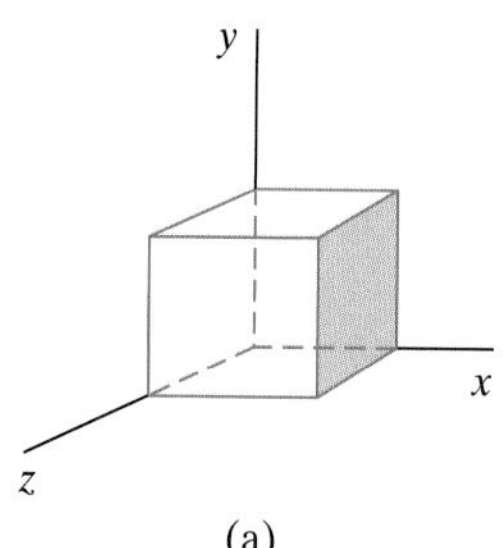

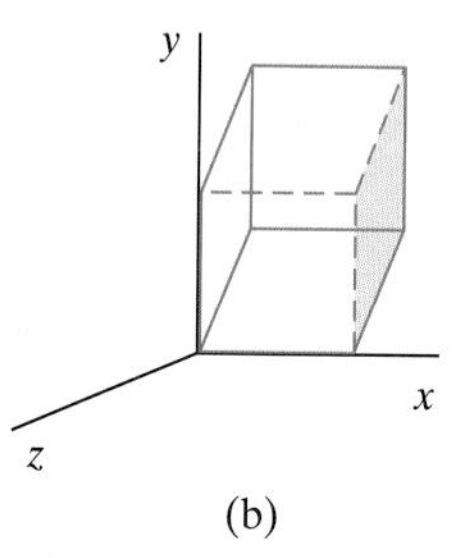

FIGURE 5-53 A unit cube (a) is sheared relative to the origin (b) by transformation matrix 5-115, with $\text{sh}_{zx} = \text{sh}_{zy} = 1$.

A general z-axis shearing transformation relative to a selected reference position is produced with the following matrix.

$$M_{\text{zshear}} = \begin{bmatrix} 1 & 0 & \text{sh}_{zx} & -\text{sh}_{zx} \cdot z_{\text{ref}} \\ 0 & 1 & \text{sh}_{zy} & -\text{sh}_{zy} \cdot z_{\text{ref}} \\ 0 & 0 & 1 & 0 \\ 0 & 0 & 0 & 1 \end{bmatrix} \qquad (5\text{-}115)$$

Shearing parameters sh_{zx} and sh_{zy} can be assigned any real values. The effect of this transformation matrix is to alter the values for the x and y coordinates by an amount that is proportional to the distance from z_{ref}, while leaving the z coordinate unchanged. Plane areas that are perpendicular to the z axis are thus shifted by an amount equal to $z - z_{\text{ref}}$. An example of the effect of this shearing matrix on a unit cube is shown in Fig. 5-53 for shearing values $\text{sh}_{zx} = \text{sh}_{zy} = 1$ and a reference position $z_{\text{ref}} = 0$. Three-dimensional transformation matrices for an x-axis shear and a y-axis shear are similar to the two-dimensional matrices. We just need to add a row and a column for the z-coordinate shearing parameters.

5-15 TRANSFORMATIONS BETWEEN THREE-DIMENSIONAL COORDINATE SYSTEMS

In Section 5-8, we examined the operations needed to transfer a two-dimensional scene description from one reference frame to another. Coordinate-system transformations are employed in computer-graphics packages to construct (model) scenes and to implement viewing routines for both two-dimensional and three-dimensional applications. As we noted in Section 5-8, a transformation matrix for transferring a two-dimensional scene description from one coordinate system to another is constructed with operations for superimposing the coordinate axes of the two systems. The same procedures apply to three-dimensional scene transfers.

We again consider only Cartesian reference frames, and we assume that an $x'y'z'$ system is defined with respect to an xyz system. To transfer the xyz coordinate descriptions to the $x'y'z'$ system, we first set up a translation that brings the $x'y'z'$ coordinate origin to the position of the xyz origin. This is followed by a sequence of rotations that align corresponding coordinate axes. If different scales are used in the two coordinate systems, a scaling transformation may also be necessary to compensate for the differences in coordinate intervals.

Figure 5-54 shows an $x'y'z'$ coordinate system with origin (x_0, y_0, z_0) and unit axis vectors defined relative to an xyz reference frame. The coordinate origin of the $x'y'z'$ system is brought into coincidence with the xyz origin using the translation matrix $\mathbf{T}(-x_0, -y_0, -z_0)$. And we can use the unit axis vectors to form

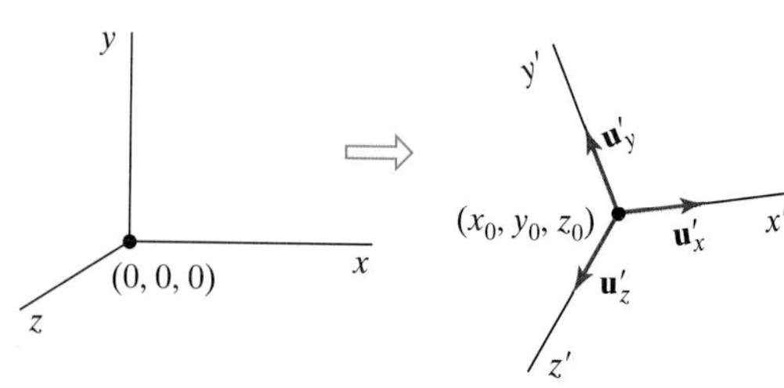

FIGURE 5-54 An $x'y'z'$ coordinate system defined within an xyz system. A scene description is transferred to the new coordinate reference using a transformation sequence that superimposes the $x'y'z'$ frame on the xyz axes.

the coordinate-axis rotation matrix

$$\mathbf{R} = \begin{bmatrix} u'_{x1} & u'_{x2} & u'_{x3} & 0 \\ u'_{y1} & u'_{y2} & u'_{y3} & 0 \\ u'_{z1} & u'_{z2} & u'_{z3} & 0 \\ 0 & 0 & 0 & 1 \end{bmatrix} \tag{5-116}$$

which transforms unit vectors $\mathbf{u}'_x$, $\mathbf{u}'_y$, and $\mathbf{u}'_z$ onto the x, y, and z axes, respectively. The complete coordinate transformation sequence is then given by the composite matrix $\mathbf{R} \cdot \mathbf{T}$. This matrix correctly transforms coordinate descriptions from one Cartesian system to another, even if one system is left-handed and the other is right-handed.

5-16 AFFINE TRANSFORMATIONS

A coordinate transformation of the form

$$\begin{aligned} x' &= a_{xx}x + a_{xy}y + a_{xz}z + b_x \\ y' &= a_{yx}x + a_{yy}y + a_{yz}z + b_y \\ z' &= a_{zx}x + a_{zy}y + a_{zz}z + b_z \end{aligned} \tag{5-117}$$

is called an **affine transformation.** Each of the transformed coordinates x', y', and z' is a linear function of the original coordinates x, y, and z, and parameters a_{ij} and b_k are constants determined by the transformation type. Affine transformations (in two dimensions, three dimensions, or higher dimensions) have the general properties that parallel lines are transformed into parallel lines and finite points map to finite points.

Translation, rotation, scaling, reflection, and shear are examples of affine transformations. We can always express any affine transformation as some composition of these five transformations. Another example of an affine transformation is the conversion of coordinate descriptions for a scene from one reference system to another, since this transformation can be described as a combination of translation and rotation. An affine transformation involving only translation, rotation, and reflection preserves angles and lengths, as well as parallel lines. For each of these three transformations, line lengths and the angle between any two lines remain the same after the transformation.

5-17 OpenGL GEOMETRIC-TRANSFORMATION FUNCTIONS

In the core library of OpenGL, a separate function is available for each of the basic geometric transformations, and all transformations are specified in three dimensions. To perform a translation, we invoke the translation routine and set the components for the three-dimensional translation vector. In the rotation function, we specify the angle and the orientation for a rotation axis that intersects the coordinate origin. And a scaling function is used to set the three coordinate scaling factors relative to the coordinate origin. In each case, the transformation routine sets up a 4 by 4 matrix that is applied to the coordinates of objects that are referenced after the transformation call.

Basic OpenGL Geometric Transformations

A 4 by 4 translation matrix is constructed with the following routine.

```
glTranslate* (tx, ty, tz);
```

Translation parameters tx, ty, and tz can be assigned any real-number values, and the single suffix code to be affixed to this function is either f (float) or d (double). For two-dimensional applications, we set tz = 0.0. And a two-dimensional position is represented as a four-element column matrix with the z component equal to 0.0. The translation matrix generated by this function is used to transform positions of objects defined after this function is invoked. As an example, we translate subsequently defined coordinate positions 25 units in the x direction and -10 units in the y direction with the statement

```
glTranslatef (25.0, -10.0, 0.0);
```

Similarly, a 4 by 4 rotation matrix is generated with

```
glRotate* (theta, vx, vy, vz);
```

where the vector v = (vx, vy, vz) can have any floating-point values for its components. This vector defines the orientation for a rotation axis that passes through the coordinate origin. If v is not specified as a unit vector, then it is automatically normalized before the elements of the rotation matrix are computed. The suffix code can be either f or d, and parameter theta is to be assigned a rotation angle in degrees, which the routine converts to radians for the trigonometric calculations. This function generates a rotation matrix using the quaternion calculations in Eq. 5-108, which is applied to positions defined after this function call. As an example, the statement

```
glRotatef (90.0, 0.0, 0.0, 1.0);
```

sets up the matrix for a 90° rotation about the z axis.

We obtain a 4 by 4 scaling matrix with respect to the coordinate origin with the following routine.

```
glScale* (sx, sy, sz);
```

The suffix code is again either f or d, and the scaling parameters can be assigned any real-number values. Therefore, this function will also generate reflections when negative values are assigned to the scaling parameters. For example, the following statement produces a matrix that scales by a factor of 2 in the x direction, scales by a factor of 3 in the y direction, and reflects with respect to the x axis.

```
glScalef (2.0, -3.0, 1.0);
```

A zero value for any scaling parameter can cause a processing error, because an inverse matrix cannot be calculated. The scale-reflect matrix is applied to subsequently defined objects.

OpenGL Matrix Operations

In Section 2-9 we noted that the `glMatrixMode` routine is used to set the *projection mode*, which designates the matrix that is to be used for the projection transformation. This transformation determines how a scene is to be projected onto the screen. We use the same routine to set up a matrix for the geometric transformations. But in this case the matrix is referred to as the *modelview matrix*, and it is used to store and combine the geometric transformations. It is also used to combine the geometric transformations with the transformation to a viewing-coordinate system. We specify the *modelview mode* with the statement

```
glMatrixMode (GL_MODELVIEW);
```

which designates the 4 by 4 modelview matrix as the **current matrix.** The OpenGL transformation routines discussed in the previous section are used to modify the modelview matrix, which is then applied to transform coordinate positions in a scene. Two other modes that we can set with the `glMatrixMode` function are the *texture mode* and the *color mode*. The texture matrix is used for mapping texture patterns to surfaces, and the color matrix is used to convert from one color model to another. We discuss viewing, projection, texture, and color transformations in later chapters. For the present, we limit our discussion to the details of the geometric transformations. The default argument for the `glMatrixMode` function is `GL_MODELVIEW`.

Once we are in the modelview mode (or any other mode), a call to a transformation routine generates a matrix that is multiplied by the current matrix for that mode. In addition, we can assign values to the elements of the current matrix, and there are two functions in the OpenGL library for this purpose. With the following function, we assign the identity matrix to the current matrix.

```
glLoadIdentity ( );
```

Alternatively, we can assign other values to the elements of the current matrix using

```
glLoadMatrix* (elements16);
```

A single-subscripted, 16-element array of floating-point values is specified with parameter `elements16`, and a suffix code of either `f` or `d` is used to designate the data type. The elements in this array must be specified in column-major order. That is, we first list the four elements in the first column, and then we list the four elements in the second column, the third column, and finally the fourth column. To illustrate this ordering, we initialize the modelview matrix with the following code.

```
glMatrixMode (GL_MODELVIEW);

GLfloat elems [16];
GLint k;

for (k = 0; k < 16; k++)
   elems [k] = float (k);
glLoadMatrixf (elems);
```

which produces the matrix

$$\mathbf{M} = \begin{bmatrix} 0.0 & 4.0 & 8.0 & 12.0 \\ 1.0 & 5.0 & 9.0 & 13.0 \\ 2.0 & 6.0 & 10.0 & 14.0 \\ 3.0 & 7.0 & 11.0 & 15.0 \end{bmatrix}$$

We can also concatenate a specified matrix with the current matrix:

```
glMultMatrix* (otherElements16);
```

Again, the suffix code is either `f` or `d`, and parameter `otherElements16` is a 16-element, single-subscripted array that lists the elements of some other matrix in column-major order. The current matrix is postmultiplied by the matrix specified in `glMultMatrix`, and this product replaces the current matrix. Thus, assuming that the current matrix is the modelview matrix, which we designate as **M**, then the updated modelview matrix is computed as

$$\mathbf{M} = \mathbf{M} \cdot \mathbf{M}'$$

where $\mathbf{M}'$ represents the matrix whose elements are specified by parameter `otherElements16` in the preceding `glMultMatrix` statement.

The `glMultMatrix` function can also be used to set up any transformation sequence with individually defined matrices. For example,

```
glMatrixMode (GL_MODELVIEW);

glLoadIdentity ( );         // Set current matrix to the identity.
glMultMatrixf (elemsM2);    // Postmultiply identity with matrix M2.
glMultMatrixf (elemsM1);    // Postmultiply M2 with matrix M1.
```

produces the following current modelview matrix.

$$\mathbf{M} = \mathbf{M}_2 \cdot \mathbf{M}_1$$

The first transformation to be applied in this sequence is the last one specified in the code. Thus, if we set up a transformation sequence in an OpenGL program, we can think of the individual transformations as being loaded onto a stack, so that the last operation specified is the first one applied. This is not what actually happens, but the stack analogy may help in remembering that, in an OpenGL program, a transformation sequence is applied in the opposite order from which it is specified.

It is also important to keep in mind that OpenGL stores matrices in column-major order. And a reference to a matrix element such as m_{jk} in OpenGL is a reference to the element in column j and row k. This is the reverse of the standard mathematical convention, where the row number is referenced first. But we can usually avoid errors in row-column references by always specifying matrices in OpenGL as 16-element, single-subscript arrays and remembering to list the elements in a column-major order.

OpenGL Matrix Stacks

For each of the four modes (modelview, projection, texture, and color) that we can select with the `glMatrixMode` function, OpenGL maintains a matrix stack. Initially, each stack contains only the identity matrix. At any time during the processing of a scene, the top matrix on each stack is called the "current matrix" for that mode. After we specify the viewing and geometric transformations, the top of the **modelview matrix stack** is the 4 by 4 composite matrix that combines the viewing transformations and the various geometric transformations that we want to apply to a scene. In some cases, we may want to create multiple views and transformation sequences, and then save the composite matrix for each. Therefore, OpenGL supports a modelview stack depth of at least 32, and some implementations may allow more than 32 matrices to be saved on the modelview stack. We can determine the number of positions available in the modelview stack for a particular implementation of OpenGL with

```
glGetIntegerv (GL_MAX_MODELVIEW_STACK_DEPTH, stackSize);
```

which returns a single integer value to array `stackSize`. The other three matrix modes have a minimum stack depth of 2, and we can determine the maximum available depth of each for a particular implementation using one of the following OpenGL symbolic constants: `GL_MAX_PROJECTION_STACK_DEPTH`, `GL_MAX_TEXTURE_STACK_DEPTH`, or `GL_MAX_COLOR_STACK_DEPTH`.

We can also find out how many matrices are currently in the stack with

```
glGetIntegerv (GL_MODELVIEW_STACK_DEPTH, numMats);
```

Initially, the modelview stack contains only the identity matrix, so the value 1 is returned by this function if we issue the query before any stack processing has occurred. Similar symbolic constants are available for determining the number of matrices currently in the other three stacks.

We have two functions available in OpenGL for processing the matrices in a stack. These stack-processing functions are more efficient than manipulating the stack matrices individually, particularly when the stack functions are implemented in hardware. For example, a hardware implementation can copy multiple matrix elements simultaneously. And we can maintain an identity matrix on the stack, so that initializations of the current matrix can be performed faster than by using repeated calls to `glLoadIdentity`.

With the following function, we copy the current matrix at the top of the active stack and store that copy in the second stack position.

```
glPushMatrix ( );
```

This gives us duplicate matrices at the top two positions of the stack. The other stack function is

```
glPopMatrix ( );
```

which destroys the matrix at the top of the stack, and the second matrix in the stack becomes the current matrix. To "pop" the top of the stack, there must be at least two matrices in the stack. Otherwise, we generate an error.

OpenGL Geometric-Transformation Programming Examples

In the following code segment, we apply each of the basic geometric transformations, one at a time, to a rectangle. Initially, the modelview matrix is the identity matrix and we display a blue rectangle. Next we reset the current color to red, specify two-dimensional translation parameters, and display the red translated rectangle (Fig. 5-55). Since we do not want to combine transformations, we next reset the current matrix to the identity. Then a rotation matrix is constructed and

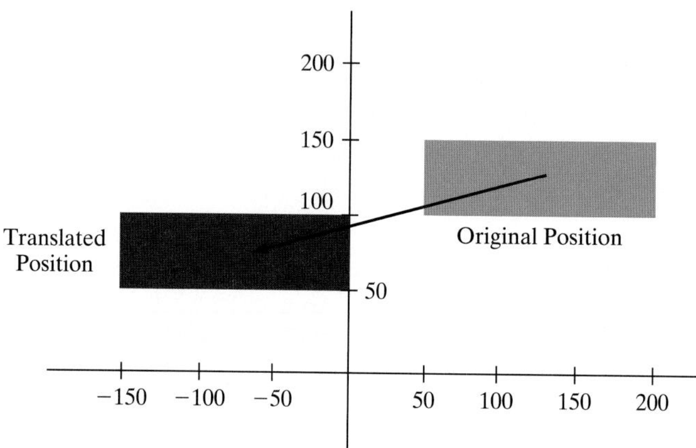

FIGURE 5-55 Translating a rectangle using the OpenGL function `glTranslatef (−200.0, −50.0, 0.0)`.

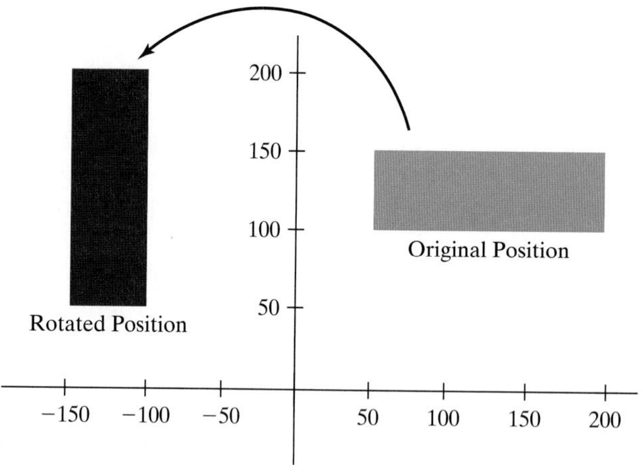

FIGURE 5-56 Rotating a rectangle about the *z* axis using the OpenGL function `glRotatef (90.0, 0.0, 0.0, 1.0)`.

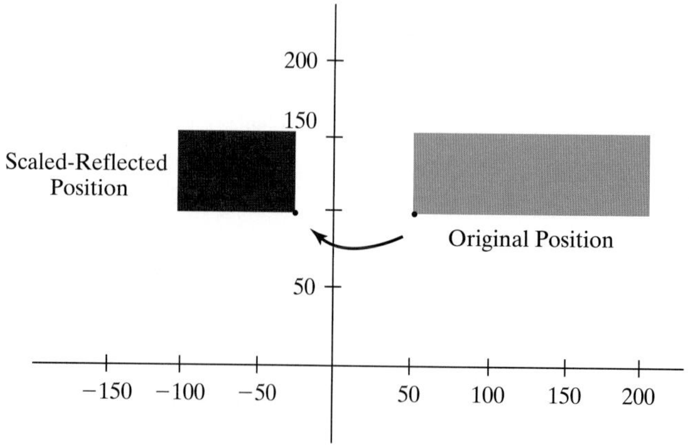

FIGURE 5-57 Scaling and reflecting a rectangle using the OpenGL function `glScalef (−0.5, 1.0, 1.0)`.

concatenated with the current matrix (the identity matrix). When the original rectangle is again referenced, it is rotated about the *z* axis and displayed in a red color (Fig. 5-56). We repeat this process once more to generate the scaled and reflected red rectangle shown in Fig. 5-57.

```
glMatrixMode (GL_MODELVIEW);

glColor3f (0.0, 0.0, 1.0);
glRecti (50, 100, 200, 150);          // Display blue rectangle.

glColor3f (1.0, 0.0, 0.0);
glTranslatef (-200.0, -50.0, 0.0); // Set translation parameters.
glRecti (50, 100, 200, 150);          // Display red, translated rectangle.

glLoadIdentity ( );                   // Reset current matrix to identity.
glRotatef (90.0, 0.0, 0.0, 1.0);     // Set 90-deg. rotation about z axis.
glRecti (50, 100, 200, 150);          // Display red, rotated rectangle.

glLoadIdentity ( );                   // Reset current matrix to identity.
glScalef (-0.5, 1.0, 1.0);            // Set scale-reflection parameters.
glRecti (50, 100, 200, 150);          // Display red, transformed rectangle.
```

Usually, it is more efficient to use the stack-processing functions than to use the matrix-manipulation functions. This is particularly true when we want to make several changes in the viewing or geometric transformations. In the following code, we repeat the rectangle transformations of the preceding example using stack processing instead of the `glLoadIdentity` function.

```
glMatrixMode (GL_MODELVIEW);

glColor3f (0.0, 0.0, 1.0);            // Set current color to blue.
glRecti (50, 100, 200, 150);          // Display blue rectangle.

glPushMatrix ( );                     // Make copy of identity (top) matrix.
glColor3f (1.0, 0.0, 0.0);            // Set current color to red.

glTranslatef (-200.0, -50.0, 0.0); // Set translation parameters.
glRecti (50, 100, 200, 150);          // Display red, translated rectangle.

glPopMatrix ( );                      // Throw away the translation matrix.
glPushMatrix ( );                     // Make copy of identity (top) matrix.

glRotatef (90.0, 0.0, 0.0, 1.0);     // Set 90-deg. rotation about z axis.
glRecti (50, 100, 200, 150);          // Display red, rotated rectangle.

glPopMatrix ( );                      // Throw away the rotation matrix.
glScalef (-0.5, 1.0, 1.0);            // Set scale-reflection parameters.
glRecti (50, 100, 200, 150);          // Display red, transformed rectangle.
```

For our final geometric-transformation programming example, we give an OpenGL version of the three-dimensional, composite-transformation code in Section 5-13. Because OpenGL postmultiplies transformation matrices as they are called, we must now invoke the transformations in the opposite order from which they are to be applied. Thus, each subsequent transformation call concatenates the designated transformation matrix on the right of the composite matrix. Since we have not yet explored the three-dimensional OpenGL viewing routines (Chapter 7), this program could be completed using two-dimensional OpenGL viewing operations and applying the geometric transformations to objects in the *xy* plane.

```
class wcPt3D {
   public:
      GLfloat x, y, z;
};

\* Procedure for generating a matrix for rotation about an
 * an axis defined with points p1 and p2.
 */
void rotate3D (wcPt3D p1, wcPt3D p2, GLfloat thetaDegrees)
{
   /*  Set up components for rotation-axis vector.  */
   float vx = (p2.x - p1.x);
   float vy = (p2.y - p1.y);
   float vz = (p2.z - p1.z);

   /* Specify translate-rotate-translate sequence in reverse order: */
   glTranslatef (p1.x, p1.y, p1.z); // Move p1 back to original position.
   /*  Rotate about axis through origin:  */
   glRotatef (thetaDegrees, vx, vy, vz);
   glTranslatef (-p1.x, -p1.y, -p1.z);  // Translate p1 to origin.
}

/*  Procedure for generating a matrix for a scaling
 *  transformation with respect to an arbitrary fixed point.
 */
void scale3D (GLfloat sx, GLfloat sy, GLfloat sz, wcPt3D fixedPt)
{
   /* Specify translate-scale-translate sequence in reverse order: */
   /* (3) Translate fixed point back to original position: */
   glTranslatef (fixedPt.x, fixedPt.y, fixedPt.z);
   glScalef (sx, sy, sz);      // (2) Scale with respect to origin.
   /* (1) Translate fixed point to coordinate origin: */
   glTranslatef (-fixedPt.x, -fixedPt.y, -fixedPt.z);
}

void displayFcn (void)
{
   /*  Input object description.  */
   /*  Set up 3D viewing-transformation routines. */
   /*  Display object.  */
```

```
   glMatrixMode (GL_MODELVIEW);

   /* Input translation parameters tx, ty, tz. */
   /* Input the defining points, p1 and p2, for the rotation axis. */
   /* Input rotation angle in degrees. */
   /* Input scaling parameters: sx, sy, sz, and fixedPt. */

   /*  Invoke geometric transformations in reverse order:  */
   glTranslatef (tx, ty, tz);      // Final transformation: Translate.
   scale3D (sx, sy, sz, fixedPt);     // Second transformation: Scale.
   rotate3D (p1, p2, thetaDegrees);   // First transformation: Rotate.

   /*  Call routines for displaying transformed objects.  */
}
```

5-18 SUMMARY

The basic geometric transformations are translation, rotation, and scaling. Translation moves an object in a straight-line path from one position to another. Rotation moves an object from one position to another along a circular path around a specified rotation axis. For two-dimensional applications, the rotation path is in the xy plane about an axis that is parallel to the z axis. Scaling transformations change the dimensions of an object relative to a fixed position.

We can express two-dimensional transformations as 3 by 3 matrix operators and three-dimensional transformations as 4 by 4 matrix operators, so that sequences of transformations can be concatenated into a single composite matrix. Or, in general, we can represent both two-dimensional and three-dimensional transformations with 4 by 4 matrices. Representing geometric-transformation operations with matrices is an efficient formulation, since it allows us to reduce computations by applying a composite matrix to an object description to obtain its transformed position. To do this, we express coordinate positions as column matrices. We choose a column-matrix representation for coordinate points because this is the standard mathematical convention, and most graphics packages now follow this convention. A three-element or four-element column matrix (vector) is referred to as a homogeneous-coordinate representation. For geometric transformations, the homogeneous coefficient is assigned the value 1.

Composite transformations are formed as matrix multiplications of translation, rotation, scaling, and other transformations. We can use combinations of translation and rotation for animation applications, and we can use combinations of rotation and scaling to scale objects in any specified direction. In general, matrix multiplications are not commutative. We obtain different results, for example, if we change the order of a translate-rotate sequence. A transformation sequence involving only translations and rotations is a rigid-body transformation, since angles and distances are unchanged. Also, the upper-left submatrix of a rigid-body transformation is an orthogonal matrix. Thus, rotation matrices can be formed by setting the upper-left, 3 by 3 submatrix equal to the elements of two orthogonal unit vectors. When the angle is small, we can reduce rotation computations by using first-order approximations for the sine and cosine functions. Over many rotational steps, however, the approximation error can accumulate to a significant value.

Other geometric transformations include reflections and shears. Reflections are transformations that rotate an object 180° about a reflection axis. This produces a mirror image of the object with respect to that axis. When the reflection axis is perpendicular to the xy plane, the reflection is obtained as a rotation in the xy plane. When the reflection axis is in the xy plane, the reflection is obtained as a rotation in a plane that is perpendicular to the xy plane. Shear transformations distort the shape of an object by shifting one or more coordinate values by an amount proportional to the distance from a shear reference line.

Transformations between Cartesian coordinate systems are accomplished with a sequence of translate-rotate transformations that brings the two systems into coincidence. We specify the coordinate origin and axis vectors for one reference frame relative to the original coordinate reference frame. For a two-dimensional system, one vector completely defines the coordinate-axis directions. But for a three-dimensional system, we must specify two of the three axis directions. The transfer of object descriptions from the original coordinate system to the second system is calculated as the matrix product of a translation that moves the new origin to the old coordinate origin and a rotation to align the two sets of axes. The rotation needed to align the two frames can be obtained from the orthonormal set of axis vectors for the new system.

Geometric transformations are affine transformations. That is, they can be expressed as a linear function of coordinate positions. Translation, rotation, scaling, reflection, and shear are affine transformations. They transform parallel lines to parallel lines and finite coordinate positions to finite positions. The geometric transformations that do not involve scaling or shear also preserve angles and lengths.

We can use raster operations for performing some simple geometric transformations on pixel arrays. For two-dimensional applications, we can use the raster operations to perform fast translations, reflections, and rotations in multiples of 90°. With a little more processing, we can perform general raster rotations and scaling.

The OpenGL basic library contains three functions for applying individual translate, rotate, and scale transformations to coordinate positions. Each function generates a matrix that is premultiplied by the modelview matrix. Thus, a sequence of geometric-transformation functions must be specified in reverse order: the last transformation invoked is the first to be applied to coordinate positions. Transformation matrices are applied to subsequently defined objects. In addition to accumulating transformation sequences in the modelview matrix, we can set this matrix to the identity or some other matrix. We can also form products with the modelview matrix and any specified matrices. All matrices are stored in stacks, and OpenGL maintains four stacks for the various types of transformations that we use in graphics applications. We can use an OpenGL query function to determine the current stack size or the maximum allowable stack depth for a system. Two stack-processing routines are available: one for copying the top matrix in a stack to the second position, and one for removing the top matrix. Several operations are available in OpenGL for performing raster transformations. A block of pixels can be translated, rotated, scaled, or reflected with these OpenGL raster operations.

Table 5-1 summarizes the OpenGL geometric-transformation functions and matrix routines discussed in this chapter. Additionally, the table lists some related functions.

TABLE 5-1

SUMMARY OF OpenGL GEOMETRIC TRANSFORMATION FUNCTIONS

Function	*Description*
`glTranslate*`	Specify translation parameters.
`glRotate*`	Specify parameters for rotation about any axis through the origin.
`glScale*`	Specify scaling parameters with respect to coordinate origin.
`glMatrixMode`	Specify current matrix for geometric-viewing transformations, projection transformations, texture transformations, or color transformations.
`glLoadIdentity`	Set current matrix to identity.
`glLoadMatrix*` (elems);	Set elements of current matrix.
`glMultMatrix*` (elems);	Postmultiply the current matrix by the specified matrix.
`glGetIntegerv`	Get max stack depth or current number of matrices in the stack for the selected matrix mode.
`glPushMatrix`	Copy the top matrix in the stack and store copy in the second stack position.
`glPopMatrix`	Erase top matrix in stack and move second matrix to top of stack.
`glPixelZoom`	Specify two-dimensional scaling parameters for raster operations.

REFERENCES

For additional techniques involving matrices and geometric transformations, see Glassner (1990), Arvo (1991), Kirk (1992), Heckbert (1994), and Paeth (1995). Discussions of homogeneous coordinates in computer graphics can be found in Blinn and Newell (1978) and in Blinn (1993, 1996, and 1998).

Additional programming examples using OpenGL geometric-transformation functions are given in Woo, Neider, Davis, and Shreiner (1999). Programming examples for the OpenGL geometric-transformation functions are also available at Nate Robins's tutorial Web site: http://www.cs.utah.edu/narobins/opengl.html. And a complete listing of OpenGL geometric-transformation functions is provided in Shreiner (2000).

EXERCISES

5-1 Write an animation program that implements the example two-dimensional rotation procedure of Section 5-1. An input polygon is to be rotated repeatedly in small steps around a pivot point in the xy plane. Small angles are to be used for each successive step in the rotation, and approximations to the sine and cosine functions are to be used to speed up the calculations. To avoid excessive accumulation of round-off errors, reset the original coordinate values for the object at the start of each new revolution.

5-2 Show that the composition of two rotations is additive by concatenating the matrix representations for $\mathbf{R}(\theta_1)$ and $\mathbf{R}(\theta_2)$ to obtain

$$\mathbf{R}(\theta_1) \cdot \mathbf{R}(\theta_2) = \mathbf{R}(\theta_1 + \theta_2)$$

5-3 Modify the two-dimensional transformation matrix (5-39), for scaling in an arbitrary direction, to include coordinates for any specified scaling fixed point (x_f, y_f).

5-4 Prove that the multiplication of transformation matrices for each of the following sequences is commutative:

(a) Two successive rotations.

(b) Two successive translations.

(c) Two successive scalings.

5-5 Prove that a uniform scaling and a rotation form a commutative pair of operations but that, in general, scaling and rotation are not commutative operations.

5-6 Multiple the individual scale, rotate, and translate matrices in Eq. 5-42 to verify the elements in the composite transformation matrix.

5-7 Modify the example program in Section 5-4 so that transformation parameters can be specified as user input.

5-8 Modify the program from the previous exercise so that the transformation sequence can be applied to any polygon, with vertices specified as user input.

5-9 Modify the example program in Section 5-4 so that the order of the geometric transformation sequence can be specified as user input.

5-10 Show that transformation matrix (5-55), for a reflection about the line $y = x$, is equivalent to a reflection relative to the x axis followed by a counterclockwise rotation of 90°.

5-11 Show that transformation matrix (5-56), for a reflection about the line $y = -x$, is equivalent to a reflection relative to the y axis followed by a counterclockwise rotation of 90°.

5-12 Show that two successive reflections about either the x axis or the y axis is equivalent to a single rotation in the xy plane about the coordinate origin.

5-13 Determine the form of the two-dimensional transformation matrix for a reflection about any line: $y = mx + b$.

5-14 Show that two successive reflections about any line in the xy plane that intersects the coordinate origin is equivalent to a rotation in the xy plane about the origin.

5-15 Determine a sequence of basic transformations that is equivalent to the x-direction shearing matrix (5-57).

5-16 Determine a sequence of basic transformations that is equivalent to the y-direction shearing matrix (5-61).

5-17 Set up a shearing procedure to display two-dimensional italic characters, given a vector font definition. That is, all character shapes in this font are defined with straight-line segments, and italic characters are formed with shearing transformations. Determine an appropriate value for the shear parameter by comparing italics and plain text in some available font. Define a simple vector font for input to your routine.

5-18 Derive the following equations for transforming a coordinate point $\mathbf{P} = (x, y)$ in one two-dimensional Cartesian system to the coordinate values (x', y') in another Cartesian system that is rotated counterclockwise by an angle θ relative to the first system. The transformation equations can be obtained by projecting point $\mathbf{P}$ onto each of the four axes and analyzing the resulting right triangles.

$$x' = x\cos\theta + y\sin\theta \qquad y' = -x\sin\theta + y\cos\theta$$

5-19 Write a procedure to compute the elements of the matrix for transforming object descriptions from one two-dimensional Cartesian coordinate system to another.

The second coordinate system is to be defined with an origin point $\mathbf{P}_0$ and a vector $\mathbf{V}$ that gives the direction for the positive y' axis of this system.

5-20 Set up procedures for implementing a block transfer of a rectangular area of a frame buffer, using one function to read the area into an array and another function to copy the array into the designated transfer area.

5-21 Determine the results of performing two successive block transfers into the same area of a frame buffer using the various Boolean operations.

5-22 What are the results of performing two successive block transfers into the same area of a frame buffer using the binary arithmetic operations?

5-23 Implement a routine to perform block transfers in a frame buffer using any specified Boolean operation or a replacement (copy) operation.

5-24 Write a routine to implement rotations in increments of 90° in frame-buffer block transfers.

5-25 Write a routine to implement rotations by any specified angle in a frame-buffer block transfer.

5-26 Write a routine to implement scaling as a raster transformation of a pixel block.

5-27 Show that rotation matrix 5-102 is equal to the composite matrix $\mathbf{R}_y(\beta) \cdot \mathbf{R}_x(\alpha)$.

5-28 By evaluating the terms in Eq. 5-106, derive the elements for the general rotation matrix given in Eq. 5-107.

5-29 Prove that the quaternion rotation matrix 5-107 reduces to the matrix representation in Eq. 5-74 when the rotation axis is the coordinate z axis.

5-30 Prove that Eq. 5-109 is equivalent to the general rotation transformation given in Eq. 5-97.

5-31 Using trigonometric identities, derive the elements of the quaternion-rotation matrix 5-108 from 5-107.

5-32 Develop a procedure for animating a three-dimensional object by incrementally rotating it about any specified axis. Use appropriate approximations to the trigonometric equations to speed up the calculations, and reset the object to its initial position after each complete revolution about the axis.

5-33 Derive the three-dimensional transformation matrix for scaling an object by a scaling factor s in a direction defined by the direction cosines α, β, and γ.

5-34 Develop a routine to reflect a three-dimensional object about an arbitrarily selected plane.

5-35 Write a procedure to shear a three-dimensional object with respect to any of the three coordinate axes, using input values for the shearing parameters.

5-36 Develop a procedure for converting an object definition in one three-dimensional coordinate reference to any other coordinate system defined relative to the first system.

5-37 Implement the example program in Section 5-17 so that the three-dimensional OpenGL geometric-transformation routines are applied to the two-dimensional triangle shown in Fig. 5-15(a) to produce the transformation shown in (b) of that figure.

5-38 Modify the program from the previous exercise so that the transformation sequence can be applied to any two-dimensional polygon, with vertices specified as user input.

5-39 Modify the example program in the previous exercise so that the order of the geometric transformation sequence can be specified as user input.

5-40 Modify the example program from the previous exercise so that the geometric transformation parameters are specified as user input.

CHAPTER 6

Two-Dimensional Viewing

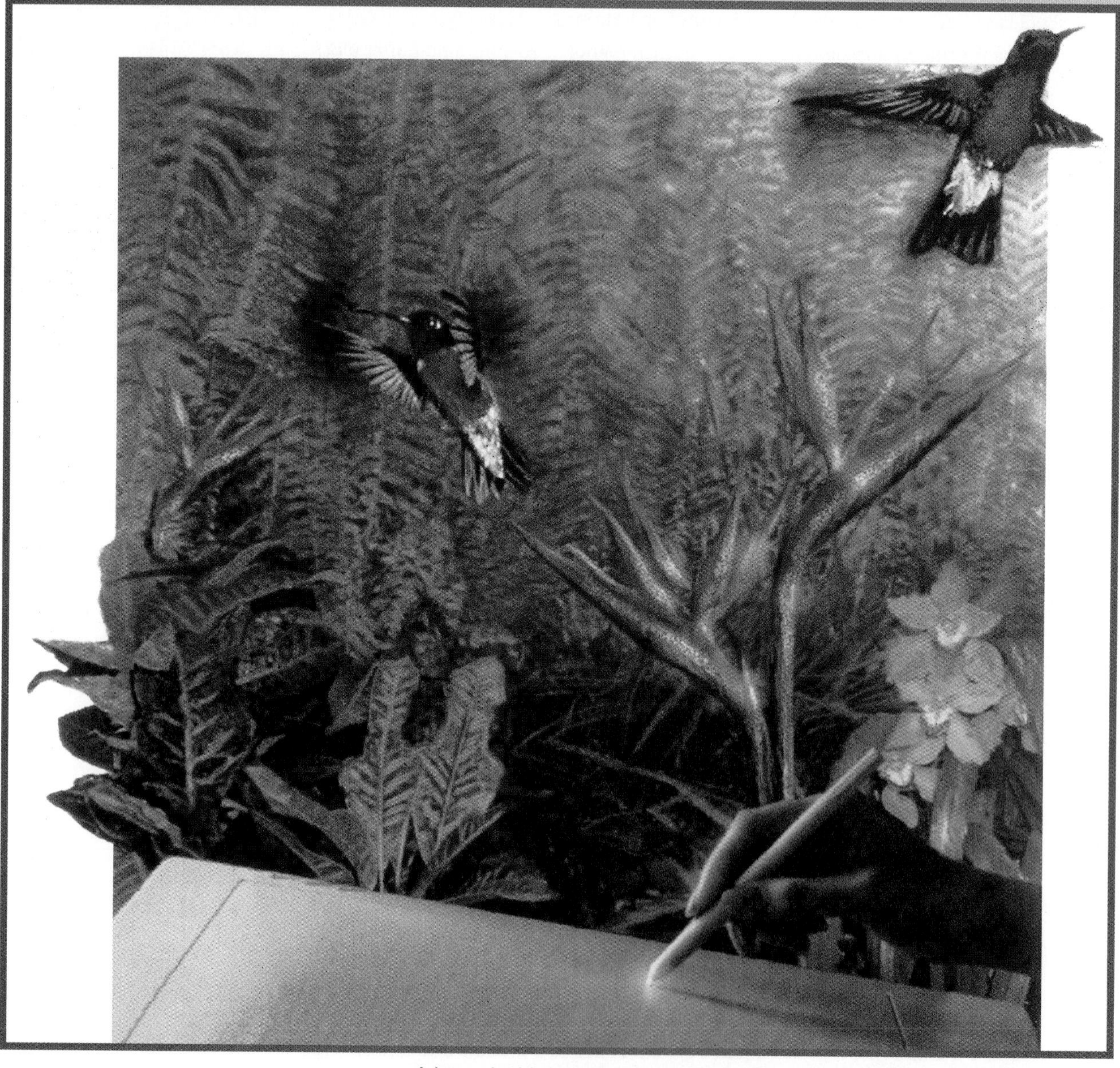

A hummingbird garden scene painted by artist John Derry of Time Arts, Inc., using a graphics tablet and cordless pressure-sensitive stylus. *(Courtesy of the Wacom Technology Corporation.)*

In Chapter 2, we briefly introduced two-dimensional viewing concepts and functions. We now examine in more detail the procedures for displaying views of a two-dimensional picture on an output device. Typically, a graphics package allows a user to specify which part of a defined picture is to be displayed and where that part is to be placed on the display device. Any convenient Cartesian coordinate system, referred to as the world-coordinate reference frame, can be used to define the picture. For a two-dimensional picture, a view is selected by specifying a region of the xy plane that contains the total picture or any part of it. A user can select a single area for display, or several areas could be selected for simultaneous display or for an animated panning sequence across a scene. The picture parts within the selected areas are then mapped onto specified areas of the device coordinates. When multiple view areas are selected, these areas can be placed in separate display locations, or some areas could be inserted into other, larger display areas. Two-dimensional viewing transformations from world to device coordinates involve translation, rotation, and scaling operations, as well as procedures for deleting those parts of the picture that are outside the limits of a selected scene area.

6-1 THE TWO-DIMENSIONAL VIEWING PIPELINE

A section of a two-dimensional scene that is selected for display is called a **clipping window,** because all parts of the scene outside the selected section are "clipped" off. The only part of the scene that shows up on the screen is what is inside the clipping window. Sometimes the clipping window is alluded to as the *world window* or the *viewing window.* And, at one time, graphics systems referred to the clipping window simply as "the window", but there are now so many windows in use on computers that we need to distinguish between them. For example, a window-management system can create and manipulate several areas on a video screen, each of which is called "a window", for the display of graphics and text (Fig. 6-1). So, we will always use the term *clipping window* to refer to a selected section of a scene that is eventually converted to pixel patterns within a display window on the video monitor. Graphics packages also allow us also to control the placement within the display window using another "window" called the **viewport.** Objects inside the clipping window are mapped to the viewport, and

FIGURE 6-1 A video screen showing multiple, simultaneous display windows. (*Courtesy of Sun Microsystems.*)

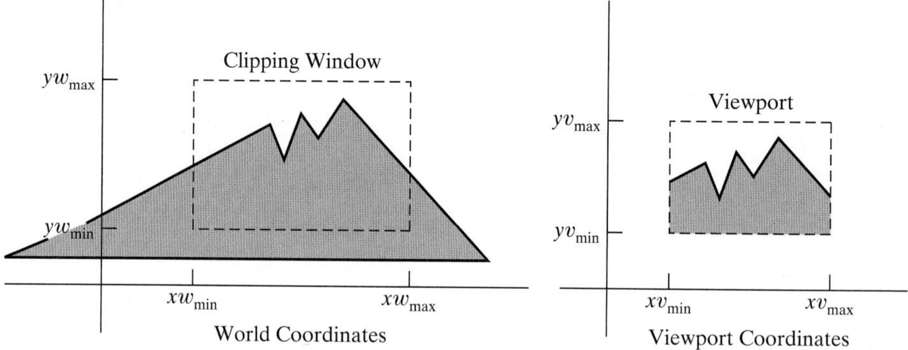

FIGURE 6-2 A clipping window and associated viewport, specified as rectangles aligned with the coordinate axes.

it is the viewport that is then positioned within the display window. The clipping window selects *what* we want to see; the viewport indicates *where* it is to be viewed on the output device.

By changing the position of a viewport, we can view objects at different positions on the display area of an output device. Multiple viewports can be used to display different sections of a scene at different screen positions. Also, by varying the size of viewports, we can change the size and proportions of displayed objects. We achieve zooming effects by successively mapping different-sized clipping windows onto a fixed-size viewport. As the clipping windows are made smaller, we zoom in on some part of a scene to view details that are not shown with the larger clipping windows. Similarly, more overview is obtained by zooming out from a section of a scene with successively larger clipping windows. And panning effects are achieved by moving a fixed-size clipping window across the various objects in a scene.

Usually, clipping windows and viewports are rectangles in standard position, with the rectangle edges parallel to the coordinate axes. Other window or viewport geometries, such as general polygon shapes and circles, are used in some applications, but these shapes take longer to process. We first consider only rectangular viewports and clipping windows, as illustrated in Figure 6-2.

The mapping of a two-dimensional, world-coordinate scene description to device coordinates is called a **two-dimensional viewing transformation.** Sometimes this transformation is simply referred to as the *window-to-viewport transformation* or the *windowing transformation.* But, in general, viewing involves more than just the transformation from clipping-window coordinates to viewport

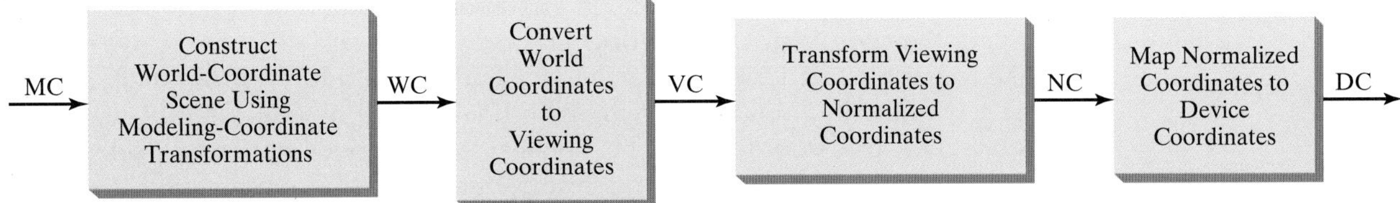

FIGURE 6-3 Two-dimensional viewing-transformation pipeline.

coordinates. In analogy with three-dimensional viewing, we can describe the steps for two-dimensional viewing as indicated in Fig. 6-3. Once a world-coordinate scene has been constructed, we could set up a separate two-dimensional, **viewing-coordinate reference frame** for specifying the clipping window. But the clipping window is often just defined in world coordinates, so that viewing coordinates for two-dimensional applications are the same as world coordinates. (For a three-dimensional scene, however, we need a separate viewing frame to specify the parameters for the viewing position, direction, and orientation.)

To make the viewing process independent of the requirements of any output device, graphics systems convert object descriptions to normalized coordinates and apply the clipping routines. Some systems use normalized coordinates in the range from 0 to 1, and others use a normalized range from −1 to 1. Depending upon the graphics library in use, the viewport is defined either in normalized coordinates or in screen coordinates after the normalization process. At the final step of the viewing transformation, the contents of the viewport are transferred to positions within the display window.

Clipping is usually performed in normalized coordinates. This allows us to reduce computations by first concatenating the various transformation matrices. Clipping procedures are of fundamental importance in computer graphics. They are used not only in viewing transformations, but also in window-manager systems, in painting and drawing packages to erase picture sections, and in many other applications.

6-2 THE CLIPPING WINDOW

To achieve a particular viewing effect in an application program, we could design our own clipping window with any shape, size, and orientation we choose. For example, we might like to use a star pattern, or an ellipse, or a figure with spline boundaries as a clipping window. But clipping a scene using a concave polygon or a clipping window with nonlinear boundaries requires more processing than clipping against a rectangle. We need to perform more computations to determine where an object intersects a circle than to find out where it intersects a straight line. And the simplest window edges to clip against are straight lines that are parallel to the coordinate axes. Therefore, graphics packages commonly allow only rectangular clipping windows aligned with the x and y axes.

If we want some other shape for a clipping window, then we must implement our own clipping and coordinate-transformation algorithms. Or we could just edit the picture to produce a certain shape for the display frame around the scene. For example, we could trim the edges of a picture with any desired pattern by overlaying polygons that are filled with the background color. In this way, we could generate any desired border effects or even put interior holes in the picture.

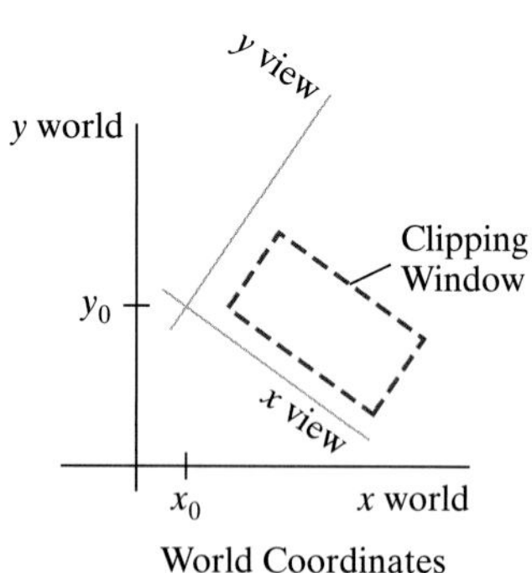

FIGURE 6-4 A rotated clipping window defined in viewing coordinates.

Rectangular clipping windows in standard position are easily defined by giving the coordinates of two opposite corners of each rectangle. If we would like to get a rotated view of a scene, we could either define a rectangular clipping window in a rotated viewing-coordinate frame or, equivalently, we could rotate the world-coordinate scene. Some systems provide options for selecting a rotated, two-dimensional viewing frame, but usually the clipping window must be specified in world coordinates.

Viewing-Coordinate Clipping Window

A general approach to the two-dimensional viewing transformation is to set up a *viewing-coordinate system* within the world-coordinate frame. This viewing frame provides a reference for specifying a rectangular clipping window with any selected orientation and position, as in Fig. 6-4. To obtain a view of the world-coordinate scene as determined by the clipping window of Fig. 6-4, we just need to transfer the scene description to viewing coordinates. Although many graphics packages do not provide functions for specifying a clipping window in a two-dimensional viewing-coordinate system, this is the standard approach for defining a clipping region for a three-dimensional scene.

We choose an origin for a two-dimensional viewing-coordinate frame at some world position $\mathbf{P}_0 = (x_0, y_0)$, and we can establish the orientation using a world vector $\mathbf{V}$ that defines the y_{view} direction. Vector $\mathbf{V}$ is called the two-dimensional **view up vector.** An alternative method for specifying the orientation of the viewing frame is to give a rotation angle relative to either the x or y axis in the world frame. From this rotation angle, we can then obtain the view up vector. Once we have established the parameters that define the viewing-coordinate frame, we use the procedures from Section 5-8 to transform the scene description to the viewing system. This involves a sequence of transformations equivalent to superimposing the viewing frame on the world frame.

The first step in the transformation sequence is to translate the viewing origin to the world origin. Next, we rotate the viewing system to align it with the world frame. Given the orientation vector $\mathbf{V}$, we can calculate the components of unit vectors $\mathbf{v} = (v_x, v_y)$ and $\mathbf{u} = (u_x, u_y)$ for the y_{view} and x_{view} axes, respectively. These unit vectors are used to form the first and second rows of the rotation matrix $\mathbf{R}$ that aligns the viewing $x_{\text{view}} y_{\text{view}}$ axes with the world $x_w y_w$ axes.

Object positions in world coordinates are then converted to viewing coordinates with the composite two-dimensional transformation matrix

$$\mathbf{M}_{WC,VC} = \mathbf{R} \cdot \mathbf{T} \qquad (6\text{-}1)$$

where $\mathbf{T}$ is the translation matrix that takes the viewing origin $\mathbf{P}_0$ to the world origin, and $\mathbf{R}$ is the rotation matrix that rotates the viewing frame of reference into coincidence with the world-coordinate system. Figure 6-5 illustrates the steps in this coordinate transformation.

World-Coordinate Clipping Window

A routine for defining a standard, rectangular clipping window in world coordinates is typically provided in a graphics-programming library. We simply specify two world-coordinate positions, which are then assigned to the two opposite corners of a standard rectangle. Once the clipping window has been established, the scene description is processed through the viewing routines to the output device.

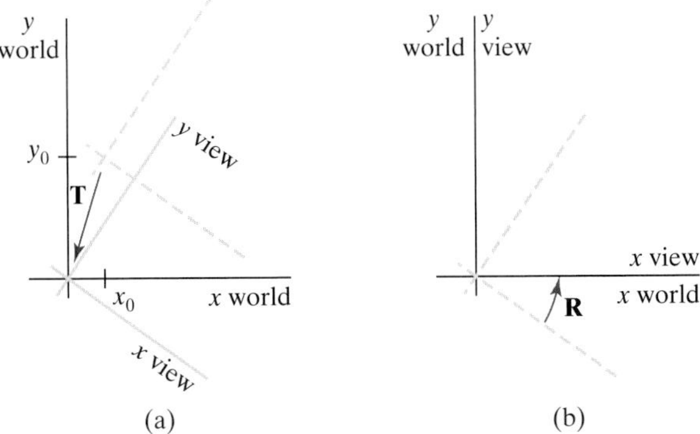

FIGURE 6-5 A viewing-coordinate frame is moved into coincidence with the world frame by (a) applying a translation matrix **T** to move the viewing origin to the world origin, then (b) applying a rotation matrix **R** to align the axes of the two systems.

If we want to obtain a rotated view of a two-dimensional scene, as discussed in the previous section, we perform exactly the same steps as described there, but without considering a viewing frame of reference. Thus, we simply rotate (and possibly translate) objects to a desired position and set up the clipping window—all in world coordinates. As an example, we could display a rotated view of the triangle in Fig. 6-6(a) by rotating it into the position we want and setting up a standard clipping rectangle. In analogy with the coordinate transformation described in the previous section, we could also translate the triangle to the world origin and define a clipping window around the triangle. In that case, we define an orientation vector and choose a reference point such as the triangle's centroid (Appendix A). Then we translate the reference point to the world origin and rotate the orientation vector onto the y_{world} axis using transformation matrix 6-1. With the triangle in the desired orientation, we can use a standard clipping window in world coordinates to capture the view of the rotated triangle. The transformed position of the triangle and the selected clipping window are shown in Fig. 6-6(b).

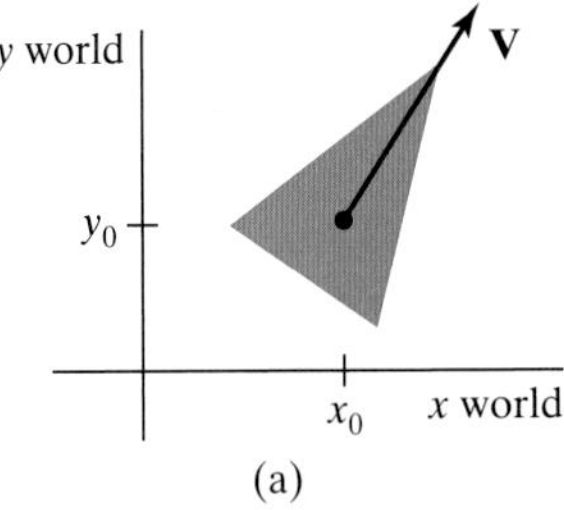

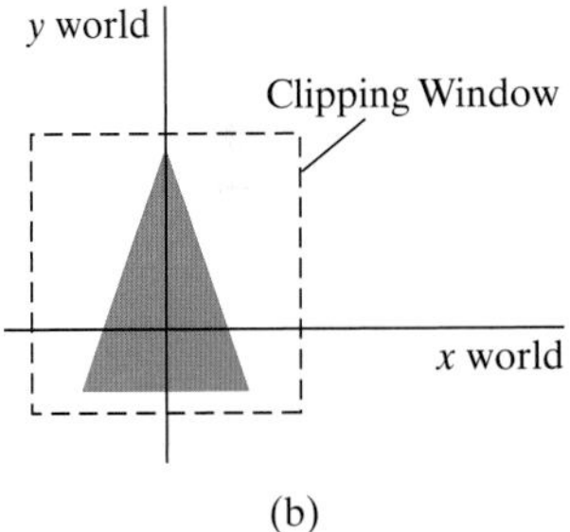

FIGURE 6-6 A triangle (a), with a selected reference point and orientation vector, is translated and rotated to position (b) within a clipping window.

6-3 NORMALIZATION AND VIEWPORT TRANSFORMATIONS

With some graphics packages, the normalization and window-to-viewport transformations are combined into one operation. In this case, the viewport coordinates are often given in the range from 0 to 1 so that the viewport is positioned within a unit square. After clipping, the unit square containing the viewport is mapped to the output display device. In other systems, the normalization and clipping routines are applied before the viewport transformation. For these systems, the viewport boundaries are specified in screen coordinates relative to the display-window position.

Mapping the Clipping Window into a Normalized Viewport

To illustrate the general procedures for the normalization and viewport transformations, we first consider a viewport defined with normalized coordinate values between 0 and 1. Object descriptions are transferred to this normalized space using a transformation that maintains the same relative placement of a point in the viewport as it had in the clipping window. If a coordinate position is at the center of the clipping window, for instance, it would be mapped to the center of

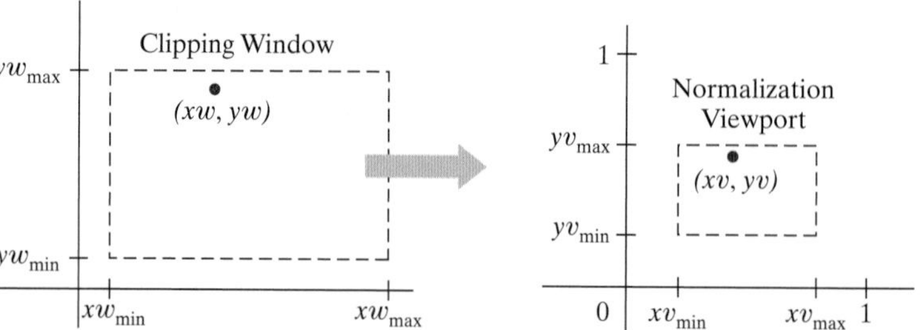

FIGURE 6-7 A point (xw, yw) in a world-coordinate clipping window is mapped to viewport coordinates (xv, yv), within a unit square, so that the relative positions of the two points in their respective rectangles are the same.

the viewport. Figure 6-7 illustrates this window-to-viewport mapping. Position (xw, yw) in the clipping window is mapped into position (xv, yv) in the associated viewport.

To transform the world-coordinate point into the same relative position within the viewport, we require that

$$
\begin{aligned}
\frac{xv - xv_{\min}}{xv_{\max} - xv_{\min}} &= \frac{xw - xw_{\min}}{xw_{\max} - xw_{\min}} \\
\frac{yv - yv_{\min}}{yv_{\max} - yv_{\min}} &= \frac{yw - yw_{\min}}{yw_{\max} - yw_{\min}}
\end{aligned}
\tag{6-2}
$$

Solving these expressions for the viewport position (xv, yv), we have

$$
\begin{aligned}
xv &= s_x xw + t_x \\
yv &= s_y yw + t_y
\end{aligned}
\tag{6-3}
$$

where the scaling factors are

$$
\begin{aligned}
s_x &= \frac{xv_{\max} - xv_{\min}}{xw_{\max} - xw_{\min}} \\
s_y &= \frac{yv_{\max} - yv_{\min}}{yw_{\max} - yw_{\min}}
\end{aligned}
\tag{6-4}
$$

and the translation factors are

$$
\begin{aligned}
t_x &= \frac{xw_{\max} xv_{\min} - xw_{\min} xv_{\max}}{xw_{\max} - xw_{\min}} \\
t_y &= \frac{yw_{\max} yv_{\min} - yw_{\min} yv_{\max}}{yw_{\max} - yw_{\min}}
\end{aligned}
\tag{6-5}
$$

Since we are simply mapping world-coordinate positions into a viewport that is positioned near the world origin, we can also derive Eqs. 6-3 using any transformation sequence that converts the rectangle for the clipping window into the viewport rectangle. For example, we could obtain the transformation from world coordinates to viewport coordinates with the sequence

(1) Scale the clipping window to the size of the viewport using a fixed-point position of $(xw_{\min}, yw_{\min})$.

(2) Translate $(xw_{\min}, yw_{\min})$ to $(xv_{\min}, yv_{\min})$.

The scaling transformation in step (1) can be represented with the two-dimensional matrix

$$\mathbf{S} = \begin{bmatrix} s_x & 0 & xw_{\min}(1 - s_x) \\ 0 & s_y & yw_{\min}(1 - s_y) \\ 0 & 0 & 1 \end{bmatrix} \qquad (6\text{-}6)$$

where s_x and s_y are the same as in Eqs. 6-4. The two-dimensional matrix representation for the translation of the lower-left corner of the clipping window to the lower-left viewport corner is

$$\mathbf{T} = \begin{bmatrix} 1 & 0 & xv_{\min} - xw_{\min} \\ 0 & 1 & yv_{\min} - yw_{\min} \\ 0 & 0 & 1 \end{bmatrix} \qquad (6\text{-}7)$$

And the composite matrix representation for the transformation to the normalized viewport is

$$\mathbf{M}_{\text{window, normviewp}} = \mathbf{T} \cdot \mathbf{S} = \begin{bmatrix} s_x & 0 & t_x \\ 0 & s_y & t_y \\ 0 & 0 & 1 \end{bmatrix} \qquad (6\text{-}8)$$

which gives us the same result as in Eqs. 6-3. Any other clipping-window reference point, such as the top-right corner or the window center, could be used for the scale–translate operations. Or, we could first translate any clipping-window position to the corresponding location in the viewport, and then scale relative to that viewport location.

The window-to-viewport transformation maintains the relative placement of object descriptions. An object inside the clipping window is mapped to a corresponding position inside the viewport. Similarly, an object outside the clipping window is outside the viewport.

Relative proportions of objects, on the other hand, are maintained only if the aspect ratio of the viewport is the same as the aspect ratio of the clipping window. In other words, we keep the same object proportions if the scaling factors sx and sy are the same. Otherwise, world objects will be stretched or contracted in either the x or y directions (or both) when displayed on the output device.

The clipping routines can be applied using either the clipping-window boundaries or the viewport boundaries. After clipping, the normalized coordinates are transformed into device coordinates. And the unit square can be mapped onto the output device using the same procedures as in the window-to-viewport transformation, with the area inside the unit square transferred to the total display area of the output device.

Mapping the Clipping Window into a Normalized Square

Another approach to two-dimensional viewing is to transform the clipping window into a normalized square, clip in normalized coordinates, and then transfer the scene description to a viewport specified in screen coordinates. This transformation is illustrated in Fig. 6-8 with normalized coordinates in the range from -1 to 1. The clipping algorithms in this transformation sequence are now standardized so that objects outside the boundaries $x = \pm 1$ and $y = \pm 1$ are detected and removed from the scene description. At the final step of the viewing transformation, the objects in the viewport are positioned within the display window.

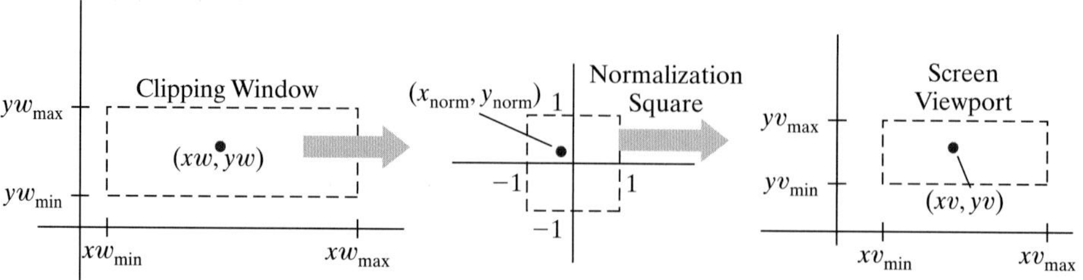

FIGURE 6-8 A point (xw, yw) in a clipping window is mapped to a normalized coordinate position (x_{norm}, y_{norm}), then to a screen-coordinate position (xv, yv) in a viewport. Objects are clipped against the normalization square before the transformation to viewport coordinates.

We transfer the contents of the clipping window into the normalization square using the same procedures as in the window-to-viewport transformation. The matrix for the normalization transformation is obtained from Eq. 6-8 by substituting -1 for xv_{min} and yv_{min} and substituting $+1$ for xv_{max} and yv_{max}. Making these substitutions in the expressions for t_x, t_y, s_x, and s_y, we have

$$\mathbf{M}_{\text{window, normsquare}} = \begin{bmatrix} \dfrac{2}{xw_{max} - xw_{min}} & 0 & -\dfrac{xw_{max} + xw_{min}}{xw_{max} - xw_{min}} \\ 0 & \dfrac{2}{yw_{max} - yw_{min}} & -\dfrac{yw_{max} + yw_{min}}{yw_{max} - yw_{min}} \\ 0 & 0 & 1 \end{bmatrix} \tag{6-9}$$

Similarly, after the clipping algorithms have been applied, the normalized square with edge length equal to 2 is transformed into a specified viewport. This time, we get the transformation matrix from Eq. 6-8 by substituting -1 for xw_{min} and yw_{min} and substituting $+1$ for xw_{max} and yw_{max}:

$$\mathbf{M}_{\text{normsquare, viewport}} = \begin{bmatrix} \dfrac{xv_{max} - xv_{min}}{2} & 0 & \dfrac{xv_{max} + xv_{min}}{2} \\ 0 & \dfrac{yv_{max} - yv_{min}}{2} & \dfrac{yv_{max} + yv_{min}}{2} \\ 0 & 0 & 1 \end{bmatrix} \tag{6-10}$$

The last step in the viewing process is to position the viewport area in the display window. Typically, the lower-left corner of the viewport is placed at a coordinate position specified relative to the lower-left corner of the display window. Figure 6-9 demonstrates the positioning of a viewport within a display window.

As before, we maintain the initial proportions of objects by choosing the aspect ratio of the viewport to be the same as the clipping window. Otherwise, objects will be stretched or contracted in the x or y directions. Also, the aspect ratio of the display window can affect the proportions of objects. If the viewport is mapped to the entire area of the display window and the size of the display window is changed, objects may be distorted unless the aspect ratio of the viewport is also adjusted.

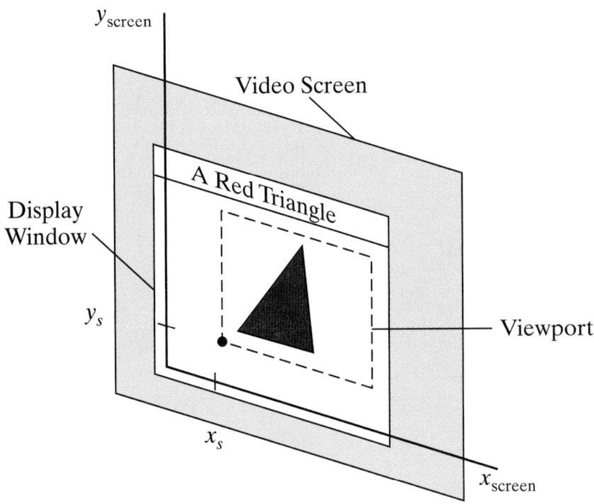

FIGURE 6-9 A viewport at coordinate position (x_s, y_s) within a display window.

Display of Character Strings

Character strings can be handled in one of two ways when they are mapped through the viewing pipeline to a viewport. The simplest mapping maintains a constant character size. This method could be employed with bitmap character patterns. But outline fonts could be transformed the same as other primitives; we just need to transform the defining positions for the line segments in the outline character shapes. Algorithms for determining the pixel patterns for the transformed characters are then applied when the other primitives in the scene are processed.

Split-Screen Effects and Multiple Output Devices

By selecting different clipping windows and associated viewports for a scene, we can provide simultaneous display of two or more objects, multiple picture parts, or different views of a single scene. And we can position these views in different parts of a single display window or in multiple display windows on the screen. In a design application, for example, we can display a wire-frame view of an object in one viewport, while also displaying a fully rendered view of the object in another viewport. And we could list other information or menus in a third viewport.

It is also possible that two or more output devices could be operating concurrently on a particular system, and we can set up a clipping-window/viewport pair for each output device. A mapping to a selected output device is sometimes referred to as a **workstation transformation.** In this case, viewports could be specified in the coordinates of a particular display device. Or each viewport could be specified within a unit square, which is then mapped to a chosen output device. Some graphics systems provide a pair of workstation functions for this purpose. One function is used to designate a clipping window for a selected output device, identified by a *workstation number*, and the other function is used to set the associated viewport for that device.

6-4 OpenGL TWO-DIMENSIONAL VIEWING FUNCTIONS

Actually, the basic OpenGL library has no functions specifically for two-dimensional viewing, since it is designed primarily for three-dimensional applications. But we can adapt the three-dimensional viewing routines to a two-dimensional scene, and the core library contains a viewport function. In addition, the OpenGL Utility (GLU) does provide a two-dimensional function for specifying the clipping window, and we have GLUT functions for handling display windows. Therefore, we can use these two-dimensional routines, along with the OpenGL viewport function, for all the viewing operations we need.

OpenGL Projection Mode

Before we select a clipping window and a viewport in OpenGL, we need to establish the appropriate mode for constructing the matrix to transform from world coordinates to screen coordinates. With OpenGL, we cannot set up a separate two-dimensional viewing-coordinate system as in Fig. 6-4, and we must set the parameters for the clipping window as part of the projection transformation. Therefore, we must first select the projection mode. We do this with the same function we used to set the modelview mode for the geometric transformations. Subsequent commands for defining a clipping window and viewport will then be applied to the projection matrix.

```
glMatrixMode (GL_PROJECTION);
```

This designates the projection matrix as the current matrix, which is originally set to the identity matrix. However, if we are going to loop back through this statement for other views of a scene, we can also set the initialization as

```
glLoadIdentity ( );
```

This ensures that each time we enter the projection mode the matrix will be reset to the identity, so that the new viewing parameters are not combined with the previous ones.

GLU Clipping-Window Function

To define a two-dimensional clipping window, we can use the OpenGL Utility function:

```
gluOrtho2D (xwmin, xwmax, ywmin, ywmax);
```

Coordinate positions for the clipping-window boundaries are given as double-precision numbers. This function specifies an orthogonal projection for mapping the scene to the screen. For a three-dimensional scene, this means that objects would be projected along parallel lines that are perpendicular to the two-dimensional xy display screen. But for a two-dimensional application, objects are already defined in the xy plane. Therefore, the orthogonal projection has no effect on our two-dimensional scene other than to convert object positions to normalized coordinates. Nevertheless, we must specify the orthogonal projection because our two-dimensional scene is processed through the full three-dimensional OpenGL viewing pipeline. In fact, we could specify the clipping window using the three-dimensional OpenGL core-library version of the `gluOrtho2D` function (Section 7-10).

Normalized coordinates in the range from -1 to 1 are used in the OpenGL clipping routines. And the `gluOrtho2D` function sets up a three-dimensional version of transformation matrix 6-9 for mapping objects within the clipping window to normalized coordinates. Objects outside the normalized square (and outside the clipping window) are eliminated from the scene to be displayed.

If we do not specify a clipping window in an application program, the default coordinates are $(xw_{\min}, yw_{\min}) = (-1.0, -1.0)$ and $(xw_{\max}, yw_{\max}) = (1.0, 1.0)$. Thus the default clipping window is the normalized square centered on the coordinate origin with a side length of 2.0.

OpenGL Viewport Function

We specify the viewport parameters with the OpenGL function

```
glViewport (xvmin, yvmin, vpWidth, vpHeight);
```

where all parameter values are given in integer screen coordinates relative to the display window. Parameters `xvmin` and `yvmin` specify the position of the lower-left corner of the viewport relative to the lower-left corner of the display window. And the pixel width and height of the viewport are set with parameters `vpWidth` and `vpHeight`. If we do not invoke the `glViewport` function in a program, the default viewport size and position are the same as the size and position of the display window.

After the clipping routines have been applied, positions within the normalized square are transformed into the viewport rectangle using matrix 6-10. Coordinates for the upper-right corner of the viewport are calculated for this transformation matrix in terms of the viewport width and height:

$$xv_{\max} = xv_{\min} + vpWidth, \qquad yv_{\max} = yv_{\min} + vpHeight \tag{6-11}$$

For the final transformation, pixel colors for the primitives within the viewport are loaded into the refresh buffer at the specified screen locations.

Multiple viewports can be created in OpenGL for a variety of applications (Section 6-3). We can obtain the parameters for the currently active viewport using the query function

```
glGetIntegerv (GL_VIEWPORT, vpArray);
```

where `vpArray` is a single-subscript, four-element array. This `Get` function returns the parameters for the current viewport to `vpArray` in the order `xvmin`, `yvmin`, `vpWidth`, and `vpHeight`. In an interactive application, for example, we can use this function to obtain parameters for the viewport that contains the screen cursor.

Creating a GLUT Display Window

In Section 2-9, we briefly introduced some of the functions in the GLUT library. Since the GLUT library interfaces with any window-management system, we use the GLUT routines for creating and manipulating display windows so that our example programs will be independent of any specific machine. To access these routines, we first need to initialize GLUT with the following function.

```
glutInit (&argc, argv);
```

Parameters for this initialization function are the same as those for the `main` procedure, and we can use `glutInit` to process command-line arguments.

We have three functions in GLUT for defining a display window and choosing its dimensions and position:

```
glutInitWindowPosition (xTopLeft, yTopLeft);
glutInitWindowSize (dwWidth, dwHeight);
glutCreateWindow ("Title of Display Window");
```

The first of these functions gives the integer, screen-coordinate position for the top-left corner of the display window, relative to the top-left corner of the screen. If either coordinate is negative, the display-window position on the screen is determined by the window-management system. With the second function, we choose a width and height for the display window in positive integer pixel dimensions. If we do not use these two functions to specify a size and position, the default size is 300 by 300 and the default position is $(-1, -1)$, which leaves the positioning of the display window to the window-management system. In any case, the display-window size and position specified with GLUT routines might be ignored, depending on the state or the other requirements currently in effect for the window-management system. Thus the window system might position and size the display window differently. The third function creates the display window, with the specified size and position, and assigns a title, although the use of the title also depends on the windowing system. At this point, the display window is defined but not shown on the screen until all the GLUT setup operations are complete.

Setting the GLUT Display-Window Mode and Color

Various display-window parameters are selected with the GLUT function

```
glutInitDisplayMode (mode);
```

We use this function to choose a color mode (RGB or index) and different buffer combinations, and the selected parameters are combined with the logical `or` operation. The default mode is single buffering and the RGB (or RGBA) color mode, which is the same as setting this mode with the statement

```
glutInitDisplayMode (GLUT_SINGLE | GLUT_RGB);
```

The color mode specification `GLUT_RGB` is equivalent to `GLUT_RGBA`. A background color for the display window is chosen in RGB mode with the OpenGL routine

```
glClearColor (red, green, blue, alpha);
```

In color-index mode, we set the display-window color with

```
glClearIndex (index);
```

where parameter `index` is assigned an integer value corresponding to a position within the color table.

GLUT Display-Window Identifier

Multiple display windows can be created for an application, and each is assigned a positive-integer **display-window identifier,** starting with the value 1 for the first window that is created. At the time that we initiate a display window, we can record its identifier with the statement

```
windowID = glutCreateWindow ("A Display Window");
```

Once we have saved the integer display-window identifier in variable name `windowID`, we can use the identifier number to change display parameters or to delete the display window.

Deleting a GLUT Display Window

The GLUT library also includes a function for deleting a display window that we have created. If we know the display window's identifier, we can eliminate it with the statement

```
glutDestroyWindow (windowID);
```

Current GLUT Display Window

When we specify any display-window operation, it is applied to the **current display window,** which is either the last display window that we created or the one we select with the following command.

```
glutSetWindow (windowID);
```

And, at any time, we can query the system to determine which window is the current display window:

```
currentWindowID = glutGetWindow ( );
```

A value of 0 is returned by this function if there are no display windows or if the current display window was destroyed.

Relocating and Resizing a GLUT Display Window

We can reset the screen location for the current display window with

```
glutPositionWindow (xNewTopLeft, yNewTopLeft);
```

where the coordinates specify the new position for the upper-left display-window corner, relative to the upper-left corner of the screen. Similarly, the following function resets the size of the current display window.

```
glutReshapeWindow (dwNewWidth, dwNewHeight);
```

And with the following command, we can expand the current display window to fill the screen.

```
glutFullScreen ( );
```

The exact size of the display window after execution of this routine depends on the window-management system. And a subsequent call to either `glutPositionWindow` or `glutReshapeWindow` will cancel the request for an expansion to full-screen size.

Whenever the size of a display window is changed, its aspect ratio may change and objects may be distorted from their original shapes. As we noted in Section 3-24, we can adjust for a change in display-window dimensions using the statement

```
glutReshapeFunc (winReshapeFcn);
```

This GLUT routine is activated when the size of a display window is changed, and the new width and height are passed to its argument: the function `winReshapeFcn`, in this example. Thus `winReshapeFcn` is the "callback function" for the "reshape event". We can then use this callback function to change the parameters for the viewport so that the original aspect ratio of the scene is maintained. In addition, we could also reset the clipping-window boundaries, change the display-window color, adjust other viewing parameters, and perform any other tasks.

Managing Multiple GLUT Display Windows

The GLUT library also has a number of routines for manipulating a display window in various ways. These routines are particularly useful when we have multiple display windows on the screen and we want to rearrange them or locate a particular display window.

We use the following routine to convert the current display window to an icon in the form of a small picture or symbol representing the window.

```
glutIconifyWindow ( );
```

This icon will be labeled with the same name that we assigned to the window, but we can change the name for the icon with

```
glutSetIconTitle ("Icon Name");
```

And we can change the name of the display window with a similar command:

```
glutSetWindowTitle ("New Window Name");
```

With multiple display windows open on the screen, some windows may overlap or totally obscure other display windows. We can choose any display window to be in front of all other windows by first designating it as the current window, then issuing the "pop-window" command:

```
glutSetWindow (windowID);
glutPopWindow ( );
```

In a similar way, we can "push" the current display window to the back, so that it is behind all other display windows. This sequence of operations is

```
glutSetWindow (windowID);
glutPushWindow ( );
```

We can also take the current window off the screen with

```
glutHideWindow ( );
```

And we can return a "hidden" display window, or one that has been converted to an icon, by designating it as the current display window and then invoking the function

```
glutShowWindow ( );
```

GLUT Subwindows

Within a selected display window, we can set up any number of second-level display windows, called *subwindows*. This provides a means for partitioning display windows into different display sections. We create a subwindow with the following function.

```
glutCreateSubWindow (windowID, xBottomLeft, yBottomLeft,
                     width, height);
```

Parameter `windowID` identifies the display window in which we want to set up the subwindow. With the remaining parameters, we specify its size and the placement of the lower-left corner of the subwindow relative to the lower-left corner of the display window.

Subwindows are assigned a positive integer identifier in the same way that first-level display windows are numbered. And we can place a subwindow inside another subwindow. Also, each subwindow can be assigned an individual display mode and other parameters. We can even reshape, reposition, push, pop, hide, and show subwindows, just as we can with first-level display windows. But we cannot convert a GLUT subwindow to an icon.

Selecting a Display-Window Screen-Cursor Shape

We can use the following GLUT routine to request a shape for the screen cursor that is to be used with the current window.

```
glutSetCursor (shape);
```

The possible cursor shapes that we can select are an arrow pointing in a chosen direction, a bidirectional arrow, a rotating arrow, a crosshair, a wristwatch, a question mark, or even a skull and crossbones. For example, we can assign the symbolic constant `GLUT_CURSOR_UP_DOWN` to parameter `shape` to obtain an up-down, bidirectional arrow. A rotating arrow is chosen with `GLUT_CURSOR_CYCLE`, a wristwatch shape is selected with `GLUT_CURSOR_WAIT`, and a skull and crossbones is obtained with the constant `GLUT_CURSOR_DESTROY`. A cursor shape can be assigned to a display window to indicate a particular kind of application, such as an animation. However, the exact shapes that we can use are system dependent.

Viewing Graphics Objects in a GLUT Display Window

After we have created a display window and selected its position, size, color, and other characteristics, we indicate what is to be shown in that window. If more than one display window has been created, we first designate the one we want as the current display window. Then we invoke the following function to assign something to that window.

```
glutDisplayFunc (pictureDescrip);
```

The argument is a routine that describes what is to be displayed in the current window. This routine, called `pictureDescrip` for this example, is referred to as a *callback function* because it is the routine that is to be executed whenever GLUT determines that the display-window contents should be renewed. Routine `pictureDescrip` usually contains the OpenGL primitives and attributes that define a picture, although it could specify other constructs such as a menu display.

If we have set up multiple display windows, then we repeat this process for each of the display windows or subwindows. Also, we may need to call `glutDisplayFunc` after the `glutPopWindow` command if the display window has been damaged during the process of redisplaying the windows. In this case, the following function is used to indicate that the contents of the current display window should be renewed.

```
glutPostRedisplay ( );
```

This routine is also used when an additional object such as a pop-up menu is to be shown in a display window.

Executing the Application Program

When the program setup is complete and the display windows have been created and initialized, we need to issue the final GLUT command that signals execution of the program:

```
glutMainLoop ( );
```

At this time, display windows and their graphic contents are sent to the screen. The program also enters the **GLUT processing loop** that continually checks for new "events", such as interactive input from a mouse or a graphics tablet.

Other GLUT Functions

The GLUT library provides a wide variety of routines to handle processes that are system dependent and to add features to the basic OpenGL library. For example, this library contains functions for generating bitmap and outline characters (Section 3-21), and it provides functions for loading values into a color table (Section 4-3). In addition, some GLUT functions, discussed in Chapter 8, are available for displaying three-dimensional objects, either as solids or in a wire-frame representation. These objects include a sphere, a torus, and the five regular polyhedra (cube, tetrahedron, octahedron, dodecahedron, and icosahedron).

Sometimes it is convenient to designate a function that is to be executed when there are no other events for the system to process. We can do that with

```
glutIdleFunc (function);
```

The parameter for this GLUT routine could reference a background function or a procedure to update parameters for an animation when no other processes are taking place.

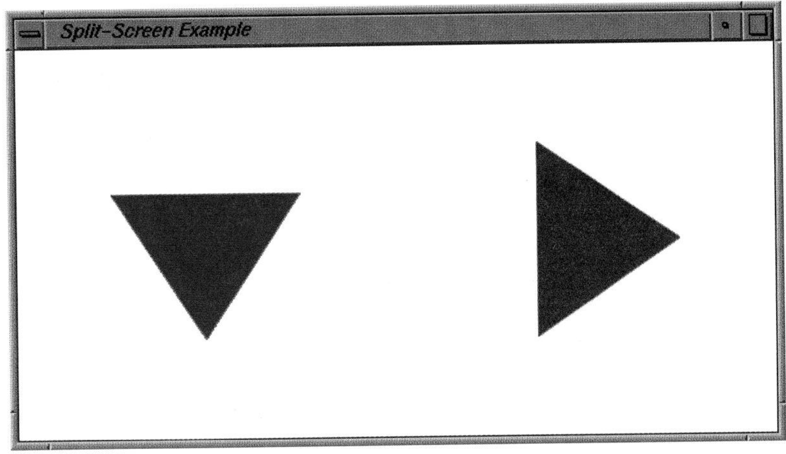

FIGURE 6-10 Split-screen effect generated within a display window by procedure `displayFcn`.

We also have Glut functions, discussed in Chapter 11, for obtaining and processing interactive input and for creating and managing menus. Individual routines are provided by GLUT for input devices such as a mouse, keyboard, graphics tablet, and spaceball.

Finally, we can use the following function to query the system about some of the current state parameters.

```
glutGet (stateParam);
```

This function returns an integer value corresponding to the symbolic constant we select for its argument. As an example, we can obtain the *x*-coordinate position for the top-left corner of the current display window, relative to the top-left corner of the screen, with the constant `GLUT_WINDOW_X`. And we can retrieve the current display-window width or the screen width with `GLUT_WINDOW_WIDTH` or `GLUT_SCREEN_WIDTH`.

OpenGL Two-Dimensional Viewing Program Example

As a demonstration of the use of the OpenGL viewport function, we use a split-screen effect to show two views of a triangle in the *xy* plane with its centroid at the world-coordinate origin. First a viewport is defined in the left half of the display window, and the original triangle is displayed there in a blue color. Using the same clipping window, we then define another viewport for the right half of the display window, and the fill color is changed to red. The triangle is then rotated about its centroid and displayed in the second viewport. Figure 6-10 shows the two triangles displayed by this example program.

```
#include <GL/glut.h>

class wcPt2D {
   public:
      GLfloat x, y;
};
```

```
void init (void)
{
   /*  Set color of display window to white.  */
   glClearColor (1.0, 1.0, 1.0, 0.0);

   /*  Set parameters for world-coordinate clipping window.  */
   glMatrixMode (GL_PROJECTION);
   gluOrtho2D (-100.0, 100.0, -100.0, 100.0);

   /*  Set mode for constructing geometric transformation matrix.  */
   glMatrixMode (GL_MODELVIEW);
}

void triangle (wcPt2D *verts)
{
   GLint k;

   glBegin (GL_TRIANGLES);
      for (k = 0; k < 3; k++)
         glVertex2f (verts [k].x, verts [k].y);
   glEnd ( );
}

void displayFcn (void)
{
   /*  Define initial position for triangle.  */
   wcPt2D verts [3] = { {-50.0, -25.0}, {50.0, -25.0}, {0.0, 50.0} };

   glClear (GL_COLOR_BUFFER_BIT);   //  Clear display window.

   glColor3f (0.0, 0.0, 1.0);       //  Set fill color to blue.
   glViewport (0, 0, 300, 300);     //  Set left viewport.
   triangle (verts);                //  Display triangle.

   /*  Rotate triangle and display in right half of display window.  */
   glColor3f (1.0, 0.0, 0.0);         //  Set fill color to red.
   glViewport (300, 0, 300, 300);     //  Set right viewport.
   glRotatef (90.0, 0.0, 0.0, 1.0);   //  Rotate about z axis.
   triangle (verts);           //  Display red rotated triangle.

   glFlush ( );
}
void main (int argc, char ** argv)
{
   glutInit (&argc, argv);
   glutInitDisplayMode (GLUT_SINGLE | GLUT_RGB);
   glutInitWindowPosition (50, 50);
   glutInitWindowSize (600, 300);
   glutCreateWindow ("Split-Screen Example");

   init ( );
   glutDisplayFunc (displayFcn);

   glutMainLoop ( );
}
```

6-5 CLIPPING ALGORITHMS

Generally, any procedure that eliminates those portions of a picture that are either inside or outside of a specified region of space is referred to as a **clipping algorithm** or simply **clipping.** Usually a clipping region is a rectangle in standard position, although we could use any shape for a clipping application.

The most common application of clipping is in the viewing pipeline, where clipping is applied to extract a designated portion of a scene (either two-dimensional or three-dimensional) for display on an output device. Clipping methods are also used to antialias object boundaries, to construct objects using solid-modeling methods, to manage a multiwindow environment, and to allow parts of a picture to be moved, copied, or erased in drawing and painting programs.

Clipping algorithms are applied in two-dimensional viewing procedures to identify those parts of a picture that are within the clipping window. Everything outside the clipping window is then eliminated from the scene description that is transferred to the output device for display. An efficient implementation of clipping in the viewing pipeline is to apply the algorithms to the normalized boundaries of the clipping window. This reduces calculations, because all geometric and viewing transformation matrices can be concatenated and applied to a scene description before clipping is carried out. The clipped scene can then be transferred to screen coordinates for final processing.

In the following sections, we explore two-dimensional algorithms for

- Point Clipping
- Line Clipping (straight-line segments)
- Fill-Area Clipping (polygons)
- Curve Clipping
- Text Clipping

Point, line, and polygon clipping are standard components of graphics packages. But similar methods can be applied to other objects, particularly conics, such as circles, ellipses, and spheres, in addition to spline curves and surfaces. Usually, however, objects with nonlinear boundaries are approximated with straight-line segments or polygon surfaces to reduce computations.

Unless otherwise stated, we assume that the clipping region is a rectangular window in standard position, with boundary edges at coordinate positions $xw_{\min}$, $xw_{\max}$, $yw_{\min}$, and $yw_{\max}$. These boundary edges typically correspond to a normalized square, in which the x and y values range either from 0 to 1 or from −1 to 1.

6-6 TWO-DIMENSIONAL POINT CLIPPING

For a clipping rectangle in standard position, we save a two-dimensional point $\mathbf{P} = (x, y)$ for display if the following inequalities are satisfied:

$$\begin{aligned} xw_{\min} &\leq x \leq xw_{\max} \\ yw_{\min} &\leq y \leq yw_{\max} \end{aligned} \tag{6-12}$$

If any one of these four inequalities is not satisfied, the point is clipped (not saved for display).

Although point clipping is applied less often than line or polygon clipping, it is useful in various situations, particularly when pictures are modeled with particle systems. For example, point clipping can be applied to scenes involving clouds, sea foam, smoke, or explosions that are modeled with "particles", such as the center coordinates for small circles or spheres.

6-7 TWO-DIMENSIONAL LINE CLIPPING

Figure 6-11 illustrates possible positions for straight-line segments in relationship to a standard clipping window. A line-clipping algorithm processes each line in a scene through a series of tests and intersection calculations to determine whether the entire line or any part of it is to be saved. The expensive part of a line-clipping procedure is in calculating the intersection positions of a line with the window edges. Therefore, a major goal for any line-clipping algorithm is to minimize the intersection calculations. To do this, we can first perform tests to determine whether a line segment is completely inside the clipping window or completely outside. It is easy to determine whether or not a line is completely inside a clipping window, but it is more difficult to identify all lines that are entirely outside the window. If we are unable to identify a line as completely inside or completely outside a clipping rectangle, we must then perform intersection calculations to determine whether any part of the line crosses the window interior.

We test a line segment to determine if it is completely inside or outside a selected clipping-window edge by applying the point-clipping tests of the previous section. When both endpoints of a line segment are inside all four clipping boundaries, such as the line from $\mathbf{P}_1$ to $\mathbf{P}_2$ in Fig 6-11, the line is completely inside the clipping window and we save it. And when both endpoints of a line segment are outside any one of the four boundaries (line $\overline{\mathbf{P}_3\mathbf{P}_4}$ in Fig. 6-11), that line is completely outside the window and it is eliminated from the scene description. But if both these tests fail, the line segment intersects at least one clipping boundary and it may or may not cross into the interior of the clipping window.

One way to formulate the equation for a straight-line segment is to use the following parametric representation, where the coordinate positions (x_0, y_0) and

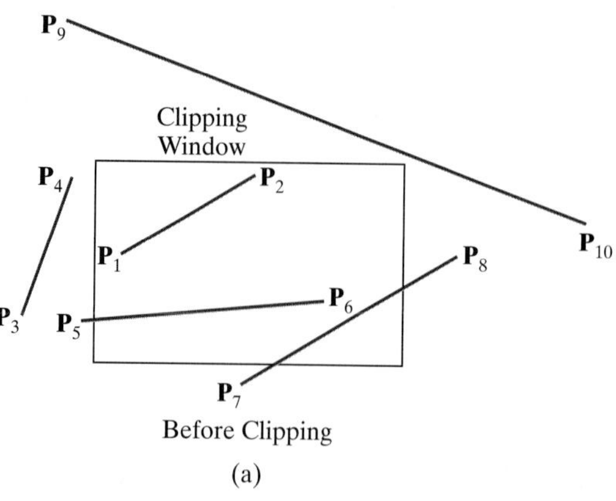

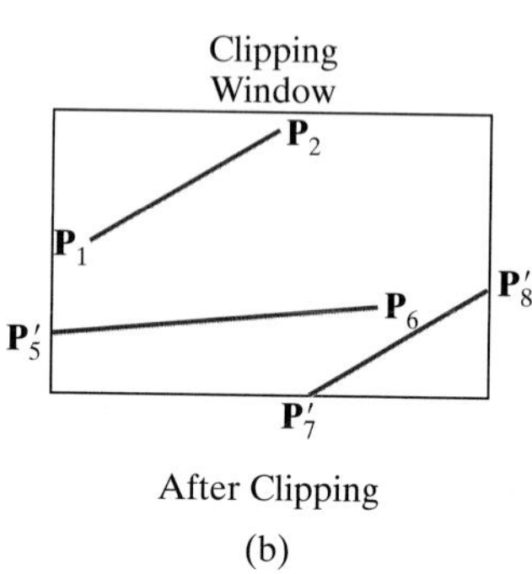

FIGURE 6-11 Clipping straight-line segments using a standard rectangular clipping window.

(x_{end}, y_{end}) designate the two line endpoints.

$$x = x_0 + u(x_{end} - x_0)$$
$$y = y_0 + u(y_{end} - y_0) \qquad 0 \le u \le 1 \tag{6-13}$$

We can use this parametric representation to determine where a line segment crosses each clipping-window edge by assigning the coordinate value for that edge to either x or y and solving for parameter u. As an example, the left window boundary is at position xw_{min}, so we substitute this value for x, solve for u, and calculate the corresponding y-intersection value. If this value of u is outside the range from 0 to 1, the line segment does not intersect that window border line. But if the value of u is within the range from 0 to 1, part of the line is inside that border. We can then process this inside portion of the line segment against the other clipping boundaries until either we have clipped the entire line or we find a section that is inside the window.

Processing line segments in a scene using the simple clipping approach described in the preceding paragraph is straightforward, but not very efficient. It is possible to reformulate the initial testing and the intersection calculations to reduce processing time for a set of line segments, and a number of faster line clippers have been developed. Some of the algorithms are designed explicitly for two-dimensional pictures and some are easily adapted to sets of three-dimensional line segments.

Cohen-Sutherland Line Clipping

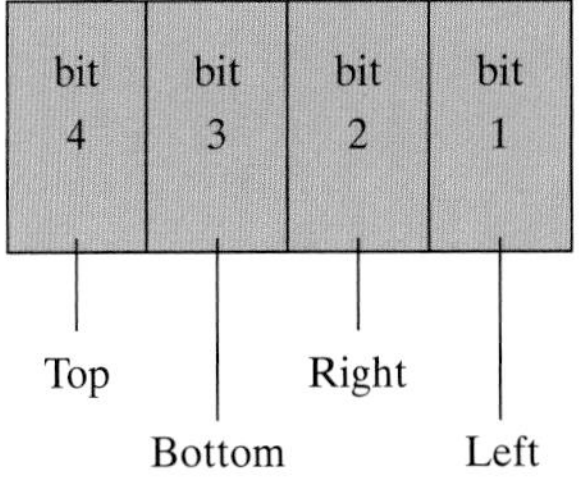

FIGURE 6-12 A possible ordering for the clipping-window boundaries corresponding to the bit positions in the Cohen-Sutherland endpoint region code.

This is one of the earliest algorithms to be developed for fast line clipping, and variations of this method are widely used. Processing time is reduced in the Cohen-Sutherland method by performing more tests before proceeding to the intersection calculations. Initially, every line endpoint in a picture is assigned a four-digit binary value, called a **region code,** and each bit position is used to indicate whether the point is inside or outside one of the clipping-window boundaries. We can reference the window edges in any order, and Fig. 6-12 illustrates one possible ordering with the bit positions numbered 1 through 4 from right to left. Thus, for this ordering, the rightmost position (bit 1) references the left clipping-window boundary, and the leftmost position (bit 4) references the top window boundary. A value of 1 (or *true*) in any bit position indicates that the endpoint is outside of that window border. Similarly, a value of 0 (or *false*) in any bit position indicates that the endpoint is not outside (it is inside or on) the corresponding window edge. Sometimes, a region code is referred to as an "**out**" **code** because a value of 1 in any bit position indicates that the spatial point is outside the corresponding clipping boundary.

Each clipping-window edge divides two-dimensional space into an inside half space and an outside half space. Together, the four window borders create nine regions, and Fig. 6-13 lists the value for the binary code in each of these regions. Thus, an endpoint that is below and to the left of the clipping window is assigned the region code 0101, and the region-code value for any endpoint inside the clipping window is 0000.

Bit values in a region code are determined by comparing the coordinate values (x, y) of an endpoint to the clipping boundaries. Bit 1 is set to 1 if $x < xw_{min}$, and the other three bit values are determined similarly. Instead of using inequality

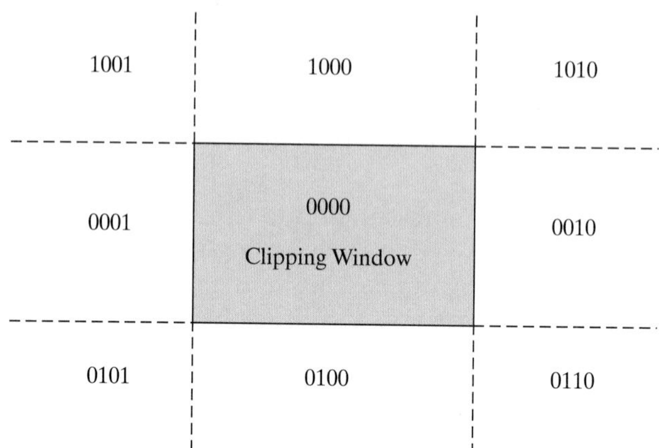

FIGURE 6-13 The nine binary region codes for identifying the position of a line endpoint, relative to the clipping-window boundaries.

testing, we can more efficiently determine the values for a region-code using bit-processing operations and the following two steps: (1) Calculate differences between endpoint coordinates and clipping boundaries. (2) Use the resultant sign bit of each difference calculation to set the corresponding value in the region code. For the ordering scheme shown in Fig. 6-12, bit 1 is the sign bit of $x - xw_{\text{min}}$; bit 2 is the sign bit of $xw_{\text{max}} - x$; bit 3 is the sign bit of $y - yw_{\text{min}}$; and bit 4 is the sign bit of $yw_{\text{max}} - y$.

Once we have established region codes for all line endpoints, we can quickly determine which lines are completely inside the clip window and which are clearly outside. Any lines that are completely contained within the window edges have a region code of 0000 for both endpoints, and we save these line segments. Any line that has a region-code value of 1 in the same bit position for each endpoint is completely outside the clipping rectangle, and we eliminate that line segment. As an example, a line that has a region code of 1001 for one endpoint and a code of 0101 for the other endpoint is completely to the left of the clipping window, as indicated by the value of 1 in the first bit position of each region code.

We can perform the inside-outside tests for line segments using logical operators. When the *or* operation between two endpoint region codes for a line segment is *false* (0000), the line is inside the clipping window. Therefore, we save the line and proceed to test the next line in the scene description. When the *and* operation between the two endpoint region codes for a line is *true* (not 0000), the line is completely outside the clipping window, and we can eliminate it from the scene description.

Lines that cannot be identified as being completely inside or completely outside a clipping window by the region-code tests are next checked for intersection with the window border lines. As shown in Fig. 6-14, line segments can intersect clipping boundary lines without entering the interior of the window. Therefore, several intersection calculations might be necessary to clip a line segment, depending on the order in which we process the clipping boundaries. As we process each clipping-window edge, a section of the line is clipped, and the remaining part of the line is checked against the other window borders. We continue eliminating sections until either the line is totally clipped or the remaining part of the line is inside the clipping window. For the following discussion, we assume that the window edges are processed in the order: left, right, bottom, top. To determine whether a line crosses a selected clipping boundary, we can check corresponding bit values in the two endpoint region codes. If one of these bit values is 1 and the other is 0, the line segment crosses that boundary.

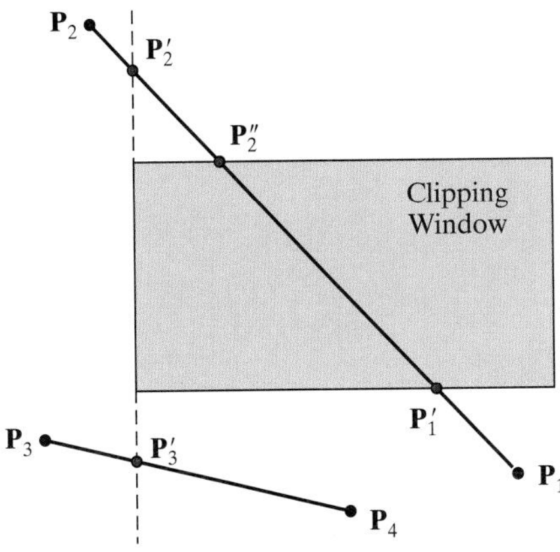

FIGURE 6-14 Lines extending from one clipping-window region to another may cross into the clipping window, or they could intersect one or more clipping boundaries without entering the window interior.

Figure 6-14 illustrates two line segments that cannot be immediately identified as completely inside or completely outside the clipping window. The region codes for the line from $\mathbf{P}_1$ to $\mathbf{P}_2$ are 0100 and 1001. Thus, $\mathbf{P}_1$ is inside the left clipping boundary and $\mathbf{P}_2$ is outside that boundary. We then calculate the intersection position $\mathbf{P}_2'$, and we clip off the line section from $\mathbf{P}_2$ to $\mathbf{P}_2'$. The remaining portion of the line is inside the right border line, and so we next check the bottom border. Endpoint $\mathbf{P}_1$ is below the bottom clipping edge and $\mathbf{P}_2'$ is above it, so we determine the intersection position at this boundary ($\mathbf{P}_1'$). We eliminate the line section from $\mathbf{P}_1$ to $\mathbf{P}_1'$ and proceed to the top window edge. There we determine the intersection position to be $\mathbf{P}_2''$. The final step is to clip off the section above the top boundary and save the interior segment from $\mathbf{P}_1'$ to $\mathbf{P}_2''$. For the second line, we find that point $\mathbf{P}_3$ is outside the left boundary and $\mathbf{P}_4$ is inside. Thus, we calculate the intersection position $\mathbf{P}_3'$ and eliminate the line section from $\mathbf{P}_3$ to $\mathbf{P}_3'$. By checking region codes for the endpoints $\mathbf{P}_3'$ and $\mathbf{P}_4$, we find that the remainder of the line is below the clipping window and can be eliminated also.

It is possible, when clipping a line segment using this approach, to calculate an intersection position at all four clipping boundaries, depending on how the line endpoints are processed and what ordering we use for the boundaries. Figure 6-15 shows the four intersection positions that could be calculated for a line segment that is processed against the clipping-window edges in the order left, right, bottom, top. Therefore, variations of this basic approach have been developed in an effort to reduce the intersection calculations.

To determine a boundary intersection for a line segment, we can use the slope-intercept form of the line equation. For a line with endpoint coordinates (x_0, y_0) and $(x_{\text{end}}, y_{\text{end}})$, the y coordinate of the intersection point with a vertical clipping border line can be obtained with the calculation

$$y = y_0 + m(x - x_0) \tag{6-14}$$

where the x value is set to either xw_{min} or xw_{max}, and the slope of the line is calculated as $m = (y_{\text{end}} - y_0)/(x_{\text{end}} - x_0)$. Similarly, if we are looking for the intersection with a horizontal border, the x coordinate can be calculated as

$$x = x_0 + \frac{y - y_0}{m} \tag{6-15}$$

with y set either to yw_{min} or to yw_{max}.

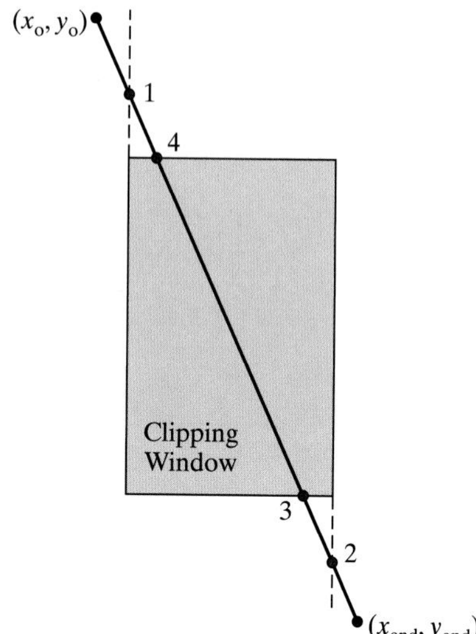

FIGURE 6-15 Four intersection positions (labeled from 1 to 4) for a line segment that is clipped against the window boundaries in the order left, right, bottom, top.

An implementation of the two-dimensional, Cohen-Sutherland line-clipping algorithm is given in the following procedures. The extension of this algorithm to three dimensions is straightforward, and we explore three-dimensional viewing methods in the next chapter.

```
class wcPt2D {
   public:
      GLfloat x, y;
};

inline GLint round (const GLfloat a)  { return GLint (a + 0.5); }

/*  Define a four-bit code for each of the outside regions of a
 *  rectangular clipping window.
 */
const GLint winLeftBitCode = 0x1;
const GLint winRightBitCode = 0x2;
const GLint winBottomBitCode = 0x4;
const GLint winTopBitCode = 0x8;

/*  A bit-mask region code is also assigned to each endpoint of an input
 *  line segment, according to its position relative to the four edges of
 *  an input rectangular clip window.
 *
 *  An endpoint with a region-code value of 0000 is inside the clipping
 *  window, otherwise it is outside at least one clipping boundary.  If
 *  the 'or' operation for the two endpoint codes produces a value of
 *  false, the entire line defined by these two endpoints is saved
 *  (accepted).  If the 'and' operation between two endpoint codes is
 *  true, the line is completely outside the clipping window, and it is
 *  eliminated (rejected) from further processing.
 */
```

```
inline GLint inside (GLint code) { return GLint (!code); }
inline GLint reject (GLint code1, GLint code2)
                        { return GLint (code1 & code2); }
inline GLint accept (GLint code1, GLint code2)
                        { return GLint (!(code1 | code2)); }

GLubyte encode (wcPt2D pt, wcPt2D winMin, wcPt2D winMax)
{
  GLubyte code = 0x00;

  if (pt.x < winMin.x)
    code = code | winLeftBitCode;
  if (pt.x > winMax.x)
    code = code | winRightBitCode;
  if (pt.y < winMin.y)
    code = code | winBottomBitCode;
  if (pt.y > winMax.y)
    code = code | winTopBitCode;
  return (code);
}

void swapPts (wcPt2D * p1, wcPt2D * p2)
{
  wcPt2D tmp;

  tmp = *p1; *p1 = *p2; *p2 = tmp;
}

void swapCodes (GLubyte * c1, GLubyte * c2)
{
  GLubyte tmp;

  tmp = *c1; *c1 = *c2; *c2 = tmp;
}

void lineClipCohSuth (wcPt2D winMin, wcPt2D winMax, wcPt2D p1, wcPt2D p2)
{
  GLubyte code1, code2;
  GLint done = false, plotLine = false;
  GLfloat m;

  while (!done) {
    code1 = encode (p1, winMin, winMax);
    code2 = encode (p2, winMin, winMax);
    if (accept (code1, code2)) {
      done = true;
      plotLine = true;
    }
    else
      if (reject (code1, code2))
        done = true;
```

```
        else {
          /* Label the endpoint outside the display window as p1. */
          if (inside (code1)) {
            swapPts (&p1, &p2);
            swapCodes (&code1, &code2);
          }
          /* Use slope m to find line-clipEdge intersection. */
          if (p2.x != p1.x)
            m = (p2.y - p1.y) / (p2.x - p1.x);
          if (code1 & winLeftBitCode) {
            p1.y += (winMin.x - p1.x) * m;
            p1.x = winMin.x;
          }
          else
            if (code1 & winRightBitCode) {
              p1.y += (winMax.x - p1.x) * m;
              p1.x = winMax.x;
            }
            else
              if (code1 & winBottomBitCode) {
                /* Need to update p1.x for nonvertical lines only. */
                if (p2.x != p1.x)
                  p1.x += (winMin.y - p1.y) / m;
                p1.y = winMin.y;
              }
              else
                if (code1 & winTopBitCode) {
                  if (p2.x != p1.x)
                    p1.x += (winMax.y - p1.y) / m;
                  p1.y = winMax.y;
                }
        }
    }
    if (plotLine)
      lineBres (round (p1.x), round (p1.y), round (p2.x), round (p2.y));
}
```

Liang-Barsky Line Clipping

Faster line-clipping algorithms have been developed that do more line testing before proceeding to the intersection calculations. One of the earliest efforts in this direction is an algorithm developed by Cyrus and Beck, which is based on analysis of the parametric line equations. Later, Liang and Barsky independently devised an even faster form of the parametric line-clipping algorithm.

For a line segment with endpoints (x_0, y_0) and $(x_{\text{end}}, y_{\text{end}})$, we can describe the line with the parametric form

$$\begin{aligned} x &= x_0 + u\Delta x \\ y &= y_0 + u\Delta y \qquad 0 \le u \le 1 \end{aligned} \tag{6-16}$$

where $\Delta x = x_{\text{end}} - x_0$ and $\Delta y = y_{\text{end}} - y_0$. In the Liang-Barsky algorithm, the parametric line equations are combined with the point-clipping conditions 6-12 to obtain the inequalities

$$\begin{aligned} xw_{\min} &\leq x_0 + u\Delta x \leq xw_{\max} \\ yw_{\min} &\leq y_0 + u\Delta y \leq yw_{\max} \end{aligned} \qquad (6\text{-}17)$$

which can be expressed as

$$u\, p_k \leq q_k, \qquad k = 1, 2, 3, 4 \qquad (6\text{-}18)$$

where parameters p and q are defined as

$$\begin{aligned} p_1 &= -\Delta x, & q_1 &= x_0 - xw_{\min} \\ p_2 &= \Delta x, & q_2 &= xw_{\max} - x_0 \\ p_3 &= -\Delta y, & q_3 &= y_0 - yw_{\min} \\ p_4 &= \Delta y, & q_4 &= yw_{\max} - y_0 \end{aligned} \qquad (6\text{-}19)$$

Any line that is parallel to one of the clipping-window edges has $p_k = 0$ for the value of k corresponding to that boundary, where k = 1, 2, 3, and 4 correspond to the left, right, bottom, and top boundaries, respectively. If, for that value of k, we also find $q_k < 0$, then the line is completely outside the boundary and can be eliminated from further consideration. If $q_k \geq 0$, the line is inside the parallel clipping border.

When $p_k < 0$, the infinite extension of the line proceeds from the outside to the inside of the infinite extension of this particular clipping-window edge. If $p_k > 0$, the line proceeds from the inside to the outside. For a nonzero value of p_k, we can calculate the value of u that corresponds to the point where the infinitely extended line intersects the extension of window edge k as

$$u = \frac{q_k}{p_k} \qquad (6\text{-}20)$$

For each line, we can calculate values for parameters u_1 and u_2 that define that part of the line that lies within the clip rectangle. The value of u_1 is determined by looking at the rectangle edges for which the line proceeds from the outside to the inside ($p < 0$). For these edges, we calculate $r_k = q_k / p_k$. The value of u_1 is taken as the largest of the set consisting of 0 and the various values of r. Conversely, the value of u_2 is determined by examining the boundaries for which the line proceeds from inside to outside ($p > 0$). A value of r_k is calculated for each of these boundaries, and the value of u_2 is the minimum of the set consisting of 1 and the calculated r values. If $u_1 > u_2$, the line is completely outside the clip window and it can be rejected. Otherwise, the endpoints of the clipped line are calculated from the two values of parameter u.

This algorithm is implemented in the following code sections. Line intersection parameters are initialized to the values $u_1 = 0$ and $u_2 = 1$. For each clipping boundary, the appropriate values for p and q are calculated and used by the function `clipTest` to determine whether the line can be rejected or whether the intersection parameters are to be adjusted. When $p < 0$, parameter r is used to update u_1; when $p > 0$, parameter r is used to update u_2. If updating u_1 or u_2 results in $u_1 > u_2$, we reject the line. Otherwise, we update the appropriate u parameter only if the new value results in a shortening of the line. When $p = 0$ and $q < 0$, we can eliminate the line since it is parallel to and outside of this boundary. If the line has not been rejected after all four values of p and q have been tested, the endpoints of the clipped line are determined from values of u_1 and u_2.

```
   class wcPt2D
   {
      private:
         GLfloat x, y;

      public:
      /*  Default Constructor: initialize position as (0.0, 0.0).  */
      wcPt3D ( ) {
         x = y = 0.0;
      }

      setCoords (GLfloat xCoord, GLfloat yCoord) {
         x = xCoord;
         y = yCoord;
      }

      GLfloat getx ( ) const {
         return x;
      }

      GLfloat gety ( ) const {
         return y;
      }
   };

inline GLint round (const GLfloat a)  { return GLint (a + 0.5); }

GLint clipTest (GLfloat p, GLfloat q, GLfloat * u1, GLfloat * u2)
{
  GLfloat r;
  GLint returnValue = true;

  if (p < 0.0) {
    r = q / p;
    if (r > *u2)
      returnValue = false;
    else
      if (r > *u1)
        *u1 = r;
  }
  else
    if (p > 0.0) {
      r = q / p;
      if (r < *u1)
        returnValue = false;
      else if (r < *u2)
        *u2 = r;
    }
    else
      /*  Thus p = 0 and line is parallel to clipping boundary.  */
      if (q < 0.0)
        /*  Line is outside clipping boundary.  */
        returnValue = false;
```

```
   return (returnValue);
}

void lineClipLiangBarsk (wcPt2D winMin, wcPt2D winMax, wcPt2D p1, wcPt2D p2)
{
   GLfloat u1 = 0.0, u2 = 1.0, dx = p2.getx ( ) - p1.getx ( ), dy;

   if (clipTest (-dx, p1.getx ( ) - winMin.getx ( ), &u1, &u2))
     if (clipTest (dx, winMax.getx ( ) - p1.getx ( ), &u1, &u2)) {
       dy = p2.gety ( ) - p1.gety ( );
       if (clipTest (-dy, p1.gety ( ) - winMin.gety ( ), &u1, &u2))
         if (clipTest (dy, winMax.gety ( ) - p1.gety ( ), &u1, &u2)) {
           if (u2 < 1.0) {
             p2.setCoords (p1.getx ( ) + u2 * dx, p1.gety ( ) + u2 * dy);
           }
           if (u1 > 0.0) {
             p1.setCoords (p1.getx ( ) + u1 * dx, p1.gety ( ) + u1 * dy);
           }
           lineBres (round (p1.getx ( )), round (p1.gety ( )),
                          round (p2.getx ( )), round (p2.gety ( )));
         }
     }
}
```

In general, the Liang-Barsky algorithm is more efficient than the Cohen-Sutherland line-clipping algorithm. Each update of parameters u_1 and u_2 requires only one division; and window intersections of the line are computed only once, when the final values of u_1 and u_2 have been computed. In contrast, the Cohen and Sutherland algorithm can repeatedly calculate intersections along a line path, even though the line may be completely outside the clip window. And, each Cohen-Sutherland intersection calculation requires both a division and a multiplication. The two-dimensional Liang-Barsky algorithm can be extended to clip three-dimensional lines (Chapter 7).

Nicholl-Lee-Nicholl Line Clipping

By creating more regions around the clipping window, the Nicholl-Lee-Nicholl (NLN) algorithm avoids multiple line-intersection calculations. In the Cohen-Sutherland method, for example, multiple intersections could be calculated along the path of a line segment before an intersection on the clipping rectangle is located or the line is completely rejected. These extra intersection calculations are eliminated in the NLN algorithm by carrying out more region testing before intersection positions are calculated. Compared to both the Cohen-Sutherland and the Liang-Barsky algorithms, the Nicholl-Lee-Nicholl algorithm performs fewer comparisons and divisions. The trade-off is that the NLN algorithm can be applied only to two-dimensional clipping, whereas both the Liang-Barsky and the Cohen-Sutherland methods are easily extended to three-dimensional scenes.

Initial testing to determine whether a line segment is completely inside the clipping window or outside the window limits can be accomplished with region-code tests, as in the previous two algorithms. If a trivial acceptance or rejection of the line is not possible, the NLN algorithm proceeds to set up additional clipping regions.

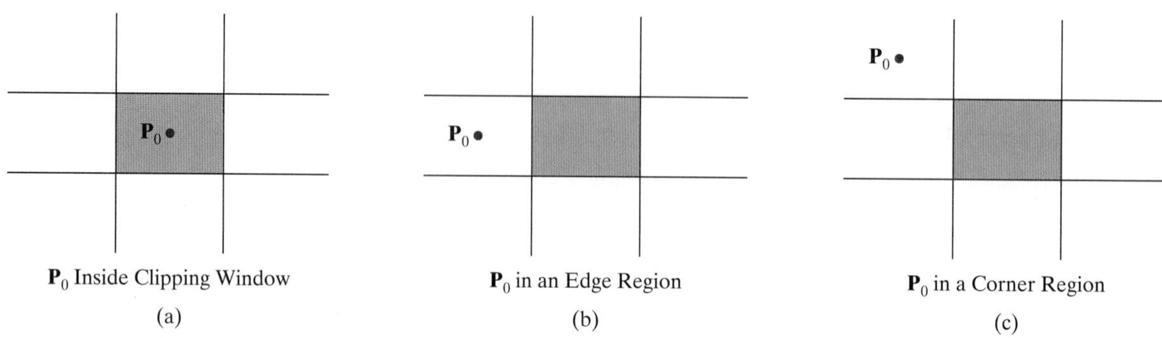

FIGURE 6-16 Three possible positions for a line endpoint $\mathbf{P}_0$ in the NLN line-clipping algorithm.

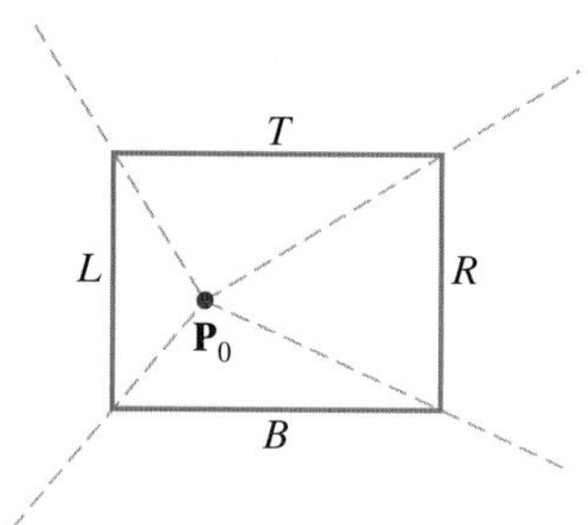

FIGURE 6-17 The four regions used in the NLN algorithm when $\mathbf{P}_0$ is inside the clipping window and $\mathbf{P}_{\text{end}}$ is outside.

For a line with endpoints $\mathbf{P}_0$ and $\mathbf{P}_{\text{end}}$, we first determine the position of point $\mathbf{P}_0$ for the nine possible regions relative to the clipping window. Only the three regions shown in Fig. 6-16 need be considered. If $\mathbf{P}_0$ lies in any one of the other six regions, we can move it to one of the three regions in Fig. 6-16 using a symmetry transformation. For example, the region directly above the clip window can be transformed to the region left of the window using a reflection about the line $y = -x$, or we could use a 90° counterclockwise rotation.

Assuming that $\mathbf{P}_0$ and $\mathbf{P}_{\text{end}}$ are not both inside the clipping window, we next determine the position of $\mathbf{P}_{\text{end}}$ relative to $\mathbf{P}_0$. To do this, we create some new regions in the plane, depending on the location of $\mathbf{P}_0$. Boundaries of the new regions are semi-infinite line segments that start at the position of $\mathbf{P}_0$ and pass through the clipping-window corners. If $\mathbf{P}_0$ is inside the clipping window, we set up the four regions shown in Fig. 6-17. Then, depending on which one of the four regions (L, T, R, or B) contains $\mathbf{P}_{\text{end}}$, we compute the line-intersection position with the corresponding window boundary.

If $\mathbf{P}_0$ is in the region to the left of the window, we set up the four regions labeled L, LT, LR, and LB in Fig. 6-18. These four regions again determine a unique clipping-window edge for the line segment, relative to the position of $\mathbf{P}_{\text{end}}$. For instance, if $\mathbf{P}_{\text{end}}$ is in any one of the three regions labeled L, we clip the line at the left window border and save the line segment from this intersection point to $\mathbf{P}_{\text{end}}$. If $\mathbf{P}_{\text{end}}$ is in region LT, we save the line segment from the left window

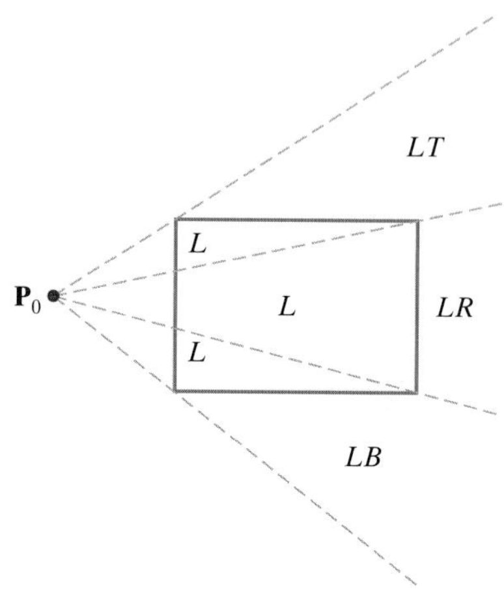

FIGURE 6-18 The four clipping regions used in the NLN algorithm when $\mathbf{P}_0$ is directly to the left of the clip window.

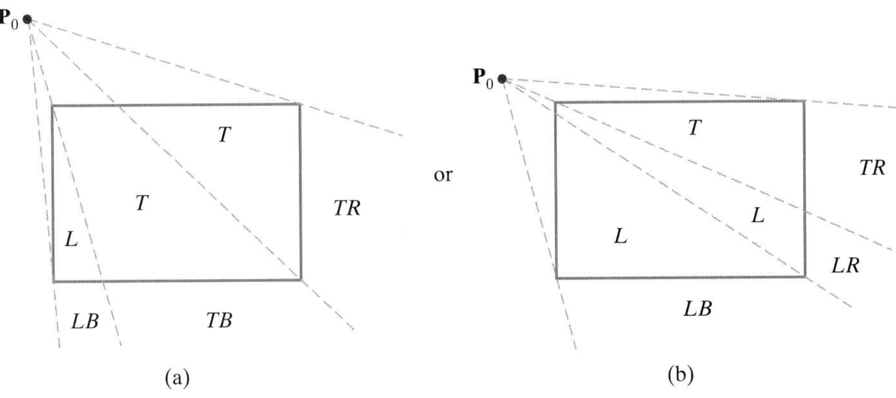

FIGURE 6-19 The two possible sets of clipping regions used in the NLN algorithm when $\mathbf{P}_0$ is above and to the left of the clipping window.

boundary to the top boundary. Similar processing is carried out for regions LR and LB. But if $\mathbf{P}_{\text{end}}$ is not in any of the four regions L, LT, LR, or LB, the entire line is clipped.

For the third case, when $\mathbf{P}_0$ is to the left and above the clipping window, we use the regions in Fig. 6-19. In this case, we have the two possibilities shown, depending on the position of $\mathbf{P}_0$ within the top-left corner of the clipping window. When $\mathbf{P}_0$ is closer to the left clipping boundary of the window, we use the regions in (a) of this figure. Otherwise, when $\mathbf{P}_0$ is closer to the top clipping boundary of the window, we use the regions in (b). If $\mathbf{P}_{\text{end}}$ is in one of the regions T, L, TR, TB, LR, or LB, this determines a unique clipping-window border for the intersection calculations. Otherwise, the entire line is rejected.

To determine the region in which $\mathbf{P}_{\text{end}}$ is located, we compare the slope of the line segment to the slopes of the boundaries of the NLN regions. For example, if $\mathbf{P}_0$ is left of the clipping window (Fig. 6-18), then $\mathbf{P}_{\text{end}}$ is in region LT if

$$\text{slope}\overline{\mathbf{P}_0\mathbf{P}_{TR}} < \text{slope}\overline{\mathbf{P}_0\mathbf{P}_{\text{end}}} < \text{slope}\overline{\mathbf{P}_0\mathbf{P}_{TL}} \qquad (6\text{-}21)$$

or

$$\frac{y_T - y_0}{x_R - x_0} < \frac{y_{\text{end}} - y_0}{x_{\text{end}} - x_0} < \frac{y_T - y_0}{x_L - x_0} \qquad (6\text{-}22)$$

And we clip the entire line if

$$(y_T - y_0)(x_{\text{end}} - x_0) < (x_L - x_0)(y_{\text{end}} - y_0) \qquad (6\text{-}23)$$

The coordinate-difference calculations and product calculations used in the slope tests are saved and also used in the intersection calculations. From the parametric equations

$$x = x_0 + (x_{\text{end}} - x_0)u$$
$$y = y_0 + (y_{\text{end}} - y_0)u$$

we calculate an x-intersection position on the left window boundary as $x = x_L$, with $u = (x_L - x_0)/(x_{\text{end}} - x_0)$, so that the y-intersection position is

$$y = y_0 + \frac{y_{\text{end}} - y_0}{x_{\text{end}} - x_0}(x_L - x_0) \qquad (6\text{-}24)$$

And an intersection position on the top boundary has $y = y_T$ and $u = (y_T - y_0)/(y_{end} - y_0)$, with

$$x = x_0 + \frac{x_{end} - x_0}{y_{end} - y_0}(y_T - y_0) \tag{6-25}$$

Line Clipping Using Nonrectangular Polygon Clip Windows

In some applications, it may be desirable to clip lines against arbitrarily shaped polygons. Methods based on parametric line equations, such as either the Cyrus-Beck algorithm or the Liang-Barsky algorithm, can be readily extended to clip lines against convex polygon windows. We do this by modifying the algorithm to include the parametric equations for the boundaries of the clipping region. Preliminary screening of line segments can be accomplished by processing lines against the coordinate extents of the clipping polygon.

For concave-polygon clipping regions, we could still apply these parametric clipping procedures if we first split the concave polygon into a set of convex polygons using one of the methods described in Section 3-15. Another approach is simply to add one or more additional edges to the concave clipping area so that it is modified to a convex-polygon shape. Then a series of clipping operations can be applied using the modified convex polygon components, as illustrated in Fig. 6-20.

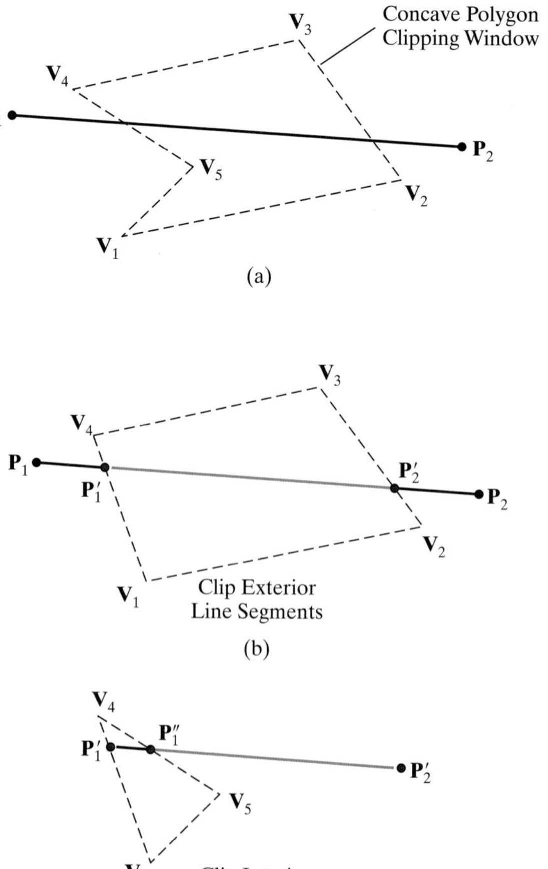

FIGURE 6-20 A concave-polygon clipping window (a), with vertex list ($\mathbf{V}_1$, $\mathbf{V}_2$, $\mathbf{V}_3$, $\mathbf{V}_4$, $\mathbf{V}_5$), is modified to the convex polygon ($\mathbf{V}_1$, $\mathbf{V}_2$, $\mathbf{V}_3$, $\mathbf{V}_4$) in (b). The external segments of line $\overline{\mathbf{P}_1\mathbf{P}_2}$ are then snipped off using this convex clipping window. The resulting line segment, $\overline{\mathbf{P}'_1\mathbf{P}'_2}$, is next processed against the triangle ($\mathbf{V}_1$, $\mathbf{V}_5$, $\mathbf{V}_4$) (c) to clip off the internal line segment $\overline{\mathbf{P}'_1\mathbf{P}''_1}$ to produce the final clipped line $\overline{\mathbf{P}''_1\mathbf{P}'_2}$.

The line segment $\overline{\mathbf{P}_1\mathbf{P}_2}$ in (a) of this figure is to be clipped by the concave window with vertices $\mathbf{V}_1$, $\mathbf{V}_2$, $\mathbf{V}_3$, $\mathbf{V}_4$, and $\mathbf{V}_5$. Two convex clipping regions are obtained, in this case, by adding a line segment from $\mathbf{V}_4$ to $\mathbf{V}_1$. Then the line is clipped in two passes: (1) Line $\overline{\mathbf{P}_1\mathbf{P}_2}$ is clipped by the convex polygon with vertices $\mathbf{V}_1$, $\mathbf{V}_2$, $\mathbf{V}_3$, and $\mathbf{V}_4$ to yield the clipped segment $\overline{\mathbf{P}'_1\mathbf{P}'_2}$ (Fig. 6-20 (b)). (2) The internal line segment $\overline{\mathbf{P}'_1\mathbf{P}'_2}$ is clipped off using the convex polygon with vertices $\mathbf{V}_1$, $\mathbf{V}_5$, and $\mathbf{V}_4$ (Fig. 6-20 (c)) to yield the final clipped line segment $\overline{\mathbf{P}''_1\mathbf{P}'_2}$.

Line Clipping Using Nonlinear Clipping-Window Boundaries

Circles or other curved-boundary clipping regions are also possible, but they require more processing because the intersection calculations involve nonlinear equations. At the first step, lines could be clipped against the bounding rectangle (coordinate extents) of the curved clipping region. Lines that are outside the coordinate extents are eliminated. To identify lines that are inside a circle, for instance, we could calculate the distance of the line endpoints from the circle center. If the square of this distance for both endpoints of a line is less than or equal to the radius squared, we can save the entire line. The remaining lines are then processed through the intersection calculations, which must solve simultaneous circle-line equations.

6-8 POLYGON FILL-AREA CLIPPING

Graphics packages typically support only fill areas that are polygons, and often only convex polygons. To clip a polygon fill area, we cannot directly apply a line-clipping method to the individual polygon edges because this approach would not, in general, produce a closed polyline. Instead, a line clipper would often produce a disjoint set of lines with no complete information about how we might form a closed boundary around the clipped fill area. Figure 6-21 illustrates a possible output from a line-clipping procedure applied to the edges of a polygon fill area. What we require is a procedure that will output one or more closed polylines for the boundaries of the clipped fill area, so that the polygons can be scan converted to fill the interiors with the assigned color or pattern, as in Fig. 6-22.

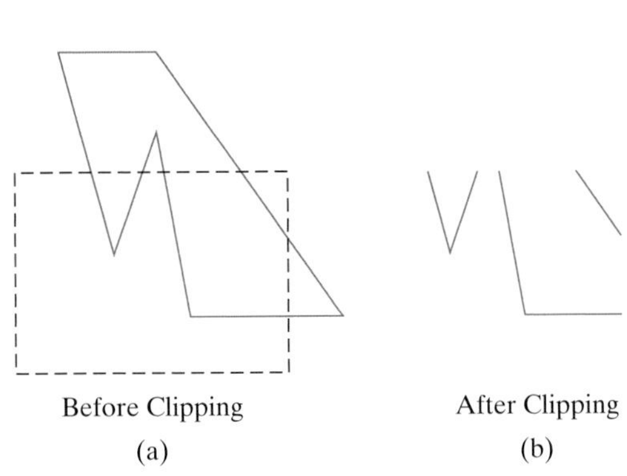

FIGURE 6-21 A line-clipping algorithm applied to the line segments of the polygon boundary in (a) generates the unconnected set of lines in (b).

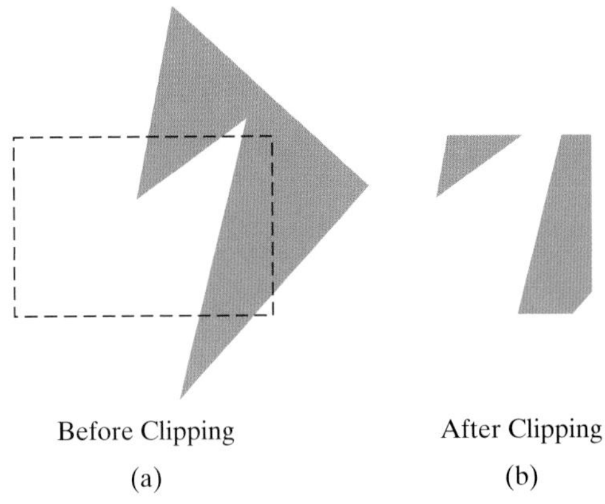

FIGURE 6-22 Display of a correctly clipped polygon fill area.

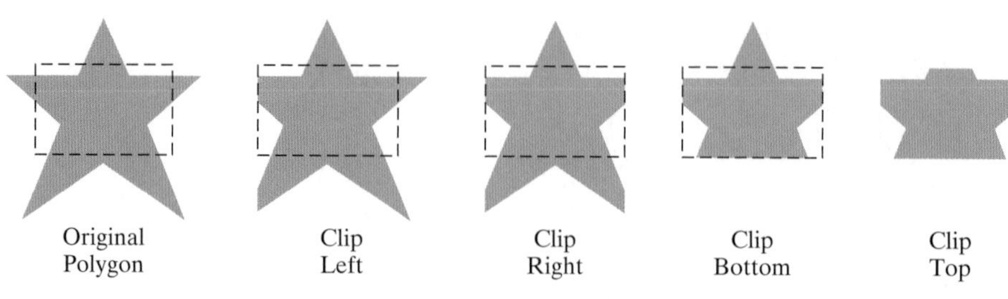

FIGURE 6-23 Processing a polygon fill area against successive clipping-window boundaries.

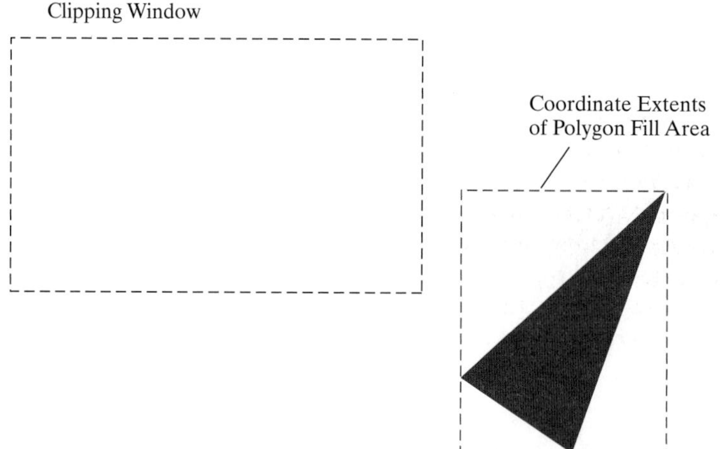

FIGURE 6-24 A polygon fill area with coordinate extents outside the right clipping boundary.

We can process a polygon fill area against the borders of a clipping window using the same general approach as in line clipping. A line segment is defined by its two endpoints, and these endpoints are processed through a line-clipping procedure by constructing a new set of clipped endpoints at each clipping-window boundary. Similarly, we need to maintain a fill area as an entity as it is processed through the clipping stages. Thus, we can clip a polygon fill area by determining the new shape for the polygon as each clipping-window edge is processed, as demonstrated in Figure 6-23. Of course, the interior fill for the polygon would not be applied until the final clipped border had been determined.

Just as we first tested a line segment to determine whether it could be completely saved or completely clipped, we can do the same with a polygon fill area by checking its coordinate extents. If the minimum and maximum coordinate values for the fill area are inside all four clipping boundaries, the fill area is saved for further processing. If these coordinate extents are all outside any one of the clipping-window borders, we eliminate the polygon from the scene description (Fig. 6-24).

When we cannot identify a fill area as being completely inside or completely outside the clipping window, we then need to locate the polygon intersection positions with the clipping boundaries. One way to implement convex-polygon clipping is to create a new vertex list at each clipping boundary, and then pass this new vertex list to the next boundary clipper. The output of the final clipping stage is the vertex list for the clipped polygon (Fig. 6-25). For concave-polygon clipping, we would need to modify this basic approach so that multiple vertex lists could be generated.

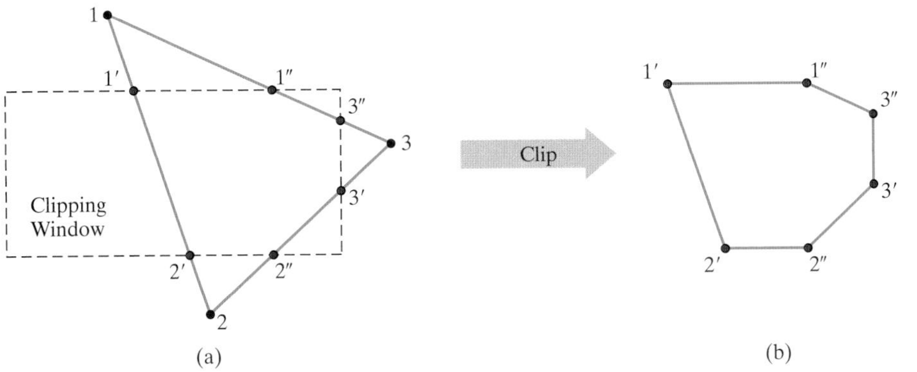

FIGURE 6-25 A convex-polygon fill area (a), defined with the vertex list $\{1, 2, 3\}$, is clipped to produce the fill-area shape shown in (b), which is defined with the output vertex list $\{1', 2', 2'', 3', 3'', 1''\}$.

Sutherland-Hodgman Polygon Clipping

An efficient method for clipping a convex-polygon fill area, developed by Sutherland and Hodgman, is to send the polygon vertices through each clipping stage so that a single clipped vertex can be immediately passed to the next stage. This eliminates the need for an output set of vertices at each clipping stage, and it allows the boundary-clipping routines to be implemented in parallel. The final output is a list of vertices that describe the edges of the clipped polygon fill area.

Since the Sutherland-Hodgman algorithm produces only one list of output vertices, it cannot correctly generate the two output polygons in Fig. 6-22(b) that are the result of clipping the concave polygon shown in (a) of that figure. However, additional processing can be amended to the Sutherland-Hodgman algorithm to obtain multiple output vertex lists, so that general concave-polygon clipping could be accommodated. And the basic Sutherland-Hodgman algorithm is able to process concave polygons when the clipped fill area can be described with a single vertex list.

The general strategy in this algorithm is to send the pair of endpoints for each successive polygon line segment through the series of clippers (left, right, bottom, and top). As soon as a clipper completes the processing of one pair of vertices, the clipped coordinate values, if any, for that edge are sent to the next clipper. Then the first clipper processes the next pair of endpoints. In this way, the individual boundary clippers can be operating in parallel.

There are four possible cases that need to be considered when processing a polygon edge against one of the clipping boundaries. One possibility is that the first edge endpoint is outside the clipping boundary and the second endpoint is inside. Or, both endpoints could be inside this clipping boundary. Another possibility is that the first endpoint is inside the clipping boundary and the second endpoint is outside. And, finally, both endpoints could be outside the clipping boundary.

To facilitate the passing of vertices from one clipping stage to the next, the output from each clipper can be formulated as shown in Fig. 6-26. As each successive pair of endpoints is passed to one of the four clippers, an output is generated for the next clipper according to the results of the following tests.

(1) If the first input vertex is outside this clipping-window border and the second vertex is inside, both the intersection point of the polygon edge with the window border and the second vertex are sent to the next clipper.

(2) If both input vertices are inside this clipping-window border, only the second vertex is sent to the next clipper.

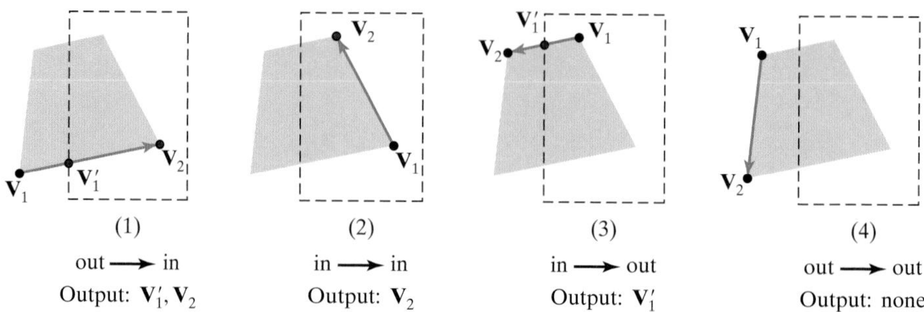

FIGURE 6-26 The four possible outputs generated by the left clipper, depending on the position of a pair of endpoints relative to the left boundary of the clipping window.

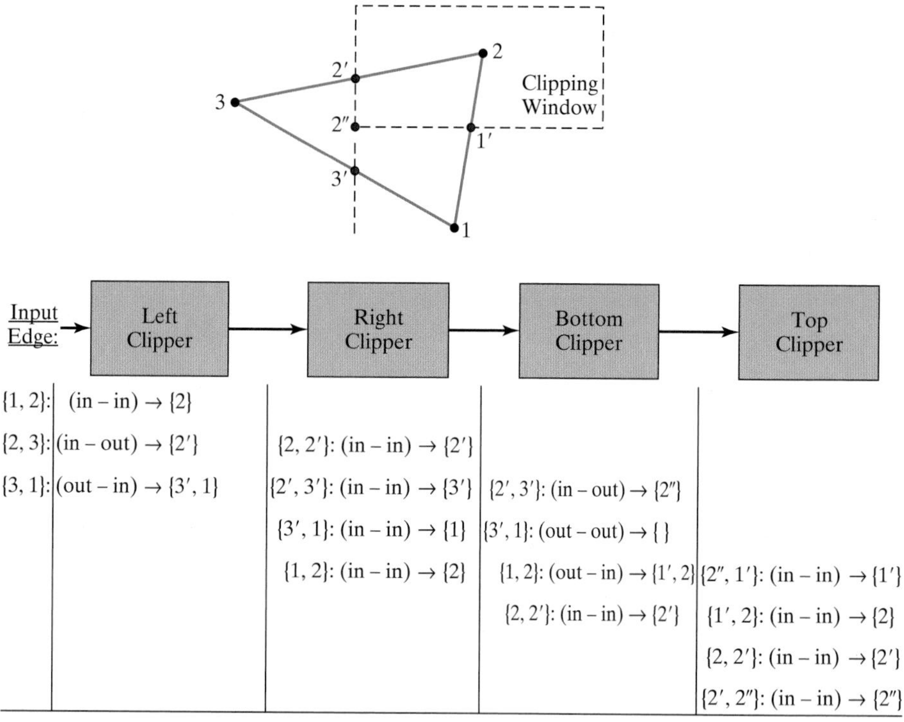

FIGURE 6-27 Processing a set of polygon vertices, {1, 2, 3}, through the boundary clippers using the Sutherland-Hodgman algorithm. The final set of clipped vertices is {1′, 2, 2′, 2″}.

(3) If the first vertex is inside this clipping-window border and the second vertex is outside, only the polygon edge-intersection position with the clipping-window border is sent to the next clipper.

(4) If both input vertices are outside this clipping-window border, no vertices are sent to the next clipper.

The last clipper in this series generates a vertex list that describes the final clipped fill area.

Figure 6-27 provides an example of the Sutherland-Hodgman polygon-clipping algorithm for a fill area defined with the vertex set {1, 2, 3}. As soon as a clipper receives a pair of endpoints, it determines the appropriate output using the tests illustrated in Fig. 6-26. These outputs are passed in succession from the left clipper to the right, bottom, and top clippers. The output from the top clipper is the set of vertices defining the clipped fill area. For this example, the output vertex list is {1′, 2, 2′, 2″}.

A sequential implementation of the Sutherland-Hodgman polygon-clipping algorithm is demonstrated in the following set of procedures. An input set of vertices is converted to an output vertex list by the left, right, bottom, and top clipping routines.

```
typedef enum { Left, Right, Bottom, Top } Boundary;
const GLint nClip = 4;

GLint inside (wcPt2D p, Boundary b, wcPt2D wMin, wcPt2D wMax)
{
  switch (b) {
  case Left:   if (p.x < wMin.x) return (false); break;
  case Right:  if (p.x > wMax.x) return (false); break;
  case Bottom: if (p.y < wMin.y) return (false); break;
  case Top:    if (p.y > wMax.y) return (false); break;
  }
  return (true);
}

GLint cross (wcPt2D p1, wcPt2D p2, Boundary winEdge, wcPt2D wMin, wcPt2D wMax)
{
  if (inside (p1, winEdge, wMin, wMax) == inside (p2, winEdge, wMin, wMax))
    return (false);
  else return (true);
}

wcPt2D intersect (wcPt2D p1, wcPt2D p2, Boundary winEdge,
                                           wcPt2D wMin, wcPt2D wMax)
{
  wcPt2D iPt;
  GLfloat m;

  if (p1.x != p2.x) m = (p1.y - p2.y) / (p1.x - p2.x);
  switch (winEdge) {
  case Left:
    iPt.x = wMin.x;
    iPt.y = p2.y + (wMin.x - p2.x) * m;
    break;
  case Right:
    iPt.x = wMax.x;
    iPt.y = p2.y + (wMax.x - p2.x) * m;
    break;
  case Bottom:
    iPt.y = wMin.y;
    if (p1.x != p2.x) iPt.x = p2.x + (wMin.y - p2.y) / m;
    else iPt.x = p2.x;
    break;
  case Top:
    iPt.y = wMax.y;
    if (p1.x != p2.x) iPt.x = p2.x + (wMax.y - p2.y) / m;
    else iPt.x = p2.x;
    break;
  }
```

```
   return (iPt);
}

void clipPoint (wcPt2D p, Boundary winEdge, wcPt2D wMin, wcPt2D wMax,
                wcPt2D * pOut, int * cnt, wcPt2D * first[], wcPt2D * s)
{
  wcPt2D iPt;

  /* If no previous point exists for this clipping boundary,
   * save this point.
   */
  if (!first[winEdge])
    first[winEdge] = &p;
  else
    /*  Previous point exists.  If p and previous point cross
     *  this clipping boundary, find intersection.  Clip against
     *  next boundary, if any.  If no more clip boundaries, add
     *  intersection to output list.
     */
    if (cross (p, s[winEdge], winEdge, wMin, wMax)) {
      iPt = intersect (p, s[winEdge], winEdge, wMin, wMax);
      if (winEdge < Top)
        clipPoint (iPt, b+1, wMin, wMax, pOut, cnt, first, s);
      else {
        pOut[*cnt] = iPt;  (*cnt)++;
      }
    }

  /*  Save p as most recent point for this clip boundary.  */
  s[winEdge] = p;

  /*  For all, if point inside, proceed to next boundary, if any.  */
  if (inside (p, winEdge, wMin, wMax))
    if (winEdge < Top)
      clipPoint (p, winEdge + 1, wMin, wMax, pOut, cnt, first, s);
    else {
      pOut[*cnt] = p;  (*cnt)++;
    }
}

void closeClip (wcPt2D wMin, wcPt2D wMax, wcPt2D * pOut,
                GLint * cnt, wcPt2D * first [ ], wcPt2D * s)
{
  wcPt2D pt;
  Boundary winEdge;

  for (winEdge = Left; winEdge <= Top; winEdge++) {
    if (cross (s[winEdge], *first[winEdge], winEdge, wMin, wMax)) {
      pt = intersect (s[winEdge], *first[winEdge], winEdge, wMin, wMax);
      if (winEdge < Top)
        clipPoint (pt, winEdge + 1, wMin, wMax, pOut, cnt, first, s);
      else {
        pOut[*cnt] = pt;  (*cnt)++;
      }
    }
  }
}
```

```
GLint polygonClipSuthHodg (wcPt2D wMin, wcPt2D wMax, GLint n, wcPt2D * pIn, wcPt2D * pOut)
{
   /*  Parameter "first" holds pointer to first point processed for
    *  a boundary; "s" holds most recent point processed for boundary.
    */
   wcPt2D * first[nClip] = { 0, 0, 0, 0 }, s[nClip];
   GLint k, cnt = 0;

   for (k = 0; k < n; k++)
     clipPoint (pIn[k], Left, wMin, wMax, pOut, &cnt, first, s);

   closeClip (wMin, wMax, pOut, &cnt, first, s);
   return (cnt);
}
```

When a concave polygon is clipped with the Sutherland-Hodgman algorithm, extraneous lines may be displayed. An example of this effect is demonstrated in Fig. 6-28. This occurs when the clipped polygon should have two or more separate sections. But since there is only one output vertex list, the last vertex in the list is always joined to the first vertex.

There are several things we can do to display clipped concave polygons correctly. For one, we could split a concave polygon into two or more convex polygons (Section 3-15) and process each convex polygon separately using the Sutherland-Hodgman algorithm. Another possibility is to modify the Sutherland-Hodgman method so that the final vertex list is checked for multiple intersection points along any clipping-window boundary. If we find more than two vertex positions along any clipping boundary, we can separate the list of vertices into two or more lists that correctly identify the separate sections of the clipped fill area. This may require extensive analysis to determine whether some points along the clipping boundary should be paired or whether they represent single vertex points that have been clipped. A third possibility is to use a more general polygon clipper that has been designed to process concave polygons correctly.

Weiler-Atherton Polygon Clipping

This algorithm provides a general polygon-clipping approach that can be used to clip a fill area that is either a convex polygon or a concave polygon. Moreover, the method was developed as a means for identifying visible surfaces in a three-dimensional scene. Therefore, we could also use this approach to clip any polygon fill area against a clipping window with any polygon shape.

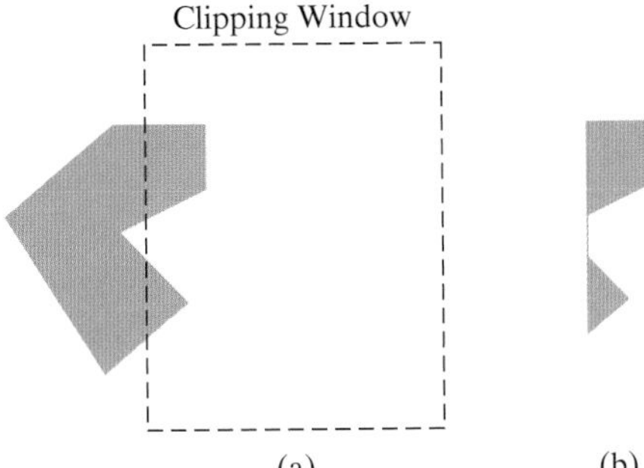

FIGURE 6-28 Clipping the concave polygon in (a) using the Sutherland-Hodgman algorithm produces the two connected areas in (b).

Instead of simply clipping the fill-area edges as in the Sutherland-Hodgman method, the Weiler-Atherton algorithm traces around the perimeter of the fill polygon searching for the borders that enclose a clipped fill region. In this way, multiple fill regions, as in Fig. 6-28(b), can be identified and displayed as separate, unconnected polygons. To find the edges for a clipped fill area, we follow a path (either counterclockwise or clockwise) around the fill area that detours along a clipping-window boundary whenever a polygon edge crosses to the outside of that boundary. The direction of a detour at a clipping-window border is the same as the processing direction for the polygon edges.

We can usually determine whether the processing direction is counterclockwise or clockwise from the ordering of the vertex list that defines a polygon fill area. In most cases, the vertex list is specified in a counterclockwise order as a means for defining the front face of the polygon. Thus, the cross product of two successive edge vectors that form a convex angle determines the direction for the normal vector, which is in the direction from the back face to the front face of the polygon. If we do not know the vertex ordering, we could calculate the normal vector, or we can use any one of the methods discussed in Section 3-15 to locate the interior of the fill area from any reference position. Then, if we sequentially process the edges so that the polygon interior is always on our left, we obtain a counterclockwise traversal. Otherwise, with the interior to our right, we have a clockwise traversal.

For a counterclockwise traversal of the polygon fill-area vertices, we apply the following Weiler-Atherton procedures.

(1) Process the edges of the polygon fill area in a counterclockwise order until an inside-outside pair of vertices is encountered for one of the clipping boundaries; that is, the first vertex of the polygon edge is inside the clip region and the second vertex is outside the clip region.

(2) Follow the window boundaries in a counterclockwise direction from the exit-intersection point to another intersection point with the polygon. If this is a previously processed point, proceed to the next step. If this is a new intersection point, continue processing polygon edges in a counterclockwise order until a previously processed vertex is encountered.

(3) Form the vertex list for this section of the clipped fill area.

(4) Return to the exit-intersection point and continue processing the polygon edges in a counterclockwise order.

Figure 6-29 illustrates the Weiler-Atherton clipping of a concave polygon against a standard, rectangular clipping window for a counterclockwise traversal of the polygon edges. For a clockwise edge traversal, we would use a clockwise clipping-window traversal.

Starting from the vertex labeled 1 in Fig. 6-29(a), the next polygon vertex to process in a counterclockwise order is labeled 2. Thus, this edge exits the clipping window at the top boundary. We calculate this intersection position (point $1'$) and make a left turn there to process the window borders in a counterclockwise direction. Proceeding along the top border of the clipping window, we do not intersect a polygon edge before reaching the left window boundary. So we label this position as vertex $1''$ and follow the left boundary to the intersection position $1'''$. We then follow this polygon edge in a counterclockwise direction, which returns us to vertex 1. This completes a circuit of the window boundaries and identifies the vertex list $\{1, 1', 1'', 1'''\}$ as a clipped region of the original fill area. Processing of the polygon edges is then resumed at point $1'$. The edge defined by

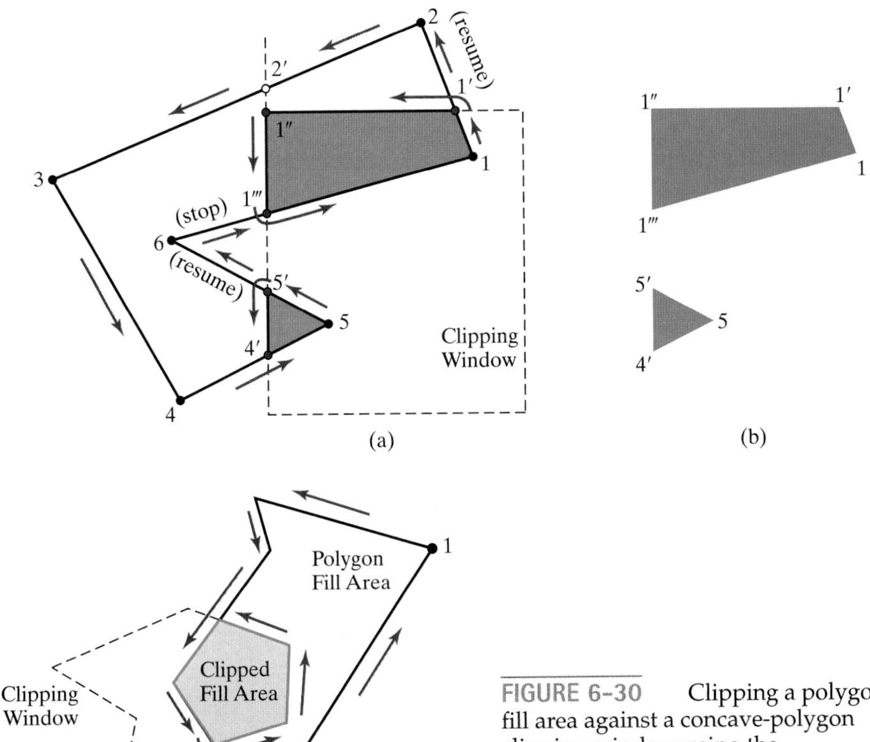

FIGURE 6-29 A concave polygon (a), defined with the vertex list $\{1, 2, 3, 4, 5, 6\}$, is clipped using the Weiler-Atherton algorithm to generate the two lists $\{1, 1', 1'', 1'''\}$ and $\{4', 5, 5'\}$, which represent the separate polygon fill areas shown in (b).

FIGURE 6-30 Clipping a polygon fill area against a concave-polygon clipping window using the Weiler-Atherton algorithm.

points 2 and 3 crosses to the outside of the left boundary, but points 2 and 2′ are above the top clipping-window border and points 2′ and 3 are to the left of the clipping region. Also the edge with endpoints 3 and 4 is outside the left clipping boundary. But the next edge (from endpoint 4 to endpoint 5) reenters the clipping region and we pick up intersection point 4′. And the edge with endpoints 5 and 6 exits the window at intersection position 5′, so we detour down the left clipping boundary to obtain the closed vertex list $\{4', 5, 5'\}$. We resume the polygon edge processing at position 5′, which returns us to the previously processed point 1‴. At this point, all polygon vertices and edges have been processed, so the fill area is completely clipped.

Polygon Clipping Using Nonrectangular Polygon Clip Windows

The Liang-Barsky algorithm and other parametric line-clipping methods are particularly well suited for processing polygon fill areas against convex-polygon clipping windows. In this approach, we use a parametric representation for the edges of both the fill area and the clipping window, and both polygons are represented with a vertex list. We first compare the positions of the bounding rectangles for the fill area and the clipping polygon. If we cannot identity the fill area as completely outside the clipping polygon, we can use inside-outside tests to process the parametric edge equations. After completing all the region tests, we solve pairs of simultaneous parametric line equations to determine the window intersection positions.

We can also process any polygon fill area against any polygon-shaped clipping window (convex or concave), as in Fig. 6-30, using the edge-traversal approach of the Weiler-Atherton algorithm. In this case, we need to maintain a vertex list for the clipping window, as well as for the fill area, with both lists arranged in a counterclockwise (or clockwise) order. And, we need to apply inside-outside tests to determine whether a fill-area vertex is inside or outside a particular clipping-window boundary. As in the previous examples, we follow the window boundaries whenever a fill-area edge exits a clipping boundary. This clipping method can also be used when either the fill area or the clipping window contains holes that are defined with polygon borders. In addition, we can use this basic approach in constructive solid-geometry applications to identify the union, intersection, or difference of two polygons. In fact, locating the clipped region of a fill area is equivalent to determining the intersection of two planar areas.

Polygon Clipping Using Nonlinear Clipping-Window Boundaries

One method for processing a clipping window with curved boundaries is to approximate the boundaries with straight-line sections and use one of the algorithms for clipping against a general polygon-shaped clipping window. Alternatively, we could use the same general procedures that we discussed for line segments. First, we can compare the coordinate extents of the fill area to the coordinate extents of the clipping window. Depending on the shape of the clipping window, we may also be able to perform some other region tests based on symmetric considerations. For fill areas that cannot be identified as completely inside or completely outside the clipping window, we ultimately need to calculate the window intersection positions with the fill area.

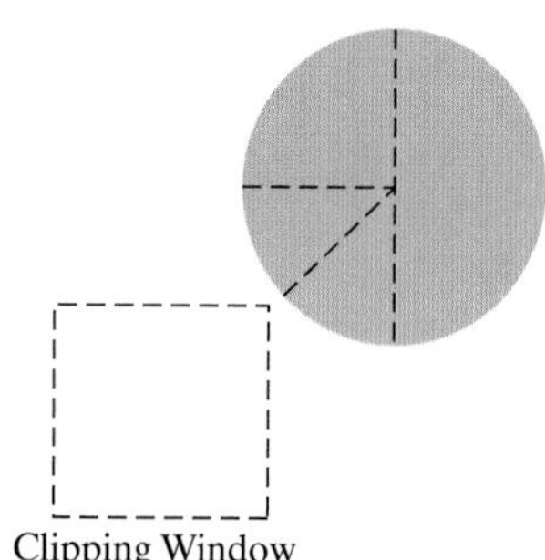

FIGURE 6-31 A circle fill area, showing the quadrant and octant sections that are outside the clipping-window boundaries.

6-9 CURVE CLIPPING

Areas with curved boundaries can be clipped with methods similar to those discussed in the previous sections. If the objects are approximated with straight-line boundary sections, we use a polygon-clipping method. Otherwise, the clipping procedures involve nonlinear equations, and this requires more processing than for objects with linear boundaries.

We can first test the coordinate extents of an object against the clipping boundaries to determine whether it is possible to trivially accept or reject the entire object. If not, we could check for object symmetries that we might be able to exploit in the initial accept/reject tests. For example, circles have symmetries between quadrants and octants, so we could check the coordinate extents of these individual circle regions. We cannot reject the complete circular fill area in Fig. 6-31 just by checking its overall coordinate extents. But half of the circle is outside the right clipping border (or outside the top border), the upper-left quadrant is above the top clipping border, and the remaining two octants can be similarly eliminated.

An intersection calculation involves substituting a clipping-boundary position (xw_{min}, xw_{max}, yw_{min}, or yw_{max}) in the nonlinear equation for the object boundary and solving for the other coordinate value. Once all intersection positions have been evaluated, the defining positions for the object can be stored for later use by the scan-line fill procedures. Figure 6-32 illustrates circle clipping against a rectangular window. For this example, the circle radius and the endpoints of the clipped arc can be used to fill the clipped region, by invoking the circle algorithm to locate positions along the arc between the intersection endpoints.

Similar procedures can be applied when clipping a curved object against a general polygon clipping region. On the first pass, we could compare the bounding rectangle of the object with the bounding rectangle of the clipping region. If this does not save or eliminate the entire object, we next solve the simultaneous line-curve equations to determine the clipping intersection points.

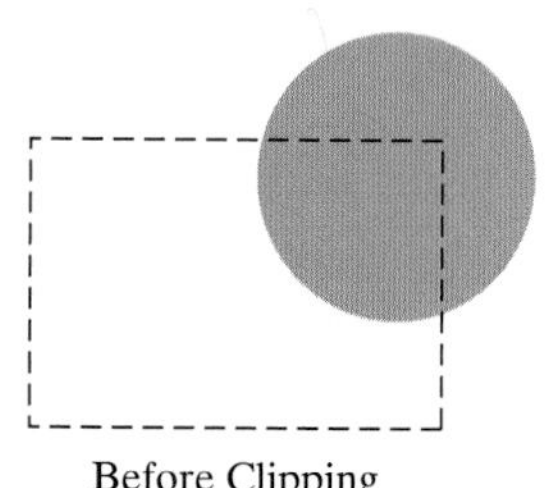

FIGURE 6-32 Clipping a circle fill area.

6-10 TEXT CLIPPING

There are several techniques that can be used to provide text clipping in a graphics package. In a particular application, the choice of clipping method depends on how characters are generated and what requirements we have for displaying character strings.

The simplest method for processing character strings relative to the limits of a clipping window is to use the *all-or-none string-clipping* strategy shown in Fig. 6-33. If all of the string is inside the clipping window, we display the entire string. Otherwise, the entire string is eliminated. This procedure is implemented by examining the coordinate extents of the text string. If the coordinate limits of this bounding rectangle are not completely within the clipping window, the string is rejected.

An alternative is to use the *all-or-none character-clipping* strategy. Here we eliminate only those characters that are not completely inside the clipping window (Fig. 6-34). In this case, the coordinate extents of individual characters are compared to the window boundaries. Any character that is not completely within the clipping-window boundary is eliminated.

A third approach to text clipping is to clip the components of individual characters. This provides the most accurate display of clipped character strings, but it requires the most processing. We now treat characters in much the same way that we treated lines or polygons. If an individual character overlaps a clipping window, we clip off only the parts of the character that are outside the window (Fig. 6-35). Outline character fonts defined with line segments are processed in this way using a polygon-clipping algorithm. Characters defined with bit maps are clipped by comparing the relative position of the individual pixels in the character grid patterns to the borders of the clipping region.

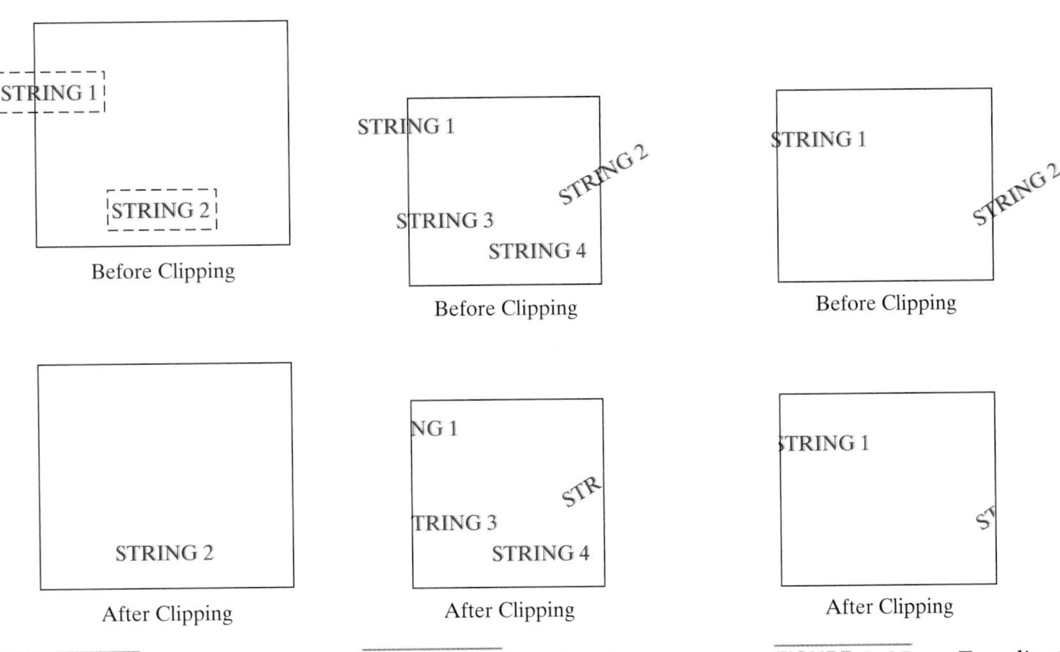

FIGURE 6-33 Text clipping using the coordinate extents for an entire string.

FIGURE 6-34 Text clipping using the bounding rectangle for individual characters in a string.

FIGURE 6-35 Text clipping performed on the components of individual characters.

6-11 SUMMARY

The two-dimensional viewing-transformation pipeline is a series of operations that result in the display of a world-coordinate picture that has been defined in the xy plane. After we construct the scene, it can be mapped to a viewing-coordinate reference frame, then to a normalized coordinate system where clipping routines can be applied. Finally, the scene is transferred to device coordinates for display. Normalized coordinates can be specified in the range from 0 to 1 or in the range from -1 to 1, and they are used to make graphics packages independent of the output-device requirements.

We select part of a scene for display on an output device using a clipping window, which can be described in the world-coordinate system or in a viewing-coordinate frame defined relative to world coordinates. The contents of the clipping window are transferred to a viewport for display on an output device. In some systems, a viewport is specified within normalized coordinates. Other systems specify the viewport in device coordinates. Typically, the clipping window and viewport are rectangles whose edges are parallel to the coordinate axes. An object is mapped to the viewport so that it has the same relative position in the viewport as it has in the clipping window. To maintain the relative proportions of an object, the viewport must have the same aspect ratio as the corresponding clipping window. And we can set up any number of clipping windows and viewports for a scene.

Clipping algorithms are usually implemented in normalized coordinates, so that all geometric transformations and viewing operations that are independent of device coordinates can be concatenated into one transformation matrix. With the viewport specified in device coordinates, we can clip a two-dimensional scene against a normalized, symmetric square, with normalized coordinates varying from -1 to 1, before transferring the contents of the normalized, symmetric square to the viewport.

All graphics packages include routines for clipping straight-line segments and polygon fill areas. Packages that contain functions for specifying single point positions or text strings also include clipping routines for those graphics primitives. Since the clipping calculations are time consuming, the development of improved clipping algorithms continues to be an area of major concern in computer graphics. Cohen and Sutherland developed a line-clipping algorithm that uses a region code to identify the position of a line endpoint relative to the clipping-window boundaries. Endpoint region codes are used to quickly identify those lines that are completely inside the clipping window and some of the lines that are completely outside. For the remaining lines, intersection positions at the window boundaries must be calculated. Liang and Barsky developed a faster line-clipping algorithm that represents line segments with parametric equations, similar to the Cyrus-Beck algorithm. This approach allows more testing to be accomplished before proceeding to the intersection calculations. And the Nicholl-Lee-Nicholl algorithm further reduces intersection calculations by using more region testing in the xy plane. Parametric line-clipping methods are easily extended to convex clipping windows and to three-dimensional scenes. However, the Nicholl-Lee-Nicholl approach applies only to two-dimensional line segments.

Algorithms for clipping straight-line segments against concave-polygon clipping windows have also been developed. One approach is to split a concave clipping window into a set of convex polygons and apply the parametric line-clipping methods. Another approach is to add edges to the concave window to modify it

TABLE 6-1

SUMMARY OF OpenGL TWO-DIMENSIONAL VIEWING FUNCTIONS

Function	Description
`gluOrtho2D`	Specify clipping-window coordinates as parameters for a two-dimensional orthogonal projection.
`glViewport`	Specify screen-coordinate parameters for a viewport.
`glGetIntegerv`	Use arguments `GL_VIEWPORT` and `vpArray` to obtain parameters for the currently active viewport.
`glutInit`	Initialize the GLUT library.
`glutInitWindowPosition`	Specify coordinates for the top-left corner of a display window.
`glutInitWindowSize`	Specify width and height for a display window.
`glutCreateWindow`	Create a display window (which is assigned an integer identifier) and specify a display-window title.
`glutInitDisplayMode`	Select parameters such as buffering and color mode for a display window.
`glClearColor`	Specify a background RGB color for a display window.
`glClearIndex`	Specify a background color for a display window using color-index mode.
`glutDestroyWindow`	Specify an identifier number for a display window that is to be deleted.
`glutSetWindow`	Specify the identifier number for a display window that is to be the current display window.
`glutPositionWindow`	Reset the screen location for the current display window.
`glutReshapeWindow`	Reset the width and height for the current display window.
`glutFullScreen`	Set current display window to the size of the video screen.
`glutReshapeFunc`	Specify a function that is to be invoked when display-window size is changed.
`glutIconifyWindow`	Convert the current display window to an icon.
`glutSetIconTitle`	Specify a label for a display-window icon.
`glutSetWindowTitle`	Specify new title for the current display window.
`glutPopWindow`	Move current display window to the "top"; i.e., in front of all other windows.
`glutPushWindow`	Move current display window to the "bottom"; i.e., behind all other windows.
`glutShowWindow`	Return the current display window to the screen.
`glutCreateSubWindow`	Create a second-level window within a display window.
`glutSetCursor`	Select a shape for the screen cursor.
`glutDisplayFunc`	Invoke a function to create a picture within the current display window.
`glutPostRedisplay`	Renew contents of current window.
`glutMainLoop`	Execute the computer-graphics program.
`glutIdleFunc`	Specify a function to execute when the system is idle.
`glutGet`	Query the system about a specified state parameter.

to a convex shape. Then a series of exterior and interior clipping operations can be performed to obtain the clipped line segment.

Although clipping windows with curved boundaries are rarely used, we can apply similar line-clipping methods. However, intersection calculations now involve nonlinear equations.

A polygon fill area is defined with a vertex list, and polygon-clipping procedures must retain information about how the clipped edges are to be connected as the polygon proceeds through the various processing stages. In the Sutherland-Hodgman algorithm, pairs of fill-area vertices are processed by each boundary clipper in turn and clipping information for that edge is immediately passed to the next clipper, which allows the four clipping routines (left, right, bottom, and top) to be operating in parallel. This algorithm provides an efficient method for clipping convex-polygon fill areas. However, when a clipped concave polygon contains disjoint sections, the Sutherland-Hodgman algorithm produces extraneous connecting line segments. Extensions of parametric line clippers, such as the Liang-Barsky method, can also be used to clip convex polygon fill areas. Both convex and concave fill areas can be correctly clipped with the Weiler-Atherton algorithm, which uses a boundary-traversal approach.

Fill areas can be clipped against convex clipping windows using an extension of the parametric line-representation approach. And the Weiler-Atherton method can clip any polygon fill area using any polygon-shaped clipping window. Fill areas can be clipped against windows with nonlinear boundaries by using a polygon approximation for the window or by processing the fill area against the curved window boundaries.

The fastest text-clipping method is the all-or-none strategy, which completely clips a text string if any part of the string is outside any clipping-window boundary. Or we could clip a text string by eliminating only those characters in the string that are not completely inside the clipping window. And the most accurate text-clipping method is to apply either point, line, polygon, or curve clipping to the individual characters in a string, depending on whether characters are defined as point grids or outline fonts.

Although OpenGL is designed for three-dimensional applications, a two-dimensional GLU function is provided for specifying a standard, rectangular clipping window in world coordinates. In OpenGL, the clipping-window coordinates are parameters for the projection transformation. Therefore, we first need to invoke the projection matrix mode. Next we can specify the viewport, using a function in the basic OpenGL library, and a display window, using GLUT functions. A wide range of GLUT functions are available for setting various display-window parameters. Table 6-1 summarizes the OpenGL two-dimensional viewing functions. Additionally, the table lists some viewing-related functions.

REFERENCES

Line-clipping algorithms are discussed in Sproull and Sutherland (1968), Cyrus and Beck (1978), Liang and Barsky (1984), and Nicholl, Lee, and Nicholl (1987). Methods for improving the speed of the Cohen-Sutherland line-clipping algorithm are given in Duvanenko (1990).

Basic polygon-clipping methods are presented in Sutherland and Hodgman (1974) and in Liang and Barsky (1983). General techniques for clipping arbitrarily shaped polygons against each other are given in Weiler and Atherton (1977) and in Weiler (1980).

Viewing operations in OpenGL are discussed in Woo, Neider, Davis, and Shreiner (1999). Display-window GLUT routines are discussed in Kilgard (1996), and additional information on GLUT can be obtained at the Web site: http://reality.sgi.com/opengl/glut3/glut3.html.

EXERCISES

6-1 Write a procedure to calculate the elements of matrix 6-1 for transforming two-dimensional world coordinates to viewing coordinates, given the viewing coordinate origin $\mathbf{P}_0$ and the view up vector $\mathbf{V}$.

6-2 Derive matrix 6-8 for transferring the contents of a clipping window to a viewport by first scaling the window to the size of the viewport, then translating the scaled window to the viewport position. Use the center of the clipping window as the reference point for the scaling and translation operations.

6-3 Write a procedure to calculate the elements of matrix 6-9 for transforming a clipping window to the symmetric normalized square.

6-4 Write a set of procedures to implement the two-dimensional viewing pipeline without clipping operations. Your program should allow a scene to be constructed with modeling-coordinate transformations, a specified viewing system, and a transformation to the symmetric normalized square. As an option, a viewing table could be implemented to store different sets of viewing transformation parameters.

6-5 Write a complete program to implement the Cohen-Sutherland line-clipping algorithm.

6-6 Carefully discuss the rationale behind the various tests and methods for calculating the intersection parameters u_1 and u_2 in the Liang-Barsky line-clipping algorithm.

6-7 Compare the number of arithmetic operations performed in the Cohen-Sutherland and the Liang-Barsky line-clipping algorithms for several different line orientations relative to a clipping window.

6-8 Write a complete program to implement the Liang-Barsky line-clipping algorithm.

6-9 Devise symmetry transformations for mapping the intersection calculations for the three regions in Fig. 6-16 to the other six regions of the xy plane.

6-10 Set up a detailed algorithm for the Nicholl-Lee-Nicholl approach to line clipping for any input pair of line endpoints.

6-11 Compare the number of arithmetic operations performed in the NLN algorithm to both the Cohen-Sutherland and Liang-Barsky line-clipping algorithms, for several different line orientations relative to a clipping window.

6-12 Adapt the Liang-Barsky line-clipping algorithm to polygon clipping.

6-13 Set up a detailed algorithm for Weiler-Atherton polygon clipping, assuming that the clipping window is a rectangle in standard position.

6-14 Devise an algorithm for Weiler-Atherton polygon clipping, where the clipping window can be any convex polygon.

6-15 Devise an algorithm for Weiler-Atherton polygon clipping, where the clipping window can be any specified polygon (convex or concave).

6-16 Write a routine to clip an ellipse in standard position against a rectangular window.

6-17 Assuming that all characters in a text string have the same width, develop a text-clipping algorithm that clips a string according to the all-or-none character-clipping strategy.

6-18 Develop a text-clipping algorithm that clips individual characters, assuming that the characters are defined in a pixel grid of a specified size.

CHAPTER 7

Three-Dimensional Viewing

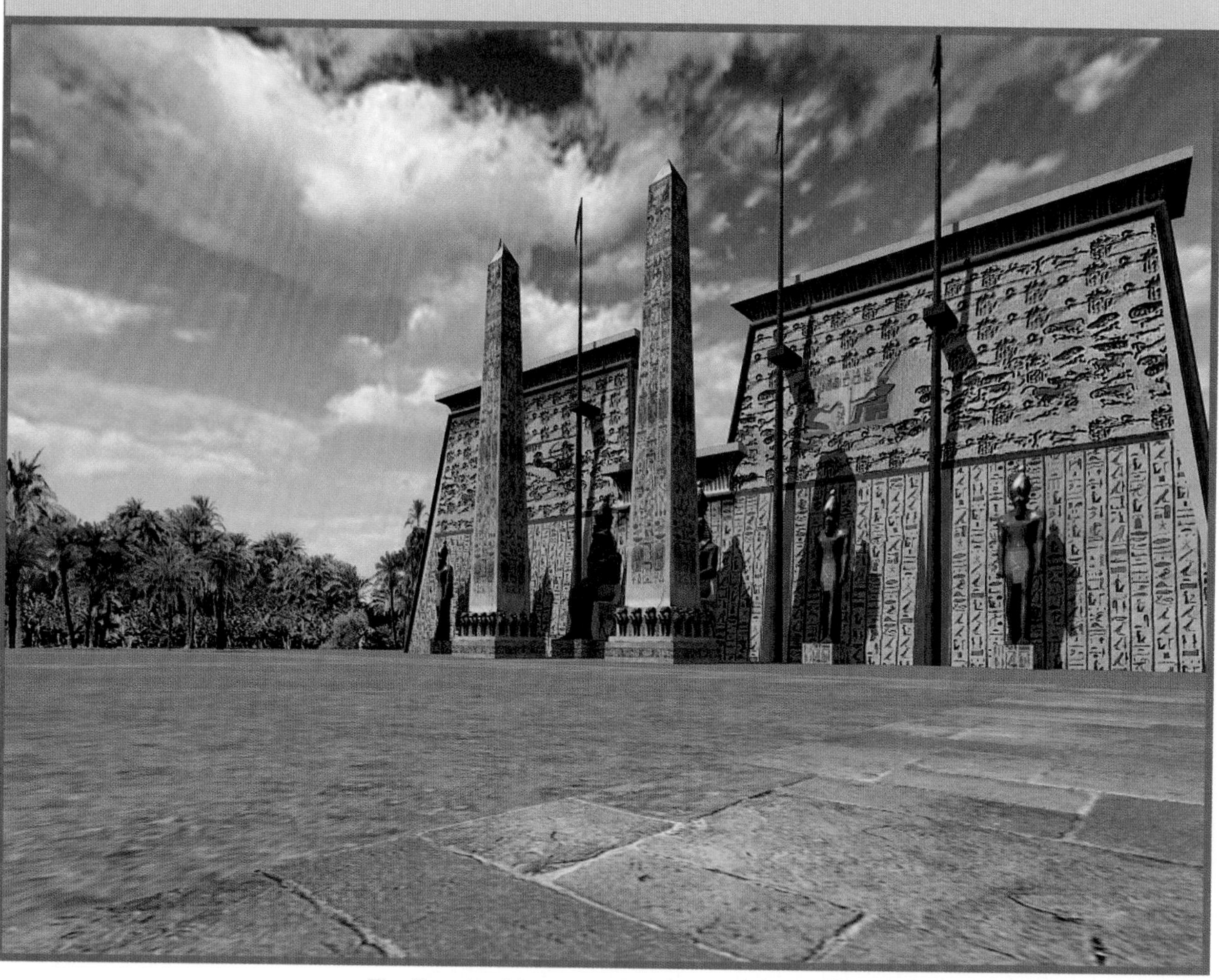

The Temple of Luxor, a scene from an E&S Digital Theater video, featuring real-time, three-dimensional, viewing and computer-animation techniques. *(Courtesy of Evans & Sutherland.)*

For two-dimensional graphics applications, viewing operations transfer positions from the world-coordinate plane to pixel positions in the plane of the output device. Using the rectangular boundaries for the clipping window and the viewport, a two-dimensional package clips a scene and maps it to device coordinates. Three-dimensional viewing operations, however, are more involved, since we now have many more choices as to how we can construct a scene and how we can generate views of the scene on an output device.

7-1 OVERVIEW OF THREE-DIMENSIONAL VIEWING CONCEPTS

When we model a three-dimensional scene, each object in the scene is typically defined with a set of surfaces that form a closed boundary around the object interior. And, for some applications, we may need also to specify information about the interior structure of an object. In addition to procedures that generate views of the surface features of an object, graphics packages sometimes provide routines for displaying internal components or cross-sectional views of a solid object. Viewing functions process the object descriptions through a set of procedures that ultimately project a specified view of the objects onto the surface of a display device. Many processes in three-dimensional viewing, such as the clipping routines, are similar to those in the two-dimensional viewing pipeline. But three-dimensional viewing involves some tasks that are not present in two-dimensional viewing. For example, projection routines are needed to transfer the scene to a view on a planar surface, visible parts of a scene must be identified, and, for a realistic display, lighting effects and surface characteristics must be taken into account.

Viewing a Three-Dimensional Scene

To obtain a display of a three-dimensional world-coordinate scene, we first set up a coordinate reference for the viewing, or "camera", parameters. This coordinate

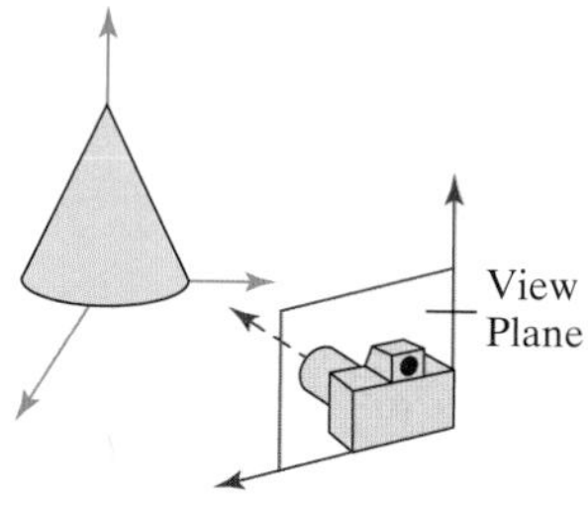

FIGURE 7-1 Coordinate reference for obtaining a selected view of a three-dimensional scene.

reference defines the position and orientation for a *view plane* (or *projection plane*) that corresponds to a camera film plane (Fig. 7-1). Object descriptions are then transferred to the viewing reference coordinates and projected onto the view plane. We can generate a view of an object on the output device in wire-frame (outline) form, as in Fig. 7-2, or we can apply lighting and surface-rendering techniques to obtain a realistic shading of the visible surfaces.

Projections

Unlike a camera picture, we can choose different methods for projecting a scene onto the view plane. One method for getting the description of a solid object onto a view plane is to project points on the object surface along parallel lines. This technique, called *parallel projection,* is used in engineering and architectural drawings to represent an object with a set of views that show accurate dimensions of the object, as in Fig. 7-3.

Another method for generating a view of a three-dimensional scene is to project points to the view plane along converging paths. This process, called a *perspective projection,* causes objects farther from the viewing position to be displayed smaller than objects of the same size that are nearer to the viewing position. A scene that is generated using a perspective projection appears more realistic, since this is the way that our eyes and a camera lens form images. In the perspective-projection view shown in Fig. 7-4, parallel lines along the viewing direction appear to converge to a distant point in the background, and the airplanes in the background are smaller than the airplane taking off in the foreground.

Depth Cueing

With few exceptions, depth information is important in a three-dimensional scene so that we can easily identify, for a particular viewing direction, which is the front

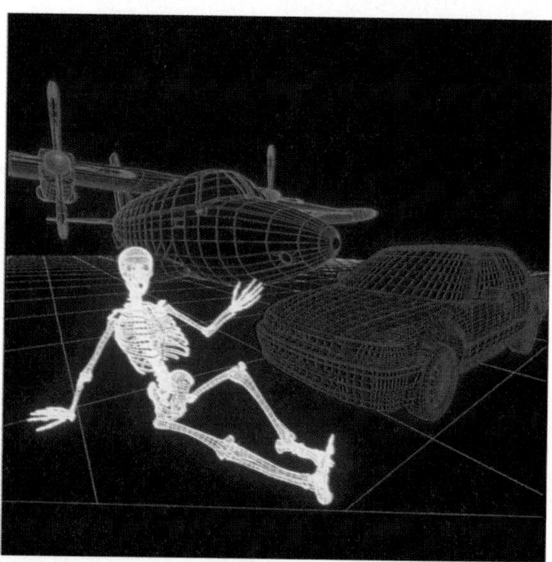

FIGURE 7-2 Wire-frame display of three objects, with back lines removed, from a commercial database of object shapes. Each object in the database is defined as a three-dimensional grid of coordinate points, which can be displayed either as a wire-frame shape or as a surface-rendered solid. (*Courtesy of Viewpoint DataLabs.*)

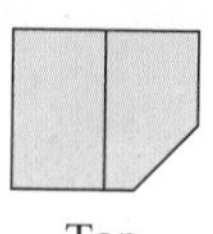

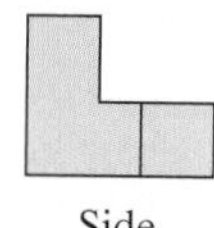

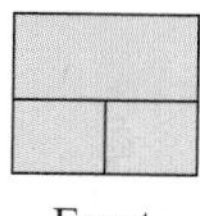

FIGURE 7-3 Three parallel-projection views of an object, showing relative proportions from different viewing positions.

FIGURE 7-4 A perspective-projection view of an airport scene. (*Courtesy of Evans & Sutherland.*)

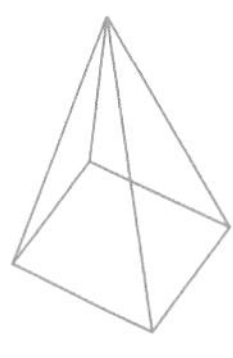

(a)

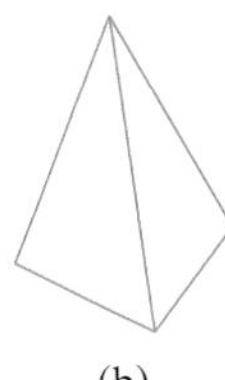

(b)

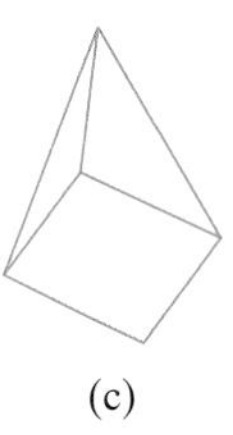

(c)

FIGURE 7-5 The wire-frame representation of the pyramid in (a) contains no depth information to indicate whether the viewing direction is (b) downward from a position above the apex or (c) upward from a position below the base.

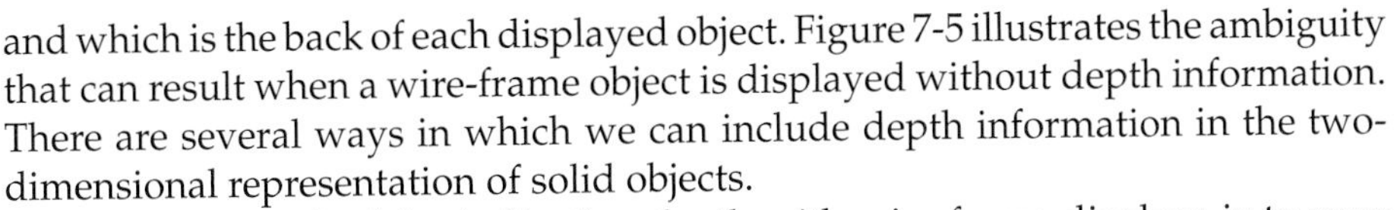

and which is the back of each displayed object. Figure 7-5 illustrates the ambiguity that can result when a wire-frame object is displayed without depth information. There are several ways in which we can include depth information in the two-dimensional representation of solid objects.

A simple method for indicating depth with wire-frame displays is to vary the brightness of line segments according to their distances from the viewing position. Figure 7-6 shows a wire-frame object displayed with *depth cueing*. The lines closest to the viewing position are displayed with the highest intensity, and lines farther away are displayed with decreasing intensities. Depth cueing is applied by choosing a maximum and a minimum intensity value and a range of distances over which the intensity is to vary.

Another application of depth cuing is modeling the effect of the atmosphere on the perceived intensity of objects. More distant objects appear dimmer to us than nearer objects due to light scattering by dust particles, haze, and smoke. Some atmospheric effects can even change the perceived color of an object, and we can model these effects with depth cueing.

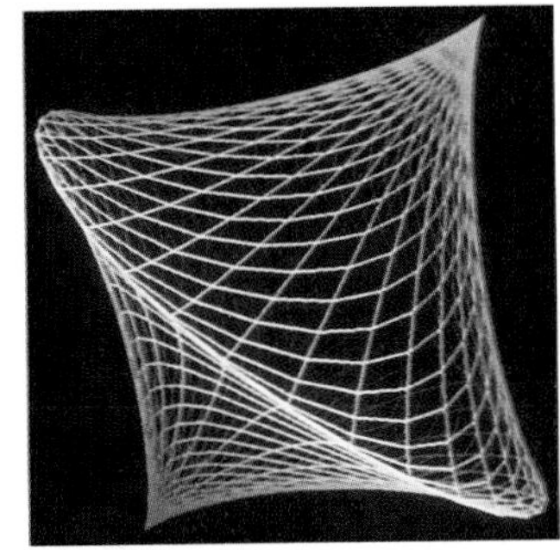

FIGURE 7-6 A wire-frame object displayed with depth cueing, so that the brightness of lines decreases from the front of the object to the back.

Identifying Visible Lines and Surfaces

We can also clarify depth relationships in a wire-frame display using techniques other than depth cueing. One approach is simply to highlight the visible lines or to display them in a different color. Another technique, commonly used for engineering drawings, is to display the nonvisible lines as dashed lines. Or we could remove the nonvisible lines from the display, as in Figs. 7-5(b) and 7-5(c). But removing the hidden lines also removes information about the shape of the back surfaces of an object, and wire-frame representations are generally used to get an indication of an object's overall appearance, front and back.

When a realistic view of a scene is to be produced, back parts of the objects are completely eliminated so that only the visible surfaces are displayed. In this

FIGURE 7-7 A realistic room display, achieved with a perspective projection, illumination effects, and selected surface properties. (*Courtesy of John Snyder, Jed Lengyel, Devendra Kalra, and Al Barr, California Institute of Technology. Copyright © 1992 Caltech.*)

case, surface-rendering procedures are applied so that screen pixels contain only the color patterns for the front surfaces.

Surface Rendering

Added realism is attained in displays by rendering object surfaces using the lighting conditions in the scene and the assigned surface characteristics. We set the lighting conditions by specifying the color and location of the light sources, and we can also set background illumination effects. Surface properties of objects include whether a surface is transparent or opaque and whether the surface is smooth or rough. We set values for parameters to model surfaces such as glass, plastic, wood-grain patterns, and the bumpy appearance of an orange. In Fig. 7-7, surface-rendering methods are combined with perspective and visible-surface identification to generate a degree of realism in a displayed scene.

Exploded and Cutaway Views

Many graphics packages allow objects to be defined as hierarchical structures, so that internal details can be stored. Exploded and cutaway views of such objects can then be used to show the internal structure and relationship of the object parts. Figure 7-8 shows several kinds of exploded displays for a mechanical design. An alternative to exploding an object into its component parts is a cutaway view, as in Fig. 7-9, which removes part of the visible surfaces to show internal structure.

Three-Dimensional and Stereoscopic Viewing

Other methods for adding a sense of realism to a computer-generated scene include three-dimensional displays and stereoscopic views. As we have seen in Chapter 2, three-dimensional views can be obtained by reflecting a raster image from a vibrating, flexible mirror. The vibrations of the mirror are synchronized with the display of the scene on the CRT. As the mirror vibrates, the focal length varies so that each point in the scene is reflected to a spatial position corresponding to its depth.

Stereoscopic devices present two views of a scene: one for the left eye and the other for the right eye. The viewing positions correspond to the eye positions of the viewer. These two views are typically displayed on alternate refresh cycles of a raster monitor. When we view the monitor through special glasses that alternately

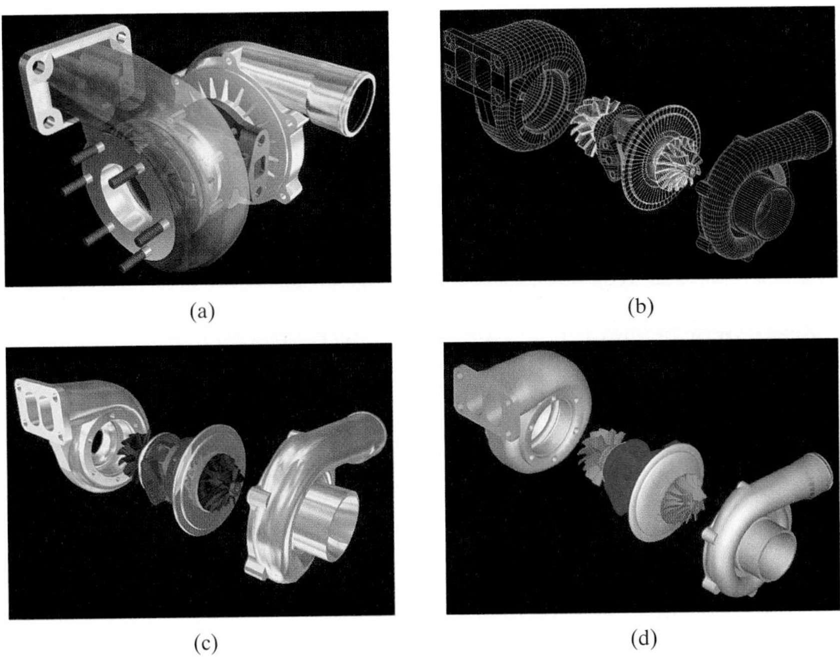
(a) (b) (c) (d)

FIGURE 7-8 A fully rendered and assembled turbine (a) can be viewed as an exploded wire-frame display (b), a surface-rendered exploded display (c), or a surface-rendered, color-coded, exploded display (d). *(Courtesy of Autodesk, Inc.)*

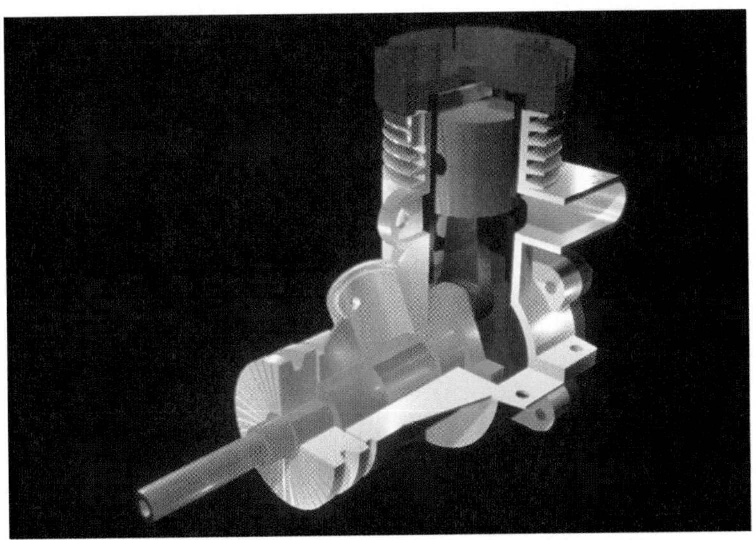

FIGURE 7-9 Color-coded cutaway view of a lawn mower engine, showing the structure and relationship of internal components. *(Courtesy of Autodesk, Inc.)*

darken first one lens then the other, in synchronization with the monitor refresh cycles, we see the scene displayed with a three-dimensional effect.

7-2 THE THREE-DIMENSIONAL VIEWING PIPELINE

Procedures for generating a computer-graphics view of a three-dimensional scene are somewhat analogous to the processes involved in taking a photograph. First of all, we need to choose a viewing position corresponding to where we would place a camera. We choose the viewing position according to whether we want to display a front, back, side, top, or bottom view of the scene. We could also

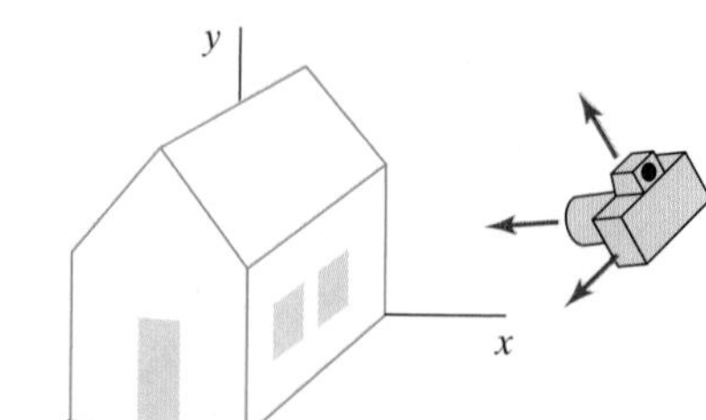

FIGURE 7-10 Photographing a scene involves selection of the camera position and orientation.

pick a position in the middle of a group of objects or even inside a single object, such as a building or a molecule. Then we must decide on the camera orientation (Fig. 7-10). Which way do we want to point the camera from the viewing position, and how should we rotate it around the line of sight to set the "up" direction for the picture? Finally, when we snap the shutter, the scene is cropped to the size of a selected clipping window, which corresponds to the aperture or lens type of a camera, and light from the visible surfaces is projected onto the camera film.

We need to keep in mind, however, that the camera analogy can be carried only so far, since we have more flexibility and many more options for generating views of a scene with a computer-graphics program than we do with a real camera. We can choose to use either a parallel projection or a perspective projection, we can selectively eliminate parts of a scene along the line of sight, we can move the projection plane away from the "camera" position, and we can even get a picture of objects in back of our synthetic camera.

Some of the viewing operations for a three-dimensional scene are the same as, or similar to, those used in the two-dimensional viewing pipeline (Section 6-1). A two-dimensional viewport is used to position a projected view of the three-dimensional scene on the output device, and a two-dimensional clipping window is used to select a view that is to be mapped to the viewport. And we set up a display window in screen coordinates, just as we do in a two-dimensional application. Clipping windows, viewports, and display windows are usually specified as rectangles with their edges parallel to the coordinate axes. In three-dimensional viewing, however, the clipping window is positioned on a selected view plane, and scenes are clipped against an enclosing volume of space, which is defined by a set of *clipping planes*. The viewing position, view plane, clipping window, and clipping planes are all specified within the viewing-coordinate reference frame.

Figure 7-11 shows the general processing steps for creating and transforming a three-dimensional scene to device coordinates. Once the scene has been modeled in world coordinates, a viewing-coordinate system is selected and the description of the scene is converted to viewing coordinates. The viewing coordinate system defines the viewing parameters, including the position and orientation of the projection plane (view plane), which we can think of as the camera film plane. A two-dimensional clipping window, corresponding to a selected camera lens, is defined on the projection plane, and a three-dimensional clipping region is established. This clipping region is called the **view volume,** and its shape and size depends on the dimensions of the clipping window, the type of projection we choose, and the selected limiting positions along the viewing direction. Projection operations are performed to convert the viewing-coordinate description of the scene to coordinate positions on the projection plane. Objects are mapped to normalized coordinates, and all parts of the scene outside the view volume are clipped off. The clipping operations can be applied after all device-independent coordinate transformations (from world coordinates to normalized coordinates)

MC → Modeling Transformation → WC → Viewing Transformation → VC → Projection Transformation → PC → Normalization Transformation and Clipping → NC → Viewport Transformation → DC

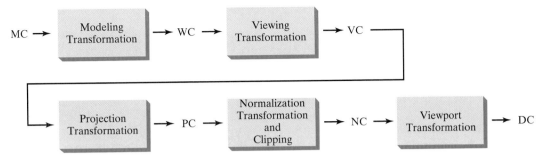

FIGURE 7-11 General three-dimensional transformation pipeline, from modeling coordinates to world coordinates to viewing coordinates to projection coordinates to normalized coordinates and, ultimately, to device coordinates.

are completed. In this way, the coordinate transformations can be concatenated for maximum efficiency.

As in two-dimensional viewing, the viewport limits could be given in normalized coordinates or in device coordinates. In developing the viewing algorithms, we will assume that the viewport is to be specified in device coordinates and that normalized coordinates are transferred to viewport coordinates, following the clipping operations. There are also a few other tasks that must be performed, such as identifying visible surfaces and applying the surface-rendering procedures. The final step is to map viewport coordinates to device coordinates within a selected display window. Scene descriptions in device coordinates are sometimes expressed in a left-handed reference frame so that positive distances from the display screen can be used to measure depth values in the scene.

7-3 THREE-DIMENSIONAL VIEWING-COORDINATE PARAMETERS

Establishing a three-dimensional viewing reference frame is similar to setting up the two-dimensional viewing reference frame discussed in Section 6-2. We first select a world-coordinate position $\mathbf{P}_0 = (x_0, y_0, z_0)$ for the viewing origin, which is called the **view point** or **viewing position.** (Sometimes the view point is also referred to as the *eye position* or the *camera position.*) And we specify a **view-up vector V,** which defines the y_{view} direction. For three-dimensional space, we also need to assign a direction for one of the remaining two coordinate axes. This is typically accomplished with a second vector that defines the z_{view} axis, with the viewing direction along this axis. Figure 7-12 illustrates the positioning of a three dimensional viewing-coordinate frame within a world system.

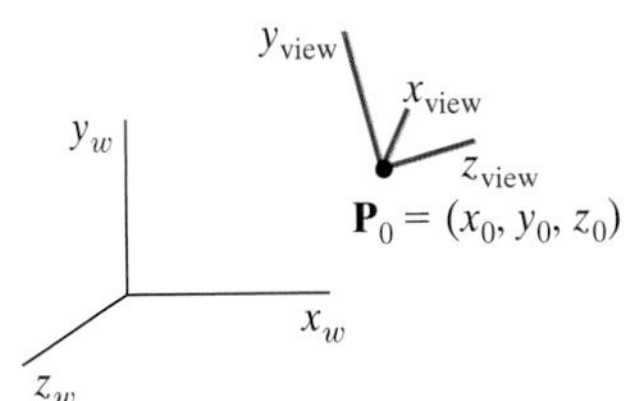

FIGURE 7-12 A right-handed viewing-coordinate system, with axes x_{view}, y_{view}, and z_{view}, relative to a right-handed world-coordinate frame.

The View-Plane Normal Vector

Because the viewing direction is usually along the z_{view} axis, the **view plane,** also called the **projection plane,** is normally assumed to be perpendicular to this axis. Thus, the orientation of the view plane, as well as the direction for the positive z_{view} axis, can be defined with a **view-plane normal vector N**, as shown in Fig. 7-13.

An additional scalar parameter is used to set the position of the view plane at some coordinate value z_{vp} along the z_{view} axis, as illustrated in Fig. 7-14. This parameter value is usually specified as a distance from the viewing origin along

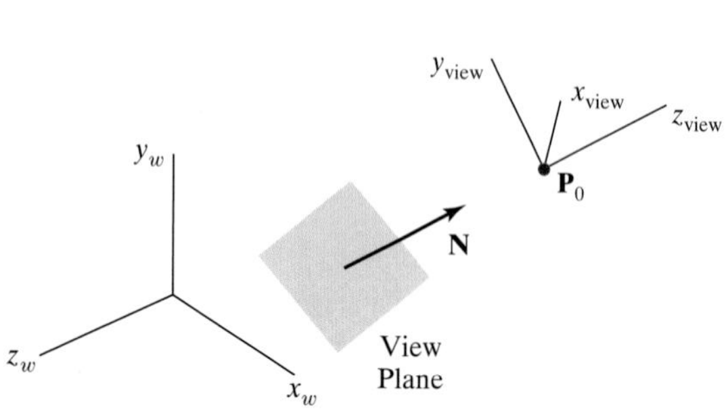

FIGURE 7-13 Orientation of the view plane and view-plane normal vector **N**.

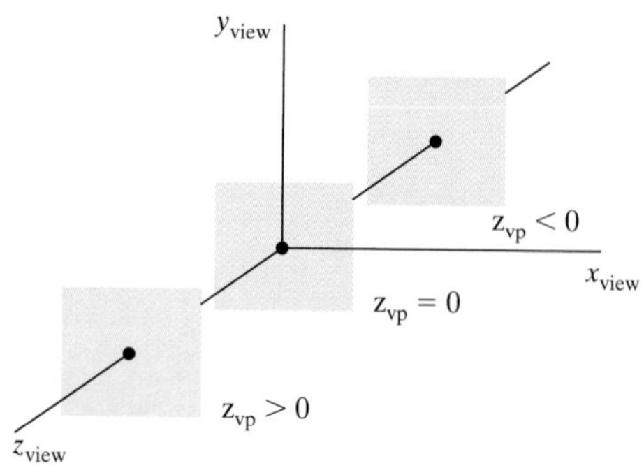

FIGURE 7-14 Three possible positions for the view plane along the z_{view} axis.

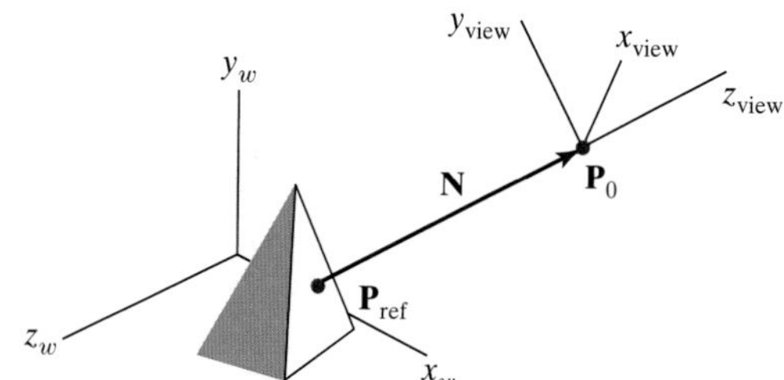

FIGURE 7-15 Specifying the view-plane normal vector **N** as the direction from a selected reference point $\mathbf{P}_{ref}$ to the viewing-coordinate origin $\mathbf{P}_0$.

the direction of viewing, which is often taken to be in the negative z_{view} direction. Thus, the view plane is always parallel to the $x_{view}y_{view}$ plane, and the projection of objects to the view plane corresponds to the view of the scene that will be displayed on the output device.

Vector **N** can be specified in various ways. In some graphics systems, the direction for **N** is defined as along the line from the world-coordinate origin to a selected point position. Other systems take **N** to be in the direction from a reference point $\mathbf{P}_{ref}$ to the viewing origin $\mathbf{P}_0$, as in Fig. 7-15. In this case, the reference point is often referred to as a *look-at point* within the scene, with the viewing direction opposite to the direction of **N**.

We could also define the view-plane normal vector, and other vector directions, using *direction angles*. These are the three angles, α, β, and γ, that a spatial line makes with the x, y, and z axes, respectively. But it is usually much easier to specify a vector direction with two point positions in a scene than with direction angles.

The View-Up Vector

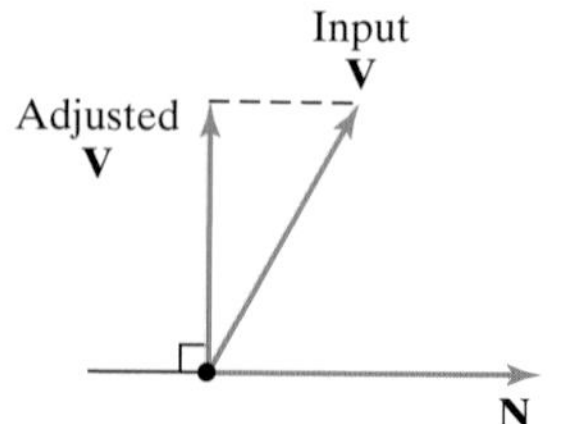

FIGURE 7-16 Adjusting the input direction of the view-up vector **V** to an orientation perpendicular to the view-plane normal vector **N**.

Once we have chosen a view-plane normal vector **N**, we can set the direction for the view-up vector **V**. This vector is used to establish the positive direction for the y_{view} axis.

Usually, **V** is defined by selecting a position relative to the world-coordinate origin, so that the direction for the view-up vector is from the world origin to this selected position. Since the view-plane normal vector **N** defines the direction for the z_{view} axis, vector **V** should be perpendicular to **N**. But, in general, it can be difficult to determine a direction for **V** that is precisely perpendicular to **N**. Therefore, viewing routines typically adjust the user-defined orientation of vector **V**, as shown in Fig. 7-16, so that **V** is projected onto a plane that is perpendicular to the view-plane normal vector.

We can choose any direction for the view-up vector **V**, as long as it is not parallel to **N**. A convenient choice is often in a direction parallel to the world y_w axis; that is, we could set $\mathbf{V} = (0, 1, 0)$.

The uvn Viewing-Coordinate Reference Frame

Left-handed viewing coordinates are sometimes used in graphics packages, with the viewing direction in the positive z_{view} direction. With a left-handed system, increasing z_{view} values are interpreted as being farther from the viewing position along the line of sight. But right-handed viewing systems are more common, since they have the same orientation as the world-reference frame. This allows a graphics package to deal with only one coordinate orientation for both world and viewing references. Although some early graphics packages defined viewing coordinates within a left-handed frame, right-handed viewing coordinates are now used by the graphics standards. However, left-handed coordinate references are often used to represent screen coordinates and for the normalization transformation.

Since the view-plane normal **N** defines the direction for the z_{view} axis and the view-up vector **V** is used to obtain the direction for the y_{view} axis, we need only determine the direction for the x_{view} axis. Using the input values for **N** and **V**, we can compute a third vector **U** that is perpendicular to both **N** and **V**. Vector **U** then defines the direction for the positive x_{view} axis. We determine the correct direction for **U** by taking the vector cross product of **V** and **N** so as to form a right-handed viewing frame. The vector cross product of **N** and **U** also produces the adjusted value for **V**, perpendicular to both **N** and **U**, along the positive y_{view} axis. Following these procedures, we obtain the following set of unit axis vectors for a right-handed viewing coordinate system.

$$
\begin{aligned}
\mathbf{n} &= \frac{\mathbf{N}}{|\mathbf{N}|} = (n_x, n_y, n_z) \\
\mathbf{u} &= \frac{\mathbf{V} \times \mathbf{n}}{|\mathbf{V}|} = (u_x, u_y, u_z) \qquad (7\text{-}1) \\
\mathbf{v} &= \mathbf{n} \times \mathbf{u} = (v_x, v_y, v_z)
\end{aligned}
$$

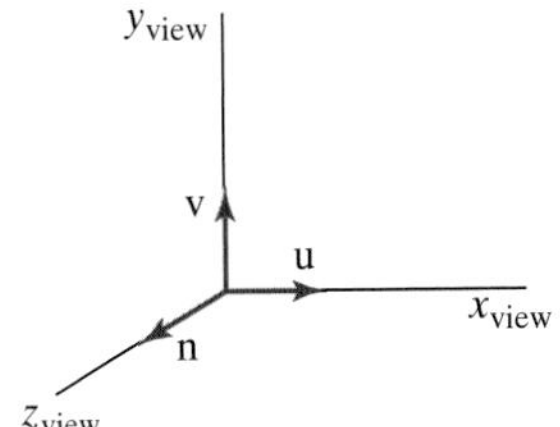

FIGURE 7-17 A right-handed viewing system defined with unit vectors **u**, **v**, and **n**.

The coordinate system formed with these unit vectors is often described as a **uvn viewing-coordinate reference frame** (Fig. 7-17).

Generating Three-Dimensional Viewing Effects

By varying the viewing parameters, we can obtain different views of objects in a scene. For instance, from a fixed viewing position, we could change the direction of **N** to display objects at positions around the viewing-coordinate origin. We could also vary **N** to create a composite display consisting of multiple views from a fixed camera position. Figure 7-18 shows a wide-angle display created for a virtual-reality environment. The wide viewing angle is attained by producing seven views of the scene from the same viewing position, but with slight shifts in the viewing direction, then the views are combined to form a composite display. Similarly, we generate stereoscopic views by shifting the viewing direction. In this case, however, we also need to shift the view point to simulate the two eye positions.

In interactive applications, the normal vector **N** is the viewing parameter that is most often changed. Of course, when we change the direction for **N**, we also have

FIGURE 7-18 A wide-angle view for a virtual-reality display generated with seven sections, each from a slightly different viewing direction. (*Courtesy of the National Center for Supercomputing Applications, University of Illinois at Urbana-Champaign.*)

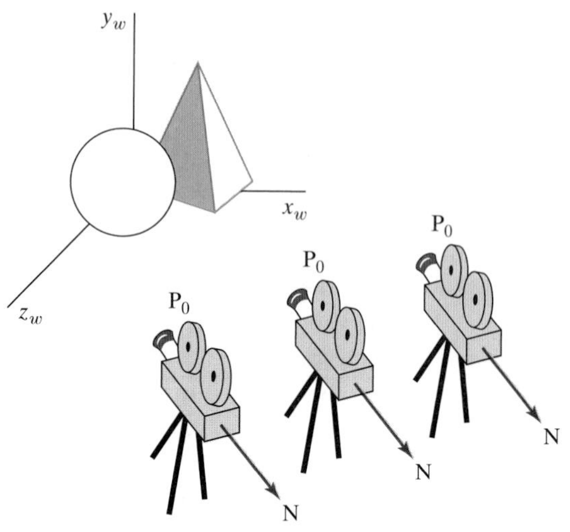

FIGURE 7-19 Panning across a scene by changing the viewing position, with a fixed direction for **N**.

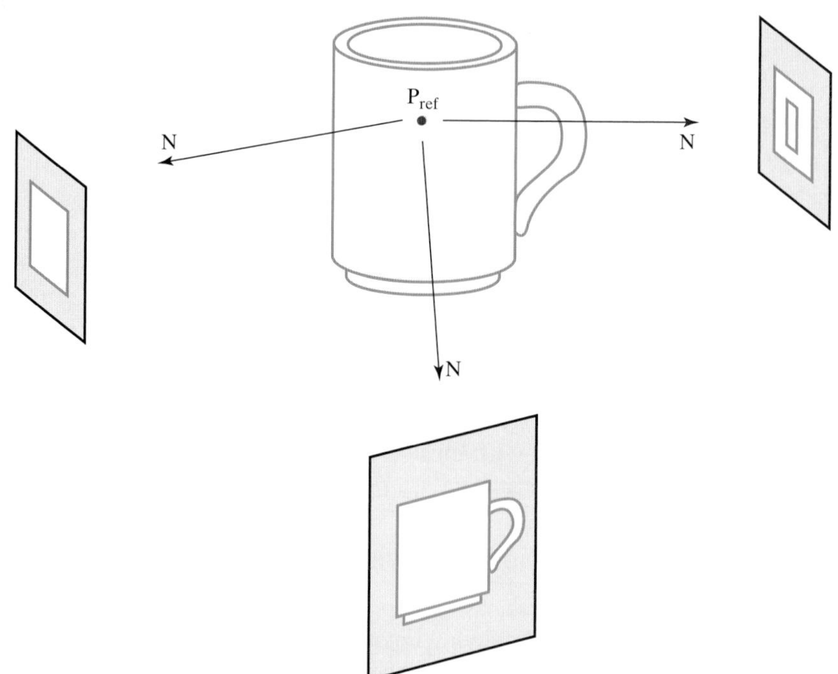

FIGURE 7-20 Viewing an object from different directions using a fixed reference point.

to change the other axis vectors to maintain a right-handed viewing-coordinate system.

If we want to simulate an animation panning effect, as when a camera moves through a scene or follows an object that is moving through a scene, we can keep the direction for **N** fixed as we move the view point, as illustrated in Fig. 7-19. And to display different views of an object, such as a side view and a front view, we could move the view point around the object, as in Fig. 7-20. Alternatively,

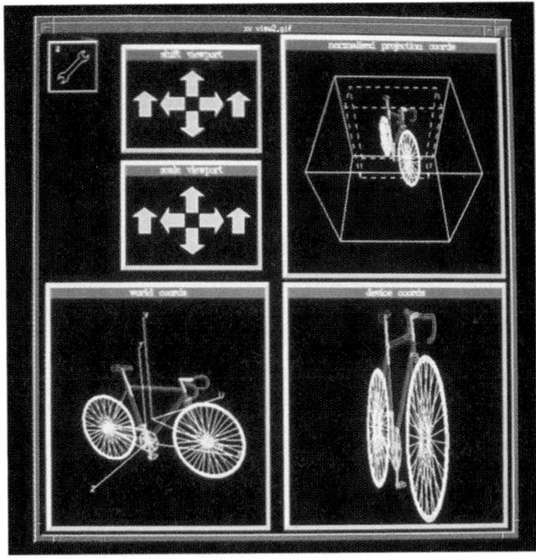

FIGURE 7-21 An interactive interface for controlling viewing parameters, developed at the University of Manchester using the PHIGS Toolkit. (*Courtesy of T. L. J. Howard, J. G. Williams, and W. T. Hewitt, Department of Computer Science, University of Manchester, United Kingdom.*)

different views of an object or group of objects can be generated using geometric transformations without changing the viewing parameters.

Figure 7-21 shows an interface developed for an interactive selection of viewing-parameter values. This software includes a viewing editor, selection of multiple display windows, menus, and other interface tools.

7-4 TRANSFORMATION FROM WORLD TO VIEWING COORDINATES

In the three-dimensional viewing pipeline, the first step after a scene has been constructed is to transfer object descriptions to the viewing-coordinate reference frame. This conversion of object descriptions is equivalent to a sequence of transformations that superimposes the viewing reference frame onto the world frame. We can accomplish this conversion using the methods for transforming between coordinate systems described in Section 5-15:

(1) Translate the viewing-coordinate origin to the origin of the world-coordinate system.

(2) Apply rotations to align the x_{view}, y_{view}, and z_{view} axes with the world x_w, y_w, and z_w axes, respectively.

The viewing-coordinate origin is at world position $\mathbf{P} = (x_0, y_0, z_0)$. Therefore, the matrix for translating the viewing origin to the world origin is

$$\mathbf{T} = \begin{bmatrix} 1 & 0 & 0 & -x_0 \\ 0 & 1 & 0 & -y_0 \\ 0 & 0 & 1 & -z_0 \\ 0 & 0 & 0 & 1 \end{bmatrix} \tag{7-2}$$

For the rotation transformation, we can use the unit vectors **u**, **v**, and **n** to form the composite rotation matrix that superimposes the viewing axes onto the world frame. This transformation matrix is

$$\mathbf{R} = \begin{bmatrix} u_x & u_y & u_z & 0 \\ v_x & v_y & v_z & 0 \\ n_x & n_y & n_z & 0 \\ 0 & 0 & 0 & 1 \end{bmatrix} \tag{7-3}$$

where the elements of matrix **R** are the components of the **uvn** axis vectors.

The coordinate transformation matrix is then obtained as the product of the preceding translation and rotation matrices:

$$\begin{aligned} \mathbf{M}_{WC,\,VC} &= \mathbf{R} \cdot \mathbf{T} \\ &= \begin{bmatrix} u_x & u_y & u_z & -\mathbf{u} \cdot \mathbf{P}_0 \\ v_x & v_y & v_z & -\mathbf{v} \cdot \mathbf{P}_0 \\ n_x & n_y & n_z & -\mathbf{n} \cdot \mathbf{P}_0 \\ 0 & 0 & 0 & 1 \end{bmatrix} \end{aligned} \tag{7-4}$$

Translation factors in this matrix are calculated as the vector dot product of each of the **u**, **v**, and **n** unit vectors with $\mathbf{P}_0$, which represents a vector from the world origin to the viewing origin. In other words, the translation factors are the negative projections of $\mathbf{P}_0$ on each of the viewing-coordinate axes (the negative components of $\mathbf{P}_0$ in viewing coordinates). These matrix elements are evaluated as

$$\begin{aligned} -\mathbf{u} \cdot \mathbf{P}_0 &= -x_0 u_x - y_0 u_y - z_0 u_z \\ -\mathbf{v} \cdot \mathbf{P}_0 &= -x_0 v_x - y_0 v_y - z_0 v_z \\ -\mathbf{n} \cdot \mathbf{P}_0 &= -x_0 n_x - y_0 n_y - z_0 n_z \end{aligned} \tag{7-5}$$

Matrix 7-4 transfers world-coordinate object descriptions to the viewing reference frame.

7-5 PROJECTION TRANSFORMATIONS

In the next phase of the three-dimensional viewing pipeline, after the transformation to viewing coordinates, object descriptions are projected to the view plane. Graphics packages generally support both parallel and perspective projections.

In a **parallel projection,** coordinate positions are transferred to the view plane along parallel lines. Figure 7-22 illustrates a parallel projection for a straight-line segment defined with endpoint coordinates $\mathbf{P}_1$ and $\mathbf{P}_2$. A parallel projection preserves relative proportions of objects, and this is the method used in computer-aided drafting and design to produce scale drawings of three-dimensional objects. All parallel lines in a scene are displayed as parallel when viewed with a parallel projection. There are two general methods for obtaining a parallel-projection view of an object: We can project along lines that are perpendicular to the view plane, or we can project at an oblique angle to the view plane.

For a **perspective projection,** object positions are transformed to projection coordinates along lines that converge to a point behind the view plane. An example of a perspective projection for a straight-line segment, defined with endpoint coordinates $\mathbf{P}_1$ and $\mathbf{P}_2$, is given in Fig. 7-23. Unlike a parallel projection, a perspective projection does not preserve relative proportions of objects. But perspective views of a scene are more realistic because distant objects in the projected display are reduced in size.

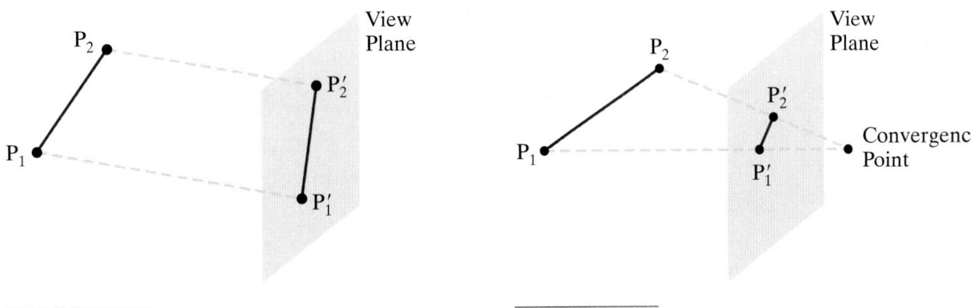

FIGURE 7-22 Parallel projection of a line segment onto a view plane.

FIGURE 7-23 Perspective projection of a line segment onto a view plane.

7-6 ORTHOGONAL PROJECTIONS

A transformation of object descriptions to a view plane along lines that are all parallel to the view-plane normal vector **N** is called an **orthogonal projection** (or, equivalently, an **orthographic projection**). This produces a parallel-projection transformation in which the projection lines are perpendicular to the view plane. Orthogonal projections are most often used to produce the front, side, and top views of an object, as shown in Fig. 7-24. Front, side, and rear orthogonal projections of an object are called *elevations;* and a top orthogonal projection is called a *plan view*. Engineering and architectural drawings commonly employ these orthographic projections, since lengths and angles are accurately depicted and can be measured from the drawings.

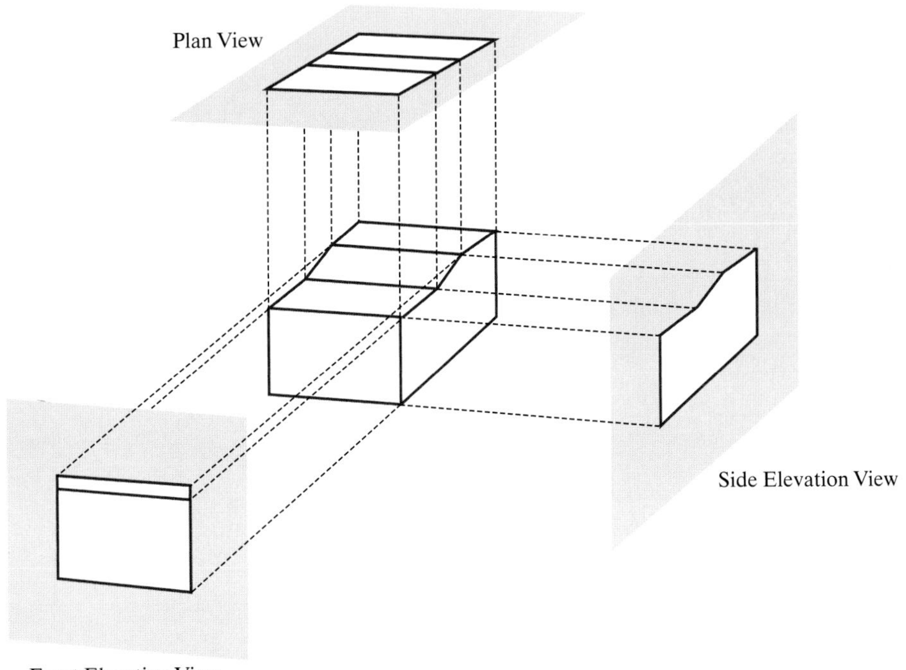

FIGURE 7-24 Orthogonal projections of an object, displaying plan and elevation views.

Axonometric and Isometric Orthogonal Projections

We can also form orthogonal projections that display more than one face of an object. Such views are called **axonometric** orthogonal projections. The most commonly used axonometric projection is the **isometric** projection, which is generated by aligning the projection plane (or the object) so that the plane intersects each coordinate axis in which the object is defined, called the *principal axes,* at the same distance from the origin. Figure 7-25 shows an isometric projection for a cube. We can obtain the isometric projection shown in this figure by aligning the view-plane normal vector along a cube diagonal. There are eight positions, one in each octant, for obtaining an isometric view. All three principal axes are foreshortened equally in an isometric projection, so that relative proportions are maintained. This is not the case in a general axonometric projection, where scaling factors may be different for the three principal directions.

Orthogonal Projection Coordinates

With the projection direction parallel to the z_{view} axis, the transformation equations for an orthogonal projection are trivial. For any position (x, y, z) in viewing coordinates, as in Fig. 7-26, the projection coordinates are

$$x_p = x, \qquad y_p = y \tag{7-6}$$

The z-coordinate value for any projection transformation is preserved for use in the visibility determination procedures. And each three-dimensional coordinate point in a scene is converted to a position in normalized space.

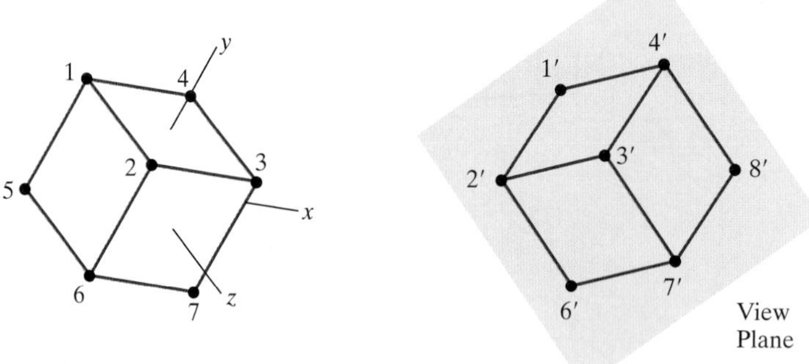

FIGURE 7-25 An isometric projection of a cube.

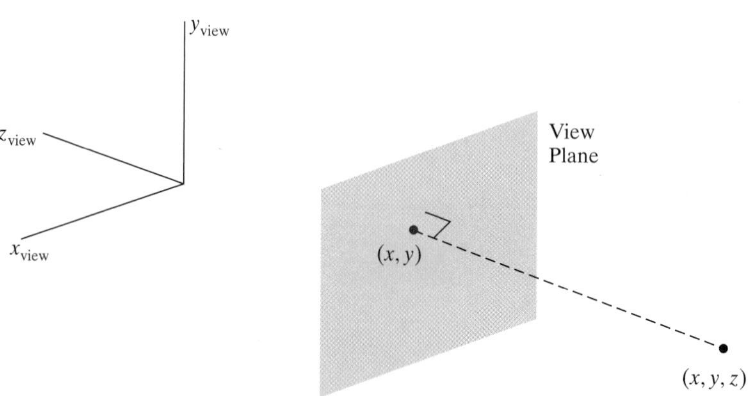

FIGURE 7-26 Orthogonal projection of a spatial position onto a view plane.

Clipping Window and Orthogonal-Projection View Volume

In the camera analogy, the type of lens is one factor that determines how much of the scene is transferred to the film plane. A wide-angle lens takes in more of the scene than a regular lens. For computer-graphics applications, we use the rectangular *clipping window* for this purpose. As in two-dimensional viewing, graphics packages typically allow only clipping rectangles in standard position. Therefore, we set up a clipping window for three-dimensional viewing, just as we did for two-dimensional viewing, by choosing two-dimensional coordinate positions for its lower-left and upper-right corners. For three-dimensional viewing, the clipping window is positioned on the view plane with its edges parallel to the x_{view} and y_{view} axes, as shown in Fig. 7-27. If we want to use some other shape or orientation for the clipping window, we must develop our own viewing procedures.

The edges of the clipping window specify the x and y limits for the part of the scene that we want to display. These limits are used to form the top, bottom, and two sides of a clipping region called the **orthogonal-projection view volume.** Since projection lines are perpendicular to the view plane, these four boundaries are planes that are also perpendicular to the view plane and that pass through the edges of the clipping window to form an infinite clipping region, as in Fig. 7-28.

We can limit the extent of the orthogonal view volume in the z_{view} direction by selecting positions for one or two additional boundary planes that are parallel to the view plane. These two planes are called the **near-far clipping planes,** or the

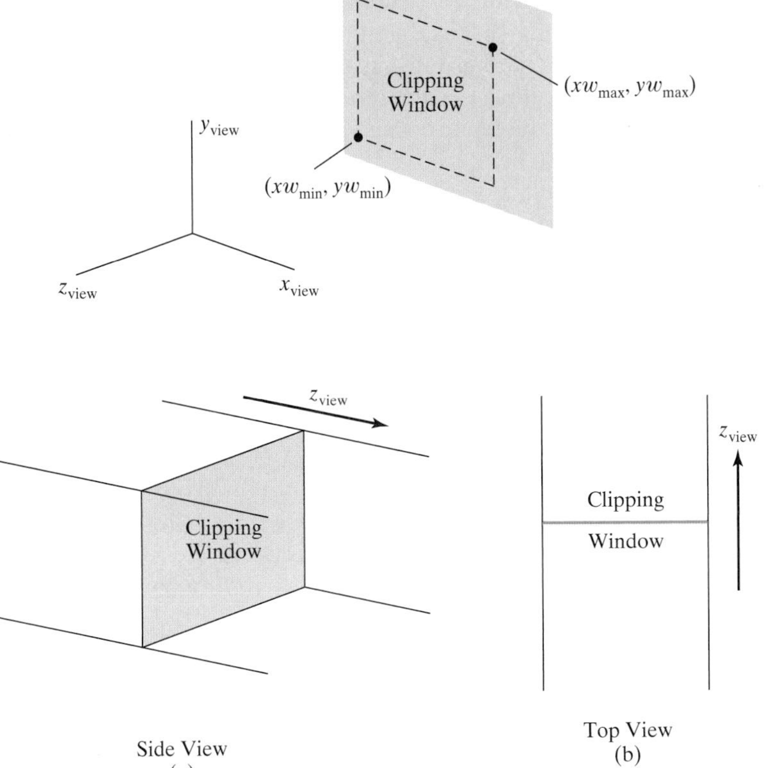

FIGURE 7-27 A clipping window on the view plane, with minimum and maximum coordinates given in the viewing reference system.

FIGURE 7-28 Infinite orthogonal-projection view volume.

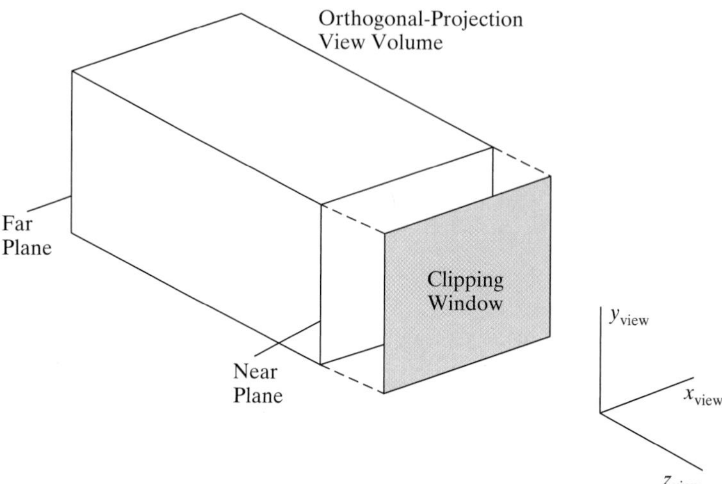

FIGURE 7–29 A finite orthogonal view volume with the view plane "in front" of the near plane.

front-back clipping planes. The near and far planes allow us to exclude objects that are in front of or behind the part of the scene that we want to display. With the viewing direction along the negative z_{view} axis, we usually have $z_{\text{far}} < z_{\text{near}}$, so that the far plane is father out along the negative z_{view} axis. Some graphics libraries provide these two planes as options, and other libraries require them. When the near and far planes are specified, we obtain a finite orthogonal view volume which is a *rectangular parallelepiped,* as shown in Fig. 7-29 along with one possible placement for the view plane. Our view of the scene will then contain only those objects within the view volume, with all parts of the scene outside the view volume eliminated by the clipping algorithms.

Graphics packages provide varying degrees of flexibility in the positioning of the near and far clipping planes, including options for specifying additional clipping planes at other positions in the scene. In general, the near and far planes can be in any relative position to each other to achieve various viewing effects, including positions that are on opposite sides of the view point. Similarly, the view plane can sometimes be placed in any position relative to the near and far clipping planes, although it is often taken to be coincident with the near clipping plane. However, providing numerous positioning options for the clipping and view planes usually results in less efficient processing of a three-dimensional scene.

Normalization Transformation for an Orthogonal Projection

Using an orthogonal transfer of coordinate positions onto the view plane, we obtain the projected position of any spatial point (x, y, z) as simply (x, y). Thus, once we have established the limits for the view volume, coordinate descriptions inside this rectangular parallelepiped are the projection coordinates, and they can be mapped into a **normalized view volume** without any further projection processing. Some graphics packages use a unit cube for this normalized view volume, with each of the x, y, and z coordinates normalized in the range from 0 to 1. Another normalization-transformation approach is to use a symmetric cube, with coordinates in the range from -1 to 1.

Since screen coordinates are often specified in a left-handed reference frame (Fig. 7-30), normalized coordinates also are often specified in a left-handed system. This allows positive distances in the viewing direction to be directly interpreted

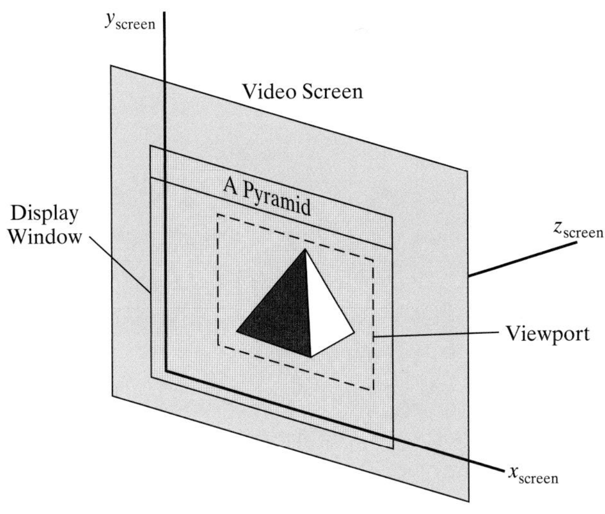

FIGURE 7-30 A left-handed screen-coordinate reference frame.

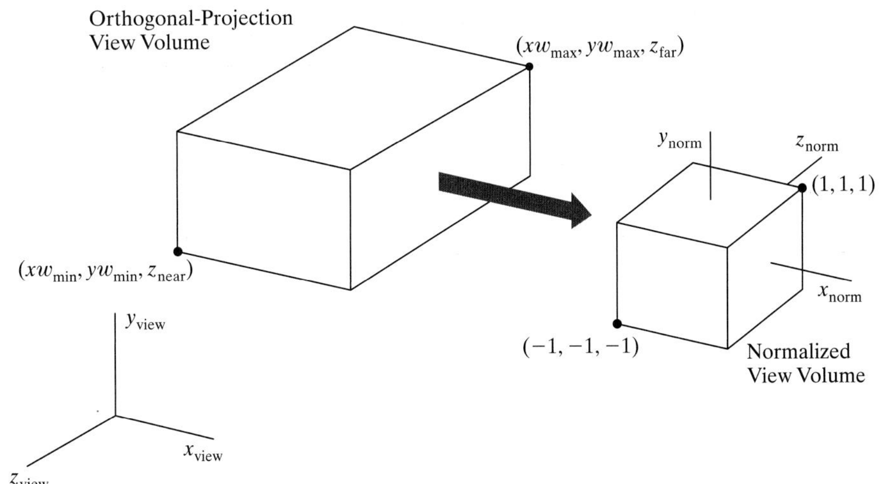

FIGURE 7-31 Normalization transformation from an orthogonal-projection view volume to the symmetric normalization cube within a left-handed reference frame.

as distances from the screen (the viewing plane). Thus, we can convert projection coordinates into positions within a left-handed normalized-coordinate reference frame, and these coordinate positions will then be transferred to left-handed screen coordinates by the viewport transformation.

To illustrate the normalization transformation, we assume that the orthogonal-projection view volume is to be mapped into the symmetric normalization cube within a left-handed reference frame. Also, z-coordinate positions for the near and far planes are denoted as z_{near} and z_{far}, respectively. Figure 7-31 illustrates this normalization transformation. Position $(x_{min}, y_{min}, z_{near})$ is mapped to the normalized position $(-1, -1, -1)$, and position $(x_{max}, y_{max}, z_{far})$ is mapped to $(1, 1, 1)$.

Transforming the rectangular-parallelepiped view volume to a normalized cube is similar to the methods discussed in Section 6-3 for converting the clipping window into the normalized symmetric square. The normalization transformation for the x and y positions within the orthogonal view volume is given by the normalization matrix 6-9. In addition, we need to transform z-coordinate values in the range from z_{near} to z_{far} to the interval from -1 to 1 using similar calculations.

Therefore, the normalization transformation for the orthogonal view volume is

$$\mathbf{M}_{\text{ortho,norm}} = \begin{bmatrix} \frac{2}{xw_{\max} - xw_{\min}} & 0 & 0 & -\frac{xw_{\max} + xw_{\min}}{xw_{\max} - xw_{\min}} \\ 0 & \frac{2}{yw_{\max} - yw_{\min}} & 0 & -\frac{yw_{\max} + yw_{\min}}{yw_{\max} - yw_{\min}} \\ 0 & 0 & \frac{-2}{z_{\text{near}} - z_{\text{far}}} & \frac{z_{\text{near}} + z_{\text{far}}}{z_{\text{near}} - z_{\text{far}}} \\ 0 & 0 & 0 & 1 \end{bmatrix} \tag{7-7}$$

This matrix is multiplied on the right by the composite viewing transformation $\mathbf{R} \cdot \mathbf{T}$ (Section 7-4) to produce the complete transformation from world coordinates to normalized orthogonal-projection coordinates.

At this stage of the viewing pipeline, all device-independent coordinate transformations are completed and can be concatenated into a single composite matrix. Thus, the clipping procedures are most efficiently performed following the normalization transformation. After clipping, procedures for visibility testing, surface rendering, and the viewport transformation can be applied to generate the final screen display of the scene.

7-7 OBLIQUE PARALLEL PROJECTIONS

In general, a parallel-projection view of a scene is obtained by transferring object descriptions to the view plane along projection paths that can be in any selected direction relative to the view-plane normal vector. When the projection path is not perpendicular to the view plane, this mapping is called an **oblique parallel projection.** Using this projection, we can produce combinations such as a front, side, and top view of an object, as in Fig. 7-32. Oblique parallel projections are defined by a vector direction for the projection lines, and this direction can be specified in various ways.

Oblique Parallel Projections in Drafting and Design

For applications in engineering and architectural design, an oblique parallel projection is often specified with two angles, α and ϕ, as shown in Fig. 7-33. A spatial position (x, y, z), in this illustration, is projected to (x_p, y_p, z_{vp}) on a view plane,

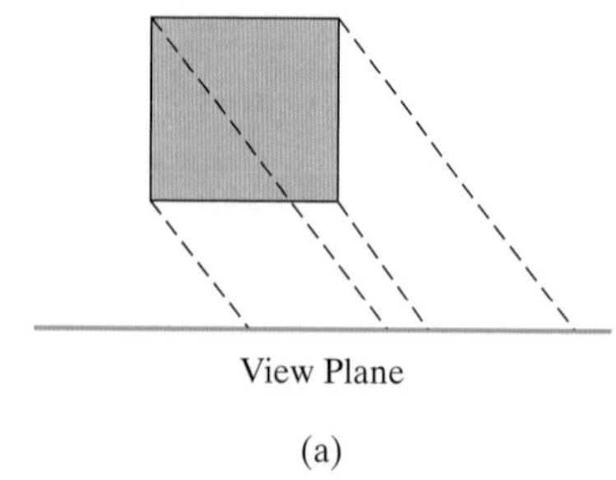

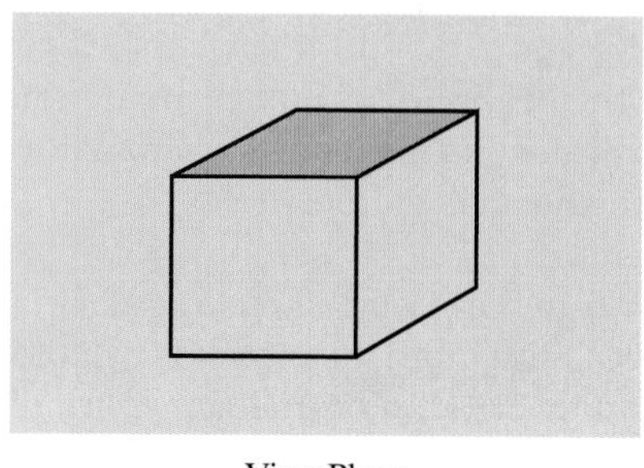

FIGURE 7-32 An oblique parallel projection of a cube, shown in a top view (a), produces a view (b) containing multiple surfaces of the cube.

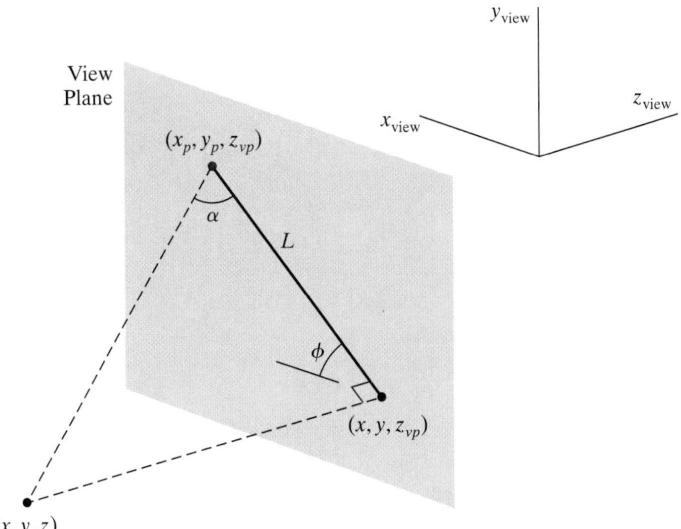

FIGURE 7-33 Oblique parallel projection of coordinate position (x, y, z) to position (x_p, y_p, z_{vp}) on a projection plane at position z_{vp} along the z_{view} axis.

which is at location z_{vp} along the viewing z axis. Position (x, y, z_{vp}) is the corresponding orthogonal-projection point. The oblique parallel projection line from (x, y, z) to (x_p, y_p, z_{vp}) has an intersection angle α with the line on the projection plane that joins (x_p, y_p, z_{vp}) and (x, y, z_{vp}). This view-plane line, with length L, is at an angle ϕ with the horizontal direction in the projection plane. Angle α can be assigned a value between 0 and 90°, and angle ϕ can vary from 0 to 360°. We can express the projection coordinates in terms of x, y, L, and ϕ as

$$
\begin{aligned}
x_p &= x + L\cos\phi \\
y_p &= y + L\sin\phi
\end{aligned}
\tag{7-8}
$$

Length L depends on the angle α and the perpendicular distance of the point (x, y, z) from the view plane:

$$
\tan\alpha = \frac{z_{vp} - z}{L} \tag{7-9}
$$

Thus

$$
\begin{aligned}
L &= \frac{z_{vp} - z}{\tan\alpha} \\
&= L_1(z_{vp} - z)
\end{aligned}
\tag{7-10}
$$

where $L_1 = \cot\alpha$, which is also the value of L when $z_{vp} - z = 1$. We can then write the oblique parallel projection equations 7-8 as

$$
\begin{aligned}
x_p &= x + L_1(z_{vp} - z)\cos\phi \\
y_p &= y + L_1(z_{vp} - z)\sin\phi
\end{aligned}
\tag{7-11}
$$

An orthogonal projection is obtained when $L_1 = 0$ (which occurs at the projection angle $\alpha = 90°$).

Equations 7-11 represent a z-axis shearing transformation (Section 5-14). In fact, the effect of an oblique parallel projection is to shear planes of constant z and project them onto the view plane. The (x, y) positions on each plane of constant z

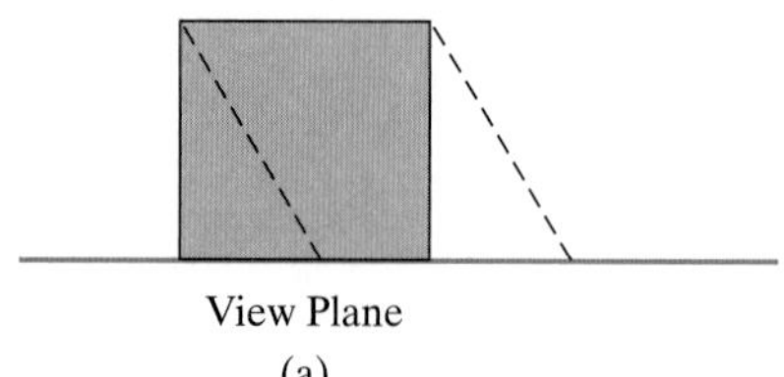

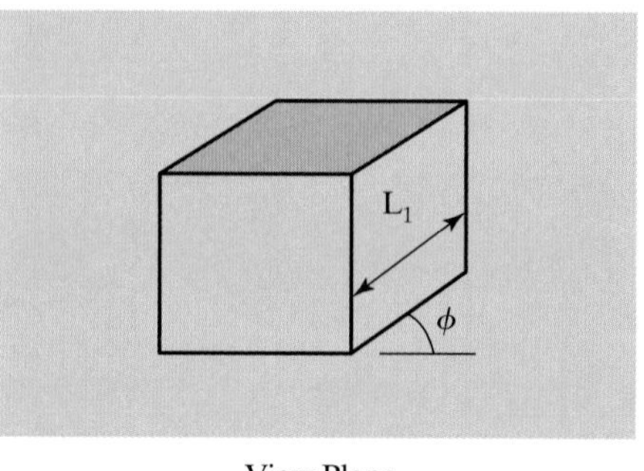

FIGURE 7-34 An oblique parallel projection (a) of a cube (top view) onto a view plane that is coincident with the front face of the cube produces the combination front, side, and top view shown in (b).

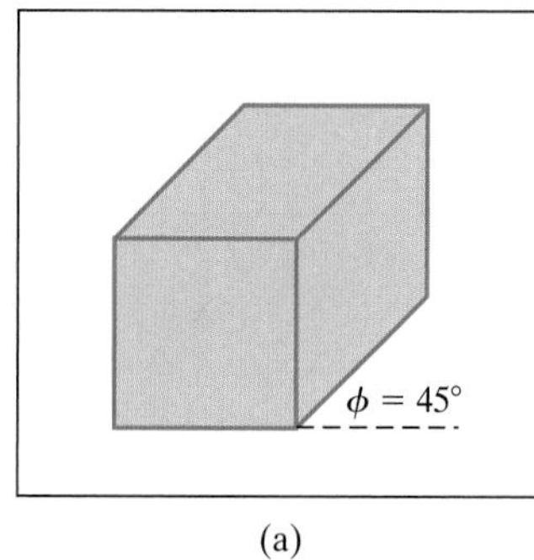

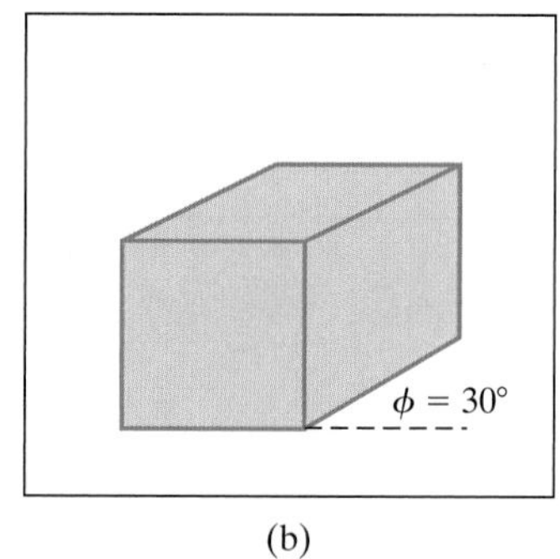

FIGURE 7-35 Cavalier projections of a cube onto a view plane for two values of angle ϕ. The depth of the cube is projected with a length equal to that of the width and height.

are shifted by an amount proportional to the distance of the plane from the view plane, so that angles, distances, and parallel lines in the plane are projected accurately. This effect is shown in Fig. 7-34, where the view plane is positioned at the front face of a cube. The back plane of the cube is sheared and overlapped with the front plane in the projection to the viewing surface. A side edge of the cube connecting the front and back planes is projected into a line of length L_1 that makes an angle ϕ with a horizontal line in the projection plane.

Cavalier and Cabinet Oblique Parallel Projections

Typical choices for angle ϕ are 30° and 45°, which display a combination view of the front, side, and top (or front, side, and bottom) of an object. Two commonly used values for α are those for which $\tan \alpha = 1$ and $\tan \alpha = 2$. For the first case, $\alpha = 45°$ and the views obtained are called **cavalier** projections. All lines perpendicular to the projection plane are projected with no change in length. Examples of cavalier projections for a cube are given in Fig. 7-35.

When the projection angle α is chosen so that $\tan \alpha = 2$, the resulting view is called a **cabinet** projection. For this angle ($\approx 63.4°$), lines perpendicular to the viewing surface are projected at half their length. Cabinet projections appear more realistic than cavalier projections because of this reduction in the length of perpendiculars. Figure 7-36 shows examples of cabinet projections for a cube.

Oblique Parallel-Projection Vector

In graphics programming libraries that support oblique parallel projections, the direction of projection to the view plane is specified with a **parallel-projection**

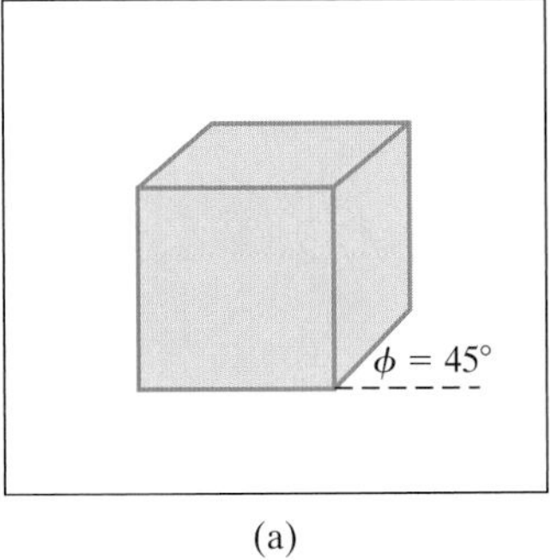

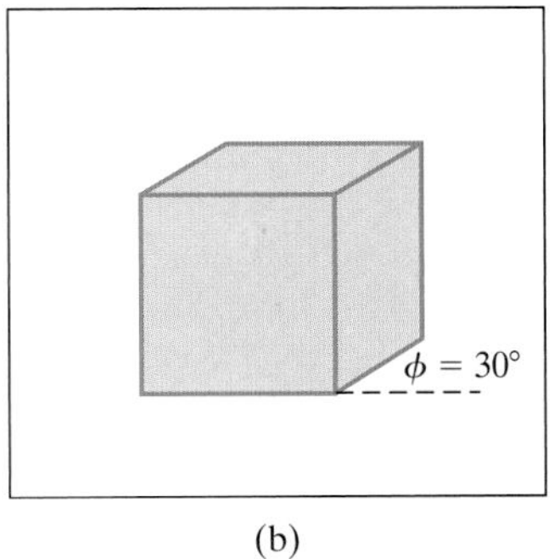

FIGURE 7-36 Cabinet projections of a cube onto a view plane for two values of angle ϕ. The depth is projected with a length that is one half that of the width and height of the cube.

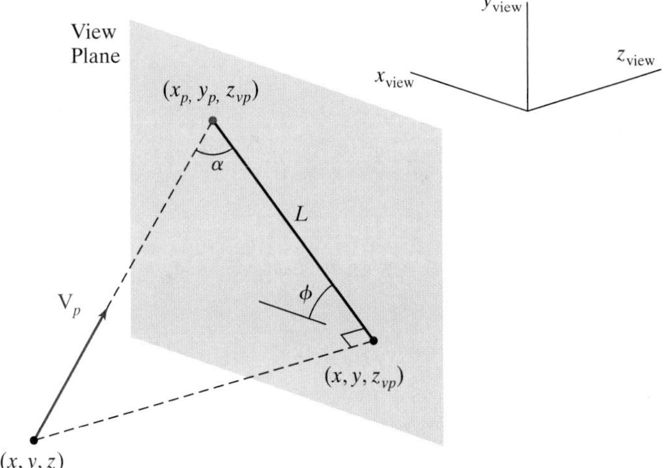

FIGURE 7-37 Oblique parallel projection of position (x, y, z) to a view plane along a projection line defined with vector $\mathbf{V}_p$.

vector, $\mathbf{V}_p$. This direction vector can be designated with a reference position relative to the view point, as we did with the view-plane normal vector, or with any other two points. Some packages use a reference point relative to the center of the clipping window to define the direction for a parallel projection. If the projection vector is specified in world coordinates, it must first be transformed to viewing coordinates using the rotation matrix discussed in Section 7-4. (The projection vector is unaffected by the translation, since it is simply a direction with no fixed position.)

Once the projection vector $\mathbf{V}_p$ is established in viewing coordinates, all points in the scene are transferred to the view plane along lines that are parallel to this vector. Figure 7-37 illustrates an oblique parallel projection of a spatial point to the view plane. We can denote the components of the projection vector relative to the viewing-coordinate frame as $\mathbf{V}_p = (V_{px}, V_{py}, V_{pz})$, where $V_{py}/V_{px} = \tan\phi$. Then, comparing similar triangles in Fig. 7-37, we have

$$\frac{x_p - x}{z_{vp} - z} = \frac{V_{px}}{V_{pz}}$$
$$\frac{y_p - y}{z_{vp} - z} = \frac{V_{py}}{V_{pz}}$$

And we can write the equivalent of the oblique parallel-projection equations 7-11

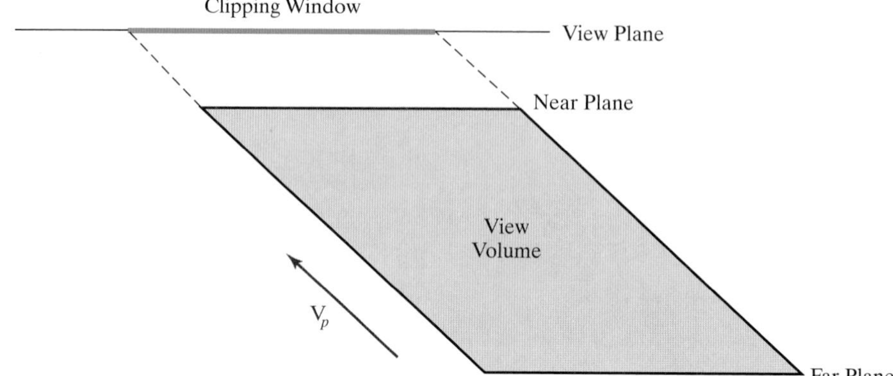

FIGURE 7-38 Top view of a finite view volume for an oblique parallel projection in the direction of vector $\mathbf{V}_p$.

in terms of the projection vector as

$$\begin{aligned} x_p &= x + (z_{vp} - z)\frac{V_{px}}{V_{pz}} \\ y_p &= y + (z_{vp} - z)\frac{V_{py}}{V_{pz}} \end{aligned} \tag{7-12}$$

The oblique parallel-projection coordinates in 7-12 reduce to the orthogonal-projection coordinates 7-6 when $V_{px} = V_{py} = 0$.

Clipping Window and Oblique Parallel-Projection View Volume

A view volume for an oblique parallel projection is set up using the same procedures as in an orthogonal projection. We select a clipping window on the view plane with coordinate positions $(xw_{\min}, yw_{\min})$ and $(xw_{\max}, yw_{\max})$, for the lower-left and upper-right corners of the clipping rectangle. The top, bottom, and sides of the view volume are then defined by the direction of projection and the edges of the clipping window. In addition, we can limit the extent of the view volume by adding a near plane and a far plane, as in Fig. 7-38. The finite oblique parallel-projection view volume is an oblique parallelepiped.

Oblique parallel projections may be affected by changes in the position of the view plane, depending on how the projection direction is to be specified. In some systems, the oblique parallel-projection direction is parallel to the line connecting a reference point to the center of the clipping window. Therefore, moving the position of the view plane or clipping window without adjusting the reference point changes the shape of the view volume.

Oblique Parallel-Projection Transformation Matrix

Using the projection-vector parameters from the equations in 7-12, we can express the elements of the transformation matrix for an oblique parallel projection as

$$\mathbf{M}_{\text{oblique}} = \begin{bmatrix} 1 & 0 & -\frac{V_{px}}{V_{pz}} & z_{vp}\frac{V_{px}}{V_{pz}} \\ 0 & 1 & -\frac{V_{py}}{V_{pz}} & z_{vp}\frac{V_{py}}{V_{pz}} \\ 0 & 0 & 1 & 0 \\ 0 & 0 & 0 & 1 \end{bmatrix} \tag{7-13}$$

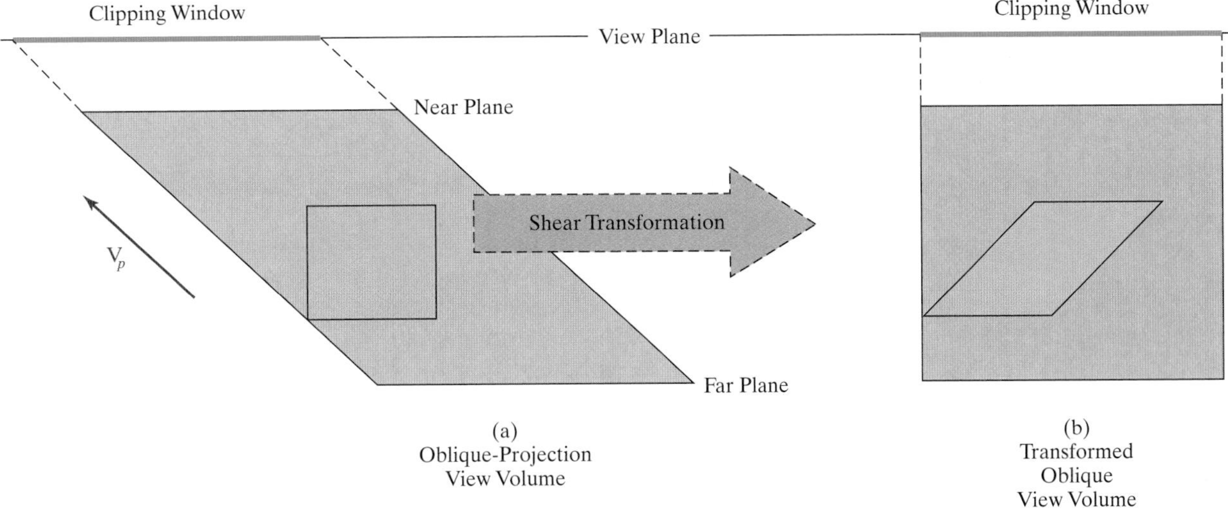

FIGURE 7-39 Top view of an oblique parallel-projection transformation. The oblique view volume is converted into a rectangular parallelepiped, and objects in the view volume, such as the green block, are mapped to orthogonal-projection coordinates.

This matrix shifts the values of the x and y coordinates by an amount proportional to the distance from the view plane, which is at position z_{vp} on the z_{view} axis. The z values of spatial positions are unchanged. If $V_{px} = V_{py} = 0$, we have an orthogonal projection and matrix 7-13 is reduced to the identity matrix.

For a general oblique parallel projection, matrix 7-13 represents a z-axis shearing transformation. All coordinate positions within the oblique view volume are sheared by an amount proportional to their distance from the view plane. The effect is to shear the oblique view volume into a rectangular parallelepiped, as illustrated in Fig. 7-39. Thus, positions inside the view volume are sheared into orthogonal-projection coordinates by the oblique parallel-projection transformation.

Normalization Transformation for an Oblique Parallel Projection

Since the oblique parallel-projection equations convert object descriptions to orthogonal-coordinate positions, we can apply the normalization procedures following this transformation. The oblique view volume has been converted to a rectangular parallelepiped, so we use the same procedures as in Section 7-6.

Following the normalization example in Section 7-6, we again map to the symmetric normalized cube within a left-handed coordinate frame. Thus, the complete transformation, from viewing coordinates to normalized coordinates, for an oblique parallel projection is

$$\mathbf{M}_{\text{oblique,norm}} = \mathbf{M}_{\text{ortho,norm}} \cdot \mathbf{M}_{\text{oblique}} \tag{7-14}$$

Transformation $\mathbf{M}_{\text{oblique}}$ is matrix 7-13, which converts the scene description to orthogonal-projection coordinates. And transformation $\mathbf{M}_{\text{ortho,norm}}$ is matrix 7-7, which maps the contents of the orthogonal view volume to the symmetric normalization cube.

To complete the viewing transformations (with the exception of the mapping to viewport screen coordinates), we concatenate matrix 7-14 to the left of the transformation $\mathbf{M}_{WC,VC}$ from Section 7-4. Clipping routines can then be applied to the normalized view volume, followed by the determination of visible objects, the surface-rendering procedures, and the viewport transformation.

7-8 PERSPECTIVE PROJECTIONS

Although a parallel-projection view of a scene is easy to generate and preserves relative proportions of objects, it does not provide a realistic representation. To simulate a camera picture, we need to consider that reflected light rays from the objects in a scene follow converging paths to the camera film plane. We can approximate this geometric-optics effect by projecting objects to the view plane along converging paths to a position called the **projection reference point** (or **center of projection**). Objects are then displayed with foreshortening effects, and projections of distant objects are smaller than the projections of objects of the same size that are closer to the view plane (Fig. 7-40).

Perspective-Projection Transformation Coordinates

We can sometimes select the projection reference point as another viewing parameter in a graphics package, but some systems place this convergence point at a fixed position, such as at the view point. Figure 7-41 shows the projection path of a

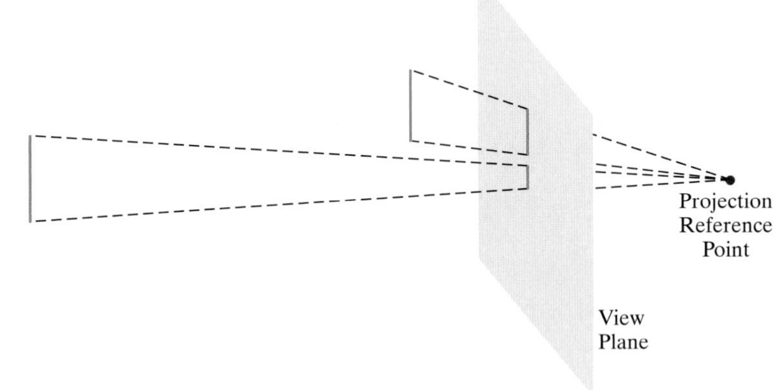

FIGURE 7-40 Perspective projection of two equal-length line segments at different distances from the view plane.

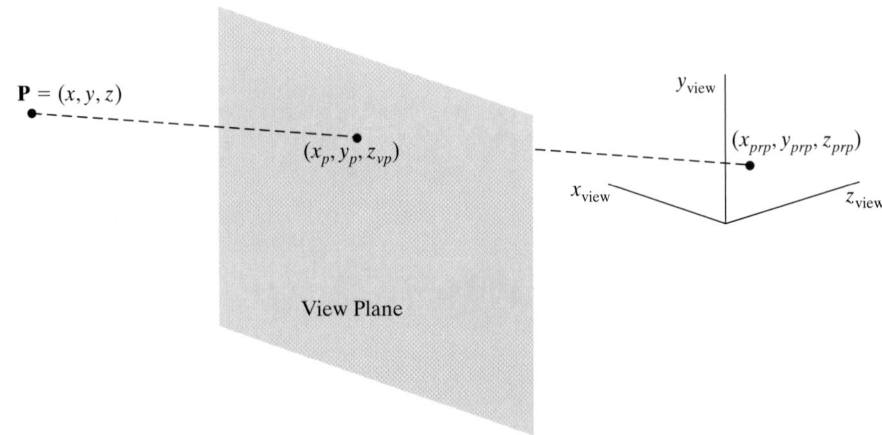

FIGURE 7-41 Perspective projection of a point **P** with coordinates (x, y, z) to a selected projection reference point. The intersection position on the view plane is (x_p, y_p, z_{vp}).

spatial position (x, y, z) to a general projection reference point at $(x_{prp}, y_{prp}, z_{prp})$. The projection line intersects the view plane at the coordinate position (x_p, y_p, z_{vp}), where z_{vp} is some selected position for the view plane on the z_{view} axis. We can write equations describing coordinate positions along this perspective-projection line in parametric form as

$$\begin{aligned} x' &= x - (x - x_{prp})u \\ y' &= y - (y - y_{prp})u \qquad 0 \le u \le 1 \\ z' &= z - (z - z_{prp})u \end{aligned} \tag{7-15}$$

Coordinate position (x', y', z') represents any point along the projection line. When $u = 0$, we are at position $\mathbf{P} = (x, y, z)$. At the other end of the line, $u = 1$ and we have the projection reference-point coordinates $(x_{prp}, y_{prp}, z_{prp})$. On the view plane, $z' = z_{vp}$ and we can solve the z' equation for parameter u at this position along the projection line:

$$u = \frac{z_{vp} - z}{z_{prp} - z} \tag{7-16}$$

Substituting this value of u into the equations for x' and y', we obtain the general perspective-transformation equations

$$\begin{aligned} x_p &= x\left(\frac{z_{prp} - z_{vp}}{z_{prp} - z}\right) + x_{prp}\left(\frac{z_{vp} - z}{z_{prp} - z}\right) \\ y_p &= y\left(\frac{z_{prp} - z_{vp}}{z_{prp} - z}\right) + y_{prp}\left(\frac{z_{vp} - z}{z_{prp} - z}\right) \end{aligned} \tag{7-17}$$

Calculations for a perspective mapping are more complex than the parallel-projection equations, since the denominators in the perspective calculations 7-17 are functions of the z coordinate of the spatial position. Therefore we now need to formulate the perspective-transformation procedures a little differently so that this mapping can be concatenated with the other viewing transformations. But first we take a look at some of the properties of equations 7-17.

Perspective-Projection Equations: Special Cases

Various restrictions are often placed on the parameters for a perspective projection. Depending on a particular graphics package, positioning for either the projection reference point or the view plane may not be completely optional.

To simplify the perspective calculations, the projection reference point could be limited to positions along the z_{view} axis, then

(1) $x_{prp} = y_{prp} = 0$:

$$x_p = x\left(\frac{z_{prp} - z_{vp}}{z_{prp} - z}\right), \qquad y_p = y\left(\frac{z_{prp} - z_{vp}}{z_{prp} - z}\right) \tag{7-18}$$

And sometimes the projection reference point is fixed at the coordinate origin, and

(2) $(x_{prp}, y_{prp}, z_{prp}) = (0, 0, 0)$:

$$x_p = x\left(\frac{z_{vp}}{z}\right), \qquad y_p = y\left(\frac{z_{vp}}{z}\right) \tag{7-19}$$

If the view plane is the uv plane and there are no restrictions on the placement of the projection reference point, then we have

(3) $z_{vp} = 0$:

$$x_p = x\left(\frac{z_{prp}}{z_{prp} - z}\right) - x_{prp}\left(\frac{z}{z_{prp} - z}\right)$$
$$y_p = y\left(\frac{z_{prp}}{z_{prp} - z}\right) - y_{prp}\left(\frac{z}{z_{prp} - z}\right) \tag{7-20}$$

With the uv plane as the view plane and the projection reference point on the z_{view} axis, the perspective equations are

(4) $x_{prp} = y_{prp} = z_{vp} = 0$:

$$x_p = x\left(\frac{z_{prp}}{z_{prp} - z}\right), \qquad y_p = y\left(\frac{z_{prp}}{z_{prp} - z}\right) \tag{7-21}$$

Of course, we cannot have the projection reference point on the view plane. In that case, the entire scene would project to a single point. The view plane is usually placed between the projection reference point and the scene, but, in general, the view plane could be placed anywhere except at the projection point. If the projection reference point is between the view plane and the scene, objects are inverted on the view plane (Fig. 7-42). With the scene between the view plane and the projection point, objects are simply enlarged as they are projected away from the viewing position onto the view plane.

Perspective effects also depend on the distance between the projection reference point and the view plane, as illustrated in Figure 7-43. If the projection reference point is close to the view plane, perspective effects are emphasized; that is, closer objects will appear much larger than more distant objects of the same size. Similarly, as the projection reference point moves farther from the view plane, the difference in the size of near and far objects decreases. When the projection reference point is very far from the view plane, a perspective projection approaches a parallel projection.

Vanishing Points for Perspective Projections

When a scene is projected onto a view plane using a perspective mapping, lines that are parallel to the view plane are projected as parallel lines. But any parallel

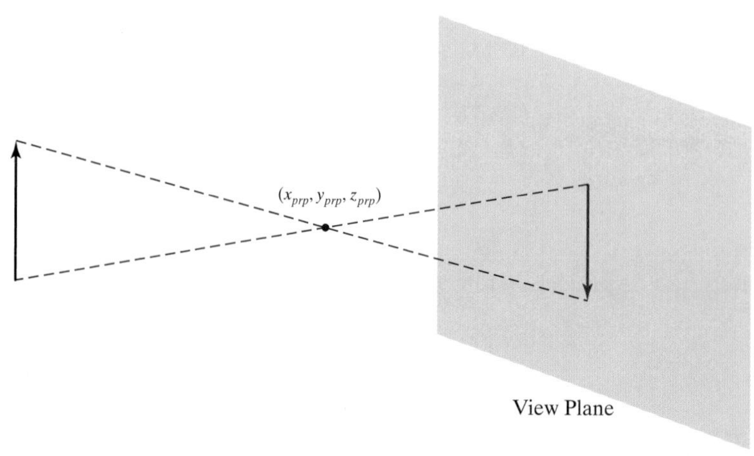

FIGURE 7-42 A perspective-projection view of an object is upside down when the projection reference point is between the object and the view plane.

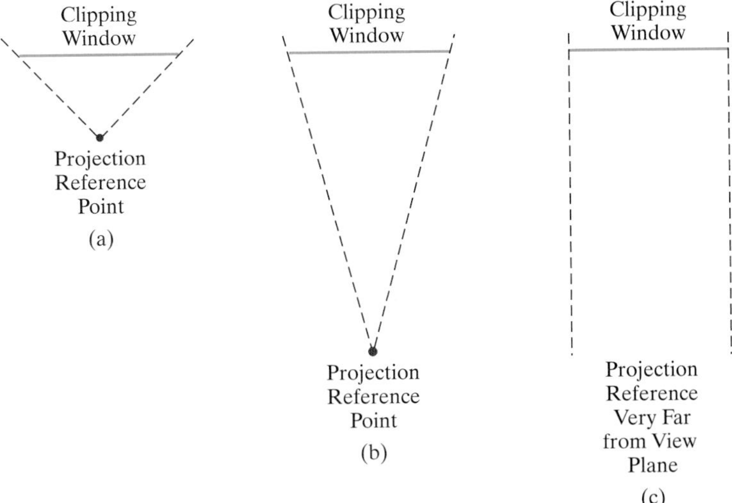

FIGURE 7-43 Changing perspective effects by moving the projection reference point away from the view plane.

lines in the scene that are not parallel to the view plane are projected into converging lines, as in Fig. 7-4. The point at which a set of projected parallel lines appears to converge is called a **vanishing point.** Each set of projected parallel lines has a separate vanishing point.

For a set of lines that are parallel to one of the principal axes of an object, the vanishing point is referred to as a **principal vanishing point.** We control the number of principal vanishing points (one, two, or three) with the orientation of the projection plane, and perspective projections are accordingly classified as one-point, two-point, or three-point projections. The number of principal vanishing points in a projection is equal to the number of principal axes that intersect the view plane. Figure 7-44 illustrates the appearance of one-point and two-point perspective projections for a cube. In the projected view (b), the view plane is aligned parallel to the xy object plane so that only the object z axis is intersected. This orientation produces a one-point perspective projection with a z-axis vanishing point. For the view shown in (c), the projection plane intersects both the x and z axes but not the y axis. The resulting two-point perspective projection contains both x-axis and z-axis vanishing points. There is not much increase in the realism of a three-point perspective projection compared to a two-point projection, so three-point projections are not used as often in architectural and engineering drawings.

Perspective-Projection View Volume

We again create a view volume by specifying the position of a rectangular clipping window on the view plane. But now the bounding planes for the view volume are not parallel, because the projection lines are not parallel. The bottom, top, and sides of the view volume are planes through the window edges that all intersect at the projection reference point. This forms a view volume that is an infinite rectangular pyramid with its apex at the center of projection (Fig. 7-45). All objects outside this pyramid are eliminated by the clipping routines. A perspective-projection view volume is often referred to as a **pyramid of vision** because it approximates the *cone of vision* of our eyes or a camera. The displayed view of a scene includes only those objects within the pyramid, just as we cannot see objects beyond our peripheral vision, which are outside the cone of vision.

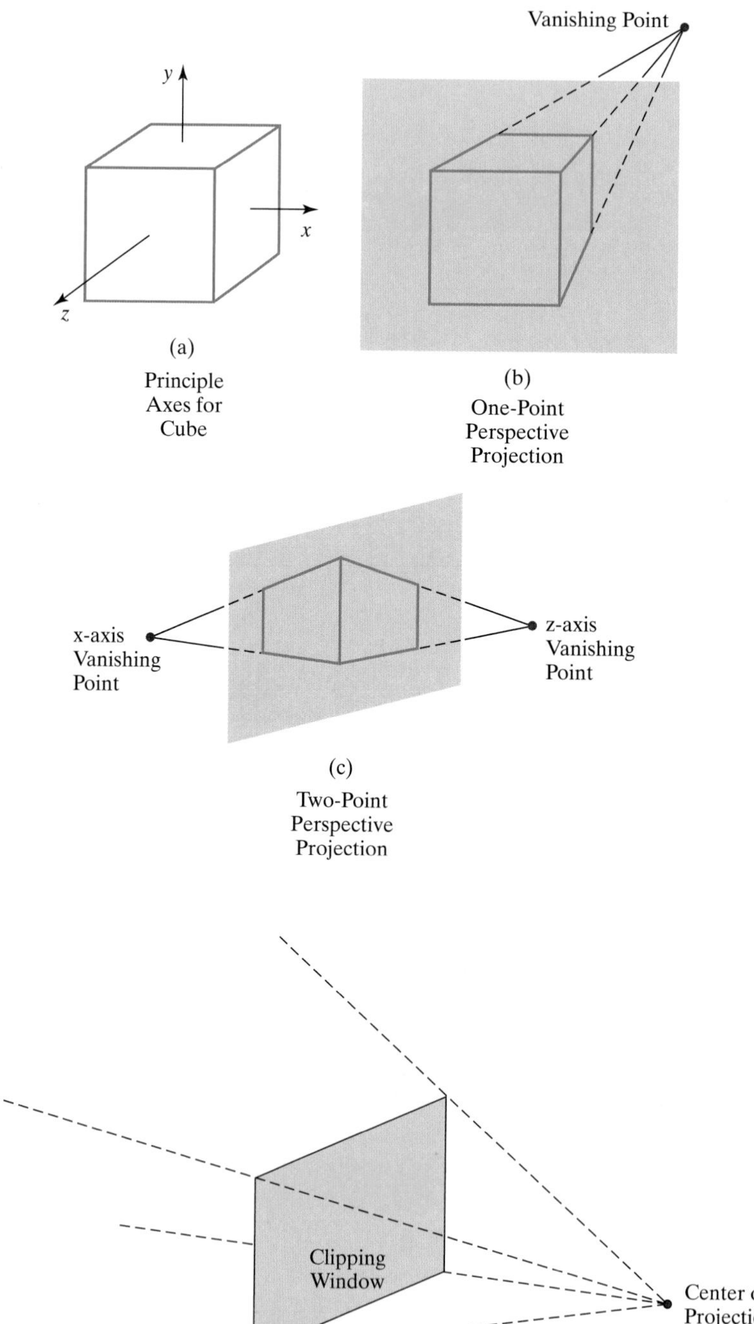

FIGURE 7-44 Principal vanishing points for perspective-projection views of a cube. When the cube in (a) is projected to a view plane that intersects only the z axis, a single vanishing point in the z direction (b) is generated. When the cube is projected to a view plane that intersects both the z and x axes, two vanishing points (c) are produced.

FIGURE 7-45 An infinite, pyramid view volume for a perspective projection.

By adding near and far clipping planes that are perpendicular to the z_{view} axis (and parallel to the view plane), we chop off parts of the infinite, perspective-projection view volume to form a truncated pyramid, or **frustum,** view volume. Figure 7-46 illustrates the shape of a finite, perspective-projection view volume with a view plane that is placed between the near clipping plane and the projection

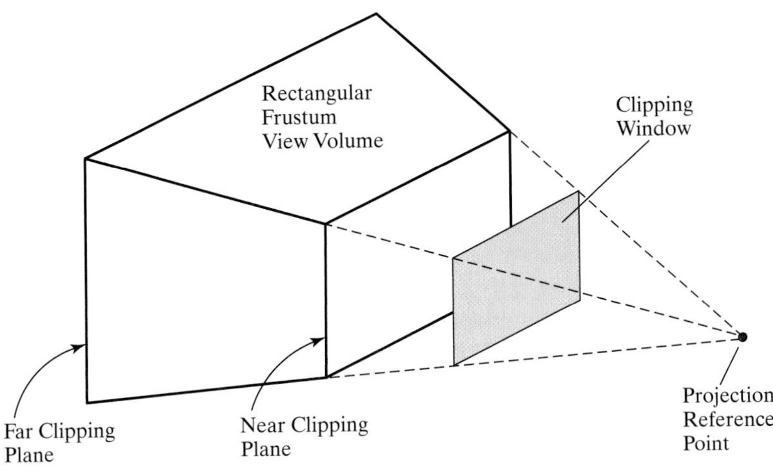

FIGURE 7-46 A perspective-projection frustum view volume with the view plane "in front" of the near clipping plane.

reference point. Sometimes the near and far planes are required in a graphics package, and sometimes they are optional.

Usually, both the near and far clipping planes are on the same side of the projection reference point, with the far plane farther from the projection point than the near plane along the viewing direction. And, as in a parallel projection, we can use the near and far planes simply to enclose the scene to be viewed. But with a perspective projection, we could also use the near clipping plane to take out large objects close to the view plane that could project into unrecognizable shapes within the clipping window. Similarly, the far clipping plane could be used to cut out objects far from the projection reference point that might project to small blots on the view plane. Some systems restrict the placement of the view plane relative to the near and far planes, and other systems allow it to be placed anywhere except at the position of the projection reference point. If the view plane is "behind" the projection reference point, objects are inverted, as shown in Fig. 7-42.

Perspective-Projection Transformation Matrix

Unlike a parallel projection, we cannot directly use the coefficients of the x and y coordinates in equations 7-17 to form the perspective-projection matrix elements, because the denominators of the coefficients are functions of the z coordinate. But we can use a three-dimensional, homogeneous-coordinate representation to express the perspective-projection equations in the form

$$x_p = \frac{x_h}{h}, \qquad y_p = \frac{y_h}{h} \tag{7-22}$$

where the homogeneous parameter has the value

$$h = z_{prp} - z \tag{7-23}$$

The numerators in 7-22 are the same as in equations 7-17:

$$\begin{aligned} x_h &= x(z_{prp} - z_{vp}) + x_{prp}(z_{vp} - z) \\ y_h &= y(z_{prp} - z_{vp}) + y_{prp}(z_{vp} - z) \end{aligned} \tag{7-24}$$

Thus, we can set up a transformation matrix to convert a spatial position to homogeneous coordinates so that the matrix contains only the perspective parameters and not coordinate values. The perspective-projection transformation of a viewing-coordinate position is then accomplished in two steps. First, we calculate the homogeneous coordinates using the perspective-transformation matrix:

$$\mathbf{P}_h = \mathbf{M}_{\text{pers}} \cdot \mathbf{P} \tag{7-25}$$

where $\mathbf{P}_h$ is the column-matrix representation of the homogeneous point (x_h, y_h, z_h, h) and $\mathbf{P}$ is the column-matrix representation of the coordinate position $(x, y, z, 1)$. (Actually, the perspective matrix would be concatenated with the other viewing-transformation matrices, and then the composite matrix would be applied to the world-coordinate description of a scene to produce homogeneous coordinates.) Second, after other processes have been applied, such as the normalization transformation and clipping routines, homogeneous coordinates are divided by parameter h to obtain the true transformation-coordinate positions.

Setting up matrix elements for obtaining the homogeneous-coordinate x_h and y_h values in 7-24 is straightforward, but we must also structure the matrix to preserve depth (z-value) information. Otherwise, the z coordinates are distorted by the homogeneous-division parameter h. We can do this by setting up the matrix elements for the z transformation so as to normalize the perspective-projection z_p coordinates. There are various ways that we could choose the matrix elements to produce the homogeneous coordinates 7-24 and the normalized z_p value for a spatial position (x, y, z). The following matrix gives one possible way to formulate a perspective-projection matrix.

$$\mathbf{M}_{\text{pers}} = \begin{bmatrix} z_{prp} - z_{vp} & 0 & -x_{prp} & x_{prp}z_{prp} \\ 0 & z_{prp} - z_{vp} & -y_{prp} & y_{prp}z_{prp} \\ 0 & 0 & s_z & t_z \\ 0 & 0 & -1 & z_{prp} \end{bmatrix} \tag{7-26}$$

Parameters s_z and t_z are the scaling and translation factors for normalizing the projected values of z-coordinates. Specific values for s_z and t_z depend on the normalization range we select.

Matrix 7-26 converts the description of a scene into homogeneous parallel-projection coordinates. However, the frustum view volume can have any orientation, so that these transformed coordinates could correspond to an oblique parallel projection. This occurs if the frustum view volume is not symmetric. If the frustum view volume for the perspective projection is symmetric, the resulting parallel-projection coordinates correspond to an orthogonal projection. We next consider these two possibilities.

Symmetric Perspective-Projection Frustum

The line from the projection reference point through the center of the clipping window and on through the view volume is the centerline for a perspective-projection frustum. If this centerline is perpendicular to the view plane, we have a **symmetric frustum** (with respect to its centerline) as in Fig. 7-47.

Since the frustum centerline intersects the view plane at the coordinate location $(x_{prp}, y_{prp}, z_{vp})$, we can express the corner positions for the clipping window

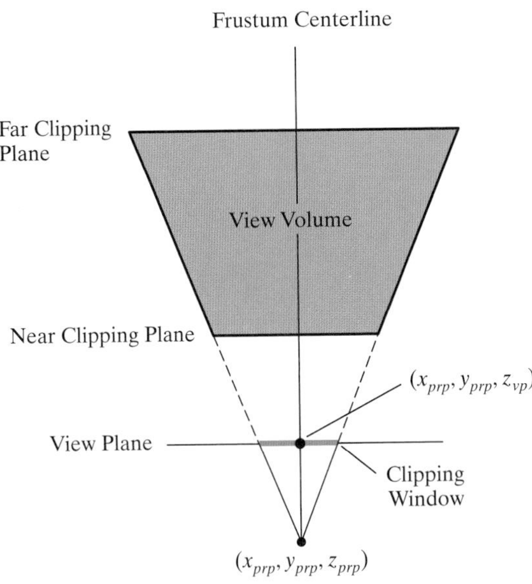

FIGURE 7-47 A symmetric perspective-projection frustum view volume, with the view plane between the projection reference point and the near clipping plane. This frustum is symmetric about its centerline when viewed from above, below, or either side.

in terms of the window dimensions:

$$xw_{\text{min}} = x_{prp} - \frac{\text{width}}{2}, \qquad xw_{\text{max}} = x_{prp} + \frac{\text{width}}{2}$$

$$yw_{\text{min}} = y_{prp} - \frac{\text{height}}{2}, \qquad yw_{\text{max}} = y_{prp} + \frac{\text{height}}{2}$$

Therefore, we could specify a symmetric perspective-projection view of a scene using the width and height of the clipping window instead of the window coordinates. This uniquely establishes the position of the clipping window, since it is symmetric about the x and y coordinates of the projection reference point.

Another way to specify a symmetric perspective projection is to use parameters that approximate the properties of a camera lens. A photograph is produced with a symmetric perspective projection of a scene onto the film plane. Reflected light rays from the objects in a scene are collected on the film plane from within the "cone of vision" of the camera. This cone of vision can be referenced with a **field-of-view angle,** which is a measure of the size of the camera lens. A large field-of-view angle, for example, corresponds to a wide-angle lens. In computer graphics, the cone of vision is approximated with a symmetric frustum, and we can use a field-of-view angle to specify an angular size for the frustum. Typically, the field-of-view angle is the angle between the top clipping plane and the bottom clipping plane of the frustum, as shown in Fig. 7-48.

For a given projection reference point and view-plane position, the field-of-view angle determines the height of the clipping window (Fig. 7-49), but not the width. We need an additional parameter to define completely the clipping-window dimensions, and this second parameter could be either the window width or the aspect ratio (width/height) of the clipping window. From the right triangles in the diagram of Fig. 7-49, we see that

$$\tan\left(\frac{\theta}{2}\right) = \frac{\text{height}/2}{z_{prp} - z_{vp}} \tag{7-27}$$

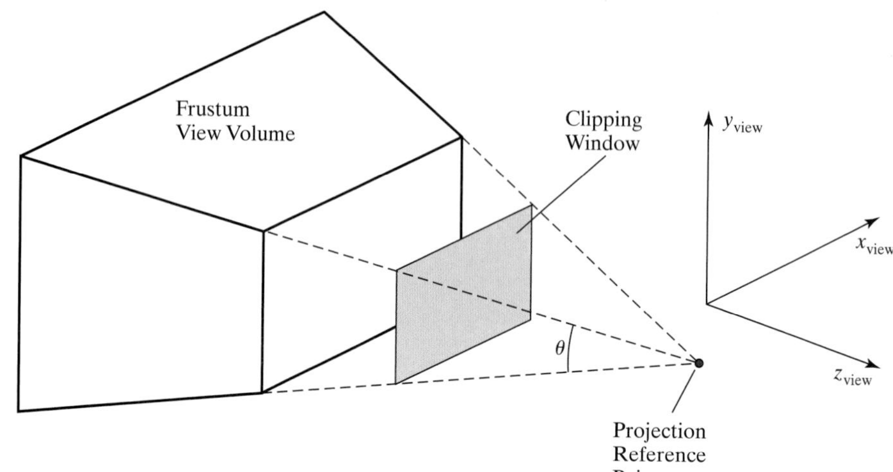

FIGURE 7-48
Field-of-view angle θ for a symmetric perspective-projection view volume, with the clipping window between the near clipping plane and the projection reference point.

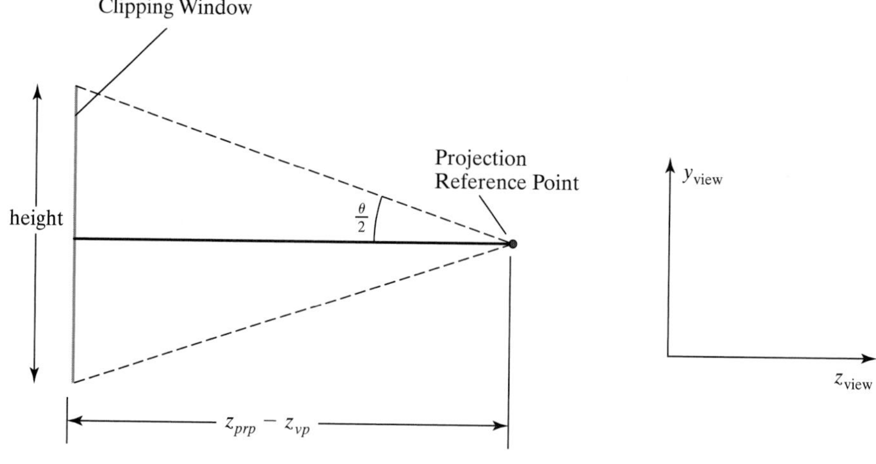

FIGURE 7-49
Relationship between the field-of-view angle θ, the height of the clipping window, and the distance between the projection reference point and the view plane.

so that the clipping-window height can be calculated as

$$\text{height} = 2(z_{prp} - z_{vp})\tan\left(\frac{\theta}{2}\right) \tag{7-28}$$

Therefore, the diagonal elements with the value $z_{prp} - z_{vp}$ in matrix 7-26 could be replaced by either of the following two expressions.

$$\begin{aligned} z_{prp} - z_{vp} &= \frac{\text{height}}{2}\cot\left(\frac{\theta}{2}\right) \\ &= \frac{\text{width} \cdot \cot(\theta/2)}{2 \cdot \text{aspect}} \end{aligned} \tag{7-29}$$

In some graphics libraries, fixed positions are used for the view plane and the projection reference point, so that a symmetric perspective projection is completely specified by the field-of-view angle, the aspect ratio of the clipping window, and the distances from the viewing position to the near and far clipping planes. The same aspect ratio is usually applied to the specification of the viewport.

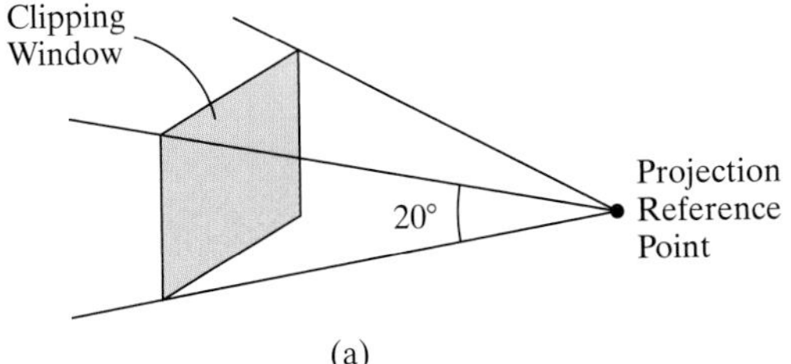

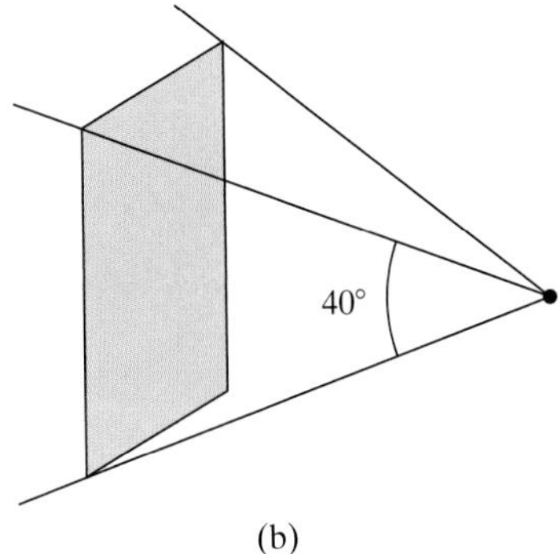

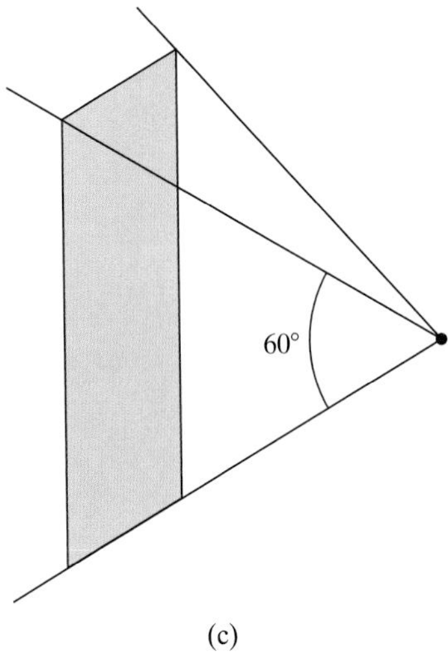

FIGURE 7-50 Increasing the size of the field-of-view angle increases the height of the clipping window and increases the perspective-projection foreshortening.

If the field-of-view angle is decreased in a particular application, the foreshortening effects of a perspective projection are also decreased. This is comparable to moving the projection reference point farther from the view plane. Also, decreasing the field-of-view angle decreases the height of the clipping window, and this provides a method for zooming in on small regions of a scene. Similarly, a large field-of-view angle results in a large clipping-window height (a zoom out), and it increases perspective effects, which is what we achieve when we set the projection reference point close to the view plane. Figure 7-50 illustrates the effects of various field-of-view angles for a fixed-width clipping window.

When the perspective-projection view volume is a symmetric frustum, the perspective transformation maps locations inside the frustum to orthogonal-projection coordinates within a rectangular parallelepiped. The centerline of the

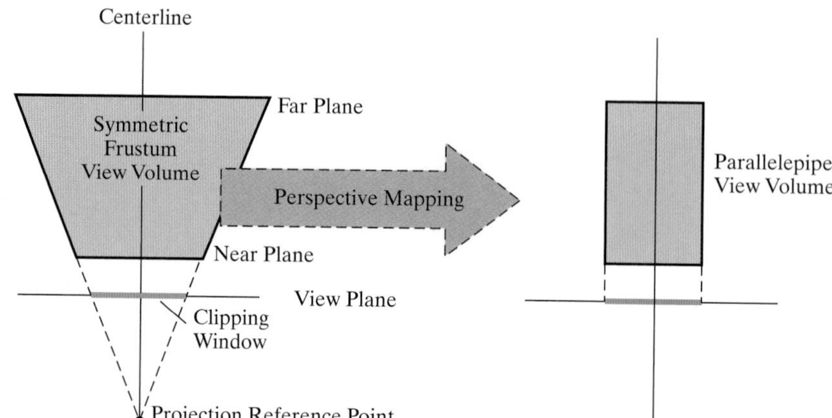

FIGURE 7-51 A symmetric frustum view volume is mapped to an orthogonal parallelepiped by a perspective-projection transformation.

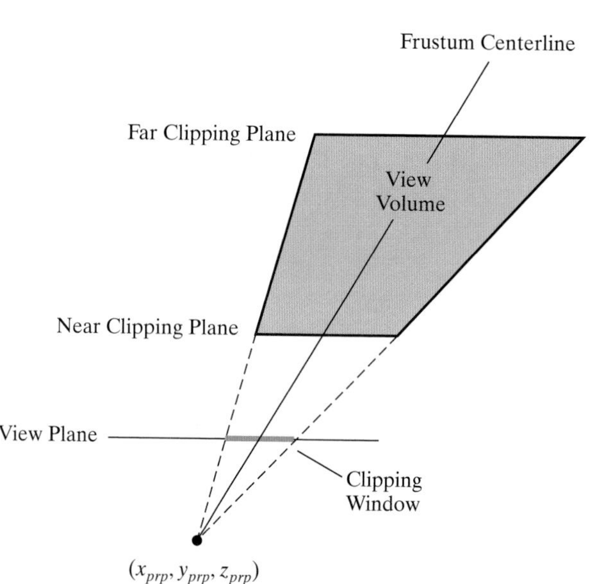

FIGURE 7-52 An oblique frustum, as viewed from at least one side or a top view, with the view plane positioned between the projection reference point and the near clipping plane.

parallelepiped is the frustum centerline, since this line is already perpendicular to the view plane (Fig. 7-51). This is a consequence of the fact that all positions along a projection line within the frustum map to the same point (x_p, y_p) on the view plane. Thus, each projection line is converted by the perspective transformation to a line that is perpendicular to the view plane and, thus, parallel to the frustum centerline. With the symmetric frustum converted to an orthogonal-projection view volume, we can next apply the normalization transformation.

Oblique Perspective-Projection Frustum

If the centerline of a perspective-projection view volume is not perpendicular to the view plane, we have an **oblique frustum.** Figure 7-52 illustrates the general appearance of an oblique perspective-projection view volume. In this case, we can first transform the view volume to a symmetric frustum and then to a normalized view volume.

An oblique perspective-projection view volume can be converted to a symmetric frustum by applying the z-axis shearing-transformation matrix 5-115. This transformation shifts all positions on any plane that is perpendicular to the z axis by an amount that is proportional to the distance of the plane from a specified z-axis reference position. In this case, the reference position is z_{prp}, which is the z coordinate of the projection reference point. And we need to shift by an amount that will move the center of the clipping window to position (x_{prp}, y_{prp}) on the view plane. Since the frustum centerline passes through the center of the clipping window, this shift adjusts the centerline so that it is perpendicular to the view plane, as in Fig. 7-47.

The computations for the shearing transformation, as well as for the perspective and normalization transformations, are greatly reduced if we take the projection reference point to be the viewing-coordinate origin. We could do this with no loss in generality by translating all coordinate positions in a scene so that our selected projection reference point is shifted to the coordinate origin. Or we could have initially set up the viewing-coordinate reference frame so that its origin is at the projection point that we want for a scene. And, in fact, some graphics libraries do fix the projection reference point at the coordinate origin.

Taking the projection reference point as $(x_{prp}, y_{prp}, z_{prp}) = (0, 0, 0)$, we obtain the elements of the required shearing matrix as

$$\mathbf{M}_{z\,\text{shear}} = \begin{bmatrix} 1 & 0 & \text{sh}_{zx} & 0 \\ 0 & 1 & \text{sh}_{zy} & 0 \\ 0 & 0 & 1 & 0 \\ 0 & 0 & 0 & 1 \end{bmatrix} \tag{7-30}$$

We can also simplify the elements of the perspective-projection matrix a bit more if we place the view plane at the position of the near clipping plane. And, since we now want to move the center of the clipping window to coordinates (0, 0) on the view plane, we need to choose values for the shearing parameters such that

$$\begin{bmatrix} 0 \\ 0 \\ z_{\text{near}} \\ 1 \end{bmatrix} = \mathbf{M}_{z\,\text{shear}} \cdot \begin{bmatrix} \dfrac{xw_{\min} + xw_{\max}}{2} \\ \dfrac{yw_{\min} + yw_{\max}}{2} \\ z_{\text{near}} \\ 1 \end{bmatrix} \tag{7-31}$$

Therefore, the parameters for this shearing transformation are

$$\begin{aligned} \text{sh}_{zx} &= -\frac{xw_{\min} + xw_{\max}}{2\,z_{\text{near}}} \\ \text{sh}_{zy} &= -\frac{yw_{\min} + yw_{\max}}{2\,z_{\text{near}}} \end{aligned} \tag{7-32}$$

Similarly, with the projection reference point at the viewing-coordinate origin and with the near clipping plane as the view plane, the perspective-projection matrix 7-26 is simplified to

$$\mathbf{M}_{\text{pers}} = \begin{bmatrix} -z_{\text{near}} & 0 & 0 & 0 \\ 0 & -z_{\text{near}} & 0 & 0 \\ 0 & 0 & s_z & t_z \\ 0 & 0 & -1 & 0 \end{bmatrix} \tag{7-33}$$

Expressions for the z-coordinate scaling and translation parameters will be determined by the normalization requirements.

Concatenating the simplified perspective-projection matrix 7-33 with the shear matrix 7-30, we obtain the following oblique perspective-projection matrix for converting coordinate positions in a scene to homogeneous orthogonal-projection coordinates. The projection reference point for this transformation is the viewing-coordinate origin, and the near clipping plane is the view plane.

$$\mathbf{M}_{\text{obliquepers}} = \mathbf{M}_{\text{pers}} \cdot \mathbf{M}_{z\,\text{shear}} = \begin{bmatrix} -z_{\text{near}} & 0 & \dfrac{xw_{\text{min}} + xw_{\text{max}}}{2} & 0 \\ 0 & -z_{\text{near}} & \dfrac{yw_{\text{min}} + yw_{\text{max}}}{2} & 0 \\ 0 & 0 & s_z & t_z \\ 0 & 0 & -1 & 0 \end{bmatrix} \tag{7-34}$$

Although we no longer have options for the placement of the projection reference point and the view plane, this matrix provides an efficient method for generating a perspective-projection view of a scene without sacrificing a great deal of flexibility.

If we choose the clipping-window coordinates so that $xw_{\text{max}} = -xw_{\text{min}}$ and $yw_{\text{max}} = -yw_{\text{min}}$, the frustum view volume is symmetric and matrix 7-34 reduces to matrix 7-33. This is because the projection reference point is now at the origin of the viewing-coordinate frame. We could also use Eqs. 7-29, with $z_{prp} = 0$ and $z_{vp} = z_{\text{near}}$, to express the first two diagonal elements of this matrix in terms of the field-of-view angle and the clipping-window dimensions.

Normalized Perspective-Projection Transformation Coordinates

Matrix 7-34 transforms object positions in viewing coordinates to perspective-projection homogeneous coordinates. When we divide the homogeneous coordinates by the homogeneous parameter h, we obtain the actual projection coordinates, which are orthogonal-projection coordinates. Thus, this perspective projection transforms all points within the frustum view volume to positions within a rectangular parallelepiped view volume. The final step in the perspective transformation process is to map this parallelepiped to a *normalized view volume*.

We follow the same normalization procedure that we used for a parallel projection. The transformed frustum view volume, which is a rectangular parallelepiped, is mapped to a symmetric normalized cube within a left-handed reference frame (Fig. 7-53). We have already included the normalization parameters for z coordinates in the perspective-projection matrix 7-34, but we still need to determine the values for these parameters when we transform to the symmetric normalization cube. Also, we need to determine the normalization transformation parameters for x and y coordinates. Since the centerline of the rectangular parallelepiped view volume is now the z_{view} axis, no translation is needed in the x and y normalization transformations: We require only the x and y scaling parameters relative to the coordinate origin. The scaling matrix for accomplishing the xy normalization is

$$\mathbf{M}_{xy\,\text{scale}} = \begin{bmatrix} s_x & 0 & 0 & 0 \\ 0 & s_y & 0 & 0 \\ 0 & 0 & 1 & 0 \\ 0 & 0 & 0 & 1 \end{bmatrix} \tag{7-35}$$

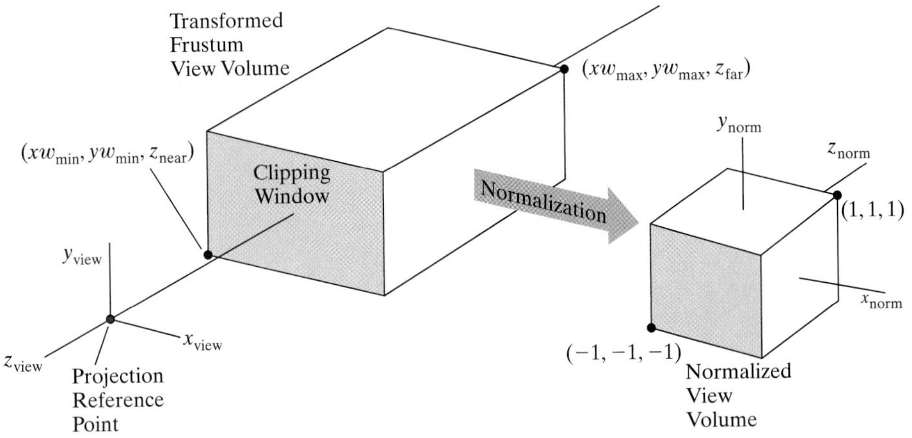

FIGURE 7-53 Normalization transformation from a transformed perspective-projection view volume (rectangular parallelepiped) to the symmetric normalization cube within a left-handed reference frame, with the near clipping plane as the view plane and the projection reference point at the viewing-coordinate origin.

Concatenating the xy-scaling matrix with matrix 7-34 produces the following normalization matrix for a perspective-projection transformation.

$$\mathbf{M}_{\text{normpers}} = \mathbf{M}_{xy\,\text{scale}} \cdot \mathbf{M}_{\text{obliquepers}}$$

$$= \begin{bmatrix} -z_{\text{near}}s_x & 0 & s_x\dfrac{xw_{\min} + xw_{\max}}{2} & 0 \\ 0 & -z_{\text{near}}s_y & s_y\dfrac{yw_{\min} + yw_{\max}}{2} & 0 \\ 0 & 0 & s_z & t_z \\ 0 & 0 & -1 & 0 \end{bmatrix} \tag{7-36}$$

From this transformation, we obtain the homogeneous coordinates:

$$\begin{bmatrix} x_h \\ y_h \\ z_h \\ h \end{bmatrix} = \mathbf{M}_{\text{normpers}} \cdot \begin{bmatrix} x \\ y \\ z \\ 1 \end{bmatrix} \tag{7-37}$$

And the projection coordinates are

$$\begin{aligned} x_p &= \frac{x_h}{h} = \frac{-z_{\text{near}}s_x x + s_x(xw_{\min} + xw_{\max})/2}{-z} \\ y_p &= \frac{y_h}{h} = \frac{-z_{\text{near}}s_y y + s_y(yw_{\min} + yw_{\max})/2}{-z} \\ z_p &= \frac{z_h}{h} = \frac{s_z z + t_z}{-z} \end{aligned} \tag{7-38}$$

To normalize this perspective transformation, we want the projection coordinates to be $(x_p, y_p, z_p) = (-1, -1, -1)$ when the input coordinates are $(x, y, z) = (xw_{\min}, yw_{\min}, z_{\text{near}})$, and we want the projection coordinates to be $(x_p, y_p, z_p) = (1, 1, 1)$ when the input coordinates are $(x, y, z) = (xw_{\max}, yw_{\max}, z_{\text{far}})$. Therefore, when we solve equations 7-38 for the normalization parameters using these conditions, we obtain

$$\begin{aligned} s_x &= \frac{2}{xw_{\max} - xw_{\min}}, & s_y &= \frac{2}{yw_{\max} - yw_{\min}} \\ s_z &= \frac{z_{\text{near}} + z_{\text{far}}}{z_{\text{near}} - z_{\text{far}}}, & t_z &= \frac{2\, z_{\text{near}}\, z_{\text{far}}}{z_{\text{near}} - z_{\text{far}}} \end{aligned} \tag{7-39}$$

And the elements of the normalized transformation matrix for a general perspective-projection are

$$\mathbf{M}_{\text{normpers}} = \begin{bmatrix} \dfrac{-2z_{\text{near}}}{xw_{\max} - xw_{\min}} & 0 & \dfrac{xw_{\max} + xw_{\min}}{xw_{\max} - xw_{\min}} & 0 \\ 0 & \dfrac{-2z_{\text{near}}}{yw_{\max} - yw_{\min}} & \dfrac{yw_{\max} + yw_{\min}}{yw_{\max} - yw_{\min}} & 0 \\ 0 & 0 & \dfrac{z_{\text{near}} + z_{\text{far}}}{z_{\text{near}} - z_{\text{far}}} & -\dfrac{2z_{\text{near}}z_{\text{far}}}{z_{\text{near}} - z_{\text{far}}} \\ 0 & 0 & -1 & 0 \end{bmatrix} \tag{7-40}$$

If the perspective-projection view volume was originally specified as a symmetric frustum, we can express the elements of the normalized perspective transformation in terms of the field-of-view angle and the dimensions of the clipping window. Thus, using Eqs. 7-29, with the projection reference point at the origin and the view plane at the position of the near clipping plane, we have

$$\mathbf{M}_{\text{normsymmpers}} = \begin{bmatrix} \dfrac{\cot\left(\frac{\theta}{2}\right)}{\text{aspect}} & 0 & 0 & 0 \\ 0 & \cot\left(\dfrac{\theta}{2}\right) & 0 & 0 \\ 0 & 0 & \dfrac{z_{\text{near}} + z_{\text{far}}}{z_{\text{near}} - z_{\text{far}}} & -\dfrac{2z_{\text{near}}\,z_{\text{far}}}{z_{\text{near}} - z_{\text{far}}} \\ 0 & 0 & -1 & 0 \end{bmatrix} \tag{7-41}$$

The complete transformation from world coordinates to normalized perspective-projection coordinates is the composite matrix formed by concatenating this perspective matrix on the left of the viewing-transformation product $\mathbf{R} \cdot \mathbf{T}$. Next, the clipping routines can be applied to the normalized view volume. The remaining tasks are visibility determination, surface rendering, and the transformation to the viewport.

7-9 THE VIEWPORT TRANSFORMATION AND THREE-DIMENSIONAL SCREEN COORDINATES

Once we have completed the transformation to normalized projection coordinates, clipping can be applied efficiently to the symmetric cube (or the unit cube). Following the clipping procedures, the contents of the normalized view volume can be transferred to screen coordinates. For the x and y positions in the normalized clipping window, this procedure is the same as the two-dimensional viewport transformation that we examined in Section 6-3. But positions throughout the three-dimensional view volume also have a depth (z coordinate), and we need to retain this depth information for the visibility testing and surface-rendering algorithms. So we can now think of the viewport transformation as a mapping to **three-dimensional screen coordinates.**

The x and y transformation equations from the normalized clipping window to positions within a rectangular viewport are given in matrix 6-10. We can adapt that matrix to three-dimensional applications by including parameters for the transformation of z values to screen coordinates. Often the normalized z values within the symmetric cube are renormalized on the range from 0 to 1.0. This allows the video screen to be referenced as $z = 0$, and depth processing can be conveniently carried out over the unit interval from 0 to 1. If we include this z renormalization, the transformation from the normalized view volume to three-dimensional screen coordinates is

$$\mathbf{M}_{\text{normviewvol,3D screen}} = \begin{bmatrix} \frac{xv_{\max} - xv_{\min}}{2} & 0 & 0 & \frac{xv_{\max} + xv_{\min}}{2} \\ 0 & \frac{yv_{\max} - yv_{\min}}{2} & 0 & \frac{yv_{\max} + yv_{\min}}{2} \\ 0 & 0 & \frac{1}{2} & \frac{1}{2} \\ 0 & 0 & 0 & 1 \end{bmatrix} \tag{7-42}$$

In normalized coordinates, the $z_{\text{norm}} = -1$ face of the symmetric cube corresponds to the clipping-window area. And this face of the normalized cube is mapped to the rectangular viewport, which is now referenced at $z_{\text{screen}} = 0$. Thus, the lower-left corner of the viewport screen area is at position $(xv_{\min}, yv_{\min}, 0)$ and the upper-right corner is at position $(xv_{\max}, yv_{\max}, 0)$.

Each xy position on the viewport corresponds to a position in the refresh buffer, which contains the color information for that point on the screen. And the depth value for each screen point is stored in another buffer area, called the *depth buffer*. In later chapters, we explore the algorithms for determining the visible surface positions and their colors.

We position the rectangular viewport on the screen just as we did for two-dimensional applications. The lower-left corner of the viewport is usually placed at a coordinate position specified relative to the lower-left corner of the display window. And object proportions are maintained if we set the aspect ratio of this viewport area to be the same as the clipping window.

7-10 OpenGL THREE-DIMENSIONAL VIEWING FUNCTIONS

The OpenGL Utility library (GLU) includes a function for specifying the three-dimensional viewing parameters and another function for setting up a symmetric perspective-projection transformation. Other functions, such as those for an orthogonal projection, an oblique perspective projection, and the viewport transformation, are contained in the basic OpenGL library. In addition, GLUT functions are available for defining and manipulating display windows (Section 6-4).

OpenGL Viewing-Transformation Function

When we designate the viewing parameters in OpenGL, a matrix is formed and concatenated with the current modelview matrix. Consequently, this viewing matrix is combined with any geometric transformations we may have also specified. This composite matrix is then applied to transform object descriptions in world coordinates to viewing coordinates. We set the modelview mode with the statement

```
glMatrixMode (GL_MODELVIEW);
```

Viewing parameters are specified with the following GLU function, which is in the OpenGL Utility library because it invokes the translation and rotation routines in the basic OpenGL library.

```
gluLookAt (x0, y0, z0, xref, yref, zref, Vx, Vy, Vz);
```

Values for all parameters in this function are to be assigned double-precision, floating-point values. This function designates the origin of the viewing reference frame as the world-coordinate position $\mathbf{P}_0$ = (`x0`, `y0`, `z0`), the reference position as $\mathbf{P}_{\text{ref}}$ = (`xref`, `yref`, `zref`), and the view-up vector as $\mathbf{V}$ = (`Vx`, `Vy`, `Vz`). The positive z_{view} axis for the viewing frame is in the direction $\mathbf{N} = \mathbf{P}_0 - \mathbf{P}_{\text{ref}}$, and the unit axis vectors for the viewing reference frame are calculated with equations 7-1.

Since the viewing direction is along the $-z_{\text{view}}$ axis, the reference position $\mathbf{P}_{\text{ref}}$ is also referred to as the "look-at point". This is usually taken to be some position in the center of the scene that we can use as a reference for specifying the projection parameters. And we can think of the reference position as the point at which we want to aim a camera that is located at the viewing origin. The up orientation for the camera is designated with vector $\mathbf{V}$, which is adjusted to a direction perpendicular to $\mathbf{N}$.

Viewing parameters specified with the `gluLookAt` function are used to form the viewing-transformation matrix 7-4 that we derived in Section 7-4. This matrix is formed as a combination of a translation, which shifts the viewing origin to the world origin, and a rotation, which aligns the viewing axes with the world axes.

If we do not invoke the `gluLookAt` function, the default OpenGL viewing parameters are

$$\mathbf{P}_0 = (0, 0, 0)$$
$$\mathbf{P}_{\text{ref}} = (0, 0, -1)$$
$$\mathbf{V} = (0, 1, 0)$$

For these default values, the viewing reference frame is the same as the world frame, with the viewing direction along the negative z_{world} axis. In many applications, we can conveniently use the default values for the viewing parameters.

OpenGL Orthogonal-Projection Function

Projection matrices are stored in the OpenGL projection mode. So, to set up a projection-transformation matrix, we must first invoke that mode with the statement

```
glMatrixMode (GL_PROJECTION);
```

Then, when we issue any transformation command, the resulting matrix will be concatenated with the current projection matrix.

Orthogonal-projection parameters are chosen with the function

```
glOrtho (xwmin, xwmax, ywmin, ywmax, dnear, dfar);
```

All parameter values in this function are to be assigned double-precision, floating-point numbers. We use `glOrtho` to select the clipping-window coordinates and the distances to the near and far clipping planes from the viewing origin. There is no option in OpenGL for the placement of the view plane. The near clipping plane is always also the view plane, and therefore the clipping window is always on the near plane of the view volume.

Function `glOrtho` generates a parallel projection that is perpendicular to the view plane (the near clipping plane). Thus, this function creates a finite orthogonal-projection view volume for the specified clipping planes and clipping window. In OpenGL, the near and far clipping planes are not optional; they must always be specified for any projection transformation.

Parameters `dnear` and `dfar` denote distances in the negative z_{view} direction from the viewing-coordinate origin. For example, if `dfar` = 55.0, then the far clipping plane is at the coordinate position $z_{\text{far}} = -55.0$. A negative value for either parameter denotes a distance "behind" the viewing origin, along the positive z_{view} axis. We can assign any values (positive, negative, or zero) to these parameters, as long as `dnear` < `dfar`.

The resulting view volume for this projection transformation is a rectangular parallelepiped. Coordinate positions within this view volume are transformed to locations within the symmetric normalized cube in a left-handed reference frame using matrix 7-7, with $z_{\text{near}} = -$ `dnear` and $z_{\text{far}} = -$ `dfar`.

Default parameter values for the OpenGL orthogonal-projection function are ± 1, which produce a view volume that is a symmetric normalized cube in the right-handed viewing-coordinate system. This default is equivalent to issuing the statement

```
glOrtho (-1.0, 1.0, -1.0, 1.0, -1.0, 1.0);
```

The default clipping window is thus a symmetric normalized square, and the default view volume is a symmetric normalized cube with $z_{\text{near}} = 1.0$ (behind the viewing position) and $z_{\text{far}} = -1.0$. Figure 7-54 shows the appearance and position of the default orthogonal-projection view volume.

For two-dimensional applications, we used the `gluOrtho2D` function to set up the clipping window. We could also have used the `glOrtho` function to specify the clipping window, as long as parameters `dnear` and `dfar` were assigned values that were on opposite sides of the coordinate origin. In fact, a call to `gluOrtho2D` is equivalent to a call to `glOrtho` with `dnear` = -1.0 and `dfar` = 1.0.

There is no OpenGL function for generating an oblique projection. To produce an oblique-projection view of a scene, we could set up our own projection matrix as in Eq. 7-14. Then we need to make this the current OpenGL projection matrix, using the matrix functions that we explored in Section 5-17. Another way to generate an oblique-projection view is to rotate the scene into an appropriate position so that an orthogonal projection in the z_{view} direction yields the desired view.

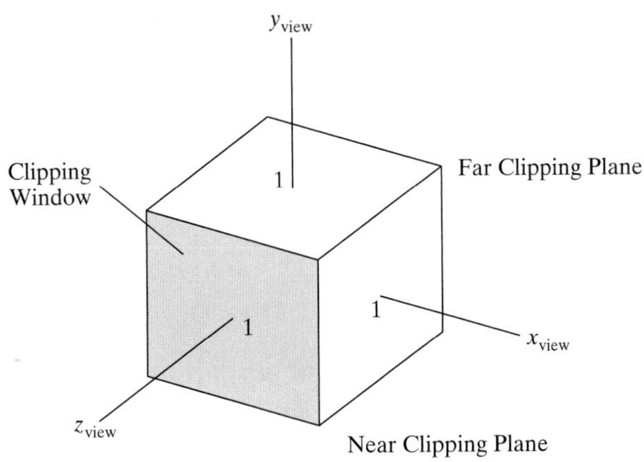

FIGURE 7-54 Default orthogonal-projection view volume. Coordinate extents for this symmetric cube are from -1 to $+1$ in each direction. The near clipping plane is at $z_{\text{near}} = 1$, and the far clipping plane is at $z_{\text{far}} = -1$.

OpenGL Symmetric Perspective-Projection Function

There are two functions available for producing a perspective-projection view of a scene. One of these functions generates a symmetric frustum view volume about the viewing direction (the negative z_{view} axis). The other function can be used for either a symmetric-perspective projection or an oblique-perspective projection. For both functions, the projection reference point is the viewing-coordinate origin and the near clipping plane is the view plane.

A symmetric, perspective-projection, frustum view volume is set up with the GLU function

```
gluPerspective (theta, aspect, dnear, dfar);
```

with each of the four parameters assigned a double-precision, floating-point number. The first two parameters define the size and position of the clipping window on the near plane, and the second two parameters specify the distances from the view point (coordinate origin) to the near and far clipping planes. Parameter `theta` represents the field-of-view angle, which is the angle between the top and bottom clipping planes (Fig. 7-48). This angle can be assigned any value from 0° to 180°. Parameter `aspect` is assigned a value for the aspect ratio (`width/height`) of the clipping window.

For a perspective projection in OpenGL, the near and far clipping planes must always be somewhere along the negative z_{view} axis; neither can be "behind" the viewing position. This restriction does not apply to an orthogonal projection, but it precludes the inverted perspective projection of an object when the view plane is behind the view point. Therefore, both `dnear` and `dfar` must be assigned positive numerical values, and the positions of the near and far planes are calculated as $z_{\text{near}} = -\texttt{dnear}$ and $z_{\text{far}} = -\texttt{dfar}$.

If we do not specify a projection function, our scene is displayed using the default orthogonal projection. In this case, the view volume is the symmetric normalized cube shown in Fig. 7-54.

The frustum view volume set up by the `gluPerspective` function is symmetric about the negative z_{view} axis. And the description of a scene is converted to normalized, homogeneous projection coordinates with matrix 7-41.

OpenGL General Perspective-Projection Function

We can use the following function to specify a perspective projection that has either a symmetric frustum view volume or an oblique frustum view volume.

```
glFrustum (xwmin, xwmax, ywmin, ywmax, dnear, dfar);
```

All parameters in this function are assigned double-precision, floating-point numbers. As in the other viewing-projection functions, the near plane is the view plane and the projection reference point is at the viewing position (coordinate origin). This function has the same parameters as the orthogonal, parallel-projection function, but now the near and far clipping-plane distances must be positive. The first four parameters set the coordinates for the clipping window on the near plane, and the last two parameters specify the distances from the coordinate origin to the near and far clipping planes along the negative z_{view} axis. Locations for the near and far planes are calculated as $z_{\text{near}} = -\texttt{dnear}$ and $z_{\text{far}} = -\texttt{dfar}$.

The clipping window can be specified anywhere on the near plane. If we select the clipping window coordinates so that $xw_{\min} = -xw_{\max}$ and $yw_{\min} = -yw_{\max}$, we obtain a symmetric frustum (about the negative z_{view} axis as its centerline).

Again, if we do not explicitly invoke a projection command, OpenGL applies the default orthogonal projection to the scene. The view volume in this case is the symmetric cube (Fig. 7-54).

OpenGL Viewports and Display Windows

After the clipping routines have been applied in normalized coordinates, the contents of the normalized clipping window, along with the depth information, are transferred to three-dimensional screen coordinates. The color value for each *xy* position on the viewport is stored in the refresh buffer (color buffer), and the depth information for each *xy* position is stored in the depth buffer.

As we noted in Section 6-4, a rectangular viewport is defined with the following OpenGL function.

```
glViewport (xvmin, yvmin, vpWidth, vpHeight);
```

The first two parameters in this function specify the integer screen position of the lower-left corner of the viewport relative to the lower-left corner of the display window. And the last two parameters give the integer width and height of the viewport. To maintain the proportions of objects in a scene, we set the aspect ratio of the viewport equal to the aspect ratio of the clipping window.

Display windows are created and managed with GLUT routines, and the various display-window functions in the GLUT library are discussed at length in Section 6-4. The default viewport in OpenGL is the size and position of the current display window.

OpenGL Three-Dimensional Viewing Program Example

A perspective-projection view of a square, as shown in Fig. 7-55, is displayed using the following program example. The square is defined in the *xy* plane, and

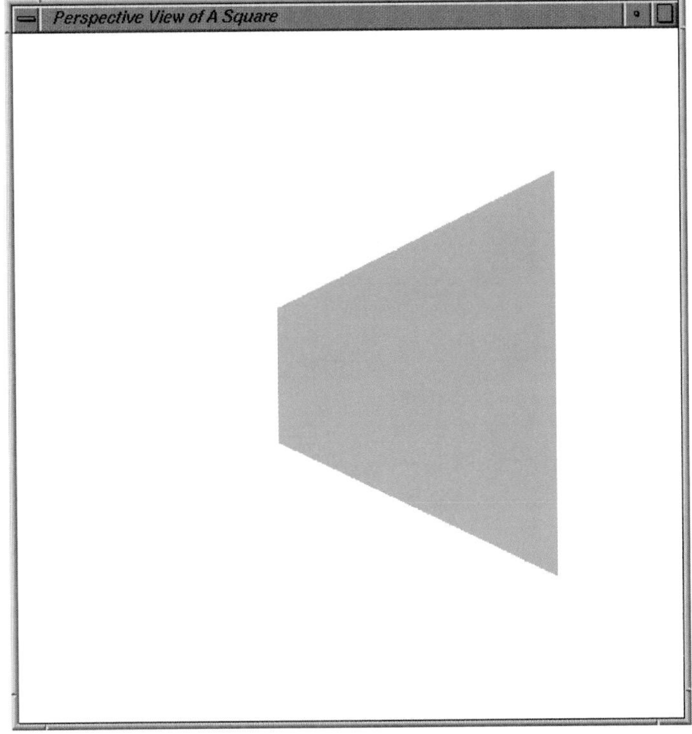

FIGURE 7-55 Output display generated by the three-dimensional viewing example program.

a viewing-coordinate origin is selected to view the front face at an angle. Choosing the center of the square as the look-at point, we obtain a perspective view using the `glFrustum` function. If we move the viewing origin around to the other side of the polygon, the back face would be displayed as a wire-frame object.

```
#include <GL/glut.h>

GLint winWidth = 600, winHeight = 600;    //  Initial display-window size.

GLfloat x0 = 100.0, y0 = 50.0, z0 = 50.0;   //  Viewing-coordinate origin.
GLfloat xref = 50.0, yref = 50.0, zref = 0.0;  //  Look-at point.
GLfloat Vx = 0.0, Vy = 1.0, Vz = 0.0;          //  View-up vector.

/*  Set coordinate limits for the clipping window:  */
GLfloat xwMin = -40.0, ywMin = -60.0, xwMax = 40.0, ywMax = 60.0;

/*  Set positions for near and far clipping planes:  */
GLfloat dnear = 25.0, dfar = 125.0;

void init (void)
{
   glClearColor (1.0, 1.0, 1.0, 0.0);

   glMatrixMode (GL_MODELVIEW);
   gluLookAt (x0, y0, z0, xref, yref, zref, Vx, Vy, Vz);

   glMatrixMode (GL_PROJECTION);
   glFrustum (xwMin, xwMax, ywMin, ywMax, dnear, dfar);
}

void displayFcn (void)
{
   glClear (GL_COLOR_BUFFER_BIT);

   /*  Set parameters for a square fill area.  */
   glColor3f (0.0, 1.0, 0.0);          //  Set fill color to green.
   glPolygonMode (GL_FRONT, GL_FILL);
   glPolygonMode (GL_BACK, GL_LINE);  //  Wire-frame back face.
   glBegin (GL_QUADS);
      glVertex3f (0.0, 0.0, 0.0);
      glVertex3f (100.0, 0.0, 0.0);
      glVertex3f (100.0, 100.0, 0.0);
      glVertex3f (0.0, 100.0, 0.0);
   glEnd ( );

   glFlush ( );
}

void reshapeFcn (GLint newWidth, GLint newHeight)
{
   glViewport (0, 0, newWidth, newHeight);

   winWidth = newWidth;
   winHeight = newHeight;
}
```

```
void main (int argc, char** argv)
{
    glutInit (&argc, argv);
    glutInitDisplayMode (GLUT_SINGLE | GLUT_RGB);
    glutInitWindowPosition (50, 50);
    glutInitWindowSize (winWidth, winHeight);
    glutCreateWindow ("Perspective View of A Square");

    init ( );
    glutDisplayFunc (displayFcn);
    glutReshapeFunc (reshapeFcn);
    glutMainLoop ( );
}
```

7-11 THREE-DIMENSIONAL CLIPPING ALGORITHMS

In Chapter 6, we discussed the advantages of using the normalized boundaries of the clipping window in two-dimensional clipping algorithms. Similarly, we can apply three-dimensional clipping algorithms to the normalized boundaries of the view volume. This allows the viewing pipeline and the clipping procedures to be implemented in a highly efficient way. All device-independent transformations (geometric and viewing) are concatenated and applied before executing the clipping routines. And each of the clipping boundaries for the normalized view volume is a plane that is parallel to one of the Cartesian planes, regardless of the projection type and original shape of the view volume. Depending on whether the view volume has been normalized to a unit cube or to a symmetric cube with edge length 2, the clipping planes have coordinate positions either at 0 and 1 or at −1 and 1. For the symmetric cube, the equations for the three-dimensional clipping planes are

$$
\begin{aligned}
xw_{\min} &= -1, \qquad & xw_{\max} &= 1 \\
yw_{\min} &= -1, \qquad & yw_{\max} &= 1 \\
zw_{\min} &= -1, \qquad & zw_{\max} &= 1
\end{aligned}
\tag{7-43}
$$

The x and y clipping boundaries are the normalized limits for the clipping window, and the z clipping boundaries are the normalized positions for the near and far clipping planes.

Clipping algorithms for three-dimensional viewing identify and save all object sections within the normalized view volume for display on the output device. All parts of objects that are outside the view-volume clipping planes are eliminated. And the algorithms are now extensions of two-dimensional methods, using the normalized boundary planes of the view volume instead of the straight-line boundaries of the normalized clipping window.

Clipping in Three-Dimensional Homogeneous Coordinates

Computer-graphics libraries process spatial positions as four-dimensional homogeneous coordinates so that all transformations can be represented as 4 by 4 matrices. As each coordinate position enters the viewing pipeline, it is converted to a four-dimensional representation:

$$(x, y, z) \rightarrow (x, y, z, 1)$$

After a position has passed through the geometric, viewing, and projection transformations, it is now in the homogeneous form

$$\begin{bmatrix} x_h \\ y_h \\ z_h \\ h \end{bmatrix} = \mathbf{M} \cdot \begin{bmatrix} x \\ y \\ z \\ 1 \end{bmatrix} \tag{7-44}$$

where matrix **M** represents the concatenation of all the various transformations from world coordinates to normalized, homogeneous projection coordinates, and the homogeneous parameter h may no longer have the value 1. In fact, h can have any real value, depending on how we represented objects in the scene and the type of projection we used.

If the homogeneous parameter h does have the value 1, the homogeneous coordinates are the same as the Cartesian projection coordinates. This is often the case for a parallel-projection transformation. But a perspective projection produces a homogeneous parameter that is a function of the z coordinate for any spatial position. The perspective-projection homogeneous parameter can even be negative. This occurs when coordinate positions are behind the projection reference point. Also, rational spline representations for object surfaces are often formulated in homogeneous coordinates, where the homogeneous parameter can be positive or negative. Therefore, if clipping is performed in projection coordinates after division by the homogeneous parameter h, some coordinate information can be lost and objects may not be clipped correctly.

An effective method for dealing with all possible projection transformations and object representations is to apply the clipping routines to the homogeneous-coordinate representations of spatial positions. And, since all view volumes can be converted to a normalized cube, a single clipping procedure can be implemented in hardware to clip objects in homogeneous coordinates against the normalized clipping planes.

Three-Dimensional Region Codes

We extend the concept of a region code (Section 6-7) to three dimensions by simply adding a couple of additional bit positions to accommodate the near and far clipping planes. Thus, we now use a six-bit region code, as illustrated in Fig. 7-56. Bit positions in this region-code example are numbered from right to left, referencing the left, right, bottom, top, near, and far clipping planes, in that order.

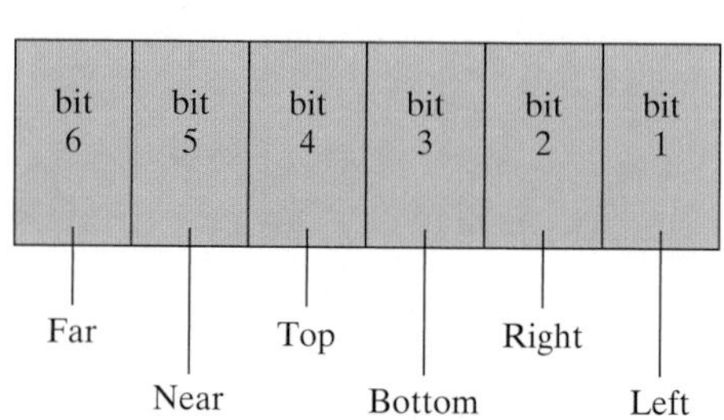

FIGURE 7-56 A possible ordering for the view-volume clipping boundaries corresponding to the region-code bit positions.

Conditions for setting the bit values in a region code are basically the same as those in Section 6-7, plus the two extra conditions for the near and far clipping planes. For a three-dimensional scene, however, we need to apply the clipping routines to the projection coordinates, which have been transformed to a normalized space. After the projection transformation, each point in a scene has the four-component representation $\mathbf{P} = (x_h, y_h, z_h, h)$. Assuming that we are clipping against the boundaries of the normalized symmetric cube (Eqs. 7-43), then a point is inside this normalized view volume if the projection coordinates of the point satisfy the following six inequalities.

$$-1 \le \frac{x_h}{h} \le 1, \qquad -1 \le \frac{y_h}{h} \le 1, \qquad -1 \le \frac{z_h}{h} \le 1 \tag{7-45}$$

Unless we have encountered an error, the value of the homogeneous parameter h is nonzero. But, before implementing region-code procedures, we can first check for the possibility of a homogeneous parameter with either a zero value or an extremely small magnitude. Also, the homogeneous parameter can be either positive or negative. Therefore, assuming $h \neq 0$, we can write the preceding inequalities in the form

$$\begin{aligned} -h \le x_h \le h, \quad & -h \le y_h \le h, \quad -h \le z_h \le h \qquad \text{if } h > 0 \\ h \le x_h \le -h, \quad & h \le y_h \le -h, \quad h \le z_h \le -h \qquad \text{if } h < 0 \end{aligned} \tag{7-46}$$

In most cases $h > 0$, and we can then assign the bit values in the region code for a coordinate position according to the tests:

$$\begin{array}{lll} \text{bit } 1 = 1 & \text{if } h + x_h < 0 & \text{(left)} \\ \text{bit } 2 = 1 & \text{if } h - x_h < 0 & \text{(right)} \\ \text{bit } 3 = 1 & \text{if } h + y_h < 0 & \text{(bottom)} \\ \text{bit } 4 = 1 & \text{if } h - y_h < 0 & \text{(top)} \\ \text{bit } 5 = 1 & \text{if } h + z_h < 0 & \text{(near)} \\ \text{bit } 6 = 1 & \text{if } h - z_h < 0 & \text{(far)} \end{array} \tag{7-47}$$

These bit values can be set using the same approach as in two-dimensional clipping. That is, we simply use the sign bit of one of the calculations $h \pm x_h$, $h \pm y_h$, or $h \pm z_h$ to set the corresponding region-code bit value. Figure 7-57 lists the 27 region codes for a view volume. In those cases where $h < 0$ for some point, we could apply clipping using the second set of inequalities in 7-46 or we could negate the coordinates and clip using the tests for $h > 0$.

Three-Dimensional Point and Line Clipping

For standard point positions and straight-line segments that are defined in a scene that is not behind the projection reference point, all homogeneous parameters are positive and the region codes can be established using the conditions in 7-47. Then, once we have set up the region code for each position in a scene, we can easily identify a point position as outside the view volume or inside the view volume. For instance, a region code of 101000 tells us that the point is above and directly behind the view volume, while the region code 000000 indicates a point within the volume (Fig. 7-57). Thus, for point clipping, we simply eliminate any individual point whose region code is not 000000. In other words, if any one of the tests in 7-47 is negative, the point is outside the view volume.

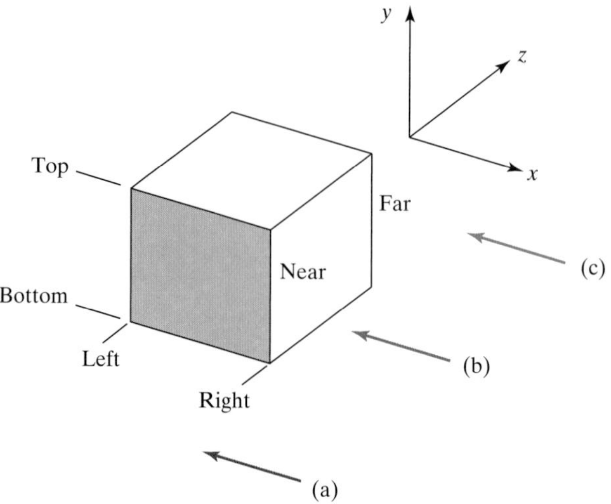

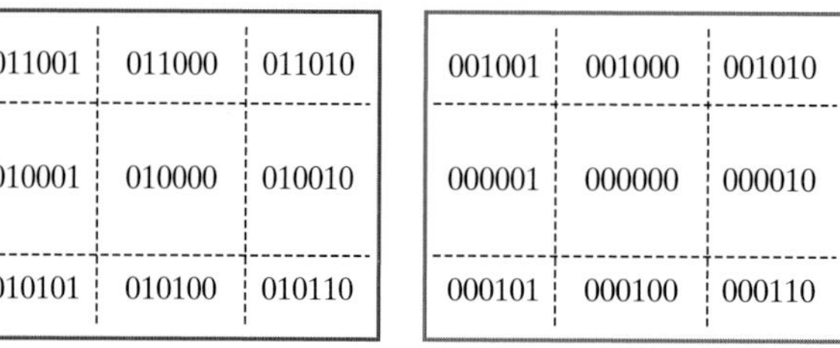

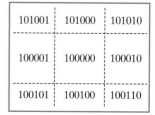

FIGURE 7-57 Values for the three-dimensional, six-bit region code that identifies spatial positions relative to the boundaries of a view volume.

Methods for three-dimensional line clipping are essentially the same as for two-dimensional lines. We can first test the line endpoint region codes for trivial acceptance or rejection of the line. If the region code for both endpoints of a line is 000000, the line is completely inside the view volume. Equivalently, we can trivially accept the line if the logical *or* operation on the two endpoint region codes produces a value of 0. And we can trivially reject the line if the logical *and* operation on the two endpoint region codes produces a value that is not 0. This nonzero value indicates that both endpoint region codes have a 1 value in the same bit position, and hence the line is completely outside one of the clipping planes. As an example of this, the line from $\mathbf{P}_3$ to $\mathbf{P}_4$ in Fig. 7-58 has the endpoint region-code values of 010101 and 100110. So this line is completely below the bottom clipping plane. If a line fails these two tests, we next analyze the line equation to determine whether any part of the line should be saved.

Equations for three-dimensional line segments are conveniently expressed in parametric form, and the clipping methods of Cyrus-Beck or Liang-Barsky (Section 6-7) can be extended to three-dimensional scenes. For a line segment with endpoints $\mathbf{P}_1 = (x_{h1}, y_{h1}, z_{h1}, h_1)$ and $\mathbf{P}_2 = (x_{h2}, y_{h2}, z_{h2}, h_2)$, we can write the parametric equation describing any point position along the line as

$$\mathbf{P} = \mathbf{P}_1 + (\mathbf{P}_2 - \mathbf{P}_1)u \qquad 0 \le u \le 1 \qquad (7\text{-}48)$$

When the line parameter has the value $u = 0$, we are at position $\mathbf{P}_1$. And $u = 1$ brings us to the other end of the line, $\mathbf{P}_2$. Writing the parametric line equation

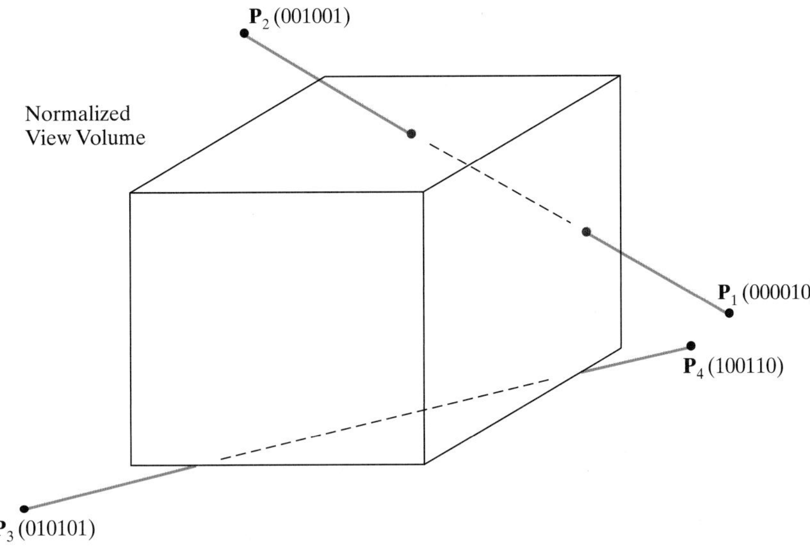

FIGURE 7-58
Three-dimensional region codes for two line segments. Line $\overline{P_1P_2}$ intersects the right and top clipping boundaries of the view volume, while line $\overline{P_3P_4}$ is completely below the bottom clipping plane.

explicitly, in terms of the homogeneous coordinates, we have

$$\begin{aligned} x_h &= x_{h1} + (x_{h2} - x_{h1})u \\ y_h &= y_{h1} + (y_{h2} - y_{h1})u \\ z_h &= z_{h1} + (z_{h2} - z_{h1})u \\ h &= h_1 + (h_2 - h_1)u \end{aligned} \qquad 0 \le u \le 1 \qquad (7\text{-}49)$$

Using the endpoint region codes for a line segment, we can first determine which clipping planes are intersected. If one of the endpoint region codes has a 0 value in a certain bit position while the other code has a 1 value in the same bit position, then the line crosses that clipping boundary. In other words, one of the tests in 7-47 generates a negative value, while the same test for the other endpoint of the line produces a nonnegative value. To find the intersection position with this clipping plane, we first use the appropriate equations in 7-49 to determine the corresponding value of parameter u. Then we calculate the intersection coordinates.

As an example of the intersection-calculation procedure, we consider the line segment $\overline{P_1P_2}$ in Fig. 7-58. This line intersects the right clipping plane, which can be described with the equation $x_{max} = 1$. Therefore, we determine the intersection value for parameter u by setting the x-projection coordinate equal to 1:

$$x_p = \frac{x_h}{h} = \frac{x_{h1} + (x_{h2} - x_{h1})u}{h_1 + (h_2 - h_1)u} = 1 \qquad (7\text{-}50)$$

Solving for parameter u, we obtain

$$u = \frac{x_{h1} - h_1}{(x_{h1} - h_1) - (x_{h2} - h_2)} \qquad (7\text{-}51)$$

Next, we determine the values y_p and z_p on this clipping plane, using the calculated value for u. In this case, the y_p and z_p intersection values are within the ± 1

boundaries of the view volume and the line does cross into the view-volume interior. So we next proceed to locate the intersection position with the top clipping plane. That completes the processing for this line segment, because the intersection points with the top and right clipping planes identify the part of the line that is inside the view volume and all the line sections that are outside the view volume.

When a line intersects a clipping boundary but does not enter the view-volume interior, we continue the line processing as in two-dimensional clipping. The section of the line outside that clipping boundary is eliminated, and we update the region-code information and the values for parameter u for the part of the line inside that boundary. Then we test the remaining section of the line against the other clipping planes for possible rejection or for further intersection calculations.

Line segments in three-dimensional scenes are usually not isolated. They are most often components in the description for the solid objects in the scene, and we need to process the lines as part of the surface-clipping routines.

Three-Dimensional Polygon Clipping

Graphics packages typically deal only with scenes that contain "graphics objects". These are objects whose boundaries are described with linear equations, so that each object is composed of a set of surface polygons. Therefore, to clip objects in a three-dimensional scene, we apply the clipping routines to the polygon surfaces. Figure 7-59, for example, highlights the surface sections of a pyramid that are to be clipped, and the dashed lines show sections of the polygon surfaces that are inside the view volume.

We can first test a polyhedron for trivial acceptance or rejection using its coordinate extents, a bounding sphere, or some other measure of its coordinate limits. If the coordinate limits of the object are inside all clipping boundaries, we save the entire object. If the coordinate limits are all outside any one of the clipping boundaries, we eliminate the entire object.

When we cannot save or eliminate the entire object, we can next process the vertex lists for the set of polygons that define the object surfaces. Applying methods similar to those in two-dimensional polygon clipping, we can clip edges to obtain new vertex lists for the object surfaces. We may also need to create some new vertex lists for additional surfaces that result from the clipping operations.

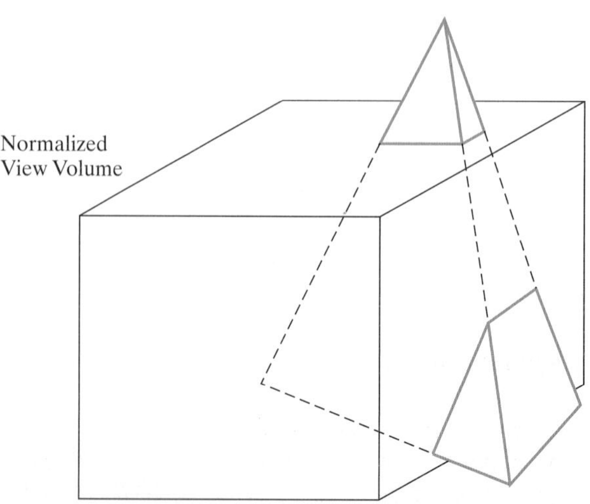

FIGURE 7-59
Three-dimensional object clipping. Surface sections that are outside the view-volume clipping planes are eliminated from the object description, and new surface facets may need to be constructed.

And the polygon tables are updated to add any new polygon surfaces and to revise the connectivity and shared-edge information about the surfaces.

To simplify the clipping of general polyhedra, polygon surfaces are often divided into triangular sections and described with triangle strips. We can then clip the triangle strips using the Sutherland-Hodgman approach discussed in Section 3-15. Each triangle strip is processed in turn against the six clipping planes to obtain the final vertex list for the strip.

For concave polygons, we can apply splitting methods (Section 3-15) to obtain a set of triangles, for example, and then clip the triangles. Alternatively, we could clip three-dimensional concave polygons using the Weiler-Atherton algorithm described in Section 6-8.

Three-Dimensional Curve Clipping

As in polyhedra clipping, we first check to determine whether the coordinate extents of a curved object, such as a sphere or a spline surface, are completely inside the view volume. Then we can check to determine whether the object is completely outside any one of the six clipping planes.

If the trivial rejection-acceptance tests fail, we locate the intersections with the clipping planes. To do this, we solve the simultaneous set of surface equations and the clipping-plane equation. For this reason, most graphics packages do not include clipping routines for curved objects. Instead, curved surfaces are approximated as a set of polygon patches, and the objects are then clipped using polygon-clipping routines. When surface-rendering procedures are applied to polygon patches, they can provide a highly realistic display of a curved surface.

Arbitrary Clipping Planes

It is also possible, in some graphics packages, to clip a three-dimensional scene using additional planes that can be specified in any spatial orientation. This option is useful in a variety of applications. For example, we might want to isolate or clip off an irregularly shaped object, eliminate part of a scene at an oblique angle for a special effect, or slice off a section of an object along a selected axis to show a cross-sectional view of its interior.

Optional clipping planes can be specified along with the description of a scene, so that the clipping operations can be performed prior to the projection transformation. However, this also means that the clipping routines are implemented in software.

A clipping plane can be specified with the plane parameters A, B, C, and D. The plane then divides three-dimensional space into two parts, so that all parts of a scene that lie on one side of the plane are clipped off. Assuming that objects behind the plane are to be clipped, then any spatial position (x, y, z) that satisfies the following inequality is eliminated from the scene.

$$Ax + By + Cz + D < 0 \tag{7-52}$$

As an example, if the plane-parameter array has the values $(A, B, C, D) = (1.0, 0.0, 0.0, 8.0)$, then any coordinate position satisfying $x + 8.0 < 0.0$ (or, $x < -8.0$) is clipped from the scene.

To clip a line segment, we can first test its two endpoints to see if the line is completely behind the clipping plane or completely in front of the plane. We can represent inequality 7-52 in a vector form using the plane normal vector

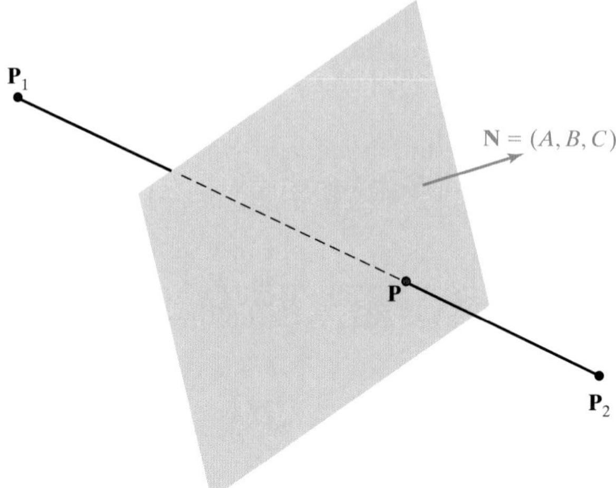

FIGURE 7-60 Clipping a line segment against a plane with normal vector **N**.

$\mathbf{N} = (A, B, C)$. Then, for a line segment with endpoint positions $\mathbf{P}_1$ and $\mathbf{P}_2$, we clip the entire line if both endpoints satisfy

$$\mathbf{N} \cdot \mathbf{P}_k + D < 0, \qquad k = 1, 2 \tag{7-53}$$

And we save the entire line if both endpoints satisfy

$$\mathbf{N} \cdot \mathbf{P}_k + D \geq 0, \qquad k = 1, 2 \tag{7-54}$$

Otherwise, the endpoints are on opposite sides of the clipping plane, as in Fig. 7-60, and we calculate the line intersection point.

To calculate the line-intersection point with the clipping plane, we can use the following parametric representation for the line segment.

$$\mathbf{P} = \mathbf{P}_1 + (\mathbf{P}_2 - \mathbf{P}_1)u, \qquad 0 \leq u \leq 1 \tag{7-55}$$

Point **P** is on the clipping plane if it satisfies the plane equation

$$\mathbf{N} \cdot \mathbf{P} + D = 0 \tag{7-56}$$

Substituting the expression for **P** from Eq. 7-55, we have

$$\mathbf{N} \cdot [\mathbf{P}_1 + (\mathbf{P}_2 - \mathbf{P}_1)u] + D = 0 \tag{7-57}$$

Solving this equation for parameter u, we obtain

$$u = \frac{-D - \mathbf{N} \cdot \mathbf{P}_1}{\mathbf{N} \cdot (\mathbf{P}_2 - \mathbf{P}_1)} \tag{7-58}$$

We then substitute this value of u into the vector parametric line representation 7-55 to obtain values for the x, y, and z intersection coordinates. For the example in Fig. 7-60, the line segment from $\mathbf{P}_1$ to **P** is clipped and we save the section of the line from **P** to $\mathbf{P}_2$.

For polyhedra, such as the pyramid in Fig. 7-61, we apply similar clipping procedures. We first test to see if the object is completely behind or completely

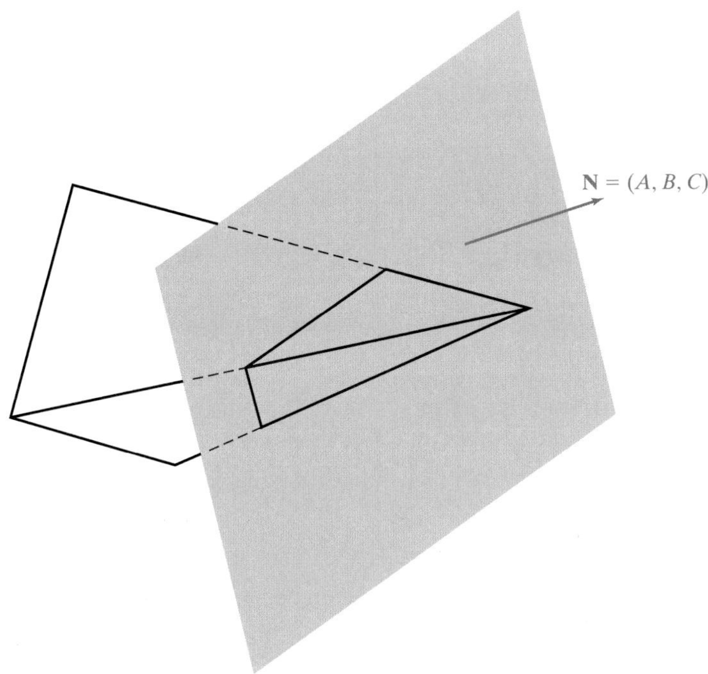

FIGURE 7-61 Clipping the surfaces of a pyramid against a plane with normal vector **N**. The surfaces in front of the plane are saved, and the surfaces of the pyramid behind the plane are eliminated.

in front of the clipping plane. If not, we process the vertex list for each polygon surface. Line-clipping methods are applied to each polygon edge in succession, just as in view-volume clipping, to produce the surface vertex lists. But in this case, we have to deal with only one clipping plane.

Clipping a curved object against a single clipping plane is easier than clipping the object against the six planes of a view volume. But we still need to solve a set of nonlinear equations to locate intersections, unless we approximate the curve boundaries with straight-line sections.

7-12 OpenGL OPTIONAL CLIPPING PLANES

In addition to the six clipping planes enclosing the view volume, OpenGL provides for the specification of additional clipping planes in a scene. Unlike the view-volume clipping planes, which are each perpendicular to one of the coordinate axes, these additional planes can have any orientation.

We designate an optional clipping plane and activate clipping against that plane with the statements

```
glClipPlane (id, planeParameters);
glEnable (id);
```

Parameter `id` is used as an identifier for a clipping plane. This parameter is assigned one of the values `GL_CLIP_PLANE0`, `GL_CLIP_PLANE1`, and so forth, up to a facility-defined maximum. The plane is then defined using the four-element array `planeParameters`, whose elements are the double-precision, floating-point values for the four plane-equation parameters A, B, C, and D. An activated clipping plane that has been assigned the identifier `id` is turned off with

```
glDisable (id);
```

The plane parameters A, B, C, and D are transformed to viewing coordinates and used to test viewing-coordinate positions in a scene. Subsequent changes in viewing or geometric-transformation parameters do not affect the stored plane parameters. Therefore, if we set up optional clipping planes before specifying any geometric or viewing transformations, the stored plane parameters are the same as the input parameters. Also, since the clipping routines for these planes are applied in viewing coordinates, and not in the normalized coordinate space, the performance of a program can be degraded when optional clipping planes are activated.

Any points that are "behind" an activated OpenGL clipping plane are eliminated. Thus, a viewing-coordinate position (x, y, z) is clipped if it satisfies condition 7-52.

Six optional clipping planes are available in any OpenGL implementation, but more might be provided. We can find out how many optional clipping planes are possible for a particular OpenGL implementation with the inquiry

```
glGetIntegerv (GL_MAX_CLIP_PLANES, numPlanes);
```

Parameter `numPlanes` is the name of an integer array that is to be assigned an integer value equal to the number of optional clipping planes that we can use.

The default for the `glClipPlane` function is that the clipping-plane parameters A, B, C, and D are each assigned a value of 0 for all optional planes. And, initially, all optional clipping planes are disabled.

7-13 SUMMARY

Viewing procedures for three-dimensional scenes follow the general approach used in two-dimensional viewing. We first create a world-coordinate scene, either from the definitions of objects in modeling coordinates or directly in world coordinates. Then we set up a viewing-coordinate reference frame and transfer object descriptions from world coordinates to viewing coordinates. Object descriptions are then processed through various routines to device coordinates.

Unlike two-dimensional viewing, however, three-dimensional viewing requires projection routines to transform object descriptions to a viewing plane before the transformation to device coordinates. Also, three-dimensional viewing operations involve more spatial parameters. We can use the camera analogy to describe three-dimensional viewing parameters. A viewing-coordinate reference frame is established with a view reference point (the camera position), a view-plane normal vector $\mathbf{N}$ (the camera lens direction), and a view-up vector $\mathbf{V}$ (the camera up direction). The view-plane position is then established along the viewing z axis, and object descriptions are projected to this plane. Either parallel-projection or perspective-projection methods can be used to transfer object descriptions to the view plane.

Parallel projections are either orthographic or oblique, and they can be specified with a projection vector. Orthographic parallel projections that display more than one face of an object are called axonometric projections. An isometric view of an object is obtained with an axonometric projection that foreshortens each principal axis by the same amount. Commonly used oblique projections are the cavalier projection and the cabinet projection. Perspective projections of objects are obtained with projection lines that meet at the projection reference point. Parallel projections maintain object proportions, but perspective projections decrease the size of distant objects. Perspective projections cause parallel lines to appear to converge to a vanishing point, provided the lines are not parallel to the view plane. Engineering and architectural displays can be generated with one-point, two-point, or three-point perspective projections, depending on the number of principal axes that intersect the view plane. An oblique perspective projection is obtained when the line from the projection reference point to the center of the clipping window is not perpendicular to the view plane.

Objects in a three-dimensional scene can be clipped against a view volume to eliminate unwanted sections of the scene. The top, bottom, and sides of the view volume are formed with planes that are parallel to the projection lines and that pass through the clipping-window edges. Near and far planes (also called front and back planes) are used to create a closed view volume. For a parallel projection, the view volume is a parallelepiped. For a perspective projection, the view volume is a frustum. In either case, we can convert the view volume to a normalized cube with boundaries either at 0 and 1 for each coordinate or at -1 and 1 for each coordinate. Efficient clipping algorithms process objects in a scene against the bounding planes of the normalized view volume. Clipping is generally carried out in graphics packages in four-dimensional homogeneous coordinates following the projection and view-volume normalization transformations. Then, homogeneous coordinates are converted to three-dimensional, Cartesian projection coordinates. Additional clipping planes, with arbitrary orientations, can also be used to eliminate selected parts of a scene or to produce special effects.

A three-dimensional viewing function is available in the OpenGL Utility library for specifying the viewing parameters (see Table 7-1). This library also includes a function for setting up a symmetric perspective-projection transformation. Three other viewing functions are available in the OpenGL basic library for specifying an orthographic projection, a general perspective projection, and

TABLE 7-1

SUMMARY OF OpenGL THREE-DIMENSIONAL VIEWING FUNCTIONS

Function	*Description*
`gluLookAt`	Specify three-dimensional viewing parameters.
`glOrtho`	Specify parameters for a clipping window and the near and far clipping planes for an orthogonal projection.
`gluPerspective`	Specify field-of-view angle and other parameters for a symmetric perspective projection.
`glFrustum`	Specify parameters for a clipping window and near and far clipping planes for a perspective projection (symmetric or oblique).
`glClipPlane`	Specify parameters for an optional clipping plane.

optional clipping planes. Table 7-1 summarizes the OpenGL viewing functions discussed in this chapter. Additionally, the table lists some viewing-related functions.

REFERENCES

Discussions of three-dimensional viewing and clipping algorithms can be found in Weiler and Atherton (1977), Weiler (1980), Cyrus and Beck (1978), and Liang and Barsky (1984). Homogeneous-coordinate clipping algorithms are described in Blinn and Newell (1978), Riesenfeld (1981), and Blinn (1993, 1996, and 1998). Various programming techniques for three-dimensional viewing are discussed in Glassner (1990), Arvo (1991), Kirk (1992), Heckbert (1994), and Paeth (1995).

A complete listing of three-dimensional OpenGL viewing functions is given in Shreiner (2000). For OpenGL programming examples using three-dimensional viewing, see Woo, Neider, Davis, and Shreiner (1999). Additional programming examples can be found at Nate Robins's tutorial Web site: http://www.cs.utah.edu/~narobins/opengl.html.

EXERCISES

7-1 Write a procedure to set up the matrix that transforms world-coordinate positions to three-dimensional viewing coordinates, given $\mathbf{P}_0$, **N**, and **V**. The view-up vector can be in any direction that is not parallel to **N**.

7-2 Write a procedure to transform the vertices of a polyhedron to projection coordinates using a parallel projection with any specified projection vector.

7-3 Write a procedure to obtain different parallel-projection views of a polyhedron by first applying a specified rotation.

7-4 Write a procedure to perform a one-point perspective projection of an object.

7-5 Write a procedure to perform a two-point perspective projection of an object.

7-6 Develop a routine to perform a three-point perspective projection of an object.

7-7 Write a routine to convert a perspective projection frustum to a regular parallelepiped.

7-8 Modify the two-dimensional Cohen-Sutherland line-clipping algorithm to clip three-dimensional lines against the normalized symmetric view volume square.

7-9 Modify the two-dimensional Liang-Barsky line-clipping algorithm to clip three-dimensional lines against a specified regular parallelepiped.

7-10 Modify the two-dimensional Liang-Barsky line-clipping algorithm to clip a given polyhedron against a specified regular parallelepiped.

7-11 Write a routine to perform line clipping in homogeneous coordinates.

7-12 Devise an algorithm to clip a polyhedron against a defined frustum. Compare the operations needed in this algorithm to those needed in an algorithm that clips against a regular parallelepiped.

7-13 Extend the Sutherland-Hodgman polygon-clipping algorithm to clip a convex polyhedron against a normalized symmetric view volume.

7-14 Write a routine to implement the preceding exercise.

7-15 Write a routine to perform polyhedron clipping in homogeneous coordinates.

7-16 Modify the program example in Section 7-10 to allow a user to specify a view for either the front or the back of the square.

7-17 Modify the program example in Section 7-10 to allow the perspective viewing parameters to be specified as user input.

7-18 Modify the program example in Section 7-10 to produce a view of any input polyhedron.

7-19 Modify the program in the preceding exercise to generate a view of the polyhedron using an orthographic projection.

7-20 Modify the program in the preceding exercise to generate a view of the polyhedron using an oblique parallel projection.

CHAPTER 8

Three-Dimensional Object Representations

A computer-generated room scene containing objects modeled with various three-dimensional representations. *(Courtesy of Autodesk, Inc.)*

Graphics scenes can contain many different kinds of objects and material surfaces: trees, flowers, clouds, rocks, water, bricks, wood paneling, rubber, paper, marble, steel, glass, plastic, and cloth, just to mention a few. So it may not be surprising that there is no single method that we can use to describe objects that will include all the characteristics of these different materials.

Polygon and quadric surfaces provide precise descriptions for simple Euclidean objects such as polyhedrons and ellipsoids; spline surfaces and constructive solid-geometry techniques are useful for designing aircraft wings, gears, and other engineering structures with curved surfaces; procedural methods, such as fractal constructions and particle systems, allow us to model terrain features, clouds, clumps of grass, and other natural objects; physically based modeling methods using systems of interacting forces can be used to describe the nonrigid behavior of a piece of cloth or a glob of jello; octree encodings are used to represent internal features of objects, such as those obtained from medical CT images; and isosurface displays, volume renderings, and other visualization techniques are applied to three-dimensional discrete data sets to obtain visual representations of the data.

Representation schemes for solid objects are often divided into two broad categories, although not all representations fall neatly into one or the other of these two categories. **Boundary representations** (**B-reps**) describe a three-dimensional object as a set of surfaces that separate the object interior from the environment. Typical examples of boundary representations are polygon facets and spline patches. **Space-partitioning representations** are used to describe interior properties, by partitioning the spatial region containing an object into a set of small, nonoverlapping, contiguous solids (usually cubes). A common space-partitioning description for a three-dimensional object is an octree representation. In this chapter, we consider the features of the various representation schemes and how they are used in computer-graphics applications.

8-1 POLYHEDRA

The most commonly used boundary representation for a three-dimensional graphics object is a set of surface polygons that enclose the object interior. Many graphics systems store all object descriptions as sets of surface polygons. This simplifies and speeds up the surface rendering and display of objects, since all surfaces are described with linear equations. For this reason, polygon descriptions are often referred to as *standard graphics objects*. In some cases, a polygonal representation is the only one available, but many packages also allow object surfaces to be described with other schemes, such as spline surfaces, which are usually converted to polygonal representations for processing through the viewing pipeline.

To describe an object as a set of polygon facets, we give the list of vertex coordinates for each polygon section over the object surface. The vertex coordinates and edge information for the surface sections are then stored in tables (Section 3-15), along with other information such as the surface normal vector for each polygon. Some graphics packages provide routines for generating a polygon-surface mesh as a set of triangles or quadrilaterals. This allows us to describe a large section of an object's bounding surface, or even the entire surface, with a single command. And some packages also provide routines for displaying common shapes, such as a cube, sphere, or cylinder, represented with polygon surfaces. Sophisticated graphics systems use fast hardware-implemented polygon renderers that have the capability for displaying a million or more shaded polygons (usually triangles) per second, including the application of surface texture and special lighting effects.

8-2 OpenGL POLYHEDRON FUNCTIONS

We have two methods for specifying polygon surfaces in an OpenGL program. Using the polygon primitives discussed in Section 3-16, we can generate a variety of polyhedron shapes and surfaces meshes. In addition, we can use GLUT functions to display the five regular polyhedra.

OpenGL Polygon Fill-Area Functions

A set of polygon patches for a section of an object surface, or a complete description for a polyhedron, can be given using the OpenGL primitive constants `GL_POLYGON`, `GL_TRIANGLES`, `GL_TRIANGLE_STRIP`, `GL_TRIANGLE_FAN`, `GL_QUADS`, and `GL_QUAD_STRIP`. For example, we could tessellate the lateral (axial) surface of a cylinder using a quadrilateral strip. Similarly, all faces of a parallelogram can be described with a set of rectangles, and all faces of a triangular pyramid could be specified using a set of connected triangular surfaces.

GLUT Regular Polyhedron Functions

Some standard shapes—the five regular polyhedra—are predefined by routines in the GLUT library. These polyhedra, also called the Platonic solids, are distinguished by the fact that all the faces of any regular polyhedron are identical regular polygons. Thus, all edges in a regular polyhedron are equal, all edge angles are equal, and all angles between faces are equal. Polyhedra are named according to the number of faces in each of the solids, and the five regular polyhedra are the regular tetrahedron (or triangular pyramid, with 4 faces), the regular hexahedron (or cube, with 6 faces), the regular octahedron (8 faces), the regular dodecahedron (12 faces), and the regular icosahedron (20 faces).

Ten functions are provided in GLUT for generating these solids: five of the functions produce wire-frame objects, and five display the polyhedra facets as shaded fill areas. The displayed surface characteristics for the fill areas are determined by the material properties and the lighting conditions that we set for a scene. Each regular polyhedron is described in modeling coordinates, so that each is centered at the world-coordinate origin.

We obtain the four-sided, regular triangular pyramid using either of the two functions:

```
glutWireTetrahedron ( );
```

or

```
glutSolidTetrahedron ( );
```

This polyhedron is generated with its center at the world-coordinate origin and with a radius (distance from the center of the tetrahedron to any vertex) equal to $\sqrt{3}$.

The six-sided regular hexahedron (cube) is displayed with

```
glutWireCube (edgeLength);
```

or

```
glutSolidCube (edgeLength);
```

Parameter `edgeLength` can be assigned any positive, double-precision floating-point value, and the cube is centered on the coordinate origin.

To display the eight-sided regular octahedron, we invoke either of the following commands.

```
glutWireOctahedron ( );
```

or

```
glutSolidOctahedron ( );
```

This polyhedron has equilateral triangular faces, and the radius (distance from the center of the octahedron at the coordinate origin to any vertex) is 1.0.

The twelve-sided regular dodecahedron, centered at the world-coordinate origin, is generated with

```
glutWireDodecahedron ( );
```

or

```
glutSolidDodecahedron ( );
```

Each face of this polyhedron is a pentagon.

And the following two functions generate the twenty-sided regular icosahedron.

```
glutWireIcosahedron ( );
```

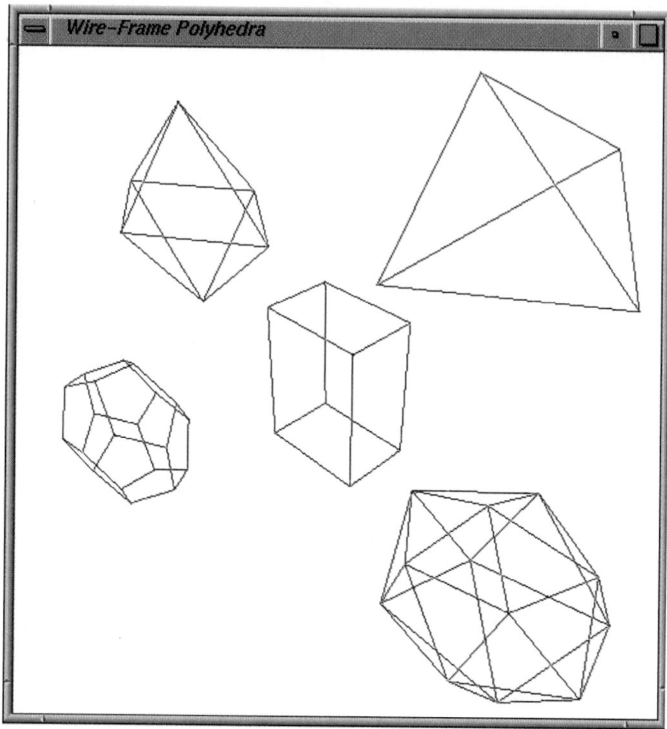

FIGURE 8-1 A perspective view of the five GLUT polyhedra, scaled and positioned within a display window by procedure `displayWirePolyhedra`.

or

```
glutSolidIcosahedron ( );
```

Default radius (distance from the polyhedron center at the coordinate origin to any vertex) for the icosahedron is 1.0, and each face is an equilateral triangle.

Example GLUT Polyhedron Program

Using the GLUT functions for the Platonic solids, the following program generates a transformed, wire-frame perspective display of these polyhedrons. All five solids are positioned within one display window (Fig. 8-1).

```
#include <GL/glut.h>

GLsizei winWidth = 500, winHeight = 500;  // Initial display-window size.

void init (void)
{
    glClearColor (1.0, 1.0, 1.0, 0.0);  // White display window.
}

void displayWirePolyhedra (void)
{
    glClear (GL_COLOR_BUFFER_BIT);  // Clear display window.

    glColor3f (0.0, 0.0, 1.0);      // Set line color to blue.
```

```
    /*  Set viewing transformation.  */
    gluLookAt (5.0, 5.0, 5.0, 0.0, 0.0, 0.0, 0.0, 1.0, 0.0);

    /*  Scale cube and display as wire-frame parallelepiped. */
    glScalef (1.5, 2.0, 1.0);
    glutWireCube (1.0);

    /*  Scale, translate, and display wire-frame dodecahedron. */
    glScalef (0.8, 0.5, 0.8);
    glTranslatef (-6.0, -5.0, 0.0);
    glutWireDodecahedron ( );

    /*  Translate and display wire-frame tetrahedron. */
    glTranslatef (8.6, 8.6, 2.0);
    glutWireTetrahedron ( );

    /*  Translate and display wire-frame octahedron. */
    glTranslatef (-3.0, -1.0, 0.0);
    glutWireOctahedron ( );

    /*  Scale, translate, and display wire-frame icosahedron. */
    glScalef (0.8, 0.8, 1.0);
    glTranslatef (4.3, -2.0, 0.5);
    glutWireIcosahedron ( );

    glFlush ( );
}

void winReshapeFcn (GLint newWidth, GLint newHeight)
{
    glViewport (0, 0, newWidth, newHeight);

    glMatrixMode (GL_PROJECTION);
    glFrustum (-1.0, 1.0, -1.0, 1.0, 2.0, 20.0);

    glMatrixMode (GL_MODELVIEW);

    glClear (GL_COLOR_BUFFER_BIT);
}

void main (int argc, char** argv)
{
    glutInit (&argc, argv);
    glutInitDisplayMode (GLUT_SINGLE | GLUT_RGB);
    glutInitWindowPosition (100, 100);
    glutInitWindowSize (winWidth, winHeight);
    glutCreateWindow ("Wire-Frame Polyhedra");

    init ( );
    glutDisplayFunc (displayWirePolyhedra);
    glutReshapeFunc (winReshapeFcn);

    glutMainLoop ( );
}
```

8-3 CURVED SURFACES

Equations for objects with curved boundaries can be expressed in either a parametric or a nonparametric form, and Appendix A gives a summary and comparison of parametric and nonparametric representations. The various objects that are often useful in graphics applications include quadric surfaces, superquadrics, polynomial and exponential functions, and spline surfaces. These input object descriptions are typically tessellated to produce polygon-mesh approximations for the surfaces.

8-4 QUADRIC SURFACES

A frequently used class of objects are the *quadric surfaces*, which are described with second-degree equations (quadratics). They include spheres, ellipsoids, tori, paraboloids, and hyperboloids. Quadric surfaces, particularly spheres and ellipsoids, are common elements of graphics scenes, and routines for generating these surfaces are often available in graphics packages. Also, quadric surfaces can be produced with rational spline representations.

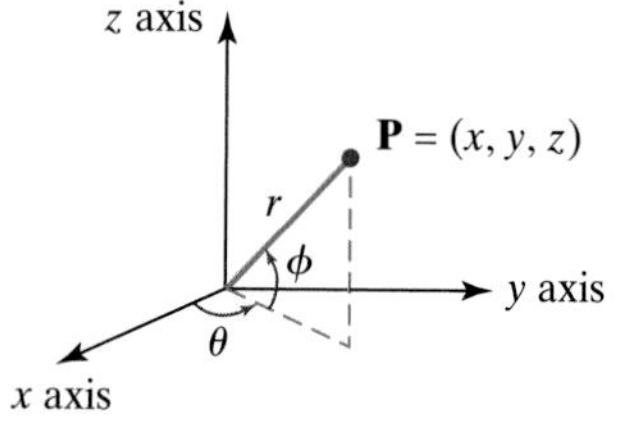

FIGURE 8-2 Parametric coordinate position (r, θ, ϕ) on the surface of a sphere with radius r.

Sphere

In Cartesian coordinates, a spherical surface with radius r centered on the coordinate origin is defined as the set of points (x, y, z) that satisfy the equation:

$$x^2 + y^2 + z^2 = r^2 \tag{8-1}$$

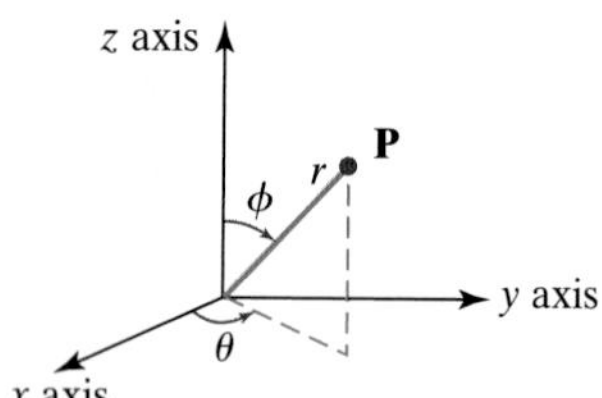

FIGURE 8-3 Spherical coordinate parameters (r, θ, ϕ), using colatitude for angle ϕ.

We can also describe the spherical surface in parametric form, using latitude and longitude angles (Fig. 8-2):

$$\begin{aligned} x &= r\cos\phi\cos\theta, \qquad -\pi/2 \le \phi \le \pi/2 \\ y &= r\cos\phi\sin\theta, \qquad -\pi \le \theta \le \pi \\ z &= r\sin\phi \end{aligned} \tag{8-2}$$

The parametric representation in Eqs. 8-2 provides a symmetric range for the angular parameters θ and ϕ. Alternatively, we could write the parametric equations using standard spherical coordinates, where angle ϕ is specified as the colatitude (Fig. 8-3). Then, ϕ is defined over the range $0 \le \phi \le \pi$, and θ is often taken in the range $0 \le \theta \le 2\pi$. We could also set up the representation using parameters u and v defined over the range from 0 to 1 by substituting $\phi = \pi u$ and $\theta = 2\pi v$.

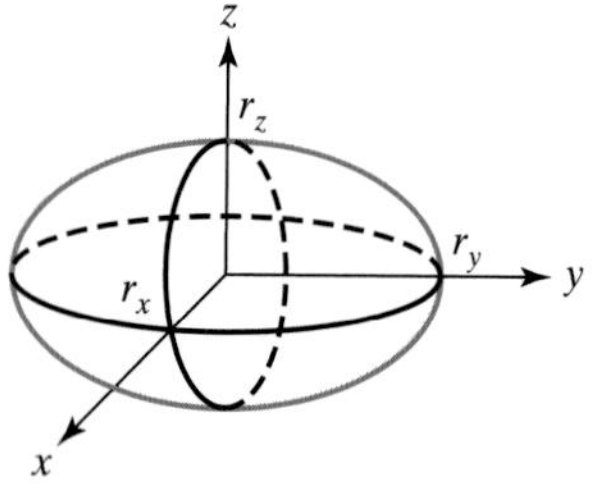

FIGURE 8-4 An ellipsoid with radii r_x, r_y, and r_z, centered on the coordinate origin.

Ellipsoid

An ellipsoidal surface can be described as an extension of a spherical surface, where the radii in three mutually perpendicular directions can have different values (Fig. 8-4). The Cartesian representation for points over the surface of an ellipsoid centered on the origin is

$$\left(\frac{x}{r_x}\right)^2 + \left(\frac{y}{r_y}\right)^2 + \left(\frac{z}{r_z}\right)^2 = 1 \tag{8-3}$$

And a parametric representation for the ellipsoid in terms of the latitude angle ϕ and the longitude angle θ in Fig. 8-2 is

$$\begin{aligned} x &= r_x \cos\phi \cos\theta, & -\pi/2 \le \phi \le \pi/2 \\ y &= r_y \cos\phi \sin\theta, & -\pi \le \theta \le \pi \\ z &= r_z \sin\phi \end{aligned} \tag{8-4}$$

Torus

A doughnut-shaped object is called a torus or anchor ring. Most often it is described as the surface generated by rotating a circle or an ellipse about a coplanar axis line that is external to the conic. The defining parameters for a torus are then the distance of the conic center from the rotation axis and the dimensions of the conic. A torus generated by the rotation of a circle with radius r in the yz plane about the z axis is shown in Fig. 8-5. With the circle center on the y axis, the axial radius, r_{axial}, of the resulting torus is equal to the distance along the y axis to the circle center from the z axis (the rotation axis). And the cross-sectional radius of the torus is the radius of the generating circle.

The equation for the cross-sectional circle shown in the side view of Fig. 8-5 is

$$(y - r_{\text{axial}})^2 + z^2 = r^2$$

Rotating this circle about the z axis produces the torus whose surface positions are described with the Cartesian equation

$$\left(\sqrt{x^2 + y^2} - r_{\text{axial}}\right)^2 + z^2 = r^2 \tag{8-5}$$

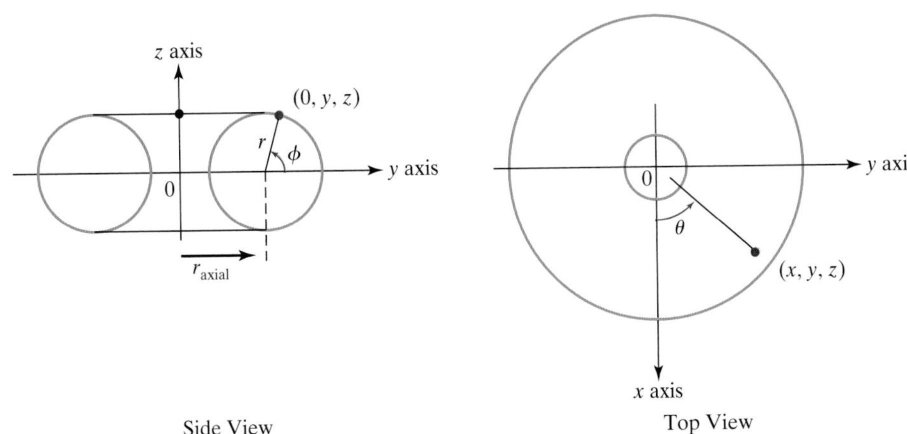

FIGURE 8-5 A torus, centered on the coordinate origin, with a circular cross section and with the torus axis along the z axis.

And the corresponding parametric equations for the torus with a circular cross section are

$$\begin{aligned} x &= (r_{\text{axial}} + r\cos\phi)\cos\theta, & -\pi \le \phi \le \pi \\ y &= (r_{\text{axial}} + r\cos\phi)\sin\theta, & -\pi \le \theta \le \pi \\ z &= r\sin\phi \end{aligned} \tag{8-6}$$

We could also generate a torus by rotating an ellipse, instead of a circle, about the z axis. For an ellipse in the yz plane with semimajor and semiminor axes denoted as r_y and r_z, we can write the ellipse equation as

$$\left(\frac{y - r_{\text{axial}}}{r_y}\right)^2 + \left(\frac{z}{r_z}\right)^2 = 1$$

where r_{axial} is the distance along the y axis from the rotation z axis to the ellipse center. This generates a torus that can be described with the Cartesian equation

$$\left(\frac{\sqrt{x^2 + y^2} - r_{\text{axial}}}{r_y}\right) + \left(\frac{z}{r_z}\right)^2 = 1 \tag{8-7}$$

The corresponding parametric representation for the torus with an elliptical cross section is

$$\begin{aligned} x &= (r_{\text{axial}} + r_y\cos\phi)\cos\theta, & -\pi \le \phi \le \pi \\ y &= (r_{\text{axial}} + r_y\cos\phi)\sin\theta, & -\pi \le \theta \le \pi \\ z &= r_z\sin\phi \end{aligned} \tag{8-8}$$

Other variations on the preceding torus equations are possible. For example, we could generate a torus surface by rotating either a circle or an ellipse along an elliptical path around the rotation axis.

8-5 SUPERQUADRICS

This class of objects is a generalization of the quadric representations. **Superquadrics** are formed by incorporating additional parameters into the quadric equations to provide increased flexibility for adjusting object shapes. One additional parameter is added to curve equations, and two additional parameters are used in surface equations.

Superellipse

We obtain a Cartesian representation for a superellipse from the corresponding equation for an ellipse by allowing the exponent on the x and y terms to be variable. One way to do this is to write the Cartesian superellipse equation in the form:

$$\left(\frac{x}{r_x}\right)^{2/s} + \left(\frac{y}{r_y}\right)^{2/s} = 1 \tag{8-9}$$

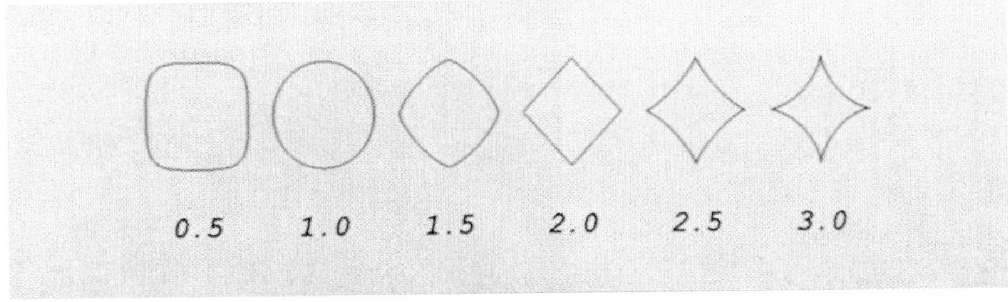

FIGURE 8-6 Superellipses plotted with values for parameter s ranging from 0.5 to 3.0 and with $r_x = r_y$.

where parameter s can be assigned any real value. When $s = 1$, we have an ordinary ellipse.

Corresponding parametric equations for the superellipse of Eq. 8-9 can be expressed as

$$\begin{aligned} x &= r_x \cos^s \theta, \qquad -\pi \le \theta \le \pi \\ y &= r_y \sin^s \theta \end{aligned} \tag{8-10}$$

Figure 8-6 illustrates superellipse shapes that can be generated using various values for parameter s.

Superellipsoid

A Cartesian representation for a superellipsoid is obtained from the equation for an ellipsoid by incorporating two exponent parameters:

$$\left[\left(\frac{x}{r_x}\right)^{2/s_2} + \left(\frac{y}{r_y}\right)^{2/s_2}\right]^{s_2/s_1} + \left(\frac{z}{r_z}\right)^{2/s_1} = 1 \tag{8-11}$$

For $s_1 = s_2 = 1$, we have an ordinary ellipsoid.

We can then write the corresponding parametric representation for the superellipsoid of Eq. 8-11 as

$$\begin{aligned} x &= r_x \cos^{s_1} \phi \cos^{s_2} \theta, \qquad -\pi/2 \le \phi \le \pi/2 \\ y &= r_y \cos^{s_1} \phi \sin^{s_2} \theta, \qquad -\pi \le \theta \le \pi \\ z &= r_z \sin^{s_1} \phi \end{aligned} \tag{8-12}$$

Figure 8-7 illustrates superellipsoid shapes that can be generated using various values for parameters s_1 and s_2. These and other superquadric shapes can be combined to create more complex structures, such as depictions of furniture, threaded bolts, and other hardware.

8-6 OpenGL QUADRIC-SURFACE AND CUBIC-SURFACE FUNCTIONS

A sphere and a number of other three-dimensional quadric-surface objects can be displayed using functions that are included in the OpenGL Utility Toolkit (GLUT) and in the OpenGL Utility (GLU). In addition, GLUT has one function

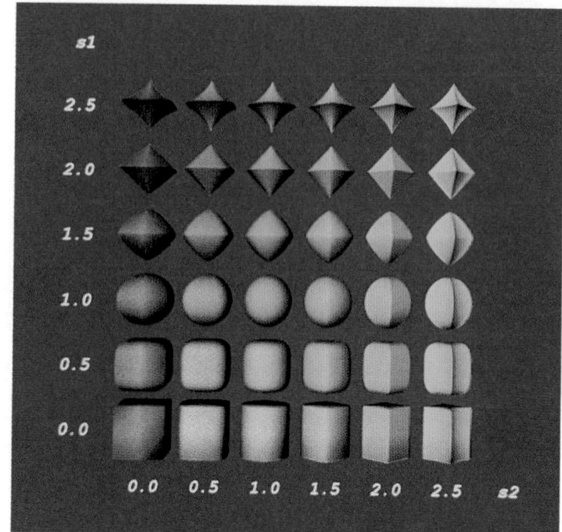

FIGURE 8-7 Superellipsoids plotted with values for parameters s_1 and s_2 ranging from 0.0 to 2.5 and with $r_x = r_y = r_z$.

for displaying a teapot shape that is defined with bicubic surface patches. The GLUT functions, which are easy to incorporate into an application program, each have two versions. One version of each function displays a wire-frame surface, and the other version displays the surface as a rendered set of fill-area polygon patches. With the GLUT functions we can display a sphere, cone, torus, or the teapot. Quadric-surface GLU functions are a little more involved to set up, but they provide a few more options. With the GLU functions, we can display a sphere, cylinder, tapered cylinder, cone, flat circular ring (or hollow disk), and a section of a circular ring (or disk).

GLUT Quadric-Surface Functions

We generate a GLUT sphere with either of the two functions:

```
glutWireSphere (r, nLongitudes, nLatitudes);
```

or

```
glutSolidSphere (r, nLongitudes, nLatitudes);
```

where the sphere radius is determined by the double-precision floating-point number assigned to parameter `r`. Parameters `nLongitudes` and `nLatitudes` are used to select the integer number of longitude and latitude lines that will be used to approximate the spherical surface as a quadrilateral mesh. Edges of the quadrilateral surface patches are straight-line approximations of the longitude and latitude lines. The sphere is defined in modeling coordinates, centered at the world-coordinate origin with its polar axis along the z axis.

A GLUT cone is obtained with

```
glutWireCone (rBase, height, nLongitudes, nLatitudes);
```

or

```
glutSolidCone (rBase, height, nLongitudes, nLatitudes);
```

We set double-precision, floating-point values for the radius of the cone base and for the cone height using parameters `rbase` and `height`, respectively. As with a GLUT sphere, parameters `nLongitudes` and `nLatitudes` are assigned integer values that specify the number of orthogonal surface lines for the quadrilateral mesh approximation. A cone longitude line is a straight-line segment along the cone surface from the apex to the base that lies in a plane containing the cone axis. Each latitude line is displayed as a set of straight-line segments around the circumference of a circle on the cone surface that is parallel to the cone base and that lies in a plane perpendicular to the cone axis. The cone is described in modeling coordinates, with the center of the base at the world-coordinate origin and with the cone axis along the world z axis.

Wire-frame or surface-shaded displays of a torus with a circular cross section are produced with

```
glutWireTorus (rCrossSection, rAxial, nConcentrics,
                    nRadialSlices);
```

or

```
glutSolidTorus (rCrossSection, rAxial, nConcentrics,
                    nRadialSlices);
```

The torus obtained with these GLUT routines can be described as the surface generated by rotating a circle with radius `rCrossSection` about the coplanar z axis, where the distance of the circle center from the z axis is `rAxial` (Section 8-4). We select a size for the torus using double-precision, floating-point values for these radii in the GLUT functions. And the size of the quadrilaterals in the approximating surface mesh for the torus is set with integer values for parameters `nConcentrics` and `nRadialSlices`. Parameter `nConcentrics` specifies the number of concentric circles (with center on the z axis) to be used on the torus surface, and parameter `nRadialSlices` specifies the number of radial slices through the torus surface. These two parameters designate the number of orthogonal grid lines over the torus surface, with the grid lines displayed as straight-line segments (the boundaries of the quadrilaterals) between intersection positions. The displayed torus is centered on the world-coordinate origin, with its axis along the world z axis.

GLUT Cubic-Surface Teapot Function

During the early development of computer-graphics methods, sets of polygon-mesh data tables were constructed for the description of several three-dimensional objects that could be used to test rendering techniques. These objects included the surfaces of a Volkswagen automobile and a teapot, developed at the University of Utah. The data set for the Utah teapot, as constructed by Martin Newell in 1975, contains 306 vertices, defining 32 bicubic Bézier surface patches (Section 8-11). Since determining the surface coordinates for a complex object is time-consuming, these data sets, particularly the teapot surface mesh, became widely used.

We can display the teapot, as a mesh of over one thousand bicubic surface patches, using either of the following two GLUT functions:

```
glutWireTeapot (size);
```

or

```
glutSolidTeapot (size);
```

The teapot surface is generated using OpenGL Bézier curve functions (Section 8-11). Parameter `size` sets the double-precision floating-point value for the maximum radius of the teapot bowl. The teapot is centered on the world-coordinate origin with its vertical axis along the y axis.

GLU Quadric-Surface Functions

To generate a quadric surface using GLU functions, we need to assign a name to the quadric, activate the GLU quadric renderer, and designate values for the surface parameters. In addition, we can set other parameter values to control the appearance of a GLU quadric surface.

The following statements illustrate the basic sequence of calls for displaying a wire-frame sphere centered on the world-coordinate origin.

```
GLUquadricObj *sphere1;

sphere1 = gluNewQuadric ( );
gluQuadricDrawStyle (sphere1, GLU_LINE);

gluSphere (sphere1, r, nLongitudes, nLatitudes);
```

A name for the quadric object is defined in the first statement, and, for this example, we have chosen the name `sphere1`. This name is then used in other GLU functions to reference this particular quadric surface. Next, the quadric renderer is activated with the `gluNewQuadric` function, then the display mode `GLU_LINE` is selected for `sphere1` with the `gluQuadricDrawStyle` command. Thus, the sphere is displayed in a wire-frame form with a straight-line segment between each pair of surface vertices. Parameter `r` is assigned a double-precision value for the sphere radius, and the sphere surface is divided into a set of polygon facets by the equally spaced longitude and latitude lines. We specify the integer number of longitude lines and latitude lines as values for parameters `nLongitudes` and `nLatitudes`.

Three other display modes are available for GLU quadric surfaces. Using the symbolic constant `GLU_POINT` in the `gluQuadricDrawStyle`, we display a quadric surface as a point plot. For the sphere, a point is displayed at each surface vertex formed by the intersection of a longitude line and a latitude line. Another option is the symbolic constant `GLU_SILHOUETTE`. This produces a wire-frame display without the shared edges between two coplanar polygon facets. And with the symbolic constant `GLU_FILL`, we display the polygon patches as shaded fill areas.

We generate displays of the other GLU quadric-surface primitives using the same basic sequence of commands. To produce a view of a cone, cylinder, or tapered cylinder, we replace the `gluSphere` function with

```
gluCylinder (quadricName, rBase, rTop, height, nLongitudes,
                nLatitudes);
```

The base of this object is in the xy plane ($z = 0$), and the axis is the z axis. We assign a double-precision radius value to the base of this quadric surface using parameter `rBase`, and we assign a radius to the top of the quadric surface using parameter `rTop`. If `rTop` $= 0.0$, we get a cone; if `rTop` $=$ `rBase`, we obtain a cylinder. Otherwise, a tapered cylinder is displayed. A double-precision height value is assigned to parameter `height`, and the surface is divided into a number of equally spaced vertical and horizontal lines as determined by the integer values assigned to parameters `nLongitudes` and `nLatitudes`.

A flat, circular ring or solid disk is displayed in the xy plane ($z = 0$) and centered on the world-coordinate origin with

```
gluDisk (ringName, rInner, rOuter, nRadii, nRings);
```

We set double-precision values for an inner radius and an outer radius with parameters `rInner` and `rOuter`. If `rInner` $= 0$, the disk is solid. Otherwise, it is displayed with a concentric hole in the center of the disk. The disk surface is divided into a set of facets with integer parameters `nRadii` and `nRings`, which specify the number of radial slices to be used in the tessellation and the number of concentric circular rings, respectively. Orientation for the ring is defined with respect to the z axis, with the front of the ring facing in the $+z$ direction and the back of the ring facing in the $-z$ direction.

We can specify a section of a circular ring with the following GLU function.

```
gluPartialDisk (ringName, rInner, rOuter, nRadii, nRings,
                    startAngle, sweepAngle);
```

The double-precision parameter `startAngle` designates an angular position in degrees in the xy plane measured clockwise from the positive y axis. Similarly, parameter `sweepAngle` denotes an angular distance in degrees from the `startAngle` position. Thus, a section of a flat, circular disk is displayed from angular position `startAngle` to `startAngle` + `sweepAngle`. For example, if `startAngle` $= 0.0$ and `sweepAngle` $= 90.0$, then the section of the disk lying in the first quadrant of the xy plane is displayed.

Allocated memory for any GLU quadric surface can be reclaimed and the surface eliminated with

```
gluDeleteQuadric (quadricName);
```

Also, we can define the front/back directions for any quadric surface with the orientation function:

```
gluQuadricOrientation (quadricName, normalVectorDirection);
```

Parameter `normalVectorDirection` is assigned either `GLU_OUTSIDE` or `GLU_INSIDE` to indicate a direction for the surface normal vectors, where "outside" indicates the **front-face direction** and "inside" indicates the **back-face direction.** The default value is `GLU_OUTSIDE`. For the flat, circular ring, the default front-face direction is in the direction of the positive z axis ("above" the disk).

Another option is the generation of surface-normal vectors.

```
gluQuadricNormals (quadricName, generationMode);
```

A symbolic constant is assigned to parameter `generationMode` to indicate how surface-normal vectors should be generated. The default is `GLU_NONE`, which means that no surface normals are to be generated, and, typically, no lighting conditions are applied to the quadric surface. For flat surface shading (a constant color value for each surface), we use the symbolic constant `GLU_FLAT`. This produces one surface normal for each polygon facet. When other lighting and shading conditions are to be applied, we use the constant `GLU_SMOOTH`, which generates a normal vector for each surface vertex position.

Other options for GLU quadric surfaces include setting surface-texture parameters. And we can designate a function that is to be invoked in the event that an error occurs during the generation of a quadric surface:

```
gluQuadricCallback (quadricName, GLU_ERROR, function);
```

Example Program Using GLUT and GLU Quadric-Surface Functions

Three quadric-surface objects (sphere, cone, and cylinder) are displayed in a wire-frame representation by the following example program. We set the view-up direction as the positive z axis so that the axis for all displayed objects is vertical. The three objects are positioned at different locations within a single display window, as shown in Fig. 8-8.

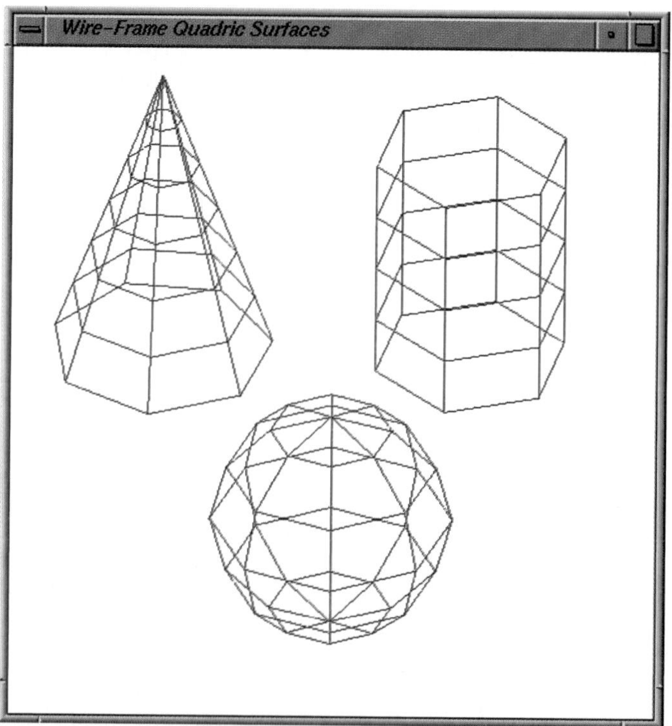

FIGURE 8-8 Display of a GLUT sphere, GLUT cone, and GLU cylinder, positioned within a display window by procedure `wireQuadSurfs`.

```
#include <GL/glut.h>

GLsizei winWidth = 500, winHeight = 500;    // Initial display-window size.

void init (void)
{
   glClearColor (1.0, 1.0, 1.0, 0.0);       // Set display-window color.
}

void wireQuadSurfs (void)
{
   glClear (GL_COLOR_BUFFER_BIT);            // Clear display window.

   glColor3f (0.0, 0.0, 1.0);                // Set line-color to blue.

   /*  Set viewing parameters with world z axis as view-up direction.  */
   gluLookAt (2.0, 2.0, 2.0, 0.0, 0.0, 0.0, 0.0, 0.0, 1.0);

   /*  Position and display GLUT wire-frame sphere.  */
   glPushMatrix ( );
   glTranslatef (1.0, 1.0, 0.0);
   glutWireSphere (0.75, 8, 6);
   glPopMatrix ( );

   /*  Position and display GLUT wire-frame cone.  */
   glPushMatrix ( );
   glTranslatef (1.0, -0.5, 0.5);
   glutWireCone (0.7, 2.0, 7, 6);
   glPopMatrix ( );

   /*  Position and display GLU wire-frame cylinder.  */
   GLUquadricObj *cylinder;   // Set name for GLU quadric object.
   glPushMatrix ( );
   glTranslatef (0.0, 1.2, 0.8);
   cylinder = gluNewQuadric ( );
   gluQuadricDrawStyle (cylinder, GLU_LINE);
   gluCylinder (cylinder, 0.6, 0.6, 1.5, 6, 4);
   glPopMatrix ( );

   glFlush ( );
}

void winReshapeFcn (GLint newWidth, GLint newHeight)
{
   glViewport (0, 0, newWidth, newHeight);

   glMatrixMode (GL_PROJECTION);
   glOrtho (-2.0, 2.0, -2.0, 2.0, 0.0, 5.0);

   glMatrixMode (GL_MODELVIEW);

   glClear (GL_COLOR_BUFFER_BIT);
}
```

```
void main (int argc, char** argv)
{
    glutInit (&argc, argv);
    glutInitDisplayMode (GLUT_SINGLE | GLUT_RGB);
    glutInitWindowPosition (100, 100);
    glutInitWindowSize (winWidth, winHeight);
    glutCreateWindow ("Wire-Frame Quadric Surfaces");

    init ( );
    glutDisplayFunc (wireQuadSurfs);
    glutReshapeFunc (winReshapeFcn);

    glutMainLoop ( );
}
```

8-7 BLOBBY OBJECTS

Various techniques have been developed for modeling nonrigid objects in computer-graphics applications, and methods for displaying the characteristics of materials such as cloth and rubber are discussed in Section 8-26. But other objects, such as molecular structures, liquids and water droplets, melting objects, and animal and human muscle shapes, exhibit a degree of fluidity. These objects change their surface characteristics in certain motions or when in proximity to other objects, and they have curved surfaces that cannot be represented easily with standard shapes. As a class, they are generally referred to as **blobby objects.**

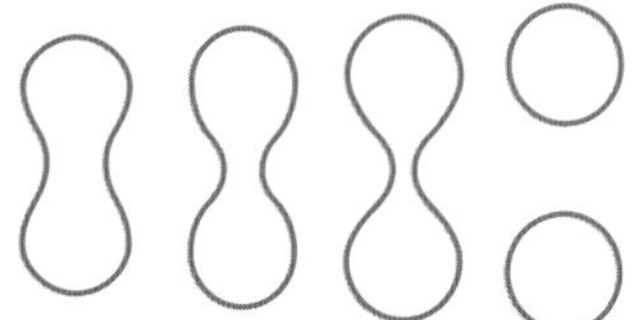

FIGURE 8-9 Molecular bonding. As two molecules move away from each other, the surface shapes stretch, snap, and finally contract into spheres.

A molecular shape, for example, can be described as spherical in isolation, but this shape changes when the molecule approaches another molecule. This is due to the fact that the shape of the electron density cloud is distorted by the presence of the other molecule, so that a bonding effect takes place between the two molecules. Figure 8-9 illustrates the stretching, snapping, and contracting effects on molecular shapes when two molecules move apart. These characteristics cannot be adequately described simply with spherical or elliptical shapes. Similarly, Fig. 8-10 shows muscle shapes in a human arm, which exhibit similar characteristics.

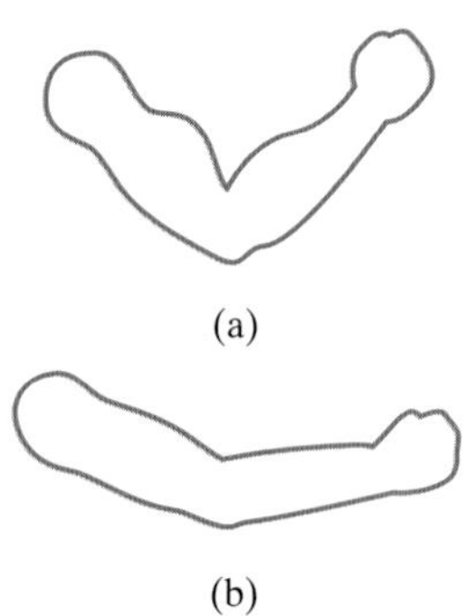

FIGURE 8-10 "Blobby" muscle shapes in a human arm.

Several models have been developed for representing blobby objects as distribution functions over a region of space. Usually the surface shapes are described so that the object volume remains constant throughout any motions or interactions. One method for modeling blobby objects is to use a combination of Gaussian density functions, or Gaussian bumps (Fig. 8-11). A surface function is then defined as

$$f(x, y, z) = \sum_k b_k e^{-a_k r_k^2} - T = 0 \tag{8-13}$$

where $r_k^2 = x_k^2 + y_k^2 + z_k^2$, parameter T is some specified threshold, and parameters a_k and b_k are used to adjust the amount of blobbiness of the individual components of the surface. Negative values for parameter b_k can be used to produce dents instead of bumps. Figure 8-12 illustrates the surface structure of a composite object modeled with four Gaussian density functions. At the threshold level, numerical

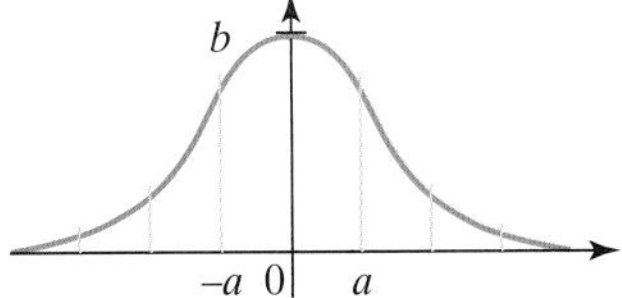

FIGURE 8-11 A three-dimensional Gaussian density function centered at position 0, with height b and standard deviation a.

FIGURE 8-12 A composite blobby object formed with four Gaussian bumps.

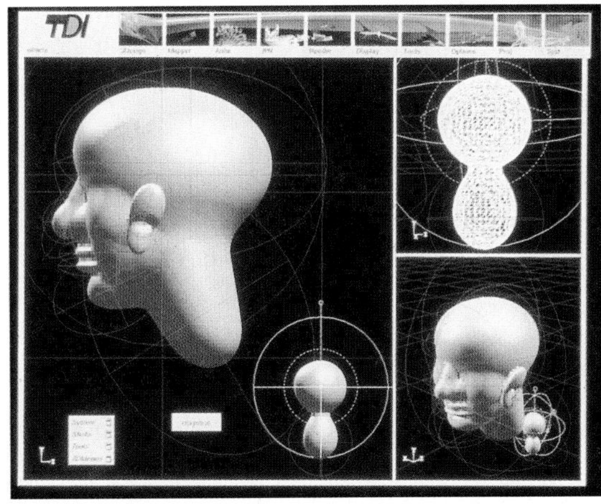

FIGURE 8-13 A screen layout, used in the Blob Modeler and the Blob Animator packages, for modeling objects with metaballs. (*Courtesy of Thomson Digital Image.*)

root-finding techniques are used to locate the coordinate intersection values. The cross sections of the individual objects are then modeled as circles or ellipses. If two cross sections are near each other, they are merged to form one blobby shape as in Figure 8-9, whose structure depends on the separation of the two objects.

Other methods for generating blobby objects use density functions that fall off to 0 in a finite interval, rather than exponentially. The **meta-ball** model describes composite objects as combinations of quadratic density functions of the form

$$f(r) = \begin{cases} b\left(1 - \dfrac{3r^2}{d^2}\right), & \text{if } 0 < r \le \dfrac{d}{3} \\ \dfrac{3}{2}b\left(1 - \dfrac{r}{d}\right)^2, & \text{if } \dfrac{d}{3} < r \le d \\ 0, & \text{if } r > d \end{cases} \tag{8-14}$$

And, the **soft object** model uses the function

$$f(r) = \begin{cases} 1 - \dfrac{22r^2}{9d^2} + \dfrac{17r^4}{9d^4} - \dfrac{4r^6}{9d^6}, & \text{if } 0 < r \le d \\ 0, & \text{if } r > d \end{cases} \tag{8-15}$$

Some design and painting packages now provide blobby function modeling for handling applications that cannot be adequately modeled with other representations. Figure 8-13 shows a user interface for a blobby object modeler using metaballs.

8-8 SPLINE REPRESENTATIONS

In drafting terminology, a spline is a flexible strip used to produce a smooth curve through a designated set of points. Several small weights are distributed along the length of the strip to hold it in position on the drafting table as the curve is drawn. The term *spline curve* originally referred to a curve drawn in this manner. We can mathematically describe such a curve with a piecewise cubic polynomial function whose first and second derivatives are continuous across the various curve sections. In computer graphics, the term **spline curve** now refers to any composite curve formed with polynomial sections satisfying any specified continuity conditions at the boundary of the pieces. A **spline surface** can be described with two sets of orthogonal spline curves. There are several different kinds of spline specifications that are used in computer-graphics applications. Each individual specification simply refers to a particular type of polynomial with certain prescribed boundary conditions.

Splines are used to design curve and surface shapes, to digitize drawings, and to specify animation paths for the objects or the camera position in a scene. Typical CAD applications for splines include the design of automobile bodies, aircraft and spacecraft surfaces, ship hulls, and home appliances.

FIGURE 8-14 A set of six control points interpolated with piecewise continuous polynomial sections.

Interpolation and Approximation Splines

We specify a spline curve by giving a set of coordinate positions, called **control points,** which indicate the general shape of the curve. These coordinate positions are then fitted with piecewise-continuous, parametric polynomial functions in one of two ways. When polynomial sections are fitted so that all the control points are connected, as in Fig. 8-14, the resulting curve is said to **interpolate** the set of control points. On the other hand, when the generated polynomial curve is plotted so that some, or all, of the control points are not on the curve path, the resulting curve is said to **approximate** the set of control points (Fig. 8-15). Similar methods are used to construct interpolation or approximation spline surfaces.

FIGURE 8-15 A set of six control points approximated with piecewise continuous polynomial sections.

Interpolation methods are commonly used to digitize drawings or to specify animation paths. Approximation methods are used primarily as design tools to create object shapes. Figure 8-16 shows the screen display of an approximation spline surface for a design application. Straight lines connect the control-point positions above the surface.

A spline curve or surface is defined, modified, and manipulated with operations on the control points. By interactively selecting spatial positions for the control points, a designer can set up an initial shape. After the polynomial fit is displayed for a given set of control points, the designer can then reposition some or all of the control points to restructure the shape of the object. And geometric transformations (translation, rotation, and scaling) are applied to the object by transforming the control points. In addition, CAD packages sometimes insert extra control points to aid a designer in adjusting the object shapes.

A set of control points forms a boundary for a region of space that is called the **convex hull.** One way to envision the shape of a convex hull for a two-dimensional curve is to imagine a rubber band stretched around the positions of the control points so that each control point is either on the perimeter of this boundary or inside it (Fig. 8-17). Thus, the convex hull for a two-dimensional spline curve is a convex polygon. In three-dimensional space, the convex hull for a set of spline control points forms a convex polyhedron. Convex hulls provide a measure for the deviation of a curve or surface from the region of space near the control points.

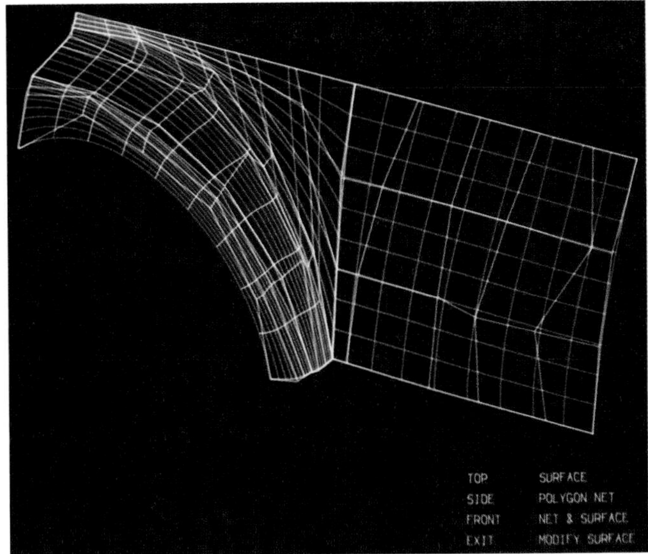

FIGURE 8-16 An approximation spline surface for a CAD application in automotive design. Surface contours are plotted with polynomial curve sections, and the surface control points are connected with straight-line segments. (*Courtesy of Evans & Sutherland.*)

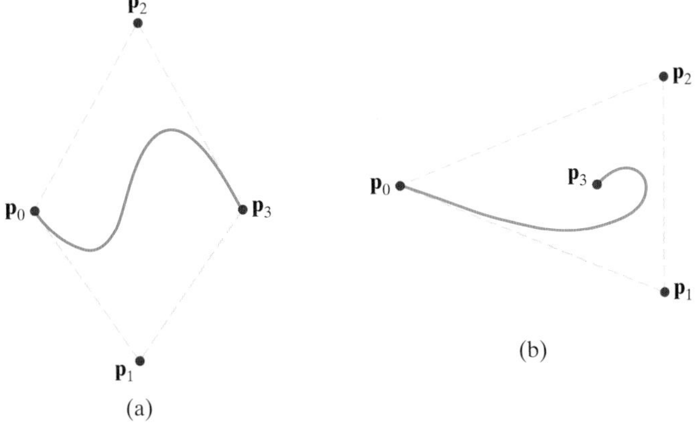

FIGURE 8-17 Convex-hull shapes (dashed lines) for two sets of control points in the xy plane.

In most cases, a spline is bounded by its convex hull, which ensures that the object shape follows the control points without erratic oscillations. Also, the convex hull provides a measure of the coordinate extents of a designed curve or surface, so it is useful in clipping and viewing routines.

A polyline connecting the sequence of control points for an approximation spline curve is usually displayed to remind a designer of the control-point positions and ordering. This set of connected line segments is called the **control graph** for the curve. Often the control graph is alluded to as the "control polygon" or the "characteristic polygon", even though the control graph is a polyline and not a polygon. Figure 8-18 shows the shape of the control graph for the control-point sequences in Fig. 8-17. For a spline surface, two sets of polyline control-point connectors form the edges for the polygon facets in a quadrilateral mesh for the surface control graph, as in Fig. 8-16.

Parametric Continuity Conditions

To ensure a smooth transition from one section of a piecewise parametric spline to the next, we can impose various **continuity conditions** at the connection points. If each section of a spline curve is described with a set of parametric coordinate

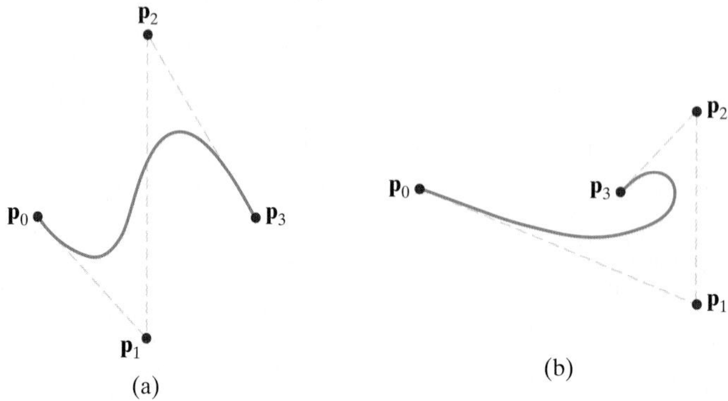

FIGURE 8-18 Control-graph shapes (dashed lines) for two sets of control points in the xy plane.

functions of the form

$$x = x(u), \qquad y = y(u), \qquad z = z(u), \qquad u_1 \le u \le u_2 \tag{8-16}$$

we set **parametric continuity** by matching the parametric derivatives of adjoining curve sections at their common boundary.

Zero-order parametric continuity, represented as C^0 continuity, means simply that the curves meet. That is, the values of x, y, and z evaluated at u_2 for the first curve section are equal, respectively, to the values of x, y, and z evaluated at u_1 for the next curve section. **First-order parametric continuity,** referred to as C^1 continuity, means that the first parametric derivatives (tangent lines) of the coordinate functions in Eq. 8-16 for two successive curve sections are equal at their joining point. **Second-order parametric continuity,** or C^2 continuity, means that both the first and second parametric derivatives of the two curve sections are the same at the intersection. Higher-order parametric continuity conditions are defined similarly. Figure 8-19 shows examples of C^0, C^1, and C^2 continuity.

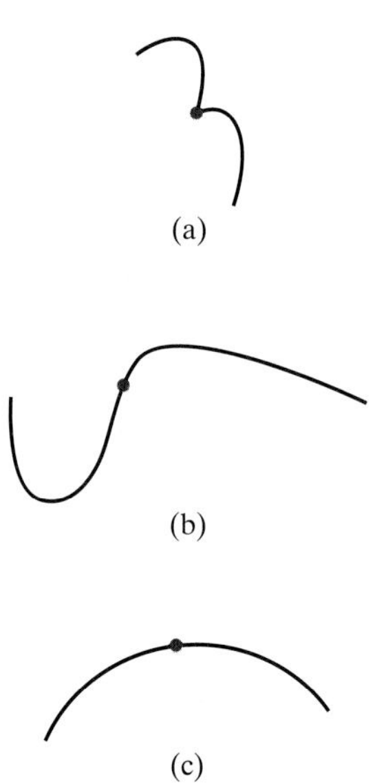

FIGURE 8-19 Piecewise construction of a curve by joining two curve segments using different orders of continuity: (a) zero-order continuity only, (b) first-order continuity, and (c) second-order continuity.

With second-order parametric continuity, the rates of change of the tangent vectors of connecting sections are equal at their intersection. Thus the tangent line transitions smoothly from one section of the curve to the next (Fig. 8-19(c)). But with first-order parametric continuity, the rate of change of tangent vectors for the two sections can be quite different (Fig. 8-19(b)), so that the general shapes of the two adjacent sections can change abruptly. First-order parametric continuity is often sufficient for digitizing drawings and some design applications, while second-order parametric continuity is useful for setting up animation paths for camera motion and for many precision CAD requirements. A camera traveling along the curve path in Fig. 8-19(b) with equal steps in parameter u would experience an abrupt change in acceleration at the boundary of the two sections, producing a discontinuity in the motion sequence. But if the camera was traveling along the path in Fig. 8-19(c), the frame sequence for the motion would smoothly transition across the boundary.

Geometric Continuity Conditions

Another method for joining two successive curve sections is to specify conditions for **geometric continuity.** In this case, we require only that the parametric derivatives of the two sections are proportional to each other at their common boundary, instead of requiring equality.

Zero-order geometric continuity, described as G^0 continuity, is the same as zero-order parametric continuity. That is, two successive curve sections must

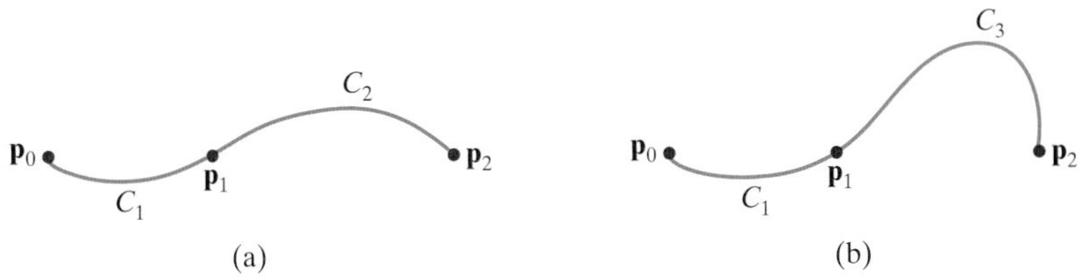

FIGURE 8-20 Three control points fitted with two curve sections joined with (a) parametric continuity and (b) geometric continuity, where the tangent vector of curve C_3 at point $\mathbf{P}_1$ has a greater magnitude than the tangent vector of curve C_1 at $\mathbf{P}_1$.

have the same coordinate position at the boundary point. **First-order geometric continuity,** or G^1 continuity, means that the parametric first derivatives are proportional at the intersection of two successive sections. If we denote the parametric position on the curve as $\mathbf{P}(u)$, the direction of the tangent vector $\mathbf{P}'(u)$, but not necessarily its magnitude, will be the same for two successive curve sections at their common point under G^1 continuity. **Second-order geometric continuity,** or G^2 continuity, means that both the first and second parametric derivatives of the two curve sections are proportional at their boundary. Under G^2 continuity, curvatures of two curve sections will match at the joining position.

A curve generated with geometric continuity conditions is similar to one generated with parametric continuity, but with slight differences in curve shape. Figure 8-20 provides a comparison of geometric and parametric continuity. With geometric continuity, the curve is pulled toward the section with the greater magnitude for the tangent vector.

Spline Specifications

There are three equivalent methods for specifying a particular spline representation, given the degree of the polynomial and the control-point positions: (1) We can state the set of boundary conditions that are imposed on the spline; or (2) we can state the matrix that characterizes the spline; or (3) we can state the set of *blending functions* (or *basis functions*) that determine how specified constraints on the curve are combined to calculate positions along the curve path.

To illustrate these three equivalent specifications, suppose we have the following parametric cubic polynomial representation for the x coordinate along the path of a spline-curve section:

$$x(u) = a_x u^3 + b_x u^2 + c_x u + d_x, \qquad 0 \le u \le 1 \tag{8-17}$$

Boundary conditions for this curve can be set for the endpoint coordinate positions $x(0)$ and $x(1)$ and for the parametric first derivatives at the endpoints: $x'(0)$ and $x'(1)$. These four boundary conditions are sufficient to determine the values of the four coefficients a_x, b_x, c_x, and d_x.

From the boundary conditions, we can obtain the matrix that characterizes this spline curve by first rewriting Eq. 8-17 as the matrix product:

$$\begin{aligned} x(u) &= [u^3 \quad u^2 \quad u \quad 1] \begin{bmatrix} a_x \\ b_x \\ c_x \\ d_x \end{bmatrix} \\ &= \mathbf{U} \cdot \mathbf{C} \end{aligned} \tag{8-18}$$

where **U** is the row matrix of powers of parameter u and **C** is the coefficient column matrix. Using Eq. 8-18, we can write the boundary conditions in matrix form and solve for the coefficient matrix **C** as

$$\mathbf{C} = \mathbf{M}_{\text{spline}} \cdot \mathbf{M}_{\text{geom}} \tag{8-19}$$

where $\mathbf{M}_{\text{geom}}$ is a four-element column matrix containing the geometric constraint values (boundary conditions) on the spline, and $\mathbf{M}_{\text{spline}}$ is the 4 by 4 matrix that transforms the geometric constraint values to the polynomial coefficients and provides a characterization for the spline curve. Matrix $\mathbf{M}_{\text{geom}}$ contains control-point coordinate values and other geometric constraints that have been specified. Thus, we can substitute the matrix representation for **C** into Eq. 8-18 to obtain

$$x(u) = \mathbf{U} \cdot \mathbf{M}_{\text{spline}} \cdot \mathbf{M}_{\text{geom}} \tag{8-20}$$

The matrix $\mathbf{M}_{\text{spline}}$, characterizing a spline representation, sometimes called the *basis matrix*, is particularly useful for transforming from one spline representation to another.

Finally, we can expand Eq. 8-20 to obtain a polynomial representation for coordinate x in terms of the geometric constraint parameters g_k, such as the control-point coordinates and slope of the curve at the control points:

$$x(u) = \sum_{k=0}^{3} g_k \cdot \text{BF}_k(u) \tag{8-21}$$

The polynomials $\text{BF}_k(u)$, for $k = 0, 1, 2, 3$, are called **blending functions** or **basis functions** because they combine (blend) the geometric constraint values to obtain coordinate positions along the curve. In subsequent sections, we explore the features of the various spline curves and surfaces that are useful in computer-graphics applications, including the specification of their matrix and blending-function representations.

Spline Surfaces

The usual procedure for defining a spline surface is to specify two sets of orthogonal spline curves using a mesh of control points over some region of space. If we denote the control-point positions as $\mathbf{p}_{k_u,k_v}$, then any point position on the spline surface can be computed as the Cartesian product of the spline-curve blending functions:

$$\mathbf{P}(u, v) = \sum_{k_u,k_v} \mathbf{p}_{k_u,k_v} \text{BF}_{k_u}(u)\text{BF}_{k_v}(v) \tag{8-22}$$

Surface parameters u and v often vary over the range from 0 to 1, but this range depends on the type of spline curves we use. One method for designating the three-dimensional control-point positions is to select height values above a two-dimensional mesh of positions on a ground plane.

Trimming Spline Surfaces

In CAD applications, a surface design may require some features that are not easily implemented simply by adjusting control-point positions. For instance, a

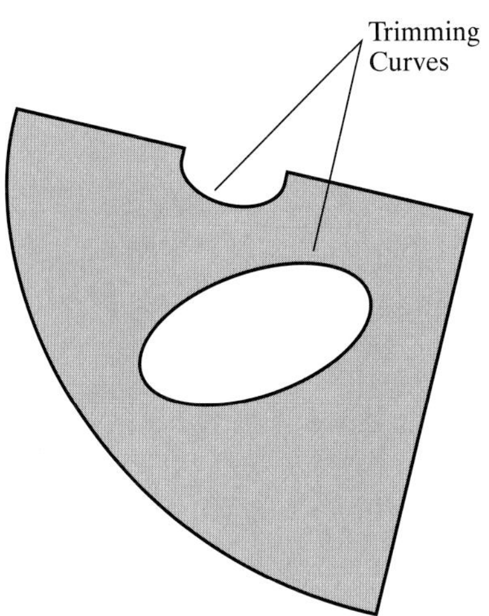

FIGURE 8-21 Modification of a surface section using trimming curves.

section of a spline surface may need to be snipped off to fit two design pieces together, or a hole may be needed so that a conduit can pass through the surface. For these applications, graphics packages often provide functions to generate **trimming curves** that can be used to take out sections of a spline surface, as illustrated in Fig. 8-21. Trimming curves are typically defined in parametric uv surface coordinates, and often they must be specified as closed curves.

8-9 CUBIC-SPLINE INTERPOLATION METHODS

This class of splines is most often used to set up paths for object motions or to provide a representation for an existing object or drawing, but interpolation splines are also used sometimes to design object shapes. Cubic polynomials offer a reasonable compromise between flexibility and speed of computation. Compared to higher-order polynomials, cubic splines require less calculations and storage space, and they are more stable. Compared to quadratic polynomials and straight-line segments, cubic splines are more flexible for modeling object shapes.

Given a set of control points, cubic interpolation splines are obtained by fitting the input points with a piecewise cubic polynomial curve that passes through every control point. Suppose we have $n+1$ control points specified with coordinates

$$\mathbf{p}_k = (x_k, y_k, z_k), \qquad k = 0, 1, 2, \ldots, n$$

A cubic interpolation fit of these points is illustrated in Fig. 8-22. We can describe the parametric cubic polynomial that is to be fitted between each pair of control

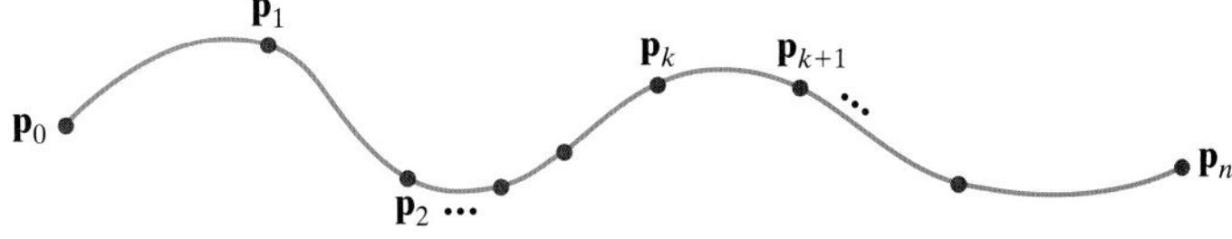

FIGURE 8-22 A piecewise continuous cubic-spline interpolation of $n+1$ control points.

points with the following set of equations

$$\begin{aligned} x(u) &= a_x\,u^3 + b_x\,u^2 + c_x\,u + d_x \\ y(u) &= a_y\,u^3 + b_y\,u^2 + c_y\,u + d_y, \qquad (0 \le u \le 1) \\ z(u) &= a_z\,u^3 + b_z\,u^2 + c_z\,u + d_z \end{aligned} \tag{8-23}$$

For each of these three equations, we need to determine the values for the four coefficients a, b, c, and d in the polynomial representation for each of the n curve sections between the $n + 1$ control points. We do this by setting enough boundary conditions at the control-point positions between curve sections so that we can obtain numerical values for all the coefficients. In the following sections, we discuss common methods for setting the boundary conditions for cubic interpolation splines.

Natural Cubic Splines

One of the first spline curves to be developed for graphics applications is the **natural cubic spline.** This interpolation curve is a mathematical representation of the original drafting spline. We formulate a natural cubic spline by requiring that two adjacent curve sections have the same first and second parametric derivatives at their common boundary. Thus, natural cubic splines have C^2 continuity.

If we have $n + 1$ control points, as in Fig. 8-22, then we have n curve sections with a total of $4n$ polynomial coefficients to be determined. At each of the $n - 1$ interior control points we have four boundary conditions: The two curve sections on either side of a control point must have the same first and second parametric derivatives at that control point, and each curve must pass through that control point. This gives us $4n - 4$ equations to be satisfied by the $4n$ polynomial coefficients. We obtain an additional equation from the first control point $\mathbf{p}_0$, the position of the beginning of the curve, and another condition from control point $\mathbf{p}_n$, which must be the last point on the curve. However, we still need two more conditions to be able to determine values for all the coefficients. One method for obtaining the two additional conditions is to set the second derivatives at $\mathbf{p}_0$ and $\mathbf{p}_n$ equal to 0. Another approach is to add two extra control points (called *dummy points*), one at each end of the original control-point sequence. That is, we add a control point labeled $\mathbf{p}_{-1}$ at the beginning of the curve and a control point labeled $\mathbf{p}_{n+1}$ at the end. Then all of the original control points are interior points, and we have the necessary $4n$ boundary conditions.

Although natural cubic splines are a mathematical model for the drafting spline, they have a major disadvantage. If the position of any one of the control points is altered, the entire curve is affected. Thus, natural cubic splines allow for no "local control", so that we cannot restructure part of the curve without specifying an entirely new set of control points. For this reason, other representations for a cubic-spline interpolation have been developed.

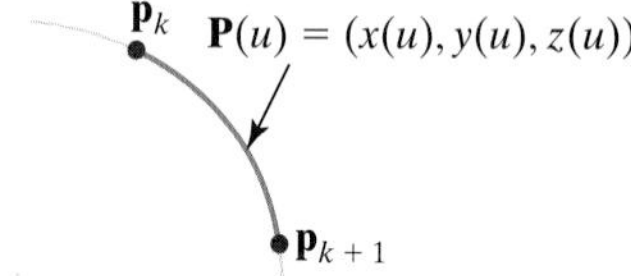

FIGURE 8-23 Parametric point function $\mathbf{P}(u)$ for a Hermite curve section between control points $\mathbf{p}_k$ and $\mathbf{p}_{k+1}$.

Hermite Interpolation

A **Hermite spline** (named after the French mathematician Charles Hermite) is an interpolating piecewise cubic polynomial with a specified tangent at each control point. Unlike the natural cubic splines, Hermite splines can be adjusted locally because each curve section is only dependent on its endpoint constraints.

If $\mathbf{P}(u)$ represents a parametric cubic point function for the curve section between control points $\mathbf{p}_k$ and $\mathbf{p}_{k+1}$, as shown in Fig. 8-23, then the boundary conditions that define this Hermite curve section are

$$\begin{aligned} \mathbf{P}(0) &= \mathbf{p}_k \\ \mathbf{P}(1) &= \mathbf{p}_{k+1} \\ \mathbf{P}'(0) &= \mathbf{Dp}_k \\ \mathbf{P}'(1) &= \mathbf{Dp}_{k+1} \end{aligned} \tag{8-24}$$

with $\mathbf{Dp}_k$ and $\mathbf{Dp}_{k+1}$ specifying the values for the parametric derivatives (slope of the curve) at control points $\mathbf{p}_k$ and $\mathbf{p}_{k+1}$, respectively.

We can write the vector equivalent of Eqs. 8-23 for this Hermite curve section as

$$\mathbf{P}(u) = \mathbf{a}\,u^3 + \mathbf{b}\,u^2 + \mathbf{c}\,u + \mathbf{d}, \qquad 0 \le u \le 1 \tag{8-25}$$

where the x component of $\mathbf{P}$(u) is $x(u) = a_x\,u^3 + b_x\,u^2 + c_x\,u + d_x$, and similarly for the y and z components. The matrix equivalent of Eq. 8-25 is

$$\mathbf{P}(u) = [u^3 \quad u^2 \quad u \quad 1] \cdot \begin{bmatrix} \mathbf{a} \\ \mathbf{b} \\ \mathbf{c} \\ \mathbf{d} \end{bmatrix} \tag{8-26}$$

and the derivative of the point function can be expressed as

$$\mathbf{P}'(u) = [3u^2 \quad 2u \quad 1 \quad 0] \cdot \begin{bmatrix} \mathbf{a} \\ \mathbf{b} \\ \mathbf{c} \\ \mathbf{d} \end{bmatrix} \tag{8-27}$$

Substituting endpoint values 0 and 1 for parameter u into the preceding two equations, we can express the Hermite boundary conditions 8-24 in the matrix form

$$\begin{bmatrix} \mathbf{p}_k \\ \mathbf{p}_{k+1} \\ \mathbf{Dp}_k \\ \mathbf{Dp}_{k+1} \end{bmatrix} = \begin{bmatrix} 0 & 0 & 0 & 1 \\ 1 & 1 & 1 & 1 \\ 0 & 0 & 1 & 0 \\ 3 & 2 & 1 & 0 \end{bmatrix} \cdot \begin{bmatrix} \mathbf{a} \\ \mathbf{b} \\ \mathbf{c} \\ \mathbf{d} \end{bmatrix} \tag{8-28}$$

Solving this equation for the polynomial coefficients, we have

$$\begin{aligned} \begin{bmatrix} \mathbf{a} \\ \mathbf{b} \\ \mathbf{c} \\ \mathbf{d} \end{bmatrix} &= \begin{bmatrix} 0 & 0 & 0 & 1 \\ 1 & 1 & 1 & 1 \\ 0 & 0 & 1 & 0 \\ 3 & 2 & 1 & 0 \end{bmatrix}^{-1} \cdot \begin{bmatrix} \mathbf{p}_k \\ \mathbf{p}_{k+1} \\ \mathbf{Dp}_k \\ \mathbf{Dp}_{k+1} \end{bmatrix} \\ &= \begin{bmatrix} 2 & -2 & 1 & 1 \\ -3 & 3 & -2 & -1 \\ 0 & 0 & 1 & 0 \\ 1 & 0 & 0 & 0 \end{bmatrix} \cdot \begin{bmatrix} \mathbf{p}_k \\ \mathbf{p}_{k+1} \\ \mathbf{Dp}_k \\ \mathbf{Dp}_{k+1} \end{bmatrix} \\ &= \mathbf{M}_H \cdot \begin{bmatrix} \mathbf{p}_k \\ \mathbf{p}_{k+1} \\ \mathbf{Dp}_k \\ \mathbf{Dp}_{k+1} \end{bmatrix} \end{aligned} \tag{8-29}$$

where $\mathbf{M}_H$, the Hermite matrix, is the inverse of the boundary constraint matrix. Equation 8-26 can thus be written in terms of the boundary conditions as

$$\mathbf{P}(u) = [u^3 \quad u^2 \quad u \quad 1] \cdot \mathbf{M}_H \cdot \begin{bmatrix} \mathbf{p}_k \\ \mathbf{p}_{k+1} \\ \mathbf{Dp}_k \\ \mathbf{Dp}_{k+1} \end{bmatrix} \tag{8-30}$$

Finally, we can determine expressions for the polynomial Hermite blending functions, $H_k(u)$ for $k = 0, 1, 2, 3$, by carrying out the matrix multiplications in Eq. 8-30 and collecting coefficients for the boundary constraints to obtain the polynomial form

$$\begin{aligned} \mathbf{P}(u) &= \mathbf{p}_k(2u^3 - 3u^2 + 1) + \mathbf{p}_{k+1}(-2u^3 + 3u^2) + \mathbf{Dp}_k(u^3 - 2u^2 + u) \\ &\quad + \mathbf{Dp}_{k+1}(u^3 - u^2) \\ &= \mathbf{p}_k H_0(u) + \mathbf{p}_{k+1} H_1 + \mathbf{Dp}_k H_2 + \mathbf{Dp}_{k+1} H_3 \end{aligned} \tag{8-31}$$

Figure 8-24 shows the shape of the four Hermite blending functions.

Hermite polynomials can be useful for some digitizing applications where it may not be too difficult to specify or approximate the curve slopes. But for

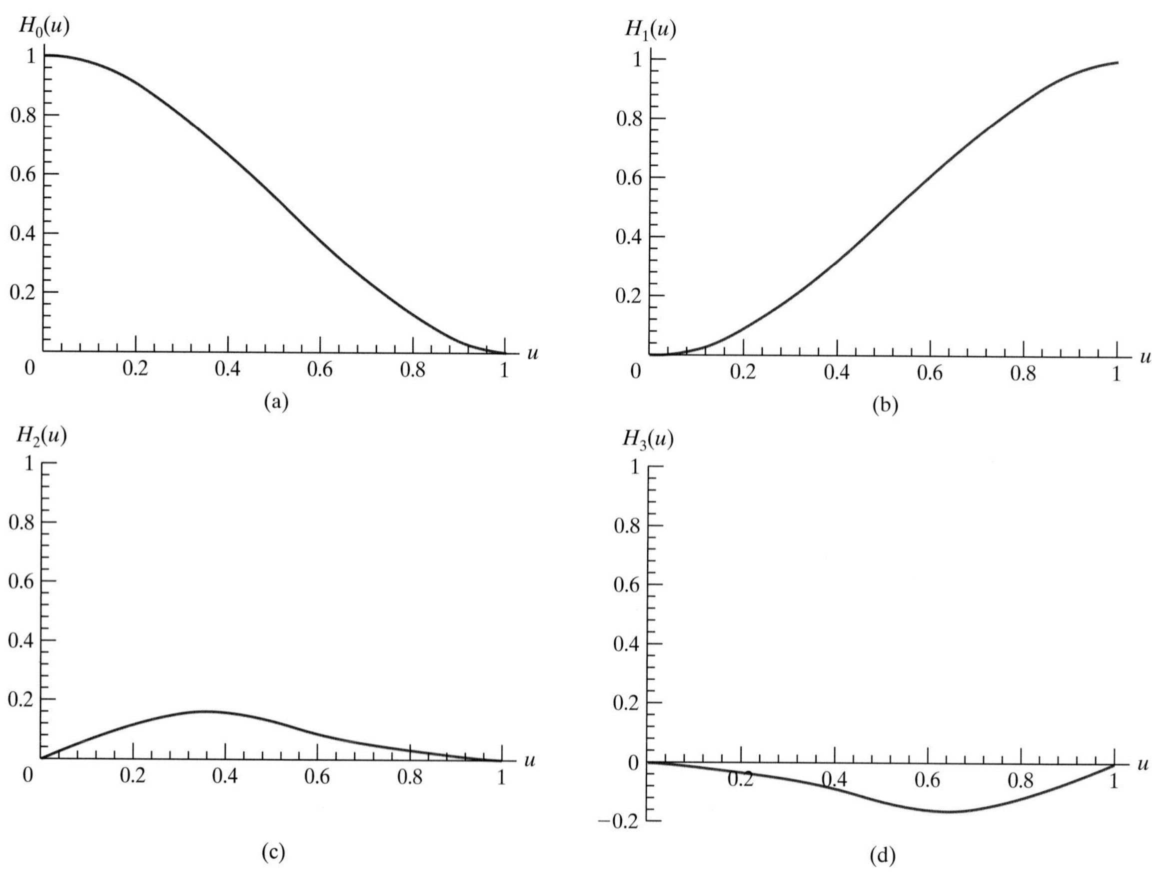

FIGURE 8-24 The Hermite blending functions.

most problems in computer graphics it is more useful to generate spline curves without requiring input values for curve slopes or other geometric information, in addition to control-point coordinates. Cardinal splines and Kochanek-Bartels splines, discussed in the following two sections, are variations on the Hermite splines that do not require input values for the curve derivatives at the control points. Procedures for these splines compute parametric derivatives from the coordinate positions of the control points.

Cardinal Splines

As with Hermite splines, the **cardinal splines** are interpolating piecewise cubic polynomials with specified endpoint tangents at the boundary of each curve section. The difference is that we do not input the values for the endpoint tangents. For a cardinal spline, the slope at a control point is calculated from the coordinates of the two adjacent control points.

A cardinal spline section is completely specified with four consecutive control-point positions. The middle two control points are the section endpoints, and the other two points are used in the calculation of the endpoint slopes. If we take $\mathbf{P}(u)$ as the representation for the parametric cubic point function for the curve section between control points $\mathbf{p}_k$ and $\mathbf{p}_{k+1}$, as in Fig. 8-25, then the four control points from $\mathbf{p}_{k-1}$ to $\mathbf{p}_{k+1}$ are used to set the boundary conditions for the cardinal-spline section as

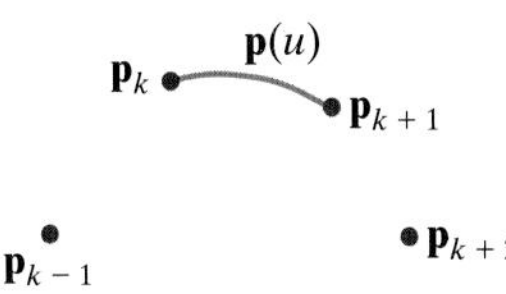

FIGURE 8-25 Parametric point function $\mathbf{P}(u)$ for a cardinal-spline section between control points $\mathbf{p}_k$ and $\mathbf{p}_{k+1}$.

$$\begin{aligned}
\mathbf{P}(0) &= \mathbf{p}_k \\
\mathbf{P}(1) &= \mathbf{p}_{k+1} \\
\mathbf{P}'(0) &= \frac{1}{2}(1-t)(\mathbf{p}_{k+1}-\mathbf{p}_{k-1}) \\
\mathbf{P}'(1) &= \frac{1}{2}(1-t)(\mathbf{p}_{k+2}-\mathbf{p}_{k})
\end{aligned} \tag{8-32}$$

Thus the slopes at control points $\mathbf{p}_k$ and $\mathbf{p}_{k+1}$ are taken to be proportional, respectively, to the chords $\overline{\mathbf{p}_{k-1}\mathbf{p}_{k+1}}$ and $\overline{\mathbf{p}_k\mathbf{p}_{k+2}}$ (Fig. 8-26). Parameter t is called the **tension** parameter since it controls how loosely or tightly the cardinal spline fits the input control points. Figure 8-27 illustrates the shape of a cardinal curve for very small and very large values of tension t. When $t = 0$, this class of curves is referred to as **Catmull-Rom splines,** or **Overhauser splines.**

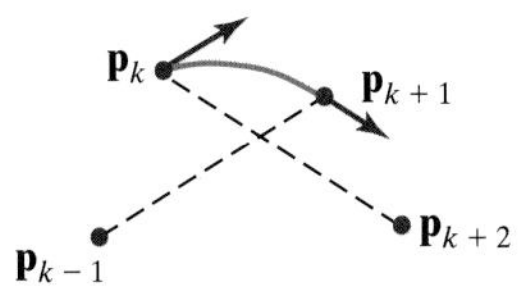

FIGURE 8-26 Tangent vectors at the endpoints of a cardinal-spline section are parallel to the chords formed with neighboring control points (dashed lines).

Using methods similar to those for Hermite splines, we can convert the boundary conditions 8-32 into the matrix form

$$\mathbf{P}(u) = [u^3 \quad u^2 \quad u \quad 1] \cdot \mathbf{M}_C \cdot \begin{bmatrix} \mathbf{p}_{k-1} \\ \mathbf{p}_k \\ \mathbf{p}_{k+1} \\ \mathbf{p}_{k+2} \end{bmatrix} \tag{8-33}$$

where the cardinal matrix is

$$\mathbf{M}_C = \begin{bmatrix} -s & 2-s & s-2 & s \\ 2s & s-3 & 3-2s & -s \\ -s & 0 & s & 0 \\ 0 & 1 & 0 & 0 \end{bmatrix} \tag{8-34}$$

with $s = (1-t)/2$.

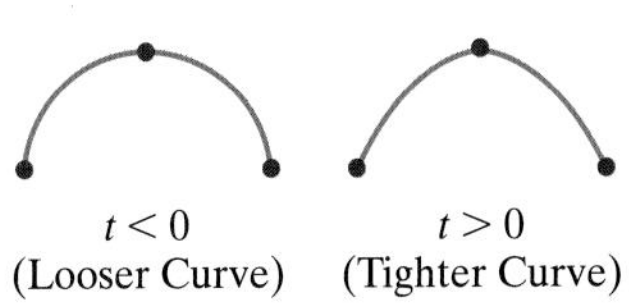

FIGURE 8-27 Effect of the tension parameter on the shape of a cardinal-spline section.

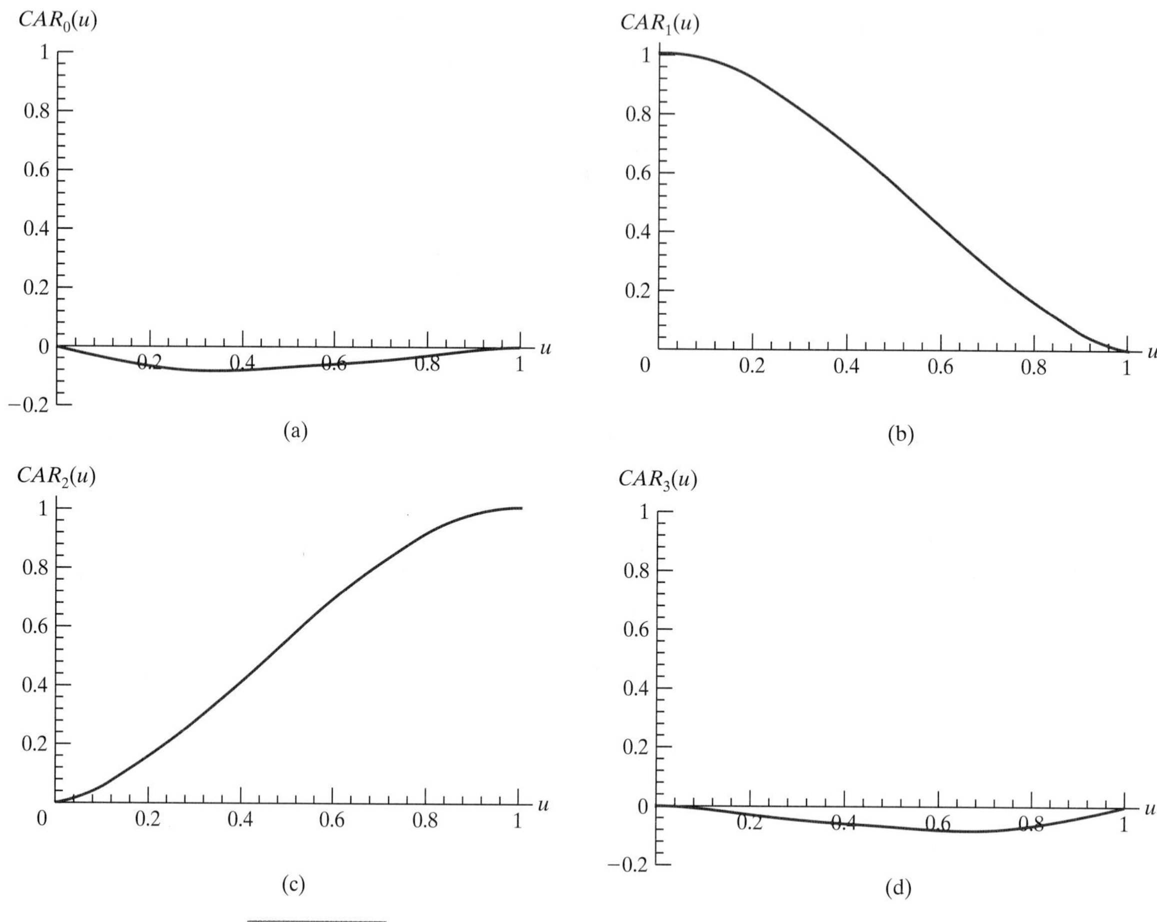

FIGURE 8-28 The cardinal-spline blending functions for $t = 0$ ($s = 0.5$).

Expanding the matrix equation 8-33 into polynomial form, we have

$$\begin{aligned}\mathbf{P}(u) &= \mathbf{p}_{k-1}(-s\,u^3 + 2s\,u^2 - s\,u) + \mathbf{p}_k[(2-s)u^3 + (s-3)u^2 + 1] \\ &\quad + \mathbf{p}_{k+1}[(s-2)u^3 + (3-2s)u^2 + s\,u] + \mathbf{p}_{k+2}(s\,u^3 - s\,u^2) \\ &= \mathbf{p}_{k-1}\,\mathrm{CAR}_0(u) + \mathbf{p}_k\,\mathrm{CAR}_1(u) + \mathbf{p}_{k+1}\,\mathrm{CAR}_2(u) + \mathbf{p}_{k+2}\,\mathrm{CAR}_3(u) \qquad (8\text{-}35)\end{aligned}$$

where the polynomials $\mathrm{CAR}_k(u)$ for $k = 0, 1, 2, 3$ are the cardinal-spline blending (basis) functions. Figure 8-28 gives a plot of the basis functions for cardinal splines with $t = 0$.

Examples of curves produced with the cardinal-spline blending functions are given in Figs. 8-29, 8-30, and 8-31. In Fig. 8-29, four cardinal-spline sections are plotted to form a closed curve. The first curve section is generated using the control-point set $\{\mathbf{p}_0, \mathbf{p}_1, \mathbf{p}_2, \mathbf{p}_3\}$, the second curve is produced with the control-point set $\{\mathbf{p}_1, \mathbf{p}_2, \mathbf{p}_3, \mathbf{p}_0\}$, the third curve section has control points $\{\mathbf{p}_2, \mathbf{p}_3, \mathbf{p}_0, \mathbf{p}_1\}$, and the final curve section has control points $\{\mathbf{p}_3, \mathbf{p}_0, \mathbf{p}_1, \mathbf{p}_2\}$. In Fig. 8-30, a closed curve is obtained with a single cardinal-spline section by setting the position of the third control point to the coordinate position of the second control point. In Fig. 8-31, a self-intersecting cardinal-spline section is produced by setting the position of the third control point very near the coordinate position of the second

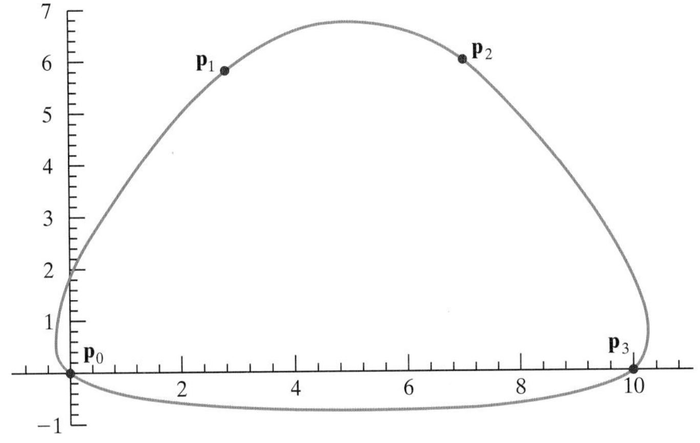

FIGURE 8-29 A closed curve with four cardinal-spline sections, obtained with a cyclic permutation of the control points and with tension parameter $t = 0$.

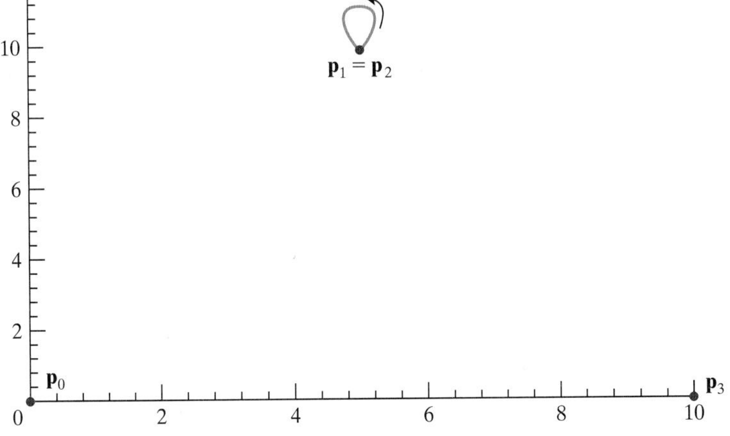

FIGURE 8-30 A cardinal-spline loop produced with curve endpoints at the same coordinate position. The tension parameter is set to the value 0.

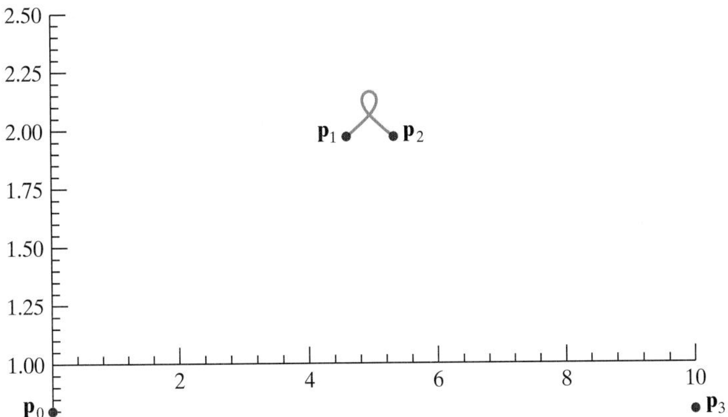

FIGURE 8-31 A self-intersecting cardinal-spline curve section produced with closely spaced curve endpoint positions. The tension parameter is set to the value 0.

control point. The resulting self-intersection is due to the constraints on the curve slope at the endpoints $\mathbf{p}_1$ and $\mathbf{p}_2$.

Kochanek-Bartels Splines

These interpolating cubic polynomials are extensions of the cardinal splines. Two additional parameters are introduced into the constraint equations defining

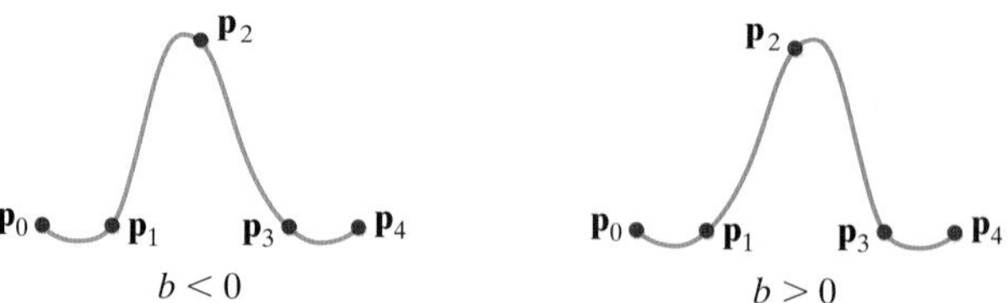

FIGURE 8-32 Effect of the bias parameter on the shape of a Kochanek-Bartels spline section.

Kochanek-Bartels splines to provide further flexibility in adjusting the shapes of curve sections.

Given four consecutive control points, labeled $\mathbf{p}_{k-1}$, $\mathbf{p}_k$, $\mathbf{p}_{k+1}$, and $\mathbf{p}_{k+2}$, we define the boundary conditions for a Kochanek-Bartels curve section between $\mathbf{p}_k$ and $\mathbf{p}_{k+1}$ as

$$\begin{aligned}
\mathbf{P}(0) &= \mathbf{p}_k \\
\mathbf{P}(1) &= \mathbf{p}_{k+1} \\
\mathbf{P}'(0)_{\text{in}} &= \frac{1}{2}(1-t)[(1+b)(1-c)(\mathbf{p}_k - \mathbf{p}_{k-1}) \\
&\qquad + (1-b)(1+c)(\mathbf{p}_{k+1} - \mathbf{p}_k)] \\
\mathbf{P}'(1)_{\text{out}} &= \frac{1}{2}(1-t)[(1+b)(1+c)(\mathbf{p}_{k+1} - \mathbf{p}_k) \\
&\qquad + (1-b)(1-c)(\mathbf{p}_{k+2} - \mathbf{p}_{k+1})]
\end{aligned} \tag{8-36}$$

where t is the **tension** parameter, b is the **bias** parameter, and c is the **continuity** parameter. In the Kochanek-Bartels formulation, parametric derivatives might not be continuous across section boundaries.

Tension parameter t has the same interpretation as in the cardinal spline formulation; that is, it controls the looseness or tightness of the curve sections. Bias, b, is used to adjust the curvature at each end of a section, so that curve sections can be skewed toward one end or the other (Fig. 8-32). Parameter c controls the continuity of the tangent vector across the boundaries of sections. If c is assigned a nonzero value, there is a discontinuity in the slope of the curve across section boundaries.

Kochanek-Bartels splines were designed to model animation paths. In particular, abrupt changes in the motion of an object can be simulated with nonzero values for parameter c. These motion changes are used in cartoon animations, for example, when a cartoon character stops quickly, changes direction, or collides with some other object.

8-10 BÉZIER SPLINE CURVES

This spline approximation method was developed by the French engineer Pierre Bézier for use in the design of Renault automobile bodies. **Bézier splines** have a number of properties that make them highly useful and convenient for curve and surface design. They are also easy to implement. For these reasons, Bézier splines are widely available in various CAD systems, in general graphics packages, and in assorted drawing and painting packages.

In general, a Bézier curve section can be fitted to any number of control points, although some graphic packages limit the number of control points to four. The degree of the Bézier polynomial is determined by the number of control points to be approximated and their relative position. As with the interpolation splines, we can specify the Bézier curve path in the vicinity of the control points using blending functions, a characterizing matrix, or boundary conditions. For general Bézier curves, with no restrictions on the number of control points, the blending-function specification is the most convenient representation.

Bézier Curve Equations

We first consider the general case of $n + 1$ control-point positions, denoted as $\mathbf{p}_k = (x_k, y_k, z_k)$, with k varying from 0 to n. These coordinate points are blended to produce the following position vector $\mathbf{P}(u)$, which describes the path of an approximating Bézier polynomial function between $\mathbf{p}_0$ and $\mathbf{p}_n$.

$$\mathbf{P}(u) = \sum_{k=0}^{n} \mathbf{p}_k \, \mathrm{BEZ}_{k,n}(u), \qquad 0 \leq u \leq 1 \tag{8-37}$$

The Bézier blending functions $\mathrm{BEZ}_{k,n}(u)$ are the *Bernstein polynomials*

$$\mathrm{BEZ}_{k,n}(u) = C(n, k) u^k (1 - u)^{n-k} \tag{8-38}$$

where parameters $C(n, k)$ are the binomial coefficients

$$C(n, k) = \frac{n!}{k!(n - k)!} \tag{8-39}$$

Vector equation 8-37 represents a set of three parametric equations for the individual curve coordinates:

$$\begin{aligned} x(u) &= \sum_{k=0}^{n} x_k \, \mathrm{BEZ}_{k,n}(u) \\ y(u) &= \sum_{k=0}^{n} y_k \, \mathrm{BEZ}_{k,n}(u) \\ z(u) &= \sum_{k=0}^{n} z_k \, \mathrm{BEZ}_{k,n}(u) \end{aligned} \tag{8-40}$$

In most cases, a Bézier curve is a polynomial of degree one less than the designated number of control points: Three points generate a parabola, four points a cubic curve, and so forth. Figure 8-33 demonstrates the appearance of some Bézier curves for various selections of control points in the xy plane ($z = 0$). With certain control-point placements, however, we obtain degenerate Bézier polynomials. For example, a Bézier curve generated with three collinear control points is a straight-line segment. And a set of control points that are all at the same coordinate position produce a Bézier "curve" that is a single point.

Recursive calculations can be used to obtain successive binomial-coefficient values as

$$C(n, k) = \frac{n - k + 1}{k} C(n, k - 1) \tag{8-41}$$

for $n \geq k$. Also, the Bézier blending functions satisfy the recursive relationship

$$\mathrm{BEZ}_{k,n}(u) = (1 - u)\mathrm{BEZ}_{k,n-1}(u) + u \, \mathrm{BEZ}_{k-1,n-1}(u), \qquad n > k \geq 1 \tag{8-42}$$

with $\mathrm{BEZ}_{k,k} = u^k$ and $\mathrm{BEZ}_{0,k} = (1 - u)^k$.

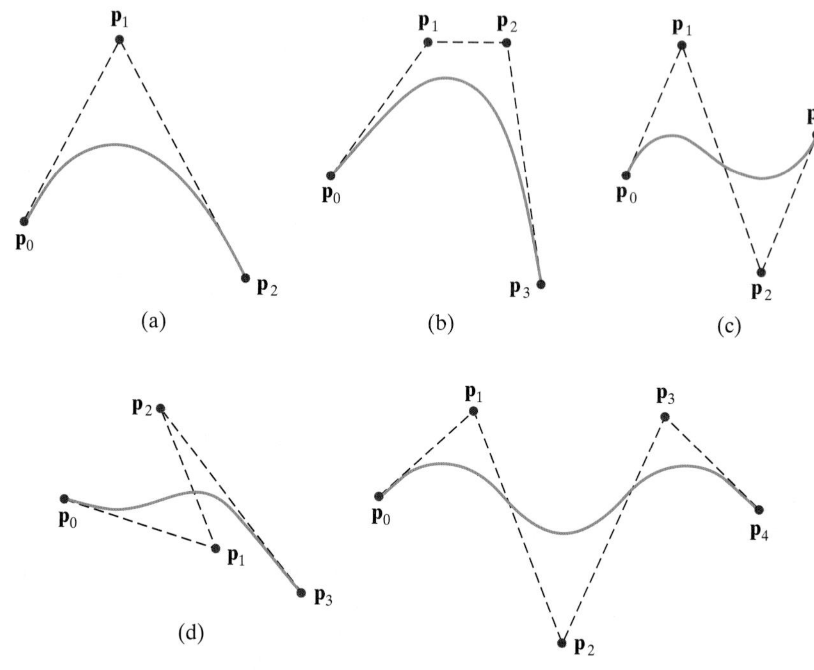

FIGURE 8-33 Examples of two-dimensional Bézier curves generated with three, four, and five control points. Dashed lines connect the control-point positions.

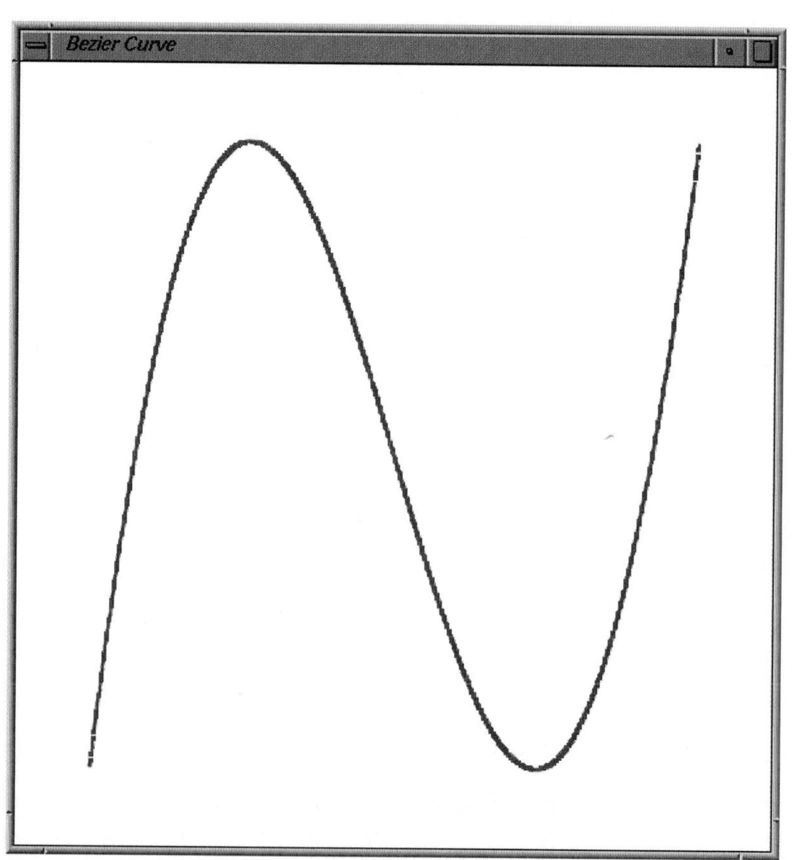

FIGURE 8-34 A Bézier curve displayed by the example program.

Example Bézier Curve-Generating Program

An implementation for calculating the Bézier blending functions and generating a two-dimensional, cubic Bézier-spline curve is given in the following program. Four control points are defined in the xy plane, and 1000 pixel positions are plotted along the curve path using a pixel width of 4. Values for the binomial coefficients are calculated in procedure `binomialCoeffs`, and coordinate positions along the curve path are calculated in procedure `computeBezPt`. These values are passed to procedure `bezier`, and pixel positions are plotted using the OpenGL point-plotting routines. Alternatively, we could have approximated the curve path with straight-line sections, using fewer points. More efficient methods for generating coordinate positions along the path of a spline curve are explored in Section 8-17. For this example, the world-coordinate limits are set so that only the curve points are displayed within the viewport (Fig. 8-34). If we wanted also to plot the control-point positions, the control graph, or the convex hull, we would need to extend the limits of the world-coordinate clipping window.

```
#include <GL/glut.h>
#include <stdlib.h>
#include <math.h>

/*  Set initial size of the display window.  */
GLsizei winWidth = 600, winHeight = 600;

/*  Set size of world-coordinate clipping window.  */
GLfloat xwcMin = -50.0, xwcMax = 50.0;
GLfloat ywcMin = -50.0, ywcMax = 50.0;

class wcPt3D {
   public:
      GLfloat x, y, z;
};

void init (void)
{
   /*  Set color of display window to white.  */
   glClearColor (1.0, 1.0, 1.0, 0.0);
}

void plotPoint (wcPt3D bezCurvePt)
{
    glBegin (GL_POINTS);
        glVertex2f (bezCurvePt.x, bezCurvePt.y);
    glEnd ( );
}

/*  Compute binomial coefficients C for given value of n.  */
void binomialCoeffs (GLint n, GLint * C)
{
   GLint k, j;

   for (k = 0;  k <= n;  k++) {
      /*  Compute n!/(k!(n - k)!).  */
```

```
         C [k] = 1;
         for (j = n;  j >= k + 1;  j--)
           C [k] *= j;
         for (j = n - k;  j >= 2;  j--)
           C [k] /= j;
      }
}

void computeBezPt (GLfloat u, wcPt3D * bezPt, GLint nCtrlPts,
                    wcPt3D * ctrlPts, GLint * C)
{
   GLint k, n = nCtrlPts - 1;
   GLfloat bezBlendFcn;

   bezPt->x = bezPt->y = bezPt->z = 0.0;

   /*  Compute blending functions and blend control points. */
   for (k = 0; k < nCtrlPts; k++) {
      bezBlendFcn = C [k] * pow (u, k) * pow (1 - u, n - k);
      bezPt->x += ctrlPts [k].x * bezBlendFcn;
      bezPt->y += ctrlPts [k].y * bezBlendFcn;
      bezPt->z += ctrlPts [k].z * bezBlendFcn;
   }
}

void bezier (wcPt3D * ctrlPts, GLint nCtrlPts, GLint nBezCurvePts)
{
   wcPt3D bezCurvePt;
   GLfloat u;
   GLint *C, k;

   /*  Allocate space for binomial coefficients  */
   C = new GLint [nCtrlPts];

   binomialCoeffs (nCtrlPts - 1, C);
   for (k = 0;  k <= nBezCurvePts;  k++) {
      u = GLfloat (k) / GLfloat (nBezCurvePts);
      computeBezPt (u, &bezCurvePt, nCtrlPts, ctrlPts, C);
      plotPoint (bezCurvePt);
   }
   delete [ ] C;
}

void displayFcn (void)
{
   /*  Set example number of control points and number of
    *  curve positions to be plotted along the Bezier curve.
    */
   GLint nCtrlPts = 4, nBezCurvePts = 1000;

   wcPt3D ctrlPts [4] = { {-40.0, -40.0, 0.0}, {-10.0, 200.0, 0.0},
                          {10.0, -200.0, 0.0}, {40.0, 40.0, 0.0} };

   glClear (GL_COLOR_BUFFER_BIT);   //  Clear display window.
```

```
   glPointSize (4);
   glColor3f (1.0, 0.0, 0.0);      //  Set point color to red.

   bezier (ctrlPts, nCtrlPts, nBezCurvePts);
   glFlush ( );
}

void winReshapeFcn (GLint newWidth, GLint newHeight)
{
   /*  Maintain an aspect ratio of 1.0.  */
   glViewport (0, 0, newHeight, newHeight);

   glMatrixMode (GL_PROJECTION);
   glLoadIdentity ( );

   gluOrtho2D (xwcMin, xwcMax, ywcMin, ywcMax);

   glClear (GL_COLOR_BUFFER_BIT);
}

void main (int argc, char** argv)
{
   glutInit (&argc, argv);
   glutInitDisplayMode (GLUT_SINGLE | GLUT_RGB);
   glutInitWindowPosition (50, 50);
   glutInitWindowSize (winWidth, winHeight);
   glutCreateWindow ("Bezier Curve");

   init ( );
   glutDisplayFunc (displayFcn);
   glutReshapeFunc (winReshapeFcn);

   glutMainLoop ( );
}
```

Properties of Bézier Curves

A very useful property of a Bézier curve is that the curve connects the first and last control points. Thus, a basic characteristic of any Bézier curve is that

$$\begin{aligned} \mathbf{P}(0) &= \mathbf{p}_0 \\ \mathbf{P}(1) &= \mathbf{p}_n \end{aligned} \tag{8-43}$$

Values for the parametric first derivatives of a Bézier curve at the endpoints can be calculated from control-point coordinates as

$$\begin{aligned} \mathbf{P}'(0) &= -n\mathbf{p}_0 + n\mathbf{p}_1 \\ \mathbf{P}'(1) &= -n\mathbf{p}_{n-1} + n\mathbf{p}_n \end{aligned} \tag{8-44}$$

From these expressions, we see that the slope at the beginning of the curve is along the line joining the first two control points, and the slope at the end of the curve is along the line joining the last two endpoints. Similarly, the parametric second derivatives of a Bézier curve at the endpoints are calculated as

$$
\begin{aligned}
\mathbf{P}''(0) &= n(n-1)[(\mathbf{p}_2 - \mathbf{p}_1) - (\mathbf{p}_1 - \mathbf{p}_0)] \\
\mathbf{P}''(1) &= n(n-1)[(\mathbf{p}_{n-2} - \mathbf{p}_{n-1}) - (\mathbf{p}_{n-1} - \mathbf{p}_n)]
\end{aligned}
\qquad (8\text{-}45)
$$

Another important property of any Bézier curve is that it lies within the convex hull (convex polygon boundary) of the control points. This follows from the fact that the Bézier blending functions are all positive and their sum is always 1,

$$\sum_{k=0}^{n} \text{BEZ}_{k,n}(u) = 1 \qquad (8\text{-}46)$$

so that any curve position is simply the weighted sum of the control-point positions. The convex-hull property for a Bézier curve ensures that the polynomial smoothly follows the control points without erratic oscillations.

Design Techniques Using Bézier Curves

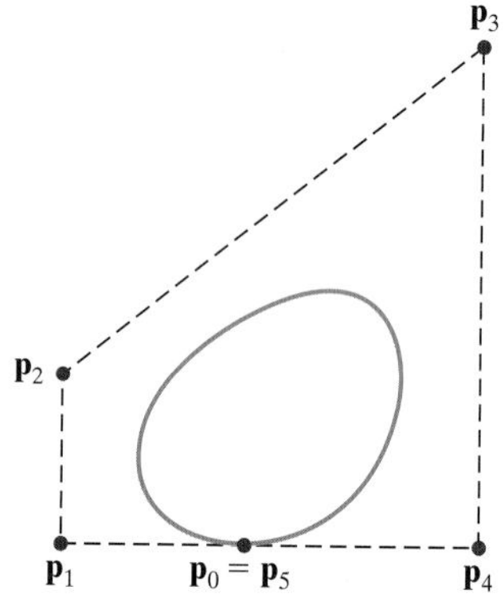

FIGURE 8-35 A closed Bézier curve generated by specifying the first and last control points at the same location.

A closed Bézier curve is generated when we set the last control-point position to the coordinate position of the first control point, as in the example shown in Fig. 8-35. Also, specifying multiple control points at a single coordinate position gives more weight to that position. In Fig. 8-36, a single coordinate position is input as two control points, and the resulting curve is pulled nearer to this position.

We can fit a Bézier curve to any number of control points, but this requires the calculation of polynomial functions of higher degree. When complicated curves are to be generated, they can be formed by piecing together several Bézier sections of lower degree. Generating smaller Bézier-curve sections also gives us better local control over the shape of the curve. Since Bézier curves connect the first and last control points, it is easy to match curve sections (zero-order continuity). Also, Bézier curves have the important property that the tangent to the curve at an endpoint is along the line joining that endpoint to the adjacent control point. Therefore, to obtain first-order continuity between curve sections, we can pick control points $\mathbf{p}_{0'}$ and $\mathbf{p}_{1'}$ for the next curve section to be along the same straight line as control points $\mathbf{p}_{n-1}$ and $\mathbf{p}_n$ of the preceding section (Fig. 8-37). If the first curve section has n control points and the next curve section has n' control points, then we match curve tangents by placing control point $\mathbf{p}_{1'}$ at the position

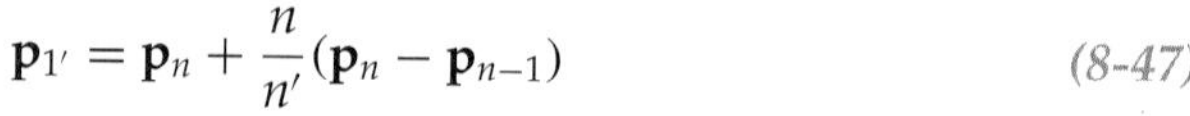

$$\mathbf{p}_{1'} = \mathbf{p}_n + \frac{n}{n'}(\mathbf{p}_n - \mathbf{p}_{n-1}) \qquad (8\text{-}47)$$

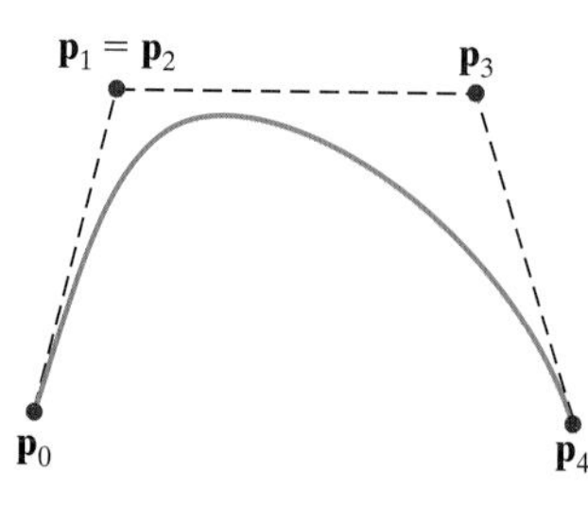

FIGURE 8-36 A Bézier curve can be made to pass closer to a given coordinate position by assigning multiple control points to that position.

To simplify the placement of $\mathbf{p}_{1'}$, we can require only geometric continuity and place $\mathbf{p}_{1'}$ anywhere along the line of $\mathbf{p}_{n-1}$ and $\mathbf{p}_n$.

We obtain C^2 continuity by using the expressions in Eqs. 8-45 to match parametric second derivatives for two adjacent Bézier sections. This establishes a coordinate position for control point $\mathbf{p}_{2'}$, in addition to the fixed positions for $\mathbf{p}_{0'}$ and $\mathbf{p}_{1'}$ that we need for C^0 and C^1 continuity. However, requiring second-order continuity for Bézier curve sections can be unnecessarily restrictive. This is particularly true with cubic curves, which have only four control points per section. In this case, second-order continuity fixes the position of the first three control points and leaves us only one point that we can use to adjust the shape of the curve segment.

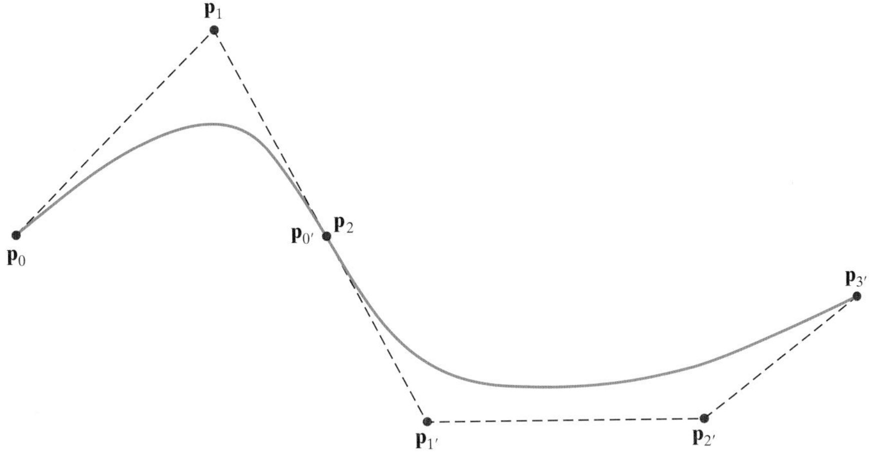

FIGURE 8-37 Piecewise approximation curve formed with two Bézier sections. Zero-order and first-order continuity is attained between the two curve sections by setting $\mathbf{p}_{0'} = \mathbf{p}_2$ and by setting $\mathbf{p}_{1'}$ along the line formed with points $\mathbf{p}_1$ and $\mathbf{p}_2$.

Cubic Bézier Curves

Many graphics packages provide functions for displaying only cubic splines. This allows reasonable design flexibility while avoiding the increased calculations needed with higher-order polynomials. Cubic Bézier curves are generated with four control points. The four blending functions for cubic Bézier curves, obtained by substituting $n = 3$ into Eq. 8-38, are

$$\begin{aligned} \text{BEZ}_{0,3} &= (1-u)^3 \\ \text{BEZ}_{1,3} &= 3u(1-u)^2 \\ \text{BEZ}_{2,3} &= 3u^2(1-u) \\ \text{BEZ}_{3,3} &= u^3 \end{aligned} \tag{8-48}$$

Plots of the four cubic Bézier blending functions are given in Fig. 8-38. The form of the blending functions determine how the control points influence the shape of the curve for values of parameter u over the range from 0 to 1. At $u = 0$, the only nonzero blending function is $\text{BEZ}_{0,3}$, which has the value 1. At $u = 1$, the only nonzero function is $\text{BEZ}_{3,3}(1) = 1$. Thus, a cubic Bézier curve always begins at control point $\mathbf{p}_0$ and ends at the position of control point $\mathbf{p}_3$. The other functions, $\text{BEZ}_{1,3}$ and $\text{BEZ}_{2,3}$, influence the shape of the curve at intermediate values of the parameter u, so that the resulting curve tends toward the points $\mathbf{p}_1$ and $\mathbf{p}_2$. Blending function $\text{BEZ}_{1,3}$ is maximum at $u = 1/3$, and $\text{BEZ}_{2,3}$ is maximum at $u = 2/3$.

We note in Fig. 8-38 that each of the four blending functions is nonzero over the entire range of parameter u between the endpoint positions. Thus, Bézier curves do not allow for *local control* of the curve shape. If we reposition any one of the control points, the entire curve is affected.

At the end positions of the cubic Bézier curve, the parametric first derivatives (slopes) are

$$\mathbf{P}'(0) = 3(\mathbf{p}_1 - \mathbf{p}_0), \qquad \mathbf{P}'(1) = 3(\mathbf{p}_3 - \mathbf{p}_2)$$

And the parametric second derivatives are

$$\mathbf{P}''(0) = 6(\mathbf{p}_0 - 2\mathbf{p}_1 + \mathbf{p}_2), \qquad \mathbf{P}''(1) = 6(\mathbf{p}_1 - 2\mathbf{p}_2 + \mathbf{p}_3)$$

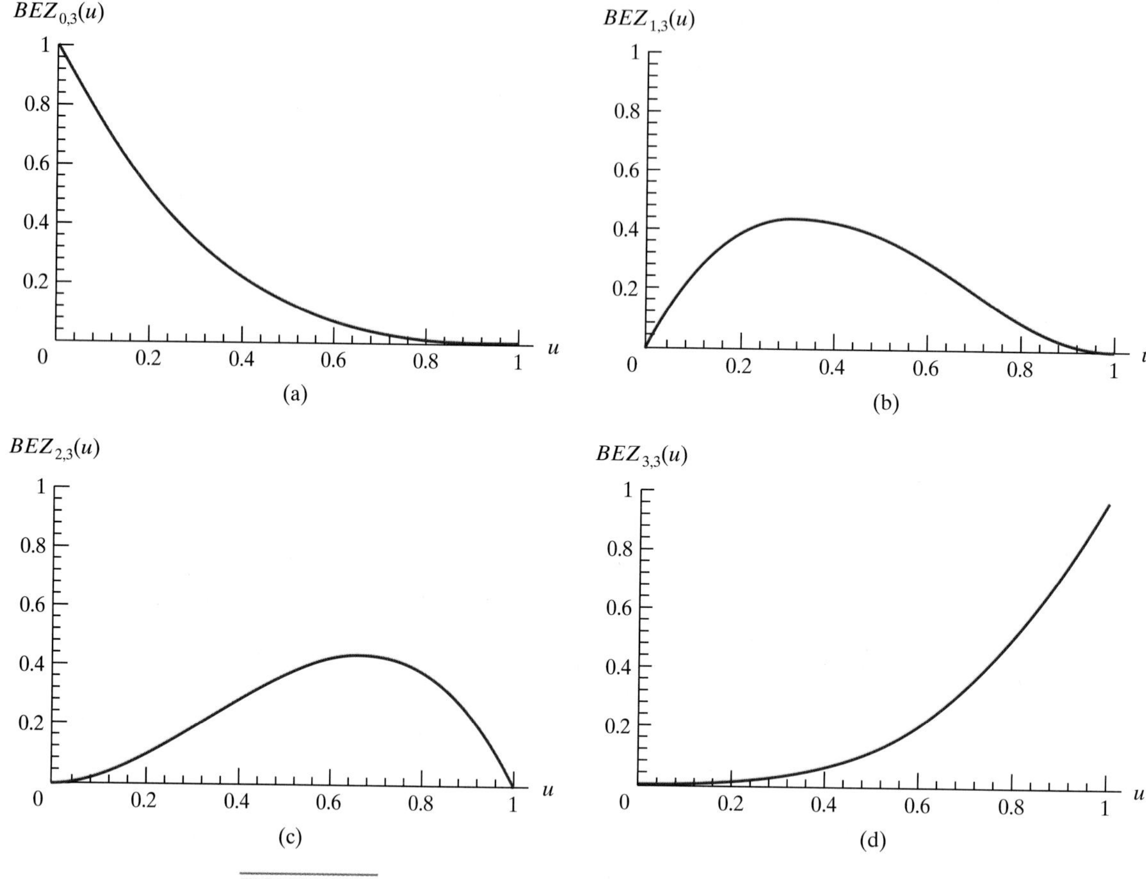

FIGURE 8-38 The four Bézier blending functions for cubic curves ($n = 3$).

We can construct complex spline curves using a series of cubic-Bézier sections. Using expressions for the parametric derivatives, we can equate curve tangents to attain C^1 continuity between the curve sections. And we could use the expressions for the second derivatives to obtain C^2 continuity, although this leaves us with no options for the placement of the first three control points.

A matrix formulation for the cubic-Bézier curve function is obtained by expanding the polynomial expressions for the blending functions and restructuring the equations as

$$\mathbf{P}(u) = [u^3 \quad u^2 \quad u \quad 1] \cdot \mathbf{M}_{\text{Bez}} \cdot \begin{bmatrix} \mathbf{p}_0 \\ \mathbf{p}_1 \\ \mathbf{p}_2 \\ \mathbf{p}_3 \end{bmatrix} \tag{8-49}$$

where the **Bézier matrix** is

$$\mathbf{M}_{\text{Bez}} = \begin{bmatrix} -1 & 3 & -3 & 1 \\ 3 & -6 & 3 & 0 \\ -3 & 3 & 0 & 0 \\ 1 & 0 & 0 & 0 \end{bmatrix} \tag{8-50}$$

We could also introduce additional parameters to allow adjustment of curve "tension" and "bias", as we did with the interpolating splines. But the more versatile B-splines, as well as β-splines, are often provided with this capability.

8-11 BÉZIER SURFACES

Two sets of orthogonal Bézier curves can be used to design an object surface. The parametric vector function for the Bézier surface is formed as the Cartesian product of Bézier blending functions:

$$\mathbf{P}(u, v) = \sum_{j=0}^{m} \sum_{k=0}^{n} \mathbf{p}_{j,k} \, \text{BEZ}_{j,m}(v) \, \text{BEZ}_{k,n}(u) \tag{8-51}$$

with $\mathbf{p}_{j,k}$ specifying the location of the $(m+1)$ by $(n+1)$ control points.

Figure 8-39 illustrates two Bézier surface plots. The control points are connected by dashed lines, and the solid lines show curves of constant u and constant v. Each curve of constant u is plotted by varying v over the interval from 0 to 1, with u fixed at one of the values in this unit interval. Curves of constant v are plotted similarly.

Bézier surfaces have the same properties as Bézier curves, and they provide a convenient method for interactive design applications. To specify the three-dimensional coordinate positions for the control points, we could first construct a rectangular grid in the xy "ground" plane. We then choose elevations above the ground plane at the grid intersections as the z-coordinate values for the control points. Surface patches can be represented with polygons and shaded using the rendering techniques discussed in Chapter 10.

Figure 8-40 illustrates a surface formed with two Bézier sections. As with curves, a smooth transition from one section to the other is assured by establishing both zero-order and first-order continuity at the boundary line. Zero-order continuity is obtained by matching control points at the boundary. First-order continuity is obtained by choosing control points along a straight line across the boundary and by maintaining a constant ratio of collinear line segments for each set of specified control points across section boundaries.

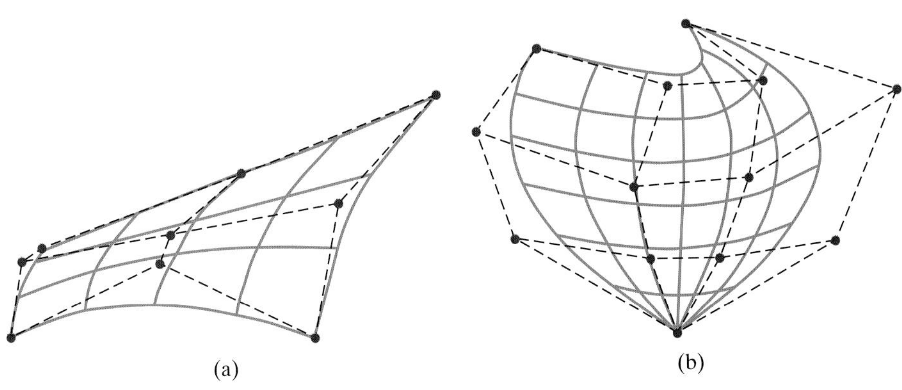

FIGURE 8-39 Wire-frame Bézier surfaces constructed with (a) nine control points arranged in a 3 by 3 mesh and (b) sixteen control points arranged in a 4 by 4 mesh. Dashed lines connect the control points.

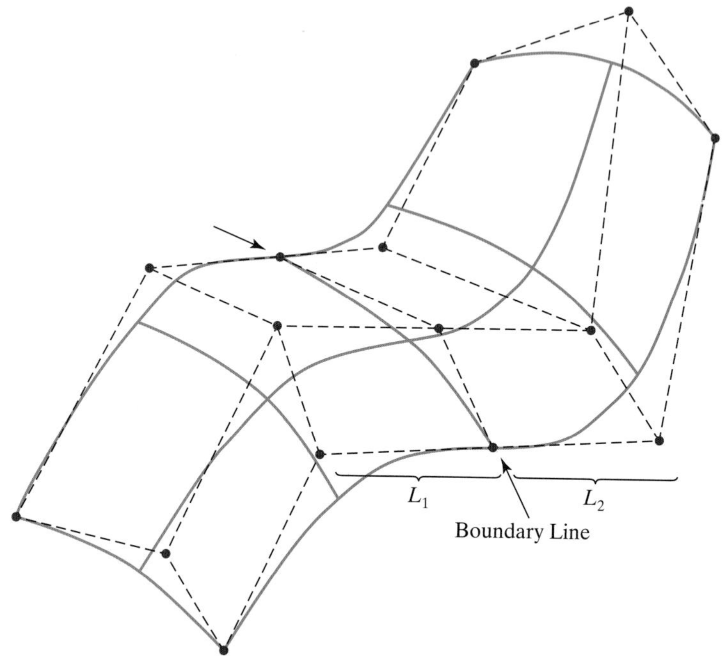

FIGURE 8-40 A composite Bézier surface constructed with two Bézier sections, joined at the indicated boundary line. The dashed lines connect the control points. First-order continuity is established by making the ratio of length L_1 to length L_2 constant for each collinear line of control points across the boundary between the surface sections.

8-12 B-SPLINE CURVES

This spline category is the most widely used, and **B-spline** functions are commonly available in CAD systems and many graphics-programming packages. Like Bézier splines, B-splines are generated by approximating a set of control points. But **B-splines** have two advantages over Bézier splines: (1) the degree of a B-spline polynomial can be set independently of the number of control points (with certain limitations), and (2) B-splines allow local control over the shape of a spline. The tradeoff is that B-splines are more complex than Bézier splines.

B-Spline Curve Equations

We can write a general expression for the calculation of coordinate positions along a B-spline curve using a blending-function formulation as

$$\mathbf{P}(u) = \sum_{k=0}^{n} \mathbf{p}_k B_{k,d}(u), \qquad u_{\min} \le u \le u_{\max}, \quad 2 \le d \le n+1 \tag{8-52}$$

where the $\mathbf{p}_k$ are an input set of $n+1$ control points. There are several differences between this B-spline formulation and the expression for a Bézier spline curve. The range of parameter u now depends on how we choose the other B-spline parameters. And the B-spline blending functions $B_{k,d}$ are polynomials of degree $d-1$, where d is the **degree parameter.** (Sometimes parameter d is alluded to as the "order" of the polynomial, but this can be misleading because the term order is also often used to mean simply the degree of the polynomial, which is $d-1$.) The degree parameter d can be assigned any integer value in the range from 2 up to the number of control points ($n+1$). Actually, we could also set the value of

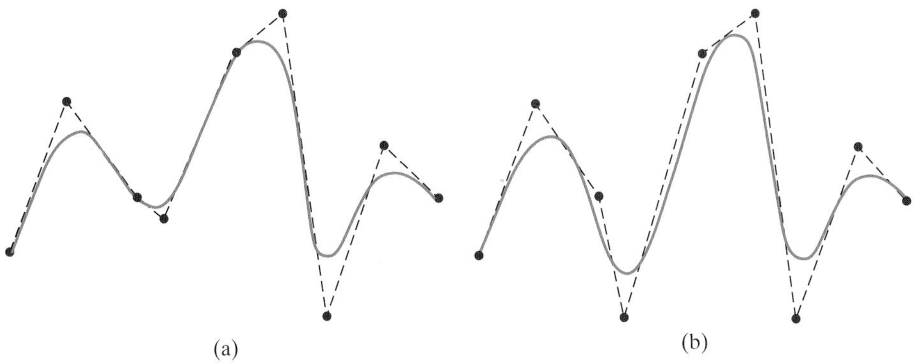

FIGURE 8-41 Local modification of a B-spline curve. Changing one of the control points in (a) produces curve (b), which is modified only in the neighborhood of the altered control point.

the degree parameter at 1, but then our "curve" is just a point plot of the control points. Local control for B-splines is achieved by defining the blending functions over subintervals of the total range of u.

Blending functions for B-spline curves are defined by the Cox-deBoor recursion formulas:

$$B_{k,1}(u) = \begin{cases} 1 & \text{if } u_k \le u \le u_{k+1} \\ 0 & \text{otherwise} \end{cases}$$

$$B_{k,d}(u) = \frac{u - u_k}{u_{k+d-1} - u_k} B_{k,d-1}(u) + \frac{u_{k+d} - u}{u_{k+d} - u_{k+1}} B_{k+1,d-1}(u) \tag{8-53}$$

where each blending function is defined over d subintervals of the total range of u. Each subinterval endpoint u_j is referred to as a **knot,** and the entire set of selected subinterval endpoints is called a **knot vector.** We can choose any values for the subinterval endpoints, subject to the condition $u_j \le u_{j+1}$. Values for $u_{\min}$ and $u_{\max}$ then depend on the number of control points we select, the value we choose for the degree parameter d, and how we set up the subintervals (knot vector). Since it is possible to choose the elements of the knot vector so that some denominators in the Cox-deBoor calculations evaluate to 0, this formulation assumes that any terms evaluated as 0/0 are to be assigned the value 0.

Figure 8-41 demonstrates the local-control characteristics of B-splines. In addition to local control, B-splines allow us to vary the number of control points used to design a curve without changing the degree of the polynomial. And we can increase the number of values in the knot vector to aid in curve design. When we do this, however, we must add control points since the size of the knot vector depends on parameter n.

B-spline curves have the following properties:

- The polynomial curve has degree $d - 1$ and C^{d-2} continuity over the range of u.
- For $n + 1$ control points, the curve is described with $n + 1$ blending functions.
- Each blending function $B_{k,d}$ is defined over d subintervals of the total range of u, starting at knot value u_k.
- The range of parameter u is divided into $n + d$ subintervals by the $n + d + 1$ values specified in the knot vector.

- With knot values labeled as $\{u_0, u_1, \ldots, u_{n+d}\}$, the resulting B-spline curve is defined only in the interval from knot value u_{d-1} up to knot value u_{n+1}. (Some blending functions are undefined outside this interval.)
- Each section of the spline curve (between two successive knot values) is influenced by d control points.
- Any one control point can affect the shape of at most d curve sections.

In addition, a B-spline curve lies within the convex hull of at most $d + 1$ control points, so that B-splines are tightly bound to the input positions. For any value of u in the interval from knot value u_{d-1} to u_{n+1}, the sum over all basis functions is 1:

$$\sum_{k=0}^{n} B_{k,d}(u) = 1 \tag{8-54}$$

Given the control-point positions and the value of the degree parameter d, we then need to specify the knot values to obtain the blending functions using the recurrence relations 8-53. There are three general classifications for knot vectors: uniform, open uniform, and nonuniform. B-splines are commonly described according to the selected knot vector class.

Uniform Periodic B-Spline Curves

When the spacing between knot values is constant, the resulting curve is called a **uniform** B-spline. For example, we can set up a uniform knot vector as

$$\{-1.5, -1.0, -0.5, 0.0, 0.5, 1.0, 1.5, 2.0\}$$

Often knot values are normalized to the range between 0 and 1, as in

$$\{0.0, 0.2, 0.4, 0.6, 0.8, 1.0\}$$

It is convenient in many applications to set up uniform knot values with a separation of 1 and a starting value of 0. The following knot vector is an example of this specification scheme.

$$\{0, 1, 2, 3, 4, 5, 6, 7\}$$

Uniform B-splines have **periodic** blending functions. That is, for given values of n and d, all blending functions have the same shape. Each successive blending function is simply a shifted version of the previous function:

$$B_{k,d}(u) = B_{k+1,d}(u + \Delta u) = B_{k+2,d}(u + 2\Delta u) \tag{8-55}$$

where Δu is the interval between adjacent knot values. Figure 8-42 shows the quadratic, uniform B-spline blending functions generated in the following example for a curve with four control points.

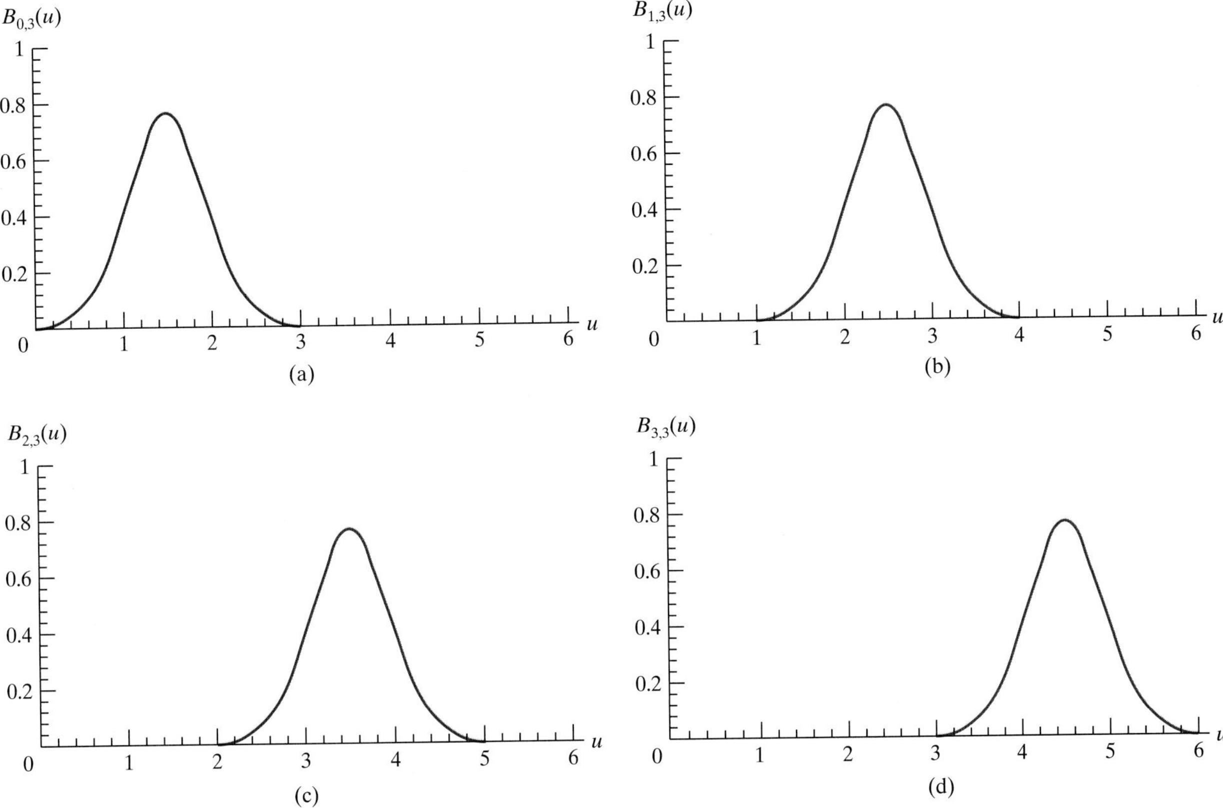

FIGURE 8-42 Periodic B-spline blending functions for $n = d = 3$ and a uniform, integer knot vector.

EXAMPLE 8-1 Uniform, Quadratic B-Splines

To illustrate the formulation of B-spline blending functions for a uniform, integer knot vector, we select parameter values $d = n = 3$. The knot vector must then contain $n + d + 1 = 7$ knot values:

$$\{0, 1, 2, 3, 4, 5, 6\}$$

and the range for parameter u is from 0 to 6, with $n + d = 6$ subintervals.

Each of the four blending functions spans $d = 3$ subintervals of the total range for u. Using the recurrence relations 8-53, we obtain the first blending function as

$$B_{0,3}(u) = \begin{cases} \frac{1}{2}u^2, & \text{for } 0 \le u < 1 \\ \frac{1}{2}u(2-u) + \frac{1}{2}(u-1)(3-u), & \text{for } 1 \le u < 2 \\ \frac{1}{2}(3-u)^2, & \text{for } 2 \le u < 3 \end{cases}$$

We obtain the next periodic blending function using relationship 8-55, substituting $u - 1$ for u in $B_{0,3}$, and shifting the starting positions up by 1:

$$B_{1,3}(u) = \begin{cases} \frac{1}{2}(u-1)^2, & \text{for } 1 \le u < 2 \\ \frac{1}{2}(u-1)(3-u) + \frac{1}{2}(u-2)(4-u), & \text{for } 2 \le u < 3 \\ \frac{1}{2}(4-u)^2, & \text{for } 3 \le u < 4 \end{cases}$$

Similarly, the remaining two periodic functions are obtained by successively shifting $B_{1,3}$ to the right:

$$B_{2,3}(u) = \begin{cases} \frac{1}{2}(u-2)^2, & \text{for } 2 \le u < 3 \\ \frac{1}{2}(u-2)(4-u) + \frac{1}{2}(u-3)(5-u), & \text{for } 3 \le u < 4 \\ \frac{1}{2}(5-u)^2, & \text{for } 4 \le u < 5 \end{cases}$$

$$B_{3,3}(u) = \begin{cases} \frac{1}{2}(u-3)^2, & \text{for } 3 \le u < 4 \\ \frac{1}{2}(u-3)(5-u) + \frac{1}{2}(u-4)(6-u), & \text{for } 4 \le u < 5 \\ \frac{1}{2}(6-u)^2, & \text{for } 5 \le u < 6 \end{cases}$$

A plot of the four periodic, quadratic blending functions is given in Fig. 8-42, which demonstrates the local feature of B-splines. The first control point is multiplied by blending function $B_{0,3}(u)$. Therefore, changing the position of the first control point only affects the shape of the curve up to $u = 3$. Similarly, the last control point influences the shape of the spline curve in the interval where $B_{3,3}$ is defined.

Figure 8-42 also illustrates the limits of the B-spline curve for this example. All blending functions are present in the interval from $u_{d-1} = 2$ to $u_{n+1} = 4$. Below 2 and above 4, not all blending functions are present. This interval, from 2 to 4, is the range of the polynomial curve, and the interval in which Eq. 8-54 is valid. Thus, the sum of all blending functions is 1 within this interval. Outside this interval, we cannot sum all blending functions, since they are not all defined below 2 and above 4.

Because the range of the resulting polynomial curve is from 2 to 4, we can determine the starting and ending position of the curve by evaluating the blending functions at these points to obtain

$$\mathbf{P}_{\text{start}} = \frac{1}{2}(\mathbf{p}_0 + \mathbf{p}_1), \qquad \mathbf{P}_{\text{end}} = \frac{1}{2}(\mathbf{p}_2 + \mathbf{p}_3)$$

Thus, the curve starts at the midposition between the first two control points and ends at the midposition between the last two control points.

We can also determine the parametric derivatives at the starting and ending positions of the curve. Taking the derivatives of the blending functions and substituting the endpoint values for parameter u, we find that

$$\mathbf{P}'_{\text{start}} = \mathbf{p}_1 - \mathbf{p}_0, \qquad \mathbf{P}'_{\text{end}} = \mathbf{p}_3 - \mathbf{p}_2$$

The parametric slope of the curve at the start position is parallel to the line joining the first two control points, and the parametric slope at the end of the curve is parallel to the line joining the last two control points.

An example plot of the quadratic periodic B-spline curve is given in Figure 8-43 for four control points selected in the xy plane. ■

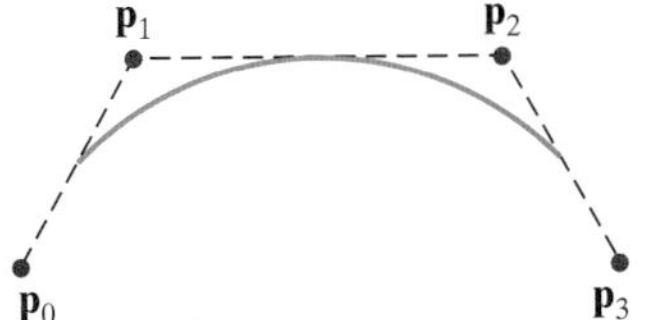

FIGURE 8-43 A quadratic, periodic B-spline fitted to four control points in the xy plane.

In the preceeding example, we noted that the quadratic curve starts between the first two control points and ends at a position between the last two control points. This result is valid for a quadratic periodic B-spline fitted to any number of distinct control points. In general, for higher-order polynomials, the start and end positions are each weighted averages of $d - 1$ control points. We can pull a spline curve closer to any control-point position by specifying that position multiple times.

General expressions for the boundary conditions for periodic B-splines can be obtained by reparameterizing the blending functions so that parameter u is mapped onto the unit interval from 0 to 1. Beginning and ending conditions are then obtained at $u = 0$ and $u = 1$.

Cubic Periodic B-Spline Curves

Since cubic periodic B-splines are commonly used in graphics packages, we consider the formulation for this class of splines. Periodic splines are particularly useful for generating certain closed curves. For example, the closed curve in Fig. 8-44 can be generated in sections by cyclically specifying four of the six control points for each section. Also, if the coordinate positions for three consecutive control points are identical, the curve passes through that point.

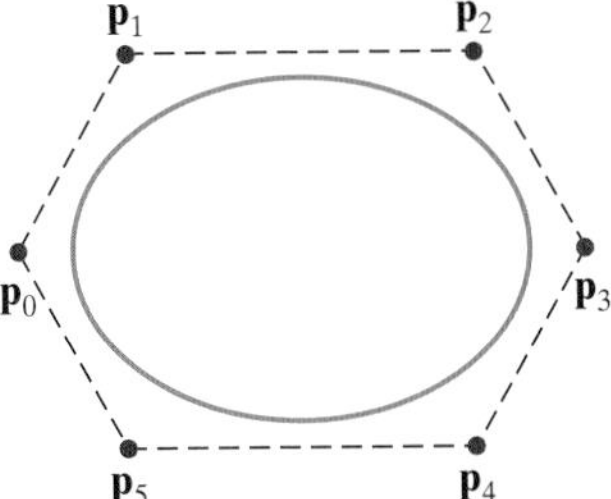

FIGURE 8-44 A closed, periodic, piecewise, cubic B-spline constructed using a cyclic specification of four control points for each curve section.

For cubic B-spline curves, $d = 4$ and each blending function spans four subintervals of the total range of u. If we are to fit the cubic to four control points, then we could use the integer knot vector

$$\{0, 1, 2, 3, 4, 5, 6, 7\}$$

and recurrence relations 8-53 to obtain the periodic blending functions, as we did in the last section for quadratic periodic B-splines.

To derive the curve equations for a periodic, cubic B-spline, we consider an alternate formulation by starting with the boundary conditions and obtaining the blending functions normalized to the interval $0 \leq u \leq 1$. Using this formulation, we can also easily obtain the characteristic matrix. The boundary conditions for periodic cubic B-splines with four control points, labeled $\mathbf{p}_0$, $\mathbf{p}_1$, $\mathbf{p}_2$, and $\mathbf{p}_3$, are

$$\begin{aligned}
\mathbf{P}(0) &= \frac{1}{6}(\mathbf{p}_0 + 4\mathbf{p}_1 + \mathbf{p}_2) \\
\mathbf{P}(1) &= \frac{1}{6}(\mathbf{p}_1 + 4\mathbf{p}_2 + \mathbf{p}_3) \\
\mathbf{P}'(0) &= \frac{1}{2}(\mathbf{p}_2 - \mathbf{p}_0) \\
\mathbf{P}'(1) &= \frac{1}{2}(\mathbf{p}_3 - \mathbf{p}_1)
\end{aligned} \tag{8-56}$$

These boundary conditions are similar to those for cardinal splines: Curve sections are defined with four control points, and parametric derivatives (slopes) at the beginning and end of each curve section are parallel to the chords joining adjacent control points. The B-spline curve section starts at a position near $\mathbf{p}_1$ and ends at a position near $\mathbf{p}_2$.

A matrix formulation for a cubic periodic B-spline with four control points can then be written as

$$\mathbf{P}(u) = [u^3 \quad u^2 \quad u \quad 1] \cdot \mathbf{M}_B \cdot \begin{bmatrix} \mathbf{p}_0 \\ \mathbf{p}_1 \\ \mathbf{p}_2 \\ \mathbf{p}_3 \end{bmatrix} \tag{8-57}$$

where the B-spline matrix for periodic cubic polynomials is

$$\mathbf{M}_B = \frac{1}{6} \begin{bmatrix} -1 & 3 & -3 & 1 \\ 3 & -6 & 3 & 0 \\ -3 & 0 & 3 & 0 \\ 1 & 4 & 1 & 0 \end{bmatrix} \tag{8-58}$$

This matrix can be obtained by solving for the coefficients in a general cubic polynomial expression, using the specified four boundary conditions.

We can also modify the B-spline equations to include a tension parameter t (as in cardinal splines). The matrix for the periodic cubic B-spline, with tension parameter t, is

$$\mathbf{M}_{B_t} = \frac{1}{6} \begin{bmatrix} -t & 12-9t & 9t-12 & t \\ 3t & 12t-18 & 18-15t & 0 \\ -3t & 0 & 3t & 0 \\ t & 6-2t & t & 0 \end{bmatrix} \tag{8-59}$$

which reduces to M_B when $t = 1$.

We obtain the periodic cubic B-spline blending functions over the parameter range from 0 to 1 by expanding the matrix representation into polynomial form. For example, using the tension value $t = 1$, we have

$$\begin{aligned} B_{0,3}(u) &= \frac{1}{6}(1-u)^3, \qquad 0 \le u \le 1 \\ B_{1,3}(u) &= \frac{1}{6}(3u^3 - 6u^2 + 4) \\ B_{2,3}(u) &= \frac{1}{6}(-3u^3 + 3u^2 + 3u + 1) \\ B_{3,3}(u) &= \frac{1}{6}u^3 \end{aligned} \tag{8-60}$$

Open Uniform B-Spline Curves

This class of B-splines is a cross between uniform B-splines and nonuniform B-splines. Sometimes it is treated as a special type of uniform B-spline, and sometimes it is considered to be in the nonuniform B-spline classification. For the **open uniform** B-splines, or simply **open** B-splines, the knot spacing is uniform except at the ends, where knot values are repeated d times.

Following are two examples of open, uniform, integer knot vectors, each with a starting value of 0.

$$\begin{array}{ll} \{0, 0, 1, 2, 3, 3\} & \text{for } d = 2 \text{ and } n = 3 \\ \{0, 0, 0, 0, 1, 2, 2, 2, 2\} & \text{for } d = 4 \text{ and } n = 4 \end{array} \quad (8\text{-}61)$$

We can normalize these knot vectors to the unit interval from 0 to 1 as

$$\begin{array}{ll} \{0, 0, 0.33, 0.67, 1, 1\} & \text{for } d = 2 \text{ and } n = 3 \\ \{0, 0, 0, 0, 0.5, 1, 1, 1, 1\} & \text{for } d = 4 \text{ and } n = 4 \end{array} \quad (8\text{-}62)$$

For any values of parameters d and n, we can generate an open uniform knot vector with integer values using the calculations

$$u_j = \begin{cases} 0 & \text{for } 0 \leq j < d \\ j - d + 1 & \text{for } d \leq j \leq n \\ n - d + 2 & \text{for } j > n \end{cases} \quad (8\text{-}63)$$

for values of j ranging from 0 to $n + d$. With this assignment, the first d knots are assigned the value 0, and the last d knots have the value $n - d + 2$.

Open uniform B-splines have characteristics that are very similar to Bézier splines. In fact, when $d = n + 1$ (degree of the polynomial is n), open B-splines reduce to Bézier splines, and all knot values are either 0 or 1. For example, with a cubic open B-spline ($d = 4$) and four control points, the knot vector is

$$\{0, 0, 0, 0, 1, 1, 1, 1\}$$

The polynomial curve for an open B-spline connects the first and last control points. Also, the parametric slope of the curve at the first control point is parallel to the straight line formed by the first two control points, and the parametric slope at the last control point is parallel to the line defined by the last two control points. Thus, the geometric constraints for matching curve sections are the same as for Bézier curves.

As with Bézier curves, specifying multiple control points at the same coordinate position pulls any B-spline curve closer to that position. Since open B-splines start at the first control point and end at the last control point, a closed curve can be generated by setting the first and last control points at the same coordinate position.

EXAMPLE 8-2 Open Uniform, Quadratic B-Splines

From conditions 8-63 with $d = 3$ and $n = 4$ (five control points), we obtain the following eight values for the knot vector:

$$\{u_0, u_1, u_2, u_3, u_4, u_5, u_6, u_7\} = \{0, 0, 0, 1, 2, 3, 3, 3\}$$

The total range of u is divided into seven subintervals, and each of the five blending functions $B_{k,3}$ is defined over three subintervals, starting at knot position u_k. Thus $B_{0,3}$ is defined from $u_0 = 0$ to $u_3 = 1$, $B_{1,3}$ is defined from $u_1 = 0$ to $u_4 = 2$, and $B_{4,3}$ is defined from $u_4 = 2$ to $u_7 = 3$. Explicit

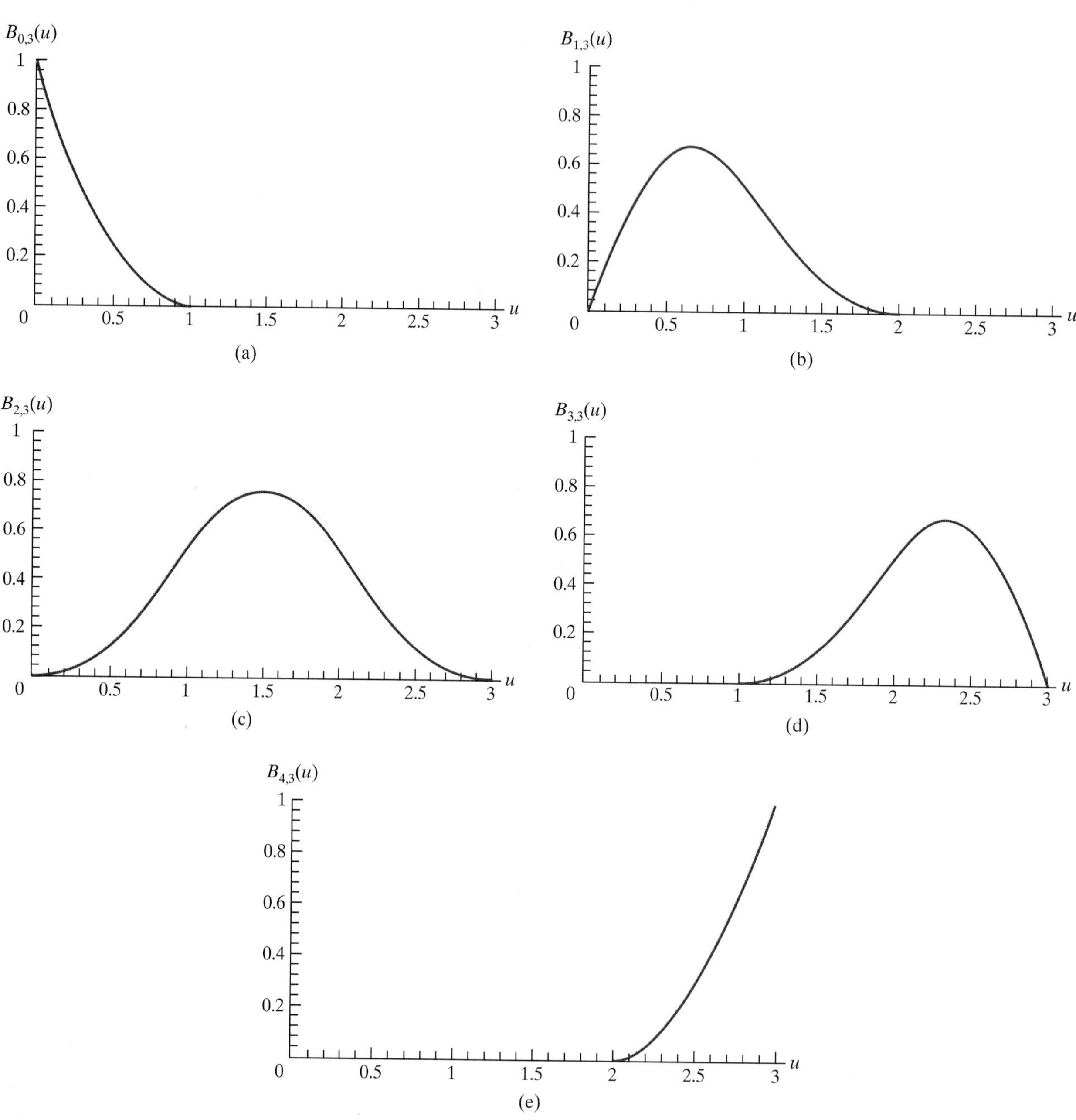

FIGURE 8-45 Open, uniform B-spline blending functions for $n = 4$ and $d = 3$.

polynomial expressions are obtained for the blending functions from recurrence relations 8-53 as

$$B_{0,3}(u) = (1-u)^2 \qquad 0 \le u < 1$$

$$B_{1,3}(u) = \begin{cases} \frac{1}{2}u(4-3u) & 0 \le u < 1 \\ \frac{1}{2}(2-u)^2 & 1 \le u < 2 \end{cases}$$

$$B_{2,3}(u) = \begin{cases} \frac{1}{2}u^2 & 0 \le u < 1 \\ \frac{1}{2}u(2-u) + \frac{1}{2}(u-1)(3-u) & 1 \le u < 2 \\ \frac{1}{2}(3-u)^2 & 2 \le u < 3 \end{cases}$$

$$B_{3,3}(u) = \begin{cases} \frac{1}{2}(u-1)^2 & 1 \le u < 2 \\ \frac{1}{2}(3-u)(3u-5) & 2 \le u < 3 \end{cases}$$

$$B_{4,3}(u) = (u-2)^2 \qquad 2 \le u < 3$$

Figure 8-45 shows the shape of the these five blending functions. The local features of B-splines are again demonstrated. Blending function $B_{0,3}$ is nonzero only in the subinterval from 0 to 1, so the first control point influences the curve only in this interval. Similarly, function $B_{4,3}$ is 0 outside the interval from 2 to 3, and the position of the last control point does not affect the shape of the beginning and middle parts of the curve. ■

Matrix formulations for open B-splines are not as conveniently generated as they are for periodic uniform B-splines. This is due to the multiplicity of knot values at the beginning and end of the knot vector.

Nonuniform B-Spline Curves

For this class of splines, we can specify any values and intervals for the knot vector. With **nonuniform** B-splines, we can choose multiple internal knot values and unequal spacing between the knot values. Some examples are

$$\{0, 1, 2, 3, 3, 4\}$$
$$\{0, 2, 2, 3, 3, 6\}$$
$$\{0, 0, 0, 1, 1, 3, 3, 3\}$$
$$\{0, 0.2, 0.6, 0.9, 1.0\}$$

Nonuniform B-splines provide increased flexibility in controlling a curve shape. With unequally spaced intervals in the knot vector, we obtain different shapes for the blending functions in different intervals, which can be used in designing the spline features. By increasing knot multiplicity, we can produce subtle variations in the curve path and introduce discontinuities. Multiple knot values also reduce the continuity by 1 for each repeat of a particular value.

We obtain the blending functions for a nonuniform B-spline using methods similar to those discussed for uniform and open B-splines. Given a set of $n + 1$ control points, we set the degree of the polynomial and select the knot values. Then, using the recurrence relations, we could either obtain the set of blending functions or evaluate curve positions directly for the display of the curve. Graphics packages often restrict the knot intervals to be either 0 or 1 to reduce computations. A set of characteristic matrices can then be stored and used to compute values along the spline curve without evaluating the recurrence relations for each curve point to be plotted.

FIGURE 8-46 A prototype helicopter, designed and modeled by Daniel Langlois of SOFTIMAGE, Inc., Montreal, Quebec, Canada, using 180,000 B-spline surface patches. The scene was then rendered using ray tracing, bump mapping, and reflection mapping. (*Courtesy of Silicon Graphics, Inc.*)

8-13 B-SPLINE SURFACES

Formulation of a B-spline surface is similar to that for Bézier splines. We can obtain a vector point function over a B-spline surface using the Cartesian product of B-spline blending functions in the form

$$\mathbf{P}(u, v) = \sum_{k_u=0}^{n_u} \sum_{k_v=0}^{n_v} \mathbf{p}_{k_u,k_v} B_{k_u,d_u}(u) B_{k_v,d_v}(v) \tag{8-64}$$

where the vector values for $\mathbf{p}_{k_u,k_v}$ specify the positions of the $(n_u + 1)$ by $(n_v + 1)$ control points.

B-spline surfaces exhibit the same properties as those of their component B-spline curves. A surface can be constructed from selected values for degree parameters d_u and d_v, which set the degrees for the orthogonal surface polynomials at $d_u - 1$ and $d_v - 1$. For each surface parameter u and v, we also select values for the knot vectors, which determines the parameter range for the blending functions. Figure 8-46 shows an object modeled with B-spline surfaces.

8-14 BETA-SPLINES

A generalization of B-splines are the **beta-splines,** also referred to as **β-splines,** that are formulated by imposing geometric continuity conditions on the first and second parametric derivatives. The continuity parameters for beta-splines are called *β parameters*.

Beta-Spline Continuity Conditions

For a specified knot vector, we designate the spline sections to the left and right of a particular knot u_j with the position vectors $\mathbf{P}_{j-1}(u)$ and $\mathbf{P}_j(u)$ (Fig. 8-47). Zero-order continuity (*positional continuity*), G^0, at u_j is obtained by requiring that

$$\mathbf{P}_{j-1}(u_j) = \mathbf{P}_j(u_j) \tag{8-65}$$

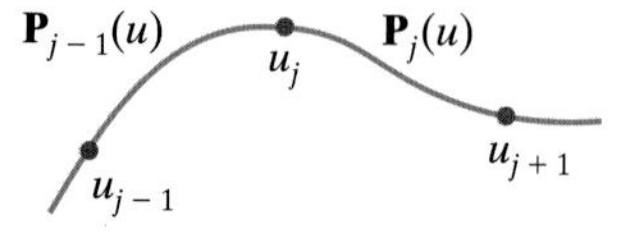

FIGURE 8-47 Position vectors along curve sections to the left and right of knot u_j.

First-order continuity (*unit tangent continuity*), G^1, is obtained by requiring tangent vectors to be proportional:

$$\beta_1 \mathbf{P}'_{j-1}(u_j) = \mathbf{P}'_j(u_j), \qquad \beta_1 > 0 \tag{8-66}$$

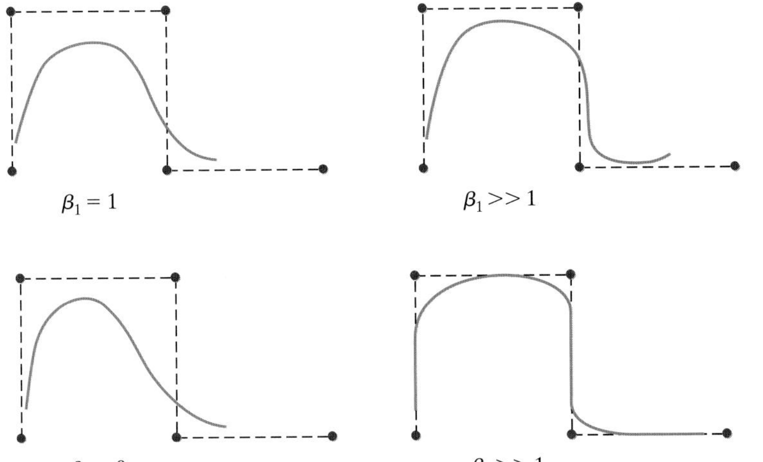

FIGURE 8-48 Effect of parameter β_1 on the shape of a beta-spline curve.

FIGURE 8-49 Effect of parameter β_2 on the shape of a beta-spline curve.

Here, parametric first derivatives are proportional, and the unit tangent vectors are continuous across the knot.

Second-order continuity (*curvature vector continuity*), G^2, is imposed with the condition

$$\beta_1^2 \mathbf{P}''_{j-1}(u_j) + \beta_2 \mathbf{P}'_{j-1}(u_j) = \mathbf{P}''_j(u_j) \qquad (8\text{-}67)$$

where β_2 can be assigned any real number and $\beta_1 > 0$. The curvature vector provides a measure of the amount of bending for the curve at position u_j. When $\beta_1 = 1$ and $\beta_2 = 0$, beta-splines reduce to B-splines.

Parameter β_1 is called the *bias parameter* since it controls the skewness of the curve. For $\beta_1 > 1$, the curve tends to flatten to the right in the direction of the unit tangent vector at the knots. For $0 < \beta_1 < 1$, the curve tends to flatten to the left. The effect of β_1 on the shape of the spline curve is shown in Fig. 8-48.

Parameter β_2 is called the *tension parameter* since it controls how tightly or loosely the spline fits the control graph. As β_2 increases, the curve approaches the shape of the control graph, as shown in Fig. 8-49.

Cubic Periodic Beta-Spline Matrix Representation

Applying the beta-spline boundary conditions to a cubic polynomial with a uniform knot vector, we obtain the matrix representation for a periodic beta-spline as

$$\mathbf{M}_\beta = \frac{1}{\delta}\begin{bmatrix} -2\beta_1^3 & 2(\beta_2 + \beta_1^3 + \beta_1^2 + \beta_1) & -2(\beta_2 + \beta_1^2 + \beta_1 + 1) & 2 \\ 6\beta_1^3 & -3(\beta_2 + 2\beta_1^3 + 2\beta_1^2) & 3(\beta_2 + 2\beta_1^2) & 0 \\ -6\beta_1^3 & 6(\beta_1^3 - \beta_1) & 6\beta_1 & 0 \\ 2\beta_1^3 & \beta_2 + 4(\beta_1^2 + \beta_1) & 2 & 0 \end{bmatrix} \qquad (8\text{-}68)$$

where $\delta = \beta_2 + 2\beta_1^3 + 4\beta_1^2 + 4\beta_1 + 2$.

We obtain the B-spline matrix M_B when $\beta_1 = 1$ and $\beta_2 = 0$. And we have the B-spline tension matrix M_{B_t} (Eq. 8-59) when

$$\beta_1 = 1, \qquad \beta_2 = \frac{12}{t}(1 - t)$$

8-15 RATIONAL SPLINES

A rational function is simply the ratio of two polynomials. Thus, a **rational spline** is the ratio of two spline functions. For example, a rational B-spline curve can be described with the position vector

$$\mathbf{P}(u) = \frac{\sum_{k=0}^{n} \omega_k \mathbf{p}_k B_{k,d}(u)}{\sum_{k=0}^{n} \omega_k B_{k,d}(u)} \tag{8-69}$$

where the $\mathbf{p}_k$ are a set of $n+1$ control-point positions. Parameters ω_k are weight factors for the control points. The greater the value of a particular ω_k, the closer the curve is pulled toward the control point $\mathbf{p}_k$ weighted by that parameter. When all weight factors are set to the value 1, we have the standard B-spline curve, since the denominator in Eq. 8-69 is then just the sum of the blending functions, which has the value 1 (Eq. 8-54).

Rational splines have two important advantages, compared to nonrational splines. First, they provide an exact representation for quadric curves (conics), such as circles and ellipses. Nonrational splines, which are polynomials, can only approximate conics. This allows graphics packages to model all curve shapes with one representation—rational splines—without needing a library of curve functions to handle different design shapes. The second advantage of rational splines is that they are invariant with respect to a perspective viewing transformation (Section 7-8). This means that we can apply a perspective viewing transformation to the control points of the rational curve, and we will obtain the correct view of the curve. Nonrational splines, on the other hand, are not invariant with respect to a perspective viewing transformation. Typically, graphics design packages use nonuniform knot vector representations for constructing rational B-splines. These splines are referred to as NURBS (*nonuniform rational B-splines*), or NURBs.

Homogeneous coordinate representations are used for rational splines, since the denominator can be treated as the homogeneous factor h in a four-dimensional representation of the control points. Thus, a rational spline can be thought of as the projection of a four-dimensional nonrational spline into three-dimensional space.

In general, constructing a rational B-spline representation is carried out using the same procedures that we employed to obtain a nonrational representation. Given the set of control points, the degree of the polynomial, the weighting factors, and the knot vector, we apply the recurrence relations to obtain the blending functions. With some CAD systems, we construct a conic section by specifying three points on an arc. A rational homogeneous-coordinate spline representation is then determined by computing control-point positions that would generate the selected conic type.

As an example of describing conic sections with rational splines, we can use a quadratic B-spline function ($d = 3$), three control points, and the open knot vector

$$\{0, 0, 0, 1, 1, 1\}$$

which is the same as a quadratic Bézier spline. We then set the weighting functions to the values

$$\begin{aligned} \omega_0 &= \omega_2 = 1 \\ \omega_1 &= \frac{r}{1-r}, \qquad 0 \le r < 1 \end{aligned} \tag{8-70}$$

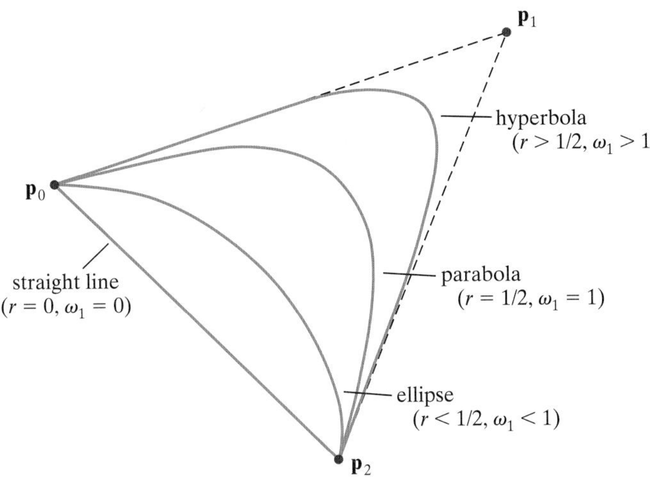

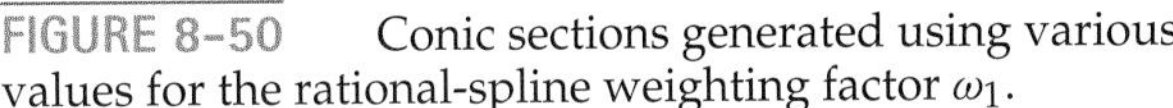

FIGURE 8-50 Conic sections generated using various values for the rational-spline weighting factor ω_1.

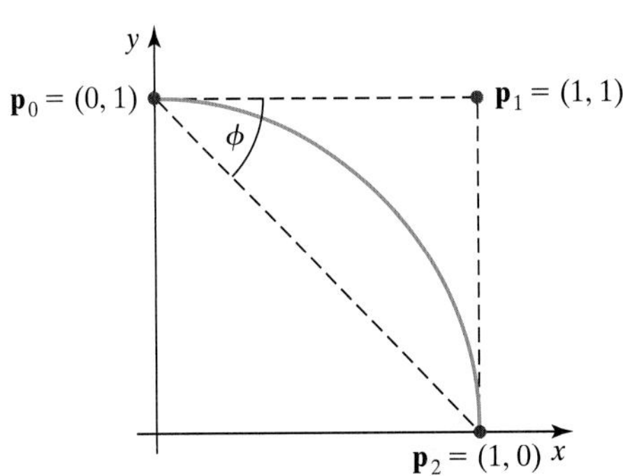

FIGURE 8-51 A circular arc in the first quadrant of the xy plane.

and the rational B-spline representation is

$$\mathbf{P}(u) = \frac{\mathbf{p}_0 B_{0,3}(u) + [r/(1-r)]\mathbf{p}_1 B_{1,3}(u) + \mathbf{p}_2 B_{2,3}(u)}{B_{0,3}(u) + [r/(1-r)]B_{1,3}(u) + B_{2,3}(u)} \tag{8-71}$$

We then obtain the various conics (Fig. 8-50) with the following values for parameter r.

$r > 1/2,$	$\omega_1 > 1$	hyperbola section
$r = 1/2,$	$\omega_1 = 1$	parabola section
$r < 1/2,$	$\omega_1 < 1$	ellipse section
$r = 0,$	$\omega_1 = 0$	straight-line segment

We can generate a one-quarter arc of a unit circle in the first quadrant of the xy plane (Fig. 8-51) by setting $\omega_1 = \cos\phi$ and by choosing the control points as

$$\mathbf{p}_0 = (0, 1), \qquad \mathbf{p}_1 = (1, 1), \qquad \mathbf{p}_2 = (1, 0)$$

A complete circle can be obtained by generating sections in the other three quadrants using similar control-point placements. Or we could produce a complete circle from the first-quadrant section using geometric transformations in the xy plane. For example, we can reflect the one-quarter circular arc about the x and y axes to produce the circular arcs in the other three quadrants.

A homogeneous representation for a unit circular arc in the first quadrant of the xy plane is

$$\begin{bmatrix} x_h(u) \\ y_h(u) \\ z_h(u) \\ h(u) \end{bmatrix} = \begin{bmatrix} 1-u^2 \\ 2u \\ 0 \\ 1+u^2 \end{bmatrix} \tag{8-72}$$

This homogeneous representation yields the parametric circle equations for the first quadrant as

$$x = \frac{x_h(u)}{h(u)} = \frac{1-u^2}{1+u^2}$$
$$y = \frac{y_h(u)}{h(u)} = \frac{2u}{1+u^2} \tag{8-73}$$

8-16 CONVERSION BETWEEN SPLINE REPRESENTATIONS

Sometimes it is desirable to be able to switch from one spline representation to another. For instance, a Bézier representation is most convenient for subdividing a spline curve, while a B-spline representation offers greater design flexibility. So we might design a curve using B-spline sections, then convert to an equivalent Bézier representation to display the object using a recursive subdivision procedure to locate coordinate positions along the curve.

Suppose we have a spline description of an object that can be expressed with the following matrix product

$$\mathbf{P}(u) = \mathbf{U} \cdot \mathbf{M}_{\text{spline1}} \cdot \mathbf{M}_{\text{geom1}} \tag{8-74}$$

where $\mathbf{M}_{\text{spline1}}$ is the matrix characterizing the spline representation and $\mathbf{M}_{\text{geom1}}$ is the column matrix of geometric constraints (for example, control-point coordinates). To transform to a second representation with spline matrix $\mathbf{M}_{\text{spline2}}$, we must determine the geometric constraint matrix $\mathbf{M}_{\text{geom2}}$ that produces the same vector point function for the object. That is,

$$\mathbf{P}(u) = \mathbf{U} \cdot \mathbf{M}_{\text{spline2}} \cdot \mathbf{M}_{\text{geom2}} \tag{8-75}$$

or

$$\mathbf{U} \cdot \mathbf{M}_{\text{spline2}} \cdot \mathbf{M}_{\text{geom2}} = \mathbf{U} \cdot \mathbf{M}_{\text{spline1}} \cdot \mathbf{M}_{\text{geom1}} \tag{8-76}$$

Solving for $\mathbf{M}_{\text{geom2}}$, we have

$$\begin{aligned}\mathbf{M}_{\text{geom2}} &= \mathbf{M}^{-1}_{\text{spline2}} \cdot \mathbf{M}_{\text{spline1}} \cdot \mathbf{M}_{\text{geom1}} \\ &= \mathbf{M}_{s1,s2} \cdot \mathbf{M}_{\text{geom1}}\end{aligned} \tag{8-77}$$

Thus, the required transformation matrix that converts from the first spline representation to the second is

$$\mathbf{M}_{s1,s2} = \mathbf{M}^{-1}_{\text{spline2}} \cdot \mathbf{M}_{\text{spline1}} \tag{8-78}$$

A nonuniform B-spline cannot be characterized with a general spline matrix. But we can rearrange the knot sequence to change the nonuniform B-spline to a Bézier representation. Then the Bézier matrix could be converted to any other form.

The following example calculates the transformation matrix for conversion from a periodic, cubic B-spline representation to a cubic Bézier spline representation.

$$\mathbf{M}_{B,\mathrm{Bez}} = \begin{bmatrix} -1 & 3 & -3 & 1 \\ 3 & -6 & 3 & 0 \\ -3 & 3 & 0 & 0 \\ 1 & 0 & 0 & 0 \end{bmatrix}^{-1} \cdot \frac{1}{6} \begin{bmatrix} -1 & 3 & -3 & 1 \\ 3 & -6 & 3 & 0 \\ -3 & 0 & 3 & 0 \\ 1 & 4 & 1 & 0 \end{bmatrix}$$

$$= \begin{bmatrix} 1 & 4 & 1 & 0 \\ 0 & 4 & 2 & 0 \\ 0 & 2 & 4 & 0 \\ 0 & 1 & 4 & 1 \end{bmatrix} \tag{8-79}$$

And the the transformation matrix for converting from a cubic Bézier representation to a periodic, cubic B-spline representation is

$$\mathbf{M}_{\mathrm{Bez},B} = \begin{bmatrix} -\frac{1}{6} & \frac{1}{2} & -\frac{1}{2} & \frac{1}{6} \\ \frac{1}{2} & -1 & \frac{1}{2} & 0 \\ -\frac{1}{2} & 0 & \frac{1}{2} & 0 \\ \frac{1}{6} & \frac{2}{3} & \frac{1}{6} & 0 \end{bmatrix}^{-1} \cdot \begin{bmatrix} -1 & 3 & -3 & 1 \\ 3 & -6 & 3 & 0 \\ -3 & 3 & 0 & 0 \\ 1 & 0 & 0 & 0 \end{bmatrix}$$

$$= \begin{bmatrix} 6 & -7 & 2 & 0 \\ 0 & 2 & -1 & 0 \\ 0 & -1 & 2 & 0 \\ 0 & 2 & -7 & 6 \end{bmatrix} \tag{8-80}$$

8-17 DISPLAYING SPLINE CURVES AND SURFACES

To display a spline curve or surface, we must determine coordinate positions on the curve or surface that project to pixel positions on the display device. This means that we must evaluate the parametric polynomial spline functions in certain increments over the range of the functions, and several methods have been developed for accomplishing this evaluation efficiently.

Horner's Rule

The simplest method for evaluating a polynomial, other than direct calculation of each term in succession, is *Horner's rule,* which performs the calculations by successive factoring. This requires one multiplication and one addition at each step. For a polynomial of degree n, there are n steps.

As an example, suppose that we have a cubic-spline representation where the x coordinate is expressed as

$$x(u) = a_x u^3 + b_x u^2 + c_x u + d_x \tag{8-81}$$

with similar expressions for the y and z coordinates. For a particular value of parameter u, we evaluate this polynomial in the following factored order.

$$x(u) = [(a_x u + b_x)u + c_x]u + d_x \tag{8-82}$$

The calculation of each x value requires three multiplications and three additions, so that the determination of each coordinate position (x, y, z) along a cubic-spline curve requires nine multiplications and nine additions.

Additional factoring manipulations could be applied to reduce the number of computations required by Horner's method, especially for higher-order polynomials (degree greater than 3). But repeated determination of coordinate positions over the range of a spline function can be computed much faster using forward-difference calculations or spline-subdivision methods.

Forward-Difference Calculations

A fast method for evaluating polynomial functions is to generate successive values recursively by incrementing previously calculated values as, for example,

$$x_{k+1} = x_k + \Delta x_k \tag{8-83}$$

Thus, once we know the increment and the value of x_k at any step, we get the next value simply by adding the increment to x_k. The increment Δx_k at each step is called the *forward difference*. For the parametric curve representation, we obtain the forward differences from the intervals we select for parameter u. If we divide the total range of u into subintervals of fixed size δ, then two successive x positions occur at $x_k = x(u_k)$ and $x_{k+1} = x(u_{k+1})$, where

$$u_{k+1} = u_k + \delta, \qquad k = 0, 1, 2, \ldots \tag{8-84}$$

and $u_0 = 0$.

As an illustration of this method, we first consider the polynomial representation $x(u) = a_x u + b_x$ for the x-coordinate position along a linear-spline curve. Two successive x-coordinate positions are represented as

$$\begin{aligned} x_k &= a_x u_k + b_x \\ x_{k+1} &= a_x(u_k + \delta) + b_x \end{aligned} \tag{8-85}$$

Subtracting the two equations, we obtain the forward difference:

$$\Delta x_k = x_{k+1} - x_k = a_x \delta \tag{8-86}$$

In this case, the forward difference is a constant. With higher-order polynomials, the forward difference is itself a polynomial function of parameter u. This forward-difference polynomial has degree one less than the original polynomial.

For the cubic-spline representation in Eq. 8-81, two successive x-coordinate positions have the polynomial representations

$$\begin{aligned} x_k &= a_x u_k^3 + b_x u_k^2 + c_x u_k + d_x \\ x_{k+1} &= a_x(u_k + \delta)^3 + b_x(u_k + \delta)^2 + c_x(u_k + \delta) + d_x \end{aligned} \tag{8-87}$$

The forward difference now evaluates to

$$\Delta x_k = 3a_x\delta\, u_k^2 + (3a_x \delta^2 + 2b_x \delta)u_k + (a_x \delta^3 + b_x \delta^2 + c_x \delta) \tag{8-88}$$

which is a quadratic function of parameter u_k. Since Δx_k is a polynomial function of u, we can use the same incremental procedure to obtain successive values of Δx_k. That is,

$$\Delta x_{k+1} = \Delta x_k + \Delta_2 x_k \tag{8-89}$$

where the second forward difference is the linear function

$$\Delta_2 x_k = 6a_x\delta^2 u_k + 6a_x\delta^3 + 2b_x\delta^2 \tag{8-90}$$

Repeating this process once more, we can write

$$\Delta_2 x_{k+1} = \Delta_2 x_k + \Delta_3 x_k \tag{8-91}$$

with the third forward difference as the constant expression

$$\Delta_3 x_k = 6a_x\delta^3 \tag{8-92}$$

Equations 8-83, 8-89, 8-91, and 8-92 provide an incremental forward-difference calculation of points along the cubic curve. Starting at $u_0 = 0$ with a constant step size δ, the initial values for the x coordinate and its first two forward differences are

$$\begin{aligned} x_0 &= d_x \\ \Delta x_0 &= a_x\delta^3 + b_x\delta^2 + c_x\delta \\ \Delta_2 x_0 &= 6a_x\delta^3 + 2b_x\delta^2 \end{aligned} \tag{8-93}$$

Once these initial values have been computed, the calculation for each successive x-coordinate position requires only three additions.

We can apply forward-difference methods to determine positions along spline curves of any degree n. Each successive coordinate position (x, y, z) is evaluated with a series of $3n$ additions. For surfaces, the incremental calculations are applied to both parameter u and parameter v.

Subdivision Methods

Recursive spline-subdivision procedures are used to repeatedly divide a given curve section in half, increasing the number of control points at each step. Subdivision methods are useful for displaying approximation spline curves since we can continue the subdivision process until the control graph approximates the curve path. Control-point coordinates can then be plotted as curve positions. Another application of subdivision is to generate more control points for shaping a curve. Thus, we could design a general curve shape with a few control points, then apply a subdivision procedure to obtain additional control points. With the added control points, we can then make fine adjustments to small sections of the curve.

Spline subdivision is most easily applied to a Bézier curve section because the curve begins at the first control point and ends at the last control point, the range of parameter u is always between 0 and 1, and it is easy to determine when the control points are "near enough" to the curve path. Bézier subdivision can be applied to other spline representations with the following sequence of operations.

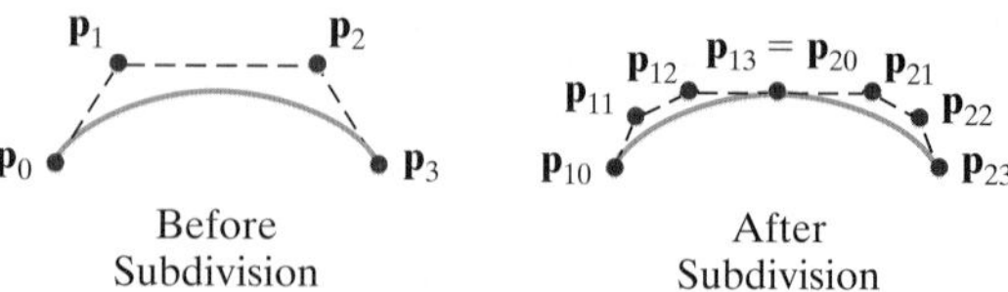

FIGURE 8-52 Subdividing a cubic Bézier curve section into two segments, each with four control points.

(1) Convert the current spline representation to a Bézier representation.

(2) Apply the Bézier subdivision algorithm.

(3) Convert the Bézier representation back to the original spline representation.

Figure 8-52 shows the first step in a recursive subdivision of a cubic Bézier curve section. Positions along the Bézier curve are described with the parametric point function $\mathbf{P}(u)$ for $0 \leq u \leq 1$. At the first subdivision step, we use the halfway point $\mathbf{P}(0.5)$ to divide the original curve into two segments. The first segment is then described with the point function $\mathbf{P}_1(s)$, and the second segment is described with $\mathbf{P}_2(t)$, where

$$
\begin{aligned}
s &= 2u, && \text{for } 0.0 \leq u \leq 0.5 \\
t &= 2u - 1, && \text{for } 0.5 \leq u \leq 1.0
\end{aligned}
\tag{8-94}
$$

Each of the two curve segments has the same number of control points as the original curve. Also, the boundary conditions (position and parametric slope) at the ends of each of the two curve segments must match the position and slope values for the original curve function $\mathbf{P}(u)$. This gives us four conditions for each curve segment that we can use to determine the control-point positions. For the first segment, the four control points are

$$
\begin{aligned}
\mathbf{p}_{1,0} &= \mathbf{p}_0 \\
\mathbf{p}_{1,1} &= \frac{1}{2}(\mathbf{p}_0 + \mathbf{p}_1) \\
\mathbf{p}_{1,2} &= \frac{1}{4}(\mathbf{p}_0 + 2\mathbf{p}_1 + \mathbf{p}_2) \\
\mathbf{p}_{1,3} &= \frac{1}{8}(\mathbf{p}_0 + 3\mathbf{p}_1 + 3\mathbf{p}_2 + \mathbf{p}_3)
\end{aligned}
\tag{8-95}
$$

And for the second segment, we obtain the four control points

$$
\begin{aligned}
\mathbf{p}_{2,0} &= \frac{1}{8}(\mathbf{p}_0 + 3\mathbf{p}_1 + 3\mathbf{p}_2 + \mathbf{p}_3) \\
\mathbf{p}_{2,1} &= \frac{1}{4}(\mathbf{p}_1 + 2\mathbf{p}_2 + \mathbf{p}_3) \\
\mathbf{p}_{2,2} &= \frac{1}{2}(\mathbf{p}_2 + \mathbf{p}_3) \\
\mathbf{p}_{2,3} &= \mathbf{p}_3
\end{aligned}
\tag{8-96}
$$

An efficient order for computing the new set of control points can be set up using only add and shift (division by 2) operations as

$$
\begin{aligned}
\mathbf{p}_{1,0} &= \mathbf{p}_0 \\
\mathbf{p}_{1,1} &= \frac{1}{2}(\mathbf{p}_0 + \mathbf{p}_1) \\
\mathbf{T} &= \frac{1}{2}(\mathbf{p}_1 + \mathbf{p}_2) \\
\mathbf{p}_{1,2} &= \frac{1}{2}(\mathbf{p}_{1,1} + \mathbf{T}) \\
\mathbf{p}_{2,3} &= \mathbf{p}_3 \\
\mathbf{p}_{2,2} &= \frac{1}{2}(\mathbf{p}_2 + \mathbf{p}_3) \\
\mathbf{p}_{2,1} &= \frac{1}{2}(\mathbf{T} + \mathbf{p}_{2,2}) \\
\mathbf{p}_{2,0} &= \frac{1}{2}(\mathbf{p}_{1,2} + \mathbf{p}_{2,1}) \\
\mathbf{p}_{1,3} &= \mathbf{p}_{2,0}
\end{aligned}
\tag{8-97}
$$

The preceding steps can be repeated any number of times, depending on whether we are subdividing the curve to gain more control points or trying to locate approximate curve positions. When we are subdividing to obtain a set of display points, we can terminate the subdivision procedure when the curve segments are small enough. One way to determine this is to check the distance from the first control point to the last control point for each segment. If this distance is "sufficiently" small, we can stop subdividing. Another test is to check the distances between adjacent pairs of control points. Or we could stop subdividing when the set of control points for each segment is nearly along a straight-line path.

Subdivision methods can be applied to Bézier curves of any degree. For a Bézier polynomial of degree $n - 1$, the $2n$ control points for each of the initial two curve segments are

$$
\begin{aligned}
\mathbf{p}_{1,k} &= \frac{1}{2^k} \sum_{j=0}^{k} C(k, j)\mathbf{p}_j, \qquad k = 0, 1, 2, \ldots, n \\
\mathbf{p}_{2,k} &= \frac{1}{2^{n-k}} \sum_{j=k}^{n} C(n-k, n-j)\mathbf{p}_j
\end{aligned}
\tag{8-98}
$$

where $C(k, j)$ and $C(n-k, n-j)$ are the binomial coefficients.

Subdivision methods can be applied directly to nonuniform B-splines by adding values to the knot vector. But, in general, these methods are not as efficient as Bézier subdivision.

8-18 OpenGL APPROXIMATION-SPLINE FUNCTIONS

Both Bézier splines and B-splines can be displayed using OpenGL functions, as well as trimming curves for spline surfaces. The core library contains the Bézier functions, and the OpenGL Utility (GLU) has the B-spline and trimming-curve functions. Bézier functions are often hardware implemented, and the GLU functions provide a B-spline interface that accesses OpenGL point-plotting and line-drawing routines.

OpenGL Bézier-Spline Curve Functions

We specify parameters and activate the routines for Bézier-curve display with the OpenGL functions

```
glMap1* (GL_MAP1_VERTEX_3, uMin, uMax, stride, nPts, *ctrlPts);
glEnable (GL_MAP1_VERTEX_3);
```

And we deactivate the routines with

```
glDisable (GL_MAP1_VERTEX_3);
```

A suffix code of `f` or `d` is used with `glMap1` to indicate either floating point or double precision for the data values. Minimum and maximum values for the curve parameter u are specified in `uMin` and `uMax`, although these values for a Bézier curve are typically set to 0 and 1.0, respectively. The three-dimensional, floating-point, Cartesian-coordinate values for the Bézier control points are listed in array `ctrlPts`, and the number of elements in this array is given as a positive integer using parameter `nPts`. Parameter `stride` is assigned an integer offset that indicates the number of data values between the beginning of one coordinate position in array `ctrlPts` and the beginning of the next coordinate position. For a list of three-dimensional control-point positions, we set `stride` = 3. A higher value for `stride` would be used if we specified the control points using four-dimensional homogeneous coordinates or intertwined the coordinate values with other data, such as color values. To express control-point positions in four-dimensional homogeneous coordinates (x, y, z, h), we need only change the value of `stride` and change the symbolic constant in `glMap1` and in `glEnable` to `GL_MAP1_VERTEX_4`.

After we have set up the Bézier parameters and activated the curve-generation routines, we need to evaluate positions along the spline path and display the resulting curve. A coordinate position along the curve path is calculated with

```
glEvalCoord1* (uValue);
```

where parameter `uValue` is assigned some value in the interval from `uMin` to `uMax`. The suffix code for this function can be either `f` or `d`, and we can also use the suffix code `v` to indicate that the value for the argument is given in an array. Function `glEvalCoord1` calculates a coordinate position using Eq. 8-37 with the parameter value

$$u = \frac{u_{\text{value}} - u_{\text{min}}}{u_{\text{max}} - u_{\text{min}}} \tag{8-99}$$

which maps the `uValue` to the interval from 0 to 1.0.

When `glEvalCoord1` processes a value for the curve parameter u, it generates a `glVertex3` function. To obtain a Bézier curve, we thus repeatedly invoke the `glEvalCoord1` function to produce a set of points along the curve path, using selected values in the range from `uMin` to `uMax`. Joining these points with straight-line segments, we can approximate the spline curve as a polyline.

As an example of the OpenGL Bézier-curve routines, the following code uses the four control-point positions from the program in Section 8-10 to generate a two-dimensional cubic Bézier curve. In this example, 50 points are plotted along the curve path, and the curve points are connected with straight-line segments.

FIGURE 8-53 A set of four control points and the associated Bézier curve, displayed with OpenGL routines as an approximating polyline.

The curve path is then displayed as a blue polyline, and the control points are plotted as red points of size 5 (Fig. 8-53).

```
GLfloat ctrlPts [4][3] = { {-40.0, 40.0, 0.0}, {-10.0, 200.0, 0.0},
                           {10.0, -200.0, 0.0}, {40.0, 40.0, 0.0} };

glMap1f (GL_MAP1_VERTEX_3, 0.0, 1.0, 3, 4, *ctrlPts);
glEnable (GL_MAP1_VERTEX_3);

GLint k;

glColor3f (0.0, 0.0, 1.0);            //  Set line color to blue.
glBegin (GL_LINE_STRIP);              //  Generate Bezier "curve".
    for (k = 0; k <= 50; k++)
        glEvalCoord1f (GLfloat (k) / 50.0);
glEnd ( );


glColor (1.0, 0.0, 0.0);              //  Set point color to red.
glPointSize (5.0);                    //  Set point size to 5.0.
glBegin (GL_POINTS);                  //  Plot control points.
    for (k = 0; k < 4; k++);
            glVertex3fv (&ctrlPts [k][0]);
glEnd ( );
```

Although the previous example generated a spline curve with evenly spaced parameter values, we can use the glEvalCoord1f function to obtain any spacing for parameter u. Usually, however, a spline curve is generated with evenly spaced parameter values, and OpenGL provides the following functions that we can use to produce a set of uniformly spaced parameter values.

```
glMapGrid1* (n, u1, u2);
glEvalMesh1 (mode, n1, n2);
```

The suffix code for glMapGrid1 can be either f or d. Parameter n specifies the integer number of equal subdivisions over the range from u1 to u2, and parameters n1 and n2 specify an integer range corresponding to u1 and u2. Parameter mode is assigned either GL_POINT or GL_LINE, depending on whether we want to display the curve using discrete points (a dotted curve) or using straight-line segments. For a curve that is to be displayed as a polyline, the output of these two functions is the same as the output from the following code, except that the argument of glEvalCoord1 is set either to u1 or to u2 if $k = 0$ or $k = n$, respectively, to avoid round-off error. In other words, with mode = GL_LINE, the preceding OpenGL commands are equivalent to

```
glBegin (GL_LINE_STRIP);
    for (k = n1; k <= n2; k++)
        glEvalCoord1f (u1 + k * (u2 - u1) / n);
glEnd ( );
```

Thus, in the previous programming example, we could replace the block of code containing the loop for generating the Bézier curve with the following statements.

```
glColor3f (0.0, 0.0, 1.0);
glMapGrid1f (50, 0.0, 1.0);
glEvalMesh1 (GL_LINE, 0, 50);
```

Using the glMapGrid1 and glEvalMesh1 functions, we can divide a curve into a number of segments and select the parameter spacing for each segment according to its curvature. Therefore, a segment with more oscillations could be assigned more intervals, and a flatter section of the curve could be assigned fewer intervals.

Instead of displaying Bézier curves, we can use the glMap1 function to designate values for other kinds of data, and seven other OpenGL symbolic constants are available for this purpose. With the symbolic constant GL_MAP1_COLOR_4, we use the array ctrlPts to specify a list of four-element (red, green, blue, alpha) colors. Then a linearly interpolated set of colors can be generated for use in an application, and these generated color values do not change the current setting for the color state. Similarly, we can designate a list of values from a color-index table with GL_MAP1_INDEX. And a list of three-dimensional, surface-normal vectors is specified in array ctrlPts when we use the symbolic constant GL_MAP1_NORMAL. The remaining four symbolic constants are used with lists of surface-texture information.

Multiple glMap1 functions can be activated simultaneously, and calls to glEvalCoord1 or to glMapGrid1 and glEvalMesh1 then produce data points for each data type that is enabled. This allows us to generate combinations of coordinate positions, color values, surface-normal vectors, and surface-texture data. But we cannot simultaneously activate GL_MAP1_VERTEX_3 and GL_MAP1_VERTEX_4, and we can only activate one of the surface-texture generators at any one time.

OpenGL Bézier-Spline Surface Functions

Activation and parameter specification for the OpenGL Bézier-surface routines are accomplished with

```
glMap2* (GL_MAP2_VERTEX_3, uMin, uMax, uStride, nuPts,
                 vMin, vMax, vStride, nvPts, *ctrlPts);
glEnable (GL_MAP2_VERTEX_3);
```

A suffix code of `f` or `d` is used with `glMap2` to indicate either floating point or double precision for the data values. For a surface, we specify minimum and maximum values for both parameter u and parameter v. The three-dimensional Cartesian coordinates for the Bézier control points are listed in the double-subscripted array `ctrlPts`, and the integer size of the array is given with parameters `nuPts` and `nvPts`. If control points are to be specified using four-dimensional homogeneous coordinates, we use the symbolic constant GL_MAP2_VERTEX_4 instead of GL_MAP2_VERTEX_3. The integer offset between the beginning of coordinate values for control point $\mathbf{p}_{j,k}$ and the beginning of coordinate values for $\mathbf{p}_{j+1,k}$ is given in `uStride`. And the integer offset between the beginning of coordinate values for control point $\mathbf{p}_{j,k}$ and the beginning of coordinate values for $\mathbf{p}_{j,k+1}$ is given in `vStride`. This allows the coordinate data to be intertwined with other data, so that we need to specify only the offsets to locate coordinate values. We deactivate the Bézier-surface routines with

```
glDisable {GL_MAP2_VERTEX_3}
```

Coordinate positions on the Bézier surface can be calculated with

```
glEvalCoord2* (uValue, vValue);
```

or with

```
glEvalCoord2*v (uvArray);
```

Parameter `uValue` is assigned some value in the interval from `uMin` to `uMax`, and parameter `vValue` is assigned some value in the interval from `vMin` to `vMax`. With the vector version, `uvArray` = (`uValue`, `vValue`). The suffix code for either function can be `f` or `d`. Function `glEvalCoord2` calculates a coordinate position using Eq. 8-51 with the parameter values

$$u = \frac{u\text{Value} - u\text{Min}}{u\text{Max} - u\text{Min}}, \qquad v = \frac{v\text{Value} - v\text{Min}}{v\text{Max} - v\text{Min}} \tag{8-100}$$

which maps each of `uValue` and `vValue` to the interval from 0 to 1.0.

To display a Bézier surface, we repeatedly invoke `glEvalCoord2`, which generates a series of `glVertex3` functions. This is similar to generating a spline curve, except that we now have two parameters, u and v. For example, a surface defined with 16 control points, arranged in a 4 by 4 grid, can be displayed as a set of surface lines with the following code. The offset for the coordinate values in the u direction is 3, and the offset in the v direction is 12. Each coordinate position is specified with three values, and the y coordinate for each group of four positions is constant.

```
GLfloat ctrlPts [4][4][3] = {
   { {-1.5, -1.5,  4.0}, {-0.5, -1.5,  2.0},
     {-0.5, -1.5, -1.0}, { 1.5, -1.5,  2.0} },
   { {-1.5, -0.5,  1.0}, {-0.5, -0.5,  3.0},
     { 0.5, -0.5,  0.0}, { 1.5, -0.5, -1.0} },
   { {-1.5,  0.5,  4.0}, {-0.5,  0.5,  0.0},
     { 0.5,  0.5,  3.0}, { 1.5,  0.5,  4.0} },
   { {-1.5,  1.5, -2.0}, {-0.5,  1.5, -2.0},
     { 0.5,  1.5,  0.0}, { 1.5,  1.5, -1.0} }
};

glMap2f (GL_MAP2_VERTEX_3, 0.0, 1.0, 3, 4,
                 0.0, 1.0, 12, 4, &ctrlPts[0][0][0]);
glEnable (GL_MAP2_VERTEX_3);

GLint k, j;

glColor3f (0.0, 0.0, 1.0);
for (k = 0; k <= 8; k++)
{
   glBegin (GL_LINE_STRIP);  // Generate Bezier surface lines.
    for (j = 0; j <= 40; j++)
       glEvalCoord2f (GLfloat (j) / 40.0, GLfloat (k) / 8.0);
    glEnd ( );
    glBegin (GL_LINE_STRIP);
    for (j = 0; j <= 40; j++)
       glEvalCoord2f (GLfloat (k) / 8.0, GLfloat (j) / 40.0);
    glEnd ( );
}
```

Instead of using the `glEvalCoord2` function, we can generate evenly spaced parameter values over the surface with

```
glMapGrid2* (nu, u1, u2, nv, v1, v2);
glEvalMesh2 (mode, nu1, nu2, nv1, nv2);
```

The suffix code for `glMapGrid2` is again either `f` or `d`, and parameter `mode` can be assigned the value `GL_POINT`, `GL_LINE`, or `GL_FILL`. A two-dimensional grid of points is produced, with `nu` equally spaced intervals between `u1` and `u2`, and with `nv` equally spaced intervals between `v1` and `v2`. The corresponding integer range for parameter `u` is `nu1` to `nu2`, and the corresponding integer range for parameter `v` is `nv1` to `nv2`.

For a surface that is to be displayed as a grid of polylines, the output of `glMapGrid2` and `glEvalMesh2` is the same as the following program sequence, except for the conditions that avoid round-off error at the beginning and ending values of the loop variables. At the beginning of the loops, the argument of glEvalCoord1 is set to (u1, v1). And at the end of the loops, the argument of glEvalCoord1 is set to (u2, v2).

```
for (k = nu1; k <= nu2; k++) {
    glBegin (GL_LINES);
        for (j = nv1; j <= nv2; j++)
            glEvalCoord2f (u1 + k * (u2 - u1) / nu,
                           v1 + j * (v2 - v1) / nv);
    glEnd ( );
}
for (j = nv1; j <= nv2; j++) {
    glBegin (GL_LINES);
        for (k = nu1; k <= nu2; k++)
            glEvalCoord2f (u1 + k * (u2 - u1) / nu,
                           v1 + j * (v2 - v1) / nv);
    glEnd ( );
}
```

Similarly, for a surface displayed as a set of filled-polygon facets (mode = GL_FILL), the output of glMapGrid2 and glEvalMesh2 is the same as the following program sequence, except for the round-off avoiding conditions for the beginning and ending values of the loop variables.

```
for (k = nu1; k < nu2; k++) {
    glBegin (GL_QUAD_STRIP);
        for (j = nv1; j <= nv2; j ++) {
            glEvalCoord2f (u1 + k * (u2 - u1) / nu,
                           v1 + j * (v2 - v1) / nv);
            glEvalCoord2f (u1 + (k + 1) * (u2 - u1) / nu,
                           v1 + j * (v2 - v1) / nv);
```

We can use the glMap2 function to designate values for other kinds of data, just as we did with glMap1. Similar symbolic constants, such as GL_MAP2_COLOR_4 and GL_MAP2_NORMAL, are available for this purpose. And we can activate multiple glMap2 functions to generate various data combinations.

GLU B-Spline Curve Functions

Although the GLU B-spline routines are referred to as "nurbs" functions, they can be used to generate B-splines that are neither nonuniform nor rational. Thus, we can use these GLU routines to display a polynomial B-spline that has uniform knot spacing. And the GLU routines can also be used to produce Bézier splines, rational or nonrational. To generate a B-spline (or Bézier spline), we need to define a name for the spline, activate the GLU B-spline renderer, and then define the spline parameters.

The following statements illustrate the basic sequence of calls for displaying a B-spline curve.

```
GLUnurbsObj *curveName;

curveName = gluNewNurbsRenderer ( );
gluBeginCurve (curveName);
    gluNurbsCurve (curveName, nknots, *knotVector, stride, *ctrlPts,
                   degParam, GL_MAP1_VERTEX_3);
gluEndCurve (curveName);
```

In the first statement, we assign a name to the curve, then we invoke the GLU B-spline rendering routines for that curve using the `gluNewNurbsRenderer` command. A value of 0 is assigned to `curveName` when there is not enough memory available to create a B-spline curve. Inside a `gluBeginCurve/gluEndCurve` pair, we next state the attributes for the curve using a `gluNurbsCurve` function. This allows us to set up multiple curve sections, and each section is referenced with a distinct curve name. Parameter `knotVector` designates the set of floating-point knot values, and integer parameter `nknots` specifies the number of elements in the knot vector. The degree of the polynomial is `degParam` − 1. We list the values for the three-dimensional, control-point coordinates in array parameter `ctrlPts`, which contains `nknots` − `degParam` elements. And the integer offset between the start of successive coordinate positions in array `ctrlPts` is specified by integer parameter `stride`. If the control-point positions are contiguous (not interspersed between other data types), the value of `stride` is set to 3. We eliminate a defined B-spline with

```
gluDeleteNurbsRenderer (curveName);
```

As an example of the use of GLU routines to display a spline curve, the following code generates a cubic, Bézier polynomial. To obtain this cubic curve, we set the degree parameter to the value 4. We use four control points, and we select an eight-element, open-uniform knot sequence with four repeated values at each end.

```
GLfloat knotVector [8] = {0.0, 0.0, 0.0, 0.0, 1.0, 1.0, 1.0, 1.0};
GLfloat ctrlPts [4][3] = { {-4.0, 0.0, 0.0}, {-2.0, 8.0, 0.0},
                           {2.0, -8.0, 0.0}, {4.0, 0.0, 0.0} };
GLUnurbsObj *cubicBezCurve;

cubicBezCurve = gluNewNurbsRenderer ( );
gluBeginCurve (cubicBezCurve);
    gluNurbsCurve (cubicBezCurve, 8, knotVector, 3, &ctrlPts [0][0],
                   4, GL_MAP1_VERTEX_3);
gluEndCurve(cubicBezCurve);
```

To create a rational B-spline curve, we replace the symbolic constant `GL_MAP1_VERTEX_3` with `GL_MAP1_VERTEX_4`. Four-dimensional, homogeneous coordinates (x_h, y_h, z_h, h) are then used to specify the control points, and the resulting homogeneous division produces the desired rational polynomial form.

We can also use the gluNurbsCurve function to specify lists of color values, normal vectors, or surface-texture properties, just as we did with the glMap1 and glMap2 functions. Any of the symbolic constants, such as GL_MAP1_COLOR_4 or GL_MAP1_NORMAL, can be used as the last argument in the gluNurbsCurve function. Each call is then listed inside the gluBeginCurve/gluEndCurve pair, with two restrictions: We cannot list more than one function for each data type, and we must include exactly one function to generate the B-spline curve.

A B-spline curve is automatically divided into a number of sections and displayed as a polyline by the GLU routines. But a variety of B-spline rendering options can also be selected with repeated calls to the following GLU function.

```
gluNurbsProperty (splineName, property, value);
```

Parameter splineName is assigned the name of a B-spline, parameter property is assigned a GLU symbolic constant that identifies the rendering property that we want to set, and parameter value is assigned either a floating-point numerical value or a GLU symbolic constant that sets the value for the selected property. Several gluNurbsProperty functions can be specified following the gluNewNurbsRenderer statement. Many of the properties that can be set using the gluNurbsProperty function are surface parameters, as described in the next section.

GLU B-Spline Surface Functions

The following statements illustrate a basic sequence of calls for generating a B-spline surface.

```
GLUnurbsObj *surfName

surfName = gluNewNurbsRenderer ( );
gluNurbsProperty (surfName, property1, value1);
gluNurbsProperty (surfName, property2, value2);
gluNurbsProperty (surfName, property3, value3);
     .
     .
     .
gluBeginSurface (surfName);
    gluNurbsSurface (surfName, nuKnots, uKnotVector, nvKnots,
                     vKnotVector, uStride, vStride, &ctrlPts [0][0][0],
                      uDegParam, vDegParam, GL_MAP2_VERTEX_3);
gluEndSurface (surfName);
```

In general, the GLU statements and parameters for defining a B-spline surface are similar to those for a B-spline curve. After invoking the B-spline rendering routines with gluNewNurbsRenderer, we could specify a number of optional surface-property values. Attributes for the surface are then set with a gluNurbsSurface call. Multiple surfaces, each with a distinct identifying name, can be defined in this way. A value of 0 is returned to variable surfName by the system when there is not enough memory available to store a B-spline object. Parameters uKnotVector and vKnotVector designate the arrays of floating-point knot values in the parametric u and v directions. We specify the number of elements in each knot vector with parameters nuKnots and nvKnots. The degree of the polynomial in parameter u is given by the value of uDegParam − 1, and the degree of the polynomial in parameter v is the value of vDegParam − 1. We list the floating-point values for the three-dimensional, control-point coordinates in array parameter ctrlPts, which contains (nuKnots − uDegParam) × (nvKnots − vDegParam) elements. The integer offset between the start of successive control points in the parametric u direction is specified with integer parameter uStride, and the offset in the parametric v direction is specified with integer parameter vStride. We erase a spline surface to free its allocated memory with the same function (gluDeleteNurbsRenderer) we used for a B-spline curve.

A B-spline surface, by default, is automatically displayed as a set of polygon fill areas by the GLU routines, but we can choose other display options and parameters. Nine properties, with two or more possible values for each property, can be set for a B-spline surface. As an example of property setting, the following statements specify a wire-frame, triangularly tessellated display for a surface.

```
gluNurbsProperty (surfName, GLU_NURBS_MODE,
                  GLU_NURBS_TESSELLATOR);
gluNurbsProperty (surfName, GLU_DISPLAY_MODE,
                  GLU_OUTLINE_POLYGON};
```

The GLU tessellating routines divide the surface into a set of triangles and display each triangle as a polygon outline. In addition, these triangle primitives can be retrieved using the gluNurbsCallback function. Other values for property GLU_DISPLAY_MODE are GLU_OUTLINE_PATCH and GLU_FILL (the default value). With the value GLU_OUTLINE_PATCH, we also obtain a wire-frame display, but the surface is not divided into triangular sections. Instead, the original surface is outlined, along with any trimming curves that have been specified. The only other value that can be set for the property GLU_NURBS_MODE is GLU_NURBS_RENDERER (the default value), which renders objects without making tessellated data available for call back.

We set the number of sampling points per unit length with the properties GLU_U_STEP and GLU_V_STEP. The default value for each is 100. To set the u or v sampling values, we also must set the property GLU_SAMPLING_METHOD to the value GLU_DOMAIN_DISTANCE. Several other values can be used with the property GLU_SAMPLING_METHOD to specify how surface tessellation is to be carried out. Properties GLU_SAMPLING_TOLERANCE and GLU_PARAMETRIC_TOLERANCE are used to set maximum sampling lengths. By setting property GLU_CULLING to the value GL_TRUE, we can improve rendering performance by not tessellating objects that are outside the viewing volume. The default value for GLU culling is GL_FALSE. And the property GLU_AUTO_LOAD_MATRIX allows the matrices for the viewing, projection, and viewport transformations to be downloaded from the OpenGL server when its value is GL_TRUE (the default value). Otherwise, if we set the value to GL_FALSE, an application must supply these matrices using the gluLoadSamplingMatrices function.

To determine the current value of a B-spline property, we use the following query function.

```
gluGetNurbsProperty (splineName, property, value);
```

For a specified `splineName` and `property`, the corresponding value is returned to parameter `value`.

When the property `GLU_AUTO_LOAD_MATRIX` is set to the value `GL_FALSE`, we invoke

```
gluLoadSamplingMatrices (splineName, modelviewMat, projMat,
                         viewport);
```

This function specifies the modelview matrix, projection matrix, and viewport that are to be used in the sampling and culling routines for a spline object. The current modelview and projection matrices can be obtained with calls to the `glGetFloatv` function, and the current viewport can be obtained with a call to `glGetIntegerv`.

Various events associated with spline objects are processed using

```
gluNurbsCallback (splineName, event, fcn);
```

Parameter `event` is assigned a GLU symbolic constant, and parameter `fcn` specifies a function that is to be invoked when the event corresponding to the GLU constant is encountered. For example, if we set parameter `event` to `GLU_NURBS_ERROR`, then `fcn` is called when an error occurs. Other events are used by the GLU spline routines to return the OpenGL polygons generated by the tessellation process. The symbolic constant `GL_NURBS_BEGIN` indicates the start of a primitive such as line segments, triangles, or quadrilaterals, and `GL_NURBS_END` indicates the end of the primitive. The function argument for the beginning of a primitive is then a symbolic constant such as `GL_LINE_STRIP`, `GL_TRIANGLES`, or `GL_QUAD_STRIP`. Symbolic constant `GL_NURBS_VERTEX` indicates that three-dimensional coordinate data are to be supplied, and a vertex function is called. Additional constants are available for indicating other data, such as color values.

Data values for the `gluNurbsCallback` function are supplied by

```
gluNurbsCallbackData (splineName, dataValues);
```

Parameter `splineName` is assigned the name of the spline object that is to be tessellated, and parameter `dataValues` is assigned a list of data values.

GLU Surface-Trimming Functions

A set of one or more two-dimensional trimming curves is specified for a B-spline surface with the following statements.

```
gluBeginTrim (surfName);
   gluPwlCurve (surfName, nPts, *curvePts, stride, GLU_MAP1_TRIM_2);
   .
   .
   .
gluEndTrim (surfName);
```

Parameter `surfName` is the name of the B-spline surface to be trimmed. A set of floating-point coordinates for the trimming curve is specified in array parameter

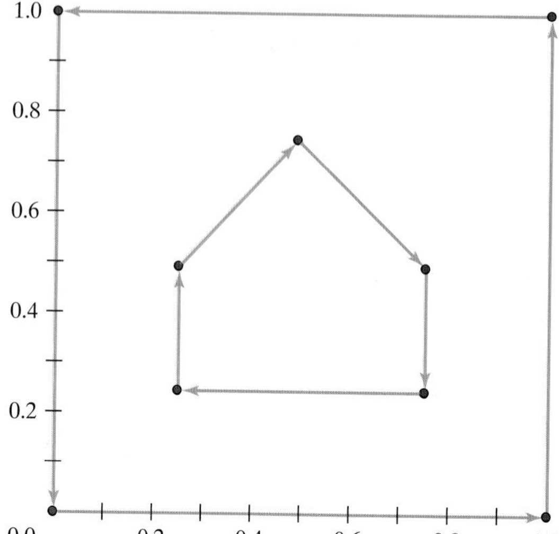

FIGURE 8-54 An outer trimming curve around the perimeter of the unit square is specified in a counterclockwise direction, and the inner trimming curve sections are defined in a clockwise direction.

curvePts, which contains nPts coordinate positions. An integer offset between successive coordinate positions is given in parameter stride. The specified curve coordinates are used to generate a piecewise linear trimming function for the B-spline surface. In other words, the generated trimming "curve" is a polyline. If the curve points are to be given in three-dimensional, homogeneous (u, v, h) parameter space, then the final argument in gluPwlCurve is set to the GLU symbolic constant GLU_MAP1_TRIM_3.

We can also use one or more gluNurbsCurve functions as a trimming curve. And we can construct trimming curves that are combinations of gluPwlCurve functions and gluNurbsCurve functions. Any specified GLU trimming "curve" must be nonintersecting, and it must be a closed curve.

The following code illustrates the GLU trimming functions for a cubic Bézier surface. We first set the coordinate points for an outermost trimming curve. These positions are specified in a counterclockwise direction completely around the unit square. Next, we set the coordinate points for an innermost trimming curve in two sections, and these positions are specified in a clockwise direction. And the knot vectors for both the surface and the first inner trim-curve section are set up to produce cubic Bézier curves. A plot of the inner and outer trimming curves on the unit square is shown in Fig. 8-54.

```
GLUnurbsObj *bezSurface;

GLfloat outerTrimPts [5][2] = { {0.0, 0.0}, {1.0, 0.0}, {1.0, 1.0),
                                {0.0, 1.0}, {0.0, 0.0} };
GLfloat innerTrimPts1 [3][2] = { {0.25, 0.5}, {0.5, 0.75},
                                {0.75, 0.5) };
GLfloat innerTrimPts2 [4][2] = { {0.75, 0.5}, {0.75, 0.25},
                                {0.25, 0.25), {0.25, 0.5} };

GLfloat surfKnots [8] = (0.0, 0.0, 0.0, 0.0, 1.0, 1.0, 1.0, 1.0);
GLfloat trimCurveKnots [8] = (0.0, 0.0, 0.0, 0.0, 1.0, 1.0, 1.0, 1.0);

bezSurface = gluNewNurbsRenderer ( );
```

```
gluBeginSurface (bezSurface);
   gluNurbsSurface (bezSurface, 8, surfKnots, 8, surfKnots, 4 * 3, 3,
                    &ctrlPts [0][0][0], 4, 4, GL_MAP2_VERTEX_3);
   gluBeginTrim (bezSurface);
      /*  Counterclockwise outer trim curve.  */
      gluPwlCurve (bezSurface, 5, &outerTrimPts [0][0], 2,
                   GLU_MAP1_TRIM_2);
   gluEndTrim (bezSurface);
   gluBeginTrim (bezSurface);
      /*  Clockwise inner trim-curve sections.  */
      gluPwlCurve (bezSurface, 3, &innerTrimPts1 [0][0], 2,
                   GLU_MAP1_TRIM_2);
      gluNurbsCurve (bezSurface, 8, trimCurveKnots, 2,
                   &innerTrimPts2 [0][0], 4, GLU_MAP1_TRIM_2):
   gluEndTrim (bezSurface);
gluEndSurface (bezSurface);
```

8-19 SWEEP REPRESENTATIONS

Solid-modeling packages often provide a number of construction techniques. **Sweep representations** are useful for constructing three-dimensional objects that possess translational, rotational, or other symmetries. We can represent such objects by specifying a two-dimensional shape and a sweep that moves the shape through a region of space. A set of two-dimensional primitives, such as circles and rectangles, can be provided for sweep representations as menu options. Other methods for obtaining two-dimensional figures include closed spline-curve constructions and cross-sectional slices of solid objects.

Figure 8-55 illustrates a translational sweep. The periodic spline curve in Fig. 8-55(a) defines the object cross section. We then perform a translational sweep for a specified distance by moving the control points $\mathbf{p}_0$ through $\mathbf{p}_3$ along a straight-line path perpendicular to the plane of the cross section. At intervals along this path, we replicate the cross-sectional shape and draw a set of connecting lines in the direction of the sweep to obtain the wire-frame representation shown in Fig. 8-55(b).

An example of object design using a rotational sweep is given in Fig. 8-56. This time, the periodic spline cross section is rotated about a specified axis in the plane of the cross section to produce the wire-frame representation shown in Fig. 8-56(b). Any axis can be chosen for a rotational sweep. If we use a rotation axis perpendicular to the plane of the spline cross section in Fig. 8-56(a), we generate

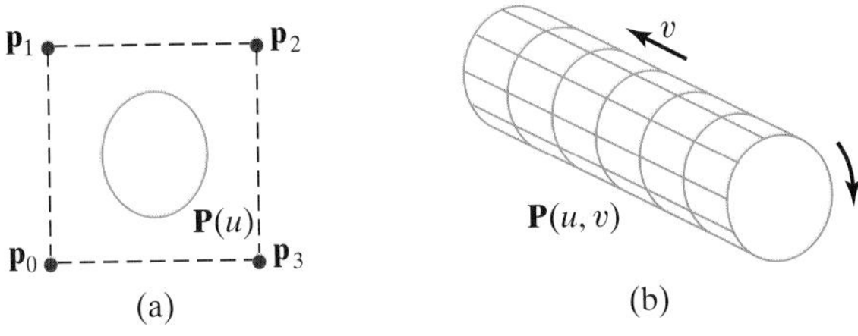

FIGURE 8-55 Constructing a solid with a translational sweep. Translating the control points of the periodic spline curve in (a) generates the solid shown in (b), whose surface can be described with the point function $\mathbf{P}(u, v)$.

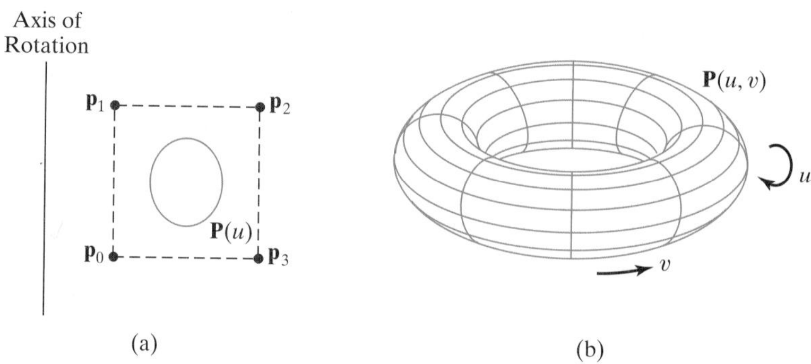

FIGURE 8-56 Constructing a solid with a rotational sweep. Rotating the control points of the periodic spline curve in (a) about the given rotation axis generates the solid shown in (b), whose surface can be described with the point function $\mathbf{P}(u, v)$.

a two-dimensional shape. But if the cross section shown in this figure has depth, then we are using one three-dimensional object to generate another.

In general, we can specify sweep constructions using any path. For rotational sweeps, we can move along a circular path through any angular distance from 0 to 360°. For noncircular paths, we can specify the curve function describing the path and the distance of travel along the path. In addition, we can vary the shape or size of the cross section along the sweep path. Or we could vary the orientation of the cross section relative to the sweep path as we move the shape through a region of space.

8-20 CONSTRUCTIVE SOLID-GEOMETRY METHODS

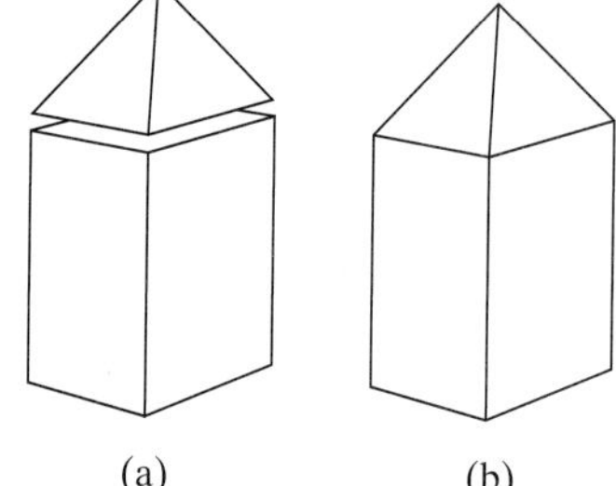

FIGURE 8-57 Combining the two objects shown in (a) using a union operation produces the new composite solid object in (b).

Another technique for solid modeling is to generate a new object from two three-dimensional objects using a set operation. This modeling method, called **constructive solid geometry** (**CSG**), creates the new object by applying the union, intersection, or difference operation to two specified solids.

Figures 8-57 and 8-58 show examples for forming new shapes using the set operations. In Fig. 8-57(a), a block and pyramid are placed adjacent to each other. With the union operation, we obtain the combined object of Fig. 8-57(b). Figure 8-58(a) shows a block and a cylinder with overlapping volumes. Using the intersection operation, we obtain the solid in Fig. 8-58(b). With a difference operation, we can display the solid shown in Fig. 8-58(c).

A CSG application starts with an initial set of three-dimensional objects, called CSG primitives, such as a block, pyramid, cylinder, cone, sphere, and perhaps some solids with spline surfaces. The primitives can be provided by the CSG package as menu selections, or the primitives themselves could be formed using sweep methods, spline constructions, or other modeling procedures. With an interactive CSG package, we can select an operation (union, intersection, or difference) and drag two primitives into position within some region of space to form a new object. This new object could then be combined with one of the existing shapes to form another new object. We can continue this process until we have the final shape for the object we are designing. An object constructed with this procedure is represented with a binary tree, as in Fig. 8-59.

Ray-casting methods are commonly used to implement constructive solid-geometry operations when objects are described with boundary representations. We apply ray casting by determining the objects that are intersected by a set of parallel lines emanating from the xy plane along the z direction. This plane is

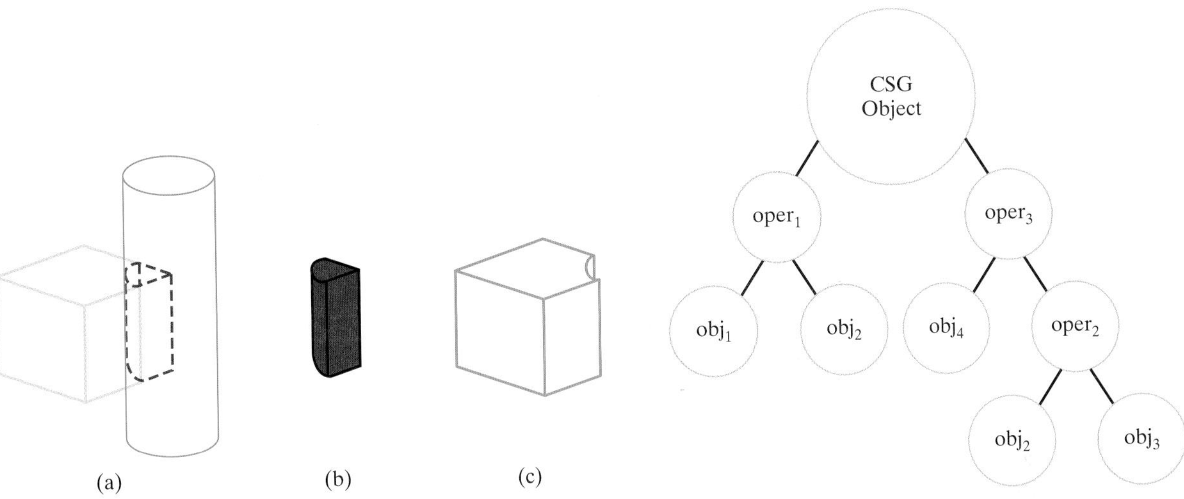

FIGURE 8-58 Two overlapping objects (a) can be combined to produce either the wedge-shaped object shown in (b), using the intersection operation, or the modified block shape shown in (c), using a difference operation.

FIGURE 8-59 An example CSG tree representation for an object.

referred to as the **firing plane,** with each ray originating from a pixel position, as illustrated in Fig. 8-60. We then calculate surface intersections along each ray path, and sort the intersection points according to the distance from the firing plane. The surface limits for the composite object are then determined by the specified set operation. An example of the ray-casting determination of surface limits for a CSG object is given in Fig. 8-61, which shows yz cross sections for two objects (a block and a sphere) and the path of a pixel ray perpendicular to the firing plane. For the union operation, the new volume is the combined interior occupied by the two objects. For the intersection operation, the new volume is the interior region common to both objects. And a difference operation subtracts the interior of one object from the other in the region where the two objects overlap.

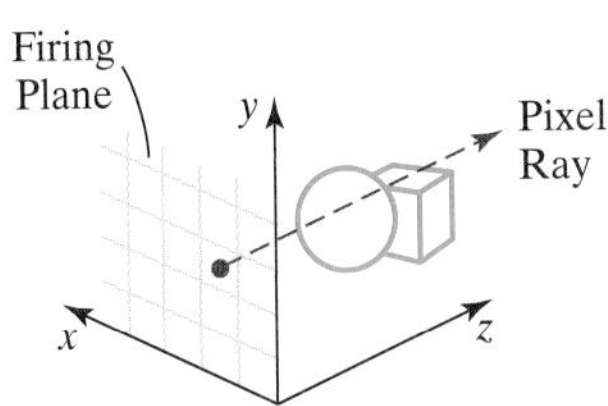

FIGURE 8-60 Implementing CSG operations using ray casting.

Each CSG primitive is typically defined in its own local (modeling) coordinates. The corresponding world-coordinate position is determined by the modeling transformation matrices used to create an overlap position with another object. The inverse of the object modeling matrices can then be used to transform the pixel rays to modeling coordinates, where the surface intersection calculations are carried out for the individual primitives. Then surface intersections for two overlapping objects are sorted according to distance along the ray path and used

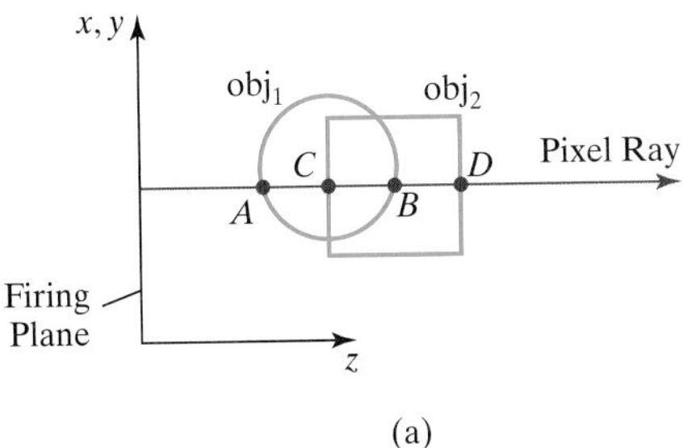

Operation	Surface Limits
Union	A, D
Intersection	C, B
Difference $(\text{obj}_2 - \text{obj}_1)$	B, D

(b)

FIGURE 8-61 Determining surface limits along a pixel ray.

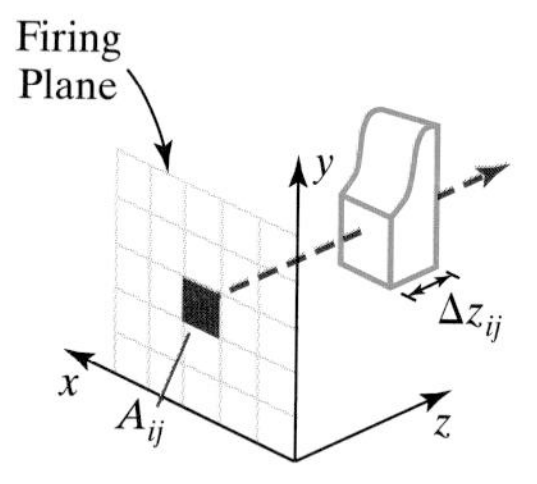

FIGURE 8-62
Determining object volume along a ray path for a pixel area A_{ij} on the firing plane.

to determine the composite object limits, according to the specified set operation. This procedure is repeated for each pair of objects that are to be combined in the CSG tree for a particular object.

Once a CSG object has been designed, ray casting is used to determine physical properties, such as volume and mass. To determine the volume of the object, we approximate the area of each pixel on the firing plane as a small square (Fig. 8-62). We can then approximate the volume V_{ij} of the object for a cross-sectional slice with area A_{ij} along the path of a ray from the pixel at position (i, j) as

$$V_{ij} \approx A_{ij} \Delta z_{ij} \tag{8-101}$$

where Δz_{ij} is the depth of the object along the ray from position (i, j). If the object has internal holes, Δz_{ij} is the sum of the distances between pairs of intersection points along the ray. We approximate the total volume of the CSG object as the sum of the individual ray-path volumes:

$$V \approx \sum_{i,j} V_{ij} \tag{8-102}$$

Given the density function, $\rho(x, y, z)$, for the object, we can approximate the mass along the ray from position (i, j) with the integration

$$m_{ij} \approx A_{ij} \int \rho(x_{ij}, y_{ij}, z)\, dz \tag{8-103}$$

where the one-dimensional integral can often be approximated without actually carrying out the integration, depending on the form of the density function. The total mass of the CSG object is then approximated as the summation

$$m \approx \sum_{i,j} m_{ij} \tag{8-104}$$

Other physical properties, such as center of mass and moment of inertia, can be obtained with similar calculations. We can improve the approximate calculations for the values of the physical properties with additional rays generated from subpixel positions on the firing plane.

If object shapes are represented with octrees, we can implement the set operations in CSG procedures by scanning the tree structure describing the contents of spatial octants. This procedure, described in the next section, searches the octants and suboctants of a unit cube to locate the regions occupied by the two objects that are to be combined.

8-21 OCTREES

Hierarchical tree structures, called **octrees,** are used to represent solid objects in some graphics systems. Medical imaging and other applications that require displays of object cross sections commonly use octree representations. The tree structure is organized so that each node corresponds to a region of three-dimensional space. This representation for solids takes advantage of spatial coherence to reduce storage requirements for three-dimensional objects. It also provides a convenient representation for storing information about object interiors.

The octree representation for a three-dimensional object is an extension of a similar two-dimensional representation scheme, called **quadtree** encoding. Quadtrees are generated by successively dividing a two-dimensional region (usually a square) into quadrants. Each node in the quadtree has four data elements, one for each of the quadrants in the region (Fig. 8-63). If all coordinate positions within a quadrant have the same color (a homogeneous quadrant), the corresponding data element in the node stores that color. In addition, a flag is set in the data element to indicate that the quadrant is homogeneous. If, for example, all points in quadrant 2 of Fig. 8-63 are red, the color code for red is then placed in data element 2 of the node. Otherwise the quadrant is heterogeneous, and it is divided into subquadrants, as shown in Fig. 8-64. The corresponding data element in the node for quadrant 2 now flags the quadrant as heterogeneous and stores the pointer to the next node in the quadtree.

An algorithm for generating a quadtree checks the color values assigned to objects within a selected two-dimensional region and sets up the quadtree nodes accordingly. If each quadrant in the original space has a single color specification, the quadtree has only one node. For a heterogeneous region of the plane, the

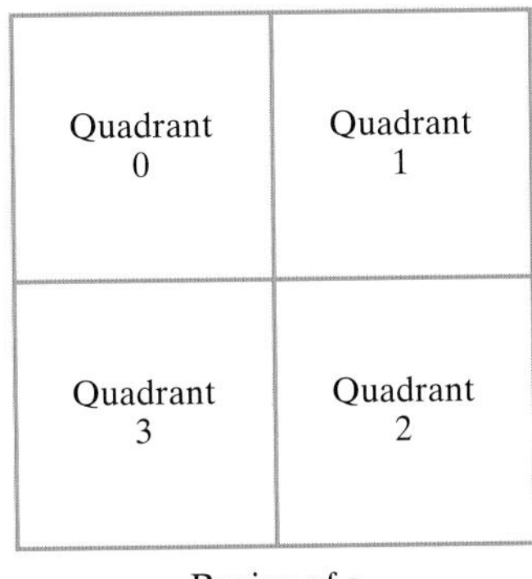

Region of a Two-Dimensional Space

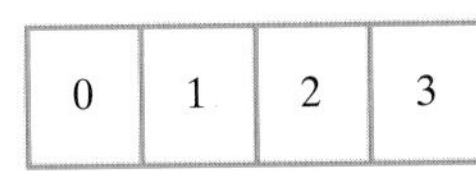

Data Elements in the Representative Quadtree Node

FIGURE 8-63 A square region of the xy plane divided into numbered quadrants and the associated quadtree node with four data elements.

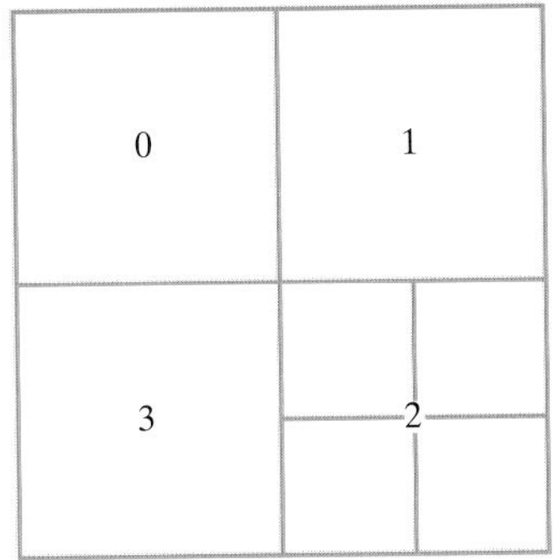

Region of a Two-Dimensional Space

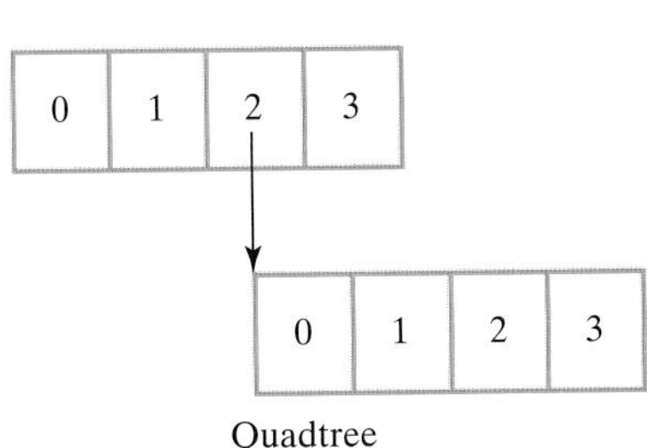

Quadtree Representation

FIGURE 8-64 A square region of the xy plane with two levels of quadrant divisions and the associated quadtree representation.

successive quadrant subdivisions continue until all sections of the subdivided region are homogeneous. Figure 8-65 shows a quadtree representation for a region containing one area with a solid color that is different from the uniform color specified for all other areas within that region.

Quadtree encodings provide considerable savings in storage when large color areas exist in a region of space, since a single node can represent a large part of the space. And this representation scheme can be used to store pixel color values. For an area containing $2n$ by $2n$ pixels, a quadtree representation contains at most n levels. And each node in the quadtree has at most four immediate descendants.

An octree encoding scheme divides a region of three-dimensional space (usually a cube) into octants and stores eight data elements in each node of the tree, as illustrated in Fig. 8-66. Individual subregions of the final subdivided three-dimensional space are called **volume elements,** or **voxels,** in analogy with the pixel components of a rectangular display area. A voxel element in the octree representation stores the property values for a homogeneous subregion of the space. Properties of the objects within a three-dimensional region of space can include color, material type, density, and other physical characteristics. For example, the objects in a selected region of space could include rocks and trees or tissue, bone, and body organs. Empty regions of the space are represented by voxel type "void". As with a quadtree representation, a heterogeneous octant in the region is subdivided until the subdivisions are homogeneous. For an octree, each node can have from zero to eight immediate descendants.

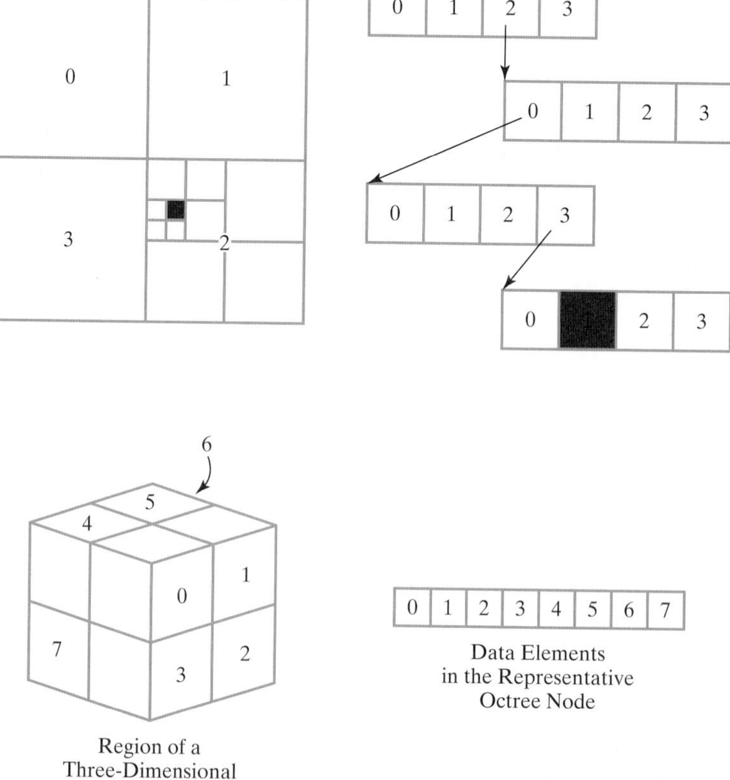

FIGURE 8-65 Quadtree representation for a square region of the xy plane that contains a single foreground-color area on a solid-color background.

FIGURE 8-66 A cube divided into numbered octants and the associated octree node with eight data elements.

Algorithms for generating octrees can be structured to accept definitions of objects in any form, such as a polygon mesh, curved surface patches, or solid-geometry constructions. For a single object, the octree can be constructed from the enclosing box (parallelepiped) determined by the coordinate extents of the object.

Once an octree representation has been established for a solid object, various manipulation routines can be applied to the object. An algorithm for performing set operations can be applied to two octree representations for the same region of space. For a union operation, a new octree is constructed using the octree nodes from each of the input trees. To set up an intersection representation for two input octrees, we construct the new tree using the octants where the two objects overlap. Similarly, for a difference operation, we look for regions occupied by one object and not the other.

A number of other octree-processing algorithms have been developed. Three-dimensional rotations, for instance, are accomplished by applying the transformations to spatial regions represented by the occupied octants. To locate the visible objects in a scene, we can first determine whether any front octants are occupied. If not, we proceed to the octants behind the front octants. This process continues until the occupied octants are located along the viewing direction. The first object detected along any viewing path through the spatial octants, front to back, is visible, and the information for that object can be transferred to a quadtree representation for display.

8-22 BSP TREES

This representation scheme is similar to octree encoding, except we now divide space into two partitions instead of eight at each step. With a **binary space-partitioning** (**BSP**) tree, we subdivide a scene into two sections at each step with a plane that can be at any position and orientation. In an octree encoding, the scene is subdivided at each step with three mutually perpendicular planes aligned with the Cartesian coordinate planes.

For adaptive subdivision of space, BSP trees can provide a more efficient partitioning, since we can position and orient the cutting planes to suit the spatial distribution of the objects. This can reduce the depth of the tree representation for a scene, compared to an octree, and thus reduce the time to search the tree. In addition, BSP trees are useful for identifying visible surfaces and for space partitioning in ray-tracing algorithms.

8-23 FRACTAL-GEOMETRY METHODS

All the object representations we have considered in the previous sections used Euclidean-geometry methods; that is, object shapes were described with equations. These methods are adequate for describing manufactured objects: those that have smooth surfaces and regular shapes. But natural objects, such as mountains and clouds, have irregular or fragmented features, and Euclidean methods do not provide realistic representations for such objects. Natural objects can be realistically described with **fractal-geometry methods,** where procedures rather than equations are used to model objects. As we might expect, procedurally defined objects have characteristics quite different from objects described with equations. Fractal-geometry representations for objects are commonly applied in many fields to describe and explain the features of natural phenomena. In computer graphics, we use fractal methods to generate displays of natural objects and visualizations of various mathematical and physical systems.

A fractal object has two basic characteristics: infinite detail at every point, and a certain *self-similarity* between the object parts and the overall features of the object. The self-similarity properties of an object can take different forms, depending on the representation we choose for the fractal. We describe a fractal object with a procedure that specifies a repeated operation for producing the detail in the object subparts. Natural objects are represented with procedures that theoretically repeat an infinite number of times. Graphics displays of natural objects are, of course, generated with a finite number of steps.

If we zoom in on a continuous Euclidean shape, no matter how complicated, we can eventually get the zoomed-in view to smooth out. But if we zoom in on a fractal object, we continue to see more and more details in the magnifications without an eventual smoothing of the object appearance. A mountain outlined against the sky continues to have the same jagged shape as we view it from a closer and closer position (Fig. 8-67). As we near the mountain, the smaller detail in the individual ledges and boulders becomes apparent. Moving even closer, we see the outlines of rocks, then stones, and then grains of sand. At each step, the outline reveals more twists and turns. If we took the grains of sand and put them under a microscope, we would again see the same detail repeated down through the molecular level. Similar shapes describe coastlines and the edges of plants and clouds.

To obtain a magnified view of a displayed fractal, we can select a section of the fractal for display within a viewing area of the same size. We then carry out the fractal-construction operations for that part of the object and display the increased detail for that level of magnification. As we repeat this process, we continue to display more and more of the object's detail. Because of the infinite detail inherent in the construction procedures, a fractal object has no definite size. When we include more of the detail in an object description, the dimensions increase without limit, but the coordinate extents for the object remain bound within a finite region of space.

We can characterize the amount of variation in object detail with a number called the *fractal dimension*. Unlike Euclidean dimension, this number is not necessarily an integer. The fractal dimension for an object is sometimes referred to as the *fractional dimension*, which is the basis for the name "fractal".

Fractal methods have proven useful for modeling a very wide variety of natural phenomena. In graphics applications, fractal representations are used to

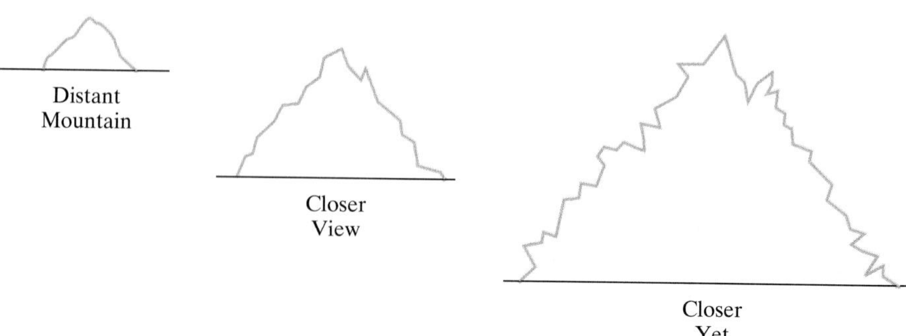

FIGURE 8-67 The ragged appearance of a mountain outline at different levels of magnification.

model terrain, clouds, water, trees and other plant life, feathers, fur, and various surface textures, and sometimes just to make pretty patterns. In other disciplines, fractal patterns have been found in the distribution of stars, river islands, and moon craters; in rain-field configurations; in stock market variations; in music; in traffic flow; in urban property utilization; and in the boundaries of convergence regions for numerical-analysis techniques.

Fractal Generation Procedures

A fractal object is generated by repeatedly applying a specified transformation function to points within a region of space. If $\mathbf{P}_0 = (x_0, y_0, z_0)$ is a selected initial position, each iteration of a transformation function F generates successive levels of detail with the calculations

$$\mathbf{P}_1 = F(\mathbf{P}_0), \qquad \mathbf{P}_2 = F(\mathbf{P}_1), \qquad \mathbf{P}_3 = F(\mathbf{P}_2), \qquad \cdots \tag{8-105}$$

In general, the transformation function can be applied to a specified point set or to an initial set of primitives, such as straight lines, curves, color areas, or surfaces. Also, we can use either deterministic or random procedures. The transformation function could be defined in terms of geometric transformations (scaling, translation, rotation), or it could involve nonlinear coordinate transformations and statistical decision parameters.

Although fractal objects, by definition, contain infinite detail, we apply the transformation function a finite number of times, and, of course, the objects we display have finite dimensions. A procedural representation approaches a "true" fractal as the number of transformations is increased to produce more and more detail. The amount of detail included in the final graphical display of an object depends on the number of iterations performed and the resolution of the display system. We cannot display detail variations that are smaller than the size of a pixel. But we can repeatedly zoom in on selected portions of an object to view more of its detail.

Classification of Fractals

Self-similar fractals have parts that are scaled down versions of the entire object. Starting with an initial shape, we construct the object subparts by apply a scaling parameter s to the overall shape. We can use the same scaling factor s for all subparts, or we can use different scaling factors for different scaled-down parts of the object. If we also apply random variations to the scaled-down subparts, the fractal is said to be *statistically self-similar*. The parts then have the same statistical properties. Statistically self-similar fractals are commonly used to model trees, shrubs, and other vegetation.

Self-affine fractals have parts that are formed with different scaling parameters, s_x, s_y, and s_z, in different coordinate directions. And we can also include random variations to obtain *statistically self-affine* fractals. Terrain, water, and clouds are typically modeled with statistically self-affine fractal construction methods.

Invariant fractal sets are formed with nonlinear transformations. This class of fractals includes *self-squaring* fractals, such as the Mandelbrot set (formed with squaring functions in complex space), and *self-inverse* fractals, constructed with inversion procedures.

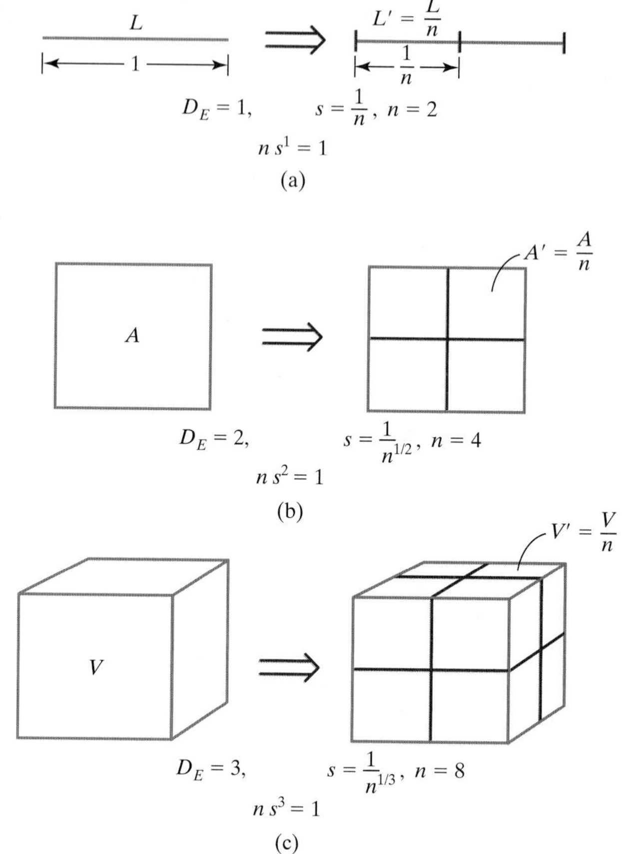

FIGURE 8-68
Subdividing a unit line (a), a unit square (b), and a unit cube (c). The Euclidean dimension is represented as D_E, and the scaling factor for each object is $s = \frac{1}{2}$.

Fractal Dimension

The amount of variation in the structure of a fractal object can be described with a number D, called the **fractal dimension,** which is a measure of the roughness, or fragmentation, of the object. More jagged-looking objects have larger fractal dimensions. One method for generating a fractal object is to set up an iterative procedure that uses a selected value for D. Another approach is to determine the fractal dimension from the desired properties of an object, although, in general, the fractal dimension can be difficult to calculate. Methods for calculating D are based on dimension concepts developed in branches of mathematics, particularly topology.

An expression for the fractal dimension of a self-similar fractal constructed with a single scalar factor s is obtained by analogy with the subdivision of a Euclidean object. Figure 8-68 shows the relationships between the scaling factor s and the number of subparts n for subdivision of a unit straight-line segment, a unit square, and a unit cube. With $s = \frac{1}{2}$, the unit line segment (Fig. 8-68(a)) is divided into two equal-length subparts. For the same scaling factor, the square in Fig. 8-68(b) is divided into four equal-area subparts, and the cube (Fig. 8-68(c)) is divided into eight equal-volume subparts. For each of these objects, the relationship between the number of subparts and the scaling factor is $n \cdot s^{D_E} = 1$. In analogy with Euclidean objects, the fractal dimension D for self-similar objects can be obtained from

$$ns^D = 1 \tag{8-106}$$

Solving this expression for D, the **fractal similarity dimension,** we have

$$D = \frac{\ln n}{\ln(1/s)} \tag{8-107}$$

For a self-similar fractal constructed with different scaling factors for the different subparts of the object, the fractal similarity dimension is obtained from the implicit relationship

$$\sum_{k=1}^{n} s_k^D = 1 \tag{8-108}$$

where s_k is the scaling factor for subpart k.

In Fig. 8-68, we considered subdivision of simple shapes (straight line, rectangle, and box). If we have more complicated shapes, including curved lines and objects with nonplanar surfaces, determining the structure and properties of the subparts is more difficult. For general object shapes, we can use *topological covering methods* that approximate object subparts with simple shapes. A subdivided curve, for example, could be approximated with straight-line sections, and a subdivided spline surface could be approximated with small squares or rectangles. Other covering shapes, such as circles, spheres, and cylinders, can also be used to approximate the features of an object divided into a number of smaller parts. Covering methods are commonly used in mathematics to determine geometric properties, such as length, area, or volume, of a complex object by summing the properties of a set of smaller covering objects. We can also use covering methods to determine the fractal dimension D of some objects.

Topological covering concepts were originally used to extend the meaning of geometric properties to nonstandard shapes. An extension of covering methods using circles or spheres led to the notion of a *Hausdorff-Besicovitch dimension,* or *fractional dimension.* The Hausdorff-Besicovitch dimension can be used as the fractal dimension of some objects, but in general, it is difficult to evaluate. More commonly, an object's fractal dimension is estimated with *box-covering methods* using rectangles or parallelepipeds. Figure 8-69 illustrates the notion of a box covering. Here, the area inside the large irregular boundary can be approximated by the sum of the areas of the small covering rectangles.

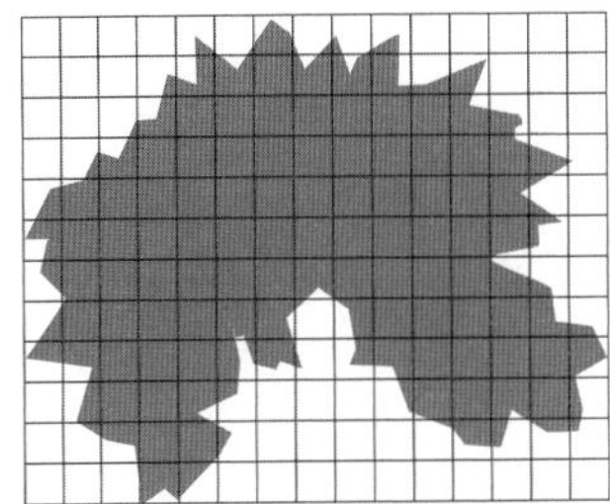

FIGURE 8-69 Box covering of an irregularly shaped object.

Box-covering methods are applied by first determining the coordinate extents of an object, then subdividing the object into a number of small boxes using the given scaling factors. The number of boxes n that it takes to cover an object is called the *box dimension,* and n is related to the fractal dimension D. For statistically self-similar objects with a single scaling factor s, we can cover the object with squares or cubes. We then count the number n of covering boxes and use Eq. 8-107 to estimate the fractal dimension. For self-affine objects, we cover the object with rectangular boxes, since different directions are scaled differently. In this case, we estimate the fractal dimension using both the number of boxes n and the affine transformation parameters.

The fractal dimension of an object is always greater than the corresponding Euclidean dimension (or topological dimension), which is simply the least number of parameters needed to specify the object. A Euclidean curve is one-dimensional since we can determine coordinate positions with one parameter, u. A Euclidean surface is two-dimensional, with surface parameters u and v. And a Euclidean solid, which requires three parameters for each coordinate specification, is three-dimensional.

For a fractal curve that lies completely within a two-dimensional plane, the fractal dimension D is greater than 1 (the Euclidean dimension of a curve). The closer D is to 1, the smoother the fractal curve. If $D = 2$, we have a *Peano curve;* that is, the "curve" completely fills a finite region of two-dimensional space. For $2 < D < 3$, the curve self-intersects and the area could be covered an infinite number of times. Fractal curves can be used to model natural object boundaries, such as shorelines.

Spatial fractal curves (those that do not lie completely within a single plane) also have fractal dimension D greater than 1, but D can be greater than 2 without self-intersecting. A curve that fills a volume of space has dimension $D = 3$, and a self-intersecting space curve has fractal dimension $D > 3$.

Fractal surfaces typically have a dimension within the range $2 < D \leq 3$. If $D = 3$, the "surface" fills a volume of space. And if $D > 3$, there is an overlapping coverage of the volume. Terrain, clouds, and water are typically modeled with fractal surfaces.

The dimension of a fractal solid is usually in the range $3 < D \leq 4$. Again, if $D > 4$, we have a self-overlapping object. Fractal solids can be used, for example, to model cloud properties such as water vapor density or temperature within a region of space.

Geometric Construction of Deterministic Self-Similar Fractals

To geometrically construct a deterministic (nonrandom) self-similar fractal, we start with a given geometric shape, called the *initiator*. Subparts of the initiator are then replaced with a pattern, called the *generator*.

As an example, if we use the initiator and generator shown in Fig. 8-70, we can construct the snowflake pattern, or Koch curve, shown in Fig. 8-71. Each straight-line segment in the initiator is replaced with the generator pattern, consisting of four equal-length line segments. Then the generator is scaled and applied to the line segments of the modified initiator, and this process is repeated for some number of steps. The scaling factor at each step is $\frac{1}{3}$, so the fractal dimension is $D = \ln 4/\ln 3 \approx 1.2619$. Also, the length of each line segment in the initiator increases by a factor of $\frac{4}{3}$ at each step, so that the length of the fractal curve tends to infinity as more detail is added to the curve (Fig. 8-72). Figure 8-73 illustrates additional generator patterns that could be used for self-similar fractal curve constructions. The generators in Fig. 8-73(b) and (c) contain more detail than the Koch curve generator, and they have higher fractal dimensions.

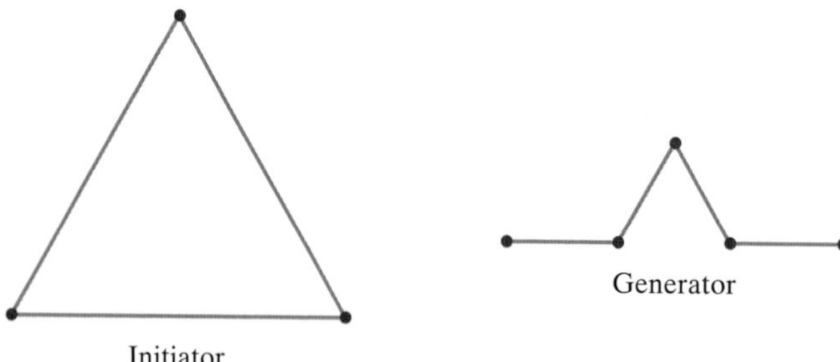

FIGURE 8-70 Initiator and generator for the Koch curve.

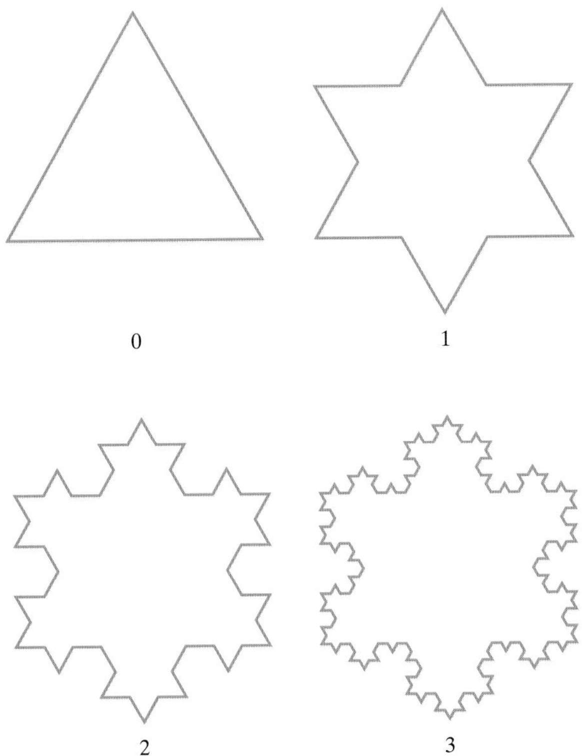

FIGURE 8-71 First three iterations in the generation of the Koch curve.

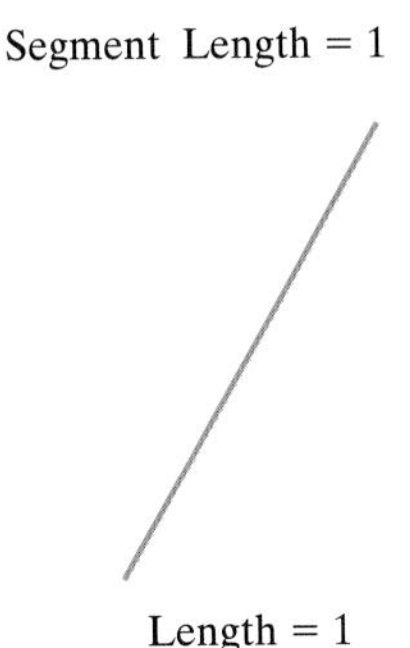

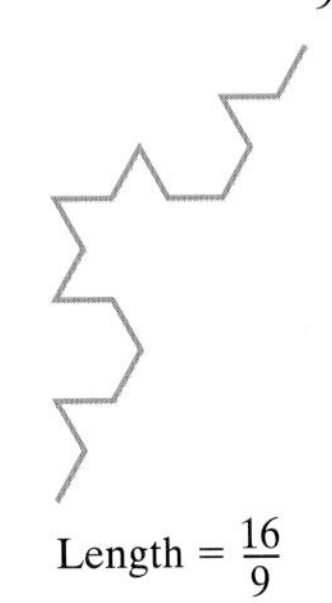

FIGURE 8-72 The length of each side of the Koch curve increases by a factor of $\frac{4}{3}$ at each step, while the line segment lengths are reduced by a factor of $\frac{1}{3}$.

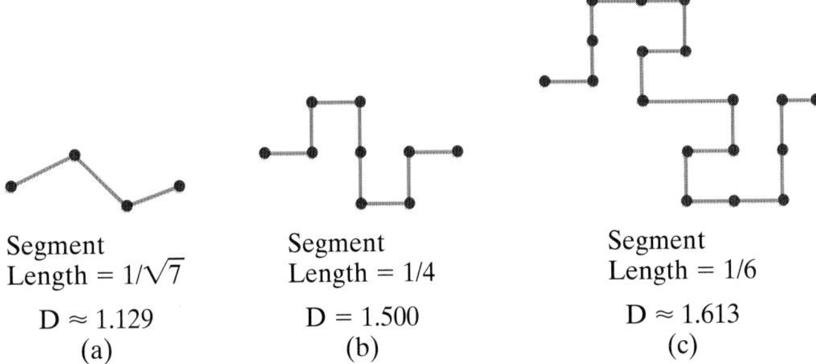

FIGURE 8-73 Generators for self-similar fractal curve constructions and their associated fractal dimensions.

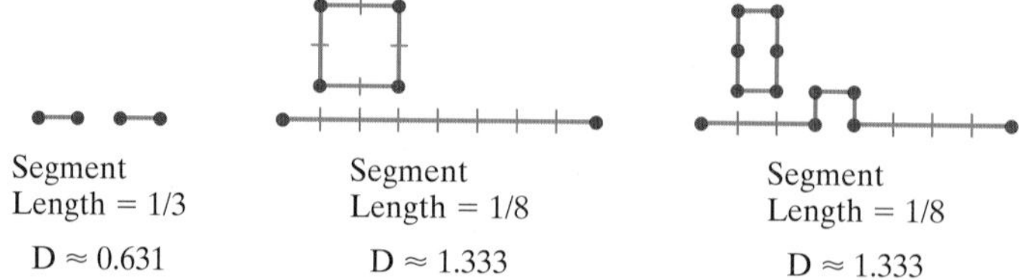

FIGURE 8-74 Fractal generators with multiple, disjoint parts.

FIGURE 8-75 Applying this generator to the edges of an equilateral triangle produces a snowflake-filling Peano curve (also called a Peano space).

We can also use generators with multiple disjoint components. Some examples of compound generators are shown in Fig. 8-74. We could combine these patterns with random variations to model various natural objects that have multiple unconnected parts, such as island distributions along a coastline.

The generator of Fig. 8-75 contains line segments with varying lengths, and multiple scaling factors are used in the construction of the fractal curve. Thus the fractal dimension of the generated curve is determined from Eq. 8-108.

Displays of trees and other plants can be constructed with self-similar geometric-construction methods. Each branch of the fern outline shown in Fig. 8-76(a) is a scaled version of the overall fern shape. In (b) of this figure, the fern is fully rendered with a twist applied to each branch.

As an example of a self-similar fractal construction for the surfaces of a three-dimensional object, we scale the regular tetrahedron shown in Fig. 8-77 by a factor of $\frac{1}{2}$, then place the scaled object on each of the original four surfaces of the tetrahedron. Each face of the original tetrahedron is converted into six smaller faces and the original face area is increased by a factor of $\frac{3}{2}$. The fractal dimension of this surface is

$$D = \frac{\ln 6}{\ln 2} \approx 2.58496$$

which indicates a fairly fragmented surface.

Another way to create self-similar fractal objects is to punch holes in a given initiator, instead of adding more surface area. Fig. 8-78 shows some examples of fractal objects created in this way.

(a)

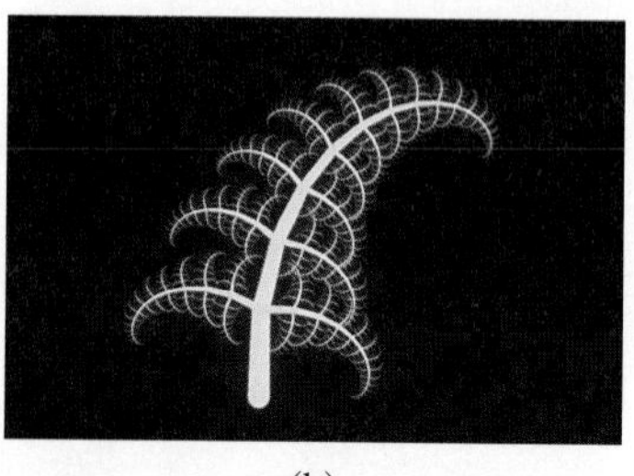

(b)

FIGURE 8-76 Self-similar constructions for a fern. *(Courtesy of Peter Oppenheimer, Computer Graphics Lab, New York Institute of Technology.)*

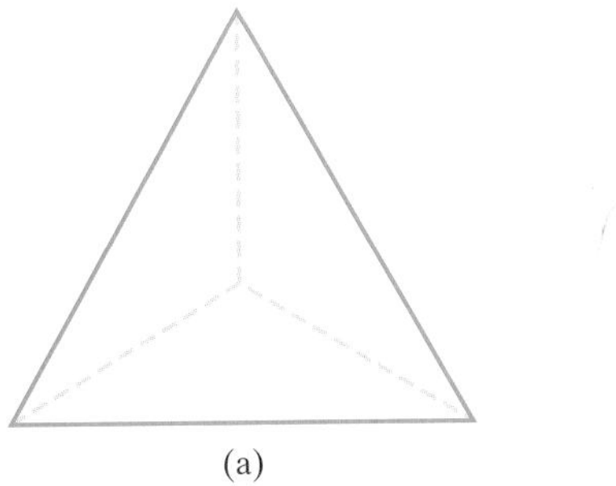

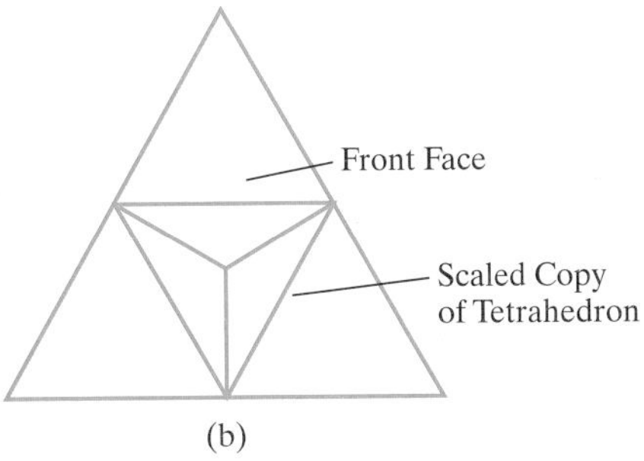

FIGURE 8-77 Scaling the tetrahedron in (a) by a factor of $\frac{1}{2}$ and positioning the scaled version on one face of the original tetrahedron produces the fractal surface (b).

FIGURE 8-78 Self-similar, three-dimensional fractals formed with generators that subtract subparts from an initiator. (*Courtesy of John C. Hart, Department of Computer Science, University of Illinois at Urbana-Champaign.*)

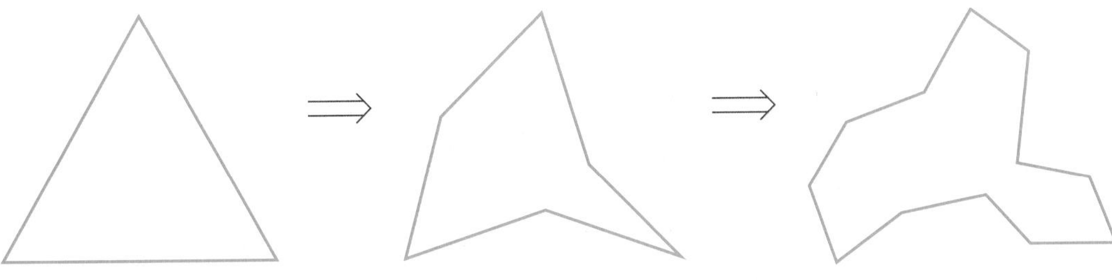

FIGURE 8-79 A modified "snowflake" pattern using random midpoint displacement.

Geometric Construction of Statistically Self-Similar Fractals

To introduce variability into the geometric construction of a self-similar fractal, we could randomly select a generator at each step from a menu of patterns. Or we could construct a self-similar fractal by computing coordinate displacements with small random variations. For example, in Fig. 8-79 we use a probability distribution function to compute variable midpoint displacements at each step in the creation of a random snowflake pattern.

Another example of this method is shown in Fig. 8-80. Random scaling parameters and branching directions are used in this display to model the vein patterns in a leaf.

Once a fractal object has been created, we can model a scene using several transformed instances of the object. Figure 8-81 illustrates instancing with random rotations of a fractal tree. In Fig. 8-82, a fractal forest is displayed using various random transformations.

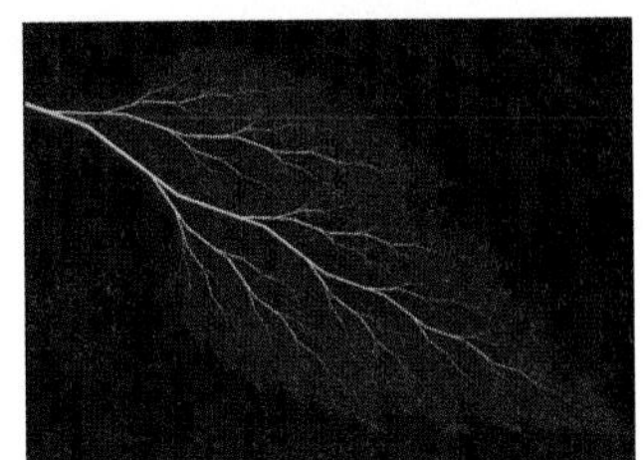

FIGURE 8-80 Random, self-similar construction of vein branching in a fall leaf. (*Courtesy of Peter Oppenheimer, Computer Graphics Lab, New York Institute of Technology.*)

FIGURE 8-81 Modeling a scene using multiple object instancing. Fractal leaves are attached to a tree in randomly transformed positions, and several rotated and scaled instances of the tree are used to form a grove. The grass is modeled with multiple instances of green cones. (*Courtesy of John C. Hart, Department of Computer Science, University of Illinois at Urbana-Champaign.*)

FIGURE 8-82 A fractal forest created with multiple instances of leaves, pine needles, grass, and tree bark. (*Courtesy of John C. Hart, Department of Computer Science, University of Illinois at Urbana-Champaign.*)

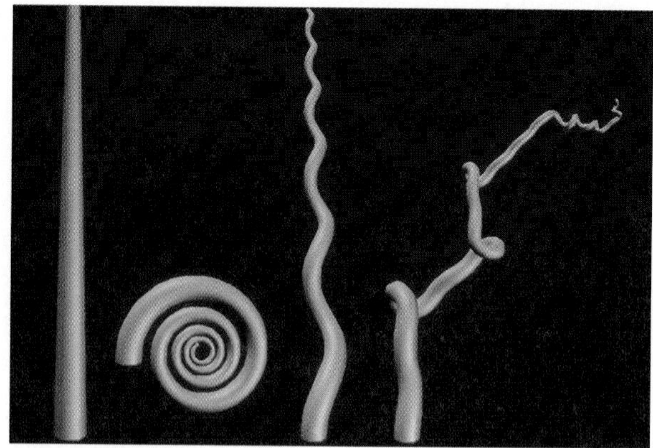

FIGURE 8-83 Modeling tree branches with spiral, helical, and random twists. (*Courtesy of Peter Oppenheimer, Computer Graphics Lab, New York Institute of Technology.*)

To model the gnarled and contorted shapes of some trees, we can apply twisting functions as well as scaling to create the random, self-similar branches. This technique is illustrated in Fig. 8-83. Starting with the tapered cylinder on the left of this figure, we can apply transformations to produce (in succession from left to right) a spiral, a helix, and a random twisting pattern. A tree modeled with

FIGURE 8-84 Tree branches modeled with random squiggles. *(Courtesy of Peter Oppenheimer, Computer Graphics Lab, New York Institute of Technology.)*

random twists is shown in Fig. 8-84. The tree bark in this display is modeled using bump mapping and fractal Brownian variations on the bump patterns. Methods for generating fractal Brownian curves are discussed in the next section, and bump-mapping methods are explored in Section 10-17.

Affine Fractal-Construction Methods

We can obtain highly realistic representations for terrain and other natural objects using affine fractal methods that model object features as *fractional Brownian motion*. This is an extension of standard Brownian motion, a form of "random walk", which describes the erratic, zigzag movement of particles in a gas or other fluid. Figure 8-85 illustrates a random-walk path in the xy plane. Starting from a given position, we generate a straight-line segment in a random direction and with a random length. Another random line is then constructed from the endpoint of this first line, and the process is repeated for a designated number of line segments. Fractional Brownian motion is obtained by adding an additional parameter to the statistical distribution describing Brownian motion. This additional parameter sets the fractal dimension for the "motion" path.

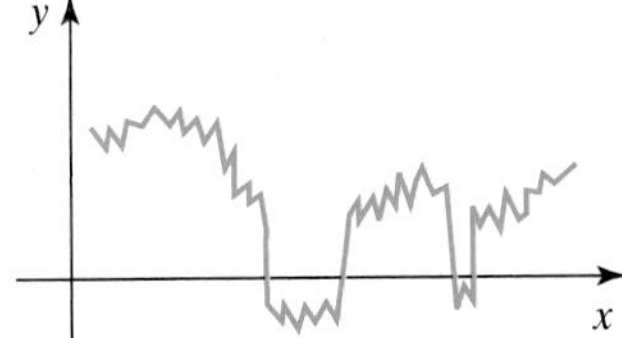

FIGURE 8-85 An example of Brownian motion (random walk) in the xy plane.

A single fractional Brownian path can be used to model a fractal curve. And with a two-dimensional array of random fractional Brownian elevations over a ground-plane grid, we can model the surface of a mountain by connecting the elevations to form a set of polygon patches. If random elevations are generated on the surface of a sphere, we can model the mountains, valleys, and oceans of a planet. In Fig. 8-86, Brownian motion was used to create the elevation variations on the planet surface. The elevations were then color coded so that lowest elevations are painted blue (the oceans) and the highest elevations white (snow on the mountains). Fractional Brownian motion was used to create the terrain features in the foreground. Craters were created with random diameters and random positions, using affine fractal procedures that closely describe the distribution of observed craters, river islands, rain patterns, and other similar systems of objects.

By adjusting the fractal dimension in the fractional Brownian-motion calculations, we can vary the ruggedness of terrain features. Values for the fractal dimension in the neighborhood of $D \approx 2.15$ produce realistic mountain features,

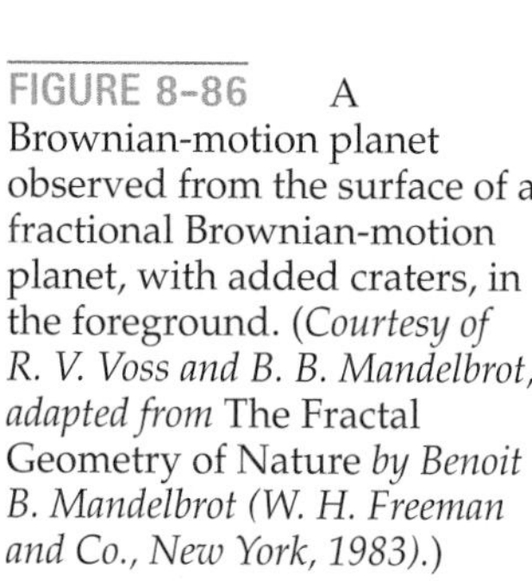

FIGURE 8-86 A Brownian-motion planet observed from the surface of a fractional Brownian-motion planet, with added craters, in the foreground. (*Courtesy of R. V. Voss and B. B. Mandelbrot, adapted from* The Fractal Geometry of Nature *by Benoit B. Mandelbrot (W. H. Freeman and Co., New York, 1983).*)

while higher values close to 3.0 can be used to create unusual-looking extraterrestrial landscapes. We can also scale the calculated elevations to deepen the valleys and increase the height of mountain peaks. Some examples of terrain features that can be modeled with fractal procedures are given in Fig. 8-87. A scene modeled with fractal clouds over a fractal mountain is shown in Fig. 8-88.

Random Midpoint-Displacement Methods

Fractional Brownian-motion calculations are time-consuming, since the elevation coordinates of the terrain above a ground plane are calculated with Fourier series, which are sums of sine and cosine terms. Fast Fourier transform (FFT) methods are typically used, but it is still a slow process to generate fractal-mountain scenes. Therefore, faster **random midpoint-displacement methods,** similar to the random displacement methods used in geometric constructions, have been developed to approximate fractional Brownian-motion representations for terrain and other natural phenomena. These methods were originally used to generate animation frames for science-fiction films involving unusual terrain and planet features. Midpoint-displacement methods are now commonly used in many other computer-graphics applications, including animations for television advertising.

Although random midpoint-displacement methods are faster than fractional Brownian-motion calculations, they produce less realistic looking terrain features. Figure 8-89 illustrates the midpoint-displacement method for generating a random-walk path in the xy plane. Starting with a straight-line segment, we calculate a displaced y value for the midposition of the line as the average of the endpoint y values plus a random offset:

$$y_{\text{mid}} = \frac{1}{2}[y(a) + y(b)] + r \tag{8-109}$$

To approximate fractional Brownian motion, we choose a value for r from a Gaussian distribution with a mean of 0 and a variance proportional to $|(b-a)|^{2H}$, where $H = 2 - D$ and $D > 1$ is the fractal dimension. Another way to obtain

(a)

(b)

(c)

FIGURE 8-87 Variations in terrain features modeled with fractional Brownian motion. (*Courtesy of (a) R. V. Voss and B. B. Mandelbrot, adapted from* The Fractal Geometry of Nature *by Benoit B. Mandelbrot (W. H. Freeman and Co., New York, 1983); and (b) and (c) Ken Musgrave and Benoit B. Mandelbrot, Mathematics and Computer Science, Yale University.*)

FIGURE 8-88 A scene modeled with fractal clouds and mountains. (*Courtesy of Ken Musgrave and Benoit B. Mandelbrot, Mathematics and Computer Science, Yale University.*)

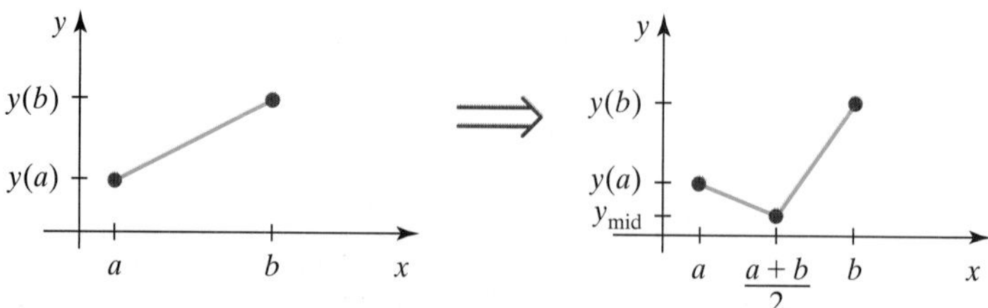

FIGURE 8-89 Random midpoint displacement of a straight-line segment.

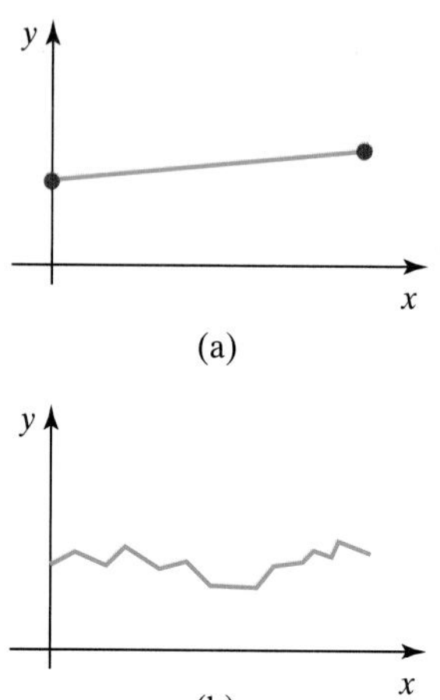

FIGURE 8-90 A random-walk path generated from a straight-line segment with four iterations of the random midpoint-displacement procedure.

a random offset is to take $r = sr_g|b - a|$, with parameter s as a selected surface "roughness" factor and r_g as a Gaussian random value with mean 0 and variance 1. Table lookups can be used to obtain the Gaussian values. The process is then repeated by calculating a displaced y value for the midposition of each half of the subdivided line. And we continue the subdivision to obtain a certain number of segments or until the lengths of the subdivided line sections are less than some selected length. At each step, the value of the random variable r decreases, since it is proportional to the width $|b - a|$ of the line section to be subdivided. Figure 8-90 shows a fractal curve obtained with this method.

Terrain features are generated by applying the random midpoint-displacement procedures to a rectangular ground plane (Fig. 8-91). We begin by assigning an elevation z value to each of the four corners (**a**, **b**, **c**, **d** in Fig. 8-91) of the ground plane. Then we divide the ground plane at the midpoint of each edge to obtain the five new grid positions: **e**, **f**, **g**, **h**, and **m**. Elevations at the midpositions **e**, **f**, **g**, and **h** of the ground-plane edges can be calculated as the average elevation of the nearest two vertices plus a random offset. For example, elevation z_e at midposition **e** is calculated using vertices **a** and **b**, while elevation at midposition **f** is calculated using vertices **b** and **c**:

$$z_e = (z_a + z_b)/2 + r_e, \qquad z_f = (z_b + z_c)/2 + r_f$$

Random values r_e and r_f can be obtained from a Gaussian distribution with mean 0 and variance proprotional to the grid separation raised to the $2H$ power, with $H = 3 - D$ and $D > 2$. Higher values for D, the surface fractal dimension, produce more jagged terrain, while lower values generate smoother terrain features. We could also calculate random offsets as the product of a surface roughness factor times the grid separation times a table lookup value for a Gaussian value with mean 0 and variance 1. The elevation z_m of the ground plane midposition **m** can be calculated using positions **e** and **g**, or positions **f** and **h**. Alternatively, we could calculate z_m using the assigned elevations of the four ground plane corners and a

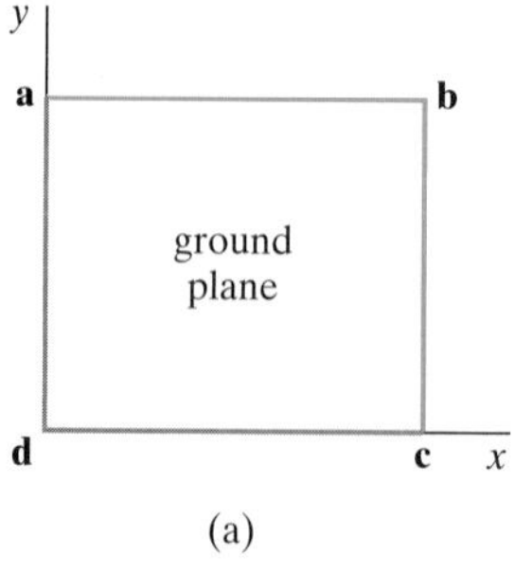

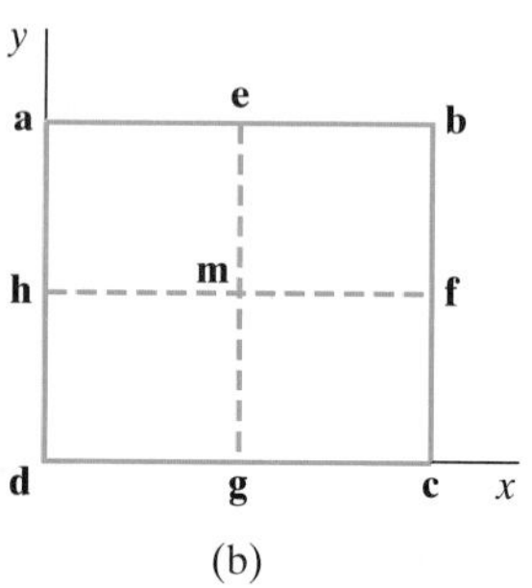

FIGURE 8-91 A rectangular ground plane (a) is subdivided into four equal grid sections (b) for the first step in a random midpoint-displacement procedure to calculate terrain elevations.

random offset as

$$z_m = (z_a + z_b + z_c + z_d)/4 + r_m$$

This process is repeated for each of the four new grid sections at each step until the grid separation becomes smaller than a selected value.

Triangular surface patches for the terrain surface can be formed as the elevations are generated. Figure 8-92 shows eight surface patches that could be constructed at the first subdivision step. At each level of recursion, the triangles are successively subdivided into smaller planar patches. When the subdivision process is completed, the patches are rendered using the positions selected for the light sources, the values of other illumination parameters, and the chosen colors and surface textures for the terrain.

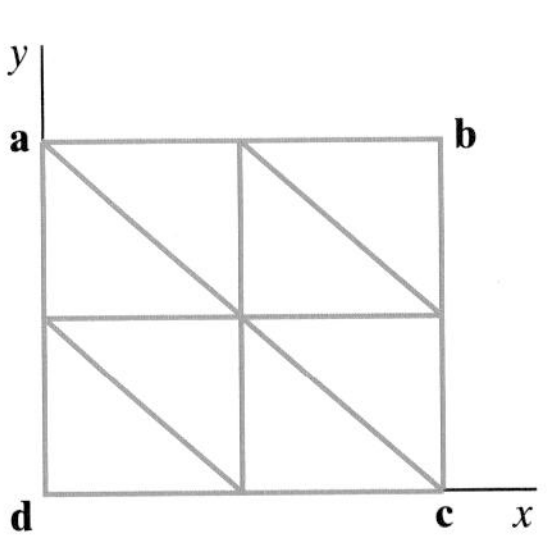

FIGURE 8-92 Eight surface patches formed over a ground plane at the first step of a random midpoint-displacement procedure for generating terrain features.

The random midpoint-displacement method can be applied to generate other components of a scene besides the terrain. For instance, we could use the same methods to obtain surface features for water waves or cloud patterns above a ground plane.

Controlling Terrain Topography

One way to control the placement of peaks and valleys in a fractal-terrain scene that is modeled with a midpoint-displacement method is to constrain the calculated elevations to certain intervals over the various sections of the ground plane. We can accomplish this by designating a set of *control surfaces* over the ground plane, as illustrated in Fig. 8-93. Then we calculate a random elevation at each midpoint grid position on the ground plane that depends on the difference between the control elevation and the average elevation calculated for that position. This procedure constrains elevations to be within a preset interval about the control-surface elevations.

Control surfaces can be used to model existing terrain features in the Rocky Mountains, or some other region, by constructing the plane facets using the elevations in a contour plot for a particular region. Or we could set the elevations for the vertices of the control polygons to design our own terrain features. Also, control surfaces can have any shape. Planes are easiest to deal with, but we could use spherical surfaces or other curve shapes.

We use the random midpoint-displacement method to calculate grid elevations, but now we select random values from a Gaussian distribution where the mean μ and standard deviation σ are functions of the control elevations. A method for obtaining the values for μ and σ is to make them both proportional to the difference between the calculated average elevation and the predefined control elevation at each grid position. For example, for grid position **e** in Fig. 8-91, we set the mean and standard deviation as

$$\mu_e = zc_e - (z_a + z_b)/2, \qquad \sigma_e = s|\mu_e|$$

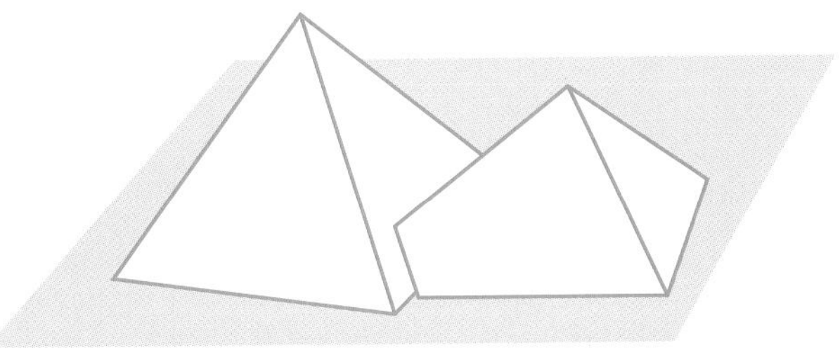

FIGURE 8-93 Control surfaces over a ground plane.

where zc_e is the control elevation for ground-plane position **e**, and $0 < s < 1$ is the scaling factor. Small values for s, such as $s < 0.1$, produce tighter conformity to the terrain envelope, and larger values for s allow greater fluctuations in terrain height.

To determine the values for the control elevations over a control-surface plane, we first determine the values for the plane parameters A, B, C, and D. For any ground-plane position (x, y), the elevation in the plane containing that control polygon is then calculated as

$$zc = (-Ax - By - D)/C$$

Incremental methods can then be used to calculate control elevations over positions in the ground-plane grid. To carry out these calculations efficiently, we subdivide the ground plane into a smaller grid of xy positions and project each polygon control surface onto the ground plane, as shown in Fig. 8-94. From this projection, we determine which grid positions are below each control polygon. This can be accomplished using procedures similar to those in scan-line area filling. That is, for each y "scan line" in the ground plane mesh that crosses the polygon edges, we calculate scan-line intersections and determine which grid positions are within the control-polygon projection. Calculations for the control elevations at these grid positions are performed incrementally as

$$zc_{i+1,j} = zc_{i,j} - \Delta x(A/C), \qquad zc_{i,j+1} = zc_{i,j} - \Delta y(B/C) \tag{8-110}$$

where Δx and Δy are the grid separations in the x and y directions. This procedure is particularly fast when parallel vector methods are applied to process the control-plane grid positions.

Figure 8-95 shows a scene constructed using control planes to structure the surfaces for the terrain, water, and clouds above a ground plane. Surface-rendering algorithms were then applied to smooth out the polygon edges and to provide the appropriate surface colors.

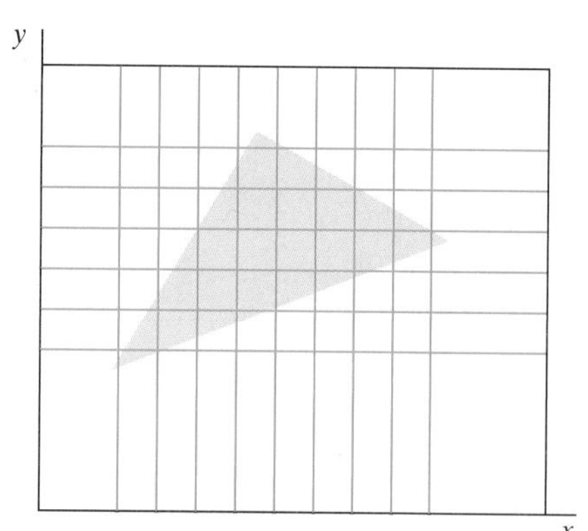

FIGURE 8-94 Projection of a triangular control surface onto a ground-plane grid.

FIGURE 8-95 A composite scene modeled with a random midpoint-displacement method and planar control surfaces over a ground plane. Surface features for the terrain, water, and clouds were modeled and rendered separately, then combined to form the composite picture. (*Courtesy of Eng-Kiat Koh, Encentuate, Inc., Cupertino, California.*)

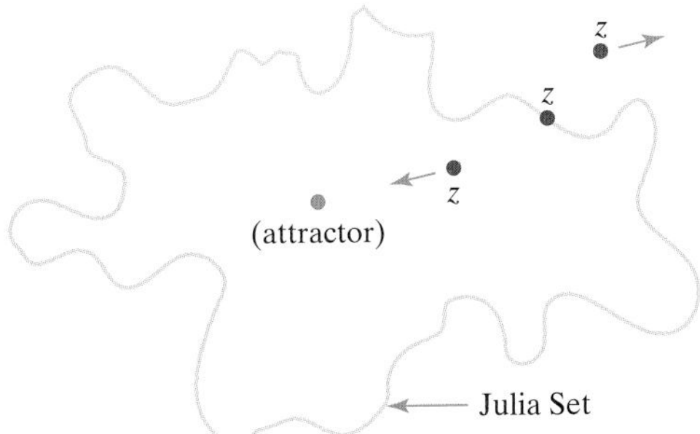

FIGURE 8-96 Possible results from repeated application of a self-squaring transformation $f(z)$ in the complex plane, depending on the position of the selected initial position.

Self-Squaring Fractals

Another method for generating fractal objects is to repeatedly apply a transformation function to points in complex space. In two dimensions, a complex number can be represented as $z = x + iy$, where x and y are real numbers and $i^2 = -1$. In three-dimensional and four-dimensional space, points are represented with quaternions. A complex squaring function $f(z)$ is one that involves the calculation of z^2, and we can use some self-squaring functions to generate fractal shapes.

Depending on the initial position selected for the iteration, repeated application of a self-squaring function will produce one of three possible outcomes (Fig. 8-96):

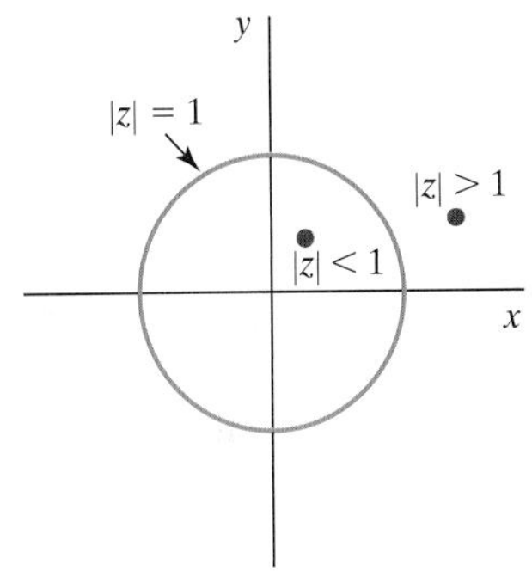

FIGURE 8-97 A unit circle in the complex plane. The nonfractal, complex squaring function $f(z) = z^2$ moves points that are inside the circle toward the origin, while points outside the circle are moved farther away from the circle. Any initial point on the circle remains on the circle.

- The transformed position can diverge to infinity.
- The transformed position can converge to a finite limit point, called an *attractor*.
- The transformed position remains on the boundary of some region.

As an example, the nonfractal squaring operation $f(z) = z^2$ in the complex plane transforms positions according to their relation to the unit circle (Fig. 8-97). Any point z whose magnitude $|z|$ is greater than 1 is transformed through a sequence of positions that tend to infinity. A point with $|z| < 1$ is transformed toward the coordinate origin. Points that are originally on the circle, $|z| = 1$, remain on the circle. Although the z^2 transformation does not produce a fractal, some complex squaring operations generate a fractal curve as the boundary between those positions that move toward infinity and those that tend toward a finite limit. A closed fractal boundary generated with a squaring operation is called a *Julia set*.

In general, we can locate the fractal boundary for a squaring function by testing the behavior of selected positions. If a position is transformed so that it either diverges to infinity or converges to an attractor point, we can try another nearby position. We repeat this process until we eventually locate a position on the fractal boundary. Then, iteration of the squaring transformation generates the fractal shape. For simple transformations in the complex plane, a quicker method for locating positions on the fractal curve is to use the inverse of the transformation function. An initial point chosen on the inside or outside of the curve will then converge to a position on the fractal curve (Fig. 8-98).

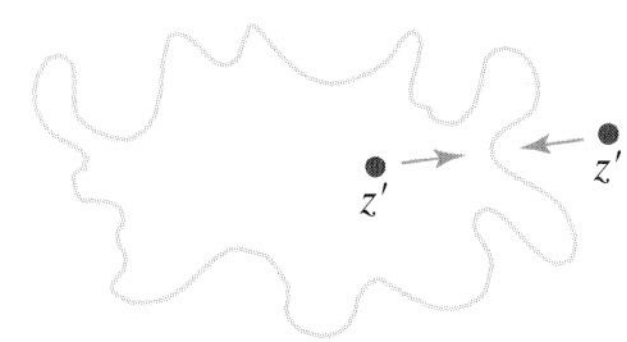

FIGURE 8-98 Locating the fractal boundary curve using the inverse, self-squaring function $z = f^{-1}(z')$.

A function that is rich in fractals is the squaring transformation

$$z' = f(z) = \lambda z(1 - z) \tag{8-111}$$

with λ as a complex constant. For this function, we can use the inverse method to locate the fractal curve. We first rearrange terms to obtain the quadratic equation:

$$z^2 - z + z'/\lambda = 0 \tag{8-112}$$

The inverse transformation is then the quadratic formula:

$$z = f^{-1}(z') = \frac{1}{2}\left(1 \pm \sqrt{1 - (4z')/\lambda}\right) \tag{8-113}$$

Using complex arithmetic operations, we solve this equation for the real and imaginary parts of z as

$$\begin{aligned} x = \text{Re}(z) &= \frac{1}{2}\left(1 \pm \sqrt{\frac{|\text{discr}| + \text{Re}(\text{discr})}{2}}\right) \\ y = \text{Im}(z) &= \pm\frac{1}{2}\sqrt{\frac{|\text{discr}| - \text{Re}(\text{discr})}{2}} \end{aligned} \tag{8-114}$$

where the discriminant of the quadratic formula is $\text{discr} = 1 - (4z')/\lambda$. A few initial values for x and y (say, 10) can be calculated and ignored before we begin to plot the fractal curve. Also, since this function yields two possible transformed (x, y) positions, we can randomly choose either the plus or the minus sign at each step of the iteration as long as $\text{Im}(\text{discr}) \geq 0$. Whenever $\text{Im}(\text{discr}) < 0$, the two possible positions are in the second and fourth quadrants. In this case, x and y must have opposite signs. The following program gives an implementation for this self-squaring function, and two example curves are plotted in Fig. 8-99.

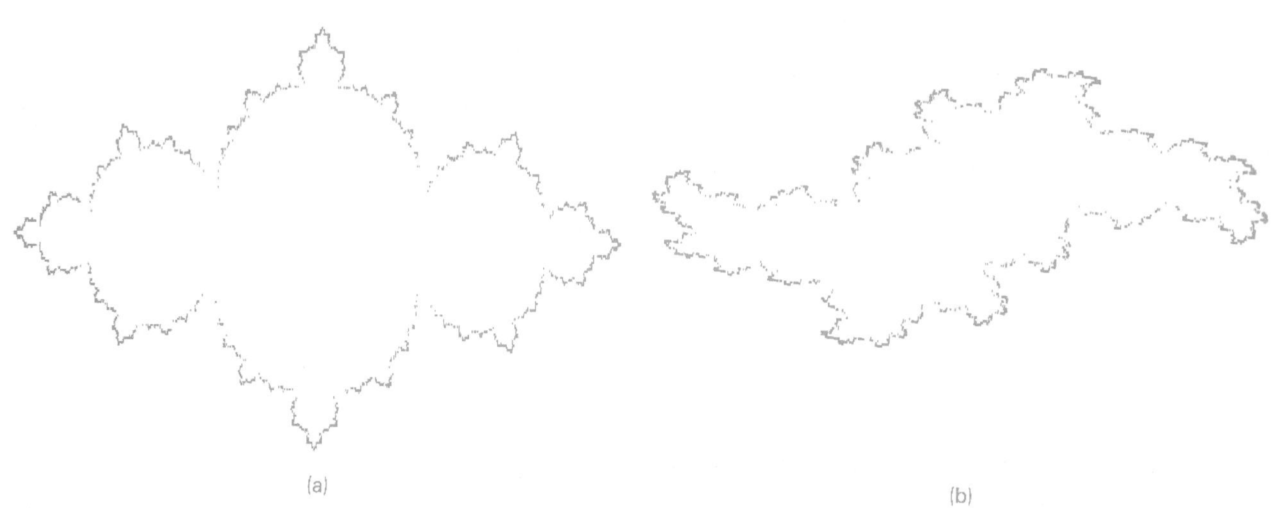

FIGURE 8-99 Two fractal curves generated with the inverse of the function $f(z) = \lambda z(1 - z)$ by procedure `selfSqTransf`, using (a) $\lambda = 3$ and (b) $\lambda = 2 + i$. Each curve is plotted with 10,000 points.

```
#include <GL/glut.h>
#include <stdlib.h>
#include <math.h>

/*  Set initial size of display window.  */
GLsizei winWidth = 600, winHeight = 600;

/*  Set coordinate limits in complex plane.  */
GLfloat xComplexMin = -0.25, xComplexMax = 1.25;
GLfloat yComplexMin = -0.75, yComplexMax = 0.75;

struct complexNum
{
   GLfloat x, y;
};

void init (void)
{
   /*  Set color of display window to white.  */
   glClearColor (1.0, 1.0, 1.0, 0.0);
}

void plotPoint (complexNum z)
{
    glBegin (GL_POINTS);
        glVertex2f (z.x, z.y);
    glEnd ( );
}

void solveQuadraticEq (complexNum lambda, complexNum * z)
{
   GLfloat lambdaMagSq, discrMag;
   complexNum discr;
   static complexNum fourOverLambda = { 0.0, 0.0 };
   static GLboolean firstPoint = true;

   if (firstPoint) {
      /*  Compute the complex number: 4.0 divided by lambda.  */
      lambdaMagSq = lambda.x * lambda.x + lambda.y * lambda.y;
      fourOverLambda.x =  4.0 * lambda.x / lambdaMagSq;
      fourOverLambda.y = -4.0 * lambda.y / lambdaMagSq;
      firstPoint = false;
   }
   discr.x = 1.0 - (z->x * fourOverLambda.x - z->y * fourOverLambda.y);
   discr.y = z->x * fourOverLambda.y + z->y * fourOverLambda.x;
   discrMag = sqrt (discr.x * discr.x + discr.y * discr.y);

   /*  Update z, checking to avoid the sqrt of a negative number.  */
   if (discrMag + discr.x < 0)
      z->x = 0;
   else
      z->x = sqrt ((discrMag + discr.x) / 2.0);
```

```
    if (discrMag - discr.x < 0)
       z->y = 0;
    else
       z->y = 0.5 * sqrt ((discrMag - discr.x) / 2.0);

    /*  For half the points, use negative root,
     *  placing point in quadrant 3.
     */
    if (rand ( ) < RAND_MAX / 2) {
       z->x = -z->x;
       z->y = -z->y;
    }

    /*  When imaginary part of discriminant is negative, point
     *  should lie in quadrant 2 or 4, so reverse sign of x.
     */
    if (discr.y < 0)
       z->x = -z->x;

    /* Complete the calculation for the real part of z. */
    z->x = 0.5 * (1 - z->x);
}

void selfSqTransf (complexNum lambda, complexNum z, GLint numPoints)
{
   GLint k;

   /*  Skip the first few points.  */
   for (k = 0;  k < 10;  k++)
      solveQuadraticEq (lambda, &z);

   /*  Plot the specified number of transformation points.  */
   for (k = 0;  k < numPoints;  k++) {
      solveQuadraticEq (lambda, &z);
      plotPoint (z);
   }
}

void displayFcn (void)
{
   GLint numPoints = 10000;          // Set number of points to be plotted.
   complexNum lambda = { 3.0, 0.0 };  //  Set complex value for lambda.
   complexNum z0 = { 1.5, 0.4 };    //  Set initial point in complex plane.

   glClear (GL_COLOR_BUFFER_BIT);   //  Clear display window.

   glColor3f (0.0, 0.0, 1.0);       //  Set point color to blue.

   selfSqTransf (lambda, z0, numPoints);
   glFlush ( );
}
```

```
void winReshapeFcn (GLint newWidth, GLint newHeight)
{
   /*  Maintain an aspect ratio of 1.0, assuming that
    *  width of complex window = height of complex window.
    */
   glViewport (0, 0, newHeight, newHeight);

   glMatrixMode (GL_PROJECTION);
   glLoadIdentity ( );

   gluOrtho2D (xComplexMin, xComplexMax, yComplexMin, yComplexMax);

   glClear (GL_COLOR_BUFFER_BIT);
}

void main (int argc, char** argv)
{
   glutInit (&argc, argv);
   glutInitDisplayMode (GLUT_SINGLE | GLUT_RGB);
   glutInitWindowPosition (50, 50);
   glutInitWindowSize (winWidth, winHeight);
   glutCreateWindow ("Self-Squaring Fractal");

   init ( );
   glutDisplayFunc (displayFcn);
   glutReshapeFunc (winReshapeFcn);

   glutMainLoop ( );
}
```

A three-dimensional plot in variables x, y, and λ of the self-squaring function $f(z) = \lambda z(1 - z)$, with $|\lambda| = 1$, is given in Fig. 8-100. Each cross-sectional slice of this plot is a fractal curve in the complex plane.

Another squaring operation that produces a variety of fractal shapes is a slightly modified z^2 transformation. In this case, the fractal is the boundary region around the set of complex values z that do not diverge under the squaring transformation

$$\begin{aligned} z_0 &= z \\ z_k &= z_{k-1}^2 + z_0 \qquad k = 1, 2, 3, \ldots \end{aligned} \tag{8-115}$$

Thus, we first select a point z in the complex plane, then we compute the transformed position $z^2 + z$. At the next step, we square this transformed position and add the original z value. We repeat this procedure until we can determine whether or not the transformation is diverging.

Mathematicians had been aware of the unusual features of such squaring functions for some time, but these functions were difficult to analyze without computing aids. After the development of the digital computer, the convergence boundary for transformation 8-115 was plotted on a line printer. As the capabilities of digital computing increased, further graphical investigation into the properties

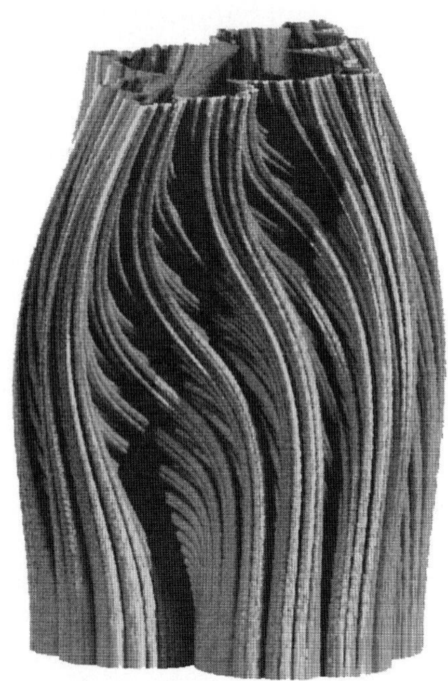

FIGURE 8-100 The function $f(z) = \lambda z(1 - z)$ plotted in three dimensions, with normalized λ values varying along the vertical axis. (*Courtesy of Alan Norton, IBM Research.*)

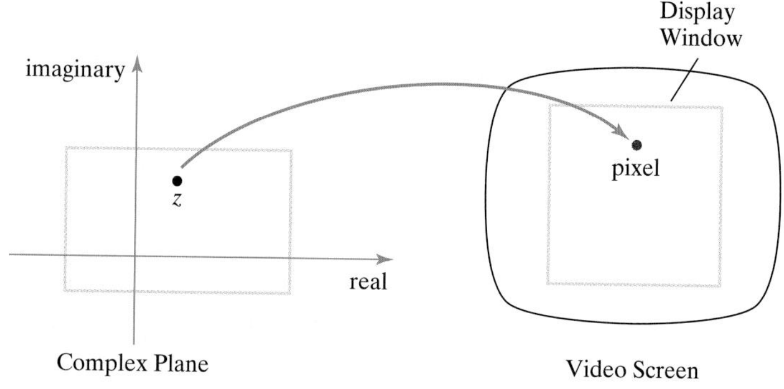

FIGURE 8-101 Mapping positions from a rectangular area in the complex plane to color-coded pixel positions within a screen display window.

of this function were possible. Subsequently, using more sophisticated computer-graphics techniques, Benoit Mandelbrot extensively studied this function, and the set of points that do not diverge under the transformation 8-115 has become known as the **Mandelbrot set.**

To implement transformation 8-115, we first choose a rectangular area in the complex plane. Positions within this area are then mapped to color-coded pixel positions within a display window on a video monitor (Fig. 8-101). The pixel colors are chosen according to the rate of divergence of the corresponding point in the complex plane under transformation 8-115. If the magnitude of a complex number is greater than 2, then it will quickly diverge as it is repeatedly squared. Therefore, we can set up a loop to repeat the squaring operations until either the magnitude of the complex number exceeds 2 or we have reached a preset number of iterations. The maximum number of iterations depends on the amount of detail we want to display and the number of points to be plotted. This value is often set to some value between 100 and 1,000, although lower values can be used to speed up the calculations. With lower settings for the iteration limit, however, we do tend to lose some detail along the boundary (Julia set) of the convergence region. At the end of the loop, we select a color value according to the number of iterations executed by the loop. For example, we can color the pixel black if the iteration count is at the maximum value (a nondiverging point), and we can color the pixel red if the iteration count is near 0. Other color values can then be chosen according to the value of the iteration count within the interval from 0 to the maximum value. By choosing different color mappings and different sections of the complex plane, we can generate a variety of dramatic displays for positions in the vicinity of the fractal boundary that encloses the nondivergent points. One

(a)

(b)

(c)

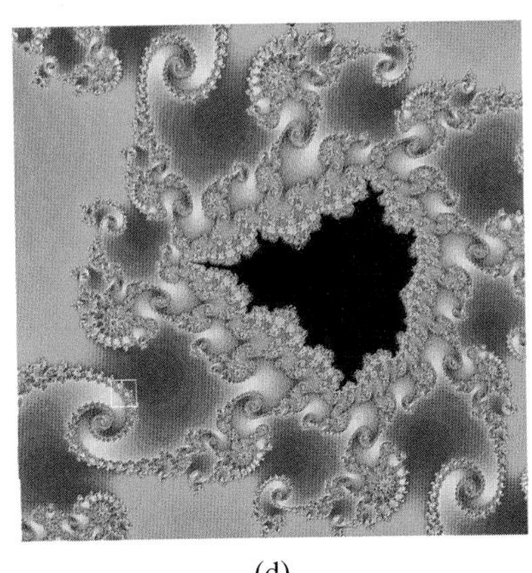

(d)

(e)

(f)

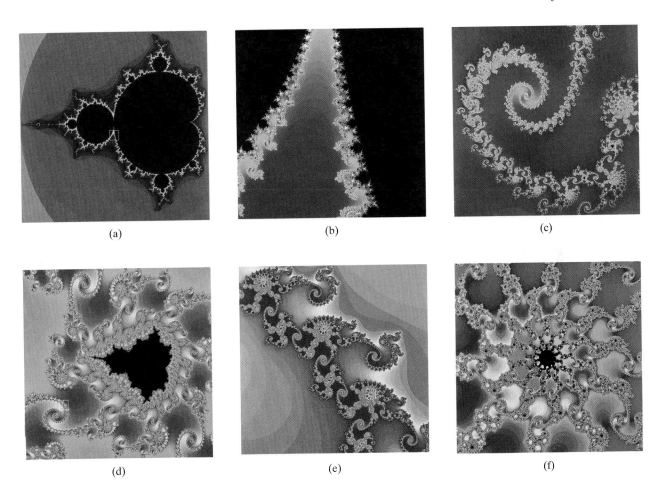

FIGURE 8-102 Zooming in on the fractal boundaries for transformation 8-115. Starting with a display of the Mandelbrot set, the black region in (a), and its surrounding areas, we zoom in on selected border regions (b) through (f). The white box outline shows the rectangular area selected for each successive zoom. Different color combinations are chosen at each step to enhance the displayed zoom patterns. (*Courtesy of Brian Evans, Vanderbilt University.*)

choice for color coding the pixel positions in the region around the Mandelbrot set is shown in Fig. 8-102(a).

An implementation of transformation 8-115 for displaying the set of convergence points and its boundaries is given in the following program. The major part of the convergence set is contained within the following region of the complex plane.

$$-2.00 \leq \text{Re}(z) \leq 0.50$$
$$-1.20 \leq \text{Im}(z) \leq 1.20$$

We can explore the details along the boundary of the Mandelbrot set by choosing successively smaller rectangular regions in the complex plane so that we can zoom in on selected areas of the display. Figure 8-102 shows a color-coded display of the region around the convergence set and a series of zooms that illustrate some of the remarkable features of this squaring transformation.

```
#include <GL/glut.h>

/*  Set initial size of the display window.  */
GLsizei winWidth = 500, winHeight = 500;

/*  Set limits for the rectangular area in complex plane.  */
GLfloat xComplexMin = -2.00, xComplexMax = 0.50;
GLfloat yComplexMin = -1.25, yComplexMax = 1.25;

GLfloat complexWidth = xComplexMax - xComplexMin;
GLfloat complexHeight = yComplexMax - yComplexMin;

class complexNum {
   public:
      GLfloat x, y;
};

struct color { GLfloat r, g, b; };

void init (void)
{
   /*  Set display-window color to white.  */
   glClearColor (1.0, 1.0, 1.0, 0.0);
}

void plotPoint (complexNum z)
{
    glBegin (GL_POINTS);
        glVertex2f (z.x, z.y);
    glEnd ( );
}

/*  Calculate the square of a complex number.  */
complexNum complexSquare (complexNum z)
{
   complexNum zSquare;

   zSquare.x = z.x * z.x - z.y * z.y;
   zSquare.y = 2 * z.x * z.y;
   return zSquare;
}

GLint mandelSqTransf (complexNum z0, GLint maxIter)
{
   complexNum z = z0;
   GLint count = 0;

   /*  Quit when z * z > 4  */
   while ((z.x * z.x + z.y * z.y <= 4.0) && (count < maxIter)) {
      z = complexSquare (z);
      z.x += z0.x;
      z.y += z0.y;
      count++;
   }
   return count;
}
```

```
void mandelbrot (GLint nx, GLint ny, GLint maxIter)
{
   complexNum z, zIncr;
   color ptColor;

   GLint iterCount;

   zIncr.x =  complexWidth / GLfloat (nx);
   zIncr.y =  complexHeight / GLfloat (ny);

   for (z.x = xComplexMin;  z.x < xComplexMax;  z.x += zIncr.x)
      for (z.y = yComplexMin;  z.y < yComplexMax;  z.y += zIncr.y) {
         iterCount = mandelSqTransf (z, maxIter);
         if (iterCount >= maxIter)
            /*  Set point color to black.  */
            ptColor.r = ptColor.g = ptColor.b = 0.0;
            else if (iterCount > (maxIter / 8)) {
                    /*  Set point color to orange.  */
                    ptColor.r = 1.0;
                    ptColor.g = 0.5;
                    ptColor.b = 0.0;
                 }
                 else if (iterCount > (maxIter / 10)) {
                         /*  Set point color to red.  */
                         ptColor.r = 1.0;
                         ptColor.g = ptColor.b = 0.0;
                      }
                      else if (iterCount > (maxIter /20)) {
                              /*  Set point color to dark blue.  */
                              ptColor.b = 0.5;
                              ptColor.r = ptColor.g = 0.0;
                           }
                           else if (iterCount > (maxIter / 40)) {
                                   /*  Set point color to yellow.  */
                                   ptColor.r = ptColor.g = 1.0;
                                   ptColor.b = 0.0;
                                }
                                else if (iterCount > (maxIter / 100)) {
                                        /*  Set point color to dark green.  */
                                        ptColor.r = ptColor.b = 0.0;
                                        ptColor.g = 0.3;
                                     }

                                     else {
                                          /*  Set point color to cyan.  */
                                          ptColor.r = 0.0;
                                          ptColor.g = ptColor.b = 1.0;
                                     }
          /*  Plot the color point.  */
          glColor3f (ptColor.r, ptColor.g, ptColor.b);
          plotPoint (z);
      }
}
```

```
void displayFcn (void)
{
   /*  Set number of x and y subdivisions and the max iterations.  */
   GLint nx = 1000, ny = 1000, maxIter = 1000;

   glClear (GL_COLOR_BUFFER_BIT);    //  Clear display window.

   mandelbrot (nx, ny, maxIter);
   glFlush ( );
}

void winReshapeFcn (GLint newWidth, GLint newHeight)
{
   /*  Maintain an aspect ratio of 1.0, assuming that
    *  complexWidth = complexHeight.
    */
   glViewport (0, 0, newHeight, newHeight);

   glMatrixMode (GL_PROJECTION);
   glLoadIdentity ( );

   gluOrtho2D (xComplexMin, xComplexMax, yComplexMin, yComplexMax);

   glClear (GL_COLOR_BUFFER_BIT);
}

void main (int argc, char** argv)
{
   glutInit (&argc, argv);
   glutInitDisplayMode (GLUT_SINGLE | GLUT_RGB);
   glutInitWindowPosition (50, 50);
   glutInitWindowSize (winWidth, winHeight);
   glutCreateWindow ("Mandelbrot Set");

   init ( );
   glutDisplayFunc (displayFcn);
   glutReshapeFunc (winReshapeFcn);

   glutMainLoop ( );
}
```

Complex-function transformations, such as Eq. 8-111, can be extended to produce fractal surfaces and fractal solids. Methods for generating these objects use *quaternion* representations (Appendix A) for transforming points in three-dimensional and four-dimensional space. A quaternion has four components, with one real-number term and three imaginary-number terms. We can represent a quaternion in the following form, as an extension of the concept of a number in the complex plane,

$$q = s + ia + jb + kc \tag{8-116}$$

where $i^2 = j^2 = k^2 = -1$. The real-number term s is also referred to as the *scalar part* of the quaternion, and the imaginary terms are called the quaternion *vector part* $\mathbf{v} = (a, b, c)$.

Using the rules for quaternion multiplication and addition discussed in Appendix A, we can apply self-squaring functions and other iteration methods to generate surfaces of fractal objects. A basic procedure is to test points in complex space until we can identify the boundary between the diverging and nondiverging positions. For example, if we first locate a nondiverging (interior) position, then we test neighboring points from that position until a diverging (exterior) point is identified. The preceding interior point is then retained as a boundary-surface position. Neighbors of this surface point are then tested to determine whether they are inside (converging) or outside (diverging). Any inside point that connects to an outside point is a surface position. In this way, the procedure threads its way along the fractal boundary without straying far from the surface. When four-dimensional fractals are generated, three-dimensional slices are projected onto the two-dimensional surface of the video monitor.

Procedures for generating self-squaring fractals in four-dimensional space require considerable computation time for evaluating the iteration function and for testing positions for convergence or divergence. Each point on a surface can be represented as a small cube, giving the inner and outer limits of the surface. Output from such programs for the three-dimensional projections of the fractal typically contain more than a million vertices for the surface cubes. We display the fractal object by applying illumination models to determine the color for each surface cube. Visible-surface detection methods are also applied so that only visible surfaces of the object are displayed. Figures 8-103 and 8-104 show examples of self-squaring, four-dimensional fractals with projections into three dimensions.

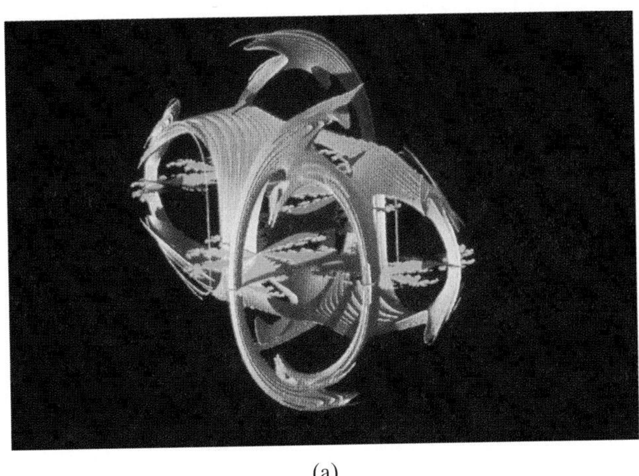

(a)

(b)

FIGURE 8-103 Three-dimensional projections of four-dimensional fractals generated with the self-squaring, quaternion function $f(q) = \lambda q(1 - q)$, using (a) $\lambda = 1.475 + 0.9061i$ and (b) $\lambda = -0.57 + i$. (*Courtesy of Alan Norton, IBM Research.*)

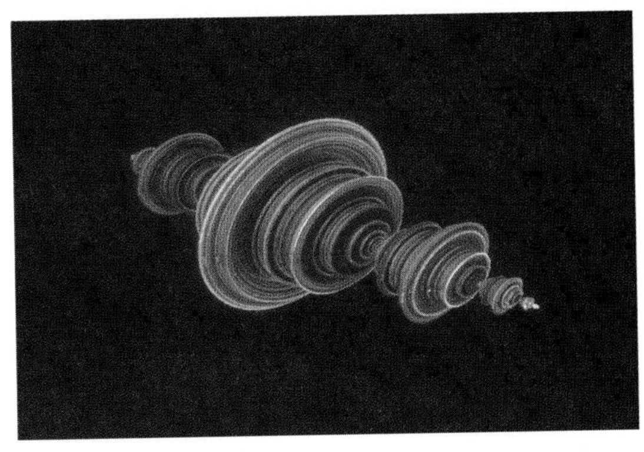

FIGURE 8-104 A three-dimensional surface projection of a four-dimensional object generated with the self-squaring, quaternion function $f(q) = q^2 - 1$. (*Courtesy of Alan Norton, IBM Research.*)

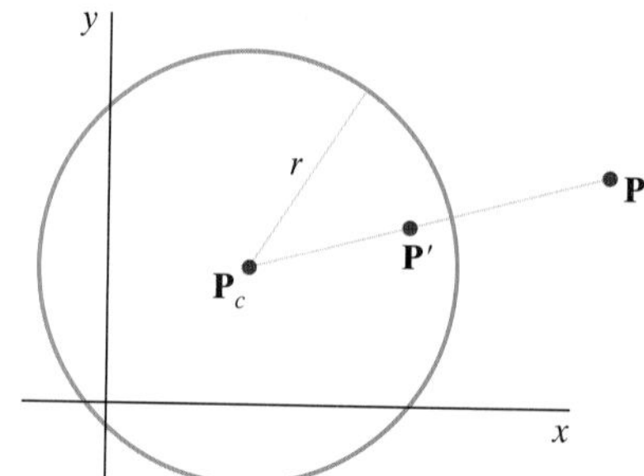

FIGURE 8-105 Inverting point **P** to a position **P′** inside a circle with radius r.

Self-Inverse Fractals

Various geometric inversion transformations can be used to create fractal shapes. Again, we start with an initial set of points, and we repeatedly apply nonlinear inversion operations to transform the initial points into a fractal.

As an example, we consider a two-dimensional inversion transformation with respect to a circle of radius r and center position $\mathbf{P}_c = (x_c, y_c)$. A point **P** outside the circle is inverted to a position **P′** inside the circle (Fig. 8-105) with the transformation

$$(\overline{\mathbf{P}_c\mathbf{P}})(\overline{\mathbf{P}_c\mathbf{P}'}) = r^2 \qquad (8\text{-}117)$$

where both **P** and **P′** lie on a straight line passing through the circle center $\mathbf{P}_c$. We can also use Eq. 8-117 to transform positions that are inside the circle. Some inside positions transform to outside positions, while other inside positions transform to inside positions.

If the coordinates of the two points are represented as $\mathbf{P} = (x, y)$ and $\mathbf{P}' = (x', y')$, we can write Eq. 8-117 as

$$[(x - x_c)^2 + (y - y_c)^2]^{1/2}[(x' - x_c)^2 + (y' - y_c)^2]^{1/2} = r^2$$

Also, since the two points are along a line passing through the circle center, we have $(y - y_c)/(x - x_c) = (y' - y_c)/(x' - x_c)$. Therefore, the transformed coordinate values for position **P′** are

$$x' = x_c + \frac{r^2(x - x_c)}{(x - x_c)^2 + (y - y_c)^2}, \qquad y' = y_c + \frac{r^2(y - y_c)}{(x - x_c)^2 + (y - y_c)^2} \qquad (8\text{-}118)$$

Thus, points outside the circle are mapped to positions within the circle circumference, with distant points ($\pm\infty$) transformed to the circle center. Conversely, points near the circle center are mapped to distant points outside the circle. As we move out from the circle center, points are mapped to outside positions closer to the circle circumference. And inside points near the circumference are transformed to inside positions closer to the circle center. For example, outside x values in the range from r to $+\infty$ map to x' values in the range from $\frac{r}{2}$ to 0, for a circle centered at the origin, $(x_c, y_c) = (0, 0)$. Inside values for x in the range from $\frac{r}{2}$ to 0 map to the x' values from r to $+\infty$, for a circle centered at the origin, and inside x values from $\frac{r}{2}$ to r are transformed to values in the range from r to $\frac{r}{2}$. Similar results are obtained for negative values of x.

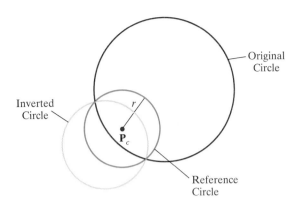

FIGURE 8-106 Inversion of a circle that does not pass through the origin of the reference circle.

We can apply this transformation to various objects, such as straight lines, circles, or ellipses. A straight line that passes through the circle center is invariant under this inversion transformation; it maps into itself. But a straight line that does not pass through the circle center inverts into a circle whose circumference contains the center point $\mathbf{P}_c$. And any circle that passes through the center of the reference circle is inverted into a straight line that does not pass through the circle center. If the circle does not intersect the center of the reference circle, it inverts into another circle, as in Fig. 8-106. Another invariant inversion is the transformation of a circle that is orthogonal to the reference circle. That is, the tangents of the two circles are perpendicular at the intersection points.

We can create various fractal shapes with this inversion transformation by starting with a set of circles and repeatedly applying the transformation using different reference circles. Similarly, we can apply circle inversion with respect to a set of straight lines. Comparable inversion methods can be developed for other two-dimensional shapes. And, we can generalize the procedure to spheres, planes, or other three-dimensional objects.

8-24 SHAPE GRAMMARS AND OTHER PROCEDURAL METHODS

A number of other procedural methods can be used to design object shapes or levels of surface detail. **Shape grammars** are sets of production rules that can be applied to an initial object to add layers of detail that are harmonious with the original shape. Transformations can be applied to alter the geometry (shape) of the object, or the transformation rules can be applied to add details for surface color or texture.

Given a set of production rules, a shape designer can experiment by applying different rules at each step of the transformation from a given initial object to the final structure. Figure 8-107 shows four geometric substitution rules for altering triangle shapes. The geometry transformations for these rules can be expressed algorithmically by the system, based on an input picture drawn with a

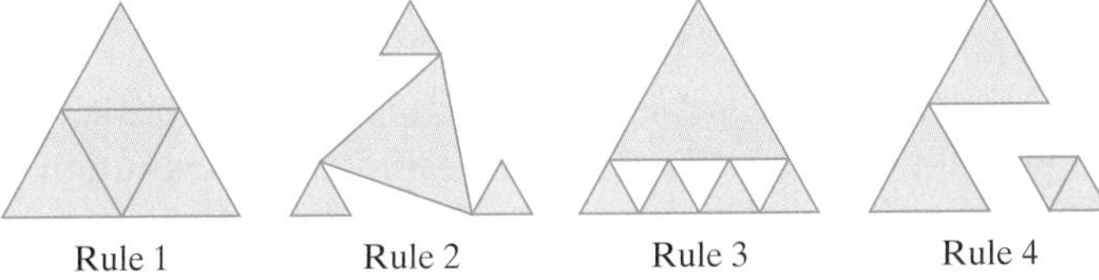

FIGURE 8-107 Four geometric substitution rules for subdividing and altering the shape of an equilateral triangle.

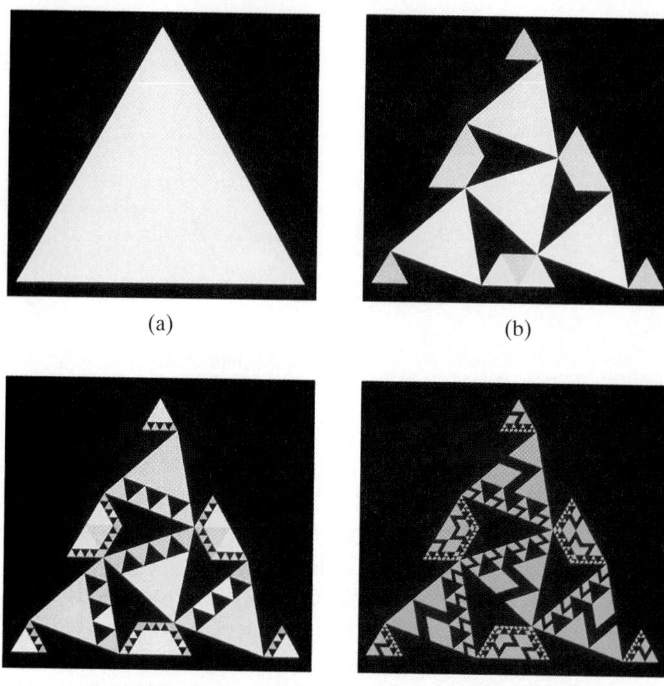

FIGURE 8-108 An equilateral triangle (a) is converted to shape (b) using substitution rules 1 and 2 in Fig. 8-107. Rule 3 is then used to convert (b) into shape (c), which in turn is transformed to (d) using rule 4. *(Courtesy of Andrew Glassner, Xerox PARC (Palo Alto Research Center). © 1992.)*

FIGURE 8-109 A design created with geometric substitution rules for altering triangle shapes. *(Courtesy of Andrew Glassner, Xerox PARC (Palo Alto Research Center). © 1992).*

production-rule editor. That is, each rule can be described graphically by showing the initial and final shapes. Implementations can then be set up in Mathematica or some programming language with graphics capability.

An application of the geometric substitutions in Fig. 8-107 is given in Fig. 8-108, where Fig. 8-108(d) is obtained by applying the four rules in succession, starting with the initial triangle in Fig. 8-108(a). Figure 8-109 shows another shape created with triangle substitution rules.

Three-dimensional shape and surface features are transformed with similar operations. Figure 8-110 shows the results of geometric substitutions applied to polyhedra. The initial shape for the objects shown in Figure 8-111 is an icosahedron

FIGURE 8-110 A design created with geometric substitution rules for altering prism shapes. The initial shape for this design is a representation of Rubik's Snake. (*Courtesy of Andrew Glassner, Xerox PARC (Palo Alto Research Center).* © *1992.*)

FIGURE 8-111 Designs created on the surface of a sphere using triangle substitution rules applied to the plane faces of an icosahedron, followed by projections to the sphere surface. (*Courtesy of Andrew Glassner, Xerox PARC (Palo Alto Research Center).* © *1992.*)

FIGURE 8-112 Realistic scenery generated with the TDI-AMAP software package, which can generate over 100 varieties of plants and trees using procedures based on botanical laws. (*Courtesy of Thomson Digital Image.*)

(a polyhedron with 20 faces). Geometric substitutions were applied to the plane faces of the icosahedron, and the resulting polygon vertices were projected to the surface of an enclosing sphere.

Another set of production rules for describing the shape of objects is called *L-grammars*, or *graftals*. These rules are typically used to generate plant displays. For instance, the topology of a tree can be described as a trunk, with some attached branches and leaves. A tree can then be modeled with rules to provide a particular connection of the branches and the leaves on the individual branches. The geometrical description is then given by placing the object structures at particular coordinate positions.

Figure 8-112 shows a scene containing various plants and trees, constructed with a commercial plant-generator package. Procedures in the software apply botanical laws to generate the shapes for the plants and trees.

8-25 PARTICLE SYSTEMS

For some applications, it is often useful to describe one or more objects using a collection of disjoint pieces, called **particle systems.** This approach can be applied to describe objects with fluid-like properties that change over time by flowing, billowing, spattering, expanding, imploding, or exploding. Objects with these characteristics include clouds, smoke, fire, fireworks, waterfalls, and water spray. Particle systems have been employed, for instance, to model the planet explosion and expanding wall of fire due to the "genesis bomb" in the motion picture *Star Trek II: The Wrath of Khan*. And particle-system methods have been used to model other kinds of objects, including clumps of grass.

In a typical application, a system of particles is defined within some spatial region and then random processes are applied to vary system parameters over time. These system parameters include the motion path for the individual particles and their color and shape. At some randomly selected time, each particle is deleted.

Particle shapes could be described with small spheres, ellipsoids, or boxes, which can vary randomly over time. Also, particle transparency, color, and movement can all be randomly chosen. Motion paths for the particles could be described kinematically or defined with forces such as a gravity field.

As each particle moves, its path is plotted and displayed in a particular color. For example, a fireworks pattern can be displayed by randomly generating particles within a spherical region of space and allowing them to move radially outward, as in Fig. 8-113. The particle paths could be color-coded from red to yellow, for instance, to simulate the temperature of the exploding particles. Similarly, realistic displays of grass clumps have been modeled with "trajectory" particles (Fig. 8-114) that are shot up from the ground and fall back to earth under gravity. In this case, the particle paths can originate within a tapered cylinder, and they might be color-coded from green to yellow.

Figure 8-115 illustrates a particle-system simulation of a waterfall. The water particles fall from a fixed elevation, are deflected by an obstacle, then splash up from the ground. Different colors are used to distinguish the particle paths at each stage. An example of an animation simulating the disintegration of an object is shown in Fig. 8-116. The object on the left disintegrates into the particle distribution on the right. A composite scene formed with a variety of representations is given in Fig. 8-117. The scene is modeled using particle-system grass and fractal mountains, in addition to texture mapping and other surface-rendering procedures.

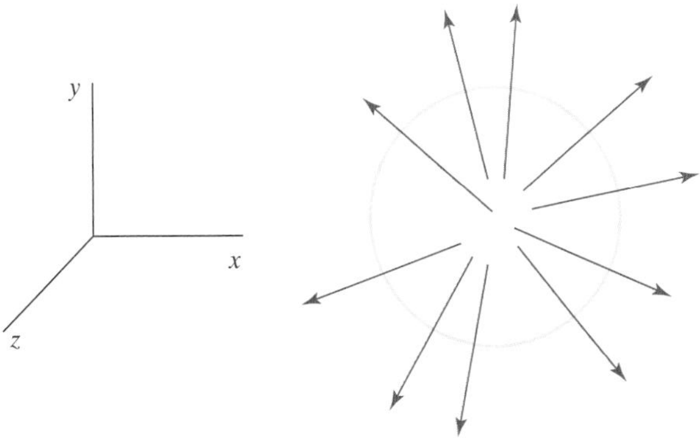

FIGURE 8-113 Modeling fireworks as a particle system with particles traveling radially outward from the center of a sphere.

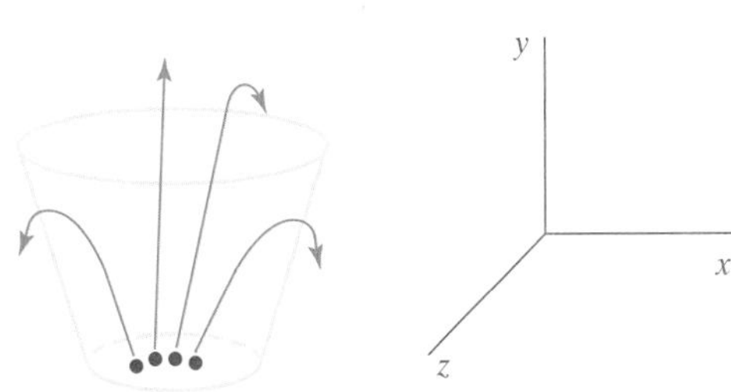

FIGURE 8-114 Modeling a clump of grass by firing particles upward within a tapered cylinder. The particle paths are parabolas due to the downward force of gravity.

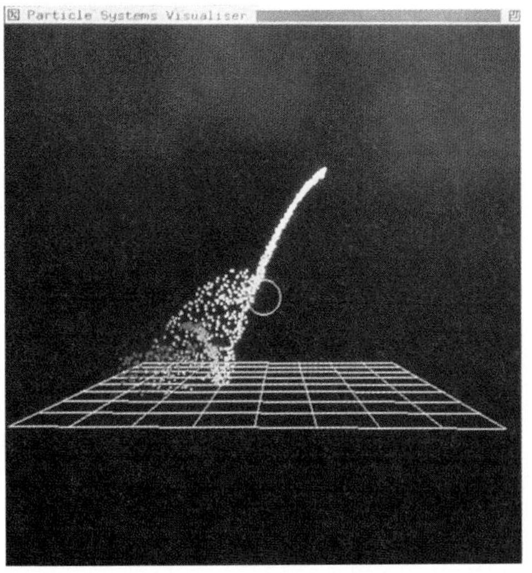

FIGURE 8-115 Simulation of the behavior of a waterfall hitting a stone (circle). The water particles are deflected by the stone and then splash up from the ground. (*Courtesy of M. Brooks and T. L. J. Howard, Department of Computer Science, University of Manchester.*)

FIGURE 8-116 An object disintegrating into a cloud of particles. (*Courtesy of Autodesk, Inc.*)

8-26 PHYSICALLY BASED MODELING

A nonrigid object, such as a rope, a cloth material, or a soft rubber ball, can be represented with **physically based modeling** methods that describe the behavior of the object in terms of the interaction of external and internal forces. An accurate description of the shape of a terry cloth towel draped over the back of a chair, for example, is obtained by considering the effect of the chair on the fabric loops in the cloth and the interaction between the cloth threads.

A common method for modeling a nonrigid object is to approximate the object with a network of point nodes with flexible connections between the nodes. One

FIGURE 8-117 A scene, entitled *Road to Point Reyes*, showing particle-system grass, fractal mountains, and texture-mapped surfaces. (*Courtesy of Pixar.* © *1983* Pixar.)

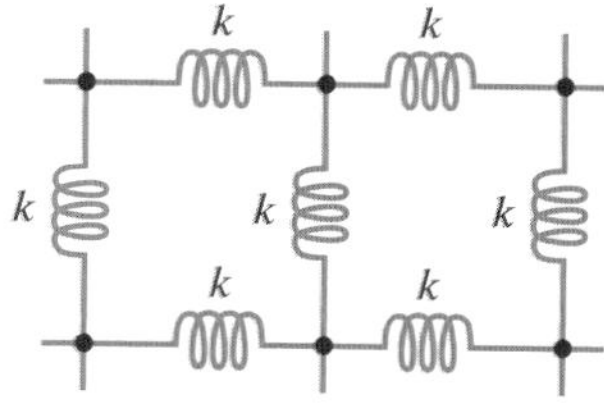

FIGURE 8-118 A two-dimensional spring network, constructed with identical spring constants k.

simple type of connection is a spring. Figure 8-118 shows a section of a two-dimensional spring network that could be used to approximate the behavior of a cloth towel or a sheet of rubber. Similar spring networks can be set up in three dimensions to model a rubber ball or a block of jello. For a homogeneous object, we can use identical springs throughout the network. If we want the object to have different properties in different directions, we can use different spring properties in different directions. When external forces are applied to a spring network, the amount of stretching or compression of the individual springs depends on the value set for the *spring constant* k, also called the *force constant* for the spring.

Horizontal displacement x of a node position under the influence of a force F_x is illustrated in Fig. 8-119. If the spring is not overstretched, we can closely approximate the amount of displacement x from the equilibrium position using Hooke's law:

$$F_s = -F_x = -kx \qquad (8\text{-}119)$$

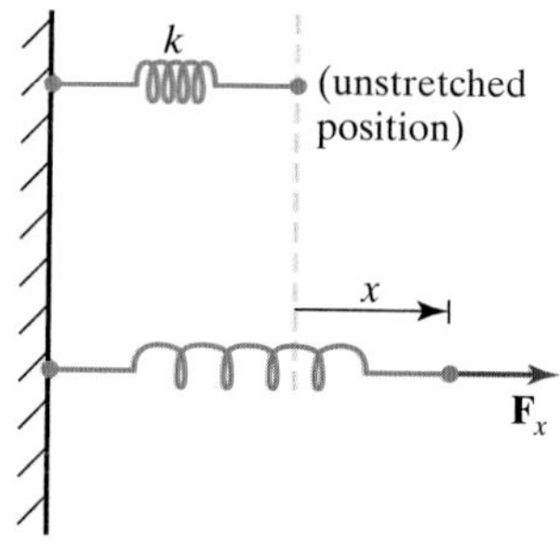

FIGURE 8-119 An external force F_x pulling on one end of a spring, with the other end rigidly fixed.

where F_s is the equal and opposite restoring force of the spring on the stretched node. This relationship holds also for horizontal compression of a spring by an amount x, and we have similar relationships for displacements and force components in the y and z directions.

If objects are completely flexible, they return to their original configuration when the external forces are removed. But if we want to model putty, or some other deformable material, we need to modify the spring characteristics so that the springs do not return to their original shape when the external forces are removed. Another set of applied forces could then deform the object in some other way.

Instead of using springs, we can also model the connections between nodes with elastic materials and minimize strain-energy functions to determine object shape under the influence of external forces. This method provides a better model for cloth, and various energy functions have been devised to describe the behavior of different cloth materials.

To model a nonrigid object, we first set up the external forces acting on the object. Then we consider the propagation of the forces throughout the network representing the object. This leads to a set of simultaneous equations that we must solve to determine the displacement of the nodes throughout the network.

Figure 8-120 shows a banana peel modeled with a spring network, and the scene in Fig. 8-121 shows examples of cloth modeling using energy functions, with a texture-mapped pattern on one cloth. By adjusting the parameters in a network using energy-function calculations, different kinds of cloth can be modeled. Figure 8-122 illustrates models for cotton, wool, and polyester cotton materials draped over a table.

Physically based modeling methods are also applied in animations to provide more accurate descriptions of motion paths. In the past, animations were often specified using spline paths and kinematics, where motion parameters are based

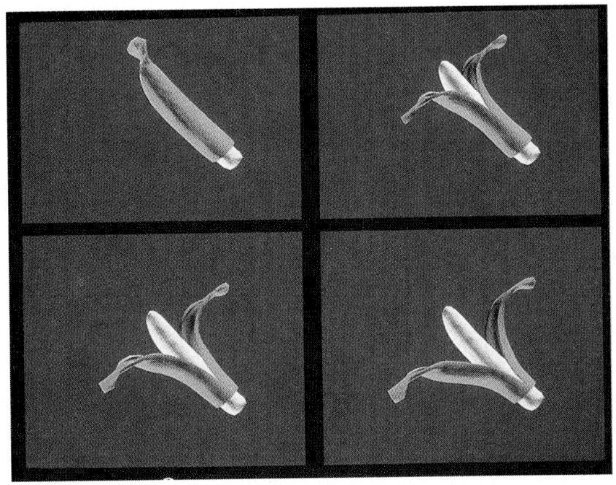

FIGURE 8-120 Modeling the flexible behavior of a banana peel with a spring network. (*Courtesy of David Laidlaw, John Snyder, Adam Woodbury, and Alan Barr, Computer Graphics Lab, California Institute of Technology.* © *1992.*)

FIGURE 8-121 Modeling the flexible behavior of cloth draped over furniture using energy-function minimization. (*Courtesy of Gene Greger and David E. Breen, Design Research Center, Rensselaer Polytechnic Institute.* © *1992.*)

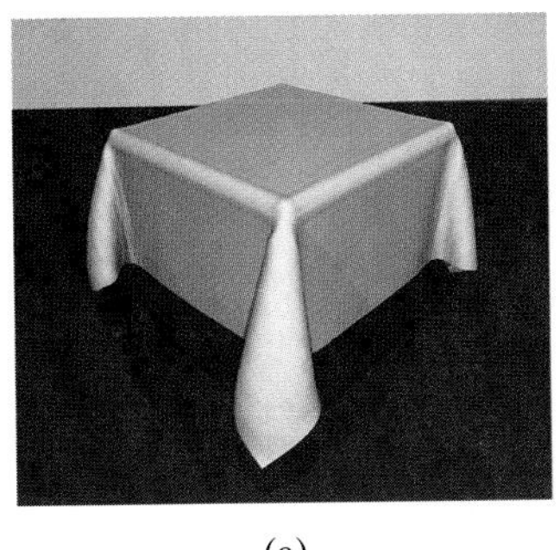

(a)

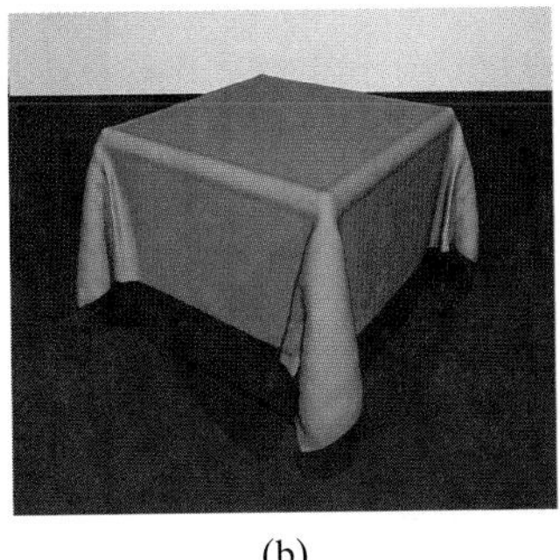

(b)

(c)

FIGURE 8-122 Modeling the characteristics of (a) cotton, (b) wool, and (c) polyester cotton using energy-function minimization. (*Courtesy of David E. Breen and Donald H. House, Design Research Center, Rensselaer Polytechnic Institute.* © *1992.*)

only on position and velocity. Physically based modeling describes motion using dynamical equations, involving forces and accelerations. Animation descriptions based on the equations of dynamics produce more realistic motions than those based on the equations of kinematics.

8-27 VISUALIZATION OF DATA SETS

The use of computer-graphics methods as an aid in scientific and engineering analysis is commonly referred to as **scientific visualization.** This involves the visualization of data sets and processes that may be difficult or impossible to analyze without graphical methods. For example, visualization techniques are needed to deal with the output of high-volume data sources such as computer monitors, satellite and spacecraft scanners, radio-astronomy telescopes, and medical scanners. Millions of data points are often generated from numerical solutions of computer simulations and from observational equipment, and it is difficult to determine trends and relationships by simply scanning the raw data. Similarly, visualization techniques are useful for analyzing processes that occur over a long time period or that cannot be observed directly, such as quantum-mechanical phenomena and special-relativity effects produced by objects traveling near the speed of light. Scientific visualization uses methods from computer graphics, image processing, computer vision, and other areas to visually display, enhance, and manipulate information to allow better understanding of the data. Similar methods employed by commerce, industry, and other nonscientific areas are sometimes referred to as **business visualization.**

Data sets are classified according to their spatial distribution and data type. Two-dimensional data sets have values distributed over a surface, and three-dimensional data sets have values distributed over the interior of a cube, a sphere, or some other region of space. Data types include scalars, vectors, tensors, and multivariate data.

Visual Representations for Scalar Fields

A scalar quantity is one that has a single value. Scalar data sets contain values that may be distributed in time, as well as over spatial positions, and the data values may also be functions of other scalar parameters. Some examples of physical scalar quantities are energy, density, mass, temperature, pressure, electric charge, electrical resistance, reflectivity, frequency, and water content.

A common method for visualizing a scalar data set is to use graphs or charts that show the distribution of data values as a function of other parameters, such as position and time. If the data are distributed over a surface, we could plot the data values as vertical bars rising from the surface, or we can interpolate the data values in some other way at selected surface positions. **Pseudo-color methods** are also used to distinguish different values in a scalar data set, and color-coding techniques can be combined with graph and chart methods. To color code a scalar data set, we choose a range of colors and map the range of data values to the color range. For example, blue could be assigned to the lowest scalar value, and red could be assigned to the highest value. Figure 8-123 gives an example of a color-coded surface plot. Color coding a data set sometimes requires careful consideration, because certain color combinations can lead to misinterpretations of the data.

FIGURE 8-123 A financial surface plot, showing stock-growth potential during the October 1987 stock-market crash. Red indicates high returns, and the plot shows that low-growth stocks performed better in the crash. (*Courtesy of Eng-Kiat Koh, Information Technology Institute, Republic of Singapore, and Encentuate, Inc., Cupertino, California.*)

Contour plots are used to display *isolines* (lines of constant value) for a scalar data set distributed over a surface. The isolines are spaced at some convenient interval to show the range and variation of the data values over the region of space. A typical application is a contour plot of elevations over a ground plane. Usually, contouring methods are applied to a set of data values that are distributed over a regular grid, as in Fig. 8-124. Regular grids have equally spaced grid lines, and data values are known at the grid intersections. Numerical solutions of computer simulations are usually set up to produce data distributions on a regular grid, while observational data sets are often irregularly spaced. Contouring methods have been devised for various kinds of nonregular grids, but nonregular data distributions are often converted to regular grids. A two-dimensional contouring algorithm traces the isolines from cell to cell within the grid by checking the four corners of grid cells to determine which cell edges are crossed by a particular isoline. The isolines are usually plotted as straight line sections across each cell, as illustrated in Fig. 8-125. Sometimes isolines are plotted with spline curves, but spline-fitting can lead to inconsistencies and misinterpretation of a data set. For example, two spline isolines could cross, or curved isoline paths might not be a true indicator of the data trends since data values are known only at the cell corners. Contouring packages can allow interactive adjustment of isolines by a researcher to correct any inconsistencies. An example of three, overlapping, color-coded contour plots in the xy plane is given in Fig. 8-126, and Fig. 8-127 shows contour lines and color coding for an irregularly shaped space.

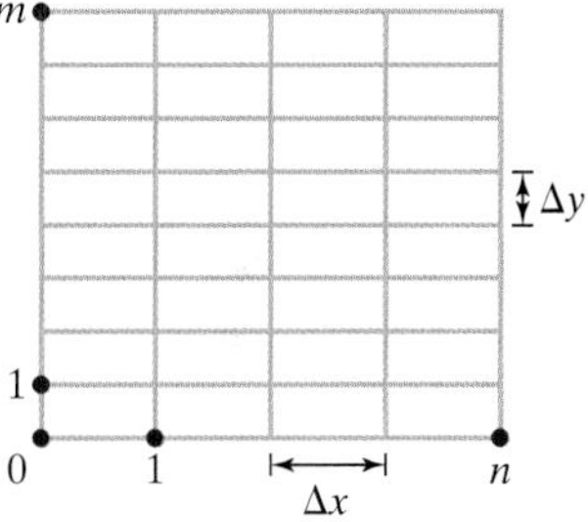

FIGURE 8-124 A regular, two-dimensional grid with data values at the intersections of the grid lines. The x grid lines have a constant Δx spacing, and the y grid lines have a constant Δy spacing, where the spacing in the x and y directions may not be the same.

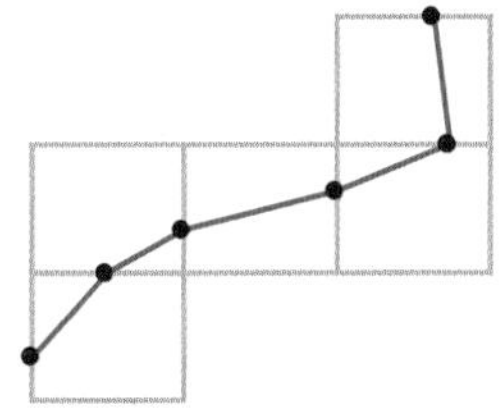

FIGURE 8-125 The path of an isoline across five grid cells.

For three-dimensional scalar data fields, we can take cross-sectional slices and display the two-dimensional data distributions over the slices. We could either color code the data values over a slice, or we could display isolines. Visualization packages typically provide a slicer routine that allows cross sections to be taken at any angle. Figure 8-128 shows a display generated by a commercial slicer-dicer package.

Instead of looking at two-dimensional cross sections, we can plot one or more **isosurfaces,** which are simply three-dimensional contour plots (Fig. 8-129). When two overlapping isosurfaces are displayed, the outer surface is made transparent so that we can view the shapes of both isosurfaces. Constructing an isosurface is similar to plotting isolines, except that now we have three-dimensional grid cells and we need to check the data values at the eight corners of a cell to locate sections of an isosurface. Figure 8-130 shows some examples of isosurface intersections with grid cells. Isosurfaces are usually modeled with triangle meshes, then surface-rendering algorithms are applied to display the final shape.

Volume rendering, which is often somewhat like an X-ray picture, is another method for visualizing a three-dimensional data set. The interior information about a data set is projected to a display screen using the ray-casting methods

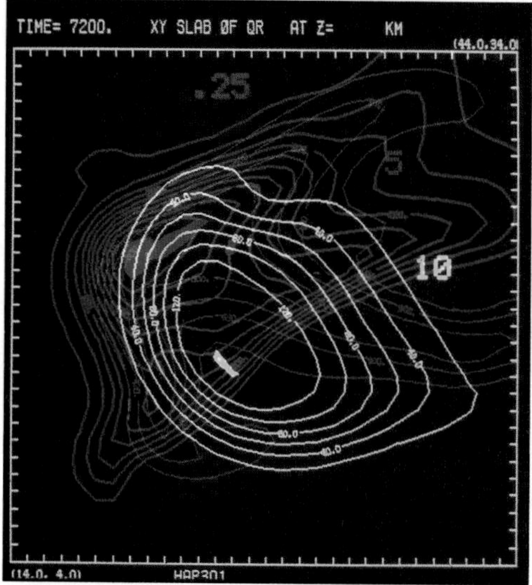

FIGURE 8-126 Color-coded contour plots for three data sets within the same region of the xy plane. (*Courtesy of the National Center for Supercomputing Applications, University of Illinois at Urbana-Champaign.*)

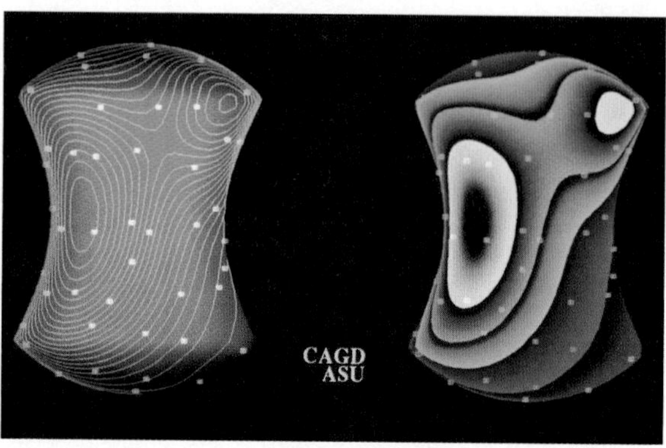

FIGURE 8-127 Color-coded contour plots over the surface of an apple-core shaped region of space. (*Courtesy of Greg Nielson, Department of Computer Science and Engineering, Arizona State University.*)

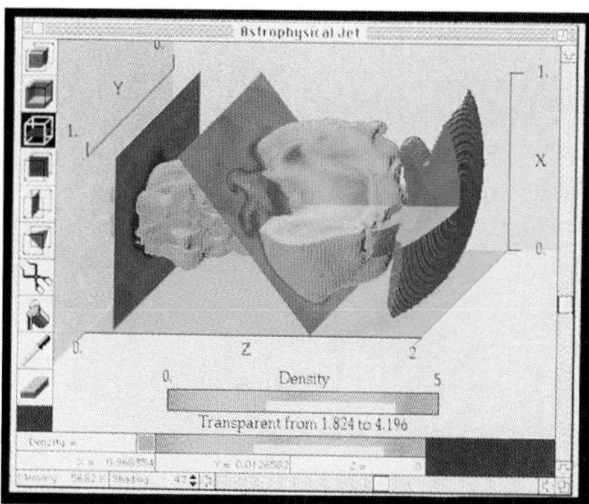

FIGURE 8-128 Cross-sectional slices of a three-dimensional data set. (*Courtesy of Spyglass, Inc.*)

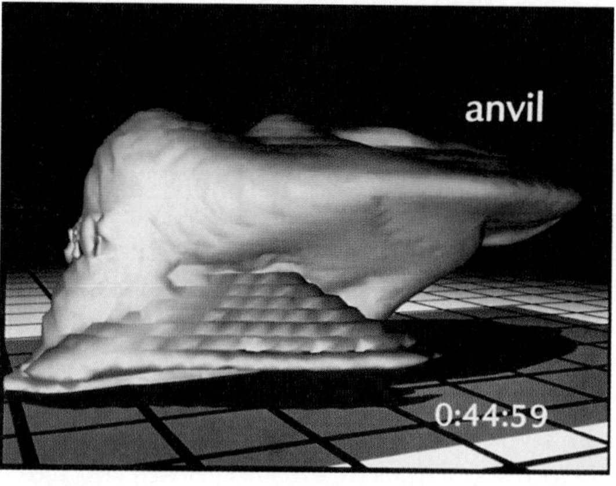

FIGURE 8-129 An isosurface generated from a set of water-content values obtained from a numerical model of a thunderstorm. (*Courtesy of Bob Wilhelmson, Department of Atmospheric Sciences and the National Center for Supercomputing Applications, University of Illinois at Urbana-Champaign.*)

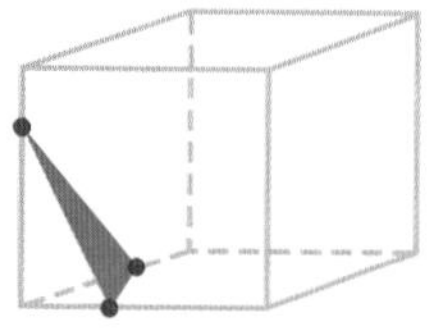
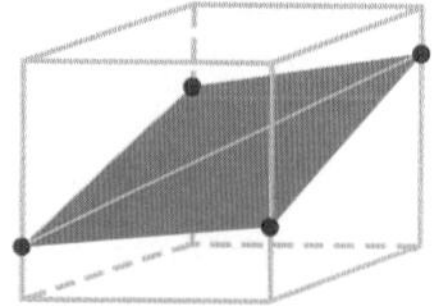
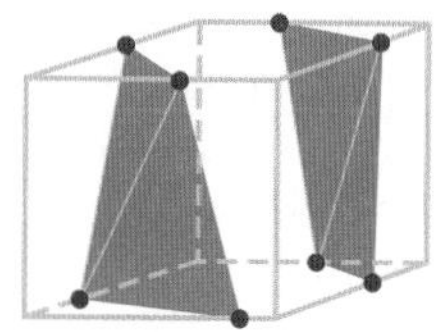
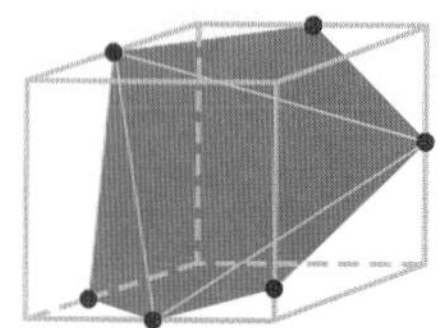

FIGURE 8-130 Isosurface intersections with grid cells, modeled with triangle patches.

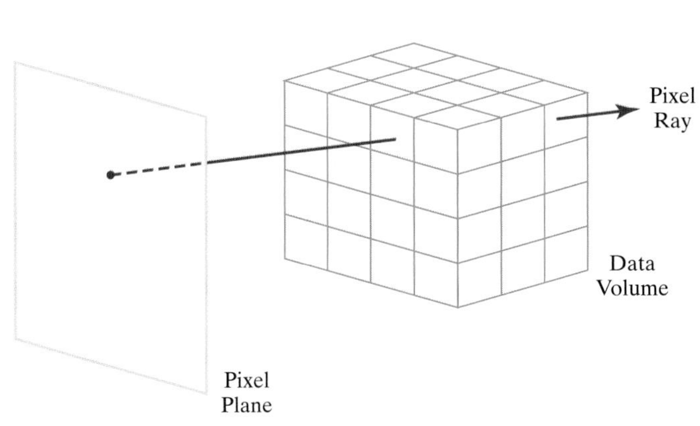

FIGURE 8-131 Volume visualization of a regular, Cartesian data grid using ray casting to examine interior data values.

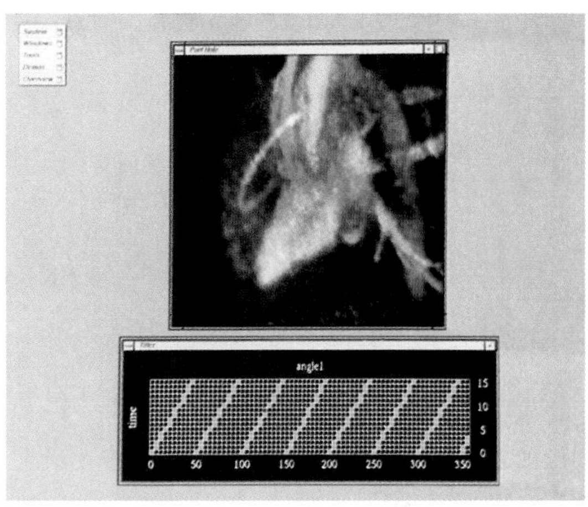

FIGURE 8-132 Volume visualization of a data set for a dog heart, obtained by plotting the color-coded distance to the maximum voxel value for each pixel. (*Courtesy of Patrick Moran and Clinton Potter, National Center for Supercomputing Applications, University of Illinois at Urbana-Champaign.*)

introduced in Section 8-20. Along the ray path from each screen pixel (Fig. 8-131), interior data values are examined and encoded for display. Often, data values at the grid positions are averaged so that one value is stored for each voxel of the data space. How the data are encoded for display depends on the application. Seismic data, for example, are often examined to find the maximum and minimum values along each ray. The values can then be color coded to give information about the width of the interval and the minimum value. In medical applications, the data values are opacity factors in the range from 0 to 1 for the tissue and bone layers. Bone layers are completely opaque, while tissue is somewhat transparent (low opacity). Along each ray, the opacity factors are accumulated until either the total is greater than or equal to 1, or until the ray exits at the back of the three-dimensional data grid. The accumulated opacity value is then encoded and displayed as a pixel color or as a gray-scale value. Figure 8-132 shows a volume visualization of a medical data set describing the structure of a dog heart. For this volume visualization, a color-coded plot of the distance to the maximum voxel value along each pixel ray was displayed.

Visual Representations for Vector Fields

A vector quantity **V** in three-dimensional space has three scalar values (V_x, V_y, V_z), one for each coordinate direction, and a two-dimensional vector has two components (V_x, V_y). Another way to describe a vector quantity is by giving its magnitude $|\mathbf{V}|$ and its direction as a unit vector **u**. As with scalars, vector quantities may be functions of position, time, and other parameters. Some examples of physical vector quantities are velocity, acceleration, force, electric current, and electric, magnetic, and gravitational fields.

One way to visualize a vector field is to plot each data point as a small arrow that shows the magnitude and direction of the vector. This method is most often used with cross-sectional slices, as in Fig. 8-133, since it can be difficult to see the data trends in a three-dimensional region that is cluttered with overlapping arrows. Magnitudes for vector values can be represented as variations in the lengths of the arrows, or we could display color-coded arrows that are all the same size.

We can also represent vector values by plotting *field lines,* also called *streamlines*. Field lines are commonly used for electric, magnetic, and gravitational fields. The magnitude of the vector values is indicated by the spacing between field lines, and the direction of the field is represented by the tangents (slopes) of the field lines, as shown in Fig. 8-134. An example of a streamline plot of a vector field is shown in Fig. 8-135. Streamlines can be displayed as wide arrows, particularly when a whirlpool, or vortex, effect is present. An example of this is given in Fig. 8-136, which displays swirling airflow patterns inside a thunderstorm. For animations of fluid flow, the behavior of the vector field can be visualized by

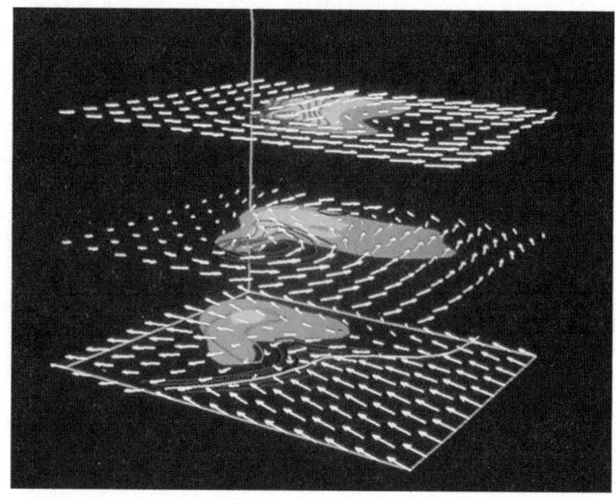

FIGURE 8-133 Arrow representation for a vector field over cross-sectional slices. *(Courtesy of the National Center for Supercomputing Applications, University of Illinois at Urbana-Champaign.)*

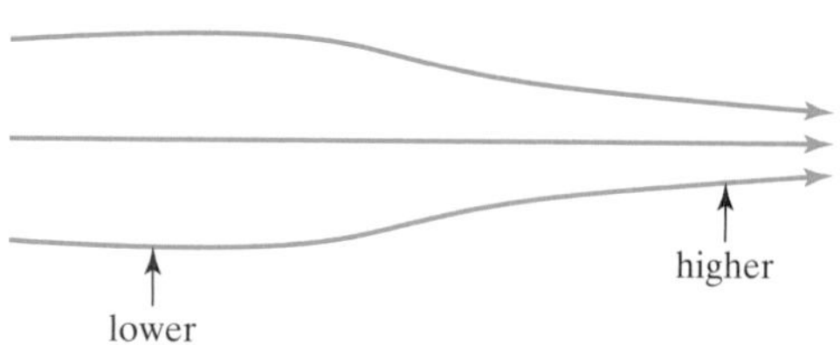

FIGURE 8-134 Field line representation for a vector data set.

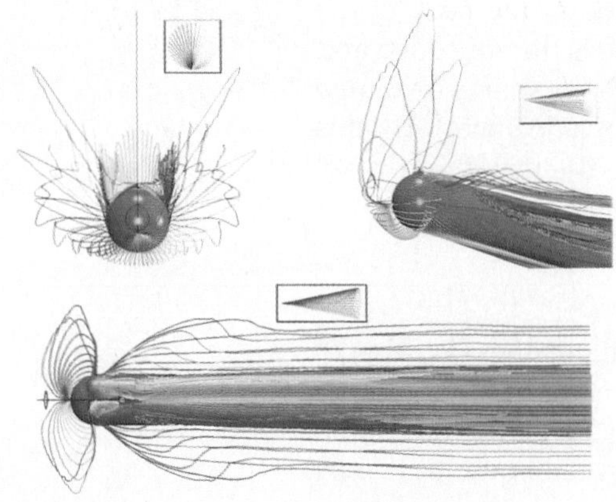

FIGURE 8-135 Visualizing airflow around a cylinder with a hemispherical cap that is tilted slightly relative to the incoming direction of the airflow. *(Courtesy of M. Gerald-Yamasaki, J. Huiltquist, and Sam Uselton, NASA Ames Research Center.)*

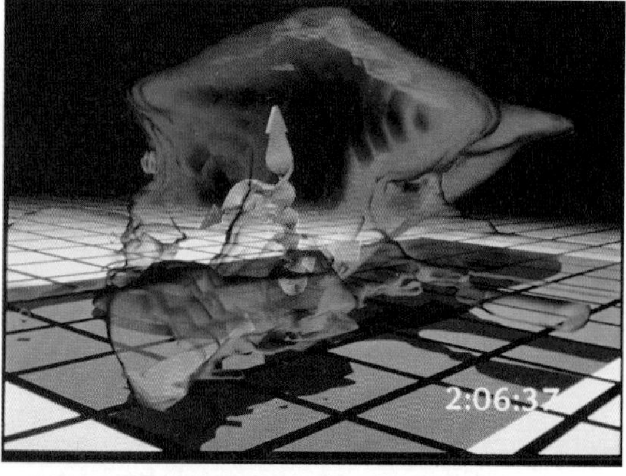

FIGURE 8-136 Twisting airflow patterns, visualized with wide streamlines inside a transparent isosurface plot of a thunderstorm. *(Courtesy of Bob Wilhelmson, Department of Atmospheric Sciences and the National Center for Supercomputing Applications, University of Illinois at Urbana-Champaign.)*

tracking particles along the flow direction. An example of a vector-field visualization using both streamlines and particles is shown in Fig. 8-137.

Sometimes, only the magnitudes of the vector quantities are displayed. This is often done when multiple quantities are to be visualized at a single position, or when the directions do not vary much in some region of space, or when vector directions are of less interest.

Visual Representations for Tensor Fields

A tensor quantity in three-dimensional space has nine components and can be represented with a 3 by 3 matrix. Actually, this representation is used for a *second-order tensor,* and higher-order tensors do occur in some applications, particularly general-relativity studies. Some examples of physical second-order tensors are stress and strain in a material subjected to external forces, conductivity (or resistivity) of an electrical conductor, and the metric tensor, which gives the properties of a particular coordinate space. The stress tensor in Cartesian coordinates, for example, can be represented as

$$\begin{bmatrix} \sigma_x & \sigma_{xy} & \sigma_{xz} \\ \sigma_{yx} & \sigma_y & \sigma_{yz} \\ \sigma_{zx} & \sigma_{zy} & \sigma_z \end{bmatrix} \tag{8-120}$$

Tensor quantities are frequently encountered in anisotropic materials, which have different properties in different directions. The x, xy, and xz elements of the conductivity tensor, for example, describe the contributions of electric-field components in the x, y, and z directions to the current in the x direction. Usually, physical tensor quantities are symmetric, so that the tensor has only six distinct values. For instance, the xy and yx components of the stress tensor have the same value.

Visualization schemes for representing all six components of a symmetric, second-order tensor quantity are based on devising shapes that have six parameters. One such graphical representation for a tensor is shown in Fig. 8-138. The

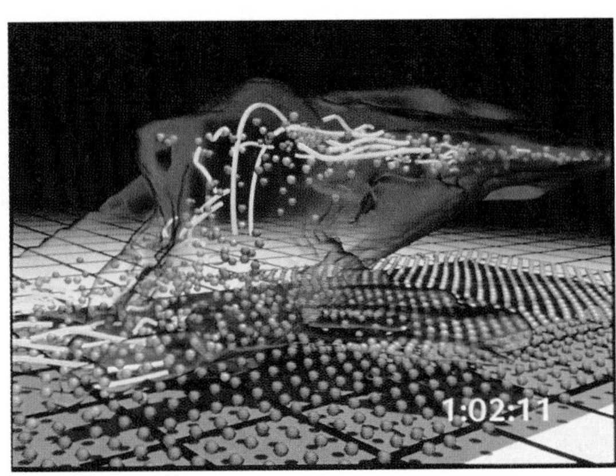

FIGURE 8-137 Airflow patterns, visualized with both streamlines and particle motion inside a transparent isosurface plot of a thunderstorm. Rising spherical particles are colored orange, and falling spherical particles are blue. (*Courtesy of Bob Wilhelmson, Department of Atmospheric Sciences and the National Center for Supercomputing Applications, University of Illinois at Urbana-Champaign.*)

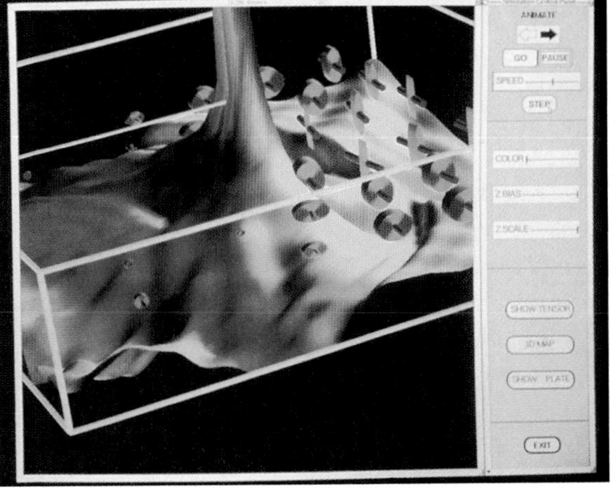

FIGURE 8-138 Representing stress and strain tensors with an elliptical disk and an arrow over the surface of a stressed material. (*Courtesy of Bob Haber, the National Center for Supercomputing Applications, University of Illinois at Urbana-Champaign.*)

three diagonal elements of the tensor are used to construct the magnitude and direction of the arrow, and the three off-diagonal terms are used to set the shape and color of the elliptical disk.

Instead of trying to visualize all six components of a symmetric tensor quantity, we can reduce the tensor to a vector or a scalar. Using a vector representation, we can simply display the values for the diagonal elements of the tensor. And by applying *tensor-contraction* operations, we can obtain a scalar representation. For example, stress and strain tensors can be contracted to generate a scalar strain-energy density that can be plotted at points in a material subject to external forces (Fig. 8-139).

Visual Representations for Multivariate Data Fields

In some applications, we may want to represent multiple data values at each grid position over some region of space. This data often contains a mixture of scalar, vector, and tensor values. As an example, fluid-flow data includes the fluid velocity, temperature, and density values at each three-dimensional position. Thus, we have five scalar values to display at each position, and the situation is similar to displaying a tensor field.

A method for displaying multivariate data fields is to construct graphical objects, sometimes referred to as **glyphs,** with multiple parts. Each part of a glyph represents a particular physical quantity. The size and color of each part can be used to display information about scalar magnitudes. To give directional information for a vector field, we can use a wedge, a cone, or some other pointing shape for the glyph part representing the vector. An example of the visualization of a multivariate data field using a glyph structure at selected grid positions is shown in Fig. 8-140.

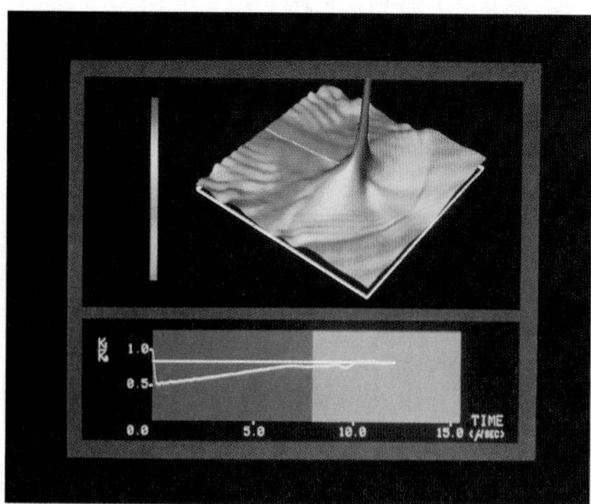

FIGURE 8-139 Representing stress and strain tensors with a strain-energy density plot in a visualization of crack propagation on the surface of a stressed material. (*Courtesy of Bob Haber, the National Center for Supercomputing Applications, University of Illinois at Urbana-Champaign.*)

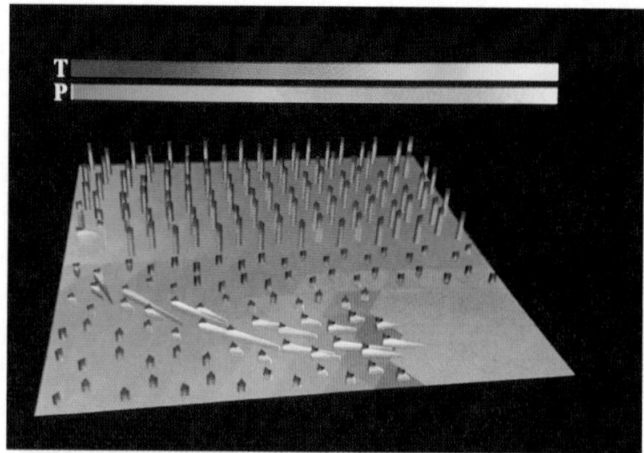

FIGURE 8-140 One frame from an animated visualization of a time-varying multivariate data field using glyphs. The wedge-shaped part of the glyph indicates the direction of a vector quantity at each point. (*Courtesy of the National Center for Supercomputing Applications, University of Illinois at Urbana-Champaign.*)

8-28 SUMMARY

Many representations have been developed for modeling the wide variety of objects and materials that we might want to display in a computer-graphics scene. In most cases, a three-dimensional object representation is rendered by a software package as a *standard graphics object,* whose surfaces are displayed as a polygon mesh.

Functions for displaying some common quadric surfaces, such as spheres and ellipsoids, are often available in graphics packages. Extensions of the quadrics, called superquadrics, provide additional parameters for creating a wider variety of object shapes. For the description of nonrigid, flexible curved surfaces we can use blobby objects to create shapes as combinations of Gaussian bumps.

The most widely used methods for CAD applications are the spline representations, which are piecewise continuous polynomial functions. A spline curve or surface is defined with a set of control points and the boundary conditions on the spline sections. Lines connecting the sequence of control points form the control graph, and all control points are within the convex hull of a spline object. The boundary conditions can be specified using parametric or geometric derivatives, and most spline representations use parametric boundary conditions. Interpolation splines connect all control points; approximation splines do not connect all control points. A spline surface can be described with the Cartesian product of two polynomials. Cubic polynomials are commonly used for the interpolation representations, which include the Hermite, cardinal, and Kochanek-Bartels splines. Bézier splines provide a simple and powerful approximation method for describing curved lines and surfaces, however the polynomial degree is determined by the number of control points and local control over curve shapes is difficult to attain. B-splines, which include Bézier splines as a special case, are a more versatile approximation representation, but they require the specification of a knot vector. Beta splines are generalizations of B-splines that are specified with geometric boundary conditions. And rational splines are formulated as the ratio of two spline representations. Rational splines can be used to describe quadrics, and they are invariant with respect to a perspective viewing transformation. A rational B-spline with a nonuniform knot vector is commonly referred to as a NURB. To determine the coordinate positions along a spline curve or surface, we can use forward-difference calculations or subdivision methods.

Other design techniques include sweep representations, constructive solid-geometry methods, octrees, and BSP trees. A sweep representation is formed with a translation or a rotation of a two-dimensional shape through a region of space. Constructive solid-geometry methods combine two or more three-dimensional shapes using the set operations: union, difference, and intersection. Octree and BSP trees use space-subdivision methods.

Fractal-geometry representations provide highly effective methods for describing natural phenomena. We can use these methods to model terrain, trees, bushes, water, and clouds, and for generating unusual graphics patterns. A fractal object can be described with a construction procedure and a fractal dimension. Fractal construction procedures include geometric constructions, midpoint-displacement methods, self-squaring operations in complex space, and inversion transformations. Other procedural methods for constructing object representations using transformation rules are shape grammars and graftals.

TABLE 8-1

SUMMARY OF OpenGL POLYHEDRON FUNCTIONS

Function	*Description*
`glutWireTetrahedron`	Display a wire-frame triangular pyramid (tetrahedron).
`glutSolidTetrahedron`	Display a surface-shaded tetrahedron.
`glutWireCube`	Display a wire-frame cube.
`glutSolidCube`	Display a surface-shaded cube.
`glutWireOctahedron`	Display a wire-frame octahedron.
`glutSolidOctahedron`	Display a surface-shaded octahedron.
`glutWireDodecahedron`	Display a wire-frame dodecahedron.
`glutSolidDodecahedron`	Display a surface-shaded dodecahedron.
`glutWireIcosahedron`	Display a wire-frame icosahedron.
`glutSolidIcosahedron`	Display a surface-shaded icosahedron.

TABLE 8-2

SUMMARY OF OpenGL QUADRIC-SURFACE AND CUBIC-SURFACE FUNCTIONS

Function	*Description*
`glutWireSphere`	Display a wire-frame GLUT sphere.
`glutSolidSphere`	Display a surface-shaded GLUT sphere.
`glutWireCone`	Display a wire-frame GLUT cone.
`glutSolidCone`	Display a surface-shaded GLUT cone.
`glutWireTorus`	Display a wire-frame GLUT torus with a circular cross section.
`glutSolidTorus`	Display a surface-shaded, circular cross section GLUT torus.
`glutWireTeapot`	Display a wire-frame GLUT teapot.
`glutSolidTeapot`	Display a surface-shaded GLUT teapot.
`gluNewQuadric`	Activate the GLU quadric renderer for an object name that has been defined with the declaration: `GLUquadricObj *nameOfObject;`
`gluQuadricDrawStyle`	Select a display mode for a predefined GLU object name.
`gluSphere`	Display a GLU sphere.
`gluCylinder`	Display a GLU cone, cylinder, or tapered cylinder.
`gluDisk`	Display a GLU flat, circular ring or solid disk.
`gluPartialDisk`	Display a section of a GLU flat, circular ring or solid disk.
`gluDeleteQuadric`	Eliminate a GLU quadric object.
`gluQuadricOrientation`	Define inside and outside orientations for a GLU quadric object.
`gluQuadricNormals`	Specify how surface-normal vectors should be generated for a GLU quadric object.
`gluQuadricCallback`	Specify a callback error function for a GLU quadric object.

TABLE 8-3

SUMMARY OF OpenGL BÉZIER FUNCTIONS

Function	*Description*
`glMap1`	Specify parameters for Bézier-curve display, color values, etc., and activate these routines using `glEnable`.
`glEvalCoord1`	Calculate a coordinate position for a Bézier curve.
`glMapGrid1`	Specify the number of equally spaced subdivisions between two Bézier-curve parameters.
`glEvalMesh1`	Specify the display mode and integer range for Bézier-curve display.
`glMap2`	Specify parameters for Bézier-surface display, color values, etc., and activate these routines using `glEnable`.
`glEvalCoord2`	Calculate a coordinate position for a Bézier surface.
`glMapGrid2`	Specify a two-dimensional grid of equally spaced subdivisions over a Bézier surface.
`glEvalMesh2`	Specify the display mode and integer range for the two-dimensional Bézier-surface grid.

Objects that exhibit fluidity, such as clouds, smoke, fire, water, and things that explode or implode, can be modeled with particle systems. Using this representation scheme, we describe an object with a set of particles and the rules that govern the particle movements.

Physically based modeling methods can be used to describe the characteristics of a flexible object, such as rope, rubber, or cloth. This scheme represents a material with a grid of spring-like sections and computes deformations using the forces acting upon the object.

Visualization techniques use computer-graphics methods to analyze data sets, which can include scalar, vector, and tensor values in various combinations. Data representations can be accomplished with color-coding or with the display of different object shapes.

Polygon surface facets for a standard graphics object can be specified in OpenGL using the polygon, triangle, or quadrilateral primitive functions. Also, GLUT routines are available for displaying the five regular polyhedra. Spheres, cones, and other quadric-surface objects can be displayed with GLUT and GLU functions, and a GLUT routine is provided for the generation of the cubic-surface Utah teapot. The core library of OpenGL contains functions for producing Bézier splines, and GLU functions are furnished for specifying B-splines and spline-surface trimming curves. Tables 8-1 through 8-4 summarize the OpenGL polyhedron, quadric, cubic, and spline functions discussed in this chapter.

TABLE 8-4

SUMMARY OF OpenGL B-SPLINE FUNCTIONS

Function	Description
`gluNewNurbsRenderer`	Activate the GLU B-spline renderer for an object name that has been defined with the declaration `GLUnurbsObj *bsplineName`.
`gluBeginCurve`	Begin assignment of parameter values for a specified B-spline curve with one or more sections.
`gluEndCurve`	Signal the end of the B-spline curve parameter specifications.
`gluNurbsCurve`	Specify the parameter values for a named B-spline curve section.
`gluDeleteNurbsRenderer`	Eliminate a specified B-spline.
`gluNurbsProperty`	Specify rendering options for a designated B-spline.
`gluGetNurbsProperty`	Determine the current value of a designated property for a particular B-spline.
`gluBeginSurface`	Begin assignment of parameter values for a specified B-spline surface with one or more sections.
`gluEndSurface`	Signal the end of the B-spline surface parameter specifications.
`gluNurbsSurface`	Specify the parameter values for a named B-spline surface section.
`gluLoadSamplingMatrices`	Specify viewing and geometric transformation matrices to be used in sampling and culling routines for a B-spline.
`gluNurbsCallback`	Specify a callback function for a designated B-spline and associated event.
`gluNurbsCallbackData`	Specify data values that are to be passed to the event callback function.
`gluBeginTrim`	Begin assignment of trimming-curve parameter values for a B-spline surface.
`gluEndTrim`	Signal the end of the trimming curve parameter specifications.
`gluPwlCurve`	Specify trimming-curve parameter values for a B-spline surface.

REFERENCES

A detailed discussion of superquadrics is contained in Barr (1981). For more information on blobby object modeling, see Blinn (1982). The meta-ball model is discussed in Nishimura (1985); the soft-object model is discussed in Wyville, Wyville, and McPheeters (1987).

Sources of information on parametric curve and surface representations include Bézier (1972), Barsky and Beatty (1983), Barsky (1984), Kochanek and Bartels (1984), Huitric and Nahas (1985), Mortenson (1985), Farin (1988), Rogers and Adams (1990), and Piegl and Tiller (1997).

Algorithms for octree and quadtree applications are given in Doctor and Torberg (1981), Yamaguchi, Kunii, and Fujimura (1984), and Brunet and Navazo (1990). Gordon and Chen (1991) present BSP-tree methods. And Requicha and Rossignac (1992) discuss solid-modeling methods.

For further information on fractal representations, see Mandelbrot (1977 and 1982), Fournier, Fussel, and Carpenter (1982), Norton (1982), Peitgen and Richter (1986), Peitgen and Saupe (1988), Hart, Sandin, and Kauffman (1989), Koh and Hearn (1992), and Barnsley (1993). Modeling methods for various natural phenomena are given in Fournier and Reeves (1986) and in Fowler, Meinhardt, and Prusinkiewicz (1992). Shape grammars are presented in Glassner (1992), and particle systems are discussed in Reeves (1983). Physically based modeling methods are presented in Barzel (1992).

A general introduction to visualization algorithms is given in Hearn and Baker (1991). Additional information on specific visualization techniques can be found in Sabin (1985), Lorensen and Cline (1987), Drebin, Carpenter, and Hanrahan (1988), Sabella (1988), Upson and Keeler (1988), Frenkel (1989), Nielson, Shriver, and Rosenblum (1990), and Nielson (1993). Guidelines for visual displays of information are given in Tufte (1990, 1997, and 2001).

Programming techniques for various representations can be found in Glassner (1990), Arvo (1991), Kirk (1992), Heckbert (1994), and Paeth (1995). Additional programming examples for the OpenGL Bézier-spline, B-spline, and trimming-curve functions can be found in Woo, Neider, Davis, and Shreiner (1999). Kilgard (1996) discusses the GLUT functions for displaying polyhedrons, quadric-surfaces, and the Utah teapot. And a complete listing of the OpenGL functions in the core library and in GLU is presented in Shreiner (2000).

EXERCISES

8-1 Set up an algorithm for converting a given sphere to a polygon-mesh representation.

8-2 Set up an algorithm for converting a given ellipsoid to a polygon-mesh representation.

8-3 Set up an algorithm for converting a given cylinder to a polygon-mesh representation.

8-4 Set up an algorithm for converting a given superellipsoid to a polygon-mesh representation.

8-5 Set up an algorithm for converting a metaball object to a polygon-mesh representation.

8-6 Write a routine to display a two-dimensional cardinal-spline curve, given an input set of control points in the xy plane.

8-7 Write a routine to display a two-dimensional Kochanek-Bartels curve, given an input set of control points in the xy plane.

8-8 What are the Bézier-curve blending functions for three control points specified in the xy plane? Plot each function and identify the minimum and maximum blending-function values.

8-9 What are the Bézier-curve blending functions for five control points specified in the xy plane? Plot each function and identify the minimum and maximum blending-function values.

8-10 Modify the program example in Section 8-10 to display any cubic Bézier curve, given a set of four input control points in the xy plane.

8-11 Modify the program example in Section 8-10 to display a Bézier curve of degree $n - 1$, given a set of n input control points in the xy plane.

8-12 Complete the OpenGL programming example in Section 8-18 to display any cubic Bézier curve, given a set of four input control points in the xy plane.

8-13 Modify the OpenGL program example in Section 8-18 to display any spatial cubic Bézier curve, given a set of four input control points in *xyz* space. Use an orthogonal projection to display the curve, with the viewing parameters specified as input.

8-14 Write a routine that can be used to design two-dimensional Bézier curve shapes that have first-order piecewise continuity. The number and position of the control points for each section of the curve are to be specified as input.

8-15 Write a routine that can be used to design two-dimensional Bézier curve shapes that have second-order piecewise continuity. The number and position of the control points for each section of the curve are to be specified as input.

8-16 Modify the program example in Section 8-10 to display any cubic Bézier curve, given a set of four input control points in the *xy* plane, using the subdivision method to calculate curve points.

8-17 Modify the program example in Section 8-10 to display any cubic Bézier curve, given a set of four input control points in the *xy* plane, using forward differences to calculate curve points.

8-18 What are the blending functions for a two-dimensional, uniform, periodic B-spline curve with $d = 5$?

8-19 What are the blending functions for a two-dimensional, uniform, periodic B-spline curve with $d = 6$?

8-20 Modify the programming example in Section 8-10 to display a two-dimensional, uniform, periodic B-spline curve, given an input set of control points, using forward differences to calculate positions along the curve path.

8-21 Modify the program in the previous example to display the B-spline curve using OpenGL functions.

8-22 Write a routine to display any specified conic in the *xy* plane using a rational Bézier-spline representation.

8-23 Write a routine to display any specified conic in the *xy* plane using a rational B-spline representation.

8-24 Develop an algorithm for calculating the normal vector to a Bézier surface at a given point $\mathbf{P}(u, v)$.

8-25 Derive expressions for calculating the forward differences for a given quadratic curve.

8-26 Derive expressions for calculating the forward differences for a given cubic curve.

8-27 Set up procedures for generating the description of a three-dimensional object from input parameters that define the object in terms of a translational sweep of a two-dimensional shape.

8-28 Set up procedures for generating the description of a three-dimensional object from input parameters that define the object in terms of a rotational sweep of a two-dimensional shape.

8-29 Devise an algorithm for generating solid objects as combinations of three-dimensional primitive shapes, such as a cube and a sphere, using constructive solid-geometry methods.

8-30 Modify the algorithm in the previous exercise so that the primitive shapes are defined in octree structures.

8-31 Develop an algorithm for encoding a two-dimensional scene as a quadtree representation.

8-32 Develop an algorithm for transforming a quadtree representation to pixel values in the frame buffer.

8-33 Write a routine to convert a polygon-mesh description of a three-dimensional object to an octree.

8-34 Using the random midpoint-displacement method, write a routine to create a mountain outline, starting with a horizontal line in the xy plane.

8-35 Write a routine to calculate elevations above a ground plane using the random midpoint-displacement method, given a set of corner elevations for the ground plane.

8-36 Write a program to display the fractal snowflake (Koch curve) for a given number of iterations.

8-37 Write a program to generate a fractal curve for a specified number of iterations using one of the generators in Fig. 8-73 or Fig. 8-74. What is the fractal dimension of the curve?

8-38 Write a program to generate fractal curves using the self-squaring function $f(z) = z^2 + \lambda$, where the complex constant λ is specified as input.

8-39 Write a program to generate a fractal curve using the self-squaring function $f(z) = i(z^2 + 1)$, where $i = \sqrt{-1}$.

8-40 Modify the programming example in Section 8-23 to use additional color levels in displaying the boundary regions around the Mandelbrot set.

8-41 Modify the program in the previous exercise to allow the colors and number of color levels to be given as input values.

8-42 Modify the program in the previous exercise to select and display any rectangular boundary region (the zoom area) around the Mandelbrot set.

8-43 Write a routine to implement point inversion, Eq. 8-118, for a specified circle and a set of point positions.

8-44 Devise a set of geometric-substitution rules for altering the shape of an equilateral triangle.

8-45 Write a program for the previous exercise that displays the stages in the conversion of the triangle.

8-46 Write a program to model and display an exploding sphere in the xy plane, using a particle system.

8-47 Modify the program of the previous exercise to explode a firecracker (cylinder).

8-48 Devise a routine for modeling a small rectangular cloth section as a grid of identical springs.

8-49 Write a routine to visualize a two-dimensional scalar data set using a pseudo-color representation.

8-50 Write a routine to visualize a two-dimensional scalar data set using contour lines.

8-51 Write a routine to visualize a two-dimensional vector data set using an arrow representation for the vector values. Use a fixed-size arrow with different color codings.

CHAPTER 9

Visible-Surface Detection Methods

A computer-graphics landscape showing the visible trees around a forest clearing.
(Courtesy of Thomson Digital Image, Inc.)

major consideration in the generation of realistic graphics displays is determining what is visible within a scene from a chosen viewing position. There are a number of approaches we can take to accomplish this, and numerous algorithms have been devised for efficient identification and display of visible objects for different types of applications. Some methods require more memory, some involve more processing time, and some apply only to special types of objects. Which method we select for a particular application can depend on such factors as the complexity of the scene, type of objects to be displayed, available equipment, and whether static or animated displays are to be generated. The various algorithms are referred to as **visible-surface detection** methods. Sometimes these methods are also referred to as **hidden-surface elimination** methods, although there can be subtle differences between identifying visible surfaces and eliminating hidden surfaces. With a wire-frame display, for example, we may not want to eliminate the hidden surfaces, but rather to display them with dashed boundaries or in some other way to retain information about their shape.

9-1 CLASSIFICATION OF VISIBLE-SURFACE DETECTION ALGORITHMS

We can broadly classify visible-surface detection algorithms according to whether they deal with the object definitions or with their projected images. These two approaches are called **object-space** methods and **image-space** methods, respectively. An object-space method compares objects and parts of objects to each other within the scene definition to determine which surfaces, as a whole, we should label as visible. In an image-space algorithm, visibility is decided point by point at each pixel position on the projection plane. Most visible-surface algorithms use image-space methods, although object-space methods can be used effectively to locate visible surfaces in some cases. Line-display algorithms, for instance, generally use object-space methods to identify visible lines in wire-frame displays, but many image-space visible-surface algorithms can be adapted easily to visible-line detection.

Although there are major differences in the basic approaches taken by the various visible-surface detection algorithms, most use sorting and coherence methods to improve performance. Sorting is used to facilitate depth comparisons by ordering the individual surfaces in a scene according to their distance from the view plane. Coherence methods are used to take advantage of regularities in a scene. An individual scan line can be expected to contain intervals (runs) of constant pixel intensities, and scan-line patterns often change little from one line to the next. Animation frames contain changes only in the vicinity of moving objects. And constant relationships can often be established between the objects in a scene.

9-2 BACK-FACE DETECTION

A fast and simple object-space method for locating the **back faces** of a polyhedron is based on the front-back tests discussed in Section 3-15. A point (x, y, z) is behind a polygon surface if

$$Ax + By + Cz + D < 0 \tag{9-1}$$

where $A, B, C,$ and D are the plane parameters for the polygon. When this position is along the line of sight to the surface, we must be looking at the back of the polygon. Therefore, we could use the viewing position to test for back faces.

We can simplify the back-face test by considering the direction of the normal vector $\mathbf{N}$ for a polygon surface. If $\mathbf{V}_{\text{view}}$ is a vector in the viewing direction from our camera position, as shown in Fig. 9-1, then a polygon is a back face if

$$\mathbf{V}_{\text{view}} \cdot \mathbf{N} > 0 \tag{9-2}$$

Furthermore, if object descriptions have been converted to projection coordinates and our viewing direction is parallel to the viewing z_v axis, then we need to consider only the z component of the normal vector $\mathbf{N}$.

In a right-handed viewing system with the viewing direction along the negative z_v axis (Fig. 9-2), a polygon is a back face if the z component, C, of its normal vector $\mathbf{N}$ satisfies $C < 0$. Also, we cannot see any face whose normal has z component $C = 0$, since our viewing direction is grazing that polygon. Thus, in general, we can label any polygon as a back face if its normal vector has a z component value that satisfies the inequality

$$C \leq 0 \tag{9-3}$$

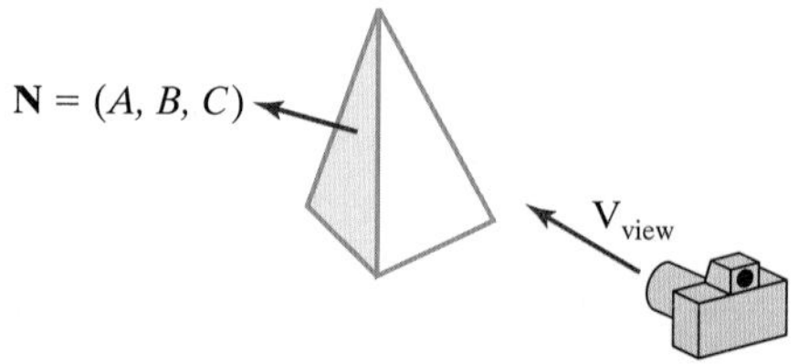

FIGURE 9-1 A surface normal vector $\mathbf{N}$ and the viewing-direction vector $\mathbf{V}_{\text{view}}$.

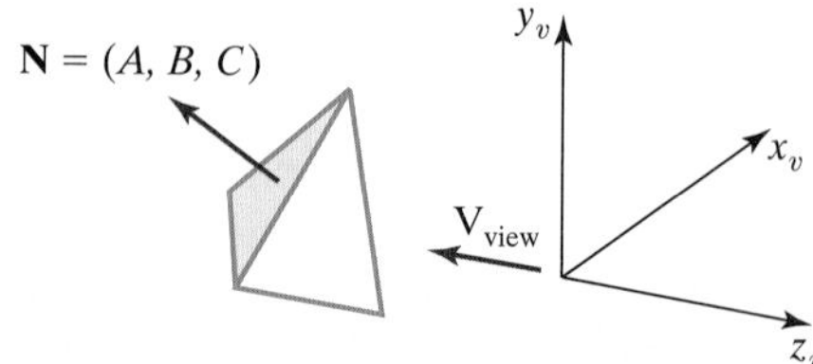

FIGURE 9-2 A polygon surface with plane parameter $C < 0$ in a right-handed viewing coordinate system is identified as a back face when the viewing direction is along the negative z_v axis.

Similar methods can be used in packages that employ a left-handed viewing system. In these packages, plane parameters A, B, C, and D can be calculated from polygon vertex coordinates specified in a clockwise direction (instead of the counterclockwise direction used in a right-handed system). Inequality 9-1 then remains a valid test for points behind the polygon. Also, back faces have normal vectors that point away from the viewing position and are identified by $C \geq 0$ when the viewing direction is along the positive z_v axis.

By examining parameter C for the different plane surfaces describing an object, we can immediately identify all the back faces. For a single convex polyhedron, such as the pyramid in Fig. 9-2, this test identifies all the hidden surfaces in the scene, since each surface is either completely visible or completely hidden. Also, if a scene contains only nonoverlapping convex polyhedra, then again all hidden surfaces are identified with the back-face method.

For other objects, such as the concave polyhedron in Fig. 9-3, more tests must be carried out to determine whether there are additional faces that are totally or partially obscured by other faces. A general scene can be expected to contain overlapping objects along the line of sight, and we then need to determine where the obscured objects are partly or completely hidden by other objects. In general, back-face removal can be expected to eliminate about half of the polygon surfaces in a scene from further visibility tests.

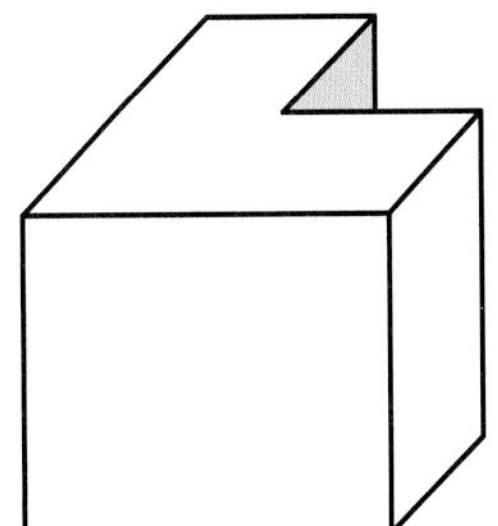

FIGURE 9-3 View of a concave polyhedron with one face partially hidden by other faces of the object.

9-3 DEPTH-BUFFER METHOD

A commonly used image-space approach for detecting visible surfaces is the **depth-buffer method,** which compares surface depth values throughout a scene for each pixel position on the projection plane. Each surface of a scene is processed separately, one pixel position at a time across the surface. The algorithm is usually applied to scenes containing only polygon surfaces, because depth values can be computed very quickly and the method is easy to implement. But we could also apply the same procedures to nonplanar surfaces. This visibility-detection approach is also frequently alluded to as the *z-buffer method,* since object depth is usually measured along the z axis of a viewing system.

Figure 9-4 shows three surfaces at varying distances along the orthographic projection line from position (x, y) on a view plane. These surfaces can be processed in any order. As each surface is processed, its depth from the view plane is compared to previously processed surfaces. If a surface is closer than any previously processed surfaces, its surface color is calculated and saved, along with its depth. The visible surfaces in a scene are represented by the set of surface colors that have been saved after all surface processing is completed. Implementation of the depth-buffer algorithm is typically carried out in normalized coordinates, so that depth values range from 0 at the near clipping plane (the view plane) to 1.0 at the far clipping plane.

As implied by the name of this method, two buffer areas are required. A depth buffer is used to store depth values for each (x, y) position as surfaces are processed, and the frame buffer stores the surface-color values for each pixel position. Initially, all positions in the depth buffer are set to 1.0 (maximum depth), and the frame buffer (refresh buffer) is initialized to the background color. Each surface listed in the polygon tables is then processed, one scan line at a time, by calculating the depth value at each (x, y) pixel position. This calculated depth is compared to the value previously stored in the depth buffer for that pixel position. If the calculated depth is less than the value stored in the depth buffer, the new

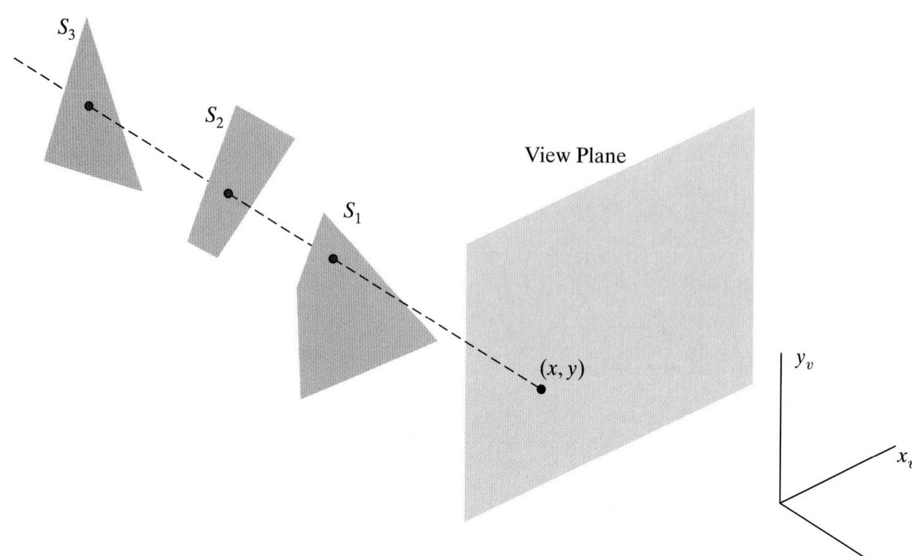

FIGURE 9-4 Three surfaces overlapping pixel position (x, y) on the view plane. The visible surface, S_1, has the smallest depth value.

depth value is stored. Then the surface color at that position is computed and placed in the corresponding pixel location in the frame buffer.

The depth-buffer processing steps are summarized in the following algorithm, assuming that depth values are normalized on the range from 0.0 to 1.0 with the view plane at depth $= 0$. We can also apply this algorithm for any other depth range, and some graphics packages allow the user to specify the depth range over which the depth-buffer algorithm is to be applied.

Depth-Buffer Algorithm

1. Initialize the depth buffer and frame buffer so that for all buffer positions (x, y),

```
depthBuff (x, y) = 1.0,    frameBuff (x, y) = backgndColor
```

2. Process each polygon in a scene, one at a time.

   - For each projected (x, y) pixel position of a polygon, calculate the depth z (if not already known).
   - If `z < depthBuff (x, y)`, compute the surface color at that position and set

```
depthBuff (x, y) = z,    frameBuff (x, y) = surfColor (x, y)
```

After all surfaces have been processed, the depth buffer contains depth values for the visible surfaces and the frame buffer contains the corresponding color values for those surfaces.

Given the depth values for the vertex positions of any polygon in a scene, we can calculate the depth at any other point on the plane containing the polygon.

At surface position (x, y), the depth is calculated from the plane equation as

$$z = \frac{-Ax - By - D}{C} \tag{9-4}$$

For any scan line (Fig. 9-5), adjacent horizontal x positions across the line differ by ± 1, and vertical y values on adjacent scan lines differ by ± 1. If the depth of position (x, y) has been determined to be z, then the depth z' of the next position $(x + 1, y)$ along the scan line is obtained from Eq. 9-4 as

$$z' = \frac{-A(x+1) - By - D}{C} \tag{9-5}$$

or

$$z' = z - \frac{A}{C} \tag{9-6}$$

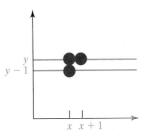

FIGURE 9-5 From position (x, y) on a scan line, the next position across the line has coordinates $(x + 1, y)$, and the position immediately below on the next line has coordinates $(x, y - 1)$.

The ratio $-A/C$ is constant for each surface, so succeeding depth values across a scan line are obtained from preceding values with a single addition.

Processing pixel positions from left to right across each scan line, we start by calculating the depth on a left polygon edge that intersects that scan line (Fig. 9-6). For each successive position across the scan line, we then calculate the depth value using Eq. 9-6.

We can implement the depth-buffer algorithm by starting at a top vertex of the polygon. Then, we could recursively calculate the x-coordinate values down a left edge of the polygon. The x value for the beginning position on each scan line can be calculated from the beginning (edge) x value of the previous scan line as

$$x' = x - \frac{1}{m}$$

where m is the slope of the edge (Fig. 9-7). Depth values down this edge are obtained recursively as

$$z' = z + \frac{A/m + B}{C} \tag{9-7}$$

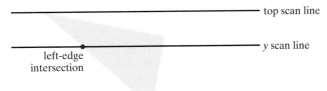

FIGURE 9-6 Scan lines intersecting a polygon surface.

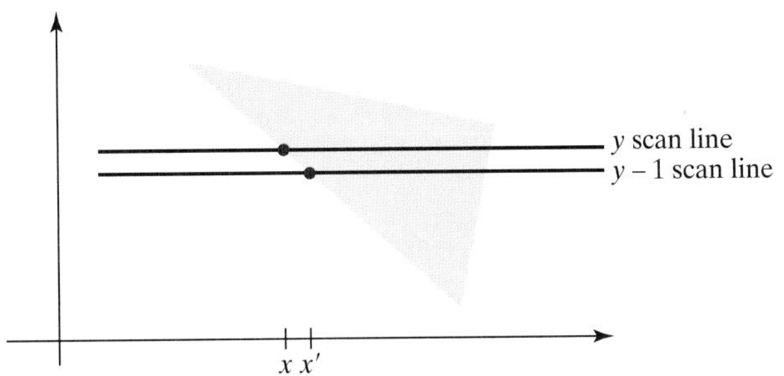

FIGURE 9-7 Intersection positions on successive scan lines along a left polygon edge.

If we are processing down a vertical edge, the slope is infinite and the recursive calculations reduce to

$$z' = z + \frac{B}{C}$$

An alternative approach is to use a midpoint method or Bresenham-type algorithm for determining the starting x values along edges for each scan line. Also, the method can be applied to curved surfaces by determining depth and color values at each surface projection point.

For polygon surfaces, the depth-buffer method is very easy to implement, and it requires no sorting of the surfaces in a scene. But it does require the availability of a second buffer in addition to the refresh buffer. A system with a resolution of 1280 by 1024, for example, would require over 1.3 million positions in the depth buffer, with each position containing enough bits to represent the number of depth increments needed. One way to reduce storage requirements is to process one section of the scene at a time, using a smaller depth buffer. After each view section is processed, the buffer is reused for the next section.

In addition, the basic depth-buffer algorithm often performs needless calculations. Objects are processed in an arbitrary order, so that a color can be computed for a surface point that is later replaced by a closer surface. To alleviate this problem, some graphics packages provide options that allow a user to adjust the depth range for surface testing. This allows distant objects, for example, to be excluded from the depth tests. Using this option, we could even exclude objects that are very close to the projection plane. Hardware implementations of the depth-buffer algorithm are typically an integral component of sophisticated computer-graphics systems.

9-4 A-BUFFER METHOD

An extension of the depth-buffer ideas is the **A-buffer** procedure (at the other end of the alphabet from "z-buffer", where z represents depth). This depth-buffer extension is an antialiasing, area-averaging, visibility-detection method developed at Lucasfilm Studios for inclusion in the surface-rendering system called REYES (an acronym for "Renders Everything You Ever Saw"). The buffer region for this procedure is referred to as the *accumulation buffer,* because it is used to store a variety of surface data, in addition to depth values.

A drawback of the depth-buffer method is that it identifies only one visible surface at each pixel position. In other words, it deals only with opaque surfaces and cannot accumulate color values for more than one surface, as is necessary if transparent surfaces are to be displayed (Fig. 9-8). The A-buffer method expands the depth-buffer algorithm so that each position in the buffer can reference a

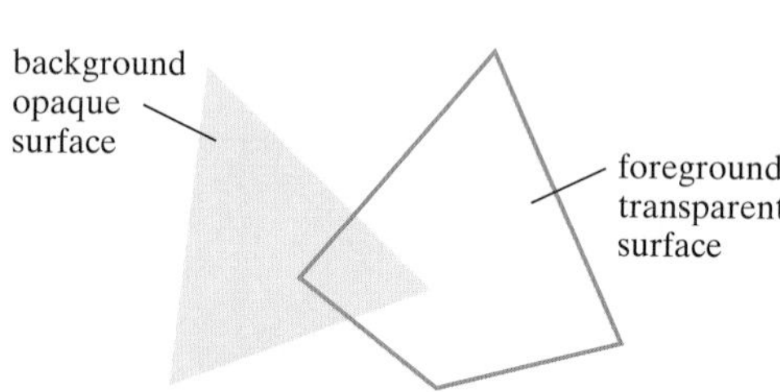

FIGURE 9-8 Viewing an opaque surface through a transparent surface requires multiple color inputs and the application of color-blending operations.

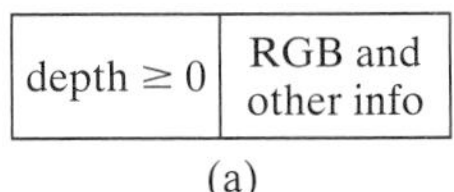

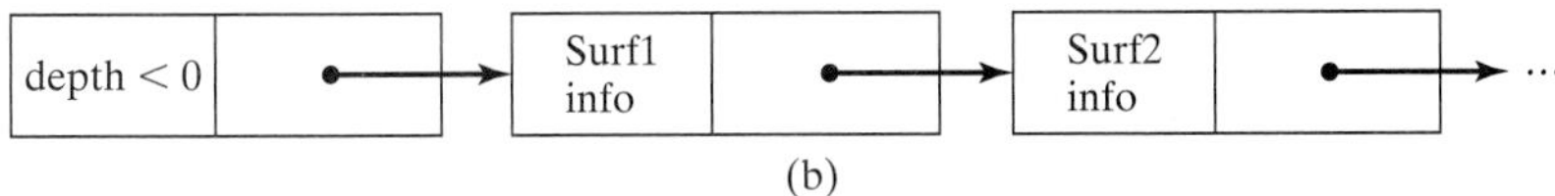

FIGURE 9-9 Two possible organizations for surface information in an A-buffer representation for a pixel position. When a single surface overlaps the pixel, the surface depth, color, and other information are stored as in (a). When more than one surface overlaps the pixel, a linked list of surface data is stored as in (b).

linked list of surfaces. This allows a pixel color to be computed as a combination of different surface colors for transparency or antialiasing effects.

Each position in the A-buffer has two fields:

- Depth Field: Stores a real-number value (positive, negative, or zero).
- Surface Data Field: Stores surface data or a pointer.

If the depth field is nonnegative, the number stored at that position is the depth of a surface that overlaps the corresponding pixel area. The surface data field then stores various surface information, such as the surface color for that position and the percent of pixel coverage, as illustrated in Fig. 9-9(a). If the depth field for a position in the A-buffer is negative, this indicates multiple-surface contributions to the pixel color. The color field then stores a pointer to a linked list of surface data, as in Fig. 9-9(b). Surface information in the A-buffer includes

- RGB intensity components
- opacity parameter (percent of transparency)
- depth
- percent of area coverage
- surface identifier
- other surface-rendering parameters

The A-buffer visibility-detection scheme can be implemented using methods similar to those in the depth-buffer algorithm. Scan lines are processed to determine how much of each surface covers each pixel position across the individual scan lines. Surfaces are subdivided into a polygon mesh and clipped against the pixel boundaries. Using the opacity factors and percent of surface coverage, the rendering algorithms calculate the color for each pixel as an average of the contributions from the overlapping surfaces.

9-5 SCAN-LINE METHOD

This image-space method for identifying visible surfaces computes and compares depth values along the various scan lines for a scene. As each scan line is processed, all polygon surface projections intersecting that line are examined to determine which are visible. Across each scan line, depth calculations are performed to determine which surface is nearest to the view plane at each pixel position. When the visible surface has been determined for a pixel, the surface color for that position is entered into the frame buffer.

Surfaces are processed using the information stored in the polygon tables (Section 3-15). The edge table contains coordinate endpoints for each line in the scene, the inverse slope of each line, and pointers into the surface-facet table to identify the surfaces bounded by each line. The surface-facet table contains the plane coefficients, surface material properties, other surface data, and possibly pointers into the edge table. To facilitate the search for surfaces crossing a given scan line, an active list of edges is formed for each scan line as it is processed. The active edge list contains only those edges that cross the current scan line, sorted in order of increasing x. In addition, we define a flag for each surface that is set to "on" or "off" to indicate whether a position along a scan line is inside or outside the surface. Pixel positions across each scan line are processed from left to right. At the left intersection with the surface projection of a convex polygon, the surface flag is turned on; at the right intersection point along the scan line, it is turned off. For a concave polygon, scan-line intersections can be sorted from left to right, with the surface flag set to "on" between each intersection pair.

Figure 9-10 illustrates the scan-line method for locating visible portions of surfaces for pixel positions along a scan line. The active list for scan line 1 contains information from the edge table for edges AB, BC, EH, and FG. For positions along this scan line between edges AB and BC, only the flag for surface S_1 is on. Therefore, no depth calculations are necessary, and color values are calculated from the surface properties and lighting conditions for surface S_1. Similarly, between edges EH and FG, only the flag for surface S_2 is on. No other positions along scan line 1 intersect surfaces, so the color for those pixels is the background color, which could be loaded into the frame buffer as part of the initialization routine.

For scan lines 2 and 3 in Fig. 9-10, the active edge list contains edges AD, EH, BC, and FG. Along scan line 2 from edge AD to edge EH, only the flag for surface S_1 is on. But between edges EH and BC, the flags for both surfaces are on. Therefore, a depth calculation is necessary, using the plane coefficients for the two surfaces, when we encounter edge EH. For this example, the depth of surface S_1 is assumed to be less than that of S_2, so the color values for surface S_1 are assigned to the pixels across the scan line until boundary BC is encountered. Then the surface flag for S_1 goes off, and the colors for surface S_2 are stored up

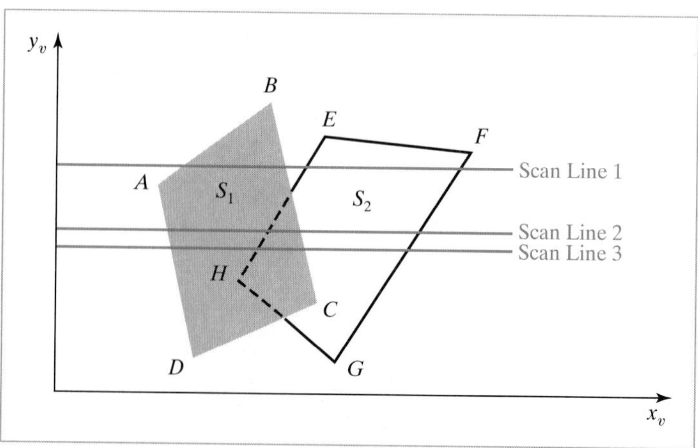

FIGURE 9-10 Scan lines crossing the view-plane projection of two surfaces, S_1 and S_2. Dashed lines indicate the boundaries of hidden surface sections.

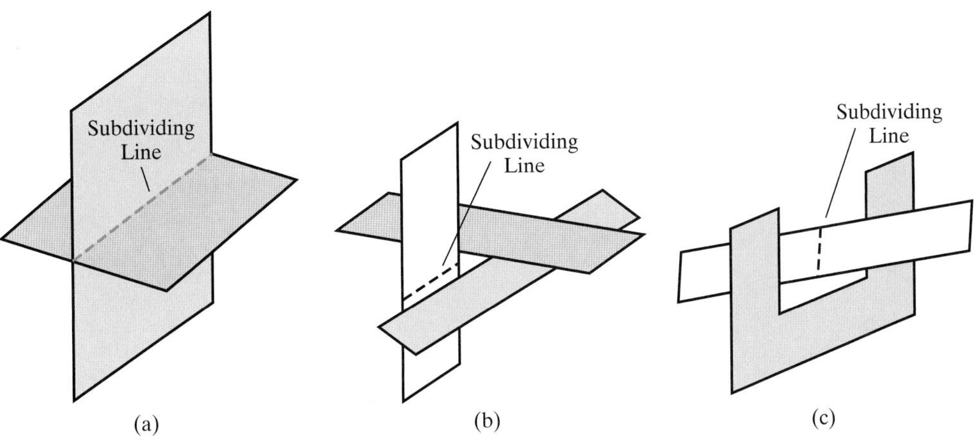

FIGURE 9-11 Intersecting and cyclically overlapping surfaces that alternately obscure one another.

to edge FG. No other depth calculations are necessary, because we assume that surface S_2 remains behind S_1 once we have determined the depth relationship at edge EH.

We can take advantage of coherence along the scan lines as we pass from one scan line to the next. In Fig. 9-10, scan line 3 has the same active list of edges as scan line 2. Since no changes have occurred in line intersections, it is again unnecessary to make depth calculations between edges EH and BC. The two surfaces must be in the same orientation as determined on scan line 2, so the colors for surface S_1 can be entered without further depth calculations.

Any number of overlapping polygon surfaces can be processed with this scan-line method. Flags for the surfaces are set to indicate whether a position is inside or outside, and depth calculations are performed only at the edges of overlapping surfaces. This procedure works correctly only if surfaces do not cut through or otherwise cyclically overlap each other (Fig. 9-11). If any kind of cyclic overlap is present in a scene, we can divide the surfaces to eliminate the overlaps. The dashed lines in this figure indicate where planes could be subdivided to form two distinct surfaces, so that the cyclic overlaps are eliminated.

9-6 DEPTH-SORTING METHOD

Using both image-space and object-space operations, the **depth-sorting** method performs the following basic functions:

(1) Surfaces are sorted in order of decreasing depth.

(2) Surfaces are scan-converted in order, starting with the surface of greatest depth.

Sorting operations are carried out in both image and object space, and the scan conversion of the polygon surfaces is performed in image space.

This visibility-detection method is often referred to as the **painter's algorithm.** In creating a watercolor or an oil painting, an artist first paints the background colors. Next, the most distant objects are added, then the nearer objects, and so forth. At the final step, the foreground is painted on the canvas over the

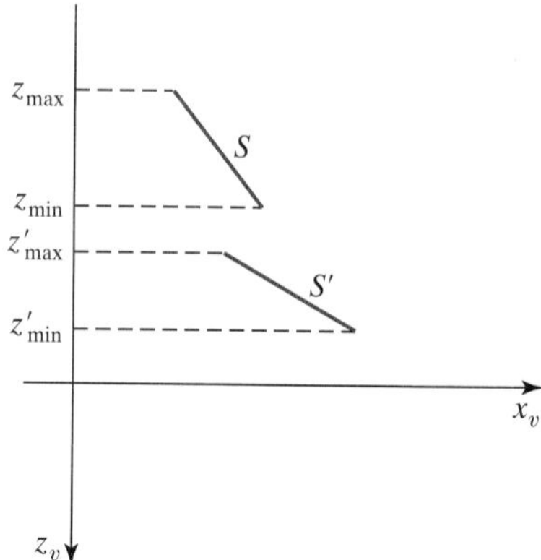

FIGURE 9-12 Two surfaces with no depth overlap.

background and the more distant objects. Each color layer covers up the previous layer. Using a similar technique, we first sort surfaces according to their distance from the view plane. The color values for the farthest surface can then be entered into the refresh buffer. Taking each succeeding surface in turn (in decreasing depth order), we "paint" the surface onto the frame buffer over the colors of the previously processed surfaces.

Painting polygon surfaces into the frame buffer according to depth is carried out in several steps. Assuming we are viewing along the z direction, surfaces are ordered on the first pass according to the smallest z value on each surface. The surface S at the end of the list (with the greatest depth) is then compared to the other surfaces in the list to determine whether there are any depth overlaps. If no depth overlaps occur, S is the most distant surface and it is scan converted. Figure 9-12 shows two surfaces that overlap in the xy plane but have no depth overlap. This process is then repeated for the next surface in the list. As long as no overlaps occur, each surface is processed in depth order until all have been scan-converted. If a depth overlap is detected at any point in the list, we need to make some additional comparisons to determine whether any of the surfaces should be reordered.

We make the following tests for each surface that has a depth overlap with S. If any one of these tests is true, no reordering is necessary for S and the surface being tested. The tests are listed in order of increasing difficulty.

(1) The bounding rectangles (coordinate extents) in the xy directions for the two surfaces do not overlap.

(2) Surface S is completely behind the overlapping surface relative to the viewing position.

(3) The overlapping surface is completely in front of S relative to the viewing position.

(4) The boundary-edge projections of the two surfaces onto the view plane do not overlap.

We perform these tests in the order listed and proceed to the next overlapping surface as soon as we find that one of the tests is true. If all the overlapping surfaces pass at least one of these tests, S is the most distant surface. No reordering is then necessary and S is scan converted.

Test 1 is performed in two parts. We check for overlap first in the x direction, then in the y direction. If there is no surface overlap in either of these directions,

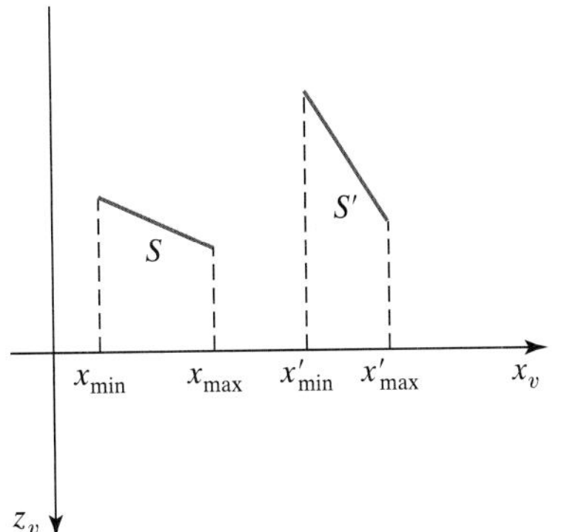

FIGURE 9-13 Two surfaces with depth overlap but no overlap in the x direction.

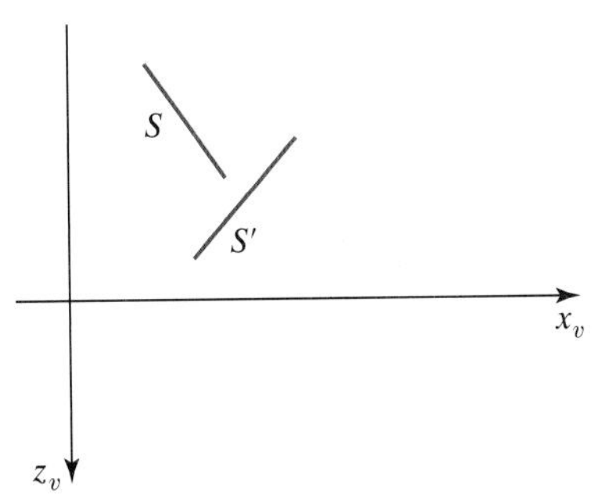

FIGURE 9-14 Surface S is completely behind the overlapping surface S'.

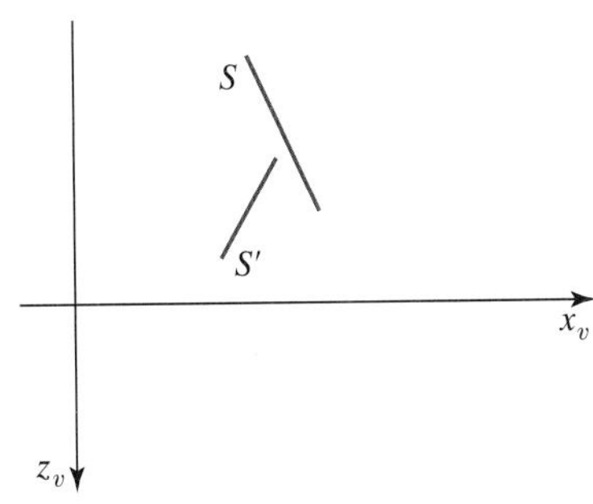

FIGURE 9-15 Overlapping surface S' is completely in front of surface S, but S is not completely behind S'.

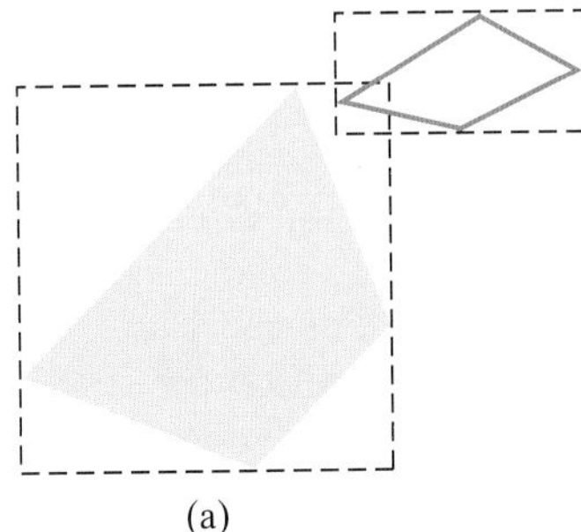

(a) (b)

FIGURE 9-16 Two polygon surfaces with overlapping bounding rectangles in the xy plane.

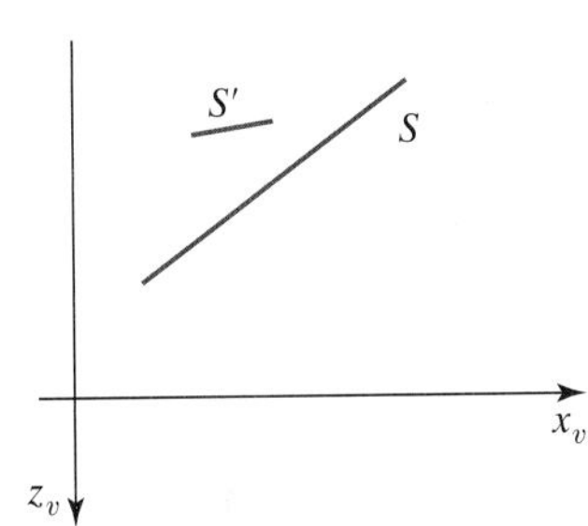

FIGURE 9-17 Surface S extends to a greater depth, but it obscures surface S'.

the two planes cannot obscure one other. An example of two surfaces that overlap in the z direction but not in the x direction is shown in Fig. 9-13.

We can perform tests 2 and 3 using back-front polygon tests. That is, we substitute the coordinates for all vertices of S into the plane equation for the overlapping surface and check the sign of the result. If the plane equations are set up so that the front of the surface is toward the viewing position, then S is behind S' if all vertices of S are in back of S' (Fig. 9-14). Similarly, S' is completely ahead of S if all vertices of S are in front of S'. Figure 9-15 shows an overlapping surface S' that is completely in front of S, but surface S is not completely behind S' (test 2 is not true).

If tests 1 through 3 have all failed, we perform test 4 to determine whether the two surface projections overlap. As demonstrated in Fig. 9-16, two surfaces may or may not intersect even though their coordinate extents overlap.

Should all four tests fail for an overlapping surface S', we interchange surfaces S and S' in the sorted list. An example of two surfaces that would be reordered with this procedure is given in Fig. 9-17. At this point, we still do not know for certain that we have found the farthest surface from the view plane. Figure 9-18 illustrates a situation in which we would first interchange S and S''. But since S'' obscures part of S', we need to interchange S'' and S' to get the three surfaces into the correct depth order. Therefore, we need to repeat the testing process for each surface that is reordered in the list.

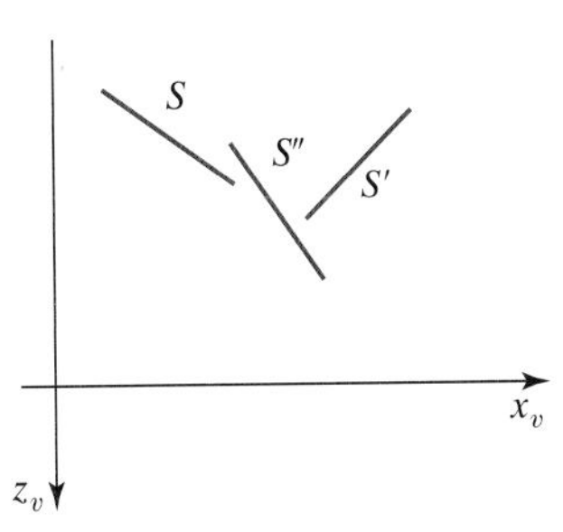

FIGURE 9-18 Three surfaces that have been entered into the sorted surface list in the order S, S', S'' should be reordered as S', S'', S.

It is possible for the algorithm just outlined to get into an infinite loop if two or more surfaces alternately obscure each other, as in Fig. 9-11. In such situations, the algorithm would continually rearrange the ordering of the overlapping surfaces. To avoid such loops, we can flag any surface that has been reordered to a farther depth position so that it cannot be moved again. If an attempt is made to switch the surface a second time, we divide it into two parts to eliminate the cyclic overlap. The original surface is then replaced by the two new surfaces, and we continue processing as before.

9-7 BSP-TREE METHOD

A **binary space-partitioning** (BSP) tree is an efficient method for determining object visibility by painting surfaces into the frame buffer from back to front, as in the painter's algorithm. The BSP tree is particularly useful when the view reference point changes, but the objects in a scene are at fixed positions.

Applying a BSP tree to visibility testing involves identifying surfaces that are behind or in front of the partitioning plane at each step of the space subdivision, relative to the viewing direction. Figure 9-19 illustrates the basic concept in this algorithm. With plane P_1, we first partition the space into two sets of objects. One set of objects is in back of plane P_1 relative to the viewing direction, and the other set is in front of P_1. Since one object is intersected by plane P_1, we divide that object into two separate objects, labeled A and B. Objects A and C are in front of P_1, and objects B and D are behind P_1. We next partition the space again with plane P_2 and construct the binary tree representation shown in Fig. 9-19(b). In this tree, the objects are represented as terminal nodes, with front objects occupying the left branches and back objects occupying the right branches.

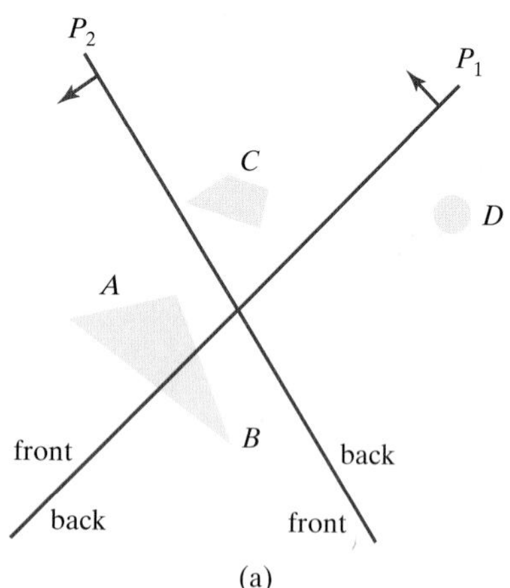

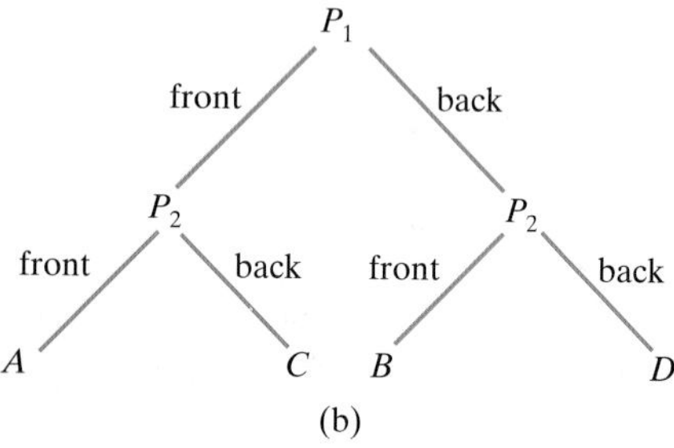

FIGURE 9-19 A region of space (a) is partitioned with two planes P_1 and P_2 to form the BSP tree representation shown in (b).

For objects described with polygon facets, we can choose the partitioning planes to coincide with polygon-surface planes. The polygon equations are then used to identify back and front polygons, and the tree is constructed with one partitioning plane for each polygon face. Any polygon intersected by a partitioning plane is split into two parts. When the BSP tree is complete, we process the tree by selecting the right nodes first, then the left nodes. Thus, the surfaces are generated for display in the order back to front, so that foreground objects are painted over the background objects. Fast hardware implementations for constructing and processing BSP trees are used in some systems.

9-8 AREA-SUBDIVISION METHOD

This technique for hidden-surface removal is essentially an image-space method, but object-space operations can be used to accomplish depth ordering of surfaces. The **area-subdivision method** takes advantage of area coherence in a scene by locating those projection areas that represent part of a single surface. We apply this method by successively dividing the total view-plane area into smaller and smaller rectangles until each rectangular area contains the projection of part of a single visible surface, contains no surface projections, or the area has been reduced to the size of a pixel.

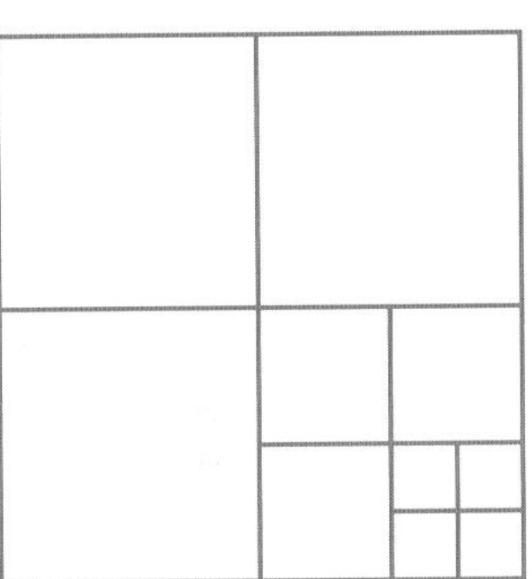

FIGURE 9-20 Dividing a square area into equal-sized quadrants at each step.

To implement this method, we need to establish tests that can quickly identify the area as part of a single surface or tell us that the area is too complex to analyze easily. Starting with the total view, we apply the tests to determine whether we should subdivide the total area into smaller rectangles. If the tests indicate that the view is sufficiently complex, we subdivide it. Next, we apply the tests to each of the smaller areas, subdividing these if the tests indicate that visibility of a single surface is still uncertain. We continue this process until the subdivisions are easily analyzed as belonging to a single surface or until we have reached the resolution limit. An easy way to do this is to successively divide the area into four equal parts at each step, as shown in Fig. 9-20. This approach is similar to that used in constructing a quadtree. A viewing area with a pixel resolution of 1024 by 1024 could be subdivided ten times in this way before a subarea is reduced to the size of a single pixel.

There are four possible relationships that a surface can have with an area of the subdivided view plane. We can describe these relative surface positions using the following classifications (Fig. 9-21).

Surrounding Surface: A surface that completely encloses the area.

Overlapping Surface: A surface that is partly inside and partly outside the area.

Inside Surface: A surface that is completely inside the area.

Outside Surface: A surface that is completely outside the area.

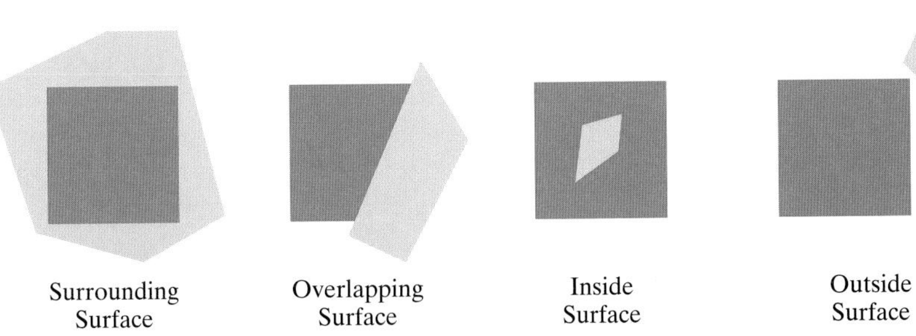

FIGURE 9-21 Possible relationships between polygon surfaces and a rectangular section of the viewing plane.

The tests for determining surface visibility within a rectangular area can be stated in terms of the four surface classifications illustrated in Fig. 9-21. No further subdivisions of a specified area are needed if one of the following conditions is true.

Condition 1: An area has no inside, overlapping, or surrounding surfaces (all surfaces are outside the area).

Condition 2: An area has only one inside, overlapping, or surrounding surface.

Condition 3: An area has one surrounding surface that obscures all other surfaces within the area boundaries.

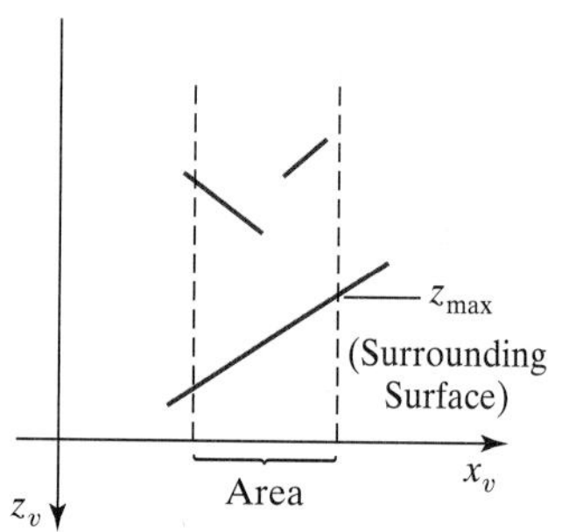

FIGURE 9-22 Within a specified area, a surrounding surface with a maximum depth of z_{max} obscures all surfaces that have a minimum depth beyond z_{max}.

Initially, we can compare the coordinate extents of each surface with the area boundaries. This will identify the inside and surrounding surfaces, but overlapping and outside surfaces usually require intersection tests. If a single bounding rectangle intersects the area in some way, additional checks are used to determine whether the surface is surrounding, overlapping, or outside. Once a single inside, overlapping, or surrounding surface has been identified, the surface color values are stored in the frame buffer.

One method for testing condition 3 is to sort the surfaces according to minimum depth from the view plane. For each surrounding surface, we then compute the maximum depth within the area under consideration. If the maximum depth of one of these surrounding surfaces is closer to the view plane than the minimum depth of all other surfaces within the area, condition 3 is satisfied. Figure 9-22 illustrates this situation.

Another method for testing condition 3 that does not require depth sorting is to use plane equations to calculate depth values at the four vertices of the area for all surrounding, overlapping, and inside surfaces. If all four depths for one of the surrounding surfaces are less than the calculated depths for all other surfaces, condition 3 is satisfied. Then the area can be displayed with the colors for that surrounding surface.

For some situations, the previous two testing methods may fail to identify correctly a surrounding surface that obscures all the other surfaces. Further testing could be carried out to identify the single surface that covers the area, but it is faster to subdivide the area than to continue with more complex testing. Once a surface has been identified as an outside or surrounding surface for an area, it will remain in that category for all subdivisions of the area. Furthermore, we can expect to eliminate some inside and overlapping surfaces as the subdivision process continues, so that the areas become easier to analyze. In the limiting case, when a subdivision the size of a pixel is produced, we simply calculate the depth of each relevant surface at that point and assign the color of the nearest surface to that pixel.

As a variation on the basic subdivision process, we could subdivide areas along surface boundaries instead of dividing them in half. If the surfaces have been sorted according to minimum depth, we can use the surface of smallest depth value to subdivide a given area. Figure 9-23 illustrates this method for subdividing areas. The projection of the boundary of surface S is used to partition the original area into the subdivisions A_1 and A_2. Surface S is then a surrounding surface for A_1, and visibility conditions 2 and 3 can be tested to determine whether further subdividing is necessary. In general, fewer subdivisions are required using this approach, but more processing is needed to subdivide areas and to analyze the relation of surfaces to the subdivision boundaries.

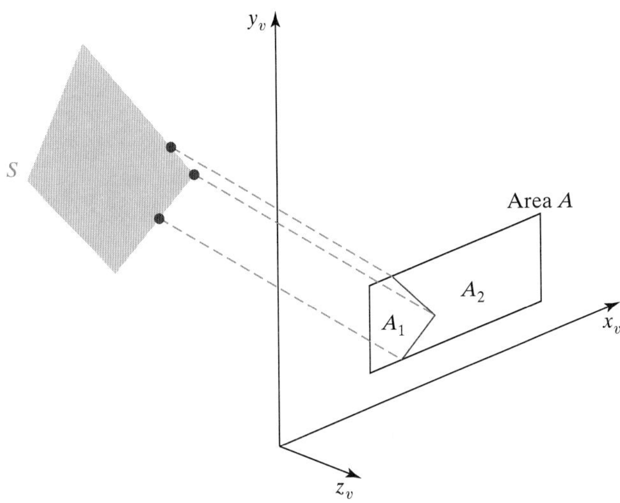

FIGURE 9-23 Area A is subdivided into A_1 and A_2 using the boundary of surface S on the view plane.

9-9 OCTREE METHODS

When an octree representation is used for the viewing volume, visible-surface identification is accomplished by searching octree nodes in a front-to-back order. In Fig. 9-24, the foreground of a scene is contained in octants 0, 1, 2, and 3. Surfaces in the front of these octants are visible to the viewer. Any surfaces toward the rear of the front octants or in the back octants (4, 5, 6, and 7) may be hidden by the front surfaces.

We can process the octree nodes of Fig. 9-24 in the order 0, 1, 2, 3, 4, 5, 6, 7. This results in a depth-first traversal of the octree, where the nodes for the four front suboctants of octant 0 are visited before the nodes for the four back suboctants. The traversal of the octree continues in this order for each octant subdivision.

When a color value is encountered in an octree node, that color is saved in the quadtree only if no values have previously been saved for the same area. In this way, only the front colors are saved. Nodes that have the value "void" are ignored. Any node that is completely obscured is eliminated from further processing, so that its subtrees are not accessed. Figure 9-25 depicts the octants in a region of space and the corresponding quadrants on the view plane. Contributions to quadrant 0 come from octants 0 and 4. Color values in quadrant 1 are obtained from surfaces

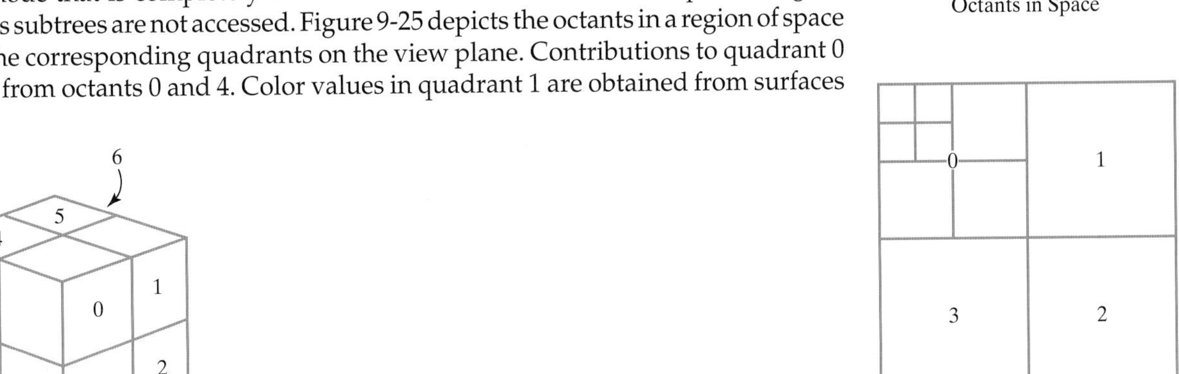

FIGURE 9-25 Octant divisions for a region of space and the corresponding quadrant plane.

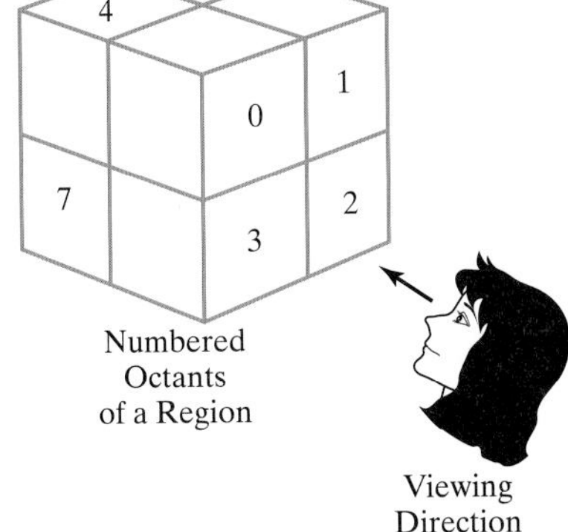

FIGURE 9-24 Objects in octants 0, 1, 2, and 3 obscure objects in the back octants (4, 5, 6, 7) when the viewing direction is as shown.

in octants 1 and 5, and values in each of the other two quadrants are generated from the pairs of octants aligned with each of these quadrants.

Effective octree visibility testing is carried out with recursive processing of octree nodes and the creation of a quadtree representation for the visible surfaces. In most cases, both a front and a back octant must be considered in determining the correct color values for a quadrant. But if the front octant is homogeneously filled with some color, we do not process the back octant. For heterogeneous regions, a recursive procedure is called, passing as new arguments the child of the heterogeneous octant and a newly created quadtree node. If the front is empty, it is necessary only to process the child of the rear octant. Otherwise, two recursive calls are made, one for the rear octant and one for the front octant.

Different views of objects represented as octrees can be obtained by applying transformations to the octree representation that reorient the object according to the view selected. Octants can then be renumbered so that the octree representation is always organized with octants 0, 1, 2, and 3 as the front face.

9-10 RAY-CASTING METHOD

If we consider the line of sight from a pixel position on the view plane through a scene, as in Fig. 9-26, we can determine which objects in the scene (if any) intersect this line. After calculating all ray-surface intersections, we identify the visible surface as the one whose intersection point is closest to the pixel. This visibility-detection scheme uses *ray casting* procedures that were introduced in Section 8-20. Ray casting, as a visibility-detection tool, is based on geometric-optics methods, which trace the paths of light rays. Since there are an infinite number of light rays in a scene and we are interested only in those rays that pass through pixel positions, we can trace the light-ray paths backward from the pixels through the scene. The ray-casting approach is an effective visibility-detection method for scenes with curved surfaces, particularly spheres.

We can think of ray casting as a variation on the depth-buffer method (Section 9-3). In the depth-buffer algorithm, we process surfaces one at a time and calculate depth values for all projection points over the surface. The calculated surface depths are then compared to previously stored depths to determine visible surfaces at each pixel. In ray casting, we process pixels one at a time and calculate depths for all surfaces along the projection path to that pixel.

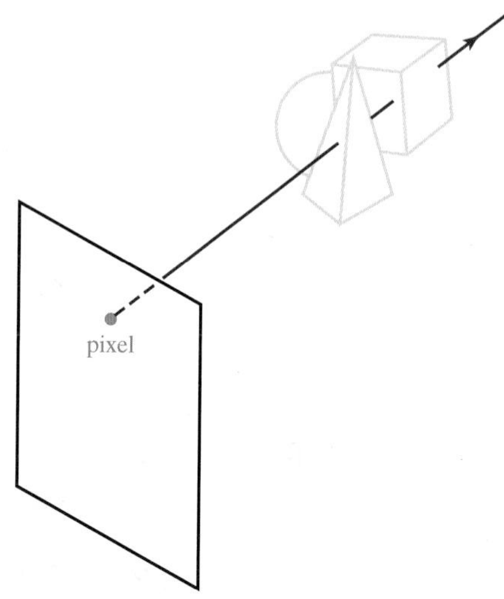

FIGURE 9-26 A ray along the line of sight from a pixel position through a scene.

Ray casting is a special case of *ray-tracing* algorithms (Section 10-11) that trace multiple ray paths to pick up global reflection and refraction contributions from multiple objects in a scene. With ray casting, we only follow a ray out from each pixel to the nearest object. Efficient ray-surface intersection calculations have been developed for common objects, particularly spheres, and we discuss these intersection methods in detail in Section 10-11.

9-11 COMPARISON OF VISIBILITY-DETECTION METHODS

The effectiveness of a visible-surface detection method depends on the characteristics of a particular application. If the surfaces in a scene are widely distributed along the viewing direction so that there is very little depth overlap, a depth-sorting or BSP-tree method is often most efficient. When there are few overlaps of the surface projections on the view plane, a scan-line or area-subdivision approach is a fast way to locate visible surfaces.

As a general rule, either the depth-sorting algorithm or the BSP-tree method is a highly effective approach for scenes with only a few surfaces. This is because these scenes usually have few surfaces that overlap in depth. The scan-line method also performs well when a scene contains a small number of surfaces. We can use the scan-line, depth-sorting, or BSP-tree method to identify visible surfaces effectively for scenes with up to several thousand polygon surfaces. With scenes that contain more than a few thousand surfaces, the depth-buffer method or octree approach performs best. The depth-buffer method has a nearly constant processing time, independent of the number of surfaces in a scene. This is because the size of the surface areas decreases as the number of surfaces in the scene increases. Therefore, the depth-buffer method exhibits relatively low performance with simple scenes and relatively high performance with complex scenes. BSP trees are useful when multiple views are to be generated using different view reference points. If a scene contains curved-surface representations, we can use octree or ray-casting methods to identify visible parts of the scene.

When octree representations are used in a system, the visibility-detection process is fast and simple. Only integer additions and subtractions are used in the process, and there is no need to perform sorting or intersection calculations. Another advantage of octrees is that they store more than just the surface geometry. The entire solid region of an object is available for display, which makes the octree representation useful for obtaining cross-sectional slices of three-dimensional objects.

It is possible to combine and implement the different visible-surface detection methods in various ways. In addition, visibility-detection algorithms are often implemented in hardware, and special systems utilizing parallel processing are employed to increase the efficiency of these methods. Special hardware systems are used when processing speed is an especially important consideration, as in the generation of animated views for flight simulators.

9-12 CURVED SURFACES

Effective methods for determining the visibility of objects with curved surfaces include ray casting and octree methods. With ray casting, we calculate ray-surface intersections and locate the smallest intersection distance along the pixel ray. With octrees, we simply search the nodes from front to back to locate the surface color values. Once an octree representation has been established from the input definition of the objects, all visible surfaces are identified with the same processing procedures. No special considerations need be given to different kinds of surfaces, curved or otherwise.

A curved surface can also be approximated as a polygon mesh, and we can then use one of the visible-surface identification methods previously discussed. But for some objects, such as spheres, it could be more efficient as well as more accurate to use ray casting and the equations describing the curved surface.

Curved-Surface Representations

We can represent a surface with an implicit equation of the form $f(x, y, z) = 0$ or with a parametric representation (Appendix A). Spline surfaces, for example, are normally described with parametric equations. In some cases, it is useful to obtain an explicit surface equation, as for example a height function over an xy ground plane:

$$z = f(x, y)$$

Many objects of interest, such as spheres, ellipsoids, cylinders, and cones, have quadratic representations. These surfaces are commonly used to model molecular structures, roller bearings, rings, and shafts.

Scan-line and ray-casting algorithms often involve numerical approximation techniques to solve the surface equation at the intersection point with a scan line or with a pixel ray. Various techniques, including parallel calculations and fast hardware implementations, have been developed for solving the curved-surface intersection equations for commonly used objects.

Surface Contour Plots

For many applications in mathematics, physical sciences, engineering, and other fields, it is useful to display a surface function with a set of contour lines that show the surface shape. The surface may be described with an equation or with data tables, such as topographic data on elevations or population density. With an explicit functional representation, we can plot the visible surface contour lines and eliminate those contour sections that are hidden by the visible parts of the surface.

To obtain an xy plot of a functional surface, we can write the surface representation in the form

$$y = f(x, z) \tag{9-8}$$

A curve in the xy plane can then be plotted for values of z within some selected range, using a specified interval Δz. Starting with the largest value of z, we plot the curves from "front" to "back" and eliminate hidden sections. We draw the curve sections on the screen by mapping an xy range for the function into an xy pixel screen range. Then, unit steps are taken in x and the corresponding y value for each x value is determined from Eq. 9-8 for a given value of z.

One way to identify the visible curve sections on the surface is to maintain a list of y_{min} and y_{max} values previously calculated for the pixel x coordinates on the screen. As we step from one pixel x position to the next, we check the calculated y value against the stored range, y_{min} and y_{max}, for the next pixel. If $y_{\text{min}} \leq y \leq y_{\text{max}}$, that point on the surface is not visible and we do not plot it. But if the calculated y value is outside the stored y bounds for that pixel, the point is visible. We then plot the point and reset the bounds for that pixel. Similar procedures can be used to project the contour plot onto the xz or yz plane. Fig. 9-27 shows an example of a surface contour plot with color-coded contour lines.

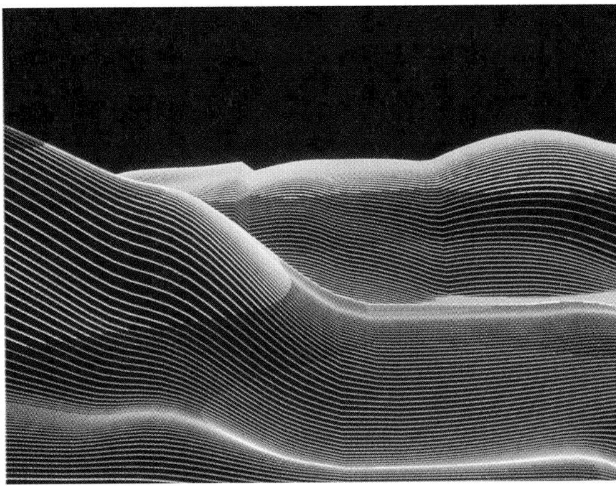

FIGURE 9-27 A color-coded surface contour plot. (*Courtesy of Los Alamos National Laboratory.*)

We can apply the same methods to a discrete set of data points by determining isosurface lines. For example, if we have a discrete set of z values for an n_x by n_y grid of xy values, we can determine the path for a line of constant z over the surface using the contour methods discussed in Section 8-27. Each selected contour line can then be projected onto a view plane and displayed with straight-line segments. Again, lines can be drawn on the display device in a front-to-back depth order, and we eliminate contour sections that pass behind previously drawn (visible) contour lines.

9-13 WIRE-FRAME VISIBILITY METHODS

Scenes usually do not contain isolated line sections, unless we are displaying a graph, diagram, or network layout. But often we want to view a three-dimensional scene in an outline form to obtain a quick display of the object features. The fastest way to generate a wire-frame view of a scene is to display all object edges. However, it may be difficult to determine the front and back features of the objects in such a display. One solution to this problem is to apply depth cueing, so that the displayed intensity of a line is a function of its distance from the viewer. Alternatively, we can apply visibility tests, so that hidden line sections can be either eliminated or displayed differently from the visible edges. Procedures for determining visibility of object edges are referred to as **wire-frame visibility methods.** They are also called **visible-line detection methods** or **hidden-line detection methods.** In addition, some of the visible-surface methods discussed in preceding sections can be used to test for edge visibility.

Wire-Frame Surface-Visibility Algorithms

A direct approach to identifying visible line sections is to compare edge positions with the positions of the surfaces in a scene. This process involves the same methods used in line-clipping algorithms. That is, we test the position of line endpoints with respect to the boundaries of a specified area, but, for visibility testing, we also need to compare edge and surface depth values. When the projected edge endpoints of a line segment are both within the projected area of a surface, we compare the depth of the endpoints to the surface depth at those (x, y) positions. If both endpoints are behind the surface, we have a hidden edge. If both endpoints are in front of the surface, the edge is visible with respect to that surface.

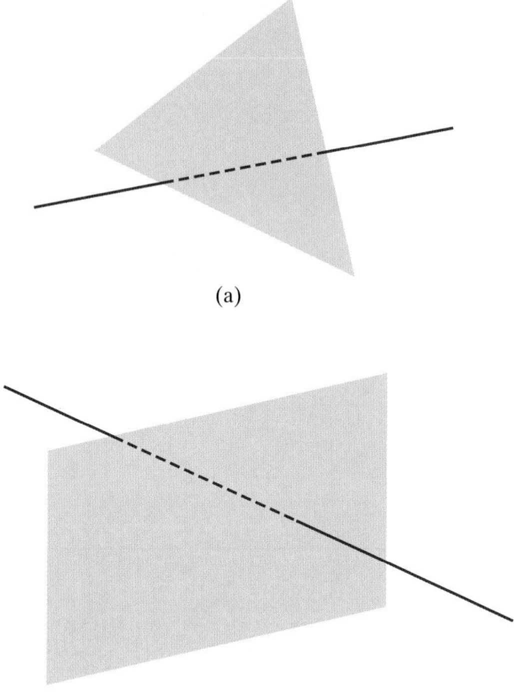

FIGURE 9-28 Hidden-line sections (dashed) for a line (a) that has greater depth than a surface and a line (b) that is partially behind a surface and partially in front of the surface.

Otherwise, we must calculate intersection positions and determine the depth values at those intersection points. If the edge has greater depth than the surface at the perimeter intersections, part of the edge is hidden by the surface, as in Fig. 9-28(a). Another possibility is that an edge has greater depth at one boundary intersection and less depth than the surface at the other boundary intersection (assuming surfaces are convex). In that case, we need to determine where the edge penetrates the surface interior, as in Fig. 9-28(b). Once we have identified a hidden section of an edge, we could eliminate it, display it as a dashed line, or display it in some other way to distinguish it from the visible sections.

Some of the visible-surface detection methods are readily adapted to wire-frame visibility testing of object edges. Using a back-face method, we could identify all the back surfaces of an object and display only the boundaries for the visible surfaces. With depth sorting, surfaces can be painted into the refresh buffer so that surface interiors are in the background color, while boundaries are in the foreground color. By processing the surfaces from back to front, hidden lines are erased by the nearer surfaces. An area-subdivision method can be adapted to hidden-line removal by displaying only the boundaries of visible surfaces. And scan-line methods can be used to display the scan-line intersection positions at the boundaries of visible surfaces.

Wire-Frame Depth-Cueing Algorithm

Another method for displaying visibility information is to vary the brightness of objects in a scene as a function of distance from the viewing position. This **depth-cueing method** is typically applied using the linear function

$$f_{\text{depth}}(d) = \frac{d_{\text{max}} - d}{d_{\text{max}} - d_{\text{min}}} \tag{9-9}$$

where d is the distance of a point from the viewing position. Values for minimum and maximum depth, d_{min} and d_{max}, can be set to convenient values for a particular application. Or the minimum and maximum depths can be set to the normalization depth range: $d_{min} = 0.0$ and $d_{max} = 1.0$. As each pixel position is processed, its color is multiplied by $f_{depth}(d)$. Thus, nearer points are displayed with higher intensities, and the points at the maximum depth have an intensity equal to 0.

The depth-cueing function can be implemented with various options. In some graphics libraries, a general atmosphere function (Section 10-3) is available, which can combine depth cueing with atmospheric effects to simulate smoke or haze, for example. Thus, an object's color could be modified by the depth-cueing function and then combined with the atmosphere color.

9-14 OpenGL VISIBILITY-DETECTION FUNCTIONS

We can apply both back-face removal and the depth-buffer visibility-testing method to our scenes using functions that are provided in the basic library of OpenGL. In addition, we can use OpenGL functions to construct a wire-frame display of a scene with the hidden lines removed, and we can display scenes with depth cueing.

OpenGL Polygon-Culling Functions

Back-face removal is accomplished with the functions

```
glEnable (GL_CULL_FACE);
glCullFace (mode);
```

where parameter `mode` is assigned the value `GL_BACK`. In fact, we could use this function to remove the front faces instead, or we could even remove both front and back faces. If our viewing position is inside a building, for example, then we want to see only the back faces (the inside of the rooms). In this case, we could either set parameter `mode` to `GL_FRONT`, or we could change the definition of front-facing polygons using the `glFrontFace` function discussed in Section 4-14. Then, if the viewing position moves outside the building, we can cull the back faces from the display. And, in some applications, we might only want to view other primitives in a scene, such as point sets and individual straight-line segments. So, to eliminate all polygon surfaces in a scene, we set parameter `mode` to the OpenGL symbolic constant `GL_FRONT_AND_BACK`.

By default, parameter `mode` in the `glCullFace` function has the value `GL_BACK`. Therefore, if we activate culling with the `glEnable` function without explicitly invoking function `glCullFace`, the back faces in a scene will be removed. The culling routine is turned off with

```
glDisable (GL_CULL_FACE);
```

OpenGL Depth-Buffer Functions

To use the OpenGL depth-buffer visibility-detection routines, we first need to modify the GLUT initialization function for the display mode to include a request for the depth buffer, as well as for the refresh buffer. We do this, for example, with the statement

```
glutInitDisplayMode (GLUT_SINGLE | GLUT_RGB | GLUT_DEPTH);
```

Depth buffer values can then be initialized with

```
glClear (GL_DEPTH_BUFFER_BIT);
```

Normally, the depth buffer is initialized with the same statement that initializes the refresh buffer to the background color. But we do need to clear the depth buffer each time we want to display a new frame. In OpenGL, depth values are normalized in the range from 0 to 1.0, so that the preceding initialization sets all depth-buffer values to the maximum value 1.0 by default.

The OpenGL depth-buffer visibility-detection routines are activated with the following function.

```
glEnable (GL_DEPTH_TEST);
```

And we deactivate the depth-buffer routines with

```
glDisable (GL_DEPTH_TEST);
```

We can also apply depth-buffer visibility testing using some other initial value for the maximum depth, and this initial value is chosen with the OpenGL function

```
glClearDepth (maxDepth);
```

Parameter `maxDepth` can be set to any value between 0 and 1.0. To load this initialization value into the depth buffer, we next must invoke the `glClear (GL_DEPTH_BUFFER_BIT)` function. Otherwise, the depth buffer is initialized with the default value (1.0). Since surface-color calculations and other processing are not performed for objects that are beyond the specified maximum depth, this function can be used to speed up the depth-buffer routines when a scene contains many distant objects that are behind the foreground objects.

Projection coordinates in OpenGL are normalized to the range from -1.0 to 1.0, and the depth values between the near and far clipping planes are further normalized to the range from 0.0 to 1.0. The value 0.0 corresponds to the near clipping plane (the projection plane), and the value 1.0 corresponds to the far clipping plane. As an option, we can adjust these normalization values with

```
glDepthRange (nearNormDepth, farNormDepth);
```

By default, `nearNormDepth` = 0.0 and `farNormDepth` = 1.0. But with the `glDepthRange` function, we can set these two parameters to any values within the range from 0.0 to 1.0, including `nearNormDepth` > `farNormDepth`. Using the `glDepthRange` function, we can restrict the depth-buffer testing to any region of the view volume, and we can even reverse the positions of the near and far planes.

Another option available in OpenGL is the test condition that is to be used for the depth-buffer routines. We specify a test condition with the following function.

```
glDepthFunc (testCondition);
```

Parameter `testCondition` can be assigned any one of the following eight symbolic constants: `GL_LESS`, `GL_GREATER`, `GL_EQUAL`, `GL_NOTEQUAL`, `GL_LEQUAL`, `GL_GEQUAL`, `GL_NEVER` (no points are processed), `GL_ALWAYS` (all points are processed). These different tests can be useful in various applications to reduce calculations in depth-buffer processing. The default value for parameter `testCondition` is `GL_LESS`, so that a depth value is processed if it has a value that is less than the current value in the depth buffer for that pixel position.

We can also set the status of the depth buffer so that it is in a read-only state or in a read-write state. This is accomplished with

```
glDepthMask (writeStatus);
```

When `writeStatus` = `GL_TRUE` (the default value), we can both read from and write to the depth buffer. With `writeStatus` = `GL_FALSE`, the write mode for the depth buffer is disabled and we can only retrieve values for comparison in depth testing. This feature is useful when we want to use the same complicated background with displays of different foreground objects. After storing the background in the depth buffer, we disable the write mode and process the foreground. This allows us to generate a series of frames with different foreground objects or with one object in different positions for an animation sequence. Thus, only the depth values for the background are saved. Another application of the `glDepthMask` function is in displaying transparency effects (Section 10-20). In this case, we want to save only the depths of opaque objects for visibility testing, and not the depths of the transparent-surface positions. So the write mode for the depth buffer is turned off when a transparent surface is processed. Similar commands are available for setting the write status for the other buffers (color, index, and stencil).

OpenGL Wire-Frame Surface-Visibility Methods

A wire-frame display of a standard graphics object can be obtained in OpenGL by requesting that only its edges are to be generated. We do this by setting the polygon-mode function (Section 4-14) as, for example

```
glPolygonMode (GL_FRONT_AND_BACK, GL_LINE);
```

But this displays both visible and hidden edges.

To eliminate the hidden lines in a wire-frame display, we can employ the depth-offset method described in Section 4-14. That is, we first specify the wire-frame version of the object using the foreground color, then we specify an interior fill version using a depth offset and the background color for the interior fill. The depth offset ensures that the background-color fill will not interfere with the display of the visible edges. As an example, the following code segment generates a wire-frame display of an object using a white foreground color and a black background color.

```
glEnable (GL_DEPTH_TEST);
glPolygonMode (GL_FRONT_AND_BACK, GL_LINE);
glColor3f (1.0, 1.0, 1.0);
\*  Invoke the object-description routine.  */

glPolygonMode (GL_FRONT_AND_BACK, GL_FILL);
glEnable (GL_POLYGON_OFFSET_FILL);
glPolygonOffset (1.0, 1.0);
glColor3f (0.0, 0.0, 0.0);
\*  Invoke the object-description routine again.  */

glDisable (GL_POLYGON_OFFSET_FILL);
```

OpenGL Depth-Cueing Function

We can vary the brightness of an object as a function of its distance from the viewing position with

```
glEnable (GL_FOG);

glFogi (GL_FOG_MODE, GL_ LINEAR);
```

This applies the linear depth function in Eq. 9-9 to object colors using $d_{min} = 0.0$ and $d_{max} = 1.0$. But we can set different values for d_{min} and d_{max} with the following function calls.

```
glFogf (GL_FOG_START, minDepth);
glFogf (GL_FOG_END, maxDepth);
```

In these two functions, parameters `minDepth` and `maxDepth` are assigned floating-point values, although integer values can be used if we change the function suffix to `i`.

In addition, we can use the `glFog` function to set an atmosphere color that is to be combined with the color of an object after applying the linear depth-cueing function. Other atmospheric effects can also be modeled, and these various options are discussed in Section 10-20.

9-15 SUMMARY

The simplest visibility test is the back-face detection algorithm, which is fast and effective as an initial screening to eliminate many polygons from further visibility tests. For a single convex polyhedron, back-face detection eliminates all hidden surfaces but, in general, back-face detection cannot completely identify all hidden surfaces.

A commonly used method for identifying all visible surfaces in a scene is the depth-buffer algorithm. When applied to standard graphics objects, this procedure is highly efficient, but it does have extra storage requirements. Two buffers are needed: one to store pixel colors and one to store the depth values for the pixel positions. Fast, incremental, scan-line methods are used to process each polygon in a scene to calculate surface depths. As each surface is processed, the two buffers are updated. An extension of the depth-buffer approach is the A-buffer, which provides additional information for displaying antialiased and transparent surfaces.

Several other visibility-detection methods have been devised. The scan-line method processes all surfaces at one time for each scan line. With the depth-sorting method (painter's algorithm), objects are "painted" into the refresh buffer according to their distances from the viewing position. Subdivision schemes for identifying visible parts of a scene include the BSP-tree method, area subdivision, and octree representations. Visible surfaces can also be detected using ray-casting methods, which project lines from the pixel plane into a scene to determine object intersection positions along these projected lines. Ray-casting methods are an integral part of ray-tracing algorithms, which allow scenes to be displayed with global-illumination effects.

Visibility-detection methods are also used in displaying three-dimensional line drawings. With curved surfaces, we can display contour plots. For wire-frame

TABLE 9-1

SUMMARY OF OpenGL VISIBILITY-DETECTION FUNCTIONS

Function	Description
`glCullFace`	Specify front or back planes of polygons for culling operations when activated with `glEnable (GL_CULL_FACE)`.
`glutInitDisplayMode`	Specify depth-buffer operations using argument `GLUT_DEPTH`.
`glClear (GL_DEPTH_BUFFER_BIT)`	Initialize depth-buffer values to the default (1.0) or a value specified by the `glClearDepth` function.
`glClearDepth`	Specify an initial depth-buffer value.
`glEnable (GL_DEPTH_TEST)`	Activate depth-testing operations.
`glDepthRange`	Specify a range for normalizing depth values.
`glDepthFunc`	Specify a depth-testing condition.
`glDepthMask`	Set write status for the depth buffer.
`glPolygonOffset`	Specify an offset to eliminate hidden lines in a wire-frame display when a background fill color is applied.
`glFog`	Specify linear depth-cueing operations and values for min and max depth in the depth-cueing calculations.

displays of polyhedrons, we search for the various edge sections of the surfaces in a scene that are visible from the viewing position.

We can implement any visibility-detection scheme in an application program by creating our own routines, but graphics libraries commonly provide functions only for back-face removal and the depth-buffer method. In high-end computer-graphics systems, the depth-buffer routines are hardware implemented.

Functions for polygon culling and for depth-buffer visibility determinations are available in the OpenGL core library. With the polygon-culling routines, we can remove the back faces of standard graphics objects, their front faces, or both. With the depth-buffer routines, we can set the range for the depth tests and the type of depth testing that is to be performed. Wire-frame displays are obtained using the OpenGL polygon-mode and polygon-offset operations. And we can also generate OpenGL scenes using depth-cueing effects. In Table 9-1, we summarize the OpenGL functions for visibility testing. The polygon-mode function and other related operations are summarized at the end of Chapter 4.

REFERENCES

Additional sources of information on visibility algorithms include Elber and Cohen (1990), Franklin and Kankanhalli (1990), Segal (1990), and Naylor, Amanatides, and Thibault

(1990). A-buffer methods are presented in Cook, Carpenter, and Catmull (1987), Haeberli and Akeley (1990), and Shilling and Strasser (1993). A summary of contouring methods is given in Earnshaw (1985).

Various programming techniques for visibility testing can be found in Glassner (1990), Arvo (1991), Kirk (1992), Heckbert (1994), and Paeth (1995). Woo, Neider, Davis, and Shreiner (1999) provide additional discussions of the OpenGL visibility-detection functions. And a complete listing of the OpenGL functions in the core library and in GLU is presented in Shreiner (2000).

EXERCISES

9-1 Set up a back-face detection procedure that will identify all the visible faces of any input convex polyhedron that has different-colored surfaces. The polyhedron is to be defined in a right-handed viewing system, and the viewing direction is specified as user input.

9-2 Implement the procedure in the preceding exercise using an orthographic parallel projection to view visible faces of the input convex polyhedron. Assume that all parts of the object are in front of the view plane.

9-3 Implement the procedure in Exercise 9-1 using a perspective projection to view visible faces of the input convex polyhedron. Assume that all parts of the object are in front of the view plane.

9-4 Write a program to produce an animation of a convex polyhedron. The object is to be rotated incrementally about an axis that passes through the object and is parallel to the view plane. Assume that the object lies completely in front of the view plane. Use an orthographic parallel projection to map the views successively onto the view plane.

9-5 Write a routine to implement the depth-buffer method for the display of the visible surfaces of any input polyhedron. The array for the depth-buffer can be set to any convenient size on your system, such as 500 by 500. How can the storage requirements for the depth buffer be determined from the definition of the objects to be displayed?

9-6 Modify the procedure in the preceding exercise to display the visible surfaces in a scene containing any number of polyhedrons. Set up efficient methods for storing and processing the various objects in the scene.

9-7 Modify the procedure of the preceding exercise to implement the A-buffer algorithm for the display of a scene containing both opaque and transparent surfaces.

9-8 Extend the procedure developed in the preceding exercise to include antialiasing.

9-9 Develop a program to implement the scan-line algorithm for displaying the visible surfaces of a given polyhedron. Use polygon tables to store the definition of the object, and use coherence techniques to evaluate points along and between scan lines.

9-10 Write a program to implement the scan-line algorithm for a scene containing several polyhedrons. Use polygon tables to store the definition of the object, and use coherence techniques to evaluate points along and between scan lines.

9-11 Set up a program to display the visible surfaces of a convex polyhedron using the painter's algorithm. That is, surfaces are to be sorted on depth and painted on the screen from back to front.

9-12 Write a program that uses the depth-sorting method to display the visible surfaces of any given object with plane faces.

9-13 Develop a depth-sorting program to display the visible surfaces in a scene containing several polyhedrons.

9-14 Write a program to display the visible surfaces of a convex polyhedron using the BSP-tree method.

9-15 Give examples of situations where the two methods discussed for condition 3 in the area-subdivision algorithm will fail to identify correctly a surrounding surface that obscures all other surfaces.

9-16 Develop an algorithm that would test a given plane surface against a rectangular area to decide whether it is a surrounding, overlapping, inside, or outside surface.

9-17 Develop an algorithm for generating a quadtree representation for the visible surfaces of an object by applying the area-subdivision tests to determine the values of the quadtree elements.

9-18 Set up an algorithm to store a quadtree representation of an object in a frame buffer.

9-19 Set up a procedure to display the visible surfaces of an object that is described with an octree representation.

9-20 Devise an algorithm for viewing a single sphere using the ray-casting method.

9-21 Discuss how antialiasing methods can be incorporated into the various hidden-surface elimination algorithms.

9-22 Write a routine to produce a surface contour plot for a given surface function $f(x, y)$.

9-23 Develop an algorithm for detecting visible line sections in a scene by comparing each line in the scene to each polygon surface facet.

9-24 Discuss how wire-frame displays might be generated with the various visible-surface detection methods discussed in this chapter.

9-25 Set up a procedure for generating a wire-frame display of a polyhedron with the hidden edges of the object shown as dashed lines.

9-26 Write a program to display a polyhedron with selected faces removed, using the OpenGL polygon-culling functions. Each face of the polygon is to be given a different color, and a face is to be selected for removal with user input. Also, a viewing position and other viewing parameters are to be specified as input values.

9-27 Modify the program in the preceding exercise to view the polyhedron from any position, using the depth-buffer routines instead of the polygon-culling routines.

9-28 Modify the program in the preceding exercise so that the depth range and the depth test condition can also be specified as user input.

9-29 Generate a wire-frame display of a polyhedron using the `glPolygonMode` and `glPolygonOffset` functions as discussed in Section 9-14.

9-30 Modify the program of the preceding exercise to display the polyhedron using the depth-cueing function `glFogi`.

9-31 Modify the program of the preceding exercise to display several polyhedrons that are distributed in depth. The depth-cueing range is to be set with user input.

CHAPTER 10

Illumination Models and Surface-Rendering Methods

A scene from the computer-animation film *Final Fantasy: The Spirits Within*, showing the illumination effects used to simulate an exploding spirit. *(Courtesy of Square Pictures, Inc. © 2001 FFFP. All rights reserved.)*

Realistic displays of a scene are obtained by generating perspective projections of objects and applying natural lighting effects to the visible surfaces. An **illumination model,** also called a **lighting model** (and sometimes referred to as a shading model), is used to calculate the color of an illuminated position on the surface of an object. A **surface-rendering method** uses the color calculations from an illumination model to determine the pixel colors for all projected positions in a scene. The illumination model can be applied to every projection position, or the surface rendering can be accomplished by interpolating colors on the surfaces using a small set of illumination-model calculations. Scan-line, image-space algorithms typically use interpolation schemes, while ray-tracing algorithms may invoke the illumination model at every pixel position. Sometimes, a surface-rendering procedure is called a shading method that calculates surface colors using a shading model, but this can lead to some confusion between the two terms. To avoid possible misinterpretations due to the use of similar terminology, we refer to the model for calculating the light intensity at a single surface point as an *illumination model* or a *lighting model*, and we use the term *surface rendering* to mean a procedure for applying a lighting model to obtain pixel colors for all projected surface positions.

Among other things, photorealism in computer graphics involves two elements: accurate representations of surface properties and good physical descriptions of the lighting effects in a scene. These surface lighting effects include light reflections, transparency, surface texture, and shadows.

In general, modeling the lighting effects that we see on an object is a complex process, involving principles of both physics and psychology. Fundamentally, lighting effects are described with models that consider the interaction of electromagnetic energy with the object surfaces in a scene. Once light reaches our eyes, it triggers perception processes that determine what we actually "see". Physical illumination models involve a number of factors, such as material properties, object position relative to light sources and other objects, and the features of the light sources. Objects can be composed of opaque materials, or they can be more or less transparent. In addition, they can have shiny or dull surfaces, and they can have a variety of surface-texture patterns. Light sources, of varying shapes, colors, and positions, can be used to provide the illumination for a scene. Given the parameters for the optical properties of surfaces, the relative positions of the surfaces in a scene, the color and positions of the light sources, the characteristics of the light sources, and the position and orientation of the viewing plane, illumination models calculate the light intensity projected from a particular surface position in a specified viewing direction.

Illumination models in computer graphics are often approximations of the physical laws that describe surface-lighting effects. To reduce computations, most packages use empirical models based on simplified photometric calculations. More accurate models, such as the radiosity algorithm, compute light intensities by considering the propagation of radiant energy between the light sources and the various surfaces in a scene. In the following sections, we first take a look at the basic lighting models often used in computer-graphics systems; then we discuss more accurate, but more complex, methods for determining the appearance of illuminated surfaces. And we explore the various surface-rendering algorithms for applying the lighting models to obtain effective displays of natural scenes.

10-1 LIGHT SOURCES

Any object that is emitting radiant energy is a **light source** that contributes to the lighting effects for other objects in a scene. We can model light sources with a variety of shapes and characteristics, and most emitters serve only as a source of illumination for a scene. In some applications, however, we may want to create an object that is both a light source and a light reflector. For example, a plastic globe surrounding a light bulb both emits and reflects light from the surface of the globe. We could also model the globe as a semitransparent surface around a light source. But for some objects, such as a large fluorescent light panel, it might be more convenient to describe the surface simply as a combination emitter and reflector.

A light source can be defined with a number of properties. We can specify its position, the color of the emitted light, the emission direction, and its shape. If the source is also to be a light-reflecting surface, we need to give its reflectivity properties. In addition, we could set up a light source that emits different colors in different directions. For example, we could define a light source that emits a red light on one side and a green light on the other side.

In most applications, and particularly for real-time graphics displays, a simple light-source model is used to avoid excessive computations. We assign light-emitting properties using a single value for each of the RGB color components, which we can describe as the amount, or the "intensity", of that color component. Color parameters and light-source models are discussed in greater detail in Chapter 12.

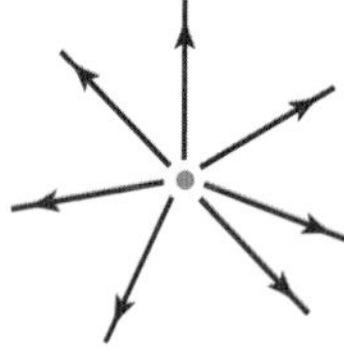

FIGURE 10-1 Diverging ray paths from a point light source.

Point Light Sources

The simplest model for an object that is emitting radiant energy is a **point light source** with a single color, specified with three RGB components. We define a point source for a scene by giving its position and the color of the emitted light. As shown in Fig. 10-1, light rays are generated along radially diverging paths from the single-color source position. This light-source model is a reasonable approximation for sources whose dimensions are small compared to the size of objects in the scene. We can also simulate larger sources as point emitters if they are not too close to a scene. We use the position of a point source in an illumination model to determine which objects in the scene are illuminated by that source and to calculate the light direction to a selected object surface position.

Infinitely Distant Light Sources

A large light source, such as the sun, that is very far from a scene can also be approximated as a point emitter, but there is little variation in its directional effects. In contrast to a light source in the middle of a scene, which illuminates objects on all sides of the source, a remote source illuminates the scene from only one direction. The light path from a distant light source to any position in the scene is nearly constant, as illustrated in Fig. 10-2.

We can simulate an infinitely distant light source by assigning it a color value and a fixed direction for the light rays emanating from the source. Only the vector for the emission direction, and not the position of the source, is needed in the illumination calculations, along with the light-source color.

Radial Intensity Attenuation

As radiant energy from a light source travels outwards through space, its amplitude at any distance d_l from the source is attenuated by the factor $1/d_l^2$. This means that a surface close to the light source receives a higher incident light intensity from that source than a more distant surface. Therefore, to produce realistic lighting effects, we should take this intensity attenuation into account. Otherwise, all surfaces are illuminated with the same intensity from a light source, and undesirable display effects can result. For example, if two surfaces with the same optical parameters project to overlapping positions, they would be indistinguishable from one another. Thus, regardless of their relative distances from the light source, the two surfaces would appear to be one surface.

In practice, however, using an attenuation factor of $1/d_l^2$ with a point source does not always produce realistic pictures. The factor $1/d_l^2$ tends to produce too much intensity variation for objects that are close to the light source, and very little

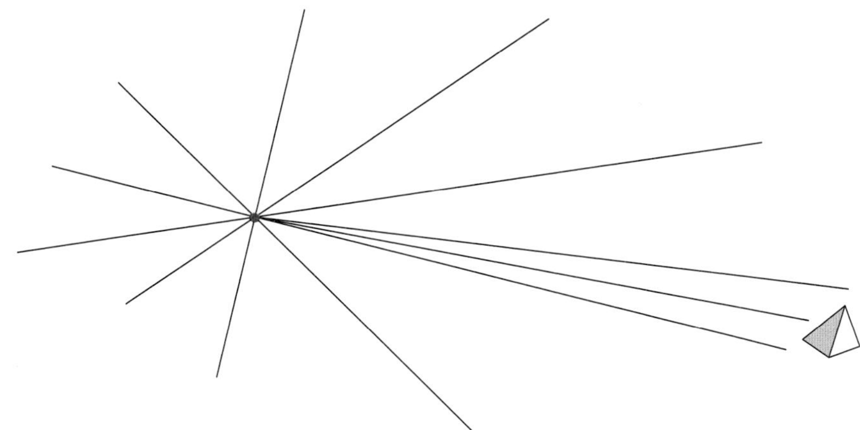

FIGURE 10-2 Light rays from an infinitely distant light source illuminate an object along nearly parallel light paths.

variation when d_l is large. This is because actual light sources are not infinitesimal points, and illuminating a scene with point emitters is only a simple approximation of true lighting effects. To generate more realistic displays using point sources, we can attenuate light intensities with an inverse quadratic function of d_l that includes a linear term:

$$f_{\text{radatten}}(d_l) = \frac{1}{a_0 + a_1 d_l + a_2 d_l^2} \tag{10-1}$$

The numerical values for the coefficients, a_0, a_1, and a_2, can then be adjusted to produce optimal attenuation effects. For instance, we can assign a large value to a_0 when d_l is very small to prevent $f_{\text{radatten}}(d_l)$ from becoming too large. As an additional option, often available in graphics packages, a different set of values for the attenuation coefficients could be assigned to each point light source in the scene.

We cannot apply the intensity-attenuation calculation 10-1 to a point source at "infinity", because the distance to the light source is indeterminate. Also, all points in the scene are at a nearly equal distance from a far-off source. To accommodate both remote and local light sources, we can express the intensity-attenuation function as

$$f_{l,\text{radatten}} = \begin{cases} 1.0, & \text{if source is at infinity} \\ \dfrac{1}{a_0 + a_1 d_l + a_2 d_l^2}, & \text{if source is local} \end{cases} \tag{10-2}$$

Directional Light Sources and Spotlight Effects

A local light source can easily be modified to produce a directional, or spotlight, beam of light. If an object is outside the directional limits of the light source, we exclude it from illumination by that source. One way to set up a directional light source is to assign it a vector direction and an angular limit θ_l measured from that vector direction, in addition to its position and color. This defines a conical region of space with the light-source vector direction along the axis of the cone (Fig. 10-3). A multicolor point light source could be modeled in this way using multiple direction vectors and a different emission color for each direction.

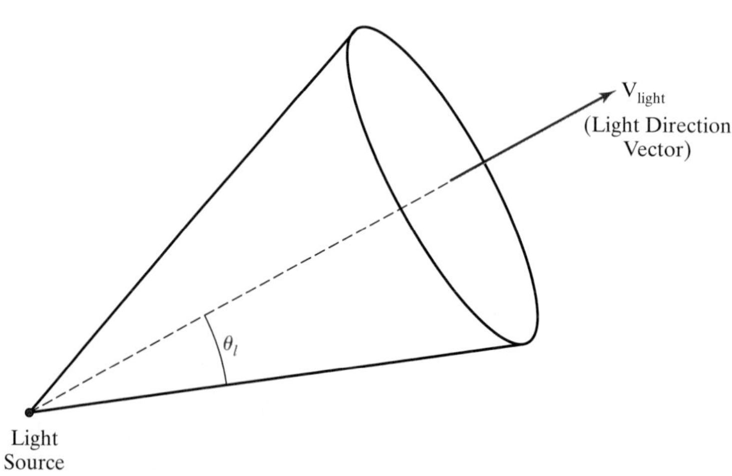

FIGURE 10-3 A directional point light source. The unit light-direction vector defines the axis of a light cone, and angle θ_l defines the angular extent of the circular cone.

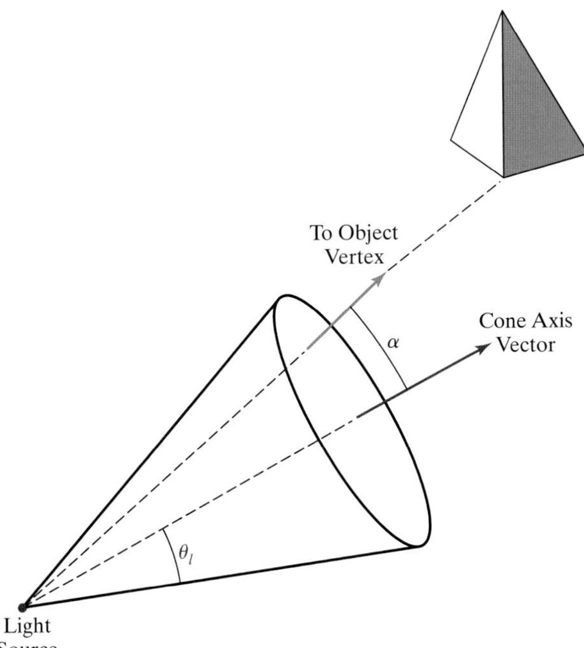

FIGURE 10-4 An object illuminated by a directional point light source.

We can denote $\mathbf{V}_{\text{light}}$ as the unit vector in the light-source direction and $\mathbf{V}_{\text{obj}}$ as the unit vector in the direction from the light position to an object position. Then

$$\mathbf{V}_{\text{obj}} \cdot \mathbf{V}_{\text{light}} = \cos\alpha \tag{10-3}$$

where angle α is the angular distance of the object from the light direction vector. If we restrict the angular extent of any light cone so that $0^\circ < \theta_l \leq 90^\circ$, then the object is within the spotlight if $\cos\alpha \geq \cos\theta_l$, as shown in Fig. 10-4. But if $\mathbf{V}_{\text{obj}} \cdot \mathbf{V}_{\text{light}} < \cos\theta_l$, the object is outside the light cone.

Angular Intensity Attenuation

For a directional light source, we can attenuate the light intensity angularly about the source as well as radially out from the point-source position. This allows us to simulate a cone of light that is most intense along the axis of the cone, with the intensity decreasing as we move farther from the cone axis. A commonly used angular intensity-attenuation function for a directional light source is

$$f_{\text{angatten}}(\phi) = \cos^{a_l}\phi, \qquad 0^\circ \leq \phi \leq \theta \tag{10-4}$$

where the attenuation exponent a_l is assigned some positive value and angle ϕ is measured from the cone axis. Along the cone axis, $\phi = 0^\circ$ and $f_{\text{angatten}}(\phi) = 1.0$. The greater the value for the attenuation exponent a_l, the smaller the value of the angular intensity-attenuation function for a given value of angle $\phi > 0^\circ$.

There are several special cases to consider in the implementation of the angular-attenuation function. There is no angular attenuation if the light source is not directional (not a spotlight). Also, an object is not illuminated by the light source if it is anywhere outside the cone of the spotlight. To determine the angular attenuation factor along a line from the light position to a surface position in a scene, we can compute the cosine of the direction angle from the cone axis using the dot product calculation in Eq. 10-3. We designate $\mathbf{V}_{\text{light}}$ as the unit vector in the light-source direction (along the cone axis) and $\mathbf{V}_{\text{obj}}$ as the unit vector in the direction from the light source to an object position. Using these two unit vectors and assuming that $0^\circ < \theta_l \leq 90^\circ$, we can express the general equation for angular attenuation as

$$f_{l,\text{angatten}} = \begin{cases} 1.0, & \text{if source is not a spotlight} \\ 0.0, & \text{if } \mathbf{V}_{\text{obj}} \cdot \mathbf{V}_{\text{light}} = \cos\alpha < \cos\theta_l \\ & \quad \text{(object is outside the spotlight cone)} \\ (\mathbf{V}_{\text{obj}} \cdot \mathbf{V}_{\text{light}})^{a_l}, & \text{otherwise} \end{cases} \tag{10-5}$$

Extended Light Sources and the Warn Model

When we want to include a large light source at a position close to the objects in a scene, such as the long neon lamp in Fig. 10-5, we can approximate it as a light-emitting surface. One way to do this is to model the light surface as a grid of directional point emitters. We can set the direction for the point sources so that objects behind the light-emitting surface are not illuminated. And we could also include other controls to restrict the direction of the emitted light near the edges of the source.

The **Warn model** provides a method for producing studio lighting effects using sets of point emitters with various parameters to simulate the barn doors, flaps, and spotlighting controls employed by photographers. Spotlighting is achieved with the cone of light discussed earlier, and the flaps and barn doors provide additional directional control. For instance, two flaps can be set up for each of the x, y, and z directions to further restrict the path of the emitted light rays. This light-source simulation is implemented in some graphics packages, and Fig. 10-6 illustrates lighting effects that can be achieved with the Warn model.

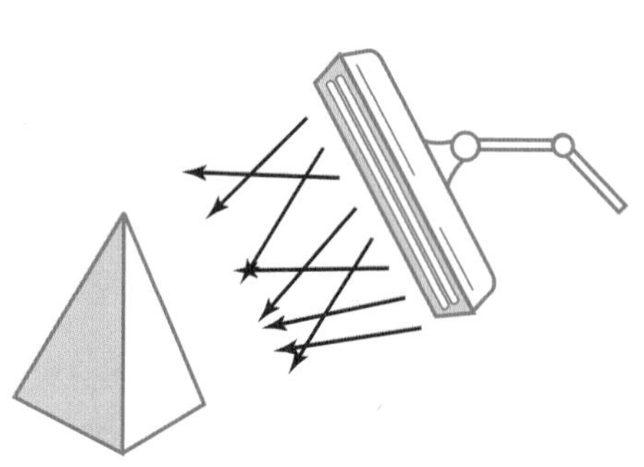

FIGURE 10-5 An object illuminated by a large nearby light source.

FIGURE 10-6 Studio lighting effects produced with the Warn model, using five extended light sources to illuminate a Chevrolet Camaro. (*Courtesy of David R. Warn, General Motors Research Laboratories.*)

10-2 SURFACE LIGHTING EFFECTS

An illumination model computes the lighting effects for a surface using the various optical properties that have been assigned to that surface. These properties include degree of transparency, color reflectance coefficients, and various surface-texture parameters.

When light is incident on an opaque surface, part of it is reflected and part is absorbed. The amount of incident light reflected by the surface depends on the type of material. Shiny materials reflect more of the incident light, and dull surfaces absorb more of the incident light. For a transparent surface, some of the incident light is also transmitted through the material.

Surfaces that are rough, or grainy, tend to scatter the reflected light in all directions. This scattered light is called **diffuse reflection.** A very rough, matte surface produces primarily diffuse reflections, so that the surface appears equally bright from any viewing angle. Figure 10-7 illustrates diffuse light scattering from a surface. What we call the color of an object is the color of the diffuse reflection when the object is illuminated with white light, which is composed of a combination of all colors. A blue object, for example, reflects the blue component of the white light and absorbs all the other color components. If the blue object is viewed under a red light, it appears black since all of the incident light is absorbed.

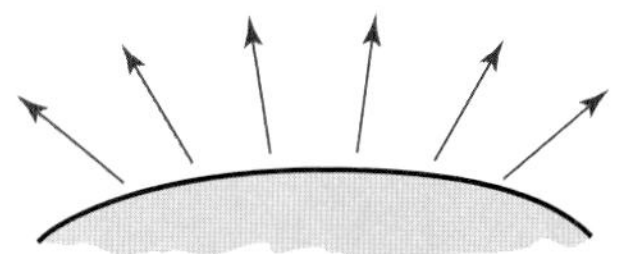

FIGURE 10-7 Diffuse reflections from a surface.

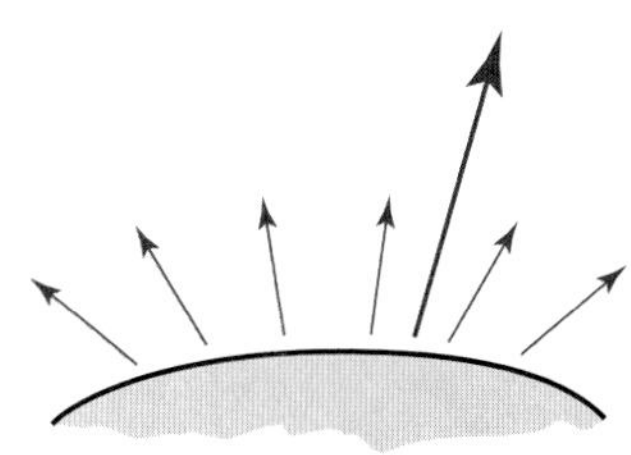

FIGURE 10-8 Specular reflection superimposed on diffuse reflection vectors.

In addition to diffuse light scattering, some of the reflected light is concentrated into a highlight, or bright spot, called **specular reflection.** This highlighting effect is more pronounced on shiny surfaces than on dull surfaces. And we can see the specular reflection when we look at an illuminated shiny surface, such as polished metal, an apple, or a person's forehead, only when we view the surface from a particular direction. A representation of specular reflection is shown in Fig. 10-8.

Another factor that must be considered in an illumination model is the **background light** or **ambient light** in a scene. A surface that is not directly exposed to a light source may still be visible due to the reflected light from nearby objects that are illuminated. Thus, the ambient light for a scene is the illumination effect produced by the reflected light from the various surfaces in the scene. Figure 10-9 illustrates this background lighting effect. The total reflected light from a surface is the sum of the contributions from light sources and from the light reflected by other illuminated objects.

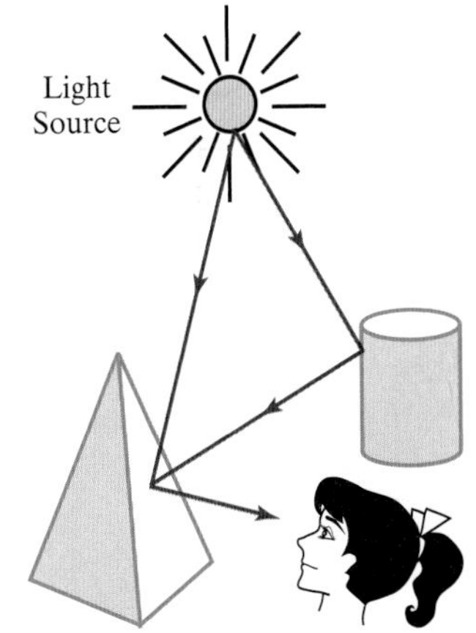

FIGURE 10-9 Surface lighting effects are produced by a combination of illumination from light sources and reflections from other surfaces.

10-3 BASIC ILLUMINATION MODELS

Accurate surface lighting models compute the results of interactions between incident radiant energy and the material composition of an object. To simplify the surface-illumination calculations, we can use approximate representations for the physical processes that produce the lighting effects discussed in the previous section. The empirical model described in this section produces reasonably good results, and it is implemented in most graphics systems.

Light-emitting objects in a basic illumination model are generally limited to point sources. However, many graphics packages provide additional functions for dealing with directional lighting (spotlights) and extended light sources.

Ambient Light

In our basic illumination model, we can incorporate background lighting by setting a general brightness level for a scene. This produces a uniform ambient lighting that is the same for all objects, and it approximates the global diffuse reflections from the various illuminated surfaces.

Assuming that we are describing only monochromatic lighting effects, such as shades of gray, we designate the level for the ambient light in a scene with an intensity parameter I_a. Each surface in the scene is then illuminated with this background light. Reflections produced by ambient-light illumination are simply a form of diffuse reflection, and they are independent of the viewing direction and the spatial orientation of a surface. However, the amount of the incident ambient light that is reflected depends on surface optical properties, which determine how much of the incident energy is reflected and how much is absorbed.

Diffuse Reflection

We can model diffuse reflections from a surface by assuming that the incident light is scattered with equal intensity in all directions, independent of the viewing position. Such surfaces are called **ideal diffuse reflectors.** They are also referred to as **Lambertian reflectors,** because the reflected radiant light energy from any point on the surface is calculated with **Lambert's cosine law.** This law states that the amount of radiant energy coming from any small surface area dA in a direction ϕ_N relative to the surface normal is proportional to $\cos \phi_N$ (Fig. 10-10). The intensity of light in this direction can be computed as the ratio of the magnitude of the radiant energy per unit time divided by the projection of the surface area in the radiation direction:

$$\begin{aligned} \text{Intensity} &= \frac{\text{radiant energy per unit time}}{\text{projected area}} \\ &\propto \frac{\cos \phi_N}{dA \cos \phi_N} \\ &= \text{constant} \end{aligned} \tag{10-6}$$

Thus, for Lambertion reflection, the intensity of light is the same over all viewing directions.

Assuming that every surface is to be treated as an ideal diffuse reflector (Lambertian), we can set a parameter k_d for each surface that determines the fraction of the incident light that is to be scattered as diffuse reflections. This parameter is called the **diffuse-reflection coefficient** or the **diffuse reflectivity.** The diffuse reflection in any direction is then a constant, which is equal to the incident light intensity multiplied by the diffuse-reflection coefficient. For a monochromatic light source, parameter k_d is assigned a constant value in the interval 0.0 to 1.0, according to the reflecting properties we want the surface to have. If we want a highly reflective surface, we set the value of k_d near 1.0. This produces a brighter

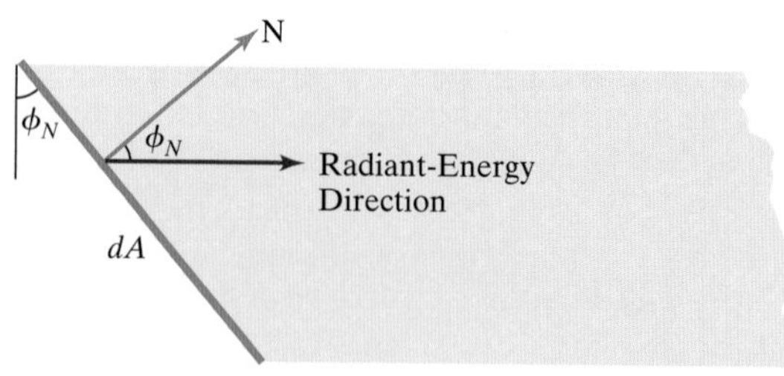

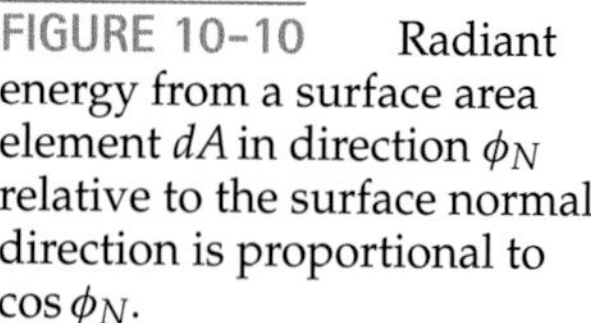
FIGURE 10-10 Radiant energy from a surface area element dA in direction ϕ_N relative to the surface normal direction is proportional to $\cos \phi_N$.

surface with the intensity of the reflected light near that of the incident light. If we want to simulate a surface that absorbs most of the incident light, we set the reflectivity to a value near 0.0.

For the background lighting effects, we can assume that every surface is fully illuminated by the ambient light I_a that we assigned to the scene. Therefore, the ambient contribution to the diffuse reflection at any point on a surface is simply

$$I_{\text{ambdiff}} = k_d I_a \tag{10-7}$$

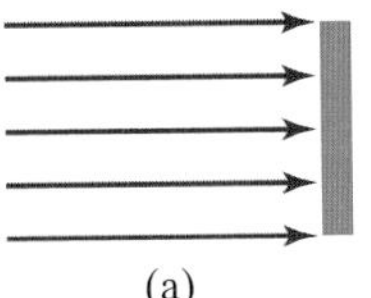

(a)

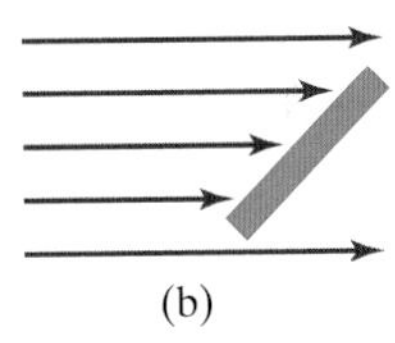

(b)

FIGURE 10-11 A surface that is perpendicular to the direction of the incident light (a) is more illuminated than an equal-sized surface at an oblique angle (b) to the incoming light direction.

Ambient light alone, however, produces a flat uninteresting shading for a surface (Fig. 10-23(b)), so scenes are rarely rendered using only ambient light. At least one light source is included in a scene, often as a point source at the viewing position.

When a surface is illuminated by a light source with an intensity I_l, the amount of incident light from the source depends on the orientation of the surface relative to the light source direction. A surface that is oriented nearly perpendicular to the illumination direction receives more light from the source than a surface that is tilted at an oblique angle to the direction of the incoming light. This illumination effect can be observed on a white sheet of paper or smooth cardboard that is placed parallel to a sunlit window. As the sheet is slowly rotated away from the window direction, the surface appears less bright. Figure 10-11 illustrates this effect, showing a beam of light rays incident on two equal-area plane surface elements with different spatial orientations relative to the illumination direction from a distant source (parallel incoming rays).

From Fig. 10-11, we see that the number of light rays intersecting a surface element is proportional to the area of the surface projection perpendicular to the incident light direction. If we denote the **angle of incidence** between the incoming light direction and the surface normal as θ (Fig. 10-12), then the projected area of a surface element perpendicular to the light direction is proportional to $\cos\theta$. Therefore, we can model the amount of incident light on a surface from a source with intensity I_l as

$$I_{l,\text{incident}} = I_l \cos\theta \tag{10-8}$$

Using Eq. 10-8, we can model the diffuse reflections from a light source with intensity I_l using the calculation

$$\begin{aligned} I_{l,\text{diff}} &= k_d I_{l,\text{incident}} \\ &= k_d I_l \cos\theta \end{aligned} \tag{10-9}$$

When the incoming light from the source is perpendicular to the surface at a particular point, $\theta = 90^\circ$ and $I_{l,\text{diff}} = k_d I_l$. As the angle of incidence increases, the illumination from the light source decreases. Furthermore, a surface is illuminated by a point source only if the angle of incidence is in the range 0° to 90° ($\cos\theta$ is in the interval from 0.0 to 1.0). When $\cos\theta < 0.0$, the light source is behind the surface.

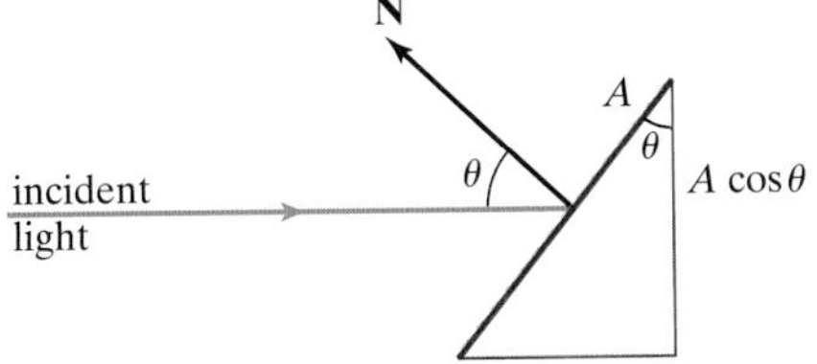

FIGURE 10-12 An illuminated area A projected perpendicular to the path of incoming light rays. This perpendicular projection has an area equal to $A\cos\theta$.

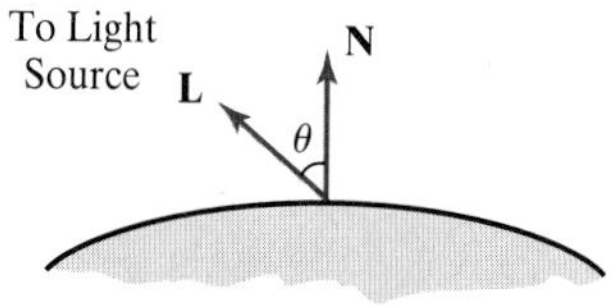

FIGURE 10-13 Angle of incidence θ between the unit light-source direction vector **L** and the unit normal vector **N** at a surface position.

At any surface position, we can denote the unit normal vector as **N** and the unit direction vector to a point source as **L**, as in Fig. 10-13. Then, $\cos\theta = \mathbf{N} \cdot \mathbf{L}$ and the diffuse reflection equation for single point-source illumination at a surface position can be expressed in the form

$$I_{l,\text{diff}} = \begin{cases} k_d I_l (\mathbf{N} \cdot \mathbf{L}), & \text{if } \mathbf{N} \cdot \mathbf{L} > 0 \\ 0.0, & \text{if } \mathbf{N} \cdot \mathbf{L} \leq 0 \end{cases} \tag{10-10}$$

The unit direction vector **L** to a nearby point light source is calculated using the surface position and the light-source position:

$$\mathbf{L} = \frac{\mathbf{P}_{\text{source}} - \mathbf{P}_{\text{surf}}}{|\mathbf{P}_{\text{source}} - \mathbf{P}_{\text{surf}}|} \tag{10-11}$$

A light source at "infinity", however, has no position, only a propagation direction. In that case, we use the negative of the assigned light-source emission direction for the direction of vector **L**.

Figure 10-14 illustrates the application of Eq. 10-10 to positions over the surface of a sphere, using selected values for parameter k_d between 0 and 1. At $k_d = 0$, no light is reflected and the object surface appears black. Increasing values for k_d increase the intensity of the diffuse reflections, producing lighter shades of gray. Each projected pixel position for the surface is assigned an intensity value as calculated by the diffuse reflection equation. The surface renderings in this figure illustrate single point-source lighting with no other lighting effects. This is what we might expect to see if we shined a very small flashlight, such as a penlight, on the object in a completely darkened room. For general scenes, however, we expect some surface reflections due to the ambient light in addition to the illumination effects produced by a light source.

We can combine the ambient and point-source intensity calculations to obtain an expression for the total diffuse reflection at a surface position. In addition, many graphics packages introduce an **ambient-reflection coefficient** k_a that can

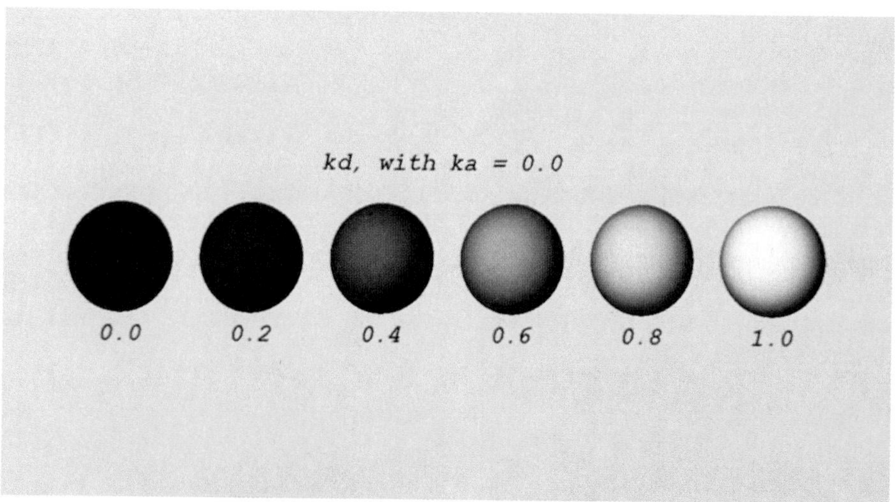

FIGURE 10-14 Diffuse reflections from a spherical surface illuminated by a point source emitting white light, with values of the diffuse reflectivity coefficient in the interval $0 \leq k_d \leq 1$.

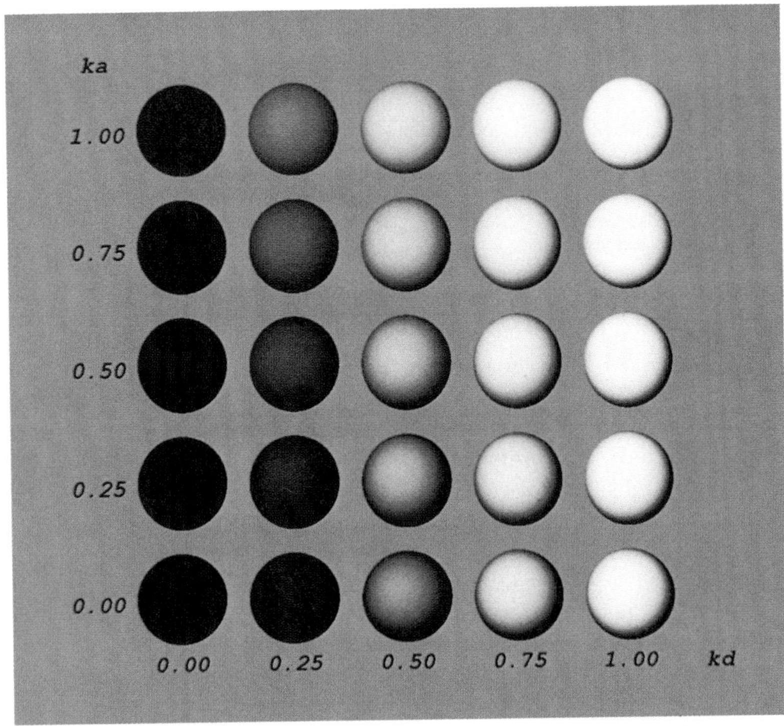

FIGURE 10-15 Diffuse reflections from a spherical surface illuminated with a dark-gray ambient light and a white point source, using five values for k_a and k_d from 0.0 to 1.0.

be assigned to each surface to modify the ambient-light intensity I_a. This simply provides us with an additional parameter for adjusting the lighting effects in our empirical model. Using parameter k_a, we can write the total diffuse-reflection equation for a single point source as

$$I_{\text{diff}} = \begin{cases} k_a I_a + k_d I_l \, (\mathbf{N} \cdot \mathbf{L}), & \text{if } \mathbf{N} \cdot \mathbf{L} > 0 \\ k_a I_a, & \text{if } \mathbf{N} \cdot \mathbf{L} \leq 0 \end{cases} \tag{10-12}$$

where both k_a and k_d depend on surface material properties and are assigned values in the range from 0 to 1.0 for monochromatic lighting effects. Figure 10-15 shows a sphere displayed with surface intensities calculated from Eq. 10-12 for values of parameters k_a and k_d between 0 and 1.0.

Specular Reflection and the Phong Model

The bright spot, or specular reflection, that we can see on a shiny surface is the result of total, or near total, reflection of the incident light in a concentrated region around the **specular-reflection angle.** Figure 10-16 shows the specular reflection direction for a position on an illuminated surface. The specular reflection angle equals the angle of the incident light, with the two angles measured on opposite sides of the unit normal surface vector **N**. In this figure, **R** represents the unit vector in the direction of ideal specular reflection, **L** is the unit vector directed toward the point light source, and **V** is the unit vector pointing to the viewer from the selected surface position. Angle ϕ is the viewing angle relative to the specular-reflection direction **R**. For an ideal reflector (a perfect mirror), incident light is reflected only in the specular-reflection direction, and we would see reflected light only when vectors **V** and **R** coincide ($\phi = 0$).

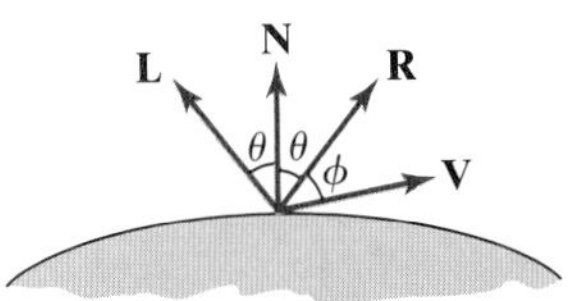

FIGURE 10-16 Specular reflection angle equals angle of incidence θ.

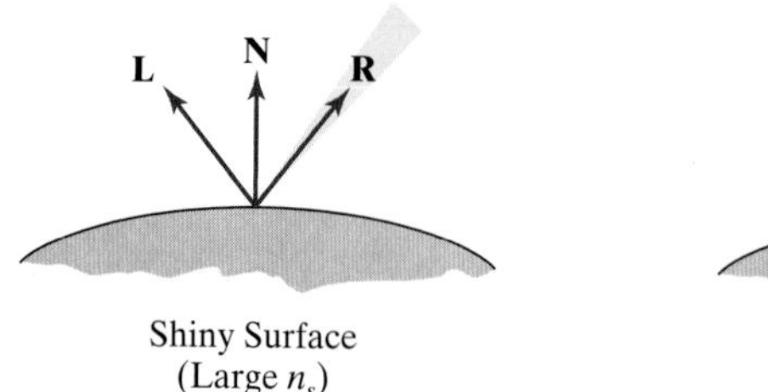

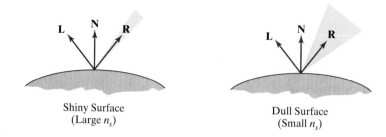

FIGURE 10-17 Modeling specular reflections (shaded area) with parameter n_s.

Objects other than ideal reflectors exhibit specular reflections over a finite range of viewing positions around vector **R**. Shiny surfaces have a narrow specular reflection range, and dull surfaces have a wider reflection range. An empirical model for calculating the specular reflection range, developed by Phong Bui Tuong and called the **Phong specular-reflection model** or simply the **Phong model,** sets the intensity of specular reflection proportional to $\cos^{n_s} \phi$. Angle ϕ can be assigned values in the range 0° to 90°, so that $\cos \phi$ varies from 0 to 1.0. The value assigned to the **specular-reflection exponent** n_s is determined by the type of surface that we want to display. A very shiny surface is modeled with a large value for n_s (say, 100 or more), and smaller values (down to 1) are used for duller surfaces. For a perfect reflector, n_s is infinite. For a rough surface, such as chalk or cinderblock, n_s is assigned a value near 1. Figures 10-17 and 10-18 show the effect of n_s on the angular range for which we can expect to see specular reflections.

The intensity of specular reflection depends on the material properties of the surface and the angle of incidence, as well as other factors such as the polarization and color of the incident light. We can approximately model monochromatic specular intensity variations using a **specular-reflection coefficient,** $W(\theta)$, for each surface. Figure 10-19 shows the general variation of $W(\theta)$ over the range $\theta = 0°$ to $\theta = 90°$ for a few materials. In general, $W(\theta)$ tends to increase as the angle of incidence increases. At $\theta = 90°$, all of the incident light is reflected ($W(\theta) = 1$). The variation of specular intensity with angle of incidence is described by *Fresnel's Laws of Reflection*. Using the spectral-reflection function $W(\theta)$, we can write the Phong specular-reflection model as

$$I_{l,\text{spec}} = W(\theta) I_l \cos^{n_s} \phi \qquad (10\text{-}13)$$

where I_l is the intensity of the light source, and ϕ is the viewing angle relative to the specular-reflection direction **R**.

As seen in Fig. 10-19, transparent materials, such as glass, exhibit appreciable specular reflections only as θ approaches 90°. At $\theta = 0°$, about 4 percent of the incident light on a glass surface is reflected. And for most of the range of θ, the reflected intensity is less than 10 percent of the incident intensity. But for many opaque materials, specular reflection is nearly constant for all incidence angles. In this case, we can reasonably model the specular effects by replacing $W(\theta)$ with a constant specular-reflection coefficient k_s. We then simply set k_s equal to some value in the range from 0 to 1.0 for each surface.

Since **V** and **R** are unit vectors in the viewing and specular-reflection directions, we can calculate the value of $\cos \phi$ with the dot product $\mathbf{V} \cdot \mathbf{R}$. In addition, no specular effects are generated for the display of a surface if **V** and **L** are on the same side of the normal vector **N** or if the light source is behind the surface. Thus, assuming the specular-reflection coefficient is a constant for any material, we can determine the intensity of the specular reflection due to a point light source at a

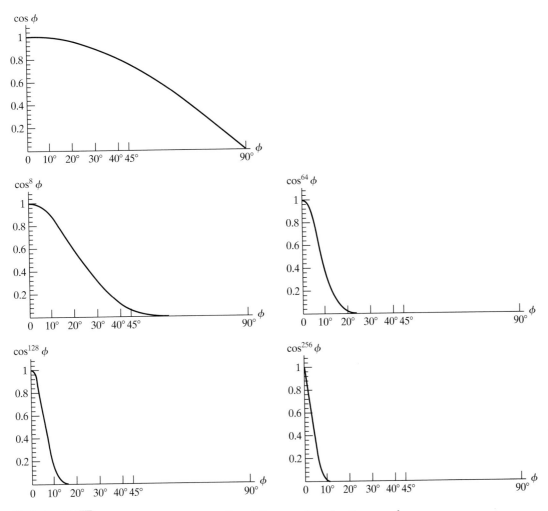

FIGURE 10-18 Plots of $\cos^{n_s}\phi$ using five different values for the specular exponent n_s.

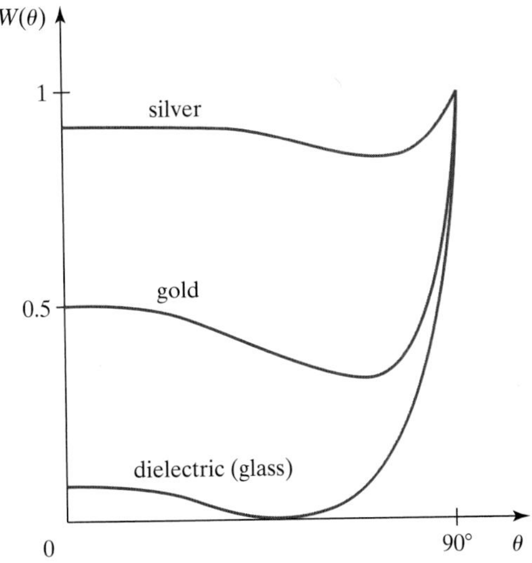

FIGURE 10-19 Approximate variation of the specular-reflection coefficient for different materials, as a function of the angle of incidence.

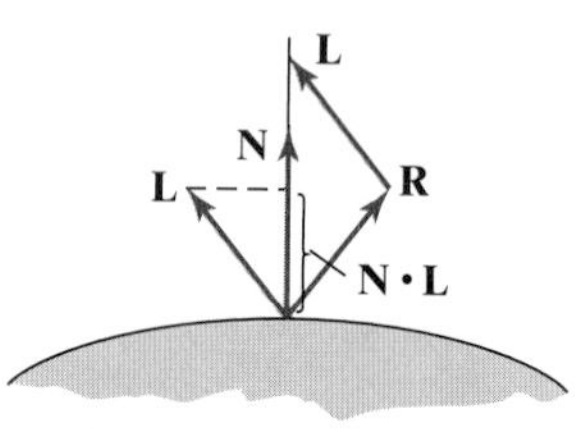

FIGURE 10-20 The projection of either **L** or **R** onto the direction of the normal vector **N** has a magnitude equal to **N** • **L**.

surface position with the calculation

$$I_{l,\text{spec}} = \begin{cases} k_s I_l (\mathbf{V} \cdot \mathbf{R})^{n_s}, & \text{if } \mathbf{V} \cdot \mathbf{R} > 0 \quad \text{and} \quad \mathbf{N} \cdot \mathbf{L} > 0 \\ 0.0, & \text{if } \mathbf{V} \cdot \mathbf{R} < 0 \quad \text{or} \quad \mathbf{N} \cdot \mathbf{L} \le 0 \end{cases} \tag{10-14}$$

The direction for **R**, the reflection vector, can be computed from the directions for vectors **L** and **N**. As seen in Fig. 10-20, the projection of **L** onto the direction of the normal vector has a magnitude equal to the dot product **N** • **L**, which is also equal to the magnitude of the projection of unit vector **R** onto the direction of **N**. Therefore, from this diagram, we see that

$$\mathbf{R} + \mathbf{L} = (2\mathbf{N} \cdot \mathbf{L})\mathbf{N}$$

and the specular-reflection vector is obtained as

$$\mathbf{R} = (2\mathbf{N} \cdot \mathbf{L})\mathbf{N} - \mathbf{L} \tag{10-15}$$

Figure 10-21 illustrates specular reflections for various values of k_s and n_s on a sphere illuminated with a single point light source.

We calculate **V** using the surface position and the viewing position, in same way that we obtained the unit vector **L** (Eq. 10-11). But if a fixed viewing direction is to be used for all positions in a scene, we can set $\mathbf{V} = (0.0, 0.0, 1.0)$, which is a unit vector in the positive z direction. Specular calculations take less time to calculate using a constant **V**, but the displays are not as realistic.

A somewhat simplified Phong model is obtained using the **halfway vector H** between **L** and **V** to calculate the range of specular reflections. If we replace **V** • **R** in the Phong model with the dot product **N** • **H**, this simply replaces the empirical

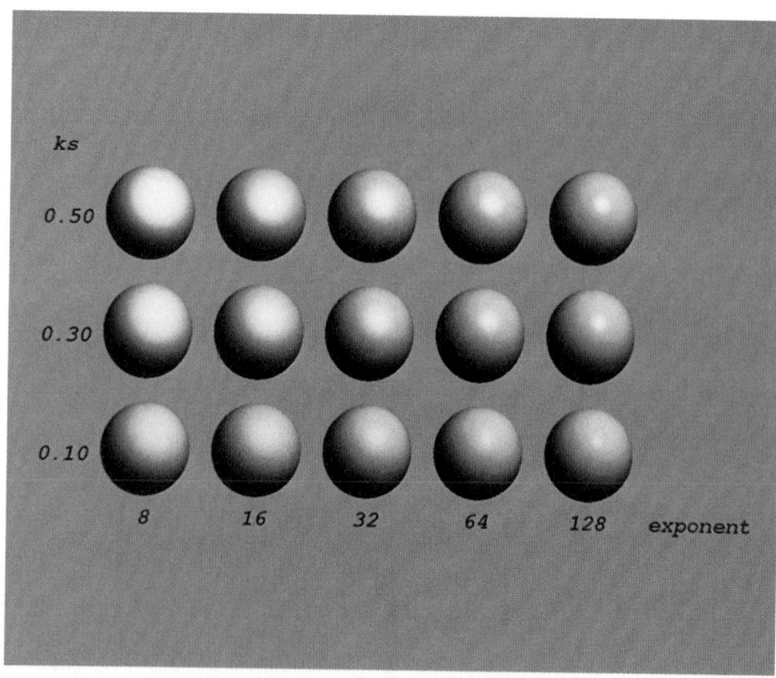

FIGURE 10-21 Specular reflections from a spherical surface for varying specular parameter values and a single light source.

$\cos\phi$ calculation with the empirical $\cos\alpha$ calculation (Fig. 10-22). The halfway vector is obtained as

$$\mathbf{H} = \frac{\mathbf{L} + \mathbf{V}}{|\mathbf{L} + \mathbf{V}|} \tag{10-16}$$

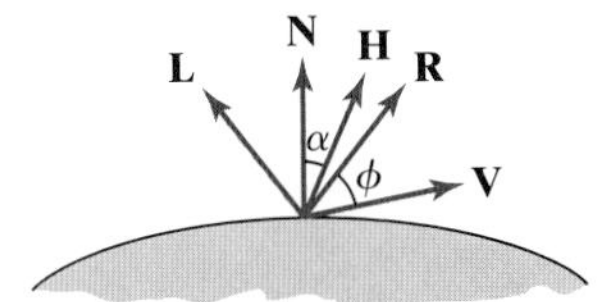

FIGURE 10-22 Halfway vector **H** along the bisector of the angle between **L** and **V**.

For nonplanar surfaces, $\mathbf{N} \cdot \mathbf{H}$ requires less computation than $\mathbf{V} \cdot \mathbf{R}$ because the calculation of **R** at each surface point involves the variable vector **N**. Also, if both the viewer and the light source are sufficiently far from the surface, vectors **V** and **L** are each constants, and thus **H** is also constant for all surface points. If the angle between **H** and **N** is greater than 90°, $\mathbf{N} \cdot \mathbf{H}$ is negative and we set the specular-reflection contribution to 0.0.

Vector **H** is the orientation direction for the surface that would produce maximum specular reflection in the viewing direction, for a given position of a point light source. For this reason, **H** is sometimes referred to as the surface orientation direction for maximum highlights. Also, if vector **V** is coplanar with vectors **L** and **R** (and thus **N**), angle α has the value $\phi/2$. When **V**, **L**, and **N** are not coplanar, $\alpha > \phi/2$, depending on the spatial relationship of the three vectors.

Combined Diffuse and Specular Reflections

For a single point light source, we can model the combined diffuse and specular reflections from a position on an illuminated surface as

$$\begin{aligned} I &= I_{\text{diff}} + I_{\text{spec}} \\ &= k_a I_a + k_d I_l (\mathbf{N} \cdot \mathbf{L}) + k_s I_l (\mathbf{N} \cdot \mathbf{H})^{n_s} \end{aligned} \tag{10-17}$$

The surface is illuminated only with ambient light if the light source is behind the surface, and there are no specular effects if **V** and **L** are on the same side of the normal vector **N**. Figure 10-23 illustrates surface lighting effects produced by the various terms in Eq. 10-17.

Diffuse and Specular Reflections from Multiple Light Sources

We can place any number of light sources in a scene. For multiple point light sources, we compute the diffuse and specular reflections as a sum of the contributions from the various sources:

$$\begin{aligned} I &= I_{\text{ambdiff}} + \sum_{l=1}^{n} [I_{l,\text{diff}} + I_{l,\text{spec}}] \\ &= k_a I_a + \sum_{l=1}^{n} I_l [k_d (\mathbf{N} \cdot \mathbf{L}) + k_s (\mathbf{N} \cdot \mathbf{H})^{n_s}] \end{aligned} \tag{10-18}$$

Surface Light Emissions

Some surfaces in a scene could be emitting light, as well as reflecting light from their surfaces. For example, a room scene can contain lamps or overhead lighting, and outdoor night scenes could include streetlights, store signs, and automobile headlights. We can empirically model surface light emissions by simply including an emission term $I_{\text{surfemission}}$ in the illumination model, in the same way that we

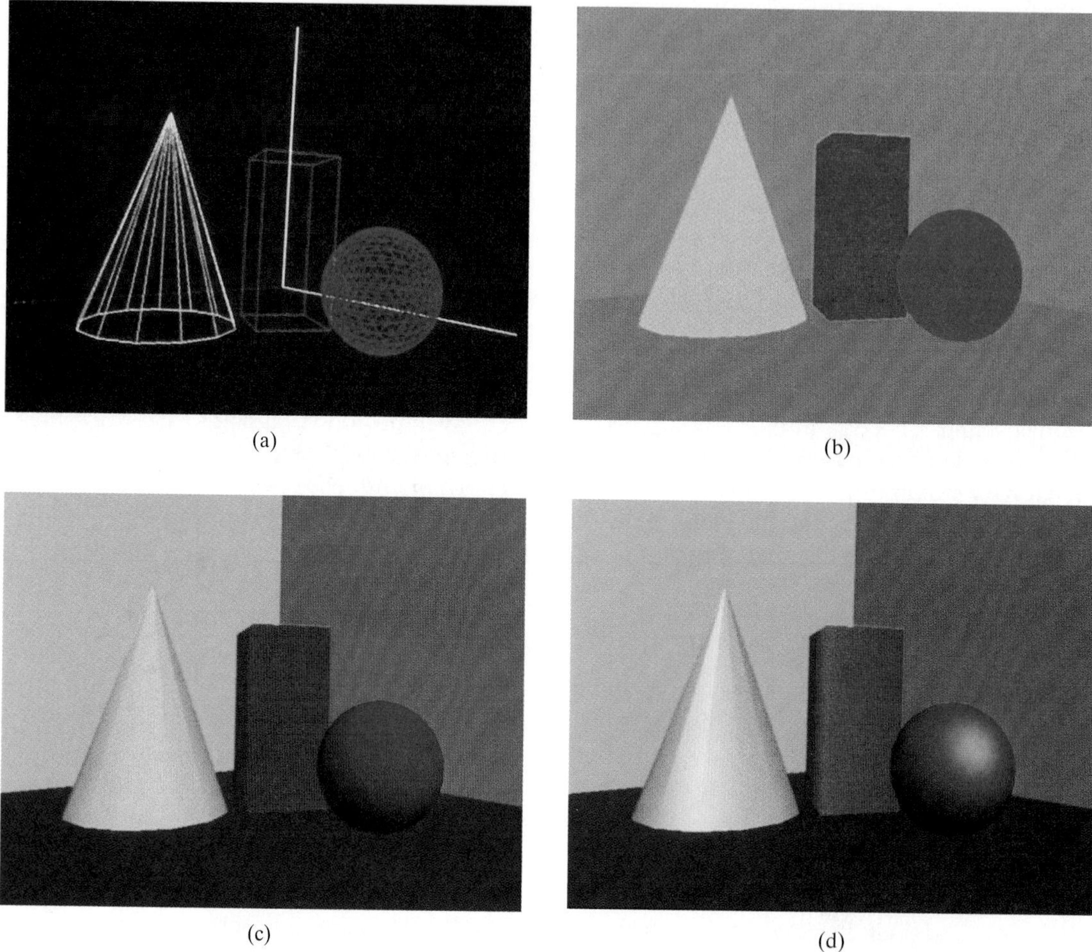

(a) (b) (c) (d)

FIGURE 10-23 A wire-frame scene (a) is displayed in (b) using ambient lighting only, with a different color for each object. Diffuse reflections resulting from illumination with ambient light and a single point source are illustrated in (c). For this display, $k_s = 0$ for all surfaces. In (d), both diffuse and specular reflections are shown for the illumination from a point source and the background lighting.

simulated background lighting using an ambient light level. This surface emission is then added to the surface reflections resulting from the light-source and the background-lighting illumination.

To illuminate other objects from a light-emitting surface, we could position a directional light source behind the surface to produce a cone of light through the surface. Or we could simulate the emission with a set of point light sources distributed over the surface. In general, however, an emitting surface is usually not used in the basic illumination model to illuminate other surfaces because of the added calculation time. Rather, surface emissions are used as a simple means for approximating the appearance of the surface of an extended light-source. This produces a glowing effect for the surface. A more realistic method for modeling surface emissions is the radiosity model discussed in Section 10-12.

Basic Illumination Model with Intensity Attenuation and Spotlights

We can formulate a general, monochromatic illumination model for surface reflections that includes multiple point light sources, attenuation factors, directional light effects (spotlight), infinite sources, and surface emissions as

$$I = I_{\text{surfemission}} + I_{\text{ambdiff}} + \sum_{l=1}^{n} f_{l,\text{radatten}} f_{l,\text{angatten}} (I_{l,\text{diff}} + I_{l,\text{spec}}) \qquad (10\text{-}19)$$

The radial attenuation function $f_{l,\text{radatten}}$ is evaluated using Eq. 10-2, and the angular attenuation function is evaluated using Eq. 10-5. For each light source, we calculate the diffuse reflection from a surface point as

$$I_{l,\text{diff}} = \begin{cases} 0.0, & \text{if } \mathbf{N} \cdot \mathbf{L}_l \leq 0.0 \text{ (light source behind object)} \\ k_d I_l (\mathbf{N} \cdot \mathbf{L}_l), & \text{otherwise} \end{cases} \qquad (10\text{-}20)$$

And the specular reflection term, due to a point-source illumination, is calculated with similar expressions:

$$I_{l,\text{spec}} = \begin{cases} 0.0, & \text{if } \mathbf{N} \cdot \mathbf{L}_l \leq 0.0 \\ & \quad \text{(light source behind object)} \\ k_s I_l \max\{0.0, (\mathbf{N} \cdot \mathbf{H}_l)^{n_s}\}, & \text{otherwise} \end{cases} \qquad (10\text{-}21)$$

To ensure that any pixel intensity does not exceed the maximum allowable value, we can apply some type of normalization procedure. A simple approach is to set a maximum magnitude for each term in the intensity equation. If any calculated term exceeds the maximum, we simply set it to the maximum value. Another way to compensate for intensity overflow is to normalize the individual terms by dividing each by the magnitude of the largest term. A more complicated procedure is to calculate all pixel intensities for the scene, then scale this set of intensities onto the intensity range from 0.0 to 1.0.

Also, the values for the coefficients in the radial attenuation function, and the optical surface parameters for a scene, can be adjusted to prevent calculated intensities from exceeding the maximum allowable value. This is an effective method for limiting intensity values when a single light source illuminates a scene. In general, however, calculated intensities are never allowed to exceed the value 1.0, and negative intensity values are adjusted to the value 0.0.

RGB Color Considerations

For an RGB color description, each intensity specification in the illumination model is a three-element vector that designates the red, green, and blue components of that intensity. Thus, for each light source, $I_l = (I_{lR}, I_{lG}, I_{lB})$. Similarly, the reflection coefficients are also specified with RGB components: $k_a = (k_{aR}, k_{aG}, k_{aB})$, $k_d = (k_{dR}, k_{dG}, k_{dB})$, and $k_s = (k_{sR}, k_{sG}, k_{sB})$. Each component of the surface color is then calculated with a separate expression. For example, the blue component of the diffuse and specular reflections for a point source are computed from modified expressions 10-20 and 10-21 as

$$I_{lB,\text{diff}} = k_{dB} I_{lB} (\mathbf{N} \cdot \mathbf{L}_l) \qquad (10\text{-}22)$$

and

$$I_{l,\text{spec}} = k_{sB} I_{lB} \max\{0.0, (\mathbf{N} \cdot \mathbf{H}_l)^{n_s}\} \tag{10-23}$$

Surfaces are most often illuminated with white light sources, but, for special effects or indoor lighting, we might use other colors for the light sources. We then set the reflectivity coefficients to model a particular surface color. For example, if we want an object to have a blue surface, we select a nonzero value in the range from 0.0 to 1.0 for the blue reflectivity component, k_{dB}, while the red and green reflectivity components are set to zero ($k_{dR} = k_{dG} = 0.0$). Any nonzero red or green components in the incident light are absorbed, and only the blue component is reflected.

In his original specular-reflection model, Phong set parameter k_s to a constant value independent of the surface color. This produces specular reflections that are the same color as the incident light (usually white), which gives the surface a plastic appearance. For a nonplastic material, the color of the specular reflection is actually a function of the surface properties and may be different from both the color of the incident light and the color of the diffuse reflections. We can approximate specular effects on such surfaces by making the specular-reflection coefficient color dependent, as in Eq. 10-23. Figure 10-24 illustrates color reflections from a matte surface, and Figs. 10-25 and 10-26 show color reflections from metal surfaces. Light reflections from object surfaces due to multiple colored light sources are shown in Fig. 10-27.

Another method for setting surface color is to specify the components of diffuse and specular color vectors for each surface, while retaining the reflectivity coefficients as single-valued constants. For an RGB color representation, for instance, the components of these two surface-color vectors could be denoted as (S_{dR}, S_{dG}, S_{dB}) and (S_{sR}, S_{sG}, S_{sB}). The blue component of the diffuse reflection (Eq. 10-22) is then calculated as

$$I_{lB,\text{diff}} = k_d S_{dB} I_{lB} (\mathbf{N} \cdot \mathbf{L}_l) \tag{10-24}$$

FIGURE 10-24 Light reflections from the surface of a black nylon cushion, modeled as woven cloth patterns and rendered using Monte-Carlo ray-tracing methods. *(Courtesy of Stephen H. Westin, Program of Computer Graphics, Cornell University.)*

FIGURE 10-25 Light reflections from a teapot with reflectance parameters set to simulate brushed aluminum surfaces and rendered using Monte-Carlo ray-tracing methods. *(Courtesy of Stephen H. Westin, Program of Computer Graphics, Cornell University.)*

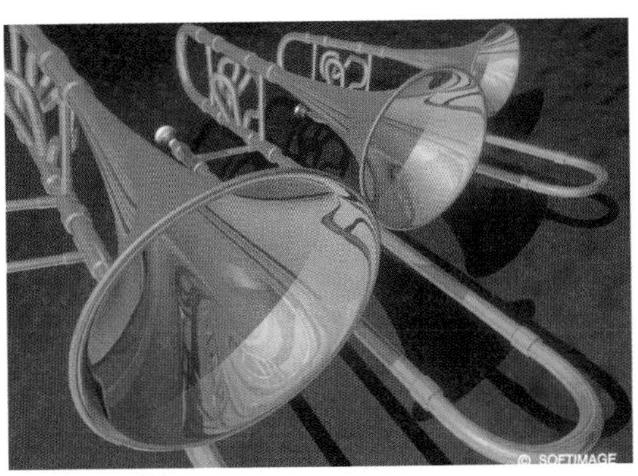

FIGURE 10-26 Light reflections from trumpets with reflectance parameters set to simulate shiny brass surfaces. (*Courtesy of SOFTIMAGE, Inc.*)

FIGURE 10-27 Light reflections due to multiple light sources of various colors. (*Courtesy of Sun Microsystems.*)

This approach provides somewhat greater flexibility, since surface color parameters and reflectivity values can be set independently.

In some graphics packages, additional lighting parameters are supplied by allowing a light source to be assigned multiple colors, where each color contributes to one of the surface lighting effects. For example, one of the colors can be used as a contribution to the general background lighting in a scene. Similarly, another light-source color can be used as the light intensity for the diffuse-reflection calculations, and a third light-source color can be used in the specular-reflection calculations.

Other Color Representations

We can describe colors using a variety of models other than the RGB representation. For example, a color can be represented using cyan, magenta, and yellow components, or a color could be described in terms of a particular hue along with the perceived brightness and saturation of the color. We can incorporate any of these representations, including color specifications with more than three components, into an illumination model. As an example, Eq. 10-24 can be expressed in terms of any spectral color with wavelength λ as

$$I_{l\lambda,\mathrm{diff}} = k_d S_{d\lambda} I_{l\lambda}(\mathbf{N} \cdot \mathbf{L}_l) \qquad (10\text{-}25)$$

The various color representations useful in computer graphics are discussed in more detail in Chapter 12.

Luminance

Another characteristic of color is **luminance,** which is sometimes also called luminous energy. Luminance provides information about the lightness or darkness level of a color, and it is a psychological measure of our perception of brightness that varies with the amount of illumination we are viewing.

Physically, color is described in terms of the frequency range for visible radiant energy (light), and luminance is calculated as a weighted sum of the intensity components in a particular illumination. Since any actual illumination contains a continuous range of frequencies, a luminance value is computed as

$$\text{luminance} = \int_{\text{visible} f} p(f)\, I(f)\, df \tag{10-26}$$

Parameter $I(f)$ in this calculation represents the intensity of the light component with a frequency f that is radiating in a particular direction. Parameter $p(f)$ is an experimentally determined proportionality function that varies with both frequency and illumination level. The integration is performed for all intensities over the frequency range contained in the light.

For gray-scale and monochromatic displays, we need only the luminance values to describe object lighting. And some graphics packages do allow the lighting parameters to be expressed in terms of luminance. Green components of a light source contribute most to the luminance, and blue components contribute least. Therefore, the luminance of an RGB color source is typically computed as

$$\text{luminance} = 0.299R + 0.587G + 0.114B \tag{10-27}$$

Sometimes, better lighting effects are achieved by increasing the contribution for the green component of each RGB color. One recommendation for this calculation is $0.2125R + 0.7154G + 0.0721B$. The luminance parameter is most often represented with the symbol Y, which corresponds to the Y component in the XYZ color model (Section 12-3).

10-4 TRANSPARENT SURFACES

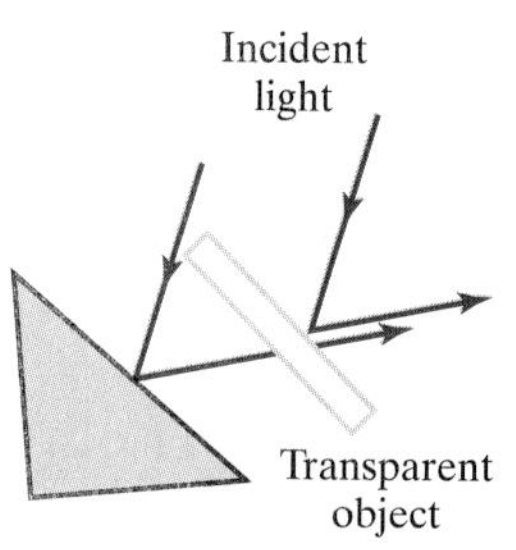

FIGURE 10-28 Light emission from a transparent surface is in general a combination of reflected and transmitted light.

We describe an object, such as a glass windowpane, as *transparent* if we can see things that are behind that object. Similarly, if we cannot see things that are behind an object, it is *opaque*. In addition, some transparent objects, such as frosted glass and certain plastic materials, are **translucent** so that the transmitted light is diffused in all directions. Objects viewed through translucent materials appear blurred and are often not clearly identifiable.

A transparent surface, in general, produces both reflected and transmitted light. The light transmitted through the surface is the result of emissions and reflections from the objects and sources behind the transparent object. Figure 10-28 illustrates the intensity contributions to the surface lighting for a transparent object that is in front of an opaque object. And Fig. 10-29 shows the transparency effects that can be displayed in a computer-generated scene.

Translucent Materials

Both diffuse and specular transmission can take place at the surfaces of a transparent object. Diffuse effects are important when translucent materials are to be modeled. Light passing through a translucent material is scattered so that background objects are seen as blurred images. We can simulate diffuse transmissions by distributing intensity contributions from background objects over a finite area, or we can use ray-tracing methods to simulate translucency. These manipulations are time-consuming, and basic illumination models ordinarily compute only specular-transparency effects.

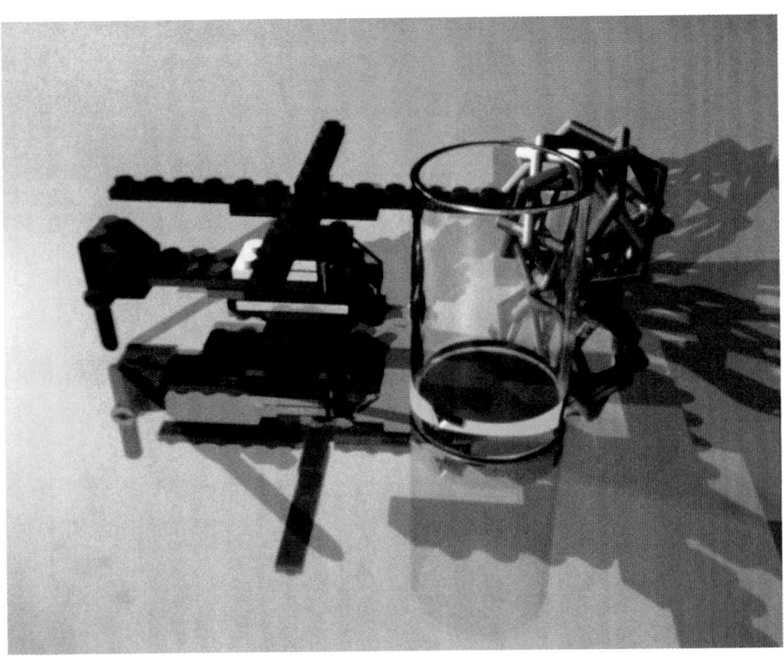

FIGURE 10-29 A ray-traced view of a scene containing a transparent drinking glass, showing both light transmissions from objects behind the glass and light reflections from the glass surface. (*Courtesy of Eric Haines, Autodesk, Inc.*)

Light Refraction

Realistic displays of a transparent material are obtained by modeling the **refraction** path of a ray of light through the material. When a light beam is incident upon a transparent surface, part of it is reflected and part is transmitted through the material as refracted light, as shown in Fig. 10-30. Because the speed of light is different in different materials, the path of the refracted light is different from that of the incident light. The direction of the refracted light, specified by the **angle of refraction** with respect to the surface normal vector, is a function of the **index of refraction** of the material and the incoming direction of the incident light. Index of refraction is defined as the ratio of the speed of light in a vacuum to the speed of light in the material. Angle of refraction θ_r is calculated from **Snell's law** as

$$\sin\theta_r = \frac{\eta_i}{\eta_r}\sin\theta_i \qquad (10\text{-}28)$$

where θ_i is the angle of incidence, η_i is the index of refraction for the incident material, and η_r is the index of refraction for the refracting material.

Actually, the index of refraction also depends on other factors, such as the temperature of the material and the wavelength of the incident light. Thus, the various color components of incident white light, for example, are refracted at different angles, which vary with temperature. Furthermore, within anisotropic materials such as crystalline quartz, the speed of light depends on direction, and some transparent materials exhibit *double refraction,* in which two refracted light rays are generated. For most applications, however, we can use a single average index of refraction for each material, as listed in Table 10-1. Using the index of refraction for air (approximately 1.0) surrounding a pane of heavy crown glass (refractive index ≈ 1.61) in Eq. 10-28, with an angle of incidence of 30°, we obtain a refraction angle of about 18° for the light passing through the crown glass.

Figure 10-31 illustrates the refraction changes for a ray of light passing through a thin sheet of glass. The overall effect of the refraction is to shift the incident light

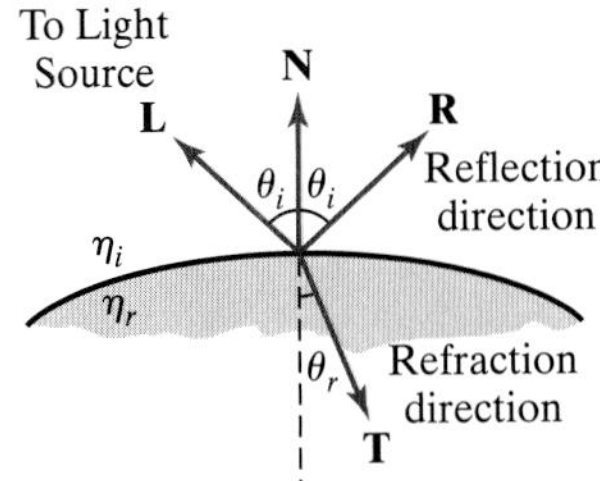

FIGURE 10-30 Reflection direction **R** and refraction (transmission) direction **T** for a ray of light incident upon a surface with index of refraction η_r.

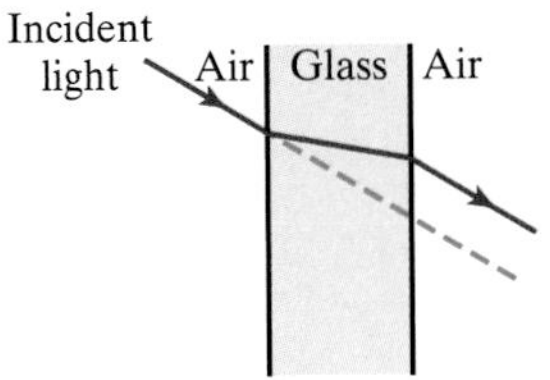

FIGURE 10-31 Refraction of light through a pane of glass. The emerging refracted ray travels along a path that is parallel to the incident light path (dashed line).

TABLE 10-1

AVERAGE INDEX OF REFRACTION FOR COMMON MATERIALS

Material	Index of Refraction
Vacuum (Air or Other Gas)	1.00
Ordinary Crown Glass	1.52
Heavy Crown Glass	1.61
Ordinary Flint Glass	1.61
Heavy Flint Glass	1.92
Rock Salt	1.55
Quartz	1.54
Water	1.33
Ice	1.31

to a parallel path as it emerges from the material. Since the evaluations for the trigonometric functions in Eq. 10-28 are time-consuming, these refraction effects could be approximated by simply shifting the path of the incident light by an appropriate amount for a given material.

From Snell's law and the diagram in Fig. 10-30, we can obtain the unit transmission vector **T** in the refraction direction θ_r as

$$\mathbf{T} = \left(\frac{\eta_i}{\eta_r}\cos\theta_i - \cos\theta_r\right)\mathbf{N} - \frac{\eta_i}{\eta_r}\mathbf{L} \tag{10-29}$$

where **N** is the unit surface normal and **L** is the unit vector in the direction from the surface position to the light source. Transmission vector **T** can be used to locate intersections of the refraction path with objects behind the transparent surface. Including refraction effects in a scene can produce highly realistic displays, but the determination of refraction paths and object intersections requires considerable computation. Most scan-line image-space methods model light transmission with approximations that reduce processing time. Accurate refraction effects are displayed using ray-tracing algorithms (Section 10-11).

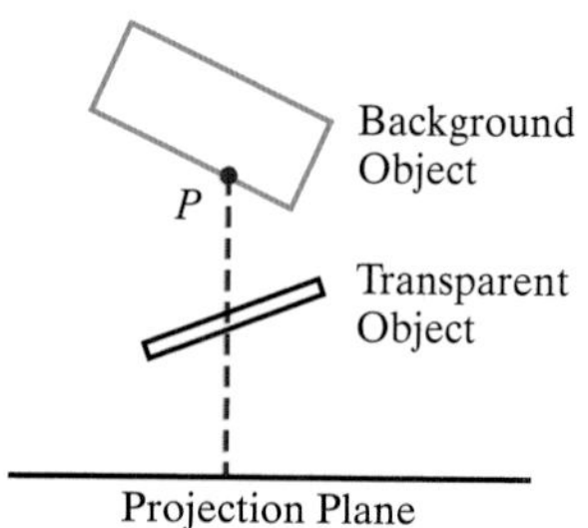

FIGURE 10-32 The intensity of a background object at point **P** can be combined with the reflected intensity off the surface of a transparent object along a perpendicular projection line (dashed).

Basic Transparency Model

A simpler procedure for modeling transparent objects is to ignore the path shifts due to refraction. In effect, this approach assumes there is no change in the index of refraction from one material to another, so that the angle of refraction is always the same as the angle of incidence. This method speeds up the calculation of intensities and can produce reasonable transparency effects for thin, polygonal surfaces.

We can combine the transmitted intensity I_{trans} through a transparent surface from a background object with the reflected intensity I_{refl} from the surface (Fig. 10-32) using a **transparency coefficient** k_t. We assign parameter k_t a value between 0.0 and 1.0 to specify how much of the background light is to be transmitted. Total surface intensity is then calculated as

$$I = (1 - k_t)I_{\text{refl}} + k_t I_{\text{trans}} \tag{10-30}$$

The term $(1 - k_t)$ is the **opacity factor.** For example, if the transparency factor is assigned the value 0.3, then 30 percent of the background light is combined with 70 percent of the reflected surface illumination.

This procedure can be used to combine the lighting effects from any number of transparent and opaque objects, as long as we process the surfaces in a depth-first order (back to front). For example, looking through the glass in Fig. 10-29, we can see the opaque objects that are behind two transparent surfaces. Similarly, when we look through the windshield of an automobile, objects inside the car are visible, as well as objects that may be behind the back window.

For highly transparent objects, we assign k_t a value near 1.0. Nearly opaque objects transmit very little light from background objects, and we can set k_t to a value near 0.0 for these materials. It is also possible to allow k_t to be a function of position over the surface, so that different parts of an object can transmit more or less of the light from the background surfaces.

A depth-sorting visibility algorithm can be modified to handle transparency by first sorting surfaces in depth order, then determining whether any visible surface is transparent. If it is, its reflected surface intensity is combined with the surface intensity of objects behind it to obtain the pixel intensity at each projected surface point.

Transparency effects could also be implemented using a modified depth-buffer approach. We can divide the surfaces in a scene into two groups so that all the opaque surfaces are processed first. At this point, the frame buffer contains the intensities of the visible surfaces, and the depth buffer contains their depths. Then, the depth positions of the transparent objects are compared to the values previously stored in the depth buffer. If any transparent surface is visible, its reflected intensity is calculated and combined with the opaque surface intensity previously stored in the frame buffer. This method can be modified to produce more accurate displays by using additional storage for the depth and other parameters of the transparent surfaces. This allows depth values for the transparent surfaces to be compared to each other, as well as to the depth values of the opaque surfaces. Visible transparent surfaces are then rendered by combining their surface intensities with those of the visible and opaque surfaces behind them.

Another approach is the A-buffer method. For each pixel position in the A-buffer, surface patches for all overlapping surfaces are saved and sorted in depth order. Then, intensities for the transparent and opaque surface patches that overlap in depth are combined in the proper visibility order to produce the final averaged intensity for the pixel.

10-5 ATMOSPHERIC EFFECTS

Another factor that is sometimes included in an illumination model is the effect of the atmosphere on an object's color. A hazy atmosphere makes colors fade and objects appear dimmer. Thus we could specify a function to modify surface colors according to the amount of dust, smoke, or smog that we want to simulate in the atmosphere. The hazy-atmosphere effect is often simulated with an exponential attenuation function such as

$$f_{\text{atmo}}(d) = e^{-\rho d} \tag{10-31}$$

or

$$f_{\text{atmo}}(d) = e^{-(\rho d)^2} \tag{10-32}$$

The value assigned to d is the distance of the object from the viewing position. And, we use parameter ρ in either of these exponential functions to set a positive density value for the atmosphere. Higher values for ρ produce a denser atmosphere and cause surface colors to be more muted. After the surface color of an object has been computed, we multiply that color by one of the atmosphere functions to decrease its intensity by an amount that depends on the value we set for the density of the atmosphere.

Instead of an exponential function, we could simplify the atmospheric attenuation calculations by using the linear depth-cueing function 9-9. This decreases the intensity of surface colors for distant objects, but we then have no provision for varying the density of the atmosphere.

Sometimes we might also want to simulate an atmosphere color. For example, the air in a smoky room could be modeled with a slate-gray color, or perhaps a pale blue. The following calculation could then be used to combine the atmosphere color with an object's color

$$I = f_{\text{atmo}}(d)I_{\text{obj}} + [1 - f_{\text{atmo}}(d)]I_{\text{atmo}} \tag{10-33}$$

where f_{atmo} is an exponential or linear atmosphere-attenuation function.

10-6 SHADOWS

Visibility detection methods can be used to locate regions that are not illuminated by light sources. With the viewing position at the location of a light source, we can determine which surface sections in the scene are not visible. These are the shadow areas. Once we have determined the shadow areas for all light sources, the shadows could be treated as surface patterns and stored in pattern arrays. Figure 10-33 illustrates shadow regions on the face of an animated character. In this image, the shadow regions are surface sections that are not visible from the position of the overhead light source. Thus, the raised hand and arm are illuminated, but the facial sections behind the arm, along the line of sight from the light source, are in shadow. The scene in Fig. 10-29 shows shadow effects produced by multiple light sources.

Shadow patterns generated by a visible-surface detection method are valid for any selected viewing position, as long as the light-source positions are not changed. Surfaces that are visible from the view position are shaded according to

FIGURE 10-33 Shadow patterns mapped onto the face of Dr. Aki Ross, an animated character in the film *Final Fantasy: The Spirits Within*. (*Courtesy of Square Pictures, Inc. © 2001 FFFP. All rights reserved.*)

the lighting model, which can be combined with texture patterns. We can display shadow areas with ambient light intensity only, or we could combine the ambient light with specified surface textures.

10-7 CAMERA PARAMETERS

The viewing and illumination procedures we have considered so far produce sharp images, which are equivalent to photographing a scene with a pinhole camera. When we photograph an actual scene, however, we can adjust the camera so that only selected objects are in focus. Other objects are then more or less out of focus, depending on the depth distribution of the objects in the scene. We can simulate the appearance of out-of-focus positions in a computer-graphics program, by projecting each position to an area covering multiple pixel positions, with the object colors merged into other objects to produce a blurred projection pattern. This procedure is similar to the methods used in antialiasing, and we can incorporate the camera effects into either a scan-line or a ray-tracing algorithm. Computer-generated scenes appear more realistic when focusing effects are included, but the focusing calculations are time consuming. Methods for setting camera and lens parameters to simulate focusing effects are discussed in Section 10-11.

10-8 DISPLAYING LIGHT INTENSITIES

A surface intensity calculated by an illumination model can have any value in the range from 0.0 to 1.0, but a computer-graphics system can display only a limited set of intensities. Therefore, a calculated intensity value must be converted to one of the allowable system values. In addition, the allowable number of system intensity levels can be distributed so that they correspond to the way that our eyes perceive intensity differences. When we display scenes on a bilevel system, we could convert calculated intensities into halftone patterns, as discussed in Section 10-9.

Distributing System Intensity Levels

For any system, the allowable number of intensity levels can be distributed over the range from 0.0 to 1.0 so that this distribution corresponds to our perception of equal intensity intervals between levels. We perceive relative light intensities the same way that we perceive relative sound intensities: on a logarithmic scale. This means that if the ratio of two intensity values is the same as the ratio of two other intensities, we perceive the difference between each pair of intensities to be the same. As an example, we perceive the difference between intensities 0.20 and 0.22 to be the same as the difference between 0.80 and 0.88. Therefore, to display $n+1$ successive intensity levels with equal perceived brightness, the intensity levels on the monitor should be spaced so that the ratio of successive intensities is constant:

$$\frac{I_1}{I_0} = \frac{I_2}{I_1} = \cdots = \frac{I_n}{I_{n-1}} = r \tag{10-34}$$

where I represents the intensity of one of the color components of a light. The lowest level that can be displayed is represented as I_0 and the highest is represented as I_n. Any intermediate intensity can then be expressed in terms of I_0 as

$$I_k = r^k I_0 \tag{10-35}$$

We can calculate the value of r, given the values of I_0 and n for a particular system, by substituting $k = n$ in the above expression. Since $I_n = 1.0$, we have

$$r = \left(\frac{1.0}{I_0}\right)^{1/n} \tag{10-36}$$

Thus, the calculation for I_k in Eq. 10-35 can be rewritten as

$$I_k = I_0^{(n-k)/n} \tag{10-37}$$

As an example, if $I_0 = \frac{1}{8}$ for a system with $n = 3$, we have $r = 2$ and the four intensity values are $\frac{1}{8}, \frac{1}{4}, \frac{1}{2}$, and 1.0.

The lowest intensity value I_0 depends on the characteristics of the monitor and is typically in the range from 0.005 to around 0.025. This residual intensity on a video monitor is due to reflected light from the screen phosphors. Therefore, a "black" region on the screen will always have some intensity value above 0.0. For a gray-scale display with 8 bits per pixel ($n = 255$) and $I_0 = 0.01$, the ratio of successive intensities is approximately $r = 1.0182$. The approximate values for the 256 intensities on this system are 0.0100, 0.0102, 0.0104, 0.0106, 0.0107, 0.0109, . . . , 0.9821, and 1.0000.

Similar methods are used with RGB color components. For example, we can express the intensity of the blue component of a color at level k in terms of the lowest attainable blue value as

$$I_{Bk} = r_B^k I_{B0} \tag{10-38}$$

where

$$r_B = \left(\frac{1.0}{I_{B0}}\right)^{1/n} \tag{10-39}$$

and n is the number of intensity levels.

Gamma Correction and Video Lookup Tables

When we display color or monochromatic images on a video monitor, the perceived brightness variations are nonlinear, but illumination models produce a linear variation for intensity values. The RGB color (0.25, 0.25, 0.25) obtained from a lighting model represents one-half the intensity of the color (0.5, 0.5, 0.5). Usually, these calculated intensities are then stored in an image file as integer values ranging from 0 to 255, with one byte for each of the three RGB components. This intensity file is also linear, so that a pixel with the value (64, 64, 64) represents one-half the intensity of a pixel with the value (128, 128, 128). The electron-gun voltages, which control the number of electrons striking the phosphor screen, produce brightness levels as determined by the **monitor response curve** shown in Fig. 10-34. Therefore, the displayed intensity value (64, 64, 64) would not appear to be half as bright as the value (128, 128, 128).

To compensate for monitor nonlinearities, graphics systems use a **video lookup table** that adjusts the linear input intensity values. The monitor response curve is described with the exponential function

$$I = a\,V^{\gamma} \tag{10-40}$$

Parameter I is displayed intensity and parameter V is the corresponding electron-gun voltage. Values for parameters a and γ depend on the characteristics of the

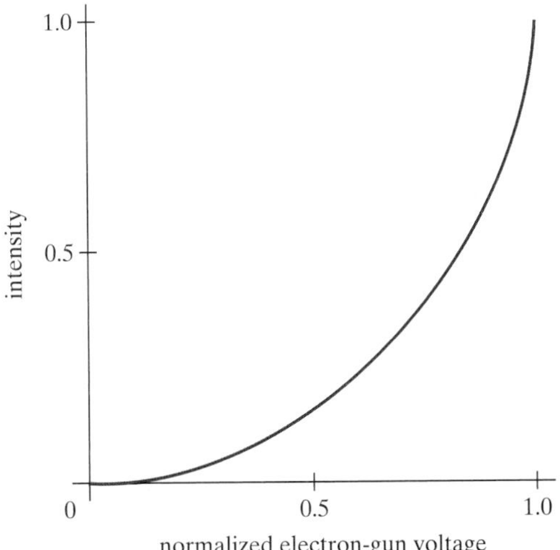

FIGURE 10-34 A typical monitor response curve, showing the variation in displayed intensity (or "brightness") as a function of the normalized electron-gun voltage.

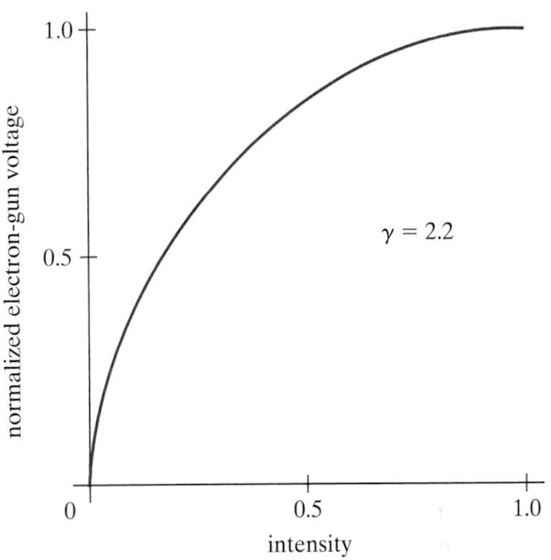

FIGURE 10-35 A video lookup correction curve for mapping a normalized intensity value to a normalized electron-gun voltage, using gamma correction with $\gamma = 2.2$.

monitor used in the graphics system. Thus, if we want to display a particular intensity value I, the voltage value to produce this intensity is

$$V = \left(\frac{I}{a}\right)^{1/\gamma} \tag{10-41}$$

This calculation is referred to as the **gamma correction** of intensity, and gamma values are typically in the range from about 1.7 to 2.3. The National Television System Committee (NTSC) signal standard is $\gamma = 2.2$. Figure 10-35 shows a gamma-correction curve using the NTSC gamma value with both intensity and voltage normalized on the interval from 0 to 1.0. Equation 10-41 is used to set up the video lookup table that converts integer intensity values in an image file to values that control the electron-gun voltages.

We can combine gamma correction with logarithmic intensity mapping to produce a lookup table. If I is an input intensity value from an illumination model, we first locate the nearest intensity I_k from a table of values created with Eq. 10-34 or Eq. 10-37. Alternatively, we could determine the level number for this intensity value with the calculation

$$k = \text{round}\left[\log_r\left(\frac{I}{I_0}\right)\right] \tag{10-42}$$

then we compute the intensity value at this level using Eq. 10-37. Once, we have the intensity value I_k, we can calculate the electron-gun voltage as

$$V_k = \left(\frac{I_k}{a}\right)^{1/\gamma} \tag{10-43}$$

Values V_k can then be placed in the lookup tables, with values for k stored in the frame-buffer pixel positions. If a particular system has no lookup table, computed values for V_k could be stored directly in the frame buffer. The combined conversion to a logarithmic intensity scale followed by calculation of the V_k using Eq. 10-43 is also sometimes referred to as gamma correction.

If the video amplifiers of a monitor are designed to convert the linear intensity values to electron-gun voltages, we cannot combine the two intensity conversion processes. In this case, gamma correction is built into the hardware, and the logarithmic values I_k must be precomputed and stored in the frame buffer (or the color table).

Displaying Continuous-Tone Images

High-quality computer graphics systems generally provide 256 intensity levels for each color component, but acceptable displays can be obtained for many applications with fewer levels. A four-level system provides minimum shading capability for continuous-tone images, while photo-realistic images can be generated on systems that are capable of from 32 to 256 intensity levels per pixel.

Figure 10-36 shows a continuous-tone photograph displayed with various intensity levels. When a small number of intensity levels are used to reproduce a

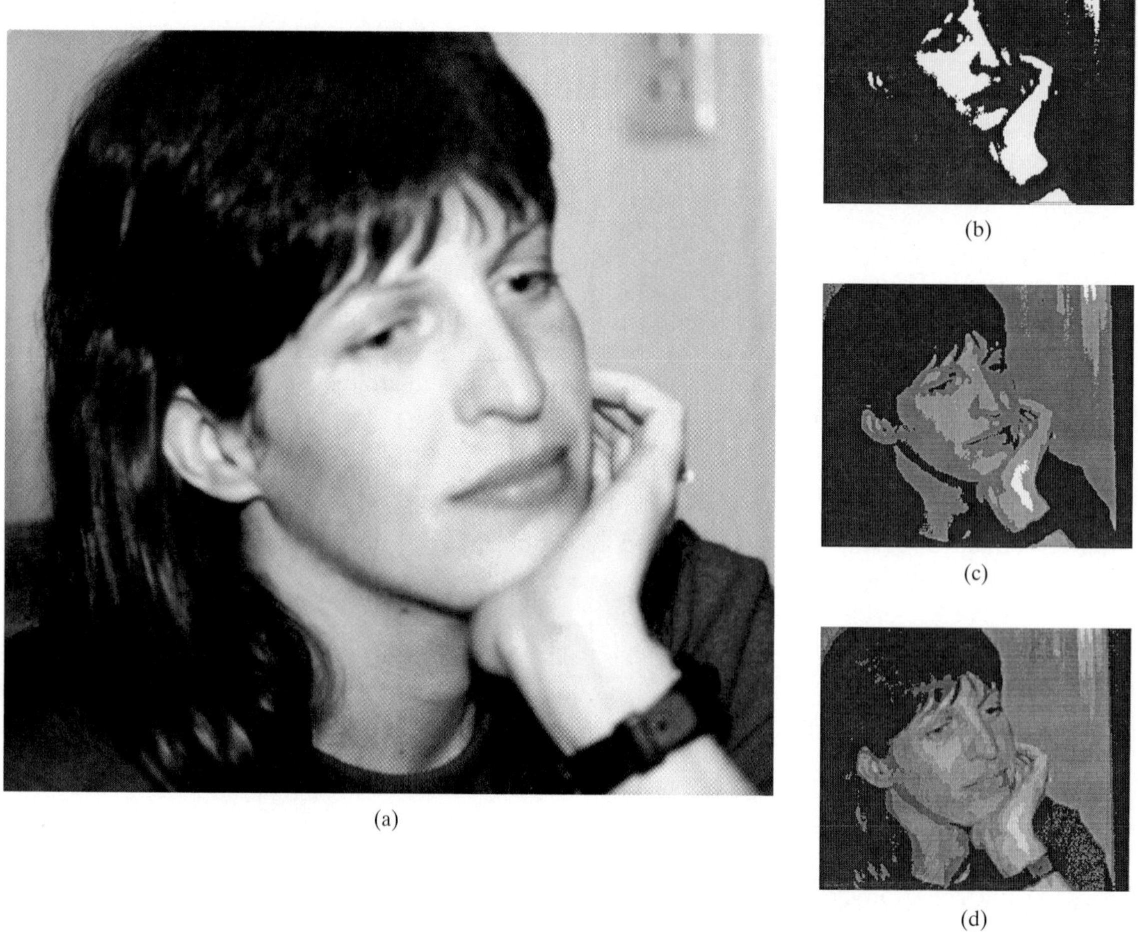

(a) (b) (c) (d)

FIGURE 10-36 A continuous-tone photograph (a) printed with 2 intensity levels (b), 4 intensity levels (c), and 8 intensity levels (d).

continuous-tone image, the borders between the different intensity regions (called *contours*) are clearly visible. In the 2-level reproduction, the facial features in the photograph are just barely identifiable. Using 4 intensity levels, we begin to identify the original shading patterns, but the contouring effects are glaring. With 8 intensity levels, contouring effects are still obvious, but we begin to have a better indication of the original shading. At 16 or more intensity levels, contouring effects diminish and the reproductions are very close to the original. Reproductions of continuous-tone images using more than 32 intensity levels show only very subtle differences from the original.

10-9 HALFTONE PATTERNS AND DITHERING TECHNIQUES

With a system that has very few available intensity levels, we can create an apparent increase in the number of available intensities by incorporating multiple pixel positions into the display of each intensity value for a scene. When we view a small region consisting of several pixel positions, our eyes tend to integrate or average the fine detail into an overall intensity. Bilevel monitors and printers, in particular, can take advantage of this visual effect to produce pictures that appear to be displayed with multiple intensity values.

Continuous-tone photographs are reproduced for publication in newspapers, magazines, and books with a printing process called **halftoning,** and the reproduced pictures are called **halftones.** For a black-and-white photograph, each constant intensity area is reproduced as a set of small black circles on a white background. The diameter of each circle is proportional to the darkness required for that intensity region. Darker regions are printed with larger circles, and lighter regions are printed with smaller circles (more white space). Figure 10-37 shows an enlarged section of a gray-scale halftone reproduction. Color halftones are printed using small circular dots of various sizes and colors, as shown in Fig. 10-38. Book and magazine halftones are printed on high-quality paper using approximately 60 to 80 circles of varying diameter per centimeter. Newspapers use lower-quality paper and lower resolution (about 25 to 30 dots per centimeter).

FIGURE 10-37 An enlarged section of a photograph reproduced with a halftoning method, showing how tones are represented with "dots" of varying sizes.

Halftone Approximations

In computer graphics, halftone reproductions are simulated using rectangular pixel regions that are called **halftone approximation patterns,** or just **pixel patterns.** The number of intensity levels that we can display with this method depends on how many pixels we include in the rectangular grids and how many levels a system can display. With n by n pixels for each grid on a bilevel system, we can represent $n^2 + 1$ intensity levels. Figure 10-39 shows one way to set up pixel patterns to represent five intensity levels that could be used with a bilevel system. In pattern 0, all pixels are turned off; in pattern 1, one pixel is turned on; and in pattern 4, all four pixels are turned on. An intensity value I in a scene is mapped to a particular pattern according to the range listed below each grid shown in the figure. Pattern 0 is used for $0.0 \leq I < 0.2$, pattern 1 for $0.2 \leq I < 0.4$, and pattern 4 is used for $0.8 \leq I \leq 1.0$.

With 3 by 3 pixel grids on a bilevel system, we can display ten intensity levels. One way to set up the ten pixel patterns for these levels is shown in Fig. 10-40. Pixel positions are chosen at each level so that the patterns approximate the increasing

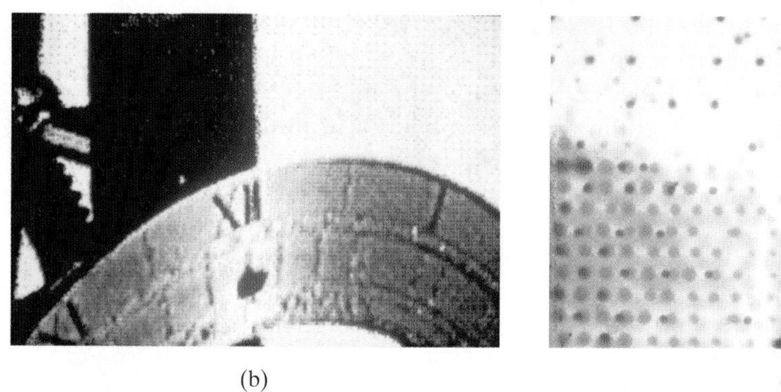

FIGURE 10-38 Color halftone dot patterns. The top of the clock dial in the color halftone (a) is enlarged by a factor of 10 in (b) and by a factor of 50 in (c). (*Courtesy of IRIS Graphics, Inc., Bedford, Massachusetts.*)

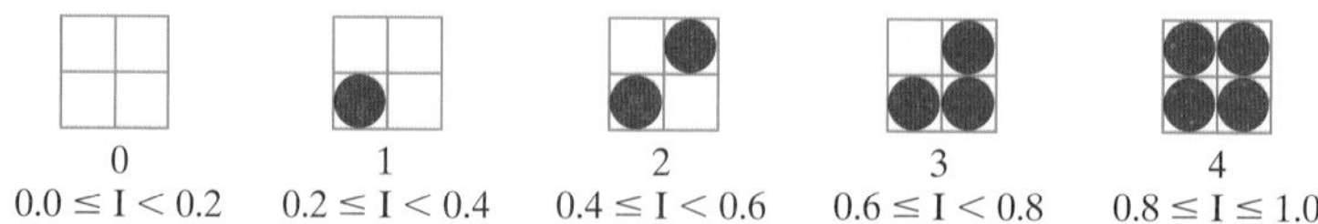

FIGURE 10-39 A set of 2 by 2 pixel grid patterns that can be used to display five intensity levels on a bilevel system, showing the "on" pixels as red circles. The intensity values that are mapped to each of the grid patterns are listed below the pixel arrays.

circle sizes used in halftone reproductions. That is, the "on" pixel positions are near the center of the grid for lower intensity levels and expand outward as the intensity level increases.

For any pixel-grid size, we can represent the pixel patterns for the various possible intensities with a mask (matrix) of pixel position numbers. As an example,

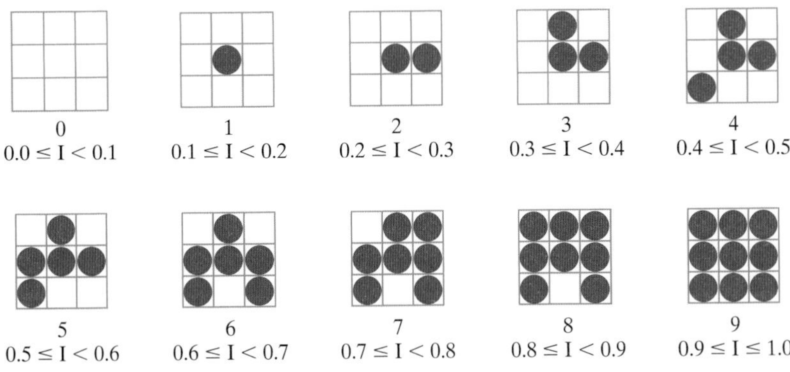

FIGURE 10-40 A set of 3 by 3 pixel grid patterns that can be used to display ten intensities on a bilevel system, showing the "on" pixels as red circles. The intensity values that are mapped to each of the grid patterns are listed below the pixel arrays.

the following mask can be used to generate the nine 3 by 3 grid patterns for intensity levels above 0 shown in Fig. 10-40.

$$\begin{bmatrix} 8 & 3 & 7 \\ 5 & 1 & 2 \\ 4 & 9 & 6 \end{bmatrix} \tag{10-44}$$

To display a particular intensity with level number k, we turn on each pixel whose position number is less than or equal to k.

Although the use of n by n pixel patterns increases the number of intensities that can be represented, the resolution of the display area is reduced by a factor of $1/n$ in the x and y directions. Using 2 by 2 grid patterns on a 512 by 512 screen area, for instance, reduces the resolution to 256 by 256 intensity positions. And with 3 by 3 patterns, we reduce the resolution of the 512 by 512 area to 128 by 128.

Another problem with pixel grids is that subgrid patterns become apparent as the grid size increases. The grid size that can be used without distorting the intensity variations depends on the size of a displayed pixel. Therefore, for systems with lower resolution (fewer pixels per centimeter), we must be satisfied with fewer intensity levels. On the other hand, high-quality displays require at least 64 intensity levels. This means that we need 8 by 8 pixel grids. And to achieve a resolution equivalent to that of halftones in books and magazines, we must display 60 dots per centimeter. Thus we need to be able to display $60 \times 8 = 480$ dots per centimeter. Some devices, for example high-quality film recorders, are able to display this resolution.

Pixel-grid patterns for halftone approximations must also be constructed to minimize contouring and other visual effects not present in the original scene. We can minimize contouring by evolving each successive grid pattern from the previous pattern. That is, we form the pattern at level k by adding an "on" position to the grid pattern used for level $k - 1$. Thus, if a pixel position is on for one grid level, it is on for all higher levels (Figs. 10-39 and 10-40). We can minimize the introduction of other visual effects by avoiding symmetrical patterns. With a 3 by 3 pixel grid, for instance, the third intensity level above zero would be better represented by the pattern in Fig. 10-41(a) than by any of the symmetrical arrangements in Fig. 10-41(b). The symmetrical patterns in this figure would produce either vertical, horizontal, or diagonal streaks in any large area shaded with intensity level 3. For hardcopy output on devices such as film recorders and some printers, isolated pixels are not effectively reproduced. Therefore a grid pattern

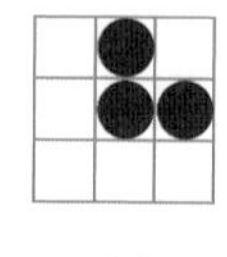

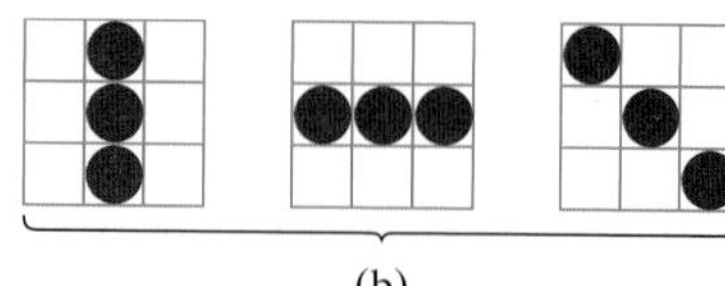

FIGURE 10-41 For a 3 by 3 pixel grid, the pattern in (a) is better than any of the symmetrical patterns in (b) for representing the third intensity level above 0.

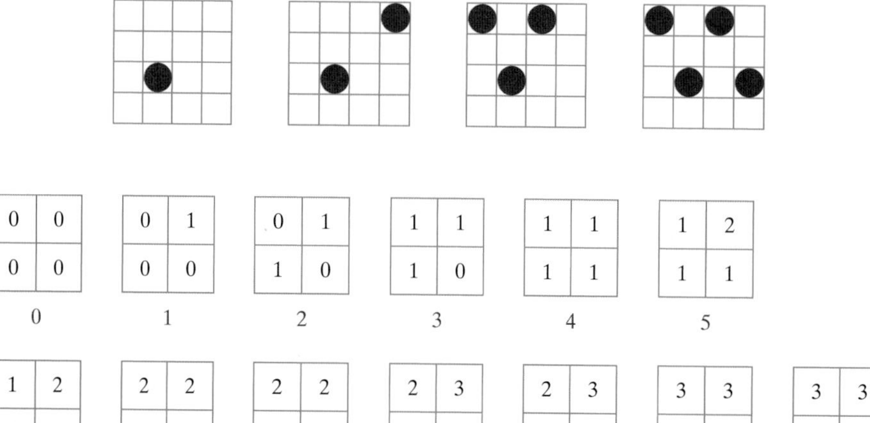

FIGURE 10-42 Halftone grid patterns with isolated pixels that cannot be reproduced effectively on some hardcopy devices.

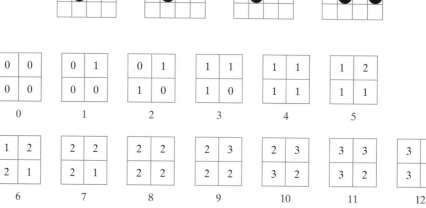

FIGURE 10-43 Intensity representations 0 through 12 obtained with halftone-approximation patterns using 2 by 2 pixel grids on a four-level system, with pixel-intensity levels labeled 0 through 3.

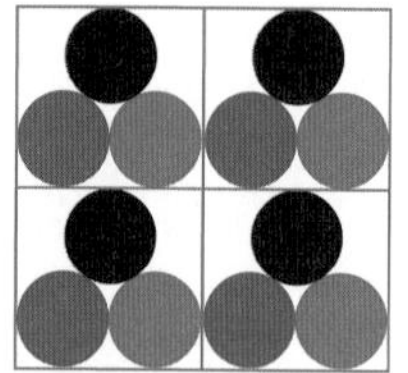

FIGURE 10-44 A 2 by 2 pixel-grid pattern for displaying RGB colors.

with a single "on" pixel or with isolated "on" pixels, as in Fig. 10-42, should be avoided.

Halftone-approximation methods can be applied also to increase the number of intensity options on systems that are capable of displaying more than two intensities per pixel. For example, on a gray-scale system that can display four intensity values per pixel, we can use 2 by 2 pixel grids to represent 13 different intensity levels. Figure 10-43 illustrates one way to set up the 13 pixel-grid patterns, where each pixel can be set to intensity level 0, 1, 2, or 3.

Similarly, we can use pixel-grid patterns to increase the number of intensities that can be represented on a color system. A three-bit per pixel RGB system, for example, uses one bit per pixel for each color gun. Thus, a pixel is displayed with three phosphor dots, so that the pixel can be assigned any one of eight different colors (including black and white). But with 2 by 2 pixel-grid patterns, we have 12 phosphor dots that we can use to represent a color, as shown in Fig. 10-44. The red electron gun can activate any combination of the four red dots in the grid pattern, and this provides five possible settings for the red color of the pattern. And the same is true for the green and blue guns, which gives us a total of 125 different color combinations that can be represented with our 2 by 2 grid patterns.

Dithering Techniques

The term **dithering** is used in various contexts. Primarily, it refers to techniques for approximating halftones without reducing resolution, as pixel-grid patterns do. But dithering is sometimes used also as a synonym for any halftone-approximation scheme, and sometimes it is used as another term for color halftone approximations.

Random values added to pixel intensities to break up contours are often referred to as **dither noise.** Various algorithms have been used to generate the random distributions. The effect is to add noise over an entire picture, which tends to soften intensity boundaries.

A method called **ordered dither** generates intensity variations with a one-to-one mapping of points in a scene to pixel positions using a **dither matrix $\mathbf{D}_n$** to select an intensity level. Matrix $\mathbf{D}_n$ contains n by n elements that are assigned distinct positive integer values in the range from 0 to $n^2 - 1$. For example, we can generate four intensity levels with

$$\mathbf{D}_2 = \begin{bmatrix} 3 & 1 \\ 0 & 2 \end{bmatrix} \tag{10-45}$$

and we can generate nine intensity levels with

$$\mathbf{D}_3 = \begin{bmatrix} 7 & 2 & 6 \\ 4 & 0 & 1 \\ 3 & 8 & 5 \end{bmatrix} \tag{10-46}$$

The matrix elements for $\mathbf{D}_2$ and $\mathbf{D}_3$ are in the same order as the pixel mask for setting up 2 by 2 and 3 by 3 pixel grids, respectively. With a bilevel system, we determine the display intensity values by comparing input intensities to the matrix elements. Each input intensity is first scaled to the range $0 \leq I \leq n^2$. If the intensity I is to be applied to screen position (x, y), we calculate the reference position (row and column) in the dither matrix as

$$j = (x \bmod n) + 1, \qquad k = (y \bmod n) + 1 \tag{10-47}$$

If $I > \mathbf{D}_n(j, k)$, we turn on the pixel at position (x, y). Otherwise, the pixel is off. For RGB color applications, this procedure is implemented for the intensity of each of the individual color components (red, green, and blue).

Elements of the dither matrix are assigned in accordance with the guidelines discussed for pixel grids. That is, we want to minimize artificial visual effects, such as contouring. Order dither produces constant intensity areas identical to those generated with pixel-grid patterns when the values of the matrix elements correspond to those in the halftone-approximation grid mask. Variations from the pixel-grid displays occur at the boundary of two different intensity areas.

Typically, the number of intensity levels is taken to be a multiple of 2. Higher-order dither matrices, $n \geq 4$, are then obtained from lower-order matrices using the recurrence relation

$$\mathbf{D}_n = \begin{bmatrix} 4\mathbf{D}_{n/2} + \mathbf{D}_2(1,1)\,\mathbf{U}_{n/2} & 4\mathbf{D}_{n/2} + \mathbf{D}_2(1,2)\,U_{n/2} \\ 4\mathbf{D}_{n/2} + \mathbf{D}_2(2,1)\,U_{n/2} & 4\mathbf{D}_{n/2} + \mathbf{D}_2(2,2)\,U_{n/2} \end{bmatrix} \tag{10-48}$$

Parameter $\mathbf{U}_{n/2}$ represents the "unity" matrix (all elements are 1). As an example, if $\mathbf{D}_2$ is specified as in Eq. 10-45, then recurrence relation 10-48 yields

$$\mathbf{D}_4 = \begin{bmatrix} 15 & 7 & 13 & 5 \\ 3 & 11 & 1 & 9 \\ 12 & 4 & 10 & 6 \\ 0 & 8 & 2 & 10 \end{bmatrix} \tag{10-49}$$

Another method for mapping a picture with m by n points to a display area with m by n pixels is **error diffusion.** Here, the error between an input intensity value and the selected intensity level at a given pixel position is dispersed, or diffused, to pixel positions to the right and below the current pixel position. Starting with a matrix **M** of intensity values obtained by scanning a photograph, we want to construct an array **I** of pixel intensity values for an area of the screen. We do this by first scanning across the rows of **M**, from left to right, starting with the top row, and determining the nearest available pixel-intensity level for each element of **M**. Then the error between the value stored in matrix **M** and the displayed intensity level at each pixel position is distributed to neighboring elements using the following simplified algorithm.

```
for (j = 0; j < m; j++)
   for (k = 0; k < n; k++) {
      \*  Determine the available system intensity value
       *  that is closest to the value of M [j][k] and
       *  assign this value to I [j][k].
       */
      error = M [j][k] - I [j][k];
      I [j][k+1]    = M [j][k+1]   + alpha * error;
      I [j+1][k-1]  = M [j+1][k-1] + beta  * error;
      I [j+1][k]    = M [j+1][k]   + gamma * error;
      I [j+1][k+1]  = M [j+1][k+1] + delta * error;
   }
```

Once the elements of matrix **I** have been assigned intensity-level values, we then map the matrix to some area of a display device, such as a printer or video monitor. Of course, we cannot disperse the error past the last matrix column ($k = n$) or below the last matrix row ($j = m$), and for a bilevel system, the system intensity values are just 0 and 1. Parameters for distributing the error can be chosen to satisfy the following relationship

$$\alpha + \beta + \gamma + \delta \leq 1 \tag{10-50}$$

One choice for the error-diffusion parameters that produces fairly good results is $(\alpha, \beta, \gamma, \delta) = (\frac{7}{16}, \frac{3}{16}, \frac{5}{16}, \frac{1}{16})$. Figure 10-45 illustrates the error distribution using these parameter values. Error diffusion sometimes produces "ghosts" in a picture by repeating, or echoing, certain parts of the picture, particularly with facial features such as hairlines and nose outlines. Ghosting can often be reduced in these cases by choosing values for the error-diffusion parameters that sum to a

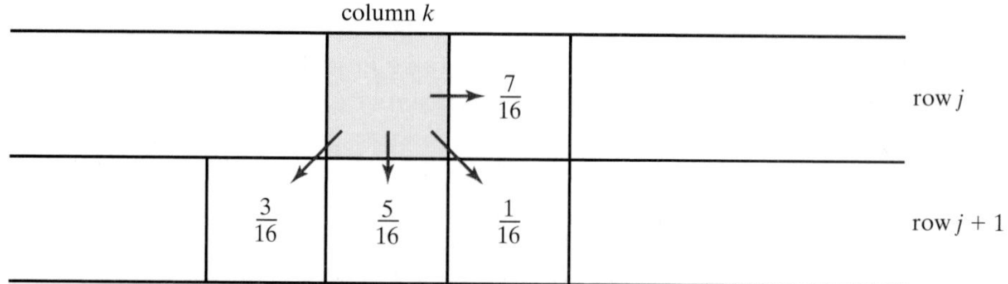

FIGURE 10-45 Fraction of intensity error that can be distributed to neighboring pixel positions using an error-diffusion scheme.

34	48	40	32	29	15	23	31
42	58	56	53	21	5	7	10
50	62	61	45	13	1	2	18
38	46	54	37	25	17	9	26
28	14	22	30	35	49	41	33
20	4	6	11	43	59	57	52
12	0	3	19	51	63	60	44
24	16	8	27	39	47	55	36

FIGURE 10-46 One possible distribution scheme for dividing the intensity array into 64 dot-diffusion classes, numbered from 0 through 63.

value less than 1 and by rescaling the matrix values after the dispersion of errors. One way to rescale is to multiply all matrix elements by 0.8 and then add 0.1. Another method for improving picture quality is to alternate the scanning of matrix rows from right-to-left and left-to-right.

A variation on the error-diffusion method is **dot diffusion.** In this method, the m by n array of intensity values is divided into 64 classes numbered from 0 to 63, as shown in Fig. 10-46. The error between a matrix value and the displayed intensity is then distributed only to those neighboring matrix elements that have a larger class number. Distribution of the 64 class numbers is based on minimizing the number of elements that are completely surrounded by elements with a lower class number, since this would tend to direct all errors of the surrounding elements to that one position.

10-10 POLYGON RENDERING METHODS

Intensity calculations from an illumination model can be applied to surface rendering in various ways. We could use an illumination model to determine the surface intensity at every projected pixel position, or we could apply the illumination model to a few selected points and approximate the intensity at the other surface positions. Graphics packages typically perform surface rendering using scan-line algorithms that reduce processing time by dealing only with polygon surfaces and by calculating surface intensity only at the vertices. The vertex intensities are then interpolated to the other positions on the polygon surface. Other, more accurate polygon scan-line rendering methods have been developed, and ray-tracing algorithms calculate the intensity at each projected surface point for curved or planar surfaces. We first consider the scan-line surface-rendering schemes that are applied to polygons. Then, in Section 10-11, we examine the methods that can be used in ray tracing.

Constant-Intensity Surface Rendering

The simplest method for rendering a polygon surface is to assign the same color to all projected surface positions. In this case, we use the illumination model to determine the intensity for the three RGB color components at a single surface position, such as a vertex or the polygon centroid. This approach, called **constant-intensity surface rendering** or **flat surface rendering,** provides a fast and simple method for displaying polygon facets on an object, which can be useful for quickly generating the general appearance of a curved surface, as in Fig. 10-50(b).

Flat rendering is also useful in design or other applications where we might want quickly to identify the individual polygonal facets used to model a curved surface.

In general, flat surface rendering of a polygon provides an accurate display of the surface if all of the following assumptions are valid.

- The polygon is one face of a polyhedron and is not a section of a curved-surface approximation mesh.
- All light sources illuminating the polygon are sufficiently far from the surface so that $\mathbf{N} \cdot \mathbf{L}$ and the attenuation function are constant over the area of the polygon.
- The viewing position is sufficiently far from the polygon so that $\mathbf{V} \cdot \mathbf{R}$ is constant over the area of the polygon.

Even if some of these conditions are not true, we can still reasonably approximate surface lighting effects using constant-intensity surface rendering if the polygon facets for an object are small.

Gouraud Surface Rendering

This scheme, devised by Henri Gouraud and referred to as **Gouraud surface rendering** or **intensity-interpolation surface rendering,** linearly interpolates vertex intensity values across the polygon faces of an illuminated object. Developed for rendering a curved surface that is approximated with a polygon mesh, the Gouraud method smoothly transitions the intensity values for each polygon facet into the values for adjacent polygons along the common edges. This interpolation of intensities across the polygon area eliminates the intensity discontinuities that can occur in flat surface rendering.

Each polygon section of a tessellated curved surface is processed by the Gouraud surface-rendering method using the following procedures.

(1) Determine the average unit normal vector at each vertex of the polygon.

(2) Apply an illumination model at each polygon vertex to obtain the light intensity at that position.

(3) Linearly interpolate the vertex intensities over the projected area of the polygon.

At each polygon vertex, we obtain a normal vector by averaging the normal vectors of all polygons in the surface mesh that share that vertex, as illustrated in Fig. 10-47. Thus, for any vertex position **V**, we obtain the unit vertex normal with the calculation

$$\mathbf{N}_V = \frac{\sum_{k=1}^{n} \mathbf{N}_k}{\left|\sum_{k=1}^{n} \mathbf{N}_k\right|} \tag{10-51}$$

Once we have obtained the normal vector at a vertex, we invoke the illumination model to obtain the surface intensity at that point.

After all vertex intensities have been computed for a polygonal facet, we can interpolate the vertex values to obtain the intensities at positions along scan lines that intersect the projected area of the polygon, as demonstrated in Figure 10-48. For each scan line, the intensity at the intersection of the scan line with a polygon edge is linearly interpolated from the intensities at the endpoints of that edge. For

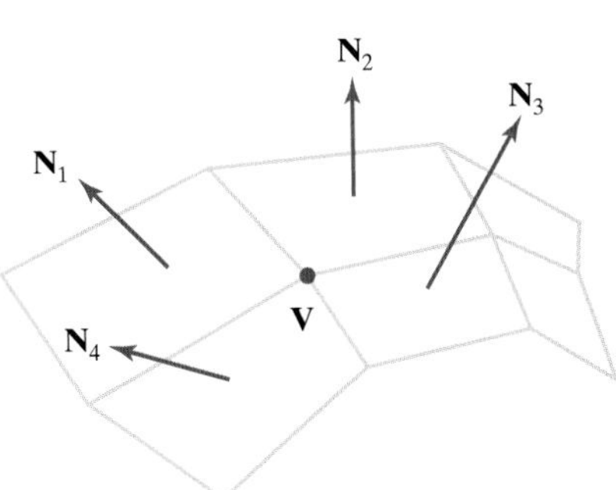

FIGURE 10-47 The normal vector at vertex **V** is calculated as the average of the surface normals for each polygon sharing that vertex.

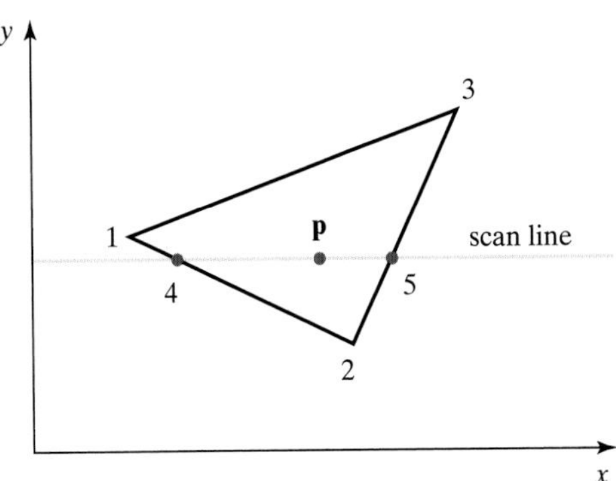

FIGURE 10-48 For Gouraud surface rendering, the intensity at point 4 is linearly interpolated from the intensities at vertices 1 and 2. The intensity at point 5 is linearly interpolated from intensities at vertices 2 and 3. An interior point **p** is then assigned an intensity value that is linearly interpolated from intensities at positions 4 and 5.

the example in Fig. 10-48, the polygon edge with endpoint vertices at positions 1 and 2 is intersected by the scan line at point 4. A fast method for obtaining the intensity at point 4 is to interpolate between the values at vertices 1 and 2 using only the vertical displacement of the scan line:

$$I_4 = \frac{y_4 - y_2}{y_1 - y_2} I_1 + \frac{y_1 - y_4}{y_1 - y_2} I_2 \qquad (10\text{-}52)$$

In this expression, the symbol I represents the intensity for one of the RGB color components. Similarly, the intensity at the right intersection of this scan line (point 5) is interpolated from intensity values at vertices 2 and 3. From these two boundary intensities, we linearly interpolate to obtain the pixel intensities for positions across the scan line. The intensity for one of the RGB color components at point **p** in Fig. 10-48, for instance, is calculated from the intensities at points 4 and 5 as

$$I_p = \frac{x_5 - x_p}{x_5 - x_4} I_4 + \frac{x_p - x_4}{x_5 - x_4} I_5 \qquad (10\text{-}53)$$

In the implementation of Gouraud rendering, we can perform the intensity calculations represented by Eqs. 10-52 and 10-53 efficiently by using incremental methods. Starting from a scan line that intersects one of the polygon vertices, we can incrementally obtain intensity values for other scan lines that intersect an edge that is connected to that vertex. Assuming that the polygon facets are convex, each scan line crossing the polygon has two edge intersections, such as points 4 and 5 in Fig. 10-48. Once we have obtained the intensities at the two edge intersections for a scan line, we apply the incremental procedures to obtain pixel intensities across the scan line.

As an example of the incremental calculation of intensities, we consider scan lines y and $y - 1$ in Fig. 10-49, which intersect the left edge of a polygon. If scan line y is the next scan line below the vertex at y_1 with intensity I_1, that is $y = y_1 - 1$,

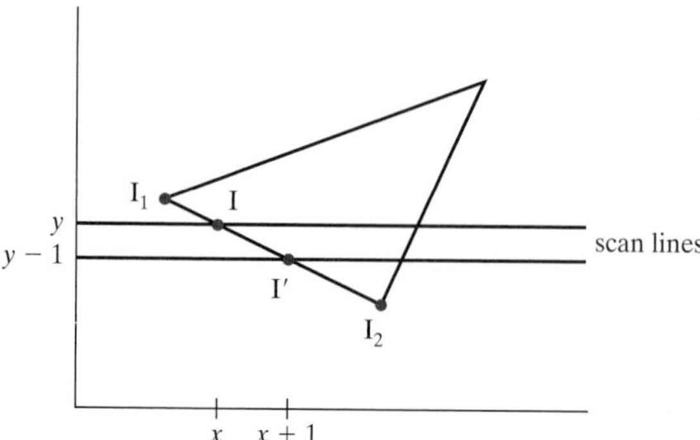

FIGURE 10-49
Incremental interpolation of intensity values along a polygon edge for successive scan lines.

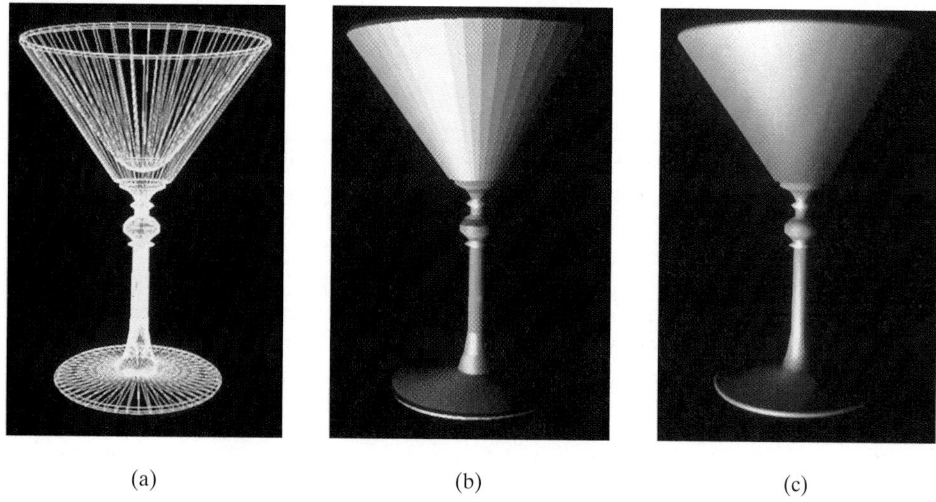

(a) (b) (c)

FIGURE 10-50 A polygon mesh approximation of an object (a) is displayed using flat surface rendering in (b) and using Gouraud surface rendering in (c).

then we can compute the intensity I on scan line y from Eq. 10-52 as

$$I = I_1 + \frac{I_2 - I_1}{y_1 - y_2} \tag{10-54}$$

Continuing on down the polygon edge, the intensity along this edge for the next scan line, $y - 1$, is

$$I' = I + \frac{I_2 - I_1}{y_1 - y_2} \tag{10-55}$$

Thus, each successive intensity value down the edge is computed simply by adding the constant term $(I_2 - I_1)/(y_1 - y_2)$ to the previous intensity value. Similar incremental calculations are used to obtain intensities at successive horizontal pixel positions along each scan line.

Gouraud surface rendering can be combined with a hidden-surface algorithm to fill in the visible polygons along each scan line. An example of a three-dimensional object rendered with the Gouraud method appears in Fig. 10-50(c).

This intensity-interpolation method eliminates the discontinuities associated with flat rendering, but it has some other deficiencies. Highlights on the surface are sometimes displayed with anomalous shapes, and the linear intensity interpolation can cause bright or dark intensity streaks, called **Mach bands,** to appear on the surface. These effects can be reduced by dividing the surface into a greater number of polygon faces or by using more precise intensity calculations.

Phong Surface Rendering

A more accurate interpolation method for rendering a polygon mesh was subsequently developed by Phong Bui Tuong. This approach, called **Phong surface rendering** or **normal-vector interpolation rendering,** interpolates normal vectors instead of intensity values. The result is a more accurate calculation of intensity values, a more realistic display of surface highlights, and a great reduction in the Mach-band effect. However, the Phong method requires more computation than the Gouraud method.

Each polygon section of a tessellated curved surface is processed by the Phong surface-rendering method using the following procedures.

(1) Determine the average unit normal vector at each vertex of the polygon.

(2) Linearly interpolate the vertex normals over the projected area of the polygon.

(3) Apply an illumination model at positions along scan lines to calculate pixel intensities using the interpolated normal vectors.

Interpolation procedures for normal vectors in the Phong method are the same as those for the intensity values in the Gouraud method. The normal vector N in Fig. 10-51 is vertically interpolated from the normal vectors at vertices 1 and 2 as

$$\mathbf{N} = \frac{y - y_2}{y_1 - y_2}\mathbf{N}_1 + \frac{y_1 - y}{y_1 - y_2}\mathbf{N}_2 \qquad (10\text{-}56)$$

And we apply the same incremental methods for obtaining normal vectors on successive scan lines and at successive pixel positions along scan lines. The difference between the two surface-rendering approaches is that we must now apply the illumination model at every projected pixel position along the scan lines to obtain the surface intensity values.

Fast Phong Surface Rendering

We can reduce processing time in the Phong-rendering method by approximating some of the illumination-model calculations. **Fast Phong surface rendering** performs the intensity calculations using a truncated Taylor-series expansion and limiting the polygon facets to triangular surface patches.

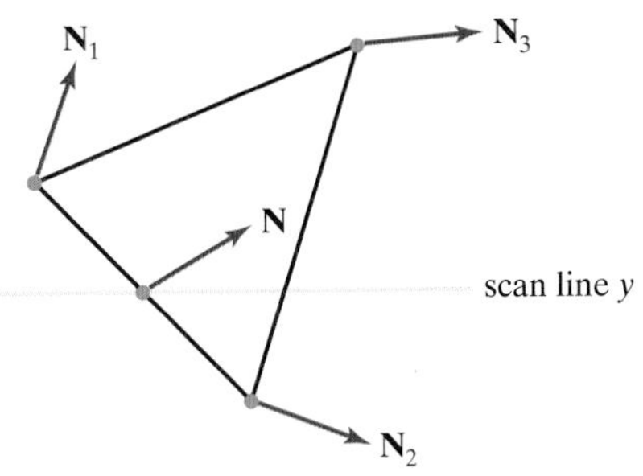

FIGURE 10-51 Interpolation of surface normals along a polygon edge.

Since the Phong method interpolates normal vectors from the vertex normals, we can write the expression for calculating the surface normal **N** at position (x, y) in a triangular patch as

$$\mathbf{N} = \mathbf{A}x + \mathbf{B}y + \mathbf{C} \tag{10-57}$$

where vectors **A**, **B**, and **C** are determined from the three vertex equations:

$$\mathbf{N}_k = \mathbf{A}x_k + \mathbf{B}y_k + \mathbf{C}, \qquad k = 1, 2, 3 \tag{10-58}$$

with (x_k, y_k) denoting a projected triangle vertex position on the pixel plane.

Omitting the reflectivity and attentuation parameters, we can write the calculation for light-source diffuse reflection from a surface point (x, y) as

$$\begin{aligned} I_{\text{diff}}(x, y) &= \frac{\mathbf{L} \cdot \mathbf{N}}{|\mathbf{L}||\mathbf{N}|} \\ &= \frac{\mathbf{L} \cdot (\mathbf{A}x + \mathbf{B}y + \mathbf{C})}{|\mathbf{L}||\mathbf{A}x + \mathbf{B}y + \mathbf{C}|} \\ &= \frac{(\mathbf{L} \cdot \mathbf{A})x + (\mathbf{L} \cdot \mathbf{B})y + \mathbf{L} \cdot \mathbf{C}}{|\mathbf{L}||\mathbf{A}x + \mathbf{B}y + \mathbf{C}|} \end{aligned} \tag{10-59}$$

This expression can be written in the form

$$I_{\text{diff}}(x, y) = \frac{ax + by + c}{[dx^2 + exy + fy^2 + gx + hy + i]^{1/2}} \tag{10-60}$$

where parameters such as a, b, c, and d are used to represent the various dot products. For example,

$$a = \frac{\mathbf{L} \cdot \mathbf{A}}{|\mathbf{L}|} \tag{10-61}$$

Finally, we can express the denominator in Eq. 10-60 as a Taylor series expansion and retain terms up to second degree in x and y. This yields

$$I_{\text{diff}}(x, y) = T_5\, x^2 + T_4\, xy + T_3\, y^2 + T_2\, x + T_1\, y + T_0 \tag{10-62}$$

where each T_k is a function of the various parameters in Eq. 10-60, such as a, b, and c.

Using forward differences, we then evaluate Eq. 10-62 with only two additions for each pixel position (x, y) once the initial forward-difference parameters have been evaluated. Although the simplifications in the fast-Phong approach reduce the Phong surface-rendering calculations, it still takes approximately twice as long to render a surface with the fast-Phong method as it does with Gouraud surface rendering. And the basic Phong method, using forward-difference calculations, takes about 6 to 7 times longer than Gouraud rendering.

Fast-Phong rendering for diffuse reflection can be extended to include specular reflections, using similar approximations for evaluating the specular terms such as $(\mathbf{N} \cdot \mathbf{H})^{n_s}$. In addition, we can generalize the algorithm to include a finite viewing position and polygons other than triangles.

10-11 RAY-TRACING METHODS

In Section 8-20, we introduced the notion of *ray casting*, which is used in constructive solid geometry for locating surface intersections along a ray from a pixel position. We also discussed ray-casting methods in Section 9-10 as a means for identifying visible surfaces in a scene. **Ray tracing** is the generalization of the basic ray-casting procedure. Instead of merely looking for the visible surface from each pixel position, we continue to bounce the pixel ray around in the scene, as illustrated in Fig. 10-52, to collect the various intensity contributions. This provides a simple and powerful rendering technique for obtaining global reflection and transmission effects. In addition, the basic ray-tracing algorithm detects visible surfaces, identifies shadow areas, provides for the rendering of transparency effects, generates perspective-projection views, and accommodates illumination effects from multiple light sources. Many extensions to the basic algorithm have been developed to produce photo-realistic displays. Ray-traced pictures of scenes can be highly realistic, particularly when the scene contains shiny objects, but ray-tracing algorithms involve considerable computation time. An example of the global reflection and transmission effects possible with ray tracing is demonstrated in Fig. 10-53.

Basic Ray-Tracing Algorithm

The coordinate system for a ray-tracing algorithm is typically set up as shown in Fig. 10-54, with the projection reference point on the z axis and the pixel positions on the xy plane. We then describe the geometry of a scene in this coordinate system and generate the pixel rays. For a perspective-projection view of the scene, each ray originates at the projection reference point (center of projection), passes through a pixel center, and continues into the scene to form the various branches of the ray along reflection and transmission paths. Contributions to the pixel intensity are then accumulated at the intersected surfaces. This rendering approach is based on the principles of geometric optics. Light rays from the surfaces in a scene emanate

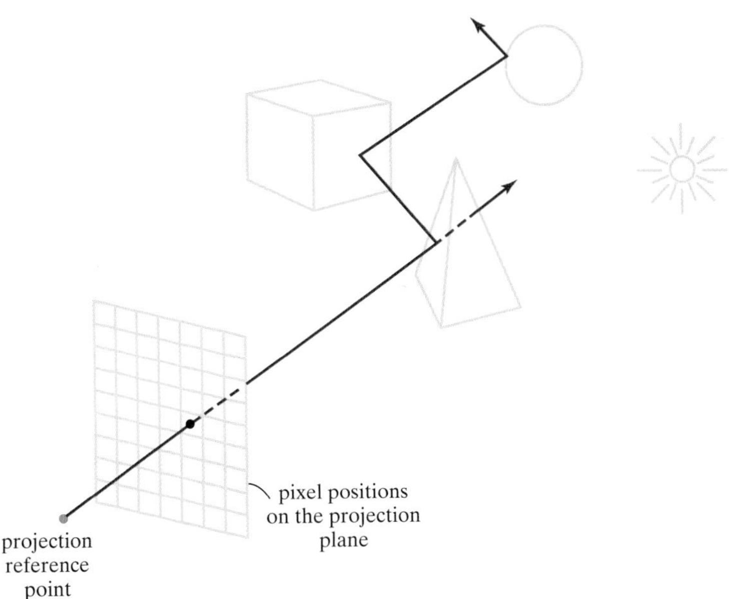

FIGURE 10-52 Multiple reflection and transmission paths for a ray from the projection reference point through a pixel position and on into a scene containing several objects.

FIGURE 10-53 A ray-traced scene, showing global reflection and transparency effects. (*Courtesy of Evans & Sutherland.*)

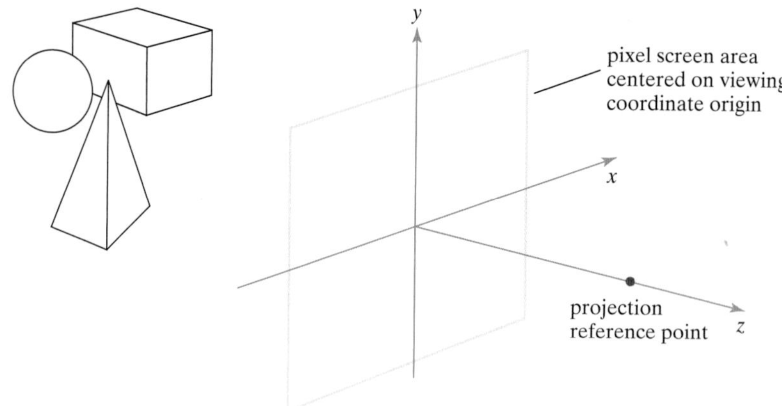

FIGURE 10-54 Ray-tracing coordinate-reference frame.

in all directions, and some pass through the pixel positions on the projection plane. Since there are an infinite number of ray emanations, we determine the intensity contributions for a particular pixel by tracing a light path backward from the pixel position into the scene. In the basic ray-tracing algorithm, one reverse light ray is generated for each pixel, which is approximately equivalent to viewing the scene through a pinhole camera.

As each pixel ray is generated, the list of surfaces in the scene is processed to determine whether there are any ray–surface intersections. If the ray does intersect a surface, we calculate the distance from the pixel to the surface intersection point. After all surfaces have been tested for a ray intersection, the smallest calculated intersection distance identifies the visible surface for that pixel. We then reflect the ray off the visible surface along a specular-reflection path (angle of reflection equals angle of incidence). For a transparent surface, we also send a ray through the surface in the refraction direction. The reflection and refraction rays are referred to as **secondary rays.**

We then repeat the ray-processing procedures for the secondary rays. Surfaces are tested for intersections, and the nearest intersected surface, if any, along a secondary ray path is used to recursively produce the next generation of reflection and refraction paths. As the rays from a pixel ricochet through the scene, each

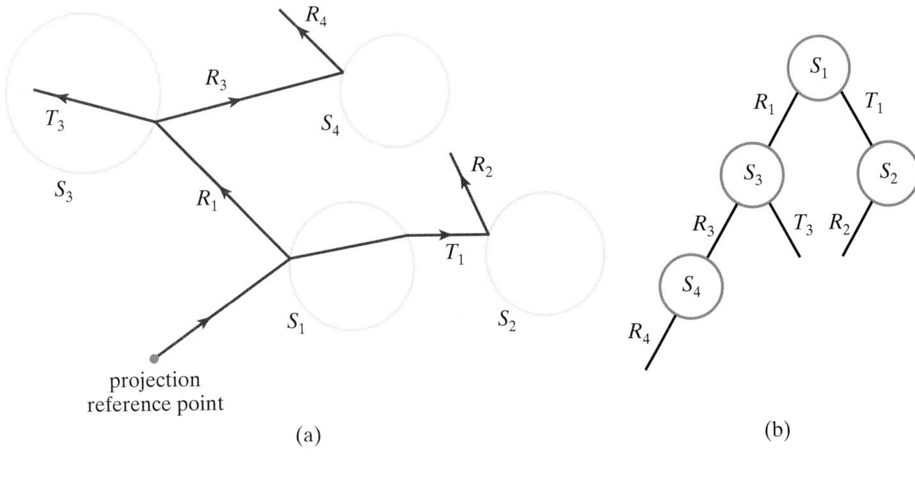

FIGURE 10-55 The reflection and refraction paths for a pixel ray traveling through a scene are shown in (a), and the corresponding binary ray-tracing tree is given in (b).

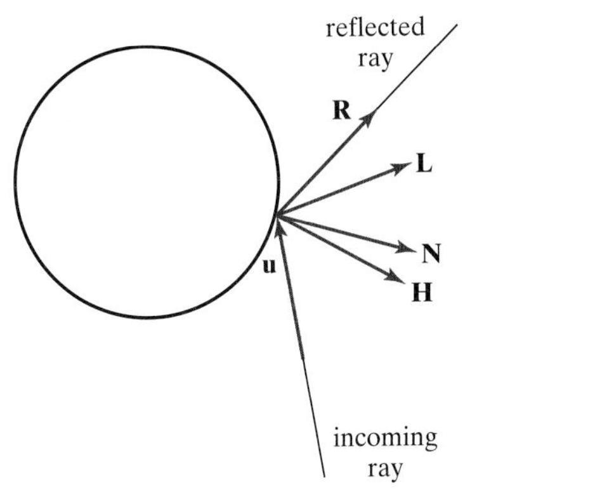

FIGURE 10-56 Unit vectors at the surface of an object intersected by an incoming ray along direction **u**.

successively intersected surface is added to a binary **ray-tracing tree,** as shown in Fig. 10-55. We use left branches in the tree to represent reflection paths and right branches to represent transmission paths. Maximum depth of the ray-tracing trees can be set as a user option, or it can be determined by the amount of storage available. We terminate a path in the binary tree for a pixel if any one of the following conditions is satisfied.

- The ray intersects no surfaces.
- The ray intersects a light source that is not a reflecting surface.
- The tree has been generated to its maximum allowable depth.

At each surface intersection, we invoke the basic illumination model to determine the surface intensity contribution. This intensity value is stored at the surface-node position in the pixel tree. A ray that intersects a nonreflecting light source can be assigned the intensity of the source, although light sources in the basic ray-tracing algorithm are usually point sources at positions beyond the coordinate limits of the scene. Figure 10-56 shows a surface intersected by a ray and the unit vectors used for the reflected light intensity calculations. Unit vector **u** is

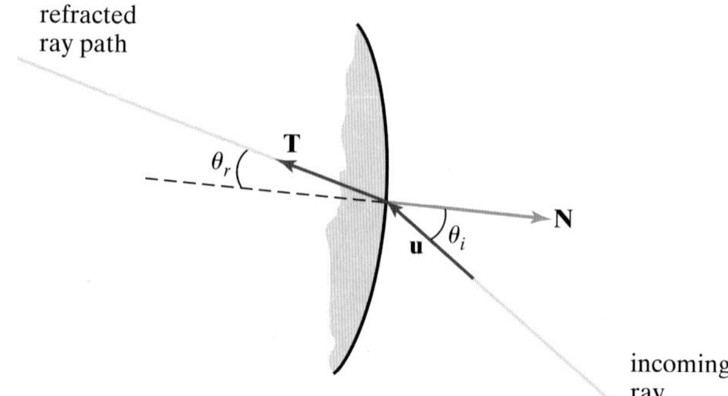

FIGURE 10-57 Refracted ray-transmission path **T** through a transparent material.

in the direction of the ray path, **N** is the unit surface normal, **R** is the unit reflection vector, **L** is the unit vector indicating the direction to a point light source, and **H** is the unit vector halfway between **L** and **V**. For the ray-tracing calculations, the viewing direction is $\mathbf{V} = -\mathbf{u}$. The path along the direction of **L** is referred to as the **shadow ray.** If any object intersects the shadow ray between the surface and the point light source, the surface position is in shadow with respect to that source. Ambient light at the surface is calculated as $k_a I_a$; diffuse reflection due to the source is proportional to $k_d(\mathbf{N} \cdot \mathbf{L})$; and the specular reflection component is proportional to $k_s(\mathbf{H} \cdot \mathbf{N})^{n_s}$. As discussed in Section 10-3, the specular-reflection direction for the secondary ray path **R** depends upon the surface normal and the incoming ray direction:

$$\mathbf{R} = \mathbf{u} - (2\mathbf{u} \cdot \mathbf{N})\mathbf{N} \tag{10-63}$$

For a transparent surface, we also need to obtain intensity contributions from light transmitted (refracted) through the material. We can locate the source of this contribution by tracing a secondary ray along the transmission direction **T**, as shown in Fig. 10-57. The unit transmission vector **T** can be obtained from vectors **u** and **N** as

$$\mathbf{T} = \frac{\eta_i}{\eta_r}\mathbf{u} - \left(\cos\theta_r - \frac{\eta_i}{\eta_r}\cos\theta_i \right)\mathbf{N} \tag{10-64}$$

Parameters η_i and η_r are the indices of refraction in the incident material and the refracting material, respectively. Angle of refraction θ_r can be calculated from Snell's law:

$$\cos\theta_r = \sqrt{1 - \left(\frac{\eta_i}{\eta_r}\right)^2 (1 - \cos^2\theta_i)} \tag{10-65}$$

After the binary tree has been completed for a pixel, the intensity contributions are accumulated, starting at the bottom (terminal nodes) of the tree. Surface intensity from each node in the tree is attenuated by the distance from the parent surface (the next node up the tree) and added to the intensity of the parent surface. The intensity assigned to the pixel is the sum of the attenuated intensities at the root node of the ray tree. If the primary ray for a pixel does not intersect an object in the scene, the ray-tracing tree is empty and the pixel is assigned the background intensity.

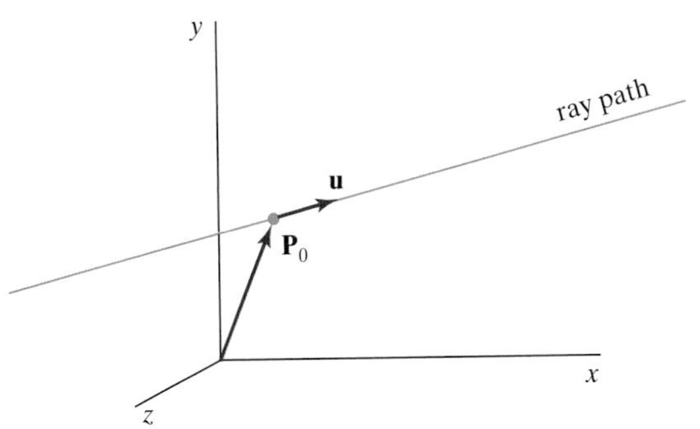

FIGURE 10-58 Describing a ray with an initial-position vector $\mathbf{P}_0$ and unit direction vector $\mathbf{u}$.

Ray–Surface Intersection Calculations

A ray can be described with an initial position $\mathbf{P}_0$ and a unit direction vector $\mathbf{u}$, as illustrated in Fig. 10-58. The coordinates for any point $\mathbf{P}$ along the ray at a distance s from $\mathbf{P}_0$ are then computed from the following **ray equation.**

$$\mathbf{P} = \mathbf{P}_0 + s\mathbf{u} \tag{10-66}$$

Initially, vector $\mathbf{P}_0$ can be set to the position $\mathbf{P}_{\text{pix}}$ of the pixel on the projection plane, or it could be chosen to be the projection reference point. Unit vector $\mathbf{u}$ is initially obtained from the position of the pixel through which the ray passes and the projection reference point:

$$\mathbf{u} = \frac{\mathbf{P}_{\text{pix}} - \mathbf{P}_{\text{prp}}}{|\mathbf{P}_{\text{pix}} - \mathbf{P}_{\text{prp}}|} \tag{10-67}$$

Although it is not necessary for $\mathbf{u}$ to be a unit vector, this will simplify some calculations.

To locate the ray-intersection position on a surface, we use the surface equation to solve for position $\mathbf{P}$, as represented by Eq. 10-66. This gives us a value for parameter s, which is the distance from $\mathbf{P}_0$ to the surface intersection point along the ray path.

At each intersected surface, vectors $\mathbf{P}_0$ and $\mathbf{u}$ are updated for the secondary rays at the ray-surface intersection point. For the secondary rays, the reflection direction for $\mathbf{u}$ is $\mathbf{R}$ and the transmission direction is $\mathbf{T}$. When a secondary ray-surface intersection is detected, we simultaneously solve the ray equation and the surface equation to obtain the intersection coordinates. We then update the binary tree and generate the next set of reflection and refraction rays.

Efficient ray-surface intersection algorithms have been devised for most commonly occurring shapes, including various spline surfaces. The general procedure is to combine the ray equation with the equations describing a surface and solve for parameter s. In many cases, numerical root-finding methods and incremental calculations are used to locate intersection points over a surface. For complex objects, it is often convenient to transform the ray equation into the local coordinate system in which an object is defined. And intersection calculations for a complex object can be simplified in many cases by transforming the object into a more congenial shape. As an example, we can ray trace an ellipsoid by transforming the ray and surface equations into a sphere-intersection problem. Figure 10-59 shows a ray-traced scene containing multiple objects and texture patterns.

FIGURE 10-59 A ray-traced scene showing global reflection of surface-texture patterns. (*Courtesy of Sun Microsystems.*)

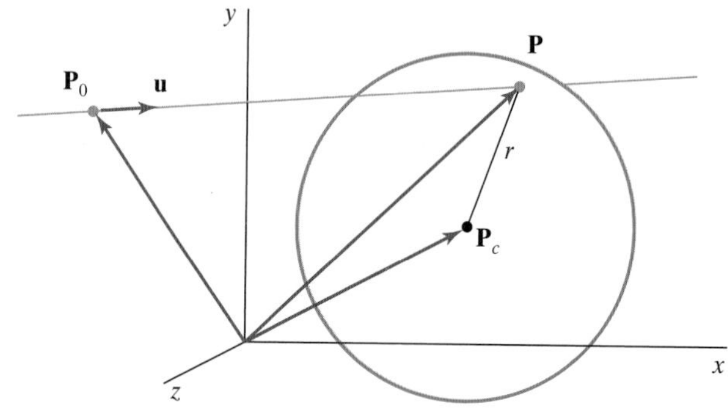

FIGURE 10-60 A ray intersecting a sphere with radius r and center position $\mathbf{P}_c$.

Ray–Sphere Intersections

The simplest objects to ray trace are spheres. If we have a sphere of radius r and center position $\mathbf{P}_c$ (Fig. 10-60), then any point $\mathbf{P}$ on the surface satisfies the sphere equation:

$$|\mathbf{P} - \mathbf{P}_c|^2 - r^2 = 0 \qquad (10\text{-}68)$$

Substituting the ray equation 10-66 for $\mathbf{P}$ in the preceding equation, we have

$$|\mathbf{P}_0 - s\mathbf{u} - \mathbf{P}_c|^2 - r^2 = 0 \qquad (10\text{-}69)$$

If we represent $\mathbf{P}_c - \mathbf{P}_0$ as $\Delta\mathbf{P}$ and expand the dot product, we obtain the quadratic equation

$$s^2 - 2(\mathbf{u} \cdot \Delta\mathbf{P})\, s + (|\Delta\mathbf{P}|^2 - r^2) = 0 \qquad (10\text{-}70)$$

whose solution is

$$s = \mathbf{u} \cdot \Delta\mathbf{P} \pm \sqrt{(\mathbf{u} \cdot \Delta\mathbf{P})^2 - |\Delta\mathbf{P}|^2 + r^2} \qquad (10\text{-}71)$$

If the discriminant is negative, either the ray does not intersect the sphere or the sphere is behind $\mathbf{P}_0$. In either case, we can eliminate the sphere from further consideration, since we assume that the scene is in front of the projection plane. When the descriminant is not negative, the surface intersection coordinates are obtained from the ray equation 10-66 using the smaller of the two values from Eq. 10-71. Figure 10-61 shows a ray-traced scene containing a snowflake pattern formed with shiny spheres, which illustrates the global surface reflections possible with ray tracing.

FIGURE 10-61 A "sphereflake" rendered with ray tracing using 7,381 spheres and 3 light sources. (*Courtesy of Eric Haines, Autodesk, Inc.*)

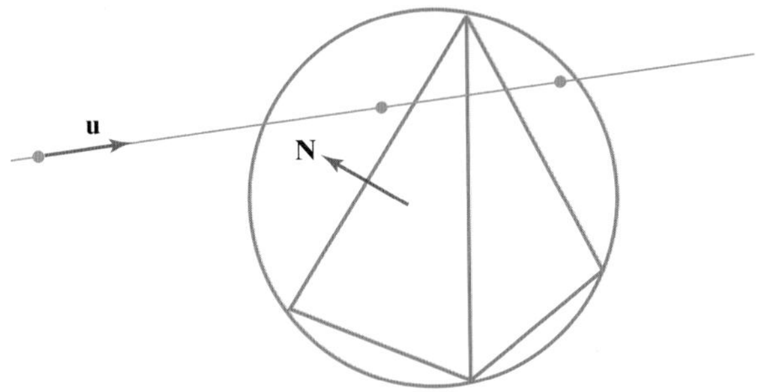

FIGURE 10-62 A polyhedron enclosed by a bounding sphere.

Some optimizations are possible in the ray–sphere intersection calculations to reduce processing time. In addition, Eq. 10-71 is susceptible to round-off errors when a small sphere far from the initial ray position is processed. That is, if

$$r^2 \ll |\Delta \mathbf{P}|^2$$

we could lose the r^2 term in the precision error of $|\Delta \mathbf{P}|^2$. We can avoid this for most cases by rearranging the calculation for distance s as

$$s = \mathbf{u} \cdot \Delta \mathbf{P} \pm \sqrt{r^2 - |\Delta \mathbf{P} - (\mathbf{u} \cdot \Delta \mathbf{P})\mathbf{u}|^2} \qquad (10\text{-}72)$$

Ray–Polyhedron Intersections

Intersection calculations for polyhedra are more complicated than the sphere-intersection procedures. Therefore, it is often more efficient to process a polyhedron by performing an initial intersection test on a bounding volume. For example, Fig. 10-62 shows a polyhedron inside a sphere. If a ray does not intersect the bounding sphere, we eliminate the polyhedron from further testing. Otherwise, we next identify the front faces of the polyhedron as those polygons that satisfy

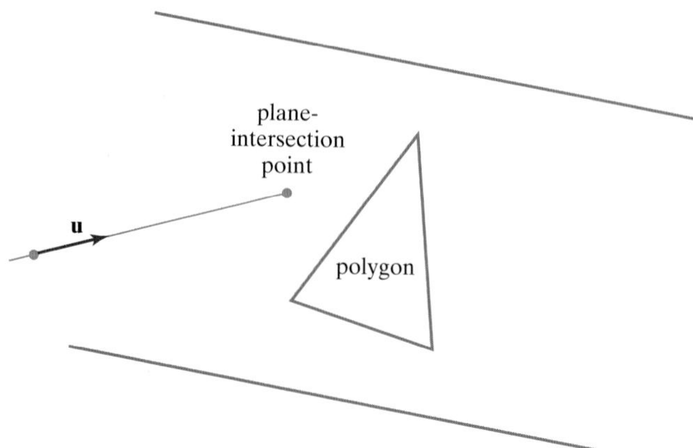

FIGURE 10-63 Ray intersection with the plane of a polygon.

the inequality

$$\mathbf{u} \cdot \mathbf{N} < 0 \tag{10-73}$$

where $\mathbf{N}$ is the surface normal for the polygon. For each face of the polyhedron that satisfies condition 10-73, we solve the plane equation

$$\mathbf{N} \cdot \mathbf{P} = -D \tag{10-74}$$

for surface position $\mathbf{P}$ that also satisfies the ray equation 10-66. Here, $\mathbf{N} = (A, B, C)$ and D is the fourth plane parameter. Position $\mathbf{P}$ is both on the plane and on the ray path if

$$\mathbf{N} \cdot (\mathbf{P}_0 + s\mathbf{u}) = -D \tag{10-75}$$

and the distance from the initial ray position to the plane is

$$s = -\frac{D + \mathbf{N} \cdot \mathbf{P}_0}{\mathbf{N} \cdot \mathbf{u}} \tag{10-76}$$

This gives us a position on the infinite plane that contains the polygon face, but this position may not be inside the polygon boundaries (Fig. 10-63). So we need to perform an inside-outside test (Section 3-15) to determine whether the ray intersected this face of the polyhedron. We perform this test for each face satisfying inequality 10-73. The smallest distance s to an intersected polygon identifies the intersection position on the polyhedron surface. If no intersection positions from Eq. 10-76 are inside points, the ray does not intersect the polyhedron.

Reducing Object-Intersection Calculations

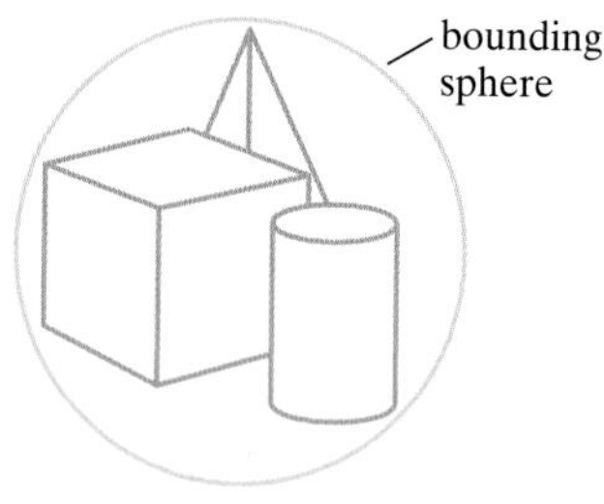

FIGURE 10-64 A group of objects inside a sphere.

Ray–surface intersection calculations can account for as much as 95 percent of the processing time in a ray tracer. For a scene with many objects, most of the processing time for each ray is spent checking objects that are not visible along the ray path. Therefore, several methods have been developed for reducing the processing time spent on these intersection calculations.

One method for reducing the intersection calculations is to enclose groups of adjacent objects within a bounding volume, such as a sphere or a box (Fig. 10-64). We can then test for ray intersections with the bounding volume. If the ray does not intersect the surface of the bounding object, we eliminate the enclosed surfaces from further intersection tests. This approach can be extended to include a hierarchy of bounding volumes. That is, we enclose several bounding volumes within a larger volume and carry out the intersection tests hierarchically. First we test the outer bounding volume; then, if necessary, we test the smaller inner bounding volumes; and so on.

Space-Subdivision Methods

Another way to reduce intersection calculations is to use **space-subdivision** procedures. We can enclose an entire scene within a cube, then we successively subdivide the cube until each subregion (cell) contains no more than a preset maximum number of surfaces. For example, we could require that each cell contain no more than one surface. If parallel and vector processing capabilities are available, the maximum number of surfaces per cell can be determined by the size of the vector registers and the number of processors. Space subdivision of the cube can be stored in an octree or in a binary-partition tree. In addition, we can perform a *uniform subdivision* by dividing the cube into eight equal size octants at each step, or we can perform an *adaptive subdivision* by subdividing only those regions of the cube that contain objects.

We then trace rays through the individual cells of the cube, performing intersection tests only within those cells containing surfaces. The first surface intersected is the visible surface for that ray. There is a trade-off, however, between the cell size and the number of surfaces per cell. As we reduce the maximum number of allowable surfaces per cell, we reduce the amount of processing needed for the surface-intersection tests, but this also reduces cell size so that more calculations are needed to determine the ray path through the cells.

Figure 10-65 illustrates the intersection of a pixel ray with the front face of a cube surrounding a scene. The intersection position on the front face of the cube identifies the initial cell that is to be traversed by this ray. We then process the ray through the cells of the cube by determining the coordinates for the entry and exit positions (Fig. 10-66). At each nonempty cell, we test for surface intersections. This processing continues until the ray intersects an object surface or exits the bounding cube.

Given a unit ray direction vector u and a ray entry position $\mathbf{P}_{\text{in}}$ for a cell, we identify the potential exit faces of a cell as those that satisfy the inequality

$$\mathbf{u} \cdot \mathbf{N}_k > 0 \qquad (10\text{-}77)$$

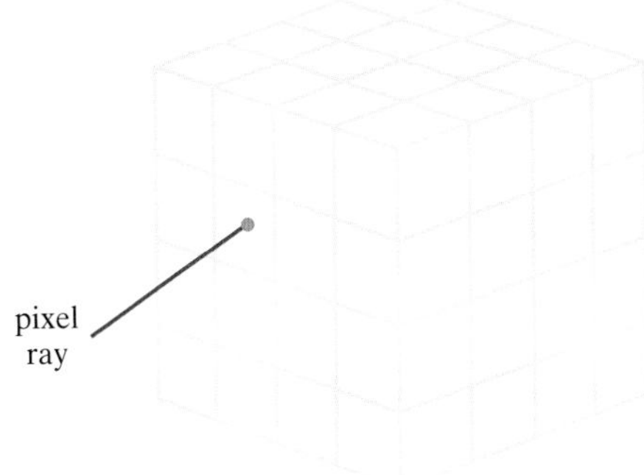

FIGURE 10-65 Ray intersection with a cube enclosing all objects in a scene.

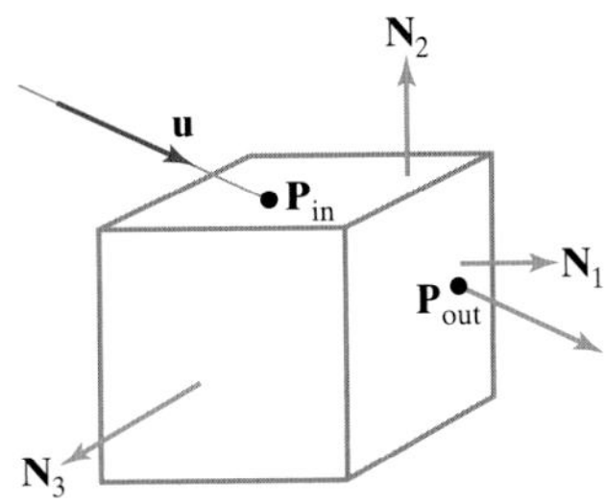

FIGURE 10-66 Ray traversal through a subregion (cell) of a cube enclosing a scene.

where $\mathbf{N}_k$ represents the unit surface normal vector for face k of the cell. If the unit normal vectors for the cell faces in Fig. 10-66 are aligned with the Cartesian-coordinate axes, then

$$\mathbf{N}_k = \begin{cases} (\pm 1, 0, 0) \\ (0, \pm 1, 0) \\ (0, 0, \pm 1) \end{cases} \tag{10-78}$$

and we can determine the three candidate exit planes merely by checking the sign of each component of $\mathbf{u}$. The exit position on each candidate plane is obtained from the ray equation:

$$\mathbf{P}_{\text{out},k} = \mathbf{P}_{\text{in}} + s_k \mathbf{u} \tag{10-79}$$

where s_k is the distance along the ray from $\mathbf{P}_{\text{in}}$ to $\mathbf{P}_{\text{out},k}$. Substituting the ray equation into the plane equation for each cell face, we have

$$\mathbf{N}_k \cdot \mathbf{P}_{\text{out},k} = -D_k \tag{10-80}$$

and the ray distance to each candidate exit face is computed as

$$s_k = \frac{-D_k - \mathbf{N}_k \cdot \mathbf{P}_{\text{in}}}{\mathbf{N}_k \cdot \mathbf{u}} \tag{10-81}$$

The smallest value computed for s_k identifies the exit face for the cell. With the cell faces aligned parallel to the Cartesian-coordinate planes, normal vectors $\mathbf{N}_k$ are the unit axis vectors 10-78, and we can simplify the calculations in Eq. 10-81. For example, if a candidate exit plane has the normal vector (1, 0, 0), then for that plane we have

$$s_k = \frac{x_k - x_0}{u_x} \tag{10-82}$$

where $\mathbf{u} = (u_x, u_y, u_z)$, $x_k = -D_k$ is the coordinate position of the candidate exit plane, and x_0 is the coordinate position of the cell entry face.

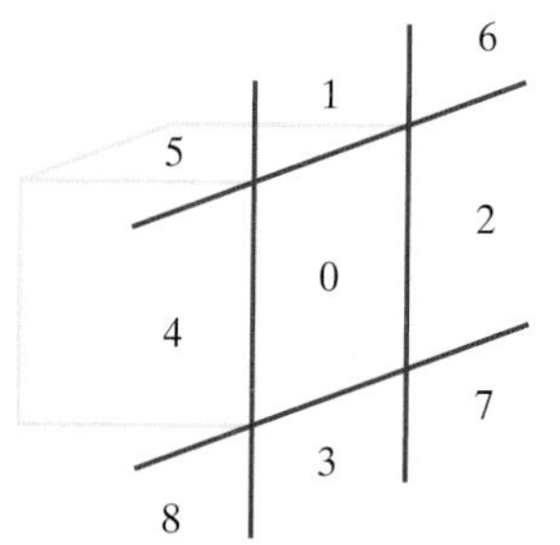

FIGURE 10-67 An example trial exit plane and its numbered sectors.

Various modifications can be made to the cell traversal procedures to speed up the processing. One possibility is to take a trial exit plane k as the one perpendicular to the direction of the largest component of $\mathbf{u}$. This trial exit plane is then divided into sectors, as shown in the example of Fig. 10-67. The sector on the trial plane containing $\mathbf{P}_{\text{out},k}$ determines the true exit plane. For example, if the intersection point $\mathbf{P}_{\text{out},k}$ is in sector 0 for the example plane of Fig. 10-67, the trial plane is the true exit plane and we are done. If the intersection point is in sector 1, the true exit plane is the top plane and we need simply calculate the exit point on the top boundary of the cell. Similarly, sector 3 identifies the bottom plane as the true exit plane; and sectors 4 and 2 identify the true exit plane as either the left or right cell plane, respectively. When the trial exit point falls in sector 5, 6, 7, or 8, we must carry out two additional intersection calculations to identify the true exit plane. Implementation of these methods on parallel vector machines provides further improvements in performance.

The scene in Fig. 10-68 was ray traced using space-subdivision methods. Without space subdivision, the ray-tracing calculations took 10 times longer. Eliminating the polygons also speeded up the processing. For a scene containing 2,048 spheres and no polygons, the same algorithm executed 46 times faster than the basic ray tracer.

FIGURE 10-68 A parallel ray-traced scene containing 37 spheres and 720 polygon surfaces. The ray-tracing algorithm used 9 rays per pixel and a tree depth of 5. Spatial-subdivision methods processed the scene 10 times faster than the basic ray-tracing algorithm on an Alliant FX/8. *(Courtesy of Lee-Hian Quek, Oracle Corporation, Redwood Shores, California.)*

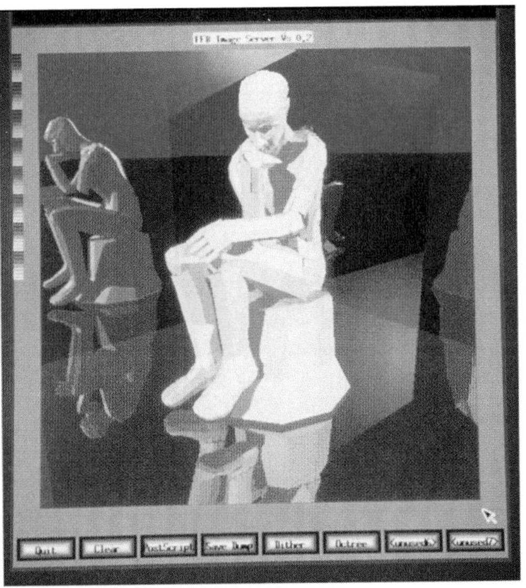

FIGURE 10-69 This ray-traced scene took 24 seconds to render on a Kendall Square Research KSR1 parallel computer with 32 processors. Rodin's sculpture *The Thinker* was modeled with 3,036 primitives. Two light sources and one primary ray per pixel were used to obtain the global illumination effects from the 1,675,776 rays processed. *(Courtesy of M. J. Keates and R. J. Hubbold, Department of Computer Science, University of Manchester, United Kingdom.)*

Figure 10-69 illustrates another ray-traced scene using spatial subdivision and parallel-processing methods. This image of Rodin's sculpture *The Thinker* was ray traced in 24 seconds using more than 1.5 million rays.

A *light-buffer* technique, which is a form of spatial partitioning, was used to render the scene in Fig. 10-70. Here, a cube is centered on each point light source, and each side of the cube is partitioned using a grid of squares. A sorted list of objects that are visible to the light through each square is then maintained by the ray tracer to speed up processing of shadow rays. As a means for determining surface illumination effects, a square for each shadow ray is computed and the shadow ray is then processed against the list of objects for that square.

Intersection tests in ray-tracing programs can also be reduced with directional subdivision procedures, by considering sectors that contain a bundle of rays. Within each sector, we can sort surfaces in depth order, as in Fig. 10-71. Each ray then needs to test only the objects within the sector that contains that ray.

Simulating Camera Focusing Effects

To model camera effects in a scene, we specify the focal length and other parameters for a convex lens (or camera aperture) that is to be positioned in front of the projection plane. Lens parameters are then set so that some objects in a scene can be in focus while other objects are out of focus. The lens focal length is the distance from the center of the lens to the focal point F, which is the convergence

(a)

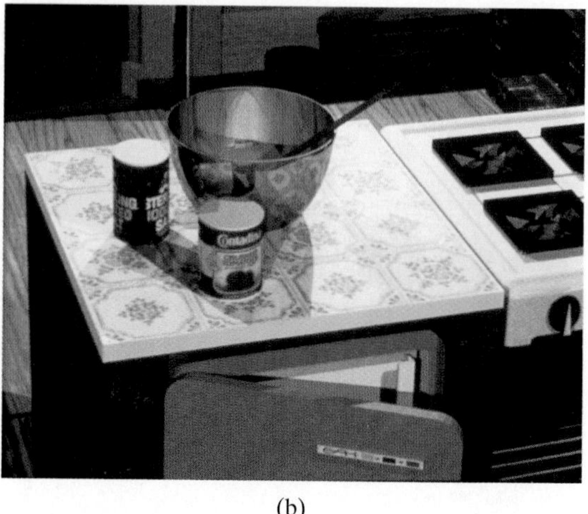

(b)

FIGURE 10-70 A room scene illuminated with 5 light sources (a) was rendered using the ray-tracing light-buffer technique to process shadow rays. A closeup (b) of part of the room shown in (a) illustrates the global illumination effects. The room is modeled with 1,298 polygons, 4 spheres, 76 cylinders, and 35 quadrics. Rendering time was 246 minutes on a VAX 11/780, compared to 602 minutes without using light buffers. (*Courtesy of Eric Haines and Donald P. Greenberg, Program of Computer Graphics, Cornell University.*)

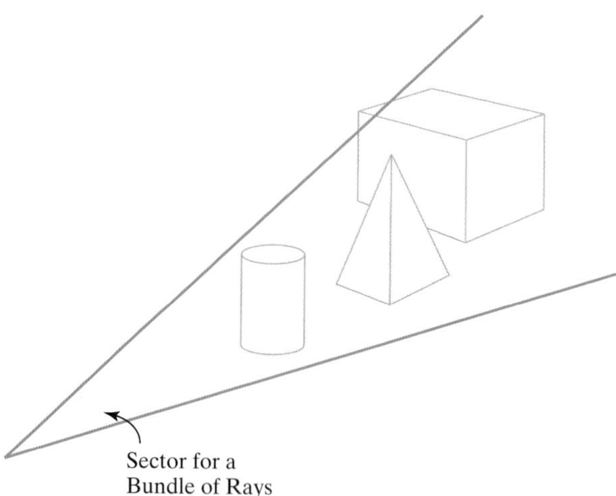

FIGURE 10-71 Directional subdivision of space. Pixel rays in the indicated sector perform intersection tests in depth order only on the surfaces within the sector.

position for a set of parallel rays passing through the lens, as illustrated in Fig. 10-72. A typical value for the focal length of a 35 mm camera is $f = 50$ mm. Camera apertures are usually described with a parameter n, called the f-number or f-stop, which is the ratio of the focal length to the aperture diameter:

$$n = \frac{f}{2r} \tag{10-83}$$

Therefore, we could use either the radius r or the f-number n, along with the focal length f, to specify the camera parameters. For a more accurate focusing model we could use the film size (width and height) and focal length to simulate the camera effects.

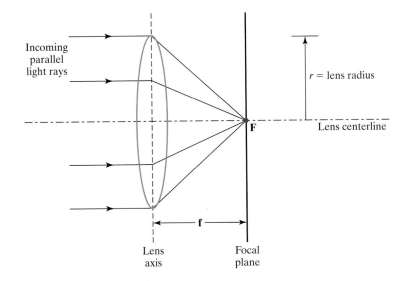

FIGURE 10-72 Side view of a thin convex lens. Parallel rays are focused by the lens at a position on the focal plane, which is at a distance f from the center of the lens.

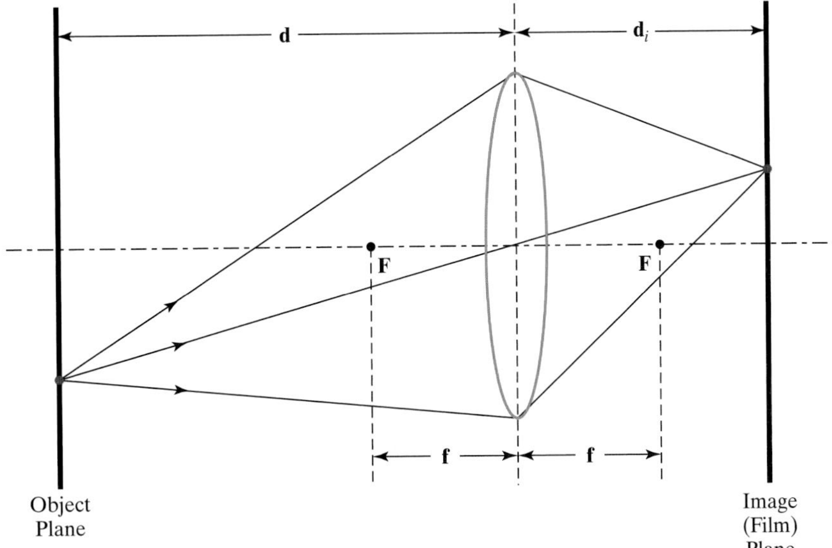

FIGURE 10-73 Thin-lens parameters. An object at a distance d from the lens is in focus on the image plane at a distance d_i from the lens.

Ray-tracing algorithms typically determine focusing effects using the **thin-lens equation** from geometric optics:

$$\frac{1}{d} + \frac{1}{d_i} = \frac{1}{f} \tag{10-84}$$

Parameter d is the distance from the lens center to an object position and d_i is the distance from the lens center to the image plane, where that object is in focus. The object point and its image are on opposite sides of the lens along a line through the lens center, and $d > f$ (Fig. 10-73). Therefore, to focus on a particular object at a distance d from the lens, we position the pixel plane at a distance d_i behind the lens.

For a scene position at some distance $d' \neq d$, the projected point will be out of focus on the image plane. If $d' > d$, the point is in focus at a position in front of the image plane; and if $d' < d$, the point is in focus at a position in back of the image

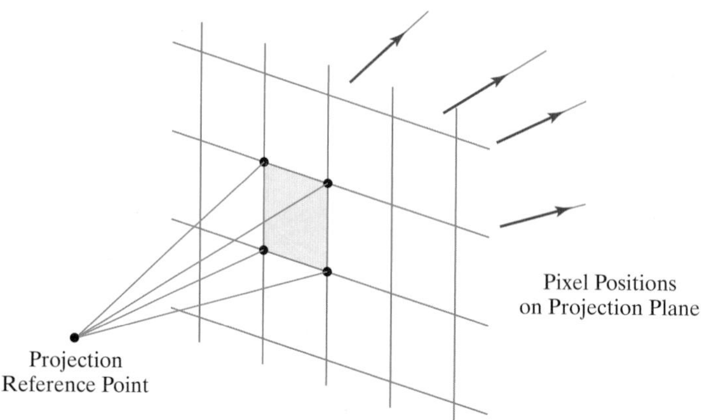

FIGURE 10-74
Supersampling with four rays per pixel, one at each pixel corner.

plane. The projection of a point at position d' on the image plane is approximately a small circle, called **the circle of confusion,** and the diameter of this circle can be computed as

$$2r_c = \frac{|d' - d|f}{nd} \qquad (10\text{-}85)$$

We can choose the camera parameters to minimize the size of the circle of confusion for a range of distances, called the **depth of field** for the camera. In addition, multiple rays are traced for each pixel to sample positions throughout the lens area, and we discuss these *distributed-ray methods* in a later section.

Antialiased Ray Tracing

Two basic antialiasing techniques employed in ray-tracing algorithms are *supersampling* and *adaptive sampling*. Sampling in ray tracing is an extension of the antialiasing methods we discussed in Section 4-17. In supersampling and adaptive sampling, the pixel is treated as a finite square area instead of a single point. Supersampling typically uses multiple, evenly spaced rays (samples) over each pixel area. Adaptive sampling uses unevenly spaced rays in some regions of the pixel area. For example, more rays can be used near object edges to obtain a better estimate of the pixel intensities. (Another method for sampling is to randomly distribute the rays over the pixel area. We discuss this approach in the next section.) When multiple rays per pixel are used, the intensities of the pixel rays are averaged to produce the overall pixel intensity.

FIGURE 10-75
Subdividing a pixel into nine subpixels with one ray at each subpixel corner.

Figure 10-74 illustrates a simple supersampling procedure. Here, one ray is generated through each corner of the pixel. If the intensities computed for the four rays are not approximately equal, or if some small object lies between the four rays, we divide the pixel area into subpixels and repeat the process. As an example, the pixel in Fig. 10-75 is divided into nine subpixels using 16 rays, one at each subpixel corner. Adaptive sampling is then used to further subdivide those subpixels that subtend a small object or do not have nearly equal-intensity rays. This subdivision process can be continued until the subpixel rays have approximately equal intensities, or until an upper bound, say 256, has been reached for the maximum number of rays per pixel.

Figure 10-76 is an example of a scene rendered with adaptive-subdivision ray tracing. An extended light source was used to provide realistic soft shadows.

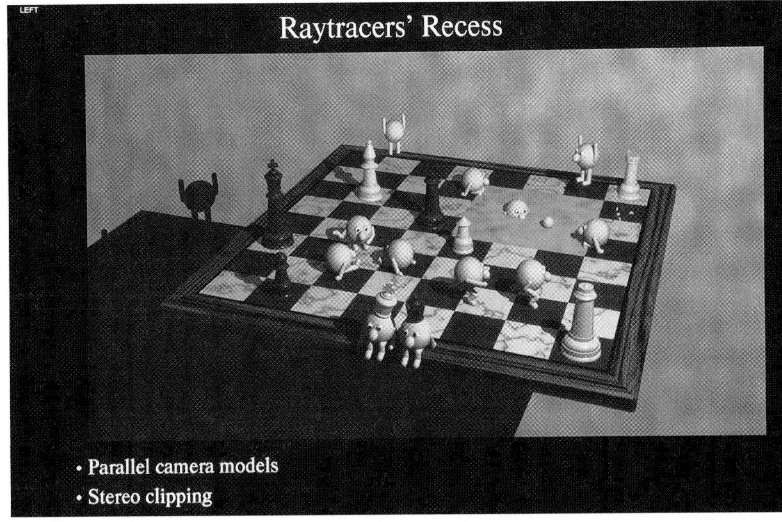

FIGURE 10-76 A scene generated with adaptive-subdivision ray tracing. *(Courtesy of Jerry Farm.)*

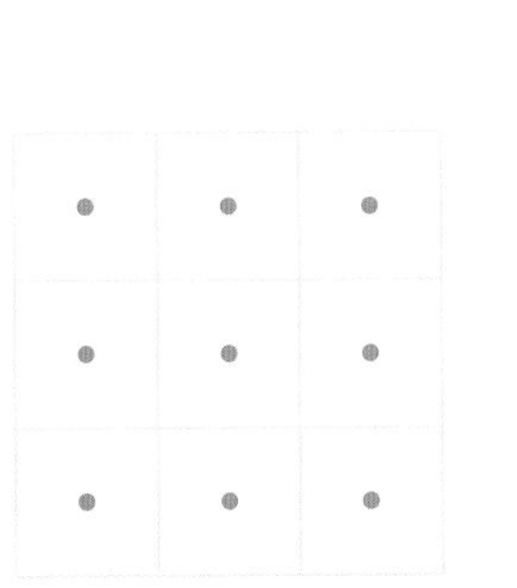

FIGURE 10-77 Ray positions centered on subpixel areas.

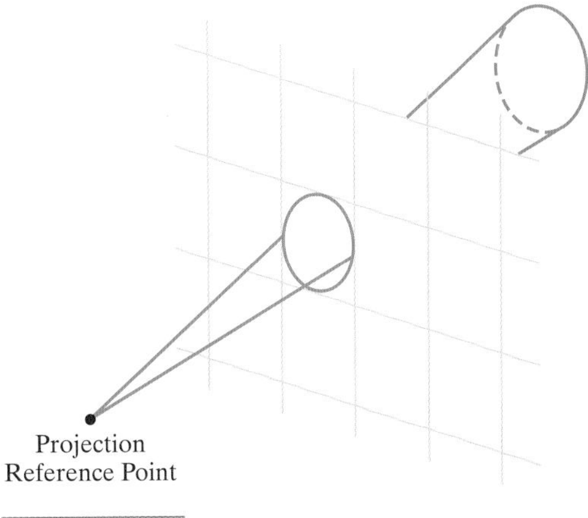

FIGURE 10-78 A pixel ray cone.

Nearly 26 million primary rays were generated, with 33.5 million shadow rays and 67.3 million reflection rays. Articulated-figure techniques (Section 13-8) were employed to develop the chess characters. Wood grain and marble surface patterns were generated using solid-texturing methods (Section 10-16) with a noise function.

Instead of passing rays through pixel corners, we can generate rays through subpixel centers, as in Fig. 10-77. With this approach, we can weight the rays according to one of the sampling schemes discussed in Section 4-17.

Another method for antialiasing displayed scenes is to treat a pixel ray as a cone, as shown in Fig. 10-78. Only one ray is generated per pixel, but the ray now has a finite cross section. To determine the percent of pixel-area coverage with objects, we calculate the intersection of the pixel cone with the object surface. For a sphere, this requires finding the intersection of two circles. For a polyhedron, we must find the intersection of a circle with a polygon.

Distributed Ray Tracing

This is a stochastic sampling method that randomly distributes rays according to the various parameters in an illumination model. Illumination parameters include pixel area, reflection and refraction directions, camera lens area, and time. Aliasing effects are thus replaced with low-level noise, which improves picture quality and allows more accurate modeling of surface gloss and translucency, finite camera apertures, finite light sources, and motion-blur displays of moving objects. **Distributed ray tracing** (also referred to as **distribution ray tracing**) essentially provides a Monte Carlo evaluation of the multiple integrals that occur in an accurate physical description of surface lighting.

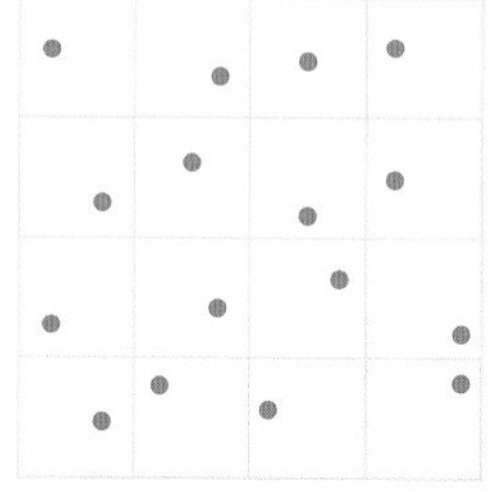

FIGURE 10-79 Pixel sampling using 16 subpixel areas and a jittered ray position from the center coordinates for each subarea.

Pixel sampling is accomplished by randomly distributing a number of rays over the pixel area. Choosing ray positions completely at random, however, can result in a clustering of rays in a small region of the pixel area, and leaving large parts of the pixel unsampled. A better approximation of the light distribution over a pixel area is obtained by using a technique called *jittering* on a regular subpixel grid. This is usually done by initially dividing the pixel area (a unit square) into the 16 subareas shown in Fig. 10-79 and generating a random *jitter position* in each subarea. The random ray positions are obtained by jittering the center coordinates of each subarea by small amounts, δ_x and δ_y, where $-0.5 < \delta_x, \delta_y < 0.5$. We then choose the jitter position as $(x + \delta_x, y + \delta_y)$, where (x, y) is the center position of the pixel.

Integer codes 1 through 16 are randomly assigned to each of the 16 rays, and a table lookup is used to obtain values for the other parameters, such as reflection angle and time. Each subpixel ray is processed through the scene to determine the intensity contribution for that ray. The 16 ray intensities are then averaged to produce the overall pixel intensity. If the subpixel intensities vary too much, we can further subdivide the pixel.

To model camera-lens effects, we process pixel rays through a lens that is positioned in front of the pixel plane. As we noted earlier, a camera is simulated using a focal length and other parameters so that selected objects will be in focus. Then we distribute subpixel rays over the aperture area. Assuming we have 16 rays per pixel, we can subdivide the aperture area into 16 zones. Each subpixel is then assigned a center position in one of the zones, and the following procedure can be used to determine the distribution sampling for the pixel. A jittered position is calculated from each zone center, and a ray is projected into the scene from this jittered zone position through the focal point of the lens. We locate the focal point for a ray at a distance f from the lens along the line from the center of the subpixel through the lens center, as shown in Fig. 10-80. With the pixel plane at a distance d_i from the lens (Fig. 10-73), positions along the ray near the object plane (the focusing plane), at a distance d in front of the lens, are in focus. Other positions along the ray are blurred. To improve the display for out-of-focus objects, we increase the number of subpixel rays.

Reflection and transmission paths are also distributed throughout a spatial region. To simulate surface gloss, rays reflected from a surface position are distributed about the specular-reflection direction **R** according to the assigned ray codes (Fig. 10-81). The maximum spread about **R** is divided into 16 angular zones, and each ray is reflected in a jittered position from the zone center corresponding to its integer code. We can use the Phong model, $\cos^{n_s}\phi$, to determine the maximum distribution for the reflection angles. If the material is transparent, refracted rays can be distributed about the transmission direction **T** in a similar manner to model translucency (Section 10-4).

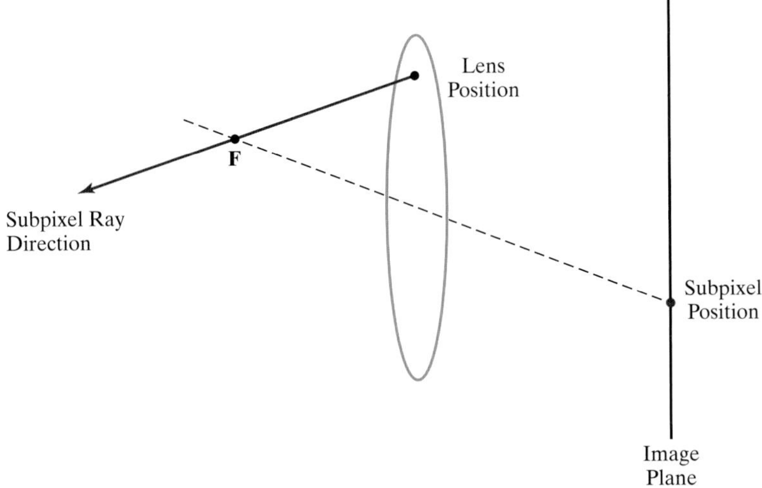

FIGURE 10-80 Distributing subpixel rays over a camera lens of focal length f.

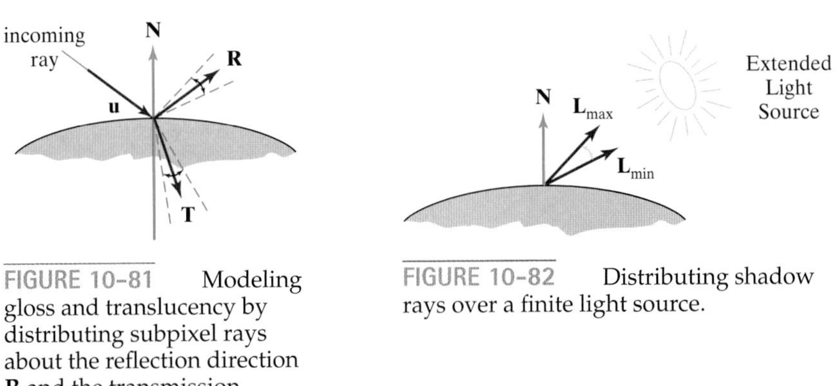

FIGURE 10-81 Modeling gloss and translucency by distributing subpixel rays about the reflection direction **R** and the transmission direction **T**.

FIGURE 10-82 Distributing shadow rays over a finite light source.

Extended light sources are handled by distributing a number of shadow rays over the area of the light source, as demonstrated in Fig. 10-82. The light source is divided into zones, and shadow rays are assigned jitter directions to the various zones. Additionally, zones can be weighted according to the intensity of the light source within that zone and the size of the projected area of the zone onto the object surface. More shadow rays are then sent to zones with higher weights. If some shadow rays intersect opaque objects between the surface and the light source, a penumbra (partly illuminated region) is generated at that surface point. But if all shadow rays are blocked, the surface point is within an umbra region (completely dark) for that light source. Figure 10-83 illustrates the regions for the umbra and penumbra on a surface partially shielded from a light source.

We create motion blur by distributing rays over time. A total frame time and the frame-time subdivisions are determined according to the motion dynamics required for the scene. Time intervals are labeled with integer codes, and each ray is assigned to a jittered time within the interval corresponding to the ray code. Objects are then moved to their positions at that time, and the ray is traced through the scene. Additional rays are used for highly blurred objects. To reduce

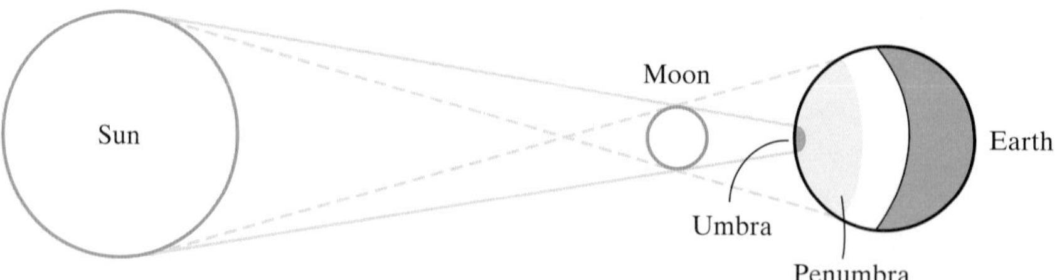

FIGURE 10-83 Umbra and penumbra regions created by a solar eclipse on the surface of the earth.

FIGURE 10-84 A scene, entitled *1984*, rendered using distributed ray tracing. Lighting effects include motion blur, penumbra, and surface reflections from multiple extended light sources. (*Courtesy of Pixar.*)

FIGURE 10-85 A brushed aluminum wheel, showing reflectance and shadow effects generated with distributed ray-tracing techniques. (*Courtesy of Stephen H. Westin, Program of Computer Graphics, Cornell University.*)

calculations, we can use bounding boxes or spheres for initial ray-intersection tests. That is, we move the bounding object according to the motion requirements and test for intersection. If the ray does not intersect the bounding object, we need not process the individual surfaces within the bounding volume. Figure 10-84 shows a scene displayed with motion blur. This image was rendered using distributed ray tracing with 4096 by 3550 pixels and 16 rays per pixel. In addition to the motion-blurred reflections, the shadows are displayed with penumbra areas resulting from the extended light sources illuminating the pool table.

Additional examples of objects rendered with distributed ray-tracing methods are given in Figs. 10-85 and 10-86. Figure 10-87 illustrates focusing, refraction, and antialiasing effects with distributed ray tracing.

FIGURE 10-86 A room scene rendered with distributed ray-tracing methods. (*Courtesy of John Snyder, Jed Lengyel, Devendra Kalra, and Al Barr, Computer Graphics Lab, California Institute of Technology. © 1988 Caltech.*)

FIGURE 10-87 A scene showing the focusing, antialiasing, and illumination effects possible with a combination of ray-tracing and radiosity methods. Realistic physical models of light illumination were used to generate the refraction effects, including the caustic in the shadow of the glass. (*Courtesy of Peter Shirley, Computer Science Department, University of Utah.*)

10-12 RADIOSITY LIGHTING MODEL

Although the basic illumination model produces reasonable results for many applications, there are a variety of lighting effects that are not accurately described by the simple approximations in this model. We can more precisely model lighting effects by considering the physical laws governing the radiant-energy transfers within an illuminated scene. This method for computing pixel color values is generally referred to as the **radiosity model.**

Radiant-Energy Terms

In the quantum model of light, the energy of the radiation is carried by the individual photons. For monochromatic light radiation, the energy of each photon is calculated as

$$E_{\text{photon},f} = hf \tag{10-86}$$

where the frequency f, measured in hertz (cycles per second), characterizes the color of the light. A blue light has a high frequency within the visible band of the electromagnetic spectrum, and a red light has a low frequency. The frequency also gives the oscillation rate for the amplitude of the electric and magnetic components of the radiation. Parameter h is *Planck's constant*, which has the value 6.6262×10^{-34} joules • sec, independently of the light frequency.

Total energy for monochromatic light radiation is

$$E_f = \sum_{\text{all photons}} hf \tag{10-87}$$

The radiant energy at a particular light frequency, is also referred to as a **spectral radiance.** However, any actual light radiations, even those from a "monochromatic" source, contain a range of frequencies. Therefore, the total radiant energy is the sum over all photons of all frequencies:

$$E = \sum_{f} \sum_{\text{all photons}} hf \tag{10-88}$$

The amount of radiant energy transmitted per unit of time is called the **radiant flux** Φ:

$$\Phi = \frac{dE}{dt} \tag{10-89}$$

Radiant flux is also referred to as **radiant power,** and it is measured in watts (joules per sec).

To obtain the lighting effects for surfaces in a scene, we calculate the radiant flux per unit area that is leaving a surface. This quantity is called the **radiosity** B, or **radiant exitance,**

$$B = \frac{d\Phi}{dA} \tag{10-90}$$

which is measured in units of watts per meter^2. And the **intensity** I is often taken to be a measure of the radiant flux in a particular direction per unit solid angle per unit projected area, with units of watts/(meter^2 • steradians). Sometimes, however, intensity is defined simply as the radiant flux in a particular direction.

Depending on the interpretation of the term intensity, the **radiance** can be defined as the intensity per unit projected area. Alternatively, we can obtain radiance from the radiant flux or the radiosity per unit solid angle.

The Basic Radiosity Model

To accurately describe diffuse reflections from a surface, the radiosity model computes radiant-energy interactions between all the surfaces in a scene. Since the

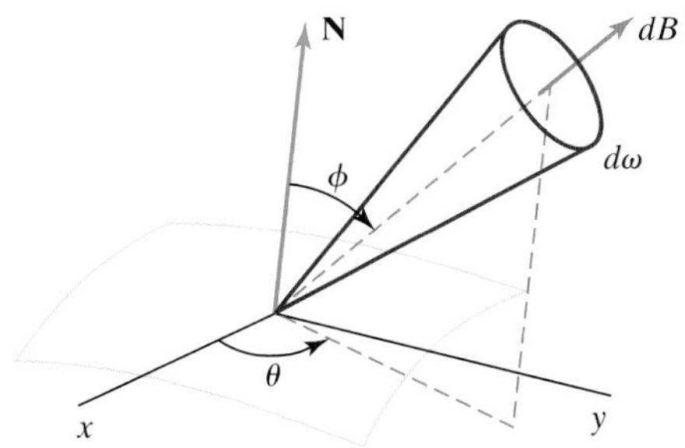

FIGURE 10-88 Visible radiant energy emitted from a surface point in direction (θ, ϕ) within solid angle $d\omega$.

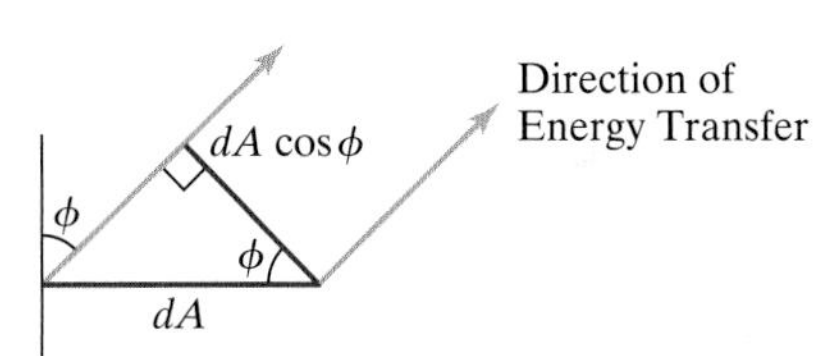

FIGURE 10-89 For a unit surface element, the projected area perpendicular to the direction of energy transfer is equal to $\cos\phi$.

resulting set of equations can be extremely difficult to solve, the basic radiosity model assumes that all surfaces are small, opaque, ideal diffuse reflectors (Lambertian).

We apply the radiosity model by determining the differential amount of radiant flux dB leaving each surface point in the scene, and then we sum the energy contributions over all surfaces to obtain the amount of energy transfer between the surfaces. In Fig. 10-88, which illustrates the radiant energy transfer from a surface, dB is the visible radiant flux emanating from the surface point in the direction given by angles θ and ϕ within a differential solid angle $d\omega$ per unit time, per unit surface area.

The intensity I for the diffuse radiation in direction (θ, ϕ) can be described as the radiant energy per unit time per unit projected area per unit solid angle, or

$$I = \frac{dB}{d\omega \cos\phi} \tag{10-91}$$

Assuming the surface is an ideal diffuse reflector (Section 10-3), we can set the intensity I to a constant for all viewing directions. Thus, $dB/d\omega$ is proportional to the projected surface area (Fig. 10-89). To obtain the total rate of energy radiation from the surface point, we need to sum the radiation for all directions. That is, we want the total energy emanating from a hemisphere centered on that surface point, as in Fig. 10-90, which is

$$B = \int_{\text{hemi}} dB \tag{10-92}$$

For a perfect diffuse reflector, I is a constant, so we can express radiant flux B as

$$B = I \int_{\text{hemi}} \cos\phi \, d\omega \tag{10-93}$$

Also, the differential element of solid angle $d\omega$ can be expressed as (Appendix A)

$$d\omega = \frac{dS}{r^2} = \sin\phi \, d\phi \, d\theta$$

so that

$$\begin{aligned} B &= I \int_0^{2\pi} \int_0^{\pi/2} \cos\phi \sin\phi \, d\phi \, d\theta \\ &= I\pi \end{aligned} \tag{10-94}$$

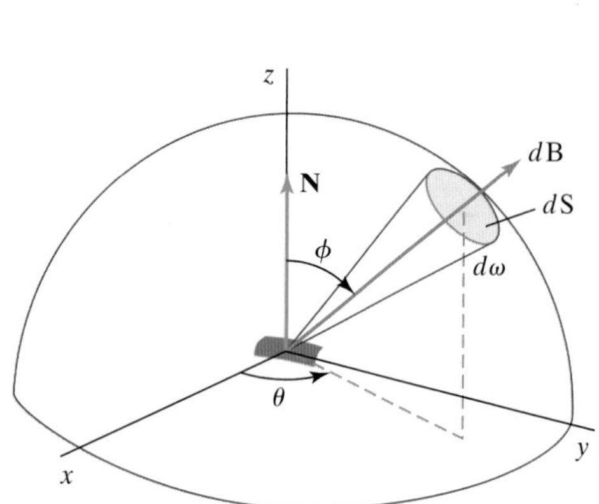

FIGURE 10-90 Total radiant energy from a surface point is the sum of the contributions in all directions over a hemisphere centered on that surface point.

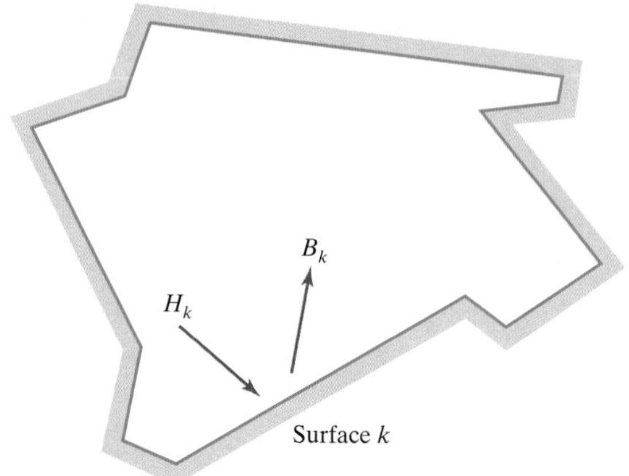

FIGURE 10-91 An enclosure of surfaces for the radiosity model.

A model for the light reflections from the various surfaces is formed by setting up an "enclosure" of surfaces (Fig. 10-91). Each surface in the enclosure is either a reflector, an emitter (light source), or a combination reflector-emitter. We designate radiosity parameter B_k as the total rate of radiant energy leaving surface k per unit area. Incident energy parameter H_k is the sum of the radiant energy contributions from all surfaces in the enclosure arriving at surface k per unit time, per unit area. That is,

$$H_k = \sum_j B_j F_{jk} \tag{10-95}$$

where parameter F_{jk} is called the *form factor* for surfaces j and k. Form factor F_{jk} is the fractional amount of radiant energy from surface j that reaches surface k.

For a scene with n surfaces in the enclosure, the radiant energy from surface k is described with the **radiosity equation:**

$$\begin{aligned} B_k &= E_k + \rho_k H_k \\ &= E_k + \rho_k \sum_{j=1}^{n} B_j F_{jk} \end{aligned} \tag{10-96}$$

If surface k is not a light source, then $E_k = 0$. Otherwise, E_k is the rate of energy emitted from surface k per unit area (watts/m^2). Parameter ρ_k is the reflectivity factor for surface k (percent of incident light that is reflected in all directions). This reflectivity factor is related to the diffuse reflection coefficient used in empirical illumination models. Plane and convex surfaces cannot "see" themselves, so that no self-incidence takes place and the form factor F_{kk} for these surfaces is 0.

To obtain the illumination effects over the various surfaces in the enclosure, we need to solve the simultaneous radiosity equations for the n surfaces, given the array values for E_k, ρ_k, and F_{jk}. That is, we must solve

$$(1 - \rho_k F_{kk}) B_k - \rho_k \sum_{j \neq k} B_j F_{jk} = E_k \qquad k = 1, 2, 3, \ldots, n \tag{10-97}$$

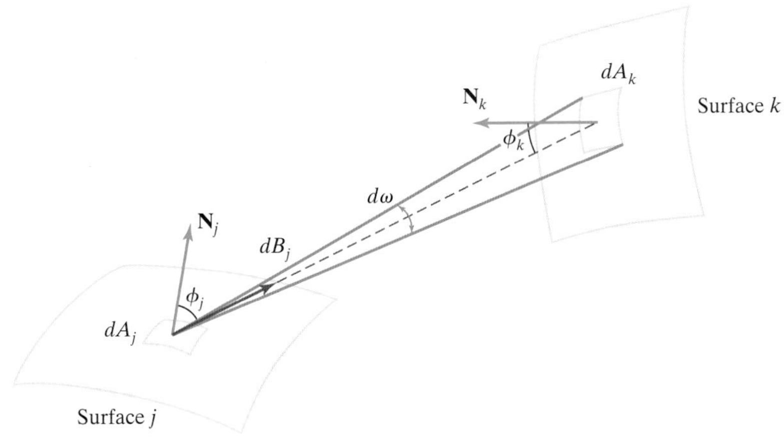

FIGURE 10-92 The transfer of a differential amount of radiant energy dB_j from a surface element with area dA_j to surface element dA_k.

or

$$\begin{bmatrix} 1-\rho_1 F_{11} & -\rho_1 F_{12} & \cdots & -\rho_1 F_{1n} \\ -\rho_2 F_{21} & 1-\rho_2 F_{22} & \cdots & -\rho_2 F_{2n} \\ \vdots & \vdots & & \vdots \\ -\rho_n F_{n1} & -\rho_2 F_{n2} & \cdots & 1-\rho_n F_{nn} \end{bmatrix} \cdot \begin{bmatrix} B_1 \\ B_2 \\ \vdots \\ B_n \end{bmatrix} = \begin{bmatrix} E_1 \\ E_2 \\ \vdots \\ E_n \end{bmatrix} \tag{10-98}$$

We then convert to intensity values I_k by dividing the radiosity values B_k by π. For color applications, we can calculate the individual RGB components of the radiosity (B_{kR}, B_{kG}, B_{kB}) using the color components for ρ_k and E_k.

Before we can solve Eq. 10-97, we must determine the values for the form factors F_{jk}. We do this by considering the energy transfer from surface j to surface k (Fig. 10-92). The rate of radiant energy falling on a small surface element dA_k from area element dA_j is

$$dB_j\, dA_j = (I_j \cos\phi_j\, d\omega)\, dA_j \tag{10-99}$$

But solid angle $d\omega$ can be written in terms of the projection of area element dA_k perpendicular to the direction dB_j as

$$d\omega = \frac{dA}{r^2} = \frac{\cos\phi_k\, dA_k}{r^2} \tag{10-100}$$

Therefore, we can express Eq. 10-99 in the form

$$dB_j\, dA_j = \frac{I_j \cos\phi_j \cos\phi_k\, dA_j\, dA_k}{r^2} \tag{10-101}$$

The form factor between the two surfaces is the percent of energy emanating from area dA_j that is incident on dA_k:

$$\begin{aligned} F_{dA_j,dA_k} &= \frac{\text{energy incident on } dA_k}{\text{total energy leaving } dA_j} \\ &= \frac{I_j \cos\phi_j \cos\phi_k\, dA_j\, dA_k}{r^2} \cdot \frac{1}{B_j\, dA_j} \end{aligned} \tag{10-102}$$

Also $B_j = \pi I_j$, so that

$$F_{dA_j,dA_k} = \frac{\cos\phi_j \cos\phi_k \, dA_k}{\pi r^2} \tag{10-103}$$

and the fraction of emitted energy from area dA_j incident on the entire surface k is

$$F_{dA_j,A_k} = \int_{\text{surf}_j} \frac{\cos\phi_j \cos\phi_k}{\pi r^2} \, dA_k \tag{10-104}$$

where A_k is the area of surface k. We can then define the form factor between the two surfaces as the area average of the above expression, which is

$$F_{jk} = \frac{1}{A_j} \int_{\text{surf}_j} \int_{\text{surf}_k} \frac{\cos\phi_j \cos\phi_k}{\pi r^2} \, dA_k \, dA_j \tag{10-105}$$

The two integrals in Eq. 10-105 are evaluated using numerical integration techniques and stipulating the following conditions

- $\sum_{k=1}^{n} F_{jk} = 1, \quad$ for all k (conservation of energy)
- $A_j F_{jk} = A_k F_{kj}$ (uniform light reflection)
- $F_{jj} = 0, \quad$ for all j (assuming only plane or convex surface patches)

To apply the radiosity model we subdivide each surface in a scene into many small polygons. The realistic appearance of the displayed scene is improved as we decrease the size of the polygon subdivisions, but more time is then needed to render the scene. We can speed up the calculation of the form factors by using a hemicube to approximate the hemisphere. This replaces the spherical surface with a set of linear (plane) surfaces. Once the form factors are evaluated, we can solve the simultaneous linear equations 10-97 using a numerical technique such as Gaussian elimination or LU decomposition (Appendix A). Alternatively, we could start with approximate values for the B_j and solve the set of linear equations iteratively using the Gauss-Seidel method. At each iteration, we calculate an estimate of the radiosity for surface patch k using the previously obtained radiosity values in the radiosity equation:

$$B_k = E_k + \rho_k \sum_{j=1}^{n} B_j F_{jk}$$

We could then display the scene at each step to observe the improvement in surface rendering. This process is repeated until there is little change in the calculated radiosity values.

Progressive Refinement Radiosity Method

Although the radiosity method produces highly realistic surface renderings, considerable processing time is needed to calculate the form factors and there are tremendous storage requirements. Using *progressive refinement*, we can restructure the iterative radiosity algorithm to speed up the calculations and reduce storage requirements at each iteration.

From the radiosity equation, the radiant energy transfer between two surface patches is calculated as

$$B_k \text{ due to } B_j = \rho_k B_j F_{jk} \tag{10-106}$$

Reciprocally,

$$B_j \text{ due to } B_k = \rho_j B_k F_{kj}, \qquad \text{for all } j \tag{10-107}$$

which we can rewrite as

$$B_j \text{ due to } B_k = \rho_j B_k F_{jk} \frac{A_j}{A_k}, \qquad \text{for all } j \tag{10-108}$$

This relationship is the basis for the progressive refinement approach to the radiosity calculations. Using a single surface patch k, we can calculate all form factors F_{jk} and consider the light transfer from that patch to all other surfaces in the environment. With this procedure, we need only compute and store parameter values for a single hemicube and the associated form factors. At the next iteration, we replace these parameter values with values for another selected patch. And we can display the progressive improvements in the surface rendering as we proceed from one selected patch to another.

Initially, we set $B_k = E_k$ for all surface patches. We then select the patch with the highest radiosity value, which is the brightest light emitter, and calculate the next approximation to the radiosity for all other patches. This process is repeated at each step, so that light sources are chosen first in order of highest radiant energy, then other patches are selected based on the amount of light received from the light sources. The steps in a simple progressive refinement approach are outlined in the following algorithm.

```
for each patch k
   \*  Set up hemicube and calculate form factors F [j][k].  */

for each patch j {
   dRad   = rho [j] * B [k] * F [j][k] * A [j] / A [k];
   dB [j] = dB [j] + dRad;
   B [j]  = B [j] + dRad;
}

dB [k] = 0;
```

At each step, the surface patch with the highest value for $\Delta B_k A_k$ is selected, since radiosity is a measure of radiant energy per unit area. Also, we choose the initial values as $\Delta B_k = B_k = E_k$ for all surface patches. This progressive refinement algorithm approximates the actual propagation of light through a scene as a function of time.

Displaying the rendered surfaces at each step produces a sequence of views that proceeds from a dark scene to a fully illuminated one. After the first step, the only surfaces illuminated are the light sources and those nonemitting patches that are visible to the chosen emitter. To produce more useful initial views of the scene, we could set an ambient light level so that all patches have some illumination. At each stage of the iteration, we then reduce the ambient light according to the amount of radiant energy transfer into the scene.

Figure 10-93 shows a scene rendered with the progressive-refinement radiosity model. Various lighting conditions in radiosity renderings are illustrated in Figs. 10-94, 10-95, and 10-96. Ray-tracing methods are often combined with the radiosity model to produce highly realistic diffuse and specular surface shadings, as in Fig. 10-87.

FIGURE 10-93 Nave of Chartres Cathedral rendered with a progressive-refinement radiosity model by John Wallace and John Lin, using the Hewlett-Packard Starbase Radiosity and Ray Tracing software. Radiosity form factors were computed with ray-tracing methods. (*Courtesy of Eric Haines, Autodesk, Inc. © 1989 Hewlett-Packard Co.*)

FIGURE 10-94 Image of a constructivist museum rendered with a progressive-refinement radiosity method. (*Courtesy of Shenchang Eric Chen, Stuart I. Feldman, and Julie Dorsey, Program of Computer Graphics, Cornell University. © 1988 Cornell University Program of Computer Graphics.*)

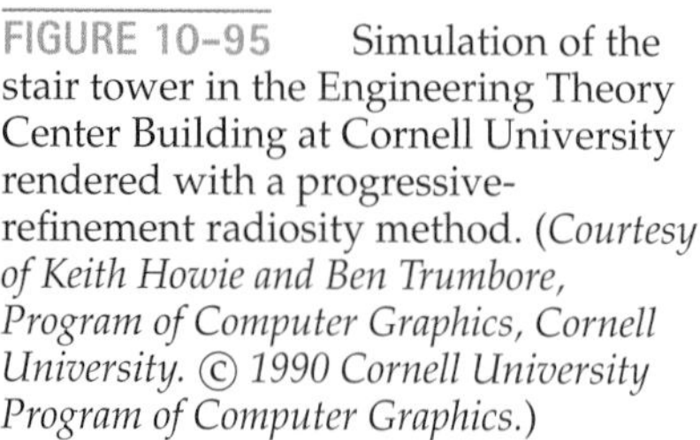

FIGURE 10-95 Simulation of the stair tower in the Engineering Theory Center Building at Cornell University rendered with a progressive-refinement radiosity method. (*Courtesy of Keith Howie and Ben Trumbore, Program of Computer Graphics, Cornell University. © 1990 Cornell University Program of Computer Graphics.*)

(a)

(b)

FIGURE 10-96 Simulation of two lighting schemes for the Parisian garret from the Metropolitan Opera's production of *La Boheme*. A fully illuminated day view of the garret is given in (a), and a night display of the garret is shown in (b). *(Courtesy of Julie Dorsey and Mark Shepard, Program of Computer Graphics, Cornell University. © 1991 Cornell University Program of Computer Graphics.)*

10-13 ENVIRONMENT MAPPING

An alternate procedure for modeling global reflections is to define an array of intensity values that describes the environment around a single object or a group of objects. Instead of using interobject ray tracing or the radiosity calculations to pick up the global specular and diffuse illumination effects, we simply map the *environment array* onto an object in relationship to the viewing direction. This procedure is called **environment mapping,** and it is sometimes referred to as **reflection mapping** (although transparency effects could also be modeled with the environment map). Another name for environment mapping is "the poor person's ray-tracing method", since it is a cheap and fast approximation of the more accurate global-illumination rendering techniques we discussed in Sections 10-11 and 10-12.

The environment map is defined over the surfaces of an enclosing universe. Information in the environment map includes intensity values for light sources, the sky, and other background objects. Figure 10-97 shows the enclosing universe

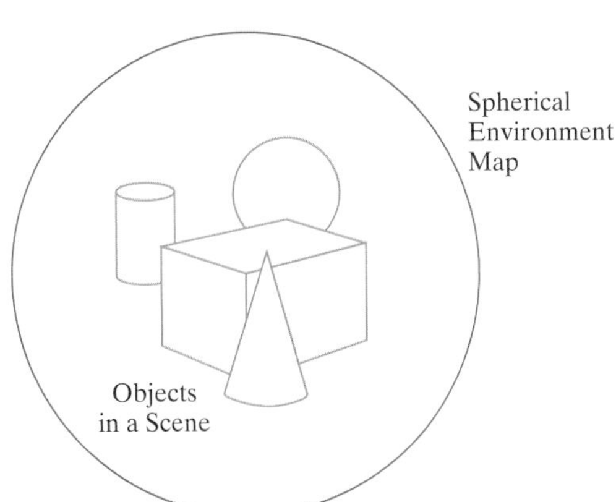

FIGURE 10-97 A spherical enclosing universe, with the environment map on the surface of the sphere.

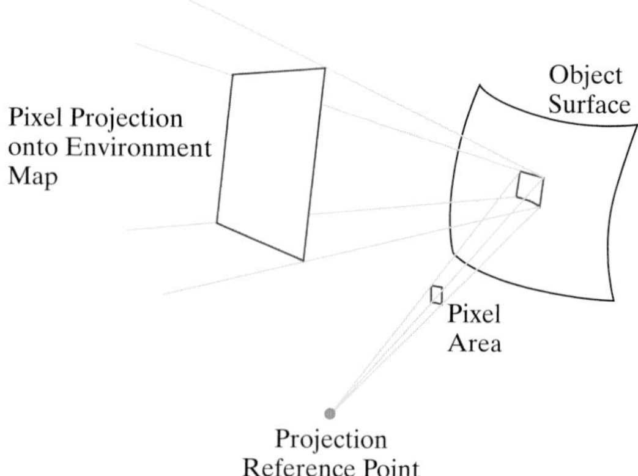

FIGURE 10-98 Projecting a pixel area to a surface, then reflecting the area to the environment map.

as a sphere, but a cube or a cylinder is often used to define the environment surfaces surrounding the objects in a scene.

To render the surface of an object, we project pixel areas onto the object surface and then reflect each projected pixel area onto the environment map to pick up the surface intensity values for the pixel. If the object is transparent, we can also refract the projected pixel area to the environment map. The environment-mapping process for reflection of a projected pixel area is illustrated in Fig. 10-98. Pixel intensity is determined by averaging the intensity values within the intersected region of the environment map.

10-14 PHOTON MAPPING

Although the radiosity method can produce accurate displays of global illumination effects for simple scenes, the method becomes more difficult to apply as the complexity of a scene increases. Both the rendering time and the storage requirements become prohibitive for very complicated scenes, and many illumination effects are difficult to model correctly. **Photon mapping** provides a general method for modeling global illumination in complex scenes that is both efficient and accurate.

The basic concept in photon mapping is to separate the illumination information from the geometry of a scene. Ray paths are traced through the scene from all light sources, and the lighting information from the ray-object intersections is stored in a **photon map.** Distributed ray-tracing methods are then applied using incremental algorithms similar to those employed in radiosity rendering.

Light sources can be designated as points, directional spotlights, or any other configuration. The assigned intensity for a light source is divided among its rays (photons), and the ray directions are distributed randomly. A point light source is modeled by generating ray paths uniformly in all directions, unless the source is directional (Section 10-1). For other light sources, random positions on the source are selected and rays are generated in random directions. More rays are generated from brighter lights than from low-power light sources. In addition, *projection maps,* which store binary information about whether or not there are objects in any region of the space, can be constructed for the light sources. Bounding spheres can also be used in the algorithm to provide object information within large spatial regions. Any number of rays can be generated for a scene, and the accuracy of the illumination effects improves as more ray paths are generated.

10-15 ADDING SURFACE DETAIL

So far we have discussed rendering techniques for displaying smooth object surfaces. However, most objects do not have smooth, even surfaces. We need surface texture to model accurately such objects as brick walls, gravel roads, shag carpets, wood, and human skin. In addition, some surfaces contain patterns that must be taken into account in the rendering procedures. The surface of a vase could contain a painted design; a water glass might have the family crest engraved into the surface; a tennis court contains markings for the alleys, service areas, and base line; and a four-lane highway has dividing lines and other markings, such as oil spills and tire skids.

Figure 10-99 illustrates the basic stages in modeling and rendering an object that is to contain surface detail. First, a wire-frame display of the object can be used to adjust the overall design. Next, surface layers are fitted over the object outline to produce a rendered, smooth-surface view of the structure. Then, surface details are added to the outer layers. For the Fig. 10-99 example, surface details include the jacket patterns, such as the seams, lettering, and cloth textures, and the skin features, such as pores, moles, freckles, and sun spots. Magnified views of the computer-generated skin features on this character are shown in Fig. 10-100, and Fig. 10-101 shows the simulated skin features for an older person. Additional examples of scenes rendered with surface detail are given in Fig. 10-102.

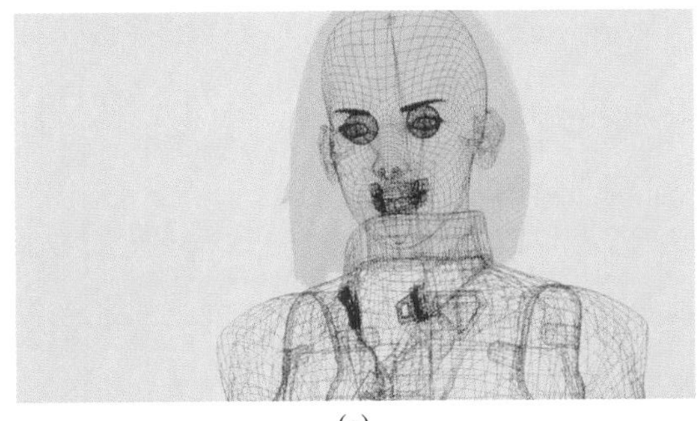

(a)

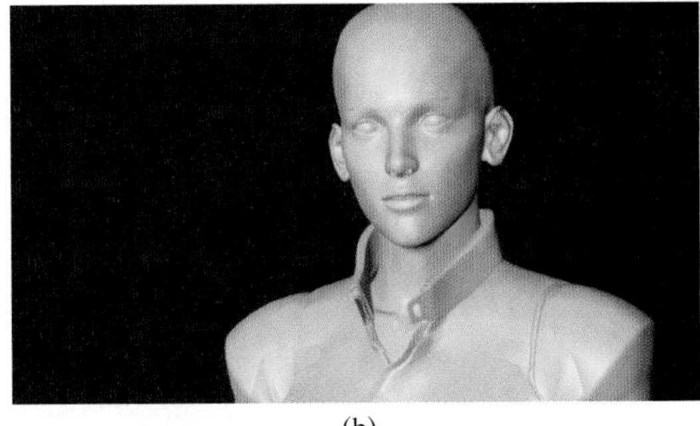

(b)

(c)

FIGURE 10-99 Modeling and rendering stages in the development of the animated character Dr. Aki Ross for the film *Final Fantasy: The Spirits Within*: (a) wire-frame model of Aki, (b) surface structure for the skin and clothing, and (c) final rendered figure, including hair and details for the skin features and clothing. (*Courtesy of Square Pictures, Inc. © 2001 FFFP. All rights reserved.*)

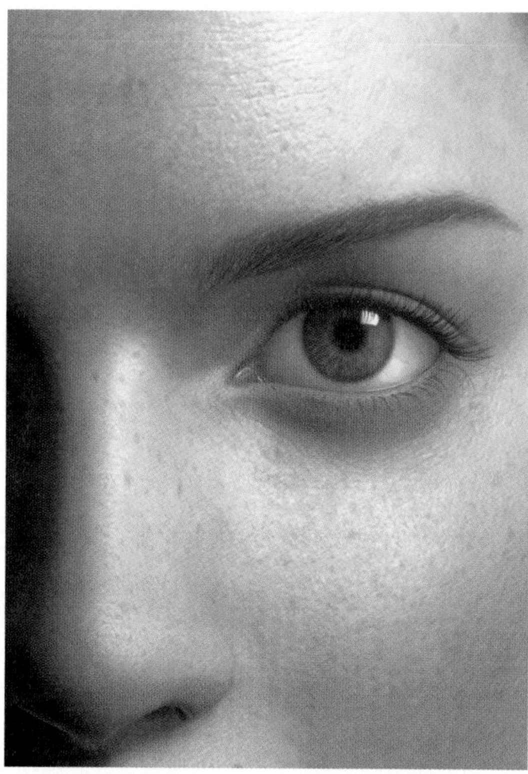

(a) (b)

FIGURE 10-100 Skin details for the animated character Dr. Aki Ross in the film *Final Fantasy: The Spirits Within.* (*Courtesy of Square Pictures, Inc.* © *2001 FFFP. All rights reserved.*)

FIGURE 10-101 Facial features and surface skin texturing for the animated character Dr. Sid, representing a man at age 70, in the film *Final Fantasy: The Spirits Within.* (*Courtesy of Square Pictures, Inc.* © *2001 FFFP. All rights reserved.*)

(a) (b) (c) (d)

FIGURE 10-102 Scenes illustrating computer-graphics generation of surface detail for various objects: (a) cactus plants with added spines and flowers (*Courtesy of Deborah R. Fowler, Przemyslaw Prusinkiewicz, and Johannes Battjes, University of Calgary. © 1992.*), (b) seashells with various patterns and fluted surfaces (*Courtesy of Deborah R. Fowler, Hans Meinhardt, and Przemyslaw Prusinkiewicz, University of Calgary. © 1992.*), (c) a table of fruit (*Courtesy of SOFTIMAGE, Inc.*), and (d) surface patterns on chess pieces and a chessboard produced with texture-mapping methods (*Courtesy of SOFTIMAGE, Inc.*).

We can add detail to surfaces using a variety of methods, including

- Pasting small objects, such as buds, flowers, or spines, onto a larger surface.
- Modeling surface patterns with small polygon areas.
- Mapping texture arrays or intensity-modifying procedures onto a surface.
- Modifying the surface normal vector to create localized bumps.
- Modifying both the surface normal vector and the surface tangent vector to display directional patterns on wood and other materials.

10-16 MODELING SURFACE DETAIL WITH POLYGONS

A simple method for adding surface detail is to model patterns or other surface characteristics using polygon facets. For large-scale detail, polygon modeling can give good results. Some examples of such large-scale detail are squares on a checkerboard, dividing lines on a highway, tile patterns on a linoleum floor, floral designs in a smooth low-pile rug, panels in a door, and lettering on the side of a panel truck. Also, we could model an irregular surface with small, randomly oriented polygon facets, provided the facets are not too small.

Surface-pattern polygons are generally overlaid on a larger surface polygon and processed along with the parent surface. The visible-surface detection algorithms process only the parent polygon, but the illumination parameters for the surface-detail polygons take precedence over the parent polygon. When intricate or fine surface detail is to be modeled, polygon methods are not practical. For example, it would be difficult to accurately model the surface structure of a raisin with polygon facets.

10-17 TEXTURE MAPPING

A common method for adding detail to an object is to map patterns onto the geometric description of the object. The texture pattern may be defined either in an array of color values or as a procedure that modifies object colors. This method for incorporating object detail into a scene is called **texture mapping** or **pattern mapping,** and the textures can be defined as one-dimensional, two-dimensional, or three-dimensional patterns. Any texture specification is referred to as a **texture space,** which is referenced with **texture coordinates** in the range from 0 to 1.0.

Texture functions in a graphics package often allow the number of color components for each position in a pattern to be specified as an option. For example, each color specification in a texture pattern could consist of four RGBA components, three RGB components, a single intensity value for a shade of blue, an index into a color table, or a single luminance value (a weighted average of the RGB components of a color). A component of a texture description is frequently alluded to as a "texel", but there is some confusion in the use of the term. Sometimes a position in texture space corresponding to a set of color components, such as an RGB triple, is called a texel, and sometimes a single texture-array element, such as the value for the red component of an RGB color, is also called a texel.

Linear Texture Patterns

A one-dimensional texture pattern can be specified in a single-subscript array of color values, which defines a sequence of colors in a linear texture space. For example, we could set up a list of 32 RGB colors, referenced with subscript values ranging from 0 to 95. The first three elements of the array store the RGB components of the first color, the next three elements store the RGB components of the second color, and so forth. This set of colors, or any contiguous subset of the colors, could then be used to form a patterned stripe across a polygon, a band around a cylinder, or a color pattern for displaying an isolated line segment.

For a linear pattern, the texture space is referenced with a single s-coordinate value. For RGB color specifications, the value $s = 0.0$ designates the first three-element RGB color in the array, the value $s = 1.0$ designates the last three RGB color components, and the value $s = 0.5$ references the middle three RGB color elements in the array. As an example, if the name of the texture array is `colorArray`, then the value $s = 0.0$ references the three array values `colorArray` [0], `colorArray` [1], and `colorArray` [2].

To map a linear texture pattern into a scene, we assign an s-coordinate value to one spatial position and another s-coordinate value to a second spatial position.

The section of the color array corresponding to the specified s-coordinate range is then used to generate a multicolored line between the two spatial positions. A texture-mapping procedure typically uses a linear function to calculate the array positions that are to be assigned to the pixels along a line segment. When the number of texture colors specified for the line is small, each color may be assigned to a large block of pixels, depending on the length of the line. For example, if the specified s-coordinate range spans a single RGB color (three RGB color elements) in the texture array, all pixels on the line are displayed in that color. But if many colors are to be mapped to the positions along the line, then fewer pixels are assigned to each color. Also, since some pixels may map to array positions between RGB colors, various schemes can be used to determine the color that is to be assigned to each pixel. A simple color-mapping method is to assign the nearest array color to each pixel. Alternatively, if a pixel is mapped to a position between the starting array elements for two colors, the pixel color could be computed as a linear combination of the nearest two color elements in the array.

Some texture-mapping procedures allow values for texture coordinates that are outside the range from 0 to 1.0. These situations might arise when we want to map multiple copies of a texture onto an object or when calculated s values could be outside the unit interval. If we want to allow texture-coordinate values outside the range from 0 to 1.0, we could just ignore the integer part of any s value. In this case, the value of -3.6, for instance, would reference the same position in texture space as the value 0.6 or the value 12.6. But if we do not want to allow values outside the range from 0 to 1.0, then we could just clamp values to this unit interval. Any computed value less than 0 is then reset to 0, and any computed value greater than 1.0 is reset to 1.0.

Surface Texture Patterns

A texture for a surface area is commonly defined with a rectangular color pattern, and positions in this texture space are referenced with two-dimensional (s, t) coordinate values. Specifications for each color in the texture pattern can be stored in a three-subscript array. If a texture pattern is defined with 16 by 16 RGB colors, for instance, then the array for this pattern contains $16 \times 16 \times 3 = 768$ elements.

Figure 10-103 illustrates a two-dimensional texture space. Values for both s and t vary from 0 to 1.0. The first row of the array lists the color values across the bottom of the rectangular texture pattern, and the last row of the array lists the color values across the top of the pattern. Coordinate position (0, 0) in texture space references the first set of color components in the first position of the first row, and position (1.0, 1.0) references the last set of color components at the last position in the last row of the array. Of course, we could list the colors in the texture array in other ways. If we listed the colors in a top-to-bottom order, the origin of the two-dimensional texture space would be at the top-left corner of the rectangular pattern. But placing the texture-space origin at the lower-left corner usually simplifies the mapping procedures to the spatial-coordinate reference for a scene.

We specify a surface-texture mapping for an object using the same procedures we used for specifying a linear-texture mapping to a scene. The (s, t) texture-space coordinates for the four corners of the texture pattern (Fig. 10-103) can be assigned to four spatial positions in the scene, and a linear transformation is used to assign color values to the projected pixel positions over the designated spatial area. Other mappings are possible. For instance, we could assign three texture-space coordinates to the vertices of a triangle.

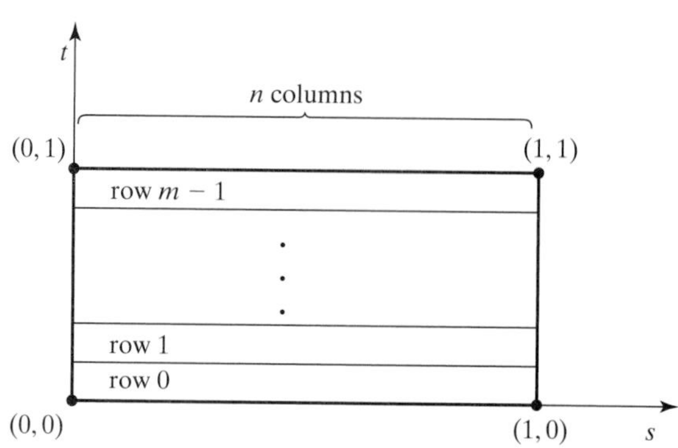

FIGURE 10-103
Two-dimensional texture-space coordinates that reference positions in an array of color values containing m rows and n columns. Each position in the array can reference multiple color components.

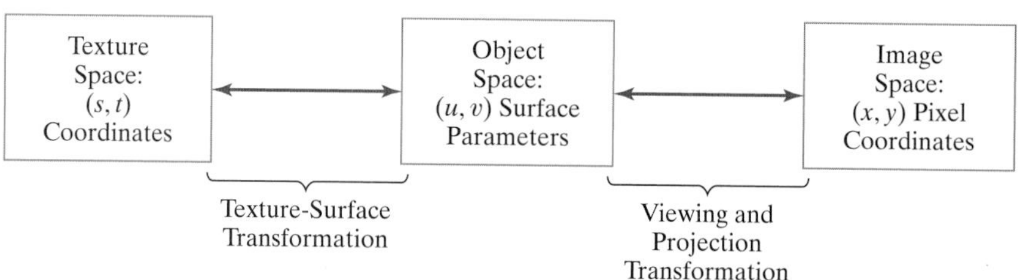

FIGURE 10-104
Coordinate reference systems for two-dimensional texture space, object space, and image space.

Surface positions on an object, such as a cubic-spline patch or a sphere section, can be described with uv object-space coordinates, and projected pixel positions are referenced in xy Cartesian coordinates. Surface texture mapping can be accomplished in one of two ways. Either we can map the texture pattern to an object surface, then to the projection plane; or we can map each pixel area onto the object surface, and then map this surface area to texture space. Mapping a texture pattern to pixel coordinates is sometimes called *texture scanning*, while the mapping from pixel coordinates to texture space is referred to as *pixel-order scanning*, *inverse scanning*, or *image-order scanning*. Figure 10-104 diagrams the two possible transformation sequences between the three spaces.

Parametric linear transformations provide a simple method for mapping positions in texture space to object space:

$$\begin{aligned} u &= u(s,t) = a_u\,s + b_u\,t + c_u \\ v &= v(s,t) = a_v\,s + b_v\,t + c_v \end{aligned} \tag{10-109}$$

The object-to-image-space transformation is accomplished with the concatenation of the viewing and projection transformations. A disadvantage of mapping from texture space to pixel space is that a selected texture patch usually does not match up with the pixel boundaries, which requires calculations to determine the fractional area of pixel coverage. Therefore, mapping from pixel space to texture space (Fig. 10-105) is the most commonly used texture-mapping method. This avoids pixel subdivision calculations, and allows antialiasing (filtering) procedures to be easily applied. An effective antialiasing procedure is to project a slightly larger pixel area that includes the centers of neighboring pixels, as shown in Fig. 10-106, and applying a pyramid function to weight the intensity values in the texture pattern. But the mapping from image space to texture space does require calculation of the inverse viewing-projection transformation $\mathbf{M}_{VP}^{-1}$ and the

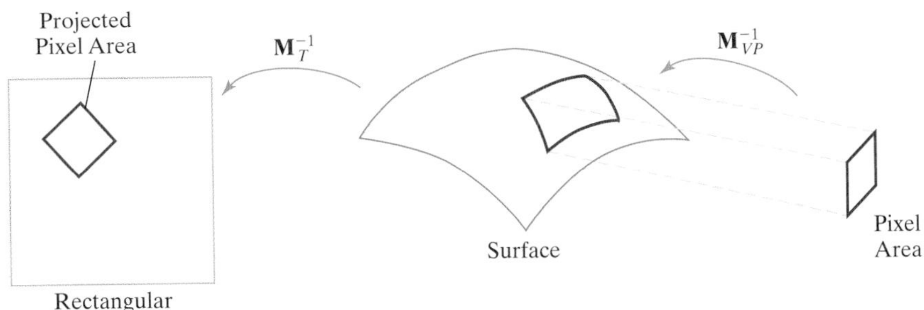

FIGURE 10-105 Texture mapping by projecting pixel areas to texture space.

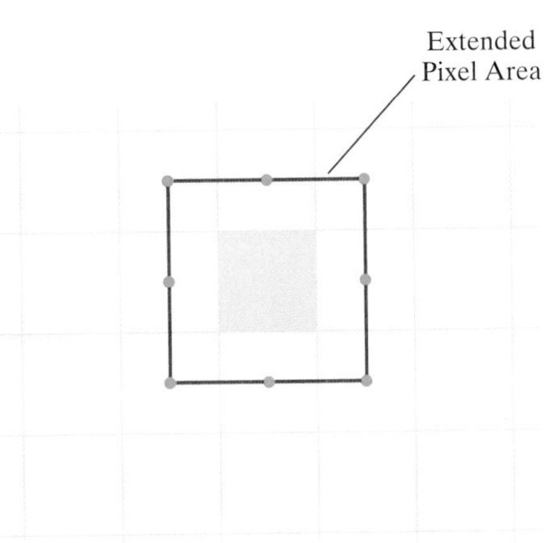

FIGURE 10-106 Extended area for a pixel that includes the center positions of adjacent pixels.

inverse texture-map transformation $\mathbf{M}_T^{-1}$. In the following example, we illustrate this approach by mapping a defined pattern onto a cylindrical surface.

EXAMPLE 10-1 Surface Texture Mapping

To illustrate the steps in surface-texture mapping, we consider the transfer of the pattern shown in Fig. 10-107(a) to a cylindrical surface. The surface parameters are the cylindrical coordinates

$$u = \theta, \qquad v = z$$

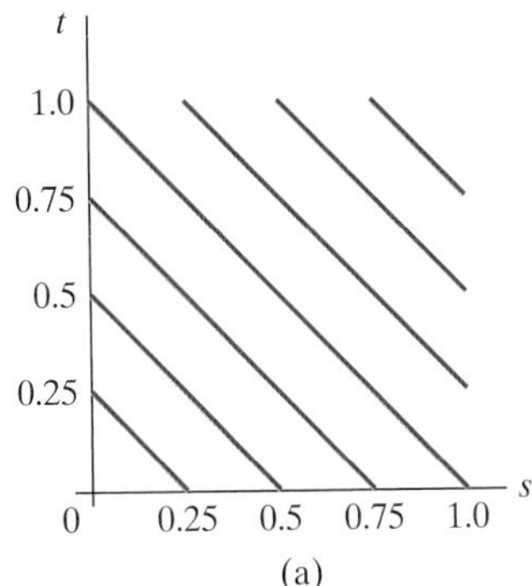

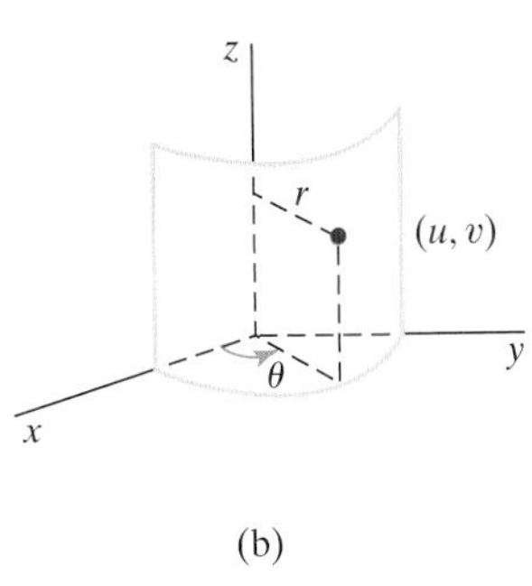

FIGURE 10-107 Mapping a texture pattern defined within a unit square (a) onto a cylindrical surface (b).

with

$$0 \leq \theta \leq \pi/2, \qquad 0 \leq z \leq 1$$

And the parametric representation for the surface in the Cartesian reference frame is

$$x = r\cos u, \qquad y = r\sin u, \qquad z = v$$

We can map the array pattern to the surface using the following linear transformation, which transforms the texture-space coordinates $(s, t) = (0, 0)$ to the lower-left corner of the surface element $(x, y, z) = (r, 0, 0)$.

$$u = s\pi/2, \qquad v = t$$

Next, we select a viewing position and perform the inverse viewing transformation from pixel coordinates to the Cartesian reference for the cylindrical surface. Then, Cartesian surface coordinates are transferred to uv surface parameters with the calculations

$$u = \tan^{-1}(y/x), \qquad v = z$$

and projected pixel positions are mapped to texture space with the inverse transformation

$$s = 2u/\pi, \qquad t = v$$

Color values in the pattern array covered by each projected pixel area are then averaged to obtain the pixel color. ■

Volume Texture Patterns

In addition to linear and surface patterns, we can designate a set of colors for positions throughout a three-dimensional region of space. These textures are often referred to as **volume texture patterns** or **solid textures.** We reference a solid texture using three-dimensional texture-space coordinates (s, t, r). And the three-dimensional texture space is defined within the unit cube, with texture coordinates ranging from 0 to 1.0.

A volume texture pattern can be stored in a four-subscript array, where the first three subscripts denote a row position, a column position, and a depth position. The fourth subscript is used to reference a component of a particular color in the pattern. For example, an RGB solid texture pattern with 16 rows, 16 columns, and 16 depth planes could be stored in an array with $16 \times 16 \times 16 \times 3 = 12{,}288$ elements.

To map the entire texture space to a three-dimensional block, we assign the coordinates for the eight corners of the texture space to eight spatial positions in a scene. Or we could map a plane section of texture space, such as a depth plane or one face of the texture cube, to a planar area in the scene. A variety of other solid-texture mapping applications are also possible.

Solid texturing allows internal views, such as cut-away displays and cross-sectional slices, for three-dimensional objects to be displayed with texture patterns. Thus bricks, cinder blocks, or wood materials can have the same texture patterns applied throughout the spatial extent of the objects. Figure 10-108 shows a scene displayed using solid textures to obtain wood grain and other material patterns.

FIGURE 10-108 A scene with object characteristics modeled using solid-texture methods. (*Courtesy of Peter Shirley, Computer Science Department, University of Utah.*)

Texture Reduction Patterns

In animations and other applications, the size of an object often changes. For objects displayed with texture patterns, we then need to apply the texture-mapping procedures to the altered dimensions of the object. When the size of a textured object is reduced, the texture pattern is applied to a smaller region and this can lead to texture distortions. To avoid this, we can create a series of **texture reduction patterns** that are to be used when the displayed size of the object is scaled down.

Typically, each reduction pattern is one half the size of the previous pattern. For example, if we have a two-dimensional 16 by 16 pattern, then we could set up four additional patterns at the reduced sizes of 8 by 8, 4 by 4, 2 by 2, and 1 by 1. For any view of an object, we can then apply an appropriate reduction pattern to minimize distortions. These reduction patterns are often referred to as **MIP maps** or **mip maps,** where the term mip is an acronym for the Latin phrase *multum in parvo*, which can be translated as "much on a small object".

Procedural Texturing Methods

Another method for adding a texture pattern to an object is to use a procedural definition for the color variations that are to be applied. This approach avoids the transformation calculations involved in mapping array patterns to object descriptions. And procedural texturing eliminates the storage requirements that are necessary when many large texture patterns, particularly solid textures, are to be applied to a scene.

We generate a procedural texture by calculating variations for the properties or characteristics of an object. Wood-grain or marble patterns, for example, can be created throughout an object using harmonic functions (sine curves)

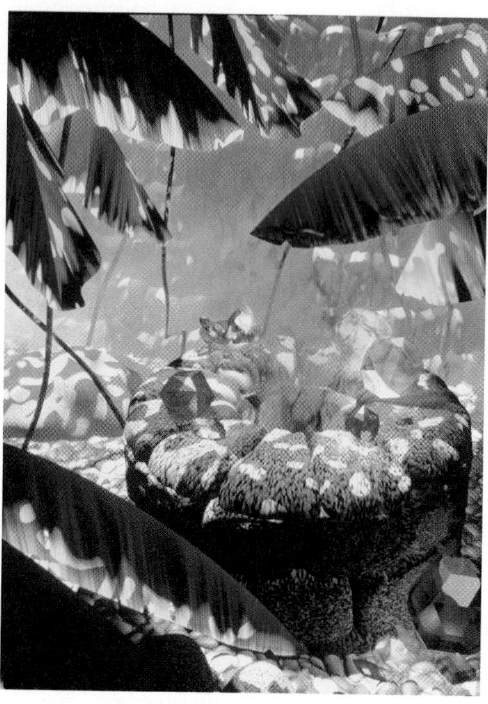

FIGURE 10-109 A scene rendered with VG Shaders and modeled with RenderMan using polygonal facets for the gem faces, quadric surfaces, and bicubic patches. In addition to texture arrays, procedural methods were used to create the steamy jungle atmosphere and the forest canopy showing a dappled lighting effect. (*Courtesy of the VALIS Group. Reprinted from* Graphics Gems III, *edited by David Kirk. © 1992 Academic Press, Inc.*)

defined in a region of three-dimensional space. Random perturbations are then superimposed on the harmonic variations to break up the symmetric patterns. The scene in Fig. 10-109 was rendered using procedural descriptions for patterns that are typical of those on the surfaces of stone masonry, polished gold, and banana leaves.

10-18 BUMP MAPPING

Although texture arrays can be used to add fine surface detail, they usually are not effective for modeling the rough surface appearance of objects such as oranges, strawberries, and raisins. The light-intensity detail that is provided in a texture array for these objects is set independently of illumination parameters such as the light-source direction. A better method for modeling surface bumpiness is to apply a perturbation function to the surface normal and then use the perturbed normal vector in the illumination-model calculations. This technique is called **bump mapping.**

If $\mathbf{P}(u, v)$ represents a position on a parametric surface, we can obtain the surface normal at that point with the calculation

$$\mathbf{N} = \mathbf{P}_u \times \mathbf{P}_v \tag{10-110}$$

where $\mathbf{P}_u$ and $\mathbf{P}_v$ are the partial derivatives of $\mathbf{P}$ with respect to parameters u and v. To provide variations in the surface normal, we can modify the surface position vector by adding a small perturbation function, called a *bump function*:

$$\mathbf{P}'(u, v) = \mathbf{P}(u, v) + b(u, v)\,\mathbf{n} \tag{10-111}$$

This adds bumps to the surface in the direction of the unit surface normal $\mathbf{n} = \mathbf{N}/|\mathbf{N}|$. The perturbed surface normal is then obtained as

$$\mathbf{N}' = \mathbf{P}'_u \times \mathbf{P}'_v \tag{10-112}$$

The partial derivative of $\mathbf{P}'$ with respect to u is

$$\begin{aligned}\mathbf{P}'_u &= \frac{\partial}{\partial u}(\mathbf{P} + b\mathbf{n}) \\ &= \mathbf{P}_u + b_u\mathbf{n} + b\mathbf{n}_u\end{aligned} \tag{10-113}$$

Assuming that the magnitude of the bump function b is small, we can neglect the last term in the above expression, so that

$$\mathbf{P}'_u \approx \mathbf{P}_u + b_u\mathbf{n} \tag{10-114}$$

Similarly,

$$\mathbf{P}'_v \approx \mathbf{P}_v + b_v\mathbf{n} \tag{10-115}$$

And the perturbed surface normal is

$$\mathbf{N}' = \mathbf{P}_u \times \mathbf{P}_v + b_v(\mathbf{P}_u \times \mathbf{n}) + b_u(\mathbf{n} \times \mathbf{P}_v) + b_u b_v(\mathbf{n} \times \mathbf{n})$$

But $\mathbf{n} \times \mathbf{n} = 0$, so that

$$\mathbf{N}' = \mathbf{N} + b_v(\mathbf{P}_u \times \mathbf{n}) + b_u(\mathbf{n} \times \mathbf{P}_v) \tag{10-116}$$

The final step is to normalize $\mathbf{N}'$ for use in the illumination-model calculations.

There are several ways in which we can specify the bump function $b(u, v)$. We could set up an analytic expression, but computations are reduced if we simply obtain bump values using table lookups. With a bump table, values for b are quickly determined using linear interpolation and incremental calculations. Then, the partial derivatives b_u and b_v are approximated with finite differences. The bump table can be set up with random patterns, regular grid patterns, or character shapes. Random patterns are useful for modeling an irregular surface, such as a raisin, while a repeating pattern could be used to model the surface of an orange, for example. To antialias, we subdivide pixel areas and average the computed subpixel intensities.

Figure 10-110 shows examples of surfaces rendered with bump mapping. An example of combined surface-rendering methods is given in Fig. 10-111. The armor for the stained-glass knight in the film *Young Sherlock Holmes* was rendered with a combination of bump mapping, environment mapping, and texture mapping. An environment map of the surroundings was combined with a bump map to produce background illumination reflections and surface roughness. Then additional color and surface illumination, bumps, spots of dirt, and stains for the seams and rivets were added to produce the overall effect shown in this figure.

(a)

(b)

FIGURE 10-110
Rendering the characteristics of rough surfaces using bump mapping. (*Courtesy of* (a) *Peter Shirley, Computer Science Department, University of Utah, and* (b) *SOFTIMAGE, Inc.*)

FIGURE 10-111 The stained-glass knight from the motion picture *Young Sherlock Holmes*. A combination of bump mapping, environment mapping, and texture mapping was used to render the armor surface. (*Courtesy of Industrial Light & Magic. © 1985 Paramount Pictures/Amblin.*)

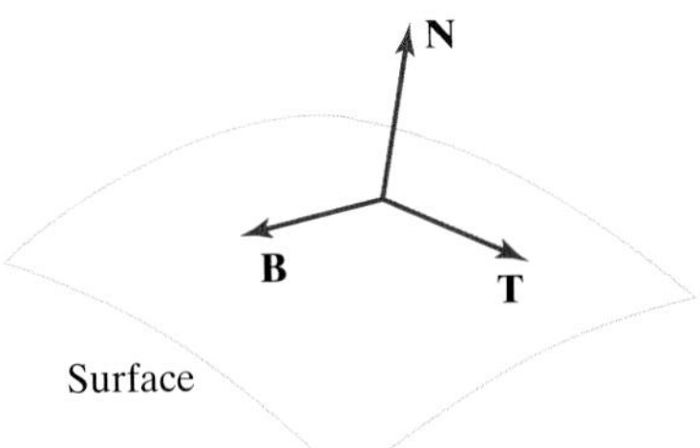

FIGURE 10-112 A local coordinate system at a surface position.

10-19 FRAME MAPPING

This method for adding surface detail is an extension of bump mapping. In **frame mapping,** we perturb both the surface normal vector **N** and a local coordinate system (Fig. 10-112) attached to **N**. The local coordinates are defined with a surface tangent vector **T** and a binormal vector $\mathbf{B} = \mathbf{T} \times \mathbf{N}$.

Frame mapping is used to model anisotropic surfaces. We orient **T** along the "grain" of the surface and apply directional perturbations, in addition to bump perturbations in the direction of **N**. In this way, we can model wood-grain patterns, cross-thread patterns in cloth, and streaks in marble or similar materials. Both bump and directional perturbations can be generated using table lookups.

10-20 OpenGL ILLUMINATION AND SURFACE-RENDERING FUNCTIONS

A variety of routines are available in OpenGL for setting up point light sources, selecting surface-reflection coefficients, and choosing values for other parameters in the basic illumination model. In addition, we can simulate transparency, and objects can be displayed using either flat surface rendering or Gouraud surface rendering.

OpenGL Point Light-Source Function

Multiple point light sources can be included in an OpenGL scene description, and various properties, such as position, type, color, attenuation, and spotlight effects, are associated with each light source. We set a property value for a light source with the function

```
glLight* (lightName, lightProperty, propertyValue);
```

A suffix code of `i` or `f` is appended to the function name, depending on the data type of the property value. For vector data, the suffix code v is also appended and parameter `propertyValue` is then a pointer to an array. Each light source is referenced with an identifier, and parameter `lightName` is assigned one of the OpenGL symbolic identifiers `GL_LIGHT0`, `GL_LIGHT1`, `GL_LIGHT2`, . . . , `GL_LIGHT7`, although some implementations of OpenGL may allow more than eight light sources. Similarly, parameter `lightProperty` must be assigned one of the ten OpenGL symbolic property constants. After all properties have been assigned to a light source, we turn on that light with the command

```
glEnable (lightName);
```

However, we also need to activate the OpenGL lighting routines, and we do that with

```
glEnable (GL_LIGHTING);
```

Object surfaces are then rendered using lighting calculations that include contributions from each light source that has been enabled.

Specifying an OpenGL Light-Source Position and Type

The OpenGL symbolic property constant for designating a light-source position is GL_POSITION. Actually, this symbolic constant is used to set two light-source properties at the same time: the light-source position and the *light-source type*. Two general classifications of light sources are available in OpenGL to illuminate a scene. A point light source can be classified as near the objects to be illuminated (a local source), or it can be treated as if it were infinitely far from the scene. And this classification is independent of the position we assign to a light source. For a nearby light source, the emitted light radiates in all directions, and the position of the light source is included in the lighting calculations. But the emitted light from a distant source is allowed to emanate in one direction only, and this direction is applied to all surfaces in the scene, independently of the assigned light-source position. The direction for the emitted rays from a light that is classified as a distant source is calculated as the direction from the assigned position of the light source to the coordinate origin.

A four-element floating-point vector is used to designate both the type of light and the coordinate values for the light position. The first three elements of this vector give the world-coordinate position, and the fourth element is used to designate the light-source type. If we assign the value 0.0 to the fourth element of the position vector, the light is considered to be a very distant source (referred to in OpenGL as a "directional" light), and the light-source position is then used only to determine the light direction. Otherwise, the light is taken to be a local point source (referred to in OpenGL as a "positional" light), and the light position is used by the lighting routines to determine the light direction to each object in the scene. In the following code example, light 1 is designated as a local source at location (2.0, 0.0, 3.0), and light 2 is a distant source with light emission in the negative y direction.

```
GLfloat light1PosType [ ] = {2.0, 0.0, 3.0, 1.0};
GLfloat light2PosType [ ] = {0.0, 1.0, 0.0, 0.0};

glLightfv (GL_LIGHT1, GL_POSITION, light1PosType);
glEnable (GL_LIGHT1);

glLightfv (GL_LIGHT2, GL_POSITION, light2PosType);
glEnable (GL_LIGHT2);
```

If we do not specify a position and type for a light source, the default values are (0.0, 0.0, 1.0, 0.0), which indicates a distant source with light rays traveling in the negative z direction.

The position of a light source is included in the scene description, and it is transformed to viewing coordinates along with the object positions by the OpenGL geometric-transformation and viewing-transformation matrices. Therefore, if we want to keep the light source at a fixed position relative to the objects in a scene, we set its position after the specification of the geometric and viewing transformations in the program. But if we want the light source to move as the view point moves, we set its position before the specification of the viewing transformation. And we can apply a translation or rotation to a light source to move it around in a stationary scene.

Specifying OpenGL Light-Source Colors

Unlike an actual light source, an OpenGL light has three different RGBA color properties. In this empirical scheme, the three light-source colors provide options for varying the lighting effects in a scene. We set these colors using the symbolic color-property constants `GL_AMBIENT`, `GL_DIFFUSE`, and `GL_SPECULAR`. Each of these colors is assigned by specifying a four-element floating-point set of values. The components for each color are specified in the order (R, G, B, A), and the alpha component is used only if the color-blending routines are activated. As we might guess from the names of the symbolic color-property constants, one of the light-source colors contributes to the background (ambient) light in a scene, another color is used in diffuse-lighting calculations, and the third color is used to compute specular-lighting effects for a surface. Realistically, a light source has just one color, but we can use the three OpenGL light-source colors to create various lighting effects. In the following code example, we set the ambient color for a local light source, labeled `GL_LIGHT3`, to black, and we set the diffuse and specular colors to white.

```
GLfloat blackColor [ ] = {0.0, 0.0, 0.0, 1.0};
GLfloat whiteColor [ ] = {1.0, 1.0, 1.0, 1.0};

glLightfv (GL_LIGHT3, GL_AMBIENT, blackColor);
glLightfv (GL_LIGHT3, GL_DIFFUSE, whiteColor);
glLightfv (GL_LIGHT3, GL_SPECULAR, whiteColor);
```

The default colors for light source 0 are black for the ambient color and white for the diffuse and specular colors. All the other light sources have a default color of black for each of the ambient, diffuse, and specular color properties.

Specifying Radial-Intensity Attenuation Coefficients for an OpenGL Light Source

We can apply radial-intensity attenuation to the light emitted from an OpenGL local light source, and the OpenGL lighting routines calculate this attenuation using Eq. 10-2, with d_l as the distance from a light-source position to an object position. The three OpenGL property constants for radial intensity attenuation are `GL_CONSTANT_ATTENUATION`, `GL_LINEAR_ATTENUATION`, and `GL_QUADRATIC_ATTENUATION`, which correspond to the coefficients a_0, a_1, and a_2 in Eq. 10-2. Either a positive integer value or a positive floating-point value can be used to set each attenuation coefficient. For example, we could assign the radial-attenuation coefficient values as

```
glLightf (GL_LIGHT6, GL_CONSTANT_ATTENUATION, 1.5);
glLightf (GL_LIGHT6, GL_LINEAR_ATTENUATION, 0.75);
glLightf (GL_LIGHT6, GL_QUADRATIC_ATTENUATION, 0.4);
```

Once the values for the attenuation coefficients have been set, the radial attenuation function is applied to all three colors (ambient, diffuse, and specular) of the light source. Default values for the attenuation coefficients are $a_0 = 1.0$, $a_1 = 0.0$, and $a_2 = 0.0$. Thus, the default is no radial attenuation: $f_{l,\text{radatten}} = 1.0$. Although radial attenuation can produce more realistic displays, the calculations are time consuming.

OpenGL Directional Light Sources (Spotlights)

For local light sources (those not considered to be at infinity), we can also specify a directional, or spotlight, effect. This limits the light that is emitted from a source to a cone-shaped region of space. We define the conical region with a direction vector along the axis of the cone and an angular spread θ_l from the cone axis, as shown in Fig. 10-113. In addition, we can specify an angular-attenuation exponent a_l for the light source that determines how much the light intensity decreases as we move from the center of the cone toward the cone surface. Along any direction within the light cone, the angular attenuation factor is $\cos^{a_l} \alpha$ (Eq. 10-5), where $\cos \alpha$ is calculated as the dot product of the cone axis vector and the vector from the light source to an object position. We compute the value for each of the ambient, diffuse, and specular light colors at angle α by multiplying the intensity components by this angular attenuation factor. If $\alpha > \theta_l$, the object is outside the light-source cone, and the object is not illuminated by this light source. For light rays within the cone, we can also attenuate the intensity values radially.

There are three OpenGL property constants for directional effects: `GL_SPOT_DIRECTION`, `GL_SPOT_CUTOFF`, and `GL_SPOT_EXPONENT`. We specify the light direction as either an integer or floating-point world-coordinate vector. The cone angle θ_l is given as an integer or floating-point value in degrees, and this angle can be either 180° or any value in the range from 0° to 90°. When the cone angle is set to 180°, the light source emits rays in all directions (360°). We set the exponent value for intensity attenuation either as an integer or floating-point number in the range from 0 to 128. The following statements set the directional effects for light

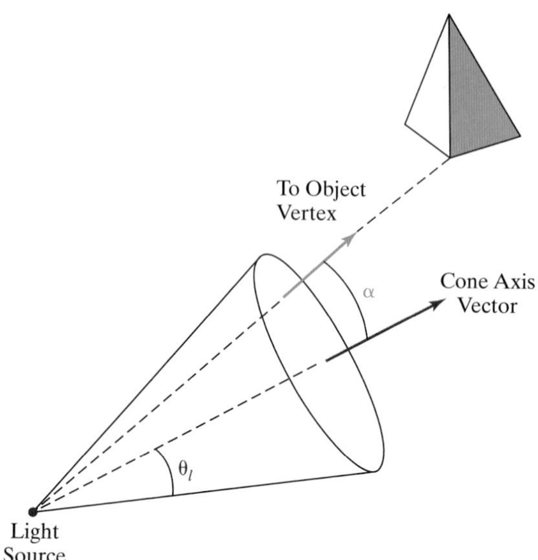

FIGURE 10-113 A circular cone of light emitted from an OpenGL light source. The angular extent of the light cone, measured from the cone axis, is θ_l, and the angle from the axis to an object direction vector is labeled as α.

source 3 so that the cone axis is in the positive x direction, the cone angle θ_l is 30°, and the attenuation exponent is 2.5.

```
GLfloat dirVector [ ] = {1.0, 0.0, 0.0};

glLightfv (GL_LIGHT3, GL_SPOT_DIRECTION, dirVector);
glLightf (GL_LIGHT3, GL_SPOT_CUTOFF, 30.0);
glLightf (GL_LIGHT3, GL_SPOT_EXPONENT, 2.5);
```

If we do not specify a direction for a light source, the default direction is parallel to the negative z axis; that is, (0.0, 0.0, −1.0). Also, the default cone angle is 180°, and the default attenuation exponent is 0. Thus, the default is a point light source that radiates in all directions, with no angular attenuation.

OpenGL Global Lighting Parameters

Several OpenGL lighting parameters can be specified at the global level. These values are used to control the way that some lighting calculations are performed, and a global parameter value is set with the following function.

```
glLightModel* (paramName, paramValue);
```

We append a suffix code of `i` or `f`, depending on the data type of the parameter value. And, for vector data, we also append the suffix code `v`. Parameter `paramName` is assigned an OpenGL symbolic constant that identifies the global property to be set, and parameter `paramValue` is assigned a single value or set of values. Using the `glLightModel` function, we can set a global ambient-light level, we can specify how specular highlights are to be calculated, and we can choose to apply the illumination model to the back faces of polygon surfaces.

In addition to the ambient color for individual light sources, we can set an independent value for the OpenGL background lighting as a global value. This provides just one more option in the empirical lighting calculations. To set this option, we use the symbolic constant `GL_LIGHT_MODEL_AMBIENT`. The following statement, for example, sets the general background lighting for a scene to a low-intensity (dark) blue color, with an alpha value of 1.0.

```
globalAmbient [ ] = {0.0, 0.0, 0.3, 1.0);

glLightModelfv (GL_LIGHT_MODEL_AMBIENT, globalAmbient);
```

If we do not set a global ambient-light level, the default is the low-intensity white (dark gray) color (0.2, 0.2, 0.2, 1.0).

Specular-reflection calculations require the determination of several vectors, including the vector **V** from a surface position to the viewing position. To speed up specular calculations, the OpenGL lighting routines can use a constant direction for vector **V**, regardless of the surface position relative to the view point. This constant unit vector is in the positive z direction, (0.0, 0.0, 1.0), and this is the default value for **V**. But if we want to turn off this default and use the actual viewing position, which is the viewing-coordinate origin, to calculate **V**, we issue the following command.

```
glLightModeli (GL_LIGHT_MODEL_LOCAL_VIEWER, GL_TRUE);
```

Although the specular calculations take more time when we use the actual viewing position to calculate **V**, we do obtain more realistic displays. We turn off the surface calculations for vector **V** when we use the default value GL_FALSE (or 0, or 0.0) for the local-viewer parameter.

When surface textures are added to the OpenGL lighting calculations, surface highlights can be dulled and the texture patterns may be distorted by the specular terms. Therefore, as an option, texture patterns can be applied only to the nonspecular terms that contribute to a surface color. These nonspecular terms include ambient effects, surface emissions, and diffuse reflections. Using this option, the OpenGL lighting routines generate two colors for each surface lighting calculation: a specular color and the nonspecular color contributions. Texture patterns are combined only with the nonspecular color, and then the two colors are combined. We select this two-color option with

```
glLightModeli (GL_LIGHT_MODEL_COLOR_CONTROL,
                    GL_SEPARATE_SPECULAR_COLOR);
```

We need not separate the color terms if we are not using texture patterns, and the lighting calculations are performed more efficiently if this option is not invoked. The default value for this property is GL_SINGLE_COLOR, which does not separate the specular color from the other surface-color components.

In some applications, we may want to display back-facing surfaces of an object. An example is the inside, cutaway view of a solid, in which some back-facing surfaces, in addition to the front-facing surfaces, are to be displayed. However, by default, the lighting calculations use the assigned material properties only for the front faces. To apply the lighting calculations to both the front and back faces, using the corresponding front-face and back-face material properties, we issue the command

```
glLightModeli (GL_LIGHT_MODEL_TWO_SIDE, GL_TRUE);
```

The surface normal vectors for the back faces are then reversed, and the lighting calculations are applied using the material properties that have been assigned to the back faces. To turn off the two-sided lighting calculations, we use the value GL_FALSE (or 0, or 0.0) in the glLightModel function, which is the default.

OpenGL Surface-Property Function

Reflection coefficients and other optical properties for surfaces are set using the function

```
glMaterial* (surfFace, surfProperty, propertyValue);
```

A suffix code of i or f is appended to the function, depending on the data type for the property value, and we also append the code v when we supply vector-valued properties. Parameter surfFace is assigned one of the symbolic constants GL_FRONT, GL_BACK, or GL_FRONT_AND_BACK; parameter surfProperty is a symbolic constant identifying a surface parameter such as I_{surf}, k_a, k_d, k_s, or n_s; and parameter propertyValue is set to the corresponding value. All properties except the specular-reflection exponent n_s are specified as vector values. We use a sequence of `glMaterial` functions to set all the illumination properties for an object, before we issue the commands that describe the object geometry.

An RGBA value for the surface emission color, I_{surf}, is selected using the OpenGL symbolic surface-property constant GL_EMISSION. As an example, the following statement sets the emission color for front surfaces to a light gray (off-white).

```
surfEmissionColor [ ] = {0.8, 0.8, 0.8, 1.0};

glMaterialfv (GL_FRONT, GL_EMISSION, surfEmissionColor);
```

The default emission color for a surface is black, (0.0, 0.0, 0.0, 1.0). Although an emission color can be assigned to a surface, this emission does not illuminate other objects in the scene. To do that, we must define the surface as a light source using the methods discussed in Section 10-3.

We use the OpenGL symbolic property names GL_AMBIENT, GL_DIFFUSE, and GL_SPECULAR to set values for the surface reflection coefficients. Realistically, the ambient and diffuse coefficients should be assigned the same vector values, and we can do that using the symbolic constant GL_AMBIENT_AND_DIFFUSE. The default values for the ambient coefficient are (0.2, 0.2, 0.2, 1.0), the default values for the diffuse coefficient are (0.8, 0.8, 0.8, 1.0), and the default values for the specular coefficient are (1.0, 1.0, 1.0, 1.0). To set the specular-reflection exponent, we use the constant GL_SHININESS. We can assign any value in the range from 0 to 128 to this property, and the default value is 0. As an example, the following statements set the values for the three reflection coefficients and the specular exponent. The diffuse and ambient coefficients are set so that the surface is displayed as a light-blue color when it is illuminated with white light; specular reflection is the color of the incident light; and the specular exponent is assigned a value of 25.0.

```
diffuseCoeff [ ] = {0.2, 0.4, 0.9, 1.0};
specularCoeff [ ] = {1.0, 1.0, 1.0, 1.0};

glMaterialfv (GL_FRONT_AND_BACK, GL_AMBIENT_AND_DIFFUSE,
                diffuseCoeff);
glMaterialfv (GL_FRONT_AND_BACK, GL_SPECULAR, specularCoeff);
glMaterialf (GL_FRONT_AND_BACK, GL_SHININESS, 25.0);
```

Components for the reflection coefficients can also be set using color-table values, and the OpenGL symbolic constant GL_COLOR_INDEXES is provided for this purpose. We assign the color-table indices as a three-element integer or floating-point array, and the default is (0, 1, 1).

OpenGL Illumination Model

Surface lighting effects are calculated by OpenGL using the basic illumination model 10-19, with some variations in the way that the parameters are specified. The ambient light level is the sum of the light-source ambient components and the global ambient setting. Diffuse-reflection calculations use the diffuse-intensity component of the light sources, and specular-reflection calculations use the specular-intensity component of each light source.

Also, the unit vector V, specifying the direction from a surface position to a viewing position, can be set to the constant value (0.0, 0.0, 0.0) if the local-viewer option is not used. For a light source positioned at "infinity", the unit light-direction vector L is in the opposite direction to the assigned direction for the light rays from that source.

OpenGL Atmospheric Effects

After the OpenGL illumination model has been applied to obtain surface colors, we can assign a color to the atmosphere in a scene and combine the surface colors with the atmosphere color. And we can use an atmosphere intensity-attenuation function to simulate viewing the scene through a hazy or smoky atmosphere. The various atmosphere parameters are set using the `glFog` function introduced in Section 9-14:

```
glEnable (GL_FOG);

glFog* (atmoParameter, paramValue);
```

A suffix code of `i` or `f` is appended to indicate data-value type, and the suffix code `v` is used with vector data.

To set an atmosphere color, we assign the OpenGL symbolic constant `GL_FOG_COLOR` to parameter `atmoParameter`. For example, we can designate the atmosphere as having a bluish-gray color with

```
GLfloat atmoColor [4] = {0.8, 0.8, 1.0, 1.0};

glFogfv (GL_FOG_COLOR, atmoColor);
```

The default value for the atmosphere color is black, (0.0, 0.0, 0.0, 0.0).

We can next choose the atmosphere-attenuation function that is to be used to combine the object color with the atmosphere color. This is accomplished using the symbolic constant `GL_FOG_MODE`:

```
glFogi (GL_FOG_MODE, atmoAttenFunc);
```

If parameter `atmoAttenFunc` is assigned the value `GL_EXP`, Eq. 10-31 is used as the atmosphere-attenuation function. With the value `GL_EXP2`, we select Eq. 10-32 as the atmosphere-attenuation function. For either of the exponential functions, we select an atmosphere density value with

```
glFog (GL_FOG_DENSITY, atmoDensity);
```

A third option for atmospheric attenuation is the linear depth-cueing function 9-13. In this case, parameter `atmoAttenFunc` is assigned the value `GL_LINEAR`. The default value for parameter `atmoAttenFunc` is `GL_EXP`.

Once an atmosphere-attenuation function has been selected, this function is used to calculate a blended atmosphere-surface color for the object. Equation 10-33 is used by the OpenGL atmosphere routines to calculate this blended color.

OpenGL Transparency Functions

Some simulated transparency effects are possible in OpenGL using the color-blending routines described in Section 4-3. However, the implementation of transparency in an OpenGL program, in general, is not straightforward. We can combine object colors for a simple scene containing a few opaque and transparent surfaces by using the alpha blending value to specify the degree of transparency and by processing surfaces in a depth-first order. But the OpenGL color-blending operations ignore refraction effects, and dealing with transparent surfaces in complex scenes with a variety of lighting conditions or animations can be formidable. Also, OpenGL provides no direct provisions for simulating the surface appearance of a translucent object (such as a grainy sheet of plastic or a pane of frosted glass), which diffusely scatters the light transmissions through the semitransparent material. Thus, to display translucent surfaces or the lighting effects resulting from refraction, we would need to write our own routines. To simulate lighting effects through a translucent object, we could use a combination of values for surface texture and material properties. For refraction effects, we could shift the pixel positions for surfaces behind a transparent object using Eq. 10-29 to calculate the amount of offset needed.

We designate objects in a scene as transparent using the alpha parameter in the OpenGL RGBA surface-color commands such as `glMaterial` and `glColor`. A surface alpha parameter can be set to the value of the transparency coefficient (Eq. 10-30) for that object. For example, if we specify the color for a transparent surface with the function

```
glColor4f (R, G, B, A);
```

then we set the alpha parameter to the value $A = k_t$. A completely transparent surface is assigned the alpha value $A = 1.0$, and an opaque surface has the alpha value $A = 0.0$.

Once we have assigned the transparency values, we activate the color-blending features of OpenGL and process the surfaces, starting with the most distant objects and proceeding in order to the objects closest to the viewing position. With color blending activated, each surface color is combined with any overlapping surfaces that are already in the frame buffer, using the assigned surface alpha values.

We set the color-blending factors so that all color components of the current surface (the "source" object) are multiplied by $(1 - A) = (1 - k_t)$, and all color components of the corresponding frame-buffer positions (the "destination") are multiplied by the factor $A = k_t$:

```
glEnable (GL_BLEND);

glBlendFunc (GL_ONE_MINUS_SRC_ALPHA, GL_SRC_ALPHA);
```

The two colors are then blended using Eq. 10-30 with the alpha parameter set to k_t, where the frame-buffer colors are those for a surface that is behind the transparent object being processed. For instance, if $A = 0.3$, then the new frame-buffer color is the sum of 30 percent of the current frame-buffer color and 70 percent of the object reflection color, for each surface position. (Alternatively, we could use the alpha color parameter as an opacity factor, instead of a transparency factor. If we set A to an opacity value, though, we also must interchange the two arguments in the function `glBlendFunc`.)

Visibility testing can be accomplished using the OpenGL depth-buffer functions from Section 9-14. As each visible opaque surface is processed, both the surface colors and the surface depth values are stored. But when we process a visible transparent surface, we want to save only its colors, because the surface does not obscure background surfaces. Therefore, as we process each transparent surface, we put the depth buffer into a read-only status using the `glDepthMask` function.

If we process all objects in depth order, the depth-buffer write mode is turned off and then back on again as we process each transparent surface. Alternatively, we could separate the two object classes, as in the following code outline.

```
glEnable (GL_DEPTH_TEST);
\*  Process all opaque surfaces.  *\

glEnable (GL_BLEND);
glDepthMask (GL_FALSE);
glBlendFunc (GL_ONE_MINUS_SRC_ALPHA, GL_SRC_ALPHA);
\*  Process all transparent surfaces.  *\

glDepthMask (GL_TRUE);
glDisable (GL_BLEND);

glutSwapBuffers ( );
```

If the transparent objects are not processed in a strictly back-to-front order, this approach will not accumulate surface colors accurately for all cases. But for simple scenes, this is a fast and effective method for generating an approximate representation for the transparency effects.

OpenGL Surface-Rendering Functions

Surfaces can be displayed with OpenGL routines using either constant-intensity surface rendering or Gouraud surface rendering. No OpenGL routines are provided for applying Phong surface rendering, ray tracing, or radiosity methods. A rendering method is selected with

```
glShadeModel (surfRenderingMethod);
```

We select constant-intensity surface rendering by assigning the symbolic value `GL_FLAT` to parameter `surfRenderingMethod`. For Gouraud shading (the default), we use the symbolic constant `GL_SMOOTH`.

When the `glShadeModel` function is applied to a tessellated curved surface, such as a sphere that is approximated with a polygon mesh, the OpenGL rendering routines use the surface-normal vectors at the polygon vertices to calculate the polygon color. The Cartesian components of a surface-normal vector in OpenGL are specified with the command

```
glNormal3* (Nx, Ny, Nz);
```

Suffix codes for this function are `b` (byte), `s` (short), `i` (integer), `f` (float), and `d` (double). In addition, we append the suffix code `v` when the vector components are designated with an array. Byte, short, and integer values are converted to floating-point values in the range from −1.0 to 1.0. The `glNormal` function sets the components for the surface-normal vector as state values that apply to all subsequent `glVertex` commands, and the default normal vector is in the positive z direction: (0.0, 0.0, 1.0).

For flat surface rendering, we need only one surface normal for each polygon. Thus, we can set each polygon normal as, for example,

```
glNormal3fv (normalVector);
glBegin (GL_TRIANGLES);
    glVertex3fv (vertex1);
    glVertex3fv (vertex2);
    glVertex3fv (vertex3);
glEnd ( );
```

If we want to apply the Gouraud surface-rendering procedure to the above triangle, we need to designate a normal vector for each vertex:

```
glBegin (GL_TRIANGLES);
    glNormal3fv (normalVector1);
    glVertex3fv (vertex1);
    glNormal3fv (normalVector2);
    glVertex3fv (vertex2);
    glNormal3fv (normalVector3);
    glVertex3fv (vertex3);
glEnd ( );
```

Although normal vectors need not be specified as unit vectors, we can reduce computations if do state all surface normals as unit vectors. Any non-unit surface normal is automatically converted to a unit normal if we have issued the command

```
glEnable (GL_NORMALIZE);
```

This command also renormalizes surface vectors if they have been modified by geometric transformations such as scaling or shear.

Another available option is the designation of a list of normal vectors that are to be combined or associated with a vertex array (Sections 3-17 and 4-3). The statements for creating an array of normal vectors are

```
glEnableClientState (GL_NORMAL_ARRAY);

glNormalPointer (dataType, offset, normalArray);
```

Parameter `dataType` is assigned the constant value `GL_BYTE`, `GL_SHORT`, `GL_INT`, `GL_FLOAT` (the default value), or `GL_DOUBLE`. The number of bytes between successive normal vectors in the array `normalArray` is given by parameter `offset`, which has a default value of 0.

OpenGL Halftoning Operations

A variety of colors and gray-scale effects are possible on some systems using OpenGL halftone routines. The halftone-approximation patterns and operations are hardware dependent, and they typically have no effect on systems with full-color graphics capabilities. However, when a system has only a small number of bits per pixel, RGBA color settings can be approximated with halftone patterns.

We activate the halftone routines with

```
glEnable (GL_DITHER);
```

which is the default, and the halftoning routines are deactivated with the function

```
glDisable (GL_DITHER);
```

10-21 OpenGL TEXTURE FUNCTIONS

An extensive set of texture functions is available in OpenGL. We can specify a pattern for a line, a surface, an interior volume of a spatial region, or as a subpattern that is to be inserted into another texture pattern. And we can apply and manipulate texture patterns in various ways. In addition, texture patterns can be used to simulate environment mapping. The OpenGL texture routines can be used only in RGB (RGBA) color mode, although some parameters can be set using a color-table index.

OpenGL Line-Texture Functions

Parameters for a one-dimensional RGBA texture pattern specified in a single-subscript color array are designated, for example, with

```
glTexImage1D (GL_TEXTURE_1D, 0, GL_RGBA, nTexColors, 0,
                dataFormat, dataType, lineTexArray);

glEnable (GL_TEXTURE_1D);
```

We have set the first argument in the `glTexImage1D` function to the OpenGL symbolic constant `GL_TEXTURE_1D` to indicate that we are defining a texture array for a one-dimensional object: a line. If we are not sure that the system will support the texture pattern with the specified parameters, we use the symbolic constant `GL_PROXY_TEXTURE_1D` for the first argument of `glTexImage1D`. This allows us to first query the system before defining the elements of the texture array, and we discuss the query procedures in a later section.

For the second and fifth arguments of this example function, we use the value 0. The first 0 value (second argument) means that this array is not a reduction of some larger texture array. For the fifth argument, the 0 value means that we do not want a border around the texture. If this fifth argument had been assigned the value 1 (the only other possibility), the texture pattern would be displayed with a one-pixel border around it, which is used to merge the pattern with adjacent texture patterns. For the third argument, the value `GL_RGBA` means that each color of the texture pattern is specified with four RGBA values. We could have just used the three RGB color values, but RGBA values are sometimes processed more efficiently because they align with processor memory boundaries. Numerous other color specifications are possible, including a single intensity or luminance value. Parameter `nTexColors`, the fourth argument, is to be assigned a positive integer indicating the number of colors in the linear texture pattern. Because a 0 value is listed for the fifth argument (the border parameter), the number of colors in the texture pattern must be a power of 2. If the fifth argument had been assigned the value 1, then the number of colors in the texture pattern would have to be 2 plus a power of 2. The two border colors are used to provide color blending with neighboring patterns. We can specify the one-subscript texture pattern with up to 64 + 2 colors, and some OpenGL implementations allow larger texture patterns. Parameters describing the texture colors and the border colors are stored in `lineTexArray`. In this example, we have no border and each successive group of four elements in the array represents one color component of the texture pattern. Therefore, the number of elements in `lineTexArray` is $4 \times$ `nTexColors`. As a specific example, if we want to define a texture pattern with 8 colors, the texture array must contain $4 \times 8 = 32$ elements.

Parameters `dataFormat` and `dataType` are similar to the arguments in the `glDrawPixels` and `glReadPixels` functions (Section 3-19). We assign an OpenGL symbolic constant to `dataFormat` to indicate how the color values are to be specified in the texture array. For instance, we could use the symbolic constant `GL_BGRA` to indicate that the color components are to be given in the order blue, green, red, alpha. To indicate the BGRA or RGBA data type, we can assign the OpenGL constant value `GL_UNSIGNED_BYTE` to parameter `dataType`. Other possible values that could be assigned to parameter `dataType`, depending on the data format we choose, include `GL_INT` and `GL_FLOAT`.

We can map multiple copies of a texture, or any contiguous subset of the texture colors, to an object in a scene. When a group of texture elements is mapped to one or more pixel areas, the boundaries of the texture elements usually do not align with the positions of the pixel boundaries. A pixel area could be contained within the boundaries of a single RGB (or RGBA) texture element or it could overlap several texture elements. To simplify the calculations in the texture mapping, we use the following functions to give each pixel the color of the nearest texture element.

```
glTexParameteri (GL_TEXTURE_1D, GL_TEXTURE_MAG_FILTER,
                        GL_NEAREST);
glTexParameteri (GL_TEXTURE_1D, GL_TEXTURE_MIN_FILTER,
                        GL_NEAREST);
```

The first function is used by the texturing routines when a section of the texture pattern must be enlarged to fit a specified coordinate range in a scene, and the second function is used when a texture pattern has to be reduced. (These two texture operations in OpenGL are referred to as magnifying, `MAG`, and minifying, `MIN`.) Although assigning the nearest texture color to a pixel can be performed quickly, it can lead to aliasing effects. To calculate the pixel color as a linear combination of overlapping texture colors, we replace the symbolic constant `GL_NEAREST` with `GL_LINEAR`. Several other parameter values can be set with the `glTexParameter` function, and we take a look at these options in a later section.

Specifying OpenGL texture patterns for a scene is somewhat similar to specifying surface-normal vectors, RGB colors, or other attributes. We need to associate the pattern with some object, but, unlike a single color setting, we now have a collection of color values. For a one-dimensional texture space, the color values are referenced with a single s coordinate that varies from 0.0 to 1.0 across the texture space (Section 10-16). Thus, the texture pattern is applied to objects in a scene by assigning texture coordinate values to object positions. A particular s-coordinate value in one-dimensional texture space is selected with the following command.

```
glTexCoord1* (sCoord);
```

Allowable suffix codes for this function are `b` (byte), `s` (short), `i` (integer), `f` (float), and `d` (double), depending on the data type for the texture coordinate parameter `sCoord`. And we can use the suffix `v` if an s-coordinate value is given in an array. As with color and other similar parameters, the s coordinate is a state parameter, which applies to all subsequently defined world-coordinate positions. The default value for the s coordinate is 0.0.

To map a linear texture pattern onto positions within a world-coordinate scene, we assign s coordinates to the endpoints of a line segment. The texture colors can be then be applied to the object in various ways, and the OpenGL default method is to multiply each pixel color value for the object by the corresponding color value in the texture pattern. If the line color is white (1.0, 1.0, 1.0, 1.0), which is the default color for objects in a scene, the line will be displayed only with the texture colors.

In the following example, we create a four-element linear texture pattern with alternating green and red colors. The entire texture pattern, from 0.0 to 1.0, is then assigned to a straight-line segment. Since the line is white, by default, it is displayed in the texture colors.

```
GLint k;
GLubyte texLine [16];   // 16-element texture array.

/*  Define two green elements for the texture pattern.
/*  Each texture color is specified in four array positions.
 */
for (k = 0; k <= 2; k += 2)
{
    texLine [4*k]    = 0;
    texLine [4*k+1]  = 255;
    texLine [4*k+2]  = 0;
    texLine [4*k+3]  = 255;
}

/*  Define two red elements for the texture pattern.   */
for (k = 1; k <= 3; k += 2)
{
    texLine [4*k]    = 255;
    texLine [4*k+1]  = 0;
    texLine [4*k+2]  = 0;
    texLine [4*k+3]  = 255;
}

glTexParameteri (GL_TEXTURE_1D, GL_TEXTURE_MAG_FILTER, GL_NEAREST);
glTexParameteri (GL_TEXTURE_1D, GL_TEXTURE_MIN_FILTER, GL_NEAREST);

glTexImage1D (GL_TEXTURE_1D, 0, GL_RGBA, 4, 0, GL_RGBA, GL_UNSIGNED_BYTE, texLine);

glEnable (GL_TEXTURE_1D);

/*  Assign the full range of texture colors to a line segment.   */
glBegin (GL_LINES);
    glTexCoord1f (0.0);
    glVertex3fv (endPt1);
    glTexCoord1f (1.0);
    glVertex3fv (endPt2);
glEnd ( );

glDisable (GL_TEXTURE_1D);
```

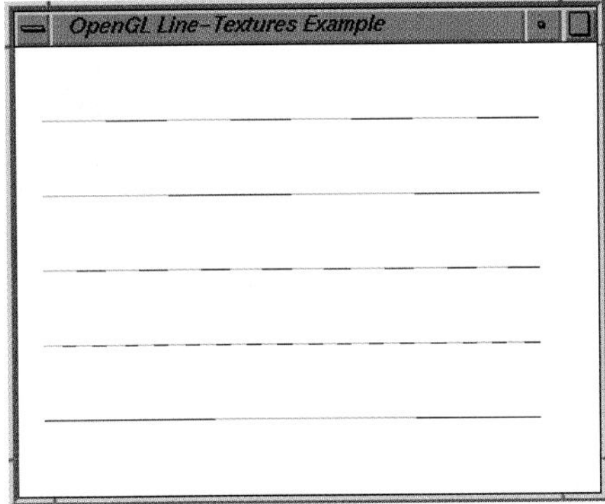

FIGURE 10-114 Examples of mapping an OpenGL single- subscript texture pattern onto a white line segment.

The line segment is displayed with alternate green and red sections along the line path. We can assign any values to the *s* coordinates. For example, the middle red and green colors of the texture pattern are mapped onto the line with the following statements.

```
glBegin (GL_LINES);
    glTexCoord1f (0.25);
    glVertex3fv (wcPt1);
    glTexCoord1f (0.75);
    glVertex3fv (wcPt2);
glEnd ( );
```

Thus, the first half of the line is red and the second half green. We could also use *s* values outside the range from 0.0 to 1.0. For instance, if we assigned the *s* value −2.0 to one endpoint of a line and the *s* value 2.0 to the other endpoint, the texture pattern would be mapped onto the line four times. The line would then be displayed with 16 green sections and 16 red sections. For *s*-coordinate values outside the unit interval, integer parts are ignored unless we specify that *s* values are to be clamped to 0 or 1.0. Figure 10-114 shows some possible line patterns that can be displayed with the array containing RGB values for two green colors and two red colors.

A vast number of parameters and options are available with OpenGL texture patterns. But, before we go into these features of the OpenGL texture routines, we first discuss the basic functions needed to generate two-dimensional and three-dimensional texture patterns.

OpenGL Surface-Texture Functions

We can set the parameters for a two-dimensional RGBA texture space using functions similar to those for our one-dimensional texture pattern example:

```
glTexImage2D (GL_TEXTURE_2D, 0, GL_RGBA, texWidth,
            texHeight, 0, dataFormat, dataType, surfTexArray);

glEnable (GL_TEXTURE_2D);
```

The only difference here is that we must specify both a width (number of columns) and a height (number of rows) for the three-subscript texture array. Both the width and height must be a power of 2, without a border, or 2 plus a power of 2, with a border. We again use RGBA color components, and we state that the pattern has no border and it is not a reduction of a larger texture pattern. Therefore the size of the array stored in `surfTexArray` is 4 × `texWidth` × `texHeight`. For two-dimensional texture patterns, we set the elements in the texture array to the color values in a bottom-to-top order. Starting at the lower-left corner of the color pattern, we set the elements in the first row of the array to the RGBA values corresponding to the bottom row of texture space, and we set the elements in the last row of the array to the RGBA values corresponding to the top of the rectangular texture space (Fig. 10-103).

As with a linear texture pattern, surface pixels in a scene can be assigned the nearest texture color or an interpolated texture color. We select one of these options with the same two `glTexParameter` functions that we used for one-dimensional textures. One function specifies the option to use when a texture pattern is enlarged to fit a coordinate range, and the other function specifies an option that is to be used with pattern reductions. And a two-dimensional texture pattern could be stretched in one direction and compressed in the other direction. For example, the following statements instruct the texturing routines to display projected surface positions using the nearest texture color.

```
glTexParameteri (GL_TEXTURE_2D, GL_TEXTURE_MAG_FILTER,
                     GL_NEAREST);
glTexParameteri (GL_TEXTURE_2D, GL_TEXTURE_MIN_FILTER,
                     GL_NEAREST);
```

To assign an interpolated texture color to surface pixels, we use the symbolic constant `GL_LINEAR` instead of `GL_NEAREST`.

A coordinate position in two-dimensional texture space is selected with

```
glTexCoord2* (sCoord, tCoord);
```

Texture space is normalized so that the pattern is referenced with coordinate values in the range from 0.0 to 1.0. However, we can use any texture-coordinate values to replicate a pattern across a surface. The texture coordinates can be specified in various formats, and we indicate a data format with a suffix code of `b`, `s`, `i`, `f`, or `d`. We also append the suffix `v` if the texture coordinates are given in an array.

To illustrate the OpenGL functions for a two-dimensional texture space, the following code segment sets up a 32 by 32 pattern and maps it onto a quadrilateral surface. Each texture color is specified with four RGBA components, and the pattern has no border.

```
GLubyte texArray [32][32][4];

/*  Next: assign the texture color components to texArray.  */

/*  Select nearest-color option.  */
glTexParameteri (GL_TEXTURE_2D, GL_TEXTURE_MAG_FILTER, GL_NEAREST);
glTexParameteri (GL_TEXTURE_2D, GL_TEXTURE_MIN_FILTER, GL_NEAREST);
```

```
glTexImage2D (GL_TEXTURE_2D, 0, GL_RGBA, 32, 32, 0, GL_RGBA,
              GL_UNSIGNED_BYTE, texArray);

glEnable (GL_TEXTURE_2D);

/*  Assign the full range of texture colors to a quadrilateral.  */
glBegin (GL_QUADS);
    glTexCoord2f (0.0, 0.0);      glVertex3fv (vertex1);
    glTexCoord2f (1.0, 0.0);      glVertex3fv (vertex2);
    glTexCoord2f (1.0, 1.0);      glVertex3fv (vertex3);
    glTexCoord2f (0.0, 1.0);      glVertex3fv (vertex4);
glEnd ( );

glDisable (GL_TEXTURE_2D);
```

OpenGL Volume-Texture Functions

Functions for a three-dimensional texture space are simple extensions of those for two-dimensional texture spaces. A four-subscript RGBA texture array with no border, for instance, can be set up with the functions

```
glTexImage3D (GL_TEXTURE_3D, 0, GL_RGBA, texWidth, texHeight,
              texDepth, 0, dataFormat, dataType, volTexArray);

glEnable (GL_TEXTURE_3D);
```

The RGBA texture colors are stored in `volTexArray`, which contains 4 × `texWidth` × `texHeight` × `texDepth` elements. And the width, height, and depth of the array must be either a power of 2 or a power of 2 plus 2.

With the following statements, we display pixels using the nearest texture color.

```
glTexParameteri (GL_TEXTURE_3D, GL_TEXTURE_MAG_FILTER,
                 GL_NEAREST);
glTexParameteri (GL_TEXTURE_3D, GL_TEXTURE_MIN_FILTER,
                 GL_NEAREST);
```

For linearly interpolated texture colors, we replace the value `GL_NEAREST` with `GL_LINEAR`.

Three-dimensional texture coordinates are selected with

```
glTexCoord3* (sCoord, tCoord, rCoord);
```

Each selected position in the texture space is then associated with a spatial coordinate position within a world-coordinate scene.

OpenGL Color Options for Texture Patterns

Elements for a texture space can be specified in many different ways. The third argument in the functions `glTexImage1D`, `glTexImage2D`, and `glTexImage1D` is used to specify the general format and number of color components for each element of a pattern. Nearly 40 symbolic constants are available for this specification. For example, each texture element could be a set of RGBA values, a set of

RGB values, a single alpha value, a single red intensity value, a single luminance value, or a luminance value paired with an alpha value. In addition, some constants also specify bit size. The OpenGL constant GL_R3_G3_B2, for instance, specifies a one-byte (8-bit) RGB color, with 3 bits allotted to the red component, 3 bits for the green component, and 2 bits for blue.

Parameter dataFormat in the texture functions is then used to specify the specific format for the texture elements. We can choose any one of eleven symbolic constants for this parameter. This allows us to specify each texture element as an index into a color table, a single alpha value, a single luminance value, a luminance-alpha pair of values, a single intensity value for one of the RGB components, the three RGB components, or the four components of an RGBA specification in the order BGRA. And the dataType parameter is assigned a value such as GL_BYTE, GL_INT, GL_FLOAT, or a symbolic constant that specifies both data type and bit size. We can choose a value from a set of 20 symbolic constants for the data-type parameter.

OpenGL Texture-Mapping Options

Texture elements can be applied to an object so that the texture values are combined with the current object color components, or the texture values can be used to replace the object color. We select a texture-mapping method with the function

```
glTexEnvi (GL_TEXTURE_ENV, GL_TEXTURE_ENV_MODE,
                applicationMethod);
```

If parameter applicationMethod is assigned the value GL_REPLACE, then the texture color, luminance, intensity, or alpha value replaces the corresponding object value. For example, a texture pattern of alpha values replaces the object alpha values. Similar replacement operations are used with a texture pattern specified with a single luminance or intensity value. A pattern of green intensity values replaces the green components of the object color.

Assigning the value GL_MODULATE to parameter applicationMethod results in a "modulation" of the object color values. That is, current object values are multiplied by the texture values. The specific results depend on the format for the elements in the texture pattern, so that, for example, alpha values modulate alpha values and intensity values modulate intensity values. The default application method for a texture pattern is GL_MODULATE. If an object's color is white (the default object color), the modulate operation produces the same result as a replace operation, depending on how the elements of the texture pattern have been specified.

We can also use the symbolic constant GL_DECAL for the texture-mapping operations, which then employ the RGBA alpha values as transparency coefficients. In this case, the object is treated as if it were transparent with the texture color in the background. If the texture pattern contains only RGB values, with no alpha component, the texture color replaces the object color. Also, in some cases, such as when the texture pattern contains only alpha values, the decal operation is undefined.

When we assign the constant GL_BLEND to parameter applicationMethod, the texture routines perform color blending using a color specified with the function

```
glTexEnv* (GL_TEXTURE_ENV, GL_TEXTURE_ENV_COLOR,
                blendingColor);
```

We append the suffix i or f according to the blending-color data type. And the suffix v is also appended if the blending color is given in an array.

OpenGL Texture Wrapping

When coordinate values in texture space are outside the range from 0 to 1.0, we can choose to replicate the patterns described in a texture array using the command

```
glTexParameter* (texSpace, texWrapCoord, GL_REPEAT);
```

Patterns are replicated using only the fractional part of a texture-space coordinate value. Parameter texSpace is assigned one of the symbolic values GL_TEXTURE_1D, GL_TEXTURE_2D, or GL_TEXTURE_3D, and parameter texWrapCoord designates a texture-space coordinate using either GL_TEXTURE_WRAP_S, GL_TEXTURE_WRAP_T, or GL_TEXTURE_WRAP_R.

To clamp a texture coordinate to the unit interval, we use the symbolic constant GL_CLAMP instead of GL_REPEAT. If a clamped texture coordinate has a value greater than 1.0, it is assigned the value 1.0. Similarly, a clamped texture coordinate that has a value less than 0.0 is assigned the value 0.0. We can specify any combination of repeating and clamping for the coordinates in a particular texture space. The default for all coordinates is GL_REPEAT.

Copying OpenGL Texture Patterns from the Frame Buffer

Either an original pattern or a subpattern can be obtained from values stored in the frame buffer. The following function sets up a two-dimensional pattern for the current texture state using a block of RGBA pixel values.

```
glCopyTexImage2D (GL_TEXTURE_2D, 0, GL_RGBA, x0, y0, texWidth,
                        texHeight, 0);
```

The two 0 values in the argument list again indicate that this pattern is not a reduction and it does not have a border. The frame-buffer position (x0, y0), relative to the lower-left corner of the buffer, references the lower-left corner of a texWidth by texHeight block of pixel colors.

A similar function is available for obtaining a block of pixel colors as a texture subpattern:

```
glCopyTexSubImage2D (GL_TEXTURE_2D, 0, xTexElement,
              yTexElement, x0, y0, texSubWidth, texSubHeight);
```

This block of pixel values is placed in the current pattern at texture-element position (xTexElement, yTexElement). Parameters texSubWidth and texSubHeight give the size of the pixel block, whose lower-left corner is at frame-buffer position (x0, y0).

OpenGL Texture-Coordinate Arrays

As with color data, surface-normal vectors, and polygon edge flags, we can specify texture coordinates in lists that can be combined or associated with vertex arrays (Sections 3-17 and 4-3).

```
glEnableClientState (GL_TEXTURE_COORD_ARRAY);

glTexCoordPointer (nCoords, dataType, offset, texCoordArray);
```

Paramenter nCoords is assigned the value 1, 2, 3, or 4, which designates the dimensionality of the texture pattern. The default value 4 is used to reference texture space in a homogeneous-coordinate form, so that a texture-space position is calculated by dividing the first three coordinate values by the fourth. This form is useful, for example, when the texture pattern is a perspective photograph. Parameter dataType is assigned the constant value GL_SHORT, GL_INT, GL_FLOAT (the default value), or GL_DOUBLE. The byte offset between coordinate positions in array texCoordArray is designated in parameter offset, which has a default value of 0.

Naming OpenGL Texture Patterns

Often it is useful to use several texture patterns in an application, so OpenGL allows multiple, named texture patterns to be created. Then we simply specify which named texture is to be applied at any time. This is a much more efficient method than invoking the glTexImage function each time, since each call to glTexImage requires that the pattern be recreated, possibly from color values in a data file. To name a texture pattern, we select a positive (unsigned) integer before the pattern is defined. As an example, the following statements name, and then activate, the green and red line pattern from our previous example as texture 3.

```
glBindTexture (GL_TEXTURE_1D, 3);
glTexImage1D (GL_TEXTURE_1D, 0, GL_RGBA, 4, 0, GL_RGBA,
                GL_UNSIGNED_BYTE, texLine);

glBindTexture (GL_TEXTURE_1D, 3);
```

The first glBindTexture statement names the pattern, and the second call to glBindTexture designates that pattern as the **current texture state.** If we have created multiple texture patterns, we could call glBindTexture again with another pattern name to activate that texture for application to some object in a scene. For a two-dimensional or three-dimensional pattern, we change the first argument of the glBindTexture function to either GL_TEXTURE_2D or GL_TEXTURE_3D. When a texture name is first invoked, a texture pattern is created using the default values for the pattern parameters.

One or more existing texture patterns are deleted with the command

```
glDeleteTextures (nTextures, texNamesArray);
```

Parameter nTextures specifies the number of pattern names that are listed in array texNamesArray.

We can also let OpenGL select a name for a pattern so that we don't have to keep track of the names that have already been used. For example,

```
static GLuint texName;

glGenTextures (1, texName);
glBindTexture (GL_TEXTURE_2D, texName);
```

As an example, the following code obtains a list of six unused texture names and uses one of them to create a pattern.

```
static GLuint texNamesArray [6];

glGenTextures (1, texNamesArray [3]);
glBindTexture (GL_TEXTURE_2D, texNamesArray [3]);
```

A query command is available in OpenGL to find out if a texture name is in use for an existing pattern:

```
glIsTexture (texName);
```

This function returns the value `GL_TRUE` if `texName` is the name of an existing pattern, otherwise the value `GL_FALSE` is returned. A `GL_FALSE` value is also returned if `texName` = 0 or if an error occurs.

OpenGL Texture Subpatterns

Once a texture pattern has been defined, we can create another pattern, called a subpattern, to modify any part, or all, of the original pattern. The texture values in the subpattern replace specified values in the original pattern. This is usually a more efficient process than recreating a texture with new elements. For example, the following function designates a set of RGBA color values that are to replace a section of a two-dimensional texture that has no border and is not a reduction of a larger pattern.

```
glTexSubImage2D (GL_TEXTURE_2D, 0, xTexElement,
           yTexElement, GL_RGBA, texSubWidth, texSubHeight,
           0, dataFormat, dataType, subSurfTexArray);
```

Parameters `xTexElement` and `yTexElement` are used to select an integer-coordinate position of a texture element within the original pattern, where position (0, 0) references the texture element at the lower-left corner of the pattern. The subpattern is pasted into the original pattern with its lower-left corner at position (`xTexElement`, `yTexElement`). Parameters `TexSubWidth` and `TexSubHeight` give the size of the subpattern. The number of color elements in the array `subSurfTexArray` for a RGBA texture pattern is 4 × `texSubWidth` × `texSubHeight`. Other parameters are the same as in the `glTexImage` function, and similar subpatterns can be set up for one-dimensional and three-dimensional textures.

OpenGL Texture Reduction Patterns

For reduced object sizes, we can use OpenGL routines to create a series of texture reduction patterns, referred to as mip maps (Section 10-17). One way to create a sequence of reduction patterns is to invoke the `glTexImage` function repeatedly using higher integer values for the second argument (the "level number") in the function. The original pattern is referenced as reduction-level number 0. A reduction pattern that is one-half the size of the original pattern is assigned the level number 1, the second one-half size reduction pattern is designated as level number 2, and so on for the other reductions. The `copyTexImage` function also generates a reduction pattern when we set the level number to 1 or higher.

Alternatively, we can have OpenGL generate reduction patterns automatically. For example, RGBA reduction patterns are obtained for a 16 by 16 surface texture using the following GLU function.

```
gluBuild2DMipmaps (GL_TEXTURE_2D, GL_RGBA, 16, 16, GL_RGBA,
                   GL_UNSIGNED_BYTE, surfTexArray);
```

A complete set of four patterns, at the reduced sizes of 8 by 8, 4 by 4, 2 by 2, and 1 by 1, is generated by this function. We can also set up selected reductions using

```
gluBuild2DMipmapLevels (GL_TEXTURE_2D, GL_RGBA, 16, 16,
            GL_RGBA, GL_UNSIGNED_BYTE, 0, minLevel, maxLevel,
            surfTexArray);
```

This function produces reduction patterns for a range of level numbers specified by parameters `minLevel` and `maxLevel`. In each case, the mip maps are constructed for the current texture pattern, specified at level number 0.

We choose a method for determining pixel colors from the reduction patterns using the `glTexParameter` function and the `GL_TEXTURE_MIN_FILTER` symbolic constant. As an example, the following function designates the mapping procedure for a two-dimensional texture pattern.

```
glTexParameter (GL_TEXTURE_2D, GL_TEXTURE_MIN_FILTER,
                GL_NEAREST_MIPMAP_NEAREST);
```

This function specifies that the texture routines should use the reduction pattern that most closely matches the pixel size (`MIPMAP_NEAREST`). A pixel is then assigned the color of the nearest texture element (`GL_NEAREST`) in that reduction pattern. With the symbolic constant `GL_LINEAR_MIPMAP_NEAREST`, we specify a linear combination of texture colors from the nearest reduction pattern. With `GL_NEAREST_MIPMAP_LINEAR` (the default value), we specify an average color calculated from the nearest texture elements in each of the reduction patterns closest to the pixel size. And `GL_LINEAR_MIPMAP_LINEAR` computes a pixel color using a linear combination of texture colors from a set of closest-size reduction patterns.

OpenGL Texture Borders

When multiple textures, or multiple copies of a single texture, are applied to an object, aliasing effects may be apparent at the edges of adjacent patterns when pixel colors are computed by linearly interpolating the texture colors. This can be avoided by including a border with each texture pattern, where border colors match the texture edge colors in the adjacent pattern.

We can designate a texture border color in several ways. The color value in an adjacent pattern can be copied to the border in another pattern using the `glTexSubImage` function, or the border colors can be directly assigned in the texture array specified with the `glTexImage` function. Another option is to set a border color using the `glTexParameter` routine. For example, we can assign a border color for a two-dimensional pattern with

```
glTexParameterfv (GL_TEXTURE_2D, GL_TEXTURE_BORDER_COLOR,
                  borderColor);
```

where parameter `borderColor` is assigned a four-element set of RGBA color components. The default border color is black (0.0, 0.0, 0.0, 0.0).

OpenGL Proxy Textures

In any of the glTexImage functions, we can set the first argument to a symbolic constant, called a texture proxy. The purpose of this constant is to hold the definition of the texture pattern until we find out if there are enough resources to handle this pattern. For a two-dimensional pattern, the proxy constant is GL_PROXY_TEXTURE_2D, and similar constants are available for linear and volumetric texture patterns. Once we have set up the texture proxy, we use glGetTexLevelFunction to determine whether specific parameter values can be accommodated.

As an example of using a texture proxy, the following statements query the system to determine whether the height specified for a two-dimensional pattern can be used.

```
GLint texHeight;

glTexImage2D (GL_PROXY_TEXTURE_2D, 0, GL_RGBA12, 16, 16, 0,
                GL_RGBA, GL_UNSIGNED_BYTE, NULL);
glGetTexLevelParameteriv (GL_PROXY_TEXTURE_2D, 0, GL_RGBA12,
                            GL_TEXTURE_HEIGHT, &texHeight);
```

If the system cannot accommodate the requested pattern height (16, in this case), a value of 0 is returned in parameter texHeight. Otherwise, the value returned is the value requested. Other pattern parameters can be queried similarly using symbolic constants such as GL_TEXTURE_WIDTH, GL_TEXTURE_DEPTH, GL_TEXTURE_BORDER, and GL_TEXTURE_BLUE_SIZE. In each case, a returned value of 0 indicates that the requested parameter value in the glTexImage function cannot be accommodated. For floating-point data values, we replace the suffix code i with the code f.

Although we might obtain an affirmative answer for a proposed texture, we still might not be able to store the pattern in memory. This can occur when another pattern is occupying the available memory.

Automatic Texturing of Quadric Surfaces

Routines are available in OpenGL for automatically generating texture coordinates in certain applications. This feature is particularly useful when it may be difficult to directly determine surface coordinates for an object, and a GLU function is available for applying these routines to quadric surfaces.

To map a texture pattern to a quadric surface, we first set up the parameters for the texture space. Then we invoke the following function and define the quadric object, as described in Section 8-6.

```
gluQuadricTexture (quadSurfObj, GL_TRUE)
```

Parameter quadSurfObj in this function is the name of the quadric object. If we want to deactivate the texturing of the quadric surface, we change the symbolic constant GL_TRUE to GL_FALSE.

Homogeneous Texture Coordinates

A four-dimensional texture-space position is specified with

```
glTexCoord4* (sCoord, tCoord, rCoord, htexCoord);
```

Texture coordinates are transformed using a 4 by 4 matrix in the same way that scene coordinates are transformed: Each coordinate is divided by the homogeneous parameter (Section 5-2). Thus, the values for the texture coordinates s, t, and r in the above function are divided by the homogeneous parameter h_{tex} to produce an actual texture-space position.

Homogeneous coordinates in texture space are useful when multiple perspective effects are combined in one display. For example, a perspective view of an object may include a texture pattern produced with a different perspective-projection transformation. The texture pattern can then be modified using homogeneous texture coordinates to adjust the texture perspective. Many other effects are possible using homogeneous texture coordinates to manipulate a texture mapping.

Additional OpenGL Texture Options

Functions are available in OpenGL for performing many other texture manipulations and applications. If we obtain a texture pattern (from a photograph or other source) that is not a power of 2, OpenGL provides a function to modify the size of the pattern. In some implementations of OpenGL, multitexturing routines are available for pasting multiple texture patterns onto an object. Environment-mapping can by simulated in OpenGL by creating a texture map in the shape of a spherical surface, and texture coordinates for spherical environment patterns, as well as other texture applications, can be automatically generated.

10-22 SUMMARY

In general, an object is illuminated with radiant energy from light emitters and from the reflective surfaces in a scene. Light sources can be modeled as point objects or they can have an extended size. In addition, light sources can be directional, and they can be treated as infinitely distant sources or as local light sources. Radial attenuation is typically applied to transmitted light using an inverse quadratic function of distance, and spotlights can be angularly attenuated as well. Reflecting surfaces in a scene are opaque, completely transparent, or partially transparent. And lighting effects are described in terms of diffuse and specular components for both reflections and refractions.

Light intensity at a surface position is calculated using an illumination model, and the basic illumination model in most graphics packages uses simplified approximations of physical laws. These lighting calculations provide a light-intensity value for each RGB component of the reflected light from a surface position, and for the transmitted light through a transparent object. The basic illumination model typically accommodates multiple light sources as point emitters, but they can be distant sources, local sources, or spotlights. Ambient light for a scene is described with a fixed intensity for each RGB color component and for all surfaces. Diffuse-intensity reflections from a surface are taken to be proportional to the cosine of the angular distance from the direction of the surface normal. Specular-intensity reflections are computed using the Phong model. And transparency effects are usually approximated using a simple transparency coefficient for a material, although accurate refraction effects can be modeled using Snell's law. Shadow effects from the individual light sources can be added by identifying the regions in a scene that are not visible from the light source. Also, the calculations necessary for obtaining light reflections and transmission effects for translucent materials are not usually part of a basic illumination model, but we can model them using methods that disperse the diffuse light components.

Intensity values calculated with an illumination model are mapped to the intensity levels available on the display system in use. A logarithmic intensity scale is used by systems to provide a set of intensity levels that increase with equal perceived brightness differentials. Gamma correction is applied to intensity values to correct for the nonlinearity of display devices. With bilevel monitors, we can use halftone patterns and dithering techniques to simulate a range of intensity values. Halftone approximations can also be used to increase the number of intensity options on systems that are capable of displaying more than two intensities per pixel. Ordered-dither, error-diffusion, and dot-diffusion methods are used to simulate a range of intensities when the number of points to be plotted in a scene is equal to the number of pixels on the display device.

Surface rendering in graphics packages is accomplished by applying the calculations from the basic illumination model to scan-line procedures that extrapolate the intensity values from a few surface points to all projected pixel positions of a surface. With constant-intensity surface rendering, also called flat rendering, we use one calculated color to display all points of a surface. Flat surface rendering is accurate for polyhedrons or curved-surface polygon meshes when the viewing and light-source positions are far from the objects in a scene. Gouraud surface rendering approximates light reflections from tessellated curved surfaces by calculating intensity values at polygon vertices and linearly interpolating these intensity values across the polygon facets. A more accurate, but slower, surface-rendering procedure is Phong surface rendering, which interpolates the average normal vectors for polygon vertices over the polygon facets. Then, the basic illumination model is employed to compute surface intensities at each projected surface position, using the interpolated values for the surface normal vectors. Fast Phong surface rendering uses Taylor series approximations to reduce processing time for the intensity calculations.

Ray tracing is a method for obtaining global, specular reflection and transmission effects by tracing light paths through a scene to pixel positions. Pixel rays are traced through a scene, bouncing from object to object while accumulating intensity contributions. A ray-tracing tree is constructed for each pixel, and intensity values are combined from the terminal nodes of the tree back up to the root. Object-intersection calculations in ray tracing can be reduced with space-subdivision methods that test for ray-object intersections only within subregions of the total space. Distributed ray tracing employs multiple rays per pixel, randomly assigning various ray parameters, such as direction and time. This provides an accurate method for modeling surface gloss and translucency, finite camera apertures, extended light sources, shadow effects, and motion blur.

Radiosity methods provide accurate modeling for diffuse-reflection effects by calculating radiant energy transfer between the various surface patches in a scene. Progressive refinement is used to speed up the radiosity calculations by considering energy transfer from one surface patch at a time. Highly photo-realistic scenes are generated using a combination of ray tracing and radiosity.

A fast method for approximating global illumination effects is environment mapping. An environment array is used to store background intensity information for a scene. This array is then mapped to the objects in a scene based on the specified viewing direction.

Photon mapping provides an accurate and efficient model for global illumination in complex scenes. Random rays are generated from the light sources, and the illumination effects for each ray are stored in a photon map, which separates the lighting information from the scene geometry. The accuracy of the illumination effects improves as more rays are generated.

Surface detail can be added to objects using polygon facets, texture mapping, bump mapping, or frame mapping. Small polygon facets can be overlaid on larger surfaces to provide various kinds of designs. Alternatively, texture patterns can be defined in one-dimensional, two-dimensional, and three-dimensional spaces, which can be used to add texture to a line, a surface, or a volume of space. Procedural texture mapping uses functions to calculate variations in object lighting effects. Bump mapping is a means for modeling surface irregularities by applying a bump function to perturb surface normal vectors. Frame mapping is an extension of bump mapping that can be used to model characteristics of anisotropic materials by allowing for horizontal surface variations, as well as vertical variations.

The core library of OpenGL contains an extensive set of functions for setting up point light sources, specifying the various parameters in the basic illumination model, selecting a surface-rendering method, activating halftone-approximation routines, and for applying texture array patterns to objects. Tables 10-2 and 10-3 provide a summary of these OpenGL illumination, surface-rendering, and texture-mapping functions.

TABLE 10-2

SUMMARY OF OpenGL ILLUMINATION AND SURFACE-RENDERING FUNCTIONS

Function	*Description*
`glLight`	Specify a light-source property value.
`glEnable (lightName)`	Activate a light source.
`glLightModel`	Specify global-lighting parameter values.
`glMaterial`	Specify a value for an optical surface parameter.
`glFog`	Specify a value for an atmosphere parameter; activate atmospheric effects with the `glEnable` function.
`glColor4f (R, G, B, A)`	Specify an alpha value for a surface to simulate transparency. In the function `glBlendFunc`, set the source blending factor to `GL_SRC_ALPHA` and the destination blending factor to `GL_ONE_MINUS_SRC_ALPHA`.
`glShadeModel`	Specify either Gouraud surface rendering or single-color surface rendering.
`glNormal3`	Specify a surface-normal vector.
`glEnable (GL_NORMALIZE)`	Specify that surface normals are to be converted to unit vectors.

Function	Description
`glEnableClientState (GL_NORMAL_ARRAY)`	Activate processing routines for an array of surface-normal vectors.
`glNormalPointer`	Create a list of surface-normal vectors that are to be used with a vertex array.
`glEnable (GL_DITHER)`	Activate operations for applying surface rendering as halftone approximation patterns.

TABLE 10-3

SUMMARY OF OpenGL TEXTURE-MAPPING FUNCTIONS

Function	Description
`glTexImage1D`	Specify parameters for setting up a one-dimensional texture space. (Activate texturing with `glEnable`.)
`glTexImage2D`	Specify parameters for setting up a two-dimensional texture space.
`glTexImage3D`	Specify parameters for setting up a three-dimensional texture space.
`glTexParameter`	Specify parameters for the texture-mapping routines.
`glTexCoord`	Specify a value for a texture coordinate in one-dimensional, two-dimensional, three-dimensional, or four-dimensional texture space.
`glTexEnv`	Specify texture-environment parameters, such as a blending color for texture mapping.
`glCopyTexImage`	Copy a block of frame-buffer pixel colors for use as a texture pattern.
`glCopyTexSubImage`	Copy a block of frame-buffer pixel colors for use as a texture subimage.
`glTexCoordPointer`	Specify texture coordinates in a list that is associated with a vertex list.
`glBindTexture`	Assign a name to a texture pattern; also used to activate a named pattern.
`glDeleteTextures`	Eliminate a list of named textures.
`glGenTextures`	Automatically generate texture names.

(continued)

Function	Description
glIsTexture	Query command to determine whether a named texture exists.
glTexSubImage	Create a texture subpattern.
gluBuild*Mipmaps	Automatic generation of texture reduction patterns for a one-dimensional, two-dimensional, or three-dimensional texture space.
gluBuild*MipmapLevels	Automatic generation of texture reduction patterns for a specified level for a one-dimensional, two-dimensional, or three-dimensional texture space.
glGetTexLevelParameter	Query the system to determine whether a texture parameter value can be accommodated.
gluQuadricTexture	Activate or deactivate texturing for a quadric surface.

REFERENCES

Basic illumination models and surface-rendering techniques are discussed in Gouraud (1971) and Phong (1975), Freeman (1980), Bishop and Wiemer (1986), Birn (2000), Akenine-Möller and Haines (2002), and Olano, Hart, Heidrich, and McCool (2002). Implementation algorithms for illumination models and rendering methods are presented in Glassner (1990), Arvo (1991), Kirk (1992), Heckbert (1994), Paeth (1995), and Sakaguchi, Kent, and Cox (2001). Halftoning methods are given in Velho and Gomes (1991). For further information on ordered dither, error diffusion, and dot diffusion see Knuth (1987).

Ray-tracing procedures are treated in Whitted (1980), Amanatides (1984), Cook, Porter, and Carpenter (1984), Kay and Kajiya (1986), Arvo and Kirk (1987), Quek and Hearn (1988), Glassner (1989), Shirley (1990 and 2000), and Koh and Hearn (1992). Algorithms for radiosity methods can be found in Goral, Torrance, Greenberg, and Battaile (1984), Cohen and Greenberg (1985), Cohen, Chen, Wallace, and Greenberg (1988), Wallace, Elmquist, and Haines (1989), Chen, Rushmeier, Miller, and Turner (1991), Dorsey, Sillion, and Greenberg (1991), Sillion, Arvo, Westin, and Greenberg (1991), He, Heynen, Phillips, Torrance, Salesin, and Greenberg (1992), Cohen and Wallace (1993), Lischinski, Tampieri, and Greenberg (1993). Schoeneman, Dorsey, Smits, Arvo, and Greenberg (1993), and Sillicon and Puech (1994). Photon-mapping algorithms are detailed in Jensen (2001). Texture-mapping methods and applications are discussed in Williams (1983), Segal, Korobkin, van Widenfelt, Foran, and Haeberli (1992), and Demers (2002). A general discussion of energy propagation, transfer equations, rendering processes, and our perception of light and color is given in Glassner (1995).

Additional programming examples using OpenGL illumination and rendering functions are given in Woo, Neider, Davis, and Shreiner (1999). Programming examples for the OpenGL lighting, rendering, and texture functions are also available at Nate Robins's tutorial Web site: http://www.cs.utah.edu/~narobins/opengl.html. And a complete listing of OpenGL illumination and rendering functions is provided in Shreiner (2000).

EXERCISES

10-1 Write a routine to implement Eq. 10-12 for diffuse reflection using a single point light source and constant surface rendering for the faces of a tetrahedron. The object description is to be given in polygon tables, including surface normal vectors for each of the polygon faces. Additional input parameters include the ambient intensity, light-source intensity, and surface reflection coefficients. All coordinate information can be specified directly in the viewing reference frame.

10-2 Modify the routine in Exercise 10-1 to render the polygon facets of a tessellated spherical surface.

10-3 Modify the routine in Exercise 10-2 to display the spherical surface using Gouraud surface rendering.

10-4 Modify the routine in Exercise 10-3 to display the spherical surface using Phong surface rendering.

10-5 Write a routine to implement Eq. 10-17 for diffuse and specular reflections using a single point light source and Gouraud surface rendering for the polygon facets of a tessellated spherical surface. The object description is to be given in polygon tables, including surface normal vectors for each of the polygon faces. Additional input includes values for the ambient intensity, light-source intensity, surface reflection coefficients, and specular-reflection parameter. All coordinate information can be specified directly in the viewing reference frame.

10-6 Modify the routine in preceding exercise to display the polygon facets using Phong surface rendering.

10-7 Modify the routine in the preceding exercise to include a linear intensity attenuation function.

10-8 Modify the routine in the preceding exercise to include two light sources in the scene.

10-9 Modify the routine in the preceding exercise so that the spherical surface is viewed through a pane of glass.

10-10 Discuss the differences you might expect to see in the appearance of specular reflections modeled with $(\mathbf{N} \cdot \mathbf{H})^{n_s}$ compared to specular reflections modeled with $(\mathbf{V} \cdot \mathbf{R})^{n_s}$.

10-11 Verify that $2\alpha = \phi$ in Fig. 10-22 when all vectors are coplanar, but that, in general, $2\alpha \neq \phi$.

10-12 Discuss how the different visible-surface detection methods can be combined with an intensity model for displaying a set of polyhedrons with opaque surfaces.

10-13 Discuss how the various visible-surface detection methods can be modified to process transparent objects. Are there any visible-surface detection methods that cannot handle transparent surfaces?

10-14 Set up an algorithm, based on one of the visible-surface detection methods, that will identify shadow areas in a scene illuminated by a distant point source.

10-15 How many intensity levels can be displayed with halftone approximations using n by n pixel grids, where each pixel can be displayed with m different intensities?

10-16 How many different color combinations can be generated using halftone approximations on a two-level RGB system with a 3 by 3 pixel grid?

10-17 Write a routine to display a given set of surface-intensity variations, using halftone approximations with 3 by 3 pixel grids and two intensity levels (0 and 1) per pixel.

10-18 Write a routine to generate ordered-dither matrices using the recurrence relation in Eq. 10-48.

10-19 Write a procedure to display a given array of intensity values using the ordered-dither method.

10-20 Write a procedure to implement the error-diffusion algorithm for a given m by n array of intensity values.

10-21 Write a program to implement the basic ray-tracing algorithm for a scene containing a single sphere hovering over a checkerboard ground square. The scene is to be illuminated with a single point light source at the viewing position.

10-22 Write a program to implement the basic ray-tracing algorithm for a scene containing any specified arrangement of spheres and polygon surfaces illuminated by a given set of point light sources.

10-23 Write a program to implement the basic ray-tracing algorithm using space-subdivision methods for any specified arrangement of spheres and polygon surfaces illuminated by a given set of point light sources.

10-24 Write a program to implement the following features of distributed ray tracing: pixel sampling with 16 jittered rays per pixel, distributed reflection directions (gloss), distributed refraction directions (translucency), and extended light sources.

10-25 Set up an algorithm for modeling the motion blur of a moving object using distributed ray tracing.

10-26 Implement the basic radiosity algorithm for rendering the inside surfaces of a rectangle when one inside face of the rectangle is a light source.

10-27 Devise an algorithm for implementing the progressive-refinement radiosity method.

10-28 Write a routine to transform an environment map to the surface of a sphere.

10-29 Write a program to map a given texture pattern onto any face of a cube.

10-30 Modify the program in the preceding exercise so that the pattern is mapped to one face of a tetrahedron.

10-31 Modify the program in the preceding exercise so that the pattern is mapped to a specified section of a spherical surface.

10-32 Write a program to map a given one-dimensional texture pattern onto a specified face of a cube as a diagonal stripe.

10-33 Modify the program in the preceding example so that the one-dimensional texture is mapped to the surface of a sphere, given two points on the spherical surface.

10-34 Given a spherical surface, write a bump-mapping procedure to simulate the bumpy surface of an orange.

10-35 Write a bump-mapping routine to produce surface-normal variations for any specified bump function.

10-36 Write an OpenGL program to display a scene containing a sphere and a tetrahedron illuminated by two light sources: one is to be a local red source and the other a distant white-light source. Set surface parameters for both diffuse and specular reflections with Gouraud surface rendering, and apply a quadratic intensity-attenuation function.

10-37 Modify the program in the preceding exercise so that the single local red source is replaced with two spotlights: one red and one blue.

10-38 Modify the program in the preceding exercise so that a smoky atmosphere is added to the scene.

10-39 Modify the program in the preceding exercise so that the scene is viewed through a semitransparent pane of glass.

10-40 Write a complete OpenGL program to display a set of diagonal lines using various one-dimensional texture patterns as in Fig. 10-114.

10-41 Write a program using a two-dimensional OpenGL texture pattern to display a black-and-white checkerboard on a blue background.

10-42 Modify the program in the preceding exercise so that the checkerboard has red and blue squares and the background is white.

10-43 Write a program using a two-dimensional OpenGL texture pattern to display a white rectangle with a set of evenly spaced diagonal red strips. Set the background color to blue.

10-44 Modify the program in the preceding exercise to map the texture pattern onto the surface of a sphere.

10-45 Modify the program in the preceding exercise to map the texture pattern onto the surface of the GLUT teapot.

CHAPTER 11

Interactive Input Methods and Graphical User Interfaces

Interactive input within the virtual-reality environment called the NCSA CAVE, which is formed with three vertical walls, a floor, a ceiling, and a stereoscopic projection system. *(Courtesy of the National Center for Supercomputing Applications, University of Illinois at Urbana-Champaign.)*

lthough we can construct programs and provide input data using the methods and program commands discussed in the previous chapters, it is often useful to be able to specify graphical input interactively. During the execution of a program, for example, we might want to change the view point or the location of an object in a scene by pointing to a screen position, or we might want to change animation parameters using menu selections. In design applications, control-point coordinates for spline constructions are chosen interactively, and pictures are often constructed using interactive painting or drawing methods. There are several kinds of data that are used by a graphics program, and a variety of interactive input methods have been devised for processing these data values. In addition, interfaces for systems now involve extensive interactive graphics, including display windows, icons, menus, and a mouse or other cursor-control devices.

11-1 GRAPHICAL INPUT DATA

Graphics programs use several kinds of input data, such as coordinate positions, attribute values, character-string specifications, geometric-transformation values, viewing conditions, and illumination parameters. Many graphics packages, including the ISO and ANSI standards, provide an extensive set of input functions for processing such data. But input procedures require interaction with display-window managers and specific hardware devices. Therefore, some graphics systems, particularly those that provide mainly device-independent functions, often include relatively few interactive procedures for dealing with input data.

A standard organization for input procedures in a graphics package is to classify the functions according to the type of data that is to be processed by each function. This scheme allows any physical device, such as a keyboard or a mouse, to input any data class, although most input devices can handle some data types better than others.

11-2 LOGICAL CLASSIFICATION OF INPUT DEVICES

When input functions are classified according to data type, any device that is used to provide the specified data is referred to as a **logical input device** for that data type. The standard logical input-data classifications are

LOCATOR	- A device for specifying one coordinate position.
STROKE	- A device for specifying a set of coordinate positions.
STRING	- A device for specifying text input.
VALUATOR	- A device for specifying a scalar value.
CHOICE	- A device for selecting a menu option.
PICK	- A device for selecting a component of a picture.

Locator Devices

Interactive selection of a coordinate point is usually accomplished by positioning the screen cursor at some location in a displayed scene, although other methods, such as menu options, could be used in certain applications. We can use a mouse, joystick, trackball, spaceball, thumbwheel, dial, hand cursor, or digitizer stylus for screen-cursor positioning. And various buttons, keys, or switches can be used to indicate processing options for the selected location.

Keyboards are used for locator input in several ways. A general-purpose keyboard usually has four cursor-control keys that move the screen cursor up, down, left, and right. With an additional four keys, we can move the cursor diagonally as well. Rapid cursor movement is accomplished by holding down the selected cursor key. Sometimes a keyboard includes a joystick, joydisk, trackball, or thumbwheels for positioning the screen cursor. For some applications, it may also be convenient to use a keyboard to type in numerical values or other codes to indicate coordinate positions.

Other devices, such as a light pen, have also been used for interactive input of coordinate positions. But light pens record screen positions by detecting light from the screen phosphors, and this requires special implementation procedures.

Stroke Devices

This class of logical devices is used to input a sequence of coordinate positions, and the physical devices used for generating locator input are also used as stroke devices. Continuous movement of a mouse, trackball, joystick, or hand cursor is translated into a series of input coordinate values. The graphics tablet is one of the more common stroke devices. Button activation can be used to place the tablet into "continuous" mode. As the cursor is moved across the tablet surface, a stream of coordinate values is generated. This procedure is used in paintbrush systems to generate drawings using various brush strokes. Engineering systems also use this process to trace and digitize layouts.

String Devices

The primary physical device used for string input is the keyboard. Character strings in computer-graphics applications are typically used for picture or graph labeling.

Other physical devices can be used for generating character patterns for special applications. Individual characters can be sketched on the screen using a stroke or locator-type device. A pattern recognition program then interprets the characters using a stored dictionary of predefined patterns.

Valuator Devices

We can employ valuator input in a graphics program to set scalar values for geometric transformations, viewing parameters, and illumination parameters. In some applications, scalar input is also used for setting physical parameters such as temperature, voltage, or stress-strain factors.

A typical physical device used to provide valuator input is a panel of control dials. Dial settings are calibrated to produce numerical values within some predefined range. Rotary potentiometers convert dial rotation into a corresponding voltage, which is then translated into a number within a defined scalar range, such as −10.5 to 25.5. Instead of dials, slide potentiometers are sometimes used to convert linear movements into scalar values.

Any keyboard with a set of numeric keys can be used as a valuator device. Although dials and slide potentiometers are more efficient for fast input.

Joysticks, trackballs, tablets, and other interactive devices can be adapted for valuator input by interpreting pressure or movement of the device relative to a scalar range. For one direction of movement, say left to right, increasing scalar values can be input. Movement in the opposite direction decreases the scalar input value. Selected values are usually echoed on the screen for verification.

Another technique for providing valuator input is to display graphical representations of sliders, buttons, rotating scales, and menus on the video monitor. Figure 11-1 illustrates some possibilities for scale representations. Cursor positioning, using a mouse, joystick, spaceball, or other device, selects a value on one of the scales. As a feedback mechanism for the user, selected colors are displayed in color bars and a selected scalar value is displayed in a small window next to each scale.

Choice Devices

Menus are typically used in graphics programs to select processing options, parameter values, and object shapes that are to be used in constructing a picture. Commonly used choice devices for selecting a menu option are cursor-positioning devices such as a mouse, trackball, keyboard, touch panel, or button box.

Keyboard function keys or separate button boxes are often used to enter menu selections. Each button or function key is programmed to select a particular

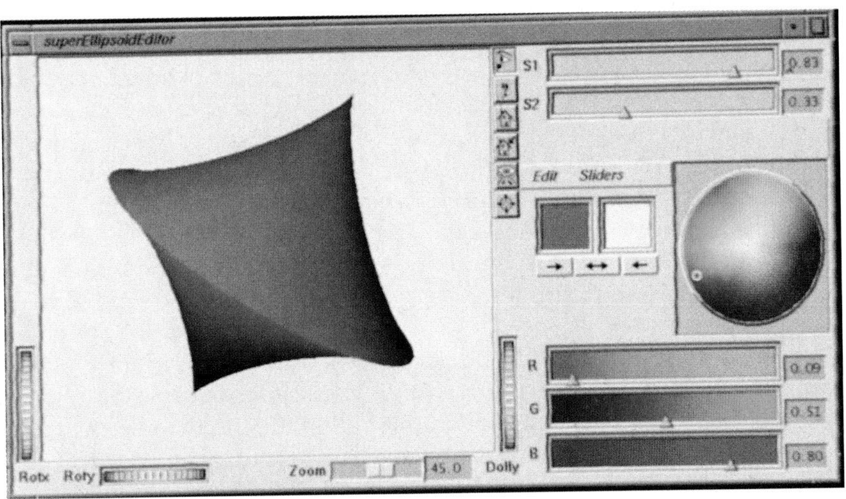

FIGURE 11-1 Graphical scale representations for valuator input. In this display, slider and thumbwheel representations are provided for selecting superellipse scalar-parameter values $s1$ and $s2$, RGB color components, rotation angles, and zoom parameters. Alternatively, a small circle can be positioned on the color wheel for selecting the three RGB components simultaneously. Keyboard arrow keys or buttons can also be used to make small changes in a selected scalar value.

operation or value, although preset buttons or keys are sometimes included on an input device.

For screen selection of listed menu options, we use a cursor-positioning device. When a screen-cursor position (x, y) is selected, it is compared to the coordinate extents of each listed menu item. A menu item with vertical and horizontal boundaries at the coordinate values x_{min}, x_{max}, y_{min}, and y_{max} is selected if the input coordinates satisfy the inequalities

$$x_{min} \leq x \leq x_{max}, \qquad y_{min} \leq y \leq y_{max} \tag{11-1}$$

For larger menus with relatively few options displayed, a touch panel is commonly used. A selected screen position is compared to the coordinate extents of the individual menu options to determine what process is to be performed.

Alternate methods for choice input include keyboard and voice entry. A standard keyboard can be used to type in commands or menu options. For this method of choice input, some abbreviated format is useful. Menu listings can be numbered or given short identifying names. A similar encoding scheme can be used with voice input systems. Voice input is particularly useful when the number of options is small (20 or fewer).

Pick Devices

We use a pick device to select a part of a scene that is to be transformed or edited in some way. Several different methods can be used to select a component of a displayed scene, and any input mechanism used for this purpose is classified as a pick device. Most often, pick operations are performed by positioning the screen cursor. Using a mouse, joystick, or keyboard, for example, we can perform picking by positioning the screen cursor and pressing a button or key to record the pixel coordinates. This screen position can then be used to select an entire object, a facet of a tessellated surface, a polygon edge, or a vertex. Other pick methods include highlighting schemes, selecting objects by name, or a combination of methods.

Using the cursor-positioning approach, a pick procedure could map a selected screen position to a world-coordinate location using the inverse viewing and geometric transformations that were specified for the scene. Then, the world-coordinate position can be compared to the coordinate extents of objects. If the pick position is within the coordinate extents of a single object, the pick object has been identified. The object name, coordinates, or other information about the object can then be used to apply the desired transformation or editing operations. But if the pick position is within the coordinate extents of two or more objects, further testing is necessary. Depending on the type of object to be selected and the complexity of a scene, several levels of search may be required to identify the pick object. For example, if we are attempting to pick a sphere whose coordinate extents overlap the coordinate extents of some other three-dimensional object, the pick position could be compared to the coordinate extents of the individual surface facets of the two objects. If this test fails, the coordinate extents of individual line segments can be tested.

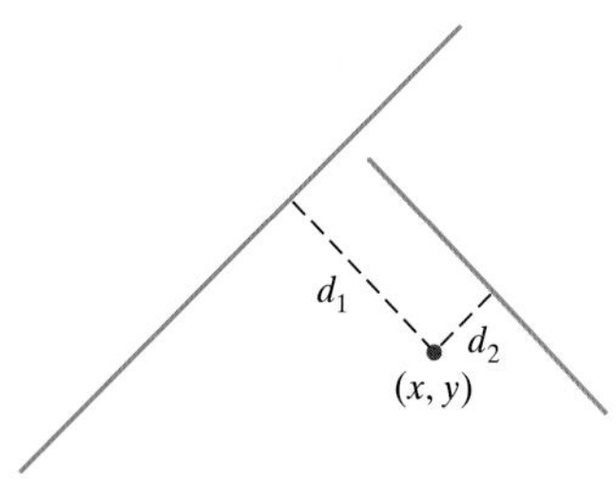

FIGURE 11-2 Distances to line segments from a pick position.

When coordinate-extent tests do not uniquely identify a pick object, the distances from the pick position to individual line segments could be computed. Figure 11-2 illustrates a pick position that is within the coordinate extents of two line segments. For a two-dimensional line segment with pixel endpoint coordinates (x_1, y_1) and (x_2, y_2), the perpendicular distance squared from a pick position

(x, y) to the line is calculated as

$$d^2 = \frac{[\Delta x(y - y_1) - \Delta y(x - x_1)]^2}{\Delta x^2 + \Delta y^2} \tag{11-2}$$

where $\Delta x = x_2 - x_1$ and $\Delta y = y_2 - y_1$. Other methods, such as comparing distances to endpoint positions, have been proposed to simplify the line-picking operations.

Pick procedures can be simplified if coordinate-extent testing is not carried out for the surface facets and line segments of an object. When the pick position is within the coordinate extents of two or more objects, the pick procedures can simply return a list of all candidate pick objects.

Another picking technique is to associate a **pick window** with a selected cursor position. The pick window is centered on the cursor position, as shown in Fig. 11-3, and clipping procedures are used to determine which objects intersect the pick window. For line picking, we can set the pick-window dimensions w and h to very small values, so that only one line segment intersects the pick window. Some graphics packages implement three-dimensional picking by reconstructing a scene using the viewing and projection transformations with the pick window as the clipping window. Nothing is displayed from this reconstruction, but clipping procedures are applied to determine which objects are within the pick view volume. A list of information for each object in the pick view volume can then be returned for processing. This list can contain information such as object name and depth range, where the depth range could be used to select the nearest object in the pick view volume.

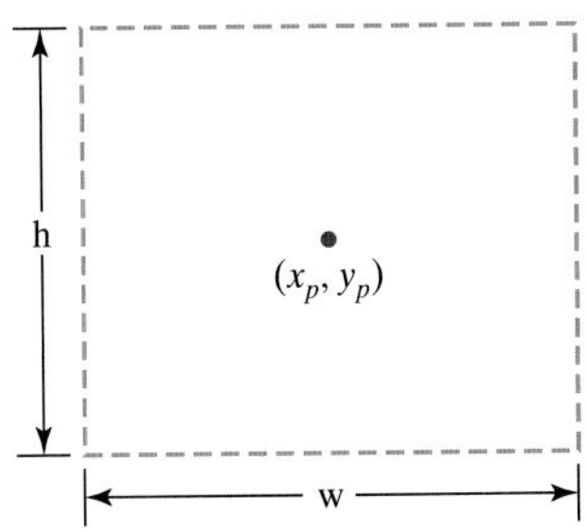

FIGURE 11-3 A pick window with center coordinates (x_p, y_p), width w, and height h.

Highlighting can also be used to facilitate picking. One way to do this is to successively highlight those objects whose coordinate extents overlap a pick position (or pick window). As each object is highlighted, a user could issue a "reject" or "accept" action using keyboard keys. The sequence stops when the user accepts a highlighted object as the pick object. Picking could also be accomplished simply by successively highlighting all objects in the scene without selecting a cursor position. The highlighting sequence can be initiated with a button or function key, and a second button can be used to stop the process when the desired object is highlighted. If very many objects are to be searched in this way, additional buttons can be used to speed up the highlighting process. One button initiates a rapid successive highlighting of structures. A second button is activated to stop the process, and a third button is used to slowly back up through the highlighting process. Finally, a stop button could be pressed to complete the pick procedure.

If picture components can be selected by name, keyboard input can be used to pick an object. This is a straightforward, but less interactive, pick-selection method. Some graphics packages allow picture components to be named at various levels down to the individual primitives. Descriptive names can be used to help a user in the pick process, but this approach has drawbacks. It is generally slower than interactive picking on the screen, and a user will probably need prompts to remember the various structure names.

11-3 INPUT FUNCTIONS FOR GRAPHICAL DATA

Graphics packages that use the logical classification for input devices provide several functions for selecting devices and data classes. These functions allow a user to specify the following options.

- The input interaction mode for the graphics program and the input devices. Either the program or the devices can initiate data entry, or both can operate simultaneously.
- Selection of a physical device that is to provide input within a particular logical classification (for example, a tablet used as a stroke device).
- Selection of the input time and device for a particular set of data values.

Input Modes

Some input functions in an interactive graphics system are used to specify how the program and input devices should interact. A program could request input at a particular time in the processing (request mode), or an input device could independently provide updated input (sample mode), or the device could independently store all collected data (event mode).

In **request mode,** the application program initiates data entry. When input values are requested, processing is suspended until the required values are received. This input mode corresponds to the typical input operation in a general programming language. The program and the input devices operate alternately. Devices are put into a wait state until an input request is made; then the program waits until the data are delivered.

In **sample mode,** the application program and input devices operate independently. Input devices may be operating at the same time that the program is processing other data. New values obtained from the input devices replace previously input data values. When the program requires new data, it samples the current values that have been stored from the device input.

In **event mode,** the input devices initiate data input to the application program. The program and the input devices again operate concurrently, but now the input devices deliver data to an input queue, also called an event queue. All input data is saved. When the program requires new data, it goes to the data queue.

Typically, any number of devices can be operating at the same time in sample and event modes. Some can be operating in sample mode, while others are operating in event mode. But only one device at a time can deliver input in request mode.

Other functions in the input library are used to specify physical devices for the logical data classes. The input procedures in an interactive package can involve complicated processing for some kinds of input. For instance, to obtain a world-coordinate position, the input procedures must process an input screen location back through the viewing and other transformations to the original world-coordinate description of a scene. And this processing also involves information from the display-window routines.

Echo Feedback

Requests can usually be made in an interactive input program for an echo of input data and associated parameters. When an echo of the input data is requested, it is displayed within a specified screen area. Echo feedback can include, for example, the size of the pick window, the minimum pick distance, the type and size of a cursor, the type of highlighting to be employed during pick operations, the range (min and max) for valuator input, and the resolution (scale) for valuator input.

Callback Functions

For device-independent graphics packages, a limited set of input functions can be provided in an auxiliary library. Input procedures can then be handled as callback functions (Section 2-9) that interact with the system software. These functions specify what actions are to be taken by a program when an input event occurs. Typical input events are moving a mouse, pressing a mouse button, or pressing a key on the keyboard.

11-4 INTERACTIVE PICTURE-CONSTRUCTION TECHNIQUES

A variety of interactive methods are often incorporated into a graphics package as aids in the construction of pictures. Routines can be provided for positioning objects, applying constraints, adjusting the sizes of objects, and designing shapes and patterns.

Basic Positioning Methods

We can interactively choose a coordinate position with a pointing device that records a screen location. How the position is used depends on the selected processing option. The coordinate location could be an endpoint position for a new line segment, or it could be used to position some object—for instance, the selected screen location could reference a new position for the center of a sphere. Or the location could be used to specify the position for a text string, which could begin at that location or it could be centered on that location. As an additional positioning aid, numeric values for selected positions can be echoed on the screen. With the echoed coordinate values as a guide, a user could make small interactive adjustments in the coordinate values using dials, arrow keys, or other devices.

Dragging

Another interactive positioning technique is to select an object and drag it to a new location. Using a mouse, for instance, we position the cursor at the object position, press a mouse button, move the cursor to a new position, and release the button. The object is then displayed at the new cursor location. Usually, the object is displayed at intermediate positions as the screen cursor moves.

Constraints

Any procedure for altering input coordinate values to obtain a particular orientation or alignment of an object is called a constraint. For example, an input line segment can be constrained to be horizontal or vertical, as illustrated in Figs. 11-4 and 11-5. To implement this type of constraint, we compare the input coordinate values at the two endpoints. If the difference in the y values of the two endpoints is smaller than the difference in the x values, a horizontal line is displayed. Otherwise, a vertical line is drawn. The horizontal-vertical constraint is useful, for instance, in forming network layouts, and it eliminates the need for precise positioning of endpoint coordinates.

Other kinds of constraints can be applied to input coordinates to produce a variety of alignments. Lines could be constrained to have a particular slant, such as 45°, and input coordinates could be constrained to lie along predefined paths, such as circular arcs.

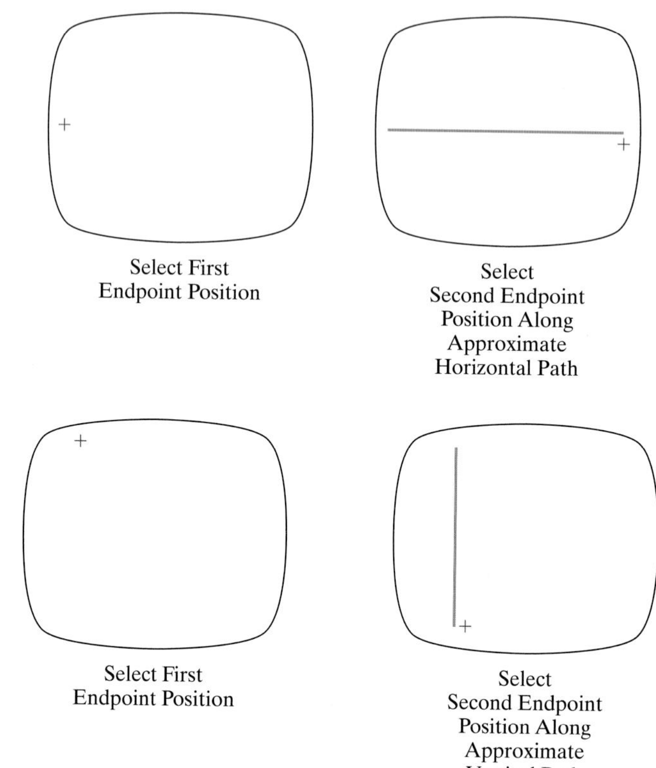

FIGURE 11-4 Horizontal line constraint.

FIGURE 11-5 Vertical line constraint.

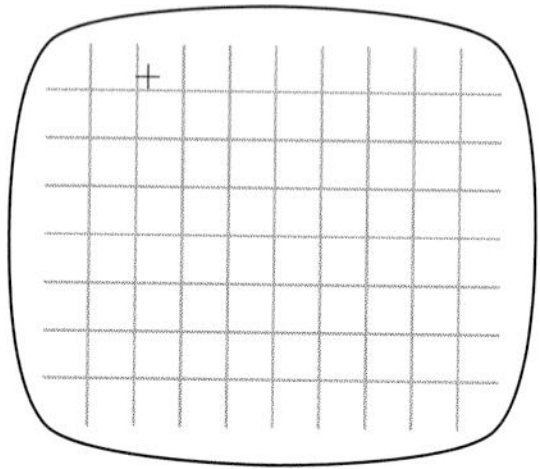

Select First Endpoint
Position Near a
Grid Intersection

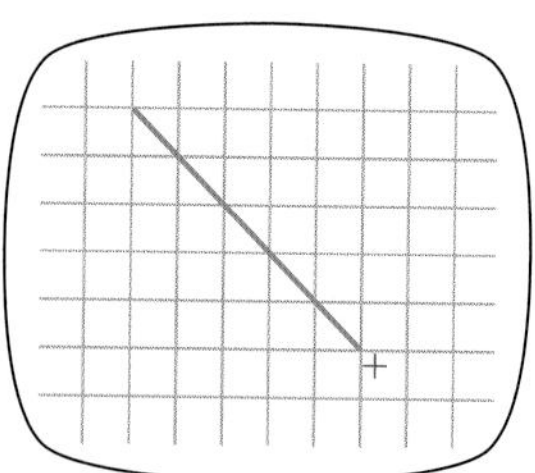

Select a Position
Near a Second
Grid Intersection

FIGURE 11-6 Construction of a line segment with endpoints constrained to grid intersection positions.

Grids

Another kind of constraint is a rectangular grid displayed in some part of the screen area. With an activated grid constraint, input coordinates are rounded to the nearest grid intersection. Figure 11-6 illustrates line drawing using a grid. Each of the cursor positions in this example is shifted to the nearest grid intersection point, and a line is drawn between these two grid positions. Grids facilitate object constructions, since a new line can be joined easily to a previously drawn line by selecting any position near the endpoint grid intersection of one end of the displayed line. Spacing between grid lines is often an option, and partial grids or grids with different spacing could be used in different screen areas.

Rubber-Band Methods

Line segments and other basic shapes can be constructed and positioned using rubber-band methods that allow the sizes of objects to be interactively stretched or contracted. Figure 11-7 demonstrates a rubber-band method for interactively specifying a line segment. First, a fixed screen position is selected for one endpoint of the line. Then, as the cursor moves around, the line is displayed from the start position to the current position of the cursor. The second endpoint of the line is input when a button or key is pressed. Using a mouse, we construct a rubber-band line while pressing a mouse key. When the mouse key is released, the line display is completed.

We can use similar rubber-band methods to construct rectangles, circles, and other objects. Figure 11-8 demonstrates rubber-band construction of a rectangle,

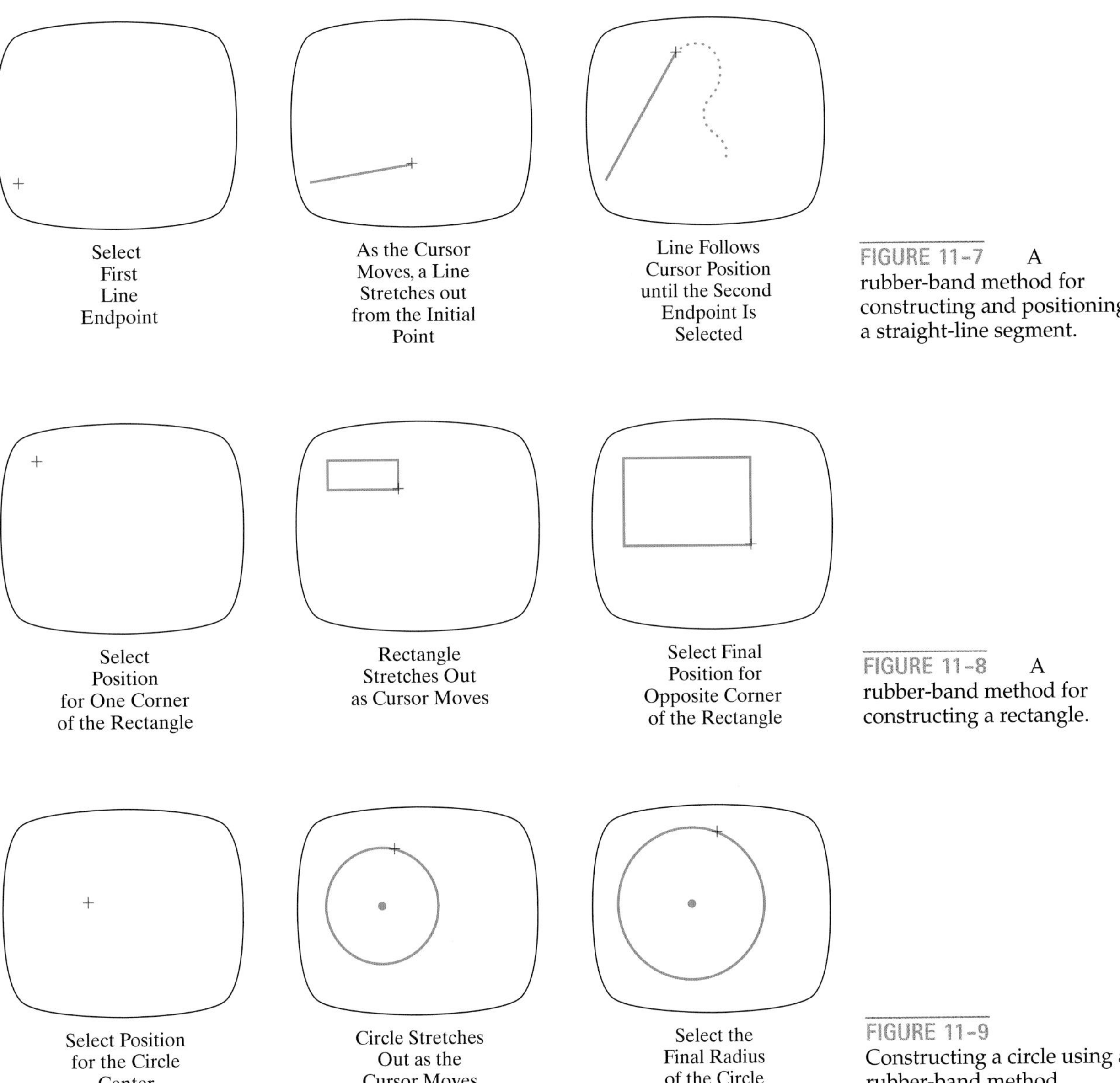
Select
First
Line
Endpoint
As the Cursor
Moves, a Line
Stretches out
from the Initial
Point
Line Follows
Cursor Position
until the Second
Endpoint Is
Selected
Select
Position
for One Corner
of the Rectangle
Rectangle
Stretches Out
as Cursor Moves
Select Final
Position for
Opposite Corner
of the Rectangle
Select Position
for the Circle
Center
Circle Stretches
Out as the
Cursor Moves
Select the
Final Radius
of the Circle

FIGURE 11-7 A rubber-band method for constructing and positioning a straight-line segment.

FIGURE 11-8 A rubber-band method for constructing a rectangle.

FIGURE 11-9 Constructing a circle using a rubber-band method.

and Fig. 11-9 shows a rubber-band circle construction. We can implement rubber-band constructions in various ways. For example, the shape and size of a rectangle can be adjusted by independently moving only the top edge of the rectangle, or the bottom edge, or one of the side edges.

Gravity Field

In the construction of figures, we sometimes need to connect lines at positions between endpoints that are not at grid intersections. Since exact positioning of the screen cursor at the connecting point can be difficult, a graphics package can include a procedure that converts any input position near a line segment into a position on the line using a *gravity field* area around the line. Any selected position

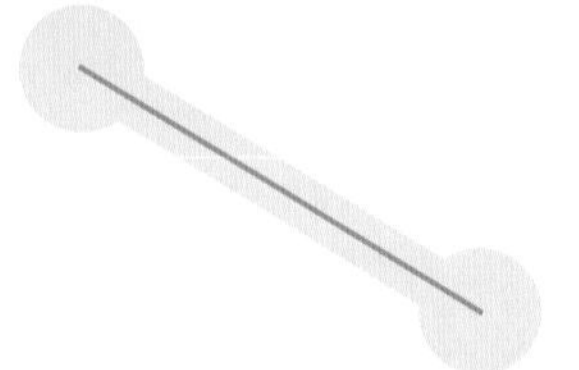

FIGURE 11-10 A gravity field around a line. Any selected point in the shaded area is shifted to a position on the line.

within the gravity field of a line is moved ("gravitated") to the nearest position on the line. A gravity field area around a line is illustrated with the shaded region shown in Fig. 11-10.

Gravity fields around the line endpoints are enlarged to make it easier for a designer to connect lines at their endpoints. Selected positions in one of the circular areas of the gravity field are attracted to the endpoint in that area. The size of gravity fields is chosen large enough to aid positioning, but small enough to reduce chances of overlap with other lines. If many lines are displayed, gravity areas can overlap, and it may be difficult to specify points correctly. Normally, the boundary for the gravity field is not displayed.

Interactive Painting and Drawing Methods

Options for sketching, drawing, and painting come in a variety of forms. Straight lines, polygons, and circles can be generated with methods discussed in the previous sections. Curve-drawing options can be provided using standard curve shapes, such as circular arcs and splines, or with freehand sketching procedures. Splines are interactively constructed by specifying a set of control points or a freehand sketch that gives the general shape of the curve. Then the system fits the set of points with a polynomial curve. In freehand drawing, curves are generated by following the path of a stylus on a graphics tablet or the path of the screen cursor on a video monitor. Once a curve is displayed, the designer can alter the curve shape by adjusting the positions of selected points along the curve path.

Line widths, line styles, and other attribute options are also commonly found in painting and drawing packages. These options are implemented with the methods discussed in Section 4-5. Various brush styles, brush patterns, color combinations, object shapes, and surface texture patterns are also available on many systems, particularly those designed as artist's workstations. Some paint systems vary the line width and brush strokes according to the pressure of the artist's hand on the stylus. Figure 11-11 shows a window and menu system used with a painting package that allows an artist to select variations of a specified object shape, different surface textures, and a variety of lighting conditions for a scene.

FIGURE 11-11 A screen layout showing one type of interface for an artist's painting package. (*Courtesy of Thomson Digital Image.*)

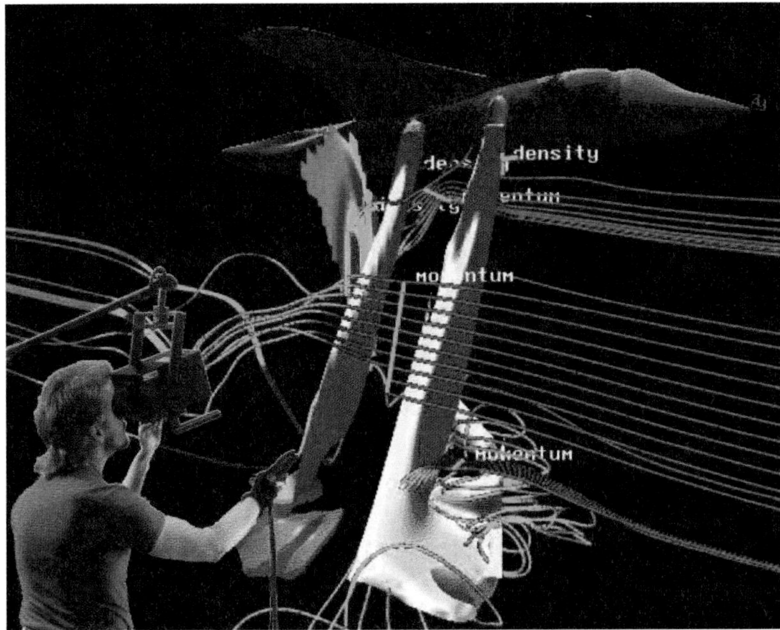

FIGURE 11-12 Using a head-tracking stereo display, called the BOOM (Fake Space Labs, Inc.), and a Dataglove (VPL, Inc.), a researcher interactively manipulates exploratory probes in the unsteady flow around a Harrier jet airplane. Software developed by Steve Bryson; data from Harrier. *(Courtesy of Sam Uselton, NASA Ames Research Center.)*

11-5 VIRTUAL-REALITY ENVIRONMENTS

A typical virtual-reality environment is illustrated in Fig. 11-12. Interactive input is accomplished in this environment with a data glove (Section 2-4), which is capable of grasping and moving objects displayed in a virtual scene. The computer-generated scene is displayed through a head-mounted viewing system (Section 2-1) as a stereographic projection. Tracking devices compute the position and orientation of the headset and data glove relative to the object positions in the scene. With this system, a user can move through the scene and rearrange object positions with the data glove.

Another method for generating virtual scenes is to display stereographic projections on a raster monitor, with the two stereographic views displayed on alternate refresh cycles. The scene is then viewed through stereographic glasses. Interactive object manipulations can again be accomplished with a data glove and a tracking device to monitor the glove position and orientation relative to the position of objects in the scene.

11-6 OpenGL INTERACTIVE INPUT-DEVICE FUNCTIONS

Interactive device input in an OpenGL program is handled with routines in the Utility Toolkit (GLUT), because these routines need to interface with a window system. In GLUT, we have functions to accept input from standard devices, such as a mouse or a keyboard, as well as from tablets, space balls, button boxes, and dials. For each device, we specify a procedure (the call-back function) that is to be invoked when an input event from that device occurs. These GLUT commands are placed in the `main` procedure along with the other GLUT statements. In addition, a combination of functions from the basic library and the GLU library can be used with the GLUT mouse function for pick input.

GLUT Mouse Functions

We use the following function to specify ("register") a procedure that is to be called when the mouse pointer is in a display window and a mouse button is pressed or released.

```
glutMouseFunc (mouseFcn);
```

This mouse callback procedure, which we named `mouseFcn`, has four arguments:

```
void mouseFcn (GLint button, GLint action, GLint xMouse,
                                          GLint yMouse)
```

Parameter `button` is assigned a GLUT symbolic constant that denotes one of the three mouse buttons, and parameter `action` is assigned a symbolic constant that specifies which button action we want to use to trigger the mouse activation event. Allowable values for `button` are GLUT_LEFT_BUTTON, GLUT_MIDDLE_BUTTON, and GLUT_RIGHT_BUTTON. (If we only have a two-button mouse, then we use just the left-button and right-button designations; with a one-button mouse, we can only assign parameter `button` the value `GLUT_LEFT_BUTTON`.) Parameter action can be assigned either `GLUT_DOWN` or `GLUT_UP`, depending on whether we want to initiate an action when we press a mouse button or when we release it. When procedure `mouseFcn` is invoked, the display-window location of the mouse cursor is returned as the coordinate position (`xMouse`, `yMouse`). This location is relative to the top-left corner of the display window, so that `xMouse` is the pixel distance from the left edge of the display window and `yMouse` is the pixel distance down from the top of the display window.

By activating a mouse button while the screen cursor is within the display window, we can select a position for displaying a primitive such as a single point, a line segment, or a fill area. We could also use the mouse as a pick device by comparing the returned screen position with the coordinate extents of displayed objects in a scene. However, OpenGL does provide routines for using the mouse as a pick device, and we discuss these routines in a later section.

As a simple example of the use of the `glutMouseFunc` routine, the following program plots a red point, with a point size equal to 3, at the position of the mouse cursor in the display window, each time that we press the left mouse button. Since the coordinate origin for the OpenGL primitive functions is the lower-left corner of the display window, we need to flip the returned `yMouse` value in the procedure `mousePtPlot`.

```
#include <GL/glut.h>

GLsizei winWidth = 400, winHeight = 300;    // Initial display-window size.

void init (void)
{
   glClearColor (0.0, 0.0, 1.0, 1.0)  // Set display-window color to blue.

   glMatrixMode (GL_PROJECTION);
   gluOrtho2D (0.0, 200.0, 0.0, 150.0);
}
```

```
void displayFcn (void)
{
   glClear (GL_COLOR_BUFFER_BIT);      //  Clear display window.

   glColor3f (1.0, 0.0, 0.0);          //  Set point color to red.
   glPointSize (3.0);                  //  Set point size to 3.0.
}

void winReshapeFcn (GLint newWidth, GLint newHeight)
{
   /*  Reset viewport and projection parameters  */
   glViewport (0, 0, newWidth, newHeight);
   glMatrixMode (GL_PROJECTION);
   glLoadIdentity ( );
   gluOrtho2D (0.0, GLdouble (newWidth), 0.0, GLdouble (newHeight));

   /*  Reset display-window size parameters.  */
   winWidth = newWidth;
   winHeight = newHeight;
}

void plotPoint (GLint x, GLint y)
{
   glBegin (GL_POINTS);
      glVertex2i (x, y);
   glEnd ( );
}

void mousePtPlot (GLint button, GLint action, GLint xMouse, GLint yMouse)
{
   if (button == GLUT_LEFT_BUTTON && action == GLUT_DOWN)
      plotPoint (xMouse, winHeight - yMouse);

   glFlush ( );
}

void main (int argc, char** argv)
{
   glutInit (&argc, argv);
   glutInitDisplayMode (GLUT_SINGLE | GLUT_RGB);
   glutInitWindowPosition (100, 100);
   glutInitWindowSize (winWidth, winHeight);
   glutCreateWindow ("Mouse Plot Points");

   init ( );
   glutDisplayFunc (displayFcn);
   glutReshapeFunc (winReshapeFcn);
   glutMouseFunc (mousePtPlot);

   glutMainLoop ( );
}
```

The next program example uses mouse input to select an endpoint position for a straight-line segment. Selected line segments are connected to demonstrate interactive construction of a polyline. Initially, two display-window locations must

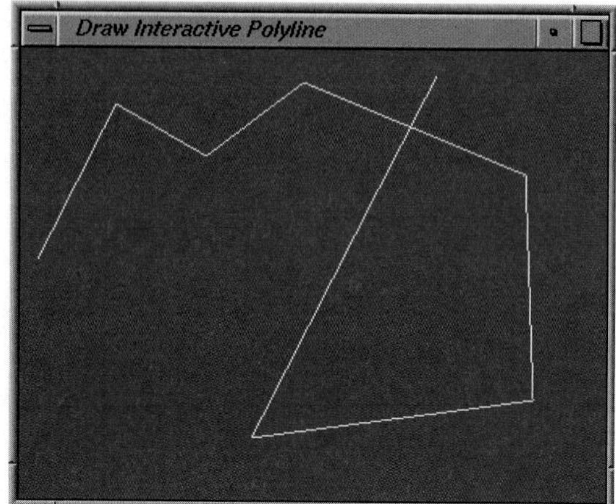

FIGURE 11-13 A sample output from the interactive mouse procedure `polyline`.

be selected with the left mouse button to generate the first line segment. Each subsequent position that we select adds another segment to the polyline. An example output from this program is given in Fig. 11-13.

```
#include <GL/glut.h>

GLsizei winWidth = 400, winHeight = 300;    // Initial display-window size.
GLint endPtCtr = 0;                        // Initialize line endpoint counter.

class scrPt {
public:
   GLint x, y;
};

void init (void)
{
   glClearColor (0.0, 0.0, 1.0, 1.0)   // Set display-window color to blue.

   glMatrixMode (GL_PROJECTION);
   gluOrtho2D (0.0, 200.0, 0.0, 150.0);
}

void displayFcn (void)
{
   glClear (GL_COLOR_BUFFER_BIT);
}

void winReshapeFcn (GLint newWidth, GLint newHeight)
{
   /*  Reset viewport and projection parameters  */
   glViewport (0, 0, newWidth, newHeight);
   glMatrixMode (GL_PROJECTION);
   glLoadIdentity ( );
   gluOrtho2D (0.0, GLdouble (newWidth), 0.0, GLdouble (newHeight));

   /*  Reset display-window size parameters.  */
   winWidth  = newWidth;
   winHeight = newHeight;
}
```

```
void drawLineSegment (scrPt endPt1, scrPt endPt2)
{
   glBegin (GL_LINES);
      glVertex2i (endPt1.x, endPt1.y);
      glVertex2i (endPt2.x, endPt2.y);
   glEnd ( );
}

void polyline (GLint button, GLint action, GLint xMouse, GLint yMouse)
{
   static scrPt endPt1, endPt2;

   if (ptCtr == 0) {
      if (button == GLUT_LEFT_BUTTON && action == GLUT_DOWN) {
         endPt1.x = xMouse;
         endPt1.y = winHeight - yMouse;
         ptCtr = 1;
      }
      else
         if (button == GLUT_RIGHT_BUTTON)          // Quit the program.
            exit (0);
   }
   else
      if (button == GLUT_LEFT_BUTTON && action == GLUT_DOWN) {
         endPt2.x = xMouse;
         endPt2.y = winHeight - yMouse;
         drawLineSegment (endPt1, endPt2);

         endPt1 = endPt2;
      }
      else
         if (button == GLUT_RIGHT_BUTTON)          // Quit the program.
            exit (0);

   glFlush ( );
}

void main (int argc, char** argv)
{
   glutInit (&argc, argv);
   glutInitDisplayMode (GLUT_SINGLE | GLUT_RGB);
   glutInitWindowPosition (100, 100);
   glutInitWindowSize (winWidth, winHeight);
   glutCreateWindow ("Draw Interactive Polyline");

   init ( );
   glutDisplayFunc (displayFcn);
   glutReshapeFunc (winReshapeFcn);
   glutMouseFunc (polyline);

   glutMainLoop ( );
}
```

Another GLUT mouse routine that we can use is

```
glutMotionFunc (fcnDoSomething);
```

This routine invokes `fcnDoSomething` when the mouse is moved within the display window with one or more buttons activated. The function that is invoked in this case has two arguments:

```
void fcnDoSomething (GLint xMouse, GLint yMouse)
```

where (`xMouse`, `yMouse`) is the mouse location in the display window relative to the top-left corner, when the mouse is moved with a button pressed.

Similarly, we can perform some action when we move the mouse within the display window without pressing a button:

```
glutPassiveMotionFunc (fcnDoSomethingElse);
```

Again, the mouse location is returned to `fcnDoSomethingElse` as coordinate position (`xMouse`, `yMouse`), relative to the top-left corner of the display window.

GLUT Keyboard Functions

With keyboard input, we use the following function to specify a procedure that is to be invoked when a key is pressed.

```
glutKeyboardFunc (keyFcn);
```

The specified procedure has three arguments:

```
void keyFcn (GLubyte key, GLint xMouse, GLint yMouse)
```

Parameter `key` is assigned a character value or the corresponding ASCII code. The display-window mouse location is returned as position (`xMouse`, `yMouse`) relative to the top-left corner of the display window. When a designated key is pressed, we can use the mouse location to initiate some action, independently of whether any mouse buttons are pressed.

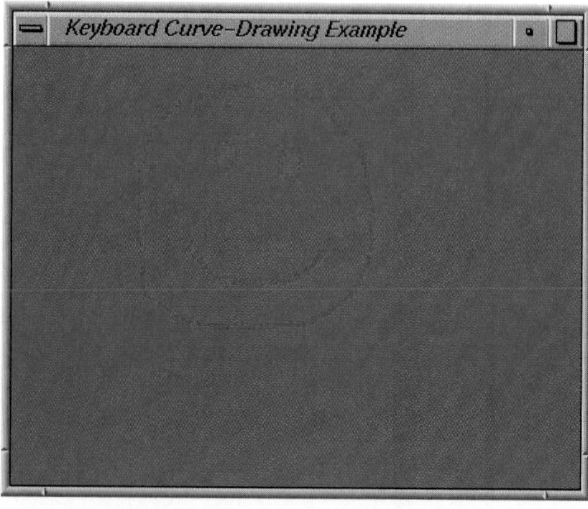

FIGURE 11-14 A sample output showing a freehand sketch using procedure `curveDrawing`.

In the following code, we present a simple curve-drawing procedure using keyboard input. A freehand curve is generated by moving the mouse within the display window while holding down the "c" key. This displays a sequence of red dots at each recorded mouse position. By slowly moving the mouse, we can obtain a solid curved line. Mouse buttons have no effect in this example. Figure 11-14 is an example output from this program.

```
#include <GL/glut.h>

GLsizei winWidth = 400, winHeight = 300;   // Initial display-window size.

void init (void)
{
   glClearColor (0.0, 0.0, 1.0, 1.0);   // Set display-window color to blue.

   glMatrixMode (GL_PROJECTION);
   gluOrtho2D (0.0, 200.0, 0.0, 150.0);
}

void displayFcn (void)
{
   glClear (GL_COLOR_BUFFER_BIT);              //  Clear display window.

   glColor3f (1.0, 0.0, 0.0);                  //  Set point color to red.
   glPointSize (3.0);                          //  Set point size to 3.0.
}

void winReshapeFcn (GLint newWidth, GLint newHeight)
{
   /*  Reset viewport and projection parameters  */
   glViewport (0, 0, newWidth, newHeight);
   glMatrixMode (GL_PROJECTION);
   glLoadIdentity ( );
   gluOrtho2D (0.0, GLdouble (newWidth), 0.0, GLdouble (newHeight));

   /*  Reset display-window size parameters.  */
   winWidth  = newWidth;
   winHeight = newHeight;
}

void plotPoint (GLint x, GLint y)
{
   glBegin (GL_POINTS);
      glVertex2i (x, y);
   glEnd ( );
}

/*  Move cursor while pressing c key enables freehand curve drawing.  */
void curveDrawing (GLubyte curvePlotKey, GLint xMouse, GLint yMouse)
{
   GLint x = xMouse;
   GLint y = winHeight - yMouse;
```

```
   switch (curvePlotKey)
   {
      case 'c':
         plotPoint (x, y);
         break;
      default:
         break;
   }
   glFlush ( );
}

void main (int argc, char** argv)
{
   glutInit (&argc, argv);
   glutInitDisplayMode (GLUT_SINGLE | GLUT_RGB);
   glutInitWindowPosition (100, 100);
   glutInitWindowSize (winWidth, winHeight);
   glutCreateWindow ("Keyboard Curve-Drawing Example");

   init ( );
   glutDisplayFunc (displayFcn);
   glutReshapeFunc (winReshapeFcn);
   glutKeyboardFunc (curveDrawing);

   glutMainLoop ( );
}
```

For function keys, arrow keys, and other special-purpose keys, we can use the command

```
glutSpecialFunc (specialKeyFcn);
```

The specified procedure has the same three arguments:

```
void specialKeyFcn (GLint specialKey, GLint xMouse,
                                     GLint yMouse)
```

but now parameter `specialKey` is assigned an integer-valued GLUT symbolic constant. To select a function key, we use one of the constants `GLUT_KEY_F1` through `GLUT_KEY_F12`. For the arrow keys, we use constants such as `GLUT_KEY_UP` and `GLUT_KEY_RIGHT`. Other keys can be designated using `GLUT_KEY_PAGE_DOWN`, `GLUT_KEY_HOME`, and similar constants for the page up, end, and insert keys. The backspace, delete, and escape keys can be designated with the `glutKeyboardFunc` routine using their ASCII codes, which are 8, 127, and 27, respectively.

An interactive program using the mouse, keyboard, and function keys is demonstrated in the following code. Mouse input is used to select a location for the lower-left corner of a red square. Keyboard input is used to scale the size of the square, and a new square is obtained with each click of the left mouse button.

```
#include <GL/glut.h>
#inclue <stdlib.h>

GLsizei winWidth = 400, winHeight = 300;   // Initial display-window size.
GLint edgeLength = 10;                     // Initial edge length for square.

void init (void)
{
   glClearColor (0.0, 0.0, 1.0, 1.0)   // Set display-window color to blue.

   glMatrixMode (GL_PROJECTION);
   gluOrtho2D (0.0, 200.0, 0.0, 150.0);
}

void displayFcn (void)
{
   glClear (GL_COLOR_BUFFER_BIT);          //  Clear display window.

   glColor3f (1.0, 0.0, 0.0);              //  Set fill color to red.
}

void winReshapeFcn (GLint newWidth, GLint newHeight)
{
   /*  Reset viewport and projection parameters  */
   glViewport (0, 0, newWidth, newHeight);
   glMatrixMode (GL_PROJECTION);
   glLoadIdentity ( );
   gluOrtho2D (0.0, GLdouble (newWidth), 0.0, GLdouble (newHeight));

   /*  Reset display-window size parameters.  */
   winWidth  = newWidth;
   winHeight = newHeight;
}

/*  Display a red square with a selected edge-length size.  */
void fillSquare (GLint button, GLint action, GLint xMouse, GLint yMouse)
{
   GLint x1, y1, x2, y2;

   /*  Use left mouse button to select a position for the
    *  lower-left corner of the square.
    */
   if (button == GLUT_LEFT_BUTTON && action == GLUT_DOWN)
   {
      x1 = xMouse;
      y1 = winHeight - yMouse;
      x2 = x1 + edgeLength;
      y2 = y1 + edgeLength;
      glRecti (x1, y1, x2, y2);
   }
   else
      if (button == GLUT_RIGHT_BUTTON)    //  Use right mouse button to quit.
         exit (0);

   glFlush ( );
}
```

```
/*  Use keys 2, 3, and 4 to enlarge the square.  */
void enlargeSquare (GLubyte sizeFactor, GLint xMouse, GLint yMouse)
{
   switch (sizeFactor)
   {
      case '2':
         edgeLength *= 2;
         break;
      case '3':
         edgeLength *= 3;
         break;
      case '4':
         edgeLength *= 4;
         break;
      default:
         break;
   }
}

/*  Use function keys F2 and F4 for reduction factors 1/2 and 1/4.  */
void reduceSquare (GLint reductionKey, GLint xMouse, GLint yMouse)
{
   switch (reductionKey)
   {
      case GLUT_KEY_F2:
         edgeLength /= 2;
         break;
      case GLUT_KEY_F3:
         edgeLength /= 4;
         break;
      default:
         break;
   }
}

void main (int argc, char** argv)
{
   glutInit (&argc, argv);
   glutInitDisplayMode (GLUT_SINGLE | GLUT_RGB);
   glutInitWindowPosition (100, 100);
   glutInitWindowSize (winWidth, winHeight);
   glutCreateWindow ("Display Squares of Various Sizes");

   init ( );
   glutDisplayFunc (displayFcn);
   glutReshapeFunc (winReshapeFcn);
   glutMouseFunc (fillSquare);
   glutKeyboardFunc (enlargeSquare);
   glutSpecialFunc (reduceSquare);

   glutMainLoop ( );
}
```

GLUT Tablet Functions

Usually, tablet activation occurs only when the mouse cursor is in the display window. A button event for tablet input is then recorded with

```
glutTabletButtonFunc (tabletFcn);
```

and the arguments for the invoked function are similar to those for a mouse:

```
void tabletFcn (GLint tabletButton, GLint action,
                    GLint xTablet, GLint yTablet)
```

We designate a tablet button with an integer identifier such as 1, 2, 3, et cetera, and the button action is again specified with either GLUT_UP or GLUT_DOWN. The returned values `xTablet` and `yTablet` are the tablet coordinates. We can determine the number of available tablet buttons with the command

```
glutDeviceGet (GLUT_NUM_TABLET_BUTTONS);
```

Motion of a tablet stylus or cursor is processed with the following function,

```
glutTabletMotionFunc (tabletMotionFcn);
```

where the invoked function has the form

```
void tabletMotionFcn (GLint xTablet, GLint yTablet)
```

The returned values `xTablet` and `yTablet` give the coordinates on the tablet surface.

GLUT Spaceball Functions

We use the following function to specify an operation when a spaceball button is activated for a selected display window.

```
glutSpaceballButtonFunc (spaceballFcn);
```

The callback function has two parameters:

```
void spaceballFcn (GLint spaceballButton, GLint action)
```

Spaceball buttons are identified with the same integer values as a tablet, and parameter `action` is assigned either the value GLUT_UP or the value GLUT_DOWN. We can determine the number of available spaceball buttons with a call to `glutDeviceGet` using the argument GLUT_NUM_SPACEBALL_BUTTONS.

Translational motion of a spaceball, when the mouse is in the display window, is recorded with the function call

```
glutSpaceballMotionFunc (spaceballTranlFcn);
```

The three-dimensional translation distances are passed to the invoked function as, for example

```
void spaceballTranslFcn (GLint tx, GLint ty, GLint tz)
```

These translation distances are normalized within the range from −1000 to 1000.

Similarly, a spaceball rotation is recorded with

```
glutSpaceballRotateFunc (spaceballRotFcn);
```

And the three-dimensional rotation angles are then available to the callback function:

```
void spaceballRotFcn (GLint thetaX, GLint thetaY, GLint thetaZ)
```

GLUT Button-Box Function

Input from a button box is obtained with the following statement.

```
glutButtonBoxFunc (buttonBoxFcn);
```

Button activation is then passed to the invoked function:

```
void buttonBoxFcn (GLint button, GLint action);
```

The buttons are identified with integer values, and the button action is specified as GLUT_UP or GLUT_DOWN.

GLUT Dials Function

A dial rotation can be recorded with the following routine.

```
glutDialsFunc (dialsFcn);
```

In this case, we use the callback function to identify the dial and obtain the angular amount of rotation:

```
void dialsFcn (GLint dial, GLint degreeValue);
```

Dials are designated with integer values, and the dial rotation is returned as an integer degree value.

OpenGL Picking Operations

In an OpenGL program, we can interactively select objects by pointing to screen positions. However, the picking operations in OpenGL are not straightforward.

Basically, we perform picking using a designated pick window to form a revised view volume. We assign integer identifiers to objects in a scene, and the identifiers for those objects that intersect the revised view volume are stored in a pick-buffer array. Thus, to use the OpenGL pick features, we need to incorporate the following procedures into a program.

- Create and display a scene.
- Pick a screen position and, within the mouse callback function, do the following:
  - Set up a pick buffer.
  - Activate the picking operations (selection mode).

- Initialize an ID name stack for object identifiers.
- Save the current viewing and geometric-transformation matrix.
- Specify a pick window for the mouse input.
- Assign identifiers to objects and reprocess the scene using the revised view volume. (Pick information is then stored in the pick buffer.)
- Restore the original viewing and geometric-transformation matrix.
- Determine the number of objects that have been picked, and return to the normal rendering mode.
- Process the pick information.

We can also use a modification of these procedures to select objects without interactive input from a mouse. This is accomplished by specifying the vertices for the revised view volume, instead of designating a pick window.

A pick-buffer array is set up with the command

```
glSelectBuffer (pickBuffSize, pickBuffer);
```

Parameter `pickBuffer` designates an integer array with `pickBuffSize` elements. The `glSelectBuffer` function must be invoked before the OpenGL picking operations (selection mode) are activated. An integer information record is stored in pick-buffer array for each object that is selected with a single pick input. Several records of information can be stored in the pick buffer, depending on the size and location of the pick window. Each record in the pick buffer contains the following information.

(1) The stack position of the object, which is the number of identifiers in the name stack up to and including the position of the picked object.
(2) The minimum depth of the picked object.
(3) The maximum depth of the picked object.
(4) The list of the identifies in the name stack from the first (bottom) identifier to the identifier for the picked object.

The integer depth values stored in the pick buffer are the original values in the range from 0 to 1.0, multiplied by $2^{32} - 1$.

The OpenGL picking operations are activated with

```
glRenderMode (GL_SELECT);
```

This places us in selection mode, which means that a scene is processed through the viewing pipeline but not stored in the frame buffer. A record of information for each object that would have been displayed in the normal rendering mode is placed in the pick buffer. In addition, this command returns the number of picked objects, which is equal to the number of information records in the pick buffer. To return to the normal rendering mode (the default), we invoke the `glRenderMode` routine using the argument `GL_RENDER`. A third option is the argument `GL_FEEDBACK`, which stores object coordinates and other information in a feedback buffer without displaying the objects. Feedback mode is used to obtain information about primitive types, attributes, and other parameters associated with the objects in a scene.

We use the following statement to activate the integer-ID name stack for the picking operations.

```
glInitNames ( );
```

The ID stack is initially empty, and this stack can be used only in selection mode. To place an unsigned integer value on the stack, we can invoke the following function.

```
glPushName (ID);
```

This places the value for parameter `ID` on the top of the stack and pushes the previous top name down to the next position in the stack. We can also simply replace the top of the stack using

```
glLoadName (ID);
```

but we cannot use this command to place a value on an empty stack. And to eliminate the top of the ID stack, we issue the command

```
glPopName ( );
```

A pick window within a selected viewport is defined using the following GLU function.

```
gluPickMatrix (xPick, yPick, widthPick, heightPick, vpArray);
```

Parameters `xPick` and `yPick` give the double-precision, screen-coordinate location for the center of the pick window relative to the lower-left corner of the viewport. When these coordinates are given with mouse input, the mouse coordinates are relative to the upper-left corner, and thus we need to invert the input `yMouse` value. The double-precision values for the width and height of the pick window are specified with parameters `widthPick` and `heightPick`. Parameter `vpArray` designates an integer array containing the coordinate position and size parameters for the current viewport. We can obtain the viewport parameters using the `glGetIntegerv` function (Section 6-4). This pick window is then used as a clipping window to construct a revised view volume for the viewing transformations. Information for objects that intersect this revised view volume is placed in the pick buffer.

We illustrate the OpenGL picking operations in the following program. The three color rectangles shown in Fig. 11-15 are displayed by this program. For this picking example, we use a 5 by 5 pick window, and the center of the pick window is given with mouse input. Therefore, we need to invert the input `yMouse` value using the viewport height, which is the fourth element of the array `vpArray`. The red rectangle is assigned ID = 30, the blue rectangle is assigned ID = 10, and the green rectangle is assigned ID = 20. Depending on the input mouse position, we can pick no rectangles, one rectangle, two of the rectangles, or all three rectangles at one time. The rectangle identifiers are entered into the ID stack in the color order: red, blue, green. Therefore, when we process a picked rectangle, we could use either its identifier or its stack position number. For example, if the stack position number, which is the first item in the pick record, is 2, then we have picked the blue rectangle and there are two rectangle identifiers listed at the end of the

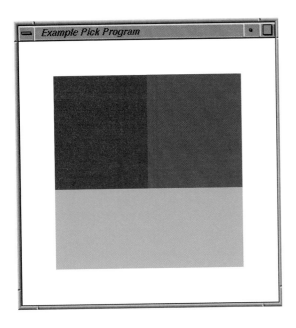

FIGURE 11-15 The three color rectangles displayed by the example pick program.

record. Alternatively, we could use the last entry in the record, which is the identifier for the picked object. In this example program, we simply list the contents of the pick buffer. The rectangles are defined in the *xy* plane, so all depth values are 0. A sample output is given in Example 11-1 for a mouse input position that is near the boundary between the red and green rectangles. No mechanism is provided for terminating the program, so any number of mouse inputs can be processed.

```
#include <GL/glut.h>
#include <stdio.h>

const GLint pickBuffSize = 32;

/*  Set initial display-window size.  */
GLsizei winWidth = 400, winHeight = 400;


void init (void)
{
   /*  Set display-window color to white.  */
   glClearColor (1.0, 1.0, 1.0, 1.0);
}

/*  Define 3 rectangles and associated IDs.  */
void rects (GLenum mode)
{
   if (mode == GL_SELECT)
      glPushName (30);          //  Red rectangle.
   glColor3f (1.0, 0.0, 0.0);
   glRecti (40, 130, 150, 260);
```

```
   if (mode == GL_SELECT)
      glPushName (10);          //  Blue rectangle.
   glColor3f (0.0, 0.0, 1.0);
   glRecti (150, 130, 260, 260);

   if (mode == GL_SELECT)
      glPushName (20);          //  Green rectangle.
   glColor3f (0.0, 1.0, 0.0);
   glRecti (40, 40, 260, 130);
}

/*  Print the contents of the pick buffer for each mouse selection.  */
void processPicks (GLint nPicks, GLuint pickBuffer [ ])
{
   GLint j, k;
   GLuint objID, *ptr;

   printf (" Number of objects picked = %d\n", nPicks);
   printf ("\n");
   ptr = pickBuffer;

   /*  Output all items in each pick record.  */
   for (j = 0; j < nPicks; j++) {
      objID = *ptr;

      printf ("   Stack position = %d\n", objID);
      ptr++;

      printf ("   Min depth = %g,", float (*ptr/0x7fffffff));
      ptr++;

      printf ("   Max depth = %g\n", float (*ptr/0x7fffffff));
      ptr++;

      printf ("   Stack IDs are: \n");
      for (k = 0; k < objID; k++) {
         printf ("   %d ",*ptr);
         ptr++;
      }
      printf ("\n\n");
   }
}

void pickRects (GLint button, GLint action, GLint xMouse, GLint yMouse)
{
   GLuint pickBuffer [pickBuffSize];
   GLint nPicks, vpArray [4];

   if (button != GLUT_LEFT_BUTTON || action != GLUT_DOWN)
      return;

   glSelectBuffer (pickBuffSize, pickBuffer);  //  Designate pick buffer.
   glRenderMode (GL_SELECT);                 //  Activate picking operations.
   glInitNames ( );                        //  Initialize the object-ID stack.
```

```
   /*  Save current viewing matrix.  */
   glMatrixMode (GL_PROJECTION);
   glPushMatrix ( );
   glLoadIdentity ( );

   /*  Obtain the parameters for the current viewport.  Set up
    *  a 5 by 5 pick window, and invert the input yMouse value
    *  using the height of the viewport, which is the fourth
    *  element of vpArray.
    */
   glGetIntegerv (GL_VIEWPORT, vpArray);
   gluPickMatrix (GLdouble (xMouse), GLdouble (vpArray [3] - yMouse),
                  5.0, 5.0, vpArray);

   gluOrtho2D (0.0, 300.0, 0.0, 300.0);
   rects (GL_SELECT);       // Process the rectangles in selection mode.

   /*  Restore original viewing matrix.  */
   glMatrixMode (GL_PROJECTION);
   glPopMatrix ( );

   glFlush ( );

   /*  Determine the number of picked objects and return to the
    *  normal rendering mode.
    */
   nPicks = glRenderMode (GL_RENDER);

   processPicks (nPicks, pickBuffer);  // Process picked objects.

   glutPostRedisplay ( );
}

void displayFcn (void)
{
   glClear (GL_COLOR_BUFFER_BIT);
   rects (GL_RENDER);                  // Display the rectangles.
   glFlush ( );
}

void winReshapeFcn (GLint newWidth, GLint newHeight)
{
   /*  Reset viewport and projection parameters.  */
   glViewport (0, 0, newWidth, newHeight);
   glMatrixMode (GL_PROJECTION);
   glLoadIdentity ( );

   gluOrtho2D (0.0, 300.0, 0.0, 300.0);
   glMatrixMode (GL_MODELVIEW);

   /* Reset display-window size parameters.  */
   winWidth  = newWidth;
   winHeight = newHeight;
}
```

```
void main (int argc, char** argv)
{
    glutInit (&argc, argv);
    glutInitDisplayMode (GLUT_SINGLE | GLUT_RGB);
    glutInitWindowPosition (100, 100);
    glutInitWindowSize (winWidth, winHeight);
    glutCreateWindow ("Example Pick Program");

    init ( );
    glutDisplayFunc (displayFcn);
    glutReshapeFunc (winReshapeFcn);
    glutMouseFunc (pickRects);

    glutMainLoop ( );
}
```

EXAMPLE 11-1 Sample Output from Procedure `pickrects`.

```
Number of objects picked = 2

  Stack position = 1
  Min depth = 0,    Max depth = 0
  Stack IDs are:
  30

  Stack position = 3
  Min depth = 0,    Max depth = 0
  Stack IDs are:
  30    10    20
```

11-7 OpenGL MENU FUNCTIONS

In addition to the input-device routines, GLUT contains various functions for adding simple pop-up menus to programs. With these functions, we can set up and access a variety of menus and associated submenus. The GLUT menu commands are placed in procedure `main` along with the other GLUT functions.

Creating a GLUT Menu

A pop-up menu is created with the statement

```
glutCreateMenu (menuFcn);
```

where parameter `menuFcn` is the name of a procedure that is to be invoked when a menu entry is selected. This procedure has one argument, which is the integer value corresponding to the position of a selected option.

```
void menuFcn (GLint menuItemNumber)
```

The integer value passed to parameter `menuItemNumber` is then used by `menuFcn` to perform some operation. When a menu is created, it is associated with the current display window.

Once we have designated the menu function that is to be invoked when a menu item is selected, we must specify the options that are to be listed in the menu. We do this with a series of statements that list the name and position for each option. These statements have the general form

```
glutAddMenuEntry (charString, menuItemNumber);
```

Parameter `charString` specifies text that is to be displayed in the menu, and parameter `menuItemNumber` gives the location for that entry in the menu. For example, the following statements create a menu with two options.

```
glutCreateMenu (menuFcn);
   glutAddMenuEntry ("First Menu Item", 1);
   glutAddMenuEntry ("Second Menu Item", 2);
```

Next, we must specify a mouse button that is to be used to select a menu option. This is accomplished with

```
glutAttachMenu (button);
```

where parameter `button` is assigned one of the three GLUT symbolic constants referencing the left, middle, or right mouse button.

To illustrate the creation and use of a GLUT menu, the following program provides two options for displaying the interior fill of a triangle. Initially, the triangle is defined with two white vertices, one red vertex, and a fill color determined by an interpolation of the vertex colors. We use the `glShadeModel` function (Sections 4-14 and 10-20) to select a polygon fill that is either a solid color or an interpolation (Gouraud rendering) of the vertex colors. A menu is created in this program that allows us to choose between these two options using the right mouse button, when the mouse cursor is inside the display window. This pop-up menu is displayed with the upper-left corner at the position of the mouse cursor, as illustrated in Fig. 11-16. A menu option is highlighted when we move

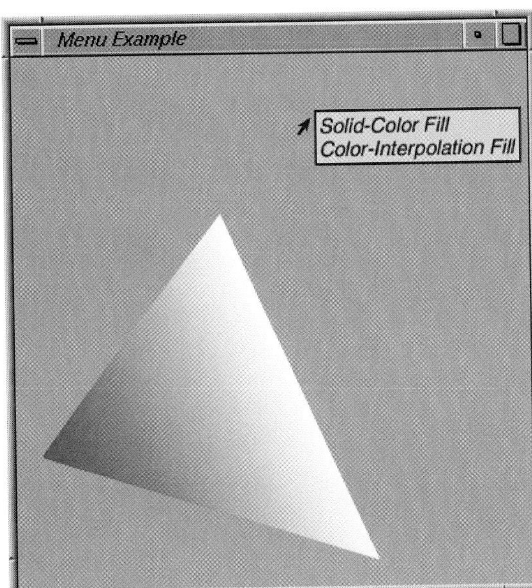

FIGURE 11-16 The OpenGL pop-up menu displayed by the example menu program.

the mouse cursor over that option. The highlighted option is then selected by releasing the right button. If the option "Solid-Color Fill" is selected, the triangle is filled with the color specified for the last vertex (which is red). At the end of the menu-display procedure, `fillOption`, we include a `glutPostRedisplay` command (Section 6-4) to indicate that the triangle should be redrawn when the menu is displayed.

```
#include <GL/glut.h>

GLsizei winWidth = 400, winHeight = 400;  // Initial display-window size.

GLfloat red = 1.0, green = 1.0, blue = 1.0;  // Initial triangle color: white.
GLenum fillMode = GL_SMOOTH;  // Initial polygon fill: color interpolation.

void init (void)
{
    glClearColor (0.6, 0.6, 0.6, 1.0);  // Set display-window color to gray.

    glMatrixMode (GL_PROJECTION);
    gluOrtho2D (0.0, 300.0, 0.0, 300.0);
}

void fillOption (GLint selectedOption)
{
    switch (selectedOption) {
        case 1:  fillMode = GL_FLAT;    break;  //  Flat surface rendering.
        case 2:  fillMode = GL_SMOOTH;  break;  //  Gouraud rendering.
    }
    glutPostRedisplay ( );
}

void displayTriangle (void)
{
    glClear (GL_COLOR_BUFFER_BIT);

    glShadeModel (fillMode);              //  Set fill method for triangle.
    glColor3f (red, green, blue);     //  Set color for first two vertices.

    glBegin (GL_TRIANGLES);
        glVertex2i (280, 20);
        glVertex2i (160, 280);
        glColor3f (red, 0.0, 0.0);      // Set color of last vertex to red.
        glVertex2i (20, 100);
    glEnd ( );

    glFlush ( );
}

void reshapeFcn (GLint newWidth, GLint newHeight)
{
    glViewport (0, 0, newWidth, newHeight);

    glMatrixMode (GL_PROJECTION);
    glLoadIdentity ( );
    gluOrtho2D (0.0, GLfloat (newWidth), 0.0, GLfloat (newHeight));
```

```
      displayTriangle ( );
      glFlush ( );
}

void main (int argc, char **argv)
{
      glutInit (&argc, argv);
      glutInitDisplayMode (GLUT_SINGLE | GLUT_RGB);
      glutInitWindowPosition (200, 200);
      glutInitWindowSize (winWidth, winHeight);
      glutCreateWindow ("Menu Example");

      init ( );
      glutDisplayFunc (displayTriangle);

      glutCreateMenu (fillOption);                    // Create pop-up menu.
          glutAddMenuEntry ("Solid-Color Fill", 1);
          glutAddMenuEntry ("Color-Interpolation Fill", 2);

      /*  Select a menu option using the right mouse button.  */
      glutAttachMenu (GLUT_RIGHT_BUTTON);

      glutReshapeFunc (reshapeFcn);

      glutMainLoop ( );
}
```

Creating and Managing Multiple GLUT Menus

When a menu is created, it is associated with the current display window (Section 6-4). We can create multiple menus for a single display window, and we can create different menus for different windows. As each menu is created, it is assigned an integer identifier, starting with the value 1 for the first menu created. The integer identifier for a menu is returned by the `glutCreateMenu` routine, and we can record this value with a statement such as

```
menuID = glutCreateMenu (menuFcn);
```

A newly created menu becomes the **current menu** for the current display window. To activate a menu for the current display window, we use the statement

```
glutSetMenu (menuID);
```

This menu then becomes the current menu, which will pop up in the display window when the mouse button that has been attached to that menu is pressed.

We eliminate a menu with the command

```
glutDestroyMenu (menuID);
```

If the designated menu is the current menu for a display window, then that window has no menu assigned as the current menu even though other menus may exist.

The following function is used to obtain the identifier for the current menu in the current display window.

```
currentMenuID = glutGetMenu ( );
```

A value of 0 is returned if no menus exist for this display window or if the previous current menu was eliminated with the `glutDestroyMenu` function.

Creating GLUT Submenus

A submenu can be associated with a menu by first creating the submenu using `glutCreateMenu`, along with a list of suboptions, and then listing the submenu as an additional option in the main menu. We can add the submenu to the option list in a main menu (or other submenu) using a sequence of statements such as

```
submenuID = glutCreateMenu (submenuFcn);
   glutAddMenuEntry ("First Submenu Item", 1);
   .
   .
   .
glutCreateMenu (menuFcn);
   glutAddMenuEntry ("First Menu Item", 1);
   .
   .
   .
   glutAddSubMenu ("Submenu Option", submenuID);
```

The `glutAddSubMenu` function can also be used to add the submenu to the current menu.

In the following program, we illustrate the creation of a submenu. This program, which is a modification of the previous menu program, displays a submenu that provides three color choices (blue, green, and white) for the first two vertices of the triangle. The main menu is now listed with three options, and the third

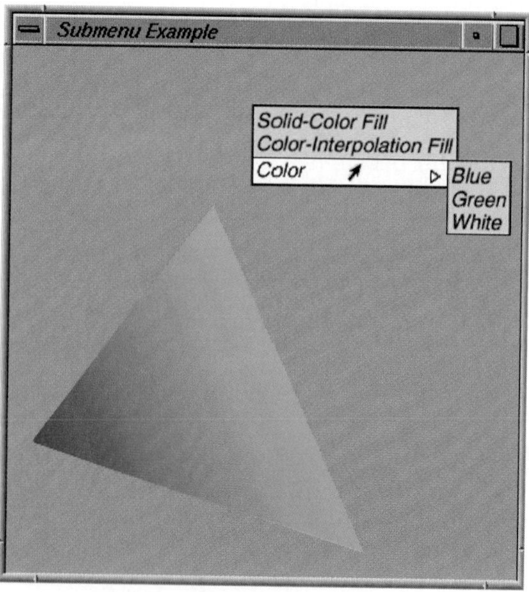

FIGURE 11-17 The OpenGL pop-up main menu and submenu displayed by the example submenu program.

option is displayed with an arrow symbol to indicate that a pop-up submenu will be displayed when that option is highlighted, as shown in Fig. 11-17. A `glutPostRedisplay` function is included at the end of both the main-menu function and the submenu function.

```
#include <GL/glut.h>

GLsizei winWidth = 400, winHeight = 400;  // Initial display-window size.

GLfloat red = 1.0, green = 1.0, blue = 1.0;      //  Initial color values.
GLenum renderingMode = GL_SMOOTH;                 //  Initial fill method.

void init (void)
{
    glClearColor (0.6, 0.6, 0.6, 1.0);  // Set display-window color to gray.

    glMatrixMode (GL_PROJECTION);
    gluOrtho2D (0.0, 300.0, 0.0, 300.0);
}

void mainMenu (GLint renderingOption)
{
    switch (renderingOption) {
        case 1:  renderingMode = GL_FLAT;    break;
        case 2:  renderingMode = GL_SMOOTH;  break;
    }
    glutPostRedisplay ( );
}

/*  Set color values according to the submenu option selected.  */
void colorSubMenu (GLint colorOption)
{
    switch (colorOption) {
        case 1:
            red = 0.0;  green = 0.0;  blue = 1.0;
            break;
        case 2:
            red = 0.0;  green = 1.0;  blue = 0.0;
            break;
        case 3:
            red = 1.0;  green = 1.0;  blue = 1.0;
    }
    glutPostRedisplay ( );
}

void displayTriangle (void)
{
    glClear (GL_COLOR_BUFFER_BIT);

    glShadeModel (renderingMode);      //  Set fill method for triangle.
    glColor3f (red, green, blue); //  Set color for first two vertices.
```

```
    glBegin (GL_TRIANGLES);
        glVertex2i (280, 20);
        glVertex2i (160, 280);
        glColor3f (1.0, 0.0, 0.0);  // Set color of last vertex to red.
        glVertex2i (20, 100);
    glEnd ( );

    glFlush ( );
}

void reshapeFcn (GLint newWidth, GLint newHeight)
{
    glViewport (0, 0, newWidth, newHeight);

    glMatrixMode (GL_PROJECTION);
    glLoadIdentity ( );
    gluOrtho2D (0.0, GLfloat (newWidth), 0.0, GLfloat (newHeight));

    displayTriangle ( );
    glFlush ( );
}

void main (int argc, char **argv)
{
    GLint subMenu;                              //  Identifier for submenu.

    glutInit (&argc, argv);
    glutInitDisplayMode (GLUT_SINGLE | GLUT_RGB);
    glutInitWindowPosition (200, 200);
    glutInitWindowSize (winWidth, winHeight);
    glutCreateWindow ("Submenu Example");

    init ( );
    glutDisplayFunc (displayTriangle);

    subMenu = glutCreateMenu (colorSubMenu);
        glutAddMenuEntry ("Blue", 1);
        glutAddMenuEntry ("Green", 2);
        glutAddMenuEntry ("White", 3);

    glutCreateMenu (mainMenu);       // Create main pop-up menu.
        glutAddMenuEntry ("Solid-Color Fill", 1);
        glutAddMenuEntry ("Color-Interpolation Fill", 2);
        glutAddSubMenu ("Color", subMenu);

    /*  Select menu option using right mouse button.  */
    glutAttachMenu (GLUT_RIGHT_BUTTON);

    glutReshapeFunc (reshapeFcn);

    glutMainLoop ( );
}
```

Modifying GLUT Menus

If we want to change the mouse button that is used to select a menu option, we first cancel the current button attachment and then attach the new button. A button attachment is cancelled for the current menu with

```
glutDetachMenu (mouseButton);
```

Parameter `mouseButton` is assigned the GLUT constant that identifies the left, right, or middle button that was previously attached to the menu.

Options within an existing menu can also be changed. For example, we can delete an option in the current menu with the function

```
glutRemoveMenuItem (itemNumber);
```

where parameter `itemNumber` is assigned the integer value of the menu option that is to be deleted.

Other GLUT routines allow us to modify the names or status of items within an existing menu. For example, we can use these routines to change the displayed name of a menu option, to change the item number of the option, or to change an option into a submenu.

11-8 DESIGNING A GRAPHICAL USER INTERFACE

All applications software now commonly include a graphical interface, composed of display windows, icons, menus, and other features to aid a user in applying the software to a particular problem. Specialized interactive dialogues are designed so that programming options are selected using familiar terms within a particular field, such as architectural and engineering design, drafting, business graphics, geology, economics, chemistry, or physics. Other considerations for a user interface are the accommodation of various skill levels, consistency, error handling, and feedback.

The User Dialogue

For any application, the *user's model* serves as the basis for the design of the dialogue by describing what the system is designed to accomplish and what operations are available. It states the type of objects that can be displayed and how the objects can be manipulated. For example, if the system is to be used as a tool for architectural design, the model describes how the package can be used to construct and display views of buildings by positioning walls, doors, windows, and other building components. A facility-layout package might include a set of furniture items along with the operations for positioning and removing different objects in a specified floor plan. And a circuit-design program provides electrical or logic symbols and the positioning operations for adding or deleting elements within a layout.

All information in the user dialogue is presented in the language of the application. In an architectural design package, this means that all interactions are described only in architectural terms, without reference to particular data structures, computer-graphics terms, or other concepts that may be unfamiliar to an architect.

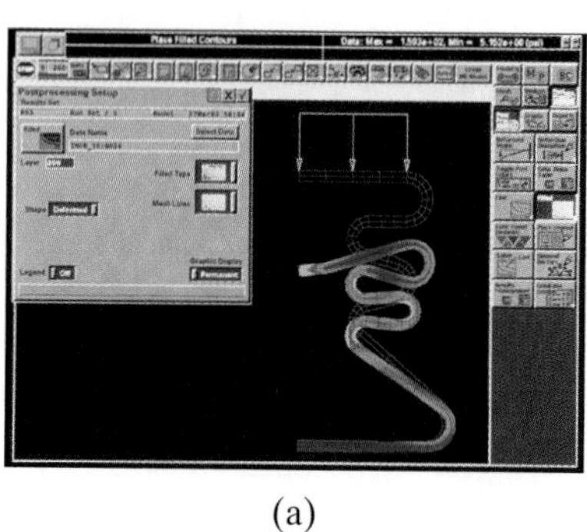

(a)

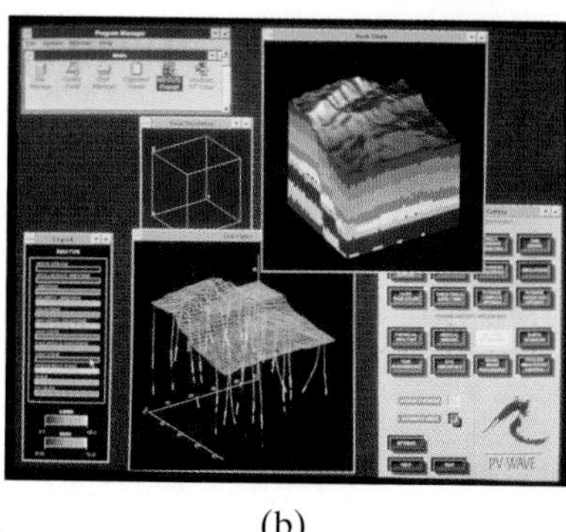

(b)

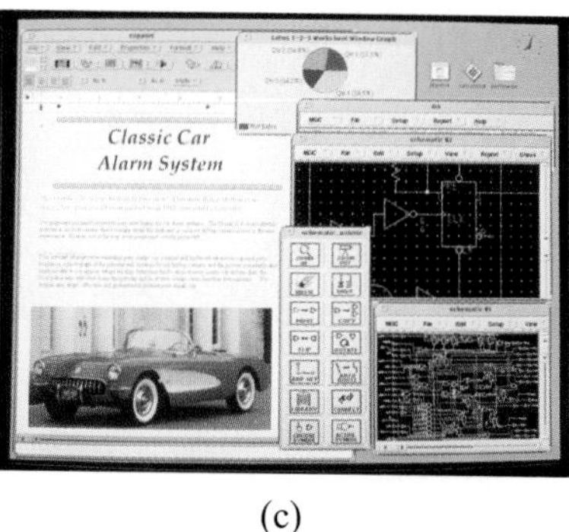

(c)

FIGURE 11-18 Examples of screen layouts using display windows, menus, and icons. (*Courtesy of (a) Intergraph Corporation; (b) Visual Numerics, Inc.; (c) Sun Microsystems.*)

Windows and Icons

Figure 11-18 shows examples of typical graphical interfaces. Visual representations are used both for the objects that are to be manipulated in an application and for the actions to be performed on the application objects.

In addition to the standard display-window operations, such as opening, closing, positioning, and resizing, other operations are needed for working with the sliders, buttons, icons, and menus. Some systems are capable of supporting multiple window managers so that different window styles can be accommodated, each with its own window manager, which could be structured for a particular application.

Icons representing objects such walls, doors, windows, and circuit elements are often referred to as **application icons.** The icons representing actions, such as rotate, magnify, scale, clip, or paste, are called **control icons,** or **command icons.**

Accommodating Multiple Skill Levels

Usually, interactive graphical interfaces provide several methods for selecting actions. For example, an option could be specified by pointing to an icon, accessing a pull-down or pop-up menu, or by typing a keyboard command. This allows a package to accommodate users that have different skill levels.

For a less experienced user, an interface with a few easily understood operations and detailed prompting is more effective than one with a large, comprehensive operation set. A simplified set of menus and options is easy to learn and remember, and the user can concentrate on the application instead of on the details of the interface. Simple point-and-click operations are often easiest for an inexperienced user of an applications package. Therefore, interfaces typically provide a means for masking the complexity of a package, so that beginners can use the system without being overwhelmed with too much detail.

Experienced users, on the other hand, typically want speed. This means fewer prompts and more input from the keyboard or with multiple mouse-button clicks. Actions are selected with function keys or with simultaneous combinations of keyboard keys, since experienced users will remember these shortcuts for commonly used actions.

Similarly, help facilities can be designed on several levels so that beginners can carry on a detailed dialogue, while more experienced users can reduce or eliminate prompts and messages. Help facilities can also include one or more tutorial applications, which provide users with an introduction to the capabilities and use of the system.

Consistency

An important design consideration in an interface is consistency. An icon shape should always have a single meaning, rather than serving to represent different actions or objects depending on the context. Some other examples of consistency are always placing menus in the same relative positions so that a user does not have to hunt for a particular option, always using the same combination of keyboard keys for an action, and always using the same color encoding so that a color does not have different meanings in different situations.

Minimizing Memorization

Operations in an interface should also be structured so that they are easy to understand and to remember. Obscure, complicated, inconsistent, and abbreviated command formats lead to confusion and reduction in the effective application of the software. One key or button used for all delete operations, for example, is easier to remember than a number of different keys for different kinds of delete procedures.

Icons and window systems can also be organized to minimize memorization. Different kinds of information can be separated into different windows so that a user can easily identify and select items. Icons should be designed as easily recognizable shapes that are related to application objects and actions. To select a particular action, a user should be able to select the icon that resembles that action.

Backup and Error Handling

A mechanism for undoing a sequence of operations is another common feature of an interface, which allows a user to explore the capabilities of a system, knowing that the effects of a mistake can be corrected. Typically, systems can now undo several operations, thus allowing a user to reset the system to some specified action. For those actions that cannot be reversed, such as closing an application without saving changes, the system asks for a verification of the requested operation.

In addition, good diagnostics and error messages help a user to determine the cause of an error. Interfaces can attempt to minimize errors by anticipating certain actions that could lead to an error. And users can be warned if they are requesting ambiguous or incorrect actions, such as attempting to apply a procedure to multiple application objects.

Feedback

Responding to user actions is another important feature of an interface, particularly for an inexperienced user. As each action is entered, some response should be given. Otherwise, a user might begin to wonder what the system is doing and whether the input should be reentered.

Feedback can be given in many forms, such as highlighting an object, displaying an icon or message, and displaying a selected menu option in a different color. When the processing of a requested action is lengthy, the display of a flashing message, clock, hourglass, or other progress indicator is important. It may also be possible for the system to display partial results as they are completed, so that the final display is built up a piece at a time. The system might also allow a user to input other commands or data while one instruction is being processed.

Standard symbol designs are used for typical kinds of feedback. A cross, a frowning face, or a thumbs-down symbol is often used to indicate an error, and some kind of time symbol or a blinking "at work" sign is used to indicate that an action is being processed. This type of feedback can be very effective with a more experienced user, but the beginner may need more detailed feedback that not only clearly indicates what the system is doing but also what the user should input next.

Clarity is another important feature of feedback. A response should be easily understood, but not so overpowering that the user's concentration is interrupted. With function keys, feedback can be given as an audible click or by lighting up the key that has been pressed. Audio feedback has the advantage that it does not use up screen space, and it does not divert the user's attention from the work area. A fixed message area can be used so that a user always know where to look for messages, but it may be advantageous in some cases to place feedback messages in the work area near the cursor. Feedback can also be displayed in different colors to distinguish it from other displayed objects.

Echo feedback is often useful, particularly for keyboard input so that errors can be quickly detected. Button and dial input can be echoed in the same way. Scalar values that are selected with dials or from displayed scales are usually echoed on the screen so that a user can check the input values for accuracy. Selection of coordinate points can be echoed with a cursor or other symbol that appears at the selected position. For more precise echoing of selected positions, the coordinate values could also be displayed on the screen.

11-9 SUMMARY

Input to graphics programs can come from many different hardware devices, with more than one device providing the same general class of input data. Graphics input functions are often designed to be independent of hardware by adopting a logical classification for input devices. A device is then specified according to the type of graphics input. The six logical devices used in the ISO and ANSI standards are locator, stroke, string, valuator, choice, and pick. Locator devices input a single coordinate position. Stroke devices input a stream of coordinates. String devices input text. Valuator devices enter a scalar value. Choice devices are used for menu selections. And pick devices allow us to select scene components. Device-independent graphics packages offer a limited set of input functions that are defined in an auxiliary library.

Three modes are commonly used for input functions. Request mode places input under the control of the application program. Sample mode allows the input devices and program to operate concurrently. Event mode allows input devices to initiate data entry and control processing of data. Once we have chosen a mode for a logical device class and the particular physical device to be used to enter this class of data, input functions are used to enter data values into the program. An application program can make simultaneous use of several physical input devices operating in different modes.

Interactive picture-construction methods are commonly used in a variety of applications, including design and painting packages. These methods provide users with the capability to specify object positions, constrain objects to predefined orientations or alignments, and interactively draw or paint objects into a scene. Grids, gravity fields, and rubber-band methods are used to aid in positioning and other picture-construction operations.

Graphical user interfaces are now standard features of applications software. A dialogue for the software is designed from the user's model, which describes the purpose and functions of the applications package. All elements of the dialogue are presented in the language of the application.

Window systems provide a typical interface with procedures for manipulating display windows, menus, and icons. General window systems can be designed to support multiple window managers.

Considerations in user-dialogue design are ease-of-use, clarity, and flexibility. Specifically, graphical interfaces are designed to maintain consistency in user interaction and to provide for different user skill levels. In addition, interfaces are designed to minimize user memorization, to provide sufficient feedback, and to provide adequate backup and error handling capabilities.

In the Utility Toolkit, GLUT, input functions are available for interactive devices, such as a mouse, tablet, spaceball, button box, and dial box. In addition, GLUT provides a function for accepting a combination of input values from a mouse and a keyboard. Picking operations can be performed using functions from the GLU library and the basic OpenGL library. We can also display pop-up menus and submenus using a set of functions in the GLUT library. A summary of the OpenGL input and menu functions is given in the Tables 11-1 and 11-2.

TABLE 11-1

SUMMARY OF OpenGL INPUT FUNCTIONS

Function	*Description*
`glutMouseFunc`	Specify a mouse callback function that is to be invoked when a mouse button is pressed.
`glutMotionFunc`	Specify a mouse callback function that is to be invoked when the mouse cursor is moved while a button is pressed.
`glutPassiveMotionFunc`	Specify a mouse callback function that is to be invoked when the mouse cursor is moved without pressing a button.
`glutKeyboardFunc`	Specify a keyboard callback function that is to be invoked when a standard key is pressed.
`glutSpecialFunc`	Specify a keyboard callback function that is to be invoked when a special-purpose key (e.g., function key) is pressed.

(*Continued*)

Function	Description
`glutTabletButtonFunc`	Specify a tablet callback function that is to be invoked when a tablet button is pressed while the mouse cursor is in a display window.
`glutTabletMotionFunc`	Specify a tablet callback function that is to be invoked when a tablet stylus or cursor is moved while the mouse cursor is in a display window.
`glutSpaceballButtonFunc`	Specify a spaceball callback function that is to be invoked when a spaceball button is pressed while the mouse cursor is in a display window, or using another display-window activation method.
`glutSpaceballMotionFunc`	Specify a spaceball callback function that is to be invoked when a spaceball translational motion occurs for an activated display window.
`glutSpaceballRotateFunc`	Specify a spaceball callback function that is to be invoked when a spaceball rotational motion occurs for an activated display window.
`glutButtonBoxFunc`	Specify a button-box callback function that is to be invoked when a button is pressed.
`glutDialsFunc`	Specify a dial callback function that is to be invoked when a dial is rotated.
`glSelectBuffer`	Specify size and name for the pick buffer.
`glRenderMode`	Activate pick operations using the argument `GL_SELECT`. This function is also used to activate the normal rendering mode or the feedback mode.
`glInitNames`	Activate the object-ID name stack.
`glPushName`	Push an object identifier onto the ID stack.
`glLoadName`	Replace the top identifier on the ID stack with a specified value.
`glPopName`	Eliminate the top item on the ID stack.
`gluPickMatrix`	Define a pick window and form a revised view volume for the picking operations.

TABLE 11-2

SUMMARY OF OpenGL MENU FUNCTIONS

Function	Description
`glutCreateMenu`	Create a pop-up menu and specify a procedure that is to be invoked when a menu item is selected; an integer identifier is assigned to the created menu.
`glutAddMenuEntry`	Specify an option that is to be listed in a pop-up menu.
`glutAttachMenu`	Specify the mouse button that is to used for selecting menu options.
`glutSetMenu`	Specify the current menu for the current display window.
`glutDestroyMenu`	Specify an identifier for a menu that is to be eliminated.
`glutGetMenu`	Returns the identifier for the current menu attached to the current window.
`glutAddSubMenu`	Specify a submenu that is to be included in a menu listing, where the indicated submenu has been set up using the `glutCreateMenu` routine.
`glutDetachMenu`	Cancel a specified mouse-button attachment for the current menu.
`glutRemoveMenuItem`	Delete a specified option in the current menu.

REFERENCES

The evolution of the concept of logical (or virtual) input devices is discussed in Wallace (1976) and in Rosenthal, Michener, Pfaff, Kessener, and Sabin (1982). Implementations for various input procedures are given in Glassner (1990), Arvo (1991), Kirk (1992), Heckbert (1994), and Paeth (1995). Additional programming examples using mouse and keyboard input can be found in Woo, Neider, Davis, and Shreiner (1999). A complete listing of the functions in the OpenGL basic library and the GLU library is given in Shreiner (2000). The GLUT input and menu functions are listed in detail in Kilgard (1996).

Guidelines for user-interface design are presented in Shneiderman (1986), Apple (1987), Bleser (1988), Brown and Cunningham (1989), Digital (1989), OSF/MOTIF (1989), and Laurel (1990). For information on the X Window System see Young (1990) and Cutler, Gilly, and Reilly (1992).

EXERCISES

11-1 Design an algorithm that allows objects to be positioned on the screen using a locator device. An object menu of geometric shapes is to be presented to a user who is to select an object and a placement position. The program should allow any number of objects to be positioned until a "terminate" signal is given.

11-2 Extend the algorithm of the previous exercise so that selected objects can be scaled and rotated before positioning. The transformation choices and transformation parameters are to be presented to the user as menu options.

11-3 Set up a procedure for interactively sketching pictures using a stroke device.

11-4 Discuss the methods that could be employed in a pattern-recognition procedure to match input characters against a stored library of shapes.

11-5 Write a routine that displays a linear scale and a slider on the screen and allows numeric values to be selected by positioning the slide along the scale line. The selected numeric value is to be echoed in a box displayed near the linear scale.

11-6 Write a routine that displays a circular scale and a pointer or a slider that can be moved around the circle to select angles (in degrees). The angular value selected is to be echoed in a box displayed near the circular scale.

11-7 Write a drawing program that allows users to create a picture as a set of straight-line segments drawn between specified endpoints. The coordinates of the individual line segments are to be selected with a locator device.

11-8 Write a drawing package that allows pictures to be created with straight-line segments drawn between specified endpoints. Set up a gravity field around each line in a picture, as an aid in connecting new lines to existing lines.

11-9 Modify the drawing package in the previous exercise so that lines can be constrained horizontally or vertically.

11-10 Develop a drawing package that can display an optional grid pattern so that selected screen positions are rounded to grid intersections. The package is to provide line-drawing capabilities, with line endpoints selected using a locator device.

11-11 Write a routine that allows a designer to create a picture by sketching straight lines using a rubber-band method.

11-12 Design a drawing package that allows straight lines, rectangles, and circles to be constructed using rubber-band methods.

11-13 Write a procedure that allows a user to pick components of a two-dimensional scene. The coordinate extents for each object are to be stored and used to identify the picked object, given an input cursor position.

11-14 Develop a procedure that allows a user to design a picture from a menu of displayed basic shapes by dragging each selected shape into position with a pick device.

11-15 Design an implementation of the input functions for request mode.

11-16 Design an implementation of the sample mode input functions.

11-17 Design an implementation of the input functions for event mode.

11-18 Design a procedure for implementing input functions for request, sample, and event mode.

11-19 Expand the OpenGL point-plotting program in Section 11-6 to include a menu that allows a user to select point size and point color.

11-20 Expand the OpenGL polyline program in Section 11-6 to include a menu that allows a user to choose the line attributes: size, color, and width.

11-21 Modify the program in the preceding exercise to allow a texture pattern to be chosen for the polyline.

11-22 Write an interactive OpenGL program to display a 100 by 100 pixel rectangle at any input position within a display window. The input position is to be the center of the rectangle. Include a menu of color options for displaying the rectangle in a solid color.

11-23 Modify the program in the preceding exercise so that the input position is rejected if all of the rectangle cannot be displayed within the display window.

11-24 Modify the program in the preceding exercise to include a menu of texture options for the rectangle. Set up a minimum of two texture patterns.

11-25 Set up an interactive OpenGL program for displaying an input character string at any position within a display window. The input position is the starting position for the text.

11-26 Write an interactive OpenGL program for positioning a single two-dimensional object at any position within a display window. The object is to be selected from a menu of basic shapes, including (minimally) a square, circle, and triangle.

11-27 Modify the program in the preceding exercise to allow any arrangement of the two-dimensional objects to be displayed, with each object selected from the menu until a quit option is chosen from the menu.

11-28 Modify the program in the preceding exercise to allow objects to be scaled or rotated. Geometric transformation operations are to be listed in a menu.

11-29 Write an interactive OpenGL program for positioning a single three-dimensional object within a display window. The object is to be selected from a menu list of GLUT wire-frame solids, such as a sphere, solid, or cylinder, and it is to be centered on an input position.

11-30 Modify the program in the preceding exercise to allow the objects to be displayed in either a wire-frame or solid form. For solid-object displays, include a point light source at the viewing position, and use default parameters for the illumination and surface shading.

11-31 Write a program to implement the OpenGL picking operations for a three-dimensional scene containing several objects. For each pick selection, create a small pick window and bring the most distant object within that pick window to the front.

11-32 Write an interactive OpenGL program to display a two-dimensional cubic Bézier curve. The four control-point positions are to be selected with mouse input.

11-33 Modify the program in the preceding exercise to display a Bézier curve with a selected degree of three, four, or five.

11-34 Write an interactive OpenGL program to display a two-dimensional cubic B-spline. The spline parameters are to be given as input, and the control points are to be selected with a mouse.

11-35 Write an interactive OpenGL program to display a cubic Bézier surface patch. The x and y coordinates for the control points can be selected with a mouse, and the z coordinate can be given as a height above a ground plane.

11-36 Select some graphics application with which you are familiar and set up a user model that will serve as the basis for the design of a user interface for graphics applications in that area.

11-37 List possible help facilities that can be provided in a user interface and discuss which types of help would be appropriate for different levels of users.

11-38 Summarize the methods for handling backup and errors. Which methods are suitable for a beginner? Which methods are better for an experienced user?

11-39 List the possible formats for presenting menus to a user, and explain under what circumstances each might be appropriate.

11-40 Discuss alternatives for feedback in terms of the various levels of users.

11-41 List the functions that must be performed by a window manager in handling screen layouts with multiple, overlapping windows.

11-42 Set up a design for a window-manager package.

11-43 Design a user interface for a painting program.

11-44 Design a user interface for a two-level hierarchical modeling package.

CHAPTER 12

Color Models and Color Applications

A computer-generated flower scene modeled with various color combinations and a basic petal shape. *(Courtesy of Przemyslaw Prusinkiewicz, University of Calgary. © 1987.)*

12-1	Properties of Light	**12-6**	The CMY and CMYK Color Models
12-2	Color Models	**12-7**	The HSV Color Model
12-3	Standard Primaries and the Chromaticity Diagram	**12-8**	The HLS Color Model
12-4	The RGB Color Model	**12-9**	Color Selection and Applications
12-5	The YIQ and Related Color Models	**12-10**	Summary

Our discussions of color up to this point have concentrated on RGB color methods, which we use for generating displays on video monitors. Several other color descriptions are useful as well in computer-graphics applications. Some methods are used to describe color output on printers and plotters, some are used for transmitting and storing color information, and others are used to provide a more intuitive color-parameter interface to a program.

12-1 PROPERTIES OF LIGHT

As we have noted in previous chapters, light exhibits many different characteristics, and we describe the properties of light in different ways in different contexts. Physically, we can characterize light as radiant energy, but we also need other concepts to describe our perception of light.

The Electromagnetic Spectrum

In physical terms, color is electromagnetic radiation within a narrow frequency band. Some of the other frequency groups in the electromagnetic spectrum are referred to as radio waves, microwaves, infrared waves, and X-rays. Figure 12-1 shows the approximate frequency ranges for these various aspects of electromagnetic radiation.

Each frequency value within the visible region of the electromagnetic spectrum corresponds to a distinct **spectral color.** At the low-frequency end (approximately 3.8×10^{14} hertz) are the red colors, and at the high-frequency end

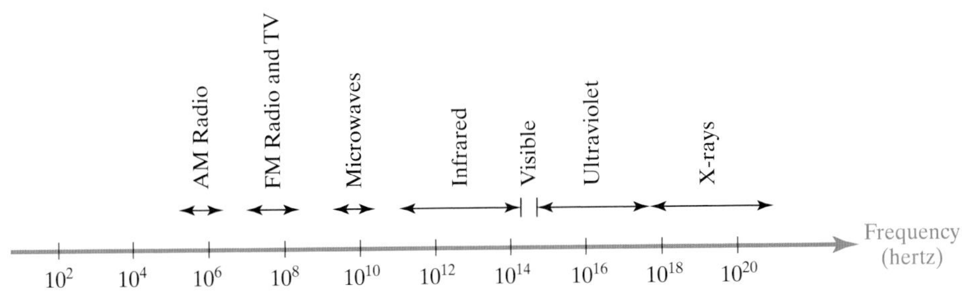

FIGURE 12-1
Electromagnetic spectrum.

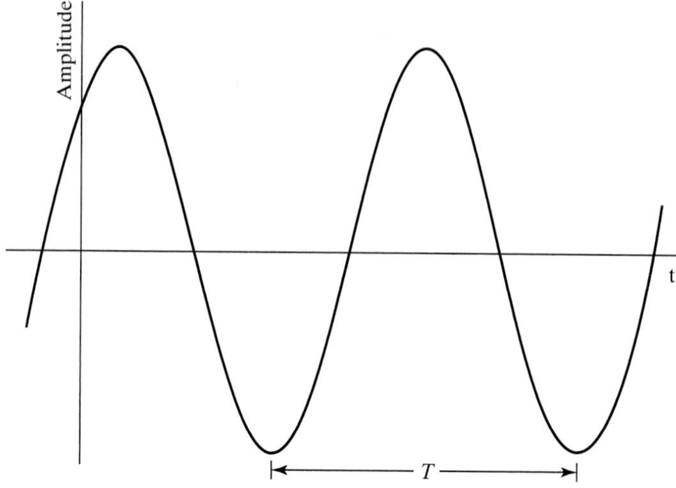

FIGURE 12-2 Time variations for the amplitude of the electric field for one frequency component of a plane-polarized electromagnetic wave. The time between two consecutive amplitude peaks or two consecutive amplitude minimums is called the period of the wave.

(approximately 7.9×10^{14} hertz) are the violet colors. Actually, the human eye is sensitive to some frequencies into the infrared and ultraviolet bands. Spectral colors range from shades of red through orange and yellow, at the low-frequency end, to shades of green, blue, and violet at the high end.

In the wave model of electromagnetic radiation, light can be described as oscillating transverse electric and magnetic fields propagating through space. The electric and magnetic fields are oscillating in directions that are perpendicular to each other and to the direction of propagation. For each spectral color, the rate of oscillation of the field magnitude is given by the frequency f. Fig. 12-2 illustrates the time-varying oscillations for the magnitude of the electric field within one plane. The time between any two consecutive positions on the wave that have the same amplitude is called the *period* $T = 1/f$ of the wave. And the distance that the wave has traveled from the beginning of one oscillation to the beginning of the next oscillation is called the *wavelength* λ. For one spectral color (a monochromatic wave), the wavelength and frequency are inversely proportional to each other, with the proportionality constant as the speed of light c:

$$c = \lambda f \tag{12-1}$$

Frequency for each spectral color is a constant for all materials, but the speed of light and the wavelength are material dependent. In a vacuum, the speed of light is very nearly $c = 3 \times 10^{10}$ cm/sec. Light wavelengths are very small, so length units for designating spectral colors are usually given in angstroms ($1\ \text{Å} = 10^{-8}$ cm) or in nanometers ($1\ \text{nm} = 10^{-7}$ cm). An equivalent term for nanometer is millimicron. Light at the low-frequency end of the spectrum (red) has a wavelength of approximately 780 nanometers (nm), and the wavelength at the other end of the spectrum (violet) is about 380 nm. Since wavelength units are somewhat more convenient to deal with than frequency units, spectral colors are typically specified in terms of the wavelength values in a vacuum.

A light source such as the sun or a standard household light bulb emits all frequencies within the visible range to produce white light. When white light is incident upon an opaque object, some frequencies are reflected and some are absorbed. The combination of frequencies present in the reflected light determines what we perceive as the color of the object. If low frequencies are predominant in the reflected light, the object is described as red. In this case, we say that the perceived light has a **dominant frequency** (or **dominant wavelength**) at the red end of the spectrum. The dominant frequency is also called the **hue,** or simply the **color,** of the light.

Psychological Characteristics of Color

Other properties besides frequency are needed to characterize our perception of light. When we view a source of light, our eyes respond to the color (or dominant frequency) and two other basic sensations. One of these we call the **brightness,** which corresponds to the total light energy and can be quantified as the luminance of the light (Section 10-3). The third perceived characteristic is called the **purity,** or the **saturation,** of the light. Purity describes how close a light appears to be to a pure spectral color, such as red. Pastels and pale colors have low purity (low saturation) and they appear to be nearly white. Another term, **chromaticity,** is used to refer collectively to the two properties describing color characteristics: purity and dominant frequency (hue).

Radiation emitted by a white light source has an energy distribution that can be represented over the visible frequencies as in Fig. 12-3. Each frequency component within the range from red to violet contributes more or less equally to the total energy, and the color of the source is described as white. When a dominant frequency is present, the energy distribution for the source takes a form such as that in Fig. 12-4. We would describe this light as a red color (the dominant frequency), with a relatively high value for the purity. The energy density of the dominant light component is labeled as E_D in this figure, and the contributions from the other frequencies produce white light of energy density E_W. We can calculate the brightness of the source as the area under the curve, which gives the total energy density emitted. Purity (saturation) depends on the difference between E_D and E_W. The larger the energy E_D of the dominant frequency compared to the white-light component E_W, the higher the purity of the light. We have a purity of 100 percent when $E_W = 0$ and a purity of 0 percent when $E_W = E_D$.

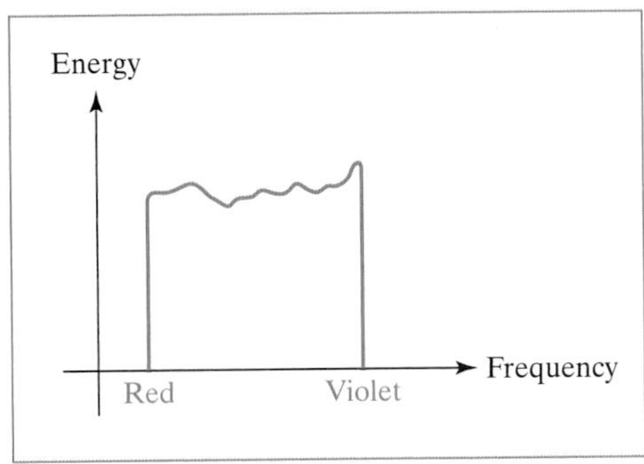

FIGURE 12-3 Energy distribution for a white light source.

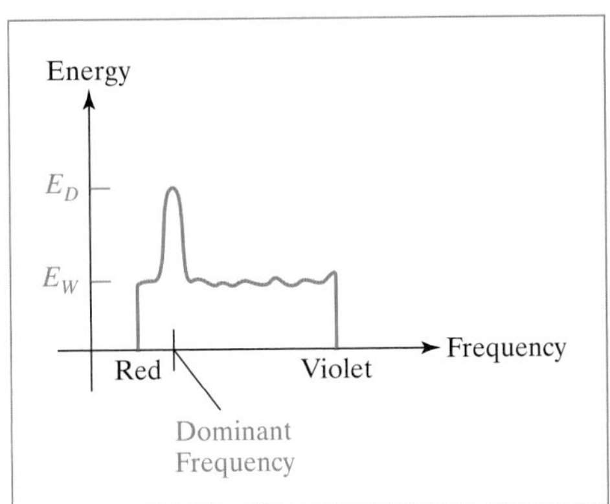

FIGURE 12-4 Energy distribution for a light source with a dominant frequency near the red end of the frequency range.

12-2 COLOR MODELS

Any method for explaining the properties or behavior of color within some particular context is called a **color model.** No single model can explain all aspects of color, so we make use of different models to help describe different color characteristics.

Primary Colors

When we combine the light from two or more sources with different dominant frequencies, we can vary the amount (intensity) of light from each source to generate a range of additional colors. This represents one method for forming a color model. The hues that we choose for the sources are called the **primary colors,** and the **color gamut** for the model is the set of all colors that we can produce from the primary colors. Two primaries that produce white are referred to as **complementary colors.** Examples of complementary color pairs are red and cyan, green and magenta, and blue and yellow.

No finite set of real primary colors can be combined to produce all possible visible colors. Nevertheless, three primaries are sufficient for most purposes, and colors not in the color gamut for a specified set of primaries can still be described using extended methods. Given a set of three primary colors, we can characterize any fourth color using color-mixing processes. Thus, a mixture of one or two of the primaries with the fourth color can be used to match some combination of the remaining primaries. In this extended sense, a set of three primary colors can be considered to describe all colors. Figure 12-5 shows a set of *color-matching functions* for three primaries and the amount of each needed to produce any spectral color. The curves plotted in Fig. 12-5 were obtained by averaging the judgments of a large number of observers. Colors in the vicinity of 500 nm can only be matched by "subtracting" an amount of red light from a combination of blue and green lights. This means that a color around 500 nm is described only by combining that color with an amount of red light to produce the blue-green combination specified in the diagram. Thus, an RGB color monitor cannot display colors in the neighborhood of 500 nm.

Intuitive Color Concepts

An artist creates a color painting by mixing color pigments with white and black pigments to form the various shades, tints, and tones in the scene. Starting with

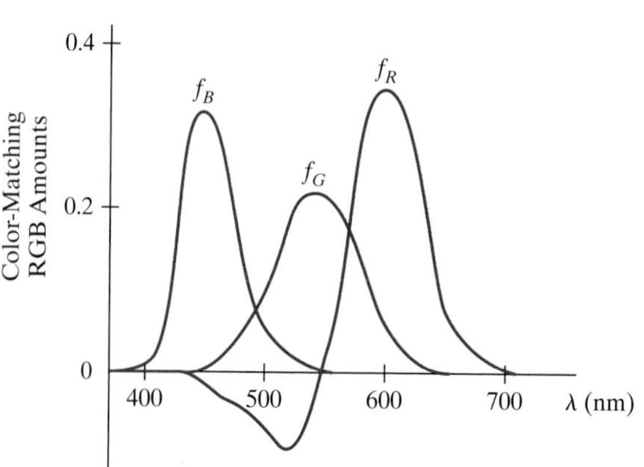

FIGURE 12-5 Three color-matching functions for displaying spectral frequencies within the approximate range from 400 nm to 700 nm.

the pigment for a "pure color" ("pure hue"), the artist adds a black pigment to produce different **shades** of that color. The more black pigment, the darker the shade. Similarly, different **tints** of the color are obtained by adding a white pigment to the original color, making it lighter as more white is added. **Tones** of the color are produced by adding both black and white pigments.

To many, these color concepts are more intuitive than describing a color as a set of three numbers that give the relative proportions of the primary colors. It is generally much easier to think of creating a pastel red color by adding white to pure red and producing a dark blue color by adding black to pure blue. Therefore, graphics packages providing color palettes to a user often employ two or more color models. One model provides an intuitive color interface for the user, and the others describe the color components for the output devices.

12-3 STANDARD PRIMARIES AND THE CHROMATICITY DIAGRAM

Since no finite set of light sources can be combined to display all possible colors, three standard primaries were defined in 1931 by the International Commission on Illumination, referred to as the CIE (Commission Internationale de l'Éclairage). The three standard primaries are imaginary colors. They are defined mathematically with positive color-matching functions (Fig. 12-6) that specify the amount of each primary needed to describe any spectral color. This provides an international standard definition for all colors, and the CIE primaries eliminate negative-value color-matching and other problems associated with selecting a set of real primaries.

The XYZ Color Model

The set of CIE primaries is generally referred to as the XYZ color model, where parameters X, Y, and Z represent the amount of each CIE primary needed to produce a selected color. Thus, a color is described with the XYZ model in the same way that we described a color using the RGB model.

In the three-dimensional XYZ color space, we represent any color $C(\lambda)$ as

$$C(\lambda) = (X, Y, Z) \tag{12-2}$$

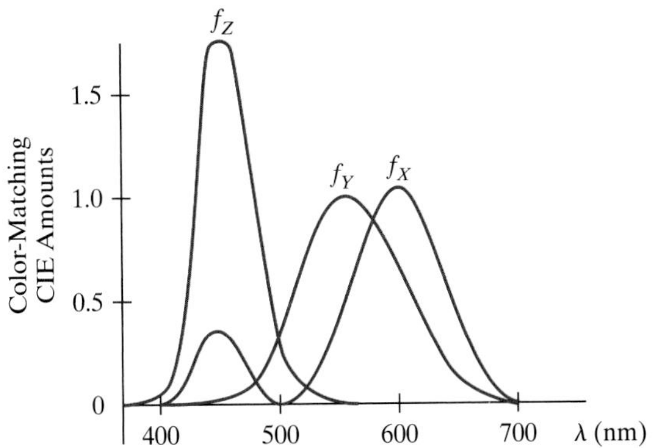

FIGURE 12-6 The three color-matching functions for the CIE primaries.

where X, Y, and Z are calculated from the color-matching functions (Fig. 12-6):

$$X = k \int_{\text{visible } \lambda} f_X(\lambda)\, I(\lambda)\, d\lambda$$
$$Y = k \int_{\text{visible } \lambda} f_Y(\lambda)\, I(\lambda)\, d\lambda \qquad (12\text{-}3)$$
$$Z = k \int_{\text{visible } \lambda} f_Z(\lambda)\, I(\lambda)\, d\lambda$$

Parameter k in these calculations has the value 683 lumens/watt, where lumen is a unit of measure for light radiation per unit solid angle from a "standard" point light source (once called a *candle*). The function $I(\lambda)$ represents the spectral radiance, which is the selected light intensity in a particular direction, and the color-matching function f_Y is chosen so that parameter Y is the luminance (Eq. 10-26) for that color. Luminance values are normally adjusted to the range from 0 to 100.0, where 100.0 represents the luminance of white light.

Any color can be represented in the XYZ color space as an additive combination of the primaries using unit vectors **X, Y, Z**. Thus, we can write Eq. 12-2 as

$$C(\lambda) = X\mathbf{X} + Y\mathbf{X} + Z\mathbf{X} \qquad (12\text{-}4)$$

Normalized XYZ Values

In discussing color properties, it is convenient to normalize the amounts in Eq. 12-3 against the sum $X + Y + Z$, which represents the total light energy. Normalized amounts are thus calculated as

$$x = \frac{X}{X+Y+Z}, \qquad y = \frac{Y}{X+Y+Z}, \qquad z = \frac{Z}{X+Y+Z} \qquad (12\text{-}5)$$

Since $x + y + z = 1$, any color can be represented with just the x and y amounts. Also, we have normalized against total energy, so parameters x and y depend only on hue and purity and they are called the **chromaticity values.** However, the x and y values alone do not allow us to completely describe all properties of the color, and we cannot obtain the amounts X, Y, and Z. Therefore, a complete description of a color is typically given with the three values x, y, and the luminance Y. The remaining CIE amounts are then calculated as

$$X = \frac{x}{y}Y, \qquad Z = \frac{z}{y}Y \qquad (12\text{-}6)$$

where $z = 1 - x - y$. Using chromaticity coordinates (x, y), we can represent all colors on a two-dimensional diagram.

The CIE Chromaticity Diagram

When we plot the normalized amounts x and y for colors in the visible spectrum, we obtain the tongue-shaped curve shown in Fig. 12-7. This curve is called the **CIE chromaticity diagram.** Points along the curve are the spectral colors (pure colors). The line joining the red and violet spectral points, referred to as the *purple line,* is not part of the spectrum. Interior points represent all possible visible color combinations. Point C in the diagram corresponds to the white-light position. Actually, this point is plotted for a white light source known as **illuminant C,** which is used as a standard approximation for average daylight.

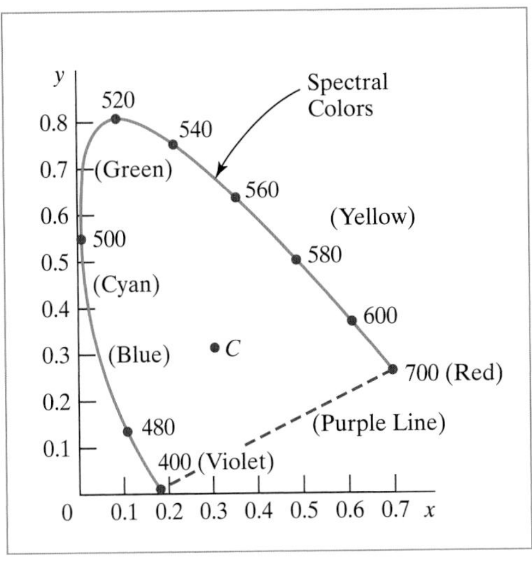

FIGURE 12-7 CIE chromaticity diagram for the spectral colors from 400 nm to 700 nm.

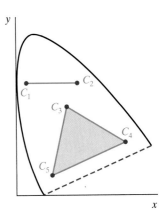

FIGURE 12-8 Color gamuts defined on the chromaticity diagram for a two-color and a three-color system of primaries.

Luminance values are not available in the chromaticity diagram because of normalization. Colors with different luminance but with the same chromaticity map to the same point. The chromaticity diagram is useful for:

- Comparing color gamuts for different sets of primaries.
- Identifying complementary colors.
- Determining purity and dominant wavelength for a given color.

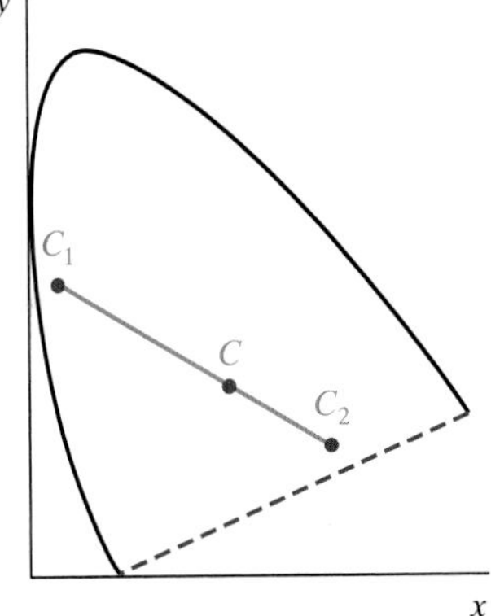

FIGURE 12-9 Representing complementary colors on the chromaticity diagram.

Color Gamuts

We identify color gamuts on the chromaticity diagram as straight-line segments or polygon regions. All colors along the straight line joining points C_1 and C_2 in Fig. 12-8 can be obtained by mixing appropriate amounts of the colors C_1 and C_2. If a greater proportion of C_1 is used, the resultant color is closer to C_1 than to C_2. The color gamut for three points, such C_3, C_4, and C_5 in Fig. 12-8, is a triangle with vertices at the three color positions. These three primaries can generate only the colors inside or on the bounding edges of the triangle. Thus, the chromaticity diagram helps us to understand why no set of three primaries can be additively combined to generate all colors, since no triangle within the diagram can encompass all colors. Color gamuts for video monitors and hard-copy devices are conveniently compared on the chromaticity diagram.

Complementary Colors

Since the color gamut for two points is a straight line, complementary colors must be represented on the chromaticity diagram as two points on opposite sides of C and collinear with C, as in Fig. 12-9. The distances of the two colors C_1 and C_2 to C determine the amounts of each needed to produce white light.

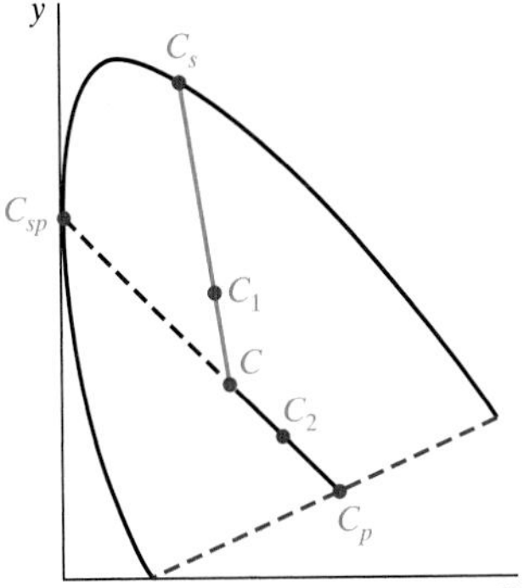

FIGURE 12-10 Determining dominant wavelength and purity using the chromaticity diagram.

Dominant Wavelength

To determine the dominant wavelength of a color, we draw a straight line from C through that color point to a spectral color on the chromaticity curve. The spectral color C_s in Fig. 12-10 is the dominant wavelength for color C_1 in this diagram. Thus, color C_1 can be represented as a combination of white light C and the spectral color C_s. This method for determining dominant wavelength will not work for color points that are between C and the purple line. Drawing a line from C through point C_2 in Fig. 12-10 takes us to point C_p on the purple line, which is not in the visible spectrum. In this case, we take the compliment of C_p on the spectral curve, which is the point C_{sp}, as the dominant wavelength. Colors such as C_2 in this diagram have spectral distributions with subtractive dominant wavelengths. We can describe such colors by subtracting the spectral dominant wavelength from white light.

Purity

For a color point such as C_1 in Fig. 12-10, we determine the purity as the relative distance of C_1 from C along the straight line joining C to C_s. If d_{c1} denotes the distance from C to C_1 and d_{cs} is the distance from C to C_s, we can represent purity as the ratio d_{c1}/d_{cs}. Color C_1 in this figure is about 25 percent pure, since it is situated at about one-fourth the total distance from C to C_s. At position C_s, the color point would be 100 percent pure.

12-4 THE RGB COLOR MODEL

According to the *tristimulus theory* of vision, our eyes perceive color through the stimulation of three visual pigments in the cones of the retina. One of the pigments is most sensitive to light with a wavelength of about 630 nm (red), another has its peak sensitivity at about 530 nm (green), and the third pigment is most receptive to light with a wavelength of about 450 nm (blue). By comparing intensities in a light source, we perceive the color of the light. This theory of vision is the basis for displaying color output on a video monitor using the three primaries red, green, and blue, which is referred to as the RGB color model.

We can represent this model using the unit cube defined on R, G, and B axes, as shown in Fig. 12-11. The origin represents black and the diagonally opposite vertex, with coordinates (1, 1, 1), is white. Vertices of the cube on the axes represent the primary colors, and the remaining vertices are the complementary color points for each of the primary colors.

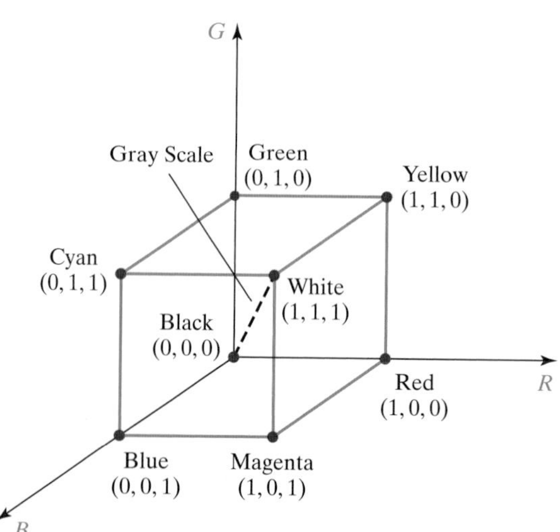

FIGURE 12-11 The RGB color model. Any color within the unit cube can be described as an additive combination of the three primary colors.

TABLE 12-1

RGB (x, y) CHROMATICITY COORDINATES

	NTSC Standard	CIE Model	Approx. Color Monitor Values
R	(0.670, 0.330)	(0.735, 0.265)	(0.628, 0.346)
G	(0.210, 0.710)	(0.274, 0.717)	(0.268, 0.588)
B	(0.140, 0.080)	(0.167, 0.009)	(0.150, 0.070)

As with the XYZ color system, the RGB color scheme is an additive model. Each color point within the unit cube can be represented as a weighted vector sum of the primary colors, using unit vectors **R**, **G**, and **B**:

$$C(\lambda) = (R,\ G,\ B) = R\,\mathbf{R} + G\,\mathbf{G} + B\,\mathbf{B} \tag{12-7}$$

where parameters R, G, and B are assigned values in the range from 0 to 1.0. For example, the magenta vertex is obtained by adding maximum red and blue values to produce the triple (1, 0, 1), and white at (1, 1, 1) is the sum of the maximum values for red, green, and blue. Shades of gray are represented along the main diagonal of the cube from the origin (black) to the white vertex. Points along this diagonal have equal contributions from each primary color, and a gray shade halfway between black and white is represented as (0.5, 0.5, 0.5). The color graduations along the front and top planes of the RGB cube are illustrated in Fig. 12-12.

Chromaticity coordinates for the National Television System Committee (NTSC) standard RGB phosphors are listed in Table 12-1. Also listed are the RGB chromaticity coordinates within the CIE color model and the approximate values used for phosphors in color monitors. Figure 12-13 shows the approximate color gamut for the NTSC standard RGB primaries.

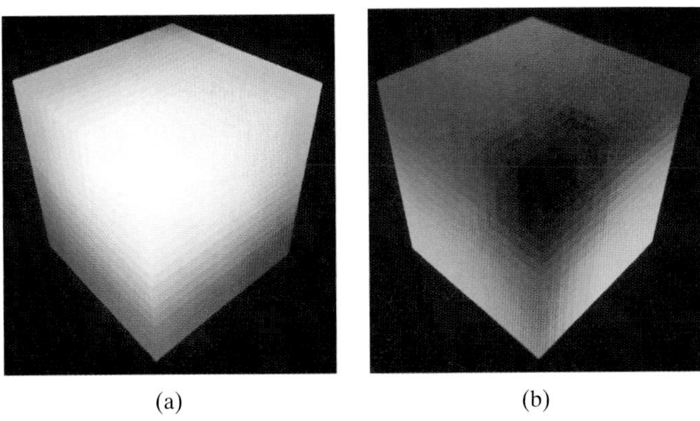

FIGURE 12-12 Two views of the RGB color cube. View (a) is along the gray-scale diagonal from white to black, and view (b) is along the gray-scale diagonal from black to white.

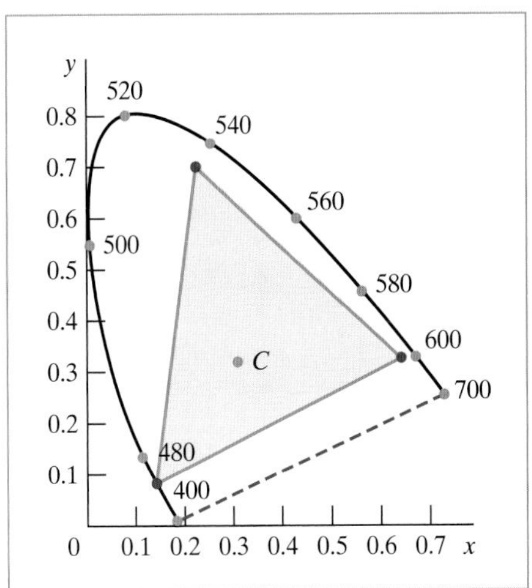

FIGURE 12-13 The RGB color gamut for NTSC chromaticity coordinates. Illuminant C is at position (0.310, 0.316), with a luminance value of $Y = 100.0$.

12-5 THE YIQ AND RELATED COLOR MODELS

Although an RGB graphics monitor requires separate signals for the red, green, and blue components of an image, a television monitor uses a composite signal. NTSC color encoding for forming the composite video signal is called the YIQ model.

The YIQ Parameters

In the YIQ color model, parameter Y is the same as the Y component in the CIE XYZ color space. Luminance (brightness) information is conveyed by the Y parameter, while chromaticity information (hue and purity) is incorporated into the I and Q parameters. A combination of red, green, and blue is chosen for the Y parameter to yield the standard luminosity curve. Since Y contains the luminance information, black-and-white television monitors use only the Y signal. Parameter I contains orange-cyan color information that provides the flesh-tone shading, and parameter Q carries green-magenta color information.

The NTSC composite color signal is designed to provide information in a form that can be received by black-and-white television monitors, which obtain gray-scale information for a picture within a 6 MHz bandwidth. Thus, the YIQ information is also encoded within a 6 MHz bandwidth, but the luminance and chromaticity values are encoded on separate analog signals. In this way, the luminance signal is unchanged for black-and-white monitors, and the color information is simply added within the same bandwidth. Luminance information, the Y value, is conveyed as an amplitude modulation on a carrier signal with a bandwidth of about 4.2 MHz. Chromaticity information, the I and Q values, is combined on a second carrier signal that has a bandwidth of about 1.8 MHz. The parameter names I and Q refer to the modulation methods used to encode the color information on this carrier. An amplitude-modulation encoding (the "in-phase" signal) transmits the I value, using about 1.3 MHz of the bandwidth. And a phase-modulation encoding (the "quadrature" signal), using about 0.5 MHz, carries the Q value.

Luminance values are encoded at a higher precision in the NTSC signal (4.2 MHz bandwidth) than the chromaticity values (1.8 MHz bandwidth), because we can more easily detect small brightness changes compared to small color changes. However, the lower precision for the chromaticity encoding does result in some degradation of the color quality for an NTSC picture.

We can calculate the luminance value for an RGB color using Eq. 10-27, and one method for producing chromaticity values is to subtract the luminance from the red and blue components of the color. Thus,

$$\begin{aligned} Y &= 0.299\,R + 0.587\,G + 0.114\,B \\ I &= R - Y \\ Q &= B - Y \end{aligned} \tag{12-8}$$

Transformations Between RGB and YIQ Color Spaces

An RGB color is converted to a set of YIQ values using an NTSC encoder that implements the calculations in Eq. 12-8 and modulates the carrier signals. The conversion from RGB space to YIQ space is accomplished using the following transformation matrix.

$$\begin{bmatrix} Y \\ I \\ Q \end{bmatrix} = \begin{bmatrix} 0.299 & 0.587 & 0.114 \\ 0.701 & -0.587 & -0.114 \\ -0.299 & -0.587 & 0.886 \end{bmatrix} \cdot \begin{bmatrix} R \\ G \\ B \end{bmatrix} \tag{12-9}$$

Conversely, an NTSC video signal is converted to RGB color values using an NTSC decoder, which first separates the video signal into the YIQ components, and then converts the YIQ values to RGB values. The conversion from YIQ space to RGB space is accomplished with the inverse of transformation 12-9:

$$\begin{bmatrix} R \\ G \\ B \end{bmatrix} = \begin{bmatrix} 1.000 & 1.000 & 0.000 \\ 1.000 & -0.509 & -0.194 \\ 1.000 & 0.000 & 1.000 \end{bmatrix} \cdot \begin{bmatrix} Y \\ I \\ Q \end{bmatrix} \tag{12-10}$$

The YUV and YC_rC_b Systems

Because of the lower bandwidth assigned to the chromaticity information in the NTSC composite analog video signal, the color quality of an NTSC picture is somewhat impaired. Therefore, variations of the YIQ encoding have been developed to improve the color quality of video transmissions. One such encoding is the YUV set of color parameters, which provides the composite color information for video transmissions by systems such as PAL (Phase Alternation Line) Broadcasting, used in most of Europe, as well as Africa, Australia, and Eurasia. Another variation of YIQ is the digital encoding called YC_rC_b. This color representation is used for digital video transformations, and it is incorporated into various graphics file formats, such as the JPEG system (Section 15-4).

12-6 THE CMY AND CMYK COLOR MODELS

A video monitor displays color patterns by combining light that is emitted from the screen phosphors, which is an additive process. However, hard-copy devices, such as printers and plotters, produce a color picture by coating a paper with color pigments. We see the color patterns on the paper by reflected light, which is a subtractive process.

The CMY Parameters

A subtractive color model can be formed with the three primary colors cyan, magenta, and yellow. As we have noted, cyan can be described as a combination of green and blue. Therefore, when white light is reflected from cyan-colored ink, the reflected light contains only the green and blue components, and the red component is absorbed, or subtracted, by the ink. Similarly, magenta ink subtracts the green component from incident light, and yellow subtracts the blue component. A unit cube representation for the CMY model is illustrated in Fig. 12-14.

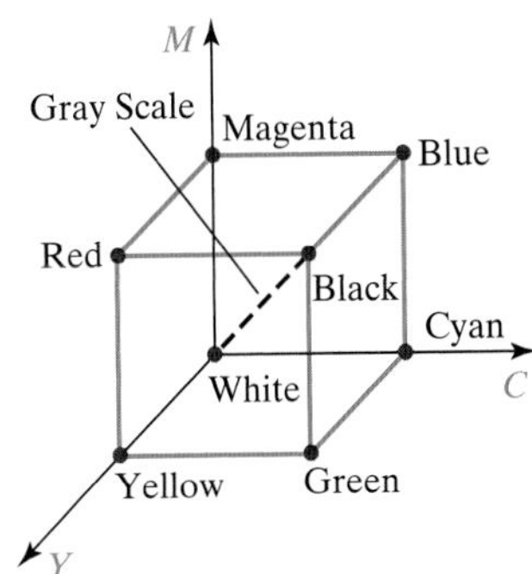

FIGURE 12-14 The CMY color model. Positions within the unit cube are described by subtracting the specified amounts of the primary colors from white.

In the CMY model, the spatial position (1, 1, 1) represents black, because all components of the incident light are subtracted. The origin represents white light. Equal amounts of each of the primary colors produce shades of gray along the main diagonal of the cube. A combination of cyan and magenta ink produces blue light, because the red and green components of the incident light are absorbed. Similarly, a combination of cyan and yellow ink produces green light, and a combination of magenta and yellow ink yields red light.

The CMY printing process often uses a collection of four ink dots, which are arranged in a close pattern somewhat as an RGB monitor uses three phosphor dots. Thus, in practice, the CMY color model is referred to as the CMYK model, where K is the black color parameter. One ink dot is used for each of the primary colors (cyan, magenta, and yellow), and one ink dot is black. A black dot is included because reflected light from the cyan, magenta, and yellow inks typically produce only shades of gray. Some plotters produce different color combinations by spraying the ink for the three primary colors over each other and allowing them to mix before they dry. For black-and-white or gray-scale printing, only the black ink is used.

Transformations Between CMY and RGB Color Spaces

We can express the conversion from an RGB representation to a CMY representation using the following matrix transformation.

$$\begin{bmatrix} C \\ M \\ Y \end{bmatrix} = \begin{bmatrix} 1 \\ 1 \\ 1 \end{bmatrix} - \begin{bmatrix} R \\ G \\ B \end{bmatrix} \tag{12-11}$$

where the white point in RGB space is represented as the unit column vector. And we convert from a CMY color representation to an RGB representation using the matrix transformation

$$\begin{bmatrix} R \\ G \\ B \end{bmatrix} = \begin{bmatrix} 1 \\ 1 \\ 1 \end{bmatrix} - \begin{bmatrix} C \\ M \\ Y \end{bmatrix} \tag{12-12}$$

In this transformation, the unit column vector represents the black point in the CMY color space.

For the conversion from RGB to the CMYK color space, we first set $K = \max(R, G, B)$. Then K is subtracted from each of C, M, and Y in Eq. 12-11. Similarly, for the transformation from CMYK to RGB, we first set $K = \min(R, G, B)$. Then K is subtracted from each of R, G, and B in Eq. 12-12. In practice, these transformation equations are often modified to improve the printing quality for a particular system.

12-7 THE HSV COLOR MODEL

Interfaces for selecting colors often use a color model based on intuitive concepts, rather than a set of primary colors. We can give a color specification in an intuitive model by selecting a spectral color and the amounts of white and black that are to be added to that color to obtain different shades, tints, and tones (Section 12-2).

The HSV Parameters

Color parameters in this model are called *hue* (H), *saturation* (S), and *value* (V). We derive this three-dimensional color space by relating the HSV parameters to the

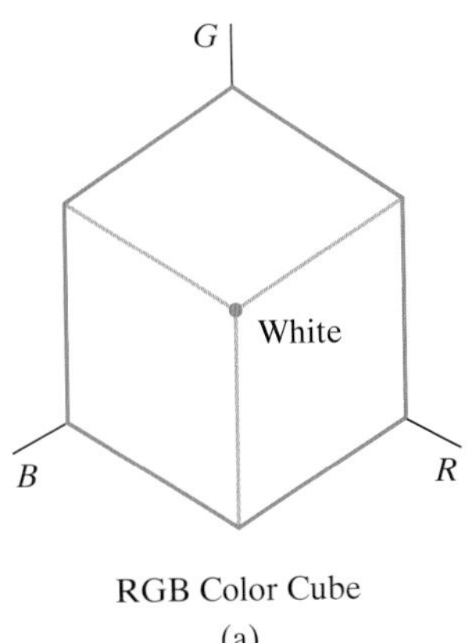

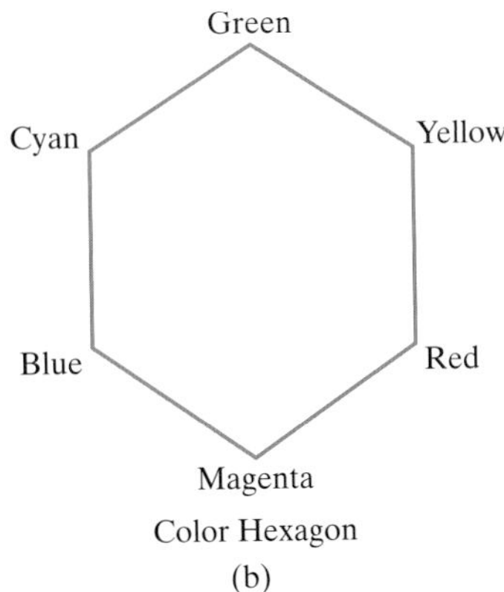

FIGURE 12-15 When the RGB color cube (a) is viewed along the diagonal from white to black, the color-cube outline is a hexagon (b).

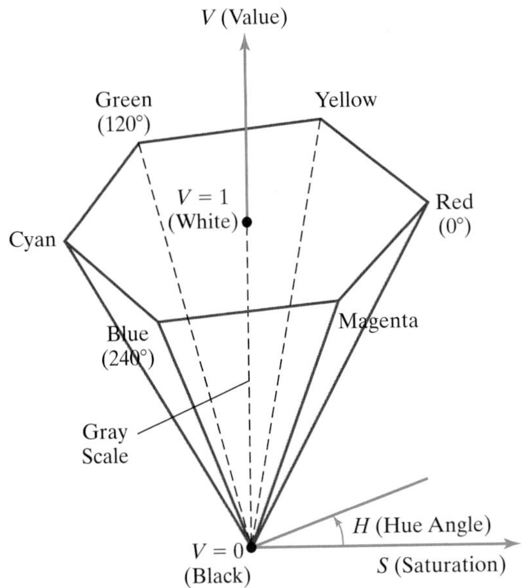

FIGURE 12-16 The HSV hexcone.

directions in the RGB cube. If we imagine viewing the cube along the diagonal from the white vertex to the origin (black), we see an outline of the cube that has the hexagon shape shown in Fig. 12-15. The boundary of the hexagon represents the various hues, and it is used as the top of the HSV hexcone (Fig. 12-16). In HSV space, saturation S is measured along a horizontal axis, and the value parameter V is measured along a vertical axis through the center of the hexcone.

Hue is represented as an angle about the vertical axis, ranging from 0° at red through 360°. Vertices of the hexagon are separated by 60° intervals. Yellow is at 60°, green at 120°, and cyan (opposite the red point) is at $H = 180^\circ$. Complementary colors are 180° apart.

Saturation parameter S is used to designate the purity of a color. A pure color (spectral color) has the value $S = 1.0$, and decreasing S values tend toward the gray-scale line ($S = 0$) at the center of the hexcone.

Value V varies from 0 at the apex of the hexcone to 1.0 at the top plane. The apex of the hexcone is the black point. At the top plane, colors have their maximum intensity. When $V = 1.0$ and $S = 1.0$, we have the pure hues. Parameter values for the white point are $V = 1.0$ and $S = 0$.

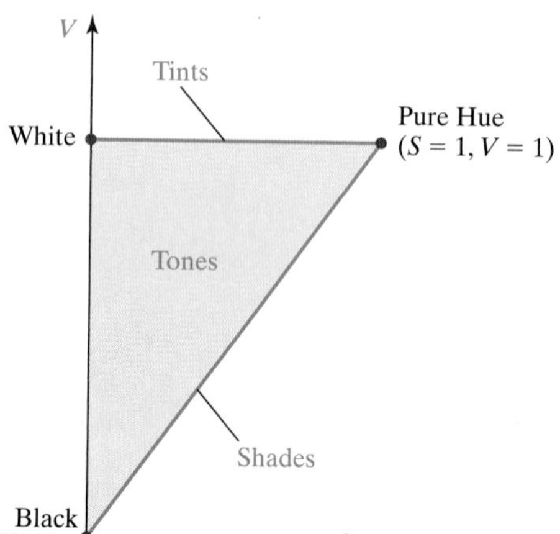

FIGURE 12-17 Cross section of the HSV hexcone, showing regions for shades, tints, and tones.

For most users, this is a more convenient model for selecting colors. Starting with a selection for a pure hue, which specifies the hue angle H and sets $V = S = 1.0$, we describe the color we want in terms of adding either white or black to the pure hue. Adding black decreases the setting for V while S is held constant. To get a dark blue, for instance, V could be set to 0.4 with $S = 1.0$ and $H = 240°$. Similarly, when white is to be added to the selected hue, parameter S is decreased while keeping V constant. A light blue could be designated with $S = 0.3$ while $V = 1.0$ and $H = 240°$. By adding some black and some white, we decrease both V and S. An interface for this model typically presents the HSV parameter choices in a color palette containing sliders and a color wheel.

Selecting Shades, Tints, and Tones

Color regions for selecting shades, tints, and tones are represented in the cross-sectional plane of the HSV hexcone shown in Fig. 12-17. Adding black to a spectral color decreases V along the side of the hexcone toward the black point. Thus, various shades are represented with the values $S = 1.0$ and $0.0 \leq V \leq 1.0$. Adding white to spectral colors produces the tints across the top plane of the hexcone, where parameter values are $V = 1.0$ and $0 \leq S \leq 1.0$. Various tones are obtained by adding both black and white to spectral colors, which generates color points within the triangular cross-sectional area of the hexcone.

The human eye can distinguish about 128 different hues and about 130 different tints (saturation levels). For each of these, a number of shades (value settings) can be detected, depending on the hue selected. About 23 shades are discernible with yellow colors, and about 16 different shades can be seen at the blue end of the spectrum. This means that we can distinguish about $128 \times 130 \times 23 = 382{,}720$ different colors. For most graphics applications, 128 hues, 8 saturation levels, and 16 value settings are sufficient. With this range of parameters in the HSV color model, 16,384 colors are available to a user. These color values can be stored in 14 bits per pixel, or we could use color-lookup tables and fewer bits per pixel.

Transformations Between HSV and RGB Color Spaces

To determine the operations required for the transformations between the HSV and RGB spaces, we first consider how the HSV hexcone can be constructed from the RGB cube. The diagonal of the RGB cube from black (the origin) to white corresponds to the V axis of the hexcone. Also, each subcube of the RGB cube corresponds to a hexagonal cross-sectional area of the hexcone. At any cross section, all sides of the hexagon and all radial lines from the V axis to any vertex have the value V. Thus, for any set of RGB values, V is equal to the value of the maximum RGB component. The HSV point corresponding to this set of RGB values lies on the hexagonal cross section at value V. Parameter S is then determined as the relative distance of this point from the V axis. Parameter H is determined by calculating the relative position of the point within each sextant of the hexagon. An algorithm for mapping any set of RGB values into the corresponding HSV values is given in the following procedure.

```
class rgbSpace {public: float r, g, b;};
class hsvSpace {public: float h, s, v;};

const float noHue = -1.0;
inline float min(float a, float b) {return (a < b)? a : b;}
inline float max(float a, float b) {return (a > b)? a : b;}

void rgbTOhsv (rgbSpace& rgb, hsvSpace& hsv)
{
   /* RGB and HSV values are in the range from 0 to 1.0 */
   float minRGB = min (r, min (g, b)), maxRGB = max (r, max (g, b));
   float deltaRGB = maxRGB - minRGB;

   v = maxRGB;
   if (maxRGB != 0.0)
      s = deltaRGB / maxRGB;
   else
      s = 0.0;
   if (s <= 0.0)
      h = noHue;
   else {
      if (r == maxRGB)
         h = (g - b) / deltaRGB;
      else
         if (g == maxRGB)
            h = 2.0 + (b - r) / deltaRGB;
         else
            if (b == maxRGB)
               h = 4.0 + (r - g) / deltaRGB;
      h *= 60.0;
      if (h < 0.0)
         h += 360.0;
      h /= 360.0;
   }
}
```

We obtain the transformation from HSV space to RGB space by determining the inverse of the operations in the preceding procedure. These inverse operations are carried out for each sextant of the hexcone, and the resulting transformation equations are summarized in the following algorithm.

```
class rgbSpace {public: float r, g, b;};
class hsvSpace {public: float h, s, v;};

void hsvTOrgb (hsvSpace& hsv, rgbSpace& rgb)
{
   /*  HSV and RGB values are in the range from 0 to 1.0  */
   int k
   float aa, bb, cc, f;

   if ( s <= 0.0)
      r = g = b = v;          //  Have gray scale if s = 0.
   else {
      if (h == 1.0)
         h = 0.0;
      h *= 6.0;
      k = floor (h);
      f = h - k;
      aa = v * (1.0 - s);
      bb = v * (1.0 - (s * f));
      cc = v * (1.0 - (s * (1.0 - f)));
      switch (k)
      {
         case 0:  r = v;   g = cc;  b = aa; break;
         case 1:  r = bb;  g = v;   b = aa; break;
         case 2:  r = aa;  g = v;   b = cc; break;
         case 3:  r = aa;  g = bb;  b = v; break;
         case 4:  r = cc;  g = aa;  b = v; break;
         case 5:  r = v;   g = aa;  b = bb; break;
      }
   }
}
```

12-8 THE HLS COLOR MODEL

Another model based on intuitive color parameters is the HLS system used by the Tektronix Corporation. This color space has the double-cone representation shown in Fig. 12-18. The three parameters in this color model are called hue (H), lightness (L), and saturation (S).

Hue has the same meaning as in the HSV model. It specifies an angle about the vertical axis that locates a hue (spectral color). In this model, $H = 0°$ corresponds to blue. The remaining colors are specified around the perimeter of the cone in the same order as in the HSV model. Magenta is at 60°, red is at 120°, and cyan is located at $H = 180°$. Again, complementary colors are 180° apart on the double cone.

The vertical axis in this model is called lightness, L. At $L = 0$, we have black, and white is at $L = 1.0$. Gray-scale values are along the L axis, and the pure colors lie on the $L = 0.5$ plane.

Saturation parameter S again specifies the purity of a color. This parameter varies from 0 to 1.0, and pure colors are those for which $S = 1.0$ and $L = 0.5$. As S decreases, more white is added to a color. The gray-scale line is at $S = 0$.

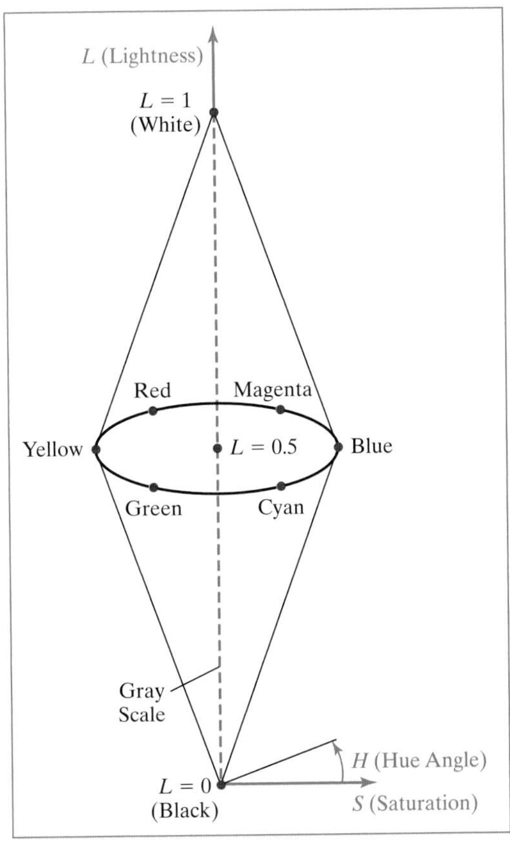

FIGURE 12-18 The HLS double cone.

To specify a color, we begin by selecting hue angle H. Then a particular shade, tint, or tone for that hue is obtained by adjusting parameters L and S. We obtain a lighter color by increasing L, and we obtain a darker color by decreasing L. When S is decreased, the spatial color point moves toward the gray-scale line.

12-9 COLOR SELECTION AND APPLICATIONS

A graphics package can provide color capabilities in a way that aids us in making color selections. For example, an interface can contain sliders and color wheels instead of requiring that all color specifications be provided as numerical values for the RGB components. In addition, some aids can be provided for choosing harmonious color combinations and for basic color selection guidelines.

One method for obtaining a set of coordinating colors is to generate the color combinations from a small subspace of a color model. If colors are selected at regular intervals along any straight line within the RGB or CMY cube, for example, we can expect to obtain a set of well-matched colors. Randomly selected hues can be expected to produce harsh and clashing color combinations. Another consideration in color displays is the fact that we perceive colors at different depths. This occurs because our eyes focus on colors according to their frequency. Blues, in particular, tend to recede. Displaying a blue pattern next to a red pattern can cause eye fatigue, since we continually need to refocus when our attention is switched from one area to the other. This problem can be reduced by separating these colors or by using colors from one-half or less of the color hexagon in the HSV model. With this technique, a display contains either blues and greens or reds and yellows.

As a general rule, the use of a smaller number of colors produces a better looking display than one with a large number of colors. Also, tints and shades tend to blend better than the pure hues. For a background, gray or the complement of one of the foreground colors is usually best.

12-10 SUMMARY

Light can be described as electromagnetic radiation with a certain energy distribution propagating through space, and the color components of light correspond to frequencies within a narrow band of the electromagnetic spectrum. However, light exhibits other properties, and we characterize the different aspects of light using a variety of parameters. With the light theories for wave-particle duality, we can explain the physical features of visible radiation. And we quantify our perceptions of a light source using terms such as dominant frequency (hue), luminance (brightness), and purity (saturation). Hue and purity are referred to collectively as the chromaticity properties of a color.

We also use color models to explain the effects of combining light sources. One method for defining a color model is to specify a set of two or more primary colors that are combined to produce various other colors. However, no finite set of primary colors is capable of producing all colors or describing all features of color. The set of colors that can be generated by a set of primaries is called a color gamut. Two colors that combine to produce white light are called complementary colors.

In 1931, the International Commission on Illumination (CIE) adopted a set of three hypothetical color-matching functions as a standard. This set of colors is referred to as the XYZ model, where X, Y, and Z represent the amounts of each color needed to match any color in the electromagnetic spectrum. The color-matching functions are structured so that all functions are positive and the Y amount for any color represents the luminance value. Normalized X and Y values, called x and y, are used to plot positions for all spectral colors on the CIE chromaticity diagram. We can use the chromaticity diagram to compare color gamuts for different color models, to identify complementary colors, and to determinant dominant frequency and purity for a specified color.

Other color models based on a set of three primaries are the RGB, YIQ, and CMY models. We use the RGB model to describe colors that are displayed on a video monitor. The YIQ model is used to describe the composite video signal for television broadcasting. And the CMY model is used to describe color on hard-copy devices.

User interfaces often provide intuitive color models, such as the HSV and HLS models, for selecting color values. With these models, we specify a color as a mixture of a selected hue and certain amounts of white and black. Adding black produces color shades, adding white produces tints, and adding both black and white produces tones.

Color selection is an important factor in the design of effective displays. To avoid clashing color combinations, we can choose adjacent colors in a display that do not differ greatly in dominant frequency. Also, we can select color combinations from a small subspace of a color model. As a general rule, a small number of color combinations formed with tints and shades, rather than pure hues, results in a more harmonious color display.

REFERENCES

A comprehensive discussion of the science of color is given in Wyszecki and Stiles (1982). Color models and color display techniques are treated in Smith (1978), Heckbert (1982), Durrett (1987), Schwartz, Cowan, and Beatty (1987), Hall (1989), and Travis (1991).

Algorithms for various color applications are presented in Glassner (1990), Arvo (1991), Kirk (1992), Heckbert (1994), and Paeth (1995). For additional information on the human visual system and our perception of light and color, see Glassner (1995).

EXERCISES

12-1 Derive the expressions for converting RGB color parameters to HSV values.

12-2 Derive the expressions for converting HSV color values to RGB values.

12-3 Design an interactive procedure that allows selection of HSV color parameters from a displayed menu; then, the HSV values are to be converted to RGB values for storage in a frame buffer.

12-4 Write a program to select colors using a set of three sliders to select values for the HSV color parameters.

12-5 Modify the program in the preceding exercise to display the numeric values for the RGB components of a selected color.

12-6 Modify the program in the preceding exercise to display the RGB color components and the combined color in small display windows.

12-7 Derive expressions for converting RGB color values to HLS color parameters.

12-8 Derive expressions for converting HLS color values to RGB values.

12-9 Write a program that will produce a set of colors that are linearly interpolated between any two specified positions in RGB space.

12-10 Write an interactive routine for selecting color values from within a specified subspace of RGB space.

12-11 Write a program that will produce a set of colors that are linearly interpolated between any two specified positions in HSV space.

12-12 Write a program that will produce a set of colors that are linearly interpolated between any two specified positions in HLS space.

12-13 Write a program to display two adjacent RGB color rectangles. Fill one rectangle with a set of randomly selected RGB color points, and fill the other rectangle with a set of color points that are selected from a small RGB subspace. Experiment with different random selections and different subspaces to compare the two color patterns.

12-14 Display the two color rectangles in the preceding exercise using color selections from either the HSV or the HLS color space.

CHAPTER 13

Computer Animation

An image of facial features transformed with morphing techniques.
(Courtesy of Vertigo Technology, Inc.)

Computer-graphics methods are now commonly used to produce animations for a variety of applications, including entertainment (motion pictures and cartoons), advertising, scientific and engineering studies, and training and education. Although we tend to think of animation as implying object motions, the term **computer animation** generally refers to any time sequence of visual changes in a picture. In addition to changing object positions using translations or rotations, a computer-generated animation could display time variations in object size, color, transparency, or surface texture. Advertising animations often transition one object shape into another: for example, transforming a can of motor oil into an automobile engine. We can also generate computer animations by varying camera parameters, such as position, orientation, or focal length. And variations in lighting effects or other parameters and procedures associated with illumination and rendering can be used to produce computer animations.

Another consideration in computer-generated animation is realism. Many applications require realistic displays. An accurate representation of the shape of a thunderstorm or other natural phenomena described with a numerical model is important for evaluating the reliability of the model. Similarly, simulators for training aircraft pilots and heavy-equipment operators must produce reasonably accurate representations of the environment. Entertainment and advertising applications, on the other hand, are sometimes more interested in visual effects. Thus, scenes may be displayed with exaggerated shapes and unrealistic motions and transformations. However, there are many entertainment and advertising applications that do require accurate representations for computer-generated scenes. And in some scientific and engineering studies, realism is not a goal. For example, physical quantities are often displayed with pseudo-colors or abstract shapes that change over time to help the researcher understand the nature of the physical process.

Two basic methods for constructing a motion sequence are **real-time animation** and **frame-by-frame animation.** In a real-time computer-animation, each stage of the sequence is viewed as it is created. Thus the animation must be generated at a rate that is compatible with the constraints of the refresh rate. For a frame-by-frame animation, each frame of the motion is separately generated and stored. Later, the frames can be recorded on film or they can be consecutively displayed on a video monitor in "real-time playback" mode. Simple animation displays are generally produced in real time, while more complex animations are constructed more slowly, frame by frame. But some applications require real-time animation, regardless of the complexity of the animation. A flight-simulator animation, for example, is produced in real time because the video displays must be generated in immediate response to changes in the control settings. In such cases, special hardware and software systems are often developed to allow the complex display sequences to be developed quickly.

13-1 RASTER METHODS FOR COMPUTER ANIMATION

Most of the time, we can create simple animation sequences in our programs using real-time methods. But, in general, we can produce an animation sequence on a raster-scan system one frame at a time, so that each completed frame could be saved in a file for later viewing. The animation can then be viewed by cycling through the completed frame sequence, or the frames could be transferred to film. If we want to generate an animation in real time, however, we need to produce the motion frames quickly enough so that a continuous motion sequence is displayed. For a complex scene, one frame of the animation could take most of the refresh cycle time to construct. In that case, objects generated first would be displayed for most of the frame refresh time, but objects generated toward the end of the refresh cycle would disappear almost as soon as they were displayed. And, for very complex animations, the frame construction time could be greater than the time to refresh the screen, which can lead to erratic motions and fractured frame displays. Since the screen display is generated from successively modified pixel values in the refresh buffer, we can take advantage of some of the characteristics of the raster screen-refresh process to produce motion sequences quickly.

Double Buffering

One method for producing a real-time animation with a raster system is to employ two refresh buffers. Initially, we create a frame for the animation in one of the buffers. Then, while the screen is being refreshed from that buffer, we construct the next frame in the other buffer. When that frame is complete, we switch the roles of the two buffers so that the refresh routines use the second buffer during the process of creating the next frame in the first buffer. This alternating buffer process continues throughout the animation. Graphics libraries that permit such operations typically have one function for activating the double-buffering routines and another function for interchanging the roles of the two buffers.

When a call is made to switch two refresh buffers, the interchange could be performed at various times. The most straightforward implementation is to switch the two buffers at the end of the current refresh cycle, during the vertical retrace of the electron beam. If a program can complete the construction of a frame within the time of a refresh cycle, say $\frac{1}{60}$ of a second, each motion sequence is displayed in synchronization with the screen refresh rate. But if the time to construct a frame is longer than the refresh time, the current frame is displayed for two or more refresh cycles while the next animation frame is being generated. For example, if the screen refresh rate is 60 frames per second and it takes $\frac{1}{50}$ of a second to construct an animation frame, each frame is displayed on the screen twice and the animation rate is only 30 frames each second. Similarly, if the frame construction time is $\frac{1}{25}$ of a second, the animation frame rate is reduced to 20 frames per second since each frame is displayed three times.

Irregular animation frame rates can occur with double buffering when the frame construction time is very nearly equal to an integer multiple of the screen refresh time. As an example of this, if the screen refresh rate is 60 frames per second, then an erratic animation frame rate is possible when the frame construction time is very close to $\frac{1}{60}$ of a second, or $\frac{2}{60}$ of a second, or $\frac{3}{60}$ of a second, and so forth. Because of slight variations in the implementation time for the routines that generate the primitives and their attributes, some frames could take a little more time to construct and some a little less time. Thus the animation frame rate can change abruptly and erratically. One way to compensate for this effect is to add a small time delay to the program. Another possibility is to alter the motions or scene description to shorten the frame construction time.

Generating Animations Using Raster Operations

We can also generate real-time raster animations for limited applications using block transfers of a rectangular array of pixel values. This animation technique is often used in game-playing programs. As we have seen in Section 5-6, a simple method for translating an object from one location to another in the xy plane is to transfer the group of pixel values that define the shape of the object to the new location. Two-dimensional rotations in multiples of 90° are also simple to perform, although we can rotate rectangular blocks of pixels through other angles using antialiasing procedures. For a rotation that is not a multiple of 90°, we need to estimate the percent of area coverage for those pixels that overlap the rotated block. Sequences of raster operations can be executed to produce real-time animation for either two-dimensional or three-dimensional objects, so long as we restrict the animation to motions in the projection plane. Then no viewing or visible-surface algorithms need be invoked.

We can also animate objects along two-dimensional motion paths using **color-table transformations.** Here we predefine the object at successive positions along the motion path, and set the successive blocks of pixel values to color-table entries. The pixels at the first position of the object are set to a foreground color, and the pixels at the other object positions are set to the background color. The animation is then accomplished by changing the color-table values so that the object color at successive positions along the animation path becomes the foreground color as the preceding position is set to the background color (Fig. 13-1).

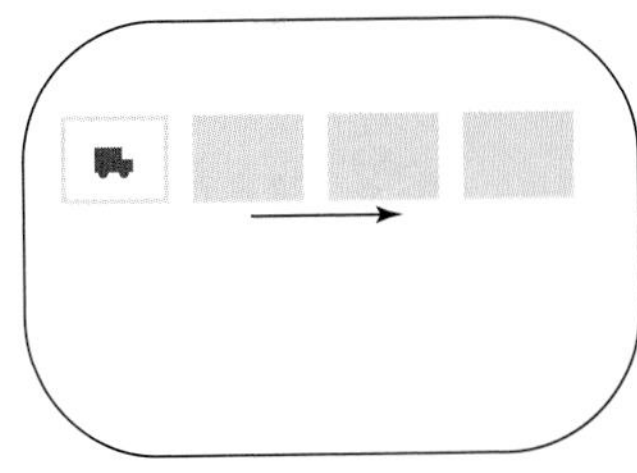

FIGURE 13-1 Real-time raster color-table animation.

13-2 DESIGN OF ANIMATION SEQUENCES

Constructing an animation sequence can be a complicated task, particularly when it involves a story line and multiple objects, each of which can move in a different way. A basic approach is to design such animation sequences using the following development stages:

- Storyboard Layout
- Object Definitions
- Key-Frame Specifications
- Generation of In-Between Frames

The **storyboard** is an outline of the action. It defines the motion sequence as a set of basic events that are to take place. Depending on the type of animation to be produced, the storyboard could consist of a set of rough sketches, along with a brief description of the motions, or it could just be a list of the basic ideas for the action. Originally, the set of motion sketches was attached to a large board that was used to present an overall view of the animation project. Hence, the name "storyboard".

An **object definition** is given for each participant in the action. Objects can be defined in terms of basic shapes, such as polygons or spline surfaces. In addition, a description is often given of the movements that are to be performed by each character or object in the story.

A **key frame** is a detailed drawing of the scene at a certain time in the animation sequence. Within each key frame, each object (or character) is positioned according to the time for that frame. Some key frames are chosen at extreme positions in the action; others are spaced so that the time interval between key frames is not too great. More key frames are specified for intricate motions than for simple, slowly varying motions. Development of the key frames is generally the responsibility of the senior animators, and often a separate animator is assigned to each character in the animation.

In-betweens are the intermediate frames between the key frames. The total number of frames, and hence the total number of in-betweens, needed for an animation is determined by the display media that is to be used. Film requires 24 frames per second, and graphics terminals are refreshed at the rate of 60 or more frames per second. Typically, time intervals for the motion are set up so that there are from three to five in-betweens for each pair of key frames. Depending on the speed specified for the motion, some key frames could be duplicated. As an example, a one-minute film sequence with no duplication requires a total of 1,440 frames. If five in-betweens are required for each pair of key frames, then 288 key frames would need to be developed.

There are several other tasks that may be required, depending on the application. These additional tasks include motion verification, editing, and the production and synchronization of a soundtrack. Many of the functions needed to produce general animations are now computer generated. Figures 13-2 and 13-3 show examples of computer-generated frames for animation sequences.

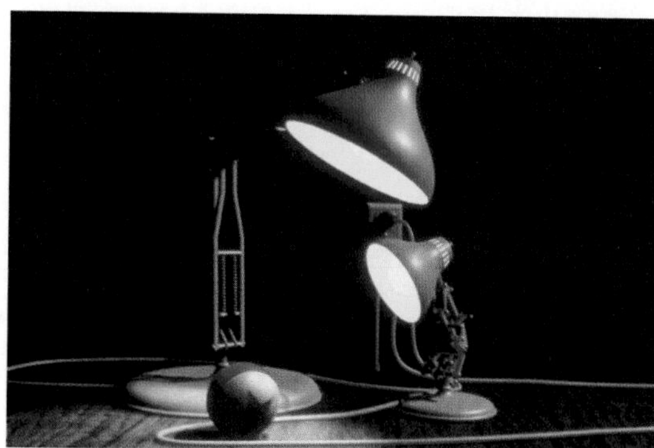

FIGURE 13-2 One frame from the award-winning computer-animated short film *Luxo Jr.* The film was designed using a key-frame animation system and cartoon animation techniques to provide lifelike actions of the lamps. Final images were rendered with multiple light sources and procedural texturing techniques. *(Courtesy of Pixar. © 1986 Pixar.)*

FIGURE 13-3 One frame from the short film *Tin Toy*, the first computer-animated film to win an Oscar. Designed using a key-frame animation system, the film also required extensive facial-expression modeling. Final images were rendered using procedural shading, self-shadowing techniques, motion blur, and texture mapping. *(Courtesy of Pixar. © 1988 Pixar.)*

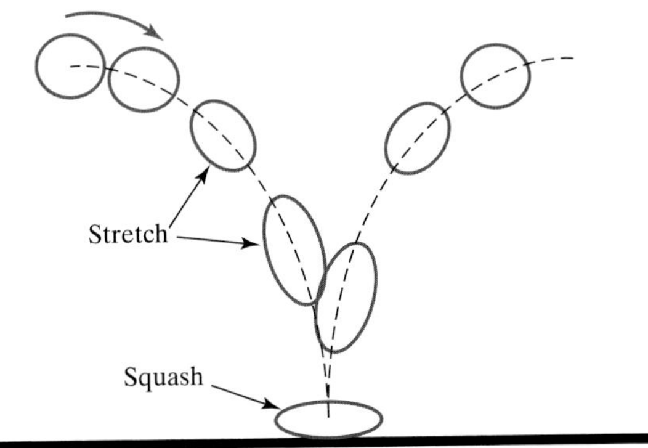

FIGURE 13-4 A bouncing-ball illustration of the "squash and stretch" technique for emphasizing object acceleration.

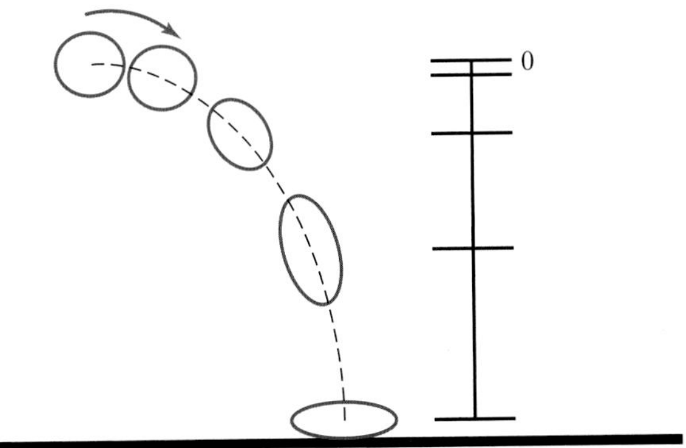

FIGURE 13-5 The position changes between motion frames for a bouncing ball increase as the speed of the ball increases.

13-3 TRADITIONAL ANIMATION TECHNIQUES

Film animators use a variety of methods for depicting and emphasizing motion sequences. These include object deformations, spacing between animation frames, motion anticipation and follow-through, and action focusing.

One of the most important techniques for simulating acceleration effects, particularly for nonrigid objects, is **squash and stretch.** Figure 13-4 shows how this technique is used to emphasize the acceleration and deceleration of a bouncing ball. As the ball accelerates, it begins to stretch. When the ball hits the floor and stops, it is first compressed (squashed) and then stretched again as it accelerates and bounces upwards.

Another technique used by film animators is **timing,** which refers to the spacing between motion frames. A slower moving object is represented with more closely spaced frames, and a faster moving object is displayed with fewer frames over the path of the motion. This effect is illustrated in Fig. 13-5, where the position changes between frames increase as a bouncing ball moves faster.

Object movements can also be emphasized by creating preliminary actions that indicate an **anticipation** of a coming motion. For example, a cartoon character might lean forward and rotate its body before starting to run. Or a character might perform a "windup" before throwing a ball. Similarly, **follow-through actions** can be used to emphasize a previous motion. After throwing a ball, a character can continue the arm swing back to its body. Or a hat can fly off a character that is stopped abruptly. And an action can be emphasized with **staging,** which refers to any method for focusing on an important part of a scene, such as a character hiding something.

13-4 GENERAL COMPUTER-ANIMATION FUNCTIONS

Many software packages have been developed either for general animation design or for performing specialized animation tasks. Typical animation functions include managing object motions, generating views of objects, producing camera motions, and the generation of in-between frames. Some animation packages, such as Wavefront for example, provide special functions for both the overall animation design and the processing of individual objects. Others are special-purpose packages for particular features of an animation, such as a system for generating in-between frames or a system for figure animation.

A set of routines is often provided in a general animation package for storing and managing the object database. Object shapes and associated parameters are stored and updated in the database. Other object functions include those for generating the object motions and those for rendering the object surfaces. Motions can be generated according to specified constraints using two-dimensional or three-dimensional transformations. Standard functions can then be applied to identify visible surfaces and apply the rendering algorithms.

Another typical function set simulates camera movements. Standard camera motions are zooming, panning, and tilting. Finally, given the specification for the key frames, the in-betweens can be automatically generated.

13-5 COMPUTER-ANIMATION LANGUAGES

We can develop routines to design and control animation sequences within a general-purpose programming language, such as C, C++, Lisp, or Fortran, but several specialized animation languages have been developed. These languages typically include a graphics editor, a key-frame generator, an in-between generator, and standard graphics routines. The graphics editor allows an animator to design and modify object shapes, using spline surfaces, constructive solid-geometry methods, or other representation schemes.

An important task in an animation specification is *scene description*. This includes the positioning of objects and light sources, defining the photometric parameters (light-source intensities and surface illumination properties), and setting the camera parameters (position, orientation, and lens characteristics). Another standard function is *action specification*, which involves the layout of motion paths for the objects and camera. And we need the usual graphics routines: viewing and perspective transformations, geometric transformations to generate object movements as a function of accelerations or kinematic path specifications, visible-surface identification, and the surface-rendering operations.

Key-frame systems were originally designed as a separate set of animation routines for generating the in-betweens from the user-specified key frames. Now, these routines are often a component in a more general animation package. In the simplest case, each object in a scene is defined as a set of rigid bodies connected at the joints and with a limited number of degrees of freedom. As an example, the single-arm robot in Fig. 13-6 has six degrees of freedom, which are referred to as arm sweep, shoulder swivel, elbow extension, pitch, yaw, and roll. We can extend

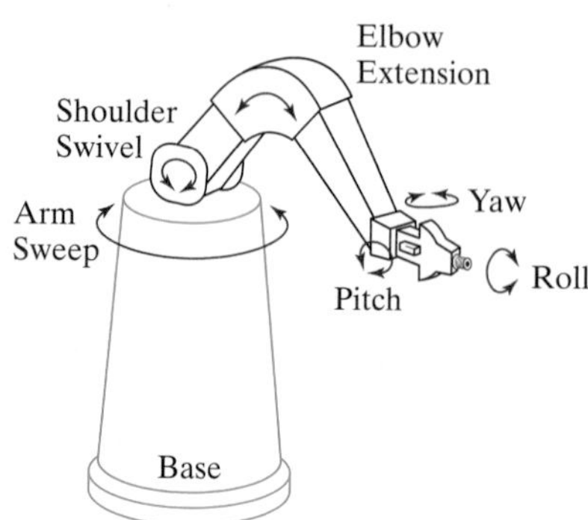

FIGURE 13-6 Degrees of freedom for a stationary, single-arm robot.

the number of degrees of freedom for this robot arm to nine by allowing three-dimensional translations for the base (Fig. 13-7). If we also allow base rotations, the robot arm can have a total of twelve degrees of freedom. The human body, in comparison, has more than 200 degrees of freedom.

Parameterized systems allow object motion characteristics to be specified as part of the object definitions. The adjustable parameters control such object characteristics as degrees of freedom, motion limitations, and allowable shape changes.

Scripting systems allow object specifications and animation sequences to be defined with a user-input *script*. From the script, a library of various objects and motions can be constructed.

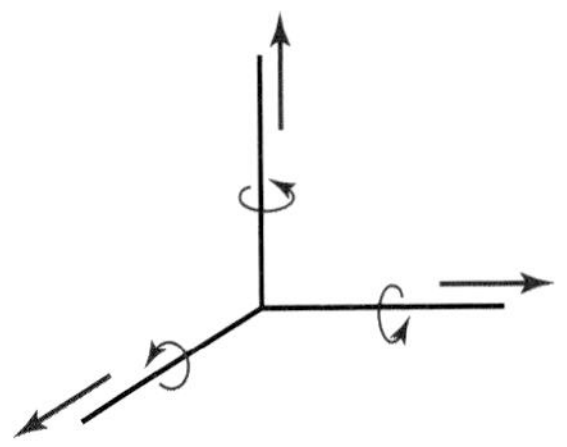

FIGURE 13-7
Translational and rotational degrees of freedom for the base of the robot arm.

13-6 KEY-FRAME SYSTEMS

A set of in-betweens can be generated from the specification of two (or more) key frames using a key-frame system. Motion paths can be given with a *kinematic description* as a set of spline curves, or the motions can be *physically based* by specifying the forces acting on the objects to be animated.

For complex scenes, we can separate the frames into individual components or objects called **cels** (celluloid transparencies). This term developed from cartoon-animation techniques, where the background and each character in a scene were placed on a separate transparency. Then, with the transparencies stacked in the order from background to foreground, they were photographed to obtain the completed frame. The specified animation paths are then used to obtain the next cel for each character, where the positions are interpolated from the key-frame times.

With complex object transformations, the shapes of objects may change over time. Examples are clothes, facial features, magnified detail, evolving shapes, and exploding or disintegrating objects. For surfaces described with polygon meshes, these changes can result in significant changes in polygon shape, so that the number of edges in a polygon could be different from one frame to the next. These changes are incorporated into the development of the in-between frames by adding or subtracting polygon edges according to the requirements of the defining key frames.

Morphing

Transformation of object shapes from one form to another is termed **morphing,** which is a shortened form of "metamorphosing". An animator can model morphing by transitioning polygon shapes through the in-betweens from one key frame to the next.

Given two key frames, each with a different number of line segments specifying an object transformation, we can first adjust the object specification in one of the frames so that the number of polygon edges (or the number of polygon vertices) is the same for the two frames. This preprocessing step is illustrated in Fig. 13-8. A straight-line segment in key frame k is transformed into two line segments in key frame $k + 1$. Since key frame $k + 1$ has an extra vertex, we add a vertex between vertices 1 and 2 in key frame k to balance the number of vertices (and edges) in the two key frames. Using linear interpolation to generate the in-betweens, we transition the added vertex in key frame k into vertex $3'$ along the straight-line path shown in Fig. 13-9. An example of a triangle linearly expanding into a quadrilateral is given in Fig. 13-10. Figures 13-11 and 13-12 show examples of morphing in television advertising.

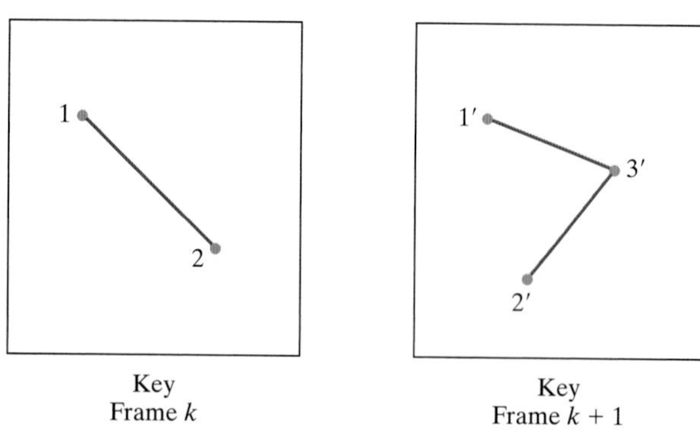

FIGURE 13-8 An edge with vertex positions 1 and 2 in key frame k evolves into two connected edges in key frame $k + 1$.

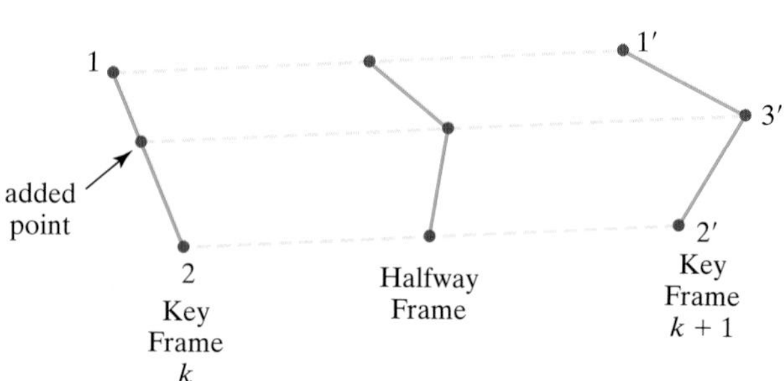

FIGURE 13-9 Linear interpolation for transforming a line segment in key frame k into two connected line segments in key frame $k + 1$.

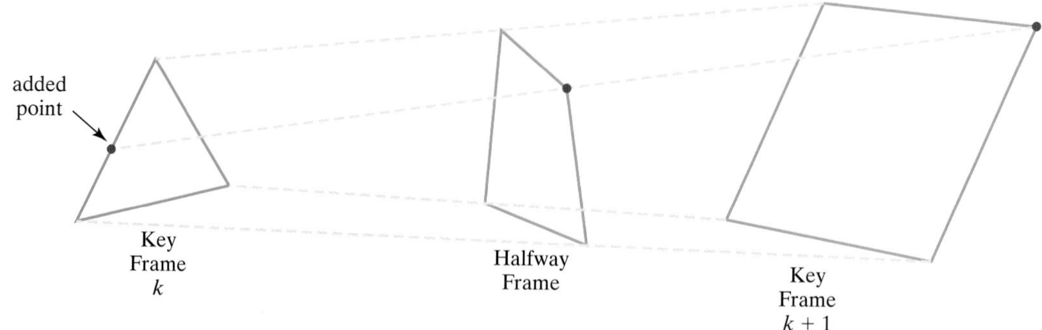

FIGURE 13-10 Linear interpolation for transforming a triangle into a quadrilateral.

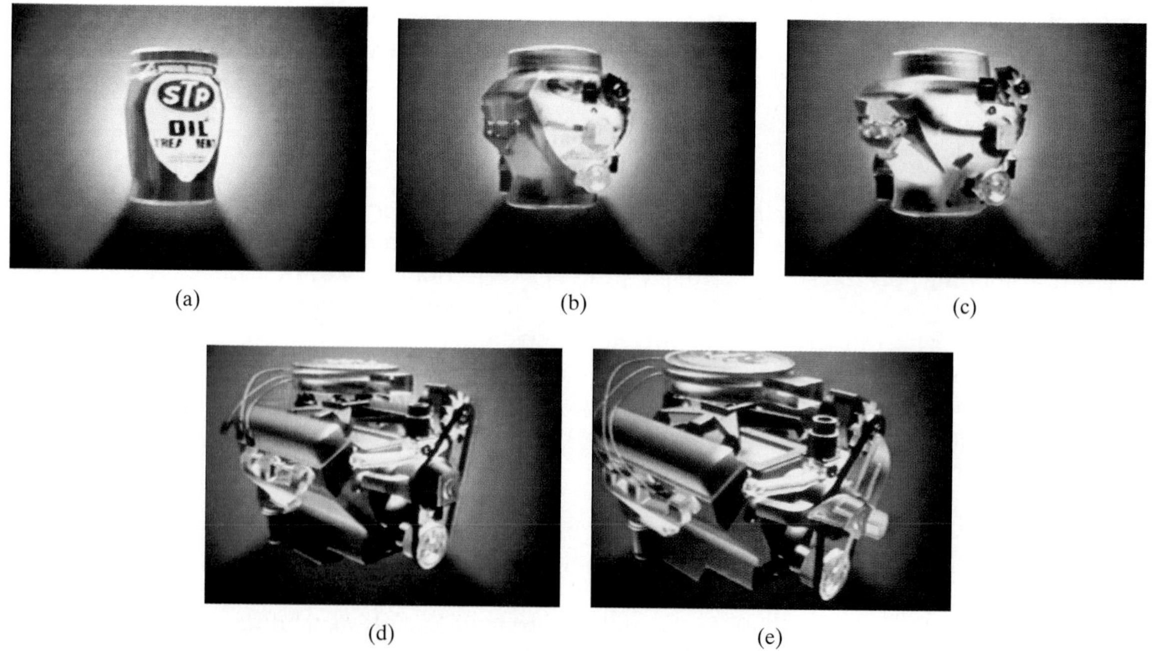

FIGURE 13-11 Transformation of an STP oil can into an automobile engine block. *(Courtesy of Silicon Graphics, Inc.)*

FIGURE 13-12
Transformation of a moving automobile into a running tiger. (*Courtesy of Exxon Company USA and Pacific Data Images.*)

We can state general preprocessing rules for equalizing key frames in terms of either the number of edges or the number of vertices to be added to a key frame. We first consider equalizing the edge count, where parameters L_k and L_{k+1} denote the number of line segments in two consecutive frames. The maximum and minimum number of lines to be equalized can be determined as

$$L_{max} = \max(L_k, L_{k+1}), \qquad L_{min} = \min(L_k, L_{k+1}) \tag{13-1}$$

Next we compute the following two quantities.

$$\begin{aligned} N_e &= L_{max} \bmod L_{min} \\ N_s &= int\left(\frac{L_{max}}{L_{min}}\right) \end{aligned} \tag{13-2}$$

The preprocessing steps for edge equalization are then accomplished with the following two procedures.

(1) Divide N_e edges of $keyframe_{min}$ into $N_s + 1$ sections.
(2) Divide the remaining lines of $keyframe_{min}$ into N_s sections.

As an example, if $L_k = 15$ and $L_{k+1} = 11$, we would divide four lines of $keyframe_{k+1}$ into two sections each. The remaining lines of $keyframe_{k+1}$ are left intact.

If we equalize the vertex count, we can use parameters V_k and V_{k+1} to denote the number of vertices in the two consecutive key frames. In this case, we determine the maximum and minimum number of vertices as

$$V_{max} = \max(V_k, V_{k+1}), \qquad V_{min} = \min(V_k, V_{k+1}) \tag{13-3}$$

Then we compute the following two values:

$$N_{ls} = (V_{\max} - 1) \bmod (V_{\min} - 1)$$
$$N_p = int\left(\frac{V_{\max} - 1}{V_{\min} - 1}\right) \tag{13-4}$$

These two quantities are then used to perform vertex equalization with the procedures:

(1) Add N_p points to N_{ls} line sections of $keyframe_{\min}$.
(2) Add $N_p - 1$ points to the remaining edges of $keyframe_{\min}$.

For the triangle-to-quadrilateral example, $V_k = 3$ and $V_{k+1} = 4$. Both N_{ls} and N_p are 1, so we would add one point to one edge of $keyframe_k$. No points would be added to the remaining lines of $keyframe_k$.

Simulating Accelerations

Curve-fitting techniques are often used to specify the animation paths between key frames. Given the vertex positions at the key frames, we can fit the positions with linear or nonlinear paths. Figure 13-13 illustrates a nonlinear fit of key-frame positions. And to simulate accelerations, we can adjust the time spacing for the in-betweens.

If the motion is to occur at constant speed (zero acceleration), we use equal-interval time spacing for the in-betweens. For instance, with n in-betweens and key-frame times of t_1 and t_2 (Fig. 13-14), the time interval between the key frames is divided into $n + 1$ equal subintervals, yielding an in-between spacing of

$$\Delta t = \frac{t_2 - t_1}{n + 1} \tag{13-5}$$

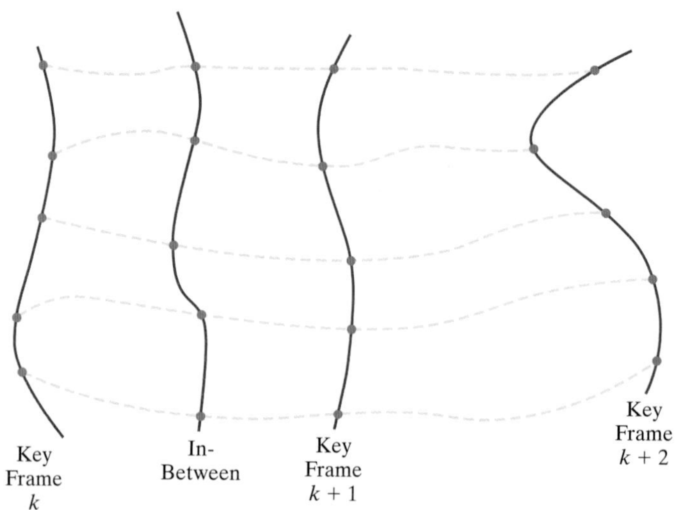

FIGURE 13-13 Fitting key-frame vertex positions with nonlinear splines.

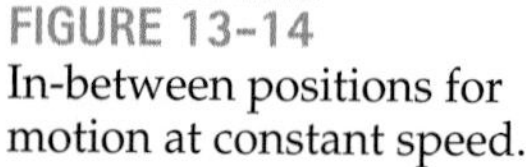

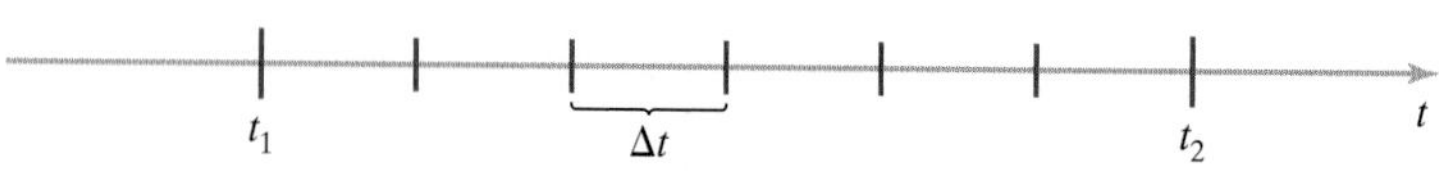

FIGURE 13-14 In-between positions for motion at constant speed.

The time for the jth in-between is

$$tB_j = t_1 + j\Delta t, \qquad j = 1, 2, \ldots, n \tag{13-6}$$

and this time value is used to calculate coordinate positions, color, and other physical parameters for that frame of the motion.

Speed changes (nonzero accelerations) are usually necessary at some point in an animation film or cartoon, particularly at the beginning and end of a motion sequence. The start-up and slow-down portions of an animation path are often modeled with spline or trigonometric functions, but parabolic and cubic time functions have been applied to acceleration modeling. Animation packages commonly furnish trigonometric functions for simulating accelerations.

To model increasing speed (positive acceleration), we want the time spacing between frames to increase so that greater changes in position occur as the object moves faster. We can obtain an increasing size for the time interval with the function

$$1 - \cos\theta, \qquad 0 < \theta < \pi/2$$

For n in-betweens, the time for the jth in-between would then be calculated as

$$tB_j = t_1 + \Delta t\left[1 - \cos\frac{j\pi}{2(n+1)}\right], \qquad j = 1, 2, \ldots, n \tag{13-7}$$

where Δt is the time difference between the two key frames. Figure 13-15 gives a plot of the trigonometric acceleration function and the in-between spacing for $n = 5$.

We can model decreasing speed (deceleration) using the function $\sin\theta$, with $0 < \theta < \pi/2$. The time position of an in-between is then determined as

$$tB_j = t_1 + \Delta t \sin\frac{j\pi}{2(n+1)}, \qquad j = 1, 2, \ldots, n \tag{13-8}$$

A plot of this function and the decreasing size of the time intervals is shown in Fig. 13-16 for five in-betweens.

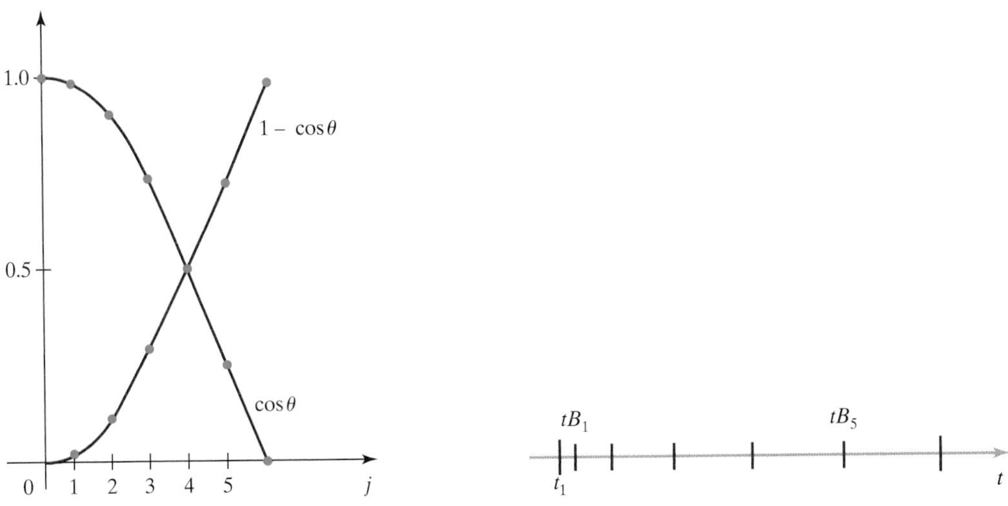

FIGURE 13-15 A trigonometric acceleration function and the corresponding in-between spacing for $n = 5$ and $\theta = j\pi/12$ in Eq. 13-7, producing increased coordinate changes as the object moves through each time interval.

Often, motions contain both speedups and slowdowns. We can model a combination of increasing–decreasing speed by first increasing the in-between time spacing, then decreasing this spacing. A function to accomplish these time changes is

$$\frac{1}{2}(1 - \cos\theta), \qquad 0 < \theta < \pi/2$$

The time for the jth in-between is now calculated as

$$tB_j = t_1 + \Delta t \left\{ \frac{1 - \cos[j\pi/(n+1)]}{2} \right\}, \qquad j = 1, 2, \ldots, n \tag{13-9}$$

with Δt denoting the time difference between the two key frames. Time intervals for a moving object first increase and then decrease, as shown in Fig. 13-17.

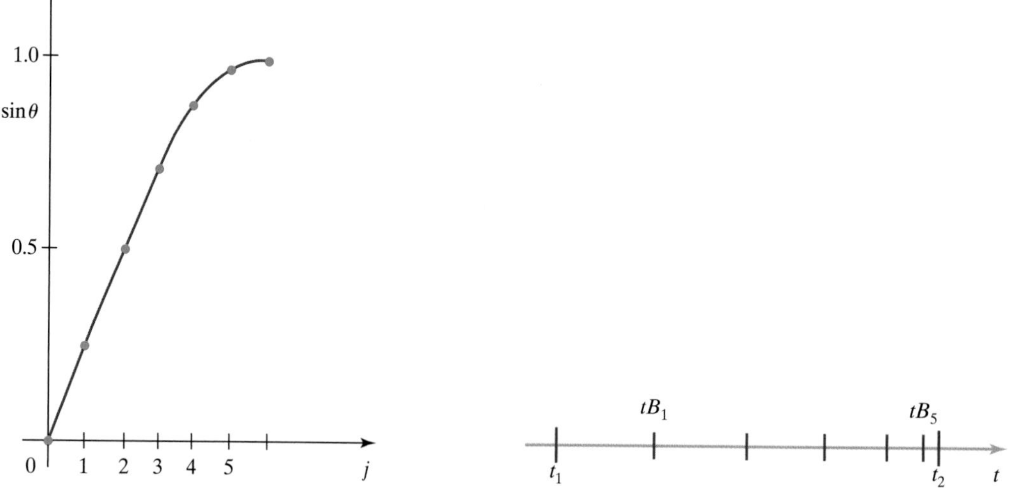

FIGURE 13-16 A trigonometric deceleration function and the corresponding in-between spacing for $n = 5$ and $\theta = j\pi/12$ in Eq. 13-8, producing decreased coordinate changes as the object moves through each time interval.

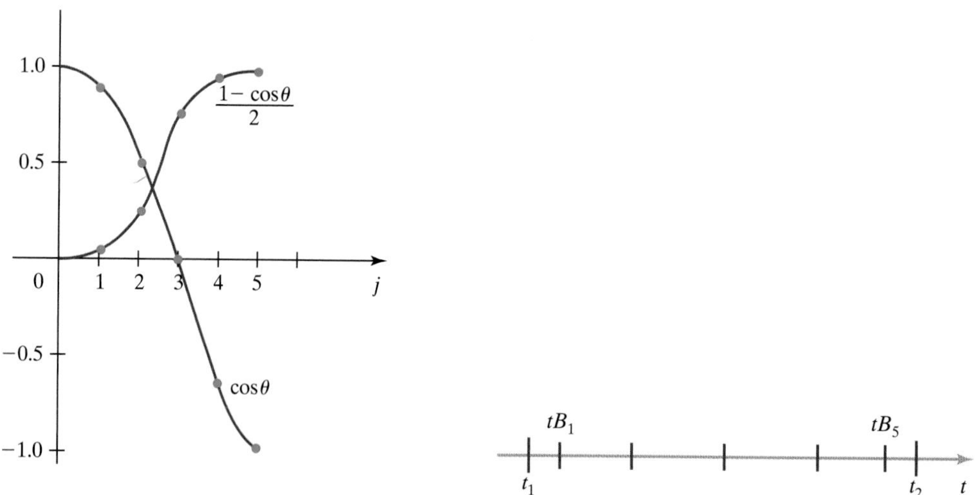

FIGURE 13-17 The trigonometric accelerate–decelerate function $(1 - \cos\theta)/2$ and the corresponding in-between spacing for $n = 5$ in Eq. 13-9.

Processing the in-betweens is simplified by initially modeling "skeleton" (wire-frame) objects, so that motion sequences can be interactively adjusted. After the animation sequence is completely defined, objects can be fully rendered.

13-7 MOTION SPECIFICATIONS

General methods for describing an animation sequence range from an explicit specification of the motion paths to a description of the interactions that produce the motions. Thus we could define how an animation is to take place by giving the transformation parameters, the motion path parameters, the forces that are to act on objects, or the details of how objects interact to produce motions.

Direct Motion Specification

The most straightforward method for defining an animation is *direct motion specification* of the geometric-transformation parameters. Here, we explicitly set the values for the rotation angles and translation vectors. Then the geometric transformation matrices are applied to transform coordinate positions. Alternatively, we could use an approximating equation involving these parameters to specify certain kinds of motions. We can approximate the path of a bouncing ball, for instance, with a damped, rectified, sine curve (Fig. 13-18):

$$y(x) = A|\sin(\omega x + \theta_0)|e^{-kx} \qquad (13\text{-}10)$$

where A is the initial amplitude (height of the ball above the ground), ω is the angular frequency, θ_0 is the phase angle, and k is the damping constant. This method for motion specification is particularly useful for simple user-programmed animation sequences.

Goal-Directed Systems

At the opposite extreme, we can specify the motions that are to take place in general terms that abstractly describe the actions in terms of the final results. In other words, an animation is specified in terms of the final state of the motions. These

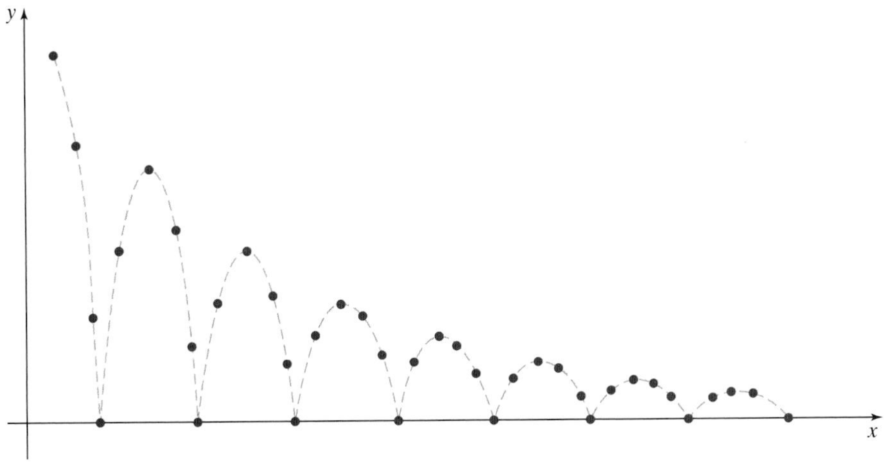

FIGURE 13-18 Approximating the motion of a bouncing ball with a damped sine function (Eq. 13-10).

systems are referred to as *goal directed,* since values for the motion parameters are determined from the goals of the animation. For example, we could specify that we want an object to "walk" or to "run" to a particular destination. Or we could state that we want an object to "pick up" some other specified object. The input directives are then interpreted in terms of component motions that will accomplish the described task. Human motions, for instance, can be defined as a hierarchical structure of submotions for the torso, limbs, and so forth. Thus, when a goal, such as "walk to the door" is given, the motions required of the torso and limbs to accomplish this action are calculated.

Kinematics and Dynamics

We can also construct animation sequences using *kinematic* or *dynamic* descriptions. With a kinematic description, we specify the animation by giving motion parameters (position, velocity, and acceleration) without reference to causes or goals of the motion. For constant velocity (zero acceleration), we designate the motions of rigid bodies in a scene by giving an initial position and velocity vector for each object. As an example, if a velocity is specified as (3, 0, −4) km per sec, then this vector gives the direction for the straight-line motion path and the speed (magnitude of velocity) is calculated as 5 km per sec. If we also specify accelerations (rate of change of velocity), we can generate speedups, slowdowns, and curved motion paths. Kinematic specification of a motion can also be given by simply describing the motion path. This is often done using spline curves.

An alternate approach is to use *inverse kinematics*. Here, we specify the initial and final positions of objects at specified times and the motion parameters are computed by the system. For example, assuming zero acceleration, we can determine the constant velocity that will accomplish the movement of an object from the initial position to the final position. This method is often used with complex objects by giving the positions and orientations of an end node of an object, such as a hand or a foot. The system then determines the motion parameters of other nodes to accomplish the desired motion.

Dynamic descriptions, on the other hand, require the specification of the forces that produce the velocities and accelerations. The description of object behavior in terms of the influence of forces is generally referred to as *physically based modeling* (Chapter 8). Examples of forces affecting object motion include electromagnetic, gravitational, frictional, and other mechanical forces.

Object motions are obtained from the force equations describing physical laws, such as Newton's laws of motion for gravitational and frictional processes, Euler or Navier-Stokes equations describing fluid flow, and Maxwell's equations for electromagnetic forces. For example, the general form of Newton's second law for a particle of mass m is

$$\mathbf{F} = \frac{d}{dt}(m\mathbf{v}) \qquad (13\text{-}11)$$

where $\mathbf{F}$ is the force vector and $\mathbf{v}$ is the velocity vector. If mass is constant, we solve the equation $\mathbf{F} = m\mathbf{a}$, with $\mathbf{a}$ representing the acceleration vector. Otherwise, mass is a function of time, as in relativistic motions or the motions of space vehicles that consume measurable amounts of fuel per unit time. We can also use *inverse dynamics* to obtain the forces, given the initial and final positions of objects and the type of motion required.

Applications of physically based modeling include complex rigid-body systems and such nonrigid systems as cloth and plastic materials. Typically, numerical methods are used to obtain the motion parameters incrementally from the dynamical equations using initial conditions or boundary values.

13-8 ARTICULATED FIGURE ANIMATION

A basic technique for animating people, animals, insects, and other critters is to model them as **articulated figures,** which are hierarchical structures composed of a set of rigid links that are connected at rotary joints (Fig. 13-19). In less formal terms, this just means that we model animate objects as moving stick figures, or simplified skeletons, that can later be wrapped with surfaces representing skin, hair, fur, feathers, clothes, or other outer coverings.

FIGURE 13-19 A simple articulated figure with nine joints and twelve connecting links, not counting the oval head.

The connecting points, or hinges, for an articulated figure are placed at the shoulders, hips, knees, and other skeletal joints, which travel along specified motion paths as the body moves. For example, when a motion is specified for an object, the shoulder automatically moves in a certain way and, as the shoulder moves, the arms move. Different types of movement, such as walking, running, or jumping, are defined and associated with particular motions for the joints and connecting links.

A series of walking leg motions, for instance, might be defined as in Fig. 13-20. The hip joint is translated forward along a horizontal line while the connecting links perform a series of movements about the hip, knee, and angle joints. Starting with a straight leg (Fig. 13-20(a)), the first motion is a knee bend as the hip moves forward (Fig. 13-20(b)). Then the leg swings forward, returns to the vertical position, and swings back, as shown in Figs. 13-20(c), (d), and (e). The final motions are a wide swing back and a return to the straight vertical position, as in Figs. 13-20(f) and (g). This motion cycle is repeated for the duration of the animation, as the figure moves over a specified distance or time interval.

As a figure moves, other motions are incorporated into the various joints. A sinusoidal motion, often with varying amplitude, can be applied to the hips so

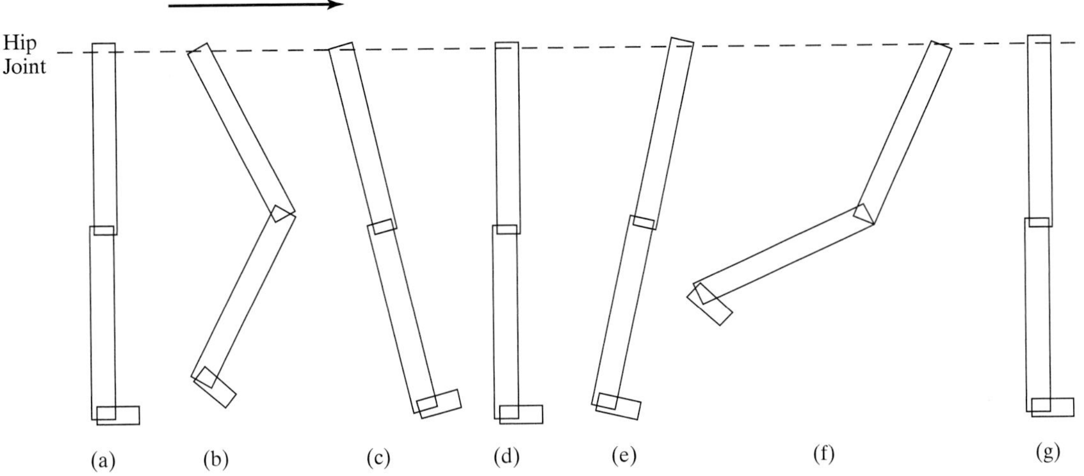

FIGURE 13-20 Possible motions for a set of connected links representing a walking leg.

that they move about on the torso. Similarly, a rolling or rocking motion can be imparted to the shoulders, and the head could bob up and down.

Both kinematic-motion descriptions and inverse kinematics are used in figure animations. Specifying the joint motions is generally an easier task, but inverse kinematics can be useful for producing simple motions over arbitrary terrain. For a complicated figure, inverse kinematics may not produce a unique animation sequence: many different rotational motions may be possible for a given set of initial and final conditions. In such cases, a unique solution may be possible by adding more constraints, such as conservation of momentum, to the system.

13-9 PERIODIC MOTIONS

When we construct an animation with repeated motion patterns, such as a rotating object, we need to be sure that the motion is sampled (Section 4-17) frequently enough to represent the movements correctly. In other words, the motion must be synchronized with the frame-generation rate so that we display enough frames per cycle to show the true motion. Otherwise, the animation may be displayed incorrectly.

A typical example of an undersampled periodic-motion display is the wagon wheel in a Western movie that appears to be turning in the wrong direction. Figure 13-21 illustrates one complete cycle in the rotation of a wagon wheel with one red spoke that makes 18 clockwise revolutions per second. If this motion is recorded on film at the standard motion-picture projection rate of 24 frames per second, then the first five frames depicting this motion would be as shown in Fig. 13-22. Since the wheel completes $\frac{3}{4}$ of a turn every $\frac{1}{24}$ of a second, only one

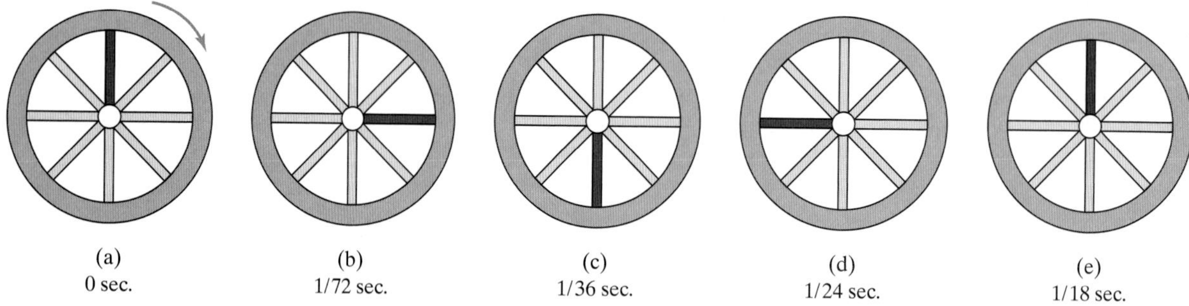

FIGURE 13-21 Five positions for a red spoke during one cycle of a wheel motion that is turning at the rate of 18 revolutions per second.

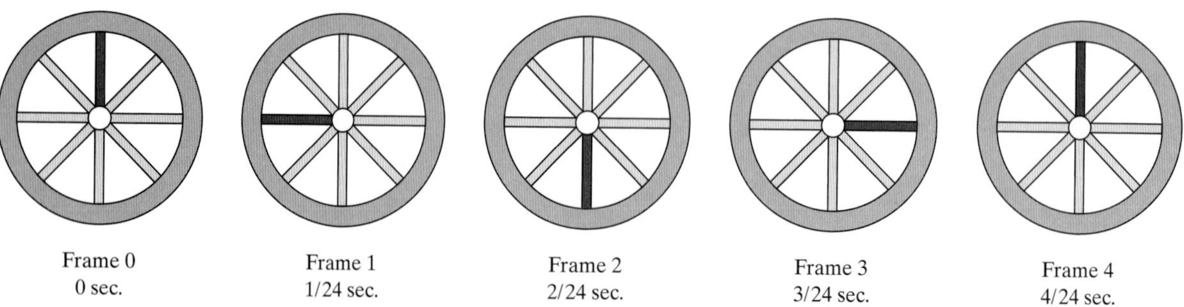

FIGURE 13-22 The first five film frames of the rotating wheel in Fig. 13-21 produced at the rate of 24 frames per second.

animation frame is generated per cycle and the wheel thus appears to be rotating in the opposite (counterclockwise) direction.

In a computer-generated animation, we can control the sampling rate in a periodic motion by adjusting the motion parameters. For example, we can set the angular increment for the motion of a rotating object so that multiple frames are generated in each revolution. Thus, a 3° increment for a rotation angle produces 120 motion steps during one revolution, and a 4° increment generates 90 positions. For faster motions, larger rotational steps could be used, as long as the number of samples per cycle is not too small and the motion is clearly displayed. When complex objects are to be animated, we also must take into account the effect that the frame construction time might have on the refresh rate, as discussed in Section 13-1. The motion of a complex object can be much slower than we want it to be if it takes too long to construct each frame of the animation.

Another factor that we need to consider in the display of a repeated motion is the effect of round-off in the calculations for the motion parameters. As we noted in Section 5-4, we can periodically reset parameter values to prevent the accumulated error from producing erratic motions. For a continuous rotation, we could reset parameter values once every cycle (360°).

13-10 OpenGL ANIMATION PROCEDURES

Raster operations (Section 5-7) and color-index assignment functions are available in the core library, and routines for changing color-table values are provided in GLUT (Section 4-3). Other raster-animation operations are available only as GLUT routines because they depend on the window system in use. In addition, computer-animation features such as double buffering may not be included in some hardware systems.

Double-buffering operations, if available, are activated using the following GLUT command.

```
glutInitDisplayMode (GLUT_DOUBLE);
```

This provides two buffers, called the *front buffer* and the *back buffer*, that we can use alternately to refresh the screen display. While one buffer is acting as the refresh buffer for the current display window, the next frame of an animation can be constructed in the other buffer. We specify when the roles of the two buffers are to be interchanged using

```
glutSwapBuffers ( );
```

To determine whether double-buffer operations are available on a system, we can issue the following query.

```
glGetBooleanv (GL_DOUBLEBUFFER, status);
```

A value of `GL_TRUE` is returned to array parameter `status` if both front and back buffers are available on a system. Otherwise, the returned value is `GL_FALSE`.

For a continuous animation, we can also use

```
glutIdleFunc (animationFcn);
```

where parameter animationFcn can be assigned the name of a procedure that is to perform the operations for incrementing the animation parameters. This procedure is continuously executed whenever there are no display-window events that must be processed. To disable the glutIdleFunc, we set its argument to the value NULL or the value 0.

An example animation program is given in the following code, which continuously rotates a regular hexagon in the xy plane about the z axis. The origin of three-dimensional screen coordinates is placed at the center of the display window, so that the z axis passes through this center position. In procedure init, we use a display list to set up the description of the regular hexagon, whose center position is originally at the screen-coordinate position (150, 150) with a radius (distance from the polygon center to any vertex) of 100 pixels. In the display function, displayHex, we specify an initial 0° rotation about the z axis and invoke the glutSwapBuffers routine. To activate the rotation, we use procedure mouseFcn which continually increments the rotation angle by 3° once we press the middle mouse button. The calculation of the incremented rotation angle is performed in procedure rotateHex, which is called by the glutIdleFunc routine in procedure mouseFcn. We stop the rotation by pressing the right mouse button, which causes the glutIdleFunc to be invoked with a NULL argument.

```
#include <GL/glut.h>
#include <math.h>
#include <stdlib.h>

const double TWO_PI = 6.2831853;

GLsizei winWidth = 500, winHeight = 500;     // Initial display window size.
GLuint regHex;                               // Define name for display list.
static GLfloat rotTheta = 0.0;

class scrPt {
public:
    GLint x, y;
};

static void init (void)
{
   scrPt hexVertex;
   GLdouble hexTheta;
   GLint k;

   glClearColor (1.0, 1.0, 1.0, 0.0);

   /*  Set up a display list for a red regular hexagon.
    *  Vertices for the hexagon are six equally spaced
    *  points around the circumference of a circle.
    */
   regHex = glGenLists (1);
   glNewList (regHex, GL_COMPILE);
      glColor3f (1.0, 0.0, 0.0);
      glBegin (GL_POLYGON);
```

```
         for (k = 0; k < 6; k++) {
            hexTheta = TWO_PI * k / 6;
            hexVertex.x = 150 + 100 * cos (hexTheta);
            hexVertex.y = 150 + 100 * sin (hexTheta);
            glVertex2i (hexVertex.x, hexVertex.y);
         }
      glEnd ( );
   glEndList ( );
}

void displayHex (void)
{
   glClear (GL_COLOR_BUFFER_BIT);

   glPushMatrix ( );
   glRotatef (rotTheta, 0.0, 0.0, 1.0);
   glCallList (regHex);
   glPopMatrix ( );

   glutSwapBuffers ( );

   glFlush ( );
}

void rotateHex (void)
{
   rotTheta += 3.0;
   if (rotTheta > 360.0)
      rotTheta -= 360.0;

   glutPostRedisplay ( );
}

void winReshapeFcn (GLint newWidth, GLint newHeight)
{
   glViewport (0, 0, (GLsizei) newWidth, (GLsizei) newHeight);

   glMatrixMode (GL_PROJECTION);
   glLoadIdentity ( );
   gluOrtho2D (-320.0, 320.0, -320.0, 320.0);

   glMatrixMode (GL_MODELVIEW);
   glLoadIdentity ( );

   glClear (GL_COLOR_BUFFER_BIT);
}

void mouseFcn (GLint button, GLint action, GLint x, GLint y)
{
   switch (button) {
      case GLUT_MIDDLE_BUTTON:           //  Start the rotation.
         if (action == GLUT_DOWN)
            glutIdleFunc (rotateHex);
         break;
      case GLUT_RIGHT_BUTTON:            //  Stop the rotation.
```

```
            if (action == GLUT_DOWN)
               glutIdleFunc (NULL);
            break;
         default:
            break;
      }
}

void main (int argc, char** argv)
{
   glutInit (&argc, argv);
   glutInitDisplayMode (GLUT_DOUBLE | GLUT_RGB);
   glutInitWindowPosition (150, 150);
   glutInitWindowSize (winWidth, winHeight);
   glutCreateWindow ("Animation Example");

   init ( );
   glutDisplayFunc (displayHex);
   glutReshapeFunc (winReshapeFcn);
   glutMouseFunc (mouseFcn);

   glutMainLoop ( );
}
```

13-11 SUMMARY

An animation sequence can be constructed frame by frame or it can be generated in real time. When separate frames of an animation are constructed and stored, the frames can later be transferred to film or displayed in rapid succession on a video monitor. Animations involving complex scenes and motions are commonly produced one frame at a time, while simpler motion sequences are displayed in real time.

On a raster system, double-buffering methods can be used to facilitate motion displays. One buffer is used to refresh the screen, while a second buffer is being loaded with the screen values for the next frame of the motion. Then the roles of the two buffers are interchanged, usually at the end of a refresh cycle.

Another raster method for displaying an animation is to perform motion sequences using block transfers of pixel values. Translations are accomplished by a simple move of a rectangular block of pixel colors from one frame-buffer position to another. And rotations in 90° increments can be performed with combinations of translations and row-column interchanges within the pixel array.

Color-table methods can be used for simple raster animations by storing an image of an object at multiple locations in the frame buffer, using different color-table values. One image is stored in the foreground color, and the copies of the image at the other locations are assigned a background color. By rapidly interchanging the foreground and background color values stored in the color table, we can display the object at various screen positions.

Several developmental stages can be used to produce an animation, starting with the storyboard, object definitions, and specification of key frames. The storyboard is an outline of the action, and the key frames define the details of the object motions for selected positions in the animation. Once the key frames have been established, in-between frames are generated to construct a smooth motion from one key frame to the next. A computer animation can involve motion specifications for the "camera", as well as motion paths for the objects and characters involved in the animation.

Various techniques have been developed for simulating and emphasizing motion effects. Squash and stretch effects are standard methods for stressing accelerations. And the timing between motion frames can be varied to produce speed variations. Other methods include a preliminary windup motion, a follow through at the end of an action, and staging methods that focus on an important action in a scene. Trigonometric functions are typically used to generate the time spacing for in-between frames when the motions involve accelerations.

Animations can be generated with special-purpose software or with a general-purpose graphics package. Systems that are available for automated computer animation include key-frame systems, parameterized systems, and scripting systems.

Many animations include morphing effects, in which one object shape is transformed into another. These effects are accomplished by using the in-between frames to transition the defining points and lines in one object into the points and lines of the other object.

Motions in an animation can be described with direct motion specifications or they can be goal directed. Thus, an animation can be defined in terms of translation and rotation parameters, or motions can be described with equations or with kinematic or dynamic parameters. Kinematic motion descriptions specify positions, velocities, and accelerations; dynamic motion descriptions are given in terms of the forces acting on the objects in a scene.

Articulated figures are often used to model the motions of people and animals. Rigid links, connected at rotary joints, are defined in a hierarchical structure. When a motion is imparted to an object, each subpart is programmed to move in a particular way in response to the overall motion.

The sampling rate for periodic motions should produce enough frames per cycle to display the animation correctly. Otherwise, erratic or misleading motions may result.

In addition to the raster ops and color-table methods, a few functions are available in the OpenGL Utility Toolkit (GLUT) for developing animation programs. These provide routines for double-buffering operations and for incrementing motion parameters during idle-processing intervals. In Table 13-1, we list the GLUT functions for producing animations with OpenGL programs.

TABLE 13-1

SUMMARY OF OpenGL ANIMATION FUNCTIONS

Function	Description
`glutInitDisplayMode (GLUT_DOUBLE)`	Activate double-buffering operations.
`glutSwapBuffers`	Interchange front and back refresh buffers.
`glGetBooleanv (GL_DOUBLEBUFFER, status)`	Query a system to determine whether double buffering is available.
`glutIdleFunc`	Specify a function for incrementing animation parameters.

REFERENCES

Computer-animation systems are discussed in Thalmann and Thalmann (1985), Watt and Watt (1992), O'Rourke (1998), Maestri (1999 and 2002), Kerlow (2000), Gooch and Gooch (2001), Parent (2002), Pocock and Rosebush (2002), and Strothotte and Schlechtweg (2002). Traditional animation techniques are explored in Lasseter (1987), Thomas, Johnston, and Johnston (1995), and Thomas and Lefkon (1997). Morphing methods are discussed in Hughes (1992), Kent, Carlson, and Parent (1992), Sederberg and Greenwood (1992), and Gomes, Darsa, Costa, and Velho (1999).

Various algorithms for animation applications are available in Glassner (1990), Arvo (1991), Kirk (1992), Gascuel (1993), Snyder, Woodbury, Fleischer, Currin, and Barr (1993), and Paeth (1995). And a discussion of animation techniques in OpenGL is given in Woo, Neider, Davis, and Shreiner (1999).

EXERCISES

13-1 Design a storyboard layout and accompanying key frames for an animation of a simple stick figure, as in Fig. 13-19.

13-2 Write a program to generate the in-betweens for the key frames specified in Exercise 13-1 using linear interpolation.

13-3 Expand the animation sequence in Exercise 13-1 to include two or more moving objects.

13-4 Write a program to generate the in-betweens for the key frames in Exercise 13-3 using linear interpolation.

13-5 Write a morphing program to transform any given polygon into another specified polygon, using five in-betweens.

13-6 Write a morphing program to transform a sphere into a specified polyhedron, using five in-betweens.

13-7 Set up an animation specification involving accelerations and implementing Eq. 13-7.

13-8 Set up an animation specification involving both accelerations and decelerations, implementing the in-between spacing calculations given in Eqs. 13-7 and 13-8.

13-9 Set up an animation specification implementing the acceleration–deceleration calculations of Eq. 13-9.

13-10 Write a program to simulate the linear, two-dimensional motion of a filled circle inside a given rectangular area. The circle is to be given an initial position and velocity, and the circle is to rebound from the walls with the angle of reflection equal to the angle of incidence.

13-11 Convert the program of the previous exercise into a ball and paddle game by replacing one side of the rectangle with a short line segment that can be moved back and forth along that rectangle edge. Interactive movement of the line segment simulates a paddle that can be positioned to prevent the bouncing ball from escaping. The game is over when the circle escapes from the interior of the rectangle. Initial input parameters include circle position, direction, and speed. The game score can include the number of times the circle is intercepted by the paddle.

13-12 Modify the ball and paddle game in the previous exercise to vary the speed of the bouncing ball. After some fixed interval, say five bounces, the speed of the ball can be incremented.

13-13 Modify the two-dimensional bouncing ball inside a rectangle to a three-dimensional motion of a sphere bouncing around inside a parallelepiped. Interactive viewing parameters can be set to view the motion from different directions.

13-14 Write a program to implement the simulation of a bouncing ball using Eq. 13-10.

13-15 Expand the program in the previous exercise to include squash and stretch effects.

13-16 Write a program to implement the motion of a bouncing ball using dynamics. The motion of the ball is to be governed by a downward gravitational force and a ground-plane friction force. Initially, the ball is to be projected into space with a given velocity vector.

13-17 Write a program to implement dynamic motion specifications. Specify a scene with two or more objects, initial motion parameters, and specified forces. Then generate the animation from the solution of the force equations. (For example, the objects could be the earth, moon, and sun with attractive gravitational forces that are proportional to mass and inversely proportional to distance squared.)

13-18 Modify the rotating hexagon program to allow a user to interactively choose an object to be rotated from a list of menu options.

13-19 Modify the rotating hexagon program so that the rotation is around an elliptical path.

13-20 Modify the rotating hexagon program to allow interactive variation of the rotation speed.

CHAPTER 14

Hierarchical Modeling

A computer-graphics scene containing a hierarchically modeled building complex.
(Courtesy of Silicon Graphics, Inc.)

In setting up the definition of a complex object or system, it is usually easiest to specify first the subparts and then describe how the subparts fit together to form the overall object or system. For instance, a bicycle can be described in terms of a frame, wheels, fenders, handlebars, seat, chain, and pedals, along with the rules for positioning these components to form the bicycle. A hierarchical description of this type can be given as a tree structure, consisting of the subparts at the tree nodes and the construction rules as the tree branches.

Architectural and engineering systems, such as building layouts, automobile design, electronic circuits, and home appliances, are now routinely developed using computer-aided design packages. And graphical design methods are used also for representing economic, financial, organizational, scientific, social, and environmental systems. Simulations are often constructed to study the behavior of a system under various conditions, and the outcome of a simulation can serve as an instructional tool or as a basis for making decisions about the system. Design packages generally provide routines for creating and managing hierarchical models, and some packages also contain predefined shapes, such as wheels, doors, gears, shafts, and electric-circuit components.

14-1 BASIC MODELING CONCEPTS

The creation and manipulation of a system representation is termed **modeling.** Any single representation is called a **model** of the system, which could be defined graphically or purely descriptively, such as a set of equations that describe the relationships between system parameters. Graphical models are often referred to as **geometric models,** because the component parts of a system are represented with geometric entities such as straight-line segments, polygons, polyhedra, cylinders, or spheres. Since we are concerned here only with graphics applications, we will use the term model to mean a computer-generated, geometric representation of a system.

System Representations

Figure 14-1 shows a graphical representation for a logic circuit, illustrating the features common to many system models. Component parts of the system are displayed as geometric structures, called **symbols,** and relationships between the symbols are represented in this example with a network of connecting lines. Three

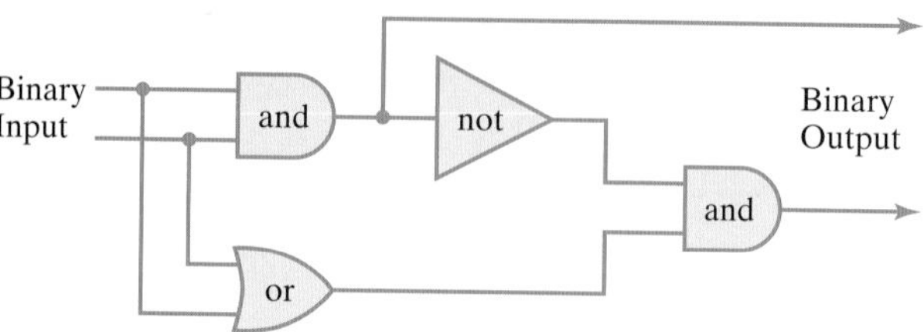

FIGURE 14-1 Model of a logic circuit.

standard symbols are used to represent logic gates for the Boolean operations: *and*, *or*, and *not*. The connecting lines define relationships in terms of input and output flow (from left to right) through the system parts. One symbol, the *and* gate, is displayed at two different positions within the logic circuit. Repeated positioning of a few basic symbols is a common method for building complex models. Each such occurrence of a symbol within a model is called an **instance** of that symbol. We have one instance for the *or* and *not* symbols in Fig. 14-1 and two instances of the *and* symbol.

In many cases, the particular graphical symbols chosen to represent the parts of a system are dictated by the system description. For circuit models, standard electrical or logic symbols are used. But with models representing abstract concepts, such as political, financial, or economic systems, symbols may be any convenient geometric pattern.

Information describing a model is usually provided as a combination of geometric and nongeometric data. Geometric information includes coordinate positions for locating the component parts, output primitives and attribute functions to define the structure of the parts, and data for constructing connections between the parts. Nongeometric information includes text labels, algorithms describing the operating characteristics of the model, and rules for determining the relationships or connections between component parts, if these are not specified as geometric data.

There are two methods for specifying the information needed to construct and manipulate a model. One method is to store the information in a data structure, such as a table or linked list. The other method is to specify the information in procedures. In general, a model specification will contain both data structures and procedures, although some models are defined completely with data structures and others use only procedural specifications. An application to perform solid modeling of objects might use mostly information taken from some data structure to define coordinate positions, with very few procedures. A weather model, on the other hand, may need mostly procedures to calculate plots of temperature and pressure variations.

As an example of how combinations of data structures and procedures can be used, we consider some alternative model specifications for the logic circuit of Fig. 14-1. One method is to define the logic components in a data table (Table 14-1), with processing procedures used to specify how the network connections are to be made and how the circuit operates. Geometric data in this table include coordinates and parameters necessary for drawing and positioning the gates. These symbols could all be drawn as polygon shapes, or they could be formed as combinations of straight-line segments and elliptical arcs. Labels for each of the component parts also have been included in the table, although the labels could be omitted if the symbols are displayed as commonly recognized shapes. Procedures would then be used to display the gates and construct the connecting lines, based on the coordinate positions of the gates and a specified order for

TABLE 14-1

DATA TABLE DEFINING THE STRUCTURE AND POSITION OF EACH GATE IN THE CIRCUIT OF FIGURE 14-1

Symbol Code	*Geometric Description*	*Identifying Label*
Gate 1	(Coordinates and other parameters)	and
Gate 2	:	or
Gate 3	:	not
Gate 4	:	and

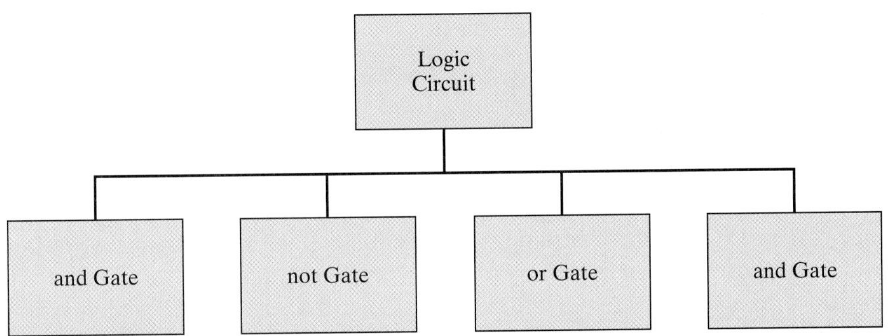

FIGURE 14-2 A one-level hierarchical description of a circuit formed with logic gates.

connecting them. An additional procedure is used to produce the circuit output (binary values) for any given input. This procedure could be set up to display only the final output, or it could be designed to display intermediate output values to illustrate the internal functioning of the circuit.

Alternatively, we might specify graphical information for the circuit model in data structures. The connecting lines, as well as the gates, could then be defined in a data table that explicitly lists endpoints for each of the lines in the circuit. A single procedure might then display the circuit and calculate the output. At the other extreme, we could completely define the model in procedures, using no external data structures.

Symbol Hierarchies

Many models can be organized as a hierarchy of symbols. The basic elements for the model are defined as simple geometric shapes appropriate to the type of model under consideration. These basic symbols can be used to form composite objects, sometimes called **modules,** which themselves can be grouped to form higher-level objects, and so on, for the various components of the model. In the simplest case, we can describe a model by a one-level hierarchy of component parts, as in Fig. 14-2. For this circuit example, we assume that the gates are positioned and connected to each other with straight lines according to connection rules that are specified with each gate description. The basic symbols in this hierarchical description are the logic gates. Although the gates themselves could be described as hierarchies—formed from straight lines, elliptical arcs, and text—that description would not be a convenient one for constructing logic circuits, in which the simplest building blocks are gates. For an application in which we were interested in designing different geometric shapes, the basic symbols could be defined as straight-line segments and arcs.

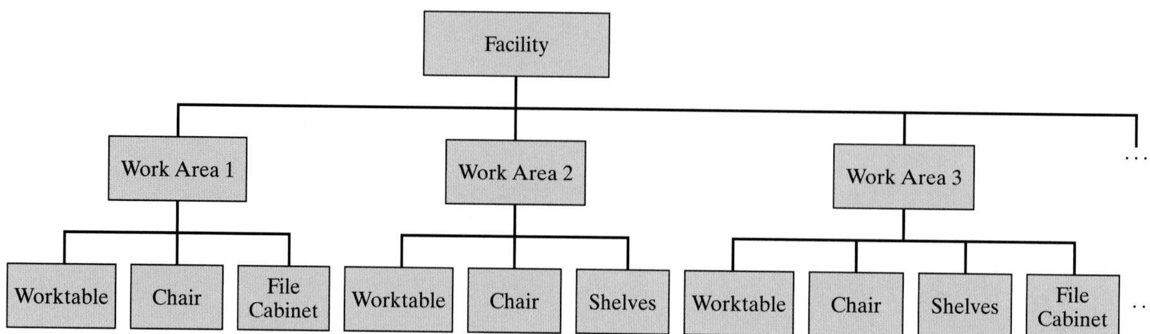

FIGURE 14-3 A two-level hierarchical description for a facility layout.

An example of a two-level symbol hierarchy appears in Fig. 14-3. Here, a facility layout is planned as an arrangement of work areas. Each work area is outfitted with a collection of furniture. The basic symbols are the furniture items: worktable, chair, shelves, file cabinet, and so forth. Higher-order objects are the work areas, which are put together with different furniture organizations. An instance of a basic symbol is defined by specifying its position, size, and orientation within each work area. Positions are given as coordinate locations in the work areas, and orientations are specified as rotations that determine which way the symbols are facing. At the first level below the root node for the facility tree, each work area is defined by specifying its position, size, and orientation within the facility layout. The boundary for each work area might be defined with a divider that encloses the work area and provides aisles within the facility.

More complex symbol hierarchies are formed with repeated groupings of symbol clusters at each higher level. The facility layout of Fig. 14-3 could be extended to include symbol clusters that form different rooms, different floors of a building, different buildings within a complex, and different complexes at widely separated geographical locations.

14-2 MODELING PACKAGES

Although system models can be designed and manipulated using a general computer-graphics package, specialized modeling systems are available to facilitate modeling in particular applications. Modeling systems provide a means for defining and rearranging model representations in terms of symbol hierarchies, which are then processed by graphics routines for display. General-purpose graphics systems often do not provide routines to accommodate extensive modeling applications. But some graphics packages, such as GL and PHIGS, do include integrated sets of modeling and graphics functions. An example of a PHIGS structure hierarchy is shown in Fig. 14-4. This display was generated using the PHIGS Toolkit software, developed at the University of Manchester, to provide an editor, windows, menus, and other interface tools for PHIGS applications.

If a graphics library contains no modeling functions, we can often use a modeling-package interface to the graphics routines. Alternatively, we could create our own modeling routines using the geometric transformations and other functions available in the graphics library.

Specialized modeling packages, such as some CAD systems, are defined and structured according to the type of application the package has been designed to

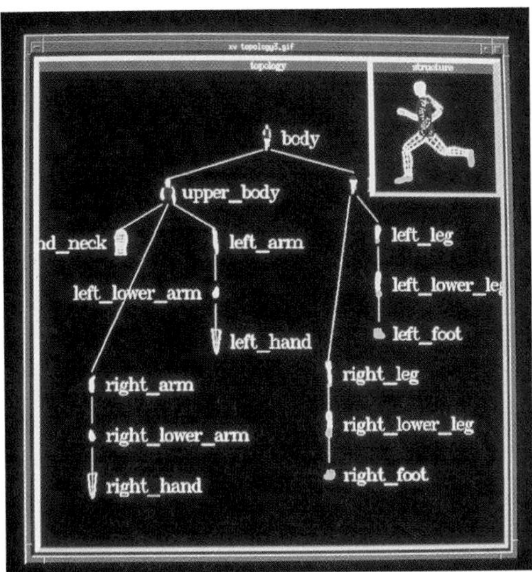

FIGURE 14-4 An object hierarchy generated using the PHIGS Toolkit package developed at the University of Manchester. The displayed object tree is itself a PHIGS structure. (*Courtesy of T. L. J. Howard, J. G. Williams, and W. T. Hewitt, Department of Computer Science, University of Manchester, United Kingdom.*)

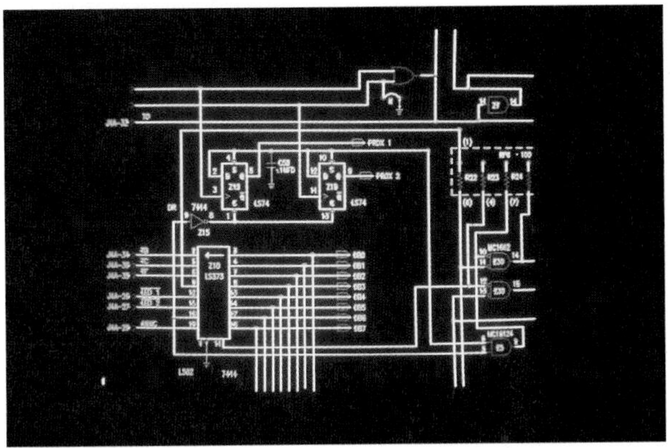

FIGURE 14-5 Two-dimensional modeling layout used in circuit design. (*Courtesy of Summagraphics.*)

FIGURE 14-6 A CAD model showing individual engine components, rendered by Ted Malone, FTI/3D-Magic. (*Courtesy of Silicon Graphics, Inc.*)

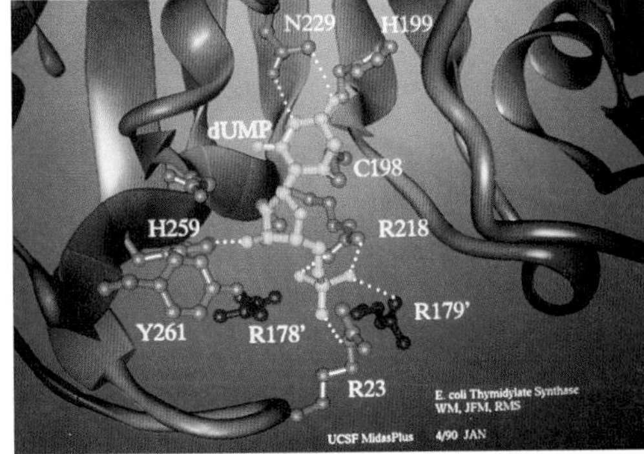

FIGURE 14-7 A ball-and-stick representation for key amino-acid residues interacting with the natural substrate of Thymidylate Synthase, modeled and rendered by Julie Newdoll, UCSF Computer Graphics Lab. (*Courtesy of Silicon Graphics, Inc.*)

handle. These packages provide menus of symbol shapes and functions for the intended application. And they can be designed for either two-dimensional or three-dimensional modeling. Figure 14-5 shows a two-dimensional layout generated by a CAD package configured for circuit design applications, and Fig. 14-6 illustrates a three-dimensional CAD application. Molecular-modeling examples are shown in Figs. 14-7 and 14-8, and a three-dimensional model of a facility layout is displayed in Fig. 14-9.

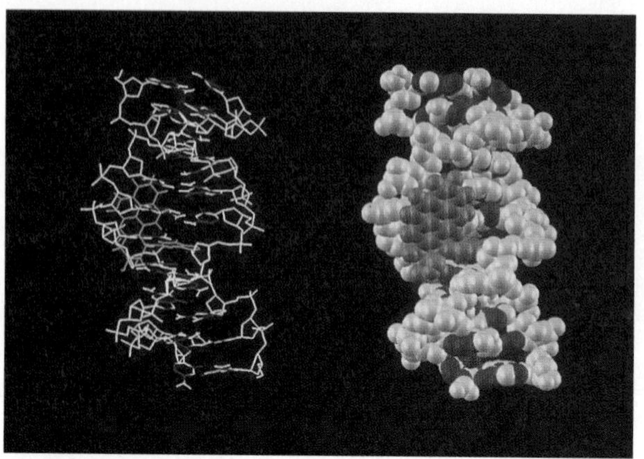

FIGURE 14-8 One half of a stereoscopic image pair showing a three-dimensional molecular model of DNA. Data supplied by Tamar Schlick, NYU, and Wilma K. Olson, Rutgers University; visualization by Jerry Greenberg, SDSC. (*Courtesy of Stephanie Sides, San Diego Supercomputer Center.*)

FIGURE 14-9 A three-dimensional view of an office layout. (*Courtesy of the Intergraph Corporation.*)

14-3 GENERAL HIERARCHICAL MODELING METHODS

We create a hierarchical model of a system by nesting the descriptions of its subparts into one another to form a tree organization. As each node is placed into the hierarchy, it is assigned a set of transformations to position it appropriately into the overall model. For an office-facility design, work areas and offices are formed with arrangements of furniture items. The offices and work areas are then placed into departments, and so forth on up the hierarchy. An example of the use of multiple coordinate systems and hierarchical modeling with three-dimensional objects is given in Fig. 14-10. This figure illustrates simulation of tractor movement. As the tractor moves, the tractor coordinate system and front-wheel coordinate system move in the world coordinate system. The front wheels rotate in the wheel system, and the wheel system rotates in the tractor system when the tractor turns.

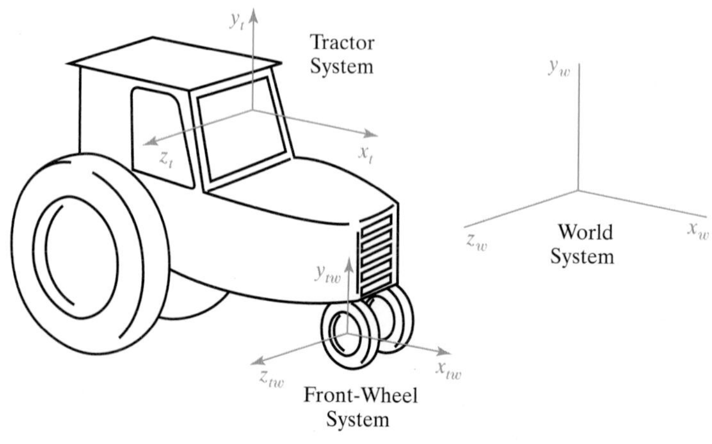

FIGURE 14-10 Possible coordinate systems used in simulating tractor movement. A rotation of the front-wheel system causes the tractor to turn. Both the wheel and tractor reference frames move in the world coordinate system.

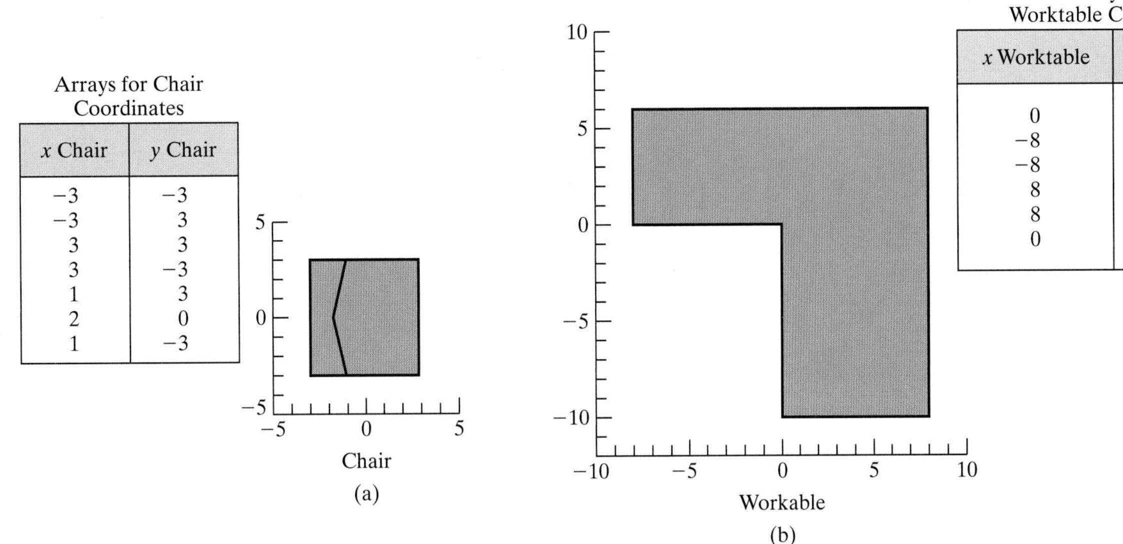

Arrays for Chair Coordinates

x Chair	y Chair
−3	−3
−3	3
3	3
3	−3
1	3
2	0
1	−3

Arrays for Worktable Coordinates

x Worktable	y Worktable
0	0
−8	0
−8	6
8	6
8	−10
0	−10

FIGURE 14-11 Objects defined in local coordinates.

Local Coordinates

In general design applications, models are constructed with instances (transformed copies) of the geometric shapes that are defined in a basic symbol set. Each instance is positioned, with the proper orientation, in the world-coordinate reference of the overall structure of the model. The various graphical objects to be used in an application are each defined relative to the world-coordinate reference system, which is referred to as the *local coordinate system* for that object. Local coordinates are also called *modeling coordinates,* or sometimes *master coordinates.* Figure 14-11 illustrates local-coordinate definitions for two symbols that could be used in a two-dimensional facility-layout application.

Modeling Transformations

To construct a graphical model, we apply transformations to the local-coordinate definitions of symbols to produce instances of the symbols within the overall structure of the model. Transformations applied to the modeling-coordinate definitions of symbols to give them a particular position and orientation within a model are referred to as *modeling transformations.* The typical transformations available in a modeling package are translation, rotation, and scaling, but other transformations might also be used in some applications.

Creating Hierarchical Structures

A first step in a hierarchical modeling application is to construct modules that are compositions of basic symbols. The modules themselves may then be combined into higher-level modules, and so on. We define each initial module as a list of symbol instances, along with appropriate transformation parameters for each symbol. At the next level, we define each higher-level module as a list of symbol and lower-level module instances along with their transformation parameters.

This process is continued up to the root of the tree, which represents the total model in world coordinates.

In a modeling package, a module is created with a sequence of commands of the form

```
createModule1
   setSymbolTransformation1
   insertSymbol1
   setSymbolTransformation2
   insertSymbol2
      .
      .
      .
closeModule1
```

Each instance of a basic symbol is assigned a set of transformation parameters for that module. Similarly, modules are combined to form higher-level modules with functions such as

```
createModule6
   setModuleTransformation1
   insertModule1
   setModuleTransformation2
   insertModule2

   setSymbolTransformation5
   insertSymbol5
      .
      .
      .
closeModule6
```

The transformation function for each module or symbol specifies how that object is to be fitted into the higher-level module. Often, options are provided so that a specified transformation matrix could premultiply, postmultiply, or replace the current transformation matrix.

Although a basic set of symbols could be available in a modeling package, the symbol set might not contain the shapes we need for a particular application. In that case, we can create additional shapes within a modeling program. As an example, the following pseudocode illustrates the specification of a simple model for a bicycle.

```
createWheelSymbol

createFrameSymbol

createBicycleModule
   setFrameTransformation
   insertFrameSymbol
```

```
    setFrontWheelTransformation
    insertWheelSymbol

    setBackWheelTransformation
    insertWheelSymbol
closeBicycleModule
```

A number of other modeling routines are usually available in a system designed for hierarchical modeling. Modules often can be selectively displayed or temporarily taken out of a system representation. This allows a designer to experiment with different shapes and design structures. And selected modules could be highlighted or moved around in the display during the design process.

14-4 HIERARCHICAL MODELING USING OpenGL DISPLAY LISTS

Complex objects can be described in OpenGL using nested display lists to form a hierarchical model. Each symbol and module for the model is created with a `glNewList` function. And we insert one display list into another display list using the `glCallList` function within the definition of the higher-order list. Geometric transformations can be associated with each inserted object to specify a position, orientation, and size within the higher-level module. As an example, the following code could be used to describe a bicycle that is simply composed of a frame and two identical wheels.

```
glNewList (bicycle, GL_COMPILE);
   glCallList (frame);

   glTranslatef (tx1, ty1, tz1);
   glCallList (wheel);

   glTranslatef (tx2, ty2, tz2);
   glCallList (wheel);
glEndList ( );
```

Similarly, the `frame` display list itself could be composed of individual display lists describing the handlebars, chain, pedals, and other components.

14-5 SUMMARY

The term "model", in computer-graphics applications, refers to a graphical representation for some system. Basic components of a system are represented as symbols, defined in local-coordinate reference frames, which are also referred to as modeling, or master, coordinates. We create a model, such as an electrical circuit, by placing instances of the symbols at selected locations with prescribed orientations.

Many models are constructed as symbol hierarchies. We can construct a hierarchical model by nesting modules, which are composed of instances of basic symbols and other modules. This nesting process may continue down to symbols that are defined with graphical output primitives and their attributes. As each symbol or module is nested within a higher-level module, an associated modeling transformation is specified for the nested structure.

A hierarchical model can be set up in OpenGL using display lists. The `glNewList` function can be used to define the overall structure of a system and its component modules. Individual symbol structures or other modules are inserted within a module using the `glCallList` function, preceded by an appropriate set of transformations to specify the position, orientation, and size of the inserted component.

REFERENCE

Examples of modeling applications using OpenGL are given in Woo, Neider, Davis, and Shreiner (1999).

EXERCISES

14-1 Discuss model representations that would be appropriate for several distinctly different kinds of systems. Also discuss how graphical representations might be implemented for each system.

14-2 Devise a two-dimensional facility layout package. A menu of furniture shapes is to be provided to a designer, who can use a mouse to select and place an object in any location within a single room (one-level hierarchy). Instance transformations can be limited to translations and rotations.

14-3 Extend the previous exercise so that furniture shapes can also be scaled.

14-4 Devise a two-dimensional facility layout package, that presents a menu of furniture shapes. A two-level hierarchy is to be used so that furniture items can be placed into various work areas, and the work areas can be arranged within a larger area. Furniture shapes are to be placed into work areas using only translation and rotation instance transformations.

14-5 Extend the previous exercise so that furniture shapes can also be scaled.

14-6 Write a set of routines for creating and displaying symbols for logic-circuit design. As a minimum, the symbol set should include the *and*, *or*, and *not* gates shown in Fig. 14-1.

14-7 Develop a modeling package for designing logic circuits that will allow a designer to position electrical symbols within a circuit network. Use the symbol set from the previous exercise, and use only translations to place an instance of one of the menu shapes into the network. Once a component has been placed in the network, it is to be connected to other specified components with straight-line segments.

14-8 Write a set of routines for editing modules that have been created in an application program. Your routines should provide for the following types of editing: appending, inserting, replacing, and deleting module elements.

14-9 Given the coordinate extents of all displayed objects in a model, write a routine to delete any selected object.

14-10 Write procedures to display and to delete a specified module in a model.

14-11 Write a routine that will selectively take modules out of a model display or return them to the display.

14-12 Write a procedure to highlight a selected module in some way. For example, the selected module could be displayed in a different color or it could be enclosed within a rectangular outline.

14-13 Write a procedure to highlight a selected module in a model by causing the module to blink on and off.

CHAPTER 15

Graphics File Formats

A computer-generated scene created with simulated watercolor brush strokes.
(Courtesy of Aydin Controls, a Division of the Aydin Corporation.)

ny stored pictorial representation is called a **graphics file** or an **image file.** For raster-graphics systems, a color screen display is represented in the frame buffer as a set of pixel RGB values. As we noted in Section 2-1, the contents of the frame buffer, or any rectangular section of it, is called a pixmap. Although monochromatic images can be stored in a bitmap form (using a single bit for each pixel), most raster pictures are now stored as pixmaps. In general, any raster representation for a picture is referred to as a **raster file.** Many formats have been developed for organizing the information in an image file in various ways, and full-color raster files can be quite large, so most file formats apply some type of compression to reduce the file size, both for archiving and for transmission. In addition, the number of color values in a full-color image file must be reduced when the picture is to be displayed on a system with limited color capabilities, or when the file is to be stored in a format that does not support 24 bits per pixel. Here, we provide a brief introduction to graphics file formats and the commonly used methods for reducing the size of both an image file and the number of colors that are to be used in the display of an image.

15-1 IMAGE-FILE CONFIGURATIONS

Pixel color values in a raster image file are typically stored as nonnegative integers, and the range of color values depends on the number of available bits per pixel position. For a full-color (24 bits per pixel) RGB image, the value for each color component is stored in one byte, with R, G, and B values ranging from 0 to 255. An uncompressed raster-graphics file composed of RGB color values is sometimes referred to as **raw data** or a **raw raster file.** Other color models, including HSV, HSB, and YC_rC_b, are used in compressed file formats. And the number of available bits per pixel depends on the format.

File formats typically include a **header** that provides information about the structure of the file. For compressed files, the header may also contain tables and other details needed to decode and display the compressed image. The header can include a variety of information, such as the file size (number of scan lines and number of pixels per scan line), the number of bits or bytes allocated per pixel, the compression method used to reduce the size of the file, the color range for the pixel values, and the image background color.

Another characteristic of raster image files is the ordering for the bytes within the file. Most computer processors store multibyte integers with the most significant byte first, but some processors store multibyte integers with the least significant byte first. The term **big endian** is used to refer to the ordering with the most significant byte first, and the term **little endian** refers to the ordering with the least significant byte first.

Some file formats store a picture in a **geometric representation,** which is a list of the coordinate positions and other information for straight-line segments, fill areas, circular arcs, spline curves, and other primitives. Geometric representations can also contain attribute information and viewing parameters. This type of image representation is commonly referred to as a *vector format* even though not all geometric structures are defined with straight-line segments. Originally, the term "vector" file was used to describe a list of line segments for display on a vector (random-scan) system. Although vector systems have been replaced by raster systems, and nonlinear object descriptions have been added to the "vector" files, the name continues to be applied to any file using a geometric representation for a picture. File formats that support both geometric and raster image representations are referred to as **hybrid formats** or **metafiles.**

Scientific-visualization applications often use an image file that is a set of data values generated from measuring instruments or from numerical computer simulations. Various programs are then used to provide particular data visualizations, such as pseudo-color displays, isosurface representations, or volume renderings.

15-2 COLOR-REDUCTION METHODS

Several methods have been devised for reducing the number of colors used in the display of an image. The most popular methods are those that attempt to generate a color sampling that closely approximates the original set of colors.

Sometimes color-reduction methods are referred to as "quantization", which is a term used in areas of physics and mathematics (such as quantum mechanics and sampling theory) for a process that produces a discrete set of values from a continuous distribution. However, a raster image file is not a continuous distribution; it contains a finite, discrete set of color values. Therefore, any color-reduction method simply replaces one discrete set of colors with a smaller discrete set of colors. Furthermore, the color-reduction processes in common use do not generate a set of colors such that each color in the set is a multiple of some selected value. In other words, color reduction does not produce a set of quantized colors.

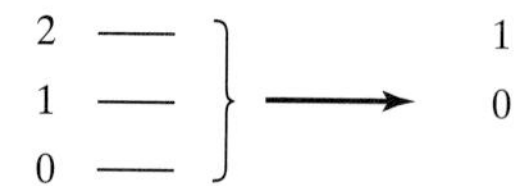

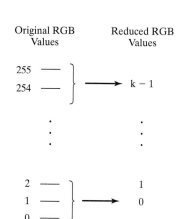

FIGURE 15-1 A uniform color reduction of the RGB values in a full-color image to k levels.

Uniform Color Reduction

A simple method for reducing colors in a raster file is to divide each of the R, G, and B color levels by an integer and truncate the result. For example, if we divide by 2, we reduce each of the R, G, and B components in a full-color representation to 128 levels. Thus, uniform color reduction replaces groups of contiguous color levels with a reduced color level, as illustrated in Fig. 15-1.

Another approach is to replace a group of pixel values with the value of the middle pixel in the group. Or, we could replace the group of pixels with the average color for the group.

In general, we can expect that not all 256 values will be present in the image file for each of the RGB components. Therefore, we can apply a uniform color-reduction method to the color levels between the minimum and maximum levels that actually occur in the image file.

We can also apply different reduction criteria to the different RGB components. For instance, we could reduce a full-color image so that the red and green

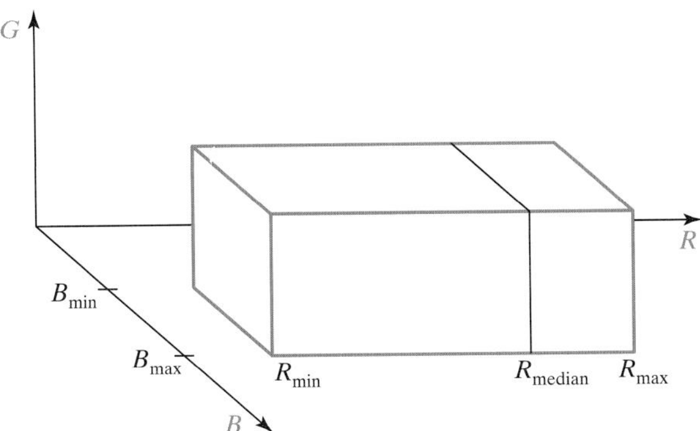

FIGURE 15-2 A block of image colors and the division of this block at the position of the median red component.

color components are represented with 3 bits each (8 levels) and the blue component is represented with 2 bits (4 levels).

Popularity Color Reduction

Another approach to color reduction is to retain only the color values that occur most frequently in an image representation. We can first process the input image file to reduce the bit representation for the individual RGB components. Then we scan this modified set of colors to produce a count, or histogram, of the frequency of occurrence for each RGB color component. To produce a reduced color file with k colors, we select the k most frequently occurring colors in the image file.

Median-Cut Color Reduction

In this algorithm, we subdivide the color space for the image file into k subregions and calculate the average color for each of the subregions. To form the subregions, we first determine the minimum and maximum values for each of the RGB components: R_{min}, R_{max}, G_{min}, G_{max}, B_{min}, and B_{max}. These values give us the bounds on the block of colors within the RGB color cube that are present in the image. For the largest of these three intervals, we determine the median value and use this value to form two smaller blocks of colors. As an example, if the red component has the largest range, we compute the value R_{median} such that half of the pixel colors are above this value and half are below. We then slice the image color block into two subblocks at the R_{median} position, as shown in Fig. 15-2. Each of the two color subblocks is then processed using the same subdivision procedure. This process continues until we have subdivided the original image color block into k subblocks. At each step, we can apply the subdivision procedure to the largest subblock. An average color at the desired precision is calculated for each subblock, and all image colors within a subblock are replaced with the average subblock color.

15-3 FILE-COMPRESSION TECHNIQUES

A variety of compression techniques are available for reducing the number of bytes in an image file, but the effectiveness of a particular compression method depends on the type of image. Simple methods that look for patterns in the image file are most effective with geometric designs that contain large single-color areas, while the more complex compression schemes produce better results with photo-realistic computer-graphics images and digitized photographs. The general technique employed to reduce the size of a graphics file is to replace the color values with an encoding that occupies fewer bytes than the original file. In addition, codes are incorporated into compressed files to indicate such things as the end of a scan line and the end of the image file.

Some compression algorithms involve floating-point operations, which can introduce round-off errors. In addition, some methods use approximations that also modify the image colors. As a result, a file that has been decoded from a compressed file often contains color values that are not exactly the same as in the original image. For instance, an integer RGB color that is specified as (247, 108, 175) in an input image file could become the color (242, 111, 177) after decoding the compressed file. But such color changes are often tolerable because our eyes are not sensitive to small color differences.

File-reduction methods that do not change the values in an image file are described as **lossless compression** techniques, and those that create color changes are referred to as **lossy compression** techniques. In most cases, lossy compression methods produce a much greater compression ratio for a file, where the compression ratio is the number of bytes in the original file divided by the number of bytes in the compressed file.

Run-Length Encoding

This compression scheme simply searches the image file for contiguous, repeated values. A reduced file is formed by storing each sequence of repeated values as the single file value along with the number of repetitions. For example, if the value 125 occurs 8 times in succession along a scan line, we store the two values 8 and 125 in the compressed file. This reduces the original eight bytes of storage to two bytes. For images with large single-color areas, this encoding scheme works well. But images such as digitized photographs have frequent color changes and few consecutive repeating values, so that many color values would be stored with a repetition factor of 1.

Variations have been developed to improve the efficiency of the basic run-length encoding algorithm. For instance, we could use a negative repetition factor to indicate a sequence of nonrepeating values, rather than just storing a repetition factor of 1 with each of the values in the nonrepeating sequence. As an example of this, the following list of values

```
{20, 20, 20, 20, 99, 68, 31, 40, 40, 40, 40, 40, 40, 40, 40, . . . }
```

could be encoded as

```
{4, 20, −3, 99, 68, 31, 8, 40, . . . }
```

which indicates that the value 20 occurs 4 times, followed by the 3 nonrepeating values 99, 68, and 31, which in turn is followed by 8 occurrences of the value 40. In this encoding example, the first 15 bytes of the input file are compressed into 8 bytes.

LZW Encoding

Developed by Lempel, Ziv, and Welch, the LZW method is a modification of the earlier LZ, LZ77, and LZ78 pattern-recognition algorithms. In the LZW scheme, repeated patterns in an image file are replaced with a code. For instance, the following list of 12 values contains two occurrences for each of the patterns {128, 96} and {200, 30, 10}:

```
{128, 96, 200, 30, 10, 128, 96, 50, 240, 200, 30, 10, . . . }
```

We can replace these two patterns with the codes $c1$ and $c2$, and the remaining pattern {50, 240} can be assign the code $c3$. This reduces the first twelve values in the input list to the following 5 bytes:

```
{c1, c2, c1, c3, c2, . . . }
```

Alternatively, any nonrepeating sequence of values, such as {50, 240} could be stored in the compressed file without assigning a code to the sequence.

Basically, the LZW algorithm searches for repeated sequences and constructs a table of such sequences along with their assigned codes. Thus, this encoding scheme is called a *substitutional algorithm* or a *dictionary-based algorithm*. The compressed file is then decoded from the code table.

Other Pattern-Recognition Compression Methods

We can use pattern-recognition schemes to locate repetitions for particular black and white or RGB color combinations throughout an image file. Duplicated scan lines and other patterns can be detected and encoded to further reduce the size of image files. In addition, fractal methods have been applied to obtain small encoded self-similar sets of color values.

Huffman Encoding

File compression is accomplished with the Huffman approach by using a variable-length code for the values in an image file. The Huffman-encoding method assigns the shortest code to the most frequently occurring value in the file, and the longest code is assigned to the least frequently occurring value.

The basic idea in the Huffman algorithm is the same as in the Morse code, which assigns variable-length character codes to letters of the alphabet. High-frequency letters in the Morse scheme are assigned one-character codes, and the lowest-frequency letters are assigned four-character codes. For example, the letter E is coded as a "dot" (·), the letter T is coded as a "dash" (–), and the letter Q is coded as a four-character sequence with one dot and three dashes (– – · –). Instead of using character codes, however, the Huffman code assigns variable-length bit codes to the values in an image file, which provides greater compression ratios.

The first step in the Huffman algorithm is to count the number of occurrences of each value in the input image file. Then, bit codes are assigned to the values according to the frequency count. One method for assigning the variable-length bit codes is to construct a binary tree with the high-frequency values near the top of the tree and the lowest-frequency values as the leaf nodes. Starting with the low-frequency values, we create the subtrees from the bottom up. Each root node of a subtree is assigned a numerical label that is the sum of the frequency counts or node labels of its two children. When the tree is complete, all left subtrees are labeled with the binary value 0, and all right trees are labeled with the binary value 1. The bit code for each file value is then formed by concatenating the branch bit labels from the top of the tree down to the node position of that file value in the tree.

TABLE 15-1

FREQUENCY COUNT FOR VALUES IN A SMALL EXAMPLE FILE

File Value	Frequency Count
96	8
177	4
141	3
85	3
210	2
43	1
Total Values in File:	21

To illustrate the general tree-construction steps, we use the set of six values in Table 15-1. This set represents a short example image file containing 21 items, with the value 96 occurring 8 times, the value 177 occurring 4 times, and so forth for the other four values in the file.

The values 210 and 43 in this table have the lowest frequency count, so we use these two values to form the first subtree (Fig. 15-3). The root of this subtree is assigned a node label that is equal to the sum of the number of occurrences of its two offspring: $3 = 2 + 1$. We delete these two file values (210 and 43) from the active list so that the next lowest frequency count is 3. But we just created a subtree that also has the node label 3. Therefore, we can form the next subtree using any two of the three items that have the label 3. We choose the two file values to form the subtree shown in Fig. 15-4, and we delete the values 141 and 85 from the active list. The next subtree is constructed with the file value 177, which has a count of 4, and the subtree whose root has the label 3 (Fig. 15-5). We delete the file value 177 and the tree node with the label 3 from the active list, and now the two lowest "counts" in the list represent subtrees. These two subtrees are then merged to produce the new subtree shown in Fig. 15-6. Finally, we complete the construction of the binary tree (Fig. 15-7) by joining the file value 96 to the last subtree we created. The value assigned to the root of the tree is the total count (21) for all values in the image file.

Now that we have all file values in a binary tree, we can label left branches in the tree with the binary value 0 and right branches with the binary value 1, as in Fig. 15-8. Starting at the root of the tree, we concatenate the branch labels down to each of the leaf nodes. This forms the set of variable-length binary codes for each of the file values, and we then set up Table 15-2, which will be stored with the compressed file. For this example, there is one file value with a one-digit

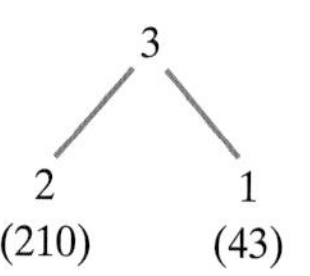

List of Remaining Frequency Labels	
96	8
177	4
141	3
85	3
node	3

FIGURE 15-3 Forming a Huffman subtree using the file values 210 and 43.

List of Remaining Frequency Labels	
96	8
node	6
177	4
node	3

FIGURE 15-4 Forming a Huffman subtree using the file values 141 and 85.

List of Remaining Frequency Labels	
96	8
node	7
node	6

FIGURE 15-5 Forming a Huffman subtree using the file value 177 and a previously created subtree.

List of Remaining Frequency Labels	
node	13
96	8

FIGURE 15-6 Forming a Huffman subtree by joining two previously created subtrees.

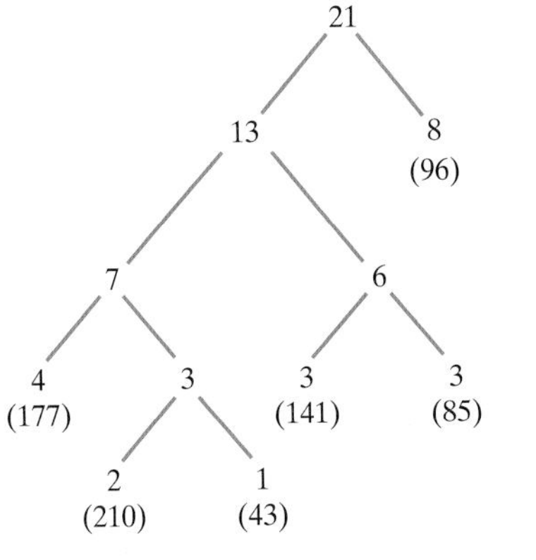

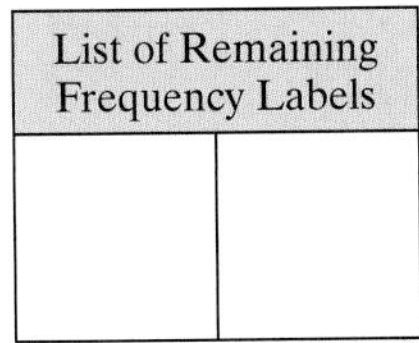

FIGURE 15-7 A complete Huffman binary tree for the file values in Table 15-1.

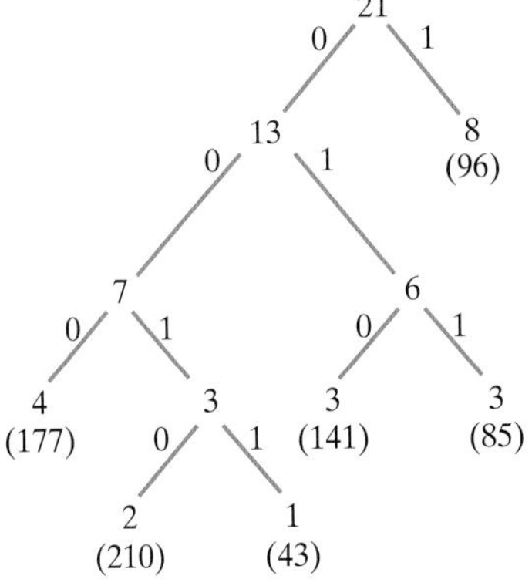

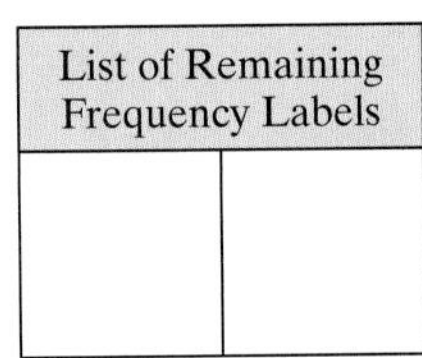

FIGURE 15-8 The complete Huffman binary tree with branch labeling.

binary code, three file values with a three-digit binary code, and two file values with a four-digit binary code. The low-frequency values have longer codes, and the higher-frequency values have shorter codes.

An important characteristic of the Huffman codes is that no bit code is a prefix for any other bit code. This allows us to decode a list of encoded file values by providing Table 15-3 along with Table 15-2. To demonstrate the decoding algorithm, we suppose that the compressed file contains the bit stream $\{100100100\ldots\}$. The first bit value in this file is 1, so it must represent the file value 96 because there is a bit code 1 and this cannot be a prefix for any other code. Next, we have a bit value of 0. There is no one-bit code other than 1 and there are no two-bit codes, so the next code must be either 001 or 0010. Checking the indexed code table, we find a file value 210 with the code 0010, which means that there cannot be a file value with the code 001. At this point, we have decoded the first two file values, 96 and 210. The next code in the bit stream must be either 010 or 0100. There is a file value with the code 010, so there cannot be a four-bit code with that prefix. Thus the third decoded file value is 141. We continue analyzing the bit stream in this manner until the compressed file has been fully decoded.

We can also use other schemes for generating and assigning Huffman bit codes. Once we have the frequency count, we could assign a code length to each file value. Using the code length and the frequency count, we can then use a list-merging algorithm to devise the specific bit codes. A predefined code set can also be used to assign codes to the file values, which eliminates the need to store the codes with the compressed file.

TABLE 15-2

INDEXED HUFFMAN CODES FOR THE EXAMPLE FILE

Index	*File Value*	*Binary Code*
1	96	1
2	177	000
3	141	010
4	85	011
5	210	0010
6	43	0011

TABLE 15-3

BIT-CODE REFERENCE TABLE

Bit-Code Length	*Min Code Value*	*Max Code Value*	*First Index*
1	1	1	1
3	000	011	2
4	0010	0011	5

TABLE 15-4

FREQUENCY COUNT AND FRACTION OF OCCURRENCES FOR VALUES IN A SMALL EXAMPLE FILE

File Value	*Frequency Count*	*File Fraction*	*Unit-Interval Range*
V_1	16	0.20	0.00–0.20
V_2	24	0.30	0.20–0.50
V_3	40	0.50	0.50–1.00
Total:	80	1.00	

Arithmetic Encoding

In this compression scheme, the frequency count in a file is used to obtain numerical codes for sequences of the file values. The arithmetic-encoding algorithm first computes the fraction of the file that is occupied by each value. This creates a set of subintervals within the unit interval from 0.0 to 1.0. Then each file fraction is repeatedly mapped onto these subintervals to establish numerical intervals for various combinations of the file values. The numerical bounds for the subintervals are used to encode these combinations.

To illustrate the method, we consider a file with 80 entries and just three distinct values. The frequency count and corresponding file fractions for the three values are listed in Table 15-4. Thus, value V_1 is associated with the subinterval from 0.00 to 0.20 within the unit interval, value V_2 is associated with the subinterval from 0.20 to 0.50, and value V_3 is associated with the subinterval from 0.50 to 1.00. In other words, 20 percent of the unit interval is associated with V_1, 30 percent with V_2, and 50 percent with V_3. If we now map V_1 onto the V_3 subinterval, it will occupy 20 percent of the top half of the unit interval. This new subinterval, with a range from 0.50 to 0.60, represents the sequence $V_3 V_1$. Similar results are obtained for the mappings of V_2 and V_3 onto the V_3 subinterval. Table 15-5 lists ranges for these three two-value sequences. Continuing in this manner, we can map the intervals for the two-value sequences onto other subintervals to obtain the sequences for longer combinations of the file values. The boundary values for the subintervals are then used to encode and decode the sequences within the file.

TABLE 15-5

UNIT-INTERVAL RANGE FOR EACH TWO-VALUE SEQUENCE STARTING WITH THE VALUE V_3

Sequence	*Unit-Interval Range*
$V_3 V_1$	0.50–0.60
$V_3 V_2$	0.60–0.75
$V_3 V_3$	0.75–1.00

Various algorithms can be used to terminate the unit-interval subdivisions and to assign numerical codes to the file-value combinations. And the arithmetic-encoding algorithm is typically implemented using binary numbers instead of the floating-point values within the unit interval. The compressed file is then a sequence of binary values.

Discrete Cosine Transform

A number of numerical transform methods, including the Fourier and Hadamard transforms, have been applied to file compression, but the discrete cosine transform is the most commonly used method. Efficient implementation algorithms for the discrete cosine transform provide faster execution and better color fidelity in a reconstructed picture at higher compression ratios.

For a list of n numerical values V_k, with $k = 0, 1, \ldots, n-1$, the discrete cosine method generates the following set of transformed values.

$$V'_j = c_j \sum_{k=0}^{n-1} V_k \cos\left[\frac{(2k+1)j\pi}{2n}\right], \qquad \text{for } j = 0, 1, \ldots, n-1 \qquad (15\text{-}1)$$

where

$$c_j = \begin{cases} \dfrac{1}{\sqrt{n}}, & \text{for } j = 0 \\ \sqrt{\dfrac{2}{n}}, & \text{for } j \neq 0 \end{cases}$$

Thus, this transform method computes a discrete sum of cosine terms with increasing frequency and with amplitudes that are proportional to the input values. Except for possible round-off errors, the original values are recovered with the inverse transformation

$$V_k = \sum_{j=0}^{n-1} c_j V'_j \cos\left[\frac{(2k+1)j\pi}{2n}\right], \qquad \text{for } k = 0, 1, \ldots, n-1 \qquad (15\text{-}2)$$

Very often, the transform values V'_j are alluded to as the "coefficients" of the cosine functions in the inverse transform equation. But this is incorrect terminology, since the coefficients of the cosine terms in the summation are the products $c_j V'_j$.

To illustrate this transform method, we consider the following list of 8 input values.

$$\{215, 209, 211, 207, 192, 148, 88, 63\}$$

The transformed values, computed to two decimal places, for this input are

$$\{471.29, 143.81, -67.76, 16.33, 7.42, -4.73, 5.49, 0.05\}$$

In this example, we note that the amplitudes of the transformed values markedly decrease, so that the higher frequency cosine terms contribute less to the recovery of the input values. This is a basic characteristic of the discrete cosine transform, which allows us to approximate closely the original values using only the first several transformed values. Therefore, to obtain a compressed image file, we could calculate and store just the first half or so of the transformation values. Table 15-6 shows the results from Eq. 15-2 when we use 4, 5, or all 8 of the transformed values to regain the input values. All calculated values in the table are rounded to two decimal places.

We can improve the efficiency of this compression technique by transforming rectangular blocks of input values, rather than transforming linear sets of values across a single scan line. For a square block of n by n input values, the transformed values are calculated as

$$V'_{lm} = c_{lm} \sum_{j=0}^{n-1} \sum_{k=0}^{n-1} V_{jk} \cos\left[\frac{(2k+1)l\pi}{2n}\right] \cos\left[\frac{(2j+1)m\pi}{2n}\right] \qquad (15\text{-}3)$$

TABLE 15-6

INVERSE DISCRETE COSINE TRANSFORMATION CALCULATIONS

Input Values:	215	209	211	207	192	148	88	63
Terms in Sum	*Inverse Discrete Cosine Transform Values:*							
4	212.63	211.85	211.53	207.42	188.43	147.65	95.47	58.02
5	215.26	209.23	208.91	210.04	191.06	145.02	92.84	60.64
8	215.00	209.00	211.00	207.00	192.00	148.00	88.00	63.00

with

$$l,\, m = 0,\, 1,\, \ldots,\, n-1$$

and

$$c_{lm} = \begin{cases} \dfrac{1}{n}, & \text{if } l = 0 \quad \text{or} \quad m = 0 \\[2ex] \dfrac{2}{n}, & \text{if } l \neq 0 \quad \text{and} \quad m \neq 0 \end{cases}$$

Also, the n by n set of input values are recovered using the inverse transformation:

$$V_{jk} = \sum_{l=0}^{n-1} \sum_{m=0}^{n-1} c_j V'_j \cos\left[\frac{(2j+1)l\pi}{2n}\right] \cos\left[\frac{(2k+1)m\pi}{2n}\right] \tag{15-4}$$

where

$$j,\, k = 0,\, 1,\, \ldots,\, n-1$$

This transform and its inverse are typically implemented using 8 by 8 groups of input values, so that groups of color values along 8 scan lines are processed simultaneously.

15-4 COMPOSITION OF THE MAJOR FILE FORMATS

Hundreds of file formats have been developed for representing graphical data within different contexts for different systems. Operating systems, for example, typically use a number of specially designed formats within the various system-processing routines. And individual formats exist for specific applications, such as three-dimensional modeling, animations, graphical user interfaces, ray-tracing software, video recording, scientific-visualization software, paint programs, word-processing systems, spreadsheet packages, internet communications, television broadcasting, and fax transmissions. In addition, the ISO and ANSI standards committees have proposed several formats and file-compression systems for general use.

Most raster file formats are designed to accommodate color images, but some apply only to bitmaps. However, the format name is often misleading, because the term bitmap is frequently used to reference color images (pixmaps). This situation is simply a result of the continued use of the older label, bitmap, for a raster file.

Before the development of color displays, all raster images were stored as bitmaps (one bit per pixel), representing the black-and-white pixel patterns in a picture. As color techniques developed, pixmap files (multiple bits per pixel) replaced the bitmaps. But very often these files were still referred to as bitmaps. As a result, many color-encoding schemes in use today for image files are labeled as "bitmap formats" even though they are actually pixmap formats (multiple bits per pixel). However, the documentation for such formats can be consulted to determine the number of bits actually allotted to each pixel position in the file.

For the most part, the file formats described in this section are not static. They undergo constant revisions and updates, and many variants often exist for a particular format.

JPEG: Joint Photographic Experts Group

In its basic form, this widely used and complex system, developed by the JPEG committee of the International Standards Organization (ISO), consists of a large collection of file-compression options. More than two dozen variations are given in the JPEG definition, so that it can be implemented in a number of different ways, from simple lossless algorithms to very high-compression lossy methods. But the basic JPEG definition does not completely specify how the compressed image file should be structured so that it can be used on different computer systems or by different applications. For instance, there is no specified organization for the header information and there is no specification for the color model that should be used in the compressed file.

The JPEG standard defines four general file-compression modes, which are called the lossless, sequential, progressive, and hierarchical modes. In the **JPEG lossless mode,** a pattern-recognition scheme is combined with either Huffman encoding or arithmetic encoding. However, the original JPEG lossless mode is not as efficient as other available lossless formats, so it is rarely implemented. The **JPEG baseline sequential mode** is the most commonly used version of JPEG. Numerical values for the color components in a picture are stored in 8 bits, and the compression algorithm combines the discrete cosine transform with either Huffman or arithmetic encoding. An *extended sequential mode* is also defined with more options than the baseline sequential mode and in which color components can be specified using 16 bits. In the **JPEG progressive mode,** an image file is processed using several passes so that "layers" of the image can be generated at varying resolutions. This mode, generally referred to as *progressive JPEG,* is becoming popular for internet applications, because a rough approximation of a picture can be viewed quickly before downloading the complete image file. Another collection of procedures for obtaining incrementally improved versions of an image is contained in the **JPEG hierarchical mode,** which divides an image into a set of subimages. This allows selected sections of a picture to be progressively constructed. Because of its complexity, hierarchical JPEG is not widely used.

Options could be provided in a large-scale JPEG implementation for the selection of both a compression mode and the compression parameters, such as the number of terms to be used in the summation calculations for the inverse, discrete cosine transform. Also, the JPEG compression definitions specify that either Huffman encoding or arithmetic encoding can be combined with the discrete cosine transform. But implementations of JPEG never use the arithmetic-encoding algorithms, because these algorithms are patented and require a licensing fee.

Although the JPEG specification does not define a specific structure for the compressed image file, implementations now use the **JPEG File Interchange**

Format (JFIF), proposed by Eric Hamilton at C-Cube Microsystems and based on suggestions from many JPEG users. In this format, the file header contains a unique JFIF identifier (referred to as the file "signature"), the version of JFIF used to set up the file, the image size (either in pixels per cm or pixels per inch), the height and width of an optional RGB preview image of the file (referred to as a "thumbnail" image), and the RGB values for the optional preview image. Pixel values in the compressed file are stored using the YC_rC_b color model, and the color components are stored in the order Y first, C_b second, and C_r third. For a gray-scale image, only the Y component is used. Other information in the file includes the tables needed by the compression algorithms. Integers are stored in JPEG files using the big-endian format.

The JPEG/JFIF baseline-sequential encoding of an image file typically consists of the following operations.

(1) **Color Conversion:** Pixel RGB color values in an image file are converted to YC_rC_b color components.

(2) **Color Sampling:** The number of color values in the file can be reduced by using only the values from selected pixels or by averaging the color components for adjacent pixel groups. A simple implementation for this sampling operation might take the color values from every other pixel, every third pixel, or every fourth pixel. Usually, the color components are sampled at different frequencies, so that more luminance values, Y components, are selected. This allows greater compression ratios to be achieved, because fewer distinct chrominance values, C_r and C_b components, are saved.

(3) **Discrete Cosine Transform:** Next, 8 by 8 groups of pixel color values are converted to discrete cosine-transform values using Eq. 15-3.

(4) **Reduction of Transformed Values:** To further compress the encoded image file, a reduced set of transform values is stored (Section 15-3). The number of values in the reduced set can be fixed, or it can be computed using an algorithm to determine the influence of the various transform terms.

(5) **Huffman Encoding:** A final compression operation is performed by converting the discrete cosine-transform values to Huffman codes, as discussed in Section 15-3.

The **Still-Picture Interchange File Format** (**SPIFF**), developed by Eric Hamilton and the ISO JPEG committee, is an extension of JFIF. This format has many more features and options than JFIF, and it is expected that SPIFF will eventually replace JFIF in JPEG implementations. However, like JPEG, this extended JFIF format contains many more options than may be practical in one implementation. For example, JFIF uses just one color model (YC_rC_b), but SPIFF provides options for thirteen different color models.

For photo-realistic computer-graphics images and digitized photographs, current JPEG implementations provide a greater compression ratio than any other system. But other formats can provide comparable compression ratios without loss of color information for simple pictures that contain large single-color areas.

CGM: Computer-Graphics Metafile Format

This format is another standard developed by ISO and ANSI. It is designed for use on any computer system and in any area of computer graphics, including scientific visualization, CAD, graphic arts, business graphics, electronic publishing, and any application using the GKS or PHIGS graphics library. Thus, CGM supports a variety of features and options.

As the designation "metafile" indicates, CGM allows an image description to be given as a pixmap or as a set of geometric definitions, including attributes such as line size, line type, fill style, and character-string specifications. Various other parameters can be included in an image file, such as the maximum value for color components, the size of a color table, list of fonts used in the file, and the bounds for a clipping window.

A character-encoding scheme is used in CGM to minimize file size, and a numerical, binary code is optimized for fast encoding and decoding of the image file. Pixel values can be given using various color schemes, such as RGB, CMYK, YC_rC_b, CIE models, and color tables. In addition, pixmap files can be compressed using variations of run-length encoding and Huffman encoding.

TIFF: Tag Image-File Format

A consortium of computer companies chaired by the Aldus Corporation developed TIFF as an efficient format for transferring raster images between different applications and computer systems. Although it is highly complex, TIFF is one of the most versatile formats and it can be customized for individual applications. It is widely used in such diverse applications as medical imaging, desktop publishing, graphical user interfaces, satellite image storage, and fax transmissions.

The TIFF format can be used with bi-level, gray-scale, and full-color images, and TIFF files are designed to store multiple raster images. Pixel color information can be provided as RGB components or as color tables. More compression alternatives are provided in TIFF than in any other system. These compression schemes include combinations of run-length encoding, LZW encoding, Huffman encoding, and the suite of JPEG methods.

PNG: Portable Network-Graphics Format

Designed by an independent group of developers, PNG provides a highly efficient lossless compression scheme for storing images. Compression algorithms in PNG include Huffman encoding and variations of LZ encoding. This format is gaining popularity on the internet for image storage and transmission. It is also useful for temporarily storing images for repeated editing. For simple computer-graphics pictures, PNG generates files with very high compression ratios, comparable to those of compressed JPEG files.

Integer values are stored in big-endian order, and color components can be specified in a precision of up to 16 bits per pixel. A number of options are supported in PNG, including RGB color components, XYZ color components, gray scale, color tables, and an alpha value for transparency information.

XBM: X Window System Bitmap Format and XPM: X Window System Pixmap Format

Unlike other formats, XBM and XPM store picture information as C or C++ code that is to be processed on workstations using the X Window system. Thus, pixel values are represented in arrays, stored in scan-line order, left to right. As the names imply, XBM is a format for bitmaps (one bit per pixel) and XPM is a format for pixmaps (multiple bits per pixel). These formats are supported by most web browsers.

The XBM and XPM formats contain no compression algorithms, but the size of the files can be reduced using specially designed compression programs. Instead of header files, these formats use *#define* preprocessor directives to specify information such as the number of pixels per scan line and the number of scan lines. In the XBM format, bit values equal to 1 represent the current foreground color and bit values equal to 0 represent the current background color. In the XPM format, pixel values can be stored in color tables using RGB or HSV components.

Adobe Photoshop Format

Widely used in image-processing applications, the Adobe Photoshop format is optimized for fast accessing of large, full-color raster images. In contrast, very little compression is achieved with the run-length encoding scheme used in Photoshop, and earlier versions of Photoshop contained no compression methods.

Pixel values are stored in big-endian order, and Photoshop provides a number of options. Photoshop supports pixmaps, bitmaps (monochrome images), and gray-scale images. Colors can be stored using RGB color components, CMYK color components, or in color tables. And various schemes are provided for representing multiple colors per pixel and halftone images, as well as transparency parameters.

MacPaint: Macintosh Paint Format

A product of the Apple Corporation, MacPaint is a standard format for all Macintosh applications. Image files for this format are bitmaps with a 0 value indicating white and a 1 value indicating black. The MacPaint format is typically used for text, line drawings, and clip art.

Pixel values are stored in big-endian order, and MacPaint files always contain 576 pixels per scan line and 720 scan lines. A run-length encoding scheme is used to compress image files.

PICT: Picture Data Format

This hybrid format is another product for Macintosh applications from the Apple Corporation. It supports images that are specified as bitmaps, pixmaps, or geometric representations. A PICT file in the geometric-representation format contains a list of Macintosh QuickDraw functions that define a picture as a set of line segments, polygons, arcs, bitmaps, other objects, clipping parameters, attributes, and other state parameters.

Images can be specified using a monochrome form (bitmap), RGB color components, or a color table. Raster files can be compressed using a run-length encoding algorithm.

BMP: Bitmap Format

Although it is called a bitmap format, BMP actually supports image files that contain multiple bits per pixel. This format was developed by the Microsoft Corporation for Windows operating-system applications. Another similar pixmap format that is also called BMP is used by the IBM OS/2 operating system.

Pixel values in a BMP file are stored in little-endian order using 1, 2, 4, 8, 16, 24, or 32 bits per pixel. The pixel color values can be specified with RGB color components or with color tables. And the pixel scan lines are stored from bottom to top, with the coordinate origin at the lower-left position of the pixmap. A BMP file is usually not compressed, but a run-length encoding algorithm can be applied to pixmaps with 4 or 8 bits per pixel.

PCX: PC Paintbrush File Format

Developed by the ZSoft Corporation, PCX is another pixmap format used by Windows operating systems. Image files in the PCX format can contain from 1 to 24 bits per pixel, and pixel values can be specified using RGB components or color tables. Values are stored in little-endian order, with the scan-line ordering from the top of the image to the bottom. And the raster files can be compressed using run-length encoding.

TGA: Truevision Graphics-Adapter Format

Developed by the Truevision Corporation for use with the Targa and Vista graphics adapters, the TGA pixmap format is also known as the **Targa format.** This format is popularly used for video editing.

In the TGA format, pixel values are stored in little-endian order, and image files can contain 8, 16, 24, or 32 bits per pixel. Pixel colors can be specified as RGB components or in tables, with two possible table formats. A single RGB color table can be used, or the R, G, and B components can be given in separate tables. Typically, TGA files are not compressed, but run-length encoding algorithms can be applied to larger image files.

GIF: Graphics Interchange Format

This format, designed for efficient telephone-line transmission of raster image files, is a product of the CompuServe Corporation. Using an LZW algorithm, GIF provides reasonably good compression ratios for simple computer-graphics pictures. But the compression ratios generated by GIF for photo-realistic images are not as good as those produced by JPEG or PNG. Although GIF has been used in many applications, its popularity has drastically declined because of the patent issues associated with the LZW compression algorithms.

Either monochrome or multicolor pictures can be processed by GIF, but pixel values can only be specified in the range from 1 to 8 bits, allowing a maximum of 256 colors. Pixel values are stored in little-endian order using RGB color tables.

15-5 SUMMARY

For a raster-graphics system, an image file is typically an RGB pixmap, which is often referred to as a raw raster file. The RGB pixel values are stored as integers in the range from 0 up to a maximum value that is determined by the number of bits available to each pixel. A picture can also be stored using a representation that contains geometric descriptions of the picture components, such as line segments, fill areas, and splines.

When raster image files are to be transferred between systems or stored in a particular form, it may be necessary to reduce the number of color values represented in the image. We can uniformly reduce the number of colors by combining color levels in various ways, such as averaging the levels. The popularity method for reducing colors selects the most frequently occurring color values. And the median-cut method subdivides the color space into a set of blocks, with all colors within each block replaced by the average block color.

Various formats have been developed for storing image files in a convenient form for particular applications or particular systems. These formats differ in the structure of the header file, the byte ordering (big endian or little endian) for integer values, and the methods used (if any) to reduce the file size for storage. The effectiveness of a file-reduction method is measured by the compression ratio, which is the ratio of the original file size to the compressed file size. File-reduction algorithms that alter the color values in an image file are described as lossy, and those that can exactly restore the color values are described as lossless. Some file formats also employ color-reduction schemes.

A common compression method for image files is run-length encoding, which replaces a sequence of repeated pixel values with the value and the run length. The LZW file-compression scheme is a variation of run-length encoding that replaces repeated patterns of pixels with a code. Other pattern-recognition compression methods include scan-line comparisons and fractal procedures for identifying self-similar sets of pixel values. In Huffman encoding, a variable-length code is assigned to color values so that the most frequently occurring values have the shortest code. Arithmetic encoding uses the frequency count for color values in an image file to create subdivisions of the unit interval from 0.0 to 1.0. The bounds on each subinterval are then used to encode the sequences of color values represented by that subinterval. The discrete cosine transform multiplies pixel color values by cosine terms with increasing frequency, and then sums these products. This summation process converts a set of pixel color values to a transformed set of values. File compression is then achieved by eliminating some of the transformed values, which produces a lossy compression of the image.

Many file formats are available for various graphics applications and for different computer systems. Some formats were developed by the standards organizations ISO and ANSI, some came from computer software or hardware companies, and some are the products of independent groups. A few of the widely used formats are JPEG, TIFF, PNG, and those for the X Window system, Apple Macintosh computers, and the Windows operating systems.

REFERENCES

Color reduction methods are presented in Heckbert (1982 and 1994), Glassner (1990), Arvo (1991), and Kirk (1992). Gonzalez and Wintz (1987) discuss transform methods and image-processing techniques in general. And various file-compression algorithms are detailed in Huffman (1952), Ziv and Lempel (1977 and 1978), Welch (1984), Rao and Yip (1990), Arvo (1991), and Barnsley and Hurd (1993).

General information on graphics file formats can be found in Brown and Shepherd (1995) and Miano (1999). For additional information on JPEG, see Taubman and Marcellin (2001). The CGM file-format standard is detailed in Henderson and Mumford (1993).

EXERCISES

15-1 Write a program to implement uniform color reduction for all color levels in a full-color system, where each RGB color component is specified in the integer range from 0 to 255. Input is to be any integer division factor d that is to be applied to each color component, and the output is the set of reduced integer color levels.

15-2 Modify the program in the previous exercise so that the input is an integer k that specifies the reduced number of levels to be generated instead of the division factor.

15-3 Modify the program in Exercise 15-2 so that a different reduction number is applied to the R, G, and B components. The reductions can be specified as the integer range for each component or the number of bits.

15-4 Write a program to implement the popularity color-reduction scheme to reduce an input image file to k colors. Input to the program is an array of pixel color values and the size of the array, specified by the number of scan lines and the number of pixel positions across each scan line.

15-5 Write a program to implement the median-cut color-reduction scheme. An image file containing n RGB pixel color values is to be reduced to k color values.

15-6 Write a program to implement run-length encoding for a single scan line containing 1024 integer values, with each value in the range from 0 to 255.

15-7 Modify the program in the previous exercise to encode a file containing n scan lines.

15-8 Write a program to implement a simplified LZ encoding algorithm for a single scan line containing 1024 integer values, with each value in the range from 0 to 255. The program should search for three-element patterns only, representing repeated RGB colors. Use integer codes for the patterns.

15-9 Expand the program in the preceding exercise to process an input file with n scan lines.

15-10 Given an input image file containing n scan lines and m RGB pixel colors on each scan line, write a program to output a table of frequency counts for the pixel colors.

15-11 Using the frequency counts from the preceding exercise, write a program to compress the image file using Huffman encoding.

15-12 Using the frequency counts from Exercise 15-10, write a program to compress the image file using arithmetic encoding.

15-13 Given a list of 32 pixel colors, with three RGB color components for each pixel, write a program to calculate the discrete cosine transform values (Eq. 15-1) for each successive group of 8 pixels in the list.

15-14 Using Eq. 15-2 and the transform values from the preceding exercise, write a program to calculate the original (restored) 32 pixel colors.

15-15 Modify the preceding exercise to calculate the inverse transform values for each set of 8 pixels, using any selected number n of the transform values; that is, n can be any value from 1 to 8, inclusive.

15-16 Given an image file containing 32 by 32 pixel colors, with three RGB color components for each pixel, write a program to calculate the discrete cosine-transform values (Eq. 15-3) for each successive group of 8 by 8 pixels.

15-17 Using Eq. 15-4 and the transform values from the preceding exercise, write a program to calculate the original (restored) 32 by 32 pixel colors.

15-18 Modify the preceding exercise to calculate the inverse transform values for each set of 8 by 8 pixels, using any selected number n by m of the transform values; that is, n and m can each be assigned any integer value from 1 to 8, inclusive.

APPENDIX A

Mathematics for Computer Graphics

A variety of mathematical concepts and techniques are employed in computer-graphics algorithms. Here, we provide a brief reference for the methods from analytic geometry, linear algebra, vector analysis, tensor analysis, complex numbers, quaternions, calculus, numerical analysis, and other areas that are referred to in the discussions throughout this book.

A-1 COORDINATE REFERENCE FRAMES

Both Cartesian and non-Cartesian reference frames are often useful in computer-graphics applications. We typically specify coordinates in a graphics program using a Cartesian reference system, but the initial specification of a scene could be given in a non-Cartesian frame of reference. Spherical, cylindrical, or other symmetries often can be exploited to simplify expressions involving object descriptions or manipulations.

Two-Dimensional Cartesian Screen Coordinates

For the device-independent commands within a graphics package, screen-coordinate positions are referenced within the first quadrant of a two-dimensional Cartesian frame in standard position, as shown in Fig. A-1(a). The coordinate origin for this reference frame is at the lower-left screen corner. Scan lines, however, are numbered from 0 at the top of the screen, so that screen positions are represented internally with respect to the upper-left corner of the screen. Therefore, device-dependent commands, such as those for interactive input and display-window manipulations, often reference screen coordinates using the inverted Cartesian frame shown in Fig. A-1(b). Horizontal coordinate values in the two systems are the same, and an inverted y value is converted to a y value measured from the bottom of the screen with the calculation

$$y = y_{\text{max}} - y_{\text{invert}} \tag{A-1}$$

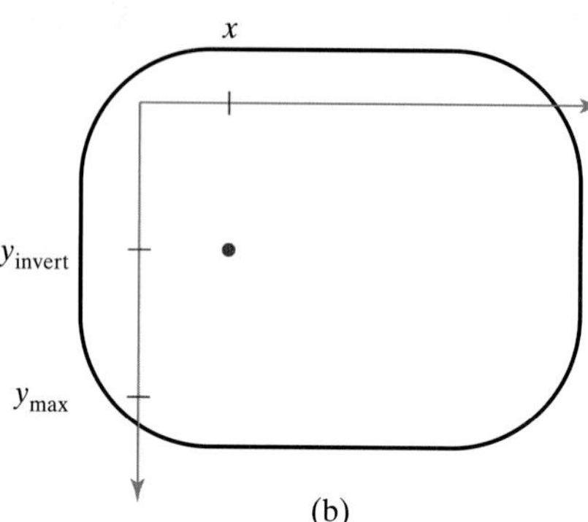

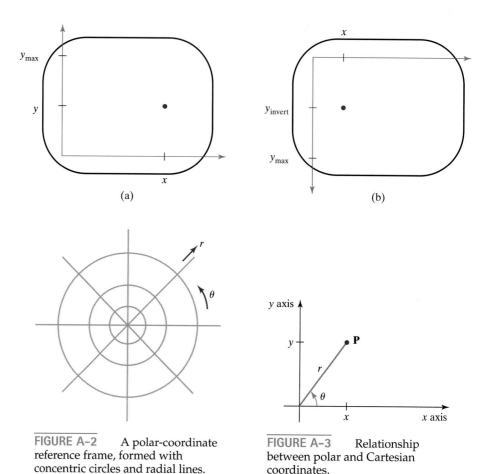

FIGURE A-1 Cartesian screen-coordinate positions are referenced with respect to the lower-left screen corner (a) or the upper-left screen corner (b).

FIGURE A-2 A polar-coordinate reference frame, formed with concentric circles and radial lines.

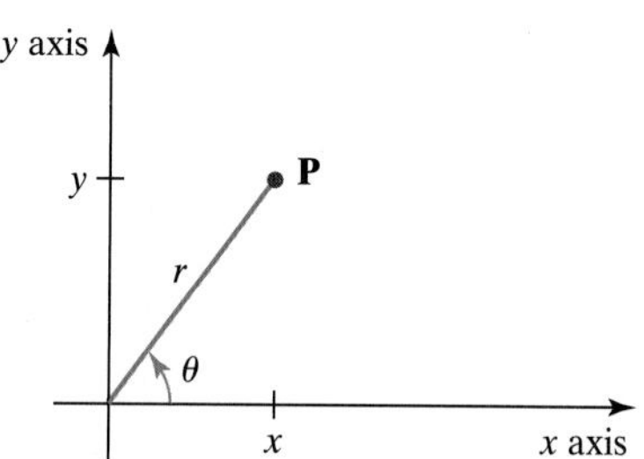

FIGURE A-3 Relationship between polar and Cartesian coordinates.

In some application packages, the screen-coordinate origin can be placed at an arbitrary position, such as the center of the screen.

Standard Two-Dimensional Cartesian Reference Frames

We use Cartesian systems in standard position for world-coordinate specifications, viewing coordinates, and other references within the two-dimensional viewing pipeline. Coordinates in these frames can be positive or negative, with any range of values. To display a view of a two-dimensional picture, we designate a clipping window and a viewport to map a section of the picture to screen coordinates.

FIGURE A-4 Right triangle with hypotenuse r, sides x and y, and an interior angle θ.

Polar Coordinates in the xy Plane

A frequently used two-dimensional non-Cartesian system is a polar-coordinate reference frame (Fig. A-2), where a coordinate position is specified with a radial distance r from the coordinate origin and an angular displacement θ from the horizontal. Positive angular displacements are counterclockwise, and negative angular displacements are clockwise. The relation between Cartesian and polar coordinates is shown in Fig. A-3. Considering the right triangle in Fig. A-4, and using the definition of the trigonometric functions, we transform from polar coordinates to Cartesian coordinates with the expressions

$$x = r\cos\theta, \qquad y = r\sin\theta \tag{A-2}$$

The inverse transformation from Cartesian to polar coordinates is

$$r = \sqrt{x^2 + y^2}, \qquad \theta = \tan^{-1}\left(\frac{y}{x}\right) \tag{A-3}$$

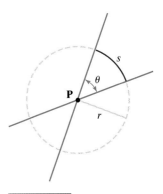

Angular values can be measured either in degrees or in dimensionless units (radians). One radian is defined as a measure for an angle that is subtended by a circular arc that has a length equal to the circle radius. This definition is illustrated in Fig. A-5, which shows two intersecting lines in a plane and a circle centered on the intersection point **P**. For any circle centered on **P**, the value of angle θ in radians is given by the ratio

$$\theta = \frac{s}{r} \qquad \text{(radians)} \tag{A-4}$$

where s is the length of the circular arc subtending θ, and r is the radius of the circle. Total angular distance around point **P** is the length of the circle perimeter ($2\pi r$) divided by r, or 2π radians. In terms of degrees, a circle circumference is divided into 360 arcs of equal length, so that each arc subtends an angle of 1 degree. Therefore, $360^\circ = 2\pi$ radians.

FIGURE A-5 An angle θ subtended by a circular arc of length s and radius r.

Other conics, besides circles, can be used to specify coordinate positions. For example, using concentric ellipses instead of circles, we can give coordinate positions in elliptical coordinates. Similarly, other types of symmetries can be exploited with hyperbolic or parabolic plane coordinates.

Standard Three-Dimensional Cartesian Reference Frames

Figure A-6(a) shows the conventional orientation for the coordinate axes in a three-dimensional Cartesian reference system. This is called a right-handed system because the right-hand thumb points in the positive z direction when we imagine grasping the z axis with the fingers curling from the positive x axis to the positive y axis (through 90°), as illustrated in Fig. A-6(b). In most computer-graphics programs, we specify object descriptions and other coordinate parameters in right-handed Cartesian coordinates. For discussions throughout this book (including the appendix), we assume that all Cartesian reference frames are right-handed unless specifically stated otherwise.

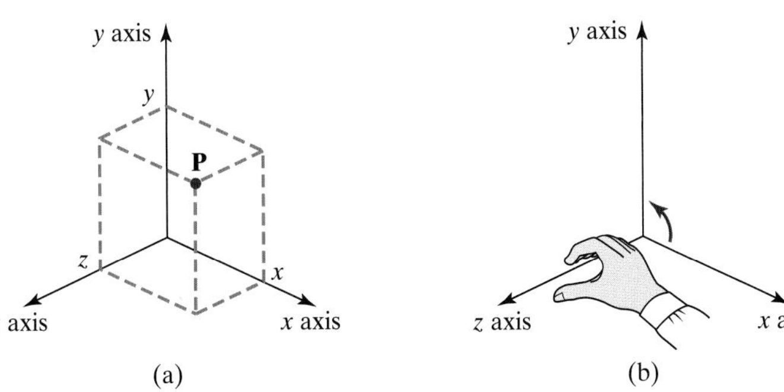

FIGURE A-6 Coordinate representation for a point **P** at position (x, y, z) in a standard right-handed Cartesian reference system.

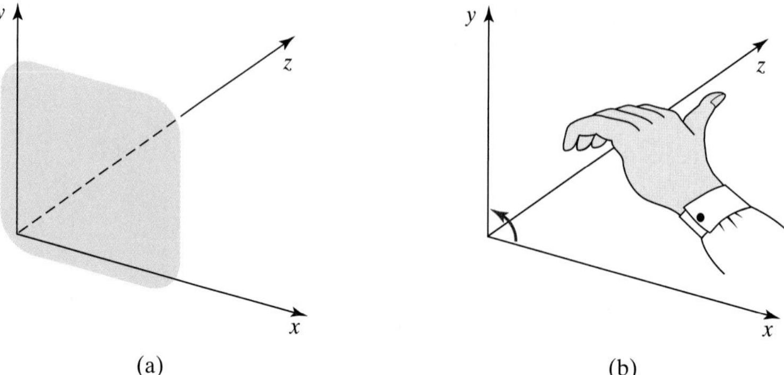

FIGURE A-7 Left-handed Cartesian coordinate system superimposed on the surface of a video monitor.

Cartesian reference frames are **orthogonal coordinate systems,** which just means that the coordinate axes are perpendicular to each other. Also, in Cartesian frames, the axes are straight lines. But coordinate systems with curved axes are useful in many applications. Most of these systems are also orthogonal in the sense that the axial directions at any point in the space are mutually perpendicular.

Three-Dimensional Cartesian Screen Coordinates

When a view of a three-dimensional scene is displayed on a video monitor, depth information is stored for each screen position. The three-dimensional position corresponding to each screen point is often referenced with the left-handed system shown in Fig. A-7. In this case, the left-hand thumb points in the positive z direction when we imagine grasping the z axis so that the fingers of the left hand curl from the positive x axis to the positive y axis through 90°. Positive z values indicate positions behind the screen for each point in the xy plane, and larger values along the positive z axis are interpreted as being farther from the viewer.

Three-Dimensional Curvilinear-Coordinate Systems

Any non-Cartesian reference frame is referred to as a **curvilinear-coordinate system.** The choice of coordinate system for a particular graphics application depends on a number of factors, such as symmetry, ease of computation, and visualization advantages. Figure A-8 shows a general curvilinear-coordinate reference frame formed with three *coordinate surfaces,* where each surface has one coordinate held constant. For instance, the x_1x_2 surface is defined with $x_3 = \text{const}_3$. *Coordinate axes* in any reference frame are the intersection curves of the coordinate surfaces. If the coordinate surfaces intersect everywhere at right angles, we have an **orthogonal curvilinear-coordinate system.** Nonorthogonal, curvilinear reference frames are useful for some applications, such as visualizations of motions governed by the laws of general relativity, but they are used less frequently in computer graphics than orthogonal systems.

A *cylindrical-coordinate* specification of a spatial position is shown in Fig. A-9 in relation to a Cartesian reference frame. The surface of constant ρ is a vertical cylinder; the surface of constant θ is a vertical plane containing the z axis; and the surface of constant z is a horizontal plane parallel to the Cartesian xy plane. We transform from a cylindrical-coordinate specification to a Cartesian reference frame with the calculations

$$x = \rho\cos\theta, \qquad y = \rho\sin\theta, \qquad z = z \tag{A-5}$$

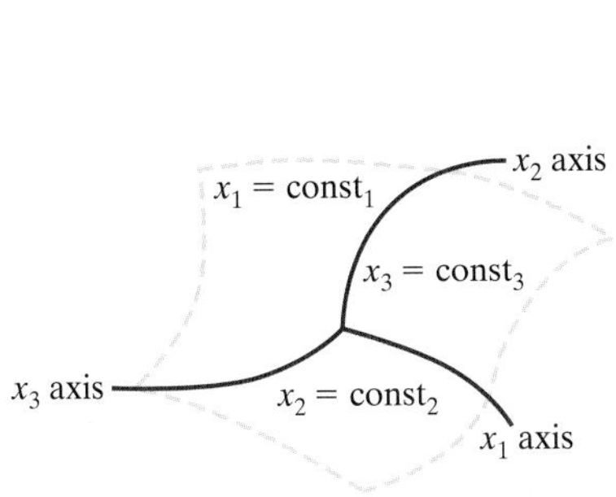

FIGURE A-8 A general curvilinear-coordinate reference frame.

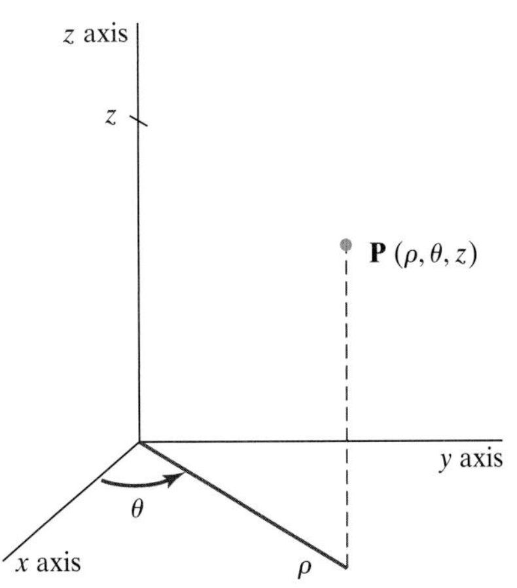

FIGURE A-9 Cylindrical coordinates ρ, θ, and z.

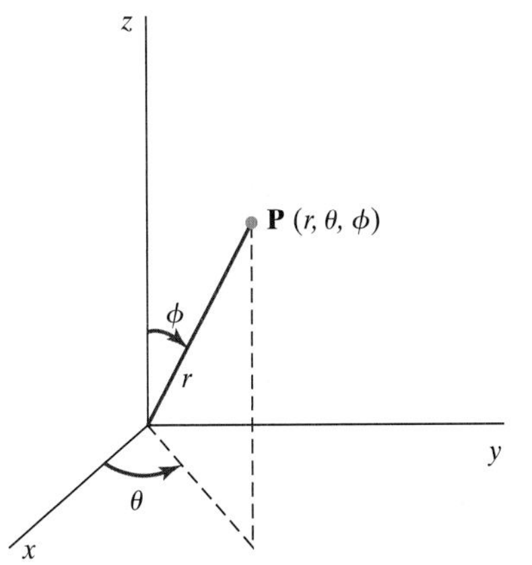

FIGURE A-10 Spherical coordinates r, θ, and ϕ.

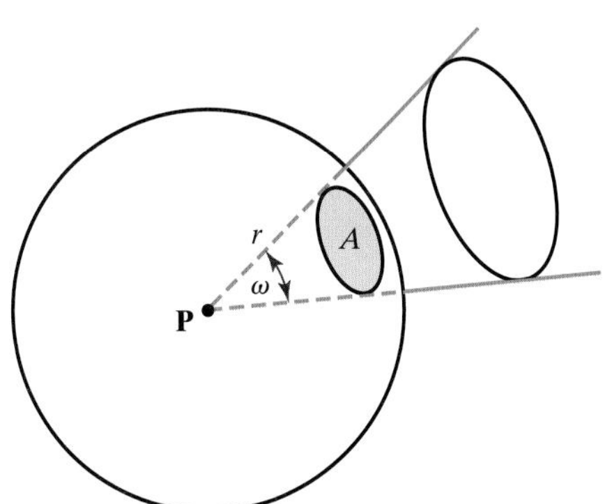

FIGURE A-11 A solid angle ω subtended by a spherical surface patch with area A and radius r.

Another commonly used curvilinear-coordinate specification is the *spherical-coordinate* system in Fig. A-10. Spherical coordinates are sometimes referred to as *polar coordinates in three-dimensional space.* The surface of constant r is a sphere; the surface of constant θ is again a vertical plane containing the z axis; and the surface of constant ϕ is a cone with apex at the coordinate origin. If $\phi < 90°$, the cone is above the xy plane. If $\phi > 90°$, the cone is below the xy plane. We transform from a spherical-coordinate specification to a Cartesian reference frame with the calculations

$$x = r\cos\theta\sin\phi, \qquad y = r\sin\theta\sin\phi, \qquad z = r\cos\phi \tag{A-6}$$

Solid Angle

The definition for a solid angle ω is formulated by analogy with the definition for a two-dimensional radian-angle θ between two intersecting lines (Eq. A-4). For a three-dimensional angle, however, we consider a cone with apex at a point **P** and a sphere centered at **P**, as shown in Fig. A-11. The solid angle ω within the cone-shaped region with apex at **P** is defined as

$$\omega = \frac{A}{r^2} \tag{A-7}$$

where A is the area of the spherical surface intersected by the cone and r is the radius of the sphere.

Also, in analogy with two-dimensional polar coordinates, the dimensionless unit for solid angles is called the **steradian.** The total solid angle about point **P** is the total area of the spherical surface ($4\pi r^2$) divided by r^2, or 4π steradians.

A-2 POINTS AND VECTORS

There is a fundamental difference between the concept of a geometric point and that of a vector. A point is a position specified with coordinate values in some reference frame, where the coordinates and other properties for the point depend on our choice for the frame of reference. A vector, on the other hand, has properties that are independent of any particular coordinate system.

Point Properties

Figure A-12 illustrates the coordinate specification for a two-dimensional point position **P** in two reference frames. In frame A, the point has coordinates that are given by the ordered pair (x, y), and its distance from the origin is $\sqrt{x^2 + y^2}$. In frame B, the same point has coordinates (0, 0), and the distance to the coordinate origin of frame B is 0.

Vector Properties

In a chosen coordinate system, we can define a vector as the difference between two point positions. Thus, for the two-dimensional points $\mathbf{P}_1$ and $\mathbf{P}_2$ in Fig. A-13, we can specify a vector as

$$\begin{aligned}\mathbf{V} &= \mathbf{P}_2 - \mathbf{P}_1 \\ &= (x_2 - x_1,\ y_2 - y_1) \\ &= (V_x, V_y)\end{aligned} \tag{A-8}$$

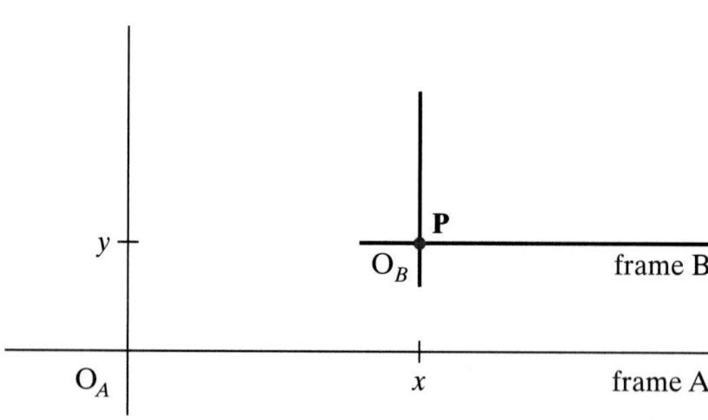

FIGURE A-12 Coordinates for a point position **P** with respect to two different Cartesian reference frames.

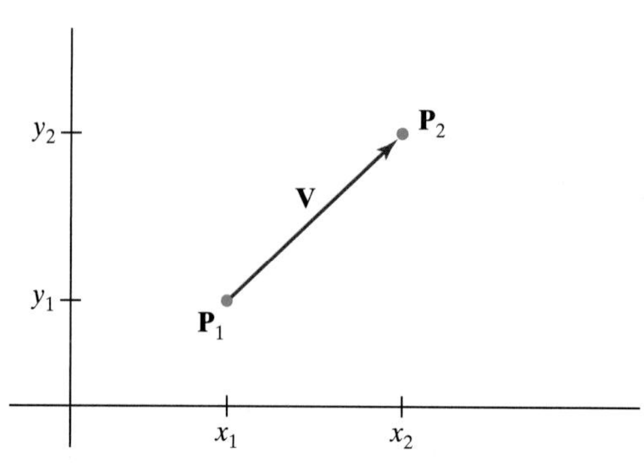

FIGURE A-13 A two-dimensional vector **V** defined in a Cartesian reference frame as the difference of two point positions.

where the Cartesian *components* (or Cartesian *elements*) V_x and V_y are the projections of **V** onto the x and y axes. We could also obtain these same vector components using two other point positions in this coordinate reference frame. In fact, there are an infinite number of point pairs that will produce the same vector components, and a vector is often defined with a single point position relative to the current frame of reference. Therefore, a vector has no fixed position within a coordinate system. Also, if we transform the representation for **V** to another reference frame, the coordinates for the positions $\mathbf{P}_1$ and $\mathbf{P}_2$ change, but the basic properties of the vector remain unchanged.

We can describe a vector as a *directed line segment* that has two fundamental properties: magnitude and direction. For the two-dimensional vector in Fig. A-13, we calculate the vector magnitude using the Pythagorean theorem, which gives us the distance along the vector direction between its two endpoint positions.

$$|\mathbf{V}| = \sqrt{V_x^2 + V_y^2} \tag{A-9}$$

We can specify the vector direction in various ways. For example, we can give the direction in terms of the angular displacement from the horizontal as

$$\alpha = \tan^{-1}\left(\frac{V_y}{V_x}\right) \tag{A-10}$$

A vector has the same magnitude and direction no matter where we position the vector within a single coordinate system. And the vector magnitude is independent of the coordinate representation. However, if we transform the vector to another reference frame, the values for its components and direction within that reference frame may change. For example, we could transform the vector to a rotated Cartesian frame so that the vector direction is along the new y direction.

For a three-dimensional Cartesian vector representation $\mathbf{V} = (V_x, V_y, V_z)$, the vector magnitude is

$$|\mathbf{V}| = \sqrt{V_x^2 + V_y^2 + V_z^2} \tag{A-11}$$

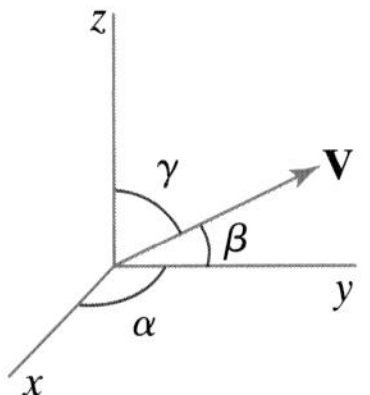

FIGURE A-14 Direction angles α, β, and γ.

And we can give the vector direction in terms of the *direction angles*, α, β, and γ, that the vector makes with each of the coordinate axes (Fig. A-14). Direction angles are the positive angles that the vector makes with each of the positive coordinate axes. We calculate these angles as

$$\cos\alpha = \frac{V_x}{|\mathbf{V}|}, \qquad \cos\beta = \frac{V_y}{|\mathbf{V}|}, \qquad \cos\gamma = \frac{V_z}{|\mathbf{V}|} \tag{A-12}$$

The values $\cos\alpha$, $\cos\beta$, and $\cos\gamma$ are called the *direction cosines* of the vector. Actually, we need specify only two of the direction cosines to give the direction of **V**, since

$$\cos^2\alpha + \cos^2\beta + \cos^2\gamma = 1 \tag{A-13}$$

Vectors are used to represent any quantities that have the properties of magnitude and direction. Two common examples are force and velocity (Fig. A-15). A force can be thought of as an amount of push or pull along a particular direction. A velocity vector specifies how fast (*speed*) an object is moving in a certain direction.

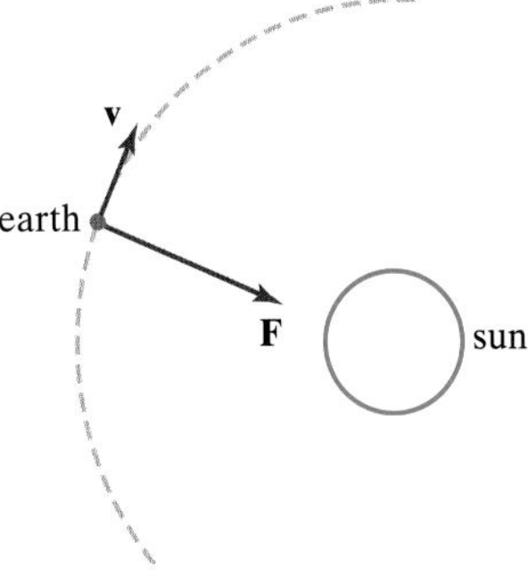

FIGURE A-15 A gravitational force vector **F** and a velocity vector **v**.

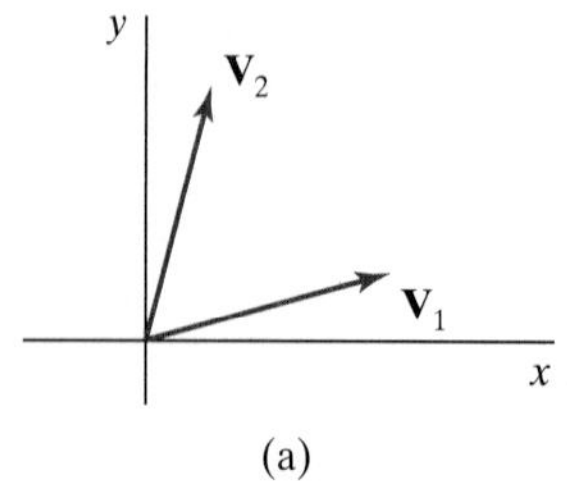

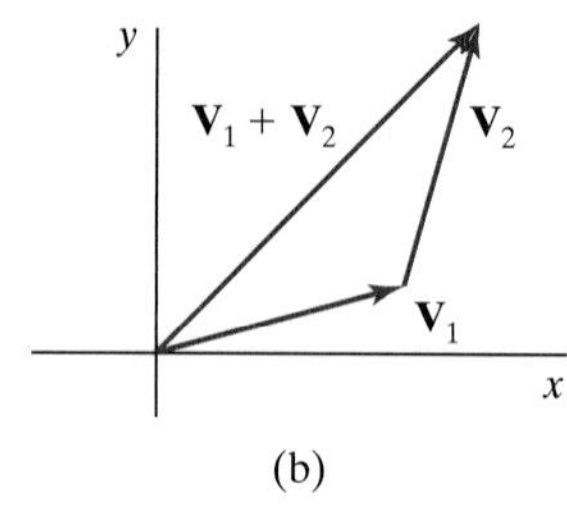

FIGURE A-16 Two vectors (a) can be added geometrically by positioning the two vectors end to end (b) and drawing the resultant vector from the start of the first vector to the tip of the second vector.

Vector Addition and Scalar Multiplication

By definition, the sum of two vectors is obtained by adding corresponding components:

$$\mathbf{V}_1 + \mathbf{V}_2 = (V_{1x} + V_{2x}, V_{1y} + V_{2y}, V_{1z} + V_{2z}) \qquad \text{(A-14)}$$

Two-dimensional vector addition is illustrated geometrically in Fig. A-16. We obtain the vector sum by placing the start position of one vector at the tip of the other vector and drawing the representation for the vector sum from the start of the first vector to the tip of the second. Addition of a vector with a scalar is undefined, since a scalar has only one numerical value while a vector has n numerical components in an n-dimensional space.

Multiplication of a vector by a scalar value s is defined as

$$s\mathbf{V} = (sV_x, sV_y, sV_z) \qquad \text{(A-15)}$$

For example, if the scalar parameter s has the value 2, each component of **V** is doubled and its magnitude is doubled.

We can also combine vectors using multiplicative processes in various ways. One highly useful method is to multiply the magnitudes of two vectors so that this product is used to form either another vector or a scalar quantity.

Scalar Product of Two Vectors

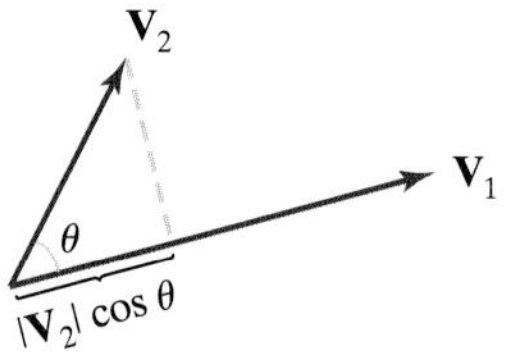

FIGURE A-17 The dot product of two vectors is obtained by multiplying parallel components.

We obtain a scalar value from two vectors with the calculation

$$\mathbf{V}_1 \cdot \mathbf{V}_2 = |\mathbf{V}_1|\,|\mathbf{V}_2| \cos\theta, \qquad 0 \le \theta \le \pi \qquad \text{(A-16)}$$

where θ is the smaller of the two angles between the vector directions (Fig. A-17). This multiplication scheme is called the **scalar product,** or **dot product,** of two vectors. It is also referred to as the *inner product,* particularly in discussing scalar products in tensor analysis. Equation A-16 is valid in any coordinate representation and can be interpreted as the product of the parallel components of the two vectors, where $|\mathbf{V}_2| \cos\theta$ is the projection of vector $\mathbf{V}_2$ in the direction of $\mathbf{V}_1$.

In addition to the coordinate-independent form of the scalar product, we can express this calculation in specific coordinate representations. For a Cartesian reference frame, the scalar product is calculated as

$$\mathbf{V}_1 \cdot \mathbf{V}_2 = V_{1x}V_{2x} + V_{1y}V_{2y} + V_{1z}V_{2z} \qquad \text{(A-17)}$$

The scalar product is a generalization of the Pythagorean theorem, and the scalar product of a vector with itself produces the square of the vector magnitude.

Also, the scalar product of two vectors is zero if and only if the two vectors are perpendicular (orthogonal).

Dot products are commutative,

$$\mathbf{V}_1 \cdot \mathbf{V}_2 = \mathbf{V}_2 \cdot \mathbf{V}_1 \tag{A-18}$$

because this operation produces a scalar. And dot products are distributive with respect to vector addition:

$$\mathbf{V}_1 \cdot (\mathbf{V}_2 + \mathbf{V}_3) = \mathbf{V}_1 \cdot \mathbf{V}_2 + \mathbf{V}_1 \cdot \mathbf{V}_3 \tag{A-19}$$

Vector Product of Two Vectors

We use the following calculation to combine two vectors to produce another vector.

$$\mathbf{V}_1 \times \mathbf{V}_2 = \mathbf{u}|\mathbf{V}_1|\,|\mathbf{V}_2| \sin\theta, \qquad 0 \le \theta \le \pi \tag{A-20}$$

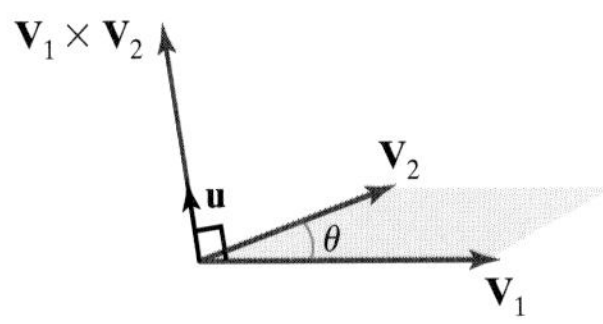

FIGURE A-18 The cross product of two vectors is a vector in a direction perpendicular to the two original vectors and with a magnitude equal to the area of the shaded parallelogram.

Parameter **u** in this expression is a unit vector (magnitude 1) that is perpendicular to both $\mathbf{V}_1$ and $\mathbf{V}_2$ (Fig. A-18). The direction for **u** is determined by the *right-hand rule:* We grasp an axis that is perpendicular to the plane containing $\mathbf{V}_1$ and $\mathbf{V}_2$ so that the fingers of the right hand curl from $\mathbf{V}_1$ to $\mathbf{V}_2$. Vector **u** is then in the direction of the right thumb. This calculation is called the **vector product,** or **cross product,** of two vectors, and Equation A-20 is valid in any coordinate representation. The cross product of two vectors is a vector that is perpendicular to the plane of the two vectors, and the magnitude of the cross-product vector is equal to the area of the parallelogram formed by the two vectors.

We can also express the cross product in terms of vector components in a specific reference frame. In a Cartesian-coordinate system, we calculate the components of the cross product as

$$\mathbf{V}_1 \times \mathbf{V}_2 = (V_{1y}V_{2z} - V_{1z}V_{2y},\, V_{1z}V_{2x} - V_{1x}V_{2z},\, V_{1x}V_{2y} - V_{1y}V_{2x}) \tag{A-21}$$

If we denote the unit vectors (magnitude 1) along the x, y, and z axes as $\mathbf{u}_x$, $\mathbf{u}_y$, and $\mathbf{u}_z$, we can write the cross product in terms of Cartesian components using a determinant notation (Section A-5):

$$\mathbf{V}_1 \times \mathbf{V}_2 = \begin{vmatrix} \mathbf{u}_x & \mathbf{u}_y & \mathbf{u}_z \\ V_{1x} & V_{1y} & V_{1z} \\ V_{2x} & V_{2y} & V_{2z} \end{vmatrix} \tag{A-22}$$

The cross product of any two parallel vectors is zero. Therefore, the cross product of a vector with itself is zero. Also, the cross product is not commutative; it is anticommutative:

$$\mathbf{V}_1 \times \mathbf{V}_2 = -(\mathbf{V}_2 \times \mathbf{V}_1) \tag{A-23}$$

And the cross product is not associative; that is,

$$\mathbf{V}_1 \times (\mathbf{V}_2 \times \mathbf{V}_3) \neq (\mathbf{V}_1 \times \mathbf{V}_2) \times \mathbf{V}_3 \tag{A-24}$$

But the cross product is distributive with respect to vector addition or subtraction:

$$\mathbf{V}_1 \times (\mathbf{V}_2 + \mathbf{V}_3) = (\mathbf{V}_1 \times \mathbf{V}_2) + (\mathbf{V}_1 \times \mathbf{V}_3) \tag{A-25}$$

A-3 TENSORS

A generalization of the concept of a vector is the class of objects called tensors. Formally, a **tensor** is defined as a quantity with a specified *rank* and with certain transformation properties when the tensor is converted from one coordinate representation to another. For orthogonal-coordinate systems, the transformation properties are straightforward and the same as those for vectors. Various physical properties of objects, such as stress, strain, and conductivity, are tensors.

The rank of a tensor, along with the dimension of the space in which the tensor is defined, determines the number of components (also called elements or coefficients) in that tensor. Scalar quantities and vectors are special cases of the more general class of tensors. A scalar is a tensor of rank zero, and a vector is a tensor of rank one. Basically, the rank of a tensor specifies the number of subscripts used to designate the tensor elements, and the spatial dimension determines the number of values that can be assigned to each subscript. Thus, a scalar quantity (tensor of rank zero) has zero subscripts, and a vector (tensor of rank one) has one subscript. Sometimes any parameter with one subscript is mislabeled as "one-dimensional", and any parameter with two subscripts is mislabeled as "two-dimensional". However, the **dimension** of a quantity depends on the spatial representation, not on the number of subscripts. In two-dimensional space, the single vector subscript can be assigned two values and the two-dimensional vector has two components. In three-dimensional space, the single vector subscript can be assigned three values and the three-dimensional vector has three components. Similarly, a tensor of rank two has two subscripts, and in three-dimensional space, this tensor has nine components (three values for each subscript).

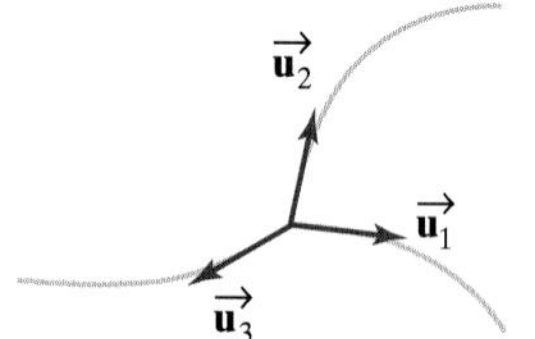

FIGURE A-19 Three-dimensional, curvilinear-coordinate axis vectors.

A-4 BASIS VECTORS AND THE METRIC TENSOR

We can specify the coordinate directions for an n-dimensional reference frame using a set of axis vectors, labeled $\vec{\mathbf{u}}_k$, where $k = 1, 2, \ldots, n$, as in Fig. A-19, which illustrates the axis vectors at the origin of a three-dimensional curvilinear space. Each coordinate-axis vector gives the direction for one of the spatial axes at any point along that axis. These axis tangent vectors form a linearly independent vector set. That is, the axis vectors cannot be written as linear combinations of each other. Also, any other vector in that space can be written as a linear combination of the axis vectors, and the set of axis vectors is called a **basis,** or a set of **base vectors,** for the space. In general, the space is referred to as a *vector space* and the basis contains the minimum number of vectors needed to represent any other vector in the space as a linear combination of the base vectors.

Determining Basis Vectors for a Coordinate Space

The basis vectors in any space are determined from the **position vector** $\vec{\mathbf{r}}$, which is the vector representation for any spatial position. For example, in three-dimensional Cartesian space, the position vector for any point (x, y, z) is

$$\vec{\mathbf{r}} = x\mathbf{u}_x + y\mathbf{u}_y + z\mathbf{u}_z \tag{A-26}$$

where $\mathbf{u}_x$, $\mathbf{u}_y$, and $\mathbf{u}_z$ are the unit base vectors for the x, y, and z axes. Unlike other coordinate representations, Cartesian basis vectors are constants that are independent of the spatial coordinates, so that we have

$$\mathbf{u}_x = \frac{\partial \vec{\mathbf{r}}}{\partial x}, \qquad \mathbf{u}_y = \frac{\partial \vec{\mathbf{r}}}{\partial y}, \qquad \mathbf{u}_z = \frac{\partial \vec{\mathbf{r}}}{\partial z} \tag{A-27}$$

Similarly, for any other three-dimensional space, we formulate the expression for the position vector $\vec{\mathbf{r}}(x_1, x_2, x_3)$ in terms of the coordinates for that space, and then we determine the basis vectors as

$$\vec{\mathbf{u}}_k = \frac{\partial \vec{\mathbf{r}}}{\partial x_k}, \qquad k = 1, 2, 3 \tag{A-28}$$

In general, the base vectors $\vec{\mathbf{u}}_k$ are neither constants nor unit vectors. They are functions of the spatial coordinates.

As an example, the position vector in two-dimensional polar-coordinate space is

$$\vec{\mathbf{r}} = r\cos\theta\,\mathbf{u}_x + r\sin\theta\,\mathbf{u}_y \tag{A-29}$$

and the polar-coordinate basis vectors are

$$\begin{aligned}\vec{\mathbf{u}}_r &= \frac{\partial \vec{\mathbf{r}}}{\partial r} = \cos\theta\,\mathbf{u}_x + \sin\theta\,\mathbf{u}_y \\ \vec{\mathbf{u}}_\theta &= \frac{\partial \vec{\mathbf{r}}}{\partial \theta} = -r\sin\theta\,\mathbf{u}_x + r\cos\theta\,\mathbf{u}_y\end{aligned} \tag{A-30}$$

In this space, $\vec{\mathbf{u}}_r$, which is a function of θ, is a unit vector. But $\vec{\mathbf{u}}_\theta$, which is a function of both r and θ, is not a unit vector.

Orthonormal Basis

Often, vectors in a basis are normalized so that each vector has a magnitude of 1. We obtain unit basis vectors in any three-dimensional space with the calculations

$$\mathbf{u}_k = \frac{\vec{\mathbf{u}}_k}{|\vec{\mathbf{u}}_k|}, \qquad k = 1, 2, 3 \tag{A-31}$$

and this set of unit vectors is called a **normal basis.** Also, for Cartesian, cylindrical, spherical, and other commonly used reference frames, including polar coordinates, the coordinate axes are mutually perpendicular at each point in space, and the set of base vectors is then referred to as an **orthogonal basis.** A set of unit, orthogonal base vectors is called an **orthonormal basis,** and these base vectors satisfy the following conditions.

$$\begin{aligned}\mathbf{u}_k \cdot \mathbf{u}_k &= 1, \qquad \text{for all } k \\ \mathbf{u}_j \cdot \mathbf{u}_k &= 0, \qquad \text{for all } j \neq k\end{aligned} \tag{A-32}$$

Although we primarily deal with orthogonal systems, nonorthogonal coordinate reference frames are useful in some applications, including relativity theory and visualization schemes for certain data sets.

A two-dimensional Cartesian system has the orthonormal basis

$$\mathbf{u}_x = (1, 0), \qquad \mathbf{u}_y = (0, 1) \tag{A-33}$$

And the orthonormal basis for a three-dimensional Cartesian reference frame is

$$\mathbf{u}_x = (1, 0, 0), \qquad \mathbf{u}_y = (0, 1, 0), \qquad \mathbf{u}_z = (0, 0, 1) \tag{A-34}$$

Metric Tensor

For "ordinary" coordinate spaces (that is, those in which we can define distances, which are formally referred to as *Riemannian spaces*), the scalar products of the basis vectors form the elements of the **metric tensor** for that space:

$$g_{jk} = \vec{\mathbf{u}}_j \cdot \vec{\mathbf{u}}_k \tag{A-35}$$

Thus, the metric tensor is of rank two and it is symmetric: $g_{jk} = g_{kj}$. Metric tensors have several useful properties. The elements of a metric tensor can be used to determine (1) the distance between two points in that space, (2) the transformation equations for conversion to another space, and (3) the components of various differential vector operators (such as gradient, divergence, and curl) within that space.

In an orthogonal space,

$$g_{jk} = 0, \qquad \text{for } j \neq k \tag{A-36}$$

For example, in a Cartesian coordinate system, where the basis vectors are constant unit vectors, the metric tensor has the components

$$g_{jk} = \begin{cases} 1, & \text{if } j = k \\ 0, & \text{otherwise} \end{cases} \qquad \text{(Cartesian space)} \tag{A-37}$$

And for the polar-coordinate basis vectors (Eqs. A-30), we can write the metric tensor in the matrix form

$$\mathbf{g} = \begin{bmatrix} 1 & 0 \\ 0 & r^2 \end{bmatrix} \qquad \text{(polar coordinates)} \tag{A-38}$$

For a cylindrical-coordinate reference frame, the base vectors are

$$\vec{\mathbf{u}}_\rho = \cos\theta\,\mathbf{u}_x + \sin\theta\,\mathbf{u}_y, \qquad \vec{\mathbf{u}}_\theta = -\rho\sin\theta\,\mathbf{u}_x + \rho\cos\theta\,\mathbf{u}_y, \qquad \vec{\mathbf{u}}_z = \mathbf{u}_z \tag{A-39}$$

And the matrix representation for the metric tensor in cylindrical coordinates is

$$\mathbf{g} = \begin{bmatrix} 1 & 0 & 0 \\ 0 & \rho & 0 \\ 0 & 0 & 1 \end{bmatrix} \qquad \text{(cylindrical coordinates)} \tag{A-40}$$

In spherical coordinates, the basis vectors are

$$\begin{aligned} \vec{\mathbf{u}}_r &= \cos\theta\sin\phi\,\mathbf{u}_x + \sin\theta\sin\phi\,\mathbf{u}_y + \cos\phi\,\mathbf{u}_z \\ \vec{\mathbf{u}}_\theta &= -r\sin\theta\sin\phi\,\mathbf{u}_x + r\cos\theta\sin\phi\,\mathbf{u}_y \\ \vec{\mathbf{u}}_\phi &= r\cos\theta\cos\phi\,\mathbf{u}_x + r\sin\theta\cos\phi\,\mathbf{u}_y - r\sin\phi\,\mathbf{u}_z \end{aligned} \tag{A-41}$$

Using these base vectors in Eq. A-35, we obtain the following matrix representation for the metric tensor.

$$\mathbf{g} = \begin{bmatrix} 1 & 0 & 0 \\ 0 & r^2 \sin^2 \phi & 0 \\ 0 & 0 & r^2 \end{bmatrix} \qquad \text{(spherical coordinates)} \tag{A-42}$$

A-5 MATRICES

A matrix is a rectangular array of quantities (numerical values, expressions, or functions), called the elements of the matrix. Some examples of matrices are

$$\begin{bmatrix} 3.60 & -0.01 & 2.00 \\ -5.46 & 0.00 & 1.63 \end{bmatrix}, \quad \begin{bmatrix} e^x & x \\ e^{2x} & x^2 \end{bmatrix}, \quad \begin{bmatrix} a_1 & a_2 & a_3 \end{bmatrix}, \quad \begin{bmatrix} x \\ y \\ z \end{bmatrix} \tag{A-43}$$

We identify matrices according to the number of rows and number of columns. For the preceding examples, the matrices in left-to-right order are 2 by 3, 2 by 2, 1 by 3, and 3 by 1. When the number of rows is the same as the number of columns, as in the second example, the matrix is called a *square matrix.*

In general, we can write an r by c matrix as

$$\mathbf{M} = \begin{bmatrix} m_{11} & m_{12} & \cdots & m_{1c} \\ m_{21} & m_{22} & \cdots & m_{2c} \\ \vdots & \vdots & & \vdots \\ m_{r1} & m_{r2} & \cdots & m_{rc} \end{bmatrix} \tag{A-44}$$

where m_{jk} represent the elements of matrix **M**. The first subscript of any element gives the row number, and the second subscript gives the column number.

A matrix with a single row or a single column represents a vector. Thus, the last two matrix examples in A-43 are, respectively, a *row vector* and a *column vector.* In general, a matrix can be viewed as a collection of row vectors or as a collection of column vectors.

When various operations are expressed in matrix form, the standard mathematical convention is to represent a vector with a column matrix. Following this convention, we write the matrix representation for a three-dimensional vector in Cartesian coordinates as

$$\mathbf{V} = \begin{bmatrix} v_x \\ v_y \\ v_z \end{bmatrix} \tag{A-45}$$

Although we use this standard matrix representation for both points and vectors, there is an important distinction between the two. The vector representation for a point always assumes that the vector is from the origin to that point. And the distance of the point from the origin is not invariant when we switch from one coordinate system to another. Also, we cannot "add" points, and we cannot apply vector operations, such as the dot product and cross product, to points.

Scalar Multiplication and Matrix Addition

To multiply a matrix **M** by a scalar value s, we multiply each element m_{jk} by the scalar. As an example, if

$$\mathbf{M} = \begin{bmatrix} 1 & 2 & 3 \\ 4 & 5 & 6 \end{bmatrix}$$

then

$$3\,\mathbf{M} = \begin{bmatrix} 3 & 6 & 9 \\ 12 & 15 & 18 \end{bmatrix}$$

Matrix addition is defined only for matrices that have the same number of rows r and the same number of columns c. For any two r by c matrices, the sum is obtained by adding corresponding elements. For example,

$$\begin{bmatrix} 1 & 2 & 3 \\ 4 & 5 & 6 \end{bmatrix} + \begin{bmatrix} 0.0 & 1.5 & 0.2 \\ -6.0 & 1.1 & -10.0 \end{bmatrix} = \begin{bmatrix} 1.0 & 3.5 & 3.2 \\ -2.0 & 6.1 & -4.0 \end{bmatrix}$$

Matrix Multiplication

The product of two matrices is defined as a generalization of the vector dot product. We can multiply an m by n matrix **A** by a p by q matrix **B** to form the matrix product **A B**, providing that the number of columns in **A** is equal to the number of rows in **B**. In other words, we must have $n = p$. We then obtain the product matrix by forming sums of the products of the elements in the row vectors of **A** with the corresponding elements in the column vectors of **B**. Thus, for the following product

$$\mathbf{C} = \mathbf{A}\,\mathbf{B} \tag{A-46}$$

we obtain an m by q matrix **C** whose elements are calculated as

$$c_{ij} = \sum_{k=1}^{n} a_{ik} b_{kj} \tag{A-47}$$

In the following example, a 3 by 2 matrix is postmultiplied by a 2 by 2 matrix to produce a 3 by 2 product matrix.

$$\begin{bmatrix} 0 & -1 \\ 5 & 7 \\ -2 & 8 \end{bmatrix} \begin{bmatrix} 1 & 2 \\ 3 & 4 \end{bmatrix} = \begin{bmatrix} 0 \cdot 1 + (-1) \cdot 3 & 0 \cdot 2 + (-1) \cdot 4 \\ 5 \cdot 1 + 7 \cdot 3 & 5 \cdot 2 + 7 \cdot 4 \\ -2 \cdot 1 + 8 \cdot 3 & -2 \cdot 2 + 8 \cdot 4 \end{bmatrix} = \begin{bmatrix} -3 & -4 \\ 26 & 38 \\ 22 & 28 \end{bmatrix}$$

Vector multiplication in matrix notation produces the same result as the dot product, provided that the first vector is expressed as a row vector and the second vector is expressed as a column vector. For example,

$$\begin{bmatrix} 1 & 2 & 3 \end{bmatrix} \begin{bmatrix} 4 \\ 5 \\ 6 \end{bmatrix} = [32]$$

This vector product results in a matrix with a single element (a 1 by 1 matrix). However, if we multiply the vectors in reverse order, we obtain the following

3 by 3 matrix.

$$\begin{bmatrix} 4 \\ 5 \\ 6 \end{bmatrix} [1 \quad 2 \quad 3] = \begin{bmatrix} 4 & 8 & 12 \\ 5 & 10 & 15 \\ 6 & 12 & 18 \end{bmatrix}$$

As the previous two vector products illustrate, matrix multiplication, in general, is not commutative. That is,

$$\mathbf{A\,B} \neq \mathbf{B\,A} \tag{A-48}$$

But matrix multiplication is distributive with respect to matrix addition:

$$\mathbf{A}(\mathbf{B} + \mathbf{C}) = \mathbf{A\,B} + \mathbf{A\,C} \tag{A-49}$$

Matrix Transpose

The **transpose** $\mathbf{M}^T$ of a matrix is obtained by interchanging rows and columns. For example,

$$\begin{bmatrix} 1 & 2 & 3 \\ 4 & 5 & 6 \end{bmatrix}^T = \begin{bmatrix} 1 & 4 \\ 2 & 5 \\ 3 & 6 \end{bmatrix}, \qquad [a \quad b \quad c]^T = \begin{bmatrix} a \\ b \\ c \end{bmatrix} \tag{A-50}$$

For a matrix product, the transpose is

$$(\mathbf{M}_1\mathbf{M}_2)^T = \mathbf{M}_2^T\mathbf{M}_1^T \tag{A-51}$$

Determinant of a Matrix

If we have a square matrix, we can combine the matrix elements to produce a single number called the **determinant** of the matrix. Determinant evaluations are useful in analyzing and solving a wide range of problems. For a 2 by 2 matrix **A**, the **second-order determinant** is defined to be

$$\det \mathbf{A} = \begin{vmatrix} a_{11} & a_{12} \\ a_{21} & a_{22} \end{vmatrix} = a_{11}a_{22} - a_{12}a_{21} \tag{A-52}$$

Higher-order determinants are obtained recursively from lower-order determinant values. To calculate a determinant of order 2 or greater, we can select any column k of an n by n matrix and compute the determinant as

$$\det \mathbf{A} = \sum_{j=1}^{n} (-1)^{j+k} a_{jk} \det \mathbf{A}_{jk} \tag{A-53}$$

where $\det \mathbf{A}_{jk}$ is the $(n-1)$ by $(n-1)$ determinant of the submatrix obtained from **A** by deleting the jth row and the kth column. Alternatively, we can select any row j and calculate the determinant as

$$\det \mathbf{A} = \sum_{k=1}^{n} (-1)^{j+k} a_{jk} \det \mathbf{A}_{jk} \tag{A-54}$$

Evaluating determinants for large matrices ($n > 4$, say) can be accomplished more efficiently using numerical methods. One way to compute a determinant is to decompose the matrix into two factors: $\mathbf{A} = \mathbf{L}\,\mathbf{U}$, where all elements of matrix **L** above the diagonal are zero, and all elements of matrix **U** below the diagonal are zero. We then compute the product of the diagonals for both **L** and **U**, and we obtain det**A** by multiplying the two diagonal products. This method is based on the following property of determinants:

$$\det(\mathbf{A}\,\mathbf{B}) = (\det \mathbf{A})(\det \mathbf{B}) \tag{A-55}$$

Another numerical method for calculating determinants is based on the Gaussian-elimination procedures discussed in Section A-14.

Matrix Inverse

With square matrices, we can obtain an *inverse matrix* if and only if the determinant of the matrix is nonzero. If an inverse exists, the matrix is said to be a **nonsingular matrix.** Otherwise, the matrix is called a **singular matrix.** For most practical applications, where a matrix represents a physical operation, we can expect the inverse to exist.

The inverse of an n by n (square) matrix **M** is denoted as $\mathbf{M}^{-1}$ and

$$\mathbf{M}\,\mathbf{M}^{-1} = \mathbf{M}^{-1}\mathbf{M} = \mathbf{I} \tag{A-56}$$

where **I** is the identity matrix. All diagonal elements of **I** have the value 1, and all other (off-diagonal) elements are zero.

Elements for the inverse matrix $\mathbf{M}^{-1}$ can be calculated from the elements of **M** as

$$m_{jk}^{-1} = \frac{(-1)^{j+k} \det \mathbf{M}_{kj}}{\det \mathbf{M}} \tag{A-57}$$

where m_{jk}^{-1} is the element in the jth row and kth column of $\mathbf{M}^{-1}$, and $\mathbf{M}_{kj}$ is the $(n-1)$ by $(n-1)$ submatrix obtained by deleting the kth row and jth column of matrix **M**. For large values of n, we can compute values for the determinants and the elements of the inverse matrix more efficiently using numerical methods.

A-6 COMPLEX NUMBERS

By definition, a **complex number** z is an ordered pair of real numbers, represented as

$$z = (x, y) \tag{A-58}$$

where x is called the **real part** of z and y is called the **imaginary part** of z. Real and imaginary parts of a complex number are designated as

$$x = \mathrm{Re}(z), \qquad y = \mathrm{Im}(z) \tag{A-59}$$

Geometrically, a complex number can be described as a point in the *complex plane,* as illustrated in Fig. A-20.

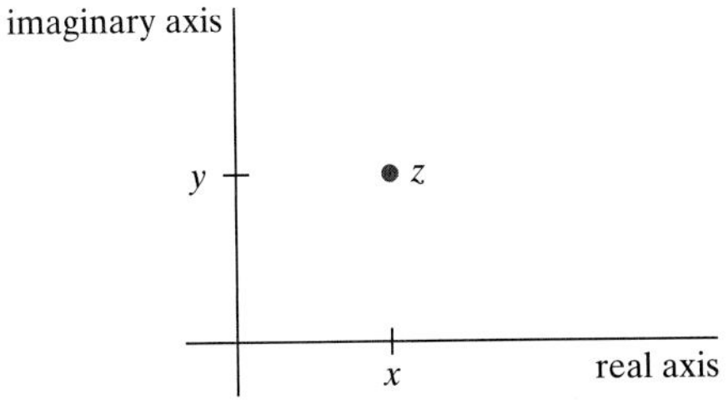

FIGURE A-20 Real and imaginary components for a point z in the complex plane.

When Re(z) = 0, the complex number z is said to be a *pure imaginary number.* Similarly, any real number can be represented as a complex number with Im(z) = 0. Thus, we can write any real number in the form

$$x = (x, 0)$$

Complex numbers arise from solutions of equations such as

$$x^2 + 1 = 0, \qquad x^2 - 2x + 5 = 0$$

which have no real-number solutions. Thus, the concept of a complex number and the rules for complex arithmetic have been devised as extensions of real number manipulations that provide solutions to such problems.

Basic Complex Arithmetic

Addition, subtraction, and scalar multiplication of complex numbers are carried out using the same rules as for two-dimensional vectors. For example, the sum of two complex numbers is

$$z_1 + z_2 = (x_1, y_1) + (x_2, y_2) = (x_1 + x_2, y_1 + y_2)$$

and we can express any complex number as the summation:

$$z = (x, y) = (x, 0) + (0, y)$$

The product of two complex numbers, z_1 and z_2, is defined as

$$(x_1, y_1)(x_2, y_2) = (x_1x_2 - y_1y_2, x_1y_2 + x_2y_1) \tag{A-60}$$

This definition for complex multiplication gives the same result as for real-number multiplication when the imaginary parts are zero:

$$(x_1, 0)(x_2, 0) = (x_1x_2, 0)$$

Imaginary Unit

The pure imaginary number with $y = 1$ is called the **imaginary unit,** and it is denoted as

$$i = (0, 1) \tag{A-61}$$

(Electrical engineers often use the symbol j for the imaginary unit, because the symbol i is used to represent electrical current.)

From the rule for complex multiplication, we have

$$i^2 = (0, 1)(0, 1) = (-1, 0)$$

Therefore, i^2 is the real number -1, and

$$i = \sqrt{-1} \tag{A-62}$$

We can represent a pure imaginary number using either of the following two forms.

$$z = iy = (0, y)$$

And a general complex number can be expressed in the form

$$z = x + iy \tag{A-63}$$

Using the definition for i, we can verify that this representation satisfies the rules for complex addition, subtraction, and multiplication.

Complex Conjugate and Modulus of a Complex Number

Another concept associated with a complex number is the *complex conjugate,* which is defined to be

$$\bar{z} = x - iy \tag{A-64}$$

Thus, the complex conjugate $\bar{z}$ is the reflection of z about the x (real) axis.

The *modulus,* or *absolute value,* of a complex number is defined as

$$|z| = \sqrt{z\bar{z}} = \sqrt{x^2 + y^2} \tag{A-65}$$

This number gives the distance in the complex plane of point z from the origin, which is sometimes referred to as the "vector length" of the complex number. Therefore, the absolute value of a complex number is simply a representation for the Pythagorean theorem in the complex plane.

Complex Division

To evaluate the ratio of two complex numbers, we can simplify the expression by multiplying the numerator and denominator by the complex conjugate of the denominator. Then we use the multiplication rules to determine the values for the components of the resulting complex number. Thus, the real and imaginary parts for the ratio of two complex numbers are obtained as

$$\begin{aligned} \frac{z_1}{z_2} &= \frac{z_1\overline{z_2}}{z_2\overline{z_2}} \\ &= \frac{(x_1, y_1)(x_2, -y_2)}{x_2^2 + y_2^2}, \\ &= \left(\frac{x_1x_2 + y_1y_2}{x_2^2 + y_2^2}, \frac{x_2y_1 - x_1y_2}{x_2^2 + y_2^2}\right) \end{aligned} \tag{A-66}$$

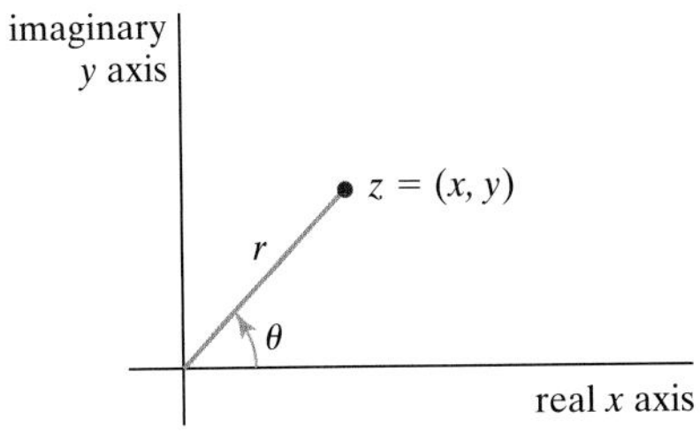

imaginary y axis

$z = (x, y)$

r θ

real x axis

FIGURE A-21 Polar-coordinate parameters in the complex plane.

Polar-Coordinate Representation for a Complex Number

Multiplication and division operations for complex numbers are greatly simplified if we express the real and imaginary parts in terms of polar coordinates (Fig. A-21):

$$z = r(\cos\theta + i\sin\theta) \tag{A-67}$$

We can also write the polar form of z as

$$z = re^{i\theta} \tag{A-68}$$

where e is the base of the natural logarithms ($e \approx 2.718281828$), and

$$e^{i\theta} = \cos\theta + i\sin\theta \tag{A-69}$$

which is *Euler's formula.*

Using the polar-coordinate form, we compute the product of two complex numbers by multiplying their absolute values and adding their polar angles. Thus,

$$z_1 z_2 = r_1 r_2 e^{i(\theta_1+\theta_2)} \tag{A-70}$$

To divide one complex number by another, we divide their absolute values and subtract the polar angles:

$$\frac{z_1}{z_2} = \frac{r_1}{r_2} e^{i(\theta_1-\theta_2)} \tag{A-71}$$

We can also use the polar representation to obtain roots of complex numbers. The nth roots of a complex number are calculated as

$$\sqrt[n]{z} = \sqrt[n]{r}\left[\cos\left(\frac{\theta + 2k\pi}{n}\right) + i\sin\left(\frac{\theta + 2k\pi}{n}\right)\right], \quad k = 0, 1, 2, \ldots, n-1 \tag{A-72}$$

These roots lie on a circle of radius $\sqrt[n]{r}$ with center at the origin of the complex plane, and they form the vertices for a regular polygon with n sides.

A-7 QUATERNIONS

Complex number concepts are extended to higher dimensions using **quaternions,** which are quantities with one real part and three imaginary parts, written as

$$q = s + ia + jb + kc \tag{A-73}$$

where the coefficients a, b, and c in the imaginary terms are real numbers, and parameter s is a real number called the *scalar part*. Parameters i, j, k are defined with the properties

$$i^2 = j^2 = k^2 = -1, \qquad ij = -ji = k \tag{A-74}$$

From these properties, it follows that

$$jk = -kj = i, \qquad ki = -ik = j \tag{A-75}$$

Scalar multiplication is defined in analogy with the corresponding operations for vectors and complex numbers. That is, each of the four components of the quaternion is multiplied by the scalar value. Similarly, quaternion addition is defined as addition of corresponding elements:

$$q_1 + q_2 = (s_1 + s_2) + i(a_1 + a_2) + j(b_1 + b_2) + k(c_1 + c_2) \tag{A-76}$$

Multiplication of two quaternions is carried out using the operations in Eqs. A-74 and A-75.

We can also use the following ordered-pair notation for a quaternion, which is similar to the ordered-pair representation for a complex number.

$$q = (s, \mathbf{v}) \tag{A-77}$$

Parameter $\mathbf{v}$ in this representation is the vector (a, b, c). Using the ordered-pair notation, we can express quaternion addition in the form

$$q_1 + q_2 = (s_1 + s_2, \mathbf{v}_1 + \mathbf{v}_2) \tag{A-78}$$

We can write the expression for quaternion multiplication relatively compactly in terms of the vector dot product and cross product operations as

$$q_1 q_2 = (s_1 s_2 - \mathbf{v}_1 \cdot \mathbf{v}_2, s_1 \mathbf{v}_2 + s_2 \mathbf{v}_1 + \mathbf{v}_1 \times \mathbf{v}_2) \tag{A-79}$$

The magnitude squared of a quaternion is defined by analogy with complex-number operations, using the following sum of the squares of the quaternion components.

$$|q|^2 = s^2 + \mathbf{v} \cdot \mathbf{v} \tag{A-80}$$

And the inverse of a quaternion is evaluated using the expression

$$q^{-1} = \frac{1}{|q|^2}(s, -\mathbf{v}) \tag{A-81}$$

so that

$$qq^{-1} = q^{-1}q = (1, 0)$$

A-8 NONPARAMETRIC REPRESENTATIONS

When we write object descriptions directly in terms of the coordinates for the reference frame in use, the representation is called **nonparametric.** For example, we can describe a surface with either of the following Cartesian functions.

$$f_1(x, y, z) = 0, \quad \text{or} \quad z = f_2(x, y) \tag{A-82}$$

The first form in A-82 is called an *implicit* expression for the surface, and the second form is called an *explicit* representation. In the explicit representation, x and y are referred to as the independent variables, and z is called the dependent variable.

Similarly, we can represent a three-dimensional curved line in nonparametric form as the intersection of two surface functions, or we could represent the curve with the pair of functions

$$y = f(x) \quad \text{and} \quad z = g(x) \tag{A-83}$$

with coordinate x as the independent variable. Values for the dependent variables y and z are then determined from Eqs. A-83 as we step through values for x for some prescribed number of intervals.

Nonparametric representations are useful in describing objects within a given reference frame, but they have some disadvantages when used in graphics algorithms. If we want a smooth plot, we must change the independent variable whenever the first derivative (slope) of either $f(x)$ or $g(x)$ becomes greater than 1. This requires continual checks on the derivative values to determine when we need to change the roles of the independent and dependent variables. Also, Eqs. A-83 provide an awkward format for representing multiple-valued functions. For instance, the implicit equation for a circle centered on the origin in the xy plane is

$$x^2 + y^2 - r^2 = 0$$

and the explicit expression for y is the multivalued function

$$y = \pm\sqrt{r^2 - x^2}$$

In general, a more convenient representation for object descriptions in graphics algorithms is in terms of parametric equations.

A-9 PARAMETRIC REPRESENTATIONS

We can classify objects according to the number of parameters needed to describe the coordinate positions on the objects. A curve, for example, in a Cartesian reference frame is classified as a one-dimensional Euclidean object, and a surface is a two-dimensional Euclidean object. When an object description is given in terms of its dimensionality parameter, the description is called a **parametric representation.**

The Cartesian description for positions along the path of a curve can be given in a parametric form using the following vector point function

$$\mathbf{P}(u) = (x(u), y(u), z(u)) \tag{A-84}$$

where each of the Cartesian coordinates is a function of parameter u. In most cases, we can normalize the three coordinate functions so that parameter u varies over the range from 0 to 1.0. For example, a circle in the xy plane with radius r and center position at the coordinate origin can be defined in parametric form with the following three functions.

$$x(u) = r\cos(2\pi u), \qquad y(u) = r\sin(2\pi u), \qquad z(u) = 0, \qquad 0 \le u \le 1 \tag{A-85}$$

Since this curve is defined in the xy plane, we could eliminate the $z(u)$ function, which has the constant value 0.

In a similar way, we can represent coordinate positions on a surface using the following Cartesian vector point function.

$$\mathbf{P}(u, v) = (x(u, v), y(u, v), z(u, v)) \tag{A-86}$$

Each of the Cartesian coordinates is now a function of the two surface parameters u and v. A spherical surface with radius r and center at the coordinate origin, for example, can be described with the equations

$$\begin{aligned} x(u, v) &= r\cos(2\pi u)\sin(\pi v) \\ y(u, v) &= r\sin(2\pi u)\sin(\pi v) \qquad 0 \le u, v \le 1 \\ z(u, v) &= r\cos(\pi v) \end{aligned} \tag{A-87}$$

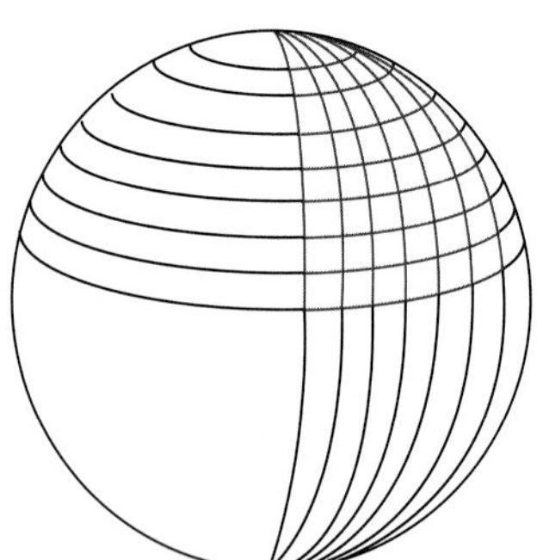

FIGURE A-22 Section of a spherical surface described by lines of constant u and lines of constant v in Eqs. A-87.

Parameter u describes lines of constant longitude over the surface, while parameter v describes lines of constant latitude. The parametric equations are again normalized so that u and v are assigned values in the range from 0 to 1.0. By keeping one of these parameters fixed while varying the other over a subrange of the unit interval, we could plot latitude and longitude lines for any spherical section (Fig. A-22).

A-10 RATE-OF-CHANGE OPERATORS

For a continuous function of a single independent variable, such as $f(x)$, we determine the rate at which the function is changing at any particular x value using a function called the *derivative of $f(x)$ with respect to x*. This derivative function is defined as

$$\frac{df}{dx} \equiv \lim_{\Delta x \to 0} \frac{f(x + \Delta x) - f(x)}{\Delta x} \tag{A-88}$$

and this definition is the basis for obtaining numerical solutions for problems involving rate-of-change operations. The functional forms for the derivatives of commonly occurring functions, such as polynomials and trigonometric functions, are available in derivative tables. And for rate-of-change problems involving simple functions, we can typically obtain closed-form solutions. But, in many cases, we need to solve rate-of-change problems using numerical methods.

When we have a function of several variables, rate-of-change operations with respect to the individual variables are called *partial derivatives*. For example, with a function such as $f(x, y, z, t)$, we can determine the rate of change of the function with respect to any one of the coordinate directions, x, y, or z, or the time parameter t. A partial derivative for a particular independent variable is defined with

Eq. A-88, where all other independent variables are held constant. Thus, for example, the partial derivative of f with respect to time is defined as

$$\frac{\partial f}{\partial t} \equiv \lim_{\Delta t \to 0} \frac{f(x, y, z, t + \Delta t) - f(x, y, z, t)}{\Delta t}$$

which is evaluated at some particular spatial position and time.

A number of partial-derivative operators occur frequently enough that they are given special names, such as gradient, Laplacian, divergence, and curl. These operators are useful in various applications, such as determining the geometry and orientation of objects, describing the behavior of objects in certain situations, calculating electromagnetic-radiation effects, and analyzing data sets in scientific visualization studies.

Gradient Operator

The vector operator with the following Cartesian components is called the *gradient operator.*

$$\text{grad} = \nabla \equiv \left(\frac{\partial}{\partial x}, \frac{\partial}{\partial y}, \frac{\partial}{\partial z} \right) \tag{A-89}$$

Symbol ∇ is referred to as *nabla, del,* or simply the *grad operator.* One important use for the gradient operator is in calculating a surface normal vector. When a surface is described with the nonparametric representation $f(x, y, z)$ = constant, the surface normal at any position is calculated as

$$\mathbf{N} = \nabla f \quad \text{(Normal Vector for a Nonparametric Surface Representation)} \tag{A-90}$$

As an example, a spherical surface with radius r can be represented in local coordinates with the nonparametric Cartesian representation $f(x, y, z) = x^2 + y^2 + z^2 = r^2$, and the gradient of f produces the surface normal vector $(2x, 2y, 2z)$. But if a surface is represented with a parametric point function $\mathbf{P}(u, v)$, then we can determine the surface normal using the vector cross-product calculation

$$\mathbf{N} = \frac{\partial \mathbf{P}}{\partial u} \times \frac{\partial \mathbf{P}}{\partial v} \quad \text{(Normal Vector for a Parametric Surface Representation)} \tag{A-91}$$

Directional Derivative

We can also use the gradient operator and the vector dot product to form a scalar product called the *directional derivative* of a function f:

$$\frac{\partial f}{\partial u} = \mathbf{u} \cdot \nabla f \tag{A-92}$$

This gives us the rate-of-change of f in a direction specified by the unit vector $\mathbf{u}$. To illustrate, we can determine the directional derivative for the spherical surface function $f = x^2 + y^2 + z^2$ in the z direction as

$$\frac{\partial f}{\partial z} = \mathbf{u}_z \cdot \nabla f = 2z$$

where $\mathbf{u}_z$ is the unit vector along the positive z direction. And for the following unit vector in the xy plane

$$\mathbf{u} = \frac{1}{\sqrt{2}}\mathbf{u}_x + \frac{1}{\sqrt{2}}\mathbf{u}_y$$

the directional derivative of f from Eq. A-92 is

$$\frac{\partial f}{\partial u} = \frac{1}{\sqrt{2}}\frac{\partial f}{\partial x} + \frac{1}{\sqrt{2}}\frac{\partial f}{\partial y} = \sqrt{2}x + \sqrt{2}y$$

General Form of the Gradient Operator

Within any three-dimensional, orthogonal-coordinate system, we obtain the components for the gradient operator using the calculations

$$\nabla = \sum_{k=1}^{3} \frac{\mathbf{u}_k}{\sqrt{g_{kk}}} \frac{\partial}{\partial x_k} \tag{A-93}$$

In this expression, each $\mathbf{u}_k$ represents the unit basis vector in the x_k-coordinate direction, and g_{kk} are the diagonal components of the metric tensor for the space.

Laplace Operator

We can use the gradient operator and the vector dot product to form a scalar differential operator called the *Laplacian* or the *Laplace operator,* which has the Cartesian-coordinate form

$$\nabla^2 = \nabla \cdot \nabla = \frac{\partial^2}{\partial x^2} + \frac{\partial^2}{\partial y^2} + \frac{\partial^2}{\partial z^2} \tag{A-94}$$

The symbol ∇^2 is often referred to as *grad squared, del squared,* or *nabla squared.* And in any three-dimensional, orthogonal-coordinate system, the Laplacian of a function $f(x, y, z)$ is computed as

$$\nabla^2 f = \frac{1}{\sqrt{g_{11}g_{22}g_{33}}} \left[\frac{\partial}{\partial x_1}\left(\frac{\sqrt{g_{22}g_{33}}}{\sqrt{g_{11}}} \frac{\partial f}{\partial x_1} \right) + \frac{\partial}{\partial x_2}\left(\frac{\sqrt{g_{33}g_{11}}}{\sqrt{g_{22}}} \frac{\partial f}{\partial x_2} \right) + \frac{\partial}{\partial x_3}\left(\frac{\sqrt{g_{11}g_{22}}}{\sqrt{g_{33}}} \frac{\partial f}{\partial x_3} \right) \right] \tag{A-95}$$

Equations involving the Laplacian arise in many applications, including the description of electromagnetic-radiation effects.

Divergence Operator

The vector dot product can also be used to combine the gradient operator with a vector function to produce a scalar quantity called the *divergence of a vector,* which has the following Cartesian form.

$$\text{div}\,\mathbf{V} = \nabla \cdot \mathbf{V} = \frac{\partial V_x}{\partial x} + \frac{\partial V_y}{\partial y} + \frac{\partial V_z}{\partial z} \tag{A-96}$$

In this expression, V_x, V_y, and V_z are the Cartesian components of the vector $\mathbf{V}$. Divergence is a measure of the rate of increase or decrease of a vector function, such as an electric field, at a point in space. In any three-dimensional, orthogonal-coordinate system, the divergence of a vector **V** is calculated as

$$\text{div}\,\mathbf{V} = \nabla \cdot \mathbf{V} = \frac{1}{\sqrt{g_{11}g_{22}g_{33}}}\left[\frac{\partial}{\partial x_1}(\sqrt{g_{22}g_{33}}V_1)+\frac{\partial}{\partial x_2}(\sqrt{g_{33}g_{11}}V_2)+\frac{\partial}{\partial x_3}(\sqrt{g_{11}g_{22}}V_3)\right] \tag{A-97}$$

with parameters V_1, V_2, and V_3 as the components of vector **V** with respect to the coordinate directions x_1, x_2, and x_3, and g_{kk} are the diagonal elements of the metric tensor.

Curl Operator

Another very useful differential operator is the *curl of a vector*, which is applied using the gradient operator and the vector cross product. The Cartesian components for the curl of a vector are

$$\text{curl}\,\mathbf{V} = \nabla \times \mathbf{V} = \left(\frac{\partial V_z}{\partial y} - \frac{\partial V_y}{\partial z}, \frac{\partial V_x}{\partial z} - \frac{\partial V_z}{\partial x}, \frac{\partial V_y}{\partial x} - \frac{\partial V_x}{\partial y}\right) \tag{A-98}$$

This operation gives us a measure of rotational effects associated with a vector quantity, such as in the scattering of electromagnetic radiation. For any three-dimensional, orthogonal-coordinate system, we can express the components of the curl in terms of the metric tensor components using the following determinant representation.

$$\text{curl}\,\mathbf{V} = \nabla \times \mathbf{V} = \frac{1}{\sqrt{g_{11}g_{22}g_{33}}}\begin{vmatrix} \sqrt{g_{11}}\,\mathbf{u}_1 & \sqrt{g_{22}}\,\mathbf{u}_2 & \sqrt{g_{33}}\,\mathbf{u}_3 \\ \dfrac{\partial}{\partial x_1} & \dfrac{\partial}{\partial x_2} & \dfrac{\partial}{\partial x_3} \\ \sqrt{g_{11}}V_1 & \sqrt{g_{22}}V_2 & \sqrt{g_{33}}V_3 \end{vmatrix} \tag{A-99}$$

Vectors $\mathbf{u}_k$ are the unit basis vectors for the space, and g_{kk} are the diagonal elements of the metric tensor.

A-11 RATE-OF-CHANGE INTEGRAL TRANSFORMATION THEOREMS

In many applications, we encounter problems that involve rate-of-change operations that are to be integrated (summed) over some region of space, which can be along a line path, across a surface, or throughout a volume of space. Often the problem can be simplified by applying a transformation theorem that converts a surface integral to a line integral, a line integral to a surface integral, a volume integral to a surface integral, or a surface integral to a volume integral. These transformation theorems are of tremendous importance in solving a wide range of practical problems.

Stokes's Theorem

For a continuous vector function $\mathbf{F}(x, y, z)$ defined over some surface region, **Stokes's theorem** states that the integral of the perpendicular component of the curl of **F** is equal to the line integral of **F** around the perimeter curve C for the

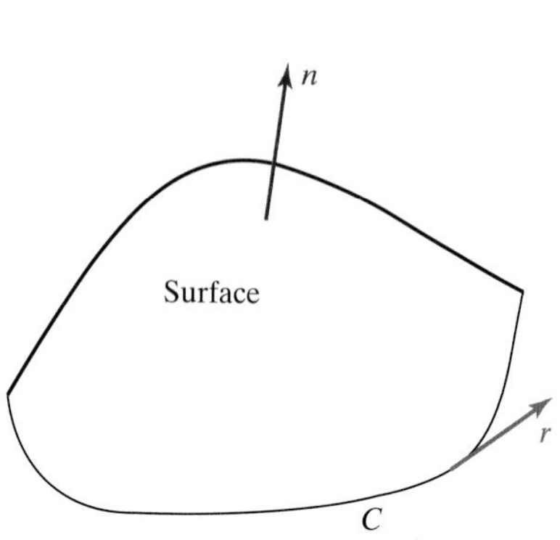

FIGURE A-23 Integration around the boundary curve C is counterclockwise in Stokes's theorem when we view the surface from the "outside" region of space.

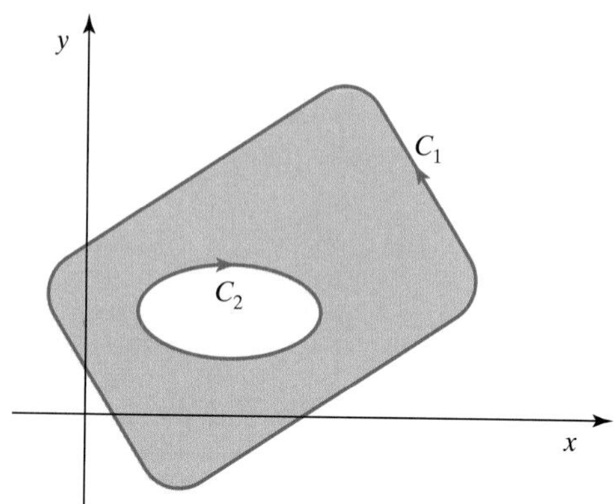

FIGURE A-24 Line integrals in Green's plane theorem are evaluated by traversing the boundary curves C_1 and C_2 so that the interior region (shaded) is always on the left.

surface. That is,

$$\iint_{\text{surf}} (\text{curl}\,\mathbf{F}) \cdot \mathbf{n}\, dA = \oint_C \mathbf{F} \cdot \mathbf{r}\, ds \qquad \text{(A-100)}$$

where the boundary C must be "piecewise smooth", which means that C must be a continuous curve or a curve composed of a finite number of continuous sections, such as circular arcs or straight-line segments. In this expression, **n** is the unit surface normal at any point, dA is a differential element of surface area, **r** is a unit tangent vector to the boundary curve C at any point, and ds is a differential line segment along C. The integration direction around C is counterclockwise when we view the front of the surface (Section 3-15), as shown in Fig. A-23.

Green's Theorem for a Plane Surface

If we consider a region of the xy plane bounded by a piecewise smooth curve C (as in Stokes's theorem), we can express **Green's plane theorem** in the Cartesian form

$$\iint_{\text{area}} \left(\frac{\partial f_2}{\partial x} - \frac{\partial f_1}{\partial y} \right) dx\, dy = \oint_C (f_1\, dx + f_2\, dy) \qquad \text{(A-101)}$$

Here, $f_1(x, y)$ and $f_2(x, y)$ are two continuous functions defined throughout the planar area bounded by curve C, and the direction of integration around C is counterclockwise. We can also apply Green's theorem to a region with internal holes, as in Fig. A-24, but we then must integrate in a clockwise direction around the interior boundary curves.

Although developed independently, Green's plane theorem is a special case of Stokes's theorem. To demonstrate this, we define a vector function **F** with Cartesian components $(f_1, f_2, 0)$. Then, Green's theorem can be written in the vector form

$$\iint_{\text{area}} (\text{curl}\,\mathbf{F}) \cdot \mathbf{u}_z\, dA = \oint_C \mathbf{F} \cdot \mathbf{r}\, ds \qquad \text{(A-102)}$$

where u_z is the unit vector perpendicular to the xy plane (in the z direction), $dA = dx\,dy$, and the other parameters are the same as in Eq. A-100.

We can use Green's plane theorem to compute the area of a planar region by setting $f_1 = 0$ and $f_2 = x$. Then, from Green's theorem, the area A of a plane figure is

$$A = \iint_{\text{area}} dx\,dy = \oint_C x\,dy \tag{A-103}$$

Similarly, if we set $f_1 = -y$ and $f_2 = 0$, we have

$$A = \iint_{\text{area}} dx\,dy = -\oint_C y\,dx \tag{A-104}$$

Adding the two previous area equations, we obtain

$$A = \frac{1}{2}\oint_C (x\,dy - y\,dx) \tag{A-105}$$

And we can also convert this Cartesian expression for the area into the following polar-coordinate form

$$A = \frac{1}{2}\oint_C r^2\,d\theta \tag{A-106}$$

Green's plane theorem can be expressed in many other useful forms. For example, if we define $f_1 = \partial f/\partial y$ and $f_2 = \partial f/\partial x$, for some continuous function f, then we have

$$\iint_{\text{area}} \nabla^2 f\,dx\,dy = \oint_C \frac{\partial f}{\partial n}\,ds \tag{A-107}$$

where $\partial f/\partial n$ is the directional derivative of f in the direction of the outward normal to the boundary curve C.

Divergence Theorem

The previous two theorems give us methods for converting between surface integrals and line integrals. The **divergence theorem** provides an equation for converting a volume integral into a surface integral, or conversely. This theorem is also known by various other names, including **Green's theorem in space** and **Gauss's theorem.** For a continuous, three-dimensional, vector function **F**, defined over a volume of space, we can express the divergence theorem in the vector form

$$\iiint_{\text{vol}} \text{div}\,\mathbf{F}\,dV = \iint_{\text{surf}} \mathbf{F}\cdot\mathbf{n}\,dA \tag{A-108}$$

where dV is a differential volume element, **n** is the normal vector for the bounding surface, and dA is a differential element of surface area.

We can use the divergence theorem to obtain several other useful integral transformations. For instance, if $\mathbf{F} = \nabla f$ for some continuous three-dimensional function f, we have the volume version of Eq. A-107, which is

$$\iiint_{\text{vol}} \nabla^2 f \, dV = \iint_{\text{surf}} \frac{\partial f}{\partial n} \, dA \tag{A-109}$$

In this equation, $\partial f/\partial n$ is the directional derivative of f in the direction of the surface normal.

From the divergence theorem, we can derive expressions for calculating the volume of a spatial region using a surface integral. Depending upon how we represent the vector function **F**, we can obtain any one of the following Cartesian forms for the surface integral.

$$\begin{aligned} V &= \iiint_{\text{vol}} dx\,dy\,dz \\ &= \iint_{\text{surf}} x\,dy\,dz = \iint_{\text{surf}} y\,dz\,dx = \iint_{\text{surf}} z\,dx\,dy \\ &= \frac{1}{3}\iint_{\text{surf}} (x\,dy\,dz + y\,dz\,dx + z\,dx\,dy) \end{aligned} \tag{A-110}$$

Green's Transformation Equations

A number of other integral transformations can be derived from the divergence theorem. The following two integral equations are generally referenced as **Green's transformation equations, Green's first and second formulas,** or **Green's identities.**

$$\iiint_{\text{vol}} (f_1 \nabla^2 f_2 + \nabla f_1 \cdot \nabla f_2) \, dV = \iint_{\text{surf}} f_1 \frac{\partial f_2}{\partial n} \, dA \tag{A-111}$$

$$\iiint_{\text{vol}} (f_1 \nabla^2 f_2 - f_2 \nabla^2 f_1) \, dV = \iint_{\text{surf}} \left(f_1 \frac{\partial f_2}{\partial n} - f_2 \frac{\partial f_1}{\partial n} \right) dA \tag{A-112}$$

In these equations, f_1 and f_2 are continuous, three-dimensional scalar functions, and $\partial f_1/\partial n$ and $\partial f_2/\partial n$ are their directional derivatives in the direction of the surface normal.

A-12 AREA AND CENTROID OF A POLYGON

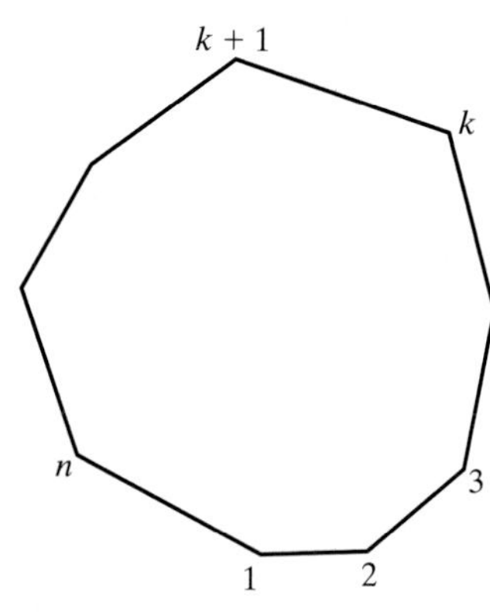

FIGURE A-25 A polygon defined with n vertices in the xy plane.

We can use the integral transformations from Section A-11 to calculate various properties of objects for computer-graphics applications. For polygons, we often use the area and the centroid coordinates in programs involving geometric transformations, simulations, system design, and animations.

Area of a Polygon

From Eq. A-103, we can compute the area of a polygon by expressing the Cartesian coordinates in parametric form and evaluating the line integral around the perimeter of the polygon. The parametric equations for the n edges of a polygon with n vertices in the xy plane (Fig. A-25) can be expressed in the form

$$\begin{aligned} x &= x_k + (x_{k+1} - x_k)u \\ y &= y_k + (y_{k+1} - y_k)u \end{aligned} \qquad 0 \le u \le 1, \qquad k = 1, 2, \ldots, n \tag{A-113}$$

where $x_{n+1} = x_1$ and $y_{n+1} = y_1$.

Substituting the differential expression $dy = (y_{k+1} - y_k)du$ and the parametric expression for x into Eq. A-103, we have

$$\begin{aligned}
A &= \oint_C x\,dy \\
&= \sum_{k=1}^{n} \int_0^1 [x_k + (x_{k+1} - x_k)u](y_{k+1} - y_k)\,du \\
&= \sum_{k=1}^{n} (y_{k+1} - y_k)[x_k + (x_{k+1} - x_k)/2] \\
&= \frac{1}{2}\sum_{k=1}^{n} (x_k y_{k+1} - x_k y_k + x_{k+1} y_{k+1} - x_{k+1} y_k)
\end{aligned} \tag{A-114}$$

For each line segment, the second and third terms in this sum are canceled by similar terms with opposite signs in the expressions for successive values of k. Therefore, the area of the polygon is computed with

$$A = \frac{1}{2}\sum_{k=1}^{n} (x_k y_{k+1} - x_{k+1} y_k) \tag{A-115}$$

Centroid of a Polygon

By definition, the centroid is the position of the center of mass for a constant-density object (all points in the object have the same mass). Thus, the coordinates for the centroid are simply the mean values for the coordinates over all positions within the object boundaries.

For some simple polygon shapes, we can obtain the centroid by averaging the vertex positions. But, in general, vertex averaging does not correctly locate the centroid, because it neglects the positions for all other points in the polygon. As illustrated in Fig. A-26, the average vertex position is near the greatest concentration of vertices, while the centroid is at the center position for the entire polygon area.

We calculate the centroid position $(\overline{x}, \overline{y})$ for a polygon in the xy plane by averaging the coordinates for all positions within the polygon boundaries:

$$\begin{aligned}
\overline{x} &= \frac{1}{A}\iint_{\text{area}} x\,dx\,dy = \frac{\mu_x}{A} \\
\overline{y} &= \frac{1}{A}\iint_{\text{area}} y\,dx\,dy = \frac{\mu_y}{A}
\end{aligned} \tag{A-116}$$

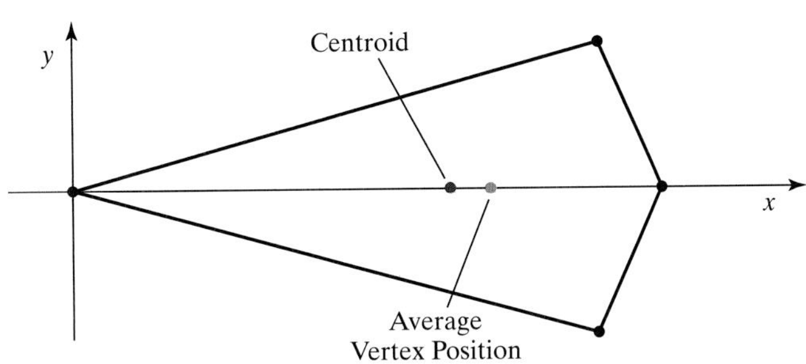

FIGURE A-26 Coordinate positions for the centroid of a polygon and the average of the vertex coordinates.

In these expressions, μ_x and μ_y are called the moments of the area with respect to the x and y axes, respectively, where the area is assumed to have unit mass per unit area.

We can evaluate each of the moments of the polygon using the same procedures we employed to compute the area of the polygon. From Green's plane theorem, we obtain a line integral equivalent to the area integral, and we evaluate the line integral using parametric representations for the Cartesian coordinates along the polygon edges. Green's theorem for a plane surface (Eq. A-101) states that

$$\iint_{\text{area}} \left(\frac{\partial f_2}{\partial x} - \frac{\partial f_1}{\partial y} \right) dx\,dy = \oint_C (f_1\,dx + f_2\,dy) \tag{A-117}$$

For the evaluation of μ_x, we can take $f_2 = \frac{1}{2}x^2$ and $f_1 = 0$ in the preceding transformation, so that

$$\mu_x = \iint_{\text{area}} x\,dx\,dy = \frac{1}{2}\oint_C x^2\,dy \tag{A-118}$$

From the parametric representations A-113 for the polygon edges, we have

$$x^2 = x_k^2 + 2x_k(x_{k+1} - x_k)u + (x_{k+1} - x_k)^2u^2$$

and

$$dy = (y_{k+1} - y_k)\,du$$

for each of the n edges, labeled $k = 1, 2, \ldots, n$. Therefore,

$$\begin{aligned} \mu_x &= \sum_{k=1}^{n} \frac{y_{k+1} - y_k}{2} \int_0^1 \left[x_k^2 + 2x_k(x_{k+1} - x_k)u + (x_{k+1} - x_k)^2u^2\right] du \\ &= \frac{1}{6}\sum_{k=1}^{n}(x_{k+1} + x_k)(x_k y_{k+1} - x_{k+1}y_k) \end{aligned} \tag{A-119}$$

For the evaluation of μ_y, we make the substitutions $f_1 = -\frac{1}{2}y^2$ and $f_2 = 0$ in Green's theorem, and we obtain

$$\mu_y = \iint_{\text{area}} y\,dx\,dy = \frac{1}{2}\oint_C y^2\,dx \tag{A-120}$$

Using the parametric representations A-113 to evaluate the line integral, we have

$$\mu_y = \frac{1}{6}\sum_{k=1}^{n}(y_{k+1} + y_k)(x_k y_{k+1} - x_{k+1}y_k) \tag{A-121}$$

Given any set of polygon vertices, we then use the expressions for A, μ_x, and μ_y in Eqs. A-116 to compute the polygon centroid coordinates. Since the expression $(x_k y_{k+1} - x_{k+1}y_k)$ appears in the calculations for all three quantities, A, μ_x, and μ_y, we compute this once for each line segment.

A-13 CALCULATING PROPERTIES OF POLYHEDRA

Methods similar to those for polygons are used to obtain polyhedra properties. But now we compute the spatial volume, instead of an area, and the centroid is obtained by averaging the coordinate positions throughout the volume of a polyhedron.

The volume of any spatial region is defined in Cartesian coordinates as

$$V = \iiint_{\text{vol}} dx\,dy\,dz \tag{A-122}$$

This integral can be converted to a surface integral using one of the transformation equations A-110. For a polyhedron, the surface integral can then be evaluated using a parametric representation for positions across each face of the solid.

We calculate the centroid positions for polyhedra using methods similar to those for polygons. By definition, the Cartesian-coordinate centroid position for a region of space (with unit mass per unit volume) is the average of all positions within the region:

$$\begin{aligned}
\overline{x} &= \frac{1}{V}\iiint_{\text{vol}} x\,dx\,dy\,dz = \frac{\mu_x}{V} \\
\overline{y} &= \frac{1}{V}\iiint_{\text{vol}} y\,dx\,dy\,dz = \frac{\mu_y}{V} \\
\overline{z} &= \frac{1}{V}\iiint_{\text{vol}} z\,dx\,dy\,dz = \frac{\mu_z}{V}
\end{aligned} \tag{A-123}$$

Again, we can convert the volume integrals to surface integrals, substitute parametric representations for the Cartesian coordinates, and evaluate the surface integrals over the faces of a polyhedron.

A-14 NUMERICAL METHODS

In computer-graphics algorithms, it is often necessary to solve sets of linear equations, nonlinear equations, integral equations, and other functional forms. Also, to visualize a discrete set of data points, it may be useful to display a continuous curve or surface function that approximates the points of the data set. In this section, we briefly summarize some common algorithms for solving various numerical problems.

Solving Sets of Linear Equations

For variables x_k, with $k = 1, 2, \ldots, n$, we can write a system of n linear equations as

$$\begin{aligned}
a_{11}x_1 + a_{12}x_2 + \cdots + a_{1n}x_n &= b_1 \\
a_{21}x_1 + a_{22}x_2 + \cdots + a_{2n}x_n &= b_2 \\
&\vdots \\
a_{n1}x_1 + a_{n2}x_2 + \cdots + a_{nn}x_n &= b_n
\end{aligned} \tag{A-124}$$

where the values for parameters a_{jk} and b_j are known. This set of equations can be expressed in the matrix form

$$\mathbf{A}\,\mathbf{X} = \mathbf{B} \tag{A-125}$$

with **A** as an n by n square matrix whose elements are the coefficients a_{jk}, **X** as the column matrix of x_j values, and **B** as the column matrix of b_j values. Solving this matrix equation for **X**, we obtain

$$\mathbf{X} = \mathbf{A}^{-1}\mathbf{B} \tag{A-126}$$

This system of equations can be solved if and only if **A** is a nonsingular matrix; that is, its determinant is nonzero. Otherwise, the inverse of matrix **A** does not exist.

One method for solving the set of equations is **Cramer's rule**:

$$x_k = \frac{\det \mathbf{A}_k}{\det \mathbf{A}} \tag{A-127}$$

where $\mathbf{A}_k$ is the matrix **A** with the kth column replaced with the elements of **B**. This method is adequate for problems with a few variables. For more than three or four variables, however, the method is extremely inefficient due to the large number of multiplications needed to evaluate each determinant. Evaluation of a single n by n determinant requires more than $n!$ multiplications.

We can solve the system of equations more efficiently using variations of **Gaussian elimination.** The basic ideas in Gaussian elimination can be illustrated with the following set of two simultaneous equations.

$$\begin{aligned} x_1 + 2x_2 &= -4 \\ 3x_1 + 4x_2 &= 1 \end{aligned} \tag{A-128}$$

To solve this set of equations, we can multiply the first equation by -3, then add the two equations to eliminate the x_1 term, yielding the equation

$$-2x_2 = 13$$

which has the solution $x_2 = -13/2$. This value is then substituted into either of the original equations to obtain the solution for x_1, which is 9. We can use this basic approach to solve any set of linear equations, but algorithms have been devised to perform the elimination and back substitution steps more efficiently.

A modification of Gaussian elimination is the **LU decomposition** (or **LU factorization**) method for solving sets of linear equations. In this algorithm, we first factor matrix **A** into two matrices, called a lower-diagonal matrix **L** and an upper-diagonal matrix **U**, such that

$$\mathbf{A} = \mathbf{L}\,\mathbf{U} \tag{A-129}$$

All elements of matrix **L** above its diagonal have the value 0, and all diagonal elements have the value 1. All elements of matrix **U** below the diagonal have the value 0. We can then write Eq. A-125 as

$$\mathbf{L}\,\mathbf{U}\,\mathbf{X} = \mathbf{B} \tag{A-130}$$

This allows us to solve the following two very much simpler sets of equations.

$$\mathbf{L}\,\mathbf{Y} = \mathbf{B}, \qquad \mathbf{U}\,\mathbf{X} = \mathbf{Y} \tag{A-131}$$

Once we have the values for the elements of matrix **Y** in Eq. A-131, we use these in the second set of equations to solve for the elements of matrix **X**. As an example, the following equation demonstrates the factorization for a 2 by 2 coefficient matrix.

$$\mathbf{A} = \begin{bmatrix} 2 & 3 \\ 8 & 5 \end{bmatrix} = \begin{bmatrix} 1 & 0 \\ 4 & 1 \end{bmatrix} \begin{bmatrix} 2 & 3 \\ 0 & -7 \end{bmatrix}$$

One method for computing the elements of the factorization matrices is given in the following set of equations, where u_{ij} are the elements for the upper-triangular matrix **U** and l_{ij} are the elements for the lower-triangular matrix **L**.

$$\begin{aligned}
u_{1j} &= a_{1j}, \qquad j = 1, 2, \ldots, n \\
l_{i1} &= \frac{a_{i1}}{u_{11}}, \qquad i = 2, 3, \ldots, n \\
u_{ij} &= a_{ij} - \sum_{k=1}^{i-1} l_{ik} u_{kj} \qquad j = i, i+1, \ldots, n; \;\; i \geq 2 \\
l_{ij} &= \frac{1}{u_{jj}} \left(a_{ij} - \sum_{k=1}^{j-1} l_{ik} u_{kj} \right) \qquad i = j+1, j+2, \ldots, n; \;\; j \geq 2
\end{aligned} \tag{A-132}$$

Gaussian elimination is sometimes susceptible to high round-off errors, and other methods might not produce an accurate solution. In such cases, we may be able to obtain a solution using the *Gauss-Seidel method*. This method is also an efficient way to solve the set of linear equations when we know the approximate values for the solution. In the Gauss-Seidel approach, we start with an initial "guess" for the values of variables x_k, then repeatedly calculate successive approximations until the difference between two successive values for each x_k is small. At each step, we calculate the approximate values for the variables as

$$\begin{aligned}
x_1 &= \frac{b_1 - a_{12}x_2 - a_{13}x_3 - \cdots - a_{1n}x_n}{a_{11}} \\
x_2 &= \frac{b_2 - a_{21}x_1 - a_{23}x_3 - \cdots - a_{2n}x_n}{a_{22}} \\
&\vdots
\end{aligned} \tag{A-133}$$

If we can rearrange matrix **A** so that each diagonal element has a magnitude greater than the sum of the magnitudes of the other elements across that row, than the Gauss-Seidel method is guaranteed to converge to a solution.

Finding Roots of Nonlinear Equations

A root of a function $f(x)$ is a value for x that satisfies the equation $f(x) = 0$. In general, the function $f(x)$ can be an algebraic expression, such as a polynomial, or it can involve transcendental functions. An algebraic expression is one that contains only the arithmetic operators, exponents, roots, and powers. Transcendental functions, such as the trigonometric functions, log functions, and exponential functions, are represented with infinite power series.

Roots of a nonlinear equation can be real numbers, complex numbers, or a combination of real and complex numbers. Sometimes we can obtain exact solutions for all roots, depending on the complexity of the equation. For example, we know how to find an exact solution for any polynomial up to degree 4, and the roots of a simple transcendental equation such as $\sin x = 0$ are known to be

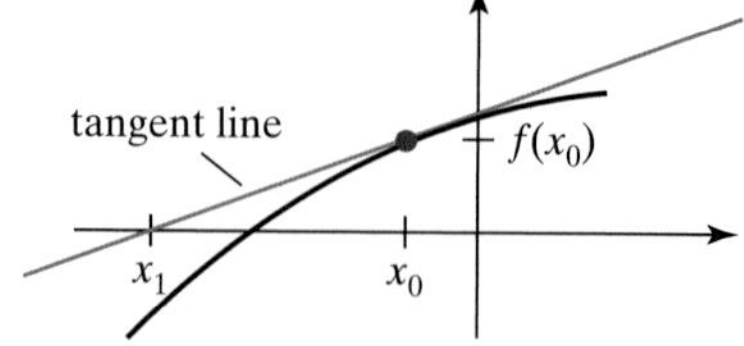

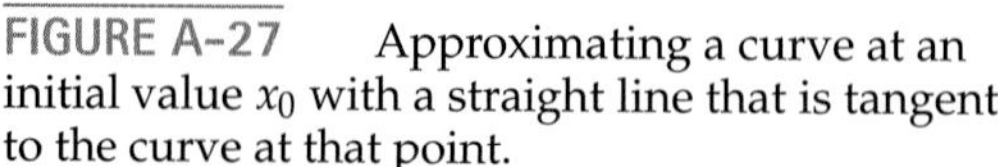
FIGURE A-27 Approximating a curve at an initial value x_0 with a straight line that is tangent to the curve at that point.

$x = k\pi$ for any integer value of k. But in most cases of practical interest, we need to apply numerical procedures to obtain the roots of a nonlinear equation.

One of the most popular methods for finding roots of nonlinear equations is the **Newton-Raphson Algorithm.** This is an iterative procedure that approximates $f(x)$ as a linear function at each step of the iteration, as shown in Fig. A-27. We start with an initial "guess" x_0 for the value of the root, then calculate the next approximation to the root, x_1, by determining where the tangent line from x_0 crosses the x axis. At x_0, the slope (first derivative) of the curve is

$$\frac{df}{dx} = \frac{f(x_0)}{x_0 - x_1} \tag{A-134}$$

Thus the next approximation to the root is

$$x_1 = x_0 - \frac{f(x_0)}{f'(x_0)} \tag{A-135}$$

where $f'(x_0)$ denotes the derivative of $f(x)$ evaluated at $x = x_0$. We repeat this procedure at each calculated approximation until the difference between successive approximations is "small enough".

In addition to solving problems involving real variables, the Newton-Raphson algorithm can be applied to a function of a complex variable $f(z)$, to a function of several variables, and to sets of simultaneous nonlinear functions, real or complex. And, if the Newton-Raphson algorithm converges to a root, it will converge faster than any other root-finding method. But it may not always converge. For example, the method fails if the derivative $f'(x)$ evaluates to 0 at some point in the iteration. Also, depending on the oscillations of the curve, successive approximations may diverge from the position of a root.

Another method, slower but guaranteed to converge, is the **bisection method.** In this algorithm, we must identify an x interval that contains a root. Then we apply a binary-search procedure within that interval to close in on the root. We first look at the midpoint of the interval to determine whether the root is in the lower or upper half of the interval. This procedure is repeated for each successive subinterval until the difference between successive midpoint positions is smaller than some preset value. A speedup can be attained by interpolating successive x positions instead of halving each subinterval (*false-position method*).

Evaluating Integrals

Integration is a summation process. For a function of a single variable x, the integral of $f(x)$ is equal to the area "under" the curve, as illustrated in Fig. A-28. For simple integrands, we can often determine a functional form for an integral, but, in general, we evaluate integrals using numerical methods.

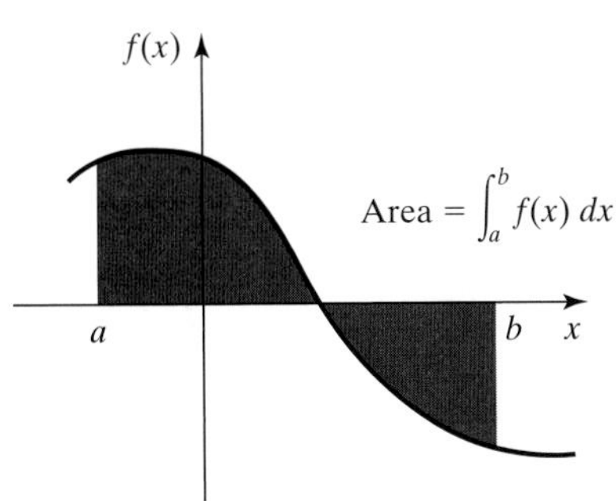

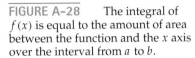

FIGURE A-28 The integral of $f(x)$ is equal to the amount of area between the function and the x axis over the interval from a to b.

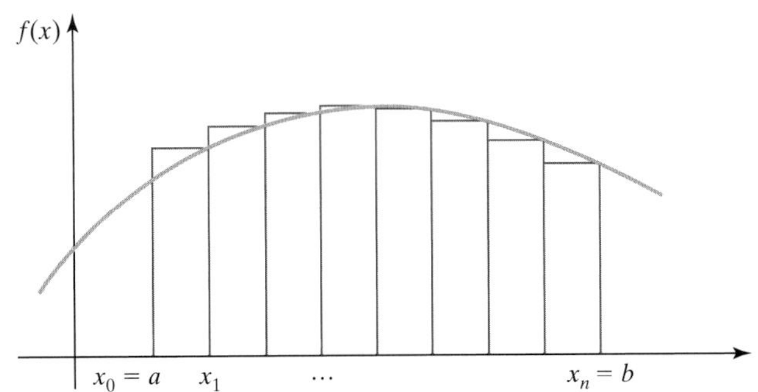

FIGURE A-29 Approximating an integral as the sum of the areas of small rectangles.

From the definition of an integral, we can form the following numerical approximation.

$$\int_a^b f(x)\,dx \approx \sum_{k=1}^{n} f_k(x)\Delta x_k \qquad \text{(A-136)}$$

The function $f_k(x)$ is an approximation to $f(x)$ over the interval Δx_k. For example, we can approximate the curve with a constant value in each subinterval and add the areas of the resulting rectangles (Fig. A-29). This approximation improves, up to a point, as we decrease the size of the subdivisions across the interval from a to b. If the subdivisions are too small, the values of successive rectangular areas can be lost in the round-off error.

Polynomial approximations for the function in each subinterval generally give better results than the rectangle approach. Using a linear approximation, the resulting subareas are trapezoids, and the approximation method is then referred to as the **trapezoid rule.** If we use a quadratic polynomial (parabola) to approximate the function in each subinterval, the method is called **Simpson's rule** and the integral approximation is

$$\int_a^b f(x)\,dx \approx \frac{\Delta x}{3}\left[f(a) + f(b) + 4\sum_{(\text{odd})k=1}^{n-1} f(x_k) + 2\sum_{(\text{even})k=2}^{n-2} f(x_k)\right] \qquad \text{(A-137)}$$

In this expression, the interval from a to b is divided into the n equal-width intervals

$$\Delta x = \frac{b-a}{n} \qquad \text{(A-138)}$$

where n is a multiple of 2, and with

$$x_0 = a, \qquad x_k = x_{k-1} + \Delta x, \qquad k = 1, 2, \ldots, n$$

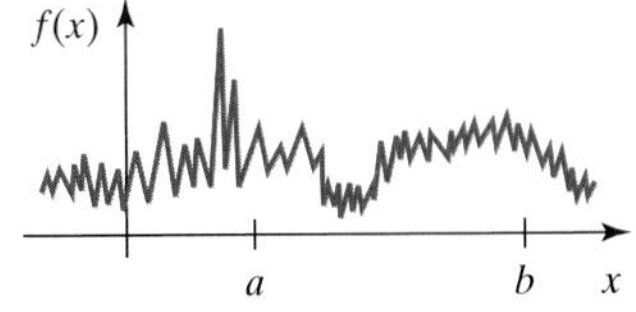

FIGURE A-30 A function with high-frequency oscillations.

For a function with a rapidly varying amplitude, such as the example in Fig. A-30, it may be difficult to accurately approximate the function over the subintervals. Also, multiple integrals (involving several integration variables) are

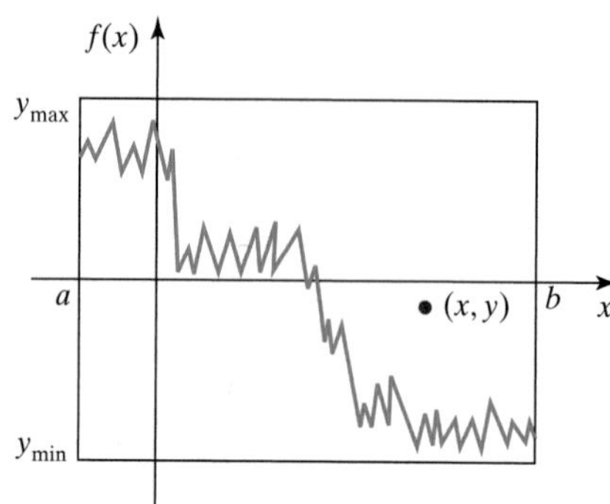

FIGURE A-31 A random position (x, y) generated within a rectangular area enclosing the function $f(x)$ over the interval from a to b.

not easy to evaluate with Simpson's rule or the other approximation methods. In these cases, we can apply **Monte Carlo** integration techniques. The term Monte Carlo is used to describe any method that employs random-number procedures to solve a deterministic problem.

We apply a Monte Carlo method to evaluate an integral by generating n random positions within a rectangular area that contains $f(x)$ over the interval from a to b (Fig. A-31). An approximation for the integral is then calculated as

$$\int_a^b f(x)\,dx \approx h(b-a)\frac{n_{\text{count}}}{n} \tag{A-139}$$

where parameter h is the rectangle height and parameter n_{count} is the number of random points that are between $f(x)$ and the x axis. A random position (x, y) in the rectangular region is computed by first generating two random numbers, r_1 and r_2, then carrying out the calculations

$$h = y_{\max} - y_{\min}, \qquad x = a + r_1(b-a), \qquad y = y_{\min} + r_2 h \tag{A-140}$$

Similar methods can be applied to multiple integrals.

In the calculations for x and y in A-140, we assume that the random numbers r_1 and r_2 are uniformly distributed over the interval (0, 1). We can obtain r_1 and r_2 from a random-number function in a mathematics or statistical library, or we can use the following algorithm, called the *linear congruential generator*:

$$\begin{aligned} i_k &= a\, i_{k-1} + c(\text{mod } m), \qquad k = 1, 2, 3, \ldots \\ r_k &= \frac{i_k}{m} \end{aligned} \tag{A-141}$$

where parameters a, c, m, and i_0 are integers, and i_0 is a starting value called the *seed*. Parameter m is chosen to be as large as possible on a particular machine, with values for a and c chosen to make the string of random numbers as long as possible before a value is repeated. For example, on a machine with 32-bit integer representations, we can set $m = 2^{32} - 1$, $a = 1664525$, and $c = 1013904223$.

Solving Ordinary Differential Equations

Any equation containing differential rate-of-change operators is referred to as a differential equation. Quantities can change values in some continuous way from one coordinate position to another. They can also change over time at a fixed position, and they can change with respect to many other parameters, such as temperature or rotational acceleration. An equation that involves derivatives of a function of a single variable is called an *ordinary differential equation.* We solve a differential equation either by determining a functional form that satisfies the equation or by using numerical approximation methods to determine the values for the quantity at selected intervals.

To solve a differential equation, we also need to know one or more starting values. An equation involving only the first derivative of a quantity, called a *first-order differential equation,* requires one starting value. An equation that contains both first and second derivatives, called a *second-order differential equation,* requires two starting values. And similarly for equations involving higher-order derivatives. There are two basic classifications for specifying starting values. An **initial-value problem** is one in which the known conditions are specified for a single value of the independent variable. A **boundary-value problem** is one in which the known conditions are specified at the boundaries for the dependent variable.

A simple example of an initial-value problem is the first-order differential equation

$$\frac{dx}{dt} = f(x, t), \qquad x(t_0) = x_0 \tag{A-142}$$

where x represents some dependent variable that varies with time t (the independent variable), $f(x, t)$ is the known time-variation function for the first derivative of x, and x_0 is the given value for x at the initial time t_0. We can also write this equation in the form

$$dx = f(x, t)\, dt$$

And, from the definition of a derivative, we can use finite intervals to approximate the differentials as

$$\Delta x_k \approx f(x_k, t_k)\Delta t_k, \qquad k = 0, 1, \ldots, n \tag{A-143}$$

where $\Delta x_k = x_{k+1} - x_k$ and $\Delta t_k = t_{k+1} - t_k$, for n time steps. Typically, we take equal time intervals and use the following incremental calculations to determine the x values at each time step, given the value of x_0 at t_0.

$$x_{k+1} = x_k + f(x_k, t_k)\Delta t \tag{A-144}$$

This numerical procedure is called the **Euler method,** and it approximates x with straight-line segments over each time interval Δt.

Although the Euler method is a simple procedure to implement, in general it is not very accurate. Improvements to this basic numerical algorithm have been developed from the following Taylor series expansion by incorporating higher-order terms into the approximation for the differential equation.

$$x(t + \Delta t) = x(t) + x'(t)\Delta t + \frac{1}{2}x''(t)\Delta t^2 + \cdots \tag{A-145}$$

Since $x'(t) = f(x, t)$, we have $x''(t) = f'(x, t)$, and so forth for the higher derivatives.

A more accurate, and more widely used, method for evaluating a first-order differential equation is the **Runge-Kutta algorithm,** also called the **fourth-order Runge-Kutta algorithm.** This procedure is based on a Taylor series expansion up to fourth order. The algorithm for the Runge-Kutta method is

$$\begin{aligned} a &= f(x_k, t_k)\Delta t \\ b &= f(x_k + a/2,\ t_k + \Delta t/2)\Delta t \\ c &= f(x_k + b/2,\ t_k + \Delta t/2)\Delta t \\ d &= f(x_k + c,\ t_k + \Delta t)\Delta t \\ t_{k+1} &= t_k + \Delta t \\ x_{k+1} &= x_k + (a + 2b + 2c + d)/6, \qquad k = 0, 1, \ldots n-1 \end{aligned} \tag{A-146}$$

We can apply similar methods to obtain solutions for ordinary differential equations of higher order. The general approach is to use the Taylor series expansion for x to include terms in x'', x''', and so forth, depending on the order of the differential equation. For example, from the Taylor series, we can obtain the following approximation for the second derivative.

$$x''(t_k) \approx \frac{x_{k+1} - 2x_k + x_{k-1}}{\Delta t^2} \tag{A-147}$$

Solving Partial Differential Equations

As we might expect, partial differential equations are generally more difficult to solve than ordinary differential equations. But we can apply similar methods and replace the partial derivatives with finite differences.

We first consider a function $f(x, t)$ that depends only on the x coordinate and time t. We can reduce a partial differential equation involving $\partial f/\partial x$ and $\partial f/\partial t$ to an ordinary differential equation by replacing the spatial derivative with finite differences. This allows us to replace the function of two variables with a one-subscript function of a single variable, time:

$$f(x, t) \rightarrow f(x_k, t) \rightarrow f_k(t) \tag{A-148}$$

The partial derivatives are then replaced with the following expressions.

$$\begin{aligned} \frac{\partial f}{\partial x} &= \frac{f_{k+1} - f_k}{\Delta x} \\ \frac{\partial f}{\partial t} &= \frac{df_k}{dt} \end{aligned} \tag{A-149}$$

Then we solve the equations at a finite number of x positions using the given initial or boundary conditions.

For higher-order derivatives, we can use Taylor series expansions to obtain the finite-difference approximations. As an example, we can use the following approximation for the second partial derivative of f with respect to x.

$$\frac{\partial^2 f(x, t)}{\partial x^2} \rightarrow \frac{f_{k+1}(t) - 2f_k(t) + f_{k-1}(t)}{\Delta x^2} \tag{A-150}$$

And when we have functions defined over surfaces or volumes of space, we can divide the space into a regular grid and use finite differences for each spatial coordinate.

Another approach that is applied to partial differential equations is the *finite-element method.* A grid of coordinate positions is set up over the domain of interest, which could be a surface or a volume of space, and then the coupled equations are solved at the node positions using variational techniques. In this method, an approximating functional solution is used instead of finite-difference equations. Depending on the problem, an integral is set up for some quantity such as potential energy or residual error. Then some procedure, such as a least-square analysis, is applied to minimize the potential energy or residual error. This minimization yields values for the unknown parameters in the approximating function for the solution.

Least-Squares Curve-Fitting Methods for Data Sets

When a computer simulation or scientific-visualization study produces a set of data values, we almost always want to determine a functional form that will describe the data set. The standard method for producing a function that fits the given data is the **least-squares algorithm.** To apply this method, we first choose a general type for the function, such as a linear function, a polynomial function, or an exponential function. We then must determine the values for the parameters in the functional form we have chosen. A two-dimensional straight-line function, for example, can be described with two parameters: the slope and the y intercept. We obtain the function parameters by minimizing the sum of the squares of the differences between the theoretical function values and the actual data values.

To illustrate this method, we first consider a two-dimensional set of n data points, labeled (x_k, y_k) with $k = 1, 2, \ldots, n$. After we have selected the functional form $f(x)$ that we want to use to describe the data distribution, we set up an expression for an error function E, which is the sum of the squares of the differences between $f(x_k)$ and the data values y_k:

$$E = \sum_{k=1}^{n} [y_k - f(x_k)]^2 \tag{A-151}$$

Parameters in the function $f(x)$ are then determined by minimizing the error expression E.

As an example, if the data set is to be described with the linear function

$$f(x) = a_0 + a_1 x$$

then

$$E = \sum_{k=1}^{n} \left[y_k^2 - 2y_k(a_0 + a_1 x_k) + a_0^2 + 2a_0 a_1 x_k + a_1^2 x_k^2\right] \tag{A-152}$$

Since the error E is a function of two variables (a_0 and a_1), we minimize E with the following two coupled equations.

$$\begin{aligned} \frac{\partial E}{\partial a_0} &= \sum_{k=1}^{n} [-2y_k + 2a_0 + 2a_1 x_k] = 0 \\ \frac{\partial E}{\partial a_1} &= \sum_{k=1}^{n} \left[-2y_k x_k + 2a_0 x_k + 2a_1 x_k^2\right] = 0 \end{aligned} \tag{A-153}$$

We can then solve this set of two linear equations using Cramer's rule, which yields

$$a_0 = \frac{(\sum_k x_k^2)(\sum_k y_k) - (\sum_k x_k)(\sum_k x_k y_k)}{D}$$
$$a_1 = \frac{n \sum_k x_k y_k - (\sum_k x_k)(\sum_k y_k)}{D} \tag{A-154}$$

where the denominator in these two expressions is

$$D = \begin{vmatrix} n & \sum_k x_k \\ \sum_k x_k & \sum_k x_k^2 \end{vmatrix} = \sum_{k=1}^{n} x_k^2 - \left(\sum_{k=1}^{n} x_k\right)^2 \tag{A-155}$$

Similar calculations are carried out for other functions. For the polynomial

$$f(x) = a_0 + a_1 x + a_2 x^2 + \cdots + a_n x^n$$

for instance, we need to solve a set of n linear equations to determine values for parameters a_k. And we can also apply least-squares fitting to functions of several variables $f(x_1, x_2, \ldots, x_m)$ which could be linear or nonlinear in each of the variables.

Bibliography

AKELEY, K. and T. JERMOLUK (1988). "High-Performance Polygon Rendering", in proceedings of SIGGRAPH '88, *Computer Graphics*, 22(4), pp. 239–246.

AKELEY, K. (1993). "RealityEngine Graphics", in proceedings of SIGGRAPH '93, *Computer Graphics*, pp. 109–116.

AKENINE-MÖLLER, T. and E. HAINES (2002). *Real-Time Rendering, Second Edition*, A. K. Peters, Natick, MA.

AMANATIDES, J. (1984). "Ray Tracing with Cones", in proceedings of SIGGRAPH '84, *Computer Graphics*, 18(3), pp. 129–135.

ANJYO, K., Y. USAMI, and T. KURIHARA (1992). "A Simple Method for Extracting the Natural Beauty of Hair", in proceedings of SIGGRAPH '92, *Computer Graphics*, 26(2), pp. 111–120.

APPLE COMPUTER, INC. (1987). *Human Interface Guidelines: The Apple Desktop Interface*, Addison-Wesley, Reading, MA.

ARVO, J. and D. KIRK (1987). "Fast Ray Tracing by Ray Classification", in proceedings of SIGGRAPH '87, *Computer Graphics*, 21(4), pp. 55–64.

ARVO, J., ed. (1991). *Graphics Gems II*, Academic Press, San Diego, CA.

ATHERTON, P. R. (1983). "A Scan-Line Hidden Surface Removal Procedure for Constructive Solid Geometry", in proceedings of SIGGRAPH '83, *Computer Graphics*, 17(3), pp. 73–82.

BARAFF, D. (1989). "Analytical Methods for Dynamic Simulation of Non-Penetrating Rigid Bodies", in proceedings of SIGGRAPH '89, *Computer Graphics*, 23(3), pp. 223–232.

BARAFF, D. and A. WITKIN (1992). "Dynamic Simulation of Non-Penetrating Flexible Bodies", in proceedings of SIGGRAPH '92, *Computer Graphics*, 26(2), pp. 303–308.

BARNSLEY, M. F., A. JACQUIN, F. MALASSENET, L. REUTER, and D. SLOAN (1988). "Harnessing Chaos for Image Synthesis", in proceedings of SIGGRAPH '88, *Computer Graphics*, 22(4), pp. 131–140.

BARNSLEY, M. F. (1993). *Fractals Everywhere, Second Edition*, Academic Press, San Diego, CA.

BARNSLEY, M. F. and L. P. HURD, (1993). *Fractal Image Compression*, AK Peters, Wellesly, MA.

BARR, A. H. (1981). "Superquadrics and Angle-Preserving Transformations", *IEEE Computer Graphics and Applications*, 1(1), pp. 11–23.

BARSKY, B. A. and J. C. BEATTY (1983). "Local Control of Bias and Tension in Beta-Splines", *ACM Transactions on Graphics*, 2(2), pp. 109–134.

BARSKY, B. A. (1984). "A Description and Evaluation of Various 3-D Models", *IEEE Computer Graphics and Applications*, 4(1), pp. 38–52.

BARZEL, R. and A. H. BARR (1988). "A Modeling System Based on Dynamic Constraints", in proceedings of SIGGRAPH '88, *Computer Graphics*, 22(4), pp. 179–188.

BARZEL, R. (1992). *Physically-Based Modeling for Computer Graphics*, Academic Press, San Diego, CA.

BAUM, D. R., S. MANN, K. P. SMITH, and J. M. WINGET (1991). "Making Radiosity Usable: Automatic Preprocessing and Meshing Techniques for the Generation of Accurate Radiosity Solutions", in proceedings of SIGGRAPH '91, *Computer Graphics*, 25(4), pp. 51–61.

BERGMAN, L. D., J. S. RICHARDSON, D. C. RICHARDSON, and F. P. BROOKS, JR. (1993). "VIEW—an Exploratory Molecular Visualization System with User-Definable Interaction Sequences", in proceedings of SIGGRAPH '93, *Computer Graphics*, pp. 117–126.

BÉZIER, P. (1972). *Numerical Control: Mathematics and Applications*, translated by A. R. Forrest and A. F. Pankhurst, John Wiley & Sons, London.

BIRN, J. (2000). *[digital] Lighting & Rendering*, New Riders Publishing, Indianapolis, IN.

BISHOP, G. and D. M. WIEMER (1986). "Fast Phong Shading", in proceedings of SIGGRAPH '86, *Computer Graphics*, 20(4), pp. 103–106.

BLAKE, J. W. (1993). *PHIGS and PHIGS Plus*, Academic Press, London.

BLESER, T. (1988). "TAE Plus Styleguide User Interface Description", NASA Goddard Space Flight Center, Greenbelt, MD.

BLINN, J. F. and M. E. NEWELL (1976). "Texture and Reflection in Computer-Generated Images", *Communications of the ACM*, 19(10), pp. 542–547.

BLINN, J. F. (1977). "Models of Light Reflection for Computer-Synthesized Pictures", in proceedings of SIGGRAPH '77, *Computer Graphics*, 11(2), pp. 192–198.

BLINN, J. F. and M. E. NEWELL (1978). "Clipping Using Homogeneous Coordinates", in proceedings of SIGGRAPH '78, *Computer Graphics*, 12(3), pp. 245–251.

BLINN, J. F. (1978). "Simulation of Wrinkled Surfaces", in proceedings of SIGGRAPH '78, *Computer Graphics*, 12(3), pp. 286–292.

BLINN, J. F. (1982). "A Generalization of Algebraic Surface Drawing", *ACM Transactions on Graphics*, 1(3), pp. 235–256.

BLINN, J. F. (1982). "Light Reflection Functions for Simulation of Clouds and Dusty Surfaces", in proceedings of SIGGRAPH '82, *Computer Graphics*, 16(3), pp. 21–29.

BLINN, J. F. (1993). "A Trip Down the Graphics Pipeline: The Homogeneous Perspective Transform", *IEEE Computer Graphics and Applications*, 13(3), pp. 75–80.

BLINN, J. (1996). *Jim Blinn's Corner: A Trip Down the Graphics Pipeline*, Morgan Kauffman, San Francisco, CA.

BLINN, J. (1998). *Jim Blinn's Corner: Dirty Pixels*, Morgan Kauffman, San Francisco, CA.

BLOOMENTHAL, J. (1985). "Modeling the Mighty Maple", in proceedings of SIGGRAPH '85, *Computer Graphics*, 19(3), pp. 305–312.

BONO, P. R., J. L. ENCARNACAO, F. R. A. HOPGOOD, et al. (1982). "GKS: The First Graphics Standard", *IEEE Computer Graphics and Applications*, 2(5), pp. 9–23.

BOUQUET, D. L. (1978). "An Interactive Graphics Application to Advanced Aircraft Design", in proceedings of SIGGRAPH '78, *Computer Graphics*, 12(3), pp. 330–335.

BOURG, D. M. (2002). *Physics for Game Developers*, O'Reilly & Associates, Sebastopol, CA.

BRESENHAM, J. E. (1965). "Algorithm for Computer Control of a Digital Plotter", *IBM Systems Journal*, 4(1), pp. 25–30.

BRESENHAM, J. E. (1977). "A Linear Algorithm for Incremental Digital Display of Circular Arcs", *Communications of the ACM*, 20(2), pp. 100–106.

BROOKS JR., F. P. (1986). "Walkthrough: A Dynamic Graphics System for Simulating Virtual Buildings", *Interactive 3D*.

BROOKS JR., F. P. (1988). "Grasping Reality Through Illusion: Interactive Graphics Serving Science", *CHI '88*, pp. 1–11.

BROOKS JR., F. P., M. OUH-YOUNG, J. J. BATTER, and P. J. KILPATRICK (1990). "Project GROPE—Haptic Display for Scientific Visualization", in proceedings of SIGGRAPH '90, *Computer Graphics*, 24(4), pp. 177–185.

BROWN, J. R. and S. CUNNINGHAM (1989). *Programming the User Interface*, John Wiley & Sons, New York.

BROWN, C. W. and B. J. SHEPHERD (1995). *Graphics File Formats*, Manning Publications, Greenwich, CT.

BRUDERLIN, A. and T. W. CALVERT (1989). "Goal-Directed, Dynamic Animation of Human Walking", in proceedings of SIGGRAPH '89, *Computer Graphics*, 23(3), pp. 233–242.

BRUNET, P. and I. NAVAZO (1990). "Solid Representation and Operation Using Extended Octrees", *ACM Transactions on Graphics*, 9(2), pp. 170–197.

BRYSON, S. and C. LEVIT (1992). "The Virtual Wind Tunnel", *IEEE Computer Graphics and Applications*, 12(4), pp. 25–34.

CALVERT, T., A. BRUDERLIN, J. DILL, T. SCHIPHORST, and C. WEILMAN (1993). "Desktop Animation of Multiple Human Figures", *IEEE Computer Graphics and Applications*, 13(3), pp. 18–26.

CAMBELL, G., T. A. DEFANTI, J. FREDERIKSEN, S. A. JOYCE, and L. A. LESKE (1986). "Two Bit/Pixel Full-Color Encoding", in proceedings of SIGGRAPH '86, *Computer Graphics*, 20(4), pp. 215–224.

CARPENTER, L. (1984). "The A-Buffer: An Antialiased Hidden-Surface Method", in proceedings of SIGGRAPH '84, *Computer Graphics*, 18(3), pp. 103–108.

CHEN, S. E., H. E. RUSHMEIER, G. MILLER, and D. TURNER (1991). "A Progressive Multi-Pass Method for Global Illumination", in proceedings of SIGGRAPH '91, *Computer Graphics*, 25(4), pp. 165–174.

CHIN, N. and S. FEINER (1989). "Near Real-Time Shadow Generation Using BSP Trees", in proceedings of SIGGRAPH '89, *Computer Graphics*, 23(3), pp. 99–106.

CHUNG, J. C., et al. (1989). "Exploring Virtual Worlds with Head-Mounted Visual Displays", *Proceedings of the SPIE (Society of Photo-Optical Instrumentation Engineers, now called the International Society for Optical Engineering) Conference on Three-Dimensional Visualization and Display Technologies*, 1083, January 1989, pp. 15–20.

COHEN, M. F. and D. P. GREENBERG (1985). "The Hemi-Cube: A Radiosity Solution for Complex Environments", in proceedings of SIGGRAPH '85, *Computer Graphics*, 19(3), pp. 31–40.

COHEN, M. F., S. E. CHEN, J. R. WALLACE, and D. P. GREENBERG (1988). "A Progressive Refinement Approach to Fast Radiosity Image Generation", in proceedings of SIGGRAPH '88, *Computer Graphics*, 22(4), pp. 75–84.

COHEN, M. F. and J. R. WALLACE (1993). *Radiosity and Realistic Image Synthesis*, Academic Press, Boston, MA.

COOK, R. L. and K. E. TORRANCE (1982). "A Reflectance Model for Computer Graphics", *ACM Transactions on Graphics*, 1(1), pp. 7–24.

COOK, R. L., T. PORTER, and L. CARPENTER (1984). "Distributed Ray Tracing", in proceedings of SIGGRAPH '84, *Computer Graphics*, 18(3), pp. 137–145.

COOK, R. L. (1984). "Shade Trees", in proceedings of SIGGRAPH '84, *Computer Graphics*, 18(3), pp. 223–231.

COOK, R. L. (1986). "Stochastic Sampling in Computer Graphics", *ACM Transactions on Graphics*, 6(1), pp. 51–72.

COOK, R. L., L. CARPENTER, and E. CATMULL (1987). "The Reyes Image Rendering Architecture", in proceedings of SIGGRAPH '87, *Computer Graphics*, 21(4), pp. 95–102.

COQUILLART, S. and P. JANCENE (1991). "Animated Free-Form Deformation: An Interactive Animation Technique", in proceedings of SIGGRAPH '91, *Computer Graphics*, 25(4), pp. 23–26.

CROW, F. C. (1977a). "The Aliasing Problem in Computer-Synthesized Shaded Images", *Communications of the ACM*, 20(11), pp. 799–805.

CROW, F. C. (1977b). "Shadow Algorithms for Computer Graphics", in proceedings of SIGGRAPH '77, *Computer Graphics*, 11(2), pp. 242–248.

CROW, F. C. (1978). "The Use of Grayscale for Improved Raster Display of Vectors and Characters", in proceedings of SIGGRAPH '78, *Computer Graphics*, 12(3), pp. 1–5.

CROW, F. C. (1981). "A Comparison of Antialiasing Techniques", *IEEE Computer Graphics and Applications*, 1(1), pp. 40–49.

CROW, F. C. (1982). "A More Flexible Image Generation Environment", in proceedings of SIGGRAPH '82, *Computer Graphics*, 16(3), pp. 9–18.

CRUZ-NEIRA, C., D. J. SANDIN, and T. A. DEFANTI (1993). "Surround-Screen Projection-Based Virtual Reality: The Design and Implementation of the CAVE", in proceedings of SIGGRAPH '93, *Computer Graphics*, pp. 135–142.

CUNNINGHAM, S., N. K. CRAIGHILL, M. W. FONG, J. BROWN, and J. R. BROWN, eds. (1992). *Computer Graphics Using Object-Oriented Programming*, John Wiley & Sons, New York.

CUTLER, E., D. GILLY, and T. O'REILLY, eds. (1992). *The X Window System in a Nutshell*, Second Edition, O'Reilly & Assoc., Inc., Sebastopol, CA.

CYRUS, M. and J. BECK (1978). "Generalized Two- and Three-Dimensional Clipping", *Computers and Graphics*, 3(1), pp. 23–28.

DAY, A. M. (1990). "The Implementation of an Algorithm to Find the Convex Hull of a Set of Three-Dimensional Points", *ACM Transactions on Graphics*, 9(1), pp. 105–132.

DEERING, M. (1992). "High Resolution Virtual Reality", in proceedings of SIGGRAPH '92, *Computer Graphics*, 26(2), pp. 195–202.

DEERING, M. F. and S. R. NELSON (1993). "Leo: A System for Cost-Effective 3D Shaded Graphics", in proceedings of SIGGRAPH '93, *Computer Graphics*, pp. 101–108.

DEMERS, O. (2002). *[digital] Texturing & Painting*, New Riders Publishing, Indianapolis, IN.

DEPP, S. W. and W. E. HOWARD (1993). "Flat-Panel Displays", *Scientific American*, 266(3), pp. 90–97.

DE REFFYE, P., C. EDELIN, J. FRANÇON, M. JAEGER, and C. PUECH (1988). "Plant Models Faithful to Botanical Structure and Development", in proceedings of SIGGRAPH '88, *Computer Graphics*, 22(4), pp. 151–158.

DEROSE, T. D. (1988). "Geometric Continuity, Shape Parameters, and Geometric Constructions for Catmull-Rom Splines", *ACM Transactions on Graphics*, 7(1), pp. 1–41.

DIGITAL EQUIPMENT CORP. (1989). "Digital Equipment Corporation XUI Style Guide", Maynard, MA.

DOCTOR, L. J. and J. G. TORBERG (1981). "Display Techniques for Octree-Encoded Objects", *IEEE Computer Graphics and Applications*, 1(3), pp. 29–38.

DORSEY, J. O., F. X. SILLION, and D. P. GREENBERG (1991). "Design and Simulation of Opera Lighting and Projection Effects", in proceedings of SIGGRAPH '91, *Computer Graphics*, 25(4), pp. 41–50.

DREBIN, R. A., L. CARPENTER, and P. HANRAHAN (1988). "Volume Rendering", in proceedings of SIGGRAPH '88, *Computer Graphics*, 22(4), pp. 65–74.

DURRETT, H. J., ed. (1987). *Color and the Computer*, Academic Press, Boston.

DUVANENKO, V. (1990). "Improved Line-Segment Clipping", *Dr. Dobb's Journal*, July 1990.

DYER, S. (1990). "A Dataflow Toolkit for Visualization", *IEEE Computer Graphics and Applications*, 10(4), pp. 60–69.

EARNSHAW, R. A., ed. (1985). *Fundamental Algorithms for Computer Graphics*, Springer-Verlag, Berlin.

EDELSBRUNNER, H. (1987). *Algorithms in Computational Geometry*, Springer-Verlag, Berlin.

EDELSBRUNNER, H. and E. P. MUCKE (1990). "Simulation of Simplicity: A Technique to Cope with Degenerate Cases in Geometric Algorithms", *ACM Transactions on Graphics*, 9(1), pp. 66–104.

ELBER, G. and E. COHEN (1990). "Hidden-Curve Removal for Free-Form Surfaces", in proceedings of SIGGRAPH '90, *Computer Graphics*, 24(4), pp. 95–104.

ENDERLE, G., K. KANSY, and G. PFAFF (1984). *Computer Graphics Programming: GKS—The Graphics Standard*, Springer-Verlag, Berlin.

FARIN, G. (1988). *Curves and Surfaces for Computer-Aided Geometric Design*, Academic Press, Boston, MA.

FARIN, G. and D. HANSFORD (1998). *The Geometry Toolbox for Graphics and Modeling*, A. K. Peters, Natick, MA.

FEDER, J. (1988). *Fractals*, Plenum Press, New York.

FEYNMAN, R. P., R. B. LEIGHTON, and M. L. SANDS (1989). *The Feynman Lectures on Physics*, Addison-Wesley, Reading, MA.

FISHKIN, K. P. and B. A. BARSKY (1984). "A Family of New Algorithms for Soft Filling", in proceedings of SIGGRAPH '84, *Computer Graphics*, 18(3), pp. 235–244.

FIUME, E. L. (1989). *The Mathematical Structure of Raster Graphics*, Academic Press, Boston.

FOLEY, J. D., A. VAN DAM, S. K. FEINER, and J. F. HUGHES (1990). *Computer Graphics: Principles and Practice, Second Edition*, Addison-Wesley, Reading, MA.

FOURNIER, A., D. FUSSEL, and L. CARPENTER (1982). "Computer Rendering of Stochastic Models", *Communications of the ACM*, 25(6), pp. 371–384.

FOURNIER, A. and W. T. REEVES (1986). "A Simple Model of Ocean Waves", in proceedings of SIGGRAPH '86, *Computer Graphics*, 20(4), pp. 75–84.

FOWLER, D. R., H. MEINHARDT, and P. PRUSINKIEWICZ (1992). "Modeling Seashells", in proceedings of SIGGRAPH '92, *Computer Graphics*, 26(2), pp. 379–387.

FRANKLIN, W. R. and M. S. KANKANHALLI (1990). "Parallel Object-Space Hidden Surface Removal", in proceedings of SIGGRAPH '90, *Computer Graphics*, 24(4), pp. 87–94.

FREEMAN, H. ed. (1980). *Tutorial and Selected Readings in Interactive Computer Graphics*, IEEE Computer Society Press, Silver Springs, MD.

FRENKEL, K. A. (1989). "Volume Rendering", *Communications of the ACM*, 32(4), pp. 426–435.

FRIEDER, G., D. GORDON, and R. A. REYNOLD (1985). "Back-to-Front Display of Voxel-Based Objects", *IEEE Computer Graphics and Applications*, 5(1), pp. 52–60.

FRIEDHOFF, R. M. and W. BENZON (1989). *The Second Computer Revolution: Visualization*, Harry N. Abrams, New York.

FU, K. S., and A. ROSENFELD (1984). "Pattern Recognition and Computer Vision", *Computer*, 17(10), pp. 274–282.

FUJIMOTO, A., and K. IWATA (1983). "Jag-Free Images on Raster Displays", *IEEE Computer Graphics and Applications*, 3(9), pp. 26–34.

FUNKHOUSER, T. A. and C. H. SEQUIN (1993). "Adaptive Display Algorithms for Interactive Frame Rates during Visualization of Complex Virtual Environments", in proceedings of SIGGRAPH '93, *Computer Graphics*, pp. 247–254.

GARDNER, T. N., and H. R. NELSON (1983). "Interactive Graphics Developments in Energy Exploration", *IEEE Computer Graphics and Applications*, 3(2), pp. 33–34.

GARDNER, G. Y. (1985). "Visual Simulation of Clouds", in proceedings of SIGGRAPH '85, *Computer Graphics*, 19(3), pp. 297–304.

GASCUEL, M.-P. (1993). "An Implicit Formulation for Precise Contact Modeling between Flexible Solids", in proceedings of SIGGRAPH '93, *Computer Graphics*, pp. 313–320.

GASKINS, T. (1992). *PHIGS Programming Manual*, O'Reilly & Associates, Sebastopol, CA.

GHARACHORLOO, N., S. GUPTA, R. F. SPROULL, and I. E. SUTHERLAND (1989). "A Characterization of Ten Rasterization Techniques", in proceedings of SIGGRAPH '89, *Computer Graphics*, 23(3), pp. 355–368.

GIRARD, M. (1987). "Interactive Design of 3D Computer-Animated Legged Animal Motion", *IEEE Computer Graphics and Applications*, 7(6), pp. 39–51.

GLASSNER, A. S. (1984). "Space Subdivision for Fast Ray Tracing", *IEEE Computer Graphics and Applications*, 4(10), pp. 15–22.

GLASSNER, A. S. (1986). "Adaptive Precision in Texture Mapping", in proceedings of SIGGRAPH '86, *Computer Graphics*, 20(4), pp. 297–306.

GLASSNER, A. S. (1988). "Spacetime Ray Tracing for Animation", *IEEE Computer Graphics and Applications*, 8(2), pp. 60–70.

GLASSNER, A. S., ed. (1989a). *An Introduction to Ray Tracing*, Academic Press, San Diego, CA.

GLASSNER, A. S. (1989b). *3D Computer Graphics: A User's Guide for Artists and Designers, Second Edition*, Design Books, Lyons & Bufford Publishers, New York.

GLASSNER, A. S., ed. (1990). *Graphics Gems*, Academic Press, San Diego, CA.

GLASSNER, A. S. (1992). "Geometric Substitution: A Tutorial", *IEEE Computer Graphics and Applications*, 12(1), pp. 22–36.

GLASSNER, A. S. (1995). *Principles of Digital Image Synthesis, Vols. 1–2*, Morgan Kaufmann, San Francisco, CA.

GLASSNER, A. S. (1999). *Andrew Glassner's Notebook: Recreational Computer Graphics*, Morgan Kaufmann, San Francisco, CA.

GLASSNER, A. S. (2002). *Andrew Glassner's Other Notebook: Further Recreations in Computer Graphics*, A. K. Peters, Natick, MA.

GLEICHER, M. and A. WITKIN (1992). "Through-the-Lens Camera Control", in proceedings of SIGGRAPH '92, *Computer Graphics*, 26(2), pp. 331–340.

GOLDSMITH, J. and J. SALMON (1987). "Automatic Creation of Object Hierarchies for Ray Tracing", *IEEE Computer Graphics and Applications*, 7(5), pp. 14–20.

GOMES, J., L. DARSA, B. COSTA, and L. VELHO (1999). *Warping and Morphing of Graphical Objects*, Morgan Kaufmann, San Francisco, CA.

GONZALEZ, R. C. and P. WINTZ (1987). *Digital Image Processing*, Addison-Wesley, Reading, MA.

GOOCH, B. and A. GOOCH (2001). *Non-Photorealistic Rendering*, A. K. Peters, Natick, MA.

GORAL, C. M., K. E. TORRANCE, D. P. GREENBERG, and B. BATTAILE (1984). "Modeling the Interaction of Light Between Diffuse Surfaces", in proceedings of SIGGRAPH '84, *Computer Graphics*, 18(3), pp. 213–222.

GORDON, D. and S. CHEN (1991). "Front-to-Back Display of BSP Trees", *IEEE Computer Graphics and Applications*, 11(5), pp. 79–85.

GORTLER, S. J., P. SCHRÖDER, M. F. COHEN, and P. HANRAHAN (1993). "Wavelet Radiosity", in proceedings of SIGGRAPH '93, *Computer Graphics*, pp. 221–230.

GOURAUD, H. (1971). "Continuous Shading of Curved Surfaces", *IEEE Transactions on Computers*, C-20(6), pp. 623–628.

GREENE, N., M. KASS, and G. MILLER (1993). "Hierarchical Z-Buffer Visibility", in proceedings of SIGGRAPH '93, *Computer Graphics*, pp. 231–238.

GROTCH, S. L. (1983). "Three-Dimensional and Stereoscopic Graphics for Scientific Data Display and

Analysis", *IEEE Computer Graphics and Applications*, 3(8), pp. 31–43.

HAEBERLI, P. and K. AKELEY (1990). "The Accumulation Buffer: Hardware Support for High-Quality Rendering", in proceedings of SIGGRAPH '90, *Computer Graphics*, 24(4), pp. 309–318.

HALL, R. A. and D. P. GREENBERG (1983). "A Testbed for Realistic Image Synthesis", *IEEE Computer Graphics and Applications*, 3(8), pp. 10–20.

HALL, R. (1989). *Illumination and Color in Computer Generated Imagery*, Springer-Verlag, New York.

HALLIDAY, D., R. RESNICK, and J. WALKER (2000). *Fundamentals of Physics, Sixth Edition*, John Wiley & Sons, New York.

HANRAHAN, P. and J. LAWSON (1990). "A Language for Shading and Lighting Calculations", in proceedings of SIGGRAPH '90, *Computer Graphics*, 24(4), pp. 289–298.

HARDY, V. J. (2000). *Java 2D API Graphics*, Sun Microsystems Press, Palo Alto, CA.

HART, J. C., D. J. SANDIN, and L. H. KAUFFMAN (1989). "Ray Tracing Deterministic 3D Fractals", in proceedings of SIGGRAPH '89, *Computer Graphics*, 23(3), pp. 289–296.

HART, J. C. and T. A. DEFANTI (1991). "Efficient Antialiased Rendering of 3-D Linear Fractals", in proceedings of SIGGRAPH '91, *Computer Graphics*, 25(4), pp. 91–100.

HAWRYLYSHYN, P. A., R. R. TASKER, and L. W. ORGAN (1977). "CASS: Computer-Assisted Stereotaxic Surgery", in proceedings of SIGGRAPH '77, *Computer Graphics*, 11(2), pp. 13–17.

HE, X. D., P. O. HEYNEN, R. L. PHILLIPS, K. E. TORRANCE, D. H. SALESIN, and D. P. GREENBERG (1992). "A Fast and Accurate Light Reflection Model", in proceedings of SIGGRAPH '92, *Computer Graphics*, 26(2), pp. 253–254.

HEARN, D. and P. BAKER (1991). "Scientific Visualization: An Introduction", *Eurographics '91 Technical Report Series*, Tutorial Lecture 6, Vienna, Austria.

HECKBERT, P. S. (1982). "Color Image Quantization for Frame Buffer Display", in proceedings of SIGGRAPH '82, *Computer Graphics*, 16(3), pp. 297–307.

HECKBERT, P. S. and P. HANRAHAN (1984). "Beam Tracing Polygonal Objects", in proceedings of SIGGRAPH '84, *Computer Graphics*, 18(3), pp. 119–127.

HECKBERT, P. S., ed. (1994). *Graphics Gems IV*, Academic Press Professional, Cambridge, MA.

HENDERSON, L. R. and A. M. MUMFORD (1993). *The CGM Handbook*, Academic Press, San Diego, CA.

HOPGOOD, F. R. A., D. A. DUCE, J. R. GALLOP, and D. C. SUTCLIFFE (1983). *Introduction to the Graphical Kernel System (GKS)*, Academic Press, London.

HOPGOOD, F. R. A. and D. A. DUCE (1991). *A Primer for PHIGS*, John Wiley & Sons, Chichester, England.

HORSTMANN, C. S. and G. CORNELL (2001). *Core Java 2, Vols. I–II*, Sun Microsystems Press, Palo Alto, CA.

HOWARD, T. L. J., W. T. HEWITT, R. J. HUBBOLD, and K. M. WYRWAS (1991). *A Practical Introduction to PHIGS and PHIGS Plus*, Addison-Wesley, Wokingham, England.

HUFFMAN, D. A. (1952). "A Method for the Construction of Minimum-Redundancy Codes", *Communications of the ACM*, 40(9), pp. 1098–1101.

HUGHES, J. F. (1992). "Scheduled Fourier Volume Morphing", in proceedings of SIGGRAPH '92, *Computer Graphics*, 26(2), pp. 43–46.

HUITRIC, H. and M. NAHAS (1985). "B-Spline Surfaces: A Tool for Computer Painting", *IEEE Computer Graphics and Applications*, 5(3), pp. 39–47.

IMMEL, D. S., M. F. COHEN, and D. P. GREENBERG (1986). "A Radiosity Method for Non-Diffuse Environments", in proceedings of SIGGRAPH '86, *Computer Graphics*, 20(4), pp. 133–142.

ISAACS, P. M. and M. F. COHEN (1987). "Controlling Dynamic Simulation with Kinematic Constraints, Behavior Functions, and Inverse Dynamics", in proceedings of SIGGRAPH '87, *Computer Graphics*, 21(4), pp. 215–224.

JARVIS, J. F., C. N. JUDICE, and W. H. NINKE (1976). "A Survey of Techniques for the Image Display of Continuous Tone Pictures on Bilevel Displays", *Computer Graphics and Image Processing*, 5(1), pp. 13–40.

JENSEN, H. W. (2001). *Realistic Image Synthesis Using Photon Mapping*, A. K. Peters, Natick, MA.

JOHNSON, S. A. (1982). "Clinical Varifocal Mirror Display System at the University of Utah", *Proceedings of SPIE*, 367, August 1982, pp. 145–148.

KAJIYA, J. T. (1983). "New Techniques for Ray Tracing Procedurally Defined Objects", *ACM Transactions on Graphics*, 2(3), pp. 161–181.

KAJIYA, J. T. (1986). "The Rendering Equation", in proceedings of SIGGRAPH '86, *Computer Graphics*, 20(4), pp. 143–150.

KAJIYA, J. T. and T. L. KAY (1989). "Rendering Fur with Three-Dimensional Textures", in proceedings of SIGGRAPH '89, *Computer Graphics*, 23(3), pp. 271–280.

KAPPEL, M. R. (1985). "An Ellipse-Drawing Algorithm for Faster Displays", in *Fundamental Algorithms for Computer Graphics*, Springer-Verlag, Berlin, pp. 257–280.

KAY, T. L. and J. T. KAJIYA (1986). "Ray Tracing Complex Scenes", in proceedings of SIGGRAPH '86, *Computer Graphics*, 20(4), pp. 269–278.

KAY, D. C. and J. R. LEVINE (1992). *Graphics File Formats*, Windcrest/McGraw-Hill, New York.

KELLEY, A. D., M. C. MALIN, and G. M. NIELSON (1988). "Terrain Simulation Using a Model of Stream Erosion", in proceedings of SIGGRAPH '88, *Computer Graphics*, 22(4), pp. 263–268.

KENT, J. R., W. E. CARLSON, and R. E. PARENT (1992). "Shape Transformation for Polyhedral Objects", in proceedings of SIGGRAPH '92, *Computer Graphics*, 26(2), pp. 47–54.

KERLOW, I. V. (2000). *The Art of 3-D Computer Animation and Imaging*, John Wiley & Sons, New York.

KILGARD, M. J. (1996). *OpenGL Programming for the X Window System*, Addison-Wesley, Reading, MA.

KIRK, D. and J. ARVO (1991). "Unbiased Sampling Techniques for Image Synthesis", in proceedings of SIGGRAPH '91, *Computer Graphics*, 25(4), pp. 153–156.

KIRK, D., ed. (1992). *Graphics Gems III*, Academic Press, San Diego, CA.

KNUDSEN, J. (1999). *Java 2D Programming*, O'Reilly & Associates, Sebastopol, CA.

KNUTH, D. E. (1987). "Digital Halftones by Dot Diffusion", *ACM Transactions on Graphics*, 6(4), pp. 245–273.

KOCHANEK, D. H. U. and R. H. BARTELS (1984). "Interpolating Splines with Local Tension, Continuity, and Bias Control", in proceedings of SIGGRAPH '84, *Computer Graphics*, 18(3), pp. 33–41.

KOH, E.-K. and D. HEARN (1992). "Fast Generation and Surface Structuring Methods for Terrain and Other Natural Phenomena", in proceedings of Eurographics '92, *Computer Graphics Forum*, 11(3), pp. C169–180.

KORIEN, J. U. and N. I. BADLER (1982). "Techniques for Generating the Goal-Directed Motion of Articulated Structures", *IEEE Computer Graphics and Applications*, 2(9), pp. 71–81.

KORIEN, J. U. and N. I. BADLER (1983). "Temporal antialiasing in Computer-Generated Animation", in proceedings of SIGGRAPH '83, *Computer Graphics*, 17(3), pp. 377–388.

KREYSZIG, E. (1998). *Advanced Engineering Mathematics, Eighth Edition*, John Wiley & Sons, New York.

LASSETER, J. (1987). "Principles of Traditional Animation Applied to 3D Computer Animation", in proceedings of SIGGRAPH '87, *Computer Graphics*, 21(4), pp. 35–44.

LATHROP, O. (1997). *The Way Computer Graphics Works*, John Wiley & Sons, New York.

LAUREL, B. (1990). *The Art of Human-Computer Interface Design*, Addision-Wesley, Reading, MA.

LENGYEL, E. (2002). *Mathematics for 3D Game Programming & Computer Graphics*, Charles River Media, Hingham, MA.

LEVOY, M. (1990). "A Hybrid Ray Tracer for Rendering Polygon and Volume Data", *IEEE Computer Graphics and Applications*, 10(2), pp. 33–40.

LEWIS, J.-P. (1989). "Algorithms for Solid Noise Synthesis", in proceedings of SIGGRAPH '89, *Computer Graphics*, 23(3), pp. 263–270.

LIANG, Y.-D. and B. A. BARSKY (1983). "An Analysis and Algorithm for Polygon Clipping." *Communications of the ACM*, 26(11), pp. 868–877.

LIANG, Y.-D. and B. A. BARSKY (1984). "A New Concept and Method for Line Clipping", *ACM Transactions on Graphics*, 3(1), pp. 1–22.

LINDLEY, C. A. (1992). *Practical Ray Tracing in C*, John Wiley & Sons, New York.

LISCHINSKI, D., F. TAMPIERI, and D. P. GREENBERG (1993). "Combining Hierarchical Radiosity and Discontinuity Meshing", in proceedings of SIGGRAPH '93, *Computer Graphics*, pp. 199–208.

LITWINOWICZ, P. C. (1991). "Inkwell: A $2^1/_2$-D Animation System", in proceedings of SIGGRAPH '91, *Computer Graphics*, 25(4), pp. 113–122.

LODDING, K. N. (1983). "Iconic Interfacing", *IEEE Computer Graphics and Applications*, 3(2), pp. 11–20.

LOKE, T.-S., D. TAN, H.-S. SEAH, and M.-H. ER (1992). "Rendering Fireworks Displays", *IEEE Computer Graphics and Applications*, 12(3), pp. 33–43.

LOOMIS, J., H. POIZNER, U. BELLUGI, A. BLAKEMORE, and J. HOLLERBACH (1983). "Computer-Graphics Modeling of American Sign Language", in proceedings of SIGGRAPH '83, *Computer Graphics*, 17(3), pp. 105–114.

LOPES, A. and K. BRODLIE (2003). "Improving the Robustness and Accuracy of the Marching-Cubes Algorithm for Isosurfaces", IEEE Transactions on Visualization and Computer Graphics, 9(1), pp. 16–29.

LORENSON, W. E. and H. CLINE (1987). "Marching Cubes: A High-Resolution 3D Surface Construction Algorithm", in proceedings of SIGGRAPH '87, *Computer Graphics*, 21(4), pp. 163–169.

MACKINLAY, J. D., S. K. CARD, and G. G. ROBERTSON (1990). "Rapid Controlled Movement Through a Virtual 3D Workspace", in proceedings of SIGGRAPH '90, *Computer Graphics*, pp. 171–176.

MACKINLAY, J. D., G. G. ROBERTSON, and S. K. CARD (1991). "The Perspective Wall: Detail and Context Smoothly Integrated", *CHI '91*, pp. 173–179.

MAESTRI, G. (1999). *[digital] Character Animation 2, Volume 1—Essential Techniques*, New Riders Publishing, Indianapolis, IN.

MAESTRI, G. (2002). *[digital] Character Animation 2, Volume 2—Advanced Techniques*, New Riders Publishing, Indianapolis, IN.

MAGNENAT-THALMANN, N. and D. THALMANN (1985). *Computer Animation: Theory and Practice*, Springer-Verlag, Tokyo.

MAGNENAT-THALMANN, N. and D. THALMANN (1987). *Image Synthesis*, Springer-Verlag, Tokyo.

MAGNENAT-THALMANN, N. and D. THALMANN (1991). "Complex Models for Animating Synthetic Actors", *IEEE Computer Graphics and Applications*, 11(5), pp. 32–45.

MANDELBROT, B. B. (1977). *Fractals: Form, Chance, and Dimension*, Freeman Press, San Francisco.

MANDELBROT, B. B. (1982). *The Fractal Geometry of Nature*, Freeman Press, New York.

MANTYLA, M. (1988). *An Introduction to Solid Modeling*, Computer Science Press, Rockville, MD.

MAX, N. L. and D. M. LERNER (1985). "A Two-and-a-Half-D Motion Blur Algorithm", in proceedings of SIGGRAPH '85, *Computer Graphics*, 19(3), pp. 85–94.

MAX, N. L. (1986). "Atmospheric Illumination and Shadows", in proceedings of SIGGRAPH '86, *Computer Graphics*, 20(4), pp. 117–124.

MAX, N. L. (1990). "Cone-Spheres", in proceedings of SIGGRAPH '90, *Computer Graphics*, 24(4), pp. 59–62.

McCARTHY, M. and A. DESCARTES (1998). *Reality Architecture: Building 3D Worlds with Java and VRML*, Prentice-Hall Europe, United Kingdom.

MEYER, G. W. and D. P. GREENBERG (1988). "Color-Defective Vision and Computer Graphics Displays", *IEEE Computer Graphics and Applications*, 8(5), pp. 28–40.

MEYERS, D., S. SKINNER, and K. SLOAN (1992). "Surfaces from Contours", *ACM Transactions on Graphics*, 11(3), pp. 228–258.

MIANO, J. (1999). *Compressed Image File Formats*, Addison-Wesley/ACM Press, New York.

MILLER, G. S. P. (1988). "The Motion Dynamics of Snakes and Worms", in proceedings of SIGGRAPH '88, *Computer Graphics*, 22(4), pp. 169–178.

MILLER, J. V., D. E. BREEN, W. E. LORENSON, R. M. O'BARA, and M. J. WOZNY (1991). "Geometrically Deformed Models: A Method for Extracting Closed Geometric Models from Volume Data", in proceedings of SIGGRAPH '91, *Computer Graphics*, 25(4), pp. 217–226.

MITCHELL, D. P. (1991). "Spectrally Optimal Sampling for Distribution Ray Tracing", in proceedings of SIGGRAPH '91, *Computer Graphics*, 25(4), pp. 157–165.

MITCHELL, D. P. and P. HANRAHAN (1992). "Illumination from Curved Reflectors", in proceedings of SIGGRAPH '92, *Computer Graphics*, 26(2), pp. 283–291.

MITROO, J. B., N. HERMAN, and N. I. BADLER (1979). "Movies from Music: Visualizing Music Compositions", in proceedings of SIGGRAPH '79, *Computer Graphics*, 13(2), pp. 218–225.

MIYATA, K. (1990). "A Method of Generating Stone Wall Patterns", in proceedings of SIGGRAPH '90, *Computer Graphics*, 24(4), pp. 387–394.

MOLNAR, S., J. EYLES, and J. POULTON (1992). "PixelFlow: High-Speed Rendering Using Image Composition", in proceedings of SIGGRAPH '92, *Computer Graphics*, 26(2), pp. 231–240.

MOON, F. C. (1992). *Chaotic and Fractal Dynamics*, John Wiley & Sons, New York.

MOORE, M. and J. WILHELMS (1988). "Collision Detection and Response for Computer Animation", in proceedings of SIGGRAPH '88, *Computer Graphics*, 22(4), pp. 289–298.

MORTENSON, M. E. (1985). *Geometric Modeling*, John Wiley & Sons, New York.

MURAKI, S. (1991). "Volumetric Shape Description of Range Data Using the 'Blobby Model' ", in proceedings of SIGGRAPH '91, *Computer Graphics*, 25(4), pp. 227–235.

MUSGRAVE, F. K., C. E. KOLB, and R. S. MACE (1989). "The Synthesis and Rendering of Eroded Fractal Terrains", in proceedings of SIGGRAPH '89, *Computer Graphics*, 23(3), pp. 41–50.

MYERS, B. A. and W. BUXTON (1986). "Creating High-Interactive and Graphical User Interfaces by Demonstration", in proceedings of SIGGRAPH '86, *Computer Graphics*, 20(4), pp. 249–258.

NAYLOR, B., J. AMANATIDES, and W. THIBAULT (1990). "Merging BSP Trees Yields Polyhedral Set Operations", in proceedings of SIGGRAPH '90, *Computer Graphics*, 24(4), pp. 115–124.

NICHOLL, T. M., D. T. LEE, and R. A. NICHOLL (1987). "An Efficient New Algorithm for 2D Line Clipping: Its Development and Analysis", in proceedings of SIGGRAPH '87, *Computer Graphics*, 21(4), pp. 253–262.

NIELSON, G. M., B. SHRIVER, and L. ROSENBLUM, ed. (1990). *Visualization in Scientific Computing*, IEEE Computer Society Press, Los Alamitos, CA.

NIELSON, G. M. (1993). "Scattered Data Modeling", *IEEE Computer Graphics and Applications*, 13(1), pp. 60–70.

NISHIMURA, H. (1985). "Object Modeling by Distribution Function and a Method of Image Generation", *Journal Electronics Comm. Conf. '85*, J68(4), pp. 718–725.

NISHITA, T. and E. NAKAMAE (1986). "Continuous-Tone Representation of Three-Dimensional Objects Illuminated by Sky Light", in proceedings of SIGGRAPH '86, *Computer Graphics*, 20(4), pp. 125–132.

NISHITA, T., T. SIRAI, K. TADAMURA, and E. NAKAMAE (1993). "Display of the Earth Taking into Account Atmospheric Scattering", in proceedings of SIGGRAPH '93, *Computer Graphics*, pp. 175–182.

NORTON, A. (1982). "Generation and Display of Geometric Fractals in 3-D", in proceedings of SIGGRAPH '82, *Computer Graphics*, 16(3), pp. 61–67.

NSF INVITATIONAL WORKSHOP (1992). "Research Directions in Virtual Environments", in proceedings of SIGGRAPH '92, *Computer Graphics*, 26(3), pp. 153–177.

OKABE, H., H. IMAOKA, T. TOMIHA, and H. NIWAYA (1992). "Three-Dimensional Apparel CAD System", in proceedings of SIGGRAPH '92, *Computer Graphics*, 26(2), pp. 105–110.

OLANO, M., J. C. HART, W. HEIDRICH, and M. McCOOL (2002). *Real-Time Shading*, A. K. Natick, MA.

OPPENHEIMER, P. E. (1986). "Real-Time Design and Animation of Fractal Plants and Trees", in proceedings of SIGGRAPH '86, *Computer Graphics*, 20(4), pp. 55–64.

O'ROURKE, M. (1998). *Principles of Three-Dimensional Computer Animation, Revised Edition*, W. W. Norton, New York.

OSF/MOTIF (1989). *OSF/Motif Style Guide*, Open Software Foundation, Prentice-Hall, Englewood Cliffs, NJ.

PAETH, A. W., ed. (1995). *Graphics Gems V*, Morgan Kaufmann, San Diego, CA.

PAINTER, J. and K. SLOAN (1989). "Antialiased Ray Tracing by Adaptive Progressive Refinement", in proceedings of SIGGRAPH '89, *Computer Graphics*, 23(3), pp. 281–288.

PALMER, I. (2001). *Essential Java 3D Fast*, Springer-Verlag, London.

PANG, A. T. (1990). "Line-Drawing Algorithms for Parallel Machines", *IEEE Computer Graphics and Applications*, 10(5), pp. 54–59.

PAO, Y. C. (1984). *Elements of Computer-Aided Design*. John Wiley & Sons, New York.

PARENT, R. (2002). *Computer Animation: Algorithms and Techniques*, Morgan Kaufmann, San Francisco, CA.

PAVLIDIS, T. (1982). *Algorithms For Graphics and Image Processing*, Computer Science Press, Rockville, MD.

PAVLIDIS, T. (1983). "Curve Fitting with Conic Splines", *ACM Transactions on Graphics*, 2(1), pp. 1–31.

PEACHEY, D. R. (1986). "Modeling Waves and Surf", in proceedings of SIGGRAPH '86, *Computer Graphics*, 20(4), pp. 65–74.

PEITGEN, H.-O. and P. H. RICHTER (1986). *The Beauty of Fractals*, Springer-Verlag, Berlin.

PEITGEN, H.-O. and D. SAUPE, eds. (1988). *The Science of Fractal Images*, Springer-Verlag, Berlin.

PENTLAND, A. and J. WILLIAMS (1989). "Good Vibrations: Modal Dynamics for Graphics and Animation", in proceedings of SIGGRAPH '89, *Computer Graphics*, 23(3), pp. 215–222.

PERLIN, K. and E. M. HOFFERT (1989). "Hypertexture", in proceedings of SIGGRAPH '89, *Computer Graphics*, 23(3), pp. 253–262.

PHONG, B. T. (1975). "Illumination for Computer-Generated Images", *Communications of the ACM*, 18(6), pp. 311–317.

PIEGL, L. and W. TILLER (1997). *The NURBS Book*, Springer-Verlag, New York.

PINEDA, J. (1988). "A Parallel Algorithm for Polygon Rasterization", in proceedings of SIGGRAPH '88, *Computer Graphics*, 22(4), pp. 17–20.

PITTEWAY, M. L. V. and D. J. WATKINSON (1980). "Bresenham's Algorithm with Gray Scale", *Communications of the ACM*, 23(11), pp. 625–626.

PLATT, J. C. and A. H. BARR (1988). "Constraint Methods for Flexible Models", in proceedings of SIGGRAPH '88, *Computer Graphics*, 22(4), pp. 279–288.

POCOCK, L. and J. ROSEBUSH (2002). *The Computer Animator's Technical Handbook*, Morgan Kaufmann, San Francisco, CA.

POTMESIL, M. and I. CHAKRAVARTY (1982). "Synthetic Image Generation with a Lens and Aperture Camera Model", *ACM Transactions on Graphics*, 1(2), pp. 85–108.

POTMESIL, M. and I. CHAKRAVARTY (1983). "Modeling Motion Blur in Computer-Generated Images", in proceedings of SIGGRAPH '83, *Computer Graphics*, 17(3), pp. 389–399.

POTMESIL, M. and E. M. HOFFERT (1987). "FRAMES: Software Tools for Modeling, Rendering and Animation of 3D Scenes", in proceedings of SIGGRAPH '87, *Computer Graphics*, 21(4), pp. 85–93.

POTMESIL, M. and E. M. HOFFERT (1989). "The Pixel Machine: A Parallel Image Computer", in proceedings of SIGGRAPH '89, *Computer Graphics*, 23(3), pp. 69–78.

PRATT, W. K. (1978). *Digital Image Processing*, John Wiley & Sons, New York.

PREPARATA, F. P. and M. I. SHAMOS (1985). *Computational Geometry*, Springer-Verlag, New York.

PRESS, W. H., S. A. TEUKOLSKY, W. T. VETTERLING, and B. P. FLANNERY (1993). *Numerical Recipes in C: The Art of Scientific Computing, Second Edition*, Cambridge University Press, Cambridge, England.

PRESS, W. H., S. A. TEUKOLSKY, W. T. VETTERLING, and B. P. FLANNERY (2002). *Numerical Recipes in C++: The Art of Scientific Computing, Second Edition*, Cambridge University Press, Cambridge, England.

PRESTON, K., FAGAN, HUANG, and PRYOR (1984). "Computing in Medicine", *Computer*, 17(10), pp. 294–313.

PRUSINKIEWICZ, P., M. S. HAMMEL, and E. MJOLSNESS (1993). "Animation of Plant Development", in proceedings of SIGGRAPH '93, *Computer Graphics*, pp. 351–360.

PRUYN, P. W. and D. P. GREENBERG (1993). "Exploring 3D Computer Graphics in Cockpit Avionics", *IEEE Computer Graphics and Applications*, 13(3), pp. 28–35.

QUEK, L.-H. and D. HEARN (1988). "Efficient Space-Subdivision Methods in Ray-Tracing Algorithms", University of Illinois, Department of Computer Science Report UIUCDCS-R-88-1468.

RAIBERT, M. H. and J. K. HODGINS (1991). "Animation of Dynamic Legged Locomotion", in proceedings of SIGGRAPH '91, *Computer Graphics*, 25(4), pp. 349–358.

RAO, K. R. and P. YIP (1990). *Discrete Cosine Transform*, Academic Press, New York.

REEVES, W. T. (1983a). "Particle Systems: A Technique for Modeling a Class of Fuzzy Objects", *ACM Transactions on Graphics*, 2(2), pp. 91–108.

REEVES, W. T. (1983b). "Particle Systems—A Technique for Modeling a Class of Fuzzy Objects", in proceedings of SIGGRAPH '83, *Computer Graphics*, 17(3), pp. 359–376.

REEVES, W. T. and R. BLAU (1985). "Approximate and Probabilistic Algorithms for Shading and Rendering Structured Particle Systems", in proceedings of SIGGRAPH '85, *Computer Graphics*, 19(3), pp. 313–321.

REEVES, W. T., D. H. SALESIN, and R. L. COOK (1987). "Rendering Antialiased Shadows with Depth Maps", in proceedings of SIGGRAPH '87, *Computer Graphics*, 21(4), pp. 283–291.

REQUICHA, A. A. G. and J. R. ROSSIGNAC (1992). "Solid Modeling and Beyond", *IEEE Computer Graphics and Applications*, 12(5), pp. 31–44.

REYNOLDS, C. W. (1982). "Computer Animation with Scripts and Actors", in proceedings of SIGGRAPH '82, *Computer Graphics*, 16(3), pp. 289–296.

REYNOLDS, C. W. (1987). "Flocks, Herds, and Schools: A Distributed Behavioral Model", in proceedings of SIGGRAPH '87, *Computer Graphics*, 21(4), pp. 25–34.

RHODES, M. L., et al. (1983). "Computer Graphics and An Interactive Stereotactic System for CT-Aided

Neurosurgery", *IEEE Computer Graphics and Applications*, 3(5), pp. 31–37.

RIESENFELD, R. F. (1981). "Homogeneous Coordinates and Projective Planes in Computer Graphics", *IEEE Computer Graphics and Applications*, 1(1), pp. 50–55.

ROBERTSON, P. K. (1988). "Visualizing Color Gamuts: A User Interface for the Effective Use of Perceptual Color Spaces in Data Displays", *IEEE Computer Graphics and Applications*, 8(5), pp. 50–64.

ROBERTSON, G. G., J. D. MACKINLAY and S. K. CARD (1991). "Cone Trees: Animated 3D Visualizations of Hierarchical Information", *CHI '91*, pp. 189–194.

ROGERS, D. F. and R. A. EARNSHAW, eds. (1987). *Techniques for Computer Graphics*, Springer-Verlag, New York.

ROGERS, D. F. and J. A. ADAMS (1990). *Mathematical Elements for Computer Graphics*, McGraw-Hill, New York.

ROGERS, D. F. (1998). *Procedural Elements for Computer Graphics*, McGraw-Hill, New York.

ROSENTHAL, D. S. H., J. C. MICHENER, G. PFAFF, R. KESSEMER, and M. SABIN (1982). "The Detailed Semantics of Graphics Input Devices", in proceedings of SIGGRAPH '82, *Computer Graphics*, 16(3), pp. 33–38.

RUBINE, D. (1991). "Specifying Gestures by Example", in proceedings of SIGGRAPH '91, *Computer Graphics*, 25(4), pp. 329–337.

RUSHMEIER, H. and K. TORRANCE (1987). "The Zonal Method for Calculating Light Intensities in the Presence of a Participating Medium", in proceedings of SIGGRAPH '87, *Computer Graphics*, 21(4), pp. 293–302.

RUSHMEIER, H. E. and K. E. TORRANCE (1990). "Extending the Radiosity Method to Include Specularly Reflecting and Translucent Materials", *ACM Transactions on Graphics*, 9(1), pp. 1–27.

SABELLA, P. (1988). "A Rendering Algorithm for Visualizing 3D Scalar Fields", in proceedings of SIGGRAPH '88, *Computer Graphics*, 22(4), pp. 51–58.

SABIN, M. A. (1985). "Contouring: The State of the Art", in *Fundamental Algorithms for Computer Graphics*, R. A. Earnshaw, ed., Springer-Verlag, Berlin, pp. 411–482.

SAKAGUCHI, H., S. L. KENT, and T. COX (2001). *The Making of Final Fantasy, The Spirits Within*, Brady Games, Indianapolis, IN.

SALESIN, D. and R. BARZEL (1993). "Adjustable Tools: An Object-Oriented Interaction Metaphor", *ACM Transactions on Graphics*, 12(1), pp. 103–107.

SAMET, H. and M. TAMMINEN (1985). "Bintrees, CSG Trees, and Time", in proceedings of SIGGRAPH '85, *Computer Graphics*, 19(3), pp. 121–130.

SAMET, H. and R. E. WEBBER (1985). "Sorting a Collection of Polygons using Quadtrees", *ACM Transactions on Graphics*, 4(3), pp. 182–222.

SAMET, H. and R. E. WEBBER (1988a). "Hierarchical Data Structures and Algorithms for Computer Graphics: Part 1", *IEEE Computer Graphics and Applications*, 8(4), pp. 59–75.

SAMET, H. and R. E. WEBBER (1988b). "Hierarchical Data Structures and Algorithms for Computer Graphics: Part 2", *IEEE Computer Graphics and Applications*, 8(3), pp. 48–68.

SCHACHTER, B. J., ed. (1983). *Computer Image Generation*, John Wiley & Sons, New York.

SCHEIFLER, R. W. and J. GETTYS (1986). "The X Window System", *ACM Transactions on Graphics*, 5(2), pp. 79–109.

SCHOENEMAN, C., J. DORSEY, B. SMITS, J. ARVO, and D. GREENBERG (1993). "Painting with Light", in proceedings of SIGGRAPH '93, *Computer Graphics*, pp. 143–146.

SCHRODER, P. and P. HANRAHAN (1993). "On the Form Factor Between Two Polygons", in proceedings of SIGGRAPH '93, *Computer Graphics*, pp. 163–164.

SCHWARTZ, M. W., W. B. COWAN, and J. C. BEATTY (1987). "An Experimental Comparison of RGB, YIQ, LAB, HSV, and Opponent Color Models", *ACM Transactions on Graphics*, 6(2), pp. 123–158.

SEDERBERG, T. W. and E. GREENWOOD (1992). "A Physically Based Approached to 2-D Shape Bending", in proceedings of SIGGRAPH '92, *Computer Graphics*, 26(2), pp. 25–34.

SEDERBERG, T. W., P. GAO, G. WANG, and H. MU (1993). "2D Shape Blending: An Intrinsic Solution to the Vertex Path Problem", in proceedings of SIGGRAPH '93, *Computer Graphics*, pp. 15–18.

SEGAL, M. (1990). "Using Tolerances to Guarantee Valid Polyhedral Modeling Results", in proceedings of SIGGRAPH '90, *Computer Graphics*, 24(4), pp. 105–114.

SEGAL, M., C. KOROBKIN, R. VAN WIDENFELT, J. FORAN, and P. HAEBERLI (1992). "Fast Shadows and Lighting Effects Using Texture Mapping", in proceedings of SIGGRAPH '92, *Computer Graphics*, 26(2), pp. 249–252.

SELMAN, D. (2002). *Java 3D Programming*, Manning Publications, Greenwich, CT.

SEQUIN, C. H. and E. K. SMYRL (1989). "Parameterized Ray-Tracing", in proceedings of SIGGRAPH '89, *Computer Graphics*, 23(3), pp. 307–314.

SHERR, S. (1993). *Electronic Displays*, John Wiley & Sons, New York.

SHILLING, A. and W. STRASSER (1993). "EXACT: Algorithm and Hardware Architecture for an Improved A-Buffer", in proceedings of SIGGRAPH '93, *Computer Graphics*, pp. 85–92.

SHIRLEY, P. (1990). "A Ray Tracing Method for Illumination Calculation in Diffuse-Specular Scenes", *Graphics Interface '90*, pp. 205–212.

SHIRLEY, P. (2000). *Realistic Ray Tracing*, A. K. Peters, Natick, MA.

SHNEIDERMAN, B. (1986). *Designing the User Interface*, Addison-Wesley, Reading, MA.

SHOEMAKE, K. (1985). "Animating Rotation with Quaternion Curves", in proceedings of SIGGRAPH '85, *Computer Graphics*, 19(3), pp. 245–254.

SHREINER, D., ed. (2000). *OpenGL Reference Manual, Third Edition*, Addison-Wesley, Reading, MA.

SIBERT, J. L., W. D. HURLEY, and T. W. BLESER (1986). "An Object-Oriented User Interface Management System", in proceedings of SIGGRAPH '86, *Computer Graphics*, 20(4), pp. 259–268.

SILLION, F. X. and C. PUECH (1989). "A General Two-Pass Method Integrating Specular and Diffuse Reflection", in proceedings of SIGGRAPH '89, *Computer Graphics*, 23(3), pp. 335–344.

SILLION, F. X., J. R. ARVO, S. H. WESTIN, and D. P. GREENBERG (1991). "A Global Illumination Solution for General Reflectance Distributions", in proceedings of SIGGRAPH '91, *Computer Graphics*, 25(4), pp. 187–196.

SILLION, F. X. and C. PUECH (1994). *Radiosity and Global Illumination*, Morgan Kaufmann, San Francisco, CA.

SIMS, K. (1990). "Particle Animation and Rendering Using Data Parallel Computation", in proceedings of SIGGRAPH '90, *Computer Graphics*, 24(4), pp. 405–413.

SIMS, K. (1991). "Artificial Evolution for Computer Graphics", in proceedings of SIGGRAPH '91, *Computer Graphics*, 25(4), pp. 319–328.

SMITH, A. R. (1978). "Color Gamut Transform Pairs", in proceedings of SIGGRAPH '78, *Computer Graphics*, 12(3), pp. 12–19.

SMITH, A. R. (1979). "Tint Fill", in proceedings of SIGGRAPH '79, *Computer Graphics*, 13(2), pp. 276–283.

SMITH, A. R. (1984). "Plants, Fractals, and Formal Languages", in proceedings of SIGGRAPH '84, *Computer Graphics*, 18(3), pp. 1–10.

SMITH, A. R. (1987). "Planar 2-Pass Texture Mapping and Warping", in proceedings of SIGGRAPH '87, *Computer Graphics*, 21(4), pp. 263–272.

SMITS, B. E., J. R. ARVO, and D. H. SALESIN (1992). "An Importance-Driven Radiosity Algorithm", in proceedings of SIGGRAPH '92, *Computer Graphics*, 26(2), pp. 273–282.

SNYDER, J. M. and J. T. KAJIYA (1992). "Generative Modeling: A Symbolic System for Geometric Modeling", in proceedings of SIGGRAPH '92, *Computer Graphics*, 26(2), pp. 369–378.

SNYDER, J. M., A. R. WOODBURY, K. FLEISCHER, B. CURRIN, and A. H. BARR (1993). "Interval Methods for Multi-Point Collisions between Time-Dependent Curved Surfaces", in proceedings of SIGGRAPH '93, *Computer Graphics*, pp. 321–334.

SOWIZRAL, H., K. RUSHFORTH, and M. DEERING (2000). *The Java 3D API Specification, Second Edition*, Addison-Wesley, Reading, MA.

SPROULL, R. F. and I. E. SUTHERLAND (1968). "A Clipping Divider", AFIPS Fall Joint Computer Conference.

STAM, J. and E. FIUME (1993). "Turbulent Wind Fields for Gaseous Phenomena", in proceedings of SIGGRAPH '93, *Computer Graphics*, pp. 369–376.

STETTNER, A. and D. P. GREENBERG (1989). "Computer Graphics Visualization for Acoustic Simulation", in proceedings of SIGGRAPH '89, *Computer Graphics*, 23(3), pp. 195–206.

STRASSMANN, S. (1986). "Hairy Brushes", in proceedings of SIGGRAPH '86, *Computer Graphics*, 20(4), pp. 225–232.

STRAUSS, P. S. and R. CAREY (1992). "An Object-Oriented 3D Graphics Toolkit", in proceedings of SIGGRAPH '92, *Computer Graphics*, 26(2), pp. 341–349.

STROTHOTTE, T. and S. SCHLECHTWEG (2002). *Non-Photorealistic Computer Graphics: Modeling, Rendering, and Animation*, Morgan Kaufmann, San Francisco, CA.

SUNG, H. C. K., G. ROGERS, and W. J. KUBITZ (1990). "A Critical Evaluation of PEX", *IEEE Computer Graphics and Applications*, 10(6), pp. 65–75.

SUTHERLAND, I. E. (1963). "Sketchpad: A Man-Machine Graphical Communication System", *AFIPS Spring Joint Computer Conference*, 23, pp. 329–346.

SUTHERLAND, I. E. and G. W. Hodgman (1974). "Reentrant Polygon Clipping", *Communications of the ACM*, 17(1), pp. 32–42.

SUTHERLAND, I. E., R. F. SPROULL, and R. SCHUMACKER (1974). "A Characterization of Ten Hidden Surface Algorithms", *ACM Computing Surveys*, 6(1), pp. 1–55.

SWEZEY, R. W. and E. G. DAVIS (1983). "A Case Study of Human Factors Guidelines in Computer Graphics", *IEEE Computer Graphics and Applications*, 3(8), pp. 21–30.

TAKALA, T. and J. HAHN (1992). "Sound Rendering", in proceedings of SIGGRAPH '92, *Computer Graphics*, 26(2), pp. 211–220.

TANNAS, JR., L. E., ed. (1985). *Flat-Panel Displays and CRTs*, Van Nostrand Reinhold, New York.

TAUBMAN, D. and M. MARCELLIN (2001). *JPEG 2000: Image-Compression Fundamentals, Standards, and Practice*, Kluwer Academic Publishers, Norwell, MA.

TELLER, S. and P. HANRAHAN (1993). "Global Visibility Algorithms for Illumination Computations", in proceedings of SIGGRAPH '93, *Computer Graphics*, pp. 239–246.

TERZOPOULOS, D., J. PLATT, A. H. BARR, et al. (1987). "Elastically Deformable Models", in proceedings of SIGGRAPH '87, *Computer Graphics*, 21(4), pp. 205–214.

THALMANN, N. M. and D. THALMANN (1985). *Computer Animation: Theory and Practice*, Springer-Verlag, Tokyo.

THALMANN, D., ed. (1990). *Scientific Visualization and Graphics Simulation*, John Wiley & Sons, Chichester, England.

THIBAULT, W. C. and B. F. NAYLOR (1987). "Set Operations on Polyhedra using Binary Space Partitioning Trees", in proceedings of SIGGRAPH '87, *Computer Graphics*, 21(4), pp. 153–162.

THOMAS, B. and W. LEFKON (1997). *Disney's Art of Animation from Mickey Mouse to Hercules*, Hyperion Press, New York.

THOMAS, F., O. JOHNSON, and C. JOHNSTON (1995). *The Illusion of Life: Disney Animation*, Hyperion Press, New York.

TORBERG, J. G. (1987). "A Parallel Processor Architecture for Graphics Arithmetic Operations", in proceedings of SIGGRAPH '87, *Computer Graphics*, 21(4), pp. 197–204.

TORRANCE, K. E. and E. M. SPARROW (1967). "Theory for Off-Specular Reflection from Roughened Surfaces", *Journal of the Optical Society of America*, 57(9), pp. 1105–1114.

TRAVIS, D. (1991). *Effective Color Displays*, Academic Press, London.

TUFTE, E. R. (1990). *Envisioning Information*, Graphics Press, Cheshire, CN.

TUFTE, E. R. (1997). *Visual Explanations: Images and Quantities, Evidence and Narrative*, Graphics Press, Cheshire, CN.

TUFTE, E. R. (2001). *The Visual Display of Quantitative Information, Second Edition*, Graphics Press, Cheshire, CN.

TURKOWSKI, K. (1982). "Antialiasing Through the Use of Coordinate Transformations", *ACM Transactions on Graphics*, 1(3), pp. 215–234.

UPSON, C. and M. KEELER (1988). "VBUFFER: Visible Volume Rendering", in proceedings of SIGGRAPH '88, *Computer Graphics*, 22(4), pp. 59–64.

UPSON, C., et al. (1989). "The Application Visualization System: A Computational Environment for Scientific Visualization", *IEEE Computer Graphics and Applications*, 9(4), pp. 30–42.

UPSTILL, S. (1989). *The RenderMan Companion*, Addison-Wesley, Reading, MA.

VAN WIJK, J. J. (1991). "Spot Noise-Texture Synthesis for Data Visualization", in proceedings of SIGGRAPH '91, *Computer Graphics*, 25(4), pp. 309–318.

VEENSTRA, J. and N. AHUJA (1988). "Line Drawings of Octree-Represented Objects", *ACM Transactions on Graphics*, 7(1), pp. 61–75.

VELHO, L. and J. D. M. GOMES (1991). "Digital Halftoning with Space-Filling Curves", in proceedings of SIGGRAPH '91, *Computer Graphics*, 25(4), pp. 81–90.

VON HERZEN, B., A. H. BARR, and H. R. ZATZ (1990). "Geometric Collisions for Time-Dependent Parametric Surfaces", in proceedings of SIGGRAPH '90, *Computer Graphics*, 24(4), pp. 39–48.

WALLACE, V. L. (1976). "The Semantics of Graphic Input Devices", in proceedings of SIGGRAPH '76, *Computer Graphics*, 10(1), pp. 61–65.

WALLACE, J. R., K. A. ELMQUIST, and E. A. HAINES (1989). "A Ray-Tracing Algorithm for Progressive Radiosity", in proceedings of SIGGRAPH '89, *Computer Graphics*, 23(3), pp. 315–324.

WALSH, A. E. and D. GEHRINGER (2002). *Java 3D*, Prentice-Hall, Upper Saddle River, NJ.

WANGER, L. R., J. A. FERWERDA, and D. P. GREENBERG (1992). "Perceiving Spatial Relationships in Computer-Generated Images", *IEEE Computer Graphics and Applications*, 12(3), pp. 44–58.

WARN, D. R. (1983). "Lighting Controls for Synthetic Images", in proceedings of SIGGRAPH '83, *Computer Graphics*, 17(3), pp. 13–21.

WATT, A. (1989). *Fundamentals of Three-Dimensional Computer Graphics*, Addison-Wesley, Wokingham, England.

WATT, M. (1990). "Light-Water Interaction Using Backward Beam Tracing", in proceedings of SIGGRAPH '90, *Computer Graphics*, 24(4), pp. 377–386.

WATT, A. and M. WATT (1992). *Advanced Animation and Rendering Techniques*, Addison-Wesley, Wokingham, England.

WEGHORST, H., G. HOOPER, and D. P. GREENBERG (1984). "Improved Computational Methods for Ray Tracing", *ACM Transactions on Graphics*, 3(1), pp. 52–69.

WEIL, J. (1986). "The Synthesis of Cloth Objects", in proceedings of SIGGRAPH '86, *Computer Graphics*, 20(4), pp. 49–54.

WEILER, K. and P. ATHERTON (1977). "Hidden-Surface Removal Using Polygon Area Sorting", in proceedings of SIGGRAPH '77, *Computer Graphics*, 11(2), pp. 214–222.

WEILER, K. (1980). "Polygon Comparison Using a Graph Representation", in proceedings of SIGGRAPH '80, *Computer Graphics*, 14(3), pp. 10–18.

WEINBERG, R. (1978) "Computer Graphics in Support of Space-Shuttle Simulation", in proceedings of SIGGRAPH '78, *Computer Graphics*, 12(3), pp. 82–86.

WELCH, T. (1984). "A Technique for High-Performance Data Compression", *IEEE Computer*, 17(6), pp. 8–19.

WERNECKE, J. (1994). *The Inventor Mentor*, Addison-Wesley, Reading, MA.

WESTIN, S. H., J. R. ARVO, and K. E. TORRANCE (1992). "Predicting Reflectance Functions from Complex Surfaces", in proceedings of SIGGRAPH '92, *Computer Graphics*, 26(2), pp. 255–264.

WESTOVER, L. (1990). "Footprint Evaluation for Volume Rendering", in proceedings of SIGGRAPH '90, *Computer Graphics*, 24(4), pp. 367–376.

WHITTED, T. (1980). "An Improved Illumination Model for Shaded Display", *Communications of the ACM*, 23(6), pp. 343–349.

WHITTED, T. and D. M. WEIMER (1982). "A Software Testbed for the Development of 3D Raster Graphics Systems", *ACM Transactions on Graphics*, 1(1), pp. 43–58.

WHITTED, T. (1983). "Antialiased Line Drawing Using Brush Extrusion", in proceedings of SIGGRAPH '83, *Computer Graphics*, 17(3), pp. 151–156.

WILHELMS, J. (1987). "Toward Automatic Motion Control", *IEEE Computer Graphics and Applications*, 7(4), pp. 11–22.

WILHELMS, J. and A. VAN GELDER (1991). "A Coherent Projection Approach for Direct Volume Rendering", in proceedings of SIGGRAPH '91, *Computer Graphics*, 25(4), pp. 275–284.

WILHELMS, J. and A. VAN GELDER (1992). "Octrees for Faster Isosurface Generation", *ACM Transactions on Graphics*, 11(3), pp. 201–227.

WILLIAMS, L. (1983). "Pyramidal Parametrics", in proceedings of SIGGRAPH '83, *Computer Graphics*, 17(3), pp. 1–11.

WILLIAMS, L. (1990). "Performance-Driven Facial Animation", in proceedings of SIGGRAPH '90, *Computer Graphics*, 24(4), pp. 235–242.

WITKIN, A. and W. WELCH (1990). "Fast Animation and Control of Nonrigid Structures", in proceedings of SIGGRAPH '90, *Computer Graphics*, 24(4), pp. 243–252.

WITKIN, A. and M. KASS (1991). "Reaction-Diffusion Textures", in proceedings of SIGGRAPH '91, *Computer Graphics*, 25(4), pp. 299–308.

WOLFRAM, S. (1984) "Computer Software in Science and Mathematics", *Scientific American*, 251(3), 188–203.

WOLFRAM, S. (1991). *Mathematica*, Addison-Wesley, Reading, MA.

WOO, A., P. POULIN, and A. FOURNIER (1990). "A Survey of Shadow Algorithms", *IEEE Computer Graphics and Applications*, 10(6), pp. 13–32.

WOO M., J. NEIDER, T. DAVIS, and D. SHREINER (1999). *OpenGL Programming Guide, Third Edition*, Addison-Wesley, Reading, MA.

WRIGHT, W. E. (1990). "Parallelization of Bresenham's Line and Circle Algorithms", *IEEE Computer Graphics and Applications*, 10(5), pp. 60–67.

WU, X. (1991). "An Efficient Antialiasing Technique", in proceedings of SIGGRAPH '91, *Computer Graphics*, 25(4), pp. 143–152.

WYSZECKI, G. and W. S. STILES (1982). *Color Science*, John Wiley & Sons, New York.

WYVILL, G., B. WYVILL, and C. McPHEETERS (1987). "Solid Texturing of Soft Objects", *IEEE Computer Graphics and Applications*, 7(12), pp. 20–26.

YAEGER, L., C. UPSON, and R. MYERS (1986). "Combining Physical and Visual Simulation: Creation of the Planet Jupiter for the Film '2010' ", in proceedings of SIGGRAPH '86, *Computer Graphics*, 20(4), pp. 85–94.

YAGEL, R., D. COHEN, and A. KAUFMAN (1992). "Discrete Ray Tracing", *IEEE Computer Graphics and Applications*, 12(5), pp. 19–28.

YAMAGUCHI, K., T. L. KUNII, and F. FUJIMURA (1984). "Octree-Related Data Structures and Algorithms", *IEEE Computer Graphics and Applications*, 4(1), pp. 53–59.

YESSIOS, C. I. (1979). "Computer Drafting of Stones, Wood, Plant, and Ground Materials", in proceedings of SIGGRAPH '79, *Computer Graphics*, 13(2), pp. 190–198.

YOUNG, D. A. (1990). *The X Window System—Programming and Applications with Xt, OSF/Motif Edition*, Prentice-Hall, Englewood Cliffs, NJ.

ZELEZNICK, R. C., et al. (1991). "An Object-Oriented Framework for the Integration of Interactive Animation Techniques", in proceedings of SIGGRAPH '91, *Computer Graphics*, 25(4), pp. 105–112.

ZELTZER, D. (1982). "Motor Control Techniques for Figure Animation", *IEEE Computer Graphics and Applications*, 2(9), pp. 53–60.

ZHANG, Y. and R. E. WEBBER (1993). "Space Diffusion: An Improved Parallel Halftoning Technique Using Space-Filling Curves", in proceedings of SIGGRAPH '93, *Computer Graphics*, pp. 305–312.

ZIV, J. and A. LEMPEL (1977). "A Universal Algorithm for Sequential Data Compression", *IEEE Transactions on Information Theory*, 23(3), pp. 337–343.

ZIV, J. and A. LEMPEL (1978). "Compression of Individual Sequences via Variable-Rate Coding", *IEEE Transactions on Information Theory*, 24(5), pp. 530–536.

Subject Index

A

D

E

F

G

H

I

J

K

L

P

Q

R

S

OpenGL Function Index

CORE LIBRARY FUNCTIONS

GLU LIBRARY FUNCTIONS

GLUT LIBRARY FUNCTIONS